MILLER'S

Antiques Shops, Fairs & Auctions in the UK & Ireland 2005

MILLER'S

Antiques Shops, Fairs & Auctions

in the UK & Ireland

2005

MILLER'S ANTIQUES SHOPS, FAIRS AND AUCTIONS IN THE UK & IRELAND 2005

Compiled, edited and designed by Miller's Publications Ltd
The Cellars, High Street, Tenterden, Kent TN30 6BN
Tel: 01580 766411 Fax: 01580 766100

Project Director Valerie Lewis
Executive Art Editor & Jacket Design Rhonda Fisher
Project Co-ordinator David Penfold, Edgerton Publishing Services
Assistant Project Co-ordinator Rosemary Cooke
Principal Researchers Victoria Lewis, Philippa Menzies,
Caroline Petherick, Carol Woodcock
Production Co-ordinator Philip Hannath
Production Controller Sarah Rogers
Advertising Co-ordinator & Administrator Melinda Williams
Advertising Executive Emma Gillingham

First published in Great Britain in 2004 by Miller's,
a division of Mitchell Beazley, imprints of Octopus Publishing Group Ltd,
2–4 Heron Quays, London E14 4JP

ISBN 1 84533 034 X

Front cover illustrations:
l. A mahogany elbow chair, inlaid with floral marquetry, Dutch, 19thC.
£200–240 / €300–360 / $360–430 ⚒ Gorringes, Lewes

r. A Staffordshire group, entitled 'London 30 Miles', c1870, 10½in (27cm) high.
£180–210 / €270–310 / $330–380 ⚒ Sworders

br. A bronze censer, cast with a dragon chasing a flaming pearl, marked, Chinese, 17thC, 5¾in (14.5cm) wide.
£300–360 / €450–540 / $540–650 ⚒ Woolley & Wallis

Printed and bound by Mackays of Chatham Ltd

2004 BACA *Winners...*

CATEGORY 1
General Antiques Dealer

UK: NORTH OF M62
Heathcote Antiques
Cross Hills, Nr Keighley, West Yorkshire BD20 7DS

M62 SOUTH, TO M4 / M25
Christopher Clarke Antiques
Stow-on-the-Wold, Gloucestershire GL54 1JS

LONDON (INSIDE M25)
sponsored by CHRISTIE'S
David Brower
113 Kensington Church Street,
London W8 7LN

SOUTH AND SOUTH-WEST OF ENGLAND
Spencer Swaffer
30 High Street, Arundel, West Sussex BN18 9AB

CATEGORY 2
Specialist Antiques Dealers

FURNITURE
Butchoff Interiors
154 Kensington Church Street, London W8 4BN

COLLECTABLES
H. Blairman & Sons Ltd
119 Mount Street, London W1K 3NL

SILVER & PLATE
Koopman Rare Art
London Silver Vaults, Chancery House,
Chancery Lane, London WC2A 1QX

ART NOUVEAU & ART DECO
Editions Graphique
3 Clifford Street, London W1S 2LF

OIL PAINTINGS
Messum's Fine Art
8 Cork Street, London W1S 3LJ

CLOCKS, WATCHES & SCIENTIFIC INSTRUMENTS
Trevor Philip & Son Ltd
75a Jermyn Street, London SW1Y 6NP

JEWELLERY
Tadema Gallery
10 Charlton Place, London N1 8AJ

CERAMICS
Brian Haughton Antiques
3b Burlington Gardens, London W1S 3EP

CATEGORY 3
Auction Houses

UK: NORTH OF M62
Lyon & Turnbull Auctioneers
33 Broughton Place, Edinburgh, Scotland
EH1 3RR

M62 SOUTH, TO M4 / M25
Bosley's Military Auctioneers
Marlow, Buckinghamshire SL7 1AH

INSIDE M25
Bonhams
101 New Bond Street, London W1S 1SR

SOUTH AND SOUTH-WEST OF ENGLAND
Dreweatt Neate
Donnington Priory, Newbury,
Berkshire RG14 2JE

CATEGORY 4
Associated Awards

AUCTIONEER OF THE YEAR
Richard Allen
Halls Fine Art Auctions, Welsh Bridge,
Shrewsbury SY3 8LA

MILLER'S CLUB BEST TOWN/VILLAGE
sponsored by MILLER'S CLUB
Petworth, West Sussex

BEST ANTIQUES CENTRE VOTED FOR BY THE READERS OF BBC HOMES & ANTIQUES
sponsored by BBC HOMES & ANTIQUES MAGAZINE
The Swan Antiques Centre, Tetsworth OX9 7AB

IN-HOUSE EXHIBITION
Art Deco Postmodernism
A Legacy of British Art Deco Glass,
10-20th September 2003, Richard Dennis Gallery,
London W8 (40pp illustrated catalogue
by Jeanette Hayhurst & Nigel Benson)

MILLER'S LIFE-TIME ACHIEVEMENT
sponsored by

Roger Warner
Burford, Oxfordshire

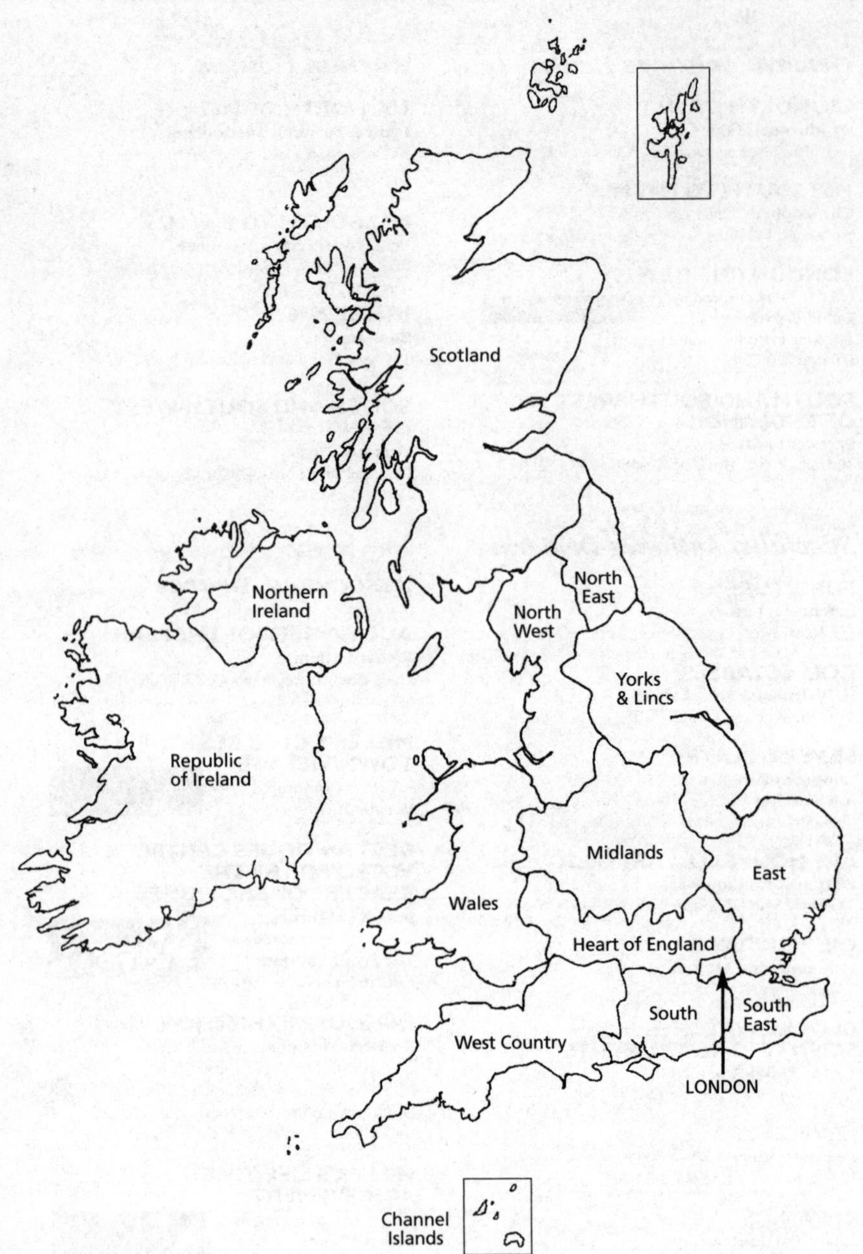
Scotland
Northern Ireland
Republic of Ireland
North East
North West
Yorks & Lincs
Midlands
East
Wales
Heart of England
South
South East
West Country
LONDON
Channel Islands

CONTENTS

HOW TO USE THIS BOOK

It is our aim to make *Miller's Antiques Shops, Fairs & Auctions in the UK & Ireland 2005* simple to use. In order to make it easier to find entries, the book has been divided into three main sections: Dealers, Antiques Centres and Auction Houses; Associated Services; and Fairs.

Key to Symbols

- ⊞ Dealer
- Auction House
- Antiques Centre
- ✉ Address
- 🅿 Parking
- ☎ Telephone No.
- Ⓜ Mobile No.
- Ⓕ Fax No.
- Ⓔ E-mail address
- Ⓦ Web Address

SOUTH EAST

SOUTH EAST

KENT • APPLEDORE

KENT

APPLEDORE

⊞ **Back 2 Wood**
Contact Richard Moate
✉ **The Old Goods Shed, Station Road, Appledore, Kent, TN26 2DF**
☎ 01233 758109
Ⓔ pine@back2wood.com
Ⓦ www.back2wood.com
Est. 1987 *Stock size* Medium
Stock Antique pine furniture
Open Mon–Fri 9am–5pm Sat 9am–4pm Sun 11am–5pm
Services Pine stripping

The Old Forge Antiques
Contact Anthony Unwin
✉ **The Old Forge, 16 The Street, Appledore, Kent, TN26 2BX** 🅿
☎ 01233 758585
Est. 2000
No. of dealers 18
Stock General antiques, china, glass, furniture, garden items
Open Mon–Sat 10am–5pm Sun 11am–5pm

ASHFORD

Hobbs Parker
Contact Alan White
✉ **Monument Way, Orbital Park, Ashford, Kent, TN24 0HB** 🅿
☎ 01233 502222 Ⓕ 01233 502211

ASHURST

⊞ **The Architectural Emporium**
Contact Michael Roberts
✉ **The Bald Faced Stag, Ashurst, Kent, TN3 9TE** 🅿
☎ 01892 740877
Ⓔ mike@architecturalemporium.com
Ⓦ www.architectural emporium.com
Est. 2000 *Stock size* Large
Stock Architectural antiques, garden statuary, sundials, fountains, fireplaces, lighting
Open Tues–Sat 9.30am–5.30pm

BARHAM

⊞ **Stablegate Antiques**
Contact Michael Giuntini
✉ **Barham, Kent, CT4 6QD** 🅿
☎ 01227 831639 Ⓕ 01227 831639
Ⓜ 07802 439777
Ⓦ www.stablegateantiques.co.uk
Est. 1981 *Stock size* Large
Stock Period furniture, pictures, silver, silver plate, ceramics, mirrors
Open Mon–Sun 10am–5pm
Fairs Claridges, NEC, Harrogate

BECKENHAM

Antiques & Collectors Market
Contact Mrs Holley

The United Kingdom has been divided into geographical regions, which are listed in the Contents on page 7. There is also a section for the Republic of Ireland. Each region is divided into counties and within each county, cities, towns and villages are listed alphabetically. Indexes to company name and place name can be found at the end of this Directory.

Each entry shows information such as address, phone number, opening hours, e-mail address and website, member organizations (eg LAPADA) and year established. Each **Dealer** entry contains details of stock and any services they provide. **Auction House** entries include information about their sales, frequency of sales and if catalogues are available. Entries for **Antiques Centres** include the number of dealers within the centre. **Associated Services** such as restorers, packers and valuers etc are listed alphabetically according to the service offered.

The **Fairs** section is divided into two parts. The first part gives an alphabetical list of fair organizers, while the second lists in date order, antiques fairs that will take place in the UK and Ireland throughout 2005. It is always advisable to contact the organizers in advance to check that information has not changed since going to press.

There are Indexes of **Specialists, Place Names** and a **General Index**, which are to be found beginning on page 564.

INTRODUCTION

It is perhaps a good thing that we do not all like the same things. I watch some of the antiques-related programmes on television and often find that things to which I would not give house room are valued very highly. On the other hand, things that I find attractive are apparently not saleable, or at least not saleable at a reasonable price. Brown furniture seems to be a current example.

The term 'current' highlights the situation. Fashions change, and they can only be fashions because the intrinsic worth of an object does not change over the years.

While all this may seem illogical from an aesthetic and even a common-sense point of view, from a collector's view point it is not a bad thing. To be able to buy at a time when prices are low can be regarded either as an ideal opportunity to enhance a collection at relatively low cost or simply as a good investment.

Of course, the best known of Miller's publications, *Miller's Antiques Price Guide*, is aimed at providing information that will help connoisseurs to purchase antiques at the right price. The *Collectables Price Guide* provides the same service for collectable items. This publication, *Miller's Antiques Shops, Fairs & Auctions in the UK & Ireland 2005*, has a different purpose, but one that is related. Knowing what to buy is, of course, most important, but knowing where to buy it comes a close second.

Miller's Antiques Shops, Fairs & Auctions in the UK & Ireland is now in its sixth edition and provides an invaluable source of information not only on where antiques shops, auction houses and antiques centres are situated, but also on what they sell and when. The index of specialists is particularly useful in this context.

The other two features of this publication are the information on associated services, which expands every year, and the fairs section. It is interesting that, although antiques shops may cease trading, it is rare for someone providing associated services to do so unless they are truly retiring, because their investment is in their skills rather than their stock.

The fairs section is a little different in this sixth edition in that the fair organizers are listed separately. This change has been made for two reasons. The first is that some organizers are unable to provide their dates in time for them to be included before the publication goes to press. The second is that lack of space has meant that it has not always been possible to include as many fairs as the editors would like. Under the old system, this meant that these fairs did not feature at all in the publication. Under the new scheme, we will include as many fair organizers as possible and we expect this section to grow in future editions.

Thus, *Miller's Antiques Shops, Fairs & Auctions in the UK & Ireland 2005* continues to provide updated information in the areas with which regular purchasers will be familar, as well as enhancing this information in new ways. If you have suggestions about ways in which this publication could be further improved, please feel free to contact us.

David Penfold

Antiques Shops, Centres & Auction Houses

If you wish your company to be entered in the next edition of the Directory, please complete the form at the end of the book or go to our website: http://www.shopsfairsauctions.com

SOUTH EAST

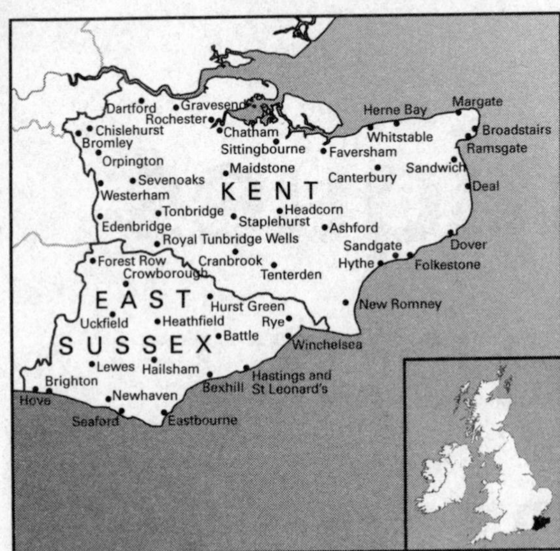

EAST SUSSEX

ALFRISTON

Alfriston Antiques
Contact John Tourell
The Square, Alfriston, East Sussex, BN26 5UD
01323 870498 01323 870498
Est. 1967 *Stock size* Large
Stock Small collectables, porcelain, silver, jewellery, clocks
Open Wed–Sat 11am–5pm Sun 2.30–4.30pm
Services Valuations

The Old Apiary
Contact Tony Phillimore
High Street, Alfriston, East Sussex, BN26 5TB
01323 870730
Est. 1995 *Stock size* Small
Stock Small furniture, decorative china
Open Mon–Sun 10am–5.30pm

BALCOMBE

Mid Sussex Auctions Ltd
Contact Lance Gibson
Glebe Farm Estate, Haywards Heath Road, Balcombe, Haywards Heath, East Sussex, RH17 6NJ
01444 819100 01444 819101
sue@midsussexauctions.fsnet.co.uk
www.midsussexauctions.fsnet.co.uk
Est. 1998
Open Mon–Fri 9am–5.30pm
Sales Antiques and general sales held at South of England Showground, Ardingly, East Sussex
Frequency Monthly
Catalogues Yes

BATTLE

Barnaby's of Battle
Contact Mr Barney Hance
50 High Street, Battle, East Sussex, TN33 0AN
01424 772221
Est. 1997 *Stock size* Medium
Stock Old pine, oak, hardwood furniture
Open Mon–Sat 10am–6pm
Services Restoration

Battle Antiques Centre
Contact Andrew Polnik or Christine Terry
91a High Street, Battle, East Sussex, TN33 0AQ
01424 773364
Est. 1963 *Stock size* Medium
No. of dealers 12
Stock General antiques
Open Mon–Sat 10am–5pm
Services Ceramic restoration, caning, rushwork, gilding, upholstery

Burstow & Hewett
Contact Mr R Ellin
Abbey Auction Galleries & Granary Salerooms, Lower Lake, Battle, East Sussex, TN33 0AT
01424 772374 01424 772302
auctions@burstowandhewett.co.uk
www.burstowandhewett.co.uk
Est. 1790
Open Mon–Fri 9am–5.30pm
Sales Sales of general antiques. Specialist sales of fine furniture, paintings and ceramics
Frequency Monthly
Catalogues Yes

Lavande
Contact Aryo Bakker or Sophie Hartley
53 High Street, Battle, East Sussex, TN33 0EN
01424 774474 01424 774474
07710 098642
info@lavande.co.uk
www.lavande.co.uk
Est. 1998 *Stock size* Medium
Stock 18th–19thC French furniture, accessories
Open Mon–Sat 9.30am–5.30pm Sun by appointment
Fairs Decorative Antiques and Textiles Fair, Battersea, Antiques & Audacity, Arundel
Services Upholstery, interior design

Spectrum Fine Jewellery Ltd (NAG, IPG)
Contact Mr Keith Ingram
46 High Street, Battle, East Sussex, TN33 0EE
01424 774404 01424 774404
Est. 1975 *Stock size* Medium
Stock Jewellery, silver
Open Tues–Sat 9.30am–5.30pm
Fairs NEC
Services Repairs, enamelling, commissions

BEXHILL-ON-SEA

Acme Inc.
Contact Mrs Ruth Hardie
42 Sackville Road, Bexhill-on-Sea,

East Sussex,
TN39 3JE P
☎ 01424 211848
Ⓜ 07973 402404
ⓔ ruth@acme-inc.com
Ⓦ www.acme-inc.com
Est. 1993 *Stock size* Large
Stock 19th–20thC decorative arts, ceramics, glass, metalware, furniture
Open Mon Thurs Fri 11am–noon 2.30–4pm Sat 3–5pm Sun 3–4pm or by appointment

Gorringes Incorporating Julian Dawson (SOFAA, ISVA)
Contact Mr Ross Mercer
✉ **Terminus Road, Bexhill-on-Sea, East Sussex, TN39 3LR** P
☎ 01424 212994 ⓕ 01424 224035
ⓔ bexhill@gorringes.co.uk
Ⓦ www.gorringes.co.uk
Est. 1926
Open Mon–Fri 8.30am–1pm 2–5pm Sat by appointment
Sales Fine art, antiques, collectables, Tues Wed 10am, viewing Fri 10am–5pm Sat 9.30am–4pm
Frequency 6 weeks
Catalogues Yes

Elizabeth Morgan Antiques
Contact Mr H Jenkins
✉ **50 Western Road, Bexhill-on-Sea, East Sussex, TN40 1DY** P
☎ 01424 218343
Est. 1983 *Stock size* Medium
Stock General antiques
Open Mon–Sat 9am–5pm

Sivyer's
Contact Mrs V Sivyer
✉ **7 Sackville Road, Bexhill-on-Sea, East Sussex, TN39 3JB** P
☎ 01424 733821
Est. 1990 *Stock size* Medium
Stock General antiques, kitchenware
Open Mon–Sat 10am–5pm

BRIGHTON

3A Antiques
Contact Daniel Brummer
✉ **3a Meeting House Lane, The Lanes, Brighton, East Sussex, BN1 1HB**
☎ 01273 220700
Est. 2003 *Stock size* Medium
Stock General antiques
Open Mon–Sun 10am–5pm
Services Restoration, silver, silver plate

Alexandria Antiques
Contact Mr A H Ahmed
✉ **3 Hanover Place, Brighton, East Sussex, BN2 2SD** P
☎ 01273 688793 ⓕ 01273 688793
Ⓜ 07880 625558
ⓔ ahahmed@ukonline.co.uk
Est. 1978 *Stock size* Medium
Stock 18th–19thC furniture, porcelain, bronzes, paintings, decorative objects
Open Mon–Fri 9.30am–5.30pm Sat Sun by appointment
Fairs Newark, Ardingly
Services Valuations, restoration

Art Deco Etc
Contact Mr J Clark
✉ **73 Upper Gloucester Road, Brighton, East Sussex, BN1 3LQ** P
Ⓜ 07971 268302
Est. 1979 *Stock size* Medium
Stock 1860–1980s pottery and glass, lighting, small furniture, metalwork
Open By appointment only
Fairs Newark, Alexandra Palace, Ardingly
Services Valuations, insurance claims

Ashton's Antiques
Contact Pearl or Bob Ashton
✉ **1 & 3 Clyde Road, Brighton, East Sussex, BN1 4NN** P
☎ 01273 605253 ⓕ 01273 605253
Ⓜ 07775 736041
Est. 1970 *Stock size* Medium
Stock Antiques, collectables
Open Thurs–Sat 10am–4pm

The Asylum Gallery
Contact Simon Etheridge
✉ **80c St James's Street, Brighton, East Sussex, BN2 1PA**
☎ 01273 626426
Est. 2001 *Stock size* Small
Stock Contemporary art, retro glassware
Open By appointment

Brighton Architectural Salvage
Contact Mr R L Legendre
✉ **33–34 Gloucester Road, Brighton, East Sussex, BN1 4AQ**
☎ 01273 681656 ⓕ 01273 681656
Ⓜ 07979 966245
Est. 1979 *Stock size* Large
Stock Restored architectural antiques, fireplaces, reclaimed flooring
Open Tues–Sat 10am–5pm
Services Fireplace installation

Brighton Books
Contact Paul Carmody
✉ **18 Kensington Gardens, Brighton, East Sussex, BN1 4AL**
☎ 01273 693845 ⓕ 01273 693845
Est. 1996 *Stock size* Large
Stock Rare, second-hand and antiquarian books
Open Mon–Sat 10am–6pm
Services Valuations, restoration

Brighton Flea Market
Contact Mr A R Wilkinson
✉ **31a Upper St James's Street, Brighton, East Sussex, BN2 1JN**
☎ 01273 624006 ⓕ 01273 328665
ⓔ arwilkinson@aol.com
Est. 1988 *Stock size* Large
Stock Antiques, bric-a-brac, collectables
Open Mon–Sat 10am–5.30pm Sun Bank Holidays 10.30am–5pm

Brighton Postcard Shop (PTA)
Contact Mr K Davies
✉ **38 Beaconsfield Road, Brighton, East Sussex, BN1 4QH** P
☎ 01273 600035 ⓕ 01273 628660
ⓔ keith@brightonpostcardshop.co.uk
Ⓦ www.postcard.co.uk/flair
Est. 1987 *Stock size* Large
Stock Postcards, ephemera, vintage glamour magazines
Open Tues–Sat 11am–4pm
Fairs Bloomsbury
Services Mail order

Tony Broadfoot Antiques
Contact Mr Tony Broadfoot
✉ **39 Upper Gardner Street, Brighton, East Sussex, BN1 4AN** P
☎ 01273 695457 ⓕ 01273 620365

SOUTH EAST

EAST SUSSEX • BRIGHTON

Est. 1982 *Stock size* Large
Stock Antique furniture
Open Mon–Fri 9am–5pm

⊞ C A R S (Classic Automobilia and Regalia Specialists)
Contact Mr G G Weiner
✉ **4–4a Chapel Terrace Mews, Kemp Town, Brighton, East Sussex, BN2 1HU** Ⓟ
☎ 01273 622722/601960
Ⓕ 01273 601960
Ⓜ 07890 836734
Ⓔ cars@kemptown-brighton.freeserve.co.uk
Ⓦ www.barcc.co.uk or www.brmmbrmm.com/barcc
Est. 1981 *Stock size* Medium
Stock Automobilia, collectors' car badges and mascots, hand-built collectors' and children's pedal cars
Open Mon–Sat 10am–6pm or by appointment
Fairs Classic car shows at NEC, Alexandra Palace
Services Valuations

⊞ Margaret Callaghan
Contact Margaret Callaghan
✉ **30A Upper St James's Street, Kemptown, Brighton, East Sussex, BN2 2JA**
☎ 01273 681384
Est. 1983 *Stock size* Medium
Stock Textiles
Open Tues Fri Sat 10.30am–5.30pm

⊞ Decorative Arts
Contact Anthony White
✉ **27 Gloucester Road, Brighton, East Sussex, BN1 4AQ** Ⓟ
☎ 01273 676486
Ⓜ 07788 107101
Ⓔ info@decarts.net
Ⓦ www.decarts.net
Est. 1996 *Stock size* Medium
Stock Oak furniture 1880–1970, decorative arts, 1970s leather furniture
Open Mon–Sat 10am–5.30pm
Sun by appointment

⊞ Enhancements
Contact Lucille Robinson
✉ **1–1a Cavendish Street, Brighton, East Sussex, BN2 1RN** Ⓟ
☎ 01273 677303
Ⓜ 07788 727878
Ⓔ luerobinson@aol.com
Est. 1992 *Stock size* Medium
Stock Kitchenware, tools, beds, pine furniture, shabby chic furniture
Open Mon–Sat 10am–5.30pm
Services Free delivery

⊞ Hallmark Jewellers
Contact Mr J Hersheson
✉ **4 Union Street, The Lanes, Brighton, East Sussex, BN1 1HA** Ⓟ
☎ 01273 725477 Ⓕ 01273 725477
Ⓜ 07885 298494
Est. 1959 *Stock size* Large
Stock Antique and modern silver, silver collectables, jewellery
Open Mon–Sat 9am–5pm
Sun 11am–4pm
Services Valuations

⊞ Dudley Hume (LAPADA)
Contact Mr D Hume
✉ **46 Upper North Street, Brighton, East Sussex, BN1 3FH**
☎ 01273 323461 Ⓕ 01273 240422
Ⓜ 07977 598627
Ⓔ dudley@dudleyhume.freeserve.co.uk
Ⓦ www.dudleyhumeantiques.co.uk
Est. 1973 *Stock size* Medium
Stock 18th–19thC furniture, decorative items
Open Mon–Fri 10.30am–4.30pm
Sat 10am–noon
Fairs Olympia

⊞ In My Room
Contact Oliver Learmonth
✉ **35 Gloucester Road, North Lane, Brighton, East Sussex, BN1 4AQ**
☎ 01273 675506 Ⓕ 01273 675506
Est. 2003 *Stock size* Medium
Stock Furniture, decorative objects
Open Mon–Sat 10am–6pm
Sun 11am–4pm closed Thurs

⊞ Jezebel
Contact Mrs A Davis
✉ **14 Prince Albert Street, Brighton, East Sussex, BN1 1HE** Ⓟ
☎ 01273 206091 Ⓕ 01273 206091
Est. 1989 *Stock size* Medium
Stock Art Deco, Art Nouveau, costumes, vintage clothing, costume jewellery
Open Mon–Sat 11am–5.30pm
Fairs Newark

⊞ The Lanes Armoury
Contact Mark or David Hawkins
✉ **26 Meeting House Lane, Brighton, East Sussex, BN1 1HB** Ⓟ
☎ 01273 321357 Ⓕ 01273 771125
Ⓔ enquiries@thelanesarmoury.co.uk
Ⓦ www.thelanesarmoury.co.uk
Est. 1992 *Stock size* Large
Stock Pre-Christian–WWII arms, armour, militaria and books
Open Mon–Sat 10am–5.15pm

⊞ Leoframes
Contact Stephen Round
✉ **70 North Road, Brighton, East Sussex, BN1 1YD** Ⓟ
☎ 01273 695862
Ⓔ stephen@leoframes.com
Est. 1985 *Stock size* Medium
Stock Antique prints, maps
Open Mon–Sat 9am–5.30pm
Services Restoration, framing

⊞ Patrick Moorhead Antiques
Contact Mr P Moorhead
✉ **15b Prince Albert Street, Brighton, East Sussex, BN1 1HF**
☎ 01273 774227 Ⓕ 01273 774227
Ⓔ patrick.moorhead@virgin.net
Est. 1985 *Stock size* Medium
Stock Furniture, decorative porcelain, bronzes
Open Mon–Fri 10am–5.30pm
Services Valuations, restoration

⊞ Patrick Moorhead Antiques
Contact Mr P Moorhead
✉ **Spring Gardens, 76 Church Street, Brighton, East Sussex, BN1 1RL** Ⓟ
☎ 01273 779696 Ⓕ 01273 220196
Ⓜ 07785 725202
Ⓔ patrick.moorhead@virgin.net
Est. 1984 *Stock size* Large
Stock 18th–19thC furniture, European and Oriental ceramics, paintings, clocks
Open Mon–Fri 10am–5.30pm
Services Valuations, restoration

⊞ Michael Norman Antiques Ltd (BADA)
Contact Michael Keehan
✉ **4 Frederick Place, Brighton, East Sussex, BN1 4EA** Ⓟ
☎ 01273 329253/326712

Ⓕ 01273 206556
Ⓔ antiques@michaelnorman.com
Ⓦ www.michaelnorman.com
Est. 1964 *Stock size* Large
Stock 18th–19thC English furniture
Open Mon–Sat 9am–5.30pm closed 1–2pm

North Laine Antiques & Flea Market
Contact Mr A Fitchett
✉ **5a Upper Gardner Street, Brighton, East Sussex, BN1 4AN** Ⓟ
☎ 01273 600894 Ⓕ 01273 600894
Ⓜ 07836 365411
Ⓔ market@fitchett.freeserve.co.uk
Est. 2002 *Stock size* Large
No. of dealers Approximately 70 including cabinets
Stock Wide range of antiques and collectables
Open Mon–Fri 10am–5.30pm Sat 9am–5.30pm Sun 10am–4pm

Oasis
Contact Mr I Stevenson
✉ **39 Kensington Gardens, Brighton, East Sussex, BN1 4AL** Ⓟ
☎ 01273 683885
Est. 1979 *Stock size* Medium
Stock Period lighting, telephones, gramophones, furniture, Art Deco, Art Nouveau, watches, lighters, glass, textiles, 1920s–1930s clothing
Open Mon–Sat 10am–5.30pm

Odin Antiques
Contact Mr A Sjovold
✉ **43 Preston Street, Brighton, East Sussex, BN1 2HP** Ⓟ
☎ 01273 732738
Est. 1979 *Stock size* Medium
Stock Antique furniture, maritime items, telescopes
Open Mon–Sat 10.30am–5.30pm

Colin Page Antiquarian Books (ABA)
Contact Mr J Loska
✉ **36 Duke Street, Brighton, East Sussex, BN1 1AG** Ⓟ
☎ 01273 325954 Ⓕ 01273 746246
Ⓔ cpage@pavilion.co.uk
Est. 1969 *Stock size* Large
Stock Antiquarian and second-hand books, antiquarian literature, natural history, plate books, bindings
Open Mon–Sat 9.30am–5.30pm
Fairs ABA, Olympia, Chelsea
Services Valuations

Dermot & Jill Palmer Antiques (LAPADA)
Contact Jill Palmer
✉ **7–8 Union Street, Brighton, East Sussex, BN1 1HA**
☎ 01273 328669 Ⓕ 01273 777641
Ⓜ 07771 614331
Ⓔ jillpalmer@maconlimited.net
Est. 1969 *Stock size* Large
Stock Mainly 19thC French and English furniture
Open Mon–Sat 9am–6pm or by appointment
Fairs Olympia, Decorative & Textile Fair Battersea

Sue Pearson Antique Dolls & Teddy Bears
Contact Sue Pearson
✉ **18 Brighton Square, Brighton, East Sussex, BN1 1HD** Ⓟ
☎ 01273 329247 Ⓕ 01273 774851
Ⓔ enquire@sue-pearson.co.uk
Ⓦ www.sue-pearson.co.uk
Est. 1981 *Stock size* Large
Stock Antique and modern bears, soft toys, dolls
Open Mon–Sun 10am–5pm
Fairs Kensington Town Hall
Services Repair of dolls and bears

Ben Ponting Antiques
Contact Michelle Ponting
✉ **53 Upper North Street, Brighton, East Sussex, BN1 3FH** Ⓟ
☎ 01273 329409 Ⓕ 01273 558749
Ⓔ pontingco@aol.com
Est. 1976 *Stock size* Large
Stock English Georgian–Edwardian antique furniture
Open Mon–Fri 9am–5pm
Services Valuations, restoration

Rainbow Books
Contact Kevin Daly
✉ **28 Trafalgar Street, Brighton, East Sussex, BN1 4ED**
☎ 01273 605101
Est. 1998 *Stock size* Large
Stock Antiquarian, second-hand books
Open Mon–Sat 10.30am–6pm

Rin-Tin-Tin (ESoc)
Contact Mr Rick Irvine
✉ **34 North Road, Brighton, East Sussex, BN1 1YB** Ⓟ
☎ 01273 672424 Ⓕ 01273 672424
Ⓔ rick@rintintin.freeserve.co.uk
Est. 1982 *Stock size* Medium
Stock Old advertising, promotional matter, magazines, early glamour, games, toys, plastics, 20thC fixtures and fittings
Open Mon–Sat 11am–5.30pm
Fairs Alexandra Palace, Juke Box Fairs
Services Framing

Savery Antiques
Contact Ann Savery
✉ **257 Ditchling Road, Fiveways, Brighton, East Sussex, BN1 6JH** Ⓟ
☎ 01273 564899
Ⓔ hjamsavery@aol.com
Est. 1968 *Stock size* Medium
Stock Small furniture, porcelain, glass, metalwork
Open Mon 10.30am–5pm Thurs–Sat 9.30am–5pm
Fairs Ardingly, Sandown Park

Snooper's Paradise
Contact Mr N Drinkwater
✉ **7–8 Kensington Gardens, Brighton, East Sussex, BN1 4AL** Ⓟ
☎ 01273 602558 Ⓕ 01273 686611
Ⓔ snoopersparadisebrighton@btinternet.com
Ⓦ www.snoopersparadise.co.uk
Est. 1994 *Stock size* Large
No. of dealers 80
Stock China, pictures, 1970s clothes and fabric, kitchenware, ephemera, jewellery, watches, records and CDs, phones and electrical, Art Deco, glass, treen, furniture, photographic, pens and lighters, militaria etc
Open Mon–Sat 9.30am–5.30pm Sun 11am–4pm

Southern Independent Auctions Ltd (NAVA)
Contact Daryl Taylor
✉ **Regent House, The Hyde Business Park, Lower Bevendean, Brighton, East Sussex, BN2 4JE** Ⓟ
☎ 01273 696545 Ⓕ 01273 624347
Ⓔ info@sia-group.co.uk

Ⓦ www.sia-groupco.uk
Est. 2000
Open Mon–Fri 9am–5pm
Sales General antiques
Catalogues Yes

⊞ Step Back In Time (PTA)
Contact Robert Jeeves
✉ **125 Queens Road, Brighton, East Sussex, BN1 3WB**
☎ 01273 731883 Ⓕ 01273 731883
Est. 1975 *Stock size* Large
Stock Postcards, prints, ephemera
Open Mon–Sat 9am–6pm
Services Valuations

⊞ Studio Bookshop
Contact Mr P Brown
✉ **68 St James's Street, Brighton, East Sussex, BN2 1PJ** Ⓟ
☎ 01273 691253
Ⓔ studiobookshop@btconnect.com
Est. 1995 *Stock size* Medium
Stock Reference books on glass, art and antiques
Open Mon–Sat 10am–5.30pm
Fairs Glass fairs
Services Catalogue, telephone orders

⊞ Trafalgar Bookshop
Contact David Boland
✉ **44 Trafalgar Street, Brighton, East Sussex, BN1 4ED**
☎ 01273 684300
Est. 1987 *Stock size* Medium
Stock Antiquarian, second-hand books
Open Mon–Sat 10am–5.30pm
Thurs 11am–5.30pm

⊞ Valelink Ltd
Contact Mr J Trory
✉ **26 Queen's Road, Brighton, East Sussex, BN1 3XA** Ⓟ
☎ 01273 202906 Ⓕ 01273 202906
Est. 1970 *Stock size* Medium
Stock Collectables
Open Mon–Sat 10am–6pm

⊞ Wardrobe
Contact Mr Clive Parks or Philip Parfitt
✉ **51 Upper North Street, Brighton, East Sussex, BN1 3FH** Ⓟ
☎ 01273 202201 Ⓕ 01273 202201
Ⓜ 07802 483056
Ⓦ www.decoratif.co.uk
Est. 1986 *Stock size* Medium
Stock Vintage clothing and accessories, textiles, jewellery, Art Deco, Bakelite, collectable plastics
Open Wed–Sat 10am–5pm or by appointment
Fairs Alexandra Palace, Sandown Park, Horticultural Hall

⊞ E & B White
Contact Elizabeth or Ben White
✉ **43 & 47 Upper North Street, Brighton, East Sussex, BN1 3FH**
☎ 01273 328706 Ⓕ 01273 207035
Est. 1965 *Stock size* Medium
Stock Antique and decorative furniture
Open Mon–Fri 9.30am–5pm
Sat 9.30am–1pm

⊞ The Witch Ball
Contact Gina Daniels
✉ **48 Meeting House Lane, Brighton, East Sussex, BN1 1HB** Ⓟ
☎ 01273 326618
Ⓜ 07889 420524
Ⓔ mg.daniels@btopenworld.com
Est. 1967 *Stock size* Large
Stock 1550–1850 prints and maps
Open Mon–Sat 10.30am–6pm
Sun by appointment
Services Lists on request

⊞ Tony Young Autographs (UACC)
Contact Tony Young
✉ **138 Edward Street, Brighton, East Sussex, BN2 0JL**
☎ 01273 732418
Est. 1984 *Stock size* Large
Stock Ephemera, autographs, general antiques
Open Mon–Fri 10am–noon 2–5pm Sat 10am–12.15pm
Fairs Autographica
Services Valuations

BURWASH

⊞ Chateaubriand Antiques
Contact William Vincent
✉ **High Street, Burwash, East Sussex, TN19 7ES** Ⓟ
☎ 01435 882535
Ⓔ info@chateaubriandantiques.co.uk
Ⓦ www.chateaubriandantiques.co.uk
Est. 1985 *Stock size* Medium
Stock Antique fine and country furniture, maps, prints, pictures, linen, lace, porcelain, Staffordshire, oil lamps, silver, rugs, carpets
Open Wed–Sat 10am–5pm
Sun noon–5pm
Services Valuations, shipping

CROWBOROUGH

⊞ Trudi's Treasures
Contact Trudi Blackman
✉ **The Old Post Office, Crowborough Hill, Jarvis Brook, Crowborough, East Sussex, TN6 2EG** Ⓟ
☎ 01892 667671
Ⓔ trudistreasures@hotmail.com
Ⓦ www.trudistreasures.co.uk
Est. 2001 *Stock size* Large
Stock Collectables, curios, pine, painted furniture, china, kitchenware
Open Mon–Sat 10am–5pm
Services Furniture painting

EASTBOURNE

⊞ 35 The Goffs
Contact Mrs Y Cole
✉ **35 The Goffs, Eastbourne, East Sussex, BN21 1HF** Ⓟ
☎ 01323 737272
Est. 2000 *Stock size* Medium
Stock Decorative antiques, furniture, chandeliers
Open Tues–Fri 1.30–4.30 pm
Sat 10.30am–4.30pm

⊞ W. Bruford
Contact John Burgess
✉ **11–13 Cornfield Road, Eastbourne, East Sussex, BN21 3NA** Ⓟ
☎ 01323 725452 Ⓕ 01323 417873
Est. 1885 *Stock size* Small
Stock Jewellery, silver
Open Mon–Sat 9.30am–5pm
Services Valuations, restoration

⊞ Camilla's Bookshop
Contact Ms C Francombe or Mr S Broad
✉ **57 Grove Road, Eastbourne, East Sussex, BN21 4TX** Ⓟ
☎ 01323 736001
Ⓔ camillas@fsnet.co.uk
Est. 1975 *Stock size* Large
Stock Antiquarian and second-

hand books, postcards, ephemera, children's books, needlework, military, aviation and nautical topics
Open Mon–Sat 10am–5.30pm
Services Valuations, book search

Collectors Dream
Contact Terence Kearns
38 Seaside, Eastbourne, East Sussex, BN22 7QJ
01323 727147
info@finechina4u.co.uk
www.finechina4u.co.uk
Est. 1986 *Stock size* Medium
Stock Collectables, Royal Doulton, vintage clockwork tin toys
Open Mon–Sat 9.30am–5.30pm
Services Valuations

John Cowderoy Antiques (LAPADA)
Contact Mr Richard Cowderoy
42 South Street, Eastbourne, East Sussex, BN21 4XB
01323 720058 01323 410163
david@cowderoyantiques.co.uk
www.cowderoyantiques.co.uk
Est. 1973 *Stock size* Large
Stock General antiques, collectables, clocks, musical boxes
Open Mon–Sat 8.30am–5pm closed Wed pm
Services Restoration

Crest Collectables
Contact Mr C Powell
54 Grove Road, Eastbourne, East Sussex, BN21 4UD
01323 721185
Est. 1986 *Stock size* Medium
Stock Teddy bears, dolls, soft toys, collectables
Open Mon–Sat 10.30am–4pm closed Wed

Crown Antiques
Contact Mark Simmons
1 Crown Street, Eastbourne, East Sussex, BN21 1NX
01323 412985
mark@crownantiques.fsnet.co.uk
Est. 1984 *Stock size* Medium
Stock Victorian–Edwardian furniture
Open Tues Thur Fri Sat 10am–5.30pm
Services Valuations, restoration

Dreweatt Neate Eastbourne Salerooms (SOFAA)
Contact Jeremy Palmer
46–50 South Street, Eastbourne, East Sussex, BN21 4XB
01323 410419 01323 416540
eastbourne@dnfa.com
www.dnfa.com
Est. 1759
Open Mon–Fri 9am–5pm
Sales Fortnightly gallery sales of general antiques, Thurs 10am, viewing Wed 9am–8pm Thurs 9–10am
Frequency Fortnightly
Catalogues Yes

Eastbourne Antiques Market
Contact Mr P C Barltrop
80 Seaside, Eastbourne, East Sussex, BN22 7QP
01323 642233
Est. 1969 *Stock size* Large
No. of dealers 25
Stock Antiques, collectables
Open Mon–Fri 10am–5.30pm Sat 10am–5pm

Eastbourne Auction Rooms
Contact Jeanette May
Auction House, Finmere Road, Eastbourne, East Sussex, BN22 8QL
01323 431444 01323 417638
enquiries@eastbourneauction.com
www.eastbourneauction.com
Est. 1994
Open Mon–Fri 9am–5pm
Sales General antiques fortnightly Sat 10am, viewing Fri 9am–7pm, antiques and collectables every six weeks Fri 10am, viewing Wed,Thurs 9am–7pm
Frequency Fortnightly
Catalogues Yes

Eastbourne Pine
Contact Mark Simmons
1 Crown Street, Eastbourne, East Sussex, BN21 1NX
01323 412985
mark@crownantiques.fsnet.co.uk
Est. 1984 *Stock size* Medium
Stock Antique pine
Open Tues Thur Fri Sat 10am–5.30pm
Services Valuations, restoration

The Enterprise Collectors Market
Contact Mr J Prysor
Enterprise Centre, Station Parade, Eastbourne, East Sussex, BN21 1BD
01323 732690
Est. 1988 *Stock size* Large
No. of dealers 15
Stock Antiques, collectables, wrist watches
Open Mon–Sat 9.30am–5pm

François
Contact François Celada
26 South Street, Eastbourne, East Sussex, BN21 4XB
01323 644464 01323 644464
Est. 1983 *Stock size* Medium
Stock Postcards, stamps, coins, militaria
Open Tues–Sat 9.30am–5pm

Charles French
Contact Mr C McCleave
2 Kings Drive, Eastbourne, East Sussex, BN21 2NU
01323 720128
Est. 1969 *Stock size* Medium
Stock General antiques
Open Mon–Fri 10am–5.30pm
Services House clearance

A & T Gibbard (PBFA)
Contact Mrs M T Gibbard or Mr A Gibbard
30 South Street, Eastbourne, East Sussex, BN21 4XB
01323 734128 01323 734128
Est. 1910 *Stock size* Large
Stock Antiquarian and second-hand books, specializing in natural history, travel, topography, leather-bound books
Open Mon–Sat 9.30am–5.30pm
Fairs Russell Hotel

More Than Music
Contact Mike Vandenbosch
PO Box 2809, Eastbourne, East Sussex, BN21 2EA
01323 649778 01323 649779
morethnmus@aol.com
www.mtmglobal.com
Est. 1995 *Stock size* Medium
Stock Vinyl, autographs, books, magazines, posters etc

SOUTH EAST
EAST SUSSEX • FOREST ROW

Open Mon–Fri 10am–5.30pm
Sat 10am–1pm
Services Worldwide mail order service

The Old Town Antiques Centre
Contact Saff Baker
52 Ocklynge Road, Eastbourne, East Sussex, BN21 1PR
01323 416016
07967 102325
Est. 1989 *Stock size* Large
No. of dealers 16
Stock Mixed antiques, furniture, fine porcelain, glass, silver, Beswick, Copenhagen figures etc
Open Mon–Sat 10am–5pm
Services Valuations, restoration

Timothy Partridge Antiques
46 Ocklynge Road, Eastbourne, East Sussex, BN21 1PP
01323 638731
07860 864709
Est. 1982 *Stock size* Medium
Stock General pre-war goods, furniture, smalls
Open Mon–Fri 10am–5pm

Seaquel Antiques & Collectors Market
Contact Mrs P Mornington-West
37 Seaside Road, Eastbourne, East Sussex, BN21 3PP
01323 645032
Est. 1998 *Stock size* Large
No. of dealers 16
Stock Furniture, collectables, bric-a-brac
Open Mon–Sat 10am–5pm
Sun 11am–4.30pm

Shine's Antiques and Collectables
Contact Brian Shine
8 Crown Street, Eastbourne, East Sussex, BN21 1NX
01323 726261
Est. 1999 *Stock size* Large
Stock Antiques, collectables
Open Mon–Sat 10am–5pm

South Coast Collectables
Contact Sylvia Redford
85 Seaside Road, Eastbourne, East Sussex, BN21 3PL
01323 648811
Est. 1997 *Stock size* Large
No. of dealers 18
Stock Antiques, collectables, Georgian–Edwardian furniture
Open Tues–Sat 10am–5pm

Tony's Antique Services Ltd
Contact Tony King
85 Seaside Road, Eastbourne, East Sussex, BN21 3PL
01323 733776 01323 733776
07752 201786
Est. 1977 *Stock size* Large
Stock Antique furniture
Open Tues–Sat 10am–5pm
Sun Mon by appointment
Services Restoration, export, search service

World of Sport
Contact Joanna Archibald
Enterprise Shopping Centre, Station Parade, Eastbourne, East Sussex, BN21 1BD
01323 411849
Est. 2002 *Stock size* Medium
Stock Sport and film memorabilia, historical prints
Open Mon–Sat 9.30am–4.30pm

FOREST ROW

The Dandelion Clock
Contact Mrs L Chapman
Lewes Road, Forest Row, East Sussex, RH18 5ES
01342 822335
www.dandelion-clock.co.uk
Est. 1994 *Stock size* Large
No. of dealers 12
Stock Pine and country furniture, antiques, collectables
Open Mon–Sat 10am–5.30pm
Services Local delivery available

Pavilion
Contact John Taylor
Country House, Lewes Road, Forest Row, East Sussex, RH18 5AN
01342 822199
Est. 1997 *Stock size* Medium
Stock Painted furniture, decorative antiques, gifts
Open Tues–Sat 10am–5.30pm

GOLDEN CROSS

Golden Cross Antiques
Contact Mrs R R Buchan
A22, Golden Cross, Hailsham, East Sussex, BN27 4AN
01825 872144 01825 872144
07957 224165
info@goldencrossantiques.co.uk
www.goldencrossantiques.co.uk
Est. 1974 *Stock size* Medium
Stock Furniture, collectables, silver
Open Mon–Sat 9am–6pm
Sun 10am–6pm

GUESTLING

Hearth & Home
Contact Mr D Hance
Rye Road, Guestling Green, Hastings, East Sussex, TN35 4LS
01424 813220 01424 813220
Est. 1984 *Stock size* Medium
Stock Original Victorian and cast-iron fireplaces
Open Mon–Sat 9am–1pm 2–5pm
Services Advice, installation

HADLOW DOWN

Hadlow Down Antiques
Contact Mr Adrian Butler
Hastingford Farm, Hastingford Lane, Hadlow Down, Uckfield, East Sussex, TN22 4DY
01825 830707
07951 817615
verandah@tesco.net
Est. 1989 *Stock size* Large
Stock Antiques, decorative furniture, accessories
Open Thurs–Sat 10am–5pm or by appointment
Services Valuations, restoration, custom-made oak furniture

HAILSHAM

Football in Focus (2001) Ltd
Contact Phil Cole
Focus House, 12 Swan Farm Business Centre, Station Road, Hailsham, East Sussex, BN27 2BY
01323 440800 01323 445138
footballinfocus@talk21.com
Est. 1998 *Stock size* Large

Stock Sporting memorabilia, film music
Open Mon–Fri 9am–5pm

Key to Symbols

- ⊞ = Dealer
- ⌂ = Antiques Centre
- ⚒ = Auction House
- ✉ = Address
- 🅿 = Parking
- ☎ = Telephone No.
- Ⓜ = Mobile tel No.
- Ⓕ = Fax No.
- Ⓔ = E-mail address
- Ⓦ = Website address

⊞ Stable Doors
Contact Mr K Skinner or Mr B Skinner
✉ **Market Street, Hailsham, East Sussex, BN27 2AE** 🅿
☎ 01323 844033
Ⓔ kevin@stabledoors.org.uk
Ⓦ www.stabledoors.org.uk
Est. 1996 *Stock size* Large
Stock Antiques, collectables
Open Mon–Sat 9am–5pm
Fairs Ardingly

⊞ Wealth of Weights (Cambridge Paperweight Circle)
Contact Mrs J Skinner or Mr K Skinner
✉ **Stable Doors, Market Street, Hailsham, East Sussex, BN27 2AE** 🅿
☎ 01323 441150
Ⓔ jaqui@weights.co.uk
Ⓦ www.weights.co.uk
Est. 1997 *Stock size* Large
Stock Largest selection of paperweights in South England. Registered PCA World Dealer
Open Mon–Sun 9am–5pm
Fairs Effingham Park, Copthorne, Woking Glass Fair
Services Valuations, collections bought

HASTINGS

⊞ Book Centre
Contact Mr R Naylor
✉ **18 West Street, Hastings, East Sussex, TN34 3AN** 🅿
☎ 01424 729866
Est. 1996 *Stock size* Large
Stock Antiquarian and second-hand books
Open Mon–Sun 9am–5pm
Services Book search

⊞ Coach House Antiques
Contact Mr R J Luck
✉ **42 George Street, Hastings, East Sussex, TN34 3EA** 🅿
☎ 01424 461849 Ⓕ 01424 461849
Ⓜ 07710 234803
Est. 1979 *Stock size* Large
Stock Longcase clocks, Victorian furniture, Dinky toys
Open Mon–Sun 10am–5pm
Services Valuations, restoration

⊞ Don't Mention The War
Contact Steve Mayne
✉ **52 High Street, Old Town, Hastings, East Sussex, TN34 3EN**
☎ 01424 442035
Ⓔ dmayne5@aol.com
Est. 2000 *Stock size* Small
Stock World War I and II memorabilia
Open Mon–Sun 10am–5pm closed Wed
Fairs War & Peace Show, Beltring
Services Lectures on Life on the Home Front

⌂ George Street Antiques Centre
Contact Mrs F Stanley
✉ **47 George Street, Hastings, East Sussex, TN34 3EA** 🅿
☎ 01424 429339
Est. 1984 *Stock size* Large
No. of dealers 8
Stock Collectables
Open Mon–Fri 9am–5pm Sat 10am–5pm Sun 11am–5pm

⊞ Howes Bookshop Ltd (ABA, PBFA)
Contact Mr M Bartley
✉ **Trinity Hall, Braybrooke Terrace, Hastings, East Sussex, TN34 1HQ** 🅿
☎ 01424 423437 Ⓕ 01424 460620
Ⓔ rarebooks@howes.co.uk
Ⓦ www.howes.co.uk
Est. 1946 *Stock size* Large
Stock Antiquarian and second-hand books, arts and humanities a speciality
Open Mon–Fri 9.30am–5pm
Fairs Olympia, Chelsea, Russell Hotel
Services Valuations

⊞ Mollycoddles Collectables
Contact Gary Baker
✉ **24 George Street, Hastings, East Sussex, TN34 3EB** 🅿
☎ 01424 433277
Est. 1995 *Stock size* Medium
Stock Collectables, pine furniture, textiles, jewellery
Open Mon–Sun 10am–5pm

⊞ Nakota Curios
Contact Mr R Kelly
✉ **12 Courthouse Street, Hastings, East Sussex, TN34 3AU** 🅿
☎ 01424 438900
Est. 1969 *Stock size* Large
Stock Chandeliers, decorative china, silverware, rugs, pictures, mirrors
Open Mon–Sat 10.30am–1pm 2pm–4.30pm

⊞ Reeves & Son
Contact Mr C Hawkins
✉ **4–6 Courthouse Street, Hastings, East Sussex, TN34 3AU** 🅿
☎ 01424 437672
Ⓜ 07778 311803
Est. 1818 *Stock size* Large
Stock Military collectables, china, smalls, books
Open Mon–Sat 9am–5pm
Services House clearance

HEATHFIELD

⊞ Botting & Berry
Contact John Botting or David Berry
✉ **31 High Street, Heathfield, East Sussex, TN21 8HU**
☎ 01435 813553
Est. 1990 *Stock size* Medium
Stock Victorian–Edwardian furniture, effects, antiquarian, second-hand books
Open Mon–Sat 10am–5pm

⌂ The Pig Sty
Contact Mrs Worton
✉ **49 High Street, Heathfield, East Sussex, TN21 8HU** 🅿
☎ 01435 866671
Est. 1997 *Stock size* Medium
No. of dealers 10

SOUTH EAST

EAST SUSSEX • HOVE

Stock General antiques and collectables
Open Mon–Sat 9am–5pm
Services Coffee shop

⊞ Graham Price Antiques Ltd
Contact Graham Price
✉ **Satinstown Farm, Burwash Road, Broad Oak, Heathfield, East Sussex, TN21 8RT** 🅿
☎ 01892 523341 ⓕ 01892 530382
ⓜ 07768 330842
ⓔ mail@upcountryantiques.co.uk
ⓦ www.upcountryantiques.co.uk
Est. 1984 *Stock size* Large
Stock Decorative and antique country furniture, rural artefacts
Open Mon–Fri 8am–5pm
Fairs Newark, Ardingly
Services Packing, shipping, courier service

Toad Hall Antique Centre
Contact Patsy Quick
✉ **55 & 57 High Street, Heathfield, East Sussex, TN21 8HU** 🅿
☎ 01435 863535 ⓕ 01435 863535
Est. 1996 *Stock size* Large
No. of dealers 16
Stock Furniture, general antiques, collectables
Open Mon–Sat 9am–5.30pm Sun 11am–4pm

HOVE

Bonhams
✉ **19 Palmeira Square, Hove, East Sussex, BN3 2JN** 🅿
☎ 01273 220000 ⓕ 01273 220335
ⓔ hove@bonhams.com
ⓦ www.bonhams.com
Est. 1793
Open Mon–Fri 9am–1pm 2–5pm
Sales Regional office. Regular house and attic sales across the country; contact London offices for further details. Free auction valuations; insurance and probate valuations

⊞ J S Carter
Contact Mr J Carter
✉ **9 Boundary Road, Hove, East Sussex, BN3 4EH** 🅿
☎ 01273 439678 ⓕ 01273 416053
Est. 1974 *Stock size* Large
Stock Victorian–Edwardian furniture
Open By appointment
Services Restoration

⊞ Simon Hunter Antique Maps (IMCOS)
Contact Mr Simon Hunter
✉ **21 St Johns Road, Hove, East Sussex, BN3 2FB** 🅿
☎ 01273 746983 ⓕ 01273 746983
ⓔ simonhunter@fastnet.co.uk
ⓦ www.antiquemaps.org.uk
Est. 1989 *Stock size* Large
Stock Antique maps
Open By appointment
Fairs London Map Fairs

Raymond P Inman
Contact Robert Inman
✉ **98a Coleridge Street, Hove, East Sussex, BN3 5AA** 🅿
☎ 01273 774777 ⓕ 01273 735660
ⓔ r.p.inman@talk21.com
Est. 1929
Open Mon–Fri 9am–5pm
Sales General antiques sales
Frequency 10 a year
Catalogues Yes

⊞ Michael Norman Antiques (BADA)
Contact John Branch or Armando Fava
✉ **61 Holland Road, Hove, East Sussex, BN3 1JB** 🅿
☎ 01273 329253 ⓕ 01273 206556
ⓔ antiques@michaelnorman.com
ⓦ www.michaelnorman.com
Est. 1965 *Stock size* Large
Stock Georgian and Regency period furniture
Open Mon–Sat 9am–1pm 2–5pm or by appointment
Services Restoration

Scarborough Perry Fine Arts
Contact Mr S Perry
✉ **Hove Auction Rooms, Hove Street, Hove, East Sussex, BN3 2GL** 🅿
☎ 01273 735266 ⓕ 01273 723813
ⓔ gspfa@pavilion.co.uk
ⓦ www.scarboroughperry.co.uk
Est. 1897
Open Mon–Fri 9am–5.30pm Sat 9am–noon
Sales General antique sales Thurs–Fri 10.30am, viewing Tues–Wed 10am–4.30pm Tues 6–8pm. Occasional special sales
Frequency 5–6 weeks
Catalogues Yes

⊞ Valentina Antique Beds
Contact Mrs Flechas
✉ **212 Church Road, Hove, East Sussex, BN3 2DJ** 🅿
☎ 01273 735035
ⓔ info@antiquebeds.com
ⓦ www.antiquebeds.com
Est. 1992 *Stock size* Large
Stock French, Victorian brass and iron bedsteads
Open Mon–Sat 10am–5pm

⊞ Yellow Lantern Antiques (LAPADA)
Contact B Higgins
✉ **34 Holland Road, Hove, East Sussex, BN3 1JL** 🅿
☎ 01273 771572 ⓕ 01273 455476
ⓜ 07860 342976
Est. 1950 *Stock size* Medium
Stock Period English town furniture pre-1840, ormolu and bronzes
Open Mon–Fri 10am–5.30pm Sat 10am–4pm
Fairs Olympia, Buxton
Services Valuations, restoration

HURST GREEN

⊞ Hurst Green Antiques
Contact Mr N Lucas
✉ **79 London Road, Hurst Green, East Sussex, TN19 7PN** 🅿
☎ 01580 860317
ⓦ www.hurstgreenantiques.com
Est. 1988 *Stock size* Large
Stock English and French period furnishings for house and garden
Open Tues–Sat 9.30am–5.30pm

LEWES

⊞ Antique Interiors for Home & Garden
Contact Mr Kevin Hillman
✉ **7 Malling Street, Lewes, East Sussex, BN7 2RA** 🅿
☎ 01273 486822
ⓜ 01273 486481
Est. 1990 *Stock size* Medium
Stock General antiques,

decorative items, garden furniture, country pine
Open Mon–Sat 9.30am–5.30pm or by appointment
Fairs Ardingly, Newark

Basically Bears
Contact Karen Goble
170a High Street, Lewes, East Sussex, BN7 1YB
☎ 01273 47887 F 01273 47887
W www.basically-bears.com
Est. 2000 *Stock size* Medium
Stock Collectable bears
Open Mon–Sat 9.30am–5pm

Bow Windows Bookshop (ABA, PBFA, ILAB)
Contact Alan or Jennifer Shelley
175 High Street, Lewes, East Sussex, BN7 1YE
☎ 01273 480780 F 01273 486686
E rarebooks@bowwindows.com
W www.bowwindows.com
Est. 1964 *Stock size* Medium
Stock General antiquarian books, all subjects
Open Mon–Sat 9.30am–5pm
Fairs Russell Hotel, International Book Fairs London
Services Valuations, 3 or 4 catalogues per year

Church Hill Antique Centre
Contact Susan Miller or Simon Ramm
6 Station Street, Lewes, East Sussex, BN7 2DA P
☎ 01273 474842 F 01273 846797
E churchhilllewes@aol.com
W www.church-hill-antiques.com
Est. 1995 *Stock size* Large
No. of dealers 60
Stock Art, collectables
Open Mon–Sat 9.30am–5pm or by appointment
Services Valuations

Cliffe Antiques Centre
Contact The Manager
47 Cliffe High Street, Lewes, East Sussex, BN7 2AN P
☎ 01273 473266 F 01273 473266
Est. 1981 *Stock size* Medium
No. of dealers 15
Stock Wide range of antiques, collectables
Open Mon–Sat 9.30am–5pm

A & Y Cumming Ltd (ABA)
Contact Andrew Cumming
84 High Street, Lewes, East Sussex, BN7 1XN P
☎ 01273 472319 F 01273 486364
E a.y.cumming@ukgateway.net
Est. 1976 *Stock size* Large
Stock Antiquarian and second-hand books on travel, natural history, colour plate books, 1st editions, leather bound
Open Mon–Fri 10am–5pm Sat 10am–5.30pm
Fairs Olympia (June), Chelsea Book Fair
Services Valuations

The Emporium Antiques Centre
Contact Michelle Doyle or Steven Madigan
42 Cliffe High Street, Lewes, East Sussex, BN7 2AN P
☎ 01273 486866
Est. 1993 *Stock size* Large
No. of dealers 60
Stock General antiques, collectables, studio ceramics, toys, textiles, silver, jewellery, books, clocks
Open Mon–Fri 9.30am–5pm Sat 9.30am–5.30pm Sun noon–4pm

The Emporium Antiques Centre Too
Contact John Evett
24 High Street, Lewes, East Sussex, BN7 2LU P
☎ 01273 477979
Est. 1989 *Stock size* Large
No. of dealers 100
Stock Antiques, collectables, furniture
Open Mon–Sat 9.30am–5pm Sun noon–5pm

The Fifteenth Century Bookshop (PBFA)
Contact Mrs Miraband
99–100 High Street, Lewes, East Sussex, BN7 1XH P
☎ 01273 474160
M 07751 487642
W www.15centurybookshop.co.uk
Est. 1930 *Stock size* Medium
Stock General stock, collectable children's books
Open Mon–Sat 10am–5.30pm Sun 10.30am–4pm
Services Book search for children's books, postal service

Gorringes Incorporating Julian Dawson (SOFAA, ISVA)
Contact Mr Julian Dawson
Garden Street, Lewes, East Sussex, BN7 1TJ P
☎ 01273 478221 F 01273 487369
E auctions@gorringes.co.uk
W www.gorringes.co.uk
Est. 1920
Open Mon–Fri 9am–5.30pm Sat 9am–12.30pm
Sales Sales of general antiques and collectables Mon (not Bank Holidays) 10am, viewing Fri 10am–5pm Sat 9am–12.30pm
Frequency Weekly
Catalogues No

Gorringes Incorporating Julian Dawson (SOFAA, ISVA, BACA Award Winner 2002)
Contact Mr P Taylor
15 North Street, Lewes, East Sussex, BN7 2PD P
☎ 01273 472503 F 01273 479559
E auctions@gorringes.co.uk
W www.gorringes.co.uk
Est. 1926
Open Mon–Fri 8.30am–5.15pm Sat 9am–11.45am
Sales Fine art and antiques 3-day sale Tues–Thurs at 10am, viewing Fri 10am–5pm Sat 9.30am–4pm prior. Occasional house sales
Frequency 6 weeks
Catalogues Yes

Ruth Kidson (ABA, PBFA)
Contact Ruth Kidson
31 Western Road, Lewes, East Sussex, BN7 1RL P
☎ 01273 487087 F 01273 487087
E ruth.kidson@virgin.net
W www.ruthkidson.co.uk
Est. 1992 *Stock size* Small
Stock Antiquarian and second-hand books
Open Tues–Thurs 11am–4pm Fri–Sat 11am–4.30pm (summer 5pm)

Lewes Antique Centre
20 Cliffe High Street, Lewes, East Sussex,

BN7 2AH P
☎ 01273 476148
Est. 1968 *Stock size* Large
No. of dealers 100
Stock Furniture, architectural salvage, bric-a-brac, china, clocks, metalware, glass
Open Mon–Sat 9.30am–5pm Sun Bank Hols 12.30–4.30pm
Services Storage, delivery, pine stripping, restoration, valuations

The Lewes Clock Shop
Contact R I McColl
4 North Street, Lewes, East Sussex, BN7 2PA P
☎ 01273 473123 F 01273 473123
E lewesclocks@btopenworld.com
Est. 1991 *Stock size* Medium
Stock Restored antique clocks
Open Mon–Sat 9am–4pm closed Wed
Services Valuations, restoration, shipping

Lewes Flea Market
Contact Mr A R Wilkinson
14a Market Street, Lewes, East Sussex, BN7 2NB P
☎ 01273 480328 F 01273 328665
M 07884 267194
E arwilkinson@aol.com
Est. 1993 *Stock size* Large
Stock Antiques, collectables, bric-a-brac
Open Mon–Fri 10am–5pm Sat Sun 10.30am–5pm

Pastorale Antiques
Contact Mr Soucek
15 Malling Street, Lewes, East Sussex, BN7 2RA P
☎ 01273 473259 F 01273 473259
Est. 1980 *Stock size* Large
Stock English, French, East European and pine furniture, garden furniture and ornaments
Open Mon–Sat 10am–5pm
Services Restoration

Potter Antiques (GADAR)
Contact Victor Potter
1 Lansdown Place, Lewes, East Sussex, BN7 2JT P
☎ 01273 487671 F 01273 330143
M 07768 274461
E cvpotter@aol.com
W www.potterantiques.com
Est. 2001 *Stock size* Small
Stock Victorian and country furniture
Open Wed–Fri 10am–5.30pm
Services Restoration

Trade Antiques Centre
Contact Amanda Tollhurst
207 High Street, Lewes, East Sussex, BN7 2NS P
☎ 01273 486688
M 08701 413783
Est. 2001 *Stock size* Large
Stock Pine, oak, mahogany furniture, enamel ware, pictures, jewellery, china and porcelain
Open Mon–Sat 10am–5.30pm Sun noon–5pm

The Treasury
Contact Pamela Marshall
89 High Street, Lewes, East Sussex, BN7 1XN P
☎ 01273 480446 F 01273 838785
Est. 1986 *Stock size* Medium
Stock Collectables, small antiques, out-of-production figurines
Open Thurs Fri 10am–5pm

Wallis & Wallis
Contact Mr Roy Butler (militaria) or Mr Glenn Butler (toys)
West Street Auction Galleries, Lewes, East Sussex, BN7 2NJ P
☎ 01273 480208 F 01273 476562
E auctions@wallisandwallis.co.uk (militaria) or grb@wallisandwallis.co.uk (toys)
W www.wallisandwallis.co.uk
Est. 1928
Open Mon–Fri 9am–5.30pm closed 1–2pm
Sales 9 militaria, medals, coins, arms and armour per annum Tues 11am, 2 connoisseur arms and armour per annum Tues Wed 11am, 8 die-cast and tinplate toys per annum Mon 10.30am, viewing prior Fri 9am–5pm Sat 9am–1pm morning of sale 9am–10.30pm. Sales dates available on request
Frequency 6 weeks
Catalogues Yes (2 to 3 weeks before sales)

Esme Walters Antiques
Contact Esme Walters
27 Station Street, Lewes, East Sussex, BN7 2BB P
☎ 01273 475476
Est. 2003 *Stock size* Small
Stock Early English oak furniture
Open Mon Wed Thurs–Sat 10am–5pm

LITTLE HORSTEAD

Pianos Galore
Contact Jason Richards
Little Horstead, East Sussex, TN22 5TT P
☎ 01825 750567 F 01825 750566
E info@pianosgalore.co.uk
W www.pianosgalore.co.uk
Est. 1982 *Stock size* Large
Stock Pianos
Open Mon–Sat 9am–5pm Sun 10am–noon

NEWHAVEN

Marion Bowen Vintage Clothes
Contact Marion Bowen
28 Manor Road, Newhaven, East Sussex, BN9 0LS P
☎ 01273 512604
Est. 1986 *Stock size* Small
Stock Victorian–1950s vintage clothes and accessories
Open By appointment
Fairs Kempton Park

Newhaven Flea Market
Contact Mrs J Mayne
28 Southway, Newhaven, East Sussex, BN9 9LA P
☎ 01273 516065
Est. 1979 *Stock size* Large
No. of dealers 40
Stock Furniture, collectables, bric-a-brac
Open Mon–Sun 10am–5.30pm

Seahaven Antiques
Contact Stephen Johnson
87 Railway Road, Newhaven, East Sussex, BN9 0AY P
☎ 01273 611899 F 01273 611899
Est. 1958 *Stock size* Medium
Stock Furniture
Trade only Yes
Open Mon–Fri 8am–6pm Sat Sun by appointment
Services Valuations, restoration, shipping

NORTHIAM

Northiam Antiques
Contact Robert Bingham
Station Road, Northiam, East Sussex, TN31 6QT P
☎ 01797 252523 Ⓕ 01797 252523
Ⓜ 07881 611157
Ⓔ robert.bingham2@btconnect.com
Est. 2004 *Stock size* Large
Stock 18th–19thC English furniture
Open Mon–Sat 10am–6pm Sun 10.30am–4pm
Fairs Ardingly, Newark
Services Valuations, shipping

NUTLEY

Nutley Antiques
Contact L Hall
Libra House, High Street, Nutley, East Sussex, TN22 3NF P
☎ 01825 713220
Est. 1986 *Stock size* Large
Stock Rustic, country and decorative items
Open Mon–Sat 10am–5pm Sun 1.30–5pm
Fairs Ardingly
Services Caning, rushing

PEACEHAVEN

Hunters Antiques
Contact Colin Ancell
348 South Coast Road, Telscombe Cliffs, Peacehaven, East Sussex, BN10 7EP P
☎ 01273 588841 Ⓕ 01273 588841
Ⓜ 07710 611311
Est. 1970 *Stock size* Large
Stock General antiques, furniture
Open Mon–Fri 10.30am–5pm Sat Sun 10.30am–2pm
Fairs Ardingly, Newark
Services Valuations

PEVENSEY

The Old Mint House
Contact Mr Andrew Nicholson
High Street, Pevensey, East Sussex, BN24 5LF P
☎ 01323 762337 Ⓕ 01323 762337
Ⓔ antiques@minthouse.co.uk
Ⓦ www.minthouse.co.uk
Est. 1903 *Stock size* Large
Stock General antiques
Open Mon–Fri 9am–5pm Sat 10.30am–4pm
Services Shipping

POLEGATE

Summers Antiques
Contact Richard Millis
87 High Street, Polegate, East Sussex, BN26 6AE P
☎ 01323 483834
Est. 2001 *Stock size* Small
Stock General antiques and collectables
Open Mon–Fri 9am–5pm Sat 9am–1pm
Fairs Ardingly

PORTSLADE

K Edwards Antiques
Contact Mr K Edwards
Unit 2, Bestwood Works, Drove Road, Portslade, Brighton, East Sussex, BN41 2PA P
☎ 01273 420866
Ⓔ kedwa31024@aol.com
Ⓦ www.kedwardsantiques.co.uk
Est. 1988 *Stock size* Large
Stock Furniture, mainly chests-of-drawers
Open Mon–Fri 7.30am–6pm
Services Restoration

ROTHERFIELD

6a Antiques
Contact Mr B Samworth
6 High Street, Rotherfield, Crowborough, East Sussex, TN6 3LL P
☎ 01892 852008
Est. 1979 *Stock size* Large
Stock Georgian–Victorian furniture, antique pine
Open Mon–Sat 10am–5pm

Forge Interiors
Contact Mr D Masham
South Street, Rotherfield, Crowborough, East Sussex, TN6 3LN P
☎ 01892 853000 Ⓕ 01892 853122
Ⓔ asiandecor@forgeinteriors.com
Ⓦ www.forgeinteriors.com
Est. 1999 *Stock size* Medium
Stock Asian and English furniture, decorative items
Open Tues–Sat 10am–1pm 2–5pm Sun 2–5pm
Services Cane and rush chairs repaired

David Hinton @ Olinda House
Contact David Hinton
South Street, Rotherfield, East Sussex, TN6 3LL P
☎ 01892 852609/852412
Ⓜ 07733 106882
Ⓔ david@olindahouse.freeserve.co.uk
Est. 1996 *Stock size* Large
Stock Furniture, china, silver, glass
Open Mon–Fri 10.30am–5pm Sat 10am–5pm Sun 11am–4pm

ROTTINGDEAN

Baba Bears
Contact Sheila Whittaker
Windmill Antiques Centre, Laureens Walk, Nevill Road, Rottingdean, East Sussex, BN2 7HG P
☎ 01273 248859
Ⓔ baba.bears@virgin.net
Ⓦ www.bababears.co.uk
Est. 1988 *Stock size* Medium
Stock Antique teddy bears and soft toys
Open By appointment

Farthings
Contact Margaret Ixer
45 High Street, Rottingdean, East Sussex, BN2 7HL P
☎ 01273 309113
Est. 1996 *Stock size* Medium
No. of dealers 40
Stock General antiques and collectables
Open Mon–Sat 9.30am–5pm Sun noon–5pm
Services Will buy and sell on behalf of a customer

Grange Antiques
Contact Richard Payne
51 Marine Drive, Rottingdean, Brighton, East Sussex, BN2 7HQ P
☎ 01273 390141
Ⓜ 07801 419620
Ⓔ richard.payne@freedom255.com
Est. 1983 *Stock size* Small
Stock General, decorative antiques
Open Mon–Sat 10am–4pm Sun by appointment
Services Watch, clock, jewellery repairs

SOUTH EAST

EAST SUSSEX • RYE

Jordans of Rottingdean
Contact Mr Jordan Payne
98 High Street, Rottingdean, Brighton, East Sussex, BN2 7HF P
01273 302003
Est. 2001 *Stock size* Medium
No. of dealers 40
Stock Antiques, collectables, fine china, jewellery
Open Mon–Sat 9.30–5pm Sun noon–5pm

Windmill Antiques & Collectables
Contact Shirley Bass
1 Laureens Walk, Nevill Road, Rottingdean, Brighton, East Sussex, BN2 7HG P
01273 308699
Est. 2002 *Stock size* Small
No. of dealers 15
Stock Antiques, collectables, furniture, garden antiques, antiquarian books, teddy bears, collectable vinyls, china, glass, eiderdowns, quilts
Open Mon–Sat 10am–5pm Sun noon–5pm or by appointment
Services House clearance, shipping

RYE

Bears Galore
Contact Richard Tatham
c/o The Corner House, 27 High Street, Rye, East Sussex, TN31 7JF
01797 223187
bearsinrye@aol.com
www.bearsgalore.co.uk
Est. 1979 *Stock size* Large
Stock Hand-made collectable teddy bears
Open Mon–Sat 10am–4.30pm Sun noon–4.30pm
Services Mail order, layaway service

Black Sheep Antiques
Contact Mrs S Wright
72 The Mint, Rye, East Sussex, TN31 7EW P
01797 224508
Est. 1991 *Stock size* Medium
Stock Victorian china and glass
Open Mon–Sun 11am–5pm
Services China matching

Bragge & Sons
Contact Mr John Bragge
Landgate House, Landgate, Rye, East Sussex, TN31 7LH P
01797 223358 F 01797 223358
Est. 1849
Stock 18thC English furniture and works of art
Open By appointment
Services Valuations, restoration

Bygones
Contact Christine Chivers
Rope Walk Shopping Centre, Rye, East Sussex, TN31 7LD P
01797 227781
Est. 1999 *Stock size* Small
Stock 1940s–1950s china, glass
Open Mon–Sat 10am–5pm

Chapter & Verse Booksellers
Contact Mr Spencer Rogers
105 High Street, Rye, East Sussex, TN31 7JE P
01797 222692
M 07970 386905
chapterandverse@btconnect.com
Est. 1976 *Stock size* Medium
Stock Antiquarian and out-of-print books
Open Mon–Sat 9.30am–5pm closed Tues
Services Free book search

Cheyne House
Contact Keith or Sue Marshall
108 High Street, Rye, East Sussex, TN31 7JE P
01797 222612
cheynehouse@ryeantiques.fsnet.co.uk
Est. 1999 *Stock size* Small
Stock Furniture, boxes
Open Mon–Sun 10am–5.30pm closed Tues

Collectors Corner
Contact Mr. Woolveridge
2 Market Road, Rye, East Sussex, TN31 7JA P
01797 225796 F 01797 229246
collectcor@hotmail.com
Est. 1994 *Stock size* Medium
Stock General antiques
Open Mon–Sun 10am–5pm

French Treasures
Contact Terri Mcloughlin
The Landgate Arch, Tower Forge, Hilders Cliff, Rye, East Sussex, TN31 7LD P
01797 229447
frenchtreasures1@aol.com
Est. 2003 *Stock size* Small
Stock Antique white French furniture, clocks, ironwork
Open Mon–Sun 10am–5pm closed Tues
Services Valuations, restoration

Herbert G Gasson
Contact Mr T J Booth
Lion Galleries, Lion Street, Rye, East Sussex, TN31 7LB P
01797 222208
M 07703 349431
hggassonantiques@hotmail.com
Est. 1909 *Stock size* Large
Stock Early oak, country, walnut, mahogany furniture
Open Mon–Sat 10am–5pm

Hope & Glory
Contact John York
Strand Quay, Rye, East Sussex, TN31 7NX P
01797 227210
Est. 2003 *Stock size* Medium
Stock Furniture, collectables, decorative items
Open Mon–Sun 10am–5pm

Ann Lingard Ropewalk Antiques (LAPADA, BACA Award Winner 2001)
Contact Ann Lingard
18–22 Ropewalk, Rye, East Sussex, TN31 7NA P
01797 223486 F 01797 224700
ann-lingard@ropewalkantiques.freeserve.co.uk
Est. 1976 *Stock size* Large
Stock English antique pine furniture, glass, copper, wooden items, garden items, kitchen shop
Open Mon–Fri 10am–5pm Sat 10am–4.30pm closed 1–2pm

Liondor Antiques
104 High Street, Rye, East Sussex, TN31 7JN P
01797 229123
john@liontech.fsnet.co.uk
Est. 2000 *Stock size* Small
Stock George III, Regency mahogany, French furniture

Open Mon–Sun 10.30am–5pm closed Tues
Fairs Newark, Ardingly

Mint Antiques
Contact Mr Charles Booth
54 The Mint, Rye, East Sussex, TN31 7EN P
☎ 01797 224055
Ⓜ 07719 547084
Est. 1984 *Stock size* Medium
Stock Antique furniture, decorative items
Open Mon–Sun 11am–4pm

Mint Arcade
Contact John Bartholomew
71 The Mint, Rye, East Sussex, TN31 7EW P
☎ 01797 225952 Ⓕ 01797 224834
Ⓔ rameses@supanet.com
Est. 1982 *Stock size* Large
No. of dealers 5
Stock Jewellery, dolls' house furniture, hand-made military figures, chess sets, picture frames and mounts, cigarette and trade cards, framed sets of cards
Open Mon–Sat 10am–4.30pm

Needles Antique Centre
Contact Jenny King
15 Cinque Ports Street, Rye, East Sussex, TN31 7AD P
☎ 01797 225064
Ⓔ needles.antiques@btinternet.com
Ⓦ www.btinternet.com/~needles_antiques_online/
Est. 1996 *Stock size* Large
No. of dealers 5
Stock Small antiques, collectables
Open Mon–Sun 10am–5pm

Quay Antiques & Collectables
Contact Norman Spratt
6 & 7 The Strand, Rye, East Sussex, TN31 7DB P
☎ 01797 227321
Est. 1977 *Stock size* Large
No. of dealers 25
Stock General antiques and collectables
Open Sun–Mon 10.30am–5.30pm

Quayside Antiques
Contact G T D Niall
The Corn Exchange, The Strand, Rye, East Sussex, TN31 7DB P
☎ 01797 227088
Ⓔ quaysideantiques@aol.com
Est. 1997 *Stock size* Large
Stock French antique furniture
Open Mon–Sun 11am–5pm closed Tues

Rye Auction Galleries
Contact Mr A Paine
Rock Channel, Rye, East Sussex, TN31 7HL P
☎ 01797 222124 Ⓕ 01797 222126
Ⓜ 07764 225457
Ⓔ sales@ryeauctions.fsnet.co.uk
Est. 1989
Open Mon–Fri 8.30am–5pm
Sales Antique and general sales 1st and 3rd Fri of each month 9.30am, viewing Thurs 9am–5pm, trade by appointment
Frequency Bi-monthly
Catalogues Yes

Rye Old Books
Contact Miss A Coleman
7 Lion Street, Rye, East Sussex, TN31 7LB P
☎ 01797 225410 Ⓕ 01797 225410
Ⓔ ryeoldbooks@aol.com
Est. 1993 *Stock size* Medium
Stock Antiquarian and second-hand books, illustrated, fine bindings
Open Mon–Sat 10.30am–5.30pm Sun 2–5pm
Services Valuations

Soldiers of Rye
Contact Chris Viner
The Mint Arcade, 71 The Mint, Rye, East Sussex, TN31 7EW
☎ 01797 225952
Ⓔ ramases@supanet.com
Ⓦ www.ryetourism.co.uk
Est. 1987 *Stock size* Medium
Stock Toy soldiers and cigarette cards
Open Mon–Sat 10am–5pm
Services Valuations

Strand House Antiques
Contact Mr D L Rodd
The Strand, Rye, East Sussex, TN31 7DB P
☎ 01797 225008
Est. 1972 *Stock size* Large
Stock Antiques and collectables, silver, china, linen, brass, jewellery
Open Mon–Sun 10.15am–5pm
Fairs Newark, Chelsea

Strand Quay Antiques
Contact Ann Marie Sutherland
1–2 The Strand, Rye, East Sussex, TN31 7DB P
☎ 01797 226790
Ⓜ 07775 602598
Est. 1994 *Stock size* Large
No. of dealers 12
Stock Victorian–Edwardian furniture, porcelain, glass, pictures, collectables
Open Mon–Sun 10am–5pm

Wish Barn Antiques
Contact Mr Robert Wheeler or Mr Joe Dearden
Wish Street, Rye, East Sussex, TN31 7DA P
☎ 01797 226797
Est. 1993 *Stock size* Large
Stock 19thC pine and country furniture, 19thC mahogany furniture
Open Mon–Sat 10am–5pm Sun 1–5pm

SEAFORD

The Barn Collectors Market & Bookshop
Contact Mr B J Wicks
Church Lane, Seaford, East Sussex, BN25 1HL P
☎ 01323 890010
Est. 1969 *Stock size* Medium
No. of dealers 20
Stock Collectables, books, militaria, jewellery
Open Mon–Sat 9.30am–5pm

Martin D Johnson Antiques
Contact Martin Johnson
14–16 High Street, Seaford, East Sussex, BN25 1PG
☎ 01323 897777 Ⓕ 01323 897777
Ⓔ antiquesbymdjohn@aol.com
Est. 1958 *Stock size* Large
Stock General antiques
Open Mon–Fri 9am–5pm Wed Sat 9am–1pm

The Little Shop
Contact Mr C Keane
6 High Street, Seaford,

East Sussex,
BN25 1PG 🅿
☎ 01323 490742
Est. 1987 *Stock size* Large
Stock General curios, collectables, dolls' house furniture
Open Tues–Sat 9.30am–6pm

The Old House (Antiques China Glass) Ltd
Contact Mr S M Barrett
✉ **18 High Street, Seaford, East Sussex, BN25 1PG** 🅿
☎ 01323 893795
Est. 1945 *Stock size* Large
Stock General antiques, furniture, china, glass, collectables
Open Mon–Sat 9am–5pm Wed 9am–1pm
Services Valuations

SEDLESCOMBE

Bridge Garage Antiques
Contact Lynn Scoones
✉ **Main Street, The Street, Sedlescombe, Battle, East Sussex, TN33 0QB** 🅿
☎ 01424 871424/870815
Est. 2000 *Stock size* Large
No. of dealers 13
Stock General antiques
Open Mon–Sun 10am–5pm

ST LEONARDS-ON-SEA

Ascent Auction Galleries
Contact Paul Turner
✉ **Mews Road, St Leonards-on-Sea, East Sussex, TN38 0EA** 🅿
☎ 01424 420275 Ⓕ 01424 460560
Ⓔ auctions@ascent01.freeserve.co.uk
Ⓦ www.invaluables.com/ascent
Est. 1848
Open Mon–Fri 9am–5pm
Sales Antiques, fine art, collectables, jewellery
Frequency Fortnightly
Catalogues Yes

Bexhill Antique Exporters
Contact Kim Abbott
✉ **78 Norman Road, St Leonards-on-Sea, East Sussex, TN38 0EJ** 🅿
☎ 01424 225103 Ⓕ 01424 225103
Ⓜ 07702 006982
Est. 1986 *Stock size* Large
Stock Furniture for the Spanish, Italian, French market
Open Mon–Fri 10am–5pm closed Wed Sat 10am–2pm
Services Exporters

The Book Jungle
Contact Mr M Gowen
✉ **24 North Street, St Leonards-on-Sea, East Sussex, TN38 0EX** 🅿
☎ 01424 421187
Est. 1990 *Stock size* Medium
Stock Antiquarian and second-hand books
Open Mon–Sat 10am–5pm closed Wed

Bookman's Halt
Contact Mr C Linklater
✉ **127 Bohemia Road, St Leonards-on-Sea, East Sussex, TN37 6RL** 🅿
☎ 01424 421413
Est. 1980 *Stock size* Medium
Stock Low-key general stock of antiquarian and second-hand books
Open Mon–Sat 10am–1pm 2.30pm–5pm closed Wed

Filsham Farmhouse Antiques
Contact John York
✉ **111 Harley Shute Road, St Leonards-on-Sea, East Sussex, TN38 8BY** 🅿
☎ 01424 433109
Ⓔ filshamfarmhouse@talk21.com
Est. 1962 *Stock size* Large
Stock Oak and shipping furniture
Open Mon–Fri 9am–5pm

Hastings Antiques Centre
Contact Mr Robert Amstad
✉ **59–61 Norman Road, St Leonards-on-Sea, East Sussex, TN38 0EG** 🅿
☎ 01424 428561 Ⓕ 01424 428561
Est. 1982 *Stock size* Large
No. of dealers 15
Stock Continental decorative furniture, sporting items, luggage, English furniture and general antiques
Open Mon–Sat 9am–5.30pm
Services Valuations

Memory Lane
Contact Mr Davis
✉ **46 Bohemia Road, St Leonards-on-Sea, East Sussex, TN37 6RQ** 🅿
☎ 01424 442333
Est. 2000 *Stock size* Small
Stock Collectables, toys, porcelain
Open Mon Tues Thurs–Sat 10am–5pm
Fairs Kempton Park Toy Fair

Monarch Antiques
Contact Mr Marcus King
✉ **371 Bexhill Road, St Leonards-on-Sea, East Sussex, TN38 8AJ** 🅿
☎ 01424 204141 Ⓕ 01424 204142
Ⓜ 07802 217842 or 07809 027930
Ⓔ monarch.antiques@virgin.net
Ⓦ www.monarch-antiques.co.uk
Est. 1981 *Stock size* Large
Stock Victorian–Edwardian furniture, pine, bamboo, decorative items
Open Mon–Sat 8.30am–5.30pm or by appointment
Fairs Newark
Services Valuations, restoration

Shabby Chic
Contact Russell Philpot
✉ **42 Norman Road, St Leonards-on-Sea, East Sussex, TN38 0EJ** 🅿
☎ 01424 440777
Ⓜ 07967 237554 or 07956 978500
Est. 2003 *Stock size* Medium
Stock Posh junk, decorative antiques
Open Mon–Sat 10am–5pm
Services Pine stripping

STAPLECROSS

Claremont Antiques
Contact Mr A Broad
✉ **Stockwood Farm, Ellenwhorne Lane, Staplecross, East Sussex, TN32 5RR** 🅿
☎ 01580 830650
Ⓜ 07786 262843
Ⓔ antclaremont@aol.com
Ⓦ www.claremontantiques.com
Est. 1995 *Stock size* Large
Stock Pine, hardwood, painted country furniture
Open By appointment

TICEHURST

Piccadilly Rare Books (ABA, PBFA)
Contact Mr P Minet
Church Street, Ticehurst, East Sussex, TN5 7AA P
☎ 01580 201221 F 01580 200957
E minet.royalty@btinternet.com
W www.picrare.com
Est. 1968 *Stock size* Large
Stock Antiquarian and second-hand books
Open Mon–Sat 10am–5pm
Fairs Chelsea, Royal National (London)
Services Valuations

UCKFIELD

Ashdown Antiques Restoration
Contact Robert Hale
Old Forge Farm, Old Forge Lane, Horney Common, Uckfield, East Sussex, TB22 3EL P
☎ 01825 713003
E roberthale.2@yahoo.com
Est. 1975 *Stock size* Medium
Stock General antiques, period furniture
Open By appointment
Services Restoration

WADHURST

Browsers Barn
Contact Brian Langridge
New Pond Farm, High Street, Wallcrouch, Wadhurst, East Sussex, TN5 7JN P
☎ 01580 200938 F 01580 200885
M 07809 836662
E brian.langridge@talk21.com
W www.browsers-barn.co.uk
Est. 1973 *Stock size* Large
Stock General antiques and collectables
Open Tues–Sat 9am–5pm Sun 10.30am–4pm
Services Shipping

Park View Antiques
Contact Bunty Ross
High Street, Durgates, Wadhurst, East Sussex, TN5 6DE P
☎ 01892 783630 F 01892 740264
M 07974 655120
E info@parkviewantiques.co.uk
W www.parkviewantiques.co.uk
Est. 1988 *Stock size* Medium
Stock Country furniture, stripped pine, artefacts, rural items, vintage tools, period oak
Open Wed–Sun 10am–4pm and by appointment
Services Restoration

WINDMILL HILL

Popes Farm Antique Pine & Stripping
Contact Peter Thompson
Popes Farm, Windmill Hill, Hailsham, East Sussex, BN27 4RS P
☎ 01323 832159
E peter@popesfarm.co.uk
W www.popesfarm.co.uk
Est. 1973 *Stock size* Medium
Stock Pine furniture
Open Mon–Fri 8.30am–6pm Sat 8.30am–4pm
Services Pine stripping

KENT

APPLEDORE

Back 2 Wood
Contact Richard Moate
The Old Goods Shed, Station Road, Appledore, Kent, TN26 2DF
☎ 01233 758109
E pine@back2wood.com
W www.back2wood.com
Est. 1987 *Stock size* Medium
Stock Antique pine furniture
Open Mon–Fri 9am–5pm Sat 9am–4pm Sun 11am–5pm
Services Pine stripping

The Old Forge Antiques
Contact Anthony Unwin
The Old Forge, 16 The Street, Appledore, Kent, TN26 2BX P
☎ 01233 758585
Est. 2000
No. of dealers 18
Stock General antiques, china, glass, furniture, garden items
Open Mon–Sat 10am–5pm Sun 11am–5pm

ASHFORD

Hobbs Parker
Contact Alan White
Monument Way, Orbital Park, Ashford, Kent, TN24 0HB P
☎ 01233 502222 F 01233 502211
E antiques@hobbsparker.co.uk
W www.hobbsparker.co.uk
Est. 1850
Open Mon–Fri 9am–5.30pm
Sales Sales of antiques and collectables every 6 weeks, monthly household sales
Frequency Monthly
Catalogues Yes

Parkinson Auctioneers
Contact Mrs L Parkinson
46 Beaver Road, Ashford, Kent, TN23 7RP P
☎ 01233 624426 F 01233 665000
E auctions@parkinson-uk.com
W www.parkinson-uk.com
Est. 1979
Open Mon–Fri 9am–5pm
Sales General sale Mon 10am, viewing Sat 9am–1pm
Frequency Monthly
Catalogues Yes

ASHURST

The Architectural Emporium
Contact Michael Roberts
The Bald Faced Stag, Ashurst, Kent, TN3 9TE P
☎ 01892 740877
E mike@architecturalemporium.com
W www.architectural emporium.com
Est. 2000 *Stock size* Large
Stock Architectural antiques, garden statuary, sundials, fountains, fireplaces, lighting
Open Tues–Sat 9.30am–5.30pm

BARHAM

Stablegate Antiques
Contact Michael Giuntini
Barham, Kent, CT4 6QD P
☎ 01227 831639 F 01227 831639
M 07802 439777
W www.stablegateantiques.co.uk
Est. 1981 *Stock size* Large
Stock Period furniture, pictures, silver, silver plate, ceramics, mirrors
Open Mon–Sun 10am–5pm
Fairs Claridges, NEC, Harrogate

SOUTH EAST

KENT • BECKENHAM

BECKENHAM

Antiques & Collectors Market
Contact Mrs Holley
Public Hall, Beckenham, Kent, BR3 5JE
020 8660 1369
Est. 1975 *Stock size* Medium
No. of dealers 12
Stock Antiques, collectables
Open Wed 8am–2pm

Pepys Antiques
Contact Sonia Elton
9 Kelsey Park Road, Beckenham, Kent, BR3 6LH
020 8650 0994
Est. 1968 *Stock size* Large
Stock Furniture, silver, porcelain, paintings
Open Mon–Sat 10am–2pm closed Wed
Services Valuations

BELLS YEW GREEN

Big Screen Collectables
Contact Earl Brown
Unit 4, Business Units, Bayham Road, Bells Yew Green, Tunbridge Wells, Kent, TN3 9BJ
01892 750066 F 01892 750077
earl.bigscreen@virgin.net
www.bigscreen.co.uk
Est. 1996 *Stock size* Medium
Stock Movie collectables
Open Mon–Fri 10am–6pm
Fairs NEC, Milton Keynes
Services Valuations

BENENDEN

Mervyn Carey
Contact Mr M Carey
Twysden Cottage, Benenden, Cranbrook, Kent, TN17 4LD
01580 240283 F 01580 240283
Est. 1991
Sales Antiques sales at Church Hall, Church Road, Tenterden, Kent. Further details by post
Frequency Five per year
Catalogues Yes

BETHERSDEN

Stevenson Brothers (British Toymakers Guild)
Contact Mark Stevenson or Sue Russell
The Workshop, Ashford Road, Bethersden, Ashford, Kent, TN26 3AP
01233 820363 F 01233 820580
sale@stevensonbros.com
www.stevensonbros.com
Est. 1982 *Stock size* Large
Stock Antique and new rocking horses
Open Mon–Fri 9am–6pm Sat 10am–1pm
Fairs The Game Fair, Burghley & Blenheim Horse Trials, Country Living
Services Restoration of rocking horses and children's classic cars

BEXLEY

Ellenor Hospice Projects
Contact Jane Heaviside
18–20 High Street, Bexley, Kent, DA5 1AD
01322 553996
Est. 1996 *Stock size* Large
Stock General antiques. All profits raised support hospice care in North West Kent and London Borough of Bexley
Open Mon–Sat 9.30am–4.30pm Thurs 9.30am–1pm

BIDDENDEN

Biddenden Antiques
Contact Jan Moloney
10 High street, Biddenden, Ashford, Kent, TN27 8AH
01580 292977 F 01634 363568
janmoloney@blueyonder.com
Est. 2000 *Stock size* Medium
Stock Silver, china, furniture, books, textiles
Open Tues–Sat 10am–5.30pm first Sun in month 11am–4.30pm

Period Piano Company
Contact David Winston
Park Farm Oast, Hareplain Road, Biddenden, Nr Ashford, Kent, TN27 8LJ
01580 291393 F 01580 291393
M 07778 652336
periodpiano@talk21.com
www.periodpiano.com
Est. 1980 *Stock size* Medium
Stock 1760–1930 pianos, piano stools, music stands, music cabinets
Open By appointment
Services Valuations, restoration, shipping

BIGGIN HILL

Aviation Antiques & Collectables
Contact Dave Sutton
2b Kings Road, Biggin Hill, Kent, TN16 3QU
01959 576424 F 01959 546424
M 07973 885754
sutt999@aol.com
Est. 1983 *Stock size* Large
Stock Aeronautica from the last 50 years
Open Mon–Sat 9am–5pm
Fairs Shoreham Aero Jumble, Biggin Hill Airshow

BILSINGTON

The Barn at Bilsington
Contact Gabrielle de Giles
Swanton Lane, Bilsington, Ashford, Kent, TN25 7JR
01233 720917 F 01233 720156
M 07721 015263
gabrielle@gabrielledegiles.com
www.gabrielledegiles.com
Est. 1985 *Stock size* Large
Stock Antique and country furniture, architectural items
Open By appointment
Fairs Battersea Decorative Antique & Textile Fair

BIRCHINGTON

Silvesters
Contact Mr S N Hartley
Albion Chambers, 1 Albion Road, Birchington, Kent, CT7 9DN
01843 841524 F 01843 845131
Est. 1954
Stock Decorative items, furniture, Georgian, Victorian, silver, porcelain, glass
Open By appointment only
Services Valuations

BLUEWATER

Bears 'n' Bunnies
Contact Mrs K Sales
Bluewater Shopping Centre, Upper Thames Walk, Greenhithe, Kent,

DA9 9SR 🅿
☎ 01322 624997
ⓔ bearsnbunnies@btopenworld.com
ⓦ www.bearsnbunnies.com
Est. 1999 *Stock size* Large
Stock Collectable bears from leading manufacturers and artists
Open Mon–Fri 10am–9pm
Sat 9am–8pm Sun 11am–5pm

Famously Yours Ltd
Contact Lee Croxon
✉ **Upper Thames Walk, Unit U090B, Bluewater, Greenhithe, Kent, DA9 9SR** 🅿
☎ 01322 427072 ⓕ 01322 427072
ⓔ enquiries@famouslyyours.com
ⓦ www.famouslyyours.com
Est. 1996 *Stock size* Large
Stock Autographed memorabilia
Open Mon–Fri 10am–9pm
Sat 9am–8pm Sun 11am–5pm

BRASTED

David Barrington
Contact Mr D Barrington
✉ **High Street, Brasted, Kent, TN16 1JL** 🅿
☎ 01959 562537
Est. 1947 *Stock size* Medium
Stock General antiques
Open Mon–Sun 9am–5pm or by appointment

Bigwood Antiques
Contact Steven Bigwood
✉ **Roshleigh, High Street, Brasted, Kent, TN16 1JA** 🅿
☎ 01959 564458 ⓕ 01959 564457
ⓔ steve@bigwoodantiques.com
ⓦ www.bigwoodantiques.com
Est. 1996 *Stock size* Medium
Stock Furniture
Open Mon–Sat 10.30am–5pm
Sun 1.30–5pm
Services Restoration, upholstery

Cooper Fine Arts
Contact Mr Jonathan Hill-Reid
✉ **Swan House, High Street, Brasted, Kent, TN16 1JJ** 🅿
☎ 01959 565818
Est. 1980 *Stock size* Medium
Stock Paintings and furniture
Open Mon–Sat 10am–6pm
Services Framing, restoration of oils and watercolours

Courtyard Antiques
Contact Gill Whyman
✉ **High Street, Brasted, Kent, TN16 1JA** 🅿
☎ 01959 564483 ⓕ 01732 454726
ⓦ www.courtyardantiques.co.uk
Est. 1982 *Stock size* Large
Stock Silver, jewellery, ceramics, 19thC furniture including extending dining tables, chairs, Tunbridge ware, glass, copper, brass, watercolours, oils, prints, objets d'art
Open Mon–Sat 10am–5pm
Sun Bank Holidays 12.30–4.30pm
Services Furniture restoration, French polishing, releathering, upholstery

G A Hill Antiques
Contact Mrs G A Hill
✉ **5 High Street, Brasted, Kent, TN16 1JA** 🅿
☎ 01959 565500
Est. 1999 *Stock size* Medium
Stock Georgian-period furniture, decorative French mirrors and chandeliers
Open Tues–Fri 10am–5pm Sat 10am–5.30pm or by appointment

Celia Jennings
Contact Celia Jennings
✉ **High Street, Brasted, Kent, TN16 1JE** 🅿
☎ 01959 563616 ⓕ 01689 853250
ⓜ 07860 483292
ⓔ celia.jennings@virgin.net
ⓦ www.early-carving.com
Est. 1965 *Stock size* Medium
Stock Early European wood carvings, sculpture
Open Mon–Sat 10am–5.30pm

Keymer Son & Co Ltd
Contact P T Keymer
✉ **Swaylands Place, The Green, High Street, Brasted, Kent, TN16 1JY** 🅿
☎ 01959 564203 ⓕ 01959 561138
Est. 1977 *Stock size* Small
Stock Small 19thC furniture
Open Mon–Fri 9.30am–5.30pm

Roy Massingham Antiques (LAPADA)
Contact Mr R Massingham
✉ **The Coach House, High Street, Brasted, Kent, TN16 1JJ** 🅿
☎ 01959 562408 ⓕ 01959 562408
Est. 1967 *Stock size* Large
Stock 18th–19thC furniture, pictures and objects
Open By appointment any time
Services Buying 'pre-valued' antiques

Old Bakery Antiques
Contact Candy Horley
✉ **High Street, Brasted, Kent, TN16 1JA**
☎ 01959 565343
Est. 2001 *Stock size* Medium
No. of dealers 5
Stock Furniture, pictures, lighting, ceramics
Open Mon–Sun 10.30am–5pm

Southdown House Antique Galleries
Contact Mr Graham Stead
✉ **High Street, Brasted, Kent, TN16 1JE** 🅿
☎ 01959 563522
Est. 1978 *Stock size* Medium
Stock 18th, 19thC and early 20thC furniture, porcelain, glass, metalware, Chinese embroidery
Open Mon–Sat 10am–5pm
Services Restoration, shipping

Dinah Stoodley
Contact Mrs D Stoodley
✉ **High Street, Brasted, Kent, TN16 1JE** 🅿
☎ 01959 563616
Est. 1965 *Stock size* Medium
Stock Early oak, country furniture
Open Mon–Sat 9.30am–5.30pm

W W Warner Antiques (BADA)
Contact Mr Chris Jowitt
✉ **The Green, High Street, Brasted, Kent, TN16 1JL** 🅿
☎ 01959 563698 ⓕ 01959 563698
Est. 1957 *Stock size* Medium
Stock 18th–19thC porcelain, glass, pottery
Open Tues–Sat 10am–5pm

BROADSTAIRS

Bee Antiques
Contact Jane Burges
✉ **23b Albion Street,**

SOUTH EAST

KENT • BROMLEY

Broadstairs, Kent,
CT10 1LU 🅿
☎ 01843 864040
ⓔ theteddymaster@aol.com
Est. 1997 *Stock size* Medium
Stock Dolls, toys, teddybears, postcards, jewellery, collectables, musical instruments
Open Mon–Sun 11am–5pm
Services Valuations, restoration, shipping, lectures

⊞ Broadstairs Antiques and Collectables

Contact Penny Law
✉ **49 Belvedere Road, Broadstairs, Kent, CT10 1PF** 🅿
☎ 01843 861965
Est. 1992 *Stock size* Large
Stock Small collectable items, medium-sized furniture
Open Tues–Sat 10am–4.30pm

⊞ Market Fayre

Contact Margaret Sage
✉ **69 High Street, Broadstairs, Kent, CT10 1NQ** 🅿
☎ 01843 862563
Est. 1989 *Stock size* Medium
Stock Antique bric-a-brac, china, glass, dolls' houses, dolls' house furniture, limited-edition bears
Open Mon–Sat 9.30am–4.30pm

⊞ Secondhand Department

Contact Mr Alan Kemp
✉ **44 Albion Street, Broadstairs, Kent, CT10 1NE** 🅿
☎ 01843 862876 ⓕ 01843 860084
Est. 1956 *Stock size* Large
Stock Antiquarian and second-hand books
Open Mon–Sat 9am–5.30pm
Sun 10.30am–4.30pm

⊞ UK Old Postcards Ltd (PTA)

Contact Clive Baker
✉ **22 Brassey Avenue, Broadstairs, Kent, CT10 2DS** 🅿
☎ 01843 862707 ⓕ 01843 862707
ⓔ info@clivebaker.co.uk
ⓦ www.ukoldpostcards.co.uk
Est. 1990 *Stock size* Medium
Stock Vintage postcards, photographs, ephemera
Open By appointment

BROMLEY

⊞ Bears 'n' Bunnies

Contact Mrs C Sales
✉ **18 The Mall, High Street, Bromley, Kent, BR1 1TS** 🅿
☎ 020 8466 9520 ⓕ 020 8466 9570
ⓔ bearsnbunnies@btinternet.com
ⓦ www.bearsnbunnies.com
Est. 1995 *Stock size* Large
Stock Collectable bears from leading manufacturers
Open Tues–Sat 10am–5pm

⊞ Patric Capon (BADA)

Contact Patric Capon
✉ **PO Box 581, Bromley, Kent, BR1 2WX** 🅿
☎ 020 8467 5722 ⓕ 020 8295 1475
ⓜ 07831 444924
ⓔ patric.capon@saqnet.co.uk
Est. 1975 *Stock size* Medium
Stock Antique clocks, marine chronometers, barometers
Open By appointment
Fairs Olympia (Summer)
Services Valuations, restoration, shipping

⊞ Peter Morris (BNTA)

Contact Mr P Morris
✉ **1 Station Concourse, Bromley North Station, Bromley, Kent, BR1 4EQ** 🅿
☎ 020 8313 3410 ⓕ 020 8466 8502
ⓔ coins@petermorris.co.uk
ⓦ www.petermorris.co.uk
Est. 1983 *Stock size* Large
Stock Coins, medals, bank notes, antiquities
Open Mon–Fri 10am–1pm 2–6pm
Sat 9am–2pm closed Wed
Fairs BNTA Coinex
Services Mail order, 4 illustrated lists, valuations

⊞ The Studio

Contact Mr Ian Burt
✉ **2 Sundridge Parade, Plaistow Lane, Bromley, Kent, BR1 4DT** 🅿
☎ 020 8466 9010
Est. 1998 *Stock size* Large
Stock Georgian–Edwardian furniture, Art Deco, ceramics
Open Tues–Sat 11am–4.30pm or by appointment closed Thurs

CANTERBURY

⊞ Antique & Design

Contact Mr S Couchman
✉ **The Old Oast, Hollow Lane, Canterbury, Kent, CT1 3SA** 🅿
☎ 01227 762871 ⓕ 01227 780970
ⓦ www.antiqueanddesign.co.uk
Est. 1987 *Stock size* Large
Stock English and Continental pine furniture
Open Mon–Sat 9am–6pm
Sun 10am–4pm

⌂ Burgate Antiques

Contact Veronica Reeves
✉ **10c Burgate, Canterbury, Kent, CT1 2HG** 🅿
☎ 01227 4546500
ⓔ vkreeves@burgate1.fsnet.co.uk
Est. 1988 *Stock size* Medium
No. of dealers 10
Stock Jewellery, furniture, silver, porcelain, Art Deco china, militaria, medals, toy soldiers, books, prints
Open Mon–Sat 10am–5pm

⊞ Bygones Reclamation (Canterbury) Ltd

Contact Bob Thorpe
✉ **Nackington Road, Canterbury, Kent, CT4 7BA** 🅿
☎ 01227 767453 ⓕ 01227 762153
ⓜ 07802 278424
ⓔ bob@bygones.net
ⓦ www.bygones.net
Est. 1991 *Stock size* Large
Stock Victorian fireplaces, cast-iron radiators, building materials, architectural salvage
Open Mon–Sun 9am–5.30pm
Services Paint stripping, spraying, sand blasting, welding repairs

The Canterbury Auction Galleries (SOFAA)

Contact Christine Wacker
✉ **40 Station Road West, Canterbury, Kent, CT2 8AN** 🅿
☎ 01227 763337 ⓕ 01227 456770
ⓔ auctions@thecanterbury auctiongalleries.com
ⓦ www.thecanterburyauction galleries.com
Est. 1911
Open Mon–Fri 9am–1pm 2–5pm
Sales 6 specialist sales a year.

Monthly sales of Victorian and later furniture
Frequency Monthly
Catalogues Yes

Canterbury Bears
Contact Maude Blackburn
1 Builders Square, Court Hill, Littlebourne, Canterbury, Kent, CT2 1XU
01227 728630 01227 728630
maude.blackburn@btinternet.com
Est. 1979 *Stock size* Medium
Stock Antique bears
Open Mon–Fri 9am–5pm
Services Restoration

The Canterbury Book Shop (PBFA, ABA, ILAB)
Contact David Miles
37 Northgate, Canterbury, Kent, CT1 1BL
01227 464773 01227 780073
canterburybookshop@btconnect.com
Est. 1980 *Stock size* Medium
Stock Antiquarian and second-hand books
Open Mon–Sat 10am–5pm
Fairs PBFA fairs, ABA London
Services Valuations

Chaucer Bookshop (ABA)
Contact Robert Sherston-Baker
6–7 Beer Cart Lane, Canterbury, Kent, CT1 2NY
01227 453912 01227 451893
chaucerbooks@btconnect.com
www.chaucer-bookshop.co.uk
Est. 1957 *Stock size* Large
Stock Antiquarian and out-of-print books
Open Mon–Sat 10am–5pm or by appointment
Services Valuations, shipping

W J Christophers
Contact Mr W Christophers
9 The Borough, Canterbury, Kent, CT1 2DR
01227 451968
Est. 1970 *Stock size* Large
Stock General antiques, 1720s–1950s, pottery, porcelain, clocks, prints, books
Open Mon–Sat 9am–5pm

The Coach House Antique Centre
Contact Manager
2a Duck Lane, Northgate, Canterbury, Kent, CT1 2AE
01227 463117
Est. 1975 *Stock size* Large
No. of dealers 5
Stock General antiques, collectables, pressed glass
Open Mon–Sat 10am–4pm

Conquest House Antiques
Contact Mrs C Hill
17 Palace Street, Canterbury, Kent, CT1 2DZ
01227 464587 01227 451375
caroline@empire-antiques.co.uk
www.empire-antiques.co.uk
Est. 1994 *Stock size* Large
Stock Georgian–Victorian furniture, small items, paintings, chandeliers, rugs
Open Mon–Sat 10am–5pm
Services Valuations, restoration

Stuart Heggie (Photographic Collectors Club)
Contact Mr Stuart Heggie
14 The Borough, Northgate, Canterbury, Kent, CT1 2DR
01227 470422 01227 470422
07833 593344
Est. 1980 *Stock size* Medium
Stock Vintage cameras, optical toys, photographic images
Open Fri–Sat 10am–5pm
Fairs South London Photographic Fair, Photographica
Services Valuations, restoration

Housepoints
Contact Mr Robin Ross Hunt
13 The Borough, Canterbury, Kent, CT1 2DR
01227 451350
07808 784638
Est. 1984 *Stock size* Large
Stock French country pine furniture, Victorian–Edwardian pieces
Open Mon–Fri 10am–5pm Sat 9.30am–5pm
Services Restoration

Nan Leith's Brocanterbury
Contact Nan Leith
68 Stour Street, Canterbury, Kent, CT1 2NZ
01227 454519
Est. 1982 *Stock size* Medium
Stock Small collectables
Open Mon Wed Fri Sat 1–6pm or by appointment

Pattinson's Galleries
Contact Mr Alan Pattinson
25 Oaten Hill, Canterbury, Kent, CT1 3HZ
01227 780365
07710 243106
alan.pattinson@tiscali.co.uk
Est. 1972 *Stock size* Medium
Stock General antiques, pine, country furniture
Open Mon–Sat 9.30am–5pm Sun 10am–3pm
Services Valuations, polishing

The Neville Pundole Gallery
Contact Neville Pundole
8a & 9 The Friars, Canterbury, Kent, CT1 2AS
01227 453471 01227 453471
07860 278774
neville@pundole.co.uk
www.pundole.co.uk
Est. 1986 *Stock size* Large
Stock William and Walter Moorcroft and contemporary pottery, glass, textiles, sculptures, pictures
Open Mon–Sat 10am–5pm or by appointment
Services Valuations

The Victorian Fireplace
Contact John Griffith
Thanet House, 92 Broad Street, Canterbury, Kent, CT1 2LU
01227 767723
info@victorianfireplace.co.uk
www.victorian fireplace.co.uk
Est. 1986 *Stock size* Large
Stock Fireplaces
Open Tue–Sat 9am–5.30pm closed Wed

Whatever Comics
Contact Mr M Armario
2 Burgate Lane, Canterbury, Kent, CT1 2HH
01227 453226
www.whatevercomics.co.uk
Est. 1988 *Stock size* Large
Stock Die-cast cars, *Star Trek*, *Star*

SOUTH EAST

KENT • CHATHAM

Wars toys, movie-related items, sci-fi collectables, Beanie Babies, action figures
Open Mon–Sat 10am–5.30pm

World Coins
Contact David Mason
35–36 Broad Street, Canterbury, Kent, CT1 2LR
01227 768887
worldcoins@bigfoot.com
www.worldcoins.freeservers.com
Est. 1970 *Stock size* Large
Stock Coins, medals, militaria, bank notes, stamps, medallions, tokens
Open Mon–Sat 9.30am–5pm closed Thurs pm
Services Valuations, identification, quarterly catalogue

CHATHAM

The American Comic Shop
Contact Mr K Earl
1 Church Street, Chatham, Kent, ME4 4BS
01634 817410
Est. 1993 *Stock size* Large
Stock American imported comics, graphic novels, collectable toys, posters
Open Mon Wed–Fri 10am–5.30pm Tues 10am–5pm Sat 9am–5.30pm
Services Valuations, mail order, standing order

CHIDDINGSTONE

Anthony Hook Antiques
Contact Mr Anthony Hook
Chiddingstone, Kent, TN8 7AE
07860 277099
Est. 1948 *Stock size* Small
Stock Period furniture
Open By appointment only

CHILHAM

Bagham Barn Antiques
Contact Peggy Boyd
Canterbury Road, Chilham, Kent, CT4 8DU
01227 732522
07780 675201
peggyboyd@baghambarn.com
www.baghambarn.com
Est. 2002 *Stock size* Large
Stock 17th–18thC furniture, ceramics, clocks, collectables, arms, coins, notes, marine
Open Tues–Sun Bank Holiday Mon 10am–5pm
Fairs Ardingly, Detling
Services Restoration

Alan Lord Antiques
Contact Mr R Lord
Bagham Barn Antiques Centre, Canterbury Road, Chilham, Kent, CT4 8DU
01303 253674 F 01303 253674
russell@lord8829.fsnet.co.uk
Est. 1953 *Stock size* Large
Stock 18th–19thC furniture, effects
Open Tues–Sun Bank Holiday Mon 10am–5pm
Services House clearance of antiques to 1930

CHISLEHURST

CCB Aviation Books and Prints
Contact Ian Brentnall
7 Holmdale Road, Chislehurst, Kent, BR6 1BY
020 8249 5540 F 020 8249 5540
07855 350145
ccbaviation@ntlworld.com
www.ccbaviation.com
Est. 1999 *Stock size* Large
Stock WWII aviation memorabilia, books, prints
Open Mon–Sat 8am–5.30pm
Services Valuations, two catalogues per year

Chislehurst Antiques (LAPADA)
Contact Margaret Crawley
7 Royal Parade, Chislehurst, Kent, BR7 6NR
020 8467 1530
07816 894210
margaret@chislehurstantiques.co.uk
www.antiquefurnishings.co.uk
Est. 1978 *Stock size* Large
Stock 1860–1910 lighting, mirrors, 1760–1900 furniture
Open Thurs–Sat Mon 10am–5pm Sun 11am–4pm or by appointment

Michael Sim
Contact Mr M Sim
1 Royal Parade, Chislehurst, Kent, BR7 6NR
020 8467 7040 F 020 8857 1313
Est. 1983 *Stock size* Large
Stock Clocks, barometers, Georgian furniture
Open Mon–Sat 9am–6pm
Services Restoration

Wrattan Antique & Craft Mews
Contact Mrs M Brown
51–53 High Street, Chislehurst, Kent, BR7 5AF
020 8295 5933
Est. 1996 *Stock size* Large
No. of dealers 45
Stock Antiques, collectables, crafts
Open Mon–Sat 9.30am–5pm
Services Café

CLIFTONVILLE

Cottage Antiques
Contact Mr D J Emsley
172 Northdown Road, Cliftonville, Margate, Kent, CT9 2RB
01843 298214/299166
07771 542872
Est. 1990 *Stock size* Large
Stock Georgian–1930s antiques, oak, china, silver, smalls
Open Mon–Sat 10am–5pm
Services Valuations

Magpies Collectables Gifts & Antiques
Contact Joanne Savage
161 North Down Road, Cliftonville, Margate, Kent, CT9 2PA
01843 223470
Est. 2003 *Stock size* Large
Stock Collectables
Open Tues–Sat 10am–5pm

COXHEATH

Farleigh Antiques
Contact John Gordon
Homestead, 107 Heath Road, Coxheath, Kent, ME17 4PP
01622 747412
Est. 1981 *Stock size* Medium
Stock Furniture
Open Fri Sat 10am–5pm Mon–Thurs by appointment
Fairs Newark, Ardingly

CRANBROOK

Antiques at Cranbrook
Contact Nick Everard
19 High Street, Cranbrook, Kent, TN17 3EE P
☎ 01580 712173
M 07885 690913
E nick@topdrawer.uk.com
Est. 1989 *Stock size* Large
No. of dealers 10
Stock 19thC country antiques, silver, small items of furniture, ceramics, prints
Open Mon–Sat 10am–5pm

Bentleys Fine Art Auctioneers (RADS)
Contact Mr Raj Bisram
The Old Granary, Waterloo Road, Cranbrook, Kent, TN17 3JQ P
☎ 01580 715857 F 01580 715857
E cranauct@aol.com
Est. 1995
Open Mon–Fri 9am–5pm
Sat by appointment
Sales 1st Sat monthly antiques and fine art sale 11am, viewing 3 days prior 10am–6.30pm. Specialist sales throughout the year
Frequency Monthly
Catalogues Yes

Bijou Art
Contact Jan Moloney
Albert House, Stone Street, Cranbrook, Kent, TN17 3HG P
☎ 01580 712720
Est. 2004 *Stock size* Medium
Stock General antiques
Open Mon–Sat 10am–5pm

Douglas Bryan (BADA, LAPADA)
Contact Douglas Bryan
The Old Bakery, St Davids Bridge, Cranbrook, Kent, TN17 3HN P
☎ 01580 713103 F 01580 712407
M 07774 737303
Est. 1980 *Stock size* Medium
Stock 17th–18thC oak furniture, associated items
Open By appointment only
Fairs Olympia, BADA

Desmond Judd Auctioneers
Contact Jude McArdle
Hazelden Farm Oast, Marden Road, Cranbrook, Kent, TN17 2LP P
☎ 01580 714522 F 01580 715266
E desjudd@dial.pipex.com
Est. 1988
Open Mon–Fri 9 am–5pm
Sat 9.30–11.30am
Sales General antiques, collectables, held at The Weald of Kent Golf Club, Headcorn, Kent Sun 11am, viewing Sat 10am–5pm
Frequency Monthly
Catalogues Yes

The Old Tackle Box
Contact Richard Dowson
PO Box 55, High Street, Cranbrook, Kent, TN17 3ZU P
☎ 01580 713979 F 01580 713979
M 07729 278293
E tackle.box@virgin.net
Est. 1994 *Stock size* Large
Stock Antique fishing tackle
Open By appointment
Services Valuations and mail order

Swan Antiques
Contact Mr Robert White
Albert House, Stone Street, Cranbrook, Kent, TN17 3HG P
☎ 01580 712720 F 01580 712720
W www.cranbrookpc.freeserve.co.uk
Est. 1979 *Stock size* Medium
Stock Folk art, country-decorated furniture
Open Thurs–Sat 10am–1pm 2–5pm
Fairs Olympia, Decorative Fair, Battersea
Services Valuations

DARTFORD

Watling Antiques
Contact John Leitch
139 Crayford Road, Dartford, Kent, DA1 4AS P
☎ 01322 523620
Est. 1970 *Stock size* Small
Stock Shipping goods, collectables
Open Mon–Sat 9.30am–5pm
Services Valuations

Wot-a-Racket (GCS [GB, USA], TCS)
Contact Mr B Casey
250 Shepherds Lane, Dartford, Kent, DA1 2PN P
☎ 01322 220619 F 01322 220619
M 07808 593467
E wot-a-racket@talk21.com
Est. 1981 *Stock size* Large
Stock Sporting memorabilia
Open By appointment
Fairs Newark, Ardingly

DEAL

Decors
Contact Nicole Loftus-Potter
67a Beach Street, Deal, Kent, CT14 6HY P
☎ 01304 368030 F 01304 368030
Est. 1990 *Stock size* Medium
Stock 17th–19thC antiques, modern St Louis, Baccarat, non-renewable pieces, textiles
Open Mon–Sun 10am–7pm or by appointment

Delpierre Antiques
Contact Margery Borley
132 High Street, Deal, Kent, CT14 6BE P
☎ 01304 371300
M 07771 864231
Est. 1998 *Stock size* Medium
Stock Individual and specialist pieces, lighting, Art Deco, Art Nouveau, Oriental, French furniture
Open Tues–Sat 9.30am–5pm or by appointment
Services Valuations

McConnell Fine Books (ABA PBFA)
Contact Mr Nick McConnell
The Golden Hind, 85 Beach Street, Deal, Kent, CT14 6JB P
☎ 01304 375086
M 07977 573766
E mcconnellbooks@aol.com
Est. 1976 *Stock size* Medium
Stock Antiquarian and second-hand books
Open By appointment
Fairs Russell Square, Olympia

Pretty Bizarre
Contact Phillip Hartley
170 High Street, Deal, Kent, CT14 6BQ P
M 07973 794537
Est. 1991 *Stock size* Medium

SOUTH EAST

KENT • EAST PECKHAM

Stock General antiques including Art Deco
Open Fri–Sat 10am–4pm

⊞ Quill Antiques
Contact Mr A J Young
✉ **12 Alfred Square, Deal, Kent, CT14 6LR** Ⓟ
☎ 01304 375958
Est. 1969 *Stock size* Small
Stock General small antiques
Open Mon–Sat 9am–5pm

⊞ Ron's Emporium
Contact Mr Ron Blown
✉ **98 Church Lane, Sholden, Deal, Kent, CT14 9QL** Ⓟ
☎ 01304 374784 Ⓕ 01304 380294
Est. 1979 *Stock size* Large
Stock Unusual items, clocks, phone boxes, antique furniture, snooker tables, collectables
Open Mon–Sat 9.30am–5.30pm closed Thurs
Services House clearance

⊞ Serendipity
Contact Marion Short or Jayne Eschalier
✉ **125 High Street, Deal, Kent, CT14 6BB** Ⓟ
☎ 01304 369165
Ⓔ dipityantiques@aol.com
Est. 1979 *Stock size* Large
Stock Small furniture, ceramics, pictures
Open Mon–Wed Fri 10am–1pm 2–4.30pm Sat 9.30am–4.30pm
Services Restoration of pictures

⊞ Toby Jug Collectables
Contact Mrs S Pettit
✉ **South Toll House, Deal Pier, Beach Street, Deal, Kent, CT14 6HZ** Ⓟ
☎ 01304 369917
Est. 1996 *Stock size* Large
Stock Royal Doulton, discontinued Toby and character jugs, other china collectables
Open Tues–Sun 11am–5.30pm closed 1.30–2.30pm
Fairs DMG Fair Detling, The Grand Hotel Folkestone

EAST PECKHAM

⊞ Desmond and Amanda North
Contact Desmond North
✉ **The Orchard, 186 Hale Street, East Peckham, Kent, TN12 5JB** Ⓟ
☎ 01622 871353 Ⓕ 01622 872998
Est. 1971 *Stock size* Medium
Stock Persian and other Oriental rugs, carpets, runners, and cushions 1800–1939
Open Mon–Sun appointment advisable
Services Valuations, restoration

EDENBRIDGE

⊞ Lennox Cato Antiques (BADA, LAPADA, WKADA, CINOA, BACA Award Winner 2003)
Contact Lennox or Susan Cato
✉ **1 The Square, Church Street, Edenbridge, Kent, TN8 5BD** Ⓟ
☎ 01732 865988 Ⓕ 01732 865988
Ⓜ 07836 233473
Ⓔ cato@lennoxcato.com
Ⓦ www.lennoxcato.com
Est. 1979 *Stock size* Medium
Stock 18th–19thC furniture, works of art, accessories
Open Mon–Fri 9.30am–5.30pm Sat 10am–5.30pm or by appointment
Fairs Olympia, BADA, Harrogate, Arundel
Services Valuations, consultancy, restoration

⊞ Chevertons of Edenbridge Ltd (LAPADA, BADA)
Contact Angus or David Adam
✉ **71–73 High Street, Edenbridge, Kent, TN8 5AL** Ⓟ
☎ 01732 863196/863358
Ⓕ 01732 864298
Ⓜ 07711 234010
Ⓔ chevertons@msn.com
Ⓦ www.chevertons.com
Est. 1959 *Stock size* Large
Stock English and Continental antique and decorative furniture, accessories
Open Mon–Sat 9am–5.30pm
Fairs NEC, Olympia (June, Nov), BADA

⊞ Yew Tree Antiques
Contact Mr Bob Carter
✉ **Crossways, Four Elms Road, Edenbridge, Kent, TN8 6AF** Ⓟ
☎ 01732 700215
Est. 1984 *Stock size* Large
Stock Small furniture, bric-a-brac, books, linen, pictures
Open Mon 1.30–5pm Tues–Sat 10am–5pm Sun 1.30–5pm
Services House clearance

ELHAM

⊞ Elham Antiques
Contact Mr Julian Chambers
✉ **High Street, Elham, Kent, CT17 9AH** Ⓟ
☎ 01303 840085
Ⓔ elhamantiques@btopenworld.com
Est. 1989 *Stock size* Large
Stock Architectural antiques, old metal toys, pine and country furniture
Open Tues–Sat 10am–5.30pm
Fairs Sandown Park, Newark
Services Valuations

⊞ Elham Valley Book Shop (PBFA)
Contact Mr Tim Parsons
✉ **St Mary's Road, Elham, Canterbury, Kent, CT4 6TH** Ⓟ
☎ 01303 840359 Ⓕ 01303 840359
Ⓔ books@elham-valley.demon.co.uk or etchinghill@hotmail.com
Ⓦ www.elham-valley.demon.co.uk
Est. 1992 *Stock size* Large
Stock Rare and second-hand books including those on art, travel, topography, modern first editions, illustrated, natural history, private press a speciality
Open Tues Thurs 2–5pm Fri 11.30am–4.30pm Sat 11am–5pm Sun noon–4pm
Services Valuations

⊞ Old Bank Antiques
Contact Mrs J Swinbourne
✉ **Bank Buildings, High Street, Elham, Kent, CT4 6TD** Ⓟ
☎ 01303 840140
Est. 2001 *Stock size* Medium
Stock General antiques, furniture, ceramics
Open Tues–Sat 10am–5.30pm Sun 11am–4.30pm

ERIDGE GREEN

⊞ Kentdale Antiques
Contact Mr Bigwood
✉ **Forge Road, Eridge Green, Eridge Green,**

Tunbridge Wells, Kent,
TN3 9LJ P
☎ 01892 863840
ⓔ kentdale.antiques@ukgateway.net
Est. 1995 *Stock size* Medium
Stock Victoriana, furniture
Open By appointment only
Services Restoration

ERITH

Belmont Jewellers
Contact Mr S J Girt
✉ 5 Belmont Road,
Northumberland Heath,
Erith, Kent,
DA8 1JY P
☎ 01322 339646
Est. 1986 *Stock size* Small
Stock Jewellery, furniture, pictures, silver, silver plate
Open Mon–Sat 9am–5pm
Fairs Ardingly
Services Valuations, jewellery repairs

FARNINGHAM

P T Beasley
Contact Mrs R Beasley
✉ Forge Yard, High Street,
Farningham, Kent,
DA4 0DB P
☎ 01322 862453
Est. 1964 *Stock size* Large
Stock 17th–19thC furniture, small items, brass, pewter
Open Mon–Sun 9am–5pm or by appointment

Farningham Pine
Contact Mr P Dzierzek
✉ The Old Bull Stores,
Farningham, Kent,
DA4 0DG P
☎ 01322 863230 ⓕ 01322 863168
Est. 1987 *Stock size* Large
Stock Pine furniture
Open Mon–Sat 10am–5pm
Sun 11am–3pm closed Wed

FAVERSHAM

Ecomerchant Ltd
Contact Paul Whitlock
or Joe Hilton
✉ The Old Filling Station,
Head Hill Road, Goodnestone,
Faversham, Kent,
ME13 9BL P
☎ 01795 530130 ⓕ 01795 530430
ⓔ sales@ecomerchant.co.uk
ⓦ www.ecomerchant.co.uk
Est. 1998 *Stock size* Medium
Stock Architectural antiques, floor boards, stone, bricks, wood/oak beams, conservation building materials
Open Mon–Fri 8am–5pm
Sat 9am–4pm

Faversham Antiques and Collectables
Contact Mr Ralph Lane
✉ 7 Court Street,
Faversham, Kent,
ME13 7AN P
☎ 01795 591471
Est. 1997 *Stock size* Large
Stock General furniture, collectables, blue and white china, Osborne plaques, jewellery, prints, books
Open Mon–Sat 10am–5pm
Fairs Ardingly

Squires Antiques
Contact Ann Squires
✉ 3 Jacob Yard, Preston Street,
Faversham, Kent,
ME13 8NY P
☎ 01795 531503 ⓕ 01795 591600
Est. 1984 *Stock size* Large
Stock General antiques
Open Mon Tues Fri Sat 10am–5pm

FOLKESTONE

Richard Amos Antiques
Contact Richard Amos
✉ 1 Darlinghurst Road, Cheriton,
Folkestone, Kent, CT19 4PL
☎ 01303 274024
Est. 1999 *Stock size* Small
Stock General antiques
Open By appointment

Hogben Auctioneers & Valuers Ltd
Contact Mr M Hogben
✉ Unit C, Highfields Industrial Estate, Warren Road,
Folkestone, Kent,
CT19 6DD P
☎ 01303 246810 ⓕ 01303 246256
ⓔ hogben.auctioneers@btconnect.com
ⓦ www.hogbenauctioneers.com
Est. 1986
Open Mon–Fri 9am–5pm
Sales 3 weekly. Sat fine art and collectables, viewing Thurs 10am–6pm Fri 10am–8pm. Specialist jewellery, ephemera, books and Art Deco sales throughout the year
Catalogues Yes

Lawton's Antiques
Contact Ian Lawton
✉ 26 Canterbury Road,
Folkestone,
Kent,
CT19 5NG P
☎ 01303 246418
Ⓜ 07833 946626
Est. 1987 *Stock size* Medium
Stock General antiques
Open Mon–Sat 9am–6pm
Services Valuations

Marrin's Bookshop (ABA, ILAB, PBFA)
Contact Patrick Marrin
or John Powell
✉ 149 Sandgate Road,
Folkestone,
Kent,
CT20 2DA P
☎ 01303 253016 ⓕ 01303 850956
Ⓜ 07765 663808 or 07905 122182
ⓔ sales@marrinbook.co.uk or marrinbook@clara.co.uk
ⓦ www.marrinbook.com, www.marrinbook.co.uk
Est. 1947 *Stock size* Medium
Stock General antiquarian and second-hand books, specializing in Kent
Open Tues–Sat 9.30am–5.30pm
Fairs PBFA London Book Fair, Russell Hotel – monthly, major events in the UK and overseas
Services Valuations

Second Treasures
Contact Allen Fairbairn
✉ 69 Tontine Street,
Folkestone, Kent,
CT20 1JB P
☎ 01303 223726 ⓕ 01303 246265
Est. 1994 *Stock size* Large
Stock General antiques
Open Mon–Fri 9am–5pm
Services Clock repairs, restoration

FOUR ELMS

Treasures
Contact Christine Evans
✉ Bough Beech Road,
Four Elms, Kent,
TN8 6NE P
☎ 01732 700363
Est. 1974 *Stock size* Large
No. of dealers 8
Stock Antiques, collectables, bric-a-brac
Open Tue–Sat 10am–5.30pm (winter 5pm) Sun 2–5pm

SOUTH EAST

KENT • GOUDHURST

GOUDHURST

Mill House Antiques
Contact Brad Russell
Unit 3, Fountain House, High Street, Goudhurst, Kent, TN17 1AL P
☎ 01580 212476
Est. 1991 *Stock size* Large
Stock Pine and country antiques, complementary items
Open Tues–Sat 10am–5pm
Services Valuations

HADLOW

Lime Tree House Antiques
Contact Wendy Thomas
Lime Tree House, 2 High Street, Hadlow, Kent, TN11 0EE P
☎ 01732 852002 F 01732 852002
Est. 1987 *Stock size* Large
Stock Oak, mahogany and decorative furniture
Open Tues–Sun 10am–4pm
Fairs Newark, Ardingly
Services Valuations, restoration

HAMSTREET

Woodville Antiques
Contact Andrew MacBean
The Street, Hamstreet, Ashford, Kent, TN26 2HG P
☎ 01233 732981 F 01233 732981
M 07932 5885979
E woodvilleantique@yahoo.co.uk
Est. 1988 *Stock size* Medium
Stock Antique and collectable tools, glass, furniture
Open Tues–Sun 10am–5.30pm
Services Valuations

HEADCORN

Headcorn Antiques
Contact Mr or Mrs Smith
61 High Street, Headcorn, Ashford, Kent, TN27 9QA P
☎ 01622 890050 F 01622 890050
Est. 1994 *Stock size* Medium
Stock General antiques, Continental pine, mahogany, oak
Open Mon–Sat 10am–5pm Sun 11am–4pm

HERNE BAY

Brigsy's Antique Centre
Contact W. Briggs
75 High Street, Herne Bay, Kent, CT6 5LQ
☎ 01227 370621
Est. 1998 *Stock size* Large
Stock General antiques
Open Mon–Sat 10am–4pm
Fairs Newark, Swinderby

HIGH HALDEN

High Halden Antiques
Contact Mr Jennings
Ashford Road, High Halden, Tenterden, Kent, TN26 3BY P
☎ 01233 850195
Est. 40 years *Stock size* Medium
Stock Victorian–Edwardian furniture, mahogany
Open Tues–Sat 10am–5pm
Services Valuations, restoration

Rother Reclamation (SALVO)
Contact Mrs Symonds
The Old Tile Centre, Ashford Road, High Halden, Tenterden, Kent, TN26 3BP P
☎ 01233 850075 F 01233 850275
M 07889 387136
Est. 1960 *Stock size* Medium
Stock Renovation materials, bricks, tiles, oak beams, flooring, doors, slate, stone, railway sleepers, garden statuary, pine furniture, sanitary ware etc
Open Mon–Sat 8am–5pm
Services Delivery (south east) & special requests

HYTHE

Malthouse Arcade
Contact Mr or Mrs Maxtone Graham
Malthouse Hill, Hythe, Kent, CT21 5BW P
☎ 01303 260103
Est. 1974 *Stock size* Large
No. of dealers 24 on two floors
Stock General antiques
Open Fri Sat Bank Holiday Mon 9.30am–5.30pm
Services Café

Owlets
Contact Mrs A Maurice
99 High Street, Hythe, Kent, CT21 5JH P
☎ 01303 230333
W www.owlets.co.uk, www.millenniumjewellers.co.uk or www.kentjewellers.co.uk
Est. 1955 *Stock size* Large
Stock Antique and estate jewellery, silver
Open Mon–Sat 9.30am–5pm closed Wed
Services Valuations, restoration, jewellery repairs

Trouvailles
Contact Mr Alan Fairbairn
18 High Street, Hythe, Kent, CT14 5AT P
☎ 01303 267801
Est. 1995 *Stock size* Large
Stock General antiques, clocks, collectables
Open Mon–Sat 10am–4.30pm closed Wed
Services Clock repair and restoration

LAMBERHURST

Forstal Farm Antique Workshops
Contact Mr D Johnstone
Forstal Farm, Goudhurst Road, Lamberhurst, Kent, TN3 8AG P
☎ 01892 891189 F 01892 891189
W www.forstalantiques.com
Est. 1997 *Stock size* Large
Stock Hand-painted beds and armoires, general bedroom furniture
Open Mon–Sat 10am–5pm or by appointment

LENHAM

Lenham Antiques
Contact Louise Kendall
13 The Square, Lenham, Kent, ME17 2PQ P
☎ 01622 858050
M 07710 434658
Est. 1998 *Stock size* Small
Stock Small furniture, collectables
Open Thurs Fri Sat 9am–4pm

LITTLEBOURNE

Good Golly Bear Dolly
Contact Kerstin Blackburn
1 Builders Square, Court Hill, Littlebourne, Canterbury, Kent, CT2 1XU P

☎ 01227 728028 Ⓕ 01227 710118
Ⓔ kerstin.blackburn@btinternet.com
Ⓦ www.goodgollybeardolly.com
Est. 2002 *Stock size* Small
Stock Antique bears, dolls, rabbits, collectables, books
Open Mon–Fri 9am–5pm
Services Restoration

Jimmy Warren
Contact Mr J Warren
✉ **Cedar Lodge, 28 The Hill, Littlebourne, Canterbury, Kent, CT3 1TA** Ⓟ
☎ 01227 721510 Ⓕ 01227 722431
Ⓔ enquiries@jimmywarren.co.uk
Ⓦ www.jimmywarren.co.uk
Est. 1973 *Stock size* Large
Stock Unusual antiques, garden ornaments
Open Mon–Sun 10am–5pm
Services Valuations

LOOSE

Loose Valley Antiques
Contact Mrs V Gibbons
✉ **Scriba House, Loose Road, Loose, Maidstone, Kent, ME15 0AA** Ⓟ
☎ 01622 743950
Est. 1998 *Stock size* Large
Stock Oak furniture, collectables, pine
Open Tues–Sat 10am–5pm Sun 10am–4pm
Services Free local delivery

LYMINGE

Valley Auctions
Contact Mr E T Hall
✉ **Claygate, Brady Road, Lyminge, Folkestone, Kent, CT18 8EU** Ⓟ
☎ 01303 862134 Ⓕ 01303 862134
Est. 1978
Open Mon–Fri 9am–5pm
Sales General antiques sale Sun 9.30am, viewing Sat 1–6pm
Frequency Monthly
Catalogues Yes

MAIDSTONE

Ad-Age Antique Advertising
Contact Mike Standen
✉ **Maidstone, Kent, ME16 8JN** Ⓟ
☎ 01622 670595
Est. 1972 *Stock size* Medium
Stock Advertising signs, enamel, tinplate, packaging, tobacco, confectionery collectables
Open By appointment

Cobnar Books (PBFA)
Contact Larry Icott
✉ **567 Red Hill, Wateringbury, Maidstone, Kent, ME18 5BE**
☎ 01622 813230
Ⓔ books@cobnar.demon.co.uk
Ⓦ www.cobnarbooks.com
Est. 1994
Stock Antiquarian and English topography books
Open Mail order only
Fairs Royal National Hotel Book Fair
Services Valuations, books on the Internet

Gem Antiques
Contact Mark Rackham
✉ **10 Gabriels Hill, Maidstone, Kent, ME15 6JG** Ⓟ
☎ 01622 763344
Ⓦ www.gemantiques.com
Est. 1994 *Stock size* Medium
Stock Jewellery, pocket watches, objets d'art
Open Mon–Sat 9.30am–5pm
Services Restoration

Stable Antiques
Contact Jan Byhurst
✉ **1a Church Street, Maidstone, Kent, ME14 1QS** Ⓟ
☎ 01622 769697
Est. 2003 *Stock size* Large
Stock Collectables, Winstanley cats
Open Mon–Sat 10am–5pm
Services Valuations – donation to charity on Thurs

Sutton Valence Antiques (LAPADA)
Contact Nigel Mullarkey or Tony Foster
✉ **Unit 4, Haslemere Parkwood Estate, Sutton Road, Maidstone, Kent, ME15 9NL** Ⓟ
☎ 01622 675332 Ⓕ 01622 692593
Ⓔ svantiques@aol.com
Ⓦ www.svantiques.co.uk
Est. 1986 *Stock size* Large
Stock 18th–19thC furniture, clocks, china, glass
Open Mon–Sat 9am–5.30pm
Services Valuations, restoration, shipping

Whatever Comics
Contact Mr M Armario
✉ **5 Middle Row, High Street, Maidstone, Kent, ME14 1TF**
☎ 01622 681041
Ⓦ www.whatevercomics.co.uk
Est. 1988 *Stock size* Medium
Stock Second-hand comics, *Star Trek* and *Star Wars* toys, movie-related items, sci-fi collectables, Beanie Babies, action figures
Open Mon–Sat 10am–5.30pm

MARGATE

Heritage Antiques
Contact Brian Selman
✉ **105 Canterbury Road, Margate, Kent, CT9 5AX**
☎ 01843 209595
Est. 2000 *Stock size* Medium
Stock Antique furniture, paintings, silver, bronzes, glass
Open Thur–Sat 10am–4pm
Services Valuations, informal lectures

NEWENDEN

Ingrid Nilson (LAPADA)
Contact Ingrid Nilson
✉ **Newenden, Kent, TN18** Ⓟ
☎ 01797 252030 Ⓕ 01797 252030
Ⓜ 07970 110370
Ⓔ ingrid@ingridnilson.com
Ⓦ www.ingridnilson.com
Est. 1989 *Stock size* Small
Stock Decorative antique prints
Open By appointment only
Fairs Claridge's Antiques Fair London, Northern Antiques Fair Harrogate
Services Framing

NORTHFLEET

Northfleet Hill Antiques
Contact Martine Kilby
✉ **36 The Hill, Northfleet, Gravesend, Kent, DA11 9EX** Ⓟ
☎ 01474 321521 Ⓕ 01474 350921
Ⓜ 07770 993906
Est. 1986 *Stock size* Medium
Stock Furniture, collectables, glass, china
Open Mon Tues Fri 10am–5pm
Fairs Mainwarings Chelsea Antiques Fair
Services Upholstery

SOUTH EAST
KENT • ORPINGTON

ORPINGTON

Curioquest
Contact Mrs B Harris
19 Crescent Way, Orpington, Kent, BR6 9LS
01689 857711
ca@curioquest.com
www.curioquest.com
Est. 1998 *Stock size* Large
Stock Victorian–modern collectables, china, glass, small items of furniture
Open Mon–Sat 10am–5pm closed Thurs
Services Valuations, auction sale agents

In Retrospect
Contact David Holman
107–109 High Street, Orpington, Kent, BR6 0LG
01689 835900 01689 891021
info@retro.fsworld.co.uk
www.awards-uk.com
Est. 1996 *Stock size* Large
Stock Antiques, collectables
Open Mon–Fri 10am–5pm Sat 9.30am–5pm closed Thur

Priory Antiques & Collectables
Contact Mahshid Travers-Spencer
89 High Street, Orpington, Kent, BR6 0LF
01689 870511 01689 824511
07785 705750
lesspencer7@hotmail.com
Est. 2003 *Stock size* Medium
Stock General antiques and collectables
Open Tues–Fri 10am–6pm Sat 9.30am–5.30pm

OTFORD

Ellenor Hospice Care Shop
Contact Mrs Gill Saunderson
11a High Street, Otford, Kent, TN14 5PG
01959 524322
Est. 1995 *Stock size* Medium
Stock General antiques
Open Mon–Sat 10am–5pm April–October 10am–4pm November–March
Services Tea rooms

Mandarin Gallery
Contact Mr Joseph Liu
The Mill Pond, 16 High Street, Otford, Sevenoaks, Kent, TN14 5PQ
01959 522778 01732 457399
Est. 1984 *Stock size* Medium
Stock Mainly Chinese Oriental furniture, ivory, wood carvings, silk, paintings
Open Tues–Sat 10am–5pm
Services Restoration

Otford Antique and Collectors Centre
Contact Mr David Lowrie
26–28 High Street, Otford, Sevenoaks, Kent, TN14 5PQ
01959 522025 01959 525858
info@otfordantiques.co.uk
www.otfordantiques.co.uk
Est. 1997 *Stock size* Large
No. of dealers 34
Stock General antiques, collectables
Open Mon–Sat 10am–5pm Sun 11am–4pm
Services Restoration, valuations, upholstery

John M Peyto & Co Ltd
Contact John Peyto
The Coach House, Rowdow Lane, Otford Hills, Sevenoaks, Kent, TN15 6XN
01959 524022 01959 522100
Est. 1992
Open Mon–Fri 7.30am–6pm
Sales General antiques 1st and 3rd Sat 10am, viewing Fri 8am–6pm
Frequency Monthly
Catalogues Yes

PETTS WOOD

The Beehive
Contact Mr Johnson
22 Station Square, Petts Wood, Kent, BR5 1NA
01689 890675
Est. 1996 *Stock size* Medium
No. of dealers 50
Stock Antiques and collectables
Open Mon–Sat 9.30am–5pm

Memory Lane
Contact Mr R K Ludlam
105 Queensway, Petts Wood, Kent, BR5 1DG
01689 826832
Est. 1972 *Stock size* Large
Stock General antiques
Open Mon–Sat 9.30am–5.30pm
Fairs Ardingly
Services House clearance

PLUCKLEY

Catchpole and Rye (SALVO)
Contact Diana Rabjohns or Tony O'Donnel
Saracen's Dairy, Pluckley Road, Pluckley, Kent, TN27 0SA
01233 840840 01233 840444
info@crye.co.uk
www.crye.co.uk
Est. 1991 *Stock size* Large
Stock Baths, basins, cisterns, taps, sanitary ware
Open Mon–Fri 9am–5pm Sat by appointment
Services Design service

RAINHAM

The Bookmark
Contact Mr G Harrison
Unit 15c, Rainham Shopping Centre, Rainham, Gillingham, Kent, ME8 7HW
01634 365987
Est. 1992 *Stock size* Large
Stock Antiquarian, second-hand, general books, fiction, non-fiction
Open Mon–Sat 9.30am–5.30pm

RAMSGATE

B & D Collectors' Toys
Contact Mr R Smith
332 Margate Road, Ramsgate, Kent, CT12 6SQ
01843 589606 01843 589606
www.banddcollectorstoys.com
Est. 1991 *Stock size* Large
Stock Old and obsolete toys, Dinky, Corgi, new collectable toys, *Star Wars*
Open Mon–Thur 9.30am–5.30pm Wed 9.30am–1pm Fri Sat 9.30am–6pm
Services Valuations, mail order

Granny's Attic
Contact Miss Penny Warn
2 Addington Street, Ramsgate, Kent,

CT11 9JL 🅿
☎ 01843 588955/596288
Ⓜ 07773 155339
Ⓔ grannysattic@amserve.com
Est. 1986 *Stock size* Large
Stock Victorian, Edwardian, pre-1930s furniture, china, silver, glass, mirrors, pictures etc
Open Mon–Wed Fri–Sat 10am–5pm closed 1–2pm
Services Free local delivery, delivery in UK and abroad can be arranged

⊞ Thanet Antiques & Marine Paraphernalia Ltd
Contact Mr Roy Fomison
✉ **Archway 8, Military Road, Ramsgate, Kent, CT11 9LG** 🅿
☎ 01843 597336 Ⓕ 01843 597336
Ⓦ www.thanetantiques.co.uk
Est. 1983 *Stock size* Large
Stock General antiques, furniture, collectables, fireplaces
Open Mon–Sun 9am–5pm

⊞ Yesteryear Railwayana
Contact Patrick or Mary Mullen
✉ **Stablings Cottage, Goodwin Road, Ramsgate, Kent, CT11 0JJ**
☎ 01843 587283 Ⓕ 01843 587283
Ⓔ mullen@yesrail.com
Ⓦ www.yesrail.com
Est. 1980 *Stock size* Medium
Stock Out-of-print and scarce books, illustrations, documentation and printed ephemera, both important and trivial, relating to some aspect of world railway history
Open Mail order only
Services Catalogue monthly

ROCHESTER

⊞ Baggins Book Bazaar
Contact Mr Godfrey George
✉ **19 High Street, Rochester, Kent, ME1 1PY** 🅿
☎ 01634 811651 Ⓕ 01634 840591
Ⓔ godfreygeorge@btinternet.com
Ⓦ www.bagginsbooks.co.uk
Est. 1986 *Stock size* Large
Stock Antiquarian, rare, second-hand books
Open Mon–Sun 10am–6pm
Services Book search, ordering service

⊞ Cathedral Antiques
Contact Jeanette Dickson
✉ **83 High Street, Rochester, Kent, ME1 1LX** 🅿
☎ 01634 842735
Ⓜ 07944 870214
Est. 1974 *Stock size* Large
Stock 17thC–1910 furniture
Open Mon–Sat 9.30am–5pm
Services Valuations for probate and insurance

⊞ City Antiques Ltd
Contact Mr Brian Ware
✉ **78 High Street, Rochester, Kent, ME1 1JY** 🅿
☎ 01634 841278
Ⓜ 07855 388620
Ⓔ wareclockmad@aol.com
Est. 1997 *Stock size* Large
Stock Clocks, barometers, Georgian, Victorian, Edwardian furniture
Open Mon–Sat 10am–5pm closed some Wed
Services Clock and barometer repair, furniture restoration

⊞ Cottage Style Antiques
Contact Mr W Miskimmin
✉ **24 Bill Street Road, Frindsbury, Rochester, Kent, ME2 4RB** 🅿
☎ 01634 717623
Est. 1982 *Stock size* Large
Stock Collectables, architectural salvage, fireplaces, interesting pieces
Open Mon–Sat 9.30am–5.30pm
Services Restoration, repairs

⊞ Dragonlee Collectables
Contact Janet Davies
✉ **Memories, 128 High Street, Rochester, Kent, ME1 1JT** 🅿
☎ 01622 729502
Ⓜ 07761 400128
Est. 1995 *Stock size* Medium
Stock Noritake, ceramic collectables, furniture
Open Mon–Sat 9am–5pm
Fairs Detling

⊞ Fieldstaff Antiques
Contact Jane Staff or Jim Field
✉ **30 High Street, Rochester, Kent, ME1 1LD** 🅿
☎ 01634 880037
Ⓔ fieldstaffantiques@supanet.com
Est. 1996 *Stock size* Large
Stock Antiques, collectables
Open Mon–Sat 10am–5pm
Services House clearance

⊞ Kaizen International Ltd
Contact Jason Hunt or Jo Olivares
✉ **88 The High Street, Rochester, Kent, ME1 1JT** 🅿
☎ 01634 814132 Ⓕ 01634 827237
Est. 1997 *Stock size* Large
Stock Jewellery, silver, furniture, wine-related items
Open Mon–Sat 10am–5.30pm
Services Valuations

Medway Auctions
Contact Mr Bill Lucas
✉ **23 High Street, Rochester, Kent, ME1 1LN** 🅿
☎ 01634 847444 Ⓕ 01634 880555
Ⓔ medauc@dircon.co.uk
Ⓦ www.medwayauctions.co.uk
Est. 1997
Open Mon–Sat 10am–4pm
Sales Two sales a month of small furniture, collectables and general effects. Spring and autumn collectors' auctions plus two or three postcard and ephemera auctions a year. Auction intake and valuation day Fri (except Good Friday) 10.30am–3pm. Contact auction office for details and viewing times
Catalogues By subscription (e-mail or post or from office Friday prior to sale)

Memories
Contact Mrs M Kilby
✉ **128 High Street, Rochester, Kent, ME1 1JT** 🅿
☎ 01634 811044
Est. 1985 *Stock size* Large
No. of dealers 12
Stock Small furniture, china, general antiques
Open Mon–Fri 9.30am–5pm Sat 9am–5pm Sun 11am–4.30pm

ROLVENDEN

⊞ Cindy's Antiques
Contact Cindy Knowles
✉ **Trafalgar Barn, Regent Street, Rolvenden, Cranbrook, Kent, TN17 4PB** 🅿

SOUTH EAST

KENT • SANDGATE

☎ 01580 240457
Ⓜ 07753 836305
Ⓔ cindysantiques@hotmail.com
Est. 2000 *Stock size* Large
Stock Furniture, bric-a-brac
Open Tues–Sat 10am–4pm
Fairs Ardingly

⊞ Falstaff Antiques
Contact C M Booth
✉ **63–67 High Street, Rolvenden, Kent, TN17 4LP** Ⓟ
☎ 01580 241234
Est. 1964 *Stock size* Medium
Stock General antiques and reproductions
Open Mon–Sat 10am–6pm

⊞ J D and R M Walters
Contact Mr John Walters
✉ **10 Regent Street, Rolvenden, Kent, TN17 4PE** Ⓟ
☎ 01580 241563
Est. 1979 *Stock size* Medium
Stock 18th–19thC furniture
Open Mon–Fri 8am–6pm Sat 11am–4.30pm or by appointment
Services Restoration

SANDGATE

⊞ Christopher Buck Antiques (BADA)
Contact Christopher Buck
✉ **56–60 Sandgate High Street, Sandgate, Folkestone, Kent, CT20 3AP** Ⓟ
☎ 01303 221229 Ⓕ 01303 221229
Ⓜ 07836 551515
Ⓔ cb@christopherbuck.co.uk
Est. 1983
Stock 18thC and early 19thC English furniture and associated items
Open Mon–Sat 9.30am–5pm
Fairs Olympia, BADA
Services Valuations, restoration

⊞ Emporium Antiques
Contact Mr West
✉ **31–33 Sandgate High Street, Sandgate, Folkestone, Kent, CT20 3AH** Ⓟ
☎ 01303 244430
Ⓜ 07860 149387
Est. 1984 *Stock size* Medium
Stock Antique and decorative furniture
Open By appointment

⊞ Finch Antiques
Contact Mr Finch
✉ **40 Sandgate High Street, Sandgate, Folkestone, Kent, CT20 3AP** Ⓟ
☎ 01303 240725
Est. 1980 *Stock size* Medium
Stock Early 18thC–1930s furniture
Open Mon–Sat 9.30am–5.30pm Sun 10.30am–4pm
Services Restoration

⊞ Michael W Fitch Antiques (LAPADA)
Contact Mr Michael Fitch
✉ **99, 97, 95 Sandgate High Street, Sandgate, Kent, CT20 3BY** Ⓟ
☎ 01303 249600 Ⓕ 01303 249600
Ⓦ www.michaelfitchantiques.co.uk
Est. 1977 *Stock size* Large
Stock 18th–19thC furniture, furnishings, clocks
Open Mon–Sat 10am–5.30pm
Services Valuations

⊞ Freeman and Lloyd Antiques (BADA, LAPADA)
Contact Mr K Freeman or Mr R Lloyd
✉ **44 Sandgate High Street, Sandgate, Folkestone, Kent, CT20 3AP** Ⓟ
☎ 01303 248986 Ⓕ 01303 241353
Ⓜ 07860 100073
Ⓔ enquiries@freemanandlloyd.com
Ⓦ www.freemanandlloyd.com
Est. 1968 *Stock size* Large
Stock 18th–early 19thC furniture, accessories, pictures, clocks, bronzes
Open Tues Thurs–Sat 10am–5pm
Fairs Olympia (February, June, November), BADA (March)
Services Valuations

⊞ David Gilbert Antiques
Contact Mr D Gilbert
✉ **30 Sandgate High Street, Sandgate, Folkestone, Kent, CT20 3AP** Ⓟ
☎ 01303 850491
Est. 1984 *Stock size* Large
Stock Edwardian–Victorian Arts and Crafts
Open Mon–Sat 9.30am–4.30pm or by appointment
Services Delivery

⊞ Gabrielle de Giles
Contact Gabrielle de Giles
✉ **21 Sandgate High Street, Sandgate, Folkestone, Kent, CT20 3BD** Ⓟ
☎ 01303 255600 Ⓕ 01233 720156
Ⓜ 07721 015263
Ⓔ gabrielle@gabrielledegiles.com
Ⓦ www.gabrielledegiles.com
Est. 2002 *Stock size* Medium
Stock Antique and country furniture, architectural items
Open Tue–Sat 10.30am–5.30pm or by appointment
Fairs Battersea Decorative Antique & Textile Fair, Antiques & Audacity, Arundel

⊞ Jonathan Greenwall Antiques (LAPADA)
Contact Mr J Greenwall
✉ **61–63 Sandgate High Street, Sandgate, Folkestone, Kent, CT20 3AH** Ⓟ
☎ 01303 248987 Ⓕ 01303 248987
Ⓜ 07799 133700
Est. 1969 *Stock size* Large
Stock Jewellery, clocks, watches, furniture, pictures, prints, glass
Open Mon–Sat 9.30am–5pm Sun Bank Holidays by appointment
Services Valuations, watch, clock and jewellery repair

⊞ David M Lancefield Antiques (LAPADA)
Contact David Lancefield
✉ **53 Sandgate High Street, Sandgate, Folkestone, Kent, CT 20 3AH** Ⓟ
☎ 01303 850149 Ⓕ 01303 850149
Ⓔ david@antiquedirect.freeserve.co.uk
Ⓦ www.davidmlancefield.co.uk
Est. 1976 *Stock size* Large
Stock General antiques
Open Mon–Sat 10am–6pm Sun Bank Holidays 11am–5pm
Services Valuations, restoration

⊞ Sandgate Passage
Contact Mr John Rendle
✉ **82 Sandgate High Street, Sandgate, Folkestone, Kent, CT20 3BX** Ⓟ
☎ 01303 850973
Est. 1987 *Stock size* Medium
Stock Old postcards, prints, books
Open Mon–Sat 10.30am–4pm
Fairs DMG Detling, York, Twickenham, Guildford, Woking
Services Valuations

SANDWICH

⊞ All Our Yesterdays
Contact Sandy Baker
✉ **3 Cattle Market,**

Sandwich, Kent,
CT13 9AE 🅿
☎ 01304 614756
ⓔ chgramophones@aol.com
Est. 1994 *Stock size* Medium
Stock General antiques, collectables, unusual items
Open Mon–Sat 10.30am–2.30pm or by appointment closed Wed
Services Gramophone repairs

Chris Baker Gramophones (CLPGS)
Contact Mr Chris Baker
✉ **3 Cattle Market, Sandwich, Kent, CT13 9AE** 🅿
☎ 01304 614756/375767
ⓕ 01304 614696
ⓜ 07808 831462
ⓔ chgramophones@aol.com
Est. 1996 *Stock size* Large
Stock Mechanical music
Open Mon–Sat 10.30am–2.30pm closed Wed
Services Repairs, stock list available on request

SEAL

Campbell and Archard (BADA)
Contact Paul Archard
✉ **Lychgate House, Church Street, Seal, Kent, TN15 0AR** 🅿
☎ 01732 761153
ⓔ campbellarchard@btclick.com
Est. 1970 *Stock size* Large
Stock Austro-Hungarian 1790–1850 clocks and regulators, English regulators and bracket clocks
Open By appointment only
Fairs Olympia, Duke of York's
Services Restoration

SEVENOAKS

Neill Robinson Blaxill (LAPADA)
Contact Neill Blaxill
✉ **21 St Johns Hill, Sevenoaks, Kent, TN13 3NX** 🅿
☎ 01732 454179
ⓦ www.hyperiondials.co.uk
Est. 2003 *Stock size* Medium
Stock Garden antiques, decorative items, clocks, barometers
Open Mon–Sat 10am–6pm or by appointment
Fairs Hampton Court
Services Clock restoration

Bonhams
✉ **49 London Road, Sevenoaks, Kent, TN13 1AR** 🅿
☎ 01732 740310 ⓕ 01732 741842
ⓔ sevenoaks@bonhams.com
ⓦ www.bonhams.com
Est. 1793
Open Mon–Fri 8.30am–5pm Sat 9am–noon
Sales Regional office. Regular house and attic sales across the country; contact London offices for further details. Free auction valuations; insurance and probate valuations
Catalogues Yes

Gem Antiques
Contact Mr M Rackham
✉ **122a High Street, Sevenoaks, Kent, TN13 1XA** 🅿
☎ 01732 743540
ⓦ www.gemasntiques.com
Est. 1994 *Stock size* Medium
Stock Jewellery, clocks
Open Mon–Sat 9.30am–5pm
Services Clock repairs

Ibbett Mosely
Contact Mr Hodge
✉ **125 High Street, Sevenoaks, Kent, TN13 1UT** 🅿
☎ 01732 456731 ⓕ 01732 740910
ⓔ auctions@ibbettmosely.co.uk
ⓦ www.ibbettmosely.co.uk
Est. 1935
Open Mon–Fri 9am–5.30pm
Sales General antiques, 9 sales a year, call for viewing times. Sales held at Otford Memorial Hall, Otford, Sevenoaks
Frequency 9 a year
Catalogues Yes

Sargeant Antiques
Contact Ann or David Sargeant
✉ **26 London Road, Sevenoaks, Kent, TN13 1AP** 🅿
☎ 01732 457304 ⓕ 01732 457688
ⓜ 07771 553632
Est. 1985 *Stock size* Medium
Stock General antiques, glass
Open Mon–Sat 9am–5pm Wed 9am–noon

SIDCUP

Memory Lane Antiques and Collectables
Contact Lynn Brackley
✉ **143 Station Road, Sidcup, Kent, DA15 7AA** 🅿
☎ 020 8300 0552
ⓜ 0794 6649843
Est. 1998 *Stock size* Medium
Stock General antiques, collectables
Open Mon–Sat 10am–5.30pm closed Wed

SISSINGHURST

Sissinghurst Antiques Gallery
Contact Jennifer Stubbs
✉ **The Street, Sissinghurst, Kent, TN17 2JG** 🅿
☎ 01580 712514
ⓜ 07786 255978
Est. 2002 *Stock size* Small
Stock Antique furniture, textiles, silver, jewellery, decorative items
Open Tues–Sat 10am–5pm
Services Valuations

SITTINGBOURNE

Past Sentence
Contact Mrs K Rowland
✉ **70 High Street, Sittingbourne, Kent, ME10 4PB** 🅿
☎ 01795 590000
ⓔ enquiries@pastsentence.com
Est. 1997 *Stock size* Medium
Stock Second-hand and antiquarian books
Open Tues Thurs–Sat 9.30am–5.30pm

SNODLAND

AJC Antiquities
Contact Andrew Cooke
✉ **73 Lucas Road, Snodland, Kent, ME6 5PZ** 🅿
☎ 01634 352383
ⓜ 07787 101472
ⓔ amjcook@blueyonder.co.uk
Est. 1999 *Stock size* Medium
Stock Art Deco, militaria, collectables, jewellery
Open Mon–Fri 9am–5pm

Amhuerst Auctions
Contact Andrew Cooke
✉ **73 Lucas Road, Snodland, Kent, ME6 5PZ** 🅿
☎ 01634 352383

SOUTH EAST

KENT • STOCKBURY

Ⓜ 07787 101472
Ⓔ amjcook@blueyonder.co.uk
Ⓦ www.amhuerstauctions.co.uk
Open Mon–Fri 9am–5pm
Sales Auction every second Saturday antiques, furniture, collectables, clocks, jewellery
Frequency Bi-monthly
Catalogues Yes

STOCKBURY

Steppes Hill Farm Antiques (BADA)
Contact Mr William Buck
✉ **Steppes Hill Farm, Stockbury, Sittingbourne, Kent, ME9 7RB** Ⓟ
☎ 01795 842205 Ⓕ 01795 842493
Ⓜ 07931 594218
Ⓔ dwabuck@btinternet.com
Stock size Small
Stock General antiques, English porcelain, collectable silver
Open Mon–Fri 9am–5pm
Fairs Olympia, International Ceramics Fair, BADA Duke of York's
Services Valuations, restoration

SUTTON VALENCE

Sutton Valence Antiques (LAPADA, CINOA)
Contact Judith Mullarkey
✉ **North Street, Sutton Valence, Maidstone, Kent, ME17 3AP** Ⓟ
☎ 01622 843333 Ⓕ 01622 843499
Ⓔ svantiques@aol.com
Est. 1978 *Stock size* Large
Stock 18th–19thC furniture, clocks, china, glass
Open Mon–Fri 9am–5pm
Sat 10am–5pm
Services Valuations, restoration, shipping, container packing

TENTERDEN

Flower House Antiques
Contact Mr Q Johnson
✉ **90 High Street, Tenterden, Kent, TN30 6JB** Ⓟ
☎ 01580 763764 Ⓕ 01580 291251 or 01797 270386
Est. 1995 *Stock size* Large
Stock 17th–early 19thC furniture, objets d'art, chandeliers, worldwide general antiques
Open Mon–Sat 9.30am–5.30pm
Sun by appointment
Services Valuations, restoration, items purchased

Gaby's Clocks and Things
Contact Gaby Gunst
✉ **140 High Street, Tenterden, Kent, TN30 6HT** Ⓟ
☎ 01580 765818
Est. 1969 *Stock size* Medium
Stock Clocks, barometers
Open Mon–Sat 10.30am–5pm
Services Clock and barometer restoration

Heirloom Antiques
Contact Jan Byhurst
✉ **68 High Street, Tenterden, Kent, TN30 6AU** Ⓟ
☎ 01580 765535
Est. 1994 *Stock size* Medium
No. of dealers 6
Stock Dolls, teddies, porcelain, prints, pictures, books, Winstanley cats and dogs, jewellery, furniture, militaria
Open Mon–Sat 10am–5pm
Sun 11am–5pm

Lambert and Foster
Contact Mrs G Brazier
✉ **102 High Street, Tenterden, Kent, TN30 6HT** Ⓟ
☎ 01580 762083 Ⓕ 01580 764317
Ⓔ saleroom@lambertandfoster.co.uk
Ⓦ www.lambertandfoster.co.uk
Est. 1830
Open Mon–Fri 9am–5.30pm
Sales General antiques sale Thurs 9.30am, viewing Sun 10.30am–4pm Tues 9.30am–4.30pm
Frequency Monthly
Catalogues Yes

Memories
Contact Mr Mark Lloyds
✉ **74 High Street, Tenterden, Kent, TN30 6AU** Ⓟ
☎ 01580 763416
Est. 1995 *Stock size* Large
Stock Antiques, collectables, small furniture
Open Mon–Sat 10am–5pm
Sun 11am–4pm

Tenterden Antique & Silver Vaults
Contact T Smith
✉ **66 High Street, Tenterden, Kent, TN30 6AU** Ⓟ
☎ 01580 765885
Est. 1991 *Stock size* Large
Stock Clocks, silver, china, glass, collectables, jewellery
Open Mon–Sat 10am–5pm
Sun 11am–4pm
Services House clearance

Tenterden Antiques Centre
Contact Mick Ellin
✉ **66a High Street, Tenterden, Kent, TN30 6AU** Ⓟ
☎ 01580 765655
Ⓜ 07776 203755
Est. 1990 *Stock size* Large
No. of dealers 7
Stock Furniture, Art Deco, china, clocks, silver, jewellery, militaria, porcelain, bric-a-brac
Open Mon–Sat 10am–5pm
Sun 11am–5pm

TEYNHAM

Jackson-Grant Antiques
Contact Mr David Jackson-Grant
✉ **133 London Road, Teynham, Sittingbourne, Kent, ME9 9QJ** Ⓟ
☎ 01795 522027
Ⓜ 07831 591881
Ⓔ david.jackson-grant@talk21.com
Ⓦ www.jackson-grantantiques.co.uk
Est. 1966 *Stock size* Large
Stock Antique furniture, small items
Open Mon–Sat 10am–5pm
Sun 1–5pm
Services Valuations

TONBRIDGE

Barden House Antiques
Contact Mrs Brenda Parsons
✉ **1 & 3 Priory Street, Tonbridge, Kent, TN2 2AP** Ⓟ
☎ 01732 350142
Est. 1959 *Stock size* Large
No. of dealers 4
Stock General antiques, prints, watercolours, jewellery, china, small pieces of furniture
Open Wed–Sat 10am–5pm

Greta May Antiques
Contact Mrs G May
✉ **The New Curiosity Shop, Tollgate Buildings, Hadlow Road, Tonbridge, Kent, TN9 1NX** Ⓟ
☎ 01732 366730
Ⓔ gretamayantiques@hotmail.com
Est. 1988 *Stock size* Medium
Stock Furniture, silver, silver plate, china, glass, teddy bears
Open Tues Thurs–Sat 10am–4.30pm
Fairs Ramada Hotel, Hollingbourne, Maidstone
Services Teddy bear repairs

Derek Roberts Antiques (BADA)
Contact Mr Paul Archard
25 Shipbourne Road, Tonbridge, Kent, TN10 3DN
01732 358986 F 01732 771842
drclocks@clara.net
www.qualityantiqueclocks.com
Est. 1968 *Stock size* Large
Stock 17th–19thC clocks, books written by Derek Roberts
Open Mon–Fri 9.30am–5pm Sat 10am–4pm
Fairs Olympia (Nov), BADA, Harrogate (Sept)
Services Valuations, annual catalogues

TUNBRIDGE WELLS

Aaron Antiques
Contact Ron Goodman
77 St Johns Road, Tunbridge Wells, Kent, TN4 9TT
01892 517644
Est. 1967 *Stock size* Large
Stock Coins, medals, clocks, china, silver, paintings, prints, scientific and musical instruments, furniture, Chinese porcelain
Open By appointment

Adams Arts & Antiques Ltd
Contact Mr M Adams
Festival House, Chapman Way, High Brooms, Tunbridge Wells, Kent, TN2 3EF
01892 557777 F 01892 557777
Est. 1998 *Stock size* Medium
Stock Garden statuary
Open Mon–Sun 9am–5pm

Amadeus Antiques
Contact Pat Davies
32 Mount Ephraim, Tunbridge Wells, Kent, TN4 8AU
01892 544406
Est. 1990 *Stock size* Medium
Stock China, lighting, furniture
Open Mon–Sat 10am–5pm

The Antiques Shop
Contact Joanne Chipchase
77a St John's Road, Tunbridge Wells, Kent, TN4 9TT
01892 676637
theantiquesshop@amserve.net
Est. 1998 *Stock size* Medium
Stock Decorative antiques and country furniture
Open Mon–Sat 10am–5pm
Fairs Ardingly

The Architectural Stores
Contact Nick Bates
55 St Johns Road, Tunbridge Wells, Kent, TN4 9TP
01892 540368
nick@thearchitecturalstores.co.uk
Est. 1987 *Stock size* Medium
Stock Antique fireplaces, period lighting, architectural
Open Tues–Sat 10am–5.30pm

Henry Baines (LAPADA)
Contact Mr H Baines
14 Church Road, Southborough, Tunbridge Wells, Kent, TN4 0RX
01892 532099 F 01892 532099
M 07973 214406
Est. 1968 *Stock size* Large
Stock Oak, country furniture
Open Prior telephone call advised

Beau Nash Antiques
Contact Mr David Wrenn
29 Lower Walk, The Pantiles, Tunbridge Wells, Kent, TN2 5TD
01892 537810
Est. 1990 *Stock size* Large
Stock Georgian–Edwardian period furniture, associated decorative items
Open Tues–Sat 11am–5pm

Calverley Antiques
Contact Mr P Nimmo
30 Crescent Road, Tunbridge Wells, Kent, TN1 2LZ
01892 538254
Est. 1984 *Stock size* Large
Stock Pine, decorative and painted furniture
Open Mon–Sun 9.30am–5.30pm
Fairs Ardingly
Services House clearance

Chapel Place Antiques
Contact Mrs J A Clare
9 Chapel Place, Tunbridge Wells, Kent, TN1 1YQ
01892 546561 F 01892 546561
Est. 1984 *Stock size* Large
Stock Antique and modern silver, hand-painted Limoges boxes, amber jewellery, silver photo frames, old silver plate, claret jugs
Open Mon–Sat 9am–5.30pm
Services Valuations

Crescent Road Antiques
Contact Mr Twiddy
36 Crescent Road, Tunbridge Wells, Kent, TN1 2LZ
01892 537815
www.crescentantiques.com
Est. 1993 *Stock size* Medium
Stock General antiques
Open Mon–Sat 9am–5pm

Culverden Antiques
Contact Mr D Mason
49 St Johns Road, Tunbridge Wells, Kent, TN4 9TP
01892 515264
Est. 1985 *Stock size* Medium
Stock 19thC furniture, decorative pieces
Open Tues–Sat 10am–5.30pm

Downlane Hall Antiques
Contact Mrs Hayes
Culverden Down, St Johns, Tunbridge Wells, Kent, TN4 9SA
01892 522440
www.downlanehallantiques.co.uk
Est. 1980 *Stock size* Large
Stock Georgian–Victorian furniture
Open Mon–Sat 9am–4pm
Services Restoration

Dreweatt Neate Tunbridge Wells Salerooms (SOFAA)
Contact Daniel Bray
Auction Hall, The Pantiles, Tunbridge Wells, Kent, TN1 1UU
01892 544500 F 01892 515191
tunbridgewells@dnfa.com
www.dnfa.com
Est. 1759
Open Mon–Fri 9am–5pm
Sales Fine art and antiques sales (7 a year), 2 Tunbridge Ware, Fri 10.30am, viewing Sat 9am–12.30pm Tues 9am–7pm Wed 9am–5pm Thurs 9am–3pm Fri 9–10am. Catalogues available on website
Frequency 7 a year
Catalogues Yes

Glassdrumman
Contact Mr or Mrs G Dyson Rooke
7 Union Square, The Pantiles, Tunbridge Wells, Kent, TN4 8HE
01892 538615

SOUTH EAST

KENT • TUNBRIDGE WELLS

Est. 1989 *Stock size* Large
Stock Georgian, Victorian, second-hand jewellery, silver, pocket watches, decorative items, furniture
Open Tues–Sat 10am–5.30pm
Services Repairs

Pamela Goodwin
Contact Pamela Goodwin
11 The Pantiles, Tunbridge Wells, Kent, TN2 5TD
☎ 01892 618200 F 01892 618200
M 07751 816443
E mail@goodwinantiques.co.uk
W www.goodwinantiques.co.uk
Est. 1998 *Stock size* Large
Stock 18th–20thC furniture, clocks, silver, English porcelain, Moorcroft, Doulton, glass, sewing collectables, Tunbridge ware, musical boxes
Open Mon–Fri 9.30am–5pm Sat 9.30am–5.30pm

Gorringes Incorporating Julian Dawson (SOFAA)
Contact Mr Leslie Gillham
15 The Pantiles, Tunbridge Wells, Kent, TN2 5TD
☎ 01892 619670 F 01892 619671
E tunbridge.wells@gorringes.co.uk
W www.gorringes.co.uk
Est. 1926
Open Mon–Fri 8.30am–5.30pm Sat 9am–noon
Sales Fine art and antiques sales every 6 weeks Tues 11.30am, viewing Mon prior noon–8pm and day of sale 8.30–11am
Frequency Quarterly
Catalogues Yes

Hall's Bookshop
Contact Sabrina Izzard
20 Chapel Place, Tunbridge Wells, Kent, TN1 1YQ
☎ 01892 527842
Est. 1898 *Stock size* Large
Stock Antiquarian and second-hand books
Open Mon–Sat 9.30am–5pm

Peter Hoare Antiques
Contact Peter Hoare
35 London Road, Southborough, Tunbridge Wells, Kent, TN4 0PB
☎ 01892 524623
E phoare@nildram.co.uk
Est. 1983 *Stock size* Medium
Stock Arts and Crafts furniture
Open Tues–Sat 10am–5.30pm
Services Valuations

Howard Neville
Contact Mr H Neville
21 The Pantiles, Tunbridge Wells, Kent, TN2 5TD
☎ 01892 511461 F 020 7491 7623
E patrickboyd_carpenter@hotmail.com
Est. 1986 *Stock size* Large
Stock Antiques and works of art
Open Mon–Sat 10am–5pm or by appointment

Old Colonial
Contact Suzy Rees or Dee Martyn
56 St Johns Road, Tunbridge Wells, Kent, TN4 9NY
☎ 01892 533993 F 01892 513281
Est. 1994 *Stock size* Large
Stock Country antiques, decorative items, painted furniture
Open Tues–Sat 10am–5.30pm or by appointment

Pantiles Antiques
Contact Mrs E M Blackburn
31 The Pantiles, Tunbridge Wells, Kent, TN2 5TD
☎ 01892 531291
Est. 1981 *Stock size* Medium
Stock Georgian and Edwardian furniture, porcelain, decorative pieces
Open Mon–Sat 9.30am–5pm
Services Restoration, upholstery

Pantiles Collectables
Contact Stephen Tewkesbury
1 The Corn Exchange, The Pantiles, Tunbridge Wells, Kent, TN2 5TE
☎ 01892 538726
E carolineannefordham@tiscali.co.uk
Est. 2001 *Stock size* Medium
Stock Post-war ceramics
Open Tues–Sat 10am–5pm Sun by appointment
Services Valuations

Pantiles Spa Antiques
Contact Mrs J A Cowpland
4, 5 & 6 Union House, The Pantiles, Tunbridge Wells, Kent, TN4 8HE
☎ 01892 541377 F 01435 865660
E psa.wells@btconnect.com
W www.pantiles-spa-antiques.co.uk
Est. 1987 *Stock size* Large
Stock Specialist dining room tables and chairs, furniture, dolls, porcelain, glass, prints, watercolours, maps, clocks, silver
Open Mon–Fri 9.30am–5pm Sat 9.30am–5.30pm
Services Free delivery within 30 mile radius

Phoenix Antiques (WKADA)
Contact Robert Pilbeam, Jane Stott or Peter Janes
51–53 St Johns Road, Tunbridge Wells, Kent, TN4 9TP
☎ 01892 549099 F 01892 549099
E shop@phoenixantiques.co.uk
W www.phoenixantiques.co.uk
Est. 1989 *Stock size* Large
Stock 18th–19thC English and French country furniture, overmantel mirrors, associated decorative items
Open Mon–Sat 10am–5.30pm or by appointment

Sporting Antiques
Contact Mr L Franklin
10 Union Square, The Pantiles, Tunbridge Wells, Kent, TN4 8HE
☎ 01892 522661 F 01892 522661
Est. 1993 *Stock size* Large
Stock Sporting antiques, arms, armour, technical instruments, tools
Open Mon–Sat 10am–5.30pm telephone call advisable

John Thompson
Contact Mr J Thompson
27 The Pantiles, Tunbridge Wells, Kent, TN2 5TD
☎ 01892 547215
Est. 1982 *Stock size* Medium
Stock 18th–early 19thC furniture, late 17th–20thC paintings, glass, porcelain
Open Mon–Sat 10am–1pm 2–5pm

Tunbridge Wells Antiques
Contact Mr Nick Harding
Union Square, The Pantiles, Tunbridge Wells, Kent, TN4 8HE
☎ 01892 533708
E nick@staffordshirefigures.com
W www.staffordshirefigures.com

Est. 1986 *Stock size* Large
Stock Tunbridge ware, Staffordshire figures, watches, clocks, silver, porcelain, pottery, furniture
Open Mon–Sat 10am–5pm
Services Valuations, restoration

Up Country Ltd
Contact Mr C Springett
The Old Corn Stores, 68 St Johns Road, Tunbridge Wells, Kent, TN4 9PE
☎ 01892 523341 F 01892 530382
E mail@upcountryantiques.co.uk
W www.upcountryantiques.co.uk
Est. 1988 *Stock size* Large
Stock Antique and decorative country furniture, rural artefacts
Open Mon–Sat 9am–5.30pm

Variety Box
Contact Penny Cogan
Tunbridge Wells, Kent, TN2
☎ 01892 531868
Est. 1982 *Stock size* Medium
Stock Tunbridge ware, hatpins, fans, sewing and collectors' items
Open By appoinment

World War Books (OMRS, PBFA)
Contact Mr Tim Harper
Oaklands, Camden Park, Tunbridge Wells, Kent, TN2 5AE
☎ 01892 538465 F 01892 538465
E wwarbooks@btinternet.com
Est. 1988 *Stock size* Large
Stock Military books including manuals, weapon books, regimental histories, maps, photographs, diaries
Open Mail order only
Fairs Arms and Armour Fair (Birmingham), World War Book Fair
Services Valuations, probate, book search, catalogue

WALMER

Grandma's Attic
Contact S J Marsh
60 The Strand, Walmer, Kent, CT14 7DP
☎ 01304 380121
Est. 1986 *Stock size* Medium
Stock Mirrors, Victoriana
Open Mon–Sat 9.45am–5.30pm closed Thurs Sun by appointment
Services Restoration, gilding

WEST KINGSDOWN

East Meets West Antiques
Contact Philippa Dudley
Unit 7, West Kingsdown Industrial Estate, London Road, West Kingsdown, Kent, TN15 6EL
☎ 01474 854807 F 01474 852839
M 07973 756302
E info@eastmeetswestantiques.co.uk
W www.eastmeetswestantiques.co.uk
Est. 2001 *Stock size* Medium
Stock Furniture
Open Fri–Sun 11am–3pm or by appointment
Services Valuations, restoration

WEST MALLING

The Old Clock Shop
63 High Street, West Malling, Kent, ME19 6NA
☎ 01732 843246 F 01732 843246
E theoldclockshop@tesco.net
W www.theoldclockshop.co.uk
Est. 1975 *Stock size* Medium
Stock Clocks, barometers
Open Mon–Sat 9am–5pm
Services Restoration

Rose and Crown Antiques
Contact Mrs Candy Lovegrove
40 High Street, West Malling, Kent, ME19 6QR
☎ 01732 872707 F 01732 872810
E jlantiques@hotmail.com
W www.antiqueswestmalling.co.uk
Est. 1995 *Stock size* Medium
Stock 18th–early 20thC furniture, small items
Open Tues–Sat 9.30am–5.30pm
Fairs Antiques for Everyone at NEC, Penman and Wakefield Fairs
Services Restoration, upholstery

WEST WICKHAM

Nightingale Antiques and Craft Centre
Contact Maureen Haggerty
89–91 High Street, West Wickham, Kent, BR4 0LS
☎ 020 8777 0335 F 020 8776 2777
Est. 1998 *Stock size* Large
No. of dealers 20
Stock Victorian–Edwardian furniture, 1930s oak, Royal Doulton, Royal Crown Derby, Moorcroft
Open Mon–Sat 10am–5pm

WESTERHAM

20th Century Marks
Contact Mr M Marks
12 Market Square, Westerham, Kent, TN16 1AW
☎ 01959 562221 F 01959 569385
M 07831 778992
E lambarda@btconnect.com
W www.20thcenturymarks.co.uk
Est. 1960 *Stock size* Large
Stock Classic 20thC designs
Open Mon–Sat 10am–5.30pm
Services Valuations, restoration

Apollo Galleries (LAPADA)
Contact Mr S M Barr
19–21 Market Square, Westerham, Kent, TN16 1AN
☎ 01959 562200 F 01959 562986
E enq@apollogalleries.com
W www.apollogalleries.com
Est. 1974 *Stock size* Large
Stock Mainly Georgian–Edwardian furniture, bronzes, oil paintings, mirrors, objets d'art
Open Mon–Sat 9.30am–5.30pm
Fairs Olympia
Services Valuations for probate and insurance

Castle Antique Centre Ltd
Contact Stewart Ward Properties
1 London Road, Westerham, Kent, TN16 1BB
☎ 01959 562492
Est. 1986 *Stock size* Large
No. of dealers 8
Stock 4 showrooms. Linen, tools, silver, jewellery, china, glass, books, 19thC clothing, chandeliers, small furniture
Open Mon–Sun 10am–5pm
Services Valuations, advice, house clearance

Clementines Antiques
Contact Jill Clark
3 The Green, Westerham, Kent, TN16 1AS
☎ 01959 562575
Est. 2000 *Stock size* Medium
Stock General antiques and collectables
Open Mon–Sat 10am–5pm Sun noon–5pm

SOUTH EAST

KENT • WESTGATE-ON-SEA

The Design Gallery
Contact Chrissie Painell or John Masters
5 The Green, Westerham, Kent, TN16 1AS
01959 561234 F 01954 561234
M 07785 503044
E sales@thedesigngallery.uk.com
W www.thedesigngallery.uk.com
Est. 2002 *Stock size* Medium
Stock Art Deco, Art Nouveau, Arts and Crafts, Gothic Revival and the Aesthetic Movement
Open Tues–Sat 10am–5.30pm Sun 1–4pm Mon by appointment
Services Valuations, restoration, shipping

The Green Antiques & Collectables
Contact Maria Lopez
3 The Green, Westerham, Kent, TN16 1AS
01959 569393
Est. 2003 *Stock size* Small
Stock Antiques, collectables, Sir Winston Churchill memorabilia
Open Mon–Sat 10am–5pm Sun noon–5pm

London House Antiques
Contact Vivienne Graham
4 Market Square, Westerham, Kent, TN16 1AW
01959 564479 F 01959 565424
Est. 1995 *Stock size* Large
No. of dealers 4
Stock Furniture, clocks, bears, dolls, porcelain, glass
Open Mon–Sat 10am–5pm or by appointment

Barbara Ann Newman
Contact Barbara Ann Newman
London House Antiques, 4 Market Square, Westerham, Kent, TN16 1AW
01959 564479
M 07850 016729
Est. 1991 *Stock size* Medium
Stock Antique dolls, teddy bears, children's antique furniture, rocking horses
Open Mon–Sat 10am–5pm
Fairs Kensington, Birmingham Doll Fair, Chelsea
Services Shipping

Regal Antiques (WKADA)
Contact Mrs T Lawrence
2 Market Square, Westerham, Kent, TN16 1AW
01959 561778 F 01959 561778
Est. 1991 *Stock size* Medium
Stock Antique jewellery, portrait miniatures, porcelain, watches, fine paintings
Open Wed–Sat 11am–5pm
Services Watch repairs

Taylor-Smith Antiques (LAPADA)
Contact Ashton Taylor-Smith
4 The Grange, High Street, Westerham, Kent, TN16 1AH
01959 563100 F 01959 565300
E mountjoy@dircon.co.uk
Est. 1974 *Stock size* Medium
Stock Fine 18th and early 19thC furniture, objets d'art, Sir Winston Churchill ephemera
Open Mon–Sat 10am–5pm closed Wed

WESTGATE-ON-SEA

Berkeley House Antiques
Contact Barbara Croall
78 St Mildreds Road, Westgate-on-Sea, Kent, CT8 8RF
01843 833458
Est. 2001 *Stock size* Medium
Stock Decorative items, small furniture, paintings, mirrors, porcelain and reproduction jewellery
Open Thurs–Sat 10am–5pm

Westgate Auctions
Contact Mr Colin Langston
Rear of 70 St Mildred's Road, Westgate-on-Sea, Kent, CT8 8RF
01843 834891
Est. 1982
Open Mon–Sat 9am–5pm, auctions on Sun
Sales Antique and modern furniture and effects Sun, viewing Sat 9.30am–5pm
Frequency Every 3 weeks
Catalogues Yes

WHITSTABLE

Bonhams
95–97 Tankerton Road, Whitstable Road, Whitstable, Kent, CT5 2AJ
01227 275007 F 01227 266443
E whitstable@bonhams.com
W www.bonhams.com
Est. 1793
Open Mon–Fri 9am–5.30pm
Sales Regional office. Regular house and attic sales across the country; contact London offices for further details. Free auction valuations; insurance and probate valuations
Catalogues Yes

Inside Out
Contact John Perry
6 Oxford Street, Whitstable, Kent, CT5 1DD
01227 280111
M 07850 365226
Est. 1985 *Stock size* Medium
Stock Country antiques, garden antiques, unusual decorative items
Open Mon–Sun 10.30am–5pm Wed 10.30am–1pm
Fairs Ardingly, Kempton Park

Laurens Antiques
Contact Mr G Laurens
2 Harbour Street, Whitstable, Kent, CT5 1AG
01227 261940
Est. 1965 *Stock size* Medium
Stock General antiques
Open Mon–Sat 10am–5pm closed Wed
Services Valuations

Tankerton Antiques (BHI)
Contact Mr Paul Wrighton
136 Tankerton Road, Whitstable, Kent, CT5 2AN
01227 266490
M 07702 244064
Est. 1985 *Stock size* Medium
Stock 18th–19thC clocks, watches, china, furniture, fabrics, ceramics
Open Thurs–Sat 10am–5pm
Fairs Brunel Clock and Watch Fair, Ardingly
Services Clock repairs

WITTERSHAM

Old Corner House Antiques
Contact Gillian Shepherd
6 Poplar Road, Wittersham, Kent, TN30 7PG
01797 270236
Est. 1986 *Stock size* Medium
Stock Early English ceramics, needleworks, carvings, country furniture
Open Wed–Sat Sat 10am–5pm

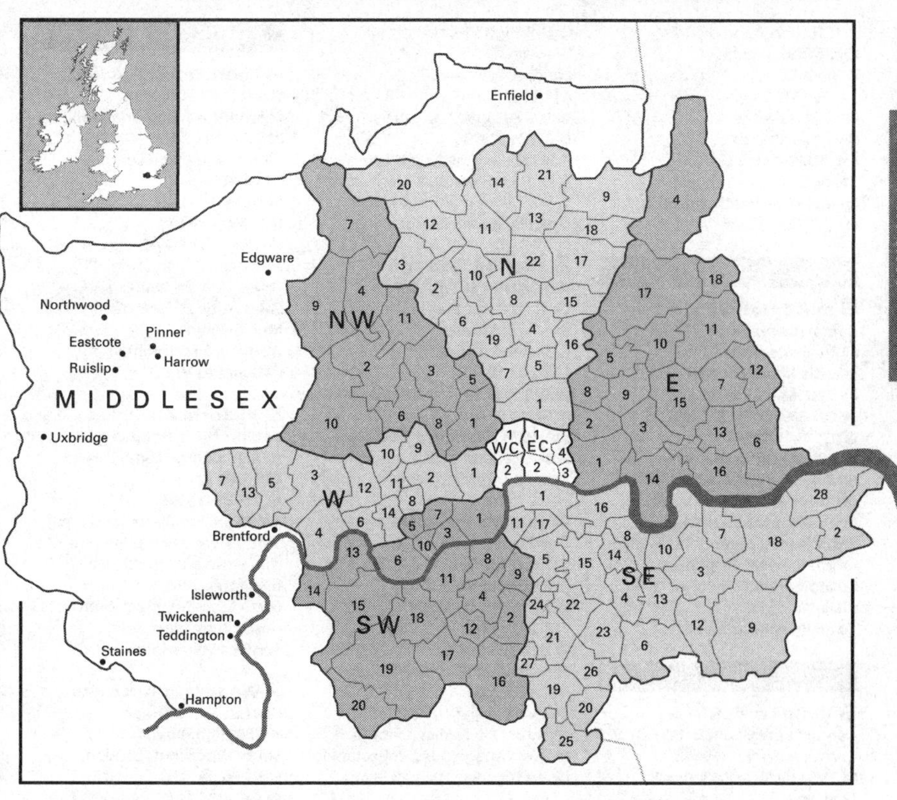

EAST

E1

AA Antiques
Contact Des King
14a Bacon Street, London, E1 6LF P
020 7739 4803
07973 324814
Est. 1996 *Stock size* Medium
Stock Antique and shipping furniture
Open Mon–Sat 10am–5pm

La Maison
Contact Mr Guillaume Bacou
107–108 Shoreditch High Street, London, E1 6JN P
020 7729 9646 F 020 7729 6399
gui@lamaison.com
www.lamaison.co.uk
Est. 1991 *Stock size* Medium
Stock French and Italian beds
Open Mon–Fri 10am–6pm
Sat 11.30am–6pm
Services Restoration, upholstery

Town House (LAPADA)
Contact Fiona Atkins
5 Fournier Street, London, E1 6QE P
020 7247 4745 F 020 7247 4745
07711 319237
fiona@townhousewindow.com
www.townhousewindow.com
Est. 1984 *Stock size* Large
Stock Early and Georgian furniture, decorative items
Open Thurs–Sat 10am–5pm or by appointment

E2

George Rankin Coin Co Ltd
Contact Mr G Rankin
325 Bethnal Green Road, London, E2 6AH P
020 7729 1280 F 020 7729 5023
Est. 1969 *Stock size* Large
Stock Jewellery, period, modern coins, medals, banknotes
Open Tues–Sat 10am–6pm closed Aug
Fairs Coinex, Cumberland and Europa
Services Valuations

E4

Record Detector
Contact Mr J Salter
3 & 4 Station Approach, Chingford, London, E4 6AL P
020 8529 6361
nick@salter.co.uk
www.salter.co.uk
Est. 1991 *Stock size* Large
Stock Second-hand records, CDs, 1950–1990s, videos, magazines
Open Mon–Sat 9.30am–6pm

Nicholas Salter Antiques
Contact Mrs S Salter

✉ 8 Station Approach, Chingford, London, E4 6AL Ⓟ
☎ 020 8529 2938
Ⓔ nick@salter.co.uk
Ⓦ www.salter.co.uk
Est. 1969 *Stock size* Large
Stock General antiques
Open Mon–Wed 10am–5pm Fri Sat 10am–6pm

E5

M A Stroh Bookseller
Contact Mr M Stroh
✉ **Riverside House, Leaside Road, London, E5 9LU** Ⓟ
☎ 020 8806 3690 Ⓕ 020 8806 3690
Ⓜ 07974 413039
Ⓔ patents@stroh.demon.co.uk
Ⓦ www.webspawner.com/users/buttonbook
Est. 1957 *Stock size* Medium
Stock Books, patents 1617–1970, journals, scientific papers, ephemera, old bindings, dissertations
Open By appointment

E9

Kelly Lordan
Contact Lesley Lordan or Christina Kelly
✉ **211a Victoria Park Road, London, E9 7JN** Ⓟ
☎ 020 8985 7550
Est. 2002 *Stock size* Small
Stock Antiques, collectables, soft furnishings
Open Mon–Sat 10am–5pm closed Thurs

E11

I D Edrich
Contact Mr I Edrich
✉ **17 Selsdon Road, London, E11 2QF** Ⓟ
☎ 020 8989 9541 Ⓕ 020 8989 9541
Ⓔ idedrich@iderich.co.uk
Ⓦ www.idedrich.co.uk
Est. 1965 *Stock size* Large
Stock First editions, antiquarian books, literary periodicals, literature a speciality
Open By appointment

Brian Hawkins Antiques (LAPADA)
Contact Brian Hawkins
✉ **6–8 High Street, Wanstead, London, E11 2AJ**
☎ 020 8989 2317 Ⓕ 020 8989 2317
Ⓜ 07831 888736
Ⓔ brianhawkinsantiques@hotmail.com
Est. 1993 *Stock size* Medium
Stock General antiques
Open By appointment

The Old Cottage Antiques (LAPADA)
Contact Peter Blake
✉ **6 High Street, Wanstead, London, E11 2AJ** Ⓟ
☎ 020 8989 2317 Ⓕ 020 8989 2317
Ⓜ 07710 031079
Est. 1973 *Stock size* Medium
Stock General antiques
Open By appointment

Wanstead Antiques Centre
Contact Mr Gill
✉ **21 High Street, Wanstead, London, E11 2AA** Ⓟ
☎ 020 8532 9844
Est. 1992 *Stock size* Medium
No. of dealers 6
Stock Georgian–Victorian furniture, ceramics, vintage radios, vintage pens, collectables
Open Tues–Sat 10am–5.30pm

E17

Peter Davis Antiques
Contact Mr P Davis
✉ **1 Georgian Village, 100 Wood Street, London, E17 3HX** Ⓟ
☎ 020 8520 6638
Est. 1972 *Stock size* Small
Stock Walking sticks, postcards, small silver, collectables
Open Mon–Wed 10.30am–4.30pm

Treasure World
Contact Ali Jewya
✉ **3 Central Parade, Hoe Street, Walthamstow, London, E17 4RT** Ⓟ
☎ 020 8521 1255 Ⓕ 020 8521 1255
Ⓜ 07957 177283
Est. 2000 *Stock size* Medium
Stock Furniture, rugs
Open Mon–Sat 9.30am–6.30pm Sun 11am–5pm

E18

Thornwood Auction
Contact Mrs D Green
✉ **Woodford Memorial Hall, 209 High Road, South Woodford, London, E18 2PA** Ⓟ
☎ 020 8553 1242
Ⓜ 07860 905667
Ⓔ greeendavolly@aol.com
Est. 1985
Open Mon–Fri 9am–5pm
Sales Antiques and general sale Mon 6.30pm
Frequency Fortnightly
Catalogues Yes

Victoria Antiques
Contact Mr M Holman
✉ **166a George Lane, London, E18 1AY** Ⓟ
☎ 020 8989 1002
Est. 1998 *Stock size* Medium
Stock Silver, silver plate, brass, china, carved items, small furniture, coins, clocks
Open Mon–Sat 11am–5pm closed Tues Thurs
Services Valuations

Woodford Auctions
Contact Mrs D Green
✉ **209 High Road, South Woodford, London, E18 2PA** Ⓟ
☎ 020 8553 1242
Ⓜ 07860 905667
Est. 1994
Open Mon 9am–5pm
Sales Antiques and general sale Mon 6.30pm, viewing Mon 4pm prior to sale
Frequency Fortnightly
Catalogues Yes

EC1

City Clocks (BHI)
Contact Jeffrey Rosson
✉ **31 Amwell Street, Clerkenwell, London, EC1R 1UN** Ⓟ
☎ 020 7278 1154 Ⓕ 020 7476 7766
Ⓜ 07074 767766
Ⓔ mail@cityclocks.co.uk
Ⓦ www.cityclocks.co.uk
Est. 1898 *Stock size* Medium
Stock Clocks
Open Tues–Fri 8.30am–5.30pm Sat 10am–3.30pm
Services Restoration, clock, watch repair

⊞ Frosts of Clerkenwell Ltd
Contact Mr G Redwood
✉ 60–62 Clerkenwell Road, London, EC1M 5PX 🅿
☎ 020 7253 0315
Ⓦ www.frostsofclerkenwell.co.uk
Est. 1938 *Stock size* Large
Stock Clocks, watches, cases, dials, movements
Open Mon–Fri 10am–5pm
Services Restoration

⊞ Hirsh London
Contact Ben Stevenson
✉ 10 Hatton Garden, London, EC1N 8AH 🅿
☎ 020 7405 6080 Ⓕ 020 7430 0107
Ⓦ www.hirsh.co.uk
Est. 1980 *Stock size* Large
Stock Fine antique jewellery, hand-made and designed diamond engagement rings
Open Mon–Fri 10am–5.30pm
Services Valuations

⊞ Andrew R Ullmann Ltd
Contact Mr J Ullmann
✉ 10 Hatton Garden, London, EC1N 8AH
☎ 020 7405 1877 Ⓕ 020 7404 7071
Ⓔ enquiries@aullmann.com
Ⓦ www.aullmann.com
Est. 1950 *Stock size* Large
Stock Antique gold and gem jewellery, clocks, silver, objets d'art, watches
Open Mon–Fri 9am–5pm
Sat 9.30am–5pm
Services Restoration

EC2

⊞ LASSCO St Michael's (LAPADA, SALVO, BACA Award Winner 2001)
Contact Ferrous Auger or Anthony Reeve
✉ St Michael's Church, Mark Street (Off Paul Street), London, EC2A 4ER 🅿
☎ 020 7749 9944 Ⓕ 020 7749 9941
Ⓔ st.michaels@lassco.co.uk
Ⓦ www.lassco.co.uk
Est. 1978 *Stock size* Large
Stock Architectural antiques, chimneypieces, overmantels, carved stonework, panelled rooms, statuary, garden ornaments and furniture, stained glass, metalwork
Open Mon–Fri 9.30am–5.30pm
Sat 10am–5pm
Services Shipping

⊞ Sport and Star Autographs (UACC, IADA)
Contact Steve Peacock
✉ 13 The Arcade, Liverpool Street, London, EC2M 7PN
☎ 020 7626 1818
Ⓦ www.autographs.me.uk
Est. 2000 *Stock size* Medium
Stock Autographs, sport, film, music, signed memorabilia
Open Mon–Fri 9am–5.45pm
Services Valuations

⊞ Westland and Co (SALVO)
Contact Mr R Muirhead
✉ St Michael's Church, Leonard Street, London, EC2A 4ER 🅿
☎ 020 7739 8094 Ⓕ 020 7729 3620
Ⓜ 07831 755566
Ⓔ westland@westland.co.uk
Ⓦ www.westland.co.uk
Est. 1969 *Stock size* Large
Stock Antique fireplaces, mantels, architectural elements, statuary, panelling
Open Mon–Fri 9am–6pm
Sat Sun 10am–5pm
Services Valuations, restoration

EC3

⊞ Halcyon Days (BADA)
Contact Georgina Foster or Cheska Moon
✉ 14 Brook Street, London, EC3V 3LL 🅿
☎ 020 7629 8811 Ⓕ 020 7283 1876
Ⓔ info@halcyondays.co.uk
Ⓦ www.halcyondays.co.uk
Est. 1950 *Stock size* Small
Stock Enamels, fans, snuff boxes, objects of virtue, tôle peinte, papier mâché, porcelain
Open Mon–Fri 10am–5.30pm
Fairs Grosvenor House

⊞ Searle & Co Ltd (NAG)
Contact Steve Carson
✉ 1 Royal Exchange, Cornhill, London, EC3V 3LL
☎ 020 7626 2456 Ⓕ 020 7283 6384
Ⓔ mail@searleandcoltd.uk
Ⓦ www.searleandcoltd.uk
Est. 1893 *Stock size* Medium
Stock General antiques
Open Mon–Fri 9am–5pm
Services Valuations

NORTH

N1

⊞ After Noah
Contact Simon Tarr
✉ 121 Upper Street, London, N1 1QP 🅿
☎ 020 7359 4281 Ⓕ 020 7359 4281
Ⓔ mailorder@afternoah.com
Ⓦ www.afternoah.com
Est. 1989 *Stock size* Medium
Stock Antique and contemporary furniture and houseware
Open Mon–Sat 10am–6pm
Sun noon–5pm
Services Restoration

⊞ Annie's Vintage Costume and Textiles
Contact Annie Moss
✉ 12 Camden Passage, Islington, London, N1 8ED 🅿
☎ 020 7359 0796 Ⓕ 020 7359 2116
Est. 1975 *Stock size* Small
Stock 1900–1940s costume, linen, textiles
Open Mon Tues Thurs Fri Sun 11am–6pm Wed Sat 9am–6pm

⊞ The Antique Trader at the Millinery Works
Contact Brian Thompson, Derek Rothera or Jeff Jackson
✉ 85–87 Southgate Road, London, N1 3JS 🅿
☎ 020 7359 2019 Ⓕ 020 7359 5792
Ⓔ antiquetrader@millinery.demon.co.uk
Ⓦ www.millineryworks.co.uk
Est. 1970 *Stock size* Large
Stock Arts and Crafts, furniture, effects
Open Tues–Sat 11am–6pm Sun noon–5pm or by appointment
Services Valuations, bi-annual exhibitions held

⊞ R Arantes
Contact R Arantes
✉ 27 The Mall, Camden Passage, Islington, London, N1 0PD 🅿
☎ 020 7226 6367 Ⓕ 020 7253 5303
Ⓜ 07712 189160
Ⓔ rlaliqueglass@btinrnet.com
Ⓦ www.laliqueglass.pnp.blueyonder.co.uk
Est. 1987 *Stock size* Large
Stock Lalique glass
Open Wed Sat 8am–5pm or by appointment
Services Valuations

Camden Passage Antiques Market
Contact Mrs S Lemkow
✉ **12 Camden Passage, London, N1 8ED** P
☎ 020 7359 0190 Ⓕ 020 7704 2095
Est. 1960 *Stock size* Large
No. of dealers 300
Stock General antiques and specialist shops
Open Wed Sat 8am–3pm stalls 8am–5pm shops

Camel Art Deco
Contact Mrs E Durack
✉ **34 Islington Green, London, N1 8DU** P
☎ 020 7359 5242
Est. 1996 *Stock size* Small
Stock Art Deco ceramics, furniture, lighting
Open Wed Sat 9am–3.30pm
Fairs Specialist Art Deco fairs
Services French polishing, upholstery of Lloyd Loom furniture

Castle Gibson
Contact Joyce Gibson
✉ **106a Upper Street, London, N1 1QN** P
☎ 020 7704 0927 Ⓕ 020 7704 0927
Stock size Large
Stock 19thC–1940s office furniture, polished metal items, 1930s leather chairs, sofas, early 20thC industrial furniture, 1920s–1940s shop fittings, garden furniture
Open Mon–Sat 10am–6pm Sun noon–5pm
Services Deliveries within London

Chancery Antiques Ltd
Contact Mr R Rote
✉ **2 The Mall, 359 Upper Street, London, N1 0PD** P
☎ 020 7359 9035 Ⓕ 020 7359 9035
Est. 1951 *Stock size* Medium
Stock Japanese porcelain, pottery, ivory, 19thC Continental works of art, cloisonné
Open Tues–Sat 10.30am–5pm or by appointment closed Thurs

Peter Chapman Antiques and Restoration (LAPADA, CINOA)
Contact Peter Chapman or Zac Chapman
✉ **10 Theberton Street, Islington, London, N1 0QX** P
☎ 020 7226 5565 Ⓕ 020 8348 4846
Ⓜ 07831 093662
Ⓔ pchapmanantiques@easynet.co.uk
Ⓦ www.antiques-peterchapman.co.uk
Est. 1971 *Stock size* Medium
Stock English and Continental furniture 1700–1900, mirrors, Grand Tour souvenirs, bronzes, spelters and other smalls, paintings, lighting, hall lanterns, stained glass, architectural, garden and decorative items
Open Mon–Sat 9.30am–6pm or by appointment
Services Valuations, restoration, shipping

Charlton House Antiques
Contact Mr S Burrows or Mr R Sims
✉ **19 Camden Passage, Islington, London, N1 8EA** P
☎ 020 7226 3141 Ⓕ 020 7226 1123
Ⓔ charlhse@aol.com
Est. 1979 *Stock size* Large
Stock Antique furniture
Open Mon–Sat 9.30am–5pm
Services Shipping

Chest of Drawers Ltd
Contact Daniel Harrison or Vincent Glanville
✉ **281 Upper Street, London, N1 2TZ**
☎ 020 7359 5909 Ⓕ 020 7704 6236
Ⓦ www.chestofdrawers.co.uk
Est. 1986 *Stock size* Large
Stock Soft and hardwood old furniture, wooden and metal beds, sofas, armchairs, chests-of-drawers, wardrobes
Open Mon–Sun 10am–6pm

Cloud Cuckoo Land
Contact Mrs C Harper
✉ **6 Charlton Place, London, N1 8AJ** P
☎ 020 7354 3141
Ⓔ cuckoolandmail@yahoo.co.uk.
Est. 1981 *Stock size* Medium
Stock Vintage clothes, accessories, 1850s–1950s, some later
Open Mon–Sat 11am–5.30pm

Rosemary Conquest
Contact Mrs R Conquest
✉ **27 Camden Passage, London, N1 8EA** P
☎ 020 7359 0616
Ⓔ rosemary@rosemaryconquest.com
Est. 1996 *Stock size* Large
Stock Continental and Dutch lighting, decorative items
Open Tue Thurs Fri 11am–5.30pm Wed Sat 9am–5.30pm

Criterion Auctioneers
Contact Daniel Webster
✉ **53 Essex Road, Islington, London, N1 2SF** P
☎ 020 7359 5707 Ⓕ 020 7354 9843
Ⓔ info@criterion-auctioneers.co.uk
Ⓦ www.criterion-auctioneers.co.uk
Est. 1989
Open Mon–Fri 9.30am–6pm
Sales Mon 5pm sale of antiques and decorative furnishings, viewing Fri 2–8pm Sat Sun 10am–6pm day of sale from 10am
Frequency Weekly
Catalogues Yes

Carlton Davidson Antiques
Contact Mr Carlton Davidson
✉ **33 Camden Passage, London, N1 8EA** P
☎ 020 7226 7491 Ⓕ 020 7226 7491
Est. 1982 *Stock size* Medium
Stock Decorative French items, including lighting
Open Wed Sat 10am–4pm

Eclectica
Contact Liz Wilson
✉ **2 Charlton Place, London, N1 8AJ** P
☎ 020 7226 5625 Ⓕ 020 7226 5625
Ⓦ www.eclectica.biz
Est. 1988 *Stock size* Large
Stock Vintage costume jewellery, 1920s–1960s
Open Sat 10am–6pm Wed 9am–6pm Mon Tues Thurs Fri 11am–6pm
Services Theatre and film hire

Fandango
Contact Jonathan Ellis or Henrietta Palmer
✉ **50 Cross Street, Islington, London, N1 2BA** P
☎ 020 7226 1777 Ⓕ 020 7226 1777
Ⓜ 07979 650805
Ⓔ shop@fandango.uk.com
Ⓦ www.fandango.uk.com
Est. 1997 *Stock size* Medium
Stock Post-war design lighting and furniture
Open Wed–Sat 11am–6pm Sun noon–5pm
Services Valuations, interior design

Feljoy Antiques
Contact Mrs Joy Humphreys
3 Angel Arcade, Camden Passage, London, N1 8EA P
020 7354 5336 F 020 7831 3485
E joy@feljoy-antiques.demon.co.uk
W www.chintz.net/feljoy
Est. 1985 *Stock size* Large
Stock Chintzware, textiles, cushions, shawls, small decorative furniture, decorative items including beadwork cushions
Open Wed 8am–3.30pm Sat 10am–4pm
Services Mail order

Vincent Freeman Antiques
Contact Vincent Freeman
1 Camden Passage, Islington, London, N1 8EA
020 7226 6178 F 020 7226 7231
E info@vincentfreemanantiques.com
W www.vincentfreemanantiques.com
Est. 1966 *Stock size* Medium
Stock 19thC music boxes
Open Wed Sat 10am–5pm or by appointment
Fairs Olympia

Furniture Vault
Contact Mr David Loveday
50 Camden Passage, London, N1 8AE
020 7354 1047 F 020 7354 1047
Est. 1984 *Stock size* Large
Stock 18th–19thC furniture
Open Tues–Sat 9.30am–4.30pm

Gateway Arcade Antiques Market
Contact Mike Spooner
357 Upper Street, Camden Passage, London, N1 0PD P
020 7351 5353 F 020 7969 1639
E antique@dial.pipex.com
Est. 2000 *Stock size* Large
No. of dealers 50
Stock Jewellery, silver, collectables, watches, militaria
Open Wed 6am–2pm Sat 8am–2pm

Get Stuffed
Contact Robert Sinclair
105 Essex Road, Islington, London, N1 2SL P
020 7226 1364 F 020 7359 8353
M 07831 260062
E taxidermy@thegetstuffed.co.uk
W www.thegetstuffed.co.uk
Est. 1913 *Stock size* Large
Stock Victorian artefacts, birds, animals, insects, butterflies and glass domes
Open Telephone for appointment

Rosemary Hart
Contact Rosemary Hart
8 Angel Arcade, 116 Islington High Street, London, N1 8EG P
M 07946 576740
E rosemaryhart@cwcom.net
Est. 1980 *Stock size* Small
Stock Small plated tableware and silver pieces, decorative pieces and mother-of-pearl
Open Wed 9am–4pm Fri Sat by appointment

Jonathan James (LAPADA)
Contact Norman Petre
52–53 Camden Passage, London, N1 8EA P
020 7704 8266
Est. 1994 *Stock size* Medium
Stock 18th–19thC English furniture
Open Tues–Sat 10am-5pm
Services Valuations

Japanese Gallery Ltd (Ukiyo-e Society)
Contact Mr C D Wertheim
23 Camden Passage, London, N1 8EA P
020 7226 3347 F 020 7229 2934
M 07930 411991
E sales@japanesegallery.co.uk
W www.japanesegallery.co.uk
Est. 1980 *Stock size* Large
Stock Japanese woodcut prints, Japanese ceramics, sword armour, Japanese dolls
Open Sun–Tues Thurs Fri 10am–6pm Wed Sat 9am–6pm
Services Restoration, free authentification

Judith Lassalle (PBFA)
Contact Mrs J Lassalle
7 Pierrepont Arcade, London, N1 8EF P
020 7607 7121
Est. 1765 *Stock size* Small
Stock Toys, games, books, optical toys, ephemera, all pre-1914
Open Wed 7.30am–4pm Sat 9.30am–4pm or by appointment
Fairs English and American ephemera fairs, PBFA Bookfair at Russell Hotel

John Laurie Antiques Ltd (LAPADA)
Contact Mr John Laurie
352 Upper Street, London, N1 0PD P
020 7226 0913 F 020 7226 4599
E rdgewirtz@aol.com
Est. 1963 *Stock size* Large
Stock Antique and modern silver, silver plate
Open Mon–Sat 9.30am–5pm
Services Restoration, replating

Leolinda
Contact Ms Leolinda Costa
3 The Mall, 359 Upper Street, Camden Passage, London, N1 0PD P
020 7226 3450 F 020 7209 0143
M 07789 162972
E leolinda@hotmail.com
W www.islington.co.uk/leolinda
Est. 1989 *Stock size* Small
Stock Old and new silver jewellery, gemstone necklaces, ethnic art, jewellery
Open Wed Sat 10am–5pm
Services After-sales service

Leons Militaria
Contact Leon
Unit 8, The Mall Antiques Arcade, 359 Upper Street, Islington, London, N1 0PD P
020 7288 1070 F 020 7288 1070
M 07989 649972
E leonsmilitaria@yahoo.co.uk
Est. 1997 *Stock size* Large
Stock Commemorative ceramics, porcelain, Victoriana, WW1, WWII
Open Tues Fri 11am–4.30pm Wed 9am–4.30pm Thur by appointment Sat 9am–5pm
Services Valuations, shipping

Leons Militaria
Contact Leon
Unit 21, The Mall Antiques Arcade, 359 Upper Street, Islington, London, N1 0PD P
020 7288 1070 F 020 7288 1070
M 07989 649972
E leonsmilitaria@yahoo.co.uk
Est. 1997 *Stock size* Large

Stock Militaria, weapons, uniforms, naval, aviation and curios, Napoleonic–WWII
Open Tues Fri 11am–4.30pm Wed 9am–4.30pm Thur by appointment Sat 9am–5pm
Services Valuations, shipping

Andrew Lineham Fine Glass (BADA, CINOA)
Contact Mr A Lineham
19 The Mall, Camden Passage, London, N1 8EA
020 7704 0195 F 01243 576241
M 07767 702722
E andrew@antiquecolouredglass.com
W www.antiquecolouredglass.com
Est. 1979 *Stock size* Large
Stock 19th–20thC coloured glass, European porcelain
Open Wed 8am–3pm Sat 10.30am–4pm or by appointment
Fairs Olympia (Nov)
Services Restoration, commission bidding, collectors services, valuations, hire

The Mall Antiques Arcade
Contact Neil Jackson
359 Upper Street, Camden Passage, London, N1 0PD
020 7351 5353 F 020 7351 5350
E antique@dial.pipex.com
W www.visitlondon.com (search for antiques)
Est. 1979 *Stock size* Large
No. of dealers 35
Stock Furniture, decorative antiques
Open Tues Thurs Fri 10am–5pm Wed 7.30am–5pm Sat 9am–6pm

Metro Retro
Contact Mr Saxon Durrant
1 White Conduit Street, London, N1 9EL
020 7278 4884 F 020 7278 4884
M 07850 319116
E sales@metroretro.co.uk
W www.metroretro.co.uk
Est. 1994 *Stock size* Large
Stock Industrial style and stripped-steel furniture, lighting and design
Open Thurs–Sat 11am–6pm
Fairs Syon Park, Jukebox Madness, Chiswick, Battersea
Services Props hire, consultancy

Michel André Morin (LAPADA, CPTA)
Contact Brian Trotman
7 Charlton Place, Islington, London, N1 8AQ
020 7226 3803 F 020 7704 0708
M 07802 832496
E michelandremorin@aol.com
Est. 1989 *Stock size* Medium
Stock French decorative furniture, chandeliers, items for interior decorators
Open Wed–Sat 7.30am–4.30pm or by appointment
Fairs Olympia, Battersea Decorative Antiques and Textiles Fair
Services Valuations, restoration

Number 19
Contact Mr D Griffith
19 Camden Passage, London, N1 8EA
020 7226 1999 F 020 7226 1126
Est. 1982 *Stock size* Large
Stock Decorative antiques, campaign furniture, vintage shop fittings, leather seating, decorative accessories
Open Tues–Sat 10am–5pm closed Thurs

Olde Hoxton Curios
Contact John Clarke
192 Hoxton Street, Shoreditch, London, N1 5LH
020 7729 7256
Est. 2003 *Stock size* Medium
Stock Antique collectables, curios
Open Mon–Fri noon–4pm Sat 10am–4.30pm

Origin Modernism
Contact Christopher Reen
25 Camden Passage, Islington, London, N1 8EA
020 7704 1326
M 07747 758852
E david@origin101.co.uk
W www.origin101.co.uk
Est. 2001 *Stock size* Medium
Stock Modernist furniture,1930s–1950s. Designers from Northern Europe, Britain and USA
Open Wed–Sat noon–6pm
Fairs 20thC Design Fair

Out of Time
Contact Mr E Farlow
110 Elmore Street, Islington, London, N1 3AH
020 7354 5755 F 020 7354 5755
E outoftime@btconnect.com
Est. 1969 *Stock size* Large
Stock 1940s–1950s homestyle furniture, glass, fridges, tables, chairs
Open Mon–Sun 10am–6pm
Fairs Jukebox Madness, Ascot
Services Valuations, restoration

Kevin Page Oriental Art Ltd (LAPADA)
Contact Mr K Page
2–6 Camden Passage, Islington, London, N1 8ED
020 7226 8558 F 020 7354 9145
E kevin@kevinpage.co.uk
W www.kevinpage.co.uk
Est. 1969 *Stock size* Large
Stock Oriental art, bronze, lacquer, porcelain, ivory
Trade only Trade and export only
Open Tues–Sat 10.30am–4.30pm

Phoenix Oriental Art (LAPADA)
Contact Elena Edwards
No 6 the Lower Mall, 359 Upper Street, Islington, London, N1 0PD
07802 763518
E okinasan@aol.com
Est. 1981 *Stock size* Large
Stock Chinese and Japanese bronze from the last 1000 years
Open Wed Sat 10am–4pm or by appointment

Piers Rankin
Contact Mr P Rankin
14 Camden Passage, Islington, London, N1 8ED
020 7354 3349 F 020 7359 8138
E rankinfamily@rankinp.fsbusiness.co.uk
Est. 1979 *Stock size* Large
Stock Silver, silver plate
Open Tues–Sat 9.30am–5.30pm
Services Packing for export

Regent Antiques
Contact Mr Tino Quaradeghini
King's Cross Freight Depot, Barpart House, York Way, London, N1 0UZ
020 7833 5545 F 020 7278 2236
M 07836 294074

ⓔ regentantiques@aol.com
Est. 1974 *Stock size* Large
Stock 18thC–Edwardian furniture
Open Mon–Fri 9am–5.30pm
Services Restoration of furniture

⊞ Rumours Decorative Arts (LAPADA)
Contact John Donovan
✉ **4 The Mall, 359 Upper Street, Camden Passage, Islington, London, N1 0PD** Ⓟ
☎ 020 7704 6549
Ⓜ 07836 277274 or 07831 103748
ⓔ rumdec@aol.com
Est. 1988 *Stock size* Large
Stock Moorcroft pottery
Open Wed Sat 8am–4pm
Sat 9am–5pm
Fairs NEC Antiques for Everyone
Services Valuations

⊞ Sugar Antiques (CPTA)
Contact Mr T Sugarman
✉ **8–9 Pierrepont Arcade, Pierrepont Row, London, N1 8EF** Ⓟ
☎ 020 7354 9896 Ⓕ 020 7931 5642
Ⓜ 07973 179980
ⓔ tony@sugar-antiques.com
Ⓦ www.sugar-antiques.com
Est. 1990 *Stock size* Large
Stock Wristwatches, pocket watches, pens, lighters, costume jewellery
Open Wed–Sat 8am–3.30pm

⊞ Tadema Gallery (BADA, LAPADA, CINOA, BACA Award Winner 2004)
Contact Sonya or David Newell-Smith
✉ **10 Charlton Place, Camden Passage, Islington, London, N1 8AJ**
☎ 020 7359 1055 Ⓕ 020 7359 1055
Ⓜ 07710 082395
ⓔ info@tademagallery.com
Ⓦ www.tademagallery.com
Est. 1978 *Stock size* Large
Stock Art Nouveau, Arts and Crafts, Art Deco jewellery
Open Wed Sat 10am–5pm or by appointment
Fairs Grosvenor House

⊞ Chris Tapsell at Christopher House (CPADA)
Contact Mr C Tapsell
✉ **5 Camden Passage, Islington, London, N1 8EA** Ⓟ
☎ 020 7354 3603
Est. 1993 *Stock size* Medium
Stock 18th–19thC English and Continental furniture, Oriental ceramics, Georgian–Victorian mirrors
Open Tues–Sat 10am–5pm closed Wed
Services Valuations, restoration

⊞ Titus Omega
Contact John Harvey
✉ **London, N1**
Ⓜ 07973 841846
ⓔ john@titusomega.com
Ⓦ www.titusomega.com
Est. 1985 *Stock size* Medium
Stock Art Nouveau, Art Deco, Arts and Crafts
Open By appointment
Fairs NEC, Olympia

⊞ Turn On Lighting
Contact Janet Holdstock
✉ **116–118 Islington High Street, Camden Passage, Islington, London, N1 8EG** Ⓟ
☎ 020 7359 7616 Ⓕ 020 7359 7616
Est. 1976 *Stock size* Large
Stock Antique lighting
Open Tues–Fri 10.30am–6pm
Sat 9.30am–4.30pm
Services Museum work, interior design

⊞ Vane House Antiques
Contact Michael Till
✉ **15 Camden Passage, Islington, London, N1 8EA**
☎ 020 7359 1343 Ⓕ 020 7359 1343
Est. 1962 *Stock size* Large
Stock 18th–early 19thC furniture
Open Tues Wed Fri and Sat 10am–5pm

⊞ The Waterloo Trading Co
Contact Robert Boys
✉ **North London Freight Centre, York Way, Kings Cross, London, N1 0AU** Ⓟ
☎ 020 7837 4806 Ⓕ 020 7837 4815
ⓔ info@robertboysshipping.co.uk
Est. 1989 *Stock size* Large
Stock 10,000 sq ft of antique furniture
Open Mon–Fri 8.30 am–5.30pm
Services Shipping

⊞ Mike Weedon (LAPADA, CPA)
✉ **7 Camden Passage, Islington, London, N1 8EA** Ⓟ
☎ 020 7226 5319/7609 6826
Ⓕ 0207 700 6389
ⓔ info@mikeweedonantiques.com
Ⓦ www.mikeweedonantiques.com
Est. 1979 *Stock size* Large
Stock Art Nouveau, Art Deco, general antiques, wholesale to Japanese trade
Open Wed 9am–5pm Sat 10am–5pm or by appointment

⊞ Agnes Wilton
Contact Agnes Wilton
✉ **3 Camden Passage, London, N1 8EA** Ⓟ
☎ 020 7226 5679 Ⓕ 020 7226 0779
Est. 1972 *Stock size* Medium
Stock Furniture, silver, decorative objects
Open Tues–Sat 10am–2pm
Services Valuations

⊞ Woodage Antiques (LAPADA)
Contact Mr C Woodage
✉ **359 Upper Street, London, N1 0PD** Ⓟ
☎ 020 7226 4173 Ⓕ 01753 529 047
ⓔ woodage.antiques@btinternet.com
Est. 1995 *Stock size* Large
Stock 18th–20thC furniture
Open Wed 7.30am–5pm
Sat 9am–5pm

⊞ www.buymeissen.com (LAPADA)
Contact Laurence Mitchell
✉ **20 The Mall, Camden Passage, Islington, London, N1 0PD**
☎ 020 7359 7579
Ⓜ 07968 065110
ⓔ laurence@buymeissen.com
Ⓦ www.buymeissen.com
Est. 1974 *Stock size* Large
Stock 19thC Meissen, European, Oriental works of art and ceramics
Open Tues–Sat 10am–5pm
Wed closed 4pm
Services Valuations, restoration

⊞ York Gallery Ltd (LAPADA)
Contact Mr G Beyer
✉ **51 Camden Passage, Islington, London, N1 8EA** Ⓟ

☎ 020 7354 8012 Ⓕ 020 7354 8012
Ⓔ prints@yorkgallery.co.uk
Ⓦ www.yorkgallery.co.uk
Est. 1989 *Stock size* Large
Stock 17th–19thC engravings
Open Wed–Sat 10am–5pm
Services Picture framing

Michael Young
Contact M Young
✉ **21 Camden Passage, London, N1 8EA** Ⓟ
Ⓜ 07768 233633
Est. 1985 *Stock size* Medium
Stock Marine models, pond yachts, general antiquities
Open Wed Sat 9am–4pm
Services Valuations

N2

Martin Henham
Contact Mr M Henham
✉ **218 High Road, London, N2 9AY** Ⓟ
☎ 020 8444 5274
Est. 1963 *Stock size* Medium
Stock Victoriana, bronzes, ceramics, porcelain
Open Mon–Sat 10am–6pm closed Thurs or by appointment
Services Furniture restoration

N3

Martin Gladman Second-hand Books
Contact Mr M Gladman
✉ **235 Nether Street, London, N3 1NT** Ⓟ
☎ 020 8343 3023
Est. 1991 *Stock size* Large
Stock Large range of rare and antiquarian books through the humanities, history, military history
Open Sat 10am–6pm
Tues–Fri 11am–8pm
Services Valuations

Intercol (ITA, Coin, Banknote and Map Collectors Societies)
Contact Mr Yasha Beresiner
✉ **43 Templars Crescent, London, N3 3QR** Ⓟ
☎ 020 8349 2207 Ⓕ 020 8346 9539
Ⓜ 07768 292066
Ⓔ yasha@compuserve.com
Ⓦ www.intercol.co.uk
Est. 1981 *Stock size* Medium
Stock Maps, charts, books, playing cards, currency
Open By appointment
Fairs Playing cards fairs, Map Society fairs (phone for details)
Services Valuations

N4

The Antique Shop
Contact Michael Slade or Michael Kairis
✉ **42 Quernmore Road, London, N4 4QP** Ⓟ
☎ 020 8341 3194 Ⓕ 020 8348 7652
Ⓜ 07973 800678
Ⓔ michael.kairis@btinternet.com or mikeslade@ntl.com
Ⓦ www.antiquesnorthlondon.co.uk
Est. 1982 *Stock size* Small
Stock Victorian–Edwardian furniture
Open Tues–Fri 10am–6pm
Sat by appointment
Fairs Alexandra Palace
Services Restoration

Kennedy Carpets
Contact Michael Kennedy or Vivien Eder
✉ **Oriental Carpet Centre, Building G, 105 Eade Road, London, N4 1TJ** Ⓟ
☎ 020 8800 4455 Ⓕ 020 8800 4466
Ⓔ kennedycarpets@ukonline.co.uk
Ⓦ www.cloudband.com/occ/kennedycarpets
Est. 1972 *Stock size* Large
Stock Antique Oriental large carpets and rugs
Open Mon–Fri 9.30am–6pm
Sat Sun by appointment
Services Valuations, restoration

Joseph Lavian
Contact Joseph Lavian
✉ **105 Eade Road, London, N4 1TJ** Ⓟ
☎ 020 8800 0707 Ⓕ 020 8800 0404
Ⓔ lavian@lavian.com
Ⓦ www.lavian.com
Est. 1962 *Stock size* Large
Stock Oriental carpets and textiles
Open Mon–Fri 9.30am–5.30pm
Services Valuations, restoration

N5

Gathering Moss
Contact Mrs S Murnane
✉ **193 Blackstock Road, London, N5 2LL** Ⓟ
☎ 020 7354 3034
Est. 1999 *Stock size* Medium
Stock Furniture, gifts, reclaimed timber items
Open Wed–Fri 10.30am–5.30pm
Sat 10am–6pm Sun 11am–4pm

Nicholas Goodyer (PBFA, ABA)
Contact Mr N Goodyer
✉ **8 Framfield Road, Highbury Fields, London, N5 1UU** Ⓟ
☎ 020 7226 5682 Ⓕ 020 7354 4716
Ⓔ email@nicholasgoodyer.com
Est. 1950 *Stock size* Medium
Stock Antiquarian and rare books on architecture, travel, design, illustrated, natural history, colour-plate books
Open Mon–Fri by appointment, prior call or e-mail advised
Fairs PBFA Russell, ABA
Services Valuations, restoration, shipping, book search

Sandby Fine Art
Contact B Ashley
✉ **72 Mountgrove Road, London, N5 2LT** Ⓟ
☎ 020 7354 4759
Est. 1989 *Stock size* Medium
Stock General antiques, fireplaces, paintings
Open Mon–Sat 9am–6pm

N6

Fisher & Sperr (ABA)
✉ **46 Highgate High Street, London, N6 5JB** Ⓟ
☎ 020 8340 7244 Ⓕ 020 8348 4293
Est. 1945 *Stock size* Large
Stock General second-hand and antiquarian books
Open Mon–Sat 10am–5pm
Services Valuations

Ripping Yarns (PBFA)
Contact Mrs C Mitchell
✉ **355 Archway Road, London, N6 4EJ** Ⓟ
☎ 020 8341 6111 Ⓕ 020 7482 5056
Ⓔ yarns@rippingyarns.co.uk
Ⓦ www.rippingyarns.co.uk
Est. 1982 *Stock size* Large
Stock General stock, antiquarian and second-hand books including children's fiction, illustrated
Open Tues–Fri 11am–5pm
Sat 10am–5pm Sun 11am–4pm
Fairs PBFA
Services Book search, French and Spanish spoken, annual catalogue

N7

Back in Time
Contact Mr Demetriou
93 Holloway Road, London, N7 8LT
020 7700 0744
mario000@btclick.com
www.backintime.com
Est. 1996 *Stock size* Large
Stock 1950s–1970s furniture, metal wardrobes, decorative items, metal kitchen furniture
Open Mon–Sat 10am–6pm
Services Valuations, restoration

Dome Antiques (LAPADA)
Contact Mr A Woolf
40 Queensland Road, London, N7 7AJ
020 7700 6266 020 7609 1692
07831 805888
info@domeantiques.com
www.domeantiques.com
Est. 1974 *Stock size* Large
Stock 19thC decorative furniture
Open Mon–Fri 9am–5pm
Fairs NEC, Olympia
Services Restoration

Ooh-La-La
Contact David or Barry
147 Holloway Road, London, N7 8LX
020 7609 6021
07970 007590
Est. 1997 *Stock size* Medium
Stock Leather chesterfields, contemporary sofas, furniture, smalls, vintage clothing
Open Mon–Thurs 11am–5pm Sat 10.30am–6pm
Services Valuations

N8

Hornsey Auctions Ltd
Contact Miss C Connoly
54–56 High Street, Hornsey, London, N8 7NX
020 8340 5334 020 8340 5334
Est. 1983
Open Thurs Fri 9.30am–5.30pm Sat 10am–4pm
Sales Antiques and general sale Wed 6.30pm, viewing Tues 5–7pm Wed 10am–6.30pm prior to sale
Frequency Weekly
Catalogues Yes

Of Special Interest
Contact Mr S Loftus
42–46 Park Road, London, N8 8TD
020 8340 0909 020 8374 6990
Est. 1988 *Stock size* Large
Stock Antique pine furniture, porcelain, fabrics, Indian items, garden furniture
Open Mon–Fri noon–7pm Sat 10am–6pm Sun noon–4pm

Solomon
Contact Solomon
49 Park Road, London, N8 8SY
020 8341 1817 020 8341 1817
solomon@solomonantiques.fsnet.co.uk
Est. 1981 *Stock size* Medium
Stock 20thC design furniture, collectables
Open Mon–Sat 9am–6pm
Services Restoration, French polishing, upholstery, hand-made furniture

N9

Anything Goes
Contact C J Bednarz
83 Bounces Road, London, N9 8LD
020 8807 9399
Est. 1978 *Stock size* Small
Stock Antiques, collectables
Open Tues–Sat 10am–5pm
Services Valuations

N10

Crafts Nouveau
Contact Laurie Strange
112 Alexandra Park Road, Muswell Hill, London, N10 2AE
020 8444 3300 020 8883 4587
07958 448380
www.craftsnouveau.co.uk
Est. 2003 *Stock size* Medium
Stock Art Nouveau, Arts and Crafts furniture, decorative arts, pewter, copperware, writing accessories
Open Wed–Sat 10.30am–6.30pm Tues Sun by appointment

N11

A Pine Romance
Contact Mrs S Gray
111 Friern Barnet Road, New Southgate, London, N11 3EU
020 8361 5860 020 8361 4697
Est. 1989 *Stock size* Medium
Stock British and Continental pine furniture, manufacturers of furniture from reclaimed timber
Open Mon–Sat 10am–5.30pm closed Wed
Services Valuations, restoration

N12

The New Curiosity Shop
Contact Mrs T Robins
211 Woodhouse Road, Friern Barnet, London, N12 9AY
020 8368 2117 020 83682117
Est. 1994 *Stock size* Medium
Stock Coins, stamps, banknotes, sci-fi memorabilia, pop memorabilia, *Star Wars* toys, Corgi, Dinky, Matchbox collectables
Open Mon–Sat 10am–5.30pm
Services Valuations

North London Auctions
Contact Mr G Flood
Lodge House, 9–17 Lodge Lane, North Finchley, London, N12 8JH
020 8445 9000 020 8446 6068
northlondonauctions@ukgateway.net
www.northlondonauctions.co.uk
Est. 1977
Open Mon–Fri 9am–5.30pm
Sales Antiques and general sale Mon 5pm, viewing Sun 9am–1pm Mon 9am–5pm
Frequency Weekly
Catalogues Yes

N13

Palmers Green Antiques Centre
Contact Michael Webb
472 Green Lane, Palmers Green, London, N13 5PA
020 8350 0878
07855 067544
Est. 1996 *Stock size* Large
No. of dealers 40+
Stock Furniture, clocks, pictures, jewellery, porcelain, china, glass, silver, lighting, general antiques
Open Mon Wed–Sat 10am–5.30pm Sun 11am–5pm
Services Valuations, house clearance

LONDON

N14

C J Martin Coins Ltd (LAPADA)
Contact Chris Martin
85 The Vale, Southgate, London, N14 6AT
020 882 1509 F 020 886 5253
ancientart@btinternet.com
www.ancientart.co.uk
Est. 1972 *Stock size* Large
Stock General antiquities and coins
Open By appointment
Services Valuations, restoration, shipping, mail order

Southgate Auction Rooms
Contact Mr J Nolan
55 High Street, Southgate, London, N14 6LD
020 8886 7888 F 020 8882 4421
www.southgateauctionrooms.com
Est. 1986
Open Mon–Fri 9am–5.30pm
Sales General and antiques sales Mon 5pm, viewing Sat 9am–1pm Mon 9am–5pm prior to sale
Frequency Weekly
Catalogues Yes

Richard Thornton Books (PBFA)
Contact Richard Thornton
116 Osidge Lane, Southgate, London, N14 5DN
020 8368 2816
richard.thorntonbooks@btinternet.com
Est. 1996 *Stock size* Medium
Stock Antiquarian, rare, used books
Open Mon–Fri 9am–6pm or by appointment
Services Valuations

N15

Krypton Komics
Contact Mr G Ochiltree
252 High Road, Tottenham, London, N15 4AJ
020 8801 5378 F 020 8376 3174
krypton.komics@virgin.net
www.kryptonkomics.com
Est. 1980 *Stock size* Large
Stock 1950s–present day American comics
Open Mon–Fri 10.30am–6pm Sat 10am–6pm
Fairs Comic Convention at the Royal National Hotel
Services Valuations, mail order catalogue

N16

The Cobbled Yard
Contact Carole Lucas
1 Bouverie Road, Stoke Newington, London, N16 0AH
020 8809 5286
info@cobbled-yard.co.uk
www.cobbled-yard.co.uk
Est. 2002 *Stock size* Medium
Stock Furniture, pine, ceramics, collectables, retro items
Open Wed–Sun 11am–6pm
Services Restoration, upholstery, carpentry

I Ehrnfeld (NAWCC)
Contact Isaac Ehrnfeld
29 Leweston Place, London, N16 6RJ
020 8802 4584 F 020 8800 1364
M 07966 136495
Est. 1989 *Stock size* Medium
Stock Watches, wristwatches
Open By appointment
Fairs Major antiques fairs, clock/watch fairs
Services Shipping

N19

Chesney's Antique Fireplace Warehouse
Contact John Norman
734–736 Holloway Road, London, N19 3JF
020 7561 8280 F 020 7561 8288
sales@chesneys.co.uk
www.chesneys.co.uk
Est. 1985 *Stock size* Large
Stock Antique fireplaces
Open Mon–Fri 9am–5.30pm Sat 10am–5pm
Services Shipping

Old School
Contact Mr F Lascelles
130c Junction Road, Tufnell Park, London, N19 5LB
020 7272 5603 F 020 7272 5603
Est. 1996 *Stock size* Large
Stock Garden furniture, statuary, antique furniture, made-to-measure furniture
Open Mon–Sun 11am–6pm

N20

The Totteridge Gallery
Contact Mrs J Clarke
61 Totteridge Lane, London, N20 0HD
020 8446 7896 F 020 8446 7541
janet@totteridgegallery.com
www.totteridgegallery.com
Est. 1987 *Stock size* Large
Stock Fine art, 18th–20thC British and Continental oil paintings, watercolours, limited edition Sir William Russell Flint prints
Open Mon–Sat 11am–6.30pm
Services Valuations, restoration

N21

Dollyland
864 Green Lanes, Winchmore Hill, London, N21 2RS
020 8360 1053 F 020 8364 1370
M 0780 821773
Est. 1986 *Stock size* Large
Stock Dolls, Steiff bears, Scalextric, trains, diecast toys
Open Tues Thurs Fri Sat 9.30am–4.30pm
Fairs Hugglets, Kensington Town Hall

Past Present Toys
Contact Mr Jim Parsons
862 Green Lanes, London, N21 2RS
020 8364 1370 F 020 8364 1370
Est. 1986 *Stock size* Large
Stock Dinkys, Hornby railways, tin-plate toys, Corgi, Matchbox
Open Tues Thurs–Sat 9.30am–4.30pm

NW1

Archive Books and Music
Contact Mr T Meaker
83 Bell Street, Marylebone, London, NW1 6TB
020 7402 8212
Est. 1975 *Stock size* Small
Stock Second-hand books, printed pop and classical music
Open Mon–Sat 10.30am–6pm

Art Furniture
Contact Liam Scanlon
158 Camden Street, London, NW1 9PA
020 7267 4324 F 020 7267 5199

Ⓔ arts-and-crafts@artfurniture.co.uk
Ⓦ www.artfurniture.co.uk
Est. 1989 *Stock size* Large
Stock Arts and Crafts furniture and objects including Liberty, Heals, Shapland and Petter
Open Mon–Sun noon–5pm
Services Shipping, restoration

Benjamin Jewellery (LAPADA)
Contact Anita Benjamin
PO Box 12656, London, NW1 4WJ
☎ 020 7486 5382 Ⓕ 020 7935 6134
Est. 1949 *Stock size* Medium
Stock Second-hand jewellery
Open By appointment
Fairs Miami Beach Show
Services Valuations

Comic Book Postal Auctions Ltd (Eagle Society)
Contact Malcolm Phillips
40–42 Osnaburgh Street, London, NW1 3ND
☎ 020 7424 0007 Ⓕ 020 7424 0008
Ⓔ comicbook@compuserve.com
Ⓦ www.compalcomics.com
Est. 1992
Open By appointment
Sales Quarterly, British and American comics, 1900–1970s, also annuals, artwork, TV-related merchandise. Sales in March, June, September, December
Frequency Quarterly
Catalogues Yes

Laurence Corner
Contact Sales Manager
62–64 Hampstead Road, London, NW1 2NU
☎ 020 7813 1010 Ⓕ 020 7813 1413
Ⓦ www.laurencecorner.com
Est. 1953 *Stock size* Large
Stock Militaria, uniforms
Open Mon–Sat 10.30am–6pm
Services Uniforms for hire

Madeline Crispin Antiques
Contact Mrs M Crispin or David Thomas
95 Lisson Grove, London, NW1 6UP
☎ 020 7402 6845
Ⓜ 07956 289906
Ⓔ david@crispinantiques.fsnet.co.uk
Est. 1979 *Stock size* Medium
Stock Furniture, decorative items
Open Mon–Fri 10am–5.30pm
Sat 10am–4pm
Services Valuations

Decorative Arts
Contact Anthony White
Unit 87, The Stables Market, Camden Market, London, NW1 8AH
☎ 01273 676486
Ⓜ 07788 107101
Ⓔ info@decarts.net
Ⓦ www.decarts.net
Est. 2002 *Stock size* Medium
Stock Oak furniture 1880–1970, decorative arts, 1970s leather furniture
Open Fri–Sun 10am–6pm

Elvisly Yours
Contact Mr Sid Shaw
233 Baker Street, London, NW1 6XE
☎ 020 7486 2005
Ⓔ elvisly@globalnet.co.uk
Ⓦ www.elvisly-yours.com
Est. 1978 *Stock size* Large
Stock Elvis memorabilia
Open Mon–Sun 11am–6.30pm

Carol Ketley Antiques (LAPADA)
Contact Carol Ketley
PO Box 16199, London, N1 7WD
☎ 020 7359 5529 Ⓕ 020 7226 4589
Ⓜ 07831 827284
Est. 1980 *Stock size* Large
Stock Drinking glasses and decanters, gilded decorative antiques including mirrors
Open By appointment
Fairs Olympia, Decorative Antiques and Textiles Fair

Planet Bazaar
Contact Maureen Silverman
149 Drummond Street, London, NW1 2PB
☎ 020 7387 8326 Ⓕ 020 7387 8326
Ⓔ info@planetbazaar.co.uk
Ⓦ www.planetbazaar.co.uk
Est. 1997 *Stock size* Medium
Stock 1950–1980 designer furniture, art, glass, lighting, ceramics, books, eccentricities
Open Tues–Sat 11.30am–7pm or by appointment

The Relic Antiques Trade Warehouse
Contact Mr Gliksten
133–135 Pancras Road, London, NW1 1JN
☎ 020 7387 6039 Ⓕ 020 7388 2691
Ⓔ malcolm.gliksten@blueyonder.co.uk
Est. 1972 *Stock size* Large
Stock Decorative antiques, folk art, fairground art, Black Forest carvings, country pieces, architectural, marine, trade signs, shop fittings
Open Mon–Fri 10am–6pm
Sat by appointment
Services Valuations, framing, mirror restoration

Travers Antiques
Contact Mr S Kluth
71 Bell Street, London, NW1 6SX
☎ 020 7723 4376
Ⓔ spkluth@aol.com
Est. 1976 *Stock size* Large
Stock 1820–1920 furniture, decorative items
Open Mon–Sat 10.30am–5pm
Services Valuations, restoration

David J Wilkins
Contact Alex Wilkins
27 Princess Road, Regents Park, London, NW1 8JR
☎ 020 7722 7608 Ⓕ 020 7483 0423
Ⓔ alexdwilkins@hotmail.com
Ⓦ www.orientalrugexperts.com
Est. 1990 *Stock size* Large
Stock Antique Oriental rugs
Open Mon–Fri by appointment

NW2

G and F Gillingham Ltd
Contact Mr Gillingham
62 Menelik Road, London, NW2 3RH
☎ 020 7435 5644 Ⓕ 020 7435 5644
Ⓜ 07958 484140
Est. 1960
Stock 1750–1950 furniture
Open By appointment
Services Valuations, exports, restoration

Quality Furniture Warehouse
Contact Mr Anthony Dwyer
Ionna House, Humber Road, London, NW2 6EN
☎ 020 8452 0074 Ⓕ 020 8450 9296
Ⓔ info@qfw.co.uk

Ⓦ www.qfw.co.uk
Est. 1981 *Stock size* Large
Stock Victorian–Edwardian furniture and earlier, quality used furniture, English and Continental, reproduction French and Italian ormolu furniture
Open Sat Sun 10.30am–5.30pm or by appointment
Fairs Newark, Wembley
Services Restoration, repairs

Sabera Trading Oriental Carpets & Rugs
Contact Nawrozzadeh
Coles Green Road, London, NW2 7EU Ⓟ
☎ 020 8450 0012 Ⓕ 020 8450 0012
Est. 1992 *Stock size* Medium
Stock Oriental carpets, rugs, Chinese porcelain, jewellery
Open Mon–Sat 10am–6pm

NW3

Keith Fawkes
Contact Keith Fawkes
1–3 Flask Walk, Hampstead, London, NW3 1HJ Ⓟ
☎ 020 7435 0614
Ⓜ 07939 000921
Est. 1967 *Stock size* Large
Stock Antiquarian and second-hand books
Open Mon–Sat 10am–5.30pm Sun 1.30–6pm
Services Valuations

Brian Fielden (BADA)
Contact Brian Fielden
7 Chalcot Gardens, London, NW3 4YB Ⓟ
☎ 020 7722 9192 Ⓕ 020 7722 9192
Est. 1965 *Stock size* Small
Stock English 18th–early 19thC furniture
Open By appointment

Gillian Gould Antiques
Contact Gill Gould
18a Belsize Park Gardens, London, NW3 4LH Ⓟ
☎ 020 7419 0500
Ⓜ 07831 150060
Ⓔ gillgould@dealwith.com
Est. 1989 *Stock size* Small
Stock Scientific, marine, general gifts
Open Mon–Wed Fri 9.30am–6.30pm Thur 9.30am–7pm Sat 9.30am–5.30pm
Services Valuations, restoration

Hampstead Antique and Craft Emporium
Contact Mrs N Apple
12 Heath Street, London, NW3 6TE Ⓟ
☎ 020 7794 3297 Ⓕ 020 7794 4620
Est. 1967 *Stock size* Large
No. of dealers 20
Stock Furniture, jewellery, first-edition teddy bears, trimmings, buttons, paintings, prints, gifts, memorabilia
Open Tues–Fri 10.30am–5pm Sat 10am–6pm Sun 11am–5.30pm

Sylvia Powell Decorative Arts (BADA, LAPADA)
Contact Mrs S Powell
400 Ceramic House, 573 Finchley Road, London, NW3 7BN Ⓟ
Ⓜ 07802 714998
Ⓔ dpowell909@aol.com
Ⓦ www.sylvia-powell.com
Est. 1987 *Stock size* Large
Stock Art pottery, 20thC decorative arts
Open By appointment
Fairs Olympia, NEC, Harrogate, BADA
Services Valuations

Recollections Antiques Ltd
Contact Mrs June Gilbert
The Courtyard, Hampstead Antique and Craft Emporium, 12 Heath Street, Hampstead, London, NW3 6TE Ⓟ
☎ 020 7431 9907 Ⓕ 020 7794 9743
Ⓜ 07930 394 014
Ⓔ junalantiques@aol.com
Est. 1991 *Stock size* Large
Stock Early 19thC blue and white transfer-printed pottery, early pine, miniature furniture, children's highchairs, kitchenware, collectors' teddy bears
Open Tues–Sat 10.30am–5pm

M & D Seligman (BADA)
Contact M or D Seligman
26 Belsize Park Gardens, London, NW3 4LH Ⓟ
☎ 020 7722 4315 Ⓕ 020 7722 4315
Ⓜ 07946 634429
Est. 1947 *Stock size* Small
Stock Sophisticated 16th–early 19thC country furniture, associated works of art, antiquities
Open By appointment

Villa Grisebach Art Auctions
Contact Mrs Sabina Fliri
27 Kemplay Road, London, NW3 1TA
☎ 020 7431 9882 Ⓕ 020 7431 9756
Ⓔ fliris@btconnect.com
Ⓦ www.villa-grisebach.de
Est. 1986
Open By appointment
Sales 19th–20thC art and photography, telephone for details
Fairs Biennale in Berlin
Catalogues Yes

NW4

Memories (PTA)
Contact Dave Smith
130–132 Brent Street, Hendon, London, NW4 2DR Ⓟ
☎ 020 8202 9080
Ⓔ dave@mempics.demon.co.uk
Ⓦ www.memoriespostcards.co.uk
Est. 1975 *Stock size* Large
Stock Postcards
Open Mon–Sat 9.30am–5.30pm
Services Valuations, price guide catalogue

Murray Cards (International) Ltd
Contact Ian Murray
51 Watford Way, Hendon, London, NW4 3JH
☎ 020 8202 5688 Ⓕ 020 8203 7878
Ⓔ murraycards@ukbusiness.com
Ⓦ www.murraycards.com
Est. 1965 *Stock size* Large
Stock Cigarette and trading cards, albums, frames, books
Open Mon–Fri 9am–5pm
Fairs Murray Fair & Auction, Royal National Hotel, London
Services Annual catalogue, auction catalogue, Fair and Auction organiser

The Talking Machine
Contact Mr D Smith
30 Watford Way, London, NW4 3AL Ⓟ
☎ 020 8202 3473
Ⓜ 07774 103139
Ⓔ davepaul50@hotmail.com
Ⓦ www.gramophones.endirect.co.uk
Est. 1975 *Stock size* Large
Stock Mechanical antiques, typewriters, radios, music boxes, photographs, sewing machines,

juke boxes, calculators, televisions
Open Variable or by appointment
Services Valuations, restoration

NW5

The Orientalist
Contact M Fadaei
✉ **74–80 Highgate Road, London, NW5 1PB** P
☎ 020 7482 0555 Ⓕ 020 7267 9603
Ⓔ orientalist74@aol.com
Ⓦ www.orientalist.demon.co.uk
Est. 1985 *Stock size* Large
Stock Hand-made antique carpets, rugs
Open Mon–Sun 10am–6pm

NW6

Frosts
Contact Mrs D Frost
✉ **205–207 West End Lane, London, NW6 1XF**
☎ 020 7372 5788 Ⓕ 020 7372 5788
Est. 1989 *Stock size* Medium
Stock Pine, painted country furniture, textiles, porcelain, blue and white china, kitchenware
Open Mon–Sat 11am–5.30pm

Gallery Kaleidoscope incorporating Scope Antiques
Contact Mr K Barrie
✉ **64–66 Willesden Lane, London, NW6 7SX** P
☎ 020 7328 5833 Ⓕ 020 7624 2913
Est. 1970 *Stock size* Large
Stock Furniture, interior decorators' pieces, paintings, prints, sculptures, glass
Open Tues–Sat 10am–6pm Thur 1–7pm
Services Valuations, framing, silverwork

NW8

Alfie's Antique Market
Contact Robin Saikia
✉ **13–25 Church Street, London, NW8 8DT** P
☎ 020 7723 6066 Ⓕ 020 7724 0999
Ⓔ alfies@clara.net
Ⓦ www.alfiesantiques.com
No. of dealers 100
Stock General antiques, collectables, 20thC design
Open Tues–Sat 10am–6pm
Services Restoration, bureau de change, rooftop restaurant

Beverley
Contact Beverley
✉ **30 Church Street, Marylebone, London, NW8 8EP** P
☎ 020 7262 1576 Ⓕ 020 7262 1576
Ⓜ 07776 136003
Est. 1958 *Stock size* Large
Stock 1850–1950 English ceramics, glass, metal, wood, pottery, collectables, decorative items
Open Mon–Fri 10.30am–6pm Sat 9.30am–6pm or by appointment
Fairs NEC, Peterborough Festival of Antiques
Services Mail order worldwide

Bizarre
Contact Mr V Conti or Mr A Taramasco
✉ **24 Church Street, London, NW8 8EP** P
☎ 020 7724 1305 Ⓕ 020 7724 1316
Ⓔ bizdec@aol.com
Ⓦ www.bizdec.co.uk
Est. 1982 *Stock size* Large
Stock Art Deco, Continental furniture, wrought iron, glass, ceramics
Open Mon–Fri 10am–5pm Sat 10am–4pm
Services Interior design

Church Street Antiques
Contact Stuart Shuster
✉ **8 Church Street, London, NW8 8ED** P
☎ 020 7723 7415 Ⓕ 020 7723 7415
Est. 1980 *Stock size* Large
Stock 18th–20thC furniture, decorative items
Open Tues–Sat 10am–6pm

Davidson Antiques
Contact Edward Davidson
✉ **5 Church Street, London, NW8 8EE** P
☎ 020 7724 9236 Ⓕ 020 7724 9387
Ⓔ enquiries@davidsonandmorgan.com
Ⓦ www.davidsonandmorgan.com
Est. 1958 *Stock size* Medium
Stock Furniture, decorative objects, clocks, chandeliers, lighting, architectural antiques
Open Mon–Sun 10am–6pm

Dodo
Contact Liz Farrow
✉ **Alfies Antique Market, FO 73, 13–25 Church Street, London, NW8 8DT** P
☎ 020 7706 1545 Ⓕ 020 7724 0999
Ⓔ liz@dodoposters.co.uk
Ⓦ www.dodoposters.com
Est. 1960 *Stock size* Large
Stock Vintage posters, card signs, labels 1920–1940, food, drink, travel, entertainment
Open Tues–Sat 10.30am–5.30pm
Fairs Ephemera Society, Russell Square Hotel
Services Restoration

Gallery of Antique Costume & Textiles
Contact L Segal
✉ **2 Church Street, London, NW8 8ED** P
☎ 020 7723 9981 Ⓕ 020 7723 9981
Ⓔ info@gact.co.uk
Ⓦ www.gact.co.uk
Est. 1980 *Stock size* Medium
Stock Antique textiles, curtains, cushions, antique costumes, mainly 1920s and 1930s, textiles by Lalya Moussa
Open Mon–Sat 10am–5.30pm
Fairs HALI Antique Textile Art Fair, Olympia

The Girl Can't Help It
Contact Sparkle Moore or Cad van Swankster
✉ **Units G80, G90 & G100 Alfie's Antique Market, 13–25 Church Street, London, NW8 8TT** P
☎ 020 7724 8984 Ⓕ 020 8809 3923
Ⓔ sparkle@sparklemoore.com
Ⓦ www.sparklemoore.com
Est. 1997 *Stock size* Medium
Stock 1930–1960 American vintage clothing, pin-up collectables
Open Tues–Sat 10am–6pm
Fairs Vintage Mayfair, Battersea Vintage Clothing Fair

Goldsmith & Perris (LAPADA)
Contact Mrs Goldsmith
✉ **Alfie's Antique Market, 13–25 Church Street, London, NW8 8DT** P
☎ 020 7724 7051 Ⓕ 020 7724 7051
Ⓜ 07831 447432
Ⓔ gandpalfies@aol.com
Est. 1975 *Stock size* Medium
Stock Antique silver, silver plate, lamps, collectables, cocktail shakers

Open Tues–Sat 10am–6pm
Fairs Portobello, Covent Garden
Services Valuations

Ora Gordon (LAPADA, CINOA)
Contact Ora Gordon
London, NW8
020 7286 1306 F 020 7286 1306
oragordon@onetel.net.uk
www.antiquesweb.co.uk
Est. 1980 *Stock size* Medium
Stock English porcelain 18th–early 20thC export Wedgwood
Open By appointment
Fairs NEC Antiques for Everyone
Services Shipping, valuations, search specific items

Patricia Harvey Antiques
Contact Mrs P Harvey
42 Church Street, London, NW8 8EP P
020 7262 8989 F 020 7262 8989
info@patriciaharveyantiques.co.uk
www.patriciaharveyantiques.co.uk
Est. 1960 *Stock size* Large
Stock 18th–19thC English, French furniture, decorative, paintings
Open Mon–Sat 10am–5.30pm
Fairs Decorative Antiques & Textiles Fair (Jan, April, Sept)
Services Valuations

Just Desks
Contact Noelle Finch
20 Church Street, London, NW8 8EP P
020 7723 7976
M 020 7402 6416
Est. 1972 *Stock size* Small
Stock Desks, tables, chairs, filing cabinets
Open Mon–Sat 9.30am–6pm

Marie Antiques
Stand G136–138, Alfie's Antique Market, 13–25 Church Street, London, NW8 8DT
020 7706 3727
marie136@globalnet.co.uk
www.marieantiques.co.uk
Est. 1987 *Stock size* Large
Stock Jewellery 1830–1930
Open Tues–Sat 10am–4.30pm
Services Valuations, restoration, shipping

Andrew Nebbett Antiques
Contact Andrew Nebbett
35–37 Church Street, Marylebone, London, NW8 8ES P
020 7723 2303
M 07768 741595
anebbett@aol.com
www.andrewnebbett.com
Est. 1999 *Stock size* Large
Stock Simple, large, English and Swedish oak furniture 17th–20thC
Open Tues–Sat 10am–5.30pm

Tara Antiques
Contact Mr G Robinson
6 Church Street, London, NW8 8ED P
020 7724 2405
Est. 1984 *Stock size* Large
Stock Eclectic mix of decorative furniture and items, ivories, sculptures
Open Tues–Fri 10am–6pm
Sat 1.30–6pm
Fairs Decorative Textile Fairs, Battersea

Tin Tin Collectables
Contact Mr P Pinnington or Mr L Verrinder
Ground Units 38–42, Alfie's Antique Market, 13–25 Church Street, London, NW8 8DT P
020 7258 1305
tin.tin@teleregion.co.uk
www.tintincollectables.com
Est. 1995 *Stock size* Large
Stock Handbags, Victorian–present day, decorative evening bags, Victorian–1940s costume
Open Tues–Sat 10am–6pm
Fairs Grays Vintage Mayfair
Services Valuations, film and TV hire

Wellington Gallery (LAPADA)
Contact Mrs M Barclay
1 St John's Wood High Street, London, NW8 7NG P
020 7586 2620 F 020 7483 0716
Est. 1979
Stock Porcelain, silver, general antiques
Open Mon–Fri 10.30am–6pm
Sat 10am–6pm

Young & Son (LAPADA)
Contact Mr Young
12 Church Street, London, NW8 8EP P
020 7723 5910
M 07958 437043
www.youngandson.com
Est. 1990 *Stock size* Medium
Stock 18th–20thC antique decorative furniture, 19thC pictures, drawings, prints, fine frames, lighting, mirrors, oddities
Open Tues–Fri 10am–5.30pm
Sat 11am–5.30pm
Services Valuations

NW10

A D Carpets (LAPADA)
Contact Ahmad Gheiace
Unit A, 1 Chandors Road, London, NW10 6NF P
020 7243 2264 F 020 8838 3191
M 07957 373457
adcarpets@aol.com
Est. 1978 *Stock size* Large
Stock Antique oriental carpets
Open Mon–Fri 9.30am–6pm

Retrouvius Architectural Reclamation (SALVO)
Contact Adam Hills
2a Ravensworth Road, Kensal Green, London, NW10 5NR P
020 8960 6060
M 07778 210855
mail@retrouvius.com
www.retrouvius.com
Est. 1992 *Stock size* Medium
Stock Architectural antiques, reclamation, design furniture
Open Thurs Fri 9.30am–6pm or by appointment
Fairs Newark, Ardingly
Services Design service

Willesden Green Architectural Salvage
Contact Mr D Harkin
189 High Road, Willesden, London, NW10 2SD P
020 8459 2947 F 020 8451 1515
Est. 1994 *Stock size* Large
Stock Radiators, stained glass windows, pine doors, lighting, architectural salvage, fireplaces
Open Mon–Sat 9am–6pm

SOUTH

SE1

LASSCO Warehouse (SALVO)
Contact Jesse Carrington

✉ **41 Maltby Street, London, SE1 3PA** 🅿
☎ 020 7394 2103
ⓔ warehouse@lassco.co.uk
ⓦ www.lassco.co.uk
Est. 1978 ***Stock size*** Large
Stock Architectural reclamation and salvage
Open Mon–Sat 10am–5pm
Services Shipping

⊞ The Antiques Exchange
Contact Ray Gibbs
✉ **170–172 Tower Bridge Road, London, SE1 3LS** 🅿
☎ 020 7403 5568 ⓕ 020 7378 8828
ⓔ info@AntiquesExchange.com
ⓦ www.AntiquesExchange.com
Est. 1966 ***Stock size*** Large
Stock Furniture, glass, china, collectables, period style lighting
Open Mon–Fri 10am–6pm Sat 10.30am–6pm Sun 11am–5pm

⊞ Sebastiano Barbagallo Antiques
Contact Mr S Barbagallo
✉ **Universal House, 294–304 St James's Road, London, SE1 5JX** 🅿
☎ 020 7231 3680 ⓕ 020 7231 3680
ⓔ sebastianobarbagallo@hotmail.com
Est. 1978 ***Stock size*** Large
Stock Chinese furniture, Indian and Tibetan antiques, crafts
Open By appointment only

⛫ Bermondsey Antiques Market
Contact Mike Spooner
✉ **Corner of Long Lane, Bermondsey Street, Bermondsey Square, London, SE1 3TQ** 🅿
☎ 020 7351 53331500
ⓕ 020 7969 1639
ⓔ antique@dial.pipex.com
Est. 1950 ***Stock size*** Large
No. of dealers 400
Stock Wide range of general antiques and collectables, including specialists in jewellery and silver
Open Fri 5am–2pm and Bank Holidays

⊞ Victor Burness Antiques
Contact Mr V Burness
✉ **241 Long Lane, Bermondsey, London, SE1 4PR** 🅿
☎ 01732 454591
Est. 1975 ***Stock size*** Medium
Stock Scientific instruments
Open Fri 6am–12.30pm
Services Valuations, restoration

⊞ Robert Bush Antiques
Contact Mr Robert Bush
✉ **The Galleries, 157 Tower Bridge Road, London, SE1 3LW**
Ⓜ 07836 236911
ⓔ bush.antiques@virgin.net
Stock Antique and decorative furniture
Open Mon–Sun 9.30am–5pm

⊞ Capital Antiques Ltd
Contact Joan Carter
✉ **168A Tower Bridge Road, London, SE1 3LS** 🅿
☎ 020 7378 7263 ⓕ 020 7378 7291
ⓔ joancarter@capitalantiques.fsbusiness.co.uk
Est. 2002 ***Stock size*** Medium
Stock 17thC–Edwardian antiques, Arts and Crafts
Open Mon–Fri 10.30am–5.30pm Sat 10.30-am–6pm Sun 11am–5pm

⛫ The Galleries Ltd
Contact Alan Bennett
✉ **157 Tower Bridge Road, London, SE1 3LW** 🅿
☎ 020 7407 5371 ⓕ 020 7403 0359
Est. 1993 ***Stock size*** Large
No. of dealers 28
Stock Victorian, Edwardian, reproduction furniture, Arts and Crafts, Art Nouveau, reproduction leather chesterfields
Open Mon–Thurs 9.30am–5.30pm Fri 8am–4pm Sat noon–6pm Sun noon–5pm

⊞ LASSCO Flooring (SALVO, Timber Trade Federation, TRADA)
Contact Hamish Urquhart
✉ **41 Maltby Street, London, SE1 3PA** 🅿
☎ 020 7237 4488 ⓕ 020 7237 2564
ⓔ flooring@lassco.co.uk
ⓦ www.lassco.co.uk
Est. 1978 ***Stock size*** Large
Stock Reclaimed timber flooring in parquet strip and board
Open Mon–Fri 9am–6pm Sat 10am–5pm
Services Shipping

⊞ LASSCO RBK (SALVO)
Contact Dan Neate
✉ **41 Maltby Street, London, SE1 3PA** 🅿
☎ 020 7394 2102 ⓕ 020 7237 8373
ⓔ rbk@lassco.co.uk
ⓦ www.lassco.co.uk
Est. 1978 ***Stock size*** Large
Stock Reclaimed radiators, bathrooms, kitchens
Open Mon–Sat 10am–5pm
Services Shipping

⊞ Mayfair Carpet Gallery Ltd
Contact Mr A H Khawaja
✉ **301–303 Borough High Street, London, SE1 1JH** 🅿
☎ 020 7403 8228 ⓕ 020 7407 1649
ⓔ aimz-kh@hotmail.com
Est. 1975 ***Stock size*** Large
Stock Fine antique Oriental carpets, rugs
Open Mon–Sat 10.30am–6.30pm
Services Valuations, restoration

⊞ Radio Days
Contact Mrs C Layzell
✉ **87 Lower Marsh, London, SE1 7AB** 🅿
☎ 020 7928 0800 ⓕ 020 7928 0800
Est. 1993 ***Stock size*** Large
Stock 1930s–1970s lighting, telephones, radios, clothing, magazines, cocktail bars
Open Mon–Sat 10am–6pm or by appointment

⊞ Tower Bridge Antiques
Contact Joan Carter
✉ **71 Tanner Street, London, SE1 3PL** 🅿
☎ 020 7403 3660 ⓕ 020 7403 6058
ⓔ towerbridgeant@aol.com
Est. 1967 ***Stock size*** Large
Stock English, French and American furniture
Open Mon–Fri 8am–5pm Sat 10am–6pm Sun 11am–5pm

⊞ G Viventi
Contact Giorgio
✉ **160 Tower Bridge Road, London, SE1 3LS** 🅿
☎ 020 7403 0022 ⓕ 020 7277 5777
ⓔ viventi@btconnect.com
Est. 2000 ***Stock size*** Large
Stock Wide range of furniture, styles and periods
Open Mon–Sat 9.30am–6pm

LONDON

SE3

Beaumont Travel Books (ABA, ILAB)
Contact Mr G Beaumont
33 Couthurst Road, Blackheath, London, SE3 8TN
020 8293 4271 Ⓕ 020 8293 4271
Ⓔ JohnGabrielB@aol.com
Ⓦ www.abebooks.com/home/beaumont
Est. 1996 *Stock size* Large
Stock Antiquarian, rare, second-hand books, anthropology, military, history, travel, exploration a speciality
Open By appointment
Services Valuations, book search

The Bookshop Blackheath Ltd
Contact Mr R Platt
74 Tranquil Vale, London, SE3 0BN
020 8852 4786
Est. 1947 *Stock size* Large
Stock Antiquarian books, prints, maps
Open Mon–Sat 10am–6pm Sun noon–6pm
Services Valuations, book search

SE5

Architectural Rescue
Contact Mr J Powell
1 Southampton Way, London, SE5 7JH
020 7277 0081 Ⓕ 020 7277 0081
Est. 1993 *Stock size* Large
Stock Flooring, radiators, sanitary ware, doors, door furniture, fireplaces a speciality, York stone
Open Mon–Sat 10am–5pm Sun 10am–2pm
Fairs Newark, Swinderby

Robert Hirschhorn (BADA, LAPADA, CINOA)
Contact Robert Hirschhorn
London, SE5
020 7703 7443
Ⓜ 07831 405937
Ⓔ hirschhornantiques@macunlimited.net
Ⓦ www.hirschhornantiques.com
Est. 1978 *Stock size* Medium
Stock 18thC and earlier country furniture, related objects
Open By appointment
Fairs Olympia, BADA
Services Valuations

SE6

The Old Mill
Contact Mr A Jackson
358 Bromley Road, Catford, London, SE6 2RT
020 8697 8006
Est. 1845 *Stock size* Medium
Stock Garden statuary, fireplaces
Open Mon–Sat 9.30am–5pm

Wilkinson PLC
Contact Jane Milnes
5 Catford Hill, London, SE6 4NU
020 8314 1080 Ⓕ 020 8690 1524
Ⓔ enquiries@wilkinson-plc.com
Ⓦ www.wilkinson-plc.com
Est. 1946 *Stock size* Large
Stock Lighting, chandeliers, candelabra
Open Mon–Fri 9am–5pm
Services Restoration

SE7

Ward's Antiques
Contact Terry or Michael Ward
267 Woolwich Road, London, SE7 7RB
020 8305 0963 Ⓕ 020 8305 2151
Ⓜ 07932 031936
Ⓦ www.wardantiquefireplaces.co.uk
Est. 1977 *Stock size* Large
Stock Victorian and Edwardian fireplaces, general antiques
Open Mon–Sat 9am–6pm Sun 11am–2pm
Services Restoration

SE8

Antique Warehouse
Contact Mrs Tillet
9–14 Deptford Broadway, London, SE8 4PA
020 8691 3062 Ⓕ 020 8469 0295
Ⓔ martin@antiquewarehouse.co.uk
Ⓦ www.antiquewarehouse.co.uk
Est. 1983 *Stock size* Large
Stock General antiques
Open Mon–Sat 10am–6pm Sun 11am–4pm
Services Valuations via website

SE10

Cassidy's Gallery (PBFA)
Contact Mr M Cassidy
20 College Approach, Greenwich, London, SE10 9HY
020 8858 7197 Ⓕ 020 8858 7197
Ⓜ 07710 012128
Ⓔ cassidysgallery@aol.com
Ⓦ www.cassidysgallery.com
Est. 1984 *Stock size* Small
Stock Antiquarian, plate books, atlases, illustrated books, maps, prints
Open By appointment

Creek Antiques
Contact Dave
23 Greenwich South Street, London, SE10 8NW
020 8293 5721
Ⓜ 07778 427521
Est. 1986 *Stock size* Medium
Stock Jewellery, silver, enamel signs, amusement machines
Open By appointment
Fairs Sandown, Newark

Decomania
Contact Mrs J Crompton
9 College Approach, London, SE10 9HY
020 8858 8180
Ⓔ deco.mania@ntlworld.com
Est. 1998 *Stock size* Large
Stock Rare pieces of 1920s–1930s Art Deco, pictures, mirrors, furniture, decorative items, jewellery
Open Wed–Sun 10.30am–5.30pm or by appointment
Services Delivery, shipping

Flying Duck Enterprises
Contact Mr J Lowe or Ms C Shrosbree
320–322 Creek Road, Greenwich, London, SE10 9SW
020 8858 1964 Ⓕ 020 8852 3215
Ⓜ 07831 273303
Ⓔ jimllkitschit@flying-duck.com
Est. 1985 *Stock size* Large
Stock 1950–1970s items, cocktail bars, furniture, lighting, fabrics, dinette sets, glassware, china, 1950s fridges
Open Tues–Fri noon–6pm Sat Sun 10.30am–6pm
Services Mail order

Greenwich Auctions Partnership
Contact Marilyn Allen
47 Old Woolwich Road, Greenwich, London, SE10 9PP

☎ 020 8853 2121 Ⓕ 020 8293 7878
Ⓔ greenwichauction@aol.com
Ⓦ www.greenwichauctions.co.uk
Est. 2000
Open Mon–Sat 9am–5pm
Sales Auction of antiques, collectables, furniture, memorabilia
Frequency Weekly
Catalogues Yes

⊞ Greenwich Gallery
Contact Richard Moy
✉ **9 Nevada Street, London, SE10 9JL** Ⓟ
☎ 020 8305 1666 ext 24
Ⓔ antiques@spreadeagle.org
Ⓦ www.spreadeagle.org
Est. 1957 *Stock size* Medium
Stock 18th–19thC watercolours, modern British art, prints
Open Mon–Sun 10.30am–5.30pm

⊞ The Junk Box
Contact Mrs M Dodd
✉ **47 Old Woolwich Road, Greenwich, London, SE10 9PP** Ⓟ
☎ 020 8293 5715
Est. 1988 *Stock size* Large
Stock Antiques, collectables, Victorian furniture, china, glass, copper, brass, kitchenware
Open Mon–Fri 10am–5pm
Services Valuations

⊞ The Junk Shop
Contact Tobias Moy
✉ **9 Greenwich South Street, London, SE10 8NW** Ⓟ
☎ 020 8305 1666 ext 25
Ⓦ www.spreadeagle.org
Est. 1985 *Stock size* Large
Stock Larger period furniture, architectural antiques, garden ornaments, decorative items
Open Mon–Sun 10.30am–5.30pm

⊞ Lamont Antiques Ltd (LAPADA)
Contact Mr F Llewellyn
✉ **Unit K, Tunnel Avenue Trading Estate, Greenwich, London, SE10 0QH** Ⓟ
☎ 020 8305 2230 Ⓕ 020 8305 1805
Ⓔ lamontantiques@aol.com
Ⓦ www.lamontantiques.com
Est. 1974 *Stock size* Large
Stock Architectural items, stained glass, pub and restaurant fixtures, fittings
Open Mon–Fri 9.30am–5pm

⊞ Marcet Books (PBFA)
Contact Mr M Kemp
✉ **4a Nelson Road, Greenwich, London, SE10 9JB** Ⓟ
☎ 020 8853 5408
Ⓔ marcetbooks@btconnect.com
Ⓦ www.marcetbooks.co.uk
Est. 1980 *Stock size* Medium
Stock Antiquarian, rare, second-hand books, maritime, foreign travel, British topography, art, natural history, poetry specialities
Open Mon–Sun 10am–5.30pm
Fairs PBFA, Russell Hotel
Services Valuations

⊞ Minerva Antiques
Contact Jonathan Atkins
✉ **90 Royal Hill, Greenwich, London, SE10 8RT** Ⓟ
☎ 020 8691 2221
Ⓔ sales@minerva-antiques.co.uk
Ⓦ www.minerva-antiques.co.uk
Est. 1989 *Stock size* Large
Stock Antique furniture, mirrors
Open Tues–Sat 10am–6pm Sun 11am–5pm
Services Restoration

⊞ Rogers Turner Books (ABA, PBFA)
Contact Mr P Rogers
✉ **23a Nelson Road, Greenwich, London, SE10 9JB** Ⓟ
☎ 020 8853 5271 Ⓕ 020 8853 5271
Ⓔ rogersturner@compuserve.com
Est. 1976 *Stock size* Medium
Stock Rare, antiquarian and second-hand books on experimental science, scientific instruments, horology, dialling a speciality
Open Thurs Fri 10am–6pm or by appointment
Fairs ABA Fairs, Olympia, PBFA London (monthly)
Services Valuations, catalogues

⊞ Spread Eagle Antiques
Contact Richard Moy
✉ **1 Stockwell Street, London, SE10 9JN** Ⓟ
☎ 020 8305 1666 ext 22
Ⓦ www.spreadeagle.org
Est. 1957 *Stock size* Medium
Stock Antique furniture, silver, decorative antiques, curios, ethnic art
Open Mon–Sun 10.30am–5.30pm

⊞ Spread Eagle Books
Contact Richard Moy
✉ **8 Nevada Street, London, SE10 9JL** Ⓟ
☎ 020 8305 1666 ext 23
Ⓦ www.spreadeagle.org
Est. 1957 *Stock size* Medium
Stock Antiquarian books, collectables, ephemera
Open Mon–Sun 10.30am–5.30pm

⊞ Unique Collections of Greenwich
Contact Glen Chapman
✉ **52 Greenwich Church Street, London, SE10 9BL** Ⓟ
☎ 020 8305 0867 Ⓕ 020 8853 1066
Ⓔ glen@uniquecollections.co.uk
Est. 1987 *Stock size* Medium
Stock Obsolete diecast Dinky toys, Corgi, Matchbox/Lesney, Tri-ang, Spot-On/Minic ships, tinplate toys, William Britains, Timpo toy soldiers, Action Man
Open Tues–Sun 11am–5pm

⊞ The Warwick Leadlay Gallery (FATG)
Contact Mr Anthony Cross
✉ **5 Nelson Road, London, SE10 9JB** Ⓟ
☎ 020 8858 0317 Ⓕ 020 8853 1773
Ⓔ wlg@ceasynet.co.uk
Ⓦ www.wlgonline.com
Est. 1974 *Stock size* Large
Stock Antique maps, decorative maritime prints, fine arts, curios
Open Mon–Sat 9.30am–5.30pm Sun 11.30am–5.30pm
Services Valuations, restoration, conservation, framing

⊞ Robert Whitfield (LAPADA)
Contact Mr R Whitfield
✉ **Unit K, Tunnel Avenue Trading Estate, Greenwich, London, SE10 0QH** Ⓟ
☎ 020 8305 2230 Ⓕ 020 8305 1805
Ⓔ robertwhitfield@btinternet.com
Est. 1974 *Stock size* Large
Stock Oak, mahogany, walnut furniture
Trade only Yes
Open Mon–Fri 9am–5pm or by appointment

SE11

⊞ Nicholas Grindley (BADA)
Contact Ms Rebecca Gardner

✉ **London, SE11**
☎ 020 7437 5449 Ⓕ 01449 614523
Ⓔ nick@nicholasgrindley.co.uk
Est. 1993 *Stock size* Small
Stock Chinese works of art, sculptures, wall paintings, furniture etc
Open By appointment
Fairs Asian Art, London (Nov), Olympia
Services Valuations by mail

⊞ Kear of Kennington Antiques
Contact Mr S A Kear
✉ **4 Windmill Row, London, SE11 5DW** Ⓟ
☎ 020 7735 1304
Est. 1968 *Stock size* Small
Stock 18thC English drinking glasses, pottery, porcelain
Open By appointment

SE13

⊞ Robert Morley & Co Ltd (BADA)
Contact Julia Morley
✉ **34 Engate Street, London, SE13 7HA** Ⓟ
☎ 020 8318 5838
Ⓔ jvm@morley-r.u-net.com
Ⓦ www.morleypianos.com
Est. 1881 *Stock size* Large
Stock Musical instruments
Open Mon–Fri 9.30am–5pm
Fairs Le Music Show
Services Restoration, tuning

⊞ The Old Station
Contact Mr R Jacob
✉ **72 Loampit Hill, Lewisham, London, SE13 7SX** Ⓟ
☎ 020 8694 6540
Ⓜ 07710 489895
Ⓔ loampit@hotmail.com
Ⓦ www.the-old-station.co.uk
Est. 1995 *Stock size* Large
Stock Large varied stock, architectural salvage, fireplaces, antique furniture, chimney pieces, sanitary ware
Open Mon–Sat 10am–5pm Sun 11am–4pm
Fairs Newark, Ardingly, Kempton
Services Door stripping, fireplace restoration

SE15

⊞ CASA
Contact Mr M Tree
✉ **155 Bellenden Road, Peckham, London, SE15 4DH** Ⓟ
☎ 020 7732 3911
Ⓜ 07957 249722
Ⓔ matt.tree@btopenworld.com
Ⓦ www.casaonline.co.uk
Est. 1993 *Stock size* Small
Stock Fireplaces, cast-iron radiators, doors, floorboards, stained glass windows, fixtures, fittings, sinks, basins, roll-top baths, taps, multi-fuel stoves, furniture, gardening antiques
Open Tues–Sat 10am–5pm or by appointement
Services Fireplace fitting, carpentry, plumbing, design

SE17

⊞ Pub Paraphernalia UK Ltd
Contact Mr M Ellis
✉ **Unit 13, Newington Industrial Estate, Crampton Street, London, SE17 3AZ** Ⓟ
☎ 020 7701 8913 Ⓕ 020 7277 4100
Ⓔ sales@pub-paraphernalia.com
Ⓦ www.pub-paraphernalia.com
Est. 1980 *Stock size* Medium
Stock Water jugs, bar towels, beer mats, glassware, ashtrays, mirrors
Open Mon–Fri 9am–5pm by appointment
Fairs NEC (Spring)

SE19

⊞ The Book Palace
Contact Mr K Harman or Mr G West
✉ **Jubilee House, Bedwardine Road, London, SE19 3AP** Ⓟ
☎ 020 8768 0022 Ⓕ 020 8768 0563
Ⓔ david@totalise.co.uk
Ⓦ www.bookpalace.com
Est. 1996 *Stock size* Large
Stock Histories of comics and popular media, art books, science fiction, film and TV biographies, Disney, animation, old US and UK comics, pulps, paperbacks, graphic novels
Open Mon–Fri 10am–6pm or by appointment
Fairs CIAMA, London Memorabilia Fair, NEC
Services Valuations, wanted titles list

SE20

⊞ Bearly Trading of London
Contact Cindy Hamilton-Aust
✉ **202 High Street, London, SE20 7QB** Ⓟ
☎ 020 8659 0500/8466 6696
Ⓕ 020 8460 3166
Ⓔ jakeaust@hotmail.com
Est. 1998 *Stock size* Large
Stock Old and new artists' teddy bears, rocking horses, antique furniture
Open Sat 10am–6pm or by appointment
Services Lay-a-way, mail order

SE21

⊞ Francis Jevons
Contact Mr F Jevons
✉ **80 Dulwich Village, London, SE21 7AJ** Ⓟ
☎ 020 8693 1991
Est. 1983 *Stock size* Small
Stock Antique furniture, china, glass, interior design items
Open Mon–Fri 9.30am–1pm 2.30–5.30pm Sat 9.30– 5pm closed Wed
Services Valuations, restoration

SE22

⊞ Browns Antiques
Contact Erica Brown
✉ **149 Lordship Lane, East Dulwich, London, SE22 8HX** Ⓟ
☎ 020 8693 3000
Est. 2002 *Stock size* Medium
Stock Fine English furniture, glass, textiles
Open Mon–Sat 11am–6pm or by appointment
Services Restoration

⊞ Melbourne Antiques & Interiors
Contact Ian Peters
✉ **8 Melbourne Grove, London, SE22 8QZ** Ⓟ
☎ 020 8299 6565 Ⓕ 020 8299 4257
Est. 1998 *Stock size* Large
Stock French furniture, mirrors, chandeliers, armoires, linens, beds, commodes, fire surrounds
Open Mon–Sat 10am–6pm or by appointment

Timothy Millett Ltd (BADA)
Contact Timothy Millett
PO Box 20851, London, SE22 0YN
020 8693 1111 020 8299 3733
07778 637898
tim@timothymillett.demon.co.uk
Est. 2000 *Stock size* Large
Stock Historical medals, works of art
Open By appointment
Fairs Olympia June, BADA

Still Useful
Contact Mr R Honour
52 Grove Vale, London, SE22 8DY
020 8299 2515
Est. 1979 *Stock size* Large
Stock Oak and mahogany furniture, decorative items, lighting
Open Mon–Sat 10am–4pm

SE26

Grenadiers
Contact Mr C Chin-See
102 Sydenham Road, London, SE26 5JX
020 8659 1588 020 8659 1588
grenadiers@btinternet.com
www.grenadiers.co.uk
Est. 1998 *Stock size* Medium
Stock Wide range of militaria
Open Mon–Fri 9.30am–6pm Sat 9.30am–5.30pm

Oola Boola Antiques London
Contact Mrs S Bramley
139–147 Kirkdale, London, SE26 4QJ
020 8291 9999 020 8291 5759
07956 261252
oola.boola@telco4u.net
Est. 1970 *Stock size* Large
Stock Victorian, Edwardian, Art Nouveau, Art Deco, Arts and Crafts furniture
Open Mon–Sat 10am–6pm Sun 11am–5pm
Services Restoration, shipping

Sydenham Antiques Centre
Contact Mr P Cockton
48 Sydenham Road, London, SE26 5QF
020 8778 1706
Est. 1996 *Stock size* Large
No. of dealers 10
Stock Antiques, china, glass, furniture, jewellery, pictures, silver
Open Mon–Sat 10am–5pm

SE27

Rosebery Fine Art Ltd (ISVA)
Contact Miss L Lloyd
74–76 Knights Hill, London, SE27 0JD
020 8761 2522 020 8761 2524
auctions@roseberys.co.uk
www.roseberys.co.uk
Est. 1987
Open Mon–Fri 9.30am–5.30pm
Sales Antiques and collectors' sale Tues Wed 11am. General sale Mon 1pm, viewing Sun 10am–2pm Mon 10am–7.30pm Tues Wed 9.30–10.45am. Quarterly select antiques, decorative arts and modern design, musical instruments, toys and collectors books
Frequency Fortnightly
Catalogues Yes

SW1

After Noah
Contact Simon Tarr
4th Floor, Harvey Nichols, London, SW1X 7RJ
020 7235 5000
mailorder@afternoah.com
www.afternoah.com
Est. 1995 *Stock size* Medium
Stock Antique and contemporary furniture and houseware
Open Mon–Fri 10am–8pm Sat 10am–7pm Sun noon–6pm
Services Restoration

Albert Amor (RWHA)
Contact Mark Law or Nicholas Lyne
37 Bury Street, London, SW1Y 6AU
020 7930 2444 020 7930 9067
info@albertamor.co.uk
www.albertamor.co.uk
Est. 1899 *Stock size* Small
Stock 18thC English porcelain
Open Mon–Thurs 10am–5pm or by appointment
Fairs Park Lane International Ceramics Fair

Anno Domini Antiques (BADA)
Contact Mr D Cohen
66 Pimlico Road, London, SW1W 8LS
020 7730 5496
Est. 1969 *Stock size* Large
Stock 18th–19thC furniture, mirrors, pictures, glass, porcelain
Open Mon–Fri 10am–1pm 2.15–5.30pm Sat 10am–3pm or by appointment
Services Valuations, restoration

Antiquus
Contact Elizabeth Amati
90–92 Pimlico Road, London, SW1W 8PL
020 7730 8681 020 7823 6409
antiquus@antiquus-london.co.uk
www.antiquus-london.co.uk
Est. 1971 *Stock size* Large
Stock Gothic, Renaissance works of art, sculpture, textiles
Open Mon–Sat 9.30am–5.30pm

The Armoury of St James (OMRS)
Contact Mr Rawlins or Mr Davis
17 Piccadilly Arcade, London, SW1Y 6NH
020 7493 5082 020 7499 4422
welcome@armoury.co.uk
www.armoury.co.uk
Est. 1969 *Stock size* Large
Stock Royal memorablilia, model soldiers, regimental brooches, side drums, bronzes
Open Mon–Fri 10am–6pm Sat noon–6pm
Services Valuations, world orders, decorations

Hilary Batstone Antiques (LAPADA)
Contact Hilary Batstone
8 Holbein Place, London, SW1W 8NL
020 7730 5335 020 7730 5335
07836 594908
hilary@batstone.com
Est. 1986 *Stock size* Medium
Stock 19th–20thC furniture, crystal chandeliers, Venetian mirrors, glass, stone, steel, natural textiles
Open Mon–Fri 10.30am–5.30pm Sat by appointment

Belgrave Carpet Gallery Ltd
Contact Mr Khawaja
91 Knightsbridge, London, SW1X 7RV
020 7235 2541 020 7407 1649

Est. 1975 *Stock size* Large
Stock Antique Oriental carpets
Open Mon–Sat 10.30am–6.30pm

Blanchard Ltd (LAPADA)
Contact Mr Piers Ingall
86–88 Pimlico Road, London, SW1W 8PL
☎ 020 7823 6310 Ⓕ 020 7823 6303
Ⓔ piers@jwblanchard.com
Est. 1950 *Stock size* Medium
Stock English and Continental furniture, decorative items, works of art, lighting
Open Mon–Fri 10am–6pm Sat 10am–3pm
Fairs Olympia (June)
Services Valuations, restoration, shipping

N Bloom and Son (1912) Ltd (LAPADA, CINOA, BACA Award Winner 2001)
Contact Ian Harris
12 Piccadilly Arcade, London, SW1Y 6NH
☎ 020 7629 5060 Ⓕ 020 7493 2528
Ⓔ nbloom@nbloom.com
Ⓦ www.nbloom.com
Est. 1912 *Stock size* Large
Stock 1860–1960 jewellery, silver
Open Mon–Fri 10.30am–5.30pm Sat 11am–5.30pm
Fairs Olympia (June), LAPADA, Claridges (April), Miami (Jan)
Services Valuations, restoration, catalogue

John Bly (BADA, CINOA)
Contact Mr John Bly or Mr James Bly
27 Bury Street, London, SW1Y 6AL Ⓟ
☎ 01442 823030
Ⓔ james@johnbly.com
Ⓦ www.johnbly.com
Est. 1891 *Stock size* Large
Stock 18th–19thC English furniture, works of art, objets d'art, paintings, silver, glass, porcelain, tapestries
Open By appointment
Fairs BADA (March), Palm Beach, Florida (Feb)
Services Valuations, restoration

J H Bourdon-Smith Ltd (BADA, CINOA)
Contact Mr J Bourdon-Smith
24 Masons Yard, Duke Street, St James's, London, SW1Y 6BU Ⓟ
☎ 020 7839 4714 Ⓕ 020 7839 3951
Est. 1953 *Stock size* Large
Stock Georgian–Victorian silver, modern reproduction silver
Open Mon–Fri 9.30am–6pm
Fairs Grosvenor House, BADA, Olympia (Nov)

John Carlton-Smith (BADA)
Contact Mr J Carlton-Smith
17 Ryder Street, London, SW1Y 6PY Ⓟ
☎ 020 7930 6622 Ⓕ 020 7930 6622
Ⓜ 07967 180682
Ⓔ jcarltonsm@aol.com
Ⓦ www.fineartantiqueclocks.com
Est. 1968 *Stock size* Large
Stock Fine antique clocks and barometers
Open Mon–Fri 9am–5.30pm
Fairs March BADA, Grosvenor House, Winter Olympia
Services Valuations

Chelsea Antique Mirrors
Contact Mr A Koll
72 Pimlico Road, London, SW1W 8LS Ⓟ
☎ 020 7824 8024 Ⓕ 020 7824 8233
Est. 1980 *Stock size* Medium
Stock 18th–19thC mirrors, furniture
Open Mon–Fri 10am–6pm Sat 10am–2pm
Services Restoration

Christie's
8 King Street, London, SW1Y 6QT Ⓟ
☎ 020 7839 9060 Ⓕ 020 7839 1611
Ⓦ www.christies.com
Est. 1766
Open Mon–Fri 9am–5pm
Sales Sales throughout the year, except Aug and Jan, viewing 4 days prior to sales and weekends, evenings. Free verbal auction estimates
Catalogues Yes

Ciancimino Ltd
Contact Mr J Ciancimino
99 Pimlico Road, London, SW1W 8PH Ⓟ
☎ 020 7730 9950 Ⓕ 020 7730 5365
Ⓔ info@ciancimino.com
Ⓦ www.ciancimino.com
Est. 1965 *Stock size* Medium
Stock Art Deco furniture, Oriental furniture, ethnography
Open Mon–Fri 10am–6pm Sat 10am–5pm
Fairs International Fine Art & Antique Dealers Show, New York

Classic Bindings (ABA)
Contact Mr S Poklewski-Koziell
61 Cambridge Street, London, SW1V 4PS Ⓟ
☎ 020 7834 5554 Ⓕ 020 7630 6632
Ⓔ info@classicbindings.net
Ⓦ www.classicbindings.net
Est. 1990 *Stock size* Large
Stock General antiquarian books, classic bindings
Open Mon–Fri 9.30am–5.30pm or by appointment
Services Valuations

Cobra & Bellamy
Contact Tanya Hunter
149 Sloane Street, London, SW1X 9BZ Ⓟ
☎ 020 7730 9993 Ⓕ 020 7824 8996
Ⓔ cobrabellamy@hotmail.com
Est. 1980 *Stock size* Medium
Stock Jewellery, amber, glass, ivory, coral
Open Mon–Fri 10.30am–6pm Sat 10.30am–5pm
Services Valuations

Peter Dale Ltd (LAPADA)
Contact Mr Robin Dale
12 Royal Opera Arcade, London, SW1Y 4UY Ⓟ
☎ 020 7930 3695 Ⓕ 020 7930 2223
Ⓜ 07785 580396
Ⓔ robin@peterdaleltd.com
Est. 1960 *Stock size* Medium
Stock European antique arms, armour
Open Mon–Fri 9.15am–5pm
Services Valuations

Kenneth Davis (Works of Art) Ltd
Contact Danielle Fluer
15 King Street, London, SW1Y 6QU Ⓟ
☎ 020 7930 0313 Ⓕ 020 7976 1306
Est. 1965 *Stock size* Medium
Stock Antique English and Continental silver, works of art
Open Mon–Fri 9.30am–5pm
Services Valuations, restoration

Alastair Dickenson Ltd (BADA)
Contact Mr A Dickenson or Mrs M Cuchet
90 Jermyn Street, London,

SW1Y 6JD P
☎ 020 7839 2808 Ⓕ 020 7839 2809
Ⓜ 07976 283530
Ⓔ adickensonsilver@btconnect.com
Est. 1996 *Stock size* Small
Stock 16th–19thC fine, rare English silver
Open Mon–Fri 9.30am–5.30pm
Services Valuations, restoration

Didier Aaron (London) Ltd (BADA)
Contact Didier Leblanc
✉ **21 Ryder Street, London, SW1Y 6PX** P
☎ 020 7839 4716 Ⓕ 020 7930 6699
Ⓔ contact@didieraaronltd.com
Est. 2985 *Stock size* Medium
Stock 18thC–early 19thC Continental furniture, old master drawings, paintings
Open Mon–Fri 11am–1pm 2–5pm and by appointment
Fairs Maastricht, Paris Biennale

Elizabeth Street Antiques and Restoration Services
Contact Mr Naik
✉ **35 Elizabeth Street, London, SW1W 9RP** P
☎ 020 7730 6777
Ⓜ 07973 909257
Est. 1993 *Stock size* Medium
Stock General antiques
Open Mon–Sat 8am–7pm
Services Restoration

Filippa & Co
Contact Filippa Naess
✉ **51 Kinnerton Street, London, SW1X 8ED** P
☎ 020 7235 1722 Ⓕ 020 7245 9160
Ⓔ filippa@dircon.co.uk
Ⓦ www.filippaandco.com
Est. 1998 *Stock size* Medium
Stock Swedish furniture, chandeliers, mirrors, decorative accessories
Open Mon–Fri 11am–5.30pm Sat Sun by appointment
Services Shipping

Un Français à Londres
Contact Mr P Sumner
✉ **202 Ebury Street, London, SW1W 8UN** P
☎ 020 7730 1771 Ⓕ 020 7730 1881
Ⓔ eburystreet@aol.com
Ⓦ www.unfrancaisalondres.com
Est. 1998 *Stock size* Large
Stock French and Continental furniture, works of art, 17th–19thC
Open Mon–Fri 10am–6pm Sat 10am–4pm or by appointment
Services Valuations, restoration, upholstery

N & I Franklin (BADA)
Contact Mr N Franklin or Mr I Franklin
✉ **11 Bury Street, London, SW1Y 6AB**
☎ 020 7839 3131 Ⓕ 020 7839 3132
Ⓔ neil@franklinsilver.com
Est. 1980 *Stock size* Large
Stock 17th–18thC English domestic silver
Open Mon–Fri 10am–5pm or by appointment
Fairs Grosvenor House
Services Valuations

J A L Franks and Co
Contact Mr G Franks
✉ **7 Allington Street, London, SW1E 5EB** P
☎ 020 7233 8433
Ⓔ jalfranks@btinternet.com
Ⓦ www.jalfranks.btinternet.co.uk
Est. 1947 *Stock size* Medium
Stock 16th–19thC antique maps
Open Mon–Fri 10am–5pm
Fairs London Map Fair, IMCOS

Victor Franses Gallery (BADA)
Contact Graham Franses
✉ **57 Jermyn Street, St James's, London, SW1Y 6LX**
☎ 020 7493 6284/7629 1144
Ⓕ 020 7495 3668
Ⓔ bronzes@vfranses.com
Ⓦ www.vfranses.com
Est. 1972 *Stock size* Large
Stock 19thC animalier sculpture, paintings, drawings, watercolours
Open Mon–Fri 10am–5pm or by appointment
Fairs Grosvenor House
Services Valuations, restoration

Christopher Gibbs Antiques (LAPADA)
Contact Richenda Symonds
✉ **3 Dove Walk, Pimlico Road, London, SW1W 8PS**
☎ 020 7730 8200 Ⓕ 020 7730 8420
Est. 1961 *Stock size* Large
Stock General antiques
Open Mon–Fri 9.30am–5.30pm

Nicholas Gifford-Mead (BADA, LAPADA)
Contact Mr N Gifford-Mead
✉ **68 Pimlico Road, London, SW1W 8LS** P
☎ 020 7730 6233 Ⓕ 020 7730 6239
Est. 1969 *Stock size* Medium
Stock Pre-1840 English and European chimneypieces, sculpture
Open Mon–Fri 9.30am–5.30pm
Services Valuations

Joss Graham Orientals
Contact Joss Graham
✉ **10 Eccleston Street, London, SW1W 9LT** P
☎ 020 7730 4370 Ⓕ 020 7730 4370
Ⓔ jossgraham@btinternet.com
Est. 1982 *Stock size* Large
Stock Oriental antiques
Open Mon–Fri 10am–6pm
Services Valuations, restoration

Nicolas Guedroitz Ltd
Contact Simon Pugh
✉ **227 Ebury Street, London, SW1W 9NF** P
☎ 020 7730 3111 Ⓕ 020 7730 1441
Ⓔ guedroitz@russianfurniture.co.uk
Ⓦ www. russianfurniture.co.uk
Est. 1996 *Stock size* Medium
Stock 18th–19thC Russian furniture
Open Mon–Fri 10am–6pm Sat 11am–3.30pm

Nicolas Guedroitz Ltd
Contact Simon Pugh
✉ **24 Pimlico Road, London, SW1W 8JA** P
☎ 020 7730 3111 Ⓕ 020 7730 1441
Ⓔ guedroitz@russianfurniture.co.uk
Ⓦ www. russianfurniture.co.uk
Est. 1996 *Stock size* Medium
Stock 18th–19thC Russian furniture
Open Mon–Fri 10am–6pm Sat 11am–3.30pm

Ross Hamilton (Antiques) Ltd (LAPADA, CINOA)
Contact Mr C M Boyce
✉ **95 Pimlico Road, London, SW1W 8PH** P
☎ 020 7730 3015 Ⓕ 020 7730 3015
Ⓦ www.lapada.co.uk/rosshamilton/
Est. 1973 *Stock size* Large
Stock 17th–19thC fine English and Continental furniture, 16th–20thC paintings, Oriental porcelain, objets d'art, bronzes
Open Mon–Fri 9am–6pm Sat 10.30am–5pm
Services Shipping worldwide

🏛 Brian Harkins

Contact Ms Erica Quan or Brian Harkins
✉ **3 Bury Street, St James's, London, SW1Y 6AB** 🅿
☎ 020 7839 3338 Ⓕ 020 7839 9339
Ⓔ info@brianharkins.co.uk
Ⓦ www.brianharkins.co.uk
Est. 1978
Stock Chinese and Japanese antiques, scholars' items, furniture, decorative items, ceramics, bronzes, rocks, baskets
Open Mon–Fri 10am–6pm

🏛 Harris Lindsay (BADA, CINOA)

Contact Jonathan Harris or Bruce Lindsay
✉ **67 Jermyn Street, London, SW1Y 6NY** 🅿
☎ 020 7839 5767 Ⓕ 020 7839 5768
Ⓦ www.harrislindsay.com
Est. 1967 *Stock size* Medium
Stock English, Continental and Oriental works of art
Open Mon–Fri 9.30am–6pm or by appointment
Fairs Grosvenor House, International Show, New York (Oct), TEFAF, Maastricht

🏛 Harvey & Gore (BADA)

Contact Brian Norman
✉ **41 Duke Street, St James's, London, SW1Y 6DF** 🅿
☎ 020 7839 4033 Ⓕ 020 7839 3313
Ⓔ norman@harveyandgore.co.uk
Ⓦ www.harveyandgore.co.uk
Est. 1723 *Stock size* Large
Stock Jewellery, bijouterie, snuff boxes, old Sheffield plate, miniatures
Open Mon–Fri 9.30am–5pm
Fairs BADA
Services Valuations, restoration, VAT margin and standard

🏛 Thomas Heneage Art Books (ABA, LAPADA)

Contact Antonia Howard-Sneyd
✉ **42 Duke Street, St James's, London, SW1Y 6DJ** 🅿
☎ 020 7930 9223 Ⓕ 020 7839 9223
Ⓔ artbooks@heneage.com
Ⓦ www.heneage.com
Est. 1988 *Stock size* Large
Stock Art reference books
Open Mon–Fri 9.30am–6pm or by appointment
Services Valuations

🏛 Hermitage Antiques PLC

Contact Mr Vieux-Pernon
✉ **97 Pimlico Road, London, SW1W 8PH** 🅿
☎ 020 7730 1973 Ⓕ 020 7730 6586
Ⓔ info@hermitage-antiques.co.uk
Ⓦ www.hermitage-antiques.co.uk
Est. 1970 *Stock size* Large
Stock Biedermeier and Russian furniture, chandeliers, oil paintings, decorative arts, bronzes
Open Mon–Fri 10am–6pm
Sat 10am–5pm
Fairs Olympia (June)
Services Consultancy

🏛 Appley Hoare Antiques

Contact Appley or Zoe Hoare
✉ **30 Pimlico Road, London, SW1W 8LJ** 🅿
☎ 020 7730 7070 Ⓕ 020 7730 8188
Ⓔ appley@appleyhoare.com
Ⓦ www.appleyhoare.com
Est. 1980 *Stock size* Large
Stock 18th–19thC French country furniture, accessories
Open Mon–Fri 10.30am–6pm
Sat 11am–5pm
Services Shipping

🏛 John Hobbs Ltd (BADA)

Contact John Hobbs, Sarah Graham or Munira Mohamed
✉ **107a Pimlico Road, London, SW1W 8PH** 🅿
☎ 020 7730 8369 Ⓕ 020 7730 0437
Ⓔ info@johnhobbs.demon.co.uk
Ⓦ www.johnhobbs.co.uk
Est. 1994 *Stock size* Large
Stock 18th–19thC Continental and English furniture, objets d'art, statuary
Open Mon–Fri 9am–6pm
Sat 11am–4pm

🏛 Christopher Hodsoll Ltd (BADA)

Contact Mr C Hodsoll
✉ **89–91 Pimlico Road, London, SW1W 8PH** 🅿
☎ 020 7730 3370 Ⓕ 020 7730 1516
Ⓔ info@hodsoll.com
Ⓦ www.hodsoll.com
Est. 1991 *Stock size* Large
Stock 18th–19thC furniture, works of art
Open Mon–Fri 9.30am–6pm
Sat 10am–4pm
Services Finders service, interior design

🏛 Hotspur Ltd (BADA)

Contact Mr R Kern
✉ **14 Lowndes Street, London, SW1X 9EX** 🅿
☎ 020 7235 1918 Ⓕ 020 7235 4371
Ⓔ robinkern@hotspurantiques.com
Est. 1924 *Stock size* Medium
Stock 18thC quality furniture, chandeliers, clocks, works of art
Open Mon–Fri 9am–6pm
Sat by appointment
Fairs Grosvenor House
Services Valuations

🏛 Christopher Howe Antiques

Contact Christopher Howe or Olivia Bishop
✉ **93 Pimlico Road, London, SW1W 8PH** 🅿
☎ 020 7730 7987 Ⓕ 020 7730 0157
Ⓔ christophe@howelondon.com
Ⓦ www.howelondon.com
Est. 1987 *Stock size* Large
Stock General antiques, furniture
Open Mon-Fri 9am–6pm
Sat 10.30am–4.30pm

🏛 Humphrey–Carrasco

Contact Mr David Humphrey or Miss Marylise Carrasco
✉ **43 Pimlico Road, London, SW1W 8NE** 🅿
☎ 020 7730 9911 Ⓕ 020 7730 9944
Ⓔ hc@humphreycarrasco.demon.co.uk
Est. 1990 *Stock size* Medium
Stock English furniture, 18th–19thC lighting
Open Mon–Fri 10am–6pm
Sat by appointment
Fairs Olympia (Nov)

🏛 Iconastas Russian Works of Art

Contact Chris Martin
✉ **5 Piccadilly Arcade, London, SW1Y 6NH**
☎ 020 7629 1433 Ⓕ 020 7408 2015
Ⓔ info@iconastas.com
Ⓦ www.iconastas.com
Est. 1972 *Stock size* Large
Stock 10thC–1974 Russian works of art
Open Mon–Fri 10am–6pm
Sat 2–5pm
Services Valuations

🏛 Isaac and Ede (BADA)

Contact David Isaac
✉ **1 Duke of York Street, London, SW1Y 6JP** 🅿
☎ 020 7925 1177 Ⓕ 020 7925 0606

Ⓔ info@isaacandede.com
Ⓦ www.isaacandede.com
Est. 1865 *Stock size* Medium
Stock Georgian, Regency prints
Open Mon–Fri 10am–5pm
appointment advisable
Fairs BADA, Olympia (June), San Francisco Fall Antiques Show
Services Framing, restoration

⊞ Jeremy Ltd (BADA)
Contact Mr M Hill
✉ **29 Lowndes Street, London, SW1X 9HX** Ⓟ
☎ 020 7823 2923 Ⓕ 020 7245 6197
Ⓔ jeremy@jeremique.co.uk
Ⓦ www.jeremy.co.uk
Est. 1946 *Stock size* Large
Stock 18th–early 19thC English and Continental furniture, works of art, clocks, antiques
Open Mon–Fri 8.30am–6pm
Sat by appointment
Fairs Grosvenor House, New York

⊞ Peter Jones/PJ2
Contact James Betts
✉ **Sloane Square, London, SW1W 8EL** Ⓟ
☎ 020 7730 3434 Ⓕ 020 7808 4006
Ⓦ www.peterjones.co.uk
Est. 1915 *Stock size* Large
Stock 18th–19thC furniture, gilt mirrors, accessories
Open Mon–Sat 9.30am–7pm
Services Shipping

⊞ Keshishian (BADA)
Contact Mr Arto or Mr Eddy Keshishian
✉ **73 Pimlico Road, London, SW1W 8NE** Ⓟ
☎ 020 7730 8810
Ⓔ rujpics@yahoo.co.uk or amale88@hotmail.com
Est. 1989 *Stock size* Large
Stock Aubussons, British Arts and Crafts, Art Deco, antique and Modernist carpets and tapestries
Open Mon–Fri 9.30am–6pm
Sat 10am–5pm

⊞ John King (BADA)
Contact Mr J King
✉ **74 Pimlico Road, London, SW1W 8LS** Ⓟ
☎ 020 7730 0427 Ⓕ 020 7730 2515
Ⓔ kingj896@aol.com
Est. 1967 *Stock size* Large
Stock Period furniture, associated items, 20thC items
Open Mon–Fri 10am–6pm or by appointment
Services Advice on furnishing homes

⊞ Knightsbridge Coins (BNTA, ANA, PNG)
Contact Mr J Brown
✉ **43 Duke Street, London, SW1Y 6DD** Ⓟ
☎ 020 7930 8215 Ⓕ 020 7930 8214
Est. 1975
Stock English and foreign medieval–present day coins
Open Mon–Fri 10.15am–6pm
Fairs Coinex, London Coin Show (Bloomsbury)
Services Valuations

⊞ Bob Lawrence Gallery
Contact Bob Lawrence
✉ **93 Lower Sloane Street, London, SW1W 8DA** Ⓟ
☎ 020 7730 5900 Ⓕ 020 7730 5902
Ⓔ bob@boblawrencegallery.fsnet.co.uk
Est. 1992 *Stock size* Medium
Stock 20thC decorative antiques and furnishings
Open Mon–Fri 10am–6pm
Sat 10am–2pm

⊞ Jeremy Mason
Contact Mr J Mason
✉ **145 Ebury Street, London, SW1W 9QN** Ⓟ
☎ 020 7730 8331 Ⓕ 020 7730 8334
Ⓜ 07939 240884
Est. 1974 *Stock size* Small
Stock Oriental works of art from all periods
Open By appointment only

⊞ Mayfair Carpet Gallery Ltd
Contact Mr A H Khawaja
✉ **91 Knightsbridge, London, SW1X 7RB** Ⓟ
☎ 020 7235 2541 Ⓕ 020 7245 9749
Ⓔ aimz-kh@hotmail.com
Est. 1975 *Stock size* Large
Stock Fine antique Oriental carpets, rugs
Open Mon–Sat 10.30am–6.30pm
Services Valuations, restoration

⊞ Alexander von Moltke
Contact Alexander von Moltke
✉ **46 Bourne Street, London, SW1W 8JD** Ⓟ
☎ 020 7730 9020 Ⓕ 020 7730 2945
Ⓔ alexvonmoltke@btinternet.com
Ⓦ www.alexandervonmoltke.com
Est. 1992 *Stock size* Large
Stock French furniture 1920–1950, Italian lighting
Open Mon–Fri 10am–6pm
Sat 10am–4pm
Fairs Olympia, Decorative Antiques & Textile Fair, Battersea

⊞ Peter Nahum at the Leicester Galleries (BADA, SLAD)
Contact Peter Nahum
✉ **5 Ryder Street, London, SW1Y 6PY** Ⓟ
☎ 020 7930 6059 Ⓕ 020 7930 4678
Ⓜ 07770 220851
Ⓔ peternahum@leicestergalleries.com
Ⓦ www.leicestergalleries.com
Est. 1984 *Stock size* Large
Stock Pre-Raphaelites, Symbolists, 19th–20thC European paintings, drawings, sculpture
Open Mon–Fri 9.30am–6pm
Fairs Grosvenor House Art and Antiques Fair and International Fine Art Fair, New York, 20/21 British Art Fair, London
Services Valuations, restoration, shipping, book search

⊞ Odyssey Fine Arts Ltd (LAPADA)
Contact Martin MacRodain
✉ **24 Holbein Place, London, SW1W 8NL**
☎ 020 7730 9942 Ⓕ 020 7259 9941
Ⓔ odysseyfineart@aol.com
Ⓦ www.odysseyart.co.uk
Est. 1993 *Stock size* Large
Stock Decorative antiques
Open Mon–Fri 10.30am–5.30pm
Sat 10.30am–3.30pm
Fairs Olympia, Decorative Antiques and Textiles

⊞ Ossowski (BADA)
Contact Mr M Ossowski
✉ **83 Pimlico Road, London, SW1W 8PH** Ⓟ
☎ 020 7730 3256 Ⓕ 020 7823 4500
Ⓔ markossowski@hotmail.com
Est. 1960 *Stock size* Large
Stock 18thC English giltwood mirrors, tables, decorative wood carving
Open Mon–Fri 10am–6pm
Sat 10am–1pm
Fairs New York International (Oct)
Services Restoration

⊞ Trevor Philip & Son Ltd (BADA, BACA Award Winner 2004)

Contact Mr T Waterman
✉ **75a Jermyn Street, St James's, London, SW1Y 6NP** P
☎ 020 7930 2954 F 020 7321 0212
E globe@trevorphilip.com
W www.trevorphilip.com
Est. 1972 *Stock size* Large
Stock Globes, ships' models, marine and navigation instruments
Open Mon–Fri 9.30am–6pm Sat by appointment only
Fairs Grosvenor House
Services Valuations, restoration

Priestley and Ferraro
Contact David Priestley
✉ **17 King Street, St James's, London, SW1Y 6QU** P
☎ 020 7930 6228 F 020 7930 6226
E info@priestleyandferraro.com
W www.priestleyandferraro.com
Est. 1994 *Stock size* Medium
Stock Early Chinese art
Open Mon–Fri 9.30am–5.30pm
Fairs International Asian Art Fair, New York, Asian Art Fair, London

Pullman Gallery Ltd
Contact Mr S Khachadourian
✉ **14 King Street, St James's, London, SW1Y 6QU** P
☎ 020 7930 9595 F 020 7930 9494
E sk@pullmangallery.com
W www.pullmangallery.com
Est. 1998 *Stock size* Large
Stock Cocktail shakers, bar accessories, smoking accessories, vintage Louis Vuitton and Hermes luggage, motor racing posters, René Lalique glass, 1900–1940
Open Mon–Fri 10am–6pm
Services Usual gallery services

Mark Ransom Ltd
Contact Mr C Walker or Mr M James
✉ **62–64 & 105 Pimlico Road, London, SW1W 8LS** P
☎ 020 7259 0220 F 020 7259 0323
E contact@markransom.co.uk
W www.markransom.co.uk
Est. 1992 *Stock size* Medium
Stock Russian and French Empire, Continental furniture, decorative items, objets d'art, prints, pictures
Open Mon–Sat 10am–6pm

Rogier Antiques
Contact Mr Elene Rogier
✉ **20a Pimlico Road, London, SW1W 8LJ** P
☎ 020 7823 4780 F 020 7823 4780
Est. 1988 *Stock size* Medium
Stock French and Continental 18th–19thC decorative furniture, unusual lamps, reproductions, lighting
Open Mon–Fri 10am–6pm Sat 11am–4pm
Services Restoration

The Silver Fund Ltd (LAPADA)
Contact A Crawford
✉ **No 1 Duke of York Street, St James's, London, SW1Y 6JP** P
☎ 020 7839 7664 F 020 7839 8935
E dealers@thesilverfund.com
W www.thesilverfund.com
Est. 1996 *Stock size* Large
Stock Georg Jensen, Tiffany, Martelé and Puiforcat silver
Open Mon–Fri 9am–6pm
Fairs Olympia June, November
Services Valuations

Sims Reed Ltd (ABA)
Contact Mr J Sims
✉ **43a Duke Street, St James's, London, SW1Y 6DD** P
☎ 020 7493 5660 F 020 7493 8468
E info@simsreed.com
W www.simsreed.com
Est. 1977 *Stock size* Large
Stock Antiquarian, rare, second-hand books, including books illustrated by artists, books on fine and applied arts
Open Mon–Fri 10am–6pm or by appointment
Fairs ABA, Olympia

Peta Smyth Antique Textiles (LAPADA, CINOA)
Contact Peta Smyth or Joseph Sullivan
✉ **42 Moreton Street, London, SW1V 2PB** P
☎ 020 7630 9898 F 020 7630 5398
E petasmyth@ukonline.co.uk
Est. 1975 *Stock size* Large
Stock 16th–19thC European textiles, needlework, silks, velvets, tapestries, hangings, cushions
Open Mon–Fri 9.30am–5.30pm
Fairs Olympia (June, Nov)
Services Valuations

Somlo Antiques Ltd (BADA)
Contact Mr Paul Symons
✉ **7 Piccadilly Arcade, London, SW1Y 6NH** P
☎ 020 7499 6526 F 020 7499 0603
E mail@somlo.com
W www.somloantiques.com
Est. 1970 *Stock size* Large
Stock Vintage wristwatches, antique pocket watches
Open Mon–Fri 10am–5.30pm
Fairs Olympia (Feb, June)
Services Valuations, repairs

Alexe Stanion Antiques
Contact Alexe Stanion
✉ **73 Elizabeth Street, London, SW1W 9PJ** P
☎ 020 7824 8808 F 020 7824 8828
E alexestanion@aol.com
W www.alexestanion.com
Est. 1999 *Stock size* Medium
Stock Mid 20thC, post-war design and Modernism
Open Mon–Sat 10am–6pm
Fairs Alexandra Palace

Westenholz Antiques Ltd
✉ **76–78 Pimlico Road, London, SW1W 8PL** P
☎ 020 7824 8090 F 020 7823 5913
E shop@westenholz.co.uk
W www.westenholz.co.uk
Stock 18th–19thC English furniture, decorative items
Open Mon–Fri 8.30am–6pm
Fairs Olympia (June, Nov)
Services Interior design

SW3

Jaki Abbott
Contact Jaki Abbott
✉ **Antiquarius, 131–141 King's Road, London, SW3 4PW** P
☎ 0777 486 4442 *Stock size* Small
Stock Antique and period jewellery
Open Mon–Sat 10am–6pm

Norman Adams Ltd (BADA, BACA Award Winner 2001)
Contact R G S Whittington or C Claxton-Stevens
✉ **8–10 Hans Road (Opposite West side of Harrods), London, SW3 1RX** P
☎ 020 7589 5266 F 020 7589 1968
E antiques@normanadams.com
W www.normanadams.com

Est. 1923 *Stock size* Large
Stock Fine 18thC English furniture, works of art, mirrors, glass, paintings, chandeliers
Open Mon–Fri 9am–5.30pm
Sat Sun by appointment
Fairs BADA (March), Grosvenor House (June)
Services Annual catalogue

Aesthetics (LAPADA)
Contact Philip A Jeffs
Stand V1, Antiquarius, 131–141 King's Road, London, SW3 4PW
020 7352 0395 020 7376 4057
Est. 1983 *Stock size* Large
Stock Ceramics and silver
Open Mon–Sat 10am–6pm
Fairs Olympia (June)
Services Shipping

After Noah
Contact Simon Tarr
261 King's Road, London, SW3 5EL
020 7351 2610
mailorder@afternoah.com
www.afternoah.com
Est. 1995 *Stock size* Medium
Stock Antique and contemporary furniture and houseware
Open Mon–Sat 10am–6pm
Sun noon–5pm
Services Restoration

Alexia Amato Antiques
Contact Alexia Amato
Stand V8, Antiquarius, 131–141 King's Road, London, SW3 4PW
020 7352 3666 020 7352 3666
07770 826254
alexia@amato.freeserve.co.uk
www.amato.freeserve.co.uk
Est. 1993 *Stock size* Medium
Stock Continental 19thC glass, especially French and Bohemian
Open Mon–Sat 10am–6pm
Services Shipping

Andipa Gallery (LAPADA)
Contact A Andipa
162 Walton Street, Knightsbridge, London, SW3 2JL
020 7589 2371 020 7225 0305
art@andipa.com
www.andipa.com
Est. 1953 *Stock size* Large
Stock Modern contemporary icons, old masters and works on paper
Open Mon–Fri 9.30am–6pm
Sat 11am–6pm
Services Valuations, restoration

Antiquarius Antique Centre
Contact Mike Spooner
131–141 King's Road, London, SW3 4PW
020 7351 5353 020 7351 5350
antique@dial.pipex.com
Est. 1969 *Stock size* Large
No. of dealers 100+
Stock General and specialist antiques of all periods
Open Mon–Sat 10am–6pm

Apter-Fredericks Ltd (BADA)
Contact Harry or Guy Apter
265–267 Fulham Road, London, SW3 6HY
020 7352 2188 020 7376 5619
antiques@apter-fredericks.com
www.apter-fredericks.com
Est. 1946 *Stock size* Large
Stock 18thC English furniture
Open Mon–Fri 9.30am–5.30pm
Fairs Grosvenor House, International Art & Antiques Fair New York

Joanna Booth (BADA, CINOA)
Contact Joanna Booth
247 King's Road, London, SW3 5EL
020 7352 8998 020 7376 7350
joanna@joannabooth.co.uk
www.joannabooth.co.uk
Est. 1966 *Stock size* Large
Stock Old master drawings, early sculptures, tapestries, oak furniture, textiles
Open Mon–Sat 10am–6pm
Fairs Olympia
Services Valuations, restoration

Bourbon Hanby Antique Centre
Contact Mr I Towning
151 Sydney Street, London, SW3 6NT
020 7352 2106/0870 142 3403
020 7565 0003
www.bourbonhanby.co.uk
Est. 1974 *Stock size* Large
No. of dealers 15
Stock China, glass, silver, porcelain, jewellery, watches, chandeliers, corkscrews
Open Mon–Sat 10am–6pm
Sun 11am–5pm
Services Restoration, jewellery manufacturing, repairs

Brown & Kingston
Contact Alan Brown or Dennis Kingston
Antiquarius, 131–141 King's Road, London, SW3 4PW
020 7376 8881 020 7376 8881
Est. 1978 *Stock size* Large
Stock Japanese Imari, oil paintings, George III furniture
Open Mon–Sat 10am–5pm
Services Shipping

Jasmin Cameron (Glass Circle)
Contact Jasmin Cameron
Stand M16, Antiquarius, 131–141 King's Road, London, SW3 4PW
0207 351 4154 0207 351 4154
07774 871257
jasmin.cameron@mail.com
Est. 1980 *Stock size* Large
Stock 18th–19thC English and Irish drinking glasses, decanters, 19thC scent bottles, paperweights
Open Mon–Fri 10am–5.30pm
Sat 10am–5.45pm
Services Valuations, restoration

Chelsea Antique Rug Gallery (LAPADA)
Contact Noah Somnez
Stand V19, Antiquarius, 131–141 King's Road, London, SW3 4PW
020 7351 6611 020 7351 6611
chelsearugs@aol.com
Est. 1978 *Stock size* Large
Stock Antique rugs, Aubusson tapestries
Open Mon–Sat 10am–6pm
Services Valuations, restoration

Chelsea Military Antiques
Contact Richard Black
Stands N13–14, Antiquarius, 131–141 King's Road, London, SW3 4PW
020 7352 0308 020 7352 0308
richard@chelseamilitaria.com
www.chelseamilitaria.com
Est. 1996 *Stock size* Large
Stock British campaign medals, 19th and 20thC Allied and Axis militaria

Open Mon–Sat 10.30am–5.30pm
Fairs Britannia and South England Miitaria Fairs
Services Valuations, medal mounting

⊞ Classic Prints
Contact Mr Paul Dowling
✉ **265 King's Road, London, SW3 5EL**
☎ 020 7376 5056 Ⓕ 020 7460 5356
Ⓜ 07770 431855
Ⓔ art@classicprints.com
Ⓦ www.classicprints.com
Est. 1983 *Stock size* Large
Stock Antique prints of all ages, maps
Open Mon–Sat 10am–6pm
Sun noon–5pm
Services Valuations

⊞ Adrian Cohen Antiques
✉ **Stand A18/19 Antiquarius, 135 Kings Road, Chelsea, London, SW3 4PW**
☎ 020 7352 7155
Ⓜ 07973 222520
Ⓔ silver@adrian-cohen.co.uk
Ⓦ www.adrian-cohen.co.uk
Est. 1987 *Stock size* Large
Stock Antique silver, silver plate
Open Mon–Sat 10am–6pm
Services Valuations, restoration

⊞ L and D Collins
Contact Louise Collins or David Collins
✉ **London, SW3**
☎ 020 7584 0712 Ⓕ 020 7584 0712
Est. 1994 *Stock size* Medium
Stock Paintings, fans, decorative objects
Open By appointment
Fairs Decorative Antiques and Textiles Fair, Penman Fairs

⊞ Richard Courtney Ltd (BADA)
Contact Mr R Courtney
✉ **114 Fulham Road, London, SW3 6HU** Ⓟ
☎ 020 7370 4020 Ⓕ 020 7370 4020
Est. 1965 *Stock size* Large
Stock Finest early 18thC English walnut furniture
Open Mon–Fri 9.30am–5.30pm
Fairs Grosvenor House, BADA Duke of York's

⊞ The Cufflink Shop
Contact Mr John Szwarc
✉ **Stand G2, Antiquarius, 131–141 King's Road, London, SW3 4PW** Ⓟ
☎ 020 7352 8201
Ⓜ 07715 381175
Est. 1990 *Stock size* Large
Stock Antique, vintage and modern cufflinks
Open Mon–Sat 10.30am–5.30pm

⊞ Jesse Davis Antiques
Contact Mr J Davis
✉ **Stands A9–11, Antiquarius, 131–141 King's Road, London, SW3 4PW** Ⓟ
☎ 020 7352 4314
Est. 1984 *Stock size* Large
Stock 19thC pottery, majolica, Staffordshire and other collectable factories, decorative objects
Open Mon–Sat 10.30am–6pm
Fairs Olympia (June), LAPADA Fair, Decorative Antiques and Textiles Fair

⊞ Robert Dickson and Lesley Rendall Antiques (BADA)
Contact Justin Keating, Robert Dickson or Lesley Rendall
✉ **263 Fulham Road, London, SW3 6HY** Ⓟ
☎ 020 7351 0330
Ⓦ www.dicksonrendallantiques.co.uk
Est. 1969 *Stock size* Large
Stock 18thC–early 19thC English furniture, works of art, lighting
Open Mon–Fri 10am–6pm
Sat 10am–4.30pm
Services Valuations, restoration

⊞ Drummonds Architectural Antiques Ltd (SALVO)
Contact Mr Drummond Shaw
✉ **78 Royal Hospital Road, Chelsea, London, SW3 4HN** Ⓟ
☎ 020 7376 4499
Ⓔ info@drummonds-arch.co.uk
Ⓦ www.drummonds-arch.co.uk
Est. 1989 *Stock size* Large
Stock Period bathrooms, oak and pine flooring, fireplaces, statues, garden furniture and lighting, brass door furniture and fittings, radiators, furniture, windows, doors, gates, railings, conservatories
Open Mon–Fri 9am–6pm
Sat 10am–5pm
Services Proper vitreous re-enamelling of cast-iron baths, restored antique bathrooms

⊞ Eclectic Antiques and Interiors
Contact Graham Tomlinson
✉ **Stands T3–4, Antiquarius, 131–141 King's Road, London, SW3 4PW** Ⓟ
☎ 020 7286 7608 Ⓕ 020 7286 7608
Ⓜ 07778 470983
Est. 1993 *Stock size* Medium
Stock English and French decorative antiques and furniture
Open Mon–Sat 10am–6pm
Services Shipping, valuations

⊞ Edge (LAPADA)
Contact Donald Edge or James Smith
✉ **Antiquarius, 131–141 King's Road, London, SW3 4PW** Ⓟ
☎ 020 7351 2333 Ⓕ 020 7352 2660
Ⓔ info@edgelondon.com
Est. 1991 *Stock size* Large
Stock Antique, bespoke jewels, diamonds set in platinum
Open Mon–Sat 11am–6pm
Services Valuations

⊞ Michael Foster (BADA)
Contact Margaret Susands
✉ **118 Fulham Road, Chelsea, London, SW3 6HU**
☎ 020 7373 3636 Ⓕ 020 7373 4042
Est. 1967 *Stock size* Medium
Stock Fine 18th–early 19thC furniture, works of art
Open Mon–Fri 9.30am–6pm
Services Valuations

⊞ Angelo Gibson
Contact Angelo Gibson
✉ **Antiquarius, 131–141 King's Road, London, SW3 4PW** Ⓟ
☎ 020 7352 4690
Ⓜ 07960 487010
Ⓔ quicksilverangelo@zoom.com
Est. 1972 *Stock size* Small
Stock Antique silver and silver plate
Open Mon–Sat 10am–6pm
Services Silver plating

⊞ Godson & Coles (BADA)
Contact Richard Godson or Richard Coles
✉ **92 Fulham Road, London, SW3 6HR** Ⓟ
☎ 020 7584 2200 Ⓕ 020 7584 2223
Ⓔ godsonandcoles@aol.com
Ⓦ www.godsonandcoles.co.uk
Stock size Medium

Stock 18th–early 19thC furniture, decorative works of art
Open Mon–Fri 9.30am–5.30pm
Fairs Grosvenor House, Olympia

James Hardy & Co
Contact Mr H P Ross
235 Brompton Road, London, SW3 2EP P
☎ 020 7589 5050 ⓕ 020 7589 9009
Est. 1853 *Stock size* Medium
Stock Silver, jewellery
Open Mon–Sat 10am–5.30pm
Services Valuations, restoration

Robin Haydock Rare Textiles (LAPADA)
Contact Robin Haydock
Antiquarius, 131–141 King's Road, London, SW3 4PW
☎ 020 7349 9110 ⓕ 020 7349 9110
ⓜ 07770 931240
ⓔ robinhaydock@talk21.com
ⓦ www.robinhaydock.com
Est. 1996 *Stock size* Medium
Stock Antique textiles, mostly 18thC European and earlier, decorative furnishings
Open Tues–Sat 10.30am–5.30pm
Fairs Olympia (June), Decorative Antiques and Textile Fairs
Services Valuations, restoration

Hayman & Hayman
Contact Georgina Hayman
Antiquarius, 131–141 King's Road, London, SW3 4PW P
☎ 020 7351 6568 ⓕ 020 8742 2262
Est. 1976 *Stock size* Large
Stock Photograph frames, Limoges boxes, scent bottles
Open Mon–Sat 10am–5.30pm
Services Valuations, restoration, shipping

Peter Herington Antiquarian Bookseller (ABA, PBFA)
Contact Kevin Finch
100 Fulham Road, Chelsea, London, SW3 6HS P
☎ 020 7591 0220 ⓕ 020 7225 7054
ⓔ mail@peter-herington-books.com
ⓦ www.peter-herington-books.com
Est. 1969 *Stock size* Large
Stock Antiquarian books, illustrated, fine bindings, English literature, travel, children's etc, modern first editions
Open Mon–Sat 10am–6pm
Fairs Olympia ABA, Chelsea ABA

Hill House Antiques & Decorative Arts
Contact S Benhalim
18 Chelsea Manor Street, London, SW3 2WR
☎ 07973 842777
ⓔ info@hillhouse-antiques.co.uk
ⓦ www.hillhouse-antiques.co.uk
Est. 1999 *Stock size* Small
Stock Arts and Crafts, Art Nouveau small furniture, metalware and decorative items of the period
Open By appointment
Fairs P & A fairs, Take Five Fairs
Services Sourcing, design consultancy

Michael Hughes (BADA)
Contact Michael Hughes
88 Fulham Road, London, SW3 6HR P
☎ 020 7589 0660 ⓕ 020 7823 7618
ⓔ antiques@michaelhughes.freeserve.com
Est. 1995 *Stock size* Large
Stock 18th–early 19thC English furniture and works of art
Open Mon–Fri 9.30am–5.30pm
Fairs Olympia

Anthony James & Son Ltd (BADA, CINOA)
Contact James Millard
88 Fulham Road, London, SW3 6HR P
☎ 020 7584 1120 ⓕ 020 7823 7618
ⓔ anthony.james10@virgin.net
ⓦ www.anthony-james.com
Est. 1949 *Stock size* Large
Stock Fine 18th–19thC English and Continental furniture, decorative items
Open Mon–Fri 9.30am–5.45pm
Fairs Olympia (June, Nov)
Services Valuations, restoration

John Keil Ltd (BADA)
Contact Diana Yates-Watson
First Floor, 154 Brompton Road, London, SW3 1HX P
☎ 020 7589 6454 ⓕ 020 7823 8235
ⓔ antiques@johnkeil.com
ⓦ www.johnkeil.com
Est. 1959 *Stock size* Medium
Stock 18thC English furniture
Open Mon–Fri 9.30am–5.30pm

M Lexton
Contact Michael Lexton
Antiquarius, 131–141 King's Road, London, SW3 4PW P
☎ 020 7351 5980 ⓕ 020 7351 5980
ⓔ mlextonltd@hotmail.com
Stock size Medium
Stock Silver
Open Tues–Sat 10.30am–6pm
Services Valuations, restoration

Peter Lipitch Ltd (BADA)
Contact Melvyn Lipitch
120–124 Fulham Road, London, SW3 6HU P
☎ 020 7373 3328 ⓕ 020 7373 8888
ⓔ antiques@peterlipitch.com
ⓦ www.peterlipitch.com
Est. 1950 *Stock size* Medium
Stock 18thC English furniture
Open Mon–Fri 9.30am–5.30pm
Sat by appointment

Little River Oriental Antiques
Contact Mr D Dykes
Antiquarius, 131–141 King's Road, London, SW3 4PW P
☎ 020 7349 9080 ⓕ 01342 300131
Est. 1997 *Stock size* Large
Stock Chinese antiquities, domestic ceramics
Open Mon–Sat 10am–6pm
Services Restoration

The Map House (BADA, ABA)
Contact Mr P Stuchlik
54 Beauchamp Place, London, SW3 1NY
☎ 020 7584 8559 ⓕ 020 7589 1041
ⓔ maps@themaphouse.com
ⓦ www.themaphouse.com
Est. 1973 *Stock size* Large
Stock 15th–19thC antique maps, 16th–19thC decorative engravings, globes, atlases
Open Mon–Fri 9.45am–5.45pm
Sat 10.30am–5pm
Services Valuations

Mariad Antiques
Contact Mrs H McClean
Antiquarius C38, 131–141 King's Road, London, SW3 4PW P
☎ 020 7351 9526
Est. 1971 *Stock size* Large
Stock Georgian, Victorian, Edwardian jewellery, cold-painted Vienna bronzes, animal subjects
Open Mon–Sun 10am–6pm
Fairs NEC
Services Valuations

⊞ Gerald Mathias
Contact Gerald Mathias
✉ **Stands R5–6, Antiquarius, 131–141 King's Road, London, SW3 4PW** 🅿
☎ 020 7351 0484
ⓔ info@geraldmathias.com
ⓦ www.geraldmathias.com
Est. 1979 *Stock size* Large
Stock Antique boxes
Open Mon–Sat 10am–5.30pm

⊞ McKenna & Co (LAPADA, NAG)
Contact Catherine McKenna
✉ **28 Beauchamp Place, London, SW3 1NJ** 🅿
☎ 020 7584 1966 ⓕ 020 7225 2893
ⓔ info@mckennajewels.com
Est. 1983 *Stock size* Large
Stock Antique, period and contemporary jewellery
Open Mon–Sat 10.15am–5.45pm
Services Valuations, restoration

⊞ C Negrillo Antiques and Jewellery
Contact C Negrillo
✉ **Stands P1–3, Antiquarius, 131–141 King's Road, London, SW3 4PW** 🅿
☎ 020 7349 0038
ⓜ 07778 336781
ⓔ negrilloc@aol.com
Est. 1994 *Stock size* Large
Stock Jewellery
Open Mon–Sat 10am–6pm

⊞ Sue Norman
Contact Sue Norman
✉ **Antiquarius, 131–141 King's Road, London, SW3 4PW** 🅿
☎ 020 7352 7217 ⓕ 020 8870 4677
ⓜ 07720 751162
ⓔ sue@sue-norman.demon.co.uk
ⓦ www.sue-norman.demon.co.uk
Est. Olympia *Stock size* Large
Stock Blue and white transfer ware
Open Mon–Sat 10.30am–5.30pm

⊞ Rogers de Rin (BADA)
Contact Mrs V de Rin
✉ **76 Royal Hospital Road, London, SW3 4HN** 🅿
☎ 020 7352 9007 ⓕ 020 7351 9407
ⓔ rogersderin@rogersderin.co.uk
ⓦ www.rogersderin.co.uk
Est. 1965 *Stock size* Medium
Stock Collectors' items, snuff boxes, enamels, Vienna bronzes, Staffordshire, Scottish Wemyss ware
Open Mon–Fri 10am–5.30pm Sat 10am–1pm
Fairs Olympia (June, Nov), BADA (March)
Services Shipping arranged

⊞ Russell Rare Books (ABA, PBFA, ILAB)
Contact Charles Russell
✉ **239a Fulham Road, Chelsea (at junction of Old Church Street), London, SW3 6HY** 🅿
☎ 020 7351 5119 ⓕ 020 7376 7227
ⓔ crussell@russellrarebooks.com
ⓦ www.russellrarebooks.com
Est. 1978 *Stock size* Medium
Stock Rare books, leather bound books, library sets, illustrated books, prints, maps
Open Mon–Fri 2am–6pm
Fairs Olympia, Russell Hotel
Services Valuations

⊞ Salamanca
Contact Mrs Martin
✉ **Stands 14–15, Antiquarius, 131–141 King's Road, London, SW3 4PW** 🅿
☎ 020 7351 5829 ⓕ 020 7351 5829
Est. 1976 *Stock size* Large
Stock Moorcroft pottery, Sabino glass, porcelain, silver
Open Mon–Sat 10.30am–5.30pm
Services Valuations, restoration

⊞ Charles Saunders Antiques
Contact Mr Charles Saunders
✉ **255 Fulham Road, London, SW3 6HY** 🅿
☎ 020 7351 5242 ⓕ 020 7352 8142
ⓔ info@charlessaundersantiques.com
ⓦ www.charlessaundersantiques.com
Est. 1987 *Stock size* Medium
Stock Antique lighting, English and Continental 18th–early 19thC furniture, objects, decorations, some 20thC furniture, lighting, decorative objects
Open Mon–Fri 9.30am–5.30pm

⊞ Christine Schell (LAPADA)
Contact Ms Christine King
✉ **15 Cale Street, London, SW3 3QS** 🅿
☎ 020 7352 5563 ⓕ 020 7589 7161
ⓜ 07836 330577
ⓔ c.schell@eidosnet.co.uk
Est. 1973 *Stock size* Medium
Stock Tortoiseshell, ivory, silver, Arts and Crafts, decorative items, mirrors
Open Mon–Sat 10am–5.30pm
Services Valuations, restoration

⊞ Snap Dragon
Contact Leonie Whittle
✉ **247 Fulham Road, London, SW3 6HY** 🅿
☎ 020 7376 8889
ⓔ snap.dragon@btconnect.com
ⓦ www.snap-dragon.net
Est. 1995 *Stock size* Large
Stock 18th–19thC Chinese furniture, chairs
Open Mon–Sat 10am–6pm

⊞ Miwa Thorpe
Contact Ms Miwa Thorpe
✉ **Stands M8–9, Antiquarius, 131–141 King's Road, London, SW3 4PW** 🅿
☎ 020 7351 2911 ⓕ 020 7351 6690
ⓜ 07768 455679
Est. 1987 *Stock size* Medium
Stock Jewellery and decorative silver
Open Mon–Sat 10am–6pm

⊞ Valerie Wade
Contact Valerie Wade
✉ **108 Fulham Road, London, SW3 6HS** 🅿
☎ 020 7225 1414 ⓕ 020 7589 9029
ⓔ info@valeriewade.com
Est. 1983 *Stock size* Medium
Stock General antiques, furniture, lighting
Open Mon–Sat 10am–6pm
Services Styling

⊞ Gordon Watson Ltd (LAPADA, BACA Award Winner 2003)
Contact Mr Sean Parks
✉ **50 Fulham Road, London, SW3 6HH** 🅿
☎ 020 7589 3108 ⓕ 020 7584 6328
ⓔ gordonwatson@btinternet.com
Stock size Medium
Stock Art Deco furniture, lighting
Open Mon–Sat 11am–6pm
Fairs Olympia

⊞ O F Wilson Ltd (BADA, LAPADA)
Contact Mr P Jackson
✉ **Queens Elm Parade, Old Church Street, Chelsea, London, SW3 6EJ** 🅿
☎ 020 7352 9554 ⓕ 020 7351 0765

ofw@email.msn.com
Est. 1949 *Stock size* Medium
Stock Continental furniture, French chimney pieces, English painted decorative furniture, mirrors
Open Mon–Fri 9.30am–5.30pm Sat 10.30am–1pm
Services Valuations

World's End Bookshop
Contact Mr S Dickson
357 King's Road, London, SW3 5ES
020 7352 9376
07961 316 918
stephen.dickson@virgin.net
Est. 1999 *Stock size* Medium
Stock Antiquarian, rare, second-hand books, non-fiction, art, literature etc
Open Mon–Sat 10am–6.30pm Sun 10am–7pm
Fairs Royal National Hotel, Bloomsbury (HD)
Services Valuations

Clifford Wright Antiques Ltd (BADA)
Contact Clifford Wright
104–106 Fulham Road, London, SW3 6HS
020 7589 0986 020 7589 3565
Est. 1960 *Stock size* Large
Stock English furniture early 18thC–Regency, English giltwood furniture, period giltwood mirrors
Open Mon–Fri 9am–6pm

SW4

Antiques and Things
Contact Mrs V Crowther
London, SW4
020 7498 1303 020 7498 1303
07767 262096
info@antiquesandthings.co.uk
www.antiquesandthings.co.uk
Est. 1985 *Stock size* Medium
Stock Lighting, chandeliers, curtain furniture, accessories, French decorative furniture, textiles
Open By appointment
Fairs Decorative Antiques and Textiles Fair

Places and Spaces
Contact Paul Carroll or Nick Hannam
30 Old Town, Clapham, London, SW4 0LB
020 7498 0998 020 7627 2625
contact@placesandspaces.com
www.placesandspaces.com
Est. 1997 *Stock size* Large
Stock 20thC classic designs, 1950s Scandinavian furniture, Italian lighting, Eames, Panton
Open Tues–Sat 10.30am–6pm Sun noon–4pm
Fairs 100% Design
Services Valuations, design consultancy

SW6

275 Antiques
Contact Mr D Fisher
275 Lillie Road, London, SW6 7LL
020 7386 7382 020 7381 8320
Est. 1991 *Stock size* Large
Stock 1880s–1930s furniture, decorative items, American Lucite furniture, lighting, 1930s–1970s
Open Mon–Sat 10am–5.30pm

291
Contact The Manager
291 Lillie Road, London, SW6 7LL
020 7381 5008 020 7388 2691
07831 785059
malcolm.gliksten@blueyonder.co.uk
Est. 1972 *Stock size* Large
No. of dealers 4
Stock Decorative and general antiques, collectables
Open Mon–Sat 10.30am–5.30pm or by appointment
Services Valuations

Artefact
Contact Victoria Davar
273 Lillie Road, Fulham, London, SW6 7LL
020 7381 2500 020 7381 8320
artefact273@mac.com
Est. 2003 *Stock size* Medium
Stock 18th–20thC French, English furniture, chandeliers
Open Mon–Sat 10.30am–5.30pm
Fairs Battersea Decorative and Textile Fair

Sebastiano Barbagallo Antiques
Contact Mr S Barbagallo
661 Fulham Road, London, SW6 5PZ
020 7751 0691 020 7751 0691
sebastianobarbagallo@hotmail.com
Est. 1978 *Stock size* Large
Stock Chinese furniture, Indian and Tibetan antiques, crafts
Open Mon–Sun 10am–6pm

Sebastiano Barbagallo Antiques
Contact Mr S Barbagallo
310 Wandsworth Bridge Road, London, SW6 2UA
020 7751 0586 020 7751 0586
sebastianobarbagallo@hotmail.com
Est. 1978 *Stock size* Medium
Stock Chinese furniture, objects
Open Mon–Sun 10am–6pm

Robert Barley
Contact Robert Barley
291 Lillie Road, London, SW6 7LL
020 7381 5008 020 7388 2691
Est. 1972 *Stock size* Medium
Stock Antiques, collectables
Open Mon–Sat 10.30am–5.30pm or by appointment

I and J L Brown Ltd
Contact Mr S Hilton
634–636 King's Road, London, SW6 2DU
020 7736 4141 020 7736 9164
enquiries@brownantiques.com
www.brownantiques.com
Est. 1978 *Stock size* Large
Stock English country, French provincial antique and reproduction furniture, extensive range of decorative items including lighting
Open Mon–Sat 9am–5.30pm or by appointment
Services Restoration, re-rushing

Alison Burdon
Contact Alison Burdon
291 Lillie Road, London, SW6 7LL
020 7381 5008 020 7388 2691
Est. 1972 *Stock size* Large
Stock Antiques, collectables
Open Mon–Sat 10.30am–5.30pm or by appointment

Aurea Carter (LAPADA)
Contact Aurea Carter
PO Box 44134, London, SW6 3YX
020 7731 3486 020 7731 3486
07815 912477
aureacarter@englishceramics.com
www.englishceramics.com
Est. 1980 *Stock size* Large
Stock 18th–early 19thC English

pottery and porcelain
Open By appointment only
Fairs Olympia, New York Ceramic Fair, Antiques for Everyone
Services Valuations, shipping

Rupert Cavendish Antiques
Contact Mr Francois Valcke
610 King's Road, London, SW6 2DX
020 7731 7041 020 7731 8302
rcavendish@aol.com
www.rupertcavendish.co.uk
Est. 1984 *Stock size* Large
Stock European 20thC paintings, Empire, Biedermeier, Art Deco furniture
Open Mon–Sat 10am–6pm

Cheyne Antiques
Contact G. Watson
314 Munster Road, London, SW6 6BH
020 7610 0247
Est. 1996 *Stock size* Small
Stock General antiques
Open Mon–Sat 9am–6pm
Services Valuations, restoration

Marc Costantini Antiques
Contact Mr M Costantini
313 Lillie Road, London, SW6 7LL
020 7610 2380 020 7610 2380
07941 075289
Est. 1999 *Stock size* Large
Stock English and Continental antique furniture
Open Mon–Sat 10.30am–5.30pm

Deans Antiques
Contact Mr D Gipson
Core One, The Gas Works, 2 Michael Road, London, SW6 2AN
020 7610 6997
07770 231687
dean.antiques@virgin.net
Est. 1988 *Stock size* Large
Stock 18th–19thC French and Italian decorative antiques
Open Wed–Fri 10am–6pm Sat 11am–4pm or by appointment
Fairs Battersea Decorative Antiques and Textiles Fair

Decorative Antiques (LAPADA)
Contact Mr T Harley
284 Lillie Road, Fulham, London, SW6 7PX
020 7610 2694 020 7386 0103
Est. 1992 *Stock size* Large
Stock 18th–19thC French provincial furniture, Irish furniture
Open Mon–Sat 10am–5.30pm

Charles Edwards (BADA, CINOA)
Contact Clare
19a Rumbold Road, London, SW6 2HX
020 7736 7172 020 7731 7388
charles@charlesedwards2.demon.co.uk
www.charlesedwards.com
Est. 1969 *Stock size* Medium
Stock Antique lighting, 18th–19thC furniture, bookcases, general antiques
Open Mon–Fri 9.30am–6pm Sat 10am–5pm

Nicole Fabre French Antiques
Contact Mrs N Fabre
592 King's Road, London, SW6 2DX
020 7384 3112 020 7610 6410
antiques@nicolefabre.com
Stock size Medium
Stock French Provençal furniture and beds, Provençal quilts, linens, textiles, 18th–19thC toiles, decorative items, antique fabrics
Open Mon–Fri 10am–6pm Sat 11am–5pm
Fairs Decorative Antiques and Textiles Fair

Hector Finch Lighting
Contact Mr H Finch
90 Wandsworth Bridge Road, London, SW6 2TF
020 7731 8886 020 7731 7408
hector@hectorfinch.com
www.hectorfinch.com
Est. 1987 *Stock size* Large
Stock Specialist period lighting shop, large range of antique and contemporary decorative lighting
Open Mon–Sat 10am–5.30pm

Floyd & James (LAPADA, CINOA)
Contact Martin James or George Floyd
592 Fulham Road, London, SW6 5NT
020 7736 0183
info@plj-antiques.com
www.plj-antiques.com
Est. 1967 *Stock size* Medium
Stock Georgian furniture, antiques and objects
Open Mon–Sat 9.30am–5.30pm
Services Valuations, restoration

Birdie Fortescue Antiques (LAPADA)
Contact Birdie Fortescue
Unit GJ, Cooper House, 2 Michael Road, London, SW6 2AD
01206 337557 01206 337557
07778 263467
bfortescueantiques@btopenworld.com
www.birdiefortescue.com
Est. 1991 *Stock size* Large
Stock 18th–early 20thC Continental furniture
Open By appointment
Fairs Olympia (Feb, June), Decorative Antiques Fair, Battersea Park (Sept)

French House Antiques
Contact Marcus Hazell
Unit A, Parsons Green Depot, Parsons Green Lane, London, SW6 4HH
020 7978 2228 020 7978 2340
info@thefrenchhouse.co.uk
www.thefrenchhouse.co.uk
Est. 1998 *Stock size* Medium
Stock French furniture, beds, mirrors
Open Mon–Sat 10am–6pm

Fulham Antiques
Contact Mr A Eves
320 Munster Road, London, SW6 6BH
020 7610 3644
fulhamantique320@aol.com
Est. 1993 *Stock size* Large
Stock Antique and decorative furniture, lighting, mirrors
Open Mon–Sat 10am–5.30pm

Ena Green
Contact Mrs Ena Green
566 King's Road, London, SW6 2DY
020 7736 2485 020 7610 9028
07831 106002
Est. 1979 *Stock size* Medium
Stock 18th–20thC painted furniture, lighting, mirrors, decorative items
Open Mon–Sat 10.30am–5.30pm

Judy Greenwood Antiques
Contact Ms J Greenwood
657–659 Fulham Road, London, SW6 5PY P
☎ 020 7736 6037 F 020 7736 1941
M 07768 347669
E judyg@dial.pipex.com
Est. 1978 *Stock size* Large
Stock 19th–20thC French decorative items, beds, textiles, lighting, furniture, mirrors, quilts
Open Mon–Fri 10am–5.30pm Sat 10am–5pm
Services Restoration, painting

Gutlin Clocks & Antiques
Contact Mr. Coxhead
606 King's Road, London, SW6 2DX P
☎ 020 7384 2439/2804
F 020 7384 2439
M 07973 123921
E mark@gutlin.com
W www.gutlin.com
Est. 1992 *Stock size* Medium
Stock Furniture, clocks, chandeliers
Open Mon–Sat 10am–6.30pm
Services Restoration

H R W Antiques Ltd (LAPADA)
Contact Mr I Henderson-Russell
26 Sulivan Road, London, SW6 3DT P
☎ 020 7371 7995 F 020 7371 9522
E ian@hrw-antiques.freeserve.co.uk
W www.hrw-antiques.com
Est. 1988 *Stock size* Large
Stock 18th–19thC English and Continental furniture and decorative items
Open Mon–Fri 9am–5pm

Nigel Hindley
Contact Mr N Hindley
281 Lillie Road, London, SW6 7LL P
☎ 020 7385 0706
Est. 1979 *Stock size* Large
Stock English period antiques, French furniture, eccentricities, lighting, mirrors
Open Mon–Sat 10.30am–5pm
Services Valuations

House of Mirrors
Contact Miss Witek
597 King's Road, London, SW6 2EL
☎ 020 7736 5885 F 020 7610 9188
E info@houseofmirrors.co.uk
W www.houseofmirrors.co.uk
Est. 1972 *Stock size* Large
Stock 19thC English mirrors
Open Mon–Fri 9am–6pm Sat 10am–6pm

Indigo
Contact Marion Bender
275 New King's Road, London, SW6 4RD P
☎ 020 7384 3101 F 020 7384 3102
E antiques@indigo-uk.com
W www.indigo-uk.com
Est. 1982 *Stock size* Large
Stock Indian, Chinese and Japanese furniture, decorative items, handicrafts, Indonesian furniture from recycled teakwood
Open Mon–Sat 10am–6pm
Fairs House and Garden Fair

Christopher Jones Antiques
Contact Rene Sanderson
618–620 King's Road, London, SW6 2DU P
☎ 020 7731 4655 F 020 7371 8682
E florehouse@msn.com
W www.christopherjones antiques.co.uk
Est. 1984 *Stock size* Large
Stock French furniture, mirrors, screens, 1860–1890 Chinese porcelain
Open Mon–Sat 10am–5.30pm

King's Court Galleries
Contact Mrs J Joel
949–953 Fulham Road, London, SW6 5HY P
☎ 020 7610 6939 F 020 7731 4737
E sales@kingscourtgalleries.co.uk
W www.kingscourtgalleries.co.uk
Est. 1984 *Stock size* Large
Stock Antique maps, engravings, sporting, decorative prints
Open Mon–Sat 10am–5.30pm
Services Framing

Graham Kirkland
Contact Mr G Kirkland
271 Lillie Road, London, SW6 7LL P
☎ 020 7381 3195 F 020 7381 3195
E sales@grahamkirkland.co.uk
W www.grahamkirkland.co.uk
Est. 1978 *Stock size* Large
Stock Religious Victoriana, statues, chalices, sanctuary lamps, crucifixes, candlesticks
Open Mon–Fri 10am–5.30pm Sat 11am–4pm

L & E Kreckovic
Contact Joanna Christopher
559 King's Road, London, SW6 2EB P
☎ 020 7736 0753 F 020 7731 5904
Est. 1969 *Stock size* Large
Stock Early 18th–19thC furniture
Open Mon–Sat 10am–6pm
Services Valuations, restoration

Lewin
Contact Harriet Lewin
638 Fulham Road, London, SW6 5RT P
☎ 027 7731 3738
W www.lewincolonial.com
Est. 1992 *Stock size* Medium
Stock Original 1829–40 Dutch colonial furniture
Open Mon–Sat 10.30am–6pm
Services Restoration

Lunn Antiques Ltd
Contact Stephen Lunn
86 New Kings Road, Fulham, London, SW6 4OU
☎ 020 7736 4638 F 020 7371 7113
E lunnantiques@aol.com
W www.lunnantiques.co.uk
Est. 1995 *Stock size* Medium
Stock Antique textiles, lace, linen
Open Mon–Sat 10am–6pm
Services Valuations, restoration

M Luther Antiques
Contact Mr M Luther
590 King's Road, Chelsea, London, SW6 2DX P
☎ 020 7371 8492 F 020 7371 8492
Est. 1992 *Stock size* Medium
Stock 18th–19thC English and Continental furniture, tables, chairs, mirrors, lighting etc
Open Mon–Sat 9.30am–6pm

David Martin-Taylor Antiques (LAPADA)
Contact Mr Cavet
558 King's Road, London, SW6 2DZ P
☎ 020 7731 4135 F 020 7371 0029
M 07889 437306
E dmt@davidmartintaylor.com
W www.davidmartintaylor.com
Est. 1965 *Stock size* Large
Stock 18th–19thC Continental and English furniture, objets d'art, decorative art, from the eccentric to the unusual
Open Mon–Fri 10am–6pm Sat 11am–4.30pm or by appointment
Fairs Olympia (June), London Decorative Arts

⊞ Ann May
Contact Mrs A May
✉ 80 Wandsworth Bridge Road, London, SW6 2TF 🅿
☎ 020 7731 0862
Est. 1969 ***Stock size*** Medium
Stock Painted French furniture, decorative items
Open Mon–Sat 10am–6pm

⊞ Mark Maynard
Contact Mr M Maynard
✉ 651 Fulham Road, London, SW6 5PU 🅿
☎ 020 7731 3533
Est. 1985 ***Stock size*** Medium
Stock Painted French furniture, decorative items
Open Mon–Sat 10am–5pm

⊞ Mora & Upham Antiques
Contact Matthew Upham or Mark Punton
✉ 584 King's Road, London, SW6 2DX 🅿
☎ 020 7731 4444 Ⓕ 020 7736 0440
Ⓔ mora.upham@talk21.com
Est. 1996 ***Stock size*** Large
Stock Gilded French chairs, antique chandeliers, 18th–19thC English and Continental furniture, mirrors
Open Mon–Sat 10am–6pm

⊞ Nimmo & Spooner
Contact Myra Spooner or Catherine Nimmo
✉ 277 Lillie Road, London, SW6 7LL 🅿
☎ 020 7385 2724 Ⓕ 020 7385 2724
Est. 1990 ***Stock size*** Medium
Stock Decorative antiques, unusual objects, 18thC French furniture
Open Mon–Sat 10.30am–5.30pm

⊞ Old World Trading Co
Contact Mr R Campion
✉ 565 King's Road, London, SW6 2EB 🅿
☎ 020 7731 4708 Ⓕ 020 7731 1291
Ⓔ oldworld@btinternet.com
Est. 1970 ***Stock size*** Large
Stock 18th–19thC English and French chimneypieces, fire dogs, grates
Open Mon–Fri 9.30am–6pm Sat 10am–3pm
Services Valuations, restoration

⊞ Orient Expressions Ltd (BABAADA)
Contact Amanda Leader or Patricia Wilkinson
✉ Studio 3M1, 3rd Floor, Cooper House, 2 Michael Road, London, SW6 2ER 🅿
☎ 020 7610 9311 Ⓕ 020 7610 6872
Ⓜ 07887 770406
Ⓔ amanda@orientexpressions.com
Ⓦ www.orientexpressions.com
Est. 1996 ***Stock size*** Medium
Stock 19th–early 20thC Chinese furniture, French, Edwardian and Art Deco pieces
Open By appointment

⊞ M Pauw Ltd
Contact M Pauw
✉ Cooper House, 2 Michael Road, Chelsea, London, SW6 2AD 🅿
☎ 020 7731 4022 Ⓕ 020 7731 7356
Ⓔ info@mpauw.com
Ⓦ www.mpauw.com
Est. 1985 ***Stock size*** Large
Stock Antique leather chairs
Open Mon–Sat 10am–6pm

⊞ Rainbow Antiques
Contact Mr Fabio Bergomi
✉ 329 Lillie Road, London, SW6 7NR 🅿
☎ 020 7385 1323 Ⓕ 020 7385 4190
Ⓔ rainbowlondon@aol.com
Ⓦ www.rainbowlondon.com
Est. 1998 ***Stock size*** Large
Stock Italian, French 1880–1940 period lighting, chandeliers, lamps, lanterns
Open Mon–Sat 10.30am–5.30pm or by appointment
Fairs Battersea Decorative Antiques Fair, House and Garden
Services Restoration, rewiring

⊞ Rankin Conn Oriental Antiques (LAPADA)
Contact Ms Sara Reynolds
✉ 608 King's Road, London, SW6 2DX 🅿
☎ 020 7384 1847 Ⓕ 020 7384 1847
Ⓜ 07774 487713
Ⓔ daphnerankin@aol.com
Ⓦ www.rankin-conn-chinatrade.com
Est. 1979 ***Stock size*** Large
Stock 17th–19thC Japanese Imari, Chinese Export porcelain, Rose Mandarin, Blue Canton, tortoiseshell tea caddies, Dutch Delft
Open Mon–Sat 10.30am–6pm or by appointment
Fairs Olympia (June, Nov)

⊞ Relic Antiques
Contact Mr Malcolm Gliksten
✉ 291 Lillie Road, London, SW6 7LL 🅿
☎ 020 7381 5008 Ⓕ 020 7388 2691
Ⓜ 07831 785059
Ⓔ malcolm.gliksten@blueyonder.co.uk
Est. 1972 ***Stock size*** Large
Stock Decorative antiques, folk art, fairground art, country pieces, marine, architectural, trade signs, shop fittings
Open Mon–Sat 10.30am–5.30pm or by appointment
Fairs Battersea Decorative, Montpellier
Services Valuations

⊞ Rogers & Co (LAPADA)
Contact Christine or Michael Rogers
✉ 604 Fulham Road, London, SW6 5RP 🅿
☎ 020 7731 8504 Ⓕ 020 7610 6040
Ⓜ 07786 540355
Ⓔ michael@sebeau.com
Est. 1971 ***Stock size*** Medium
Stock 19thC English antiques
Open Mon–Fri 10am–6pm Sat 10am–5pm
Services Interior design, consultancy

⊞ Soo San
Contact Suzanna Murray
✉ 598a King's Road, London, SW6 2DX
☎ 020 7731 2063 Ⓕ 020 7311 1566
Ⓔ suze@soosan.co.uk
Ⓦ www.soosan.co.uk
Est. 1995 ***Stock size*** Large
Stock Oriental antiques and interiors
Open Mon–Sat 10am–6pm

⊞ Stephen Sprake Antiques
Contact Mr S Sprake
✉ 283 Lillie Road, London, SW6 7LL 🅿
☎ 020 7381 3209 Ⓕ 020 7381 9502
Ⓜ 07710 922225
Est. 1998 ***Stock size*** Medium
Stock 18th–20thC English and French furniture, lighting, unusual architectural pieces
Open Mon–Sat 10.30am–5.30pm

Suzie Simons
Contact Suzie Simons
291 Lillie Road, London, SW6 7LL
020 7381 5008 020 7388 2691
Est. 1972 *Stock size* Medium
Stock Antiques, collectables
Open Mon–Sat 10.30am–5.30pm or by appointment

Trowbridge Gallery (LAPADA)
Contact Martin
555 King's Road, London, SW6 2EB
020 7731 8733 020 7371 8138
gallery@trowbridge.com
www.trowbridge.com
Est. 1983 *Stock size* Large
Stock Antique prints
Open Mon–Sat 9.30am–6pm

Leigh Warren
Contact Mr F Cochrane
565 King's Road, London, SW6 2EB
020 7736 9166
020 77361 1291
Est. 1979 *Stock size* Large
Stock 19th–20thC lighting
Open Mon–Fri 10am–5pm Sat 10am–4pm

York Gallery Ltd
Contact Mr G Beyer
569 King's Road, London, SW6 2EB
020 7736 2260 020 7736 2260
prints@yorkgallery.co.uk
www.yorkgallery.co.uk
Est. 1989 *Stock size* Large
Stock Antique prints
Open Mon–Sat 10.30am–6pm
Services Picture framing

SW7

Atlantic Bay Gallery (BADA)
Contact Mr Wojtek Grodzinski
35 Thurloe Place, London, SW7 2HJ
020 7589 8489 020 7589 8189
07831 455492
atlanticbaygallery@btinternet.com
www.atlanticbaycarpet.com
Est. 1945 *Stock size* Large
Stock Oriental and European carpets and textiles, Islamic and Indian art
Open Mon–Fri 9am–5.30pm
Services Valuations, restoration

Bonhams
Montpelier Street, London, SW7 1HH
020 7393 3900 020 7393 3905
info@bonhams.com
www.bonhams.com
Est. 1793
Open Mon–Fri 9am–4.30pm Sun 11am–3pm
Sales Regular sales of antique and modern guns and militaria, antiquities, clocks and watches, coins, collectables, including toys, scientific instruments and entertainment memorabilia, carpets and rugs, contemporary ceramics, ceramics and glass, decorative arts, design, furniture, Islamic works of art, jewellery, pictures, frames, Oriental works of art, silver and tribal art. In addition to general sales, regional salerooms offer more specialized areas of interest including sporting memorabilia, collectables and textiles. Regular house and attic sales across the country; contact London offices for further details. Free auction valuations; insurance and probate valuations
Catalogues Yes

Christie's South Kensington (BACA Award Winner 2002)
85 Old Brompton Road, London, SW7 3LD
020 7930 6074 020 7321 3311
www.christies.com
Est. 1766
Open Tues–Fri 9am–5pm Mon 9am–7.30pm
Sales Weekly furniture sale Wed 10.30am. Fortnightly sale of silver Tues 2pm and ceramics Tues 10.30am and 2pm. Fortnightly jewellery sale Tues 2pm and pictures Thurs 10.30am, viewing Sun 1–4pm Mon 9am–7.30pm Tues–Fri 9am–5pm
Catalogues Yes

Gloucester Road Bookshop
Contact Vivi Gregory
123 Gloucester Road, London, SW7 4TE
020 7370 3503 020 7373 0610
manager@gloucesterbooks.co.uk
www.gloucesterbooks.co.uk
Est. 1983 *Stock size* Large
Stock Antiquarian, rare, second-hand books, modern literature, academic, art, first editions
Open Mon–Fri 9.30am–10.30pm Sat Sun 10.30am–6.30pm
Services Catalogues, shipping, book search

M P Levene Ltd (BADA)
Contact Mr Martin Levene
5 Thurloe Place, London, SW7 2RR
020 7589 3755 020 7589 9908
silver@mplevene.co.uk
www.mplevene.co.uk
Est. 1889 *Stock size* Medium
Stock Antique and modern English silver, silver cufflinks, cutlery sets, hand-made silver scale models
Open Mon–Fri 9am–6pm Sat 9am–1.30pm
Services Valuations

Robert Miller
Contact Robert Miller
15 Glendower Place, South Kensington, London, SW7 3DR
020 7584 4733
07771 2657259
Est. 1968 *Stock size* Medium
Stock Furniture, pictures and works of art
Open Mon–Fri 9am–5pm Sat 2–6pm or by appointment
Fairs Olympia

Shanxi Ltd
Contact Gail Davidner
60 Gloucester Road, Kensington, London, SW7 4QT
020 7581 3456
info@shanxi.co.uk
www.shanxi.co.uk
Est. 1994 *Stock size* Medium
Stock Antique Chinese furniture and decorative items
Open Mon–Sat 10am–6pm Sun 11am–5pm

SW8

Davies Antiques (LAPADA)
Contact Hugh Davies
c/o The Packing House, 6–12 Ponton Road, Battersea, London, SW8 5BA
020 8947 1902 020 8947 1902
hugh.davies@btconnect.com

Ⓦ www.antique-meissen.com
Est. 1975 *Stock size* Large
Stock Meissen porcelain 18thC–Art Deco period
Open By appointment

Paul Orssich (PBFA)
Contact Paul Orssich
2 St Stephens Terrace, South Lambeth, London, SW8 1DH Ⓟ
☎ 020 7787 0030 Ⓕ 020 7735 9612
Ⓔ paulo@orssich.com
Ⓦ www.orssich.com
Est. 1980 *Stock size* Large
Stock Antiquarian, rare and out-of-print books on Hispanic topics
Open By appointment
Services Valuations, book search

SW9

Collectable Furniture
Contact Robert Beckford
11 Rushcroft Road, Brixton, London, SW9 8LQ Ⓟ
☎ 020 7738 4141
Ⓔ robert@soulsofblackfolk.com
Ⓦ www.soulsofblackfolk.com
Est. 1998 *Stock size* Large
Stock 1950s–1970s collectables
Open Mon–Sat noon–8pm Sun noon–5pm
Services Valuations

More Than Just Furniture
Contact Robert Beckford
407 Coldharbour Lane,Brixton, London, SW9 8LQ Ⓟ
☎ 020 7738 4141
Ⓔ robert@soulsofblackfolk.com
Ⓦ www.soulsofblackfolk.com
Est. 1998 *Stock size* Large
Stock 1960s furniture, lighting
Open Mon–Sat noon–8pm Sun noon–5pm
Services Valuations

SW10

Adam & Eve Books
Contact Mr S Dickson
18a Basement, Redcliffe Square, London, SW10 9JZ Ⓟ
☎ 020 7370 4535
Ⓜ 07961 316 918
Ⓔ stevdcksn@btinternet.com
Est. 1999 *Stock size* Small
Stock Antiquarian books, Middle East, travel, first editions, modern first editions a speciality
Open By appointment
Fairs Royal National Hotel Book Fair

Paul Andrews Antiques
Contact Paul or Tycho Andrews
The Furniture Cave, 533 King's Road, London, SW10 0TZ Ⓟ
☎ 020 7352 4584 Ⓕ 020 7351 7815
Ⓔ mail@paulandrews.co.uk
Ⓦ www.paulandrewsantiques.co.uk
Est. 1969 *Stock size* Large
Stock Eclectic furniture, sculpture, paintings, works of art, modern design
Open Mon–Sat 10am–6pm Sun noon–5pm
Fairs Olympia Spring and Summer

Alasdair Brown
Contact Mr A Brown
Suite 150, 405 Kings Road, London, SW10 0BB Ⓟ
Ⓕ 020 7384 3334
Ⓜ 07836 672857
Ⓔ ab@ajcb.demon.co.uk
Ⓦ www.alasdairbrown.com
Est. 1984 *Stock size* Medium
Stock 19th–20thC furniture, lighting, upholstery, unusual items
Open By appointment
Fairs Olympia
Services Valuations

Chelsea Gallery (LAPADA)
Contact Mr S Toscani
The Plaza, 535 King's Road, Chelsea, London, SW10 0SZ Ⓟ
☎ 020 7823 3248 Ⓕ 020 7352 1579
Ⓔ info@chelseagallery.co.uk
Ⓦ www.chelseagallery.co.uk
Est. 1978 *Stock size* Medium
Stock Antique illustrated books, literature, prints, maps, specializing in natural history, travel, architecture, history
Open Mon–Sat 10.30am–7pm
Services Framing

The Classic Library
Contact Gerry Freeman
1st floor, 533 King's Road, London, SW10 0TZ
☎ 020 7376 7653 Ⓕ 020 7376 7653
Stock size Large
Stock Antiquarian books, bookcases, library furniture, prints
Open Mon–Sat 10am–6pm Sun noon–5pm

L'Encoignure
Contact Thomas Kerr
517 King's Road, London, SW10 0TX Ⓟ
☎ 020 7351 6465 Ⓕ 020 7351 4744
Ⓔ kerrant@globalnet.co.uk
Ⓦ www.thomaskerrantiques.com
Est. 1994 *Stock size* Large
Stock 18th–19thC French furniture, decorative items, Continental furniture
Open Mon–Sat 10am–6pm
Services Interior design

First Floor
Contact Mr N McAuliffe
The Furniture Cave, 533 King's Road, London, SW10 0TZ Ⓟ
☎ 020 7352 2046
Ⓔ mail@firstfloor.co.uk
Ⓦ www.firstfloor.co.uk
Est. 1972 *Stock size* Medium
Stock 18th–20thC furniture, chandeliers, lighting, tapestries, furniture, accessories
Open Mon–Sat 10am–6pm Sun noon–5pm

Kenneth Harvey Antiques (LAPADA)
Contact Mr K Harvey
The Furniture Cave, 533 King's Road, London, SW10 0TZ Ⓟ
☎ 020 7352 3775 Ⓕ 020 7352 3759
Ⓔ mail@kennethharvey.com
Ⓦ www.kennethharvey.com
Est. 1982 *Stock size* Large
Stock English–French furniture, chandeliers, mirrors, late 17th–20thC, leather armchairs
Open Mon–Sat 10am–6pm Sun 11am–5pm

Simon Hatchwell Antiques
Contact Mr A Hatchwell
533 King's Road, London, SW10 0TZ Ⓟ
☎ 020 7351 2344 Ⓕ 020 7351 3520
Ⓔ hatchwells@btconnect.com
Est. 1961 *Stock size* Large
Stock English and Continental furniture, early 19th–20thC chandeliers, lighting, bronzes, barometers, clocks including longcase clocks
Open Mon–Sat 10am–6pm Sun 11.30am–5pm
Fairs Olympia (June)
Services Valuations, restoration

Langfords Marine Antiques (BADA, LAPADA)
Contact Mrs J Langford
The Plaza, 535 King's Road, London, SW10 0SZ
020 7351 4881 020 7352 0763
langford@dircon.co.uk
www.langfords.co.uk
Est. 1950 *Stock size* Large
Stock Ship's models, nautical artefacts, steam engines
Open Mon–Fri 10am–5.30pm Sat by appointment

Stephen Long
Contact Mr S Long
348 Fulham Road, London, SW10 9UH
020 7352 8226
Est. 1966 *Stock size* Medium
Stock Painted furniture, small decorative items, English pottery, 1780–1850
Open Mon–Fri 9.30am–1pm 2.15–5pm occasional Sat 10am–12.30pm

Lots Road Galleries
Contact Melina Papadopolous
71–73 Lots Road, Chelsea, London, SW10 0RM
020 7351 7771 020 7376 6899
info@lotsroad.com
www.lotsroad.com
Est. 1979
Open Mon–Wed 9am–6pm Thurs 9am–7pm Fri 9am–4pm Sat 10am–4pm Sun 10am–7pm
Sales 2 sales each Sunday, 2pm modern and reproduction furnishings, 4.30pm antiques, viewing Thurs 2–7pm Fri–Sat 10am–4pm Sun 10am
Frequency 2 per month
Catalogues Yes

James McWhirter
Contact James McWhirter
22 Park Walk, London, SW10 0AQ
020 7351 5399 020 7352 9821
mail@jamesmcwhirter.com
www.jamesmcwhirter.com
Est. 1988 *Stock size* Medium
Stock 17th–20thC unusual objects and furniture
Open Mon–Fri 9am–5.30pm

John Nicholas Antiques Ltd
Contact John or Nicholas McAuliffe
First Floor, The Furniture Cave, 533 King's Road, London, SW10 0TZ
020 7352 2046 020 7352 3654
mail@firstfloor.co.uk
Est. 1980 *Stock size* Large
No. of dealers 20
Stock 18th–19thC decorative furniture
Open Mon–Sat 10am–6pm Sun noon–5pm

John Nicholas Antiques Ltd
Contact John or Nicholas McAuliffe
First Floor, 533 King's Road, London, SW10 0TZ
020 7352 2046 020 7352 3654
www.thecave.co.uk
Est. 1999 *Stock size* Medium
Stock Dining chairs, tables and library furniture
Open Mon–Sat 10am–6pm Sun noon–5pm

Phoenix Trading Co
Contact Mr T Shalloe
The Furniture Cave, 533 King's Road, London, SW10 0TZ
020 7351 6543 020 7352 9803
07768 825626
mail@phoenixtrading.co.uk
www.phoenixtrading.co.uk.
Est. 1979 *Stock size* Large
Stock Antique and reproduction decorative accessories, furniture, porcelain, bronze, marble
Open Mon–Sat 10am–6pm Sun 11am–5pm

H W Poulter & Son
Contact Mr D Poulter
279 Fulham Road, London, SW10 9PZ
020 7352 7268 020 7351 0984
hwpoulterandson@btconnect.com
www.hwpoulterandson.co.uk
Est. 1946 *Stock size* Large
Stock 18th–19thC marble, wooden, stone fireplaces, accessories
Open Mon–Fri 9am–5pm Sat 9am–noon
Services Restoration of marble

Christopher Preston Ltd (LAPADA)
Contact Christopher Preston
The Furniture Cave, 553 King's Road, Chelsea, London, SW10 0TZ
020 7352 8587 020 7376 3627
christopherpreston@yahoo.co.uk
www.antiquebrasshandles.co.uk
Est. 1973 *Stock size* Large
Stock 18th–19thC furniture, fireguards, fenders, brass door furniture
Open Mon–Sat 10am–6pm
Services Restoration

Jane Sacchi Linens Ltd (LAPADA)
Contact Jane Sacchi
World's End Studios, 132–134 Lots Road, Chelsea, London, SW10 0RJ
020 7349 7020 020 7349 7049
enquiries@janesacchi.com
www.janesacchi.com
Est. 1989 *Stock size* Medium
Stock 19thC–early 20thC bed and table linen, 1930s furniture
Open Mon–Fri 10am–5pm

Francis Smith Ltd
Contact Mr Norman Ashford
107 Lots Road, Chelsea, London, SW10 0RN
020 7349 0011 020 7349 0770
www.wbauctioneers.com
Est. 1835
Open Mon–Fri 9am–6pm
Sales Antiques and general sale Tues 6pm, viewing Sun 11am–4pm Mon 9am–7pm Tues 9am–6pm prior to sale
Frequency Fortnightly
Catalogues Yes

John Thornton
Contact John or Caroline Thornton
455 Fulham Road, London, SW10 9UZ
020 7352 8810
Est. 1964 *Stock size* Medium
Stock Antiquarian and second-hand books, Catholic and Anglo-Catholic theology
Open Mon–Sat 10am–5.30pm

SW11

Banana Dance Ltd (LAPADA)
Contact Mr J Daltrey
Unit 20, Northcote Road Antiques Market, 155a Northcote Road, Battersea, London,

SW11 2QB 🅿
☎ 01634 364539
ⓔ jonathan@bananadance.com
ⓦ www.bananadance.com
Est. 1988 *Stock size* Large
Stock Clarice Cliff, Art Deco, ceramics, silver, silver plate
Open Mon–Sat 10am–6pm Sun noon–5pm
Fairs Alexandra Palace
Services Valuations, mail order

Battersea Collectables
Contact Mr David Nurse
✉ **495 Battersea Park Road, London, SW11 4LW** 🅿
☎ 020 7228 8820 ⓕ 020 7978 6188
ⓜ 07939 087757
ⓔ revdavidnurse@onetel.net.uk
Est. 1998 *Stock size* Medium
Stock China, clocks, furniture, pictures, mirrors, collectables, Asian, Far East furniture
Open Mon–Sat 10am–6pm
Services Valuations, shipping

Braemar Antiques
Contact Mrs Marlis Ramos de Deus
✉ **Braemar Villas, 113 Northcote Road, London, SW11 6PW** 🅿
☎ 020 7924 5628
Est. 1994 *Stock size* Medium
Stock Decorative antiques, furniture, chandeliers, mirrors, fabrics
Open Mon–Sat 10am–5.30pm
Fairs Chelsea Brocante

Chesney's Antique Fireplaces
Contact Henry Masterton
✉ **194–202 Battersea Park Road, London, SW11 4ND** 🅿
☎ 020 7627 1410 ⓕ 020 7622 1078
ⓔ sales@chesneys.co.uk
ⓦ www.chesneys.co.uk
Est. 1985 *Stock size* Large
Stock Antique and reproduction fireplaces
Open Mon–Fri 9am–5.30pm Sat 10am–5pm
Fairs Decorex

Criterion Riverside Auctions
Contact Addison Gelpey
✉ **41–47 Catford Road, Chatfield Road, London, SW11 3SE** 🅿
☎ 020 7924 1723
ⓔ info@criterionriversideauctions.co.uk
ⓦ www.criterionriversideauctions.co.uk
Est. 1990
Open Mon–Sun 10am–6pm
Sales General antiques
Frequency Weekly
Catalogues Yes

Eccles Road Antiques
Contact Mrs H Rix
✉ **60 Eccles Road, London, SW11 1LX** 🅿
☎ 020 7228 1638 ⓕ 020 8767 5313
ⓜ 07885 172087
Est. 1985 *Stock size* Large
Stock Victoriana, pine and mahogany furniture, collectables, kitchenware
Open Tues–Sat 10am–5pm Sun noon–5pm
Fairs Ardingly

Garland Antiques
Contact Mrs Garland Beech
✉ **74 Chatham Road, London, SW11 6HG** 🅿
☎ 020 7924 4284 ⓕ 020 7924 4284
Est. 1998 *Stock size* Medium
Stock English and Continental furniture, decorative items
Open Tues–Sat 10am–6pm Sun noon–5pm
Services Pine stripping

Gideon Hatch Rugs & Carpets
Contact Gideon Hatch
✉ **1 Port House, Plantation Wharf, London, SW11 3GY** 🅿
☎ 020 7223 3996
ⓜ 07801 748962
ⓦ www.gideonhatch.co.uk
Est. 1998 *Stock size* Medium
Stock Rugs and carpets
Open By appointment
Fairs Olympia
Services Restoration, cleaning

Jenny Hicks Beach
Contact Jenny Hicks Beach
✉ **7 Battersea Church Road, London, SW11 3LY**
☎ 020 7228 6900 ⓕ 020 7228 6900
ⓜ 07778 794832 *Stock size* Small
Stock Rugs, carpets
Fairs Olympia, Battersea Decorative Antiques and Textiles, HALI Antique Textile Art Fair
Services Search service

The House Hospital
Contact Mr J Brunton
✉ **15 Winders Road, London, SW11 3HE** 🅿
☎ 020 8870 8202
Est. 1983 *Stock size* Medium
Stock Fireplaces, cast-iron radiators, doors, handles, general architectural salvage
Open Mon–Sat 10am–5pm

Northcote Road Antiques Market
Contact Mrs Gill Wilkins
✉ **155a Northcote Road, London, SW11 6QB** 🅿
☎ 020 7228 6850
Est. 1986 *Stock size* Large
No. of dealers 40
Stock Jewellery, prints, pictures, glass, Victoriana, Art Deco, furniture, lighting, silver, plate, textiles
Open Mon–Sat 10am–6pm Sun noon–5pm
Services Café

Overmantels
Contact Seth Taylor
✉ **66 Battersea Bridge Road, London, SW11 3AG** 🅿
☎ 020 7223 8151 ⓕ 020 7924 2283
ⓔ seth@overmantels.co.uk
ⓦ www.overmantels.co.uk
Est. 1982 *Stock size* Small
Stock Mirrors, console tables
Open Mon–Sat 9.30am–5.30pm

Kate Thurlow and David Alexander Antiques (LAPADA, CINOA)
Contact Kate Thurlow or Rodney Robertson
✉ **29A Battersea Bridge Road, London, SW11 3BA** 🅿
☎ 020 7738 0792
ⓜ 07836 588776
ⓔ katethurlow@onetel.com
Est. 1978 *Stock size* Medium
Stock 16th–17thC Continental, English furniture, associated wares
Open By appointment
Fairs Olympia
Services Restoration

Wood Pigeon
Contact Mr J Taylor or Mrs B Cunnell
✉ **71 Webb's Road, London, SW11 6SD** 🅿
☎ 020 7223 8668 ⓕ 020 8647 8790

Ⓜ 07958 787676 or 07932 780707
Est. 1996 ***Stock size*** Medium
Stock French, country, painted, upholstered furniture, decorative items
Open Tues–Sat 10.30am–5.30pm
Services Decorative furniture painting, upholstery

www.antiques.co.uk
Contact Iain Brunt
✉ **c14 The Old Imperial Laundry, 71–73 Warriner Gardens, Battersea, London, SW11 4XW** Ⓟ
☎ 020 7622 6446 Ⓕ 020 7622 3663
Ⓔ mail@antiques.co.uk
Ⓦ www.antiques.co.uk
Est. 1995 ***Stock size*** Large
Stock Varied
Open By appointment

Robert Young Antiques (BADA)
Contact Robert or Josyane Young
✉ **68 Battersea Bridge Road, London, SW11 3AG** Ⓟ
☎ 020 7228 7847 Ⓕ 020 7585 0489
Ⓔ office@robertyoungantiques.com
Ⓦ robertyoungantiques.com
Est. 1975 ***Stock size*** Medium
Stock Country furniture, folk art, treen, naive and primitive paintings, Scandinavian objects
Open Tues–Fri 9.30am–6pm
Sat 10am–5pm
Fairs Olympia (June), San Francisco Fall, The New York Winter Antiques Show
Services In-house annual exhibition of Folk Art, May

SW13

Christine Bridge Antiques (BADA, LAPADA, CINOA)
Contact Christine Bridge or Darryl Bowles
✉ **78 Castelnau, London, SW13 9EX** Ⓟ
☎ 020 8741 5501 Ⓕ 020 8255 0172
Ⓜ 07831 126668
Ⓔ christine@bridge-antiques.com
Ⓦ www.bridge-antiques.com or www.antiqueglass.co.uk
Est. 1970 ***Stock size*** Medium
Stock 18thC collectors' glass, 19thC coloured and decorative glass
Open By appointment only
Fairs BADA, Olympia, fairs in USA and Far East
Services Glass restoration, repairs, polishing, cleaning, web site design (www.ABAC11.com)

Simon Coleman Antiques
Contact Simon Coleman
✉ **40 White Hart Lane, Barnes, London, SW13 0PZ** Ⓟ
☎ 020 8878 5037
Est. 1977 ***Stock size*** Large
Stock Fully restored farmhouse tables, narrow serving tables
Open Mon–Fri 9.30am–6pm
Sat 9.30am–5pm

The Dining Room Shop
Contact David Hur
✉ **62–64 White Hart Lane, Barnes, London, SW13 0PZ** Ⓟ
☎ 020 8878 1020 Ⓕ 020 8876 2367
Ⓔ enquiries@thedining roomshop.co.uk
Ⓦ www.thediningroomshop.co.uk
Est. 1985 ***Stock size*** Medium
Stock Everything for formal and country dining rooms, furniture, china, glass, silver, linens, lighting, prints
Open Mon–Sat 10am–5.30pm
Fairs Olympia June
Services Valuations, restoration

Joy McDonald Antiques
Contact Ms Angela McDonald
✉ **50 Station Road, Barnes, London, SW13 0LP** Ⓟ
☎ 020 8876 6184 Ⓕ 020 8876 6184
Est. 1966 ***Stock size*** Medium
Stock 18th–20thC mirrors, chandeliers, lighting, upholstered chairs, decorative items
Open Tues–Sat 10.30am–5.30pm

Tobias & The Angel
Contact Angel Hughes
✉ **68 White Hart Lane, London, SW13 0PZ** Ⓟ
☎ 020 8878 8902 Ⓕ 020 8296 0058
Est. 1985 ***Stock size*** Large
Stock Country antiques, furniture, lampshades, pictures, mirrors, linen, pretty, useful objects for the home
Open Mon–Sat 10am–6pm
Services Mail order, bespoke furniture

SW14

The Arts and Crafts Furniture Co Ltd
Contact Mr P Rogers
✉ **49 Sheen Lane, East Sheen, London, SW14 8AB** Ⓟ
☎ 020 8876 6544 Ⓕ 020 8876 6544
Ⓔ acfc@49sheen.fsnetco.uk
Ⓦ www.acsc.co.uk
Est. 1989 ***Stock size*** Large
Stock Arts and Crafts furniture, copperware, ceramics, fabrics, artworks
Open Mon–Fri 10am–6pm
Sat 10am–5pm
Services Restoration

Mary Cooke Antiques Ltd (BADA)
Contact Mary Cooke or Neil Shepperson
✉ **12 The Old Power Station, 121 Mortlake High Street, London, SW14 8SN** Ⓟ
☎ 020 8876 5777 Ⓕ 020 8876 1652
Ⓜ 07836 521103
Ⓔ silver@marycooke.co.uk
Ⓦ www.marycooke.co.uk
Est. 1967 ***Stock size*** Medium
Stock 18th–early 19thC silver
Open By appointment
Fairs Olympia, BADA

Paul Foster Books (ABA, PBFA)
Contact Paul Foster
✉ **119 Sheen Lane, East Sheen, London, SW14 8AE** Ⓟ
☎ 020 8876 7424 Ⓕ 020 8876 7424
Ⓔ paulfosterbooks@btinternet.com
Est. 1990 ***Stock size*** Medium
Stock Antiquarian, rare, second-hand, out-of-print books
Open Wed–Sat 10.30am–6pm
Fairs Olympia, Chelsea

Pamela Godwin
Contact Pamela Godwin
✉ **136 Upper Richmond Road West, East Cheam, London, SW14 8DS** Ⓟ
☎ 020 8878 8988
Est. 1964 ***Stock size*** Large
Stock General antiques, Georgian, second-hand furniture
Open Mon–Sat 11am–5pm closed Wed or by appointment
Services Valuations

SW15

30th Century Comics
Contact Mr W Morgan
✉ **18 Lower Richmond Road,**

London, SW15 1JP 🅿
☎ 020 8788 2052
Ⓔ rob@thirtiethcentury.free-online.co.uk
Ⓦ www.thirtiethcentury.free-online.do.uk
Est. 1994 ***Stock size*** Large
Stock Vintage and new British and American comics, annuals
Open Mon–Wed Sat 10.30am–6pm Thurs Fri 10.30am–7pm Sun 11am–5pm
Services Mail order, twice yearly catalogue, valuations

⊞ The Clock Clinic Ltd (LAPADA)
Contact Mr R Pedler FBHI
✉ **85 Lower Richmond Road, Putney, London, SW15 1EU** 🅿
☎ 020 8788 1407 Ⓕ 020 8780 2838
Ⓔ clockclinic@btconnect.com
Ⓦ www.clockclinic.co.uk
Est. 1971 ***Stock size*** Medium
Stock Antique clocks, barometers, all overhauled and guaranteed
Open Tues–Fri 9am–6pm Sat 9am–1pm
Fairs Olympia (Feb, June, Nov)
Services Valuations, restoration, repairs

⊞ Hanshan Tang Books (ABA)
Contact Mr J Cayley
✉ **Unit 3, Ashburton Centre, 276 Cortis Road, London, SW15 3AY** 🅿
☎ 020 8788 4464 Ⓕ 020 8780 1565
Ⓔ hst@hanshan.com
Ⓦ www.hanshan.com
Est. 1974 ***Stock size*** Medium
Stock East Asian art, archaeology
Open By appointment
Services Book search, library purchases

SW16

⊞ H C Baxter & Sons (BADA, LAPADA)
Contact Mr G Baxter
✉ **40 Drewstead Road, London, SW16 1AB** 🅿
☎ 020 8769 5969 Ⓕ 020 8769 0898
Ⓔ partners@hcbaxter.co.uk
Ⓦ www.hcbaxter.co.uk
Est. 1928 ***Stock size*** Medium
Stock 18th–19thC English furniture, decorative items
Trade only Public by appointment only
Open Wed Thurs 9am–5pm
Fairs Olympia (Nov) BADA, Duke of York, Grosvenor House
Services Valuations

⊞ A and J Fowle
Contact Mr A Fowle
✉ **542 Streatham High Road, London, SW16 3QF** 🅿
☎ 020 8764 2896
Ⓜ 0796 8058790
Est. 1950 ***Stock size*** Medium
Stock General antiques, furniture, silver, china, paintings
Open Mon–Sun 9am–6pm or by appointment
Fairs Ardingly

⊞ Kantuta
Contact Mrs N Wright
✉ **1d Gleneagle Road, London, SW16 6AX** 🅿
☎ 020 8677 6701
Est. 1986 ***Stock size*** Medium
Stock Antique furniture
Open Mon–Sat 10am–6pm
Services Restoration

SW17

⊞ Hudson Bay Trading Co Antiques
Contact David Hudson
✉ **6 Khama Road, Tooting, London, SW17 0EL** 🅿
Ⓜ 07915 557700
Ⓦ www.hbtc.co.uk
Est. 1969 ***Stock size*** Medium
Stock General antiques, English furniture, silver, collectables
Open By appointment
Services Valuations, restoration

⊞ Roger Lascelles Clocks
Contact Mr R Lascelles
✉ **Unit 11, Wimbledon Stadium Business Centre, Riverside Road, London, SW17 0BA** 🅿
☎ 020 8879 6011 Ⓕ 020 8879 1818
Ⓔ info@rogerlascelles.com
Ⓦ www.rogerlascelles.com
Est. 1974 ***Stock size*** Large
Stock Longcase, mantel and traditional reproduction clocks
Open Mon–Fri 10am–5pm (telephone first) or by appointment

SW18

⊞ Bertie's
Contact Mrs B Ferguson
✉ **1st Floor, 284 Merton Road, London, SW18 5JN** 🅿
☎ 020 8874 2520
Est. 1985 ***Stock size*** Small
Stock Antique and reproduction pine furniture, china, collectables
Open Tues–Sat 9.30am–5.30pm
Services Bespoke pine furniture

⊞ The Earlsfield Bookshop
Contact Mr C Dixon
✉ **513 Garratt Lane, Wandsworth, London, SW18 4SW** 🅿
☎ 020 8946 3744
Est. 1994 ***Stock size*** Medium
Stock General books
Open Mon–Thurs 4–6pm Fri 11am–6pm Sat 10am–5pm
Fairs Kempton Park, Bloomsbury
Services Valuations

⊞ Just a Second
Contact Mr J Ferguson
✉ **284 Merton Road, London, SW18 5JN** 🅿
☎ 020 8874 2520
Est. 1980 ***Stock size*** Medium
Stock General antiques, good quality furniture
Open Tues–Sat 9.30am–5.30pm
Services Valuations, restoration

Lloyds International Auction Galleries Ltd
Contact Mr Mick Bown
✉ **9 Lydden Road, Earlsfield, London, SW18 4LT** 🅿
☎ 020 8788 7777 Ⓕ 020 8874 5390
Ⓔ lloyd_international@compuserve.com
Ⓦ www.lloyds-auction.co.uk
Est. 1944
Open Mon–Fri 9.30am–5.30pm
Sales Furniture, paintings and collectables sale Sat 11am, viewing Fri 10.30am–7.30pm Sat 9am prior to sale. Jewellery sale Tues 11am, viewing Mon 9.30am–4pm. General Met Police 'Lost Property' sale Wed 3pm, viewing Wed 10.30am–2.45pm prior to sale
Frequency Fortnightly all sales
Catalogues Yes

SW19

⊞ Corfield Potashnick (LAPADA)
Contact Jonathan Fry
✉ **39 Church Road, Wimbledon Village, London,**

SW19 5DG
☎ 020 8944 9022
Ⓜ 07974 565659
Ⓔ jonfry@btopenworld.com
Est. 1997 *Stock size* Medium
Stock 18th–19thC furniture
Open Mon–Sat 10am–6pm
Fairs LAPADA, Commonwealth Institute, London
Services Valuations, restoration

Mark J West (BADA)
Contact Mr M West
Cobb Antiques Ltd, 39b High Street, London, SW19 5BY Ⓟ
☎ 020 8946 2811
Ⓔ westglass@aol.com
Ⓦ www.markjwest-glass.com
Est. 1977 *Stock size* Large
Stock 18th–early 20thC English and Continental table glass
Open Mon–Sat 10am–5.30pm
Fairs Olympia, Grosvenor House

SW20

W F Turk Fine Antique Clocks (BADA, LAPADA, CINOA)
Contact Mr W Turk
355 Kingston Road, London, SW20 8JX Ⓟ
☎ 020 8543 3231 Ⓕ 020 8543 3231
Ⓔ sales@wfturk.com
Ⓦ www.fwturk.com
Est. 1979 *Stock size* Large
Stock Antique clocks, 17th–19thC longcase and bracket clocks, French decorative mantel and carriage clocks
Open Tues–Fri 9am–5.30pm
Sat 9am–4pm
Fairs Olympia, LAPADA, NEC
Services Valuations, restoration, repairs, sales

WEST

W1

David Aaron
Contact Mr David Aaron
22 Berkeley Square, London, W1J 6EH Ⓟ
☎ 020 7491 9588 Ⓕ 020 7491 9522
Ⓔ david_aaron@hotmail.com
Est. 1910 *Stock size* Large
Stock Worldwide ancient art, rare carpets
Open Mon–Fri 9am–6pm
Sat by appointment only
Services Valuations, restoration

Aaron Gallery (ADA)
Contact Simon Aaron
125 Mount Street, London, W1K 3NS Ⓟ
☎ 020 7499 9434 Ⓕ 020 7499 0072
Ⓔ simon@aarongallery.com
Ⓦ www.aarongallery.com
Est. 1910 *Stock size* Large
Stock Islamic, near Eastern, Greek, Roman, Egyptian ancient art
Open Mon–Fri 10am–5.30pm
Services Valuations, restoration

ADC Heritage Ltd (BADA)
Contact Francis Raeymaekers or Elisabeth Bellord
90 Mount Street, London, W1K 2ST Ⓟ
☎ 020 7355 1444 Ⓕ 020 7355 2444
Ⓜ 07747 692554
Ⓔ raeymaekers@aol.com
elbellord@btinternet.com
Est. 1980 *Stock size* Small
Stock Antique English silver and old Sheffield plate
Open By appointment only
Services Valuations, restoration

Adrian Alan Ltd (BADA, LAPADA)
Contact Miss H Alan
66–67 South Audley Street, London, W1YK 2QX Ⓟ
☎ 020 7495 2324 Ⓕ 020 7495 0204
Ⓔ enquiries@adrianalan.com
Ⓦ www.adrianalan.com
Est. 1964 *Stock size* Large
Stock Furniture, light fittings, mirrors, objets d'art, paintings, statues, garden furniture, pianos, 19thC Continental furniture a speciality
Open Mon–Fri 9.30am–6pm
Fairs Olympia (June)
Services Restoration, shipping, storage

Altea Maps and Books (PBFA, ABA)
Contact Mr M De Martini
3rd Floor, 91 Regent Street, London, W1RB 4EL Ⓟ
☎ 020 7494 9060 Ⓕ 020 7287 7938
Ⓔ info@alteamaps.com
Ⓦ www.alteamaps.com
Est. 1993 *Stock size* Medium
Stock 15th–19thC maps, atlases, travel books
Open By appointment
Fairs London Map Fairs, ABA Olympia (June)
Services Valuations, sale on commission

Argyll Etkin Ltd (PTS)
Contact Jim Hanson or Ian Shapiro
1–9 Hills Place, Oxford Circus, London, W1F 7SA Ⓟ
☎ 020 7437 7800
Ⓔ royalty@argyll-etkin.com
Ⓦ www.argyll-etkin.com
Est. 1950 *Stock size* Large
Stock Royal memorabilia, manuscripts, autographs, history of the posts
Open Mon–Fri 8.30am–5pm
Fairs Olympia, Stampex

Victor Arwas Gallery (BACA Award Winner 2004)
Contact Greta or Victor Arwas
3 Clifford Street, London, W1S 2LF Ⓟ
☎ 020 7734 3944 Ⓕ 020 7437 1859
Ⓔ art@victorarwas.com
Ⓦ www.victorarwas.com
Est. 1965 *Stock size* Large
Stock Original paintings, water colours and graphics 1880–1980, Art Nouveau, Art Deco, Arts and Crafts
Open Mon–Fri 11am–6pm
Sat 11am–2pm
Services Valuations, restoration, Victor Arwas is author of about 25 books on decorative arts and related topics

ATLAS
Contact Mr B Burdett
49 Dorset Street, London, W1U 7NF Ⓟ
☎ 020 7224 4192 Ⓕ 020 7224 3351
Ⓔ info@atlasgallery.com
Ⓦ www.atlasgallery.com
Est. 1993 *Stock size* Medium
Stock Antiquarian, rare, second-hand books, travel a speciality. Fine art photographs from vintage prints to limited edition modern prints
Open Mon–Fri 9am–5.30pm
Fairs Bloomsbury, Phillips
Services Valuations, book search

Aytac Antiques (NAWCC)
Contact Mr O Aytac
Grays Antiques Market, Unit 331–332, 58 Davies Street,

London,
W1Y 1LB 🅿
☎ 020 7629 7380 Ⓕ 020 7629 7380
Ⓔ ossiemania@aol.com
Est. 1982 *Stock size* Large
Stock Vintage wristwatches, clocks, 19thC French bronzes
Open Mon–Fri 10.30am–5pm
Services Wristwatch restoration, repair

⊞ J and A Beare Ltd (BADA)
Contact Simon Morris or Frances Gilham
✉ **30 Queen Anne Street, London, W1G 8HX** 🅿
☎ 020 7307 9666 Ⓕ 020 7307 9651
Ⓔ violins@beares.com
Ⓦ www.beares.com
Est. 1892 *Stock size* Large
Stock Musical instruments of the violin family
Open Mon–Fri 10am–12.30pm 1.30pm–5pm
Services Valuations

⊞ Linda Bee
Contact Linda Bee
✉ **The Mews Antique Market, 1–7 Davies Mews, London, W1K 5AB** 🅿
☎ 020 7629 5921 Ⓕ 020 7629 5921
Ⓜ 07956 276384
Ⓦ www.emews.com
Est. 1992 *Stock size* Large
Stock Vintage fashion accessories, handbags, perfume bottles, powder compacts, costume jewellery
Open Mon–Fri 1–6pm or by appointment
Fairs Alexandra Palace
Services Valuations

⊞ Paul Bennett (LAPADA)
Contact Mr Dubiner
✉ **48A George Street, London, W1H 5RF**
☎ 020 7935 1555
Ⓔ paulbennet@ukgateway.net
Ⓦ www.paulbennet.ukgateway.net
Est. 1967
Stock Antique and modern silver, Sheffield plate
Open Mon–Fri 10am–6pm
Fairs Olympia, Claridges
Services Valuations

⊞ Daniel Bexfield Antiques (LAPADA, BADA, CINOA)
Contact Mr D Bexfield
✉ **26 Burlington Arcade, Mayfair, London, W1J 0PU** 🅿
☎ 020 7491 1720 Ⓕ 020 7491 1730
Ⓔ antiques@bexfield.co.uk
Ⓦ www.bexfield.co.uk
Est. 1981 *Stock size* Large
Stock 17th–20thC quality silver, objects of virtue
Open Mon–Sat 9am–6pm
Services Valuations, restoration

⌂ Biblion Ltd
Contact Leo Harrison or Stephen Poole
✉ **Grays Antique Market, 1–7 Davies Mews, London, W1Y 2LP** 🅿
☎ 020 7629 1374 Ⓕ 020 7493 7158
Ⓔ info@biblion.co.uk
Ⓦ www.biblion.com
Est. 1999 *Stock size* Large
No. of dealers 100
Stock Antiquarian, rare books, prints, modern first editions, children's
Open Mon–Sat 10am–6pm
Services Book binding, book search, shipping

⊞ H Blairman & Sons Ltd (BADA, BACA Award Winner 2004)
Contact Martin Levy, Patricia Levy or Sara Sowerby
✉ **119 Mount Street, London, W1K 3NL** 🅿
☎ 020 7493 0444 Ⓕ 020 7495 0766
Ⓔ blairman@atlas.co.uk
Ⓦ www.blairman.co.uk
Est. 1884 *Stock size* Large
Stock 18th–19thC furniture, works of art
Open Mon–Fri 9am–6pm or by appointment
Fairs Grosvenor House Fair, International Fine Art & Antique Dealers Show, New York
Services Catalogues

⊞ Blunderbuss Antiques
Contact Mr C Greenaway
✉ **29 Thayer Street, London, W1U 2QW** 🅿
☎ 020 7486 2444 Ⓕ 020 7935 1645
Ⓔ mail@blunderbuss-antiques.co.uk
Ⓦ www.blunderbuss-antiques.co.uk
Est. 1968 *Stock size* Large
Stock 16thC–WWII weapons, militaria
Open Tues–Fri 9.30am–4.30pm

⌂ The Bond Street Antiques Centre
Contact Neil Jackson
✉ **124 New Bond Street, London, W1Y 9AE** 🅿
☎ 020 7969 1500 Ⓕ 020 7351 5350
Ⓔ antique@dial.pipex.com
Est. 1968 *Stock size* Large
No. of dealers 35
Stock Jewellery, silver, fine vintage watches
Open Mon–Fri 10am–6.45pm Sat 11am–5.30pm
Services Valuations

⚒ Bonhams (BACA Award Winner 2004)
✉ **101 New Bond Street, London, W1S 1SR** 🅿
☎ 020 7629 6602 Ⓕ 020 7629 8876
Ⓔ info@bonhams.com
Ⓦ www.bonhams.com
Est. 1793
Open Mon–Fri 9am–4.30pm Sun 11am–3pm
Sales Regular sales of furniture and works of art, pictures, books, maps and manuscripts, clocks and watches, coins and medals, carpets and rugs, contemporary ceramics, ceramics and glass, Decorative Arts, design, jewellery, musical instruments, Oriental works of art, wine and silver. In addition to general sales, the regional salerooms offer more specialized areas of interest including sporting memorabilia, collectables and textiles. Regular house and attic sales across the country; contact London offices for further details. Free auction valuations, insurance and probate valuations
Catalogues Yes

⊞ David Bowden Chinese and Japanese Art
Contact David Bowden
✉ **Grays Antique Market, 58 Davies Street, London, W1K 5LP** 🅿
☎ 020 7495 1773
Est. 1980 *Stock size* Large
Stock Japanese netsuke, works of art, Chinese works of art
Open Mon–Fri 10am–6pm
Fairs NEC

⊞ Patrick Boyd-Carpenter and Howard Neville
Contact Mr P Boyd-Carpenter or Mr H Neville

✉ **Grays Antique Market, 58 Davies Street, London, W1Y 2LP** 🅿
☎ 020 7491 7623 Ⓕ 020 7491 7623
Ⓔ patrickboyd_carpenter@hotmail.com
Est. 1986 *Stock size* Large
Stock Wide range of antiques, 16th–18thC sculpture, paintings, prints
Open Mon–Fri 10.30am–5.30pm or by appointment
Services Valuations, restoration

🏛 Brandt Oriental Antiques (BADA)
Contact Robert Brandt
✉ **1st Floor, 29 New Bond Street, London, W1S 2RL** 🅿
☎ 020 7499 8835 Ⓕ 020 7409 1882
Ⓜ 07774 989661
Ⓔ brandt@nildram.co.uk
Est. 1980 *Stock size* Medium
Stock Japanese metalwork and screens, the China trade
Open By appointment
Fairs June Olympia, New York

🏛 John Bull (Antiques) Ltd (LAPADA)
Contact Elliot or Ken Bull
✉ **139a New Bond Street, London, W1S 2TN** 🅿
☎ 020 7629 1251 Ⓕ 020 7495 3001
Ⓔ sales@jbsilverware.co.uk
Ⓦ www.antique-silver.co.uk
Est. 1952 *Stock size* Medium
Stock Antique silver giftware
Open Mon–Fri 9am–5pm
Fairs Antiques for Everyone

🏛 C and L Burman (BADA)
Contact Charles Truman or Lucy Burniston
✉ **5 Vigo Street, London, W1S 3HF** 🅿
☎ 020 7439 6604 Ⓕ 020 7439 6605
Ⓔ charles-truman@lineone.net
Est. 2001 *Stock size* Medium
Stock Antiques and works of art including silver, glass, ceramics, furniture, sculpture
Open By appointment
Fairs March BADA, Grosvenor House, Winter Olympia, New York Ceramics Fair
Services Valuations, restoration

🏛 The Button Queen Ltd
Contact Martin Frith
✉ **19 Marylebone Lane, London, W1U 2NF**
☎ 020 7935 1505 Ⓕ 020 7935 1505
Ⓦ www.thebuttonqueen.co.uk
Est. 1950 *Stock size* Large
Stock Buttons
Open Mon–Wed 10am–5pm Thur–Fri 10am–6pm Sat 10am–4pm

🏛 Paul Champkins Oriental Art (BADA)
Contact Mr P Champkins
✉ **41 Dover Street, London, W1X 3RB** 🅿
☎ 020 7495 4600 Ⓕ 01235 751658
Ⓔ pc@paulchampkins.demon.co.uk
Est. 1995 *Stock size* Medium
Stock Chinese, Korean, Japanese porcelain, works of art
Open By appointment
Fairs Grosvenor House, New York Ceramics Fair, Olympia (winter)
Services Valuations, restoration, auction purchasing advice

🏛 Jocelyn Chatterton (LAPADA)
Contact Jocelyn Chatterton
✉ **126 Grays Antique Market, 58 Davies Street, London, W1Y 2LP**
Ⓜ 07798 804853
Ⓔ jocelyn@cixi.demon.co.uk
Ⓦ www.cixi.demon.co.uk
Est. 1997 *Stock size* Medium
Stock Oriental textiles, sewing tools
Open Mon–Fri 10am–5.30pm or by appointment

🏛 Antoine Chenevière Fine Arts Ltd (BADA)
Contact Mr Chenevière
✉ **27 Bruton Street, London, W1X 7DB** 🅿
☎ 020 7491 1007 Ⓕ 020 7495 6173
Ⓔ finearts@antoinecheneviere.com
Stock size Medium
Stock 18th–19thC Russian, Austrian, German and Italian furniture, objets d'art
Open Mon–Sat 9.30am–6pm
Fairs Grosvenor House, The Armoury Fair

🏛 Classical Numismatic Group Inc. (BNTA)
Contact Irene Tilmont
✉ **14 Old Bond Street, London, W1S 4PP** 🅿
☎ 020 7495 1888 Ⓕ 020 7499 5916
Ⓔ cng@cngcoins.com
Ⓦ www.cngcoins.com
Est. 1990 *Stock size* Large
Stock Coins, Greek, Roman, Medieval, European to end of 18thC
Open Mon–Fri 9.30am–5.30pm
Fairs Coinex
Services Valuations, auctions, phone for details

🏛 Sibyl Colefax & John Fowler (LAPADA)
Contact Roger Jones
✉ **39 Brook Street, London, W1K 4JE** 🅿
☎ 020 7493 2231 Ⓕ 020 7355 4037
Ⓔ antiques@sibylcolefax.com
Ⓦ www.colefaxantiques.com
Stock size Large
Stock 18th–19thC Continental and English furniture, objects, pictures
Open Mon–Fri 9.30am–5.30pm
Fairs Olympia

🏛 Sandra Cronan Ltd (BADA)
Contact Sandra Cronan
✉ **18 Burlington Arcade, London, W1J 0PN** 🅿
☎ 020 7491 4851 Ⓕ 020 7493 2758
Ⓔ enquiries@sandracronan.com
Ⓦ www.sandracronan.com
Est. 1978 *Stock size* Medium
Stock 18th–early 20thC jewellery
Open Mon–Fri 10am–5pm
Fairs Grosvenor House, March BADA
Services Valuations, restoration, repairs, design commission

🏛 Adèle De Havilland
Contact Adèle De Havilland
✉ **The Bond Street Antique Centre, 124 New Bond Street, London, W1S 1DX**
☎ 020 7499 7127
Est. 1971 *Stock size* Medium
Stock Oriental porcelain, netsuke, jade, ivory carvings, bronze figures, objects of virtue
Open Mon–Sat 10am–4pm
Services Valuations

🔨 Dix Noonan Webb (BNTA, ANA, OMRS, OMSA)
Contact Mr C Webb
✉ **16 Bolton Street, Piccadilly, London, W1J 8BQ** 🅿
☎ 020 7016 1700 Ⓕ 020 7016 1799
Ⓔ auction@dnw.co.uk
Ⓦ www.dnw.co.uk

LONDON

Est. 1991
Open Mon–Fri 9am–5.30pm
Sales Coins, tokens, commemmorative and war medals, orders, decorations, militaria, banknotes
Frequency 8 per annum
Catalogues Yes

Charles Ede Ltd (BADA, ADA, IADA)
Contact Mr J Ede
20 Brook Street, London, W1K 5DE P
020 7493 4944 F 020 7491 2548
info@charlesede.com
www.charlesede.com
Est. 1976 *Stock size* Medium
Stock Egyptian, Greek, Roman classical and pre-classical antiquities
Open Tues–Fri 12.30–4.30pm or by appointment
Fairs Grosvenor House
Services Valuations, bidding at auction, mail order

Editions Graphiques (BACA Award Winner 2004)
Contact Gretha or Victor Arwas
3 Clifford Street, London, W1S 2LF P
020 7734 3944 F 020 7437 1859
art@victorarwas.com
www.victorarwas.com
Est. 1965 *Stock size* Large
Stock Original paintings, water colours and graphics 1880–1980, Art Nouveau, Art Deco, Arts and Crafts
Open Mon–Fri 11am–6pm Sat 11am–2pm
Services Valuations, restoration, Victor Arwas is author of about 25 books on decorative arts and related topics

Peter Edwards
Contact Mr P Edwards
31 Burlington Arcade, London, W1J 0PY P
020 7491 1589 F 020 7408 2405
peter@peter-edwards-jewels.co.uk
www.peter-edwards-jewels.co.uk
Est. 1966 *Stock size* Medium
Stock 20thC jewellery, signed pieces
Open Mon–Sat 10am–6pm
Fairs Olympia, Harrogate
Services Valuations, restoration

Elisabeth's Antiques Ltd (LAPADA)
Contact Elisabeth Hage
Bond Street Antiques Centre, 124 New Bond Street, London, W1S 1DX
020 7491 1723 F 020 7629 8910
Stock size Medium
Stock Antique and period jewellery
Open Mon–Sat 10.30am–5.30pm
Fairs Olympia fairs

Emanouel Corporation (UK) Ltd (LAPADA)
Contact Emanouel Naghi
64–64a South Audley Street, London, W1K 2QT P
020 7493 4350 F 020 7629 3125
Est. 1975 *Stock size* Large
Stock General antiques, works of art
Open Mon–Fri 10am–6pm
Services Valuations, shipping

Eskenazi Ltd (BADA)
Contact Mr J Eskenazi
10 Clifford Street, London, W1S 2LJ P
020 7493 5464 F 020 7499 3136
gallery@eskenazi.co.uk
www.eskenazi.co.uk
Est. 1960 *Stock size* Medium
Stock Early Chinese works of art
Open Mon–Fri 9am–5.30pm

John Eskenazi Ltd (BADA)
Contact Kate Cook
15 Old Bond Street, London, W1S 4AX P
020 7409 3001 F 020 7629 2146
john.eskenazi@john-eskenazi.com
www.john-eskenazi.com
Est. 1994 *Stock size* Medium
Stock South East Asian, Himalayan and Indian works of art, Oriental textiles and carpets
Open Mon–Fri 9.30am–6pm or by appointment
Fairs International Asian Art Fair

Essie Carpets
Contact Mr Essie
62 Piccadilly, London, W1J 0DZ P
020 7493 7766 F 020 7495 3456
Est. 1766 *Stock size* Large
Stock Persian, Oriental rugs, tapestries
Open Mon–Fri 9.30am–6pm Sun Bank Holidays 10.30am–5.30pm

Simon Finch Rare Books (ABA, PBFA)
Contact Mr S Finch
53 Maddox Street, London, W1S 2PN P
020 7499 0974 F 020 7499 0799
rarebooks@simonfinch.com
www.simonfinch.com
Est. 1982 *Stock size* Medium
Stock 15th–20thC books art, architecture, literature, science, medicine
Open Mon–Fri 10am–6pm
Fairs Olympia, Chelsea, Grosvenor House
Services Valuations, library advice

Matthew Foster
Contact Mr M Foster or Mr J Silver
Units 5 & 6, Bond Street Antiques Centre, 124 New Bond Street, London, W1S 1DX P
020 7629 4977 F 020 7629 4977
info@matthew-foster.com
www.matthew-foster.com
Est. 1987 *Stock size* Large
Stock Large stock of Victorian gold jewellery, Edwardian, Art Deco gem set jewellery
Open Mon–Fri 10am–5.30pm Sat 11am–5.30pm
Fairs Olympia (June)

Peter Gaunt
Contact Mr P Gaunt
Stand 120, Grays Antique Market, 58 Davies Street, London, W1K 5JF P
020 7629 1072 F 020 7629 5253
Est. 1978 *Stock size* Large
Stock Antique silver including Georgian teaspoons, 17thC candlesticks
Open Mon–Fri 10am–5.30pm
Services Valuations

The Gilded Lily Jewellery Ltd (LAPADA, CINOA)
Contact Ms Korin Harvey
Stand 145–146, Grays Antique Market, 58 Davies Street, London, W1K 5LP P
020 7499 6260 F 020 7499 6260
jewellery@gilded-lily.co.uk
www.graysantiques.com
Est. 1970 *Stock size* Large
Stock Glamorous jewellery, signed pieces

Open Mon–Fri 10am–6pm
Fairs Olympia, LAPADA, Miami Beach, Hong Kong

Glendining's (BNTA, SOFAA)
Contact Mr A Litherland
101 New Bond Street, London, W1S 1SR
020 7493 2445
Est. 1900
Open Mon–Fri 8.30am–5pm
Sales 4 coin sales, 3 medal sales, also arms, armour, militaria
Frequency 7 per annum
Catalogues Yes

Gordon's Medals (OMRS)
Contact Mr M Gordon
Stand G14–16, The Mews Antique Market, Davies Mews, London, W1K 5AB
020 7495 0900 020 7495 0115
07976 266293
malcolm@gordonsmedals.co.uk
www.gordonsmedals.co.uk
Est. 1979 *Stock size* Large
Stock Militaria, uniforms, headgear, badges, medals, documents
Open Mon–Fri 10.30am–6pm
Fairs Brittania Fair, OMRS
Services Valuations

Graham & Oxley Ltd (BADA)
Contact Michael Graham
49 Hallam Street, London, W1W 6JW
020 7436 7030 020 7436 0098
mg@grahamandoxley.com
www.grahamandoxley.com
Est. 1968 *Stock size* Medium
Stock General decorative antiques
Open By appointment
Fairs Spring Olympia, Battersea Antiques & Textiles
Services Valuations

The Graham Gallery (LAPADA)
Contact Mr G Whittall
60 South Audley Street, Mayfair, London, W1K 2QW
020 7495 3151 020 7495 3171
Est. 1979 *Stock size* Large
Stock 18th–19thC furniture, 19thC oil paintings, objets d'art, Art Deco furniture
Open Mon–Fri 10.30am–6pm or by appointment
Fairs Olympia (June), LAPADA

Graus Antiques
Contact Jackie Stern
139A New Bond Street, London, W1S 2TN
020 7629 6680 020 7499 8774
eric@graus-antiques.com
Est. 1945 *Stock size* Large
Stock Antique pocket watches, jewellery
Open Mon–Fri 9am–5pm

Anita Gray (LAPADA)
Contact Mrs A Gray
Grays Antique Market, 58 Davies Street, London, W1K 5LP
020 7408 1638 020 7495 0707
info@chinese-porcelain.com
www.chinese-porcelain.com
Est. 1975 *Stock size* Medium
Stock Asian and European porcelain, works of art, 16th–18thC
Open Mon–Fri 10am–6pm
Fairs Olympia (June)

Grays Antique Market
Contact William Griffith or Kirstine Wallace
58 Davies Street, London, W1K 5AB
020 7629 7034 020 7629 3279
grays@clara.net
www.graysantiques.com
Est. 1977 *Stock size* Large
No. of dealers 150
Stock Automata, British and Oriental ceramics, gems, precious stones, glass, Islamic jewellery, objects, prints, paintings, silver, textiles, lace, linen, watches
Open Mon–Fri 10am–6pm special hours at Christmas
Services Café, bureau de change, jewellery repair, glass and metal engraving, pearl stringing

Simon Griffin Antiques Ltd
Contact Mr S Griffin
3 Royal Arcade, 28 Old Bond Street, London, W1S 4SB
020 7491 7367
Est. 1979 *Stock size* Medium
Stock Antique, modern silverware, old Sheffield plate
Open Mon–Sat 10.30am–5.30pm

Sarah Groombridge (LAPADA)
Contact Sarah Groombridge
Stand 335, Grays Antique Market, 58 Davies Street, London, W1K 5LP
020 7629 0225 01252 616201
07770 920277
sarah.groombridge@totalise.co.uk
Est. 1974 *Stock size* Medium
Stock Fine antique jewellery, Georgian–1920s, including natural pearls, cameos
Open Mon–Fri 10am–6pm
Fairs Olympia (Nov, June) LAPADA, Antiques for Everyone, Miami (Jan)

Guest and Gray
Contact Anthony Gray
The Mews Antique Market, 1–7 Davies Mews, London, W1K 5AB
020 7408 1252 020 7499 1445
07968 719496
info@chinese-porcelain-art.com
www.chinese-porcelain-art.com
Est. 1970 *Stock size* Large
Stock Asian and European ceramics, works of art, reference books
Open Mon–Fri 10am–6pm
Fairs International Ceramics Fair, Olympia
Services Valuations

Claire Guest at Thomas Goode & Co. Ltd
Contact Claire Guest
19 South Audley Street, London, W1Y 6BH
020 7499 2823/7243 1423
020 7629 4230/7792 5450
07974 767851
claireguest130@hotmail.co.uk
Est. 1969 *Stock size* Medium
Stock Antique furniture, silver, silver plate, glass, china
Open Mon–Sat 10am–6pm

Hadji Baba Ancient Art Ltd (IADA)
Contact R Soleimani
34a Davies Street, London, W1K 4NE
020 7499 9363 020 7493 5504
info@hadjibaba.co.uk
www.hadjibaba.co.uk
Est. 1979 *Stock size* Medium
Stock Islamic and Asian art
Open Mon–Fri 10am–6pm
Services Valuations

Robert Hall (BADA)
Contact Mr R Hall
15c Clifford Street, London,

W1X 1RF P
☎ 020 7734 4008 F 020 7734 4408
E roberthall@snuffbottle.com
W www.snuffbottle.com.
Est. 1976 *Stock size* Large
Stock 18th–19thC Chinese snuff bottles
Open Mon–Fri 10am–5.30pm or by appointment
Fairs Grosvenor House
Services Valuations, bi-annual catalogues

Hallmark Antiques
Contact Mr Ralph
✉ **Stands 319 & 356, Grays Antique Market, Davies Street, London, W1K 5LP** P
☎ 0207 629 8757
Est. 1979 *Stock size* Medium
Stock Victorian–Edwardian jewellery, amber, silver, silver photo frames
Open Mon–Fri 10am–6pm

Hancocks and Co (Jewellers) Ltd (BADA)
Contact Steven Burton, Duncan Semmens or Ian Morton
✉ **52–53 Burlington Arcade, London, W1J 0HH**
☎ 020 7493 8904 F 020 7493 8905
E info@hancockslondon.com
W www.hancockslondon.com
Est. 1849 *Stock size* Large
Stock Jewellery, silver
Open Mon–Fri 9.30am–5pm Sat by appointment
Fairs Grosvenor House, Maastricht, The Armoury, Palm Beach
Services Valuations, restoration, purchase of second-hand items

Brian Haughton Antiques (BACA Award Winner 2004)
Contact Brian Haughton
✉ **3b Burlington Gardens, London, W1S 3EP** P
☎ 020 7734 5491 F 020 7494 4604
E info@haughton.com
W www.haughton.com
Est. 1965 *Stock size* Large
Stock 18th–19thC English and Continental ceramics
Open Mon–Fri 10am–5pm
Fairs International Ceramics Fair and Seminar (June), The International Fine Art & Antique Dealers Show, New York (Oct)

Gerard Hawthorn Ltd (BADA)
Contact Mr G Hawthorn
✉ **104 Mount Street, London, W1K 2TL** P
☎ 020 7409 2888 F 020 7409 2777
M 07775 917487
E mail@gerardhawthorn.com
Est. 1996 *Stock size* Medium
Stock Chinese, Japanese, Korean ceramics, works of art
Open Mon–Fri 10am–late
Fairs 2 exhibitions at gallery (June, Nov), International Asian Art Fair, New York (March)
Services Valuations, restoration, photography

G Heywood Hill Ltd (ABA)
Contact Mr John Saumarez Smith
✉ **10 Curzon Street, London, W1J 5HH** P
☎ 020 7629 0647 F 020 7408 0286
E books@gheywoodhill.com
W www.gheywoodhill.com
Est. 1936 *Stock size* Medium
Stock Fiction, history, travel, memoirs, children's antiquarian, second-hand, new books
Open Mon–Fri 9am–5.30pm Sat 9am–12.30pm
Services Book search

Hirsh London
Contact Ben Stevenson
✉ **56–57 Burlington Arcade, London, W1J 0QN** P
☎ 020 7499 6814 F 020 7629 9946
W www.hirsh.co.uk
Est. 1980 *Stock size* Large
Stock Fine antique jewellery, hand-made and designed diamond engagement rings
Open Mon–Fri 10am–5.30pm
Services Valuations

Brian and Lynn Holmes (LAPADA)
Contact Brian or Lynn Holmes
✉ **Stand 304–306, Grays Antique Market, 58 Davies Street, London, W1Y 2LP** P
☎ 020 7629 7327 F 020 7629 7327
W www.graysantiques.com
Est. 1971 *Stock size* Large
Stock Antique Georgian, Victorian silver, gold and jewellery, Scottish antique jewellery
Open Mon–Fri 10am–6pm
Services Valuations, restoration

Holmes Ltd
Contact Mr Eldred
✉ **24 Burlington Arcade, London, W1J 0PS**
☎ 020 7629 8380
Est. 1923 *Stock size* Small
Stock Antique, modern jewellery and silver
Open Mon–Sat 9.45am–5pm

C John Ltd (BADA)
Contact Mr L Sassoon
✉ **70 South Audley Street, London, W1K 2RA** P
☎ 020 7493 5288 F 020 7409 7030
E cjohn@dircom.co.uk
Est. 1948 *Stock size* Large
Stock Persian, French, Russian, Caucasian tapestries, Indian, Turkish, Chinese carpets, rugs, textiles
Open Mon–Fri 9.30am–5pm
Fairs Grosvenor House
Services Valuations, restoration

Johnson Walker Ltd (BADA)
Contact Miss R Gill
✉ **64 Burlington Arcade, London, W1J 0QT** P
☎ 020 7629 2615/6
F 020 7409 0709
Est. 1849 *Stock size* Medium
Stock Jewellery, bijouterie
Open Mon–Sat 9.30am–5.30pm
Services Valuations, repairs

John Joseph (LAPADA, LJAJDA)
Contact Mr J Joseph
✉ **Stand 345–346, Grays Antique Market, 58 Davies Street, London, W1Y 2LP** P
☎ 020 7629 1140 F 020 7629 1140
E jewellery@john-joseph.co.uk
W www.john-joseph.co.uk
Est. 1985 *Stock size* Large
Stock Victorian, Edwardian, Art Deco jewellery, gem set, gold, platinum
Open Mon–Fri 10am–6pm
Fairs Olympia (June)

M & A Kaae
Contact Minoo Kaae
✉ **The Mews Antique Market, 1–7 Davies Mews, London, W1Y 2LP**
☎ 020 7629 1200
Est. 1981 *Stock size* Large
Stock Diamonds
Open Mon–Fri 10am–6pm

⊞ Daniel Katz Ltd (SLAD)
Contact Daniel Katz or Stuart Lochhead
✉ **13 Old Bond Street, London, W1S 4SX**
☎ 020 7493 0688 Ⓕ 020 7499 7493
Ⓔ info@katz.co.uk
Ⓦ www.katz.co.uk
Est. 1969 *Stock size* Large
Stock European sculpture
Open Mon–Fri 9am–6pm

⊞ Roger Keverne Ltd (BADA)
Contact Mr R Keverne
✉ **2nd Floor, 16 Clifford Street, London, W1S 3RG** Ⓟ
☎ 020 7434 9100 Ⓕ 020 7434 9101
Ⓔ rogerkeverne@keverne.co.uk
Ⓦ www.keverne.co.uk
Est. 1996 *Stock size* Large
Stock Chinese ceramics, jade, lacquer, bronzes, enamels, hard stones, ivory, bamboo
Open Mon–Fri 9.30am–5.30pm Sat for exhibitions
Fairs Exhibition at 16 Clifford Street (Jun, Nov), International Asian Art Fair, New York (March)
Services Valuations, restoration

⊞ D S Lavender Antiques Ltd (BADA)
Contact Mr D Lavender
✉ **26 Conduit Street, London, W1S 2XX** Ⓟ
☎ 020 7629 1782 Ⓕ 020 7629 3106
Ⓔ dslavender@clara.net
Est. 1946 *Stock size* Large
Stock Gold, silver, enamel fine snuff boxes, fine jewels, 16th–early 19thC portrait miniatures
Open Mon–Fri 9.30am–5pm
Fairs Grosvenor House
Services Valuations, restoration

⊞ Michael Lipitch Ltd (BADA)
Contact Mr M Lipitch
✉ **Mayfair, PO Box 3146, London, EN4 0BP** Ⓟ
Ⓜ 07730 954347
Ⓔ michaellipitch@hotmail.com
Est. 1960 *Stock size* Large
Stock 18thC fine furniture and objects
Open By appointment
Fairs Grosvenor House, BADA, Olympia (Nov)
Services Specialist advice on forming collections

⊞ Sanda Lipton (BADA, CINOA, BACA Award Winner 2003)
Contact Sanda Lipton
✉ **3rd Floor, Elliott House, 28A Devonshire Street, London, W1G 6PS** Ⓟ
☎ 020 7431 2688 Ⓕ 020 7431 3224
Ⓜ 07836 660008
Ⓔ sanda@antique-silver.com
Ⓦ www.antique-silver.com
Est. 1979 *Stock size* Medium
Stock 16th–mid 19thC silver, collectors items, early English spoons, historical medals
Open By appointment
Fairs Olympia, March BADA
Services Valuations, restoration, consultancy, bidding at auction

⊞ Michael Longmore and Trianon Antiques Ltd (LAPADA)
Contact Mr Bruce Rowley
✉ **Stand 378, Grays Antique Market, 58 Davies Street, London, W1K 5LP** Ⓟ
☎ 020 7491 2764 Ⓕ 020 7409 1587
Ⓔ michaellongmore@aol.com
Est. 1974 *Stock size* Large
Stock Fine jewellery, objets d'art
Open Mon–Fri 10am–5.30pm

⊞ Maggs Bros Ltd (ABA, BADA, PBFA)
Contact Mr Edward F Maggs
✉ **50 Berkeley Square, London, W1J 5BA** Ⓟ
☎ 020 7493 7160 Ⓕ 020 7499 2007
Ⓔ ed@maggs.com
Ⓦ www.maggs.com
Est. 1853 *Stock size* Large
Stock Military history, travel, natural history, science, modern literature, early English and Continental books, illustrated manuscripts, autographed letters
Open Mon–Fri 9.30am–5pm
Fairs Olympia
Services Catalogues issued by all departments

⊞ Mallett at Bourdon House Ltd (BADA, SLAD, CINOA. BACA Award Winner 2003)
✉ **2 Davies Street, London, W1K 3DJ** Ⓟ
☎ 020 7629 2444 Ⓕ 020 7499 2670
Ⓔ info@mallettantiques.com
Ⓦ www.mallettantiques.com
Est. 1860 *Stock size* Large
Stock 18th–19thC English, continental furniture, objets d'art, glass, needlework, 18th–19thC pictures
Open Mon–Fri 9am–6pm Sat by appointment
Fairs Grosvenor House, Asian & Ceramics Fair, Olympia, Miami, New York, Maastricht, San Francisco
Services Restoration

⊞ Mallett & Son (Antiques) Ltd (BADA, SLAD, CINOA. BACA Award Winner 2003)
✉ **141 New Bond Street, London, W1S 2BS** Ⓟ
☎ 020 7499 7411 Ⓕ 020 7495 3179
Ⓔ info@mallettantiques.com
Ⓦ www.mallettantiques.com
Est. 1865 *Stock size* Large
Stock 18th–19thC English, continental furniture, objet d'art, glass, needlework, 18th–19thC pictures
Open Mon–Fri 9am–6pm Sat 10am–4pm
Fairs Grosvenor House, Asian & Ceramics Fair, Olympia, Miami, New York
Services Restoration

⊞ Map World (LAPADA)
Contact Jeffrey Sharpe
✉ **25 Burlington Arcade, Piccadilly, London, W1V 9AD**
☎ 020 7495 5377 Ⓕ 020 7495 5377
Ⓔ info@map-world.com
Ⓦ www.map-world.com
Est. 1982 *Stock size* Large
Stock 15th–19thC antique maps
Open Mon–Sat 10am–5.30pm
Services Valuations

⊞ Marks Antiques (BADA, LAPADA)
Contact Anthony Marks
✉ **49 Curzon Street, London, W1J 7UN**
☎ 020 7499 1788 Ⓕ 020 7409 3183
Ⓔ marks@marksantiques.com
Ⓦ www.marksantiques.com
Est. 1921 *Stock size* Large
Stock Antique silver, Russian works of art
Open Mon–Fri 9.30am–6pm Sat 9.30am–5pm
Fairs Olympia, Grosvenor House
Services Valuations, Shipping

Marlborough Rare Books Ltd (ABA)
Contact Jonathan Gestetner
✉ **4th Floor, 144–146 New Bond Street, London, W1S 2TR**
☎ 020 7493 6993 Ⓕ 020 7499 2479
Ⓔ sales@mrb-books.co.uk
Est. 1948 *Stock size* Medium
Stock Antiquarian and rare art, architecture, illustrated, colour plate, fine bindings, English literature, topography, London
Open Mon–Fri 9.30am–5.30pm
Fairs Olympia, Chelsea, California, New York
Services Valuations

Massada Antiques (LAPADA, LJAJDA)
Contact Mr B Yacobi
✉ **Bond Street Antiques Centre, 124 New Bond Street, London, W1S 1DX** Ⓟ
☎ 020 7493 5610 Ⓕ 020 7491 9852
Est. 1970 *Stock size* Large
Stock Georgian–Edwardian wearable, decorative jewellery
Open Mon–Sat 10am–5.30pm
Fairs Olympia (June, Nov)
Services Valuations, repairs

Mayfair Gallery Ltd
Contact Mrs C Giese
✉ **39 South Audley Street, London, W1K 2PP** Ⓟ
☎ 020 7491 3435/3436
Ⓕ 020 7491 3437
Ⓔ mayfairgallery@mayfairgallery.com
Est. 1974 *Stock size* Large
Stock 19thC antiques, decorative arts, bronzes, marbles, Continental porcelain, furniture
Open Mon–Fri 9.30am–6pm Sat by appointment
Fairs Olympia, Miami Beach
Services Valuations, restoration

Theresa McCullough Ltd (BADA)
Contact Theresa McCullough
✉ **35 Dover Street (1st Floor Mezzanine), London, W1S 4NQ** Ⓟ
☎ 020 7499 2243 Ⓕ 020 7491 0042
Ⓜ 07958 992374
Ⓔ theresamccullough@asianart.org
Ⓦ www.theresamccullough.com
Est. 2000 *Stock size* Medium
Stock Indian, South East Asian works of art
Open By appointment
Fairs International Asian Art Fair New York and London

Melton's
Contact Cecilia Neale
✉ **27 Bruton Place, London, W1J 6NQ**
☎ 020 7409 2938 Ⓕ 020 7495 3196
Ⓔ sales@meltons.co.uk
Ⓦ www.meltons.co.uk
Est. 1980 *Stock size* Medium
Stock Antiques and collectables
Open Mon–Fri 9.30am–5.30pm

The Mews Antique Market
Contact William Griffith or Kirstine Wallace
✉ **1–7 Davies Mews, London, W1K 5AB** Ⓟ
☎ 020 7629 7034 Ⓕ 020 7493 9344
Ⓔ grays@clara.net
Ⓦ www.graysantiques.com
Est. 1978 *Stock size* Large
No. of dealers 150
Stock Asian, Islamic antiquities, books, perfume bottles, Bohemian glass, ceramics, handbags, carpets, jewellery, militaria, pewter, teddy bears, dolls, toys, clocks, timepieces
Open Mon–Fri 10am–6pm
Services Restoration, repairs, restaurant

Michael's Boxes (PADA)
Contact Michael Cassidy
✉ **Unit L15, The Mews Antique Market, 1–7 Davies Mews, London, W1K 5AB** Ⓟ
☎ 020 7629 5716 Ⓕ 020 8930 8318
Ⓔ info@michaelsboxes.com
Ⓦ www.michaelsboxes.com
Est. 1997 *Stock size* Large
Stock Limoges, enamel and porcelain antique boxes
Open Mon–Fri 10am–5pm
Fairs Portobello
Services Personalized boxes

Moira
Contact Mrs S Lauder
✉ **11 New Bond Street, London, W1S 3SR**
☎ 020 7629 0160 Ⓕ 020 7495 3343
Ⓔ info@moira-jewels.com
Est. 1970 *Stock size* Large
Stock Antique, modern and own design jewellery
Open Mon–Sat 10am–5pm

Sydney L Moss Ltd (BADA)
Contact Paul G Moss or Mr M Rutherston
✉ **51 Brook Street, London, W1Y 1AU** Ⓟ
☎ 020 7629 4670 Ⓕ 020 7491 9278
Ⓔ pasi@slmoss.com
Ⓦ www.slmoss.com
Est. 1904 *Stock size* Large
Stock Chinese and Japanese antiques, works of art, paintings
Open Mon–Fri 10am–5.30pm
Fairs International Asian Art Fair New York
Services Valuations

Morris Namdar
Contact Mr Morris Namdar
✉ **Stand B18, The Mews Antique Market, 1–7 Davies Mews, London, W1K 5AB** Ⓟ
☎ 020 7629 1183
Est. 1979 *Stock size* Medium
Stock Chinese, Japanese, European ceramics, glass, textiles
Open Mon–Fri 10am–6pm

Richard Ogden Ltd (BADA)
Contact Robert Ogden
✉ **28–29 Burlington Arcade, London, W1J 0NX** Ⓟ
☎ 020 7493 9136 Ⓕ 020 7355 1508
Ⓔ admin@richardogden.com
Est. 1948 *Stock size* Medium
Stock Traditional antiques, jewellery
Open Mon–Sat 9.30am–5pm
Services Valuations

Pelham Galleries Ltd (BADA, CINOA)
Contact Mr Alan Rubin
✉ **24 & 25 Mount Street, London, W1K 2RR** Ⓟ
☎ 020 7629 0905 Ⓕ 020 7495 4511
Ⓔ antiques@pelhamgalleries.com
Ⓦ www.pelhamgalleries.com
Est. 1928 *Stock size* Large
Stock English and European furniture, 16th–19thC works of art, early keyboard instruments
Open Mon–Fri 9am–5.30pm Sat by appointment
Fairs Grosvenor House
Services Valuations, shipping

Pendulum of Mayfair
Contact Mr J D Clements
✉ **King House,**

51 Maddox Street, London, W1R 9LA 🅿
☎ 020 7629 6606
ⓦ www.pendulumofmayfair.co.uk
Est. 1995 *Stock size* Large
Stock Clocks, including longcase, bracket, wall, Georgian period furniture
Open Mon–Fri 10am–6pm Sat 10am–5pm or by appointment

⊞ Ronald Phillips Ltd (BADA)
Contact Mr S Phillips
✉ **26 Bruton Street, London, W1J 6QL** 🅿
☎ 020 7493 2341 ⓕ 020 7495 0843
ⓔ email@ronaldphillipsltd.co.uk
Est. 1952 *Stock size* Large
Stock 18thC English furniture, glass, clocks, barometers, mirrors
Open Mon–Fri 9am–5.30pm Sat by appointment
Fairs Grosvenor House

⊞ S J Phillips Ltd (BADA)
✉ **139 New Bond Street, London, W1A 3DL**
☎ 020 7629 6261 ⓕ 020 7495 6180
ⓔ enquiries@sjphillips.com
ⓦ www.sjphillips.com
Est. 1869 *Stock size* Large
Stock Antique–20thC jewellery, 18thC silver
Open Mon–Fri 10am–5pm
Fairs Grosvenor House, TEFAF, Maastricht
Services Restoration

⊞ Pickering and Chatto (ABA, PBFA)
Contact Mr J Hudson
✉ **36 St George Street, London, W1R 9FA** 🅿
☎ 020 7491 2656 ⓕ 020 7491 9161
ⓔ rarebook@pickering-chatto.com
ⓦ www.pickering-chatto.com
Est. 1820 *Stock size* Medium
Stock Antiquarian, rare, second-hand books on economics, philosophy, medicine, general literature
Open Mon–Fri 9.30am–5.30pm or by appointment
Fairs Olympia
Services Book search valuations

⊞ Pieces of Time (BADA)
Contact Mr J Wachsmann
✉ **Units 17–19, The Mews Antique Market, 1–7 Davies Mews, London, W1Y 2LP** 🅿
☎ 020 7629 2422 ⓕ 020 7409 1625
ⓔ info@antique-watch.com
ⓦ www.antique-watch.com
Est. 1973 *Stock size* Large
Stock Antique pocket watches, Judaica
Open Mon–Fri 10.30am–5pm
Services Valuations

⊞ Nicholas S Pitcher Oriental Art
Contact Mr N S Pitcher
✉ **1st Floor, 29 New Bond Street, London, W1S 2RL** 🅿
☎ 020 7499 6621 ⓕ 020 7499 6621
ⓜ 07831 391574
ⓔ nickpitcher@caol.com
ⓦ www.asianart.com/pitcher
Est. 1990 *Stock size* Medium
Stock Early Chinese ceramics, works of art
Open By appointment
Fairs Arts of Pacific Asia Show, New York, London (June)
Services Valuations

⊞ Jonathan Potter Ltd (ABA, BADA, LAPADA, PBFA)
Contact Mr J Potter
✉ **125 New Bond Street, London, W1S 1DY** 🅿
☎ 020 7491 3520 ⓕ 020 7491 9754
ⓔ jpmaps@attglobal.net
ⓦ www.jpmaps.co.uk
Est. 1974 *Stock size* Large
Stock History of cartography books, atlases, maps, reproduction globes
Open Mon–Fri 10am–6pm Sat by appointment
Fairs ABA, Olympia, IMCoS, International Map Fair
Services Valuations, restoration, framing

⊞ Nick Potter Ltd
Contact Nick Potter
✉ **34 Sackville Street, Mayfair, London, W1S 3ED** 🅿
☎ 020 7439 4029 ⓕ 020 7439 4027
ⓔ art@nickpotter.com
ⓦ www.nickpotter.com
Est. 1997 *Stock size* Medium
Stock Fine sporting pictures 1750–1940, prints, memorabilia
Open Mon–Fri 10am–5.30pm or by appointment
Services Valuations, restoration

⊞ Pullman Gallery Ltd
Contact Mr S Khachadourian
✉ **116 Mount Street, Mayfair, London, W1K 3NH** 🅿
☎ 020 7499 8080 ⓕ 020 7499 9090
ⓔ sk@pullmangallery.com
ⓦ www.pullmangallery.com
Est. 1998 *Stock size* Large
Stock Automobilia, vintage luggage
Open Mon–Fri 10am–6pm

⊞ Bernard Quaritch Ltd (PBFA, ABA, BADA)
Contact Mr I Smith
✉ **5–8 Lower John Street, London, W1R 4AU**
☎ 020 7734 2983 ⓕ 020 7734 0967
ⓔ rarebooks@quaritch.com
ⓦ www.quaritch.com
Est. 1847 *Stock size* Large
Stock Antiquarian books
Open Mon–Fri 9am–5.30pm
Fairs Olympia
Services Valuations

⊞ Rare Jewellery Collections Ltd (LAPADA, CINOA)
Contact Elizabeth Powell
✉ **45–46 New Bond Street, London, W1S 2SF** 🅿
☎ 020 7499 5414 ⓕ 020 7499 6906
ⓔ info@rarejewelcollections.com
ⓦ www.rarejewelcollections.com
Est. 1983 *Stock size* Medium
Stock Vintage jewellery
Open By appointment only

⊞ David Richards & Sons
Contact Mr Richards
✉ **10 New Cavendish Street, London, W1G 8UL** 🅿
☎ 020 7935 3206/0322
ⓕ 020 7224 4423
Est. 1970 *Stock size* Large
Stock Modern and antique silver plate, decorative items, flatware
Open Mon–Fri 9.30am–5.30pm
Services Valuations, restoration

⊞ Rossi & Rossi Ltd
Contact Mr Fabio Rossi
✉ **13 Old Bond Street, London, W1S 4SX** 🅿
☎ 020 7355 1804 ⓕ 020 7355 1806
ⓔ info@rossirossi.com
ⓦ www.asianart.com/rossi
Est. 1986 *Stock size* Medium
Stock Asian art, sculpture, paintings from India, the Himalayas, Chinese textiles
Open Mon–Fri 10.30am–5.30pm

Samiramis (LAPADA)
Contact Mr H Ismael
M14–16, The Mews Antique Market, 1–7 Davies Mews, London, W1Y 1FH
☎ 020 7629 1161 Ⓕ 020 7493 5106
Est. 1978 *Stock size* Medium
Stock Islamic pottery, silver, Eastern items, calligraphy
Open Mon–Fri 10am–6pm

Alistair Sampson Antiques Ltd (BADA, BACA Award Winner 2002)
Contact Mr A Sampson or Mr C Banks
120 Mount Street, London, W1K 3NN
☎ 020 7409 1799 Ⓕ 020 7409 7717
Ⓔ info@alistairsampson.com
Ⓦ www.alistairsampson.com
Est. 1969 *Stock size* Large
Stock English pottery, oak, country furniture, metalwork, needlework, pictures, 17th–18thC decorative items
Open Mon–Fri 9.30am–5.30pm Sat by appointment
Fairs Olympia, Grosvenor House

Seaby Antiquities (ADA)
Contact Peter Clayton
14 Old Bond Street, London, W1S 4PP
☎ 020 7495 2590 Ⓕ 020 7491 1595
Ⓔ minerva@minervamagazine.com
Ⓦ www.royalathena.com
Est. 1942 *Stock size* Small
Stock Museum quality antiquities
Open Mon–Fri 10am–5pm
Services Valuations

Bernard J Shapero Rare Books (ABA, PBFA, BADA)
Contact Lucinda Boyle
32 St George Street, London, W1S 2EA
☎ 020 7493 0876 Ⓕ 020 7229 7860
Ⓔ rarebooks@shapero.com
Ⓦ www.shapero.com
Est. 1979 *Stock size* Large
Stock 16th–20thC guide books, antiquarian and rare books, English and Continental literature, specializing in travel, natural history, colour plate
Open Mon–Fri 9.30am–6.30pm Sat 11am–5pm August Mon–Fri 10am–5pm
Fairs Olympia
Services Valuations, restoration

Shapiro & Co. (LAPADA)
Contact Sheldon Shapiro
Stand 380, Grays Antique Market, 58 Davies Street, London, W1K 5LP
☎ 020 74912710 Ⓕ 020 74912710
Ⓜ 07768 840930
Est. 1982
Stock Jewellery, silver, objets d'art, Imperial Russian works of art
Open Mon–Fri 10am–6pm
Fairs Olympia, NEC

Shiraz Antiques (BADA)
Contact Mr Reza Kiadeh
1 Davies Mews, London, W1K 5AB
☎ 020 7495 0635 Ⓕ 020 7495 0635
Est. 1990 *Stock size* Medium
Stock Asian art, antiquities, glass, marble, pottery
Open Mon–Fri 10am–6pm
Fairs BADA

W Sitch (Antique) Co Ltd
Contact Mr Sitch
48 Berwick Street, London, W1V 4JD
☎ 020 7437 3776 Ⓕ 020 7437 5707
Ⓔ wsitch-co@hotmail.com
Ⓦ www.wsitch.co.uk
Est. 1776 *Stock size* Large
Stock Lighting
Open Mon–Sat 8am–6pm
Services Valuations, restoration, shipping

R Solaimany
Contact Mr R Solaimany
Unit A16, The Mews Antique Market, 1–7 Davies Mews, London, W1K 5AB
☎ 020 7491 2562 Ⓕ 020 7493 9344
Est. 1981 *Stock size* Medium
Stock Oriental ceramics, bronzes, Roman glass
Open Mon–Fri 10am–6pm

Sotheby's (BACA Award Winner 2003)
34–35 New Bond Street, London, W1A 2AA
☎ 020 7293 5000
Ⓦ www.sothebys.com
Est. 1744
Open Mon–Fri 9am–5.30pm
Sales International auctioneer of fine art, furniture, jewellery, decorative arts, collectables and more. Services include restoration, valuation, financial service, picture library, on-line auctions, Sotheby's International Realty and Sotheby's Bookshop
Frequency Varies by month
Catalogues Yes

Henry Sotheran Ltd (ABA, PBFA, ILAB)
Contact Mr A McGeachin
2 Sackville Street, Piccadilly, London, W1S 3DP
☎ 020 7439 6151 Ⓕ 020 7434 2019
Ⓔ sotherans@sotherans.co.uk
Ⓦ www.sotherans.co.uk
Est. 1761 *Stock size* Large
Stock Antiquarian books on English literature, natural history, travel, children's illustrated, modern first editions, prints, art, architecture
Open Mon–Fri 9.30am–6pm Sat 10am–4pm

Spectrum
Contact Mrs S Spectrum
Stand 372, Grays Antique Market, 58 Davies Street, London, W1K 5LP
☎ 020 7629 3501 Ⓕ 020 8883 5030
Ⓜ 07770 753302
Est. 1979 *Stock size* Large
Stock Georgian seedpearl necklaces, brooches, Georgian–Victorian jewellery, Georg Jensen jewellery
Open Mon–Fri 10am–6pm
Services Valuations, repairs, stringing, designing

A and J Speelman Ltd (BADA)
Contact Mr J Speelman or J Mann
129 Mount Street, London, W1K 3NX
☎ 020 7499 5126 Ⓕ 020 7355 3391
Ⓔ enquiries@ajspeelman.com
Est. 1976 *Stock size* Large
Stock Oriental furniture, porcelain, works of art
Open Mon–Fri 10am–6pm
Fairs New York, Asian Art Fair
Services Valuations, restoration

St. Petersburg Collection Ltd
Contact Mr B Lynch
42 Burlington Arcade, London, W1J 0QG
☎ 020 7495 2883 Ⓕ 01895 810566

ⓔ creations@stpetersburg collection.com
ⓦ www.stpetersburgcollection.com
Est. 1989 *Stock size* Medium
Stock English and French objets d'art, boxes, 19th–20thC silver, glass, ormolu
Open Mon–Sat 10am–5pm

Stair & Company Ltd (BADA, CINOA)
Contact Mr R Luck
✉ **14 Mount Street, London, W1K 2RF** Ⓟ
☎ 020 7499 1784 ⓕ 020 7269 1050
ⓔ stairandcompany@talk21.com
ⓦ www.stairandcompany.com
Est. 1911 *Stock size* Large
Stock 18thC fine English furniture, works of art
Open Mon–Fri 9.30am–5.30pm or by appointment
Fairs Grosvenor House, BADA
Services Valuations, restoration

Jacob Stodel (BADA)
Contact Jacob Stodel
✉ **Flat 53, Macready House, 75 Crawford Street, London, W1H 5LP** Ⓟ
☎ 020 7723 3732
ⓔ jacobstodel@aol.com
Stock 18thC English and Continental furniture, 17th–early 19thC Oriental and European ceramics and works of art
Open By appointment
Fairs Maastricht
Services Valuations

June and Tony Stone Fine Antique Boxes (LAPADA)
Contact Tony Stone
✉ **5 Burlington Arcade, Bond Street, London, W1J 0PD** Ⓟ
☎ 07092 106600 or 020 7493 9495
ⓕ 07092 106611 or 020 7493 9496
ⓜ 07739 800908
ⓔ jts@boxes.co.uk
ⓦ www.boxes.co.uk
Est. 1990 *Stock size* Large
Stock 18th–19thC boxes, rare and unusual tea caddies
Open Mon–Sat 10am–6pm
Fairs Olympia June, Fairs in New York, Miami
Services Shipping included in prices

E Swonnell Ltd
Contact Miss S Swonnell
✉ **37 South Audley Street, London, W1K 2PN** Ⓟ
☎ 020 7629 9649 ⓕ 020 7629 9649
Est. 1957 *Stock size* Large
Stock 17th–19thC silver and plate, large decorative items
Open Mon–Fri 9am–6pm
Services Valuations, restoration

Tagore Ltd
Contact Mr R Falloon
✉ **Stand 302, Grays Antique Market, 58 Davies Street, London, W1Y 2LP** Ⓟ
☎ 020 7499 0158 ⓕ 020 7499 0158
ⓔ grays@clara.net
Est. 1977 *Stock size* Large
Stock 20thC drinking, smoking, gambling collectors' items, silver, glass, gentlemen's gifts
Open Mon–Fri 10am–6pm
Services Valuations

Textile-Art: The Textile Gallery (BADA)
Contact Michael Franses or Nicholas Waterhouse
✉ **12 Queen Street, Mayfair, London, W1J 5PG** Ⓟ
☎ 020 7499 7979 ⓕ 020 7409 2596
ⓜ 07836 321461
ⓔ post@textile-art.com
ⓦ www.textile-art.com
Est. 1972
Stock Textile art from China, Central Asia, India and Ottoman Empire, 300BC–1800AD, classical carpets,1400–1700
Open Mon–Fri by appointment 10.30am–6pm
Fairs The European Fine Art Fair, Maastricht, Summer Olympia
Services Conservation of important textiles to museum standards

Toynbee-Clarke Interiors Ltd
Contact Mrs Daphne Toynbee-Clarke
✉ **95 Mount Street, London, W1K 2TA** Ⓟ
☎ 020 7499 4472 ⓕ 020 7495 1204
Est. 1959 *Stock size* Medium
Stock Continental furniture, works of art, 18th–19thC Chinese hand-painted export wallpapers, early 19thC French panoramic papers
Open Mon–Fri 11am–5.30pm or by appointment
Services Restoration

Trianon Antiques Ltd (LAPADA, LJAJDA)
Contact Miss L Horton
✉ **Bond Street Antiques Centre, 124 New Bond Street, London, W1S 1DX** Ⓟ
☎ 020 7629 6678 ⓕ 020 7355 2055
ⓔ trianonantiques@hotmail.com
Est. 1974 *Stock size* Large
Stock Fine jewellery, objets d'art
Open Mon–Sat10am–5.30pm
Fairs Olympia (June), Miami

Jan Van Beers Oriental Art (BADA)
Contact Mr J Van Beers
✉ **34 Davies Street, London, W1Y 1LG** Ⓟ
☎ 020 7408 0434 ⓕ 020 7355 1397
ⓔ jan@vanbeers.demon.co.uk
ⓦ www.janvanbeers.com
Est. 1978 *Stock size* Large
Stock Chinese and Japanese antiques, ceramics, works of art
Open Mon–Fri 10am–6pm
Fairs Asian Art Fair New York
Services Valuations

Vigo Carpet Gallery (LAPADA)
Contact Nadia Mair
✉ **6a Vigo Street, London, W1S 3HF** Ⓟ
☎ 020 7439 6971 ⓕ 020 7439 2353
ⓔ vigo@btinternet.com
Est. 1980 *Stock size* Large
Stock Hand-made antique carpets
Open Mon–Fri 10am–6pm Sat 11am–5pm
Fairs HALI Antique Textile Art Fair

Vinci Antiques
Contact Mr A Vinci
✉ **27 Avery Row, London, W1X 9HD** Ⓟ
☎ 020 7499 1041
Est. 1974 *Stock size* Large
Stock Objets d'art, objects of virtue, silver, porcelain, glass, paintings, jewellery, bronzes
Open Mon–Sat 9am–7pm

Rupert Wace Ancient Art Ltd (ADA, IADAA, BADA)
Contact Mr R Wace
✉ **14 Old Bond Street, London,**

W1X 3DB P
☎ 020 7495 1623 ⓕ 020 7495 8495
ⓔ info@rupertwace.co.uk
ⓦ www.rupertwace.co.uk
Est. 1987 *Stock size* Large
Stock Antiquities, Greek, Roman, ancient Egyptian, Near Eastern, Celtic, Dark Ages
Open Mon–Fri 10am–5pm or by appointment
Services Valuations

⊞ Westminster Group Antique Jewellery (LAPADA)
Contact Mr R Harrison
✉ **Stand 150, Grays Antique Market, 58 Davies Street, London, W1K 2LP** P
☎ 020 7493 8672 ⓕ 020 7493 8672
Est. 1976 *Stock size* Large
Stock Victorian–Edwardian second-hand jewellery, watches
Open Mon–Fri 10am–6pm

⊞ Wheels of Steel
Contact Jeff Williams
✉ **Stand A12–13, Unit B10, Basement, The Mews Antique Market, 1–7 Davies Mews, London, W1Y 2LP**
☎ 020 7629 2813
Est. 1976 *Stock size* Large
Stock Model trains
Open Mon–Fri 10.30am–6pm

⊞ Wilkinson PLC
Contact Mark Savin
✉ **1 Grafton Street, London, W1S 4EA** P
☎ 020 7495 2477 ⓕ 020 7491 1737
ⓔ enquiries@wilkinson-plc.com
ⓦ www.wilkinson-plc.com
Est. 1946 *Stock size* Large
Stock Lighting, chandeliers, candelabra
Open Mon–Fri 9.30am–5pm
Services Restoration

⊞ Wimpole Antiques (LAPADA)
Contact Lyn Lindsay
✉ **Stand 349, Grays Antique Market, Davies Street, London, W1Y 1LB** P
☎ 020 7499 2889 ⓕ 020 7499 2889
ⓔ WimpoleAntiques@compuserve.com
Est. 1977 *Stock size* Large
Stock Affordable, wearable jewellery, 1780–1960, Victorian jewellery
Open Mon–Fri 10am–6pm
Fairs Olympia, NEC, LAPADA
Services Valuations, repairs

⊞ Windsor House Antiques Ltd (LAPADA)
Contact Dr Kevin Smith
✉ **28–29 Dover Street, London, WIS 4NA**
☎ 020 7659 0340 ⓕ 020 7499 6728
ⓔ sales@windsorhouseantiques.co.uk
ⓦ www.windsorhouseantiques.co.uk
Est. 1958 *Stock size* Large
Stock 18th & 19thC English furniture, decorative accessories
Open Mon–Fri 9.30am–6pm or by appointment
Fairs Claridges

⊞ Linda Wrigglesworth Ltd
Contact Gary Dickinson
✉ **34 Brook Street, London, W1K 5DN** P
☎ 020 7486 8990 ⓕ 020 7935 1511
ⓔ info@lindawrigglesworth.com
ⓦ www.lindawrigglesworth.com
Est. 1977
Stock Chinese court costumes, Tibetan and Korean textiles
Open Mon–Fri 11am–7pm by appointment
Fairs Grosvenor House

⊞ Grace Wu Bruce Ltd (BADA)
Contact Grace Wu or Rebecca Feng
✉ **12a Balfour Mews, London, W1K 2BJ** P
☎ 020 7499 3750 ⓕ 020 7491 3896
ⓔ art@grace-wu-bruce.com
Est. 1987 *Stock size* Medium
Stock Chinese furniture, works of art
Open By appointment
Fairs Grosvenor House, New York Asian Art Fair

⊞ Yamamoto Antiques
Contact Mrs M Yamamoto
✉ **Units 14 & 15, Bond Street Antique Centre, 124 New Bond Street, London, W1Y 9AE**
☎ 0207 491 0983 ⓕ 0207 491 0983
ⓔ m@bondst.plus.com
Est. 1995 *Stock size* Medium
Stock Jewellery, porcelain
Open Mon–Fri 10am–5.30pm Sat 10.30am–5.30pm
Services Shipping

W2

⊞ Sean Arnold Sporting Antiques (PADA)
Contact Sean Arnold
✉ **21–22 Chepstow Corner, off Westbourne Grove, London, W2 4XE** P
☎ 020 7221 2267 ⓕ 020 7221 5464
Est. 1977 *Stock size* Large
Stock Sporting antiques, luggage, globes
Open Mon–Sat 10am–6pm or by appointment
Services Valuations, restoration

Bonhams
✉ **10 Salem Road, London, W2 4DL** P
☎ 020 7313 2700 ⓕ 020 7313 2701
ⓔ info@bonhams.com
ⓦ www.bonhams.com
Est. 1793
Open Mon–Fri 9am–5pm
Sales Regular house and attic sales across the country; contact London offices (SW7) for further details. Free auction valuations; insurance and probate valuations
Catalogues Yes

⊞ Mark Gallery (BADA, CINOA)
Contact Helen Mark
✉ **9 Porchester Place, Marble Arch, London, W2 2BS** P
☎ 020 7262 4906 ⓕ 020 7224 9416
Est. 1970
Stock 16th–19thC Russian and Greek icons, contemporary and modern French lithographs and etchings
Open Mon–Fri 10am–1pm 2–6pm Sat by appointment 11am–1pm
Fairs Olympia, Cologne
Services Valuations, restoration

⊞ Reel Poster Gallery
Contact Mr Tony Nourmand
✉ **72 Westbourne Grove, London, W2 5SH** P
☎ 020 7727 4488 ⓕ 020 7727 4499
ⓔ info@reelposter.com
ⓦ www.reelposter.com
Est. 1989
Stock Original vintage film posters
Open Mon–Fri 11am–7pm Sat noon–6pm
Services Valuations, annual catalogue

W3

Chiswick and West Middlesex Auctions
Contact Mr D Wells or Mr T Keane
1 Colville Road, London, W3 8BL P
020 8992 4442 F 020 8896 0541
www.chiswickauctions.co.uk
Est. 1992
Open Mon–Fri 10am–6pm
Sales Antiques and general effects Tues noon, viewing Sun noon–6pm Mon 10am–6pm Tues 10am–noon
Frequency Weekly
Catalogues Yes

W4

The Chiswick Fireplace Co
Contact Rosemary O'Grady
68 Southfield Road, London, W4 1BD P
020 8995 4011 F 020 8995 4012
Est. 1990 *Stock size* Medium
Stock Original Art Nouveau, Edwardian, Victorian fireplaces, marble, limestone and wood surrounds
Open Mon–Sat 9.30am–5pm

Chiswick Park Antiques
Contact Mr Azzariti
2 Chiswick Park Station, London, W4 5EB P
020 8995 8930
Est. 1965 *Stock size* Medium
Stock Mirrors, furniture, clocks
Open Mon–Sat 11am–6pm
Services Restoration

David Edmonds Indian Furniture
1–4 Prince of Wales Terrace, London, W4 2EY P
020 8742 1920 F 020 8742 3030
M 07831 666436
E dareindia@aol.com
Est. 1987 *Stock size* Large
Stock Fine quality Indian furniture, antiques, architectural items
Open Mon–Sat 10am–5pm Sun by appointment
Services Valuations, repairs

W A Foster (PBFA)
Contact Mr Foster
183 Chiswick High Road, London, W4 2DR P
020 8995 2768
Est. 1968 *Stock size* Medium
Stock Antiquarian, rare, second-hand books, fine bindings, illustrated children's books
Open Thurs–Sat 10.30am–5.30pm
Fairs PBFA Hotel Russell

Harmers of London Stamp Auctioneer Ltd (PTS)
Contact Mr G Childs
111 Power Road, Chiswick, London, W4 5PY P
020 8747 6100 F 020 8996 0649
E auctions@harmers.demon.co.uk
www.harmers.com
Est. 1918
Open Mon–Fri 9am–5pm (valuations 9.30am–4pm)
Sales Philatelic auctions every 6 weeks, ring for details
Frequency Every 6 weeks
Catalogues Yes

The Old Cinema
Contact Mr K Norris
160 Chiswick High Road, London, W4 1PR P
020 8995 4166 F 020 8995 4167
E theoldcinema@antiques-uk.co.uk
www.antiques-uk.co.uk/theoldcinema
Est. 1980 *Stock size* Large
Stock Georgian–Art Deco furniture, large items of furniture, clocks, silver
Open Mon–Sat 9.30am–6pm Sun noon–5pm

Strand Antiques
Contact Mrs A Brown
46 Devonshire Road, London, W4 2HD P
020 8994 1912
Est. 1977 *Stock size* Large
Stock English and French furniture, glass, lighting, jewellery, silver, garden items, kitchenware, books, prints, textiles, collectables
Open Tues–Sat 10.30am–5.30pm
Services Furniture restoration

W5

Harold's Place
Contact Miss Warner
148 South Ealing Road, Ealing, London, W5 4QJ P
020 8579 4825
Est. 1976 *Stock size* Medium
Stock Antique china, glass, decorative items
Open Mon–Sat 9.30am–5.30pm

W8

Abstract/Noonstar (LAPADA)
Contact Galya Aytac or Juliette Boagers
58–60 Kensington Church Street, London, W8 4DB
020 7376 2652 F 020 7376 2652
M 07770 281301
E galya53@aol.com
www.abstract-antiques.com
Est. 1980 *Stock size* Medium
Stock 20thC decorative arts, Art Nouveau, Art Deco
Open Mon–Sat 11am–5pm
Services Valuations, shipping

Antik West Oriental Art & Antiques (CINOA)
Contact Mr J Robinson or B Gremner
at Patrick Sandberg Antiques, 150–152 Kensington Church Street, London, W8 4BH P
020 7229 4115 F 020 7792 3467
E china@antikwest.com
www.antikwest.com
Est. 1980 *Stock size* Large
Stock Oriental porcelain, pottery
Open Mon–Fri 10am–6pm Sat 10am–4pm
Fairs Gothenburg, Sweden (Oct), Asian Art in London (Nov)
Services Valuations, restoration

Artemis Decorative Arts Ltd (LAPADA)
Contact Mr M Jones
36 Kensington Church Street, London, W8 4BX P
020 7376 0377 F 020 7376 0377
E artemis.w8@btinternet.com
Est. 1994 *Stock size* Medium
Stock Art Nouveau, Art Deco, glass, bronze, ivory, furniture
Open Mon–Sat 10am–6pm

Garry Atkins
Contact Mr G Atkins
107 Kensington Church Street, London, W8 7LN P

☎ 020 7727 8737 Ⓕ 020 7792 9010
Ⓔ garry.atkins@englishpottery.com
Ⓦ www.englishpottery.com
Est. 1983 *Stock size* Large
Stock English and Continental pottery, 18thC and earlier
Open Mon–Fri 10am–5.30pm
Fairs New York Ceramics Fair

⊞ Gregg Baker Asian Art (BADA, LAPADA, CINOA)
Contact Mr G Baker
✉ **132 Kensington Church Street, London, W8 4BH** Ⓟ
☎ 020 7221 3533 Ⓕ 020 7221 4410
Ⓔ gregg@japanesescreens.com
Ⓦ www.japansesescreens.com
Est. 1984 *Stock size* Medium
Stock Japanese screens, Japanese and Chinese works of art
Open Mon–Fri 10am–6pm Sat 11am–4pm or by appointment
Fairs Grosvenor House, International Asian Art Fair, New York

⊞ Eddy Bardawil (BADA)
Contact Mr E Bardawil
✉ **106 Kensington Church Street, London, W8 4BH** Ⓟ
☎ 020 7221 3967 Ⓕ 020 7221 5124
Est. 1982 *Stock size* Medium
Stock 18th–19thC English furniture, works of art
Open Mon–Fri 10am–6pm Sat 10am–1pm
Services Restoration

⊞ Berwald Oriental Art (BADA, CINOA)
Contact Isabella Corble
✉ **101 Kensington Church Street, London, W8 7LN** Ⓟ
☎ 020 7229 0800 Ⓕ 020 7229 1101
Ⓔ info@berwald-oriental,com
Ⓦ www.berwald-oriental.com
Est. 1986 *Stock size* Medium
Stock Fine Chinese pottery and porcelain, Han to Qing and Chinese works of art
Open Mon–Fri 10am–6pm or by appointment

⊞ Nicolaus Boston Antiques
Contact Mr N Boston
✉ **58–60 Kensington Church Street, London, W8 4DB** Ⓟ
☎ 020 7937 2237 Ⓕ 020 8874 0033
Ⓔ sales@majolica.co.uk
Ⓦ www.majolica.co.uk
Est. 1983 *Stock size* Large
Stock Majolica, Christopher Dresser, aesthetic pottery
Open Fri 10am–6pm or by appointment
Fairs Olympia, Ceramic Fair, New York

⊞ David Brower (KCSADA, BACA Award Winner 2004)
Contact Mr D Brower
✉ **113 Kensington Church Street, London, W8 7LN** Ⓟ
☎ 020 7221 4155 Ⓕ 020 7221 6211
Ⓜ 07831 234343
Ⓔ David@davidbrower-antiques.com
Ⓦ www.davidbrower-antiques.com
Est. 1969 *Stock size* Large
Stock Meissen, KPM, European and Asian porcelain, French bronzes, Japanese works of art
Open Mon–Fri 10am–6pm Sat by appointment
Fairs Olympia (June)

⊞ Butchoff Interiors (LAPADA, BACA Award Winner 2004)
Contact Mr A Kaye
✉ **154 Kensington Church Street, London, W8 4BN** Ⓟ
☎ 020 7221 8174 Ⓕ 020 7792 8923
Ⓔ enquiries@butchoff.com
Ⓦ www.butchoff.com
Est. 1999 *Stock size* Medium
Stock One-off items, textiles, collectables, dining tables, chairs, consoles, accessories
Open Mon–Fri 9.30am–6pm Sat 9.30am–5pm

⊞ Cohen & Cohen (BADA, KCSADA)
Contact Mr M Cohen or Mrs E Cohen
✉ **101b Kensington Church Street, London, W8 7LN** Ⓟ
☎ 020 7727 7677 Ⓕ 020 7229 9653
Ⓔ info@cohenandcohen.co.uk
Est. 1973 *Stock size* Large
Stock Chinese export porcelain, works of art
Open Mon–Fri 10am–6pm Sat by appointment
Fairs Grosvenor House

⊞ Barry Davies Oriental Art (BADA)
Contact Barry Davies
✉ **PO Box 34867, London, W8 6WH** Ⓟ
☎ 020 7408 0207 Ⓕ 020 7493 3422
Ⓔ bdoa@btopenworld.com
Ⓦ www.barrydavies.com
Est. 1976 *Stock size* Large
Stock Japanese works of art
Open By appointment

⊞ Decor Antique Chandeliers (KCSADA)
Contact John Slattery
✉ **125 Kensington High Street, London, W8 7LP**
☎ 020 7221 1080 Ⓕ 020 7792 3404
Stock size Large
Stock Chandeliers

⊞ Denton Antiques
Contact Mr N Denton
✉ **156 Kensington Church Street, London, W8 4BN** Ⓟ
☎ 020 7229 5866 Ⓕ 020 7792 1073
Est. 1897 *Stock size* Large
Stock French and English chandeliers, lighting, table lamps, 1750–1920
Open Mon–Fri 9.30am–5.30pm

⊞ Didier Antiques (LAPADA)
Contact Didier Haspeslagh
✉ **58–60 Kensington Church Street, Kensington, London, W8 4DB** Ⓟ
☎ 020 7938 2537 Ⓕ 020 7938 2537
Ⓜ 07973 800415
Ⓔ didier.antiques@virgin.net.
Ⓦ www.didierantiques.com
Est. 1989 *Stock size* Large
Stock Late 19th–early 20thC Arts and Crafts, Art Nouveau, jewellery, silver, 1960s–1970s designer jewellery
Open By appointment
Fairs Olympia (June, Nov)

⊞ C. Fredericks and Son (BADA, KCSADA)
Contact Richard Fredericks
✉ **142 Kensington Church Street, London, W8 4BN** Ⓟ
☎ 020 7727 2240 Ⓕ 020 7727 2240
Ⓔ antiques@cfredericksandson.freeserve.co.uk
Est. 1947 *Stock size* Medium
Stock 18thC English furniture
Open Mon–Fri 9.30am–5.30pm
Fairs BADA Olympia (Nov)
Services Restoration

Michael German Antiques Ltd (BADA, LAPADA)
Contact Mr M German or Mr D Strickland
38b Kensington Church Street, London, W8 4BX P
020 7937 2771 F 020 7937 8566
E info@antiquecanes.com or info@antiqueweapons.com
W www.antiquecanes.com or www.antiqueweapons.com
Est. 1973 *Stock size* Large
Stock Antique walking canes, antique arms, armour
Open Mon–Fri 10am–5pm Sat 10am–1pm

Green's Antique Galleries
Contact Sidney Green
117 Kensington Church Street, London, W8 7LN
020 7229 9618
Est. 1952 *Stock size* Medium
Stock General antiques
Open Mon–Sat 9.30am–5.30pm

Adrian Harrington (ABA, PBFA, ILAB)
Contact Adrian Harrington, Jon Gilbert or Pierre Lambardini
64a Kensington Church Street, London, W8 4DB P
020 7937 1465 F 020 7368 0912
E rare@harringtonbooks.co.uk
W www.harringtonbooks.co.uk
Est. 1964 *Stock size* Large
Stock Antiquarian and rare books, specializing in literature, modern first editions, children's books, library sets, travel
Open Mon–Sat 10am–6pm
Fairs Olympia, Chelsea Town Hall
Services Valuations

Haslam & Whiteway
Contact Helen Duntan
105 Kensington Church Street, London, W8 7LN
020 7229 1145
Est. 1972 *Stock size* Medium
Stock 19thC British design
Open Mon–Fri 10am–6pm Sat 10am–4pm

Jeanette Hayhurst (BADA)
Contact Mrs J Hayhurst
32a Kensington Church Street, London, W8 4HA P
020 7938 1539
Est. 1979 *Stock size* Medium
Stock 18thC glass, specializing in English drinking glasses
Open Mon–Fri 10am–5pm Sat noon–5pm or by appointment
Fairs BADA, Harrogate, NEC

D Holmes
Contact Mr D Holmes
47c Earls Court Road, in Abingdon Villas, London, W8 6EE P
020 7937 6961
M 07790 431895
Est. 1965 *Stock size* Small
Stock 18th–19thC English mahogany furniture
Open Fri 9am–7pm Sat 9am–3pm
Services Also showrooms at Oudenaarde, Belgium

Hope & Glory
Contact Mr J Pym
131a Kensington Church Street (Entrance in Peel Street), London, W8 7LP P
020 7727 8424
Est. 1982 *Stock size* Large
Stock Commemorative ceramics, Royal, political etc
Open Mon–Sat 10am–5pm

Jonathan Horne (BADA, CINOA)
Contact Mr S Westman or Jonathan Horne
66c Kensington Church Street, London, W8 4BY P
020 7221 5658 F 020 7792 3090
E jh@jonathanhorne.co.uk
W www.jonathanhorne.co.uk
Est. 1968 *Stock size* Large
Stock Early English pottery, medieval–1820
Open Mon–Fri 9.30am–5.30pm
Fairs BADA, Olympia (June, Nov), Buxton (May)
Services Valuations

Iona Antiques (BADA)
Contact Stephen Joseph
PO Box 285, London, W8 6HZ P
020 7602 1193
F 020 7371 2843
E iona@ionaantiques.com
W www.ionaantiques.com
Est. 1974 *Stock size* Large
Stock 19thC paintings of animals
Open By appointment
Fairs Grosvenor House, Olympia (June)

J A N Fine Art (KCSADA)
Contact F K Shimizu
134 Kensington Church Street, Kensington, London, W8 4BH P
020 7792 0736 F 020 7221 1380
E fusashimizu@aol.com
Est. 1979 *Stock size* Medium
Stock Japanese, Chinese, Korean ceramics, bronzes, works of art
Open Mon–Fri 10am–6pm Sat by appointment

Jag Applied and Decorative Arts (Decorative Arts Society)
Contact C A Warner, G J Morgan or G S Strickland
58–60 Kensington Church Street, London, W8 4DB P
020 7938 4404 F 020 7938 4404
M 07974 567507
E jag@jagdecorativearts.com
W www.jagdecorativearts.com
Est. 1990 *Stock size* Medium
Stock Liberty pewter and silver, Art Nouveau metal, glass decorative items
Open Mon–Sat 11am–5pm

Japanese Gallery Ltd (Ukiyo-e Society)
Contact Mr C D Wertheim
66d Kensington Church Street, London, W8 4BY P
020 7229 2934 F 020 7229 2934
M 07930 411991
E sales@japanesegallery.co.uk
W www.japanesegallery.co.uk
Est. 1978 *Stock size* Large
Stock Japanese woodcut prints, Japanese ceramics, sword armour, Japanese dolls
Open Mon–Sat 10am–6pm
Services Exhibitions every 3 months of Japanese print, Japanese-speaking staff

Roderick Jellicoe (BADA, KCSADA, BACA Award Winner 2001)
3a Campden Street, off Kensington Church Street, London,

W8 7EP 🅿
☎ 020 7727 1571 Ⓕ 020 7727 1805
Ⓔ jellicoe@englishporcelain.com
Ⓦ www.englishporcelain.com
Est. 1975
Stock 18thC English porcelain
Open Mon–Fri 10am–5.30pm
Sat by appointment
Fairs NY Ceramics fair

John Jesse
Contact John Jesse
✉ **160 Kensington Church Street, London, W8 4BN** 🅿
☎ 020 7229 0312 Ⓕ 020 7229 4732
Ⓜ 07767 497880
Ⓔ jj@johnjesse.com
Est. 1963 *Stock size* Medium
Stock 20thC decorative arts, sculpture, glass, ceramics, silver, jewellery
Open Mon–Fri 10am–5.30pm
Sat 11am–4pm

Howard Jones, The Silver Shop (LAPADA)
Contact Howard Jones
✉ **43 Kensington Church Street, London, W8 4BA** 🅿
☎ 020 7937 4359 Ⓕ 020 7937 4359
Ⓔ sjsilvershop@aol.com
Ⓦ www.silvershop.com
Est. 1979 *Stock size* Small
Stock Antique and modern silver, trinket boxes, picture frames, cufflinks, jewellery
Open Tues–Sat 10am–5.30pm

Peter Kemp
Contact Mr P Kemp
✉ **170 Kensington Church Street, London, W8 4BN** 🅿
☎ 020 7229 2988 Ⓕ 020 7229 2988
Ⓜ 07836 282285
Ⓔ peterkemp@btinternet.com
Est. 1971 *Stock size* Large
Stock 18thC Oriental, European porcelain, works of art
Open Mon–Fri 10.30am–5.30pm or by appointment

The Lacquer Chest
Contact Mrs G Andersen
✉ **75 Kensington Church Street, London, W8 4BG** 🅿
☎ 020 7937 1306 Ⓕ 020 7376 0223
Ⓔ email@laquerchest.freeserve.co.uk
Est. 1959 *Stock size* Large
Stock Military chests, china, clocks, samplers, lamps
Open Mon–Fri 9.30am–5.30pm
Sat 10.30am–4.30pm
Services Prop hire of antiques

Lev Antiques Ltd
Contact Alyson Lawrence
✉ **97a Kensington Church Street, London, W8 7LN** 🅿
☎ 020 7727 9248 Ⓕ 020 7727 9248
Ⓜ 07768 470473
Ⓔ alyson@richardlawrence.co.uk
Est. 1882 *Stock size* Medium
Stock Jewellery, silver, paintings, objets d'art, antiquities
Open Tues–Sat 10.30am–5.45pm
Mon noon–5.30pm
Services Oil painting restoration

Libra Antiques
Contact Mrs A Wolsey
✉ **131d Kensington Church Street, London, W8 7PT** 🅿
☎ 020 7727 2990
Est. 1979 *Stock size* Large
Stock English blue and white pottery 1790–1820, creamware
Open Mon–Fri 10am–5pm
Sat 10am–4pm

London Antique Gallery
Contact Mr C D Wertheim
✉ **66e Kensington Church Street, London, W8 4BY** 🅿
☎ 020 7229 2934 Ⓕ 020 7229 2934
Ⓜ 07930 411991
Ⓔ sales@japanesegallery.co.uk
Est. 1996 *Stock size* Medium
Stock Meissen, Dresden, Worcester, Minton, Shelley, Sèvres, Lalique, bisque dolls
Open Mon–Sat 10am–6pm
Services Restoration, framing

Mah's Antiques
Contact Mr Mah
✉ **141 Kensington Church Street, London, W8 7LP** 🅿
☎ 020 7229 9047 Ⓕ 020 7354 1860
Est. 1994 *Stock size* Large
Stock Oriental and European porcelain, works of art
Open Mon–Fri 10.30am–5.30pm
Services Valuations, restoration

E and H Manners (BADA)
Contact Errol Manners
✉ **66a Kensington Church Street, London, W8 4BY** 🅿
☎ 020 7229 5516 Ⓕ 020 7229 5516
Ⓜ 07767 250763
Ⓔ manners@europeanporcelain.com
Ⓦ www.europeanporcelain.com
Est. 1986 *Stock size* Medium
Stock 18thC European porcelain, pottery
Open Mon–Fri 10am–5.30pm
Fairs International Ceramics Fair

S Marchant & Son (BADA, KCSADA)
Contact Mr S Marchant or Mr R Marchant
✉ **120 Kensington Church Street, London, W8 4BH** 🅿
☎ 020 7229 5319 Ⓕ 020 7792 8979
Ⓔ gallery@marchantasianart.com
Ⓦ www.marchantasianart.com
Est. 1925 *Stock size* Large
Stock Chinese porcelain, works of art, snuff bottles, jade
Open Mon–Fri 9.30am–5.30pm
Fairs Grosvenor House, International Asian Art
Services Valuations

R & G McPherson Antiques (BADA)
Contact Robert McPherson
✉ **40 Kensington Church Street, London, W8 4BX** 🅿
☎ 020 7937 0812 Ⓕ 020 7938 2032
Ⓜ 07768 432630
Ⓔ robertmcpherson@orientalceramics.com
Ⓦ www.orientalceramics.com
Est. 1987 *Stock size* Medium
Stock Chinese, Japanese ceramics before 1820
Open Mon–Fri 10.30am–5.30pm
Sat 10am–1pm
Fairs Olympia June
Services Valuations

Michael Coins
Contact Mr M Gouby
✉ **6 Hillgate Street, London, W8 7SR** 🅿
☎ 020 7727 1518 Ⓕ 020 7727 1518
Ⓔ michael@michael-coins.co.uk
Ⓦ www.michael-coins.co.uk
Est. 1966 *Stock size* Medium
Stock English and foreign, medieval–present day coins, banknotes
Open Mon–Fri 10am–5pm

Colin D Monk
Contact Mr C Monk
✉ **58–60 Kensington Church Street, London,**

W8 4DB
☎ 020 7229 3727 ⓕ 020 7376 1501
ⓔ colindmonk@yahoo.co.uk
Stock size Medium
Stock Oriental porcelain
Open Mon–Sat 11am–5pm

Nassirzadeh Antiques
Contact Mr Houshang
✉ **178 Kensington Church Street, London, W8 4DP**
☎ 020 7243 8262 ⓕ 020 7243 8262
ⓜ 07958 626777
Est. 1984 *Stock size* Large
Stock Porcelain, glass, textiles
Open Mon–Sat 11am–6pm

Pruskin Galleries
Contact Michael Pruskin
✉ **50 & 73 Kensington Church High Street, London, W8 4BG**
☎ 020 7937 1994 ⓕ 020 7376 1285
ⓔ pruskin@pruskingallery.demon.co.uk
Est. 1977 *Stock size* Large
Stock Decorative art, paintings, furniture, ceramics, jewellery, glass
Open Mon–Fri 10am–6pm
Sat 11am–5pm

Mrs Quick Chandeliers
Contact Mr N Denton
✉ **166 Kensington Church Street, London, W8 4BN**
☎ 020 7229 1338 ⓕ 020 7792 1073
Est. 1897 *Stock size* Large
Stock French and English chandeliers, lighting, table lamps, 1750–1920
Open Mon–Fri 9.30am–5.30pm

Raffety & Walwyn Ltd (BADA, CINOA, LAPADA)
Contact Nigel Raffety or Howard Walwyn
✉ **79 Kensington Church Street, London, W8 4BG**
☎ 020 7938 1100 ⓕ 020 7938 2519
ⓔ raffety@globalnet.co.uk
ⓦ www.raffetyantiqueclocks.com
Est. 1982 *Stock size* Medium
Stock Late 17th–18thC clocks, barometers, furniture
Open Mon–Fri 10am–6pm Sat by appointment
Fairs BADA, Grosvenor House, Olympia (June)

Paul Reeves
Contact Mr P Reeves or Mr S Barrett
✉ **32b Kensington Church Street, London, W8 4HA**
☎ 020 7937 1594 ⓕ 020 7938 2163
Est. 1976 *Stock size* Large
Stock Victorian–Edwardian furniture, artefacts, textiles, glass, ceramics, metalwork, Arts and Crafts, Aesthetic movement, Gothic revival
Open Mon–Fri 10am–5.30pm
Sat 11am–4pm

Reindeer Antiques Ltd (BADA, LAPADA)
Contact Adrian Butterworth
✉ **81 Kensington Church Street, London, W8 4BG**
☎ 020 7937 3754 ⓕ 020 7937 7199
ⓔ pejwal@hotmail.com
ⓦ www.reindeerantiques.co.uk
Est. 1969 *Stock size* Large
Stock Fine period English furniture, 17th–19thC mahogany, walnut, oak mirrors, paintings, objets d'art
Open Mon–Sat 9.30am–6pm
Fairs BADA (March), LAPADA (Oct), NEC
Services Valuations, restoration

Roderick Antique Clocks (LAPADA, KCSADA)
Contact Mr R Mee
✉ **23 Vicarage Gate, (Junction Kensington Church Street), London, W8 4AA**
☎ 020 7937 8517 ⓕ 020 7937 8517
ⓔ rick@roderickantiqueclocks.com
ⓦ www.roderickantiqueclocks.com
Est. 1975 *Stock size* Large
Stock Antique clocks, 1700–1900, including bracket, Vienna, longcase, carriage, English, French, German
Open Mon–Fri 10am–5.30pm
Sat 10am–4pm
Services Valuations, repairs

Brian Rolleston Antiques Ltd (BADA)
Contact Mr B Rolleston
✉ **104a Kensington Church Street, London, W8 4BU**
☎ 020 7229 5892 ⓕ 020 7229 5892
Est. 1955 *Stock size* Medium
Stock 18thC English furniture
Open Mon–Fri 10am–1pm
2–5.30pm
Fairs Grosvenor House, Olympia (Nov), BADA

Dyala Salam Antiques (KCSADA)
Contact Miss Dyala Salam
✉ **174a Kensington Church Street, London, W8 4DP**
☎ 020 7370 2078 ⓕ 020 7229 2433
Est. 1991 *Stock size* Large
Stock 18th–19thC Ottoman antiques, textiles, Bohemian glass, Islamic furniture
Open Mon–Fri 11am–6pm
Sat 11.30am–3.30pm

Patrick Sandberg Antiques (BADA, CINOA)
Contact Mr C Radford
✉ **150–152 Kensington Church Street, London, W8 4BH**
☎ 020 7229 0373 ⓕ 020 7792 3467
ⓔ psand@antiquefurniture.net
ⓦ www.antiquefurniture.net
Est. 1983 *Stock size* Large
Stock 18th–19thC English furniture, mirrors, accessories
Open Mon–Fri 10am–6pm
Sat 10am–4pm
Fairs Olympia

Santos (BADA)
Contact Mr A Santos
✉ **21 Old Court House, London, W8 4PD**
☎ 020 7937 6000 ⓕ 020 7937 3351
ⓦ www.santoslondon.com
Est. 1979 *Stock size* Small
Stock 17th–18thC Chinese export porcelain
Open By appointment only
Fairs International Ceramics Fair & Seminar London, The International Asian Art Fair, The New York Ceramics Fair, Lisbon International Fair

B Silverman (BADA)
Contact Robin Silverman or Bill Brackenbury
✉ **4 Campden Street, Off Kensington Church Street, London, W8 7EP**
☎ 020 7985 0555 ⓕ 020 7985 0556
ⓔ silver@silverman-london.com
ⓦ www.silverman-london.com
Est. 1925 *Stock size* Large
Stock 17th–19thC fine English silverware, silver flatware
Open Mon–Fri 10am–5pm
Sat 10am–4pm
Fairs Olympia, BADA, Harrogate
Services Valuations

⊞ Simon Spero (BACA Award Winner 2003)
Contact Mr S Spero
✉ **109 Kensington Church Street, London, W8 7LN** 🅿
☎ 020 7727 7413 Ⓕ 020 7727 7414
Est. 1964 *Stock size* Large
Stock 18thC English porcelain, enamels
Open Mon–Fri 10am–5pm closed 1–2pm
Services Valuations, author of 5 reference books, lecturer

⊞ Stockspring Antiques (BADA, KCSADA)
Contact Mrs F Marno
✉ **114 Kensington Church Street, London, W8 4BH**
☎ 020 7727 7995 Ⓕ 020 7727 7995
Ⓔ stockspring@antique-porcelain.co.uk
Ⓦ www.antique-porcelain.co.uk
Est. 1979 *Stock size* Large
Stock 18th–early 19thC English porcelain
Open Mon–Fri 10am–5.30pm Sat 10am–1pm
Fairs Olympia (Nov, June)
Services Packing, shipping

⊞ Through The Looking Glass
Contact Sarah Link
✉ **137 Kensington Church Street, London, W8 7LP** 🅿
☎ 020 7221 4026 Ⓕ 020 7602 3678
Est. 1988 *Stock size* Large
Stock 19thC mirrors
Open Mon–Sat 10am–5.30pm

⊞ Geoffrey Waters Ltd (BADA)
Contact Geoffrey Waters
✉ **133 Kensington Church Street, London, W8 7LP** 🅿
☎ 020 7243 6081
Ⓔ info@antique-chinese-porcelain.com
Ⓦ www.antique-chinese-porcelain.com
Est. 1992 *Stock size* Medium
Stock 16th–18thC Chinese porcelain
Open Mon–Fri 10.15am–5.30pm Sat 10.15am–4.30pm

⊞ Jorge Welsh (BADA)
Contact Mr J Welsh
✉ **116 Kensington Church Street, London, W8 4BH** 🅿
☎ 020 7229 2140 Ⓕ 020 7792 3535
Ⓜ 07831 186224
Ⓔ uk@jorgewelsh.com
Ⓦ www.jorgewelsh.com
Est. 1997 *Stock size* Large
Stock Chinese porcelain, particularly Chinese Export, porcelain, Indo-Portugese art, Namban, Japanese export works of art
Open Mon–Fri 10am–5.30pm
Fairs Olympia (June), Asian Art in London

⊞ Mary Wise & Grosvenor Antiques (BADA)
Contact Mrs M Wise
✉ **27 Holland Street, London, W8 4NA** 🅿
☎ 020 7937 8649 Ⓕ 020 7937 7179
Ⓜ 07850 863050
Ⓔ info@wiseantiques.com
Ⓦ www.wiseantiques.com
Est. 1970 *Stock size* Small
Stock Porcelain, small bronzes, works of art, Chinese watercolours on pith paper
Open Mon–Fri 10am–5pm
Fairs New York Ceramics Fair, San Francisco Fall Antiques Show
Services Bid at auction

⊞ Zeitgeist Antiques
Contact Mr A Self
✉ **58 Kensington Church Street, London, W8 4DB** 🅿
☎ 020 7938 4817 Ⓕ 020 7938 4817
Ⓔ adself@btinternet.com
Ⓦ www.zeitgeistantiques.com
Est. 1988 *Stock size* Small
Stock Art Nouveau, Art Deco, glass, ceramics, metalware
Open Mon–Sat 10am–6pm
Fairs 20thC Olympia, Great Antiques Fair

W9

⊞ Fluss and Charlesworth
Contact John Charlesworth
✉ **London, W9**
Ⓜ 07831 830323
Est. 1973 *Stock size* Small
Stock 18thC English, Continental furniture
Open By appointment
Fairs Olympia

⊞ Vale Antiques
Contact Mr P Gooley
✉ **245 Elgin Avenue, Maida Vale, London, W9 1NJ** 🅿
☎ 020 7328 4796
Est. 1973 *Stock size* Large
Stock Eclectic mix of antiques, Victorian–1950s, pictures, mirrors, silver, silver plate, china, etc
Open Mon–Sat 10am–6pm
Services Restoration, pearl stringing, clock and watch repairs

W10

⊞ 88 Antiques
Contact Mr D Lucas
✉ **88 Golborne Road, London, W10 5PS** 🅿
☎ 020 8960 0827
Est. 1977 *Stock size* Large
Stock Antique pine, country furniture
Open Tues–Sat 10am–6pm
Services Makers of tables from reclaimed 100-year-old wood

⊞ Bazar
Contact Ms M Davis or Ms C Rogers
✉ **82 Golborne Road, London, W10 5PS** 🅿
☎ 020 8969 6262
Est. 1992 *Stock size* Medium
Stock French decorative country furniture, beds, tables, armchairs, kitchenware, garden furniture
Open Tues–Thurs 10am–5pm Fri 9.30am–5.30pm Sat 10am–5.30pm

W11

⊞ 51 Antiques
Contact Mr Justin Raccanello
✉ **51 Ledbury Road, London, W11 2AA** 🅿
☎ 020 7229 6153 Ⓕ 020 7229 6153
Est. 1975 *Stock size* Medium
Stock Italian ceramics, 1500–1900, Venetian glass
Open Mon–Fri 9.30am–5.30pm Sat 9.30am–1pm

⌂ 75 Portobello Road
Contact Gavin Douglas
✉ **75 Portobello Road, London, W11 2QB**
☎ 020 7221 1121 Ⓕ 01825 724418
Ⓔ gavin@antique-clocks.co.uk
Stock size Medium
No. of dealers 5
Stock 18th–19thC Continental clocks, decorative gilt bronzes, porcelain, 19th–20thC animal

subjects, Vienna, French bronzes, Staffordshire, terracotta, tobacco jars, chess sets, paperweights
Open Mon–Fri 10.30am–4.30pm Sat 7.30am–5pm

Admiral Vernon Antiques Market (PADA)
Contact Angelo Soteriades
141–149 Portobello Road, London, W11 2DY
☎ 020 7727 5242 Ⓕ 020 7727 5242
Ⓜ 07956 277077
Ⓔ info@portobello-antiques.com
Ⓦ www.portobello-antiques.com
Est. 1983 *Stock size* Large
No. of dealers over 200
Stock Glass, treen, works of art, Art Deco, Art Nouveau, jewellery
Open Sat 6am–5pm
Services Valuations

Chloe Alberry
Contact Chloe or Theo
84 Portobello Road, London, W11 2QD
☎ 020 7727 0707
Ⓦ www.alberry.co.uk
Est. 2002 *Stock size* Small
Stock Antique and old furniture, decorative items from India, Indonesia, China
Open Mon–Sun 9am–6pm
Services Delivery

Alice's
Contact Mrs D Carter
86 Portobello Road, London, W11 2QD P
☎ 020 7229 8187 Ⓕ 020 7792 2456
Est. 1887 *Stock size* Large
Stock Painted furniture, decorative items, general antiques
Open Tues–Fri 9am–5pm Sat 7am–4pm

Anthea's Antiques
Contact A Mcilroy
Burton's Arcade, 296 Westbourne Grove, Portobello Market, London, W11 2PS P
☎ 020 8690 7207
Ⓜ 07961 838780
Est. 1985 *Stock size* Medium
Stock 19thC English and Continental glass and ceramics
Trade only Yes
Open Sat 7am–4pm
Fairs Newark, Ardingly
Services Will arrange shipping if required

Appleby Antiques (PADA)
Contact Mike or Sue Witts
Geoffrey Van Gallery, 105–107 Portobello Road, London, W11 2QB P
☎ 01453 753126
Ⓜ 07778 282532
Ⓔ mike@applebyantiques.net
Ⓦ www.applebyantiques.net
Est. 1986 *Stock size* Medium
Stock English pottery,1750–1930, specializing in Wedgwood, Lustreware, culinary moulds in pewter, copper, ceramic
Open Sat 6.45am–4pm
Fairs NEC
Services Shipping

Arbras Gallery
Contact Sandy
292 Westbourne Grove, London, W11 2PS P
☎ 020 7229 6772 Ⓕ 020 7229 6772
Ⓔ info@arbrasgallery.co.uk
Ⓦ www.arbrasgallery.co.uk
Est. 1973 *Stock size* Large
Stock Silver picture frames, giftware
Open Mon–Fri 10am–4.30pm Sat 7am–4.30pm
Services Mail order

Atlam Sales and Service (PADA)
Contact B Skogland-Kirk
111 Portobello Road, London, W11 2QB P
☎ 020 7602 7573 Ⓕ 020 7602 2997
Ⓔ info@atlam-watches.co.uk
Ⓦ www.atlam-watches.co.uk www.atlamsilver.com
Est. 1979 *Stock size* Large
Stock Silver and antique pocket watches, decorative silver
Open Mon–Fri 9am–5pm Sat 8am–5pm

B and T Antiques Ltd (LAPADA)
Contact Bernadette Lewis or Vigi Sawdon
79–81 Ledbury Road, London, W11 2AG P
☎ 020 7229 7001 Ⓕ 020 7229 2033
Ⓔ bt.antiques@virgin.net
Est. 1994 *Stock size* Large
Stock Decorative antiques, Art Deco furniture and objects
Open Mon–Sat 10am–6pm
Services Restoration, gilding

Sebastiano Barbagallo Antiques
Contact Mr S Barbagallo
15 Pembridge Road, London, W11 3HG P
☎ 020 7792 3320 Ⓕ 020 7792 3320
Ⓔ sebastianobarbagallo@hotmail.com
Est. 1978 *Stock size* Large
Stock Chinese furniture, Indian and Tibetan antiques, crafts
Open Mon–Fri 10.30am–6pm Sat 9am–7pm Sun 10.30am–5pm

Barham Antiques (PADA)
Contact Mr M Barham
83 Portobello Road, London, W11 2QB P
☎ 020 7727 3845 Ⓕ 020 7727 3845
Ⓔ mchlbarham@aol.com
Ⓦ www.barhamantiques.co.uk
Est. 1970 *Stock size* Large
Stock Boxes, caddies, inkwells, clocks, glassware, inkstands, small furniture, silver plate
Open Mon–Fri 10am–4.30pm Sat 7am–5pm
Services Valuations, restoration

Beagle Gallery and Asian Antiques
Contact Mr Beagle
303 Westbourne Grove, London, W11 2QA P
☎ 020 7229 9524 Ⓕ 020 7792 0333
Est. 1984 *Stock size* Medium
Stock Oriental furniture, sculpture
Open By appointment

Book and Comic Exchange
Contact Mr R Brown
14 Pembridge Road, London, W11 3HL P
☎ 020 7229 8420
Ⓦ www.buy-sell-trade.co.uk
Est. 1967 *Stock size* Medium
Stock Modern first editions, cult books, comics
Open Mon–Sun 10am–8pm

F E A Briggs Ltd
Contact Joan Wilson
77 Ledbury Road, London, W11 2AG P
☎ 020 7727 0909 Ⓕ 023 8081 2595
Ⓔ feabriggs@aol.com
Est. 1966 *Stock size* Small
Stock Victorian furniture
Open Mon–Fri 9am–5.30pm
Fairs Newark
Services Restoration

Jack Casimir Ltd (BADA, LAPADA)
23 Pembridge Road, London, W11 3HG
020 7727 8643
Est. 1931 *Stock size* Large
Stock 16th–19thC British and European domestic brass, copper, pewter, paktong
Open Mon–Sat 9.30am–5pm
Services Shipping

Chamade Antiques
Contact George Walters
65 Portobello Road, London, W11 2QB
020 8446 0130
Est. 1994 *Stock size* Medium
Stock Antique Rolex watches
Open Sat 7am–3pm

Chelsea Clocks and Antiques
Contact Mr Donald Lynch
73 Portobello Road, Notting Hill, London, W11 2QB
020 7229 7762 F 020 7274 5198
E info@chelseaclocks.co.uk
W www.chelseaclocks.co.uk
Est. 1979 *Stock size* Medium
Stock Clocks, scales, boxes, collectables, ink stands and wells
Open Mon–Sat 10am–5pm

Sheila Cook Textiles
Contact Mrs S Cook
184 Westbourne Grove, London, W11 2RH
020 7792 8001 F 020 7243 1744
E sheilacook@sheilacook.co.uk
W www.sheilacook.co.uk
Est. 1970 *Stock size* Small
Stock Mid-18thC–1970s European costume, textiles, accessories
Open By appointment
Services Valuations

Julia Craig (PADA, BABAADA, PRADA)
Contact Julia Craig
Harris's Arcade, 163–165 Portobello Road, London, W11 2DY
01225 448202
M 07771 786846
E julia@juliacraigcostume.com
W www.juliacraigcostume.com
Est. 1980 *Stock size* Large
Stock Antique lace and linen, costumes, costume accessories
Open Fri–Sat 10am–5pm
Fairs P & A Fairs, Hammersmith
Services Valuations

Stuart Craig (PADA)
Contact Stuart Craig
Unit 72, Ground Floor, Admiral Vernon Antiques Market, 141–149 Portobello Road, London, W11 2DY
020 7221 8662
M 07947 889012
Est. 1991 *Stock size* Medium
Stock Early 19thC–1950s antique ladies' clothing, accessories
Open Sat 8.30am–4pm or by appointment

Crown Arcade (ADA)
Contact Angelo Soteriades
119 Portobello Road, London, W11 2DY
020 7727 5242 F 020 7727 5242
M 07956 277077
E info@portobello-collections.co.uk
W www.portobello-antiques.com
Est. 1983 *Stock size* Large
No. of dealers 21
Stock Glass, treen, works of art, jewellery, Art Deco, Art Nouveau
Open Sat 6am–5pm
Services Valuations

Cura Antiques
Contact Mr Cura
34 Ledbury Road, London, W11 2AB
020 7229 6880 F 020 7792 3731
E mail@cura-antiques.com
W www.cura-antiques.com
Est. 1969 *Stock size* Medium
Stock Continental works of art, furniture, old master paintings
Open Mon–Fri 10.30am–5.30pm Sat 10.30am–1pm
Fairs Olympia (June)
Services Restoration

John Dale Antiques (PADA)
Contact Mrs Jo Cairns
87 Portobello Road, London, W11 2QB
020 7727 1304
Est. 1960 *Stock size* Medium
No. of dealers 4
Stock Decorative antiques, books, prints
Open Sun Mon Fri 10am–5pm Sat 7am–6pm

Gavin Douglas (LAPADA, PADA)
Contact Gavin Douglas
75 Portobello Road, London, W11 2QB
020 7221 1121 F 01825 724418
E gavin@antique-clocks.co.uk
W www.antique-clocks.co.uk
Est. 1992 *Stock size* Large
Stock Antique clocks, ormolu, bronzes and porcelain
Open Mon–Sat 10.30am–4.30pm Sat 7.30am–5pm
Fairs Olympia, LAPADA
Services Valuations, restoration

Simon Finch (ABA, PBFA)
Contact Simon Finch
61a Ledbury Road, London, W11 2AL
020 7792 3303
E rarebooks@simonfinch.com
W www.simonfinch.com
Est. 1982 *Stock size* Medium
Stock Modern first editions, art and photography
Open Mon–Sat 10am–6pm
Fairs Olympia, Chelsea, Grosvenor House

Fleurdelys Antiquités
Contact Ms Laurence Paul
Gallery 289, 289 Westbourne Grove, London, W11 2QA
0207 636 2327 F 0207 636 2327
M 07798 600437
E info@fleurdelys.com
Est. 1997 *Stock size* Large
Stock Chinese antique wood stands, Chinese porcelain
Open Sat 7am–5pm or by appointment

Good Fairy Antique Market (PADA)
Contact Derek E Carter
100 Portobello Road, London, W11 2DY
01634 233900 F 01634 268154
M 07704 32169
E derekcarter@yahoo.com
W www.goofairyantiques.co.uk
Est. 1975 *Stock size* Large
No. of dealers 50
Stock Stamps, silver, glass, small antiques, collectables, memorabilia
Open Sat 4am–5pm

Henry Gregory (PADA)
Contact Camy Gregory
82E Portobello Road, London, W11 2QD
020 7792 9221
Est. 1970 *Stock size* Medium
Stock Silver plate, silver, sporting goods, decorative antiques

Open Mon–Fri 10am–4.30pm
Sat 8am–4.30pm
Services Shipping

Hampton Antiques (PADA)
Contact Mark Goodger
119 Portobello Road, Crown Arcade, London, W11 2DY
☎ 01604 863979 Ⓕ 01604 863979
Ⓜ 07779 654879
Ⓔ info@hamptonantiques.co.uk
Ⓦ www.hamptonantiques.co.uk
Est. 1981 *Stock size* Large
Stock Boxes and tea caddies
Open Sat 6.30am–3pm
Fairs NEC, Penman Fairs, Earls Court

Harris's Arcade
Contact Angelo Soteriades
161–163 Portobello Road, London, W11 2DY
☎ 020 7727 5242
Ⓜ 07956 277077
Ⓔ info@portobello-antiques.com
Ⓦ www.portobello-antiques.com
Est. 2003 *Stock size* Medium
No. of dealers 35
Stock Collectables, textiles. Oriental, English porcelain, antiquities, travel
Open Sat 5am–5pm

Hart & Rosenberg
Contact Mrs E Hart
Units L52–L53, Lower Trading Hall, Admiral Vernon Antiques Market, 141–149 Portobello Road, London, W11 2DY Ⓟ
☎ 020 8874 5250
Est. 1968 *Stock size* Large
Stock Oriental and Continental ceramics, decorative items
Open Sat 9am–4pm
Services Valuations, restoration

Helios Gallery (ADA, PADA, BABAADA)
Contact Rolf Kiaer
292 Westbourne Grove, London, W11 2PS Ⓟ Ⓕ 01225 336097
Ⓜ 07711 955997
Ⓔ heliosgallery@btinternet.com
Ⓦ www.heliosgallery.com
Est. 1995 *Stock size* Medium
Stock Roman, Greek, Egyptian, Chinese, ancient art
Open Sat 8am–4pm or by appointment
Fairs ADA Fair
Services Valuations, restoration, shipping

Hirst Antiques
Contact Mrs S Hirst
59 Pembridge Road, London, W11 3HN Ⓟ
☎ 020 7727 9364 Ⓕ 020 7460 6480
Est. 1969 *Stock size* Large
Stock General antique furniture, antique beds, bronzes, sculpture, pictures
Open Mon–Sat 10am–6pm

Erna Hiscock (PADA)
Contact Erna Hiscock
Chelsea Galleries, 69 Portobello Road, London, W11 2PS
☎ 01233 661407 Ⓕ 01233 661407
Ⓔ erna@ernahiscockantiques.com
Ⓦ www.ernahiscockantiques.com
Est. 1975 *Stock size* Large
Stock 17th–19thC samplers, needlework
Open Sat 7am–3pm
Fairs NEC
Services Valuations

Humbleyard Fine Art (PADA)
Contact James Layte
Unit 32, Admiral Vernon Arcade, Portobello Road, London, W11 2DY Ⓟ
☎ 01362 637793 Ⓕ 01362 637793
Ⓜ 07836 349416
Est. 1974 *Stock size* Medium
Stock Scientific, medical, decorative and collectors' items
Open Sat 6am–1.30pm
Fairs Olympia
Services Valuations

Kleanthous Antiques Ltd (LAPADA)
Contact Mr C Kleanthous
144 Portobello Road, London, W11 2DZ Ⓟ
☎ 020 7727 3649 Ⓕ 020 7243 2488
Ⓜ 07850 375501
Ⓔ antiques@kleanthaus.com
Ⓦ www.kleanthous.com
Est. 1969 *Stock size* Medium
Stock Jewellery, wristwatches, furniture, clocks, pocket watches, porcelain, china, silver, works of art, 20thC decorative items
Open Sat 8.30am–4pm or by appointment
Fairs Olympia

Lenson-Smith (LAPADA)
Contact Millie Lenson-Smith
153 Portobello Road, London, W11 2DY
☎ 020 8340 8767 Ⓕ 020 8340 8767
Stock size Medium
Stock Unusual collectables, furniture
Fairs Olympia, Battersea

M & D Lewis (PADA)
Contact Mr M Lewis
1 Lonsdale Road, London, W11 2BY Ⓟ
☎ 020 7727 3908 Ⓕ 020 7727 3908
Est. 1959 *Stock size* Large
Stock English and Continental furniture, Oriental porcelain
Open Mon–Fri 10am–5pm
Sat 10am–4pm

Lunn Antiques Ltd
Contact Stephen Lunn
Unit 8, Admiral Vernon Arcade, Portobello Road, London, W11 2DY
☎ 020 7736 4638 Ⓕ 020 7371 7113
Ⓔ lunnantiques@aol.co,
Ⓦ www.lunnantiques.co.uk
Est. 1995 *Stock size* Medium
Stock 17thC needlepoint, Mechlin, 18thC Brussels, Valenciennes
Open By appointment
Services Valuations, restoration

Caira Mandaglio
Contact Anne or Sharon
31 Pembridge Road, London, W11 3HG Ⓟ
☎ 020 7727 5496 Ⓕ 020 7229 4889
Ⓜ 07836 354632
Ⓔ caira_mandaglio@btopenworld.com
Ⓦ www.cairamandaglio.co.uk
Est. 1998 *Stock size* Large
Stock 20thC furniture, lighting, glassware, objets d'art, chandeliers
Open Wed–Fri 11am–5pm
Sat 10.30am–5.30pm

Mario's Antiques (LAPADA, PADA)
Contact M Barazi
115 Portobello Road, London, W11 2DY Ⓟ
☎ 07919 254000 Ⓕ 020 8900 0810
Ⓜ 07956 580772
Ⓔ marwan@barazi.screaming.net
Ⓦ www.marios-antiques.com
Est. 1986 *Stock size* Medium
Stock Porcelain, Meissen, Sèvres, Vienna

Open Wed Fri 10am–4pm
Sat 7am–5pm
Fairs Olympia, LAPADA, NEC

Robin Martin Antiques
Contact Mr P Martin
44 Ledbury Road, London, W11 2AB
020 7727 1301 020 7727 1301
paul.martin11@btconnect.com
Est. 1971 *Stock size* Medium
Stock Mirrors, Regency furniture, Continental furniture, works of art, lighting
Open Mon–Fri 10am–6pm
Sat 10am–1pm
Fairs Olympia (June, Nov)

Mayflower Antiques (PADA)
Contact Mr John Odgers
117 Portobello Road, London, W11 2DY
020 7727 0381
07860 843569
antiques@johnodgers.com
Est. 1970 *Stock size* Medium
Stock Music boxes, clocks, dolls, scientific instruments, pistols, collectable items
Open Sat 7am–4pm
Fairs Newark, Ardingly

MCN Antiques
Contact Makoto Umezawa
183 Westbourne Grove, London, W11 2SB
020 7727 3796 020 7229 8839
Est. 1980 *Stock size* Large
Stock Japanese porcelain, works of art
Open Mon–Fri 10am–6pm
Sat 11am–3pm

Mimi Fifi
Contact Rita Delaforge
27 Pembridge Road, Notting Hill Gate, London, W11 3HG
020 7243 3154 020 7938 4222
07956 222238
www.mimififi.com
Est. 1992 *Stock size* Large
Stock Collectors' and vintage toys, Coca-Cola memorabilia, Pokemon, perfume-related items, vintage badges, tobacco memorabilia, Michelin memorabilia, Kewpie dolls, Japanese collectables
Open Mon–Sat 11am–6pm
Services Overseas postal service

Myriad Antiques
Contact Mrs S Nickerson
131 Portland Road, London, W11 4LW
020 7229 1709 020 7221 3882
Est. 1975 *Stock size* Large
Stock French painted furniture, garden furniture, bamboo, Victorian–Edwardian upholstered chairs, mirrors, objets d'art
Open Tues–Sat 11am–6pm

Polly Pallister (PADA)
Contact Polly Pallister
Geoffrey Van Gallery, 105–107 Portobello Road, London, W11 2QB
020 7267 7864
www.polly-pallister-antiques.com
Est. 1996 *Stock size* Medium
Stock 18th–19thC decorative antiques, 18thC engravings, creamware, silk patchworks, textiles
Open Sat 7am–2.30pm or by appointment

Portobello Antique Store
Contact Mr J Ewing
79 Portobello Road, London, W11 2QB
020 7221 1994 020 7221 1994
Est. 1984 *Stock size* Large
Stock Silver, silver plate, decorative items, flatware
Open Tues–Fri 10am–4pm
Sat 8.15am–4pm

Portobello Studios (PADA)
Contact Angelo Soteriades
101–103 Portobello Road, London, W11 2QB
020 7727 5242 020 7727 5242
07956 277077
info@portobello-antiques.com
www.portobello-antiques.co.uk
Est. 1983
No. of dealers 40
Stock Treen, glass, works of art, Art Deco, Art Nouveau, jewellery
Open Sat 6am–5pm
Services Valuations

Red Lion Antiques Market (PADA)
Contact Angelo Soteriades
165–169 Portobello Road, London, W11 2DY
020 7436 9416 020 7727 5242
07956 277077
info@portobello-collections.co.uk
www.portobello-antiques.co.uk
Est. 1983 *Stock size* Large
No. of dealers 40
Stock Glass, treen, Art Deco, Art Nouveau, jewellery, cameras, collectables, Oriental, African art, jewellery
Open Sat 6am–5pm
Services Valuations, café

The Red Teapot Arcade
Contact Angelo Soteriades
101/103 Portobello Road, London, W11 2QB
020 7727 5242
07956 277077
info@portobello-antiques.com
www.portobello-antiques.com
Est. 2003 *Stock size* Medium
No. of dealers 40
Stock High quality antiques, watches, lighters, pens, silver
Open Sat 6am–5pm

Rogers Antiques Gallery
Contact Mike Spooner
65 Portobello Road, London, W11 2QB
020 7969 1500 020 7969 1639
Est. 1969 *Stock size* Large
No. of dealers 65
Stock Wide range of antiques and collectables, specialist dealers in most fields
Open Sat 7am–4.30pm
Services Valuations

Schredds of Portobello (LAPADA, CINOA)
Contact George R Schrager
107 Portobello Road, London, W11 2QB
020 8348 3314 020 8341 5971
silver@schredds.demon.co.uk
www.schredds.com
Est. 1972 *Stock size* Large
Stock Small pieces of pre-1880 silver
Open Sat 7am–2.30pm
Fairs Antiques for Everyone, Earl's Court, Penman fairs
Services Valuations, shipping

Justin F Skrebowski Prints (PBFA, PADA)
Contact Mr J Skrebowski
Ground Floor, 177 Portobello Road, London,

W11 2DY
☎ 020 7792 9742 Ⓕ 020 7792 9742
Ⓜ 07774 612474
Ⓔ justin@skreb.co.uk
Ⓦ www.skreb.co.uk
Est. 1979 *Stock size* Large
Stock 18th–19thC decorative prints, 18th–20thC frames for prints and watercolours, oils, watercolours
Open Sat 9am–4pm or by appointment
Fairs PBFA, Russell Hotel
Services Folio stands, easels, display equipment

Pam Taylor Antiques (PADA)
Contact Mrs P Taylor
Portobello Studios, The Red Teapot, 101 Portobello Road, London, W11 2QB
Ⓜ 07850 416717
Ⓔ pamlet@globalnet.co.uk
Est. 1982 *Stock size* Medium
Stock Late 19th–early 20thC ceramics, glass, oil lamps
Open Sat 6.30am–3.30pm
Fairs Antiques for Everyone

Themes and Variations
Contact Liliane Fawcett
231 Westbourne Grove, London, W11 2SE
☎ 020 7727 5531 Ⓕ 020 7221 6378
Ⓔ go@themesandvariations.com
Ⓦ www.themesandvariations.com
Est. 1984 *Stock size* Large
Stock Post-war Scandinavian, Italian furniture, decorative arts
Open Mon–Fri 10am–2pm Sat 2–6pm

Philip Thomas Design
Contact Philip Thomas
4a Ladbroke Grove, London, W11 3BG
☎ 020 7229 4044 Ⓕ 020 7229 4044
Ⓔ info@pjthomas.com
Est. 1990 *Stock size* Medium
Stock Eclectic Continental furniture and design
Open Tues–Sat 10am–6pm

Anthony Thompson Ltd
7 Kensington Park Gardens, Notting Hill, London, W11 3HB
☎ 020 7221 7729
Ⓔ at@anthonythompsonltd.co.uk
Ⓦ www.anthonythompsonltd.co.uk
Est. 1990 *Stock size* Small
Stock Antique rugs, carpets
Open By appointment
Services Valuations, restoration, packing, shipping

Virginia
Contact Mrs V Bates
98 Portland Road, London, W11 4LQ
☎ 020 7727 9908 Ⓕ 020 7229 2198
Est. 1971 *Stock size* Medium
Stock Vintage clothes, late 19thC–late 1930s
Open 11am–6pm by appointment only

Trude Weaver (LAPADA)
Contact Mr B Weaver
71 Portobello Road, London, W11 2QB
☎ 020 7229 8738 Ⓕ 020 7229 8738
Ⓜ 07768 551269
Est. 1968 *Stock size* Large
Stock 18th–19thC English and Continental furniture, complementary accessories
Open Wed–Sat 9.30am–5.30pm
Fairs Olympia (June, Nov)

W12

Neil Freeman Angling Auctions
Contact Mr N Freeman
PO Box 2095, London, W12 8RU
☎ 020 8749 4175 Ⓕ 020 8743 4855
Ⓜ 07785 281349
Ⓔ neil@anglingauctions.demon.co.uk
Ⓦ www.thesaurus.co.uk/angling-auctions/
Est. 1990
Sales Angling auctions twice yearly, first Sat April noon, first Sat October noon, viewing The Grand Hall, Chiswick Town Hall, Heathfield Terrace, London W4 Fri 1.30–7pm Sat 8.30am to sale
Frequency Twice yearly
Catalogues yes

W14

Asenbaum Fine Arts Ltd
Contact Mrs C Fells
10 Carlton Mansions, Holland Park Gardens, London, W14 8DW
☎ 020 7602 5373 Ⓕ 020 7602 5373
Est. 1998 *Stock size* Medium
Stock English and Viennese silver, Viennese furniture, Victorian jewellery
Trade only Yes
Open By appointment only

WC1

Afribilia Ltd
Contact Dave Saffery
16 Bury Place, Bloomsbury, London, WC1A 2JL
☎ 020 7404 7137 Ⓕ 020 7404 7138
Ⓔ sales@afribilia.com
Ⓦ www.afribilia.com
Est. 2001 *Stock size* Medium
Stock African memorabilia
Open Tues–Sat 10.30am–5.30pm
Services Valuations

Steven Burak Books
Contact Steven Burak
Ground Floor Shop, 18 Leigh Street, Bloomsbury, London, WC1H 9EW
☎ 020 7388 1153
Ⓔ stevenburaklondon@yahoo.com
Est. 2002 *Stock size* Medium
Stock Antiquarian, rare, out of print books, ephemera, manuscripts
Open Mon–Sat 11am–7pm
Services Valuations

George & Peter Cohn
Contact Peter Cohn
Unit 21, 21 Wren Street, London, WC1X 0HF
☎ 020 7278 3749
Est. 1947 *Stock size* Medium
Stock Chandeliers, wall lights, lanterns, chandelier parts
Open Mon–Fri 9.30am–4pm
Services Restoration

Coincraft (ADA, IBNS, PNG, ANA)
Contact Mr B Clayden
44 & 45 Great Russell Street, London, WC1B 3LU
☎ 020 7636 1188 Ⓕ 020 7323 2860
Ⓔ info@coincraft.com
Ⓦ ww.coincraft.com
Est. 1955
Stock Greek, Roman, English, medieval–present day coins, British and foreign banknotes, ancient artefacts
Open Mon–Fri 9.30am–5pm Sat 10am–2.30pm or by appointment
Fairs Marriott, Cumberland
Services Catalogue of British coins

⊞ Collinge & Clark (PBFA)
Contact Mr O Clark
✉ **13 Leigh Street, London, WC1H 9EW** P
☎ 020 7387 7105 F 020 7388 1315
Est. 1989 *Stock size* Medium
Stock Antiquarian, rare, second-hand books, private press books, limited editions, 18th–19thC political and social history, typography
Open Mon–Fri 11am–6.30pm
Sat 11am–3.30pm

⊞ Fine Books Oriental Ltd (PBFA)
Contact Mr J Somers
✉ **38 Museum Street, London, WC1A 1LP** P
☎ 020 7242 5288 F 020 7242 5344
E oriental@finebooks.demon.co.uk
W www.finebooks.demon.co.uk
Est. 1977 *Stock size* Medium
Stock Oriental, Middle Eastern, South Asian and Indian, out-of-print, rare books
Open Mon–Fri 9.30am–6pm
Sat 11am–6pm
Fairs PBFA, Russell Hotel
Services Valuations

⊞ Robert Frew Ltd (PBFA, ABA)
Contact Mr R Frew
✉ **106 Great Russell Street, London, WC1B 3NB** P
☎ 020 7580 2311 F 020 7580 2313
E shop@robertfrew.com
W www.robertfrew.com
Est. 1976 *Stock size* Medium
Stock Antiquarian and rare books, travel, literature, classics, maps, prints
Open Mon–Fri 10am–6pm
Sat 10am–2pm
Fairs PBFA Bookfairs, Russell Hotel, ABA Olympia Chelsea

⊞ R A Gekoski Booksellers (ABA, ILAB)
Contact Rick Gekoski or Peter Grogan
✉ **Pied Bull Yard, 15a Bloomsbury Square, London, WC1A 2LP** P
☎ 020 7404 6676 F 020 7404 6595
E gekoski@dircon.co.uk
Est. 1984 *Stock size* Small
Stock First editions, letters, paintings, manuscripts
Open Mon–Fri 10am–5.30pm
Fairs ABA
Services Valuations

⊞ Griffith & Partners Ltd
Contact David Griffith
✉ **31–35 Great Ormond Street, London, WC1N 3HZ** P
☎ 020 7430 1394
Est. 1992 *Stock size* Medium
Stock Antiquarian, rare, second-hand books, London topography, Middle East, poetry, Anglo and Welsh topics a speciality
Open Mon–Fri noon–6pm
occasional Sat or by appointment
Services Valuations, book search, catalogues, mail order

⊞ Jarndyce Antiquarian Booksellers (ABA, PBFA)
Contact Mr B Lake or Ms Janet Nassau
✉ **46 Great Russell Street, London, WC1B 3PA** P
☎ 020 7631 4220 F 020 7631 1882
E books@jarndyce.com
W www.jarndyce.com
Est. 1969 *Stock size* Large
Stock Antiquarian, rare, second-hand books on English language, English literature, Dickens, 18th–20thC economic and social history
Open Mon–Fri 10.30am–5.30pm
Fairs Olympia, Chelsea ABA, York PBFA
Services Valuations, catalogues

⊞ Jessop Classic Photographic
Contact Martin Frost or Steve Johnson
✉ **67 Great Russell Street, London, WC1B 3BN** P
☎ 020 7831 3640 F 020 7831 3956
W www.jessops.com/classic
Est. 1989 *Stock size* Large
Stock 1900–1970 classic cameras
Open Mon–Sat 9am–5.30pm
Services Repairs

⊞ Photo Books International (PBFA)
Contact Bill Herbert
✉ **99 Judd Street, London, WC1H 9NE** P
☎ 020 7813 7363 F 020 7813 7363
E pbi@britishlibrary.net
W www.pbi-books.com
Est. 1997 *Stock size* Large
Stock Books on photography
Open Wed–Sat 11am–6pm
Fairs London Photographs Fairs

⊞ Rennies (ESoc)
Contact Mr P Rennie
✉ **13 Rugby Street, London, WC1N 3QT** P
☎ 020 7405 0220
E info@rennart.co.uk
W www.rennart.co.uk
Est. 1990 *Stock size* Small
Stock 20thC art and design, inter-war period posters, graphics
Open Tues–Fri noon–6.30pm
Sat noon–6pm
Services Valuations

⊞ Roe and Moore
Contact Mr T Roe
✉ **29 Museum Street, London, WC1A 1LH** P
☎ 020 7636 4787
E roe&moore@fsbdial.co.uk
W www.abebooks.com
Est. 1992 *Stock size* Medium
Stock Prints, posters, 19th–20thC rare books, children's books, photography, European language books
Open Mon–Sat 10.30am–6pm

⊞ Unsworths Booksellers Ltd (ABA, PBFA)
Contact Mr Charlie Unsworth
✉ **12 Bloomsbury Street, London, WC1B 3QA**
☎ 020 7436 9836 F 020 7637 7334
E books@unsworths.com
W www.unsworths.com
Est. 1986 *Stock size* Large
Stock Antiquarian, second-hand and remainder books on the humanities
Open Mon–Sat 10.30am–8pm
Sun 11am–7pm
Fairs See website for details

⊞ Vortex Books
Contact Stephen Lowe
✉ **The Aquarium, 10 Woburn Walk, London, WC1H 0JL**
☎ 020 7387 8417
E info@aquariumgallery.co.uk
W www.aquariumgallery.co.uk
Est. 1993 *Stock size* Medium
Stock Books, posters
Open Mon–Sat 11am–6pm

WC2

⊞ Anchor Antiques Ltd
Contact Mrs Samne
✉ **26 Charing Cross Road, London, WC2H 0DG**
☎ 020 7836 5686

Est. 1964 *Stock size* Medium
Stock European and Oriental ceramics
Trade only Yes
Open By appointment

Any Amount of Books (PBFA, ABA, ILAB)
Contact Nigel Burwood
56 Charing Cross Road, London, WC2H 0QA
020 7836 3597 020 7240 1769
charingx@anyamountofbooks.com
www.anyamountofbooks.com
Est. 1975 *Stock size* Large
Stock Antiquarian, rare, second-hand books
Open Mon–Sat 10.30am–9.30pm Sun 11.30am–8.30pm
Fairs PBFA Russell Hotel, Olympia
Services Shipping, appraisals, book hire

The Apple Market
Contact Kate Lockyer
Covent Garden Market, London, WC2E 8RF
020 7836 9136
www.coventgardenmarket.co.uk
Est. 1980 *Stock size* Small
No. of dealers 40
Stock 40 traders use the traditional wrought iron stalls of the original Covent Garden, jewellery, china, small collectable items
Open Mon 10am–6pm

Argenteus Ltd (LAPADA)
Contact Mr M Feldman
Vault 2, The London Silver Vaults, 53 Chancery Lane, London, WC2A 1QS
020 7831 3637 020 7430 0126
Est. 1991 *Stock size* Medium
Stock Antique silver, Sheffield plate, flatware
Open Mon–Fri 9am–5.30pm Sat 9am–1pm

A H Baldwin and Son (BADA, IAPN, BNTA)
Contact Tim Wilkes
11 Adelphi Terrace, London, WC2N 6BJ
020 7930 6879 020 7930 9450
coins@baldwin.sh
www.baldwin.sh
Est. 1872
Stock Coins, commemorative medals, numismatic books
Open Mon–Fri 9am–5pm
Services Valuations

Malcolm Bord
Contact Mr M Bord
16 Charing Cross Road, London, WC2H 0HR
020 7836 0631 020 7240 1920
Est. 1970 *Stock size* Large
Stock Worldwide old silver and bronze coins
Open Mon–Sat 10.30am–5.30pm
Services Valuations

Charing Cross Markets
Contact Rodney Bolwell
1 Embankment Place, London, WC2N 6NN
01483 281771 01483 281771
rodney@chicane.fsbusiness.co.uk
Est. 1974 *Stock size* Large
No. of dealers 35
Stock Stamps, postcards, coins
Open Sat 7.30am–3pm

Coins and Bullion (BNTA, ANA)
Contact Mr P Cohen
20 Cecil Court, London, WC2N 4HE
020 7379 0615
Est. 1977
Stock British coins from 1500, world coins
Open Mon–Fri 10.30am–5.30pm Sat noon–5pm
Services Valuations

Paul Daniel (LSVA)
Contact Paul Daniel
51 & 68 The London Silver Vaults, Chancery Lane, London, WC2A 1QS
020 7430 1327 020 7430 1327
07831 338461
paveldaniel@aol.com
Est. 1979 *Stock size* Medium
Stock Commercial English and Continental silver
Open Mon–Fri 10am–4pm
Services Valuations, restoration

Bryan Douglas (LAPADA)
Contact Mr B Douglas
12 & 14 The London Silver Vaults, Chancery Lane, London, WC2A 1QS
020 7242 7073 020 7242 7073
sales@bryandouglas.co.uk
www.bryandouglas.co.uk
Est. 1971 *Stock size* Large
Stock Antique, vintage, modern silver, silver plate, old Sheffield plate
Open Mon–Fri 9.30am–5pm Sat 9.30am–1pm
Services Valuations

Eat My Handbag Bitch
Contact George or Georgina Enoch
37 Drury Lane, Covent Garden, London, WC2B 5RR
020 7836 0830 020 7836 0890
gallery@eatmyhandbagbitch.co.uk
www.eatmyhandbagbitch.co.uk
Est. 1998 *Stock size* Large
Stock Design of the Modern movements, 1840–1985, rare furniture, decorative items, ceramics, glass, art
Open Mon–Sat 11am–6pm or by appointment
Fairs Olympia Fine Art (Spring)
Services Valuations, interior design, shipping

R Feldman Ltd Antique Silver (LAPADA)
Contact Mr R Feldman
4 & 6 The London Silver Vaults, 53 Chancery Lane, London, WC2A 1QS
020 7405 6111 020 7430 0126
rfeldman@rfeldman.co.uk
www.rfeldman.co.uk
Est. 1954 *Stock size* Large
Stock Antique Victorian silver, old Sheffield plate
Open Mon–Fri 9am–5.30pm Sat 9am–1pm
Services Valuations, repairs

I Franks (LAPADA)
Contact Eric Franks
The Vaults, 9–11 The London Silver Vaults, Chancery Lane, London, WC2A 1QS
020 7242 4035 020 7242 4035
sales@ifranks.com
www.ifranks.com
Est. 1958 *Stock size* Large
Stock Silver
Open Mon–Fri 9.30am–5pm Sat 10am–1pm

Fraser's Autographs (UACC)
Contact Kerry Watson
399 The Strand, London, WC2R 0LX

☎ 020 7557 4404 Ⓕ 020 7836 7342
Ⓔ sales@frasersautographs.co.uk
Ⓦ www.frasersautographs.com
Est. 1978 *Stock size* Large
Stock Signed photos, letters, documents, stage and film costumes and props, signed guitars, sports equipment
Open Mon–Sat 9.30am–5.30pm
Fairs Stanley Gibbons Fairs
Services Valuations, want list, bi-monthly postal Internet autograph auction, lifetime authenticity guarantee

Stanley Gibbons Auctions Ltd (PTS, ASDA)
Contact Mr Colin Avery
✉ **399 Strand, London, WC2R 0LX**
☎ 020 7836 8444 Ⓕ 020 7836 7342
Ⓔ auctions@stanleygibbons.co.uk
Ⓦ www.stanleygibbons.com/auction
Est. 1856
Open Mon–Fri 9am–5pm
Sales 6 Postbid sales per year, 6 Collections & Ranges sales, occasional Web-only sales, viewing for all sales by appointment
Frequency Every 4–6 weeks
Catalogues Yes

Gillian Gould Antiques
Contact Gill Gould
✉ **Ocean Leisure, 11–14 Northumberland Avenue, London, WC2N 5AQ** Ⓟ
☎ 020 7419 0500
Ⓜ 07831 150060
Ⓔ gillgould@dealwith.com
Est. 1989 *Stock size* Small
Stock Scientific, marine, general gifts
Open Mon–Fri 9.30am–6.30pm closed Wed Sat 9.30am–5.30pm
Services Valuations, restoration

Anthony Green Antiques (NAWCC)
Contact Anthony Green
✉ **Vault 54, The London Silver Vaults, Chancery Lane, London, WC2A 1QS** Ⓟ
☎ 0207 430 0038 Ⓕ 0207 430 0046
Ⓜ 07900 681469
Ⓔ vintagewatches@hotmail.com
Ⓦ www.anthonygreen.com
Est. 1985 *Stock size* Large
Stock Vintage wristwatches and antique pocket watches
Open Mon–Fri 10am–5pm Sat 11am–5pm

Grosvenor Prints
Contact Ms McDiarmid
✉ **28 Shelton Street, London, WC2H 9JE** Ⓟ
☎ 020 7836 1979 Ⓕ 020 7379 6695
Ⓔ grosvenorprints@btinternet.com
Ⓦ www.grosvenorprints.com
Est. 1976 *Stock size* Large
Stock Topographical, sporting, dogs, portraits, decorative prints
Open Mon–Fri 10am–6pm Sat 11am–4pm
Fairs ABA Olympia, London

Hamiltons
Contact Mr M Hamilton
✉ **25 The London Silver Vaults, Chancery Lane, London, WC2A 1QS** Ⓟ
☎ 020 7831 7030 Ⓕ 020 7831 5483
Stock size Large
Stock Antique silver, flatware services a speciality
Open Mon–Fri 9.30am–5.30pm Sat 9.30am–1pm

P J Hilton Books
Contact Mr P Hilton
✉ **12 Cecil Court, London, WC2N 4HE** Ⓟ
☎ 020 7379 9825
Ⓔ paul.hilton@rarebook.globalnet.co.uk
Ⓦ www.rarebookweb.com
Est. 1986 *Stock size* Medium
Stock Antiquarian, second-hand, rare books, pre-1700 a speciality
Open Mon–Fri 10.30am–6pm Sat 10.30am–5pm
Services Book search

Raymond D Holdich (OMRS)
Contact Mr R Holdich
✉ **7 Whitcomb Street, London, WC2H 7HA** Ⓟ
☎ 020 7930 1979 Ⓕ 020 7930 1152
Ⓜ 07774 133493
Ⓔ rdhmedals@aol.com
Ⓦ www.rdhmedals.com
Est. 1969 *Stock size* Large
Stock Cap badges, militaria including medals, orders, decorations
Open Mon–Fri 9.30am–3.30pm
Services Valuations, restoration

Stephen Kalms Antiques (LAPADA)
Contact Mr S Kalms
✉ **The London Silver Vaults, Chancery Lane, London, WC2A 1QS** Ⓟ
☎ 020 7430 1254 Ⓕ 020 7405 6206
Ⓔ stephen@kalms.freeserve.co.uk
Est. 1990 *Stock size* Large
Stock Victorian–Edwardian silver, silver plate, decorative items
Open Mon–Fri 9am–5.30pm Sat 9am–1pm
Fairs Olympia (June)
Services Valuations, restoration, repairs

Koopman/Rare Art (London) Ltd (BADA, BACA Award Winner 2004)
Contact Mr L Smith
✉ **The London Silver Vaults, Chancery Lane, London, WC2A 1QS** Ⓟ
☎ 020 7242 7624 Ⓕ 020 7831 0221
Ⓔ rareart@compuserve.com
Ⓦ www.rareartlondon.com
Est. 1984 *Stock size* Large
Stock Antique silver
Open Mon–Fri 9am–5.30pm Sat 10am–1pm
Fairs Olympia (June), IFAADS, New York

Langfords (LAPADA)
Contact Adam Langford
✉ **8 & 10 The London Silver Vaults, 53–64 Chancery Lane, London, WC2A 1QS** Ⓟ
☎ 020 7242 5506 Ⓕ 020 7405 0431
Ⓔ vault@longfords.com
Ⓦ www.langfords.com
Est. 1940 *Stock size* Medium
Stock Silver
Open Mon–Fri 9am–5.30pm Sat 9am–1pm
Services Valuations, restoration, commissions, buys silver

Nat Leslie Ltd
Contact Mr M Hyams
✉ **21 The London Silver Vaults, 53 Chancery Lane, London, WC2A 1QS** Ⓟ
☎ 020 7242 4787
Est. 1947 *Stock size* Large
Stock Modern, antique, contemporary silverware, silver plate, flatware a speciality
Open Mon–Fri 9.30am–4.30pm

Linden & Co (Antiques) Ltd
Contact Mr S or Mr H Linden
✉ **Vault 7, London Silver Vaults, Chancery Lane, London, WC2A 1QS** Ⓟ
☎ 020 7242 4863 Ⓕ 020 7405 9946

Ⓔ lindenandco@aol.com
Ⓦ www.lindenantiquessilver.co.uk
Est. 1960 *Stock size* Medium
Stock Silver, silver plate
Open Mon–Fri 10am–5.30pm
Services Engraving

C and T Mammon (LSVA)
Contact Mr C Mammon
✉ **55 & 64 The London Silver Vaults, Chancery Lane, London, WC2A 1QT** Ⓟ
☎ 020 7405 2397 Ⓕ 020 7405 4900
Ⓜ 07785 325642
Ⓔ claudemammon@btinternet.com
Ⓦ www.candtmammon.com
Est. 1969 *Stock size* Large
Stock Decorative silver, silver-plate items
Open Mon–Fri 9am–5.30pm or by appointment
Services Valuations

E W Marchpane Ltd (ABA, PBFA)
Contact K Fuller
✉ **16 Cecil Court, Charing Cross Road, London, WC2N 4HE** Ⓟ
☎ 020 7836 8661 Ⓕ 020 7497 0567
Ⓔ k_fuller@btclick.com
Est. 1989 *Stock size* Medium
Stock Antiquarian, rare, second-hand books, children's and illustrated books a speciality
Open Mon–Sat 10.30am–6pm

Arthur Middleton Ltd (SIS)
Contact Mr A Middleton or Miss Morgan
✉ **12 New Row, London, WC2N 4LF** Ⓟ
☎ 020 7836 7042 Ⓕ 020 7497 2486
Ⓔ arthur@antique-globes.com
Ⓦ www.antique-globes.com
Est. 1978 *Stock size* Medium
Stock Marine and scientific instruments, globes
Open Mon–Fri 10am–6pm
Services Valuations

Colin Narbeth and Son (IBNS)
Contact Mr Simon Narbeth
✉ **20 Cecil Court, London, WC2N 4HE**
☎ 020 7379 6975 Ⓕ 017 2 811244
Ⓔ colin.narbeth@btinternet.com
Ⓦ www.colin-narbeth.com
Est. 1982 *Stock size* Large
Stock Banknotes, bonds, shares of all countries and periods
Open Mon Sat 10.30am–4pm Tues–Fri 10am–5pm
Fairs Bonnington Paper Money Fair, IBNS (Oct)

Jeffrey Neal & Lynn Bloom (LAPADA)
Contact Jeffrey Neal or Lynn Bloom
✉ **Vault 27, The London Silver Vaults, Chancery Lane, London, WC2A 1QS** Ⓟ
☎ 020 7242 6189 Ⓕ 020 8421 8848
Ⓜ 07768 533055
Ⓔ sales@bloomvault.com
Ⓦ www.bloomvault.com
Est. 1923 *Stock size* Large
Stock Silver, centrepieces, napkins, cutlery, miniature toys, collectables
Open Mon–Fri 10am–5pm Sat 10am–1pm
Fairs NEC
Services Valuations, restoration

Notions Antiquaria
Contact T Alena Brett
✉ **24 Cecil Court, Charing Cross Road, London, WC2N 4HE**
☎ 020 7836 8222
Est. 1989 *Stock size* Medium
Stock Antiquarian books, maps, prints, early documents
Open By appointment

Percy's Ltd (LAPADA)
Contact Mr D Simons
✉ **16 The London Silver Vaults, Chancery Lane, London, WC2A 1QS** Ⓟ
☎ 020 7242 3618 Ⓕ 020 7831 6541
Ⓔ sales@percys-silver.com
Ⓦ www.percys-silver.com
Est. 1935 *Stock size* Large
Stock 18th–19thC decorative silver and plate
Open Mon–Fri 9.30am–5pm Sat 10am–1pm
Fairs Olympia (June, Nov)
Services Valuations, repairs

Henry Pordes Books Ltd
Contact Mr G Della-Ragione
✉ **58–60 Charing Cross Road, London, WC2H 0BB**
☎ 020 7836 9031 Ⓕ 020 7240 4232
Ⓔ henrypordes@clara.net
Ⓦ www.henrypordes.clara.net
Est. 1983 *Stock size* Medium
Stock Remainders, second-hand, antiquarian books, art, literature, film, theatre, music Judaica a speciality
Open Mon–Sat 10am–7pm

Quinto Bookshop
Contact Mrs Rebecca De Miguel
✉ **48a Charing Cross Road, London, WC2H 0BB** Ⓟ
☎ 020 7379 7669
Est. 1979 *Stock size* Medium
Stock General second-hand, antiquarian books
Open Mon–Sat 9am–9pm Sun noon–7pm

Bertram Rota Ltd (ABA, ILAB)
Contact Mr J Rota
✉ **1st Floor, 31 Long Acre, London, WC2E 9LT** Ⓟ
☎ 020 7836 0723 Ⓕ 020 7497 9058
Ⓔ bertramrota@compuserve.com
Ⓦ www.bertramrota.co.uk
Est. 1923 *Stock size* Small
Stock Antiquarian, rare, second-hand books, 1890–present day first editions of English and American literature
Open Mon–Fri 9.30am–5.30pm
Services Valuations, book search, catalogues (4–6 a year)

Silstar Antiques Ltd
Contact Mr B Stern
✉ **29 The London Silver Vaults, Chancery Lane, London, WC2A 1QS** Ⓟ
☎ 020 7242 6740 Ⓕ 020 7430 1745
Ⓔ antique@silstar.fsnet.co.uk
Est. 1955 *Stock size* Large
Stock Antique and modern silver of all descriptions
Open Mon–Fri 10am–5pm

Jack Simons Antiques Ltd (LAPADA)
Contact Mr J Simons
✉ **16 The London Silver Vaults, Chancery Lane, London, WC2A 1QS** Ⓟ
☎ 020 7242 3221 Ⓕ 020 7831 6541
Est. 1955 *Stock size* Large
Stock Fine antique English and Continental silver, objets d'art
Open Mon–Fri 9.30am–5pm Sat 10am–1pm
Services Valuations, restoration

Star Signings
Contact John or Mark
✉ **8 Upper St Martin's Lane,**

Covent Garden, London,
WC2H 9DL
☎ 020 7836 3013
Ⓔ starsignings@btconnect.com
Est. 1998 *Stock size* Large
Stock Signed memorabilia, photographs, programmes, shirts, sporting, films, music
Open Mon–Sat 11am–6pm
Services Valuations

⊞ S & J Stodel (BADA)
Contact Mr S Stodel
✉ **24 The London Silver Vaults, Chancery Lane, London, WC2A 1QS** Ⓟ
☎ 020 7405 7009 Ⓕ 020 7242 6366
Ⓔ stodel@msn.com
Ⓦ www.chinesesilver.com
Est. 1973
Stock Chinese export silver, Art Deco silver, antique silver flatware
Open Mon–Fri 9.30am–5.30pm Sat 9.30am–1pm
Fairs Olympia (June)

⊞ Storeys Ltd
Contact T Kingswood
✉ **3 Cecil Court, Charing Cross, London, WC2N 4EZ**
☎ 020 7836 3777 Ⓕ 020 7836 3788
Ⓔ storeysltd@btinternet.com
Est. 1984 *Stock size* Large
Stock Antiquarian prints
Open Mon–Sat 10am–6pm

⊞ Tindley & Chapman
Contact James Tindley
✉ **4 Cecil Court, London, WC2N 4HE** Ⓟ
☎ 020 7240 2161 Ⓕ 020 7379 1062
Est. 1972 *Stock size* Medium
Stock Antiquarian, second-hand, 20thC first editions, literature, novels, poetry
Open Mon–Fri 10am–5.30pm Sat 11am–4pm
Services Valuations

⊞ Tom Tom
Contact Gary Mitchell
✉ **42 New Compton Street, London, WC2H 8DA** Ⓟ
☎ 020 7240 7909 Ⓕ 020 7240 7909
Ⓔ mail@tomtom.biz
Ⓦ www.tomtom.biz
Est. 1993 *Stock size* Large
Stock Post-war designer furniture and technology, classics by Eames, Jacobsen, Saarinen
Open Tues–Fri noon–7pm Sat 11am–6pm or by appointment
Services Valuations

⊞ Travis & Emery Music Bookshop (ABA, PBFA)
Contact Mr Coleman
✉ **17 Cecil Court, off Charing Cross Road, London, WC2N 4EZ**
☎ 020 7240 2129 Ⓕ 020 7497 0790
Ⓔ maenq@travis-and-emery.com
Est. 1960 *Stock size* Medium
Stock Antiquarian sheet music, prints, ephemera, books on music
Open Mon–Sat 11am–6pm Sun noon–4pm or by appointment
Services Valuations

⊞ William Walter Antiques Ltd (BADA, LAPADA)
Contact Miss E Simpson
✉ **3 The London Silver Vaults, Chancery Lane, London, WC2A 1QS** Ⓟ
☎ 020 7242 3248 Ⓕ 020 7404 1280
Ⓔ enq@wwantiques.prestel.co.uk
Ⓦ www.williamwalter.co.uk
Est. 1949 *Stock size* Large
Stock Georgian silver, decorative silver, flatware etc
Open Mon–Fri 9.30am–5.30pm Sat 9.30am–1pm
Services Valuations, repairs

⊞ Watkins Books Ltd
Contact Jeremy Cranswick or Ricky James
✉ **19 Cecil Court, London, WC2N 4EZ** Ⓟ
☎ 020 7836 2182
Ⓔ service@watkinsbooks.com
Ⓦ www.watkinsbooks.com
Est. 1894 *Stock size* Large
Stock Antiquarian books specializing in mystical, occult, Eastern religions
Open Mon–Fri 10am–8pm Sat 10.30am–6pm
Services Shipping

⊞ Peter K Weiss
Contact Mr P Weiss
✉ **18 The London Silver Vaults, Chancery Lane, London, WC2A 8QS** Ⓟ
☎ 020 7242 8100
Ⓔ peterweiss@mymailstation.com
Est. 1958 *Stock size* Large
Stock Antique clocks, watches, objets d'art
Open Mon–Fri 10am–4pm Sat 10am–1pm
Services Valuations, restoration

⊞ Nigel Williams Rare Books (PBFA, ABA)
Contact Mr Nigel Williams
✉ **25 Cecil Court, Charing Cross Road, London, WC2N 4EZ** Ⓟ
☎ 020 7836 7757 Ⓕ 020 7379 5918
Ⓔ sales@nigelwilliams.com
Ⓦ www.nigelwilliams.com
Est. 1989 *Stock size* Medium
Stock Antiquarian, rare, second-hand books, collectable children's, illustrated, 19th–20thC first editions
Open Mon–Sat 10am–6pm
Fairs Olympia, Russell Hotel
Services Monthly catalogue

⊞ The Witch Ball
Contact Rosslyn Glassman
✉ **2 Cecil Court, London, WC2N 4HE**
☎ 020 7836 2922 Ⓕ 020 7836 2922
Ⓔ thewitchball@btinternet.com
Ⓦ www.thewitchball.co.uk
Est. 1967 *Stock size* Medium
Stock Antique prints, posters of the performing arts
Open Mon–Sat 10.30am–7pm

MIDDLESEX

ASHFORD

⊞ Magnet Antiques
Contact Mr Ted Pullen
✉ **23 Woodthorpe Road, Ashford, Middlesex, TW15 2RP** Ⓟ
☎ 01784 253107
Ⓦ www.magnetantiques.co.uk
Est. 1989 *Stock size* Medium
Stock Edwardian, Victorian, reproduction furniture, Doulton, Beswick, Kevin Francis ceramics, Sally Tuffin
Open Mon–Sat 10am–5pm

EASTCOTE

⊞ Eastcote Bookshop (PBFA)
Contact Mrs E May
✉ **156–160 Field End Road, Eastcote, Middlesex, HA5 1RH** Ⓟ
☎ 020 8866 9888 Ⓕ 020 8985 9383
Est. 1994 *Stock size* Large
Stock Antiquarian, rare, second-hand books
Open Tues Wed noon–4pm Fri Sat 10.30am–5pm
Fairs Russell Hotel

ENFIELD

Designer Classics
Contact Mr L Wilkin
70 Goat Lane, Enfield, Middlesex, EN1 4UB
020 8366 6006 F 020 8366 8786
designerclassics@btconnect.com
www.designerclassic.co.uk
Est. 1998 *Stock size* Large
Stock 1950s–present day classics by famous designers, Bellini, Herman Miller, Verner Panton, computers, hi-fi, radios etc
Open By appointment or mail order via Internet

Gallerie Veronique
Contact Ms V Aslangul
66 Chase Side, Enfield, Middlesex, EN2 6NJ P
020 8342 1005 F 020 8342 1005
M 07770 410041
antiques@gallerieveronique.co.uk
Est. 1993 *Stock size* Large
Stock Victorian, Edwardian, 1970s furniture
Open Mon–Fri 10am–3pm Sat 10am–5pm closed Wed
Services Restoration, upholstery

Griffin Antiques
Contact Mr J Gardner
6 Chase Side, Enfield, Middlesex, EN2 6NF P
020 8366 5959
Est. 1970 *Stock size* Medium
Stock Wide range of antiques, porcelain, silver, metalware, scales, weights, measures, candlesticks
Open Mon–Fri 10.30am–6pm Sat 4.30am–6pm
Fairs Newark
Services Valuations

Period Style Lighting (Lighting Association)
Contact Gillian Day
8–9 East Lodge Lane, Botany Bay, Enfield, Middlesex, EN2 8AS
020 8363 9789
Est. 1991 *Stock size* Large
Stock Antique, period lighting, chandeliers
Open Tues–Sun 10am–5pm
Services Valuations, restoration

HAREFIELD

David Ansell (BHI, BAFRA)
Contact David Ansell
48 Dellside, Harefield, Middlesex, UB9 6AX P
01895 824648
M 07812 841993
davidansell@globalnet.co.uk
Est. 1990 *Stock size* Medium
Stock Clocks, photographic items
Open Mon–Sun 8.30am–5.30pm or by appointment
Fairs NEC, Newark
Services Restoration

HARROW

The Collectors Shop (PTA, ESoc)
Contact Mr I Crawford
16 Village Way East, Rayners Lane, Harrow, Middlesex, HA2 7LU P
020 8866 1053
Est. 1992 *Stock size* Large
Stock Postcards, cigarette cards, illustrated sheet music, toys, sporting items, records, illustrated song sheets, film memorabilia, militaria, china, collectables
Open Mon–Sat 9.30am–4.30pm closed Wed
Services Valuations

HATCH END

A & C Antiques & Collectables
Contact Mrs Chris Stevens
266–268 Uxbridge Road, Hatch End, Middlesex, HA5 4HS P
020 8421 1653
Est. 1994 *Stock size* Large
No. of dealers 26
Stock Doulton, Art Deco, ceramics, small furniture, collectables
Open Mon–Sat 10am–5.30pm Sun 11.30am–4pm
Services Ceramic repairs

ISLEWORTH

Antique Traders
Contact Mr T Keane
156 London Road, Isleworth, Middlesex, TW7 5BG P
020 8847 1020
Est. 1997 *Stock size* Large
Stock Wide range of antiques, furniture, porcelain, glass, pictures, mirrors
Open Mon–Sat 10.30am–6pm
Services Valuations

LALEHAM

Laleham Antiques
Contact Mrs H Potter
23 Shepperton Road, Laleham, Middlesex, TW18 1SE P
01784 450353
Est. 1973 *Stock size* Medium
Stock Antique and reproduction furniture, silver, plated items, pictures, brass, copper, jewellery, collectables
Open Mon Tues Thurs Fri 11am–4pm

RUISLIP

Alberts of Kensington
Contact Mr J A Wooster
PO Box 147, Ruislip, Middlesex, HA4 9WD
020 8869 9292 F 020 8869 9393
Est. 1964
Open Tues–Fri 10am–6pm Sat 10am–4pm postal only
Sales 10–12 postal auctions of cigarette cards and ephemera per year
Catalogues Yes

The Old Trinket Box
Contact Eilleen Cameron
1b High Street, Ruislip, Middlesex, HA4 7AU P
01895 675658
Est. 1995 *Stock size* Medium
No. of dealers 10
Stock Wide range of collectables, antiques
Open Mon–Sat 10am–5pm Sun 11am–4pm

STAINES

K W Dunster Antiques
Contact Mr K W Dunster
23 Church Street, Staines, Middlesex, TW18 4EN P
01784 453297 F 01784 483146
M 07831 649626
Est. 1973 *Stock size* Medium

Stock Brass, furniture, jewellery, marine items
Open Mon–Sat 9am–4pm
Services Valuations, house clearance

Staines Antiques
Contact Mr D Smith
145–147 Kingston Road, Staines, Middlesex, TW18 1PD
01784 461306 F 01784 461306
Est. 1978 *Stock size* Large
Stock Furniture, ceramics
Open Mon–Sat 9am–5.30pm
Services Valuations, restoration

TEDDINGTON

Waldegrave Antiques
Contact Mrs J Murray
197 Waldegrave Road, Teddington, Middlesex, TW11 8LX
020 8404 0162
M 07946 506145
Est. 1997 *Stock size* Large
Stock Wide selection of antiques, furniture, silver, porcelain, glass
Open Mon–Sat 10.30am–5.30pm
Fairs Kempton Park

TWICKENHAM

Antique Interiors
Contact Mr A Mundy
93 Crown Road, Twickenham, Middlesex, TW1 3EX
020 8607 9853
Est. 1995 *Stock size* Medium
Stock English, French and 19thC mahogany and old pine furniture, other quality English items, garden items
Open Tues–Sat 10am–5.30pm
Services Restoration, upholstery

Cheyne Galleries
Contact Mrs C Cox
8 Crown Road, Twickenham, Middlesex, TW1 3EE
020 8892 6932
Est. 1977 *Stock size* Medium
Stock Wide range of antique and second-hand items, collectables
Open Tues–Sat 10am–6pm
Services Valuations, house clearance

Anthony C Hall (ABA, PBFA)
Contact Mr A C Hall
30 Staines Road, Twickenham, Middlesex, TW2 5AH
020 8898 2638 F 020 8893 8855
E achallbooks@internet.co.uk
W www.hallbooks.co.uk
Est. 1966 *Stock size* Large
Stock Out-of-print and rare books, Russian and eastern European topics a speciality, mail order
Open Mon–Fri 9am–5.30pm closed Wed
Fairs Richmond Book Fair

John Ives (PBFA)
Contact Mr J Ives
5 Normanhurst Drive, Twickenham, Middlesex, TW1 1NA
020 8892 6265 F 020 8744 3944
E jives@btconnect.com
W www.ukbookworld.com/members/johnives
Est. 1979
Stock Reference books on antiques and collecting, 1,000s of titles in stock including scarce items
Open By appointment
Services Mail order only, catalogue

David Morley Antiques
Contact Mr D Morley
371 Richmond Road, Twickenham, Middlesex, TW1 2EF
020 8892 2986
Est. 1968 *Stock size* Large
Stock Wide range of antiques including small furniture, silver, porcelain, silver plate, telephones, old toys
Open Mon–Sat 10am–1pm 2–5pm closed Wed
Services Valuations

The Twickenham Antiques Warehouse
Contact Mr A Clubb
80 Colne Road, Twickenham, Middlesex, TW2 6QE
020 8894 5555
M 07973 132847
E and.clubb@aol.com
Est. 1984 *Stock size* Large
Stock English and Continental furniture, 1700–1930s, decorative items
Open Mon–Sat 9.30am–5pm
Services Valuations, restoration

UXBRIDGE

Antiques Warehouse & Restoration
Contact Mr M Allenby
34 Rockingham Road, Uxbridge, Middlesex, UB8 2TZ
01895 256963
Est. 1979 *Stock size* Large
Stock 1800–1950 furniture, collectables
Open Mon–Sat 10am–5pm
Services Restoration

Anthony Smith
Contact Mr Anthony Smith
45 Windsor Street, Uxbridge, Middlesex, UB8 1AB
01895 814442 F 01895 253756
E smith45@supanet.com
Est. 1997 *Stock size* Large
Stock Georgian–Edwardian furniture
Open Mon–Sat 10am–6pm Sun 11am-4pm
Services Restoration, upholstery

WEST RUISLIP

A Bainbridge & Co
Contact Mr P Bainbridge
The Auction House, Ickenham Road, West Ruislip, Middlesex, HA4 7DL
01895 621991 F 01895 623621
Est. 1979
Open Mon–Fri 9am–5pm
Sales Antiques and general effects Thurs 11am, viewing Wed 1–7pm Thurs from 9.30am
Frequency Monthly. Please call to confirm
Catalogues Yes

WRAYSBURY

Wyrardisbury Antiques
Contact Mr C Tuffs
23 High Street, Wraysbury, Staines, Middlesex, TW19 5DA
01784 483225 F 01784 483225
Est. 1978 *Stock size* Medium
Stock All types, ages of clocks up to Edwardian, small furniture, barometers
Open Tues–Sat 10am–5pm
Services Valuations, repairs

BERKSHIRE

ALDERMASTON

Village Antiques Aldermaston
Contact Mrs Vivian Green
The Old Dispensary, The Street, Aldermaston, Reading, Berkshire, RG7 4LW P
☎ 0118 971 2370
Est. 1997 *Stock size* Large
Stock Clocks, architectural antiques, furniture, china, glass, silver, garden items
Open Tues–Sun 10am–5.30pm

ASCOT

Edwards and Elliott
Contact Mr Francis Ogley
32 High Street, Ascot, Berkshire, SL5 7HG P
☎ 01344 872588 F 01344 624700
M 07885 333627
E edwards2@netcomuk.co.uk
W www.edwardsandelliott.co.uk
Est. 1994
Open Mon–Fri 9am–5.30pm Sat 10am–4pm Sun 10am–2pm
Sales Wed Thurs every 5–6 weeks antiques and modern, viewing day of sale 9am–noon. Held at Silver Ring Grandstand, Ascot Racecourse
Frequency Every 5–6 weeks
Catalogues Yes

Melnick House Antiques (ESoc)
Contact Mrs J Collins
306 Kings Road, Sunninghill, Ascot, Berkshire, SL5 8TS P
☎ 01344 628383 F 01344 291800
E antiquarian@melnick-house.demon.co.uk
Est. 1972 *Stock size* Large
Stock Antique maps, prints, decorative antiques
Open Mon–Sat 10am–5pm
Services Restoration, free postage worldwide

ASHMORE GREEN

Law Fine Art Ltd
Contact Mr Mark Law
Ash Cottage, Ashmore Green Road, Ashmore Green, Berkshire, RG18 9ER P
☎ 01635 860033 F 01635 860036
E info@lawfineart.co.uk
W www.lawfineart.co.uk
Est. 2000
Open Mon–Fri 9am–5.30pm
Sales Eight sales a year including five specialist ceramics and glass sales
Frequency Monthly
Catalogues Yes

CAVERSHAM

Amber Antiques
Contact Clair Hughes
12 Bridge Street, Caversham, Berkshire, RG4 8AA
☎ 01189 541394 F 01189 499234
M 07977 499234
W www.amberantiques.co.uk
Est. 1995 *Stock size* Medium
Stock French antiques, decorative items
Open Mon–Sat 10.30am–5.30pm
Services Restoration, in-house traditional upholstery

D Card
Contact D Card
1a Chester Street, Caversham, Reading, Berkshire, RG4 8JH P
☎ 01189 470777 F 01189 470777
E d.card@ntlworld.com
Est. 1971 *Stock size* Small
Stock Longcase, carriage, table clocks and music boxes
Open Mon–Fri 9am–5pm appointment preferred
Services Valuations, restoration

The Clock Workshop (LAPADA, TVADA, BHI)
Contact Mr J Yealland
17 Prospect Street, Caversham, Reading, Berkshire, RG4 8JB P
☎ 01189 470741
E theclockworkshop@hotmail.com
W www.lapada.co.uk
Est. 1981 *Stock size* Medium
Stock English clocks, French carriage, mantel clocks, barometers
Open Mon–Fri 9.30am–5.30pm

Sat 10am–1pm
Fairs Olympia, LAPADA, TVADA
Services Valuations, restoration

COOKHAM

Cookham Antiques
Contact Mr G Wallis
35 Station Parade, Cookham, Maidenhead, Berkshire, SL6 9BR
01628 523224
07778 020536
Est. 1989 *Stock size* Large
Stock Furniture, decorative items, architectural
Open Mon–Sat 10am–5pm Sun 11am–5pm
Services Valuations

DONNINGTON

Dreweatt Neate (SOFAA, ARVA, BACA Award Winner 2004)
Contact Clive Stewart-Lockhart
Donnington Priory, Donnington, Newbury, Berkshire, RG14 2JE
01635 553553 01635 553599
donnington@dnfa.com
www.dnfa.com
Est. 1759
Open Mon–Fri 9.30am–6pm Sat 9am–12.30pm
Sales General sales fortnightly Tues at 10am, antiques sales every six weeks Wed 10am, viewing Sat prior 9am–12.30pm Mon 9.30am–7pm and 9.30am–4pm for Wed sales Catalogues available on website
Catalogues Yes

ETON

Art and Antiques (Eton Traders)
Contact Mrs V Rand
69 High Street, Eton, Windsor, Berkshire, SL4 6AA
01753 855727
07903 921168
Est. 1982 *Stock size* Large
Stock Furniture, china, brass, silver plate, jewellery, collectors' items
Open Mon–Fri 10.30am–5.30pm Sat 10.30am–6pm Sun 2.30–6pm

Roger Barnett
Contact Roger Barnett
91 High Street, Eton, Windsor, Berkshire, SL4 6AF
01753 867785
Est. 1976 *Stock size* Medium
Stock Brown furniture, brass, longcase clocks
Open Variable

Eton Antiques
Contact Mr M Procter
80 High Street, Eton, Windsor, Berkshire, SL4 6AF
01753 860752 01753 818222
www.etonantiques.com
Est. 1969 *Stock size* Large
Stock 18th–19thC English furniture
Open Mon–Sat 10am–5.30pm
Services Valuations, restoration, shipping

Marcelline Herald Antiques (LAPADA, TVADA)
Contact Marcelline Herald
41 High Street, Eton, Windsor, Berkshire, SL4 6BD
01753 833924
07774 607443
www.tvada.co.uk
Est. 1998 *Stock size* Medium
Stock 17thC shop in historic Eton High Street selling18th–19thC furniture, mirrors and decorative items
Open Tues–Sat 10am–5pm
Fairs Decorative Fair Battersea, TVADA
Services Valuations

Peter J Martin and Son (TVADA, LAPADA)
Contact Mr P Martin
40 High Street, Eton, Windsor, Berkshire, SL4 6BD
01753 864901
07850 975889
pjmartin.antiques@btopenworld.com
www.pjmartin-antiques.co.uk
Est. 1967 *Stock size* Large
Stock 18th–20thC furniture, copper, brass, mirrors
Open Mon–Fri 9am–5pm closed 1–2pm Sat 10am–1pm or by appointment
Services Restoration

Mostly Boxes
Contact Mr G Munday
93 High Street, Eton, Windsor, Berkshire, SL4 6AF
01753 858470 01753 857212
Est. 1982 *Stock size* Large
Stock Ivory, tortoiseshell, wooden decorative antique boxes
Open Mon–Sat 10am–6.30pm
Fairs K & M London

Studio 101
Contact Anthony Cove
101 High Street, Eton, Windsor, Berkshire, SL4 6AF
01753 863333
Est. 1959 *Stock size* Small
Stock General antiques
Open By appointment

Times Past Antiques (MBHI)
Contact Mr P Jackson
59 High Street, Eton, Windsor, Berkshire, SL4 6BL
01753 856392 01753 856392
07768 454444
phillipstimespast@aol.com
Est. 1974 *Stock size* Medium
Stock Clocks, barometers, small furniture
Open By appointment
Services Valuations, restoration

Turks Head Antiques
Contact Mrs A Baillie or Mr A Reeve
98 High Street, Eton, Windsor, Berkshire, SL4 6AF
01753 863939
Est. 1975 *Stock size* Medium
Stock Porcelain, silver, glass, pictures
Open Mon–Sat 10am–5pm
Services Restoration of porcelain, silver-plating

Windsor & Eton Antiques Centre
Contact Mrs Thomas
17 High Street, Eton, Windsor, Berkshire, SL4 6AX
01753 840412 01628 630041
Est. 2000 *Stock size* Medium
No. of dealers 22
Stock General antiques and collectables
Open Mon–Fri 10.30am–5pm Sun 1–5pm
Services Valuations

FIFIELD

Jan Hicks Antiques (TVADA, LAPADA)
Contact Jan Hicks
Fifield, Nera Windsor, Glouc, SL4
☎ 01488 683986 Ⓕ 01488 681222
Ⓜ 07770 230686
Ⓔ antiques@janhicks.com
Est. 1987 *Stock size* Large
Stock French and English country furniture, 18thC and earlier, oil paintings
Open By appointment
Fairs TVADA, Antiques & Audacity (Arundel Castle)

GORING-ON-THAMES

Barbara's Antiques and Bric-a-Brac
Contact Mrs M Bateman
Wheel Orchard, Station Road, Goring on Thames, Reading, Berkshire, RG8 9HB
☎ 01491 873032
Est. 1981 *Stock size* Large
Stock Furniture, linen, lace, jewellery, china, brass, silver, plate, railwayana
Open Mon–Sat 10am–1pm 2.15–5pm

HUNGERFORD

Beedham Antiques Ltd (BADA)
Contact Herbert or Paul Beedham
26 Charnham Street, Hungerford, Berkshire, RG17 0EJ
☎ 01488 684141 Ⓕ 01488 684050
Est. 1971 *Stock size* Medium
Stock 16th–17thC English and Continental oak furniture
Open Mon–Sat 11am–5pm or by appointment
Fairs Olympia June, Nov

Below Stairs of Hungerford
Contact Stewart Hofgartner
103 High Street, Hungerford, Berkshire, RG17 0NB
☎ 01488 682317 Ⓕ 01488 684294
Ⓔ hofgartner@belowstairs.co.uk
Ⓦ www.belowstairs.co.uk
Est. 1972 *Stock size* Large
Stock Collectables, furniture, taxidermy, garden items, kitchenware, lighting, interior fittings, no reproductions
Open Mon–Sun 10am–6pm
Services Valuations

Sir William Bentley Billiards
Contact Travers Mettleton
Standen Manor Farm, Hungerford, Berkshire, RG17 0RB
☎ 01488 681711 Ⓕ 01488 685197
Ⓦ www.billiards.co.uk
Est. 1976 *Stock size* Large
Stock Billiard tables, accessories, build contemporary and traditional billiard tables including convertible dining and billiard tables
Open Mon–Sun or by appointment
Fairs Daily Telegraph House and Garden, Ideal Homes
Services Valuations, restoration

Bowhouse Antiques
Contact Jo Preston
3–4 Faulkener Square, Charnham Street, Hungerford, Berkshire, RG17 0EP
☎ 01488 680826
Ⓜ 07710 921331
Est. 2000 *Stock size* Large
Stock 19thC decorative interiors
Open Mon–Sat 9.30am–5.30pm Sun 11am–4pm
Services Upholstery

Bridge House Antiques & Interiors
Contact Kate Pols
7 Bridge Street, Hungerford, Berkshire, RG17 0EH
☎ 01488 681999 Ⓕ 01488 681999
Ⓔ bridgehouse@kpols.fsnet.co.uk
Est. 1992 *Stock size* Large
Stock Antiques, decorative items for interiors
Open Tues–Sat 10am–5.30pm
Services Shipping

Barry Cotton Antiques
Contact Barry Cotton
Great Grooms Antique Centre, Riverside House, Charnham Street, Hungerford, Berkshire, RG17 0EP
☎ 020 8563 9899 Ⓕ 020 8563 9899
Ⓔ enquiries@barrycottonantiques.com
Ⓦ www.barrycottonantiques.com
Est. 1998 *Stock size* Medium
Stock 18th–19thC period furniture, associated items
Open Mon–Sat 9.30–5.30pm Sun 10am–4pm
Services Valuations

Countryside Books (PBFA)
Contact Mr Martin Smith
The Hungerford Antiques Centre, High Street, Hungerford, Berkshire, RG17 0NB
☎ 01264 773943
Est. 1980 *Stock size* Medium
Stock Antiquarian, rare, second-hand books
Open Mon–Fri 9.15am–5.30pm Sat 9.15am–6pm Sun 11am–5pm
Fairs PBFA fair, Russell Hotel

Franklin Antiques
Contact Mrs L Franklin
25 Charnham Street, Hungerford, Berkshire, RG17 0EJ
☎ 01488 682404 Ⓕ 01488 686069
Ⓔ antiques@lyndafranklin.com
Est. 1974 *Stock size* Large
Stock 18th–19thC Continental furniture
Open Mon–Sat 10am–5.30pm
Services Interior decoration and sourcing

Garden Art
Contact Mr Arnie Knowles
Barrs Yard, 1 Bath Road, Hungerford, Berkshire, RG17 0HE
☎ 01488 681881 Ⓕ 01488 681882
Ⓔ garden.art@dial.pipex.com
Est. 1976 *Stock size* Large
Stock Architectural antiques for the garden including gates, neo-classical statuary, bronze
Open Mon–Sat 10am–6pm Sun 11am–4pm or by appointment
Services Valuations, restoration, garden design

Great Grooms of Hungerford
Contact Mr J Podger
Riverside House, Charnham Street, Hungerford, Berkshire, RG17 0EP
☎ 01488 682314 Ⓕ 01488 686677
Ⓔ antiques@great-grooms.co.uk
Ⓦ www.great-grooms.co.uk
Est. 1998 *Stock size* Large

No. of dealers 65
Stock General antiques, furnishings, country furniture, porcelain, clocks, silver, rugs, glass, bronzes, lighting, pictures
Open Mon–Sat 9.30am–5.30pm Sun 10am–4pm
Services Valuations, restoration

Hungerford Arcade
Contact Trevor Butcher
26 High Street, Hungerford, Berkshire, RG17 0ER
01488 683701
Est. 1978 ***Stock size*** Large
No. of dealers 80
Stock General antiques and collectables
Open Mon–Sun 9.15am–5.30pm

Roger King Antiques
Contact Mrs A King
111 High Street, Hungerford, Berkshire, RG17 0NB
01488 682256
www.kingantiques.co.uk
Est. 1974 ***Stock size*** Large
Stock Furniture, George III–Edwardian
Open Mon–Sat 9.30am–5pm Sun 11am–5pm

M J M Antiques (Arms & Armour Society)
Contact Michael Mancey
13 Bridge Street, Hungerford, Berkshire, RG17 0EH
01488 684905 01488 684090
07774 479997
mike@oldguns.co.uk
www.oldguns.co.uk
Est. 1999 ***Stock size*** Medium
Stock Fine antique arms
Open Mon–Sat 10am–5pm or by appointment
Fairs Arms & armour fairs
Services Valuations

The Old Malthouse (BADA, CINOA)
Contact Mr or Mrs P Hunwick
15 Bridge Street, Hungerford, Berkshire, RG17 0EG
01488 682209 01488 682209
07771 862257
hunwick@oldmalthouseantiques.co.uk
Est. 1959 ***Stock size*** Large
Stock 18th–19thC furniture, brass, mirrors, paintings, decorative items
Open Mon–Sat 10am–5.30pm
Fairs Olympia, Chelsea
Services Valuations

Principia Fine Art
Contact Mr M Forrer
111d High Street, Hungerford, Berkshire, RG17 0NF
01488 682873
07899 926020
www.antiquesportfolio.com
Est. 1970 ***Stock size*** Large
Stock Scientific instruments, small furniture, Oriental art, books, paintings, works of art
Open Mon–Fri 10.30am–5pm Sat 2.30–5pm
Services Valuations, restoration, shipping, book search

Styles Silver (LAPADA)
Contact Mr or Mrs Styles
12 Bridge Street, Hungerford, Berkshire, RG17 0EH
01488 683922 01488 683488
07778 769559
dpgstyles@btinternet.com
www.styles-silver.co.uk
Est. 1974 ***Stock size*** Large
Stock Silver of all periods, flatware services a speciality, collectables, christening, wedding presents
Open Mon–Sat 9am–5.30pm or by appointment
Services Restoration

Turpins Antiques (BADA, CINOA)
Contact Mrs J Sumner
17 Bridge Street, Hungerford, Berkshire, RG17 0EG
01488 681886
Est. 1959 ***Stock size*** Medium
Stock 18thC English and Regency walnut furniture
Open Wed Fri Sat 10am–5pm or by appointment
Fairs Olympia

Youll's Antiques
Contact Mr B Youll
27–28 Charnham Street, Hungerford, Berkshire, RG17 0EJ
01488 682046 01488 684335
bruce.youll@virgin.net
www.youll.com
Est. 1935 ***Stock size*** Large
Stock 17th–20thC English and French furniture, porcelain, silver, decorative items
Open Mon–Sun 10.30am–5.30pm
Fairs Newark
Services Valuations, restoration

KINGSCLERE

Wyseby House Books (PBFA)
Contact Dr Tim Oldham
Kingsclere Old Bookshop, 2a George Street, Kingsclere, Newbury, Berkshire, RG20 5NQ
01635 297995 01635 297677
info@wyseby.co.uk
www.wyseby.co.uk
Est. 1977 ***Stock size*** Large
Stock General antiquarian, rare, second-hand books, fine art, decorative arts, architecture a speciality
Open Mon–Sat 9am–5pm
Services Catalogue 10 times a year

LECKHAMPSTEAD

Hill Farm Antiques
Contact Mr M Beesley
Hill Farm, Shop Lane, Leckhampstead, Newbury, Berkshire, RG20 8QG
01488 638541/638361
01488 638541
beesley@hillfarmantiques.demon.co.uk
www.hillfarmantiques.co.uk
Est. 1987 ***Stock size*** Large
Stock 19thC extending dining tables in mahogany, oak, walnut
Open By appointment

MIDGHAM

Berkshire Antiques Centre
Contact Mrs J Bradley
Unit 1, Kennet Holme Farm Buildings, Bath Road, Midgham, Berkshire, RG7 5UX
01189 710477 01189 710477
enquiries@berkshire-antiques.fsnet.co.uk
Est. 2000 ***Stock size*** Large
No. of dealers 10
Stock Furniture, general antiques and collectables
Open Mon–Sun 10.30am–4.30pm closed Wed

Cameo
Contact Chris Hart or Jon King
Kennet Home farm, Bath Road, Midgham, Reading, Berkshire, RG7 5UX P
☎ 01189 713772 F 01189 710330
W www.cameo-auctioneers@lineone.net
Open Mon–Fri 9am–5pm Sat by appointment
Sales Two day sale of antiques, furniture, collectables, pictures
Frequency Monthly
Catalogues Yes

Special Auction Services
Contact Andrew Hilton
Kennetholme, Bath Road, Midgham, Reading, Berkshire, RG7 5UX P
☎ 0118 971 2949 F 0118 971 2420
E commemorative@aol.com
W www.invaluable.com/sas
Est. 1991
Open 9am–5pm by appointment
Sales Special auctions of commemoratives, pot lids, Prattware, fairings, Goss & Crested, Baxter and Le Blond prints, toys for the collector. Held at The Courtyard Hotel, Padworth, Nr Reading. Please telephone for details
Frequency 8 per annum
Catalogues Yes

MORTIMER

Frank Milward (BNTA, ANA)
Contact Mr F Milward
2 Ravensworth Road, Mortimer, Reading, Berkshire, RG7 3UU P
☎ 0118 933 2843 F 0118 933 2843
Est. 1975 *Stock size* Medium
Stock English and foreign coins, banknotes
Open By appointment
Fairs International Coin Fair, Coinex, London
Services Valuations

NEWBURY

Invicta Bookshop (PBFA)
Contact Mr S Hall
8 Cromwell Place, Newbury, Berkshire, RG14 1AF P
☎ 01635 31176
Est. 1969 *Stock size* Medium
Stock Antiquarian, rare, second-hand books, cookery, cricket, military topics a speciality
Open Mon–Sat 10.30am–5.30pm closed Wed
Fairs Oxford, Bath, York PBFA
Services Book search

Newbury Salvage Ltd
Contact Mr A Bromhead
Kelvin Road, Newbury, Berkshire, RG14 2DB P
☎ 01635 528120 F 01635 551007
M 07776 174875
Est. 1988 *Stock size* Large
Stock Bricks, tiles, slates, chimney pots, fireplaces, doors, windows, statuary, sanitary ware, oak beams
Open Mon–Fri 8am–5pm Sat 9am–1pm

Alan Walker (BADA, TVADA)
Contact Mr A Walker
Halfway Manor, Halfway, Newbury, Berkshire, RG20 8NR P
☎ 01488 657670 F 01488 657670
W www.alanwalker-barometers.com
Est. 1987 *Stock size* Large
Stock 18th–19thC barometers, barographs, related instruments
Open By appointment
Fairs Olympia, BADA, Duke of York's
Services Valuations, restoration, barometers purchased

PANGBOURNE

R Butler
Contact Rita Butler
4 Station Road, Pangbourne, Reading, Berkshire, RG8 7AN P
☎ 0118 984 5522 F 0118 984 4520
Est. 1999 *Stock size* Medium
No. of dealers 4
Stock Small to medium-sized furniture 17th–20thC, Art Deco, decorative interiors, Georgian and other glass
Open Tues–Sat 10am–5pm

READING

Addington Antiques
Contact Paul Schneiderman
41 Addington Road, Reading, Berkshire, RG1 5PZ P
☎ 0118 935 3435
Est. 1996 *Stock size* Small
Stock General antiques 18thC–1960s design
Open Thurs–Sat 10am–6pm
Fairs Newark, Ardingly

Fanny's Antiques
Contact Fanny Lyons
1 Lynmouth Road, Reading, Berkshire, RG1 8DE P
☎ 0118 950 8261
Est. 1993 *Stock size* Large
No. of dealers 29
Stock General antiques, furniture, smalls, garden antiques
Open Mon–Sat 10.30am–4pm Sun noon–4pm

Graham Gallery
Contact John Steeds
Highwoods, Burghfield Common, Reading, Berkshire, RG7 3BG P
☎ 01189 831070 F 01189 831070
E jfsteeds@aol.com
Est. 1975 *Stock size* Medium
Stock 19th–20thC oils, watercolours, prints
Open By appointment

Reading Collectors Centre
Contact John Willcocks
Unit 14–15, Harris Arcade, Station Road, Reading, Berkshire, RG1 1DN
☎ 0118 932 0111 F 0118 958 8666
Est. 2000 *Stock size* Medium
No. of dealers 3
Stock General antiques, memorabilia, records, toys, model railways, militaria
Open Mon–Sat 10am–5.15pm
Services Valuations

Retro Centre
Contact Al Baynham
11 Bristol & West Arcade, Reading, Berkshire, RG1 1JL
☎ 0118 958 1058
E info@retro-centre.co.uk
W www.retro-centre.co.uk
Est. 2003 *Stock size* Medium
Stock Mid-20thC design, homewares, collectables
Open Mon–Sat 10am–6pm
Services Book search

SLOUGH

Randtiques
Contact Mr Tony Lowe
23 Stoke Road, Slough, Berkshire, SL2 5AH
01753 572512
07770 407005
Est. 1984 *Stock size* Medium
Stock Furniture, china, glass, pine, prints, watercolours
Open Mon–Sat 10am–5pm closed Wed
Services Framing, paint stripping

Randtiques
Contact Mr Tony Lowe
The Lady Hague, Stoke Road Legion, Slough, Berkshire, SL2 5AH
07770 407005
Est. 2003
Sales General antiques every Tues 6.30pm, viewing 2–6.30pm
Frequency Weekly
Catalogues No

SONNING-ON-THAMES

Cavendish Fine Art (BADA)
Contact Janet Middlemiss
Dower House, Pearson Road, Sonning-on-Thames, Berkshire, RG4 6UL
0118 969 1904
07831 295575
info@cavendishfineart.com
www.cavendishfineart.com
Est. 1973 *Stock size* Large
Stock Georgian furniture
Open By appointment
Fairs Olympia, BADA

TWYFORD

Bell Antiques
Contact Mr N Timms
2b High Street, Twyford, Reading, Berkshire, RG10 9AE
0118 934 2501
Est. 1989 *Stock size* Large
Stock General antiques, collectables
Open Mon–Sat 9.30am–5.30pm Sun 10am–5.30pm

Stephen Brown Antiques
Contact Stephen Brown
Unit 6, Three Bridge Mill, Twyford, Berkshire, MK18 4DY
01296 730130 01296 730196
07770 380133
sbrownantiques@btopenworld.com
www.stephenbrownantiques.co.uk
Est. 1997 *Stock size* Large
Stock Victorian–Edwardian furniture
Trade only Yes
Open Mon–Fri 10am–5pm or by appointment
Services Shipping

WARFIELD

Moss End Antiques Centre (TVADA)
Contact Maureeen Staite or Maura Dorrington
Moss End, Warfield, Berkshire, RG42 6EJ
01344 861942
www.mossendantiques.co.uk
Est. 1988 *Stock size* Large
No. of dealers 20
Stock Antique furniture, clocks, silver, glass, porcelain, linen, collectables, Oriental furniture
Open Tues–Sun 10.30am–5pm
Services Restoration, coffee shop

WARGRAVE

Ferry Antiques
Contact Peter or Kate Turner
70 High Street, Wargrave, Berkshire, RG10 8BY
0118 940 4415
07778 615975
Est. 1993 *Stock size* Medium
Stock 18th–19thC furniture, general antiques, glass, porcelain, silver, decorative objects
Open Wed–Sun 10am–5.30pm
Fairs The East Berkshire Antiques Fair
Services Valuations, restoration

Rosina Antiques
Contact Maxine Lucas
64 High Street, Wargrave, Berkshire, RG10 8BY
0118 947 3011 0118 940 6299
rosina-antiques@yahoo.com
www.rosina-antiques.co.uk
Est. 2001 *Stock size* Small
Stock General antiques, musical instruments
Open Wed–Sun 10am–5pm

Wargrave Antiques
Contact Mr J Connell
66 High Street, Wargrave, Berkshire, RG10 8BY
0118 940 2914
Est. 1979 *Stock size* Large
Stock Furniture, porcelain, glass, silver, copper, brass, 19thC furniture a speciality
Open Wed–Sun 10am–5pm
Services Valuations, restoration

WINDSOR

Berkshire Antiques Co Ltd
Contact Mr Sutton
42 Thames Street, Windsor, Berkshire, SL4 1PR
01753 830100 01753 832278
b.antiques@btconnect.com
www.jewels2go.co.uk
Est. 1981 *Stock size* Large
Stock Silver, dolls, jewellery, furniture, pictures, porcelain, Art Deco, Art Nouveau, commemorative memorabilia, royal commemoratives
Open Mon–Sat 10.30am–5.30pm Sun by appointment
Services Valuations, restoration, antique dolls hospital

Dee's Antique Pine
Contact Mrs Dee Waghorn
89 Grove Road, Windsor, Berkshire, SL4 1HT
01753 865627
dee@deesantiquepine.co.uk
www.deesantiquepine.co.uk
Stock size Large
Stock Antique pine wardrobes, chests-of-drawers
Open Tues–Sat 10am–6pm Sun 11am–3pm or by appointment

Norah's Antique Shoppe
Contact Norah Brooks
51 Thames Street, Windsor, Berkshire, SL4 1TU
01753 851958
Est. 1987 *Stock size* Large
Stock General antiques, collectables
Open Mon–Sat 10am–5.30pm Sun noon–3pm
Services Valuations, restoration

Old Barn Antiques
Contact Mrs Sue Lakey
Wyevale Garden Centre, Dedworth Road, Windsor, Berkshire, SL4 4LH
01753 833099
www.estories.co.uk
Est. 1991 *Stock size* Large
Stock Furniture, porcelain, jewellery, garden antiquities, militaria, silver, dolls, glassware, collectables
Open Mon–Sat 10am–5pm Sun 10.30am–4.30pm

Rule's Antiques (TVADA)
Contact Miss Sue Rule
39 St Leonards Road, Windsor, Berkshire, SL4 3BP
01753 833210
Est. 1995 *Stock size* Medium
Stock Decorative pieces, brass, lighting, door furniture and fittings, retro 1930–1979
Open Mon–Sat 10am–6pm
Fairs TVADA

Supatra
Contact Colin Macintosh
The Old Coach House, Trinity Yard, 59 St Leonards Road, Windsor, Berkshire, SL4 3BX
01753 858885 F 0870 62232
info@supatra.com
www.supatra.com
Est. 2001 *Stock size* Large
Stock Antique Oriental furniture
Open Mon–Sat 10.30am–5.30pm Sun 11am–4pm
Services Restoration

WOKINGHAM

Barkham Antiques Centre
Contact Len or Mary Collins
Barkham Street, Wokingham, Berkshire, RG40 4PJ
0118 976 1355
www.neatsite.com
Est. 1984 *Stock size* Large
No. of dealers 40
Stock Collectables, toy specialists, Doulton, general antiques, architectural salvage
Open Mon–Sun 10.30am–5pm
Services Restoration

K Faulkner
Contact Kenneth Faulkner
65 Brookside, Wokingham, Berkshire, RG41 2ST
0118 978 5255
kfaulkner@bowmore.demon.co.uk
www.bowmore.demon.co.uk
Est. 1995 *Stock size* Medium
Stock Sale and purchase of sporting memorabilia, specializing in cricket
Open By appointment
Services Valuations, mail order

Martin & Pole
Contact Mr G J R Lewis
The Auction House, Milton Road, Wokingham, Berkshire, RG40 1DB
0118 979 0460 F 0118 977 6166
a@martinpole.co.uk
www.martinpole.co.uk
Est. 1846
Open Mon–Fri 9am–5pm
Sales Monthly antiques and collectables, also modern and household. No sales in August. Telephone for details
Frequency 2 per month
Catalogues Yes

WOOLHAMPTON

The Old Bakery Antiques
Contact Susan Everard
Bath Road, Woolhampton, Reading, Berkshire, RG10 8BY
0118 971 2116
Est. 1974 *Stock size* Medium
Stock Antiques and collectables
Open Mon–Sat 10am–5pm Sun 1–5pm
Fairs Newark, Ardingly

HAMPSHIRE

ALDERSHOT

Aldershot Antiques
Contact Mr N Powell-Pelly
2a Elms Road, Aldershot, Hampshire, GU11 1LJ
01252 408408 F 01252 408408
M 07768 722152
Est. 1979 *Stock size* Small
Stock Period furniture
Open By appointment
Services Valuations

Traders Antiques and Country Pine Centre
Contact Mrs J Burns
Norfolk House, 131 Grosvenor Road, Aldershot, Hampshire, GU11 3ER
01252 322055
Est. 1969 *Stock size* Large
Stock Furniture, fireplaces, doors, pine, mahogany, oak, collectables
Open Mon–Sat 10am–5.30pm
Services Restoration, French polishing

ALRESFORD

Artemesia
Contact Mr Tim Wright
16 West Street, Alresford, Hampshire, SO24 9AT
01962 732277
Est. 1969 *Stock size* Large
Stock English and Continental furniture, ceramics, works of art
Open Mon–Sat 10am–1pm 2–5pm
Services Valuations

Laurence Oxley Ltd (ABA, FATG)
Contact Anthony Oxley
17 Broad Street, Alresford, Hampshire, SO24 9AW
01962 732188 F 01962 732998
M 07769 715510
aoxley@freenet.co.uk
Est. 1950
Stock Victorian watercolours, old maps, antiquarian books
Open Mon–Sat 9am–5pm
Fairs Chelsea Book Fair
Services Restoration, picture framing

Pineapple House
Contact Peter Radford
49 Broad Street, Alresford, Hampshire, SO24 9AS
01962 736575
M 07973 254749
Est. 1979 *Stock size* Small
Stock 19th–20thC general antiques especially walnut and mahogany furniture
Open Thur 11am–3pm Fri Sat 11am–5pm Sun 11am–4pm or by appointment

SOUTH

ALTON

Appleton Eves Ltd
Contact Richard Eves
30 Normandy Street, Alton, Hampshire, GU34 1BX
☎ 01420 84422 Ⓕ 01420 84422
Est. 2001 *Stock size* Small
Stock Antiques, collectables, gifts
Open Mon–Sat 10am–5pm

Jardinique (SALVO)
Contact Mr Edward Neish
Old Park Farm, Kings Hill, Beech, Alton, Hampshire, GU34 4AW
☎ 01420 560055
Ⓔ enquiries@jardinique.co.uk
Ⓦ www.jardinique.co.uk
Est. 1994 *Stock size* Large
Stock Statuary, sundials, urns, garden items, seats, fountains, stone troughs, staddle stones
Open Tues–Sat 10am–5pm or by appointment
Services Valuations

ANDOVER

May and Son
Contact Mr J May
Unit 3, The Old Hatchery, Upper Clatford, Andover, Hampshire, SP11 7LW
☎ 01264 323417 Ⓕ 01264 338841
Ⓜ 07710 001660
Ⓔ office@mayandson.com
Ⓦ www.mayandson.com
Est. 1925
Open Mon–Fri 9am–5pm
Sat 9am–noon
Sales Antique furniture and effects 3rd Wed of the month at 10.30am, viewing Tues 8.30am–6pm morning of sale from 8.30am. Sales take place in Village Hall, Penton Mewsey, Andover. Periodic specialist auctions
Frequency Monthly
Catalogues Yes

Pearsons Auction Rooms
Contact Dominic Foster
41a London Street, Andover, Hampshire, SP10 2NU
☎ 01264 364820 Ⓕ 01264 323402
Ⓦ www.pearsons.com
Est. 1979
Open Mon–Fri 8.30am–6pm
Sales Fortnightly antique and general, pictures, prints, silver and jewellery Mon 10am, viewing Fri 9am–8pm
Sat 9am–5pm
Frequency Fortnightly
Catalogues Yes

ASH

Secondhand Land
Contact Elaine Barker
47 Ash Street, Ash, Hampshire, GU12 6OF
☎ 01252 332330
Est. 1992 *Stock size* Large
Stock General antiques
Open Mon–Sat 10am–5pm closed Wed
Services Valuations

ASH VALE

The House of Christian
Contact Mrs Bail
5 Vale Road, Ash Vale, Aldershot, Hampshire, GU12 5HH
☎ 01252 314478
Est. 1975 *Stock size* Medium
Stock Pine furniture, general antiques and collectables
Open Mon–Fri 10am–5pm
Sat 12.30–3.30pm
Services Valuations, restoration

ASHURST

Nova Foresta Books (PBFA)
Contact Mr Peter Roberts
185 Lyndhurst Road, Ashurst, Southampton, Hampshire, SO40 7AR
☎ 023 8029 3389
Ⓦ www.novaforestabooks.co.uk
Est. 1994 *Stock size* Medium
Stock Antiquarian, rare, second-hand books, New Forest, 20thC literature and art a speciality
Open Tues–Sat 10am–5.30pm
Fairs PBFA fairs
Services Valuations, book search

BASINGSTOKE

Hickley's Autographs & Memorabilia
Contact Mr R Hickley
PO Box 6090, Basingstoke, Hampshire, RG23 8YR
☎ 01256 411893 Ⓕ 01256 411894
Ⓔ sales@hickleysautographs.com
Ⓦ www.hickleysautographs.com
Est. 1993 *Stock size* Large
Stock Worldwide memorabilia
Open By appointment only
Services Valuations, search service

The Squirrel Antique & Collectors Centre
Contact Alan Stone
Joyce's Yard, 9a New Street, Basingstoke, Hampshire, RG21 7DE
☎ 01256 464885
Ⓔ ahs@squirrelsuk.fsnet.co.uk
Est. 1981 *Stock size* Large
Stock Antique jewellery, silver, dolls, teddy bears, Art Deco ceramics, china, furniture
Open Mon–Sat 10am–5.30pm
Services Valuations

BISHOPS WALTHAM

Something Else Antiques
Contact Selina Simpson
4 Basing Mews, Lower Basingwell Street, Bishops Waltham, Hampshire, SO32 1PA
☎ 01489 892179
Est. 1969 *Stock size* Large
Stock General antiques, collectables
Open Mon–Sat 10am–5pm or by appointment
Services Valuations, restoration

BOTLEY

The Furniture Trading Co
Contact Mr Davies
The Old Flour Mills, Mill Hill, Botley, Hampshire, SO30 2GB
☎ 01489 788194 Ⓕ 01489 797337
Ⓔ mail@furnituretradingco.co.uk
Ⓦ www.furnituretradingco.co.uk
Est. 1984 *Stock size* Large
Stock General antiques, antique and contemporary furniture, accessories, porcelain, lighting, mirrors
Open Mon–Sat 10am–5pm
Sun 11am–4pm
Services Restoration

BROCKENHURST

Antiquiteas
Contact Mr R Wolstenholme
37 Brockley Road,

Brockenhurst, Hampshire, SO42 7RB 🅿
☎ 01590 622120
ⓔ antiquiteas@aol.com
Ⓦ www.antiquiteas.co.uk
Est. 1999 *Stock size* Medium
Stock Pine furniture, copper, brass, porcelain
Open Mon–Sat 10am–5pm
Sun 10am–4pm

Squirrels
Contact Sue Crocket
✉ **Lyndhurst Road, Brockenhurst, Hampshire, SO42 7RL** 🅿
☎ 01590 622433
Est. 1989 *Stock size* Medium
Stock Antiques, collectables, stripped pine, furniture, Victoriana, Art Deco, Art Nouveau, kitchenware, garden items, pictures, mirrors
Open Wed–Sun 10am–5pm
winter 10am–4pm

BROOK

F E A Briggs Ltd
Contact Frank Briggs
✉ **Birchenwood Farm, Brook, Hampshire, SO43 7JA** 🅿
☎ 023 8081 2595 ⓕ 023 8081 2595
Ⓜ 07831 315838
ⓔ feabriggs@aol.com
Est. 1966 *Stock size* Large
Stock Victorian furniture
Open Mon–Fri 9am–5.30pm
Fairs Newark
Services Restoration

CHANDLERS FORD

Bonan's Antique Glass
Contact Elaine Bonan
✉ **Chandlers Ford, Hampshire, SO53** 🅿
☎ 023 8027 3900
ⓔ info@bonansantglass.co.uk
Ⓦ www.bonansantglass.co.uk
Est. 1999 *Stock size* Small
Stock 18th–19thC glass
Open By appointment
Fairs NEC
Services Mail order

Boris Books (PBFA)
Contact Mrs P Stevenson
✉ **2 Holland Close, Chandlers Ford, Eastleigh, Hampshire, SO53 3NA** 🅿
☎ 023 8027 5496
Ⓜ 07789 790949
ⓔ pam@borisbooks.fsnet.co.uk
Est. 1995 *Stock size* Small
Stock Antiquarian, rare, collectable, second-hand books, specializing in literature, music, children's, illustrated
Open By appointment
Fairs PBFA Bookfairs
Services Book search

CRAWLEY

The Pine Barn
Contact Mr P Chant
✉ **Folly Farm, Crawley, Winchester, Hampshire, SO21 2PH** 🅿
☎ 01962 776687 ⓕ 01962 776687
Est. 1987 *Stock size* Large
Stock Furniture made from reclaimed pine, antique, reproduction pine and oak furniture
Open Mon–Sat 9am–5pm
Sun by appointment
Services Valuations, restoration, shipping

EAST COSHAM

Wayne Buckner Antiques
Contact Audrey Buckner
✉ **Medina, East Cosham, Portsmouth, Hampshire, PO6 2AJ** 🅿
☎ 02392 385835 ⓕ 02392 327584
Ⓜ 07801 254494
ⓔ wayne.buckner@virgin.net
Est. 1996 *Stock size* Medium
Stock Collectables, clocks, small items of furniture, music boxes, barometers, china toys, Meccano, steam engines, china, glassware, jewellery
Open Mon–Sat by appointment
Fairs Kempton, Goodwood
Services Valuations, restoration, house clearance

EMSWORTH

Antique Bed Company
Contact Mr I Trewick
✉ **32 North Street, Emsworth, Hampshire, PO10 7DG** 🅿
☎ 01243 376074 ⓕ 01243 376074
ⓔ antiquebeds@aol.com
Ⓦ www.antiquebedsemsworth.co.uk
Est. 1992 *Stock size* Large
Stock Victorian–Edwardian brass, iron and wooden beds
Open Mon–Sat 9am–5.30pm
Services Valuations, restoration

Bookends
Contact Mrs C Waldron
✉ **7 High Street, Emsworth, Hampshire, PO10 7AQ** 🅿
☎ 01243 372154
Ⓜ 07796 263508
ⓔ cawaldron@tinyworld.co.uk
Est. 1982 *Stock size* Medium
Stock Antiquarian, rare, second-hand books, sheet music
Open Mon–Sat 9.30am–5pm
Sun 10.30am–3pm
Services Valuations, book search

Dolphin Quay Antique Centre
Contact Christopher or Lisa Creamer
✉ **Queen Street, Emsworth, Hampshire, PO10 7BU** 🅿
☎ 01243 379994
ⓔ chrisdqantiquesaol.com
Est. 1969 *Stock size* Large
No. of dealers 40+
Stock Fine antique furniture, porcelain, clocks, watches, jewellery, silver
Open Mon–Sat 10am–5pm
Sun 10am–4pm
Services Restoration, furniture upholstery, clock clinic Wed 4–6pm

Tiffins Antiques
Contact Phyl Hudson
✉ **12 Queen Street, Emsworth, Hampshire, PO10 7BL** 🅿
☎ 01243 372497
Est. 1989 *Stock size* Small
Stock General antiques, silver, oil lamps
Open Wed–Sat 9am–5pm

EVERSLEY

Eversley Antiques
Contact Hilary Craven
✉ **Church Lane, Eversley, Hampshire, RG27 0PX** 🅿
☎ 0118 932 8518 ⓕ 01252 622576
Ⓜ 07811 934905
Est. 1998 *Stock size* Large
No. of dealers 20
Stock General antiques, collectables
Open Mon–Sun 10am–5pm
Services Delivery

FARNBOROUGH

Clarice Cliff Ltd (ADDA)
Contact Mr J Motley
The Clarice Cliff Nostalgia Store, Kingsmead, Farnborough, Hampshire, GU14 7SL
☎ 01252 372188 ℱ 01252 513671
ⓔ admin@claricecliff.net
ⓦ www.claricecliff.co.uk
Est. 1973 *Stock size* Large
Stock Clarice Cliff, English 20thC ceramics
Open Mon–Sat 10am–5pm
Services Valuations, archive information, gallery

FORDINGBRIDGE

Bristow and Garland
Contact Mr David Bristow
45–47 Salisbury Street, Fordingbridge, Hampshire, SP6 1AB
☎ 01425 657337 ℱ 01425 657337
ⓔ davidbristow@bristowand garland.fonet.co.uk
Est. 1960 *Stock size* Small
Stock Antiquarian, rare, second-hand books, manuscripts, ephemera
Open Mon–Sat 9.30am–5pm closed Thurs pm

Quatrefoil
Contact C D Aston
Burgate, Fordingbridge, Hampshire, SP6 1LX
☎ 01425 653309 ℱ 01425 653309
Ⓜ 07802 361804
ⓔ coaston@quatrefoil.plus.com
Est. 1972 *Stock size* Medium
Stock 17th–18thC oak furniture, 15th–17thC oak carvings and sculpture
Open Mon–Sun 9am–8pm

West Essex Coin Investments (BNTA, IBNS)
Contact Mr R Norbury
Croft Cottage, Station Road, Alderholt, Fordingbridge, Hampshire, SP6 3AZ
☎ 01425 656459 ℱ 01425 656459
Est. 1977 *Stock size* Medium
Stock English coinage medieval–present day including English milled, British colonial, coins of the USA
Open By appointment only
Fairs York Racecourse, BNTA Fairs
Services Valuations

GOSPORT

Easter Antiques
Contact Mr R Easter
333 Forton Road, Gosport, Hampshire, PO12 3HF
☎ 023 9250 3621
Est. 1984 *Stock size* Small
Stock Small decorative items
Open Thurs–Sat 10am–5pm
Services Valuations, restoration

Former Glory
Contact Mr L Brannon
49 Whitworth Road, Gosport, Hampshire, PO12 3NJ
☎ 023 9250 4869
Est. 1986 *Stock size* Medium
Stock Victorian–Edwardian furniture, china
Open Mon–Sat 9am–5pm closed Wed
Services Restoration, traditional upholstery

HARTLEY WINTNEY

Nicholas Abbott (LAPADA)
Contact Mr C N Abbott
High Street, Hartley Wintney, Hook, Hampshire, RG27 8NY
☎ 01252 842365 ℱ 01252 842365
ⓔ nicholasabbott@web-hq.com
ⓦ nicholasabbott.com
Est. 1964 *Stock size* Medium
Stock 18thC furniture
Open Mon–Sat 9.30am–5.30pm
Services Valuations, restoration

Anvil Antiques
Contact Andrew Pitter
The Old Forge Cottage, The Green, Hartley Wintney, Hampshire, RG27 8PG
☎ 01252 845403
Ⓜ 07778 934938
Est. 1980 *Stock size* Large
Stock General antiques
Open Mon–Sat 10am–5pm
Services Restoration china, pottery, porcelain

Cedar Antiques Centre Ltd
Contact Derek Green
High Street, Hartley Wintney, Hampshire, RG27 8NY
☎ 01252 843222 ℱ 01252 842111
ⓔ ca@cedar-antiques.com
ⓦ www.cedar-antiques.com
Est. 1998 *Stock size* Large
No. of dealers 38
Stock Early English furniture, silver, glass, water colours, carpets
Open Mon–Sat 10am–5.30pm Sun 11am–5pm
Services Café, Museum of T G Green pottery

Cedar Antiques Ltd
Contact Sally Green
High Street, Hartley Wintney, Hampshire, RG27 8NT
☎ 01252 843252 ℱ 01252 842111
ⓔ ca@cedar-antiques.com
ⓦ www.cedar-antiques.com
Est. 1964 *Stock size* Large
Stock 17th–20thC English and Continental country furniture with colour
Open Mon–Sat 10am–5.30pm Sun 11am–5pm
Services Valuations, restoration

Bryan Clisby
Contact Mr B Clisby
Cedar Antique Centre, High Street, Hartley Wintney, Hampshire, RG27 8NY
☎ 01252 716436/843222
ⓔ bryanclisby@boltblue.co.uk
Est. 1978 *Stock size* Large
Stock Longcase, bracket, wall clocks, mantel clocks, barometers
Open Mon–Sun 10am–5.30pm
Services Restoration

Deva Antiques
Contact Mr A Gratwick
High Street, Hartley Wintney, Hook, Hampshire, RG27 8NY
☎ 01252 843538 ℱ 01252 842946
ⓔ devaants@aol.com
ⓦ www.deva-antiques.com
Est. 1986 *Stock size* Medium
Stock 18th–19thC mahogany, walnut, country furniture, decorative accessories
Open Mon–Sat 9am–5.30pm
Services Collection from BR station by arrangement

Graham Dobinson Antiques
Contact Graham Dobinson
The Old Workshops, Cricket Green, Hartley Wintney,

Hampshire,
RG27 8QB P
☎ 01252 842115
Est. 1982 *Stock size* Small
No. of dealers 20
Stock Antique furniture
Open Mon–Fri 8.30am–5.30pm
Services Restoration

Sally Green Designs
Contact Sally Green
✉ **63 High Street,**
Hartley Wintney, Hampshire,
RG27 8NT P
☎ 01252 843252 F 01252 842111
E sg@cedar-ltd.demon.co.uk
W www.cedar-antiques.com
Est. 1965 *Stock size* Medium
Stock 18th–19thC English and Continental country furniture
Open Mon–Sat 10am–5.30pm
Sun 11am–5pm

David Lazarus Antiques (BADA)
Contact Mr D Lazarus
✉ **High Street, Hartley Wintney,**
Hook, Hampshire,
RG27 8NS P
☎ 01252 842272 F 01252 842272
Est. 1973 *Stock size* Medium
Stock Furniture, sculpture, objets d'art
Open Mon–Sat 9.30am–5.30pm

HEADLEY

Victorian Dreams
Contact Mrs S Kay
✉ **The Old School, Crabtree Lane,**
Headley, Bordon, Hampshire,
GU35 8QH P
☎ 01428 717000 F 01428 717111
E sales@victorian-dreams.co.uk
W www.victorian-dreams.co.uk
Est. 1985 *Stock size* Large
Stock Brass, iron, wooden, upholstered and caned bedsteads
Open Mon–Sat 9am–5.30pm
Sun 10am–4pm
Fairs Newark, Ardingly
Services Valuations, restoration, world and nationwide delivery

HIGHBRIDGE

Brambridge Antiques
Contact Mr D May
✉ **Bugle Farm, Highbridge Road,**
Highbridge, Eastleigh,
Hampshire,
SO50 6HS P
☎ 01962 714386
Est. 1973 *Stock size* Medium
Stock Mahogany, walnut furniture
Open Mon–Sat 9am–5pm
Services Restoration

HORNDEAN

The Goss & Crested China Club
Contact Lynda Pine
✉ **62 Murray Road,**
Horndean, Hampshire,
PO8 9JL P
☎ 023 9259 7440 F 023 9259 1975
E info@gosschinaclub.demon.co.uk
W www.gosscrestedchina.co.uk
Est. 1969 *Stock size* Large
Stock Over 5,000 pieces of Goss and crested china
Open Mon–Sat 9am–5pm
Services Monthly mail order catalogue, museum on site, search service for wants lists

LISS

Plestor Barn Antiques
Contact Mr McCarthy
✉ **Farnham Road, Liss,**
Hampshire, GU33 6JQ P
☎ 01730 893922
M 07850 539998
E craigmccarthy@btopenworld.com
Est. 1984 *Stock size* Medium
Stock Victorian–Edwardian stripped pine, 1920s furniture, used and reproduction soft furnishings
Open Mon–Fri 10am–4pm
Sat 10am–2pm
Services Light removals service

LYMINGTON

Carlsen's Antiques and Fine Arts
Contact Mr D Carlsen
✉ **8 St Thomas Street,**
Lymington, Hampshire,
SO41 9NA P
☎ 01590 676370
Est. 1987 *Stock size* Large
Stock Watercolours, pencils, etchings, mirrors, small Georgian–Victorian furniture
Open Mon–Sat 9.30am–5.30pm
Fairs Winchester, Lymington
Services Valuations

Century Fine Arts
Contact Victoria Roberts
✉ **120 High Street,**
Lymington, Hampshire,
SO41 9AQ P
☎ 01590 673532 F 01590 678855
Est. 1995 *Stock size* Large
Stock Antique furniture, period paintings, prints, lamps, decorative items
Open Mon–Sat 9.30am–5.30pm

Corfield Ltd
Contact Mr A Roberts
✉ **120 High Street,**
Lymington, Hampshire,
SO41 9AQ P
☎ 01590 673532 F 01590 678855
Est. 1995 *Stock size* Medium
Stock Decorative items, paintings, Regency, Georgian, Victorian furniture
Open Mon–Sat 9.30am–5.30pm
Services Restoration

Godleton Barn Antiques
Contact R Belfield
✉ **Godleton farm, Silver Street,**
Sway, Lymington, Hampshire,
SO41 6DJ P
☎ 0203 8033 2293
Est. 1978 *Stock size* Medium
Stock Antique pine, salvage
Open Mon–Sat 9am–5pm
Services Restoration, paint stripping

George Kidner
Contact Mrs K Chamberlain
✉ **The Old School, The Square,**
Pennington, Lymington,
Hampshire,
SO41 8GN P
☎ 01590 670070 F 01590 675167
E info@georgekidner.co.uk
W www.georgekidner.co.uk
Est. 1991
Open Mon–Fri 9am–5pm
Sales Furniture and decorative items, silver, jewellery, paintings, collectors items. Sales Wed, viewing Sat 9.30am–1pm
Mon 9.30am–4.30pm
Tues 9.30am–7pm
Frequency Quarterly
Catalogues Yes

Lymington Antique Centre
Contact Lisa Reeves
✉ **76 High Street,**
Lymington, Hampshire,
SO41 9AL
☎ 01590 670934
Est. 1990 *Stock size* Large
No. of dealers 30

Stock Furniture, porcelain, books, jewellery, silver, pictures
Open Mon–Fri 10am–5pm Sat 9am–5pm
Services Restoration

Barry Papworth (NAG)
Contact Steve Park
28 St Thomas Street, Lymington, Hampshire, SO41 9NE
01590 676422
Est. 1978 *Stock size* Medium
Stock Jewellery and silver
Open Mon–Sat 9.15am–5.15pm
Services Valuations, restoration

Pennyfarthing Antiques
Contact Roberta Payne
Lymington Antiques Centre, 76 High Street, Lymington, Hampshire, SO41 9AL
023 8086 0846
07970 847690
bobbypayne@lineone.net
Est. 1996 *Stock size* Large
Stock Georgian–Edwardian furniture, clocks, Oriental items, watches, barometers
Open Mon–Sat 10am–5pm
Services Valuations, restoration

Pod Interior Style
Contact Miss Polly Sturgess
15 St Thomas Street, Lymington, Hampshire, SO41 9NB
01590 688769
Est. 1997 *Stock size* Medium
Stock Furniture, upholstery service
Open Mon–Fri 10am–6pm Sat 10am–5pm

Wick Antiques (LAPADA, CINOA)
Contact Mr Charlie Wallrock
Fairlea House, 110–112 Marsh Lane, Lymington, Hampshire, SO4 19EE
01590 677558 01590 677558
charles@wickantiques.co.uk
www.wickantiques.co.uk
Est. 1984 *Stock size* Large
Stock 18th–19thC English and French furniture
Open Mon–Fri 9am–5pm Sat by appointment
Fairs Olympia Fine Arts Fair, Fall Fair New York
Services Restoration

LYNDHURST

Lita Kaye Antiques
Contact Mr S Ferder
13 High Street, Lyndhurst, Hampshire, SO43 7BB
023 8028 2337
Est. 1950 *Stock size* Large
Stock English period, 18thC Regency furniture, porcelain, decorative items
Open Mon–Sat 9.30am–5.30pm

Lyndhurst Antique Centre
Contact Mrs G Ashley
19–21 High Street, Lyndhurst, Hampshire, SO43 7BB
023 8028 4000
Est. 1998 *Stock size* Large
No. of dealers 50
Stock Collectables, furniture, militaria
Open Mon–Sun 10am–5pm

MATTINGLEY

Odiham Auction Sales
Contact Mr S R Thomas
Unit 4, Priors Farm, West Green Road, Mattingley, Hampshire, RG29 8JU
01189 326824 01189 326797
07836 201764
auction@dircon.co.uk
Est. 1989
Open Mon–Fri 9.30am–4pm
Sales General antiques sales Wed. Smalls sales at 2pm, furniture sales at 6.30pm, viewing Tues 6–9pm Wed 9am–2pm
Frequency Monthly
Catalogues Yes

MILFORD-ON-SEA

Carringtons Antiques
Contact Kerry Lee
100 High Street, Milford-on-Sea, Hampshire, SO41 0QE
01590 644665
Est. 2000 *Stock size* Medium
Stock General antiques, oil lamps and accessories
Open Mon–Sat 10am–5pm
Fairs Ardingly, Sandown Park, Newark
Services Oil lamp restoration

NEW MILTON

Forest House Antiques
Contact Mr K Plater
4 Winston Parade, Lymington Road, New Milton, Hampshire, BH25 6PT
01425 614441
Est. 1984 *Stock size* Large
Stock 18th–19thC English furniture, ceramics, collectables
Open Mon–Fri 9am–4.30pm
Fairs Antiques for Everyone, Newark
Services Valuations, restoration

NORTH WARNBOROUGH

Second Chance Antique Centre
Contact David Myers
Dunleys Hill, Hook Road, North Warnborough, Near Odiham, Hampshire, RG25 1DX
01256 704273
07932 664086 *Stock size* Large
No. of dealers 20
Stock General antiques
Open Mon–Sat 10am–5.30pm Sun 11am–5.30pm

OLD BEDHAMPTON

J F F Militaria & Fire Brigade Collectables
Contact Mr J Franklin
Ye Olde Coach House, Mill Lane, Old Bedhampton, Hampshire, PO9 3JH
023 9248 6485
07786 012316
Est. 1995 *Stock size* Medium
Stock Militaria, brass fire helmets, medals, badges, cloth insignia, equipment, buttons
Open By appointment only
Fairs Stoneleigh, Beltring
Services Valuations

PETERSFIELD

Folly Four Antiques & Collectables
Contact Diane
10–12 College Street, Petersfield, Hampshire, GU31 4AD
01730 266650
Est. 1999 *Stock size* Small
Stock Antiques and collectables
Open Mon–Sat 10am–4.30pm

Jacobs and Hunt Fine Art Auctioneers
26 Lavant Street, Petersfield, Hampshire, GU32 3EF
01730 233933 01730 262323
www.jacobsandhunt.co.uk
Est. 1895
Open Mon–Fri 9am–5pm
Sales General antiques sales Fri, viewing Wed 10am–4.30pm Thurs 10am–6.30pm morning of sale from 9am
Frequency Monthly
Catalogues Yes

The Petersfield Bookshop (ABA, PBFA)
Contact Frank Westwood
16a Chapel Street, Petersfield, Hampshire, GU32 3DS
01730 263438 01730 269426
sales@petersfieldbookshop.com
www.petersfieldbookshop.com
Est. 1918 *Stock size* Large
Stock Antiquarian and modern books
Open Mon–Sat 9am–5.30pm
Fairs ABA, Olympia, Chelsea
Services Valuations, quarterly catalogues

PORTSMOUTH

The Architectural Warehouse
Contact Mrs Byng
17 Beck Street, Portsmouth, Hampshire, PO1 3AN
023 9287 7070 023 9229 4777
des_res@hotmail.com
Est. 2000 *Stock size* Large
Stock Architectural antiques, Victorian fireplaces, doors, baths, pine furniture, radiators, stained glass
Open Mon–Sat 10am–5pm
Services Paint stripping

Good Day Antiques and Decor
Contact Mrs G Day
22 The Green, Rowlands Castle, Portsmouth, Hampshire, PO9 6AB
023 9241 2924
0795 8619413
Gillday@aol.com
Est. 1979 *Stock size* Medium
Stock Victorian furniture, small cabinets, jewellery, silver, porcelain, pottery, pictures
Open Thurs–Sun 11am–4pm
Services Silver-plating, gilding, engraving

Alexandra Gray Antiques & Decorative Ideas
Contact Alexandra Gray
129–131 Havant Road, Drayton, Portsmouth, Hampshire, PO6 2AA
023 9237 6379
07752 781835
Est. 1997 *Stock size* Large
No. of dealers 15
Stock General antiques, chandeliers, French beds, china, especially Crown Derby, clocks, oil lamps
Open Mon–Sat 10am–5pm Sun noon–4pm closed Wed
Services Upholstery

RINGWOOD

E Chalmers Hallam (PBFA)
Contact Mrs L Hiscock
9 Post Office Lane, St Ives, Ringwood, Hampshire, BH24 2PG
01425 470060 01425 470060
laura@chalmershallam.freeserve.co.uk
Est. 1946 *Stock size* Large
Stock Antiquarian, rare, second-hand books, angling, field sports, travel, Africana
Open By appointment
Services Valuations

The Magpie's Nest
Contact Mrs Favia Lister
Ringwood Road, Burley, Ringwood, Hampshire, BH24 4BU
01425 402404
Est. 1974 *Stock size* Small
Stock Porcelain, small collectables, jewellery
Open Mon–Sun 10am–5pm
Services Repairs to jewellery including re-threading, plating, silver, small furniture

Millers Antiques Ltd (LAPADA)
Contact Mr A J Miller
Netherbrook House, Christchurch Road, Ringwood, Hampshire, BH24 1DR
01425 472062 01425 472727
07806 711280
mail@millers-antiques.co.uk
www.millers-antiques.co.uk
Est. 1897 *Stock size* Large
Stock English and Continental country furniture, 19thC majolica, Quimper, treen, decorative items
Open Mon 9.30am–1.30pm Tue–Fri 9.30am–5pm Sat 10am–3pm
Fairs Decorative Antiques and Textiles Fair, Great Antiques Fair
Services Valuations, restoration, packing, shipping

Sci-Fi World
Contact Mr J Wilson
42a High Street, Ringwood, Hampshire, BH24 1AG
01425 474506
jameswilsonfive@aol.com
Est. 1996 *Stock size* Medium
Stock Cards, badges, mugs, videos, books, toys
Open Mon–Sat 10am–5pm
Services Valuations

Lorraine Tarrant Antiques
Contact Mrs L Tarrant
23 Market Place, Ringwood, Hampshire, BH24 1AN
01425 461123
Est. 1991 *Stock size* Medium
Stock Furniture, carved oak, old pine, bears, collectors' items, tapestry cushions
Open Tues–Sat 10am–5pm

ROMSEY

Antique Enterprises
Contact Mr M Presterfield
19 Cavendish Close, Romsey, Hampshire, SO51 7HT
01794 515589
07803 552992
Est. 1976 *Stock size* Medium
Stock Furniture, china, glass, collectables
Open By appointment

Bell Antiques (Gemmological Association)
Contact Mr M Gay

✉ **8 Bell Street, Romsey, Hampshire, SO51 8GA** 🅿
☎ 01794 514719
Est. 1979 ***Stock size*** Large
Stock Jewellery, silver, glass, china, small furniture, maps, topographical prints
Open Mon–Sat 9.30am–5.30pm closed Wed in winter

⊞ Rick Hubbard Art Deco
Contact Rick Hubbard
✉ **3 Tee Court, Bell Street, Romsey, Hampshire, SO51 8GY** 🅿
☎ 01794 513133
Ⓜ 07767 267607
Ⓦ www.rickhubbard-artdeco.co.uk
Est. 1995 ***Stock size*** Large
Stock 20thC ceramics
Open Tues–Sat 10am–4pm
Fairs Alexander Palace, Shelley Collectors Fair

SOUTHAMPTON

⊞ Amber Antiques
Contact Mr R Boyle
✉ **115 Portswood Road, Portswood, Southampton, Hampshire, SO17 2FX** 🅿
☎ 023 8058 3645 Ⓕ 023 8058 3645
Est. 1970 ***Stock size*** Large
Stock Furniture
Open Mon–Sun 9am–5pm
Services Restoration

⊞ Cobwebs
Contact Mr P Boyd-Smith
✉ **78 Northam Road, Southampton, Hampshire, SO14 0PB** 🅿
☎ 023 8022 7458 Ⓕ 023 8022 7458
Ⓦ www.cobwebs.uk.com
Est. 1974 ***Stock size*** Large
Stock Ocean liner memorabilia, *Titanic* and White Star Line, aviation items, Royal and Merchant Navy items
Open Mon–Sat 10am–4pm closed Wed
Fairs Transportation 2000, British Titanic Convention
Services Valuations

⊞ Peter Rhodes Books
Contact Peter Rhodes
✉ **21 Portswood Road, Southampton, Hampshire, SO17 2ES** 🅿
☎ 023 8039 9003
Ⓔ peterrhodes.book@virgin.net
Est. 1997 ***Stock size*** Large
Stock Antiquarian, rare, second-hand books, travel, history, archaeology
Open Mon–Sat 11am–5pm
Fairs HD Fairs
Services Valuations, book search

SOUTHSEA

⊞ The Clock Shop
Contact M J Childs
✉ **155 Highland Road, Southsea, Hampshire, PO4 9EY** 🅿
☎ 023 9285 1649
Ⓜ 07905 059783
Est. 1999 ***Stock size*** Large
Stock Clocks, watches, jewellery general antiques
Open Wed–Sat 9am–5pm
Fairs Kempton Park, DMG
Services Valuations, clock restoration

⊞ Design Explosion
Contact Susan Mosely
✉ **2 Exmouth Road, Southsea, Hampshire, PO5 2QL** 🅿
☎ 023 9229 3040
Ⓜ 07850 131414
Ⓔ sue.moseley@btconnect.com
Ⓦ www.ianparmiter.co.uk
Est. 1998 ***Stock size*** Medium
Stock 1950s–1970s china, glass, lighting, furniture
Open Fri Sat 9am–5pm
Fairs Ardingly, Kempton, Newark

⊞ A Fleming (Southsea) Ltd
Contact Mr Alfred Fleming
✉ **The Clock Tower, Castle Road, Southsea, Hampshire, PO5 3DE** 🅿
☎ 023 9282 2934 Ⓕ 023 9229 3501
Ⓜ 07885 334545
Ⓔ mail@flemingsantiques.fsnet.co.uk
Ⓦ www.flemingsantiques.com
Est. 1908 ***Stock size*** Medium
Stock 18th–19thC English and Continental furniture, silver, boxes, barometers
Open Wed–Fri 9.30am–5.30pm Sat 9.30am–1pm or by appointment
Fairs Goodwood, Petersfield
Services Valuations, furniture and silver restoration

⊞ Langford Antiques
Contact Mr I Langford
✉ **70 Albert Road, Southsea, Hampshire, PO5 2SL** 🅿
☎ 023 9283 0517
Est. 1982 ***Stock size*** Medium
Stock Victorian–20thC furniture, collectables, silver, costume jewellery
Open Mon–Fri 11am–5pm Sat 10am–6pm closed Wed

🔨 D M Nesbit & Co
Contact John Cameron MRICS, ANAVA
✉ **7 Clarendon Road, Southsea, Hampshire, PO5 2ED** 🅿
☎ 023 9286 4321 Ⓕ 023 9229 5522
Ⓔ auctions@nesbits.co.uk
Ⓦ www.nesbits.co.uk
Est. 1921
Open Mon–Fri 9.30am–5pm
Sales General antiques sale monthly. Telephone for details
Catalogues Yes

⊞ Oldfield Gallery
Contact Ann Downs
✉ **76 Elm Grove, Southsea, Hampshire, PO5 1LN** 🅿
☎ 023 9283 8042
Ⓔ oldfield-gallery@ntlworld.com
Ⓦ www.oldfield-antiquemaps.co.uk
Est. 1972 ***Stock size*** Large
Stock Antique maps and prints
Open Tues–Sat 10am–5pm
Fairs London Map Fairs
Services Valuations, framing

⊞ Ian Parmiter
Contact Mr I Parmiter
✉ **18a Albert Road, Southsea, Hampshire, PO5 2SH** 🅿
☎ 023 9229 3040 Ⓕ 023 9229 3040
Ⓔ ian.parmiter@btconnect.com
Ⓦ www.ianparmiter.co.uk
Est. 1987 ***Stock size*** Medium
Stock Architectural antiques, unusual items
Open Mon 11am–2.30pm Fri Sat 9am–5pm or by appointment

STOCKBRIDGE

🔨 Evans and Partridge
Contact John Partridge
✉ **Agriculture House, Stockbridge, Hampshire, SO20 6HF** 🅿
☎ 01264 810702 Ⓕ 01264 810944
Ⓔ auctions@evansandpartridge.co.uk
Est. 1973
Open Mon–Fri 9am–5.30pm

Sat 9am–4pm
Sales Sales of early and modern fishing tackle, sporting guns, antique weapons, steam, tractors and farming bygones
Frequency Annual
Catalogues Yes

Lane Antiques
Contact Mrs E Lane
High Street, Stockbridge, Hampshire, SO20 6EU
01264 810435
Est. 1982 *Stock size* Medium
Stock 18th–19thC porcelain, silver, glass, small furniture, objets d'art, fine art
Open By appointment

Stockbridge Antiques Centre
Contact Tim Baker
Old London Road, Stockbridge, Hampshire, SO20 6EJ
01264 811008
rona@oakchairs.com
www.oakchairs.com
Est. 1978 *Stock size* Medium
Stock Pine and oak country furniture
Open Mon–Sat 10am–5pm
Sun 11am–2pm closed Wed

Elizabeth Viney (BADA)
Contact Miss E A Viney MBE
Jacobs House, High Street, Stockbridge, Hampshire, SO20 6HF
01264 810761
Est. 1967 *Stock size* Small
Stock 18th–19thC furniture, treen, domestic metalware, brass, candlesticks, police truncheons
Open By appointment only

Fizzy Warren Decorative Antiques
Contact Fizzy Warren
High Street, Stockbridge, Hampshire, SO20 6EY
01264 811137
Est. 1998 *Stock size* Medium
Stock Decorative antiques, 19thC French chandeliers, mirrors, furniture, fabrics
Open Mon–Sat 10.30am–5pm

WICKHAM

Brighthouse Antiques and Fine Contemporary Arts
Contact Peter Heselwood or Skye Holland
Bridge Street, Wickham, Hampshire, PO17 5JA
01329 836677 F 01329 836636
M 07712 899599
brighthouse@btconnect.com
Est. 2004 *Stock size* Large
No. of dealers 60
Stock General antiques, art gallery, objets d'art, clocks, jewellery,
Open Mon–Sat 10am–5pm
Sun 11am–3pm
Services Valuations, restoration, shipping, house clearance

Solent Railwayana Auctions
Contact Nigel Maddock
Community Centre, Mill Lane, Wickham, Hampshire, PO17 5AL
01489 574029
nigel@solentrailwayana.com
www.solentrailwayana.com
Est. 1992
Open Sale 11am–5pm
Sales Railwayana auctions. Dates for 2005 19 March, 18 June, 15 October
Frequency 3 per annum
Catalogues Yes

WINCHESTER

Bonhams
The Red House, Hyde Street, Winchester, Hampshire, SO23 7DX
01962 862515 F 01962 865166
winchester@bonhams.com
www.bonhams.com
Est. 1793
Open Mon–Fri 8.30am–5pm
Sales Regional office. Regular house and attic sales across the country; contact London offices for further details. Free auction valuations; insurance and probate valuations

Burgess Farm Antiques
Contact Mr Brown
39 Jewry Street, Winchester, Hampshire, SO23 8RY
01962 777546
Est. 1982 *Stock size* Large
Stock Antique pine and country furniture, general antiques
Open Mon–Sat 9.30am–5pm
Services Valuations, restoration

The Clock-Work-Shop (Winchester) (BHI, AHS)
Contact Mr P Ponsford-Jones
6a Parchment Street, Winchester, Hampshire, SO23 8AT
01962 842331 F 01962 878775
M 07973 736155
www.clock-work-shop.co.uk
Est. 1994 *Stock size* Large
Stock Clocks, barometers, furniture
Open Mon–Sat 9am–5pm
Services Restoration of clocks and barometers

G E Marsh (Antique Clocks) Ltd (BADA, CINOA, CC, BHI, NAWCC)
Contact Mr D Dipper
32a The Square, Winchester, Hampshire, SO23 9EX
01962 844443 F 01962 844443
gem@marshclocks.co.uk
www.marshclocks.co.uk
Est. 1947 *Stock size* Medium
Stock Carriage clocks, English longcase clocks, Continental clocks
Open Mon–Fri 9.30am–5pm
Sat 9.30am–1pm 2–5pm
Services Valuations, restoration, home visits

The Pine Cellars
Contact Mr N Brain
39 Jewry Street, Winchester, Hampshire, SO23 8RY
01962 777546
Est. 1971 *Stock size* Large
Stock Antique pine, country furniture
Open Mon–Sat 9am–5.30pm
Services Restoration

Studio Coins (BNTA)
Contact Mr S Mitchell
16 Kilham Lane, Winchester, Hampshire, SO22 5PT
01962 853156 F 01962 624246
Est. 1987
Stock Old English coins
Open By appointment only
Fairs Coinex, Cumberland, York
Services Free bi-monthly list

Todd & Austin Antiques & Fine Art
Contact Gerald Austin
2 Andover Road, Winchester,

Hampshire, SO23 7BS P
☎ 01962 869824
Est. 1974 *Stock size* Medium
Stock 18th–early 20thC pottery, porcelain, glass paperweights 1845–60, decorative silver, boxes, silver plate, Oriental arts, 18th–19thC glass, objets d'art
Open Tues–Fri 9.30am–5pm Sat 9am–noon
Services Valuations

⊞ Irene S Trudgett Collectables
Contact Irene S Trudgett
✉ **3 Andover Road, Winchester, Hampshire, SO23 7BS** P
☎ 01962 854132/862070
Est. 1966 *Stock size* Medium
Stock Pottery, porcelain, cigarette cards, Goss and crested china, glass, collectables
Open Mon–Fri 9.30am–4pm Thurs Sat 9.30am–noon
Services Valuations, restoration, book search

⊞ Webb Fine Arts
Contact Mr Webb
✉ **38 Jewry Street, Winchester, Hampshire, SO23 8RY** P
☎ 01962 842273 Ⓕ 01962 880602
Ⓔ davieswebb@hotmail.com
Ⓦ www.webbfinearts.co.uk
Est. 1972 *Stock size* Large
Stock Victorian paintings
Open Mon–Fri 9.30am–5pm Sat 9.30am–2pm
Services Valuations, restoration

⊞ The Winchester Bookshop (PBFA)
Contact Mr M Green
✉ **10a St Georges Street, Winchester, Hampshire, SO23 8BG** P
☎ 01962 855630
Est. 1991 *Stock size* Medium
Stock Antiquarian, rare, second-hand books, topography, archaeology, travel, literature a speciality
Open Mon–Sat 10am–5.15pm
Fairs PBFA fairs
Services Valuations, book search

ISLE OF WIGHT

BEMBRIDGE

⊞ Cobwebs Antiques and Collectables (GADAR)
Contact Mrs Sue Williams
✉ **Foreland Road, Bembridge, Isle of Wight, PO35 5XN** P
☎ 01983 874487
Est. 1997 *Stock size* Medium
Stock Bunnykins, Beatrix Potter, Doulton
Open Tues–Sat 10am–5pm

COWES

⊞ Copperwheat Restoration (RICS)
Contact Carole Copperwheat
✉ **Rear of Pascall Atkey, 29–30 High Street, Cowes, Isle of Wight, PO31 7RX** P
☎ 01983 281011
Ⓜ 07720 399670
Est. 1985 *Stock size* Small
Stock 17th–18thC furniture, metalware, ceramics
Open Any time by prior telephone call
Services Valuations, restoration

⊞ Flagstaff Antiques
Contact Mr T A M Cockram
✉ **Tudor House, Bath Road, Cowes, Isle of Wight, PO31 7RH** P
☎ 01983 200138
Est. 1995 *Stock size* Medium
Stock Jewellery, porcelain, silver
Open Mon–Sat 10.30am–4pm closed Wed
Fairs Miami, Florida
Services Valuations

⊞ Gaby Goldscheider
Contact Miss G Goldscheider
✉ **The Library, Deep Eene, Baring Road, Cowes, Isle of Wight, PO31 8DB**
☎ 01983 293598
Est. 1974 *Stock size* Large
Stock Second-hand, antiquarian, rare books, prints, children's books, literature, fiction, topography, travel, nautical a speciality. About 15,000 books in stock
Open By appointment

⊞ Royal Standard Antiques
Contact Mrs C Bradbury
✉ **70–72 Park Road, Cowes, Isle of Wight, PO31 7LY** P
☎ 01983 281672
Ⓜ 07890 962262
Ⓔ caroline@royalstandardantiques.fsbusiness.co.uk
Ⓦ www.royalstandardantiques.fsbusiness.co.uk
Est. 1994 *Stock size* Medium
Stock Georgian–Edwardian English and French furniture, pictures, engravings, commemoratives, architectural antiques
Open Mon–Sat 10.30am–5.30pm Wed 10.30am–1pm or by appointment
Services Furniture restoration, stained glass restoration, upholstery, chair caning

FRESHWATER

⊞ The Old Village Clock Shop
Contact Mr R Taylor
✉ **3 Moa Place, Freshwater, Isle of Wight, PO40 9DS** P
☎ 01983 754193
Est. 1970 *Stock size* Medium
Stock 17th–19thC English longcase and dial clocks, Vienna regulators, early German, English bracket, French ormolu, carriage clocks
Open Wed Fri Sat 9.30am–1pm or by appointment
Services Valuations

GODSHILL

⊞ Style
Contact Mrs R Brooks
✉ **High Street, Godshill, Isle of Wight, PO38 3HH** P
☎ 01983 840194 Ⓕ 01983 840194
Est. 1992 *Stock size* Large
Stock China, glass, collectables, items of interest, furniture
Open Mon–Sun 10am–5pm

NEWPORT

⊞ Mike Heath Antiques
Contact Mr M Heath
✉ **3–4 Holyrood Street, Newport, Isle of Wight, PO30 5AU** P
☎ 01983 525748
Est. 1979 *Stock size* Medium
Stock Furniture, oil lamps, porcelain, glass, collectables
Open Mon–Sat 10am–5pm Thurs 1–5pm
Services Metal restoration, polishing

Lugley Street Antiques
Contact Mr D Newman
13 Lugley Street, Newport, Isle of Wight, PO30 5HD
01983 523348
Est. 1986 *Stock size* Large
Stock Furniture, clocks, china, collectables, 19thC furniture a speciality
Open Mon–Sat 9.30am–5pm closed Thurs

Online Antiques
Contact Kim or Steve Snow
5 Watchbell Lane, Newport, Isle of Wight, PO30 5XU
01983 526282
vintage.uk@virgin.net
www.vintage-uk.com
Est. 2001 *Stock size* Small
Stock Anything old and interesting
Open Mon–Sat 10am–4pm
Services Online auction service

RYDE

Heritage Books
Contact Rev D H Nearn
7 Cross Street, Ryde, Isle of Wight, PO33 2AD
01983 562933 01983 812634
dhnearn.heritagebooksryde@virgin.net
Est. 1977 *Stock size* Medium
Stock General, Isle of Wight antiquarian prints, books on modern theology, history, culture of Africa a speciality
Open Mon–Sat 10am–5pm closed Thurs
Fairs Guildford Book Fair
Services Book search

Nooks and Crannies
Contact Mr D Burnett
60 High Street, Ryde, Isle of Wight, PO33 2RJ
01983 568984
Est. 1986 *Stock size* Medium
Stock Collectables, lamps, 78 rpm records, telephones, radios, glass, china, furniture
Open Mon–Sat 9.30am–1.30pm 2.30–5pm closed Thurs pm
Fairs Ardingly

Ryde Antiques
Contact Caroline Meeus
61 High Street, Ryde, Isle of Wight, PO33 2RJ
01983 615025
Est. 1968 *Stock size* Medium
Stock General antiques
Open Mon–Sat 10am–4.30pm

Ways
Contact Mr T L Smith
The Auction House, Garfield Road, Ryde, Isle of Wight, PO33 2PT
01983 562255 01983 565108
www.waysauctionrooms.fsbusiness.co.uk
Est. 1815
Open Mon–Fri 9am–5pm
Sales Antique and modern furnishings sale on Thurs, viewing day prior 10am–6pm. No buyer's premium
Frequency Every 5 weeks
Catalogues Yes

SANDOWN

Lake Antiques
Contact Mrs J Marchant
18 Sandown Road, Sandown, Isle of Wight, PO36 9JP
01983 406888
07710 067678
Est. 1982 *Stock size* Medium
Stock Antique furniture, clocks, pictures, decorative items
Open Mon–Sat 10am–4pm closed Wed or by appointment
Services Valuations, mainland deliveries arranged

SHANKLIN

Shanklin Auction Rooms (NAVA)
Contact Mr H Riches
79 Regent Street, Shanklin, Isle of Wight, PO37 7AP
01983 863441 01983 863890
sales@shanklinauctionrooms.co.uk
www.shanklinauctionrooms.co.uk
Est. 1850
Open Mon–Fri 9am–5pm
Sales Collectables monthly, antiques quarterly. Telephone for details
Frequency Monthly
Catalogues Yes

VENTNOR

Curios
Contact Mr M Gregory
3 Church Place, Chale, Ventnor, Isle of Wight, PO38 2HA
01983 730230
07811 835159
Est. 1995 *Stock size* Large
Stock Taxidermy, architectural antiques, fireplaces, staddle stones, unusual curiosities
Open Mon–Sun noon–5.30pm
Services Valuations

Plumridge Antiques
Contact Mr R Plumridge
Unit 2, Caxton House, Ventnor Industrial Estate, Ventnor, Isle of Wight, PO38 1DX
01983 856666 01983 855325
07855 649297
acornpianos@aol.com
Est. 1999 *Stock size* Large
Stock Pianos, furniture
Open Mon–Fri 8.30am–5pm Sat 8.30am–1pm
Services Packers, shippers

Ultramarine
Contact Mrs M Stevens
40b High Street, Ventnor, Isle of Wight, PO38 1RZ
01983 854062
Est. 1999 *Stock size* Large
Stock Collectables, costume jewellery, china, stoneware, glass
Open Mon Tues 10am–1pm Thurs Fri Sat 10am–2pm closed Wed

Ventnor Antiques Centre
Contact Mrs P Huntley
66 High Street, Ventnor, Isle of Wight, PO38 1LU
01983 855302 01983 855325
Est. 1994 *Stock size* Medium
No. of dealers 4
Stock General antiques, collectables, furniture
Open Mon–Sat 10am–5pm
Services Delivery

Ventnor Junction
Contact Mr or Mrs P Dolby
48 High Street, Ventnor, Isle of Wight, PO38 1LT
01983 853996
shop@ventjunc.freeserve.co.uk
www.ventjunc.freeserve.co.uk
Est. 1987 *Stock size* Large
Stock Old toys, collectables, tin trains

Open Most mornings or by appointment
Fairs Sandown Park Toy Fair, Esher
Services Mail order

YARMOUTH

Yarmouth Antiques and Books
Contact Mrs V Blakeley or Mr M Coyle
The House, The Square, Yarmouth, Isle of Wight, PO41 0NP
☎ 01983 760046
yarmouth-antiquesiow@btopenworld.com
Est. 1996 *Stock size* Medium
Stock Antiquarian, second-hand books, china, collectables
Open Mon–Sun 10am–5pm
Fairs Kempton Park, February

SURREY

ABINGER HAMMER

Stirling Antiques
Contact Mr U Burrell
Aberdeen House, Guildford Road, Abinger Hammer, Dorking, Surrey, RH5 6RY
☎ 01306 730706 F 01306 731575
M 07748 005619
Est. 1968 *Stock size* Medium
Stock Architectural stained glass, metalware, furniture, jewellery, silver, curios
Open Mon–Sat 9.30am–6pm closed Thurs

ADDLESTONEMOOR

Small Wood Ltd
Contact Julian Faulkner
The Elephant House, Addlestonemoor, Surrey, KT15 2QF
☎ 01932 848122 F 01932 831690
enquiries@small-wood.com
Est. 1998 *Stock size* Medium
Stock Architectural salvage, contemporary furniture, art and antiques
Open Mon–Sat 10am–5pm

ASHTEAD

Bumbles
Contact Mrs B Kay
90 The Street, Ashtead, Surrey, KT21 1AW
☎ 01372 276219 F 01798 875545
Est. 1978 *Stock size* Medium
Stock General furniture, clocks, porcelain, silver, coins, cigarette cards, lighting, oil-lamp parts
Open Mon–Sat 10am–5.30pm
Services Furniture restoration, upholstery

BETCHWORTH

Stoneycroft Farm (LAPADA, DADA)
Contact J G Elias
Reigate Road, Betchworth, Surrey, RH3 7EY
☎ 01737 845215 F 01737 845215
W www.desk.uk.com
Est. 1987 *Stock size* Large
Stock Country furniture, bookcases, linen presses, dining room tables
Open Mon–Fri 8am–5.30pm Sat 10am–3pm

BLETCHINGLEY

John Anthony
Contact Mrs N Hart
71 High Street, Bletchingley, Redhill, Surrey, RH1 4LJ
☎ 01883 743197 F 01883 742108
M 07836 221689
johnanthonyantiques@hotmail.com
Est. 1974 *Stock size* Medium
Stock 18th–19thC furniture
Open By appointment only

Lawrences Auctioneers Ltd
Contact Miss S Debnam
Norfolk House, High Street, Bletchingley, Redhill, Surrey, RH1 4PA
☎ 01883 743323 F 01883 744578
W www.lawrencesbletchingley.co.uk
Est. 1960
Open Mon–Fri 9am–5pm
Sales General antiques sales on Tues Wed Thurs, viewing Fri Sat 10am–5pm
Frequency Every 6 weeks
Catalogues Yes

Post House Antiques
Contact Mr P Bradley
High Street, Bletchingley, Surrey, RH1 4PA
☎ 01883 743317 F 01883 743317
Est. 1975 *Stock size* Large
Stock Antique lighting
Open Mon–Sat 10am–5pm
Services Restoration

Quill Antiques
Contact Mrs J Davis
86 High Street, Bletchingley, Surrey, RH1 4PA
☎ 01883 743755
Est. 1973 *Stock size* Large
Stock Agricultural, rural bygones, copper, brass, glass, porcelain
Open Tues–Sat 10am–5.30pm
Fairs Dorking

BRAMLEY

Memories Antiques
Contact Mrs P S Kelsey
High Street, Bramley, Guildford, Surrey, GU5 0HB
☎ 01483 892205
M 07774 885014
Est. 1985 *Stock size* Medium
No. of dealers 8
Stock Georgian–Victorian French, pine furniture, silver, jewellery, porcelain, collectables, garden items, kitchenware, French antiques
Open Mon–Sat 10am–5pm
Services ëWanted' service

BROCKHAM

Cartels Auctioneers and Valuers
Contact Mr Carter
2 Tanners Court, Middle Street, Brockham, Dorking (on A25), Surrey, RH3 7NH
☎ 01737 844646 F 01737 844646
M 07768 004293
cartels@onetel.net.uk
Est. 1978
Open Mon–Fri 9.30am–5pm
Sales General antiques, fine art, pre-1930s, viewing all day Fri 10am–7pm and morning of sale 8.30–10am
Frequency Monthly excluding August
Catalogues Yes

CARSHALTON

Cherub Antiques
Contact Mr M Wisdom
312 Carshalton Road,

Carshalton, Surrey,
SM5 3QB 🅿
☎ 020 8643 0028
Ⓜ 07764 275778
Est. 1985 *Stock size* Large
Stock Continental and English antique pine, mahogany
Open Mon–Sat 10am–5.30pm
Services Pine stripping, French polishing

The Clock House (BWCG)
Contact Mark Cocklin
✉ **75 Pound Street, Carshalton, Surrey, SM5 3PG** 🅿
☎ 020 8773 4844
Ⓜ 07850 363317
Ⓔ mark@theclockhouse.co.uk
Ⓦ www.theclockhouse.co.uk
Est. 1989 *Stock size* Medium
Stock Antiquarian horology, longcase clocks
Open Tues–Fri 9.30am–4.30pm Sat 9am–6pm or by appointment
Fairs Brunel University
Services Valuations, restoration, spares

CATERHAM

Chaldon Books and Records
Contact Mr K Chesson
✉ **1 High Street, Caterham, Surrey, CR3 5UE** 🅿
☎ 01883 348583
Est. 1994 *Stock size* Medium
Stock Rare and second-hand books
Open Mon Tues 10am–2pm Thurs–Sat 10am–5pm
Services Book search

CHEAM

Parkins
Contact Miss Wendy Zenthon
✉ **18 Malden Road, Cheam, Surrey, SM3 8QF** 🅿
☎ 020 8644 6633 Ⓕ 020 8255 4703
Ⓔ info@parkinsauction.co.uk
Ⓦ www.parkinsauction.co.uk
Est. 1945
Open Mon–Fri 9am–1pm 2–5pm
Sales Antique furniture and effects 1st Mon of month 10am, general furniture and effects 2nd and 4th Mon of month 10am, viewing Fri 2–4pm Sat 10am–4pm. Smaller fine antiques and collectables monthly evening sale, viewing 2–7pm
Catalogues Yes

Village Antiques
Contact Miss S Jenner
✉ **16 Malden Road, Cheam, Sutton, Surrey, SM3 8QF** 🅿
☎ 020 8644 8567 Ⓕ 020 8644 8567
Est. 1986 *Stock size* Large
Stock Furniture, lighting, porcelain, glass, silver, jewellery, collectors' items
Open Mon–Sat 11am–5pm closed Tues Thurs
Services House clearance

CHERTSEY

D'Eyncourt Antiques
Contact Mr G D H Davies
✉ **21 Windsor Street, Chertsey, Surrey, KT16 8AY** 🅿
☎ 01932 563411
Est. 1970 *Stock size* Large
Stock Furniture, jewellery, china, collectables, fireplaces
Open Mon–Fri 10am–5.15pm Sat 7am–5.30pm Sun 11am–4pm
Fairs London Photographic Fair
Services Valuations

CHOBHAM

Chobham Antique Clocks (BHI)
Contact Mike Morris
✉ **73–75 High Street, Chobham, Woking, Surrey, GU24 8AF** 🅿
☎ 01276 682560
Est. 1989 *Stock size* Medium
Stock Antique clocks, barometers
Open Tues–Sat 10am–5pm
Services Valuations, restoration

Mimbridge Antiques and Collectables
Contact Mrs J Monteath Scott
✉ **Mimbridge Garden Centre, Station Road, Chobham, Woking, Surrey, GU24 8AS** 🅿
☎ 01276 855736
Ⓜ 0771 862284
Est. 1987 *Stock size* Medium
Stock Small antiques, pictures, prints, maps, garden items, period furniture, decorative items, porcelain, glass, dolls
Open Mon–Sun 10am–5pm
Fairs Kempton
Services Picture framing

What-Not Antiques
Contact Carole Fisher
✉ **82 High Street, Chobham, Surrey, GU24 8AF** 🅿
☎ 01276 857622 Ⓕ 01276 856766
Est. 1984 *Stock size* Medium
Stock Antique pine and oak furniture, collectables, Disney
Open Mon–Sat 9am–5.30pm Sun 10.30am–4pm

CHURT

Churt Curiosity Shop
Contact Mrs G Gregory
✉ **Crossways, Churt, Farnham, Surrey, GU10 2JE** 🅿
☎ 01428 714096
Est. 1995 *Stock size* Medium
Stock Victorian–Edwardian small furniture, Victorian china, glass, collectables
Open Tues–Sat 10.15am–5pm closed Wed

COBHAM

Village Antiques
Contact Mr N Tsangari
✉ **38 Portsmouth Road, Cobham, Surrey, KT11 1HZ** 🅿
☎ 01932 589841
Ⓜ 07973 549221
Est. 1998 *Stock size* Medium
Stock General antiques, small furniture, pictures, porcelain, glass
Open Mon–Fri 10am–6pm or by appointment
Services Picture restoration

COMPTON

Country Rustics
Contact Veronica Dewey
✉ **45 The Street, Compton, Guildford, Surrey, GU3 1EG** 🅿
☎ 01483 810505
Est. 2001 *Stock size* Small
Stock Rustic furniture and collectables
Open Tues–Sun 10am–6pm

Old Barn Antiques
Contact Mrs Chris Thurner
✉ **Old Barn, The Street,**

Compton, Guildford, Surrey, GU3 1EB P
☎ 01483 810819
Est. 1993 *Stock size* Small
No. of dealers 6
Stock Country items, blue and white, Victoriana, china, glass, collectables
Open Mon–Sat 10am–4pm

COULSDON

⊞ Decodream
Contact David Mobbs
✉ **233 Chipstead Valley Road, Coulsdon, Surrey, CR5 3BY** P
☎ 020 8668 5534 ⓕ 01737 556079
Est. 1987 *Stock size* Large
Stock Art Deco pottery
Open Mon–Sat by appointment
Services Valuations

CRANLEIGH

⊞ Dingly Dell Antiques & Collectables
Contact Susanna Wadey
✉ **8 Smithbrook Kilns (A281), Cranleigh, Surrey, GU6 8JJ** P
☎ 01483 268868
Est. 2002 *Stock size* Large
Stock Antiques, collectables
Open Tues–Sat 10am–5pm
Services Coffee shop

CROYDON

Croydon Coin Auctions
Contact Mr G J Monk
✉ **PO Box 201, Croydon, Surrey, CR9 7AQ** P
☎ 020 8656 4583 ⓕ 020 8656 4583
ⓔ graeme@croydoncoinauctions.co.uk
ⓦ www.croydoncoinauctions.co.uk
Est. 1983
Open Mon–Fri 9am–5pm
Sales 6 sales a year of English, foreign and ancient coins, medallions, tokens and bank notes. Held at the United Reformed Church Hall, East Croydon Tues noon
Frequency Bi-monthly

⊞ Oscar Dahling Antiques
Contact Oscar Dahling
✉ **87 Cherry Orchard Road, East Croydon, Surrey, CR0 6BE**
☎ 0208 8681 8090
ⓔ oscar.dahling@virgin.net
Est. 1991 *Stock size* Medium
Stock General antiques
Open Tues–Thur 10.30am–6pm Sat 10.30am–4.30pm
Services Valuations

⊞ McNally Antiques
Contact I McNally
✉ **322 Brighton Road, South Croydon, Surrey, CR2 6AJ** P
☎ 020 8686 8387 ⓕ 020 8686 8387
Est. 1972 *Stock size* Large
Stock Oak, walnut, mahogany furniture
Open Mon–Fri 9am–5pm Sat 9.30am–1pm or by appointment
Services Shipping

DORKING

⊞ Antique Clocks by Patrick Thomas
Contact Mr P Thomas
✉ **62a West Street, Dorking, Surrey, RH4 1BS** P
☎ 01306 743661 ⓕ 01306 743661
ⓜ 07976 971024
ⓦ www.antiqueclockshop.co.uk
Est. 1992 *Stock size* Large
Stock Clocks, scientific instruments, sporting antiques
Open Mon–Sat 9.30am–5.30pm Sun 11am–4pm
Services Valuations, restoration

⊞ Nicholas Arkell Antiques Ltd (LAPADA)
Contact Nicholas Arkell
✉ **64–65 West Street, Dorking, Surrey, RH4 1BS** P
☎ 01306 742152 ⓕ 01306 742152
ⓜ 07973 819783
ⓔ nick@arkellantiques.co.uk
ⓦ www.arkellantiques.com
Est. 1978 *Stock size* Large
Stock Georgian and Edwardian satinwood furniture, silver, lighting, garden statuary
Open Mon–Sat 10am–5pm
Fairs LAPADA, Guildford, Olympia

⊞ G D Blay Antiques (BADA)
Contact Geoffrey Blay
✉ **56 West Street, Dorking, Surrey, RH4 1BS** P
ⓜ 07785 767718
ⓔ gdblay@gdblayantiques.com
ⓦ www.gdblayantiques.com
Stock size Medium
Stock Pre-1830s furniture, clocks, mirrors
Open Tues–Sat 10am–5pm or by appointment
Fairs Summer and Winter Olympia, BADA Chelsea

⊞ J and M Coombes (DADA)
Contact Mr M Coombes
✉ **44 West Street, Dorking, Surrey, RH4 1BU** P
☎ 01306 885479 ⓕ 01306 885479
Est. 1967 *Stock size* Large
Stock Victorian–Edwardian furniture
Open Mon–Fri 9am–5pm Sat 10am–5pm Sun 11am–4pm

Crows Auction Gallery
Contact Crows Auction Gallery
✉ **Rear of Dorking Halls, Reigate Road, Dorking, Surrey, RH4 1SG** P
☎ 01306 740382 ⓕ 01306 881672
ⓜ 07713 382446
ⓔ enquiriescrows.co.uk
ⓦ www.crowsauctions.co.uk
Est. 1988
Open Mon–Fri 9am–4pm Sat 9.30am–noon
Sales Antiques and collectables sale last Wed in month 10am, viewing Sat 9am–1pm Mon–Tues 9am–4pm and morning of sale
Frequency Monthly
Catalogues Yes

⊞ Dolphin Square Antiques
Contact Diana James
✉ **42 West Street, Dorking, Surrey, RH4 1BU** P
☎ 01306 887901
Est. 1995 *Stock size* Medium
Stock Georgian–Edwardian furniture, clocks, mirrors, Staffordshire, porcelain, glass, copper, brass ware, bronzes
Open Tues–Sat 10am–5.30pm

⊞ Dorking Desk Shop (LAPADA, DADA)
Contact J G Elias
✉ **41 West Street, Dorking, Surrey, RH4 1BU**
☎ 01306 883327 ⓕ 01306 875363
ⓦ www.desk.uk.com
Est. 1973 *Stock size* Large

Stock Library and writing furniture, pedestal and partner's desks, bookcases, dining tables, oak and country furniture, wardrobes
Open Mon–Fri 8am–5.30pm Sat 10.30am–5.30pm
Services Desk finding service

Dorking House Antiques
Contact Mrs G Emburey
17–18 West Street, Dorking, Surrey, RH4 1BS
01306 740915
Est. 1988 *Stock size* Large
No. of dealers 25
Stock Period furniture, silver, porcelain, paintings, collectables, treen, clocks
Open Mon–Sat 10am–5pm

Gallery Eleven (LAPADA)
11 West Street, Dorking, Surrey, RH4 1BL
01306 887771 Ⓕ 01306 887771
Est. 1990 *Stock size* Large
Stock Fine 18th–19thC furniture, quality ceramics, decorative items, contemporary pieces, glassware, gardenware
Open Tues Wed Fri Sat 11.30am–4pm
Services Valuations, display on commission basis

Great Grooms of Dorking
Contact Mr J Podger
50–52 West Street, Dorking, Surrey, RH4 1BU
01306 887076 Ⓕ 01306 881029
Ⓔ laurence@hampshires.co.uk or antiques@great-grooms.co.uk
Ⓦ www.great-grooms.co.uk
Est. 1993 *Stock size* Large
No. of dealers 25
Stock Antique furniture, collectables, jewellery, silver, china, glass, pictures, lighting
Open Mon–Sat 9.30am–5.30pm Sun 10am–4pm
Services Valuations, restoration, interior design

Harmans Antiques (LAPADA)
Contact Mr P Harman
19 West Street, Dorking, Surrey, RH4 1QH
01306 743330 Ⓕ 01306 742593
Ⓔ enquiries@harmans-antiques.uk.com
Ⓦ www.harmans-antiques.uk.com
Est. 1956 *Stock size* Large
Stock Georgian–Edwardian furniture
Open Mon–Sat 10am–5pm Sun 11am–4pm
Fairs Guildford
Services Restoration

The Howard Gallery (LAPADA)
Contact Mrs F Howard
5 West Street, Dorking, Surrey, RH4 1BL
01306 880022
Ⓦ www.thehowardgallery.co.uk
Est. 1989 *Stock size* Medium
Stock 17th–18thC early Georgian, Queen Anne, Regency, oak, country furniture, longcase, bracket clocks
Open Tues–Sat 11am–5pm
Services Restoration, shipping

King's Court Galleries (FATG)
Contact Mrs J Joel
54 West Street, Dorking, Surrey, RH4 1BS
01306 881757 Ⓕ 01306 875305
Ⓔ sales@kingscourtgalleries.co.uk
Ⓦ www.kingscourtgalleries.co.uk
Est. 1984 *Stock size* Large
Stock Antique maps, engravings, sporting and decorative prints
Open Mon–Sat 9.30am–5.30pm
Services Bespoke framing, mounting

Malthouse Antiques
Contact Mr C Waters
49 West Street, Dorking, Surrey, RH4 1BU
01306 886169
Est. 1993 *Stock size* Large
No. of dealers 5
Stock 17th–20thC antiques
Open Mon–Sat 10am–5pm
Services Valuations, restoration, shipping

Mayfair Antiques
43 West Street, Dorking, Surrey, RH4 1BU
01306 885007 Ⓕ 01306 742636
Est. 1968 *Stock size* Medium
Stock General antiques, furniture
Open Mon–Sat 10am–5.30pm
Services Restoration

Bruce Moss Antiques
Contact Bruce Moss
Hampshires of Dorking Antique Centre, 50–52 West Street, Dorking, Surrey, RH4 1BU
01306 887076
Est. 2004 *Stock size* Medium
Stock Georgian furniture, silver
Open Mon–Sat 9.30am–5.30pm Sun & Bank Holidays 10am–4pm

Pilgrims Antique Centre
Contact Mrs M Pritchard
7 West Street, Dorking, Surrey, RH4 1BL
01306 875028
Est. 1990 *Stock size* Medium
No. of dealers 10
Stock Glass, furniture, paintings, books, Art Deco, barometers, Jobling glass, collectables
Open Mon–Fri 10am–5pm Sat 10am–5.30pm
Services Restaurant

The Refectory
Contact Mr Chris Marks
38 West Street, Dorking, Surrey, RH4 1BU
01306 742111 Ⓕ 01306 742111
Est. 1995 *Stock size* Medium
Stock 16th–19thC English country furniture, refectory tables, coffers, Windsor chairs, country items
Open Mon–Sat 10.30am–5.30pm Sun by appointment

Eric Tombs
Contact Mr Eric Tombs
62a West Street, Dorking, Surrey, RH4 1BS
01306 743661
Ⓜ 07720 561680
Ⓔ ertombs@aol.com
Est. 1992 *Stock size* Medium
Stock Scientific instruments
Open Mon–Sat 9.30am–5.30pm Sun 11am–4pm
Fairs Scientific Instruments Fair
Services Valuations, restoration

The Vinery Antiques
Contact Cindy King or Pauline Schwarz

✉ 55 West Street, Dorking, Surrey, RH4 1BS P
☎ 01306 743440 *Stock size* Medium
Stock 18th–19thC mahogany, walnut furniture, upholstery, early porcelain, decorative items
Open Tues–Sat 10.30am–5pm Wed closed 2pm or by appointment
Services Valuations, restoration, furniture search

West Street Antiques
Contact Mr J G Spooner
✉ 63 West Street, Dorking, Surrey, RH4 1BS P
☎ 01306 883487 F 01306 883487
E weststant@aol.com
W antiquearmsandarmour.com
Est. 1986 *Stock size* Medium
Stock English furniture, arms, armour. Comprehensive on-line catalogue
Open Mon–Sat 9.30am–1pm 2.15–5.30pm or by appointment
Fairs London Arms Fair, Park Lane Arms Fair
Services Valuations

P F Windibank
Contact Mr S Windibank
✉ Dorking Halls, Reigate Road, Dorking, Surrey, RH4 1SG P
☎ 01306 884556 F 01306 884669
E sjw@windibank.co.uk
W www.windibank.co.uk
Est. 1945
Open Mon–Fri 9am–5pm Sat 10am–1pm
Sales Antique and quality sales on Sat, viewing Thurs 5–9pm Fri 9am–5pm
Frequency 4–6 weeks
Catalogues Yes

EAST MOLESEY

Books Bought and Sold Ltd
Contact Mr P Sheridan
✉ 68 Walton Road, East Molesey, Surrey, KT8 0DL P
☎ 020 8224 3232 F 020 8224 3576
E booksbought@yahoo.co.uk
Est. 1973 *Stock size* Medium
Stock Antiquarian, rare, second-hand books, transport, collectable children's books a speciality
Open Tues–Sat 10am–5pm
Fairs HD Book Fairs

Elizabeth R Antiques
Contact E L Mallah
✉ 39 Bridge Road, Hampton Court, East Molesey, Surrey, KT8 9ER P
☎ 020 8979 4004 F 020 8979 4004
E lizaantiques@hotmail.com
Est. 1994 *Stock size* Large
Stock 18th–19thC furniture, porcelain, glass, jewellery, 20thC dolls and toys
Open Tues–Sat 10am–4.30pm Sun 11am–3pm closed Wed
Fairs Alexandra Palace, Sandown
Services Valuations, restoration

The Hampton Court Emporium
Contact Mr A Smith
✉ 52–54 Bridge Road, East Molesey, Surrey, KT8 9HA P
☎ 020 8941 8876
W www.hamptoncourtemporium.com
Est. 1992 *Stock size* Large
No. of dealers 38
Stock Cameras, books, jewellery, lace, silver, brass, copper, toys, war ephemera, French arts, furniture
Open Mon–Sat 10am–5.30pm Sun 11am–5.30pm

Journeyman Antique Centre
Contact Mr or Mrs A Caplan
✉ 77 Bridge Road, East Molesey, Surrey, KT8 9WH
☎ 0208 979 7954
Est. 1974 *Stock size* Large
No. of dealers 9
Stock General antiques, collectables, furniture, jewellery
Open Mon–Sat 10.30am–5.30pm Sun noon–5pm

Nostradamus Centre
Contact Kristina Carson
✉ 53 Bridge Road, East Molesey, Surrey, KT8 9HA P
☎ 020 8783 0595
Est. 1980 *Stock size* Medium
No. of dealers 20
Stock Furniture, crystal, silver, old toys, Art Deco, jewellery
Open Tues–Mon 10am–5.30pm

Palace Antiques
Contact John Prince
✉ 29–31 Bridge Road, East Molesey, Surrey, KT8 9ER P
☎ 020 8979 2182 F 020 8949 1153
Est. 2000 *Stock size* Large
No. of dealers 15
Stock General antiques and bronzeware
Open Mon–Sun 10am–6pm

Rhombus
Contact Jackie Griffin
✉ 28 Bridge Road, East Molesey, Surrey, KT8 9HA P
☎ 020 8224 5035
M 07941 292049
Est. 2000 *Stock size* Medium
No. of dealers 2
Stock Art Deco centre
Open Wed–Sun 11am–5.30pm closed Fri

Alexis F J Turner Antiques
Contact Mr Turner
✉ Antiques at 144a Bridge Road, East Molesey, Surrey, KT8 9HW P
☎ 020 8542 5926
M 07770 880960
Est. 1992 *Stock size* Medium
Stock Natural history, taxidermy, gentlemen's effects, curiosities
Open Sat 10am–2pm or by appointment

EPSOM

Gavantiques
Contact Gavin Taylor
✉ 20 Stoneleigh Broadway, Epsom, Surrey, KT17 2HU P
☎ 0208 786 3484
M 07836 561612
Est. 1988 *Stock size* Medium
Stock General antiques
Open Mon–Sat 10am–4pm closed Thur

ESHER

Memento
Contact Michael Coshall
✉ 8B Church Street, Esher, Surrey, KT10 8QS
☎ 01372 462121 F 01372 462121
Est. 2004 *Stock size* Medium
Stock Decorative antiques,

including statues, for house and garden
Open Tue–Sun 11am–6pm
Services Sourcing items for clients

EWELL

J W McKenzie Ltd
Contact John
12 Stoneleigh Park Road, Ewell, Surrey, KT19 0QR
0208 393 7700 0208 393 1694
jwmck@net.comuk.co.uk
www.mckenzie-cricket.co.uk
Est. 1972 *Stock size* Large
Stock Antiquarian, rare books, memorabilia
Open Mon–Fri 9am–5pm or by appointment
Services Four catalogues per year

FARNHAM

Annie's Antiques
Contact Annie
1 Ridgway Parade, Frensham Road, Farnham, Surrey, GU9 8UZ
01252 713447
Est. 1982 *Stock size* Medium
Stock General antiques
Open Mon–Sat 10am–5.30pm

Bourne Mill Antiques
Contact Mrs Vicky Bowers
39–43 Guildford Road, Farnham, Surrey, GU9 9PY
01252 716663
07808 628440
Est. 1960 *Stock size* Large
No. of dealers 70
Stock Antiques, collectables in 38 rooms
Open Mon–Sat 9.30am–5pm Sun 10am–5pm

Casque and Gauntlet Militaria
Contact R L Colt or A Colt
55–59 Badshot Lea Road, Badshot Lea, Farnham, Surrey, GU9 9LP
01252 320745
www.armsandarmour.co.uk/dealers/casque/casque.htm
Est. 1972 *Stock size* Large
Stock Militaria, 15thC–modern times including swords, bayonets, armour
Open Mon–Sat 11am–5pm
Services Restoration of antique weapons

Christopher's Antiques
Contact Mr C Booth
39a West Street, Farnham, Surrey, GU9 7DX
01252 713794 01252 713266
cbooth7956@aol.com
Est. 1972 *Stock size* Large
Stock French provincial country furniture
Open Mon–Fri 8am–5.30pm Sat 8am–noon
Services Valuations, restoration

FERNHURST

John Nicholson Fine Art Auctioneers
Contact Mr G Nugent
The Auction Rooms, Longfield, Midhurst Road, Fernhurst, Surrey, GU27 3HA
01428 653727 01428 641509
sales@johnnicholsons.com
www.johnnicholsons.com
Est. 1992
Open Mon–Fri 9am–5.30pm
Sales Fine art auctions 6 weekly Wed Thurs. Paintings, prints, antiquarian books 3–4 times a year
Catalogues Yes

GODALMING

E Bailey
Contact E Bailey
Portsmouth Road, Milford, Godalming, Surrey, GU8 5DR
01483 422943
Est. 1978 *Stock size* Medium
Stock General antiques, collectables, curios, golf clubs, woodworking, engineering tools
Open Mon–Sat 8.30am–5pm closed Thurs

Hamptons International Auctioneers and Valuers
Contact Liz Bryder
Baverstock House, 93 High Street, Godalming, Surrey, GU7 1AL
01483 423567 01483 426392
fineartauctions@hamptons-int.com
www.hamptons.co.uk/fineart
Est. 1996
Open Mon–Fri 9am–5.30pm
Sales Sales of antiques, furniture, carpets, pictures, clocks, china, glass, jewellery, silver, objects of virtue take place on Wed and Thurs at 11am, viewing Sat 9.30am–12.30pm Mon 9.30am–7pm Tues 9.30am–3pm day of sale up to 10.30am
Frequency 4 sales every 6–8 weeks
Catalogues Yes

Heath-Bullocks (BADA)
Contact Mrs Mary Heath-Bullock
8 Meadrow, Godalming, Surrey, GU7 3HN
01483 422562 01483 426077
heathbullocks@aol.com
www.heath-bullocks.com or www.antiquescare.com
Est. 1925 *Stock size* Large
Stock 17th–19thC furniture
Open Mon–Sat 10am–4pm and by appointment
Fairs BADA, The Surrey Antiques Fair, The Buxton Antiques Fair
Services Valuations, restoration, upholstery

Honeypot Antiques
Contact Bob Holroyd
Milford Road, Elstead, Godalming, Surrey, GU8 6HR
01252 703614
www.honeypotantiques.co.uk
Est. 1996 *Stock size* Large
No. of dealers 25
Stock General antiques and collectables
Open Mon–Sat 10am–5pm Sun 11am–5pm

GOMSHALL

The Coach House Antiques (LAPADA)
Contact Paul or Louise Reeves
60 Station Road, Gomshall, Guildford, Surrey, GU5 9NP
01483 203838 01483 202999
coach_house.antiques@virgin.net
www.coachhouseantiques.com
Est. 1987 *Stock size* Medium
Stock Regency–William IV furniture, clocks
Open Mon–Sat 9.30am–5pm Sun noon–5pm closed Thurs
Fairs Guildford
Services Restoration

The Studio
Contact Mrs M Ellenger
Station Road, Gomshall, Guildford, Surrey, GU5 9LQ
01483 202449
Est. 1984 *Stock size* Large
Stock Furniture, china, silver, pictures
Open Mon–Sun noon–5pm

GREAT BOOKHAM

Roger A Davis Antiquarian Horologist
Contact Roger Davis
19 Dorking Road, Great Bookham, Surrey, KT23 4PU
01372 457655
Est. 1972 *Stock size* Medium
Stock Antique clocks
Open Tues Thurs Sat 9.30am–12.30pm 2–5pm
Services Restoration

Memory Lane Antiques
Contact Mrs J Westwood
30 Church Road, Great Bookham, Leatherhead, Surrey, KT23 3PW
01372 459908
Est. 1984 *Stock size* Medium
Stock Antiques, toys
Open Mon–Fri 10am–5pm Sat 10am–2pm closed Wed

GUILDFORD

Bonhams
Millmead, Guildford, Surrey, GU2 4BE
01483 504030 F 01483 450205
E guildford@bonhams.com
W www.bonhams.com
Est. 1793
Open Mon–Fri 9am–1pm 2–5pm
Sales Regional office. Regular house and attic sales across the country; contact London offices for further details. Free auction valuations; insurance and probate valuations

Clarke Gammon Wellers Auctioneers & Valuers (RICS)
Contact Gordon Patrick or Sarah Moran
Bedford Road, Guildford, Surrey, GU1 4SJ
01483 880915 F 01483 880918
W www.invaluable.com/wellers
Est. 1919
Open Mon–Fri 9am–5.30pm
Sales Fine art, antiques and collectors' sales, viewing Sat 9am–noon Mon 9am–7pm prior to sale
Frequency 6 weeks
Catalogues Yes

Denning Antiques
Contact Mrs C Denning
1 Chapel Street, Guildford, Surrey, GU1 3UH
01483 539595
Est. 1984 *Stock size* Large
Stock Silver, textiles, jewellery
Open Mon–Sat 10am–5pm

Horological Workshops (BADA, BHI)
Contact Mr M D Tooke
204 Worplesdon Road, Guildford, Surrey, GU2 9UY
01483 576496 F 01483 452212
E enquiries@horological workshops.com
W www.horologicalworkshops.com
Est. 1968 *Stock size* Large
Stock Clocks, watches, barometers
Open Tues–Fri 8.30am–5.30pm Sat 9am–12.30pm
Services Valuations, restoration, shipping, collection, delivery

Pew Corner Ltd (SALVO)
Contact David Bouldin
Artington Manor Farm, Old Portsmouth Road, Guildford, Surrey, GU3 1LP
01483 533337 F 01483 535554
E pewcorner@pewcorner.co.uk
W www.pewcorner.co.uk
Est. 1988 *Stock size* Large
Stock Reclaimed church interiors furniture, hand-made solid oak furniture
Open Mon–Sat 10am–5pm

Wellers Auctioneers
Contact Mr Glen Snelgar FRICS or Mr Mark Longson
70 Guildford Street, Chertsey, Surrey, KT16 9BB
01932 568678 F 01932 568626
E auctions@wellers.co.uk
W www.wellers.co.uk
Est. 1980
Open Mon–Fri 9am–5pm
Sales Antique sales 2nd Sat monthly at 9.30am
Frequency Monthly
Catalogues Yes

HAM COMMON

Glencorse Antiques (LAPADA)
Contact Mr Prydal
321 Richmond Road, Ham Parade, Ham Common, Surrey, KT2 5QU
020 8541 0871
M 07740 779917
Est. 1983 *Stock size* Medium
Stock 19thC furniture, Victorian, modern British paintings
Open Mon–Sat 10am–5.30pm
Fairs Olympia (Spring), Claridges (April)

HAMPTON WICK

The Rug Studio
Contact Rachel Bassill
34 High Street, Hampton Wick, Surrey, KT1 4DB
020 8977 4403 F 020 8977 4408
E info@therugstudio.co.uk
W www.therugstudio.co.uk
Est. 1994 *Stock size* Medium
Stock Antique, Oriental and contemporary rugs
Open Tues–Fri 10am–5.30pm Sat 10am–4pm Sun 11am–4pm (excluding August)
Fairs Country Living, Antiques for Everyone
Services Restoration, rug search

HASLEMERE

Serendipity
Contact Mrs E Moore
7 Petworth Road, Haslemere, Surrey, TU27 2BJ
01428 642682
Est. 1997 *Stock size* Medium
No. of dealers 12
Stock Furniture, china, glass, books, maps, pictures, collectables
Open Mon–Sat 10am–5pm Sun 10.30am–4.30pm

West Street Antiques (LAPADA)
Contact Mr M Holden

✉ 8–10 West Street,
Haslemere, Surrey,
GU27 2AB 🅿
☎ 01428 644911 ⓕ 01428 645201
ⓔ info@weststreetantiques.co.uk
ⓦ www.weststreetantiques.co.uk
Est. 1998 *Stock size* Medium
Stock 17thC–early 20thC furniture, dinner services, maps, prints, Georgian and Victorian silver
Open Mon–Sat 9.30am–5pm
Services Valuations, restoration

Woods Wharf Antiques Market
Contact Mrs C Lunnon
✉ 56 High Street,
Haslemere, Surrey,
GU27 2LA 🅿
☎ 01428 642125 ⓕ 01428 642125
Est. 1975 *Stock size* Medium
No. of dealers 8
Stock Antiques, collectables
Open Mon–Sat 9.30am–5pm

HINDHEAD

Albany Antiques
Contact Mr T Winstanley
✉ 8–10 London Road,
Hindhead, Surrey,
GU26 6AF 🅿
☎ 01428 605528 ⓕ 01428 605528
ⓜ 07931 672345
Est. 1949 *Stock size* Large
Stock Georgian furniture, 18thC brass, Victorian antiques, porcelain, statuary
Open Mon–Sat 9.30am–5pm or by appointment

Book Academy
✉ Crossways House,
Crossways Road, Grayshott,
Hindhead, Surrey,
GU26 6HJ 🅿
☎ 01428 609910 ⓕ 01428 609904
Est. 1970 *Stock size* Large
Stock Antiquarian and new, reformed theology books including bibles, prayer, hymn books, Dickens, Hampshire a speciality
Open Mon–Fri 9.30am–4.30pm
Services Valuations, book repair, rebinding

M J Bowdery (BADA)
Contact Mr Malcolm John Bowdery
✉ 12 London Road,
Hindhead, Surrey,
GU26 6AF 🅿
☎ 01428 606376
ⓜ 07774 821444
Est. 1970 *Stock size* Small
Stock 18th–19thC furniture
Open Mon–Sat 9am–1pm or by appointment
Services Valuations

Drummonds Architectural Antiques Ltd (SALVO)
Contact Mr Drummond Shaw
✉ The Kirkpatrick Buildings,
25 London Road,
Hindhead, Surrey,
GU26 6AB 🅿
☎ 01428 609444 ⓕ 01428 609445
ⓔ info@drummonds-arch.co.uk
ⓦ www.drummonds-arch.co.uk
Est. 1989 *Stock size* Large
Stock Period bathrooms, oak and pine flooring, fireplaces, statues, garden furniture and lighting, brass door furniture and fittings, radiators, furniture, windows, doors, gates, railings, conservatories
Open Mon–Fri 9am–6pm
Sat 10am–5pm
Services Proper vitreous re-enamelling of cast-iron baths, restored antique bathrooms

HORLEY

Surrey Antiques
Contact Mr M Bradnum
✉ 3 Central Parade,
Massetts Road, Horley, Surrey,
RH6 7PP 🅿
☎ 01293 775522
Est. 1989 *Stock size* Large
Stock Antiques, collectables, furniture, silver, china, glass, brass, linen, pictures, books
Open Mon–Sat 10am–5pm
Services House clearance

KINGSTON-UPON-THAMES

Glydon and Guess (NAG, NPA)
Contact Mr A Fleckney
✉ 14 Applemarket,
Kingston-upon-Thames, Surrey,
KT1 1JE 🅿
☎ 020 8546 3758 ⓕ 020 8541 5743
ⓔ glydonandguess@finegem.co.uk
ⓦ www.finegem.co.uk
Est. 1940 *Stock size* Medium
Stock Jewellery, antique and modern furniture, clocks, barometers
Open Mon–Sat 9.30am–5pm
Services Valuations, restoration, pawnbrokers

The Kingston Antiques Centre
✉ 29–31 Old London Road,
Kingston-upon-Thames, Surrey,
KT2 6ND 🅿
☎ 020 8549 2004 ⓕ 020 8549 3839
ⓔ enquiries@antiquesmarket.co.uk
ⓦ www.kingstonantiquescentre.co.uk
Est. 1996 *Stock size* Large
No. of dealers 80+
Stock Furniture, jewellery, porcelain, silver, pictures, 20thC design, lighting, Oriental
Open Mon–Sat 9.30am–6pm
Sun 10.30am–6pm

MERSTHAM

Geoffrey Van-Hay Antiques
Contact Geoffrey Van-Hay
✉ The Old Smithy,
7 High Street,
Merstham, Surrey,
RH1 3BA 🅿
☎ 01737 645131 ⓕ 01737 645131
ⓔ olliev@hotmail.com
Est. 1992 *Stock size* Medium
Stock General antiques
Open Mon–Sat 9.30am–5.30pm
Services Valuations, restoration

OXTED

The Second-Hand Bookshop
Contact Mr David Neal
✉ 27 Station Road West,
Oxted, Surrey,
RH8 9EE 🅿
☎ 01883 715755
Est. 1994 *Stock size* Medium
Stock Rare, second-hand books, mainly non-fiction
Open Mon–Sat 10am–5pm
Fairs HD, Titlepage

REDHILL

F G Lawrence and Son
Contact Mr C Lawrence
✉ Rear of 89 Brighton Road,
Redhill, Surrey,
RH1 6PS 🅿
☎ 01737 764196 ⓕ 01737 764196
ⓜ 07850 787873
ⓔ fglawrence@btopenworld.com
Est. 1890 *Stock size* Large
Stock Georgian, Edwardian,

1920s furniture
Open Mon–Fri 9am–5pm
Sat 9am–1pm
Fairs Newark, Ardingly
Services Valuations, restoration

REIGATE

The Gallery (LAPADA, CINOA)
Contact Jeffrey S Cohen
3–5 Church Street, Reigate, Surrey, RH2 0AA
☎ 01737 242813 Ⓕ 01737 362819
Ⓜ 07711 670676
Ⓔ the.gallery@virgin.net
Ⓦ www.thegallery.uk.com
Est. 1990 *Stock size* Large
Stock Modern British paintings 1850–1960, French post impressionist, 18th–19thC Regency, Georgian, Sheraton revival furniture
Open Mon–Sat 10am–5pm
Services Conservation

Knoller, Bertram
Contact Bertram Knoller
14a London Road, Reigate, Surrey, RH2 9HY
☎ 01737 242548
Est. 1970 *Stock size* Small
Stock Copper, brass, silver, fireplace accessories, lighting
Open Tues Thurs Sat 10am–5pm
Services Clock repairs, metal repairs and polishing

Reigate Galleries (PBFA)
Contact J S Morrish
45a Bell Street, Reigate, Surrey, RH2 7AQ
☎ 01737 246055
Est. 1958 *Stock size* Large
Stock Antiquarian, rare, second-hand books, antique engravings
Open Mon–Sat 9am–5.30pm
Wed 9am–1pm
Fairs PBFA fairs in London

M & M White Antiques and Reproduction Centre
Contact Mr M White
57 High Street, Reigate, Surrey, RH2 9AE
☎ 01737 222331
Ⓜ 07974 172801
Est. 1994 *Stock size* Medium
Stock Regency, Victorian, reproduction furniture
Open Mon–Sat 10am–5.30pm
Fairs Newark, Ardingly

RICHMOND

Antigone
Contact Mr S Bolster
3 Brewers Lane, Richmond, Surrey, TW9 1HH
☎ 020 8940 6894
Ⓜ 07785 222082
Est. 1982 *Stock size* Large
Stock Antique jewellery, objects of virtue
Open Mon–Sat 10am–5pm
Services Valuations, probate

Antique Mart
Contact Mr G Katz
72–74 Hill Rise, Richmond, Surrey, TW10 6UB
☎ 020 8940 6942 Ⓕ 020 8715 4668
Ⓜ 07775 626423
Est. 1963 *Stock size* Medium
Stock 18th–19thC furniture
Open Thurs–Sun 2–5.15pm or by appointment

Hugo Austin Antiques
Contact Hugo Austin
128 Kew Road, Richmond, Surrey, TW9 2PN
☎ 0208 332 2316
Est. 1993 *Stock size* Medium
Stock French country furniture
Open Mon–Sat 10.30am–6.30pm
Sun 2–6pm
Services Restoration

Andrew Davis Antiques
Contact Mr A Davis
6 Mortlake Terrace, Kew Green, Richmond, Surrey, TW9 3DT
☎ 020 8948 4911
Ⓜ 07768 904041
Est. 1969 *Stock size* Medium
Stock General antiques, pictures, prints
Open Open most days and by appointment
Services Valuations, house clearance

The Gooday Gallery
Contact Mrs D Gooday
14 Richmond Hill, Richmond, Surrey, TW10 6QX
☎ 020 8940 8652
Ⓜ 07710 124540
Ⓔ goodaygallery@aol.com
Est. 1971 *Stock size* Medium
Stock Arts and Crafts, Art Nouveau, Art Deco, post-modernism, tribal art, African and Oceanic masks
Open Thurs–Sat 11am–5pm or by appointment
Services Valuations

Horton (LAPADA)
Contact David Horton
2 Paved Court, Richmond, Surrey, TW9 1LZ
☎ 020 8832 1775
Ⓔ richmond@hortonlondon.co.uk
Ⓦ www.hortonlondon.co.uk
Est. 1978 *Stock size* Small
Stock Antique jewellery
Open Mon–Sat 10am–5pm
Services Repairs

Lionel Jacobs (NAG)
Contact Tom French
12–14 Brewers Lane, Richmond, Surrey, TW9 1HH
☎ 020 8940 8069 Ⓕ 020 8332 1841
Ⓔ lioneljacobs@lioneljacobs.com
Ⓦ www. lioneljacobs.com
Est. 1977 *Stock size* Medium
Stock Antique fine jewellery, silver, watches
Open Tues–Sat 10am–5pm
Services Valuations, jewellery and watch repair

Linden Antique Prints
Contact Mr M Synan
1a Church Court, Richmond, Surrey, TW9 1JL
☎ 01959 574306 Ⓕ 020 8223 26516
Ⓔ martin@lindenprints.com
Ⓦ www.lindenprints.com
Est. 1997 *Stock size* Medium
Stock Antique prints, maps, watercolours
Open Mon–Fri 10.30am–5.30pm or by appointment
Fairs Royal National

Marryat Antiques Ltd (LAPADA)
Contact Mrs M Samuels
88 Sheen Road, Richmond, Surrey, TW9 1UF
☎ 020 8332 0262
Est. 1990 *Stock size* Large

Stock Furniture, pictures, silver, porcelain, Oriental antiques
Open Mon–Fri 10am–5.30pm Sat 9.30am–5.30pm Sun by appointment
Services Restoration

Richmond Hill Antiques
Contact Mrs M Hobson
82 Hill Rise, Richmond, Surrey, TW10 6UB
020 8940 5755 020 8940 5755
07909 912382
richmondhillant@hotmail.com
Est. 1970 *Stock size* Medium
Stock Georgian and Victorian furniture
Open Mon Thurs Fri noon–4pm Sat 10.30am–5.30pm Sun 1.30–5.30pm Tues Wed by appointment
Services Valuations, restoration, shipping

Vellantiques
Contact S Vella
127 Kew Road, Richmond, Surrey, TW9 2PN
020 8940 5392
07960 897075
Est. 1983 *Stock size* Large
Stock Furniture, pictures, jewellery
Open Mon–Sat 10am–6pm
Fairs Ardingly, Kempton
Services Valuations

RIPLEY

J Hartley Antiques Ltd (LAPADA)
Contact Mr J Hartley
186 High Street, Ripley, Woking, Surrey, GU23 6BB
01483 224318
Est. 1973 *Stock size* Medium
Stock Antique furniture
Open Mon–Fri 9am–6pm Sat 9.30am–5pm
Services Free local delivery

The Lamp Gallery
Contact Graham Jones
Talbot Walk Antique Centre, Talbot Hotel, High Street, Ripley, Surrey, GU23 6BB
01483 211724 01483 211724
Est. 1986 *Stock size* Medium
Stock Interior lighting, including Art Nouveau and Art Deco lamps
Open Mon–Sat 10am–5pm Sun 11am–4pm or by appointment
Services Valuations, shipping

Sage Antiques & Interiors (LAPADA)
Contact Mr H Sage
High Street, Ripley, Surrey, GU23 6BB
01483 224396 01483 211996
Est. 1973 *Stock size* Large
Stock 18thC mahogany, oak, walnut furniture
Open Mon–Sat 9am–5.30pm

Talbot Walk Antique Centre
Contact Graham Jones
Talbot Hotel, High Street, Ripley, Surrey, GU23 6BB
01483 211724 01483 211724
Est. 1999 *Stock size* Medium
No. of dealers 40
Stock Interior lighting, including Art Nouveau and Art Deco lamps, general antiques, furniture
Open Mon–Sat 10am–5pm Sun 11am–4pm
Services Valuations, restoration, shipping

Anthony Welling (BADA)
Contact Mr A Welling
Broadway Barn, High Street, Ripley, Woking, Surrey, GU23 6AQ
01483 225384 01483 225384
Est. 1970 *Stock size* Medium
Stock Large 17th–18thC oak, country furniture
Open Mon–Sat 10am–4.30pm Sun and evenings by appointment
Services Valuations, restoration

RUNFOLD

The Antiques Warehouse
Contact Mrs H Burroughs
Badshot Farm, St Georges Road, Runfold, Farnham, Surrey, GU9 9HY
01252 317590 01252 879751
07971 973289
www.theantiqueswarehouse.co.uk
Est. 1995 *Stock size* Large
No. of dealers 40
Stock Wide variety of antiques including glass, silver, china, 17thC–1930s furniture, paintings, prints, garden artefacts
Open Mon–Sun 10am–5.30pm including Bank Holidays
Services Restoration, upholstery

The Packhouse Antiques Centre
Contact Alison Hougham
Hewetts Kilns, Tongham Road, Runfold, Farnham, Surrey, GU10 1PJ
01252 781010 01252 783876
www.packhouse.com
Est. 1990 *Stock size* Large
No. of dealers 109
Stock Furniture, collectables, garden artefacts, clocks, paintings, mirrors
Open Mon–Fri 10.30am–5.30pm Sat–Sun 10am–5.30pm
Services Delivery service, finders file

Runfold Collectables Ltd
Contact Bernard Green
Old Guildford Road, Runfold, Surrey, GU10 1PN
01252 781124
Est. 1995 *Stock size* Large
Stock Furniture
Open Tue–Fri 10am–5.30pm Sat Sun noon–5pm
Services Valuations, upholstery

SHERE

Helena's Collectables
Contact Mrs H Lee
Middle Street, Shere, Guildford, Surrey, GU5 9HF
01483 203039 01483 203039
helena@collectables.demon.co.uk
www.collectables.demon.co.uk
Est. 1996 *Stock size* Large
Stock Royal Worcester, Wedgwood, Coalport, Doulton, Beswick, classic Disney, porcelain, collectable ceramics
Open Mon–Sat 9.30am–5.30pm Sun 10.30am–4.30pm
Services Mail order service

Shere Antiques Centre
Contact Mrs Jean Watson
Middle Street, Shere, Guildford, Surrey, GU5 9HF
01483 202846 01483 830762
Est. 1987 *Stock size* Large
Stock Ceramics, clocks, chandeliers, furniture, garden tools

Open Mon–Fri 11am–5pm
Sat Sun 11am–5pm or by appointment
Services Restoration, shipping, house clearance

SOUTH HOLMWOOD

Holmwood Antiques
Contact R Dewdney
Charlwyns, Norfolk Road, South Holmwood, Dorking, Surrey, RH5 4LA
☎ 01306 888468 Ⓕ 01306 742636
Est. 1968 *Stock size* Medium
Stock General antiques
Open Mon–Fri 9am–6pm or by appointment
Services Restoration

SURBITON

Cockrell Antiques
Contact Peter or Sheila Cockrell
278 Ewell Road, Surbiton, Surrey, KT6 7AG
☎ 020 8390 8290
Ⓦ www.cockrellantiques.co.uk
Est. 1984 *Stock size* Large
Stock General antiques, mainly furniture
Open Mon–Sat 9am–6pm
Services Valuations

Maple Antiques
Contact Lynda or Geof Morris
4 Maple Road, Surbiton, Surrey, KT6 4AB
☎ 020 8399 6718
Est. 1981 *Stock size* Medium
Stock Mahogany, pine, oak, walnut furniture, mirrors, rugs, garden art
Open Mon–Sat 10am–5.30pm
Fairs Ardingly, Kempton Park

Laurence Tauber Antiques
Contact Laurence Tauber
131 Ewell Road, Surbiton, Surrey, KT6 6AL
☎ 020 8390 0020
Ⓜ 07710 443293
Est. 1973 *Stock size* Large
Stock 19thC–1930s Continental and decorative items
Open By appointment

TADWORTH

Ian Caldwell (LAPADA)
Contact Mr I Caldwell
9a The Green, Dorking Road, Tadworth, Surrey, KT20 5SQ
☎ 01737 813969
Ⓔ caldwell.antiques@virgin.net
Ⓦ www.lapada.co.uk/homepages/2486.htm
Est. 1978 *Stock size* Medium
Stock Town furniture William and Mary–Edwardian
Open Mon–Sat 10am–5pm closed Wed
Services Valuations, restoration

Restore
Contact Mr G R Fisher
37 Walton Street, Tadworth, Surrey, KT20 7RR
☎ 01737 817866 Ⓕ 01737 819518
Ⓜ 07970 186769
Ⓔ info@restoreltd.co.uk
Ⓦ www.restoreltd.co.uk
Est. 1999 *Stock size* Medium
Stock Antique and contemporary design furniture
Open Mon–Fri 9am–5pm

THAMES DITTON

Clifford and Roger Dade
Contact Mr R Dade
Boldre House, Weston Green, Hampton Court Way, Thames Ditton, Surrey, KT7 0JP
☎ 020 8398 6293 Ⓕ 020 8398 6293
Ⓔ roger@dadeantiques.com
Est. 1937 *Stock size* Medium
Stock Georgian furniture, particularly mahogany
Open By appointment

WALLINGTON

An-Toy-Ques
Contact Mrs Britt Grace
85 Stafford Road, Wallington, Surrey, SM6 9AP
☎ 020 8288 8124
Ⓔ antoyques@tinyworld.co.uk
Est. 1994 *Stock size* Large
Stock Old toys including dolls, dolls' houses, bears, trains, lead figures
Open Tues–Sat 10.30am–5pm closed Wed
Fairs Sandown Park, Train fairs, Reading Vintage
Services Valuations, restoration

WALTON-ON-THAMES

Antique Church Furnishings (SALVO)
Contact Mr L Skilling
Rivernook Farm, Sunnyside, Walton-on-Thames, Surrey, KT12 2ET
☎ 01932 252736 Ⓕ 01932 252736
Ⓔ info@churchantiques.com
Ⓦ www.churchantiques.com
Est. 1989 *Stock size* Large
Stock Church furniture, fixtures and fittings
Open Mon–Fri 10am–6pm

Chancellors Church Furnishings (SALVO)
Contact Mr S Williams
Rivernook Farm, Sunnyside, Walton-on-Thames, Surrey, KT12 2ET
☎ 01932 230284 Ⓕ 01932 252736
Ⓜ 07973 139308
Ⓔ info@churchantiques.com
Ⓦ www.churchantiques.com
Est. 1992 *Stock size* Large
Stock All pre-war church furnishings, fixtures and fittings
Open Mon–Fri 10am–6pm

S & H Jewell Ltd
Contact Mr R Jewell or Mr G Korkis
17 Wolsey Drive, Walton-on-Thames, Surrey, KT12 3AY
☎ 01932 222690
Ⓜ 07973 406 255
Est. 1830 *Stock size* Large
Stock Quality English antique and period style 19th–20thC furniture
Open By appointment
Fairs Newark
Services Valuations, restoration

WEST BYFLEET

Academy Billiard Company
Contact Robert Donachie
5 Camp Hill Industrial Estate, Camp Hill Road, West Byfleet, Surrey, KT14 6EW
☎ 01932 352067 Ⓕ 01932 353904
Ⓔ academygames@fsbdial.co.uk
Ⓦ www.games-room.com
Est. 1983 *Stock size* Large
Stock Antique and modern games room equipment

Open By appointment
Services Valuations, restoration, shipping

WEYBRIDGE

⊞ Antiques & Decor
Contact Frances Jackson
✉ **8 York Road, Weybridge, Surrey, KT13 9DT** P
☎ 01932 855427 ℱ 01932 855427
Est. 1999 *Stock size* Medium
Stock Antiques, decor
Open Mon–Sat 9am–5pm

⊞ Church House Antiques
Contact Mary Foster
✉ **42 Church Street, Weybridge, Surrey, KT13 8DP** P
☎ 01932 842190
Est. 1886 *Stock size* Medium
Stock Antique jewellery, furniture, silver, decorative accessories
Open Thurs–Sat 10am–5.30pm

⊞ The Clockshop
Contact Mr A Forster
✉ **64 Church Street, Weybridge, Surrey, KT13 8DL** P
☎ 01932 855503 ℱ 01932 840407
Est. 1969 *Stock size* Large
Stock Antique clocks, barometers
Open Mon–Sat 10am–6pm closed Wed
Services Restoration

⊞ Not Just Silver (NAG, RJA)
Contact Susan Hughes
✉ **16 York Road, Weybridge, Surrey, KT13 9DT** P
☎ 01932 842468 ℱ 01932 830054
Ⓜ 07774 298151
ⓔ sales@not-just-silver.com
ⓦ www.not-just-silver.com
Est. 1969 *Stock size* Medium
Stock Silver
Open Mon–Sat 9.30am–5.30pm
Services Valuations, restoration, silver and gold plating, watch repairs

⊞ Village Antiques
Contact Barry Mulvany
✉ **39 St Marys Road, Weybridge, Surrey, KT13 9PT** P
☎ 01932 846554
Ⓜ 07803 372399
ⓦ www.villageantiques.biz
Est. 1980 *Stock size* Medium
Stock Mahogany, pine furniture, silver
Open Mon–Sat 10am–3pm
Services Restoration, valuations

WOKING

⌂ Aspidistra Antique Centre
Contact Mrs Caswell
✉ **Wych Hill, Woking, Surrey, GU22 0EU** P
☎ 01483 771117 ℱ 01483 771117
Ⓜ 07990 615637
ⓔ info@aspidistraantiques.co.uk
ⓦ www.aspidistra-antiques.co.uk
Est. 2000 *Stock size* Medium
No. of dealers 20
Stock Regency and Art Deco furniture
Open Mon–Sat 10am–4.30pm
Services Restoration of upholstery, paintings

⚒ Barbers Fine Art Auctioneers (West Sussex Estate Agents, Surveyors and Auctioneers)
Contact Mr K Mansfield
✉ **Mayford Centre, Mayford Green, Woking, Surrey, GU22 0PP** P
☎ 01483 728939 ℱ 01483 762552
ⓔ barbersfineart@btconnect.com
ⓦ www.invaluable.com/barbers
Est. 1971
Open Mon–Sat 9am–1pm
Sales General and fine art sales. Please telephone for further details
Frequency Every 5–6 weeks
Catalogues Yes

⚒ Ewbank Fine Art Auctioneers (SOFAA)
Contact Mr C T J Ewbank RICS
✉ **Burnt Common Auction Rooms, London Road, Send, Woking, Surrey, GU23 7LN** P
☎ 01483 223101 ℱ 01483 222171
ⓔ antiques@ewbankauctions.co.uk
ⓦ www.ewbankauctions.co.uk
Est. 1990
Open Mon–Fri 9.30am–5pm
Sales 4 antiques sales and 14 sales of Victorian and later furnishings annually, viewing Tues week of sale 2–5pm and Wed 10am–8pm. Telephone for sale details
Frequency Monthly
Catalogues Yes

⊞ Goldsworth Books and Prints (PBFA)
Contact Mr Brian Hartles
✉ **47 Goldsworth Road, Woking, Surrey, GU21 6JY** P
☎ 01483 767670 ℱ 01483 767670
ⓔ brian@goldsworthbooks.com
Est. 1986 *Stock size* Medium
Stock Antiquarian, rare, second-hand books, antiquarian maps, books illustrated by Arthur Rackham a speciality
Open Tues–Fri 10am–5pm Sat 9.30am–4.30pm
Fairs Russell Hotel, London, York National
Services Worldwide book search

WEST SUSSEX

ARDINGLY

⊞ Ardingly Antiques
Contact Mary Burke
✉ **64 High Street, Ardingly, West Sussex, RH 17 6TD** P
☎ 01444 892680
Est. 1990 *Stock size* Medium
Stock General antiques and collectables
Open Mon–Sun 2–5.30pm closed Tues
Fairs Ardingly, Sandown Park, Alexandra Palace

⌂ Rocking Horse Antique Market
Contact Mrs J Livett or Mr P Livett
✉ **16 High Street, Ardingly, West Sussex, RH17 7TD** P
☎ 01444 892205
Est. 1993 *Stock size* Large
No. of dealers 20
Stock Antiques, collectables, books, ephemera
Open Mon–Sat 9.30am–5.30pm Sun 10am–5.30pm 5pm during winter

ARUNDEL

⊞ Antiquities
Contact Mr Ian Fenwick or Mrs Christina Fenwick
✉ **5–7 Tarrant Street, Arundel,**

West Sussex,
BN18 9DG
☎ 01903 884355 Ⓕ 01903 884355
Ⓔ antiquities@btconnect.com
Est. 1991 *Stock size* Large
Stock 19thC English and French furniture, decorative items, majolica, blue and white, pond boats, French mirrors, chandeliers, lighting
Trade only Trade and export, public by appointment
Open Mon–Sat 10am–5pm or by appointment
Services Shipping, major credit cards accepted

Arundel Antiques Centre
✉ **51 High Street, Arundel, West Sussex, BN18 9AJ**
☎ 01903 882749
Est. 1975
No. of dealers 30
Stock Furniture, china, silver, porcelain, general antiques
Open Mon–Sun 10am–5pm
Services Valuations

Arundel Antiques Gallery
Contact Herbert Smith
✉ **Castle Mews, Tarrant Street, Arundel, West Sussex, BN18 9DG**
☎ 01903 883066/882048
Est. 1978 *Stock size* Large
Stock Georgian–Victorian furniture, paintings, longcase clocks
Open By appointment

The Arundel Bookshop
Contact G or A Shepherd
✉ **10 High Street, Arundel, West Sussex, BN18 9AB**
☎ 01903 882680
Est. 1977 *Stock size* Medium
Stock Rare, antiquarian, second-hand books
Open Mon–Sat 10am–5pm Sun 10.30am–5pm

Arundel Bridge
Contact Lesley Barrett
✉ **6 High Street, Arundel, West Sussex, BN18 9AB**
☎ 01903 884164
Est. 1980 *Stock size* Medium
Stock General antiques
Open Mon–Sun 10am–5pm

Baynton-Williams
Contact Sarah or Roger Baynton-Williams
✉ **37A High Street, Arundel, West Sussex, BN18 9AG**
☎ 01903 883588
Ⓔ gallery@baynton-williams.freeserve.co.uk
Ⓦ www.baynton-williams.com
Est. 1946 *Stock size* Medium
Stock Antiquarian maps, prints, decorative and botanical
Open Mon–Sat 10am–6pm or by appointment
Services Valuations

DecoGraphic Collectors Gallery
Contact G Cox
✉ **Arundel Antiques Centre, 51 High Street, Arundel, West Sussex, BN18 9AJ**
☎ 01243 787391
Est. 1994 *Stock size* Medium
Stock 1880–1960 toys, cameras, wirelesses, gramophones
Open Mon–Sun 10am–5pm
Services Restoration

Decorum
Contact Caroline Baker
✉ **9 Tarrant Street, Arundel, West Sussex, BN18 9DG**
☎ 01903 884436 Ⓕ 01903 889527
Ⓔ caroline@decorum-arundel.co.uk
Est. 1989 *Stock size* Medium
Stock French furniture and antiques
Open Mon–Sun 10am–5pm

The Jolly Pedlars
Contact Mr Travers
✉ **43 High Street, Arundel, West Sussex, BN18 9AG**
☎ 01903 884401 Ⓕ 01903 723381
Est. 1982 *Stock size* Medium
Stock General antiques, collectables, toys, dolls
Open Mon–Sun 10.30am–4.30pm

Mermaid Vintage
Contact Lisa Roake
✉ **Ninevah House Antique Centre, Tarrant Street, Arundel, West Sussex, BN18 9DG**
☎ 07979 906511
Ⓔ enquiries@mermaidvintage.co.uk
Ⓦ www.mermaidvintage.co.uk
Est. 2000 *Stock size* Medium
Stock Vintage clothes, 1890–1960, costume jewellery
Open Wed–Fri 10am–2.30pm Sat 10am–4pm or by appointment
Fairs Goodwood, vintage clothing fairs

Ninevah House Antique Centre
Contact Peter Munday
✉ **Tarrant Street, Arundel, West Sussex, BN18 9DG**
☎ 01322 287181
Est. 1989 *Stock size* Large
No. of dealers 15
Stock Antiques, craft and collectables
Open Mon–Fri 10am–5pm Sat 9.30am–5pm Sun 11am–5pm

The Old Cornstore Antiques Centre
Contact Peter Francis
✉ **31 High Street, Arundel, West Sussex, BN18 9AG**
☎ 01903 885456 Ⓕ 01903 885456
Est. 2001 *Stock size* Large
No. of dealers 30
Stock Georgian–Edwardian furniture, jewellery ceramics, silver, paintings, clocks
Open Mon–Sat 10am–5pm Sun 11am–5pm closed Wed
Services Valuations, shipping

Old Maps
Contact Mr K R Goddard
✉ **59 High Street, Arundel, West Sussex, BN18 9AJ**
☎ 01903 882522
Est. 1975 *Stock size* Medium
Stock Maps, prints
Open Mon–Sun 10am–5pm
Services Valuations

Passageway Antiques
Contact J Saxon
✉ **18 High Street, Arundel, West Sussex, BN18 9AB**
☎ 01903 884602 Ⓕ 01903 884602
Est. 1994 *Stock size* Large
Stock Antiques, collectables
Open Mon–Sat 10am–5pm Sun 11am–5pm
Services Valuations

Spencer Swaffer (LAPADA, BACA Award Winner 2004)

Contact Spencer Swaffer
30 High Street, Arundel, West Sussex, BN18 9AB
01903 882132 01903 884564
spencerswaffer@btconnect.com
www.spencerswaffer.com
Est. 1974 *Stock size* Large
Stock Eclectic mix of decorative items
Open Mon–Fri 9am–6pm Sun 10am–6pm

The Walking Stick Shop
Contact Stuart Thompson
8 & 9 The Old Printing Works, Tarrant Street, Arundel, West Sussex, BN18 9JH
01903 883796
www.walkingsticks.uk.com
Est. 1978 *Stock size* Large
Stock Walking sticks
Open Mon–Sat 9am–5.30pm

BALCOMBE

Woodall & Emery Ltd
Contact Mrs Chinn
Haywards Heath Road, Balcombe, Haywards Heath, West Sussex, RH17 6PG
01444 811608 01444 819365
enquiries@woodallandemery.co.uk
www.woodallandemery.co.uk
Est. 1860 *Stock size* Large
Stock Antique lighting, chandeliers, table lights, lanterns
Open Mon–Sat 10am–5pm
Services Restoration, rewiring

BARNHAM

Howard's Reclamation
Contact Craig Howard
Longfield Timber Mill, Lake Lane, Barnham, West Sussex, PO22 0AE
01243 552095
chowardsreclaim@aol.com
Est. 1971 *Stock size* Large
Stock Old and new planked timber floors, oak beams, oak sleepers, telegraph poles, bricks, doors, stone, fireplaces and architectural antiquities
Open Mon–Fri 9am–1pm 2–5pm Sat 8am–1pm closed Wed

BILLINGSHURST

Hereford House
Contact J Preedy
55 Station Road, Billingshurst, West Sussex, RH14 9SE
01403 785379 01403 785379
Antiquelighting@herefordhse.fsnet.co.uk
Est. 1996 *Stock size* Medium
Stock Antique furniture, lighting, mirrors
Open Wed–Fri 10am–6pm Sat 10am–1pm or by appointment
Services Electric lighting restoration

Sotheby's South
Summers Place, Billingshurst, West Sussex, RH14 9AD
01403 833500 01403 833696
www.sothebys.com
Est. 1744
Open Mon–Fri 9.30am–1pm 2.15–4.30pm (valuations Tues 9.30am–1pm)
Sales Garden statuary sales in May and September. Valuations given for items to be sold in London saleroom
Frequency Twice a year
Catalogues Yes

BOGNOR REGIS

Memory Lane
Contact David Crack
79 Aldwick Road, Bognor Regis, West Sussex, PL21 2NW
01243 841412
Est. 2004 *Stock size* Medium
Stock General antiques, collectables
Open Mon–Sat 9.30am–5.30pm

BOSHAM

Mr Pickett's
Contact Mr M Pickett
Top Barn, Old Park Lane, Bosham, Nr Chichester, West Sussex, PO18 8EX
01243 574573 02392 410009
07779 997012
info@mrpicketts.com
www.mrpicketts.com
Est. 1991 *Stock size* Large
Stock Victorian pine furniture
Open By appointment
Services Stripping, restoration, bespoke pine furniture

BUCKS GREEN

Music Room Antiques (BADA)
Contact Andrew Lancaster
School House, Bucks Green, Horsham, West Sussex, RH12 3JP
01403 822189 01403 823089
07744 986926
andrew@squarepiano.net
www.squarepiano.net
Est. 1986 *Stock size* Medium
Stock Square pianos and associated music-related antiques
Open By appointment
Fairs BADA, Harrogate Antique Fair
Services Restoration

BURGESS HILL

British Antique Replicas
22 School Close, Queen Elizabeth Avenue, Burgess Hill, West Sussex, RH15 9RX
01444 245577 01444 232014
www.1760.com
Est. 1963 *Stock size* Large
Stock English antique replica furniture
Open Mon–Sat 9am–5.30pm
Services Restoration of antique furniture

Recollect The Dolls Hospital
Contact Paul Jago
17 Junction Road, Burgess Hill, West Sussex, RH15 0HR
01444 871052 01444 871052
dollshopuk@aol.com
Est. 1973 *Stock size* Medium
Stock Antique dolls
Open Tues–Fri 10am–4pm Sat 10am–1pm or by appointment
Services Restoration of dolls

CHICHESTER

Henry Adams Fine Art Auctioneers (ARVA, SOFAA)
Contact Kate Lawson-Paul
Baffins Hall, Baffins Lane, Chichester, West Sussex, PO19 1UA
01243 532223 01243 532299
enquiries@henryadamsfineart.co.uk
www.henryadamsfineart.co.uk
Est. 2000

Open Mon–Fri 9am–5.30pm
Sales Antiques and fine art
Frequency Six weekly
Catalogues Yes

Antics
Contact Peter German
19 The Hornet, Chichester, West Sussex, PO19 4JL P
01243 786327
Est. 1981 *Stock size* Small
Stock General antiques
Open Mon–Sat 9am–4pm

Antiques and Bygones
Contact Mrs M Haydon
24 The Buttermarket, North Street, Chichester, West Sussex, PO19 1LQ
01243 788071
Est. 1975 *Stock size* Medium
Stock China, glass, collectors' items
Open Tues–Sat 10am–4pm

Barnett Antiques
Contact Mrs B Barnett
Unit 1, Almshouse Arcade, 19 The Hornet, Chichester, West Sussex, PO19 4JL P
01243 528089
Est. 1970 *Stock size* Medium
Stock Bric-a-brac, toys
Open Mon–Sat 10am–4.30pm

Canon Gate Bookshop (PBFA)
Contact P Pegler
28 South Street, Chichester, West Sussex, PO19 1EL P
01243 778477
Est. 1980 *Stock size* Medium
Stock Rare, antiquarian, second-hand books
Open Mon–Sat 10.30am–5pm

Canute Antiques
Contact Wendy Rowden
Bosham Walk, Bosham Lane, Chichester, West Sussex, PO18 8HX P
01243 576111
Est. 1977 *Stock size* Small
Stock Silver, jewellery, porcelain and collectors' items
Open Mon–Sun 10am–5.30pm

Chichester Antiques Centre
Contact Michael Carter
46–48 The Hornet, Chichester, West Sussex, PO19 4JG P
01243 530100
Est. 1994 *Stock size* Large
No. of dealers 40
Stock General antiques, collectables, 18th–20thC furniture, gramophones
Open Mon–Sat 10am–5pm Sun 11am–4pm closed Tues
Services Valuations

The Chichester Bookshop
Contact Mr N Howell
39 Southgate, Chichester, West Sussex, PO19 1DP P
01243 785473
chibooks@fsbdial.co.uk
Est. 1965 *Stock size* Large
Stock Rare, second-hand books, specialists in railway books, Sussex books, maps, prints
Open Mon–Sat 9.30am–5pm
Services Book search

Collectors Corner
Contact Vivienne Barnett
Almshouse Arcade, 19 The Hornet, Chichester, West Sussex, PO19 7JL
01243 778126
Est. 1983 *Stock size* Medium
Stock Antiques, collectables, toys, furniture, bric-a-brac
Open Mon–Sat 9am–4.30pm

Gems
Contact Maureen Hancock
39 West Street, Chichester, West Sussex, PO19 1RP P
01243 786173 F 01243 778865
Est. 1985 *Stock size* Large
Stock Edwardian furniture, Staffordshire figures, European porcelain
Open Tues–Sat 10am–1pm 2.30–5pm or by other appointment
Services Restoration

Peter Hancock
Contact Peter Hancock
40 West Street, Chichester, West Sussex, PO19 1RP P
01243 786173 F 01243 778865
Est. 1965 *Stock size* Large
Stock A comprehensive range of antiques and collectables
Open Tues–Sat 10am–1pm 2.15–5.30pm or by appointment
Services Restoration

Heirloom Antiques
Contact Alan Hayes
57–58 Pound Farm Road, Chichester, West Sussex, PO19 2LU P
01243 530489
M 07970 396265
Est. 1986 *Stock size* Large
Stock Furniture, collectables, curios
Open Mon–Sat 9.30am–5pm
Fairs Goodwood, Kempton

Heritage Antiques
Contact Mr D Grover
83 & 84 St Pancras, Chichester, West Sussex, PO19 4NL P
01243 783796
Est. 1987 *Stock size* Medium
Stock Georgian–Edwardian, 1920s furniture
Open Mon–Sat 9am–5.30pm

W D Priddy Antiques, Chichester Furniture Warehouse
Contact Mr W D Priddy
Unit 6, Terminus Mill, Terminus Road, Chichester, West Sussex, PO19 2UN P
01243 783960 F 01243 783960
M 07712 002371
bill@priddyantiques.fsnet.co.uk
www.priddyantiques.co.uk
Est. 1983 *Stock size* Medium
Stock Georgian–Edwardian furniture
Open Mon–Fri 10am–4pm Sat 10am–5pm variable Sundays 11am–4pm or by appointment

Squirrel Antiques
Contact Lesley Hampshire
44 The Hornet, Chichester, West Sussex, PO19 7JG P
01243 790904
Est. 1990 *Stock size* Small
Stock Collectables, curios
Open Mon–Sat 10am–12.30pm 1.30–4pm
Fairs Sandown Park

St Pancras Antiques
Contact Mr R Willatt
150 St Pancras,

Chichester, West Sussex,
PO19 5SH P
☎ 01243 787645
Est. 1980 *Stock size* Medium
Stock Arms, armour, pre-1800 furniture, ceramics, numismatics, militaria
Open Mon–Sat 9.30am–5pm Thurs 9.30am–1pm
Services Valuations

Stride & Son
Contact Mr M Hewitt or Mr K Warne
✉ **Southdown House, St Johns Street, Chichester, West Sussex, PO19 1XQ** P
☎ 01243 780207 Ⓕ 01243 786713
Ⓔ enquiries@stridesauctions.co.uk
Ⓦ www.stridesauctions.co.uk
Est. 1890
Open Mon–Fri 9am–5.30pm closed 1–2pm
Sales Monthly sale of general antiques, periodic book auctions
Frequency Monthly
Catalogues Yes

Whitestone Farm Antiques
Contact Carey Mordue
✉ **Whitestone Farm, Main Road, Birdham, Chichester, West Sussex, PO20 7HU** P
☎ 01243 513706
Ⓔ antiques@whitestonefarm.force9.co.uk
Est. 1970 *Stock size* Medium
Stock 18th–20thC furniture, shabby chic
Open Mon–Sat 10am–5.30pm
Services Restoration

COCKING

The Victorian Brass Bedstead Co
Contact David Woolley
✉ **Hoe Copse, Cocking, Midhurst, West Sussex, GU29 0HL** P
☎ 01730 812287
Ⓔ toria@netcomuk.co.uk
Est. 1982 *Stock size* Large
Stock Brass and iron bedsteads, mattresses, bases, quilts
Open Mon–Sun By appointment
Services Valuations, restoration

CUCKFIELD

David Foord-Brown Antiques (LAPADA, BADA)
Contact David Foord-Brown
✉ **3 Bank Buildings, High Street, Cuckfield, West Sussex, RH17 5JU** P
☎ 01444 414418
Ⓜ 07850 188250
Est. 1988 *Stock size* Large
Stock 18th–19thC furniture, porcelain, silver, glass
Open Mon–Sat 10am–5.30pm and by appointment
Fairs BADA Fair

DITCHLING

Dycheling Antiques
Contact Mrs E A Hudson
✉ **34 High Street, Ditchling, West Sussex, BN6 8TA** P
☎ 01273 842929
Ⓜ 07785 456341
Ⓔ hudson@icsgroup.demon.co.uk
Est. 1979 *Stock size* Large
Stock Sets of Georgian–Victorian dining furniture, upholstered furniture, chiffoniers
Open Tues Thurs–Sat 10.30am–5.30pm or by appointment
Services Chair search service

HAYWARDS HEATH

Roundabout Antiques
Contact Angie Craik
✉ **7 Commercial Square, Haywards Heath, West Sussex, RH16 1DW** P
☎ 01273 835926 Ⓕ 01273 835659
Ⓔ roundabout@mistral.co.uk
Est. 1993 *Stock size* Medium
Stock Collectables, silver, jewellery, furniture, musical instruments
Open Mon–Sat 9.30am–5.30pm

HENFIELD

Ashcombe Coach House Antiques (BADA, CINOA)
Contact Mr Roy Green
✉ **PO Box No 2527, Henfield, West Sussex, BN5 9SU** P
☎ 01273 491630 Ⓕ 01273 492681
Ⓜ 07803 180098
Ⓔ sharon@anglocontinental.fsnet.co.uk
Est. 1953 *Stock size* Large
Stock 18th–early 19thC furniture, decorative objects
Open By appointment only
Fairs Olympia, BADA

Henfield Antiques and Collectables
Contact Mrs D Evans
✉ **2 Commercial Buildings, High Street, Henfield, West Sussex, BN5 9DE** P
☎ 01273 495300
Est. 1999 *Stock size* Large
Stock Kitchenware, pine furniture, Beswick, Wade
Open Mon–Sun 10.30am–5pm
Services Verbal valuations

HORSHAM

Denham's
Contact Kate Tyekiff or Louise Shelley
✉ **The Auction Galleries, Dorking Road (A24), Warnham, Horsham, West Sussex, RH12 3RZ** P
☎ 01403 255699 Ⓕ 01403 253837
Ⓔ enquiries@denhams.com
Ⓦ www.invaluable.com/denhams
Est. 1884
Open Mon–Thurs 9am–5.30pm Fri 9am–5pm Sat 9am–noon
Sales Sales of antiques and collectors' items every four weeks
Frequency Every 4 weeks
Catalogues Yes

Horsham Bookshop (PBFA)
Contact Mr Nick Costin
✉ **4 Park Place (Off Piries Place), Horsham, West Sussex, RH12 1DG** P
☎ 01403 252187
Ⓜ 07941 802954
Ⓔ sales@horshambookshop.com
Ⓦ www.horshambookshop.com
Est. 1986 *Stock size* Large
Stock Rare, antiquarian, second-hand books, bindings, children's books, military, transport and collectable books
Open Tues–Sat 9.30am–5pm
Fairs PBFA
Services Valuations, book search

Murray and Kemmett
Contact J Murray
✉ **102 Bishopric, Horsham, West Sussex,**

RH12 1QN 🅿
☎ 01403 254847
ⓔ jcwm@onetel.net.uk
ⓦ www.murraryandkemmett.co.uk
Est. 1980 *Stock size* Medium
Stock Rare, second-hand books, crime fiction, religious books a speciality
Open Mon–Sat 9.15am–1pm 2–5pm
Services Book search

HOUGHTON

Stable Antiques at Houghton
Contact Ian Wadey
✉ **Main Road (B2139), Houghton, West Sussex, BN18 9LW** 🅿
☎ 01798 839555 or 01903 740555
ⓦ www.stableantiques.co.uk
Est. 2000 *Stock size* Medium
No. of dealers 12
Stock Antiques, furniture and design
Open Tues–Sat 11am–4pm

HUNSTON

J and M Riley
Contact Mr J Riley
✉ **Frensham House, Hunston, Chichester, West Sussex, PO20 6NX** 🅿
☎ 01243 782660
Est. 1966 *Stock size* Medium
Stock 18thC English furniture
Open Mon–Sat 9am–6pm and by appointment

HURSTPIERPOINT

Heather Boardman Antiques
Contact Heather Boardman
✉ **40 High Street, Hurstpierpoint, West Sussex, BN16 9RG** 🅿
☎ 01273 832101
Est. 1987 *Stock size* Small
Stock Decorative items, collectables
Open Mon–Sat 9.30am–5pm closed Wed
Fairs Ardingly

Graham Foster Antiques
Contact Graham Foster
✉ **The Old Telephone Exchange, 41 Cuckfield Road, Hurstpierpoint, West Sussex, BN6 9RW** 🅿
☎ 01273 833099
ⓜ 07850 576434
ⓔ graham.foster-antiques@ukonline.co.uk
Est. 1982 *Stock size* Large
Stock Iron gates, furniture
Open Mon–Sat 8.30am–6pm
Fairs Ardingly, Newark
Services Valuations, restoration

Julian Antiques
Contact Mrs C Ingram or Mr J Ingram
✉ **124 High Street, Hurstpierpoint, West Sussex, BN6 9PX** 🅿
☎ 01273 832145
Est. 1969 *Stock size* Medium
Stock 19thC French mirrors, clocks, candelabra, fireplaces, bronzes, sculptures, fenders, furniture
Open By appointment
Services Shipping

Samuel Orr (LAPADA)
Contact Mr S Orr
✉ **34–36 High Street, Hurstpierpoint, West Sussex, BN6 9RG** 🅿
☎ 01273 832081 ⓕ 01273 832081
ⓜ 07860 230888
ⓔ clocks@samorr.co.uk
ⓦ www.samorr.co.uk
Est. 1977 *Stock size* Large
Stock Antique clocks, barometers
Open Mon–Sat 10am–6pm or by appointment
Services Clock restoration

LINDFIELD

Lindfield Galleries (BADA)
Contact David Adam
✉ **62 High Street, Lindfield, West Sussex, RH16 2HL** 🅿
☎ 01444 483817 ⓕ 01444 484682
ⓔ david@orientalandantiquerugs.com
ⓦ www.orientalandantiquerugs.com
Est. 1973 *Stock size* Large
Stock Oriental carpets and tapestries
Open Tues–Fri 9.30am–5pm Sat 10am–4pm
Services Valuations, restoration

Spongs Antique Centre
Contact Ashley or Karen Richardson
✉ **102 High Street, Lindfield, West Sussex, RH16 2HS** 🅿
☎ 01444 487566
Est. 2000 *Stock size* Medium
No. of dealers 34
Stock Furniture, china, silver, ceramics, Carlton ware
Open Mon–Fri 10am–5pm Sun 2–5pm
Services Restoration

Stable Antiques
Contact Adrian Hoyle
✉ **98a High Street, Lindfield, West Sussex, RH16 2HP** 🅿
☎ 01444 483662
Est. 1989 *Stock size* Large
Stock George III–Edwardian furniture, antique country pine 1850–1920, some porcelain
Open Mon–Sat 10am–5.30pm Sun 2–5.30pm
Services Free local delivery

LITTLEHAMPTON

Peter Cheney Auctioneers and Valuers (SSA)
Contact Mr P Cheney
✉ **Western Road Auction Rooms, Western Road, Littlehampton, West Sussex, BH17 5NP** 🅿
☎ 01903 722264/713418
ⓕ 01903 713418
Est. 1940
Open Mon–Fri 9am–1pm 2–5pm
Sales Monthly auction sales of antiques, furniture, pictures, silver, porcelain and collectors items. Valuations for insurance and probate. No buyer's premium
Frequency Monthly
Catalogues Yes

Joan's Antiques
Contact Mrs J Walkden
✉ **1 New Road, Littlehampton, West Sussex, BN17 5AX** 🅿
☎ 01903 722422
Est. 1977 *Stock size* Large
Stock China, glass, 1930s items, Victoriana, collectables
Open Thurs–Sat 10.30am–4.30pm
Fairs Goodwood

MIDHURST

Churchill Clocks (BHI)
Contact Mr W P Tyrell
✉ **Rumbolds Hill,**

Midhurst, West Sussex, GU29 9BZ 🅿
☎ 01730 813891
ⓔ info@churchillclocks.co.uk
ⓦ www.churchillclocks.co.uk
Est. 1970 *Stock size* Medium
Stock Clocks, longcase, mantel, French bracket etc
Open Mon–Sat 9am–5pm closed Wed pm
Services Valuations, restoration, shipping

PETWORTH

Angel Antiques
Contact Nick or Barbara Swanson
✉ **Church Street, Petworth, West Sussex, GU28 0AD** 🅿
☎ 01798 343306 ⓕ 01798 342665
ⓔ swansonantiques@aol.com
ⓦ www.angel-antiques.com
Est. 1991 *Stock size* Medium
Stock Oak and country furniture, Mason's, ceramics, decorative items
Open Mon–Sat 10am–5.30pm or by appointment

Antiquated (PAADA)
Contact Vicki Emery
✉ **10 New Street, Petworth, West Sussex, GU28 OAS** 🅿
☎ 01798 344011 ⓕ 01798 344011
Est. 1989 *Stock size* Medium
Stock 18th–19thC painted furniture, 19thC rocking horses
Open Mon–Sat 10am–5.30pm

Baskerville Antiques (BADA)
Contact Mr B Baskerville
✉ **Saddlers House, Saddlers Row, Petworth, West Sussex, GU28 0AH** 🅿
☎ 01798 342067 ⓕ 01798 343956
ⓔ brianbaskerville@aol.com
Est. 1971 *Stock size* Medium
Stock Antiquarian horologist, clocks, barometers
Open Tues–Sat 10am–6pm

John Bird Antiques (PAADA)
Contact Mr Ian Miller
✉ **High Street, Petworth, West Sussex, GU28 0AU** 🅿
☎ 01798 343250 ⓕ 01798 343250
ⓜ 07966 279761
Est. 1985 *Stock size* Large
Stock Furniture, fine art, decorative antiques
Open Mon–Sat 10.15am–5.15pm

Bradley's Past and Present Shop
Contact Mr & Mrs M Bradley
✉ **21 High Street, Petworth, West Sussex, GU28 0AU** 🅿
☎ 01798 343533
ⓜ 07941 506232
Est. 1979 *Stock size* Medium
Stock Furniture and bygones, gramophones
Open Tues–Sat 10am–1pm 2–5pm
Services Restoration of furniture, gramophones

Callingham Antiques Ltd
Contact Nigel Callingham
✉ **Northchapel, Petworth, West Sussex, GU28 9HL** 🅿
☎ 01428 707379
ⓔ antiques@callingham.freeserve.co.uk
Est. 1979 *Stock size* Medium
Stock 17th–18thC English furniture
Open Mon–Sat 9am–5.30pm closed Wed
Services Restoration

Ronald G Chambers – Fine Antiques (LAPADA, CINOA, PAADA)
Contact Mr R G Chambers or Mrs J F Tudor
✉ **Market Square, Petworth, West Sussex, GU28 0AH** 🅿
☎ 01798 342305 ⓕ 01798 342724
ⓜ 07932 161968
ⓔ jackie@ronaldchambers.com
ⓦ www.ronaldchambers.com
Est. 1985 *Stock size* Large
Stock Fine-quality antique furniture and objets d'art 1700–1910 Queen Anne–Edwardian period, paintings, longcase clocks, gilded mirrors, bronze statuary and decorative items, jewellery
Open Mon–Sat 10am–5.30pm Sun 10am–4.30pm
Services Valuations, restoration, exchange and finder service, shipping

Oliver Charles Antiques Ltd (PAADA)
Contact Mr A Gardner
✉ **Lombard Street, Petworth, West Sussex, GU28 0AG** 🅿
☎ 01798 344443
ⓔ olivercharles@aol.com
ⓦ www.olivercharles.com
Est. 1987 *Stock size* Medium
Stock 18th–19thC English furniture, related items, 19thC paintings
Open Mon–Sat 10am–5.30pm Sun by appointment

Cleall Antiques
Contact John Bird
✉ **2 Leppards, High Street, Petworth, West Sussex, GU28** 🅿
☎ 01798 343933 ⓕ 01798 343933
ⓜ 07831 869955
ⓔ damiancleall@hotmail.com
Est. 1976 *Stock size* Medium
Stock Decorative objects and furniture
Open Mon–Sat 10.15am–5.15 pm
Fairs Olympia

Du Cros Antiques
Contact Mr J Du Cros
✉ **1 Pound Street, Petworth, West Sussex, GU28 0DX** 🅿
☎ 01798 342071
ⓜ 07870 740245
Est. 1982 *Stock size* Medium
Stock 17th–19thC English furniture, metalware
Open Mon–Sat 10am–5.30pm
Services Verbal valuations

Elliott's (PAADA)
Contact Mrs P Elliott
✉ **19 East Street, Petworth, West Sussex, GU28 0AB** 🅿
☎ 01798 343408
Est. 1993 *Stock size* Large
Stock Georgian–Edwardian furniture
Open Thur–Sat 10am–5pm

Richard Gardner Antiques (LAPADA, CINOA, PAADA, BACA Award Winner 2002)
Contact Richard Gardner
✉ **Market Square, Petworth, West Sussex, GU28 0AN** 🅿
☎ 01798 343411
ⓔ rg@richardgardnerantiques.co.uk
ⓦ www.richardgardnerantiques.co.uk
Est. 1990 *Stock size* Large
Stock Fine period furniture,

works of art including bronzes, Staffordshire figures, paintings, silver, mirrors, 18th–19thC porcelain, etchings
Open Mon–Sat 10am–5.30pm Sun 10am–5pm

⊞ John Giles (LAPADA)
Contact John Giles
✉ **High Street, Petworth, West Sussex, GU28 0AU** 🅿
☎ 01798 342136
Ⓜ 07770 873689
Ⓔ gilesandhart@btinternet.com
Est. 1963 *Stock size* Medium
Stock 18th–early 20thC furniture, decorative items,
Open Mon–Sat 10am–5.30pm
Fairs Olympia June

⊞ John Harris Antiques and Restorations
Contact Mr J Harris
✉ **Stables, London Road, Northchapel, Petworth, West Sussex, GU28 9EQ** 🅿
☎ 01428 707667
Est. 1976 *Stock size* Medium
Stock 18th–19thC furniture, decorative items
Open Mon–Sat 8am–5pm
Services Restoration

⊞ William Hockley Antiques
Contact Val Thrower
✉ **Tudor Rose Antique Centre, East Street, Petworth, West Sussex, GU28 0AB** 🅿
☎ 01403 701917 Ⓕ 01403 701917
Ⓔ williamhockley@ocsl.co.uk
Ⓦ www.tudor-rose-antiques.co.uk
Est. 1982 *Stock size* Medium
Stock Early English oak, country furniture and interiors
Open Mon–Sun 10am–5.30pm
Services Interior design

⊞ Obelisk Antiques Petworth
Contact Paul Tanserell or Heather Denham
✉ **6 High Street, Petworth, West Sussex, GU28 0AU** 🅿
☎ 01798 344622
Ⓔ all@obeliskantiques.com
Est. 1981 *Stock size* Medium
Stock Decorative, painted furniture, garden furniture
Open Mon–Sat 10am–5pm

⊞ Octavia Antiques (PAADA)
Contact Aline Bell
✉ **East Street, Petworth, West Sussex, GU28 0AB** 🅿
☎ 01798 342771
Est. 1972 *Stock size* Small
Stock Decorative antiques, small furniture, mirrors, lamps, chairs, blue and white china
Open Mon–Sat 10.30am–5.30pm closed Fri

⊞ Petworth Antique Centre & Market
Contact Mrs D M Rayment
✉ **East Street, Petworth, West Sussex, GU28 0AB** 🅿
☎ 01798 342073 Ⓕ 01798 344566
Est. 1974 *Stock size* Large
Stock English oak furniture, silver, linen, books, soft furnishings, porcelain, glass, fans, general antiques
Open Mon–Sat 10am–5.30pm

⊞ Petworth Collectables and Bookshop
Contact Mr Hanson
✉ **Middle Street, Petworth, West Sussex, GU28 0BE** 🅿
☎ 01798 342154
Est. 1987 *Stock size* Large
Stock Rare, second-hand, out-of-print books and collectables
Open Mon–Sat 10am–6pm

⊞ Red Lion Antiques (LAPADA)
Contact Mr R Wilson
✉ **New Street, Petworth, West Sussex, GU28 0AS** 🅿
☎ 01798 344485 Ⓕ 01798 344439
Ⓔ rod@redlion-antiques.com
Ⓦ www.redlion-antiques.com
Est. 1980 *Stock size* Large
Stock 17th–19thC furniture
Open Mon–Sat 10am–5.30pm or by appointment
Fairs LAPADA

⊞ Riverbank Gallery Ltd
Contact Linda Burke White
✉ **High Street, Petworth, West Sussex, GU28 0AU** 🅿
☎ 01798 344401 Ⓕ 01798 343135
Ⓔ rvrbnkg@aol.com
Est. 1997 *Stock size* Large
Stock Large English 18th–19thC furniture, decorative items, garden furniture, decorative paintings, marine antiques
Open Mon–Sat 10am–5.30pm

⊞ Nicholas Shaw Antiques (BADA, LAPADA, CINOA)
Contact Nicholas Shaw
✉ **Virginia Cottage, Petworth, West Sussex, GU28 0AG** 🅿
☎ 01798 345146 Ⓕ 01798 345157
Ⓜ 07885 643000
Ⓔ silver@nicholas-shaw.com
Ⓦ www.nicholas-shaw.com
Est. 1992 *Stock size* Large
Stock Fine and rare antique silver
Open Tues–Sat 10am–5.30pm or by appointment
Fairs BADA Fair, Olympia, Antiques for Everyone, LAPADA
Services Valuations, restoration

⊞ Thakeham Furniture
Contact Tim and Belinda Chavasse
✉ **Golden Square, Petworth, West Sussex, GU28 0AP** 🅿
☎ 01798 432333
Ⓦ www.thakehamfurniture.com
Est. 1979 *Stock size* Medium
Stock 18th–19thC English furniture
Open Mon–Sat 10am–5pm
Services Restoration

⌂ Tudor Rose Antique Centre
Contact Elizabeth Lee
✉ **East Street, Petworth, West Sussex, GU28 0AB** 🅿
☎ 01798 343621 Ⓕ 01798 344951
Ⓜ 07980 927331
Ⓔ info@tudor-rose-antiques.co.uk
Ⓦ www.tudor-rose-antiques.co.uk
Est. 2001 *Stock size* Large
No. of dealers 12
Stock General antiques, brown and decorative furniture, silver, porcelain, blue and white, books, reclamation, including William Hockley, early country furniture and interiors
Open Mon–Sat 10am–5.15pm Sun 11am–4.15pm

⊞ T G Wilkinson Antiques Ltd (BADA, PAADA)
Contact Mr Wilkinson
✉ **Swan House, Market Square, Petworth, West Sussex,**

GU28 0AH 🅿
☎ 01798 343638
Est. 1987 *Stock size* Large
Stock Oak, walnut, mahogany furniture, country furniture, silver, porcelain, decorative items, paintings
Open Mon–Sat 10am–5pm
Services Valuations, restoration

PULBOROUGH

⊞ Barn Antiques
Contact Pam Borham
✉ **Wyevale Garden Centre, Storham Road, Pulborough, West Sussex, RH20 1DS** 🅿
☎ 01798 874782
Est. 1996 *Stock size* Large
Stock Bric-a-brac, pictures, books
Open Mon–Sat 10am–5pm
Sun 10.30am–4.30pm

Rupert Toovey & Co (RICS)
Contact Alan Toovey
✉ **Spring Gardens, Washington, Pulborough, West Sussex, RH20 3BS** 🅿
☎ 01903 891955 Ⓕ 01903 891966
Ⓔ auctions@rupert-toovey.com
Ⓦ www.rupert-toovey.com
Est. 1995
Open Mon–Fri 9am–5pm
Sales Monthly sales of antiques, fine art, collectables, silver, jewellery, clocks and furniture. Sales of books and postcards 2–3 times a year
Frequency Monthly
Catalogues Yes

SHOREHAM BY SEA

⊞ Rodney Arthur Classics
Contact Rodney Oliver
✉ **Unit 5, Riverbank Business Centre, Old Shoreham Road, Shoreham by Sea, West Sussex, BN43 5FL** 🅿
☎ 01273 441606 Ⓕ 01273 441977
Est. 1979 *Stock size* Medium
Stock 19thC furniture
Open Mon–Sat 9am–5pm
Services Restoration

⊞ Bookworms of Shoreham
Contact Mrs P A Liddell
✉ **4 High Street, Shoreham by Sea, West Sussex, BN43 5DA**
☎ 01273 453856
Est. 1992 *Stock size* Medium
Stock Rare, second-hand books, military, modern art
Open Tues–Sat 10am–5pm

SMALL DOLE

⊞ Alexander Antiques
Contact Judith Goodinge
✉ **Small Dole, Henfield, West Sussex, BN5 9XE** 🅿
☎ 01273 493121
Est. 1972 *Stock size* Medium
Stock Country furniture, treen, boxes, brass, copper
Open Telephone call advisable
Fairs Petersfield

STEYNING

⊞ Curiouser & Curiouser
Contact Deborah Pepper
✉ **50 The High Street, Steyning, West Sussex, BN44 3RD**
☎ 01903 879483
Est. 1963 *Stock size* Medium
Stock General antiques
Open Mon–Sat 10.30am–5pm closed Thurs

STORRINGTON

Stable Antiques
Contact Ian Wadey
✉ **46 West Street, Storrington, West Sussex, RH20 4EE** 🅿
☎ 01903 740555 or 01798 839555
Ⓕ 01903 740441
Ⓦ www.stableantiques.co.uk
Est. 1993 *Stock size* Large
No. of dealers 35
Stock Antiques, furniture and bric-a-brac
Open Mon–Sun 10am–6pm

STREAT

⊞ Fisher Nautical (PBFA)
Contact S D Fisher
✉ **Huntswood House, St Helena Lane, Streat, Hassocks, West Sussex, BN6 8SD**
☎ 01273 890273 Ⓕ 01273 891439
Ⓔ fishernautical@seabooks.fsnet.co.uk
Ⓦ www.fishernautical.co.uk
Est. 1963 *Stock size* Large
Stock Rare, antiquarian, second-hand nautical books
Open Mail order Mon–Fri 9am–5pm
Services Mail order

TURNERS HILL

⊞ Albion House Antiques
Contact Janet Avery
✉ **Albion House, North Street, Turners Hill, West Sussex, RH10 4NS** 🅿
☎ 01342 715670
Est. 1971 *Stock size* Large
Stock 18th–19thC brass, copper, furniture, collectables
Open Mon–Sun 9am–6pm summer 9am–7pm

WEST GRINSTEAD

⊞ Bedouin Antiques (SALVO)
Contact Chris Thornton
✉ **Partridge Barns, Floodgates Farm, West Grinstead, West Sussex, RH13 8LH** 🅿
☎ 01403 711441 Ⓕ 01403 713382
Ⓔ info@bedouin.uk.com
Ⓦ www.bedouin.uk.com
Est. 2003 *Stock size* Small
Stock Unusual, decorative antiques
Open Tues–Sat 10am–4pm
Fairs Battersea Decorative Antiques

WISBOROUGH GREEN

John Bellman Ltd
Contact John Ireland
✉ **New Pound, Wisborough Green, West Sussex, RH14 0AZ** 🅿
☎ 01403 700858 Ⓕ 01403 700059
Ⓔ enquiries@bellmans.co.uk
Ⓦ www.bellmans.co.uk
Est. 1989
Open Mon–Fri 9am–5pm
Sales Monthly sales of antiques and collectables Wed 1pm Thurs 10am and 2pm Fri 10am, viewing Sat prior 9am–noon Mon 9am–4pm Tues 9am–7pm Wed 9am–1pm
Frequency Monthly
Catalogues Yes

WORTHING

⊞ Acorn Antiques
Contact Henry Nicholls
✉ **91 Rowlands Road,**

SOUTH

Worthing, West Sussex,
BN11 3JX P
☎ 01903 216926
e hnick@ntlworld.com
Est. 1992 *Stock size* Large
Stock Georgian–Edwardian furniture, china, silver, jewellery
Open Mon–Sat 9am–5.30pm
Services Valuations, restoration

⊞ Badgers Books
Contact Ray Potter
✉ **8–10 Gratwicke Road, Worthing, West Sussex, BN11 4BH** P
☎ 01903 211816
Est. 1982 *Stock size* Large
Stock Rare, antiquarian, second-hand books
Open Mon–Sat 9am–5.30pm

⊞ Chloe Antiques
Contact Mrs Dorothy Peters
✉ **61 Brighton Road, Worthing, West Sussex, BN11 3EE** P
☎ 01903 202697
Est. 1967 *Stock size* Large
Stock Small collectables, jewellery, china, glass
Open Mon–Sat 10am–4.30pm closed Wed

⊞ Corner Antiques
Contact Richard Mihok
✉ **9–10 Havercroft Building, North Street, Worthing, West Sussex, BN11 1DY** P
☎ 01903 537669
Est. 1997 *Stock size* Small
Stock General antiques, textiles, collectables
Open Mon–Sat 10am–5pm
Fairs Charmandan Centre Worthing

Gorringes
Contact Clifford Lansberry
✉ **44–46 High Street, Worthing, West Sussex, BN11 1LL** P
☎ 01903 238999
e worthing@gorringes.co.uk
w www.gorringes.co.uk
Est. 1928
Open Mon–Fri 9am–1pm 2–5pm
Sales Auctions of Edwardian–Victorian furniture and collectables, silver, paintings, Oriental and rugs Thurs 10am, viewing Sat 9am–12.30pm Mon–Wed 9am–5pm day of sale 9–10am
Frequency Every 6 weeks
Catalogues Yes

⊞ Interiors and Antiques
Contact Pat or Janet Cassie
✉ **162 Findon Road, Worthing, West Sussex, BN14 0EL** P
☎ 01903 261134
e janet.cassie@btopenworld.com
Est. 1998 *Stock size* Medium
Stock Furniture, china, glass, garden statues, bird baths
Open Mon–Sun 10am–6pm closed Wed 10am–1pm

⊞ Wilsons Antiques (LAPADA)
Contact Mr F Wilson
✉ **45–47 New Broadway, Tarring Road, Worthing, West Sussex, BN11 4HS** P
☎ 01903 202059
M 07778 813395
e frank@wilsons-antiques.com
w www.wilsons-antiques.com
Est. 1936 *Stock size* Medium
Stock Georgian–Edwardian formal English furniture
Open Mon–Fri 10am–4.30pm or by appointment
Fairs Olympia, NEC Antiques for Everyone

Worthing Auction Galleries Ltd
Contact Mr R Rood
✉ **Fleet House, Teville Gate, Worthing, West Sussex, BN11 1UA** P
☎ 01903 205565 F 01903 214365
e info@worthing-auctions.co.uk
w www.worthing-auctions.co.uk
Est. 1964
Open Mon–Fri 8.30am–5pm closed 1–2pm
Sales Monthly sales of general antiques
Frequency Monthly
Catalogues Yes

WEST COUNTRY

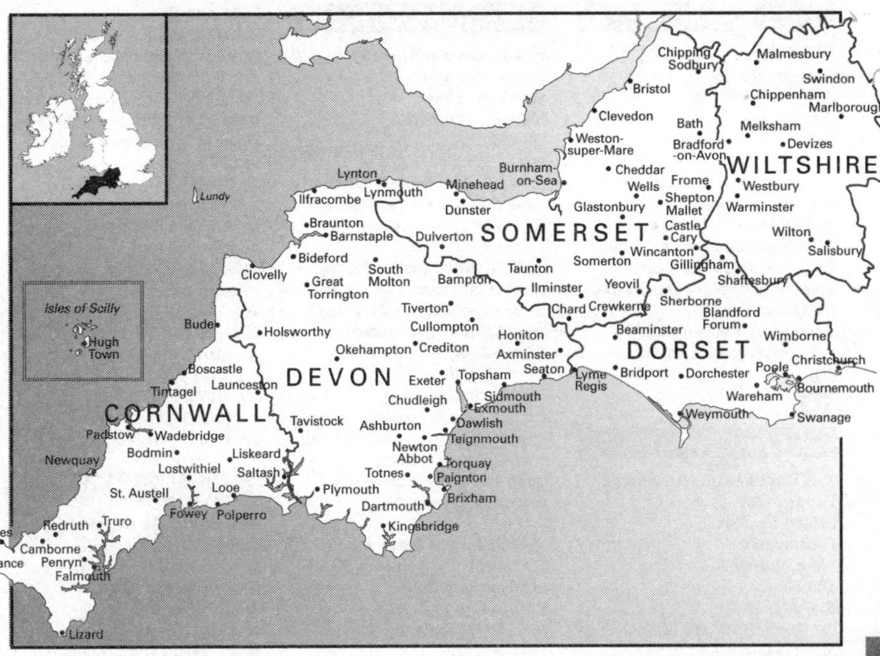

CORNWALL

BODMIN

Bodmin Antiques Centre
Contact Ralph Solomons
Townend, Bodmin, Cornwall, PL31 2LN P
01208 78661
0771 2431837
bodminantiques@hotmail.com
www.bodminantiquescentre.co.uk
Est. 1996 *Stock size* Large
No. of dealers 7
Stock General antiques, small items, porcelain, pottery, commemoratives, jewellery, collectables, glass, toys
Open Mon–Sat 10am–4pm
Services Valuations

BOSCASTLE

Atique
Contact Amanda Dawson
Boscastle Old Mill, Boscastle, Cornwall, PL35 0AQ P
01840 250230
www.boscastleoldmill.com
Est. 1999 *Stock size* Medium
Stock English, Continental antiques and linens
Open Mon–Sun 10am–5pm Nov–Feb by appointment

BUDE

Bluebells
Contact Denise Osbourne
36 Lansdown Road, Bude, Cornwall, EX23 8BA P
01288 350230
bluebellantiques@hotmail.com
Est. 2002 *Stock size* Medium
Stock Antiques, collectables, gifts
Open Mon–Sat 10am–4pm or by appointment

CALLINGTON

Country Living Antiques
Contact Ian Baxter CBE
Weston House, Haye Road, Callington, Cornwall, PL17 7JJ P
01579 382245
Est. 1988 *Stock size* Medium
Stock Country furniture and effects
Open Mon–Sat 9.30am–5.30pm
Services Free valuations

CALSTOCK

Collectable Adge
Contact Adrian Jones
14 Church Lane, Calstock, Cornwall, PL18 9QH
01822 832231 01822 832231
ag-jones1@talk21.com
Est. 1997 *Stock size* Large
Stock Football memorabilia
Open By appointment only
Fairs International Programme Fair London
Services New catalogue every two months

CAMELFORD

Corner Shop Antiques and Gallery
Contact Mr P J Tillett
68 Fore Street, Camelford, Cornwall, PL32 9PG P
01840 212573
07884 456247
tillett18@aol.com
Est. 1989 *Stock size* Medium
Stock General antiques, collectables, Victorian watercolours
Open Mon–Sat 10am–5.30pm

CARLYON BAY

L Edscer
Contact L Edscer
91 Sea Road, Carlyon Bay, St Austell, Cornwall, PL25 3SH
01726 810070 Ⓕ 01726 810070
Ⓔ lawrenceedscer@prs17495.demon.co.uk
Ⓦ www.autosportcollector.com
Est. 1989 *Stock size* Large
Stock Motor racing and rallying memorabilia
Open Mon–Sun 9am–6pm
Fairs Goodwood events, Beaulieu Fair
Services Valuations

CHACEWATER

Chacewater Antiques
Contact Mrs J Bateman
5 Fore Street, Chacewater, Truro, Cornwall, TR4 8PS
01872 561411
Est. 1992 *Stock size* Medium
Stock Georgian–Edwardian furniture, paintings, 19thC brassware, jewellery, silver
Open Tues–Sat 10am–5pm

CHARLESTOWN

Charlestown Trading
Contact Pippa Kennedy
The Old Gun Store, Charlestown, Cornwall, PL25 3NJ
01726 76018
Est. 1997 *Stock size* Medium
Stock General antiques, garden statuary, original fireplaces, Cornish ranges
Open Mon–Sun 10am–4.30pm

Once Upon a Time
Contact Pippa and Graham Kennedy
The Old Workshop, Charlestown, St Austell, Cornwall, PL25 3NJ
01726 76018 Ⓕ 01872 262520
Est. 1992 *Stock size* Large
Stock China, furniture, garden statuary, coins, general antiques
Open Mon–Sun 10am–4.30pm
Services Valuations, house clearances

FALMOUTH

Arcade Antiques
Contact G Springfield
19 High Street, Falmouth, Cornwall, TR11 2AB
01326 212472
Est. 1995 *Stock size* Medium
Stock General antiques, clocks
Open Mon–Sat 10.30am–5pm

Browsers Bookshop
Contact Mr Floyd
13–15 St George's Arcade, Church Street, Falmouth, Cornwall, TR11 3DH
01326 313464
Est. 1981 *Stock size* Medium
Stock Antiquarian, second-hand books, printed music
Open Mon–Sat 9.30am–5pm
Services Valuations

Isabelline Books
Contact Mr M Whetman
2 Highbury House, 8 Woodlane Crescent, Falmouth, Cornwall, TR11 4QS
01326 210412 Ⓕ 0870 051 6387
Ⓔ mikann@beakbook.demon.co.uk
Ⓦ www.beakbook.demon.co.uk
Est. 1997 *Stock size* Small
Stock Antiquarian books on ornithology
Open By appointment
Services Valuations, 3 catalogues a year

Marine Instruments
Contact Alistair Heane
The Wheelhouse, Upton Slip, Falmouth, Cornwall, TR11 3DQ
01326 312414 Ⓕ 01326 211414
Ⓔ info@marineinstruments.co.uk
Ⓦ www.marineinstruments.co.uk
Est. 1960 *Stock size* Large
Stock Marine-related charts, publications, sextants, compasses
Open Mon–Fri 9am–5pm Sat 9am–1pm
Services Worldwide mail order, valuations, repair of sextants and compasses

Old Town Hall Antiques
Contact Terry Brandreth or Mary Sheppard
Old Town Hall, 3 High Street, Falmouth, Cornwall, TR11 2AB
01326 319437
Ⓦ www.oldtownhallantiques.co.uk
Est. 1986 *Stock size* Large
Stock 17th–early 20thC furniture, general antiques and collectables
Open Mon–Sat 10am–5.30pm Sun 10am–4pm
Services Deliveries abroad

P S I Collectables
Contact Phil Hart
2a Berkeley Court, Falmouth, Cornwall, TR11 3XE
01326 212540 Ⓕ 01326 212540
Ⓔ psico@tiscali.co.uk
Est. 1998 *Stock size* Medium
Stock Wade, American comics, collectable bears, annuals
Open Mon–Sat 10am–5pm

FOWEY

Bookends of Fowey
Contact Mrs C Alexander
4 South Street, Fowey, Cornwall, PL23 1AR
01726 833361
Ⓔ info@bookendsoffowey.com
Ⓦ www.bookendsoffowey.com
Est. 1987 *Stock size* Large
Stock Antiquarian, second-hand books
Open Mon–Sat 10am–5.30pm Apr–Oct Sun 10am–5.30pm
Services Valuations, book search, publishers of Cornish literature books

GRAMPOUND

Pine & Period Furniture
Contact Simon Payne
Fore Street, Grampound, Cornwall, TR2 4QT
01726 883117
Ⓜ 07850 318298
Est. 1971 *Stock size* Medium
Stock Pine and period furniture
Open Mon–Sat 10.30am–5pm

Radnor House Antiques
Contact Geoff or Penny Hodgson
Fore Street, Grampound, Truro, Cornwall, TR2 4QT
01726 882921
Est. 1975 *Stock size* Medium
Stock Victorian, Edwardian and Georgian oak, pine and mahogany furniture
Open Mon–Sat 10am–6pm

HAYLE

⊞ Copperhouse Gallery
Contact Paul Dyer
✉ **14 Fore Street, Copperhouse, Hayle, Cornwall, TR27 4DY** P
☎ 01736 752787
Est. 1900 *Stock size* Large
Stock Victorian and early 20thC watercolours, art pottery
Open Tues–Sat 9am–5pm

HELSTON

⊞ Butchers Antiques
Contact Howard Jones
✉ **Rear of 12 Wendron Street, Helston, Cornwall, TR13 8PS** P
☎ 01326 565117
Est. 1991 *Stock size* Medium
Stock Country and pine furniture, cottageware and very unusual items
Open Mon–Sat 8am–5pm

⊞ The Helston Bookworm (PBFA)
Contact Mr and Mrs Summers
✉ **9 Church Street, Helston, Cornwall, TR13 8TA** P
☎ 01326 565079
Est. 1994 *Stock size* Medium
Stock Antiquarian and second-hand books
Open Mon–Fri 10am–5.30pm Sat 10am–2pm
Fairs PBFA, local fairs (telephone for details)
Services Restoration, book search

LAUNCESTON

⊞ Antique Chairs and Museum
Contact Alice or Tom Brown
✉ **Colhay Farm, Polson, Launceston, Cornwall, PL15 9QS** P
☎ 01566 777485 Ⓕ 01566 777485
Est. 1987 *Stock size* Large
Stock Period chairs
Open Mon–Sun 9am–5.30pm
Services Restoration, upholstery

⊞ Todd's Antiques
Contact Mr T Mead
✉ **2 High Street, Launceston, Cornwall, PL15 8ER** P
☎ 01566 775007 Ⓕ 01566 775007
Est. 1997 *Stock size* Large
Stock Small furniture, collectables, ceramics
Open Mon–Fri 9am–5pm Thurs–Sat 9am–4pm

LELANT

⊞ Mike Read Antique Sciences
Contact Mr M Read
✉ **1 Abbey Meadow, Lelant, St Ives, Cornwall, TR26 3LL** P
☎ 01736 757237 Ⓕ 01736 757237
Ⓔ mikeread@macmail.com
Est. 1978 *Stock size* Medium
Stock Scientific instruments, maritime works of art and nautical artefacts
Open By appointment
Fairs International Antique Scientific and Medical Instruments Fair, Portman Square
Services Valuations

LISKEARD

⊞ Olden Days
Contact Hazel Young
✉ **Five Lanes, Dobwalls, Liskeard, Cornwall, PL14 6JD** P
☎ 01579 321577 Ⓕ 01579 321804
Ⓜ 07879 814815
Est. 1989 *Stock size* Medium
Stock General antiques, old furniture, new pine
Open Mon–Sat 9.30am–5.30pm Sun 10am–4pm
Services Bespoke furniture, upholstery, restoration

LOOE

⊞ Abbey Bears
Contact Alex Hall
✉ **Fore Street, Looe, Cornwall, PL13 1DT** P
☎ 01503 265441
Est. 1999 *Stock size* Large
Stock Teddy bears
Open Mon–Sun 10am–6pm

⊞ Tony Martin
Contact Mr Tony Martin
✉ **Fore Street, East Looe, Looe, Cornwall, PL13 1AE** P
☎ 01503 262734
Est. 1965 *Stock size* Medium
Stock General small furniture, china, ceramics, pictures
Open Appointment advisable

LOSTWITHIEL

⊞ John Bragg Antiques
Contact Ann Bragg
✉ **35 Fore Street, Lostwithiel, Cornwall, PL22 0BN** P
☎ 01208 872827
Ⓜ 07798 941484
Est. 1973 *Stock size* Large
Stock Period furniture
Open Mon–Sat 10am–5pm closed Wed pm
Services Valuations

⊞ Deja-Vu Antiques & Collectables
Contact Adrian or Marianne Barratt
✉ **31 Fore Street, Lostwithiel, Cornwall, PL22 0BN** P
☎ 01208 873912
Ⓔ antiquedejavu@hotmail.com
Est. 1998 *Stock size* Medium
Stock Furniture, pictures, collectables, curios, silver, large selection of books
Open Mon–Sat 10am–5pm closed Wed pm
Services Book search

⊞ The Furniture Store
Contact Mike Edwards
✉ **2 Queen Street, Lostwithiel, Cornwall, PL22 0AB**
☎ 01208 873408 Ⓕ 01208 873408
Ⓜ 07790 759540
Est. 1986 *Stock size* Large
Stock Pine furniture, turn-of-the-century oak, Bakelite radios
Open Mon–Sat 10am–5.30pm Wed closed 1pm

⊞ The Higgins Press
Contact Doris Roberts
✉ **South Street, Lostwithiel, Cornwall, PL22 0BZ** P
☎ 01208 872755
Est. 1980 *Stock size* Medium
Stock Antiques and collectables
Open Mon–Sat 10am–4pm closed Wed pm

Jefferys
Contact Ian Morris
✉ **5 Fore Street, Lostwithiel, Cornwall, PL22 0BP** P
☎ 01208 872245 Ⓕ 01208 873260
Ⓔ jefferys.lostwithiel@btinternet.com

Ⓦ www.jefferys.uk.com
Est. 1865
Open Mon–Fri 9am–5.30
Sales Antique and fine art sales every two months Wed 10am, viewing prior Mon 2–7pm Tues 10am–1pm 2–5pm. General household sales fortnightly Wed 10am, viewing prior Tues 10am–1pm 2–5pm
Catalogues Yes

The Old Palace Antiques
Contact Mr J Askew
✉ **Quay Street, Lostwithiel, Cornwall, PL22 0BS** Ⓟ
☎ 01208 872909
Est. 1979 *Stock size* Medium
Stock Pine furniture, china, brass, prints, postcards
Open Tues–Sun 9am–5pm

Yesterdays
Contact John Faircloth
✉ **9 Fore Street, Lostwithiel, Cornwall, PL22 0BP** Ⓟ
☎ 01208 872344 Ⓕ 01208 872344
Ⓔ jfaircloth@onetel.net
Est. 1997 *Stock size* Medium
Stock Old pine and country furniture, rural bygones, general antiques, complementary items
Open Tues–Sat 10am–5pm
Services Picture framing

MARAZION

Antiques
Contact Andrew S Wood
✉ **The Shambles, Market Place, Marazion, Cornwall, TR17 0AR** Ⓟ
☎ 01736 711381
Est. 1988 *Stock size* Medium
Stock General antiques and collectors' items particularly 19th–20thC pottery, porcelain and glass
Open 1 Apr–31 Oct Mon–Fri 10.15am–5.30pm 1 Nov–31 Mar Mon–Sat 10.15am–5pm

MEVAGISSEY

Cloud Cuckoo Land
Contact Paul Mulvey
✉ **12 Fore Street, Mevagissey, St Austell, Cornwall, PL26 6UQ** Ⓟ
☎ 01726 842364
Ⓔ paul@cloudcuckooland.biz
Ⓦ www.cloudcuckooland.biz
Est. 1993 *Stock size* Medium
Stock Autographs
Open Mon–Sun 11am–6pm

PADSTOW

Jacob & His Fiery Angel
Contact Mrs Sonya Fancett
✉ **7 Middle Street, Padstow, Cornwall, PL28 8AP** Ⓟ
☎ 01841 532130 or 01209 831616
Ⓕ 01841 532130
Ⓔ debbiemorriskirby@tesco.net
Ⓦ www.jacobandhisfieryangel.com
Est. 1992 *Stock size* Large
Stock Antiques, eccentricities, eg angels, chandeliers, cats, curiosities, taxidermy (birds)
Open Mon–Sat 11am–5pm winter Mon Thurs Sat noon–4pm or by appointment

PAR

Bonhams
✉ **Cornubia Hall, Eastcliffe Road, Par, Cornwall, PL24 2AQ**
☎ 01726 814047 Ⓕ 01726 817979
Ⓔ par@bonhams.com
Ⓦ www.bonhams.com
Open Mon–Fri 9am–5.30pm
Sales Regional Saleroom. Frequent sales. Regular house and attic sales across the country; contact London offices for further details. Free auction valuations; insurance and probate valuations

Tinkers Pine Stripping & Antiques
Contact Mark or Heidi Chapman
✉ **Unit 9, The Roundhouse, Harbour Road, Par, Cornwall, PL24 2BB** Ⓟ
☎ 01726 812812
Est. 2001 *Stock size* Medium
Stock Doors, architraves, skirting boards, fire surrounds, bannisters, spindles, cupboard doors, mouldings, odd pieces of furniture, stripped doors
Open Tues–Sat 9am–5pm
Services Pine stripping

PENRYN

The Old School Antiques
Contact Mr J Gavin
✉ **The Old School, Church Road, Penryn, Cornwall, TR10 8DA** Ⓟ
☎ 01326 375092
Ⓜ 07789 698303
Est. 1985 *Stock size* Large
Stock Antique furniture, glass, china, clocks
Open Mon–Sun 9am–5.30pm
Services Clock repairs and furniture restoration

Leon Robertson Antiques
Contact Mr L Robertson
✉ **Unit 2, The Old School, Church Road, Penryn, Cornwall, TR10 8DA** Ⓟ
☎ 01326 372767
Ⓜ 07971 171909
Est. 1973 *Stock size* Medium
Stock Furniture, paintings, general antiques
Open Mon–Sun 9am–5.30pm
Services Valuations

PENZANCE

Antiques and Fine Art
Contact Elinor Davies or Geoffrey Mills
✉ **1–3 Queens Buildings, The Promenade, Penzance, Cornwall, TR18 4HH** Ⓟ
☎ 01736 350509
Ⓦ www.antiquesfineart.co.uk
Est. 1994 *Stock size* Medium
Stock 17th–19thC furniture
Open Mon–Sat 10am–4pm
Services Valuations, restoration, upholstery

Chapel Street Arcades
Contact Mr Bentley
✉ **61–62 Chapel Street, Penzance, Cornwall, TR18 4AE** Ⓟ
Ⓜ 07890 542708
Est. 1984 *Stock size* Medium
No. of dealers 25
Stock Furniture, brass, copper, silver, glass, porcelain, pictures, prints, linen, collectors' items
Open Mon–Sat 10am–5pm

R W Jeffery
Contact Mr R W Jeffery
✉ **Trebehor, St Levan, Penzance, Cornwall, TR19 6LX** Ⓟ
☎ 01736 871263
Est. 1968 *Stock size* Large
Stock Coins, banknotes
Open By appointment
Services Mail order

Peter Johnson
Contact Mr P Johnson
62 Chapel Street, Penzance, Cornwall, TR18 4AE
01736 363267
Est. 1992 *Stock size* Medium
Stock Period lighting, Oriental ceramics, furniture, hand-made silk lampshades
Open Tues–Sat 9.30am–5pm
Services Valuations

W H Lane & Son, Fine Art Auctioneer and Valuers
Contact Graham J Bazley
Jubilee House, Queen Street, Penzance, Cornwall, TR18 4DF
01736 361447 F 01736 350097
E info@whlane.co.uk
Est. 1934
Open Mon–Fri 9am–1pm 2–5.30pm
Sales 6 major picture sales per annum, occasional country house sales
Catalogues Yes

David Lays (BACA Award Winner 2003)
Contact Mr D Lay FRICS
The Penzance Auction House, Alverton, Penzance, Cornwall, TR18 4RE
01736 361414 F 01736 360035
E david.lays@btopenworld.com
W www.invaluable.com/davidlay
Est. 1985
Open Mon–Fri 9am–5pm
Sales Auctioneers and valuers General sales every 3 weeks Tues 10am, viewing Sat 9am–1pm Mon 9am–5pm. Bi-monthly 2-day antiques auctions Thurs Fri 10am, viewing Sat, day prior and day of sale 8.30–10am. Traditional contemporary art auctions 3 per annum Feb June Oct Thurs 11am, viewing Sat 9am–1pm, day prior 9am–5pm day of sale 8.30–11am. Book and Collectors' sales 2 per annum Aug and Dec Tues 10am, viewing Sat 9am–1pm day prior 9am–5pm morning of sale 8.30–10am
Catalogues Yes

New Street Books
Contact Mr K Hearn
4 New Street, Penzance, Cornwall, TR18 2LZ
01736 362758
E eankelvin@yahoo.com
Est. 1991 *Stock size* Medium
Stock Antiquarian and second-hand books, Cornish topics a speciality
Open Mon–Sat 10am–5pm
Fairs Morrab Library Book Fair
Services Book search

The Old Custom House
Contact Mr M Bauer
53 Chapel Street, Penzance, Cornwall, TR18 4AF
01736 331030 F 01736 331030
Est. 1997 *Stock size* Medium
Stock Glass, china
Open Mon–Sat 9am–5.30pm Sun by appointment

Penzance Rare Books
Contact Pat Johnstone
43 Causewayhead, Penzance, Cornwall, TR18 2SS
01736 362140
E pat@boscathnoe.free-online.co.uk
Est. 1991 *Stock size* Large
Stock Antiquarian and second-hand books
Open Mon–Sat 10am–5pm
Services Valuations

Tony Sanders Gallery
Contact Mr Tony Sanders
14 Chapel Street, Penzance, Cornwall, TR18 4AW
01736 366620
Est. 1969 *Stock size* Large
Stock Antique furniture, paintings, silver, glass, Newlyn copper
Open Mon–Sat 9am–5.30pm

Shiver Me Timbers
Contact Mr T R E Gray
Station Road, Long Rock, Penzance, Cornwall, TR20 9TT
01736 711338
Est. 1983 *Stock size* Medium
Stock Reclaimed materials
Open Mon–Sat 10am–5pm
Services Hire of materials to film companies, makes reproduction furniture

POLPERRO

Expectations
Contact John Walker
Fore Street, Polperro, Cornwall, PL13 2QR
01503 272631
Est. 2001 *Stock size* Medium
Stock Furniture, lamps, brass, copper
Open Summer Mon–Sun winter Sat–Mon 10.30am–5.30pm
Services Search service for oil lamp parts

Gentry Antiques
Contact Pauline Black
Little Green, Polperro, Cornwall, PL13 2RF
01503 272361
E info@gentryantiques.co.uk
Est. 1998 *Stock size* Medium
Stock Pottery, porcelain and decorative items
Open Mon–Sun 10am–5pm
Fairs Battersea Antiques and Decorators Fair

REDRUTH

La Belle
Contact Danny Everard
52 Fore Street, Redruth, Cornwall, TR15 2AE
01209 216228
Est. 1991 *Stock size* Medium
Stock General antiques
Open Mon–Sat 9am–5pm
Services Valuations

Evergreen Antiques & Interiors
Contact Michele Jelf
38 Fore Street, Redruth, Cornwall, TR15 2AE
01209 215634
E evergreen@forestreet38.freeserve.co.uk
Est. 2000 *Stock size* Medium
Stock General antiques, interiors
Open Mon–Sat 10am–4.30pm

The Old Steam Bakery
Contact Mr Stephen Phillips
60a Fore Street, Redruth, Cornwall, TR15 2AF
01209 315099
Est. 1994 *Stock size* Large
Stock Late Victorian and Edwardian oak and pine furniture
Open Mon–Sat 10.30am–5pm

Pool Auctions
Contact Mr or Mrs Duncan
✉ **Unit 1, Trevenson Road, Pool, Redruth, Cornwall, TR15 3PH** P
☎ 01209 717111
Est. 1995
Open Mon–Fri 9am–3pm
Sales Antiques and general household sale Tues 6pm, viewing Tues 9am–6pm prior to sale
Frequency Weekly
Catalogues No

Richards Son & Murdoch
Contact Mr Eddy
✉ **Alma Place, Redruth, Cornwall, TR15 2AT** P
☎ 01209 216367 F 01209 314959
Est. 1876
Open Mon–Fri 9am–1pm 2–5pm Sat 9am–noon
Sales Tuesday, general antiques, household furniture, 11am
Frequency Every 5–6 weeks
Catalogues Yes

Romantiques
Contact Patrick Ludford
✉ **Old Rectory, Churchtown, Redruth, Cornwall, TR15 3BT** P
M 07980 500490
Est. 1999 *Stock size* Medium
Stock Period antiques and ornamental garden antiques, staddle stones, troughs
Open Mon–Sat 10am–5pm or by appointment

Thornleigh Trading Antique Lighting
Contact Mr Duncan
✉ **46 Fore Street, Redruth, Cornwall, TR15 2AE** P
☎ 01209 315454
Est. 1992 *Stock size* Large
Stock Antique lighting, Victorian oil lamps
Open Mon–Sat 9.30am–5pm

ST COLUMB

M R Dingle
Contact Mr Dingle
✉ **Station Yard, Station Approach, St Columb Road, St Columb, Cornwall, TR9 6QR** P
☎ 01726 861119
Est. 1989 *Stock size* Large
Stock Architectural antiques including reclaimed timber
Open Mon–Fri 8am–5pm Sat 8am–noon

ST IVES

The Bear Shop
Contact John Barnes
✉ **13 Fore Street, St Ives, Cornwall, TR26 1AB** P
☎ 01736 798586
E enquiries@cornwallbearshop.co.uk
W www.cornwallbearshop.co.uk
Est. 2000 *Stock size* Large
Stock Teddy bears
Open Mon–Sun 9am–5pm
Fairs Totally Teddies and Hugglets

The Book Gallery
Contact David and Tina Wilkinson
✉ **The Old Post Office Garage, St Ives, Cornwall, TR26 2LR**
☎ 01736 793545
Est. 1991 *Stock size* Medium
Stock Antiquarian and second-hand books, art on St Ives a speciality
Open By appointment
Services Book search and catalogue of St Ives books

Courtyard Collectables
Contact Janice Mosedale
✉ **Cyril Noall Square, Fore Street, St Ives, Cornwall, TR26 1HE**
☎ 01736 798809
Est. 1994 *Stock size* Large
Stock General collectables
Open May–October Mon–Sun 10am–10pm Nov–April Mon–Sat 10am–5pm Sun noon–5pm

Dragons Hoard
Contact Chris Prescott
✉ **2 Tre-Pol-Pen, Street-an-Pol, St Ives, Cornwall, TR26 2DS**
☎ 01736 798484 F 01736 798417
E dragonshoard@dragonshoard.ws
W www.dragonshoard.ws
Est. 1985 *Stock size* Small
Stock Collectables old and new, Britain's figures, farm animals, diecast models, Corgi, Matchbox, playing cards, Kinder Surprise, storage systems, advertising, ephemera, curios
Open Mon–Fri 10.30am–5pm Sat 10.30am–4pm
Fairs Newark

Tremayne Applied Arts
Contact Roger or Anne Tonkinson
✉ **Street-an-Pol, St Ives, Cornwall, TR26 2DS**
☎ 01736 797779 F 01736 793222
E tomkinson@btinternet.com
Est. 1997 *Stock size* Large
Stock 20thC antiques, 1960s, Arts and Crafts, Art Deco, Art Nouveau
Open Mon–Fri 10.30am–4.30pm Sat 10am–1.30pm closed Wed

ST JUST

St Just Bygones
Contact H I Whitelaw
✉ **30 Fore Street, St Just, Penzance, Cornwall, TR19 7LX** P
☎ 01736 787860
Est. 1990 *Stock size* Large
Stock Furniture, general antiques, bric-a-brac
Open Mon–Sat 10am–5.30pm
Services House clearance

TIDEFORD

Cutcrew Antiques
Contact Miss Nicola Stewart
✉ **Cutcrew Sawmills, Tideford, Cornwall, PL12 5JS** P
☎ 01752 851402
Est. 1984 *Stock size* Large
Stock Georgian–Edward furniture situated in an 18thC water mill
Open Mon–Sun 9am–5.30pm

TINTAGEL

Atique
Contact Amanda Dawson
✉ **Bath House, Fore Street, Tintagel, Cornwall, PL34 0DD** P
☎ 01840 779009
E antique.interiors@virgin.net
W www.boscastleoldmill.com
Est. 1999 *Stock size* Medium
Stock English, Continental antiques and linens, contemporary art
Open Mon–Sun 10am–5pm Nov–Feb by appointment

The House That Jack Built
Contact Sam Rowe
✉ **Hollybush Studio, Fore Street,**

Tintagel, Cornwall,
PL34 0DB
☎ 01840 770055
Est. 2003 *Stock size* Small
Stock Antiques, collectables
Open By appointment

TRURO

Alan Bennett Ltd
Contact Mr Alan Bennett or Justin Bennett
24 New Bridge Street, Truro, Cornwall, TR1 2AA P
☎ 01872 273296
Est. 1954 *Stock size* Large
Stock Furniture pre-1910, general antiques
Open Mon–Sat 9am–5.30pm
Services Valuations

Blackwater Pine Antiques
Contact Linda Cropper
Blackwater, Truro, Cornwall, TR4 8ET P
☎ 01872 560919
Est. 1989 *Stock size* Large
Stock Antique pine and country furniture
Open Mon–Sat 10am–5.30pm closed Wed
Services Valuations, restoration

Bonython Bookshop
Contact Mrs R Carpenter
16 Kenwyn Street, Truro, Cornwall, TR1 3BU
☎ 01872 262886
bonythonbooks@btconnect.com
Est. 1996 *Stock size* Small
Stock Antiquarian, second-hand and art books, Cornish interest a speciality
Open Mon–Sat 10.30am–4.30pm
Services Valuations, book search

Bric-a-Brac
Contact Richard Bonehill
16a Walsingham Place, Truro, Cornwall, TR1 2RP P
☎ 01872 225200
richard@bonehill3.freeserve.co.uk
www.bonehill3.freeserve.co.uk
Est. 1974 *Stock size* Large
Stock Militaria, small collectables, royal commemorative china
Open Mon–Sat 9.30am–5pm
Fairs Lostwithiel
Services Research into WWI and WWII war deaths

Philip Buddell
Contact Linda Buddell
The Elms, Tresillian, Truro, Cornwall, TR2 4BA
☎ 01872 250173
07974 022893
lulubudd@aol.com
Est. 1989
Open Mon–Sat 10am–5pm
Sales Auctions and viewing at a hall in Ladock. Antiques and general household sale 3-weekly on Sat 10am, viewing Fri 2–8pm. Specialist wine, toy and book sales quarterly. Telephone for details
Catalogues Yes

Philip Buddell Antiques
Contact Philip or Linda Buddell
The Elms, Tresillian, Truro, Cornwall, TR2 4BA P
☎ 01872 520173
07974 022893
lulubudd@aol.com
Est. 2000 *Stock size* Medium
Stock Fine furniture, paintings
Open Mon–Sat 10am–5pm
Services Valuations, auctions

Coinage Hall Antique Centre
Contact David Taylor
1 Princes Street, Truro, Cornwall, TR1 2QU P
☎ 01872 262336
Est. 1996 *Stock size* Medium
No. of dealers 3
Stock Fine furniture, collectables, general antiques, fabrics, fine art, postcards, cigarette cards
Open Mon–Sat 10am–3.30pm
Services Valuations

Collectors Corner
Contact Alan McLoughlin
Unit 45–46, Pannier Market, Back Quay, Truro, Cornwall, TR1 2LL P
☎ 01872 272729
almacmedal@aol.com
www.militarycollectables.co.uk
Est. 1997 *Stock size* Medium
Stock Coins, banknotes, medals, militaria, stamps, postcards, cigarette cards
Open Mon–Sat 9.30am–4.30pm
Services Valuations, medal mounting

Count House Antiques
Contact Mrs M Such
Coinage Hall, 1 Princes Street, Truro, Cornwall, TR1 2ES P
☎ 01872 264269
Est. 1998 *Stock size* Medium
Stock General antiques
Open Mon–Sat 10am–4.30pm
Fairs Exeter

Just Books
Contact Jenny Wicks
9 Pydar Mews, Truro, Cornwall, TR1 2UX P
☎ 01872 242532
Est. 1986 *Stock size* Medium
Stock Antiquarian, collectable, second-hand and out-of-print books, Cornwall a speciality
Open Mon–Sat 10am–5pm
Services Valuations, book search, repairs referral

Lodge and Thomas
Contact Mr Lodge
58 Lemon Street, Truro, Cornwall, TR1 2PY
☎ 01872 272722 01872 223665
info@lodgeandthomas.co.uk
www.lodgeandthomas.co.uk
Est. 1892
Open Mon–Fri 9am–5.30pm Sat 9am–noon
Sales General antiques and collectables sale, viewing 9–11am prior to sale. Telephone for details. Sales held at Ludgvan Community Hall, Ludgvan, Penzance, Cornwall
Frequency 8 per year
Catalogues Yes

Once Upon A Time
Contact Graham Kennedy
The Coinage Hall, 1 Princes Street, Truro, Cornwall, TR1 2QU P
☎ 01872 262520
pbootantiques@btconnect.com
Est. 1996 *Stock size* Medium
Stock General antiques, English, French and Continental furniture, paintings, sculpture
Open Mon–Sat 10am–4pm
Services Restoration, upholstery

⊞ Taylor's Collectables
Contact Mr D Taylor
✉ **The Coinage Hall, 1 Princes Street, Truro, Cornwall, TR1 2QU** Ⓟ
☎ 01872 262336
Ⓜ 07775 811686
Est. 1994 *Stock size* Medium
Stock Postcards, cigarette cards, toys, general antiques
Open Mon–Sat 10am–3.30pm
Fairs Newark, West Point, Twickenham
Services Valuations

VERYAN

⊞ Granny's Attic
Contact A K Gray
✉ **Village Centre, Veryan, Truro, Cornwall, TR2 5QA** Ⓟ
☎ 01872 501637
Est. 2000 *Stock size* Medium
Stock Antiques, country items, collectables, second-hand clothes
Open Fri Sat 10am–4.30pm or by appointment

WADEBRIDGE

⊞ Acorn Antique Interiors
Contact Brian or Margaret
✉ **Eddystone Road, Wadebridge, Cornwall, PL27 7AL** Ⓟ
☎ 01208 812815
Est. 1982 *Stock size* Medium
Stock Antique pine furniture
Open Mon–Sat 9am–5pm
Services Restoration

Lambrays
Contact Richard J Hamm
✉ **Polmorla Walk, The Platt, Wadebridge, Cornwall, PL27 7AE** Ⓟ
☎ 01208 813593 Ⓕ 01208 814986
Ⓔ lambrays@freeuk.com
Est. 1981
Open Mon–Fri 9am–5.30pm Sat 9am–noon (prior to sale)
Sales Quarterly specialist antique sales. Victoriana sales fortnightly Mon 11am
Catalogues Yes

⊞ Polmorla Bookshop
Contact Joan Buck
✉ **1 Polmorla Road, Wadebridge, Cornwall, PL27 7NB** Ⓟ
☎ 01208 814399
Est. 1991 *Stock size* Large
Stock Antiquarian, rare, second-hand and out-of-print books
Open Mon–Sat 10.30am–5pm
Services Valuations, book search

⊞ Relics
Contact Mr K Brenton
✉ **4 Polmorla Road, Wadebridge, Cornwall, PL27 7NB** Ⓟ
☎ 01208 815383
Est. 1991 *Stock size* Large
Stock Furniture, china, brass, kitchenware, pictures
Open Mon–Sat 10am–5pm

⊞ Victoria Antiques
Contact Mr Daly
✉ **21 Molesworth Street, Wadebridge, Cornwall, PL27 7DD** Ⓟ
☎ 01208 814160 Ⓕ 01208 814160
Est. 1974 *Stock size* Large
Stock General antiques, clocks, barometers, period furniture
Open Mon–Sat 9am–5pm

DEVON

ASHBURTON

⊞ Adrian Ager
Contact Adrian Ager
✉ **Ashburton Marbles, Great Hall, North Street, Ashburton, Newton Abbott, Devon, TQ13 7QD** Ⓟ
☎ 01364 653189 Ⓕ 01364 653189
Ⓔ afager@tinyworld.co.uk
Ⓦ www.adrianager.co.uk
Est. 1975 *Stock size* Large
Stock Victorian furnishings, interior fittings, fireplaces, dining room tables, garden statuary, garden ornaments
Open Mon–Fri 8am–5pm Sat 10am–4pm
Services Valuations, restoration

⊞ The Dartmoor Bookshop Ltd (PBFA)
Contact Mr Paul Heatley
✉ **2 Kingsbridge Lane, Ashburton, Newton Abbot, Devon, TQ13 7DX** Ⓟ
☎ 01364 653356
Ⓔ Dartmoorbks@aol.com
Ⓦ www.dartmoorbks.dabsol.co.uk
Est. 1974 *Stock size* Large
Stock Antiquarian, second-hand, rare and out-of-print books
Open Wed–Sat 9.30am–5.30pm

⊞ Kessler Ford Antiques
Contact Matthew Ford or Elizabeth Kessler
✉ **9 North Street, Ashburton, Newton Abbot, Devon, TQ13 7QJ** Ⓟ
☎ 01364 654310 Ⓕ 01364 654141
Ⓜ 07770 782402
Ⓔ kessler.ford@netmatters.co.uk
Est. 1998 *Stock size* Medium
Stock 17th–18thC English oak and mahogany furniture
Open Tues–Sat 10am–5pm or by appointment

⊞ Memories
Contact Julia Walters
✉ **Globe Buildings, 15 North Street, Ashburton, Newton Abbot, Devon, TQ13 7QH** Ⓟ
☎ 01364 654681
Ⓜ 07773 795777
Ⓔ julieann.walters@btopenworld.com
Est. 1996 *Stock size* Medium
Stock A varied range of Georgian–Edwardian furniture, collectables
Open Mon–Sat 10am–4pm closed Wed pm
Fairs Westpoint, Exeter

⊞ Moor Antiques
Contact Mr or Mrs Gatland
✉ **19a North Street, Ashburton, Newton Abbot, Devon, TQ13 7QH** Ⓟ
☎ 01364 653767
Ⓜ 07720 183414
Ⓔ moorantiques@aol.com
Est. 1984 *Stock size* Medium
Stock 18th–19thC furniture, silver, glass, porcelain, clocks, jewellery
Open Mon–Sat 10am–4pm Wed 10am–1pm
Services Valuations

⊞ Pennsylvania Pine Company
Contact Stephen Robinson
✉ **18 East Street, Ashburton, Devon, TQ13 7AZ**
☎ 01364 652244 Ⓕ 01364 652244
Ⓦ www.pennsylvaniapine.co.uk
Est. 2000 *Stock size* Medium
Stock Antique English pine
Open Mon–Sat 10.30am–4.30pm closed Wed
Services Valuations, restoration

Rendells (RICS, CAAV)
Contact Mr Clive Morgan
Stonepark, Ashburton, Newton Abbot, Devon, TQ13 7RH
01364 653017 01364 654251
stonepark@rendells.co.uk
www.rendells.co.uk
Est. 1816
Open Mon–Fri 9am–5.30pm
Sales Antiques and selected items monthly Thurs Fri 10am, viewing Tues 10am–7pm Wed 10am–5pm
Catalogues Yes

The Shambles
Contact Mrs Spendlove or Mrs Keith
24 North Street, Ashburton, Newton Abbot, Devon, TQ13 7QD
01364 653848
Est. 1986 *Stock size* Large
No. of dealers 6
Stock Furniture, collectables, marine antiques, textiles, pictures, rugs, silver, Staffordshire figures
Open Mon–Sat 10am–5pm

The Snug
Contact Ros Gregg or Carol Dant
15 North Street, Ashburton, Newton Abbot, Devon, TQ13 7QH
01364 653096
Est. 1991 *Stock size* Medium
Stock Antiques, textiles, interiors
Open Mon–Sat 10am–4.30pm

Taylors
Contact Wendy Taylor
5 North Street, Ashburton, Newton Abbot, Devon, TQ13 7QJ
01364 652631
Est. 1985 *Stock size* Medium
Stock 18thC–Edwardian oak furniture, 18thC blue and white Chinese porcelain
Open Mon–Sat 10am–5pm

AXMINSTER

Axminster Auctions
Contact John Bloxham
Coombe Lane, Axminster, Devon, EX13 5AY
01297 35693 01297 35693
Est. 1858
Open Mon–Fri 9am–5pm
Sales General antiques sale second Wed of the month 10am, viewing Tues 10am–8pm
Frequency Monthly

South Street Antiques
Contact Philip Atkins
South Street, Axminster, Devon, EX13 5AD
01297 33701
Est. 1987 *Stock size* Medium
Stock General antiques
Open Mon–Sat 9.30am–4.30pm closed Wed pm
Fairs Shepton Mallet
Services Valuations

BAMPTON

Bampton Gallery
Contact Gerald Chidwick
2–4 Brook Street, Bampton, Devon, EX16 9LY
01398 331119/331354
01398 331119
bampton.gallery@bampton.org.uk
www.bampton.org.uk
Est. 1997 *Stock size* Medium
Stock Antique porcelain, glass, small furniture, pictures
Open Mon–Thurs 9.30am–3pm Sat 9am–noon or by appointment
Services Restoration, upholstery

BARNSTAPLE

The Barn Antiques
Contact Mr T Cusack
73 Newport Road, Barnstaple, Devon, EX32 9BG
01271 323131
Est. 1987 *Stock size* Large
Stock General antiques
Open Mon–Sat 9.30am–5pm closed Wed pm
Services Valuations, restoration

Barnstaple Auctions
Contact Mr Mugleston
Pilton Quay, Barnstaple, Devon, EX31 1PB
01271 342952 01271 342952
Est. 1993
Open Mon–Fri 9am–5pm Sat 10am–2pm
Sales General antiques sale last Thurs of month 6.30pm, viewing Wed 4–7pm
Frequency Monthly
Catalogues Yes

Medina Gallery
Contact Richard Jennings
80 Boutport Street, Barnstaple, Devon, EX31 1SR
01271 371025
Est. 1973 *Stock size* Medium
Stock Antique prints, maps, oils, watercolours
Open Mon–Sat 9.30am–5pm

North Devon Antiques Centre
Contact Patrick Broome
The Old Church, Cross Street, Barnstaple, Devon, EX31 1BD
01271 375788 01271 375788
07967 930917
partick-broome@top-finish-designs.freeserve.co.uk
Est. 1998 *Stock size* Large
No. of dealers 27
Stock Georgian to contemporary furniture, Royal Worcester, Clarice Cliff, crested china ware, Barum and Brannam, militaria, clocks, architectural salvage, pictures and prints, Art Deco
Open Mon–Sat 10am–4.30pm
Services Restoration, café also open 6 days

Tarka Books (BA)
Contact Fiona Broster
5 Bear Street, Barnstaple, Devon, EX32 7BU
01271 374997
info@tarkabooks.co.uk
www.tarkabooks.co.uk
Est. 1987 *Stock size* Large
Stock Second-hand books, Henry Williamson titles a speciality
Open Mon–Sat 9.45am–5pm
Services Book search

BEER

Beer Collectables
Contact Mr Forkes
Dolphin Hotel, Fore Street, Beer, Seaton, Devon, EX12 3EQ
01297 24362
Est. 1993 *Stock size* Medium
Stock Collectables, china, glass, fishing tackle, jewellery

Open Mon–Sun 10am–5pm
Fairs Exeter Livestock, Salisbury, T&T Fairs

BIDEFORD

J Collins & Son (BADA, LAPADA, CINOA)
Contact Mr John Biggs
28 High Street, Bideford, Devon, EX39 2AN
01237 473103 01237 475658
biggs@collinsantiques.co.uk
www.collinsantiques.co.uk
Est. 1953 *Stock size* Large
Stock Georgian and Regency furniture, Victorian oil paintings, watercolours
Open By appointment
Fairs BADA, Olympia (Nov)
Services Restoration of English furniture, watercolours and oil paintings

Peter Hames (PBFA)
Contact Mr P Hames
Old Bridge Antiques Centre, Market Place, Bideford, Devon, EX39 2DR
01237 421065 01237 421065
peterhames@hotmail.com
www.members.aol.com/tarkabooks
Est. 1979 *Stock size* Medium
Stock Small selection of general books, jazz and North Devon books a speciality
Open Mon–Sat 9am–5.30pm
Fairs PBFA

Medina Gallery
Contact Caroline Jennings
55 Mill Street, Bideford, Devon, EX39 2JR
01237 476483
Est. 1973 *Stock size* Medium
Stock Antique prints, maps, oils, watercolours
Open Mon–Sat 9.30am–5pm

BOVEY TRACEY

Albion House Antiques
Contact Anthony Seed
75a Fore Street, Bovey Tracey, Devon, TQ13 9HB
01626 835650
antseeds@aol.com
Est. 1998 *Stock size* Medium
Stock Antiques, collectables
Open By appointment
Services Valuations

BRAUNTON

Book Cellar
Contact Mr Dennis Stow
5a The Square, East Street, Braunton, Devon, EX33 2JD
01271 815655 01271 815655
Est. 1988 *Stock size* Large
Stock Antiquarian and second-hand books
Open Summer Mon–Sat 10am–5pm closed Wed winter Tues Thurs Fri Sat 10am–4pm

BRIXHAM

Antique, Electric & Turret Clocks
Contact Dr Paul Strickland
Ye Olde Coffin House, King Street, Brixham, Devon, TQ5 9TF
01803 856307
clocks@forall.fsnet.co.uk
www.forall.fsnet.co.uk
Est. 2002 *Stock size* Large
Stock Clocks, related tools, books
Open Mon–Sun 9am–5pm
Services Restoration

Brixham's King Street Rooms
Contact Mr Dean
King Street Rooms, King Street, Brixham, Devon, TQ5 9TF
01803 858303
Est. 1971 *Stock size* Medium
Stock Early motoring, clocks, general antiques
Open Mon–Sat 10am–5pm

John Prestige Antiques
Contact Mr Prestige
Greenswood Court, Greenswood Road, Brixham, Devon, TQ5 9HN
01803 856141 01803 851649
sales@john-prestige.co.uk
www.john-prestige.co.uk
Est. 1971 *Stock size* Large
Stock Furniture, pictures, mirrors, ceramics
Trade only Yes
Open Mon–Fri 8.45am–6pm or by appointment
Services Valuations, restoration

BUDLEIGH SALTERTON

B & T Thorn and Son
Contact Mr Thorn
2 High Street, Budleigh Salterton, Devon, EX9 6LQ
01395 442448
Est. 1950 *Stock size* Medium
Stock Ceramics, English pottery and porcelain
Open Tues Fri Sat 10am–1pm
Services Valuations

CATTEDOWN

Plymouth Auction Rooms
Contact Mr P Keen
Edwin House, St John's Road, Cattedown, Plymouth, Devon, PL4 0NZ
01752 254740 01752 254740
info@plymouthauctions.co.uk
www.plymouthauctions.co.uk
Est. 1992
Open Mon–Thur 9am–1pm 2–5pm Fri 9am–1pm
Sales Antiques and collectables three weekly Wed 10.30am, viewing Tues 10am–7pm Wed 9–10.30am.
Catalogues Yes

CLYST HONITON

Pennies Antiques
Contact Mrs Clark
Home Farm, Clyst Honiton, Devon, EX25 2LX
01392 444491
www.penniesantiques.co.uk
Est. 1979 *Stock size* Medium
Stock General antiques
Open Mon–Sat 10am–5pm

COLYTON

Colyton Antique Centre
Contact R C Hunt
Dolphin Street, Colyton, Devon, EX24 6LU
01297 552339 01297 552339
07973 678989
colytonantiques@modelgarage.co.uk
www.modelgarage.co.uk
Est. 1988 *Stock size* Medium
No. of dealers 30
Stock Antiques and collectables
Open Summer Mon–Sat

10am–5pm Sun Bank Holidays 11am–4pm winter Mon–Sat 10am–4pm Sun 11am–4pm

COMBE MARTIN

Combe Martin Clock Shop
Contact Robin Westcott
1 High Street, Combe Martin, Ilfracombe, Devon, EX34 0EP
01271 882607
robin@robinw.force9.co.uk
www.robinw.force9.co.uk
Est. 1980 *Stock size* Medium
Stock Clocks from longcase to mantel and barometers
Open Mon–Sat 9am–6pm
Services Restoration of clocks

Selectables
Contact Mr T Pickard
2 Hangman Pass, Combe Martin, Ilfracombe, Devon, EX34 0DN
01271 889060
0788 7806493
trevor@sherbrook1.fsbusiness.co.uk
Est. 2000 *Stock size* Medium
Stock General antiques, glass, ceramics, small furniture
Open Mon–Sun 10am–5.30pm closed Wed
Services Valuations

CREDITON

Mid Devon Antiques
Contact Colin Knowles
The Corn Store, Morchard Road, Copplestone, Crediton, Devon, EX17 5LP
01363 84066
07718 583086
Est. 1965 *Stock size* Medium
Stock Country furniture, tables, beds
Open By appointment
Services Restoration, repairs

Musgrave Bickford Antiques (BHI)
Contact Dennis Bickford
15 East Street, Crediton, Devon, EX17 3AT
01363 775042
Est. 1987 *Stock size* Medium
Stock Clocks, barometers
Open By appointment
Fairs Westpoint
Services Valuations, restoration

CULLOMPTON

Cobweb Antiques
Contact Richard Holmes
The Old Tannery, Exeter Road, Cullompton, Devon, EX15 1DT
01884 38476 01884 38476
tannery@cullompton-antiques.co.uk
www.cullompton-antiques.co.uk
Est. 1986 *Stock size* Large
Stock General antiques, country furniture
Open Mon–Sat 10am–5pm

Cullompton Old Tannery Antiques
Contact George Mills
The Old Tannery, Exeter Road, Cullompton, Devon, EX15 1DT
01884 38476 01884 38476
tannery@cullompton-antiques.co.uk
www.cullompton-antiques.co.uk
Est. 1987 *Stock size* Large
Stock Antique country furniture, English, French and European clocks, mirrors, decorative items
Open Mon–Sat 10am–5pm
Services Shipping, courier

Oaks & Partners
The Old Tannery, Exeter Road, Cullompton, Devon, EX15 1DT
01884 35848 01884 38000
auctionsoaksandpartners.co.uk
www.invaluable.com/oaksandpartners
Est. 1979
Open Mon–Fri 9am–4pm closed Wed
Sales Antiques and general sale Sat 10.30am, viewing Thurs 9am–5pm Fri 9am–8pm
Frequency 3-weekly
Catalogues Yes

DARTMOUTH

Looking Back
Contact Paddy Distin
32 Lower Street, Dartmouth, Devon, TQ6 9AN
01803 832615
Est. 1990 *Stock size* Medium
Stock General antiques
Open Summer Mon–Sun 10am–5.30pm
Services House clearance

Pennyfarthing Antiques
Contact Jill Williams
11 Lower Street, Dartmouth, Devon, TQ6 9AN
01803 839411
Est. 2000 *Stock size* Medium
Stock Antique furniture, ceramics, prints, collectables of interest
Open Mon–Fri 10am–4.30pm Sat 10am–5pm Sun 11am–4pm

DAWLISH

Emporium
Contact Michael Peters
40b The Strand, Dawlish, Devon, EX7 9PT
01626 862222 01626 774689
07768 076360
Est. 1983 *Stock size* Medium
Stock General antiques
Open Tues–Sat 10am–5pm
Fairs West Point, Shepton Mallet
Services Valuations

EXETER

Bearnes (SOFAA)
Contact N J Saintey
St Edmund's Court, Okehampton Street, Exeter, Devon, EX4 1DU
01392 207007 01392 207007
enquiries@bearnes.co.uk
www.bearnes.co.uk
Est. 1945
Open Mon–Fri 9.30am–5pm
Sales General sale Tues am, viewing Sat 9.30am–noon Mon 9.30am–7pm. 17–20 general and 3 specialist sales a year Tues Wed. Telephone for details
Catalogues Yes

Lisa Cox Music (ABA)
Contact Lisa Cox
The Coach House, Colleton Crescent, Exeter, Devon, EX2 4DJ
01392 490290 01392 277336
music@lisacoxmusic.co.uk
www.lisacoxmusic.co.uk
Est. 1984 *Stock size* Large
Stock Antiquarian music, pictures, ephemera, autographs
Open By appointment
Services Valuations

Eclectique
Contact Sue Bellamy
26–27 Commercial Road,

The Quay, Exeter, Devon,
EX2 4AE 🅿
☎ 01392 250799
Est. 1994 *Stock size* Medium
Stock Antique and painted furniture, ceramics, lamps, objets d'art, collectables
Open Mon–Sun 11am–5.30pm
Services Interior design

Exeter Antique Lighting
Contact Julian Wood
✉ **Cellar 15, The Quay, Exeter, Devon, EX2 4AP** 🅿
☎ 01392 490848
Ⓜ 07702 969438
Est. 1990 *Stock size* Large
Stock Antique lighting, fireplaces, iron beds
Open Mon–Sun 11am–5pm or by appointment
Fairs Newark, Ardingly
Services Valuations, restoration

Exeter Rare Books (ABA, PBFA)
Contact Mr R C Parry
✉ **13a Guildhall Shopping Centre, Exeter, Devon, EX4 3HG** 🅿
☎ 01392 436021
Est. 1974 *Stock size* Medium
Stock Antiquarian, rare, second-hand books
Open Mon–Sat 10am–1pm 2–5pm
Fairs Chelsea ABA

Exeter's Antiques Centre on the Quay
Contact Patsy Bliss
✉ **The Quay, Exeter, Devon, EX2 4AN** 🅿
☎ 01392 493501
Ⓦ www.exeterquayantiques.co.uk
Est. 1984 *Stock size* Large
No. of dealers 21
Stock Antiques, collectables, books, postcards, jewellery, tools, records, coins
Open Mon–Sun summer 10am–6pm winter 10am–5pm
Services Restaurant

McBains Antiques (LAPADA)
Contact Mr Martin McBain
✉ **Exeter Airport Industrial Estate, Exeter, Devon, EX5 2BA** 🅿
☎ 01392 446304 Ⓕ 01392 446304
Ⓜ 07831 381236
Ⓔ mcbain.exports@zetnet.co.uk
Est. 1980 *Stock size* Large
Stock Georgian, Victorian, Edwardian furniture, also selection of French and Continental furniture
Open Mon–Fri 9am–6pm Sat 10am–1pm closed Bank Holiday weekends
Fairs Newark
Services Shipping, full container and export facility

Mortimers
Contact Ian Watson
✉ **87 Queen Street, Exeter, Devon, EX4 3RP** 🅿
☎ 01392 279994
Ⓜ 07812 998896
Est. 1970 *Stock size* Large
Stock Antique jewellery, watches, clocks and silver
Open Mon–Sat 9.30am–5pm
Services Valuations, restoration

Pennies Antiques
Contact Mrs Clark
✉ **6 Marsh Green Road, Marsh Barton, Exeter, Devon, EX2 8NY** 🅿
☎ 01392 276532
Ⓦ www.penniesantiques.co.uk
Est. 1979 *Stock size* Medium
Stock General antiques
Open Mon–Sun 10am–5pm

Phantique
Contact Mrs Bliss
✉ **Unit 5–7, 47 The Quay, Exeter, Devon, EX2 4AN** 🅿
☎ 01392 498995
Ⓦ www.phantique.co.uk
Est. 1996 *Stock size* Large
No. of dealers 9
Stock General antiques and collectables, prints, books, Torquay pottery, Dinky toys, costume jewellery, Oriental ceramics
Open Summer Mon–Fri 10.30am–5.30pm Sat Sun 10.30am–6pm winter 10.30am–5pm

The Quay Gallery Antiques Emporium
Contact Mark Davis
✉ **43 The Quay, Exeter, Devon, EX2 4AN** 🅿
☎ 01392 213283
Est. 1984 *Stock size* Large
Stock Fine mahogany and oak furniture, porcelain, silver, glass, paintings, prints, general antiques, antiquities, clocks, Art Deco, 20thC furniture
Open Mon–Sun 10am–5pm
Fairs West Point, Shepton Mallet, Cooper Fairs
Services Valuations

Tredantiques (LAPADA)
Contact Jon Tredant
✉ **The Antiques Complex, Exeter Airport Industrial Estate, Exeter, Devon, EX5 2BA** 🅿
☎ 01392 447082
Ⓜ 07967 447082
Ⓦ www.tredantiques.com
Est. 1982 *Stock size* Large
Stock Good quality furniture and decorative items
Open Mon–Fri 9am–5.30pm Sat 10am–1.30pm

Victoriana Antiques and Kents Jewellers
Contact Mr Kent
✉ **68 Sidwell Street, Exeter, Devon, EX4 6PH** 🅿
☎ 01392 275204/275291
Est. 1945 *Stock size* Medium
Stock General antiques, porcelain, jewellery, silver
Open Mon Tues Thurs–Sat 9.30am–5pm
Services Jewellery, silver and porcelain restoration and repair

EXMINSTER

Tobys (SALVO)
Contact Mr P Norrish
✉ **Station House, Station Road, Exminster, Exeter, Devon, EX6 8DZ** 🅿
☎ 01392 833499 Ⓕ 01392 833429
Ⓦ www.tobysreclamation.co.uk
Est. 1983 *Stock size* Large
Stock Architectural antiques, sanitary ware, fireplaces, reclaimed building materials
Open Mon–Fri 8.30am–5pm Sat 9.30am–4.30pm Sun Bank Holidays 10.30am–4.30pm
Services House clearance, nationwide delivery

EXMOUTH

Browsers
Contact Mr or Mrs Spiller
✉ **1–2 The Strand, Exmouth,**

Devon, EX8 1HL
☎ 01395 265010
Est. 1988 *Stock size* Large
Stock Collectables, toys, advertising, books, china
Open Mon–Sat 10.30am–6pm

Martin Spencer-Thomas (NAVA)
Contact Mr M Spencer-Thomas
Bicton Street Auction Rooms, Bicton Street, Exmouth, Devon, EX8 2RT
☎ 01395 267403 F 01395 222598
E martin@martinspencer thomas. co.uk
W www.martinspencerthomas.co.uk
Est. 1984
Open Mon–Fri 9am–5pm
Sales Antiques sale Mon 1.30pm, viewing Thurs 9am–5pm Fri 9am–5pm Sat 10am–4pm
Frequency 5 weeks
Catalogues Yes

HATHERLEIGH

Hatherleigh Antiques (BADA)
Contact Michael Dann
15 Bridge Street, Hatherleigh, Devon, EX20 3HU P
☎ 01837 810159
Est. 1980 *Stock size* Large
Stock Gothic and Renaissance furniture
Open By appointment
Services Valuations, restoration

HELE

Fagins Antiques
Contact Jean Pearson
Old Whiteways Cider Factory, Hele, Exeter, Devon, EX5 4PW P
☎ 01392 882062 F 01392 882194
E cstrong@fagins-antiques.co.uk
W www.fagins-antiques.co.uk
Est. 1978 *Stock size* Large
Stock Stripped pine, dark wood, general antiques, china, architectural antiques
Open Mon–Fri 9.15am–5pm Sat 11am–5pm Sun Bank Holidays 11am–4pm
Services Pine stripping

HOLSWORTHY

Baileys
Contact Sarah Stewart
Bude Road, Holsworthy, Devon, EX22 6HZ P
☎ 01409 254800
Est. 1996 *Stock size* Large
Stock Pine, mahogany and oak furniture, general antiques
Open Mon–Sat 9.30am–5pm
Services Restoration, pine stripping, upholstery

HONITON

Antique Toys
38 High Street, Honiton, Devon, EX14 1PJ P
☎ 01404 41194
E honitonantiquetoys38@hotmail.com
Est. 1976 *Stock size* Large
Stock Toys, teddies, dolls
Open Wed Fri Sat 10.30am–5pm
Services Dolls' hospital

Asian Art.co.uk Ltd
Contact The Manager
Yarrow, 155 High Street, Honiton, Devon, EX14 1LJ P
☎ 01404 44399
E james@asianart.co.uk
W www.asianart.co.uk
Est. 1982 *Stock size* Large
Stock Oriental antiques, furniture, kilims, carpets
Open By appointment

Jane Barnes Antiques and Interiors
Contact Mrs Barnes
35 High Street, Honiton, Devon, EX14 1PW P
☎ 01404 41712/861300
F 01404 861300
M 07971 328618
Est. 1985 *Stock size* Medium
Stock General antiques, Victorian and Edwardian
Open Mon–Sat 10am–4pm closed Wed or by appointment
Services Chairs copied to order

Bell Antiques (LAPADA)
Contact Nick Ball
The Grove Antiques Centre, High Street, Honiton, Devon, EX14 1PW P
☎ 01404 890185 F 01404 890185
E nick.ball2@tesco.net
Est. 1983 *Stock size* Medium
Stock Glass
Open Mon–Sat 10am–5pm
Services Valuations

Bonhams
Dowell Street, Honiton, Devon, EX14 1LX
☎ 01404 41872 F 01404 43137
E honiton@bonhams.com
W www.bonhams.com
Open Mon–Fri 9am–5.30pm
Sales Regional Saleroom. Frequent sales. Regular house and attic sales across the country; contact London offices for further details. Free auction valuations; insurance and probate valuations

Roderick Butler (BADA)
Contact Mr R Butler or Mrs V Butler
Marwood House, Honiton, Devon, EX14 1PY P
☎ 01404 42169
Est. 1948 *Stock size* Large
Stock 17th–18thC Regency furniture, works of art and metalwork
Open Mon–Sat 9.30am–5pm August by appointment only
Services Restoration

C J Button-Stephens Antiques
Contact Christopher Button-Stephens
59 High Street, Honiton, Devon, EX14 1PW
☎ 01404 42640
Est. 1966 *Stock size* Small
Stock General antiques
Open Mon–Sat 10am–4pm

Collectables
Contact Mr Chris Guthrie
134B High Street, Honiton, Devon, EX14 1JP P
☎ 01404 47024
E chris@collectableshoniton.co.uk
W www.collectableshoniton.co.uk
Est. 1995 *Stock size* Medium
Stock Annuals, breweriana, cameras, ceramics, cigarette cards, commemorative, militaria, mugs, phonecards, postcards, railwayana, toys, games
Open Mon–Sat 10am–4.45pm closed Thurs

Colystock Antiques
Contact Dave McCollum
Rising Sun Farm, Stockland,

Honiton, Devon,
EX14 9NH P
☎ 01404 861271 F 01404 861271
Est. 1985 *Stock size* Large
Stock 18th–19thC pine and reproduction furniture, reclaimed pine kitchens
Open Mon–Sat 8.30am–6pm Sun 1–4pm

Dreweatt Neate Honiton Salerooms (SOFAA)
Contact Nigel Trevelyan
✉ **205 High Street, Honiton, Devon, EX14 1LQ** P
☎ 01404 42404 F 01404 46510
E honiton@dnfa.com
W www.dnfa.com
Est. 1759
Open Mon–Fri 9am–5pm
Sales Monthly fine art & antiques Fri 10.30am, viewing Mon–Thurs 9am–5pm Thurs Fri 9–10am. Twice yearly sales of steam, model engineering, works of art & railwayana. Twice yearly sales of West Country pictures. Catalogues available on website
Catalogues Yes

Evans Emporium
Contact Bob Evans
✉ **140 High Street, Honiton, Devon, EX14 1JP** P
☎ 01404 47869
Est. 2002 *Stock size* Medium
Stock Antiques, collectables, music and instruments
Open Mon–Sat 10am–5pm

Leigh Extence Antique Clocks (BHI)
Contact Mr Leigh Extence
✉ **The Grove, 55 High Street, Honiton, Devon, EX14 1PW** P
☎ 01404 549047
M 07967 802160
E clocks@extence.co.uk
W www.extence.co.uk
Est. 1981 *Stock size* Medium
Stock Antique clocks and barometers
Open By appointment or telephone call
Services Valuations, restoration, clock research

Fountain Antiques
Contact J Palmer or G York
✉ **132 High Street, Honiton, Devon, EX14 1JP** P
☎ 01404 42074 F 01404 44993
M 07831 138011
E antiques@gyork.co.uk
Est. 1988 *Stock size* Large
No. of dealers 15
Stock Linen, books, cutlery, telephones, china, furniture, lighting
Open Mon–Sat 9.30am–5.30pm

The Globe Antiques & Art Centre
Contact A J Littler
✉ **165 High Street, Honiton, Devon, EX14 1LQ** P
☎ 01404 549372 F 01404 41465
E theglobe@honitonantiques.com
W www.honitonantiques.com
Est. 2000 *Stock size* Large
No. of dealers 25
Stock Period furniture, Art Deco, silver, porcelain, glass, corkscrews, lamps, ephemera, collectables, bespoke furniture, Oriental rugs, clocks, barometers, jewellery, permanent art exhibition, pictures
Open Mon–Sat 10am–5pm
Services Restoration

The Grove Antique Centre
Contact Lesley Phillips
✉ **55 High Street, Honiton, Devon, EX14 1PW** P
☎ 01404 43377 F 01404 43390
M 07866 440408
E info@groveantiquescentre.com
W www.groveantiquescentre.com
Est. 1998 *Stock size* Medium
Stock Bears, silver, porcelain, 18th–20thC furniture, collectables, paintings, clocks, barometers, rugs, decorative items, china, glassware, beds
Open Mon–Sat 10am–5pm
Services Shipping deliveries

Hermitage Antiques
Contact Christian Giltsoff
✉ **37 High Street, Honiton, Devon, EX14 8PW** P
☎ 01404 44406 F 01404 42471
M 07768 960144
E antiquesmerchant@ndirect.co
Est. 1980 *Stock size* Large
Stock General antiques, furniture
Open Mon–Sat 10am–5pm
Services Valuations, buying and selling

High Street Books (PBFA)
Contact Geoff Tyson
✉ **150 High Street, Honiton, Devon, EX14 8JX** P
☎ 01404 45570 F 01404 45570
M 07930 171380
E tysonsbooks@hotmail.com
Est. 1982 *Stock size* Medium
Stock Antiquarian, books, maps and prints
Open Mon–Sat 10am–5pm
Fairs PBFA
Services Valuations

Honiton Antique Centre
Contact Nick Thompson
✉ **Abingdon House, 136 High Street, Honiton, Devon, EX14 8JP** P
☎ 01404 42108
Est. 1982 *Stock size* Large
No. of dealers 20
Stock Early 17th–20thC furniture, metalware, sporting, ceramics, china, glass, paintings, militaria
Open Mon–Sat 9.30am–5.30pm Sun 11am–4pm
Services Valuations, restoration, delivery

Honiton Old Book Shop (PBFA, ABA)
Contact Roger Collicott or Adele
✉ **Felix House, 51 High Street, Honiton, Devon, EX14 1PW** P
☎ 01404 47180 F 01404 47180
Est. 1978 *Stock size* Medium
Stock Antiquarian, rare and second-hand books, leather bindings, antiquarian maps and prints
Open Mon–Sat 10am–5pm
Fairs PBFA, Russell, ABA, Chelsea Town Hall, Olympia (June)
Services Valuations

Kingsway House Antiques
Contact Mrs M Peache
✉ **3 High Street, Honiton, Devon, EX14 8PR** P
☎ 01404 46213
W www.kingsway-antiques.com
Est. 1981 *Stock size* Medium
Stock Georgian furniture, china, clocks
Open Mon–Sat 10am–5.30pm or by appointment

Merchant House Antiques
Contact Christian Giltsoff
19 High Street, Honiton, Devon, EX14 1PR
01404 42694 F 01404 42471
E antiquesmerchant@ndirect.co.uk
Est. 1980 *Stock size* Large
Stock Fine furniture, general antiques and collectables
Open Mon–Sat 10am–5pm
Services Valuations and interior design

Otter Antiques
Contact Kate Skailes
69 High Street, Honiton, Devon, EX14 1PW
01404 42627 F 01404 43337
E otterantiques@jspencer.co.uk
W www.jspencer.co.uk
Est. 1979 *Stock size* Large
Stock Fine and antique silver, silver plate
Open Mon–Sat 9.30am–5pm Thurs 9.30am–1.30pm
Services Valuations, restoration, silver plating, engraving

Alexander Paul Restorations
Contact Dave Steele
Fenny Bridges, Honiton, Devon, EX14 1PJ
01404 850881 F 01404 850881
E alexanderpaulre@aol.com
W www.alexanderpaulantiques.com
Est. 2000 *Stock size* Medium
Stock French and English country furniture
Open Mon–Fri 9am–5.30pm Sat 10am–4pm
Services Restoration

Pilgrim Antiques (LAPADA)
Contact Mrs Mills
145 High Street, Honiton, Devon, EX14 1LJ
01404 41219 F 01404 45317
E pilgrimantiques@globalnet.co.uk
W www.pilgrimantiques.co.uk
Est. 1971 *Stock size* Large
Stock 17th–18thC English and French oak and country furniture, longcase clocks
Open Mon–Sat 9am–5.30pm
Services Valuations, shipping

Plympton Antiques
Contact Mr Button-Stephens
59 High Street, Honiton, Devon, EX14 8PW
01404 42640
Est. 1966 *Stock size* Medium
Stock Mostly mahogany furniture, copper, brass, porcelain
Open Mon–Sat 10am–4.30pm closed Thurs

Portland House Antiques and Collectables
Contact Mrs Gunilla Tanner
149 High Street, Honiton, Devon, EX14 1LJ
01404 45700
E jgtanner@btinternet.com
Est. 2002 *Stock size* Large
Stock Furniture, pictures, china, clocks, glass, Beswick, antique Honiton lace, kitchenware, all in a Georgian House fitted in period style
Open Mon–Sat 10am–5pm Sun in summer 11am–4pm
Services Restoration, upholstery, lacemaking demonstrations

Staffordshire Pride
Contact Sharon Racklyeft
Abingdon House Antique Centre, 136 High Street, Honiton, Devon, EX14 1JP
01404 42108
M 07958 453295
Est. 1975 *Stock size* Large
Stock 1790–1900 Staffordshire figures
Open Mon–Sun 9.30am–5.30pm

Jane Strickland & Daughters (LAPADA)
Contact Jane Strickland
71 High Street, Honiton, Devon, EX14 1PW
01404 44221
E JSandDaughtersUK@aol.com
Est. 1980 *Stock size* Medium
Stock 18th–19thC English and Continental furniture, upholstery, mirrors, lights, Aubussons, needlepoints
Open Mon–Sat 10am–5pm

ILFRACOMBE

Relics
Contact Nicola Bradshaw
113 High Street, Ilfracombe, Devon, EX34 9ET
01271 865486
M 07817 114989
Est. 1980 *Stock size* Medium
Stock General antiques and collectables
Open Mon–Sat 10am–5pm

KINGSBRIDGE

Avon House Antiques
Contact Mr or Mrs Hayward
13 Church Street, Kingsbridge, Devon, TQ7 1BT
01548 853718
M 07977 451223
E daymor@btopenworld.com
Est. 1969 *Stock size* Medium
Stock General antiques and collectables
Open Mon–Sat 10am–5pm Thurs Sat closed pm
Fairs Devon County Antiques Fairs
Services Valuations, restoration

Haywards Antiques & Avon House Antiques
Contact Mr D Hayward
13 Church Street, Kingsbridge, Devon, TQ7 1BT
01548 853718
M 07977 451223
W www.haywardsantiques.fsbusiness.co.uk
Est. 1985 *Stock size* Large
Stock General antiques and collectables
Open Mon–Wed 10am–5pm Thurs–Sat 10am–1pm
Fairs West Point, Exeter
Services Valuations

Salters Bookshelf 'The Bookshelf at the Top'
Contact Steve Salter
89 Fore Street, Kingsbridge, Devon, TQ7 1AB
01548 856176/857503 F 01548 857503
Est. 1997 *Stock size* Medium
Stock Old picture postcards, postal history, postal stationery, accessories, ephemera
Open Mon–Sat 9am–5.30pm summer Sun 10am–2.30pm
Services Picture framing, booksearch agents

LYNTON

Farthings
Contact Jane or Lucy Farthing
Church Hill House, Church Hill, Lynton, Devon, EX35 6HY P
☎ 01598 753744 F 01598 753483
E jane@farthings1.freeserve.co.uk
W www.farthings.antiques.com
Est. 1984 *Stock size* Large
Stock Antiques, Oriental, Vienna bronzes, bronzes, 18th–20thC sporting art, Moorcroft, Mulberry bears, collectables, crafts
Open Mon–Sun 10am–4.30pm
Fairs Westpoint, Antiques for Everyone
Services Search service, delivery

Wood's Antiques
Contact Mr or Mrs Wood
29a Lee Road, Lynton, Devon, EX35 6BS P
☎ 01598 752722
Est. 1995 *Stock size* Medium
Stock Antiques, collectables, furniture, clocks
Open Mon–Sun 9am–6pm closed Thurs

MERTON

Barometer World
Contact Phiip Collins
Quicksilver Barn, Merton, Okehampton, Devon, EX20 3DS P
☎ 01805 603443 F 01805 603344
E enquiries@barometerworld.co.uk
W www.antiquebarometers.org.uk
Est. 1979 *Stock size* Large
Stock 1780–1930s barometers
Open Tues–Sat 9am–5pm
Services Valuations, restoration

MODBURY

Collectors Choice
Contact Allan Jenkins
27 Church Street, Modbury, Ivybridge, Devon, PL21 0QR P
☎ 01548 831111
M 07884 365361
Est. 1994 *Stock size* Medium
Stock Small furniture, ceramics, Bakelite, radios, general antiques
Open Mon–Sat 10am–5.30pm
Services Valuations, clock restoration

Wild Goose Antiques
Contact Kay or Ty Freeman
34 Church Street, Modbury, Devon, PL21 0QR P
☎ 01548 830715
E wildgooseantiques@tiscali.co.uk
Est. 2000 *Stock size* Medium
Stock Antique pine, country furniture, decorative items, brass, iron beds
Open Mon–Sat 10am–5.30pm

MONKTON

Pughs Antiques
Contact Mr Guy Garner
Pughs Farm, Monkton, Honiton, Devon, EX14 9QH P
☎ 01404 42860 F 01404 47792
E sales@pughsantiques.com
W www.pughsantiques.com
Est. 1986 *Stock size* Large
Stock Victorian–Edwardian furniture in mahogany, oak, walnut and pine, French furniture, antique beds
Open Mon–Sat 9am–5.30pm
Services Export

NEWTON ABBOT

The Attic
Contact Mr Gillman
9 Union Street, Newton Abbot, Devon, TQ12 2JX P
☎ 01626 355124
Est. 1976 *Stock size* Large
Stock General antiques and small furniture
Open Tues–Sat 9am–5.30pm closed Thurs

Michael J Bowman
Contact Mr M Bowman ARICS
6 Haccombe House, Netherton, Newton Abbot, Devon, TQ12 4SJ P
☎ 01626 872890 F 01626 872890
W www.ukauctioneers.co.uk
Est. 1986
Open By appointment
Sales 7 antiques and effects sales per annum Sat 2pm, viewing Fri 4.30–8.30pm. Held at Chudleigh Town Hall, also free valuations Mon 2–5pm at same venue
Catalogues Yes

St Leonard's Antiques and Craft Centre
Contact Mr Derick Wilson
St Leonard's, Wolborough Street, Newton Abbot, Devon, TQ12 1JQ P
☎ 01626 335666 F 01626 335666
M 07860 178969
E leonardsantique@tiscali.co.uk
Est. 1999 *Stock size* Large
No. of dealers 32
Stock General antiques, furniture, jewellery
Open Mon–Sun 10am–4.30pm

Tobys (SALVO)
Contact Mr P Norrish
Brunel Road, Newton Abbot, Devon, TQ12 4PB P
☎ 01626 351767 F 01626 336788
W www.tobysreclamation.co.uk
Est. 1985 *Stock size* Large
Stock General antiques, reclaimed material
Open Mon–Fri 8.30am–5pm Sat 9.30am–5pm Sun 10.30am–4.30pm
Fairs Exeter Ideal Home, Devon County Show
Services House clearance

OKEHAMPTON

Past & Present
Contact P Roche
14 & 15 The Victorian Arcade, Okehampton, Devon, EX20 1EX
☎ 01837 659238
Est. 1999 *Stock size* Medium
Stock General antiques, collectables
Open Mon–Sat 10am–4pm closed Wed

St James Street Antiques
Contact Jo Catling
1 St James Street, Okehampton, Devon, EX20 1DW P
☎ 01837 659623
M 07775 853583
Est. 2001 *Stock size* Medium
Stock General antiques, books
Open Mon–Sat 10am–4.30pm
Services Valuations

PAIGNTON

The Pocket Bookshop
Contact Mr L Corrall
159 Winner Street,

Paignton, Devon,
TQ3 3BP
☎ 01803 529804
Est. 1985 *Stock size* Large
Stock Antiquarian, second-hand and out-of-print books
Open Summer Mon–Sat 10.30am–5.30pm
winter Tues–Sat 10.30am–5.30pm

PLYMOUTH

Anita's Antiques
Contact Anita Walker
27 New Street, Plymouth, Devon, PL1 2NB
☎ 01752 269622
Est. 1984 *Stock size* Large
Stock Furniture, silver, china, jewellery, lighting, glass, clocks, barometers, general antiques
Open Mon–Sat 9am–5pm

Annterior Antiques
Contact Anne Tregenza
22 Molesworth Road, Stoke, Plymouth, Devon, PL1 5LZ
☎ 01752 558277 F 01752 564471
M 07815 618659
E sales@annterior.co.uk
W www.annterior.co.uk
Est. 1984 *Stock size* Medium
Stock 19th–early 20thC country furniture, stripped pine, small accessories
Open Mon–Fri 9.30am–5.30pm
Sat 10am–5pm closed Tues
Services Restoration, finding service

Barbican Antique Centre
Contact Tony Cremer-Price
82–84 Vauxhall Street, Plymouth, Devon, PL4 0EX
☎ 01752 201752 F 020 8546 1618
M 07836 291791
Est. 1971 *Stock size* Large
No. of dealers 60
Stock Silver, jewellery, porcelain, glass, pictures, furniture, collectables
Open Mon–Sat 9.30am–5pm Sun 10am–5pm

Eric Distin Auctioneers & Chartered Surveyors (RICS)
Contact Mr E Distin
72 Mutley Plain, Plymouth, Devon, PL4 6LF
☎ 01752 663046 F 01752 257342
E eric@distin.fsbusiness.co.uk
Est. 1973
Sales Antiques and collectables Sat 10.30am, viewing morning of sale or afternoon prior
Frequency Fortnightly
Catalogues Yes

Grosvenor Chambers Restoration
Contact Robert Miller
180 Rendle Street, Plymouth, Devon, PL1 1UQ
☎ 01752 257544
E robbie@grosvenor-restoration.co.uk
Est. 1989 *Stock size* Large
Stock General architectural antiques, pine furniture, lighting
Open Mon–Sat 9am–5.30pm
Services Valuations, restoration, wood and metal stripping

Frederick Harrison
Contact Mr Harrison
43 Bridwell Road, Weston Mill, Plymouth, Devon, PL5 1AB
☎ 01752 365595
Est. 1974 *Stock size* Large
Stock Antiquarian, rare and second-hand books, particularly on diving, Dartmoor and local topography
Open By appointment
Services Valuations

New Street Antique and Craft Centre
Contact Mrs Cuthill
27 New Street, Barbican, Plymouth, Devon, PL1 2NB
☎ 01752 256265 F 01752 256265
Est. 1980 *Stock size* Large
No. of dealers 11
Stock General collectables, books, stamps, postcards, craft materials, locally made crafts
Open Mon–Sat Sun during holiday season 10am–5pm
Services Café

Parade Antiques
Contact Mr Cabello
17 The Parade, The Barbican, Plymouth, Devon, PL1 2JW
☎ 01752 221443
Est. 1992 *Stock size* Large
Stock General antiques, militaria
Open Mon–Sun 10am–5pm

G S Shobrook and Co incorporating Fieldens (RICS)
Contact Roger Shobrook
20 Western Approach, Plymouth, Devon, PL1 1TG
☎ 01752 663341 F 01752 255157
E info@shobrook.co.uk
W www.shobrook.co.uk
Est. 1920
Open Mon–Fri 9am–5pm
Sat 9–11am
Sales Monthly antiques and collectables sale Wed 1.30pm, viewing Tues 9am–5pm or by appointment. Weekly general household sale Wed 10am, viewing Tues 9am–5pm
Catalogues Yes

Michael Wood Fine Art
Contact Mr M Wood
The Gallery, 1 Southside Ope, The Barbican, Plymouth, Devon, PL1 2LL
☎ 01752 225533 F 01752 225533
M 07764 377899 or 07971 847722
E michael@michaelwoodfineart.com
W www.michaelwoodfineart.com
Est. 1967 *Stock size* Large
Stock 1850–present day paintings, watercolours, original prints, sculptures, art pottery, studio glass
Open Tues–Sat 10am–5pm
Fairs NEC
Services Valuations, picture presentation and conservation

Woodford Antiques & Collectables
Contact Mr Bill Humphries
17–18 New Street, The Barbican, Plymouth, Devon, PL1 2NA
☎ 01752 344562 F 01752 344562
M 07711 723006
Est. 1996 *Stock size* Medium
Stock Ceramics, kitchenware, general antiques and Torquay pottery
Open Mon–Sat 10am–4.30pm
Sun noon–4.30pm
Services Shipping

PLYMPTON

Eldreds Auctioneers and Valuers
Contact Anthony Eldred

13–15 Ridge Park Road, Plympton, Plymouth, Devon, PL7 2BS
☎ 01752 340066 Ⓕ 01752 341760
Ⓔ enquiries@eldreds.net
Ⓦ www.eldreds.net
Est. 1992
Open Mon–Fri 8.30am–5pm
Sales Fortnightly 19th–20thC sales, 6–8 weekly antiques and specialist sales, telephone for details
Catalogues Yes

SEATON

Etcetera Antiques
Contact Mrs Rymer
12 Beer Road, Seaton, Devon, EX12 2PA
☎ 01297 21965
Ⓜ 07780 840507
Est. 1965 *Stock size* Large
Stock Furniture and small items
Trade only Yes
Open By appointment
Services Restoration, house clearances, shipping

The Green Dragon
Contact Mrs Denning
4 Marine Crescent, Seaton, Devon, EX12 2QN
☎ 01297 22039
Est. 2001 *Stock size* Large
No. of dealers 38
Stock Antiques, collectables, English ceramics, Oriental, lace, books
Open Mon–Sun 10am–5pm

SIDMOUTH

The Lantern Shop Gallery
Contact Julia Creeke
5 New Street, Sidmouth, Devon, EX10 8AP
☎ 01395 578462 Ⓕ 01395 578462
Est. 1977 *Stock size* Medium
Stock Porcelain, watercolours, oils
Open Mon–Sat 9.45am–4.45pm

The Old Curiosity Shop
Contact Mr or Mrs T Koch
Old Fore Street, Sidmouth, Devon, EX10 8LP
☎ 01395 515299
Est. 1995 *Stock size* Large
Stock General collectables
Open Mon–Sat 10am–5pm Sun 11am–5pm

Sidmouth Antiques Centre
Contact Mr R Hair
Devonshire House, All Saints Road, Sidmouth, Devon, EX10 8ES
☎ 01395 512588
Ⓜ 07714 376918
Ⓦ www.sidmouthantiques.com
Est. 1994 *Stock size* Medium
No. of dealers 10
Stock General antiques, antiquarian books
Open Mon–Sat 10am–5pm summer Sun 2–5pm

The Vintage Toy & Train Shop
Contact David Salisbury
Devonshire House, All Saints Road, Sidmouth, Devon, EX10 8ES
☎ 01395 512588 Ⓕ 01395 513399
Est. 1982 *Stock size* Medium
Stock Hornby Gauge O and Dublo trains, original Meccano, Dinky toys
Open Mon–Sat 10am–5pm

Sue Wilde
Contact Sue Wilde
Ashcroft, Milford Road, Sidmouth, Devon, EX10 8DR
☎ 01395 577966 Ⓕ 01395 577988
Ⓔ compacts@wildewear.co.uk
Ⓦ www.wildewear.co.uk
Est. 1980 *Stock size* Medium
Stock Vintage fashion accessories, Art Deco period, beaded bags
Open By appointment

SOUTH BRENT

Patrick Pollak Rare Books (ABA)
Contact Patrick Pollak
Moorview, Plymouth Road, South Brent, Devon, TQ10 9HT
☎ 01364 73457 Ⓕ 01364 649126
Ⓔ patrick@rarevols.co.uk
Ⓦ www.rarevols.co.uk
Est. 1973 *Stock size* Large
Stock Rare, antiquarian scholarly books
Open By appointment
Services Mail order

SOUTH MOLTON

C R Boumphrey
Contact Mr Boumphrey
Finehay, Mariansleigh, South Molton, Devon, EX36 4LL
☎ 01769 550419
Est. 1969 *Stock size* Medium
Stock 17th–18thC furniture
Open By appointment
Services Finds and orders stock

The Dragon
Contact Gerald Harris or Jenny Aker
77 South Street, South Molton, Devon, EX36 4AG
☎ 01769 572374
Ⓜ 07712 079818
Ⓔ snapdragonantiques@hotmail.com
Ⓦ www.nd1.co.uk/smtic/dragon.htm
Est. 1998 *Stock size* Medium
Stock Pine and country furniture, books, farming bygones, kitchenware
Open Mon–Sat 9.30am–5pm

Furniture Antique Market
Contact Mr P Soton
14a Barnstaple Street, South Molton, Devon, EX36 3BQ
☎ 01769 573401
Est. 1990 *Stock size* Large
No. of dealers 10
Stock General antiques, furniture, clocks, bric-a-brac
Open Mon–Sat 9am–4pm

Snapdragon
Contact Gerald Harris or Jenny Aker
80 South Street, South Molton, Devon, EX36 4AG
☎ 01769 572374
Ⓜ 07712 079818
Ⓔ snapdragonantiques@hotmail.com
Ⓦ www.snapdragoncdevon.co.uk.
Est. 1998 *Stock size* Medium
Stock Pine and country furniture, roll-top baths, fireplaces, agricultural bygones
Open Mon–Sat 9.30am–5pm

R M Young Bookseller
Contact Mr M Young
17 Broad Street, South Molton, Devon, EX36 3AQ

☎ 01769 573350
ⓔ rdyoung@lineone.net
Est. 1985 *Stock size* Large
Stock Antiquarian, second-hand, rare and out-of-print books, Countryside topics a speciality
Open Mon–Sat 10am–5pm
Services Book search, book binding

TAVISTOCK

Archways
Contact Mrs Diana Hunter
✉ **Court Gate, Bedford Square, Tavistock, Devon, PL19 0AE**
☎ 01822 612773
Est. 1989 *Stock size* Medium
Stock General antiques, small items, clocks
Open Tues–Sat 10am–4pm closed Thurs

Den of Antiquity
Contact Shelly Barlow
✉ **7 Pixon Lane, Crelake Industrial Estate, Tavistock, Devon, PL19 8DH** P
☎ 01822 610274
ⓜ 07971 182381
Est. 1999 *Stock size* Large
Stock Georgian–Edwardian and French furniture
Open Mon–Sat 10am–5.30pm Sun 2–5pm

Tavistock Furniture Store
Contact Shelley Barlow
✉ **7 Pixon Lane, Tavistock, Devon, PL19 9AZ** P
☎ 01822 610274
ⓔ doa@pixonlane.fsnet.co.uk
Est. 1999 *Stock size* Large
Stock English and French country furniture and decorative items
Open Mon–Sat 10am–5pm

Ward and Chowen Auction Rooms
Contact Mrs Pat Smith
✉ **Market Road, Tavistock, Devon, PL19 0BW** P
☎ 01822 612603 ⓕ 01822 617311
ⓔ tavistockauctionrooms@wardchowen.co.uk
Est. 1830
Open Mon–Fri 8.30am–4.30pm
Sales Quarterly antiques sale Tues, viewing Mon 10am–6pm. Fortnightly general household sale Thurs 10am (no catalogue), viewing Wed 1–6pm
Catalogues Yes

TEDBURN ST MARY

A E Wakeman and Sons Ltd
Contact Mr Wakeman
✉ **Newhouse Farm, Tedburn St Mary, Exeter, Devon, EX6 6AL** P
☎ 01647 61254 ⓕ 01647 61254
ⓜ 07836 284765/636525
Est. 1971 *Stock size* Medium
Stock 19thC furniture
Trade only Yes
Open Mon–Fri 8.30am–5.30pm or by appointment
Fairs Newark

TEIGNMOUTH

Extence Antiques
Contact Mr T E or L E Extence
✉ **2 Wellington Street, Teignmouth, Devon, TQ14 8HH** P
☎ 01626 773353 ⓕ 01626 777789
Est. 1928 *Stock size* Large
Stock Jewellery, silver and objets d'art
Open Tues–Sat 10am–5pm
Services Valuations, repair and restoration of jewellery and silver

Timepiece Antiques
Contact Clive or Willow Pople
✉ **125 Bitton Park Road, Teignmouth, Devon, TQ14 9BZ** P
☎ 01626 770275
Est. 1988 *Stock size* Medium
Stock Country, mahogany and oak furniture, longcase clocks, brass, copper, metalware, gramophones, general antiques
Open Tues–Sat 9.30am–5.30pm

TIVERTON

Judith Christie
Contact Judith Christie
✉ **42 Gold Street, Tiverton, Devon, EX16 6PX** P
☎ 01884 258795
ⓜ 07770 741885
Est. 1974 *Stock size* Medium
Stock General antiques, interiors and decorative arts
Open Tues Fri Sat 10.30am–5pm

Magnolia House Antiques
Contact Paul or Sarah
✉ **Morley House, Angel Hill, Tiverton, Devon, EX16 6PE**
☎ 01844 252649
Est. 1983 *Stock size* Large
Stock Victorian furniture
Open Mon–Sat 10am–6pm
Services Restoration

TOPSHAM

Bizarre!
Contact Alexandra Fairweather
✉ **The Quay Antiques Centre, The Quay, Topsham, Exeter, Devon, EX3 OJA** P
☎ 01392 874006
ⓔ office@antiquesattopshamquay.co.uk
ⓦ www.antiquesattopshamquay.co.uk
Est. 1991 *Stock size* Large
Stock Vintage clothes, textiles and accessories
Open Mon–Sun 10am–5pm
Fairs Hammersmith Textile and Costume, Hyson Textile Fair

Bounty Antiques
Contact J Harding or J Purves
✉ **76 Fore Street, Topsham, Devon, EX3 0HQ** P
☎ 01392 875007
ⓜ 07939 526504
Est. 1997 *Stock size* Large
No. of dealers 18
Stock General antiques, collectables, scientific instruments, maritime items
Open Mon–Sat 9.30am–5pm
Services Valuations

Charis
Contact Chris Evans
✉ **The Quay Antiques Centre, The Quay, Topsham, Exeter, Devon, EX3 OJA** P
☎ 01392 874006
ⓔ office@antiquesattopshamquay.co.uk
ⓦ www.antiquesattopshamquay.co.uk
Est. 1993 *Stock size* Medium
Stock Old glass, crystal, china, jewellery
Open Mon–Sun 10am–5pm

Curzon Pictures
✉ **The Quay Antiques Centre, The Quay, Topsham, Exeter, Devon,**

EX3 OJA 🅿
☎ 01392 874006
ⓔ office@antiquesattopshamquay.co.uk
ⓦ www.antiquesattopshamquay.co.uk
Est. 1993 *Stock size* Medium
Stock Prints, Louis Wain, Sir Russell Flint
Open Mon–Sun 10am–5pm

⊞ Gudrun Doel
Contact Gudrun (Goody) Doel
✉ **The Quay Antiques Centre, The Quay, Topsham, Exeter, Devon, EX3 OJA** 🅿
☎ 01392 874006
ⓔ office@antiquesattopshamquay.co.uk
ⓦ www.antiquesattopshamquay.co.uk
Est. 1993 *Stock size* Medium
Stock Decorative items, porcelain, glass, pictures, silver, textiles
Open Mon–Sun 10am–5pm
Fairs Livestock Centre, Exeter

⊞ Domani Antique & Contemporary
Contact Caro Brewster or Jonathan Cull
✉ **48 Fore Street, Topsham, Devon, EX3 0HY**
☎ 01392 877899 ⓕ 01392 877899
ⓔ shop@domani-topsham.com
ⓦ www.domani-topsham.com
Est. 2003 *Stock size* Small
Stock Unusual antique and contemporary furniture, contemporary art, ceramics and glass
Open Tues–Sat 10am–5.30pm or by appointment
Fairs Olympia (Cull Antiques)

⊞ Farthings
✉ **The Quay Antiques Centre, The Quay, Topsham, Exeter, Devon, EX3 OJA** 🅿
☎ 01392 874006
ⓔ office@antiquesattopshamquay.co.uk
ⓦ www.antiquesattopshamquay.co.uk
Est. 1993 *Stock size* Medium
Stock Ceramics, commemorative china
Open Mon–Sun 10am–5pm

⊞ Rob Gee
Contact Rob Gee
✉ **The Quay Antiques Centre, The Quay, Topsham, Exeter, Devon, EX3 OJA** 🅿
☎ 01392 874006
ⓔ office@antiquesattopshamquay.co.uk
ⓦ www.antiquesattopshamquay.co.uk
Est. 1993
Stock Pot lids, Pratt ware, chemist items, steam and toy locomotives
Open Mon–Sun 10am–5pm

⊞ Nicky Gowing
Contact Nicky Gowing
✉ **The Quay Antiques Centre, The Quay, Topsham, Exeter, Devon, EX3 OJA** 🅿
☎ 01392 874006
ⓔ office@antiquesattopshamquay.co.uk
ⓦ www.antiquesattopshamquay.co.uk
Est. 1993 *Stock size* Medium
Stock Decorative china, character jugs, Toby jugs
Open Mon–Sun 10am–5pm

⊞ Sheila Hyson
Contact Sheila Hyson
✉ **The Quay Antiques Centre, The Quay, Topsham, Exeter, Devon, EX3 OJA** 🅿
☎ 01392 874006
ⓜ 07798 808701
ⓔ shyson@freenetname.co.uk
ⓦ www.antiquesattopshamquay.co.uk
Est. 1993 *Stock size* Large
Stock Kitchenware
Open Mon–Sun 10am–5pm
Fairs Hyson Fairs, Deco 1950s and 1960s Fair, Exmouth Fair

⊞ Robin Jeffreys
Contact Robin Jeffreys
✉ **The Quay Antiques Centre, The Quay, Topsham, Exeter, Devon, EX3 OJA** 🅿
☎ 01392 874006
ⓔ office@antiquesattopshamquay.co.uk
ⓦ www.antiquesattopshamquay.co.uk
Est. 1966 *Stock size* Large
Stock Ceramics and Oriental ware
Open Mon–Sun 10am–4pm
Fairs Hyson Pottery and Glass Fair, Chafford Antiques and Collectors' Fair

⊞ Bart and Julie Lemmy
Contact Bart or Julie Lemmy
✉ **The Quay Antiques Centre, The Quay, Topsham, Exeter, Devon, EX3 OJA** 🅿
☎ 01392 874006
ⓜ 07809 172468
ⓔ rosettibrides@btinternet.com
ⓦ www.antiquesattopshamquay.co.uk
Est. 1993
Stock Royal Doulton figurines
Open Mon–Sun 10am–5pm
Services Shipping furniture

⊞ Betty Lovell
Contact Betty Lovell
✉ **The Quay Antiques Centre, The Quay, Topsham, Exeter, Devon, EX3 OJA** 🅿
☎ 01392 874006
ⓔ office@antiquesattopshamquay.co.uk
ⓦ www.antiquesattopshamquay.co.uk
Est. 1993 *Stock size* Medium
Stock Linen and Lace
Open Mon–Sun 10am–5pm
Fairs Hysons Textile Fair

⊞ D Lovell
Contact D Lovell
✉ **The Quay Antiques Centre, The Quay, Topsham, Exeter, Devon, EX3 OJA** 🅿
☎ 01392 874006
ⓔ office@antiquesattopshamquay.co.uk
ⓦ www.antiquesattopshamquay.co.uk
Est. 1986 *Stock size* Medium
Stock Silver and silver plate
Open Mon–Sun 10am–5pm

⊞ Mere Antiques (LAPADA)
Contact Mrs M Hawkins or Mrs M Reed
✉ **13 Fore Street, Topsham, Exeter, Devon, EX3 0HF** 🅿
☎ 01392 670373
ⓜ 07957 867751
ⓔ bob@ntlbusiness.com
ⓦ info@mereantiques.com
Est. 1986 *Stock size* Medium
Stock 18th–19thC porcelain, Japanese Satsuma ware, period furniture, paintings, silver
Open Mon–Sat 9.30am–5.30pm
Fairs NEC (LAPADA and Antiques for Everyone), Olympia
Services Appraisals, deliveries

⊞ Number 38
Contact Stuart Westaway
✉ **The Quay Antiques Centre, The Quay, Topsham, Exeter, Devon, EX3 OJA** 🅿
☎ 01392 874006
ⓔ office@antiquesattopshamquay.co.uk

www.antiquesattopshamquay.co.uk
Est. 1993 *Stock size* Medium
Stock Restored period lighting
Open Mon–Sun 10am–5pm
Services Restoration

Old Tools Feel Better!
Contact Barry Cook
The Quay Antiques Centre, The Quay, Topsham, Exeter, Devon, EX3 OJA P
01392 874006 F 01392 874006
M 07799 054565
E office@antiquesattopshamquay.co.uk
W www.antiquesattopshamquay.co.uk
Est. 1993 *Stock size* Large
Stock Antique and collectable quality used tools
Open Mon–Sun 10am–5pm

Pennies Antiques
Contact Mrs Clark
40 Fore Street, Topsham, Exeter, Devon, EX3 0HU P
01392 877020
W www.penniesantiques.co.uk
Est. 1979 *Stock size* Medium
Stock General antiques
Open Mon–Sat 10am–5pm Sun 11am–4pm

The Quay Centre
Contact Beverley Cook
The Quay, Topsham, Exeter, Devon, EX3 OJA P
01392 874006
E office@antiquesattopshamquay.co.uk
W www.antiquesattopshamquay.co.uk
Est. 1993 *Stock size* Large
No. of dealers 80
Stock Furniture, collectables, ephemera, Exeter silver, Torquay ware, studio pottery, jewellery, tools, period lighting, textiles
Open Mon–Sun 10am–5pm
Services Cards accepted, online buying, shipping advice

Joel Segal Books
Contact Mrs Neal
27 Fore Street, Topsham, Exeter, Devon, EX3 0HD
01392 877895
Est. 1993 *Stock size* Large
Stock Antiquarian, rare and second-hand books
Open Mon–Sat 10.30am–5pm

The Venerable Bead
Contact Daphne King
The Quay Antiques Centre, The Quay, Topsham, Exeter, Devon, EX3 OJA P
01392 874006
M 07787 561681
E office@antiquesattopshamquay.co.uk
W www.antiquesattopshamquay.co.uk
Est. 1993 *Stock size* Large
Stock Costume jewellery
Open Mon–Sun 10am–4pm
Fairs Westpoint, Shepton Mallet

S Vye
Contact S Vye
The Quay Antiques Centre, The Quay, Topsham, Exeter, Devon, EX3 OJA P
01392 874006
E s.vye@virgin.net
W www.antiquesattopshamquay.co.uk
Est. 1993 *Stock size* Medium
Stock Furniture, ceramics, paintings, samplers
Open Mon–Sun 10am–5pm

Yesteryears
Contact Paul Gowing
The Quay Antiques Centre, The Quay, Topsham, Exeter, Devon, EX3 OJA P
01392 874006
M 07813 569391
W www.antiquesattopshamquay.co.uk
Est. 1993 *Stock size* Medium
Stock Furniture, including compactums, wardrobes, dressing tables
Open Mon–Sun 10am–5pm

TORQUAY

About Time Antiques (BWCG)
Contact David Jacobs
96 Belgrave Road, Torquay, Devon, TQ2 5HZ P
01803 200680 F 01803 200680
M 07771 580509
E clockrepairs@hotmail.com
W www.torbay.antiques.co.uk
Est. 1990 *Stock size* Medium
Stock Antique clocks, jewellery, gold, silver, glass, lighting, porcelain
Open Mon–Sat 9am–5pm
Services Longcase clock restoration

The Old Cop Shop
Contact Mr L Rolfe or Brian Harper
Castle Lane, Torquay, Devon, TQ1 3AN P
01803 294484
Est. 1974 *Stock size* Large
Stock General antiques
Open Mon–Sat 9am–5pm
Services Valuations

Tobys (SALVO)
Contact Mr P Norrish
Newton Road, Torquay, Devon, TQ2 5DD P
01803 212222 F 01803 200523
W www.tobysreclamation.co.uk
Est. 1985 *Stock size* Large
Stock General antiques, furniture, architectural antiques, gifts
Open Mon–Sat 8.30am–5pm Sun Bank Holidays 10.30am–4.30pm
Fairs Exeter Ideal Home, Devon County Show
Services House clearance, nationwide delivery

Upstairs Downstairs
Contact Ms Linda Nicholls
53 Fore Street, St Marychurch, Torquay, Devon, TQ1 4PR P
01803 313010
Est. 1997 *Stock size* Large
Stock Antique and modern jewellery, glass, rocking horses, paintings, china, furniture
Open Mon–Sat 9am–5pm
Services Valuations

West Country Old Books (PBFA)
Contact Mr D Neil
215 Babbacombe Road, Torquay, Devon, TQ1 3SX P
01803 322712
Est. 1989 *Stock size* Small
Stock Antiquarian and good quality second-hand books, specializing in topography, and literature
Open By appointment only
Fairs PBFA
Services Valuations and books bought

West of England Auctions
Contact Mr Warren Hunt
3 Warren Road, Torquay, Devon, TQ2 5TQ P

☎ 01803 211266 Ⓕ 01803 212286
Est. 1949
Open Mon–Fri 9am–1pm 2–5pm
Sales Sales of antiques, silver, jewellery Mon 11am, viewing Sat 9am–noon Sun 1–5pm
Mon 9–11am prior to sale
Frequency Fortnightly
Catalogues yes

TOTNES

Bogan House Antiques
Contact Mr M Mitchell
✉ **43 High Street, Totnes, Devon, TQ9 5NP** Ⓟ
☎ 01803 862075
Est. 1989 *Stock size* Large
Stock Silver, wood, brass, glass, Japanese woodblock prints
Open Tues noon–4.30pm
Fri 10am–4.30pm
Sat 10.30am–4.30pm

The Exchange
Contact John Caley
✉ **76 High Street, Totnes, Devon, TQ9 5SN**
☎ 01803 866836
Ⓔ bookworm1700@yahoo.com
Est. 1996 *Stock size* Large
No. of dealers 7
Stock Books, printed ephemera, tools, brass, china, stamps, toys, records, musical instruments, postcards, second-hand videos, spiritual items, music books
Open Mon–Sat 10am–5pm
5.30pm in summer
Services Valuations, restoration to instruments

Fine Pine Antiques
Contact Nick or Linda Gildersleve
✉ **Woodland Road, Harbertonford, Totnes, Devon, TQ9 7SU** Ⓟ
☎ 01803 732465
Ⓔ info@fine-pine-antiques.co.uk
Ⓦ www.fine-pine-antiques.co.uk
Est. 1973 *Stock size* Medium
Stock Pine and country antiques
Open Mon–Sat 9.30am–5pm
Sun 11am–4pm
Services Valuations, restoration and stripping

Pandora's Box
Contact Sarah Mimpriss
✉ **5b High Street, Totnes, Devon, TQ9 5NN** Ⓟ
☎ 01803 867799
Est. 1999 *Stock size* Small
Stock Georgian–Edwardian furniture, mirrors, china, collectables
Open Fri Sat 10.30am–4pm

Pedlar's Pack Books
Contact Brenda Greysmith or Andy Collins
✉ **4 The Plains, Totnes, Devon, TQ9 5DR** Ⓟ
☎ 01803 866423
Ⓔ books@thepedlarspack.co.uk
Est. 1983 *Stock size* Medium
Stock Antiquarian, second-hand, rare and modern books, art and history books a speciality
Open Mon–Sat 9am–5pm
Services Valuations, book search

TYTHERLEIGH

The Trading Post Antique Centre
Contact Mr M Remfry
✉ **Main Road, Tytherleigh, Axminster, Devon, EX13 7BE** Ⓟ
☎ 01460 221330
Est. 1987 *Stock size* Large
No. of dealers 30
Stock General antiques, furniture, collectables
Open Mon–Sat 10am–4.30pm
Sun 10am–4pm closed Tues
Services Valuations, restoration, clock repairs, repair of cane chairs, house clearance

UFFCULME

Country Antiques & Interiors
Contact Mr M C Mead
✉ **The Old Brewery, High Street, Uffculme, Cullompton, Devon, EX15 3AB** Ⓟ
☎ 01884 841770 Ⓕ 01884 841770
Ⓜ 07768 328433
Ⓔ mike@englishcountryantiques.co.uk
Ⓦ www.englishcountryantiques.co.uk
Est. 1994 *Stock size* Medium
Stock Country furniture, decorative items, contemporary
Open By appointment
Services Shipping arranged

YEALMPTON

Carnegie Paintings & Clocks
Contact Chris Carnegie
✉ **15 Fore Street, Yealmpton, Plymouth, Devon, PL8 2JN** Ⓟ
☎ 01752 881170
Ⓦ www.paintingsandclocks.com
Est. 1996 *Stock size* Medium
Stock Pre-1940s paintings, clocks, barometers
Open Thurs–Sat 10am–5.30pm
Services Restoration

DORSET

BERE REGIS

Dorset Reclamation (SALVO)
Contact David Kirk
✉ **Cow Drove, Bere Regis, Wareham, Dorset, BH20 7JZ** Ⓟ
☎ 01929 472200 Ⓕ 01929 472292
Ⓔ info@dorsetrec.u-net.com
Ⓦ www.dorset-reclamation.co.uk
Est. 1992 *Stock size* Large
Stock Decorative architectural and garden antiques including flagstones, flooring, bathrooms, fittings, radiators, chimney pieces, traditional building materials
Open Mon–Fri 8am–5pm
Sat 9am–4pm
Services Delivery

Legg of Dorchester
Contact Mrs H Legg
✉ **The Old Mill, West Street, Bere Regis, Wareham, Dorset, BH20 7HS** Ⓟ
☎ 01929 472051
Ⓔ jerry@leggofdorchester.co.uk
Ⓦ www.leggofdorchester.co.uk
Est. 1930 *Stock size* Large
Stock General, mostly furniture
Open Mon–Sat telephone to check times

BLANDFORD FORUM

Milton Antiques & Restoration
Contact Nigel Church
✉ **Bere's Yard, Market Place, Blandford Forum, Dorset, DT11 7HV** Ⓟ
☎ 01258 450100
Est. 1989 *Stock size* Medium
Stock Period furniture
Open Mon–Sat 9am–5pm
Services Restoration

Robert A Warry Auctioneer (FNAVA)
Contact Mr R Warry
✉ **1a Alfred Street,**

Blandford Forum, Dorset, DT11 7JJ P
☎ 01258 452454 Ⓕ 01258 452454
Ⓔ auctioneers@rwarry.freeserve.co.uk
Ⓦ www.rwarry.freeserve.co.uk
Est. 1956
Open Mon–Fri 9am–5pm
Sales Antique and collectables sale every three weeks, Fri 10am, viewing Wed 2–5pm Thurs 9.30am–7.30pm morning of sale
Frequency Every 3 weeks
Catalogues Yes

BOURNEMOUTH

Abbey Models
Contact Nick Powner
✉ **42 Littledown Drive, Littledown, Bournemouth, Dorset, BH7 7AQ** P
☎ 01202 395999 Ⓕ 01202 395999
Ⓔ npowner@bournemouth.demon.co.uk
Ⓦ www.the-internet-agency.com/abbeymodels
Est. 1992 *Stock size* Large
Stock Old toys, Dinky, Corgi, Matchbox
Open By appointment
Fairs Sandown Park, NEC Toys
Services Valuations, mail-order catalogues available

Aladdins Antiques
Contact Paul
✉ **Flat 3, 54 Lansdowne Road, Bournemouth, Dorset, BH1 1RS** P
☎ 01202 298805
Ⓜ 07779 250940
Ⓔ paulboysen@cwcom.net
Ⓦ www.aladdinsantiques.cwc.net
Est. 1992 *Stock size* Small
Stock Furniture, ceramics
Open Mon–Sat 9am–6pm closed Wed

Altamira Deco
Contact Mr Ganley
✉ **14 Seamoor Road, Bournemouth, Dorset, BH4 9AR** P
☎ 01202 766444
Ⓜ 07885 778342
Ⓔ gallery@altamiradeco.com
Ⓦ www.altamiradeco.com
Est. 1992 *Stock size* Large
Stock Art Deco furniture, glass, ceramics, bronze, modern design 1950–80s
Open Tues–Sat 10am–5.30pm
Services Valuations

Books & Maps
Contact Mr R J Browne
✉ **1–3 Jewelbox Buildings, Cardigan Road, Winton, Bournemouth, Dorset, BH9 1BB** P
☎ 01202 521373 Ⓕ 01202 529403
Ⓔ sales@booksandmaps.freeserve.co.uk
Ⓦ www.booksandmaps.freeserve.co.uk
Est. 1984 *Stock size* Large
Stock Antiquarian, rare, second-hand books, maps, books on Africa and dogs a speciality
Open Mon–Sat 9am–5.30pm
Fairs Russell Hotel
Services Valuations

Boscombe Militaria
Contact Mr E A Browne
✉ **86 Palmerston Road, Bournemouth, Dorset, BH1 4HU** P
☎ 01202 304250 Ⓕ 01202 733696
Est. 1982 *Stock size* Medium
Stock 20thC militaria, uniforms, medals, badges
Open Mon–Sat 10am–1pm 2–5pm closed Wed
Fairs Farnham, Beltring

Boscombe Stamp Company
Contact Philip Clarke
✉ **20 North Road, Bournemouth, Dorset, BH7 6ET** P
☎ 01202 268672 Ⓕ 01202 466205
Est. 2002 *Stock size* Large
Stock World wide stamps
Open Mon–Sat 8am–5.30pm
Services Valuations

Boscombe Toy Collectors
Contact Mr Harvey
✉ **802b Somerset Road, Boscombe, Bournemouth, Dorset, BH7 6DD** P
☎ 01202 398884
Est. 2001 *Stock size* Medium
Stock Trains, Action Man, *Star Wars*, die-cast and Dragon figures
Open Mon–Sat 10am–5pm closed Wed

Chorley-Burdett Antiques
Contact Ray Burdett
✉ **828 Christchurch Road, Bournemouth, Dorset, BH7 6DF** P
☎ 01202 423363 Ⓕ 01202 423363
Est. 1992 *Stock size* Medium
Stock Victorian–Edwardian furniture, new and reclaimed pine
Open Mon–Sat 9am–5.30pm

Claire's Collectables
Contact Claire Castle
✉ **Shop 6, Royal Arcade, Christchurch Road, Boscombe, Bournemouth, Dorset, BH1 4BT** P
☎ 01202 397558
Est. 1995 *Stock size* Large
Stock Collectables, china
Open Mon 10am–4pm Thurs–Sat 10am–5pm
Services Valuations, Poole pottery replacements

Clobber
Contact Richard Mason
✉ **874 Christchurch Road, Bournemouth, Dorset, BH7 6DJ** P
☎ 01202 429794
Ⓜ 07779 324109
Ⓔ richard@clobber.freeserve.co.uk
Est. 1997 *Stock size* Medium
Stock 1920–70s clothing
Open Mon–Sat 10.30am–5.30pm
Services Valuations

Dalkeith Auctions Bournemouth
Contact Mr P Howard
✉ **Dalkeith Hall, Dalkeith Steps, rear of 81 Old Christchurch Road, Bournemouth, Dorset, BH1 1YL** P
☎ 01202 292905 Ⓕ 01202 292931
Ⓔ how@dalkeith-auctions.co.uk
Ⓦ www.dalkeith-auctions.co.uk
Est. 1992
Open Mon–Sat 9am–3pm
Sales Collectors' sales of ephemera and other collectors' items 1st Sat of month 11am, viewing week before 9am–3pm
Frequency Monthly
Catalogues Yes

The Emporium Antiques Centre
Contact Rebecca Hood
✉ **908 Christchurch Road, Boscombe, Bournemouth, Dorset, BH7 6DL** P
☎ 01202 422380 Ⓕ 01202 433348
Est. 1996 *Stock size* Large
No. of dealers 10
Stock General antiques, decorative arts
Open Mon–Sat 9.30am–5.30pm

Lionel Geneen Ltd (LAPADA)
Contact Mr Robert Geneen
811 Christchurch Road, Boscombe, Bournemouth, Dorset, BH7 6AP P
☎ 01202 422961/520417
F 01202 422961
M 07770 596781
Est. 1902 *Stock size* Medium
Stock 19thC English, Continental, Oriental furniture, porcelain, bronzes, glass, ornamental decorative pieces, dessert services, tea and dinner services
Open Mon–Fri 9am–1pm 2–5pm Sat 9am–noon or by appointment
Services Valuations

Hardy's Collectables
Contact Mr J Hardy
Boscombe, Bournemouth, Dorset, BH7 P
☎ 01202 473744
M 07970 056858/613077
Est. 1987 *Stock size* Large
Stock 20thC collectables, mainly smalls, toys, metalware, ceramics
Open By appointment
Fairs Alexandra Palace, Kempton

Kebo Antiques Market
Contact Mr K Lawrence
823a Christchurch Road, Bournemouth, Dorset, BH7 6AP P
☎ 01202 417052
Est. 1989 *Stock size* Small
No. of dealers 5
Stock General antiques
Open Mon–Sat 10am–5pm
Services Valuations

Manor Antiques
Contact D R or T W Vendy
739 Christchurch Road, Bournemouth, Dorset, BH7 6AN P
☎ 01202 392779
Est. 1969 *Stock size* Large
Stock General antiques, furniture, silver, porcelain
Open Mon–Sat 10am–1pm 2–5pm

Modern and Antique Fire Arms (GTA)
Contact Val O'Donovan
147 Tuckton Road, Saltbourne, Bournemouth, Dorset, BH6 3JZ P
☎ 01202 429369 F 01202 426926
Est. 1997 *Stock size* Medium
Stock Firearms and accessories
Open Mon–Sat 9.30am–1pm 2–5.30pm Wed by appointment
Fairs Midland Game Fair, Bisley Fair

Mussenden & Sons, GB
Contact Gordon or David Mussenden
24 Seamoor Road, Westbourne, Bournemouth, Dorset, BH4 9AR
☎ 01202 764462
Est. 1970 *Stock size* Medium
Stock Antiques, jewellery, silver
Open Mon–Sat 9am–5pm closed Wed

Norman D Landing Militaria
Contact Mr Kenneth Lewis
76 Alma Road, Winton, Bournemouth, Dorset, BH9 1AN P
☎ 01202 521944 F 01202 521944
M 07711 790044
E kenneth@44doughboy.fsnet.co.uk
W norman-d-landing.com
Est. 1995 *Stock size* Large
Stock US uniforms and equipment (1900–1945). US Army uniforms and equipment 1910–1945.
Open Thurs–Sat 10am–5pm, Mon–Wed by appointment
Fairs Stoneleigh, Warwicks (January), Beltring, Kent (July)
Services Valuations, mail order, hires to film and TV. Author of *Doughboy to GI*

George A Payne & Son Ltd
Contact Mr Payne
742 Christchurch Road, Boscombe, Bournemouth, Dorset, BH7 6BZ P
☎ 01202 394954
Est. 1900 *Stock size* Medium
Stock Jewellery and silver
Open Mon–Sat 9.15am–5.30pm
Services Valuations, restoration

Pokesdown Antique Centre
Contact Mr C Lane
848 Christchurch Road, Boscombe, Bournemouth, Dorset, BH7 6AP P
☎ 01202 433263
Est. 1989 *Stock size* Large
No. of dealers 10
Stock Decorative antiques, wristwatches, lighting, pine, collectables (Georgian to modern), paintings
Open Mon–Sat 9am–5.30pm
Services Valuations, delivery, wristwatch repairs

Poole Pottery China Matching Service
Contact Claire Castle
Shop 6, Royal Arcade, Christchurch Road, Boscombe, Bournemouth, Dorset, BH1 4BT P
☎ 01202 397558
Est. 1995 *Stock size* Medium
Stock Poole, Denby, Masons, Royal Albert, Royal Doulton, Wedgwood,
Open Mon 10am–4pm Thurs–Sat 10am–5pm
Services China matching service

R E Porter
2–6 Post Office Road, Bournemouth, Dorset, BH1 1BA P
☎ 01202 554289
Est. 1930 *Stock size* Large
Stock Silver, Baxter prints
Open Mon–Sat 9.30am–5pm
Services Valuations, restoration

Rawlinsons
Contact Mr M Rawlinson
884 Christchurch Road, Bournemouth, Dorset, BH7 6DJ P
☎ 01202 433394
Est. 1983 *Stock size* Large
Stock General, smalls, furniture, glass, china, metalware, clocks, Art Deco
Open Mon–Sat 10am–5.30pm

H Rowan
Contact Mr H Rowan
459 Christchurch Road, Boscombe, Bournemouth, Dorset, BH1 4AD P
☎ 01202 398820
Est. 1968 *Stock size* Large
Stock Antiquarian and second-hand books, maps, prints, local interest, art and antiques topics a speciality
Open Mon–Sat 9.30am–5.30pm
Services Valuations

The Sage Door
Contact Philip Richards
920 Christchurch Road, Bournemouth, Dorset, BH7 6DL P
01202 434771
07713 335851
Est. 1975 *Stock size* Large
Stock Antique and decorative furniture, lighting, soft furnishings
Open Mon–Sat 10am–5pm

Sainsburys of Bournemouth Ltd (LAPADA)
Contact Jonathan Sainsbury
23–25 Abbott Road, Bournemouth, Dorset, BH9 1EU P
01202 529271 F 01202 510028
sales@sainsburys-antiques.com
www.sainsburys-antiques.com
Est. 1918 *Stock size* Large
Stock Antique furniture and accessories, exceptional replica chairs
Open By appointment
Services Antique timbers used to create replica furniture

Sandy's Antiques
Contact Michael Sandy
790–792 Christchurch Road, Boscombe, Bournemouth, Dorset, BH7 6DD P
01202 301190 F 01202 301190
07836 367384
Est. 1970 *Stock size* Large
Stock Edwardian, Victorian, shipping, furniture
Open Mon–Sat 10am–5.30pm
Services Packing containers for export

Smith & Sons
Contact Matthew Smith
903 Christchurch Road, Bournemouth, Dorset, BH7 6AX P
01202 429523/01425 476705
enquiries@dsmithandsons.demon.co.uk
www.dsmithandsons.demon.co.uk
Est. 1968 *Stock size* Medium
Stock Country furniture and china, books
Open Mon–Sat 10am–5pm
Services Restoration

Sterling Coins and Medals (OMRS)
Contact Mr V Henstridge
2 Somerset Road, Boscombe, Bournemouth, Dorset, BH7 6JH P
01202 423881 F 01202 423881
agagia@aol.com
Est. 1985 *Stock size* Medium
Stock Coins and medals
Open Mon–Sat 9am–3.30pm Wed 9am–12.30pm
Services Valuations and medal mounting

Victorian Chairman
Contact Mrs M Leo
883 Christchurch Road, Bournemouth, Dorset, BH7 6AU P
01202 420996
Est. 1977 *Stock size* Medium
Stock Victorian tables and chairs, wrought iron, glass tables
Open Mon–Sat 10am–5pm
Services Restoration of upholstery, French polishing

Volume One Books and Records
Contact Richard Cargill
1073 Christchurch Road, Boscombe East, Bournemouth, Dorset, BH7 6BE P
01202 417652 F 01202 483686
Est. 1989 *Stock size* Large
Stock Books, LP records, and CDs (classical, easy listening, jazz, stage and screen, country, rock and pop)
Open Mon Tues Fri 10am–5.30pm Wed 10am–1pm Sat 10am–1pm closed 3rd Sat in each month
Fairs Midhurst Monthly Market, Sussex; others – please phone
Services Record search and mail order

Wonderworld
Contact Mr David Hern
540 Christchurch Road, Boscombe, Bournemouth, Dorset, BH1 4BE P
01202 394918
davejh4000@aol.com
www.wonderworld.uk.com
Est. 1977 *Stock size* Large
Stock Modern collectables, *Star Wars*, comics, Beanie Babies
Open Mon–Sat 9.30am–5.30pm

Yesterdays Books (PBFA)
Contact David Weir
6 Cecil Avenue, Bournemouth, Dorset, BH8 9EH P
01202 522442
07946 548420
djl.weir@btinternet.com
Est. 1974 *Stock size* Medium
Stock Antiquarian books, African topics a speciality
Open By appointment
Fairs PBFA at London, Oxford and elsewhere, the London Travel Bookfair
Services Valuations, book search

BRIDPORT

The Auction House Bridport
Contact Michael Dark
38a St Michael's Trading Estate, Bridport, Dorset, DT6 3RR P
01308 459400 F 01308 459685
07905 481388
sales@theauctionhouse.dabsol.co.uk
www.theauctionhouse.dabsol.co.uk
Est. 1998
Open Mon–Fri 9.30am–5pm
Sales Antiques and modern sale last Fri each month 10am, viewing prior Wed Thurs 10am–5pm
Frequency Monthly
Catalogues Yes

Batten's Jewellers
Contact Gemma Batten
26 South Street, Bridport, Dorset, DT6 3NQ P
01308 456910
Est. 1978 *Stock size* Medium
Stock Jewellery, clocks, watches, silver
Open Mon–Fri 9am–5pm Thurs Sat 9am–1pm

P E L Bedford
Contact Patrick Bedford
81 East Street, Bridport, Dorset, DT6 3LB P
01308 421370
Est. 1956 *Stock size* Large
Stock Oriental and general antiques, porcelain, paintings, jewellery
Open Variable, telephone call advisable

Benchmark Antiques
Contact Meg Standage
West Allington,

Bridport, Dorset,
DT6 5BG 🅿
☎ 01308 420941 ⓕ 01308 420941
ⓔ hohobird@netscape.net
Est. 1992 *Stock size* Medium
Stock 18thC furniture and related items
Open By appointment
Fairs NEC
Services Valuations

⊞ Bridport Old Books (PBFA)
Contact Ms C MacTaggart
✉ **11 South Street, Bridport, Dorset, DT6 3NR** 🅿
☎ 01308 425689
Est. 1998 *Stock size* Medium
Stock Antiquarian and second-hand books, children's illustrated, WWI, T E Lawrence, modern first editions
Open Mon–Sat 10am–5pm
Services Valuations

⊞ Cast From The Past
Contact David Coxhead
✉ **Unit 57, Redbrick Studio, St Michael's Trading Estate, Bridport, Dorset, DT6 3RR** 🅿
☎ 01308 426400
Est. 2002 *Stock size* Large
Stock Architectural antiques
Open Mon–Sat 8am–5pm
Services Valuations, restoration, demolition, clearance

⊞ Jack's
Contact D Skeels
✉ **24 South Street, Bridport, Dorset, DT6 3NQ** 🅿
☎ 01308 420700
Est. 1985 *Stock size* Medium
Stock Oriental rugs, furniture, antiques, collectables
Open Mon–Sat 9am–5pm
Services Restoration (rugs), cleaning

⊞ Ann Quested Antiques
Contact Ann Quested
✉ **59 East Street, Bridport, Dorset, DT6 3LB** 🅿
☎ 01308 422576/421551
Est. 1990 *Stock size* Medium
Stock Pine and country furniture, brass
Open Wed–Sat 10.30am–5pm
Services Valuations

CHRISTCHURCH

⊞ Classic Pictures (PTA)
Contact Betty Underwood
✉ **12a Castle Street, Christchurch, Dorset, BH23 1DT** 🅿
☎ 01202 470276
ⓔ enquiries@classic-pictures.com
Est. 1989 *Stock size* Large
Stock Old postcards, Edwardian pictures, prints
Open Tues–Sat 9.30am–5pm
Fairs New Forest Show, Bournemouth International Centre
Services Valuations

⊞ H L B Antiques
Contact Mr H L Blechman
✉ **139 Barrack Road, Christchurch, Dorset, BH23 2AW** 🅿
☎ 01202 429252
Est. 1967 *Stock size* Medium
Stock General collectables, gramophones, postcards, walking sticks, Art Deco, ivory
Open Sat 9am–5pm or by appointment
Fairs New Caledonian Market in Bermondsey
Services Valuations, restoration

⊞ Gerald Hampton
Contact Gerald Hampton
✉ **12 Purewell, Christchurch, Dorset, BH23 1EP** 🅿
☎ 01202 484000
Est. 1930 *Stock size* Medium
Stock General antiques
Trade only Yes
Open By appointment

⊞ M & R Lankshear Antiques
Contact Mike Lankshear
✉ **18 Plantation Drive, Walkford, Christchurch, Dorset, BH23 5SA** 🅿
☎ 01425 277332
ⓜ 07811 018476
Est. 1977 *Stock size* Medium
Stock General antiques, military items
Open Mon–Sat 9.30am–5pm
Services Valuations

⊞ Past 'n' Present
Contact Pete Woodford
✉ **4 St Catherine's Parade, Fairmile Road, Christchurch, Dorset, BH23 2LQ** 🅿
☎ 01202 478900
Est. 1997 *Stock size* Large
Stock Collectables
Open Mon–Sat 9.30am–5pm closed Wed pm
Services Valuations, restoration

⊞ Tudor House Antiques (LAPADA)
Contact Mrs P Knight or Mrs D Burton
✉ **420 Lymington Road, Highcliffe, Christchurch, Dorset, BH23 5HE** 🅿
☎ 01425 280440
Est. 1940 *Stock size* Medium
Stock General
Open Tues–Sat 10am–5pm closed Wed

CRANBORNE

⊞ Tower Antiques
Contact Mr P White
✉ **The Square, Cranbourne, Dorset, BH21 5PR** 🅿
☎ 01725 517552
Est. 1973 *Stock size* Small
Stock Georgian, Victorian furniture
Open Mon–Sat 8.30am–5.30pm

DORCHESTER

⊞ The Antiques Emporium
Contact Bruce Clarke-Williams
✉ **9 High East Street, Dorchester, Dorset, DT1 1HS** 🅿
☎ 01305 261546
Est. 1997 *Stock size* Medium
Stock General antiques
Open Tues–Sat 9.30am–5.30pm

⊞ Box of Porcelain
Contact Robert Lunn
✉ **51d Icen Way, Dorchester, Dorset, DT1 1EW** 🅿
☎ 01305 267110 ⓕ 01305 263201
ⓜ 07786 802113
ⓔ rlunn@boxofporcelain.com
ⓦ www.boxofporcelain.com
Est. 1987 *Stock size* Large
Stock Collectables, Doulton, Beswick, Royal Worcester, Spode, Coalport, Lladrow, Moorcroft
Open Mon–Sat 10.30am–5pm closed Thurs

Chattels
Colliton Antique Centre, 3 Colliton Street, Dorchester, Dorset, DT1 1XH
01305 263620
Est. 1993 *Stock size* Large
Stock General, Edwardian, Victorian furniture
Open Mon–Sat 9am–4pm

Colliton Antique Centre
Contact Tony Phillips
3a Colliton Street, Dorchester, Dorset, DT1 1XH
01305 269398/260115
Est. 1983 *Stock size* Large
No. of dealers 6
Stock General Victorian, Georgian, Edwardian furniture, jewellery, silver, old pine
Open Mon–Sat 9am–5pm Sun by appointment
Services Restoration of metalwork, silver and jewellery valuations

De Danann Antiques Centre
Contact Mr J Burton
27 London Road, Dorchester, Dorset, DT1 1NF
01305 250066/264123
01305 250113
www.dedanann.co.uk
Est. 1994 *Stock size* Medium
No. of dealers 20
Stock General antiques
Open Mon–Sat 9am–5pm

The Dorchester Bookshop
Contact Michael Edmonds
3 Nappers Court, Charles Street, Dorchester, Dorset, DT1 1EE
01305 269919
Est. 1993 *Stock size* Medium
Stock Second-hand, antiquarian books
Open Tues–Sat 10am–5pm
Services Valuations, restoration and book search

Hy Duke & Son (SOFAA)
Contact Mr Guy Schwinge or Mr Gary Batt
The Dorchester Fine Art Salerooms, Weymouth Avenue, Dorchester, Dorset, DT1 1QS
01305 265080 01305 260101
07778 523962
enquiries@dukes-auctions.com
www.dukes-auctions.com
Est. 1823
Open Mon–Fri some Sats 9am–1pm 2–5.30pm
Sales Specialist sales of paintings, furniture, ceramics, silver, jewellery and furniture, viewing week prior Sat 9.30am–noon Mon 9.30am–5pm Tues 9.30am–7pm Wed 9.30am–5pm morning of sale
Frequency 9 per annum
Catalogues Yes

Legg of Dorchester
Contact Mrs H Legg
Regency House, 51 High East Street, Dorchester, Dorset, DT1 1HU
01305 264964
jerry@leggdorchester.co.uk
www.leggofdorchester.co.uk
Est. 1930 *Stock size* Large
Stock General, mostly furniture
Open Mon–Sat 9.45am–4.45pm

John Walker Antiques (BADA, BACA Award Winner 2002)
Contact Mr J Walker
52 High West Street, Dorchester, Dorset, DT1 1UT
01305 260324
07880 528436
Est. 1973 *Stock size* Medium
Stock Early oak, textiles, ceramics, metalwork
Open Tues–Sat 9.30am–5pm

GILLINGHAM

Talisman (LAPADA)
Contact Mr Ken Bolan
The Old Brewery, Wyke Road, Gillingham, Dorset, SP8 4NW
01747 824423 01747 823544
arcadia@talisman-antiques.co.uk
www.talisman-antiques.co.uk
Est. 1979 *Stock size* Large
Stock Antiques and garden statuary
Open Mon–Fri 9am–5pm Sat 10am–4pm
Fairs Olympia June November

LYME REGIS

The Commemorative Man
Contact Mr Harris
Lyme Regis Antique & Craft Centre, Marine Parade, Lyme Regis, Dorset, DT7 3JH
01297 32682
Est. 1994 *Stock size* Large
Stock Political, royal and sporting commemoratives
Open April–Oct Mon–Sun 11am–6.30pm Nov–Mar Fri Sat Sun 11am–4.30pm
Services Mail order and search service

Lyme Regis Antique & Craft Centre
Contact Mr C Willis
Marine Parade, Lyme Regis, Dorset, DT7 3JH
01297 445053
Est. 1995 *Stock size* Large
No. of dealers 35
Stock Commemoratives, stamps, coins, toys, linen, brass taps, Art Deco, lamps, lighting
Open Apr–Oct Mon–Sun 11am–6.30pm Nov–Mar Fri Sat Sun 11am–4.30pm

LYTCHETT MINSTER

Old Button Shop
Contact Thelma Johns
Dorchester Road, Lytchett Minster, Dorset, BH16 6JF
01202 622169
info@oldbuttonshop.fsnet.co.uk
Est. 1970 *Stock size* Small
Stock General and cottage antiques, antique and Dorset buttons
Open Tues–Fri 2–5pm Sat 11am–1pm
Services Valuations, restoration

MAIDEN NEWTON

Dynasty Antiques
Contact Nigel Hirst
Newton Hall, Dorchester Road, Maiden Newton, Dorchester, Dorset, DT2 0BD
01300 321313
07787 561586
www.dynastyantiques.co.uk

Est. 2000 *Stock size* Medium
Stock Chinese, Tibetan antique furniture
Open Mon–Sat 10am–5pm closed Wed or by appointment

MELBURY OSMOND

Hardy Country
Contact Mr S Groves
Meadow View, Drive End, Melbury Osmond, Dorchester, Dorset, DT2 0NA
☎ 01935 83440
Ⓜ 07814 048449
Est. 1972 *Stock size* Large
Stock Old pine
Open Mon–Sat 9am–6pm Sun by appointment
Services Valuations, restoration

POOLE

Branksome Antiques
Contact Brian Neal
370 Poole Road, Branksome, Poole, Dorset, BH12 1AW
☎ 01202 763324 Ⓕ 01202 763324
Est. 1972 *Stock size* Medium
Stock General antiques, scientific, medical, marine, silver, brass, copper
Open Mon Tues Thur Fri 10am–5pm
Fairs Scientific Fair, Portman Hotel

Castle Books
Contact Mr Clark
2 North Street, Poole, Dorset, BH15 1NX
☎ 01202 660295
Est. 1980 *Stock size* Medium
Stock Antiquarian, modern second-hand, collectable books
Open Mon–Sat 10am–5pm
Services Valuations

Davey & Davey (NAVA)
Contact Neil Davey
13 St Peters Road, Parkstone, Poole, Dorset, BH14 0NZ
☎ 01202 748567 Ⓕ 01202 716258
Ⓦ www.daveyanddavey.com
Est. 1946
Open Mon–Fri 9am–1pm 2–5.30pm
Sales General antiques and collectables every 2 months Tues 10am, viewing Mon 10am–4pm
Catalogues Yes

Down To The Woods Ltd
Contact Vanessa Harris
92 The Dolphin Centre, Poole, Dorset, BH15 1SR
☎ 01202 669448
Ⓔ downttw@globalnet.co.uk
Est. 1998 *Stock size* Large
Stock Bears, soft toys, bean-bag collections, dolls' houses
Open Mon–Sat 9.30am–5.30pm
Services Layaway, mail order

Fireplaces 'n' Things
Contact Mr D L Shackford
87–89 Alder Road, Parkstone, Poole, Dorset, BH12 2AB
☎ 01202 735301 Ⓕ 01202 735301
Est. 1980 *Stock size* Large
Stock Antique and reproduction fireplaces
Open Mon–Sat 10am–4pm closed Wed
Services Valuations, restoration

Grand Prix Top Gear
Contact Mr N Grint
160 Ashley Road, Parkstone, Poole, Dorset, BH14 9BY
☎ 07000 553949 Ⓕ 01202 710104
Ⓔ f1@topgear.org
Ⓦ www.topgear.org
Est. 1989 *Stock size* Large
Stock Memorabilia. Formula One collectables including car body parts, original team clothing, signed photos, models, caps
Open Mon–Sat 9am–6pm telephone first
Fairs Autosport Show NEC, Silverstone GP
Services Mail order and trade suppliers

Great Expectations
Contact Mr Carter
115 Penn Hill Avenue, Lower Parkstone, Poole, Dorset, BH14 9LY
☎ 01202 740645
Est. 2000 *Stock size* Medium
Stock General antiques, paintings, prints, objets d'art
Open Wed–Sat 10.30am–5pm

W A Howe
Contact Mr W A Howe
23 Cooke Road, Branksome, Poole, Dorset, BH12 1QB
☎ 01202 743350
Est. 1999 *Stock size* Small
Stock Antiquarian, second-hand books, modern first editions, cookery, golf
Open Mon–Sun 8am–8pm
Fairs Local book fairs
Services Valuations

Laburnum Antiques & Interiors
Contact Mrs D Mills
Lonbourne House, 250 Bournemouth Road, Poole, Dorset, BH14 9HZ
☎ 01202 746222 Ⓕ 01202 736777
Ⓔ enquiries@laburnumantiques.co.uk
Ⓦ www.laburnumantiques.co.uk
Est. 1997 *Stock size* Medium
Stock Georgian–Edwardian furniture, accessories, ottomans, stools and cushions, full range of interiors, soft furnishings
Open Tues–Sat 10am–5.30pm
Services Complete home furnishing service, fully qualified furniture restoration

Stocks and Chairs
Contact Mrs Carole Holding-Parsons
11 Bank Chambers, Penn Hill Avenue, Poole, Dorset, BH14 9NB
☎ 01202 718618
Ⓦ www.stockandchairsantiques.com
Est. 1979 *Stock size* Large
Stock 18th–19thC furniture, some smalls
Open Mon–Sat 11am–5pm closed Wed
Services Restoration of hand-dyed leather

Stocks and Chairs
Contact Mrs Carole Holding-Parsons
The Old Church Hall, Hardy Road, Poole, Dorset, BH14 9HN
☎ 01202 718418 Ⓕ 01202 718918
Ⓦ www.stockandchairsantiques.com
Est. 1979 *Stock size* Large
Stock Antique leather chairs and settees
Open Mon–Fri 8.30am–5.30pm and by appointment
Services Restoration of hand-dyed leather

PUDDLETOWN

Antique Map and Bookshop (PBFA, ABA)
Contact Mrs H M Proctor
32 High Street, Puddletown, Dorchester, Dorset, DT2 8RU P
01305 848633
proctor@puddletown.demon.co.uk
www.puddletownbookshop.co.uk
Est. 1976 *Stock size* Medium
Stock Antique maps, antiquarian, second-hand books
Open Mon–Sat 9am–5pm
Fairs Oxford, Russell Hotel (June) – PBFA
Services Valuations, restoration, book catalogues (4–6 a year)

PYMORE

William Morey & Son
Contact Malcolm Wilson
The Sale Room, Unit 3, Pymore Mills Estate, Pymore, Dorset, DT6 5PJ P
01308 422078 F 01308 422078
M 07748 356376
enquiries@wmoreyandson.co.uk
www.wmoreyandson.co.uk
Est. 1870
Open Mon–Fri 9am–5pm
Sales Antiques auction every 3 weeks Thurs 9.30am, viewing Wed 9am–4pm
Catalogues Yes

SEMLEY

Dairy House Antiques
Contact Andrew Stevenson
Station Road, Semley, Shaftesbury, Dorset, SP7 9AN P
01747 853317
Est. 1998 *Stock size* Large
No. of dealers 9
Stock Antiques and collectables
Open Mon–Sat 9am–5pm

Semley Auctioneers
Contact Mr Simon Pearce
Station Road, Semley, Shaftesbury, Dorset, SP7 9AN P
01747 855122 F 01747 855222
simon.pearce@semley auctioneers.com
www.semleyauctioneers.com
Est. 1990
Open Mon–Fri 9am–5pm
Sales Sat 10am, viewing Friday prior 9am–9pm morning of sale. Items of higher quality appear in these sales about every 6 weeks
Frequency Fortnightly
Catalogues Yes

SHAFTESBURY

Robert Morgan Antiques
Contact Robert Morgan
Unit 1a, Station Road, Semley, Shaftesbury, Dorset, SP7 8AH P
01747 858770
M 07767 416106
bobkate@barnhouse2.fsnet.co.uk
www.robertmorganantiques.co.uk
Est. 1985 *Stock size* Medium
Stock Small furniture, unusual items, medals, coins
Open By appointment
Fairs Kempton Park, Newark
Services Valuations

Mr Punch's Antique Market
Contact Mr C Jolliffe
33 Bell Street, Shaftesbury, Dorset, SP7 8AE P
01747 855775 F 01747 855775
www.mrpunchs.co.uk
Est. 1994 *Stock size* Large
No. of dealers 20
Stock General, furniture, collectables, militaria, maps
Open Tue–Sat 10am–6pm
Services Valuations, restoration, pine stripping, house clearance, Punch museum

Shaston Antiques
Contact Mr J D Hine
14 & 16a Bell Street, Shaftesbury, Dorset, SP7 8AE
01747 850405
Est. 1996 *Stock size* Medium
Stock Georgian–Victorian quality furniture
Open Mon Tues Thurs Sat 9am–5pm Wed 9am–1pm
Services Restoration

SHERBORNE

Abbas Antiques
Contact Trevor F J Jeans
Sherborne World of Antiques & Fine Art, Long Street, Sherborne, Dorset, DT9 3BS P
01935 816451 F 01935 816240
Est. 1991 *Stock size* Medium
Stock 19thC furniture and smalls
Open Tue–Sat 9.30am–5pm
Services Valuations, restoration

Antiques of Sherborne (LAPADA, SAADA)
Contact Clive or Linda Greenslade
1 The Green, Sherborne, Dorset, DT9 3HZ P
01935 816549 F 01935 816549
M 07971 019173
clive@antiquesofsherborne. fsnet.co.uk
Est. 1988 *Stock size* Medium
Stock Georgian–Edwardian period town and country furniture, dining tables, chairs, sofas, wing chairs, linen, chess and mah jong sets
Open Mon–Sat 10am–5pm
Fairs Shepton Mallet
Services Upholstery, restoration, deliveries worldwide

Chapter House Books
Contact Mr or Mrs Hutchison
Trendle Street, Sherborne, Dorset, DT9 3NT
01935 816262
chapterhousebooks@tiscali.co.uk
Est. 1988 *Stock size* Large
Stock Antiquarian books (mostly hardback), out-of-print, paperbacks
Open Mon–Sat 10am–5pm
Services Valuations, book repair, book search

Greystoke Antiques
Contact Mr F Butcher
4 Swan Yard, Cheap Street, Sherborne, Dorset, DT9 3AX P
01935 812833
Est. 1974 *Stock size* Large
Stock Silver, Georgian and Victorian, English blue transfer-printed pottery 1800–1850
Open Mon–Sat 10am–4.30pm closed Wed
Services Valuations, restoration

Pastimes
Contact Oliver Chisholm
Digby Road, Sherborne, Dorset, DT9 3NL P
01593 389666

ⓔ info@pastimes-toys.co.uk
Est. 2000 *Stock size* Large
Stock Antique and collectable toys
Open Thurs–Sat 9am–5pm

Phoenix Antiques (SAADA)
Contact Neil or Sally Brent Jones
21 Cheap Street, Sherborne, Dorset, DT9 3PU Ⓟ
☎ 01935 812788
ⓔ phoenixantique@aol.com
Est. 1982 *Stock size* Medium
Stock 18th–20thC English and Continental furniture, mahogany, rosewood, painted country furniture, furnishings and lighting
Open Mon–Sat 9.30am–5.30pm or by appointment

Piers Pisani Ltd Antiques (SAADA)
Contact Mr Piers Pisani
The Court Yard, Newland, Sherborne, Dorset, DT9 3JG Ⓟ
☎ 01935 815209 ⓕ 01935 815209
ⓔ antiques@pierspisani.sagehost.co.uk
ⓦ www.pierspisani.com
Est. 1987 *Stock size* Large
Stock English and French furniture, upholstery
Open Mon–Sat 10am–5pm
Services Valuations, restoration, furniture copy

Renaissance
Contact Malcolm Heygate Browne
South Street, Sherborne, Dorset, DT9 3NG Ⓟ
☎ 01935 815487 ⓕ 01935 815487
Est. 1984 *Stock size* Large
Stock 18th–19thC English furniture, pottery, porcelain, Middle Eastern carpets
Open Mon–Sat 10am–5pm Sun 11am–3pm
Services Valuations, restoration

Sherborne World of Antiques
Contact Mr T F J Jeans
Long Street, Sherborne, Dorset, DT9 3BS Ⓟ
☎ 01935 816451 ⓕ 01935 816240
ⓔ info@sherborneworldof antiques.co.uk
ⓦ www.sherborneworldof antiques.co.uk
Est. 2000 *Stock size* Large
No. of dealers 20
Stock General antiques, fine art, jewellery, clocks, porcelain
Open Tues–Sat 9.30am–5pm
Services Valuations, restoration, shipping, book search

Timecraft Clocks (BHI)
Contact Mr G Smith
Unit 2, 24 Cheap Street, Sherborne, Dorset, DT9 3PX Ⓟ
☎ 01935 817771
Est. 1994 *Stock size* Small
Stock Clocks, barometers, musical boxes
Open Tue–Fri 10.30am–5.30pm Sat 10.30am–5pm
Services Restoration, repairs

Wessex Antiques (SAADA)
Contact Frances Bryant
6 Cheap Street, Sherborne, Dorset, DT9 3PX Ⓟ
☎ 01935 816816 ⓕ 01935 816816
ⓔ drucie.bryant@virgin.co.uk
Est. 1986 *Stock size* Small
Stock Furniture, Staffordshire figures, 19thC glass, Oriental rugs
Open Tues–Sat 10am–5pm

Henry Willis (Antique Silver)
Contact Henry Willis
38 Cheap Street, Sherborne, Dorset, DT9 3PX Ⓟ
☎ 01935 816828
Ⓜ 07971 171818
Est. 1975 *Stock size* Medium
Stock English silver medieval–1940
Open Mon–Sat 10am–5pm
Fairs Olympia (June)

STOURPAINE

Onslow Auctions Ltd
Contact Patrick Bogue
The Coach House, Manor Road, Stourpaine, Dorset, DT11 8TQ Ⓟ
☎ 01258 488838
ⓔ onslow.auctions@btinternet.com
ⓦ www.onslows.uk
Est. 1984
Open Mon–Fri 9.30am–5pm by appointment
Sales Collectors' sales, vintage travel, aeronautical, posters, railways, motoring, Titanic, ocean liners, advisable to telephone for details
Frequency 4 per annum
Catalogues Yes

SWANAGE

New, Secondhand & Antiquarian Books
Contact Mrs J Blanchard
35 Station Road, Swanage, Dorset, BH19 1AD Ⓟ
☎ 01929 424088 ⓕ 01929 424088
ⓦ www.editionone.co.uk
Est. 1987 *Stock size* Large
Stock New, second-hand, antiquarian books. First and pocket editions
Open Summer Mon–Sun 9.30am–5.00pm winter closed Sun

WAREHAM

Cottees of Wareham
Contact Mr Bullock
The Market, East Street, Wareham, Dorset, BH20 4NR Ⓟ
☎ 01929 552826 ⓕ 01929 554916
ⓔ auctions@cottees.fsnet.co.uk
ⓦ www.auctionsatcottees.co.uk
Est. 1902
Open Mon–Fri 9am–5pm closed 1–2pm
Sales General antique sales fortnightly Tues 10am and 2pm, viewing Mon 10am–1pm 2–5pm 6–8pm. Regular quality antique and fine art sales. Poole pottery, Clarice Cliff, Moorcroft pottery, Art Deco and collectable toy sales
Catalogues Yes

Heirlooms Antique Jewellers & Silversmiths
Contact Mr or Mrs Young
21 South Street, Wareham, Dorset, BH20 4LR Ⓟ
☎ 01929 554207 ⓕ 01929 554207
Est. 1985 *Stock size* Small
Stock Antique and period jewellery and silver
Open Mon–Sat 9.30am–5pm closed Wed
Services Jewellery, silver, watch, clock repair

WEYMOUTH

Books Afloat
Contact John Ritchie
66 Park Street, Weymouth,

Dorset, DT4 7DE P
☎ 01305 779774
Est. 1983 *Stock size* Large
Stock Antiquarian, rare and second-hand books. Shipping, naval antiques and memorabilia, old postcards, ship models, paintings
Open Mon–Sat 9.30am–5.30pm

Books & Bygones
Contact Denise Nash
✉ **26 Great George Street, Weymouth, Dorset, DT4 7AS** P
☎ 01305 777231
Est. 1985 *Stock size* Medium
Stock Antiques, collectables, out of print, rare and antiquarian books
Open Mon–Sun 2–5pm
Services Valuations

The Crows Nest
Contact Julia Marko
✉ **3 Hope Square, Weymouth, Dorset, DT4 8TR** P
☎ 01305 786930 F 01305 786930
Est. 1992 *Stock size* Large
Stock China, glass, pictures, farming, ships' lamps, nautical, collectables
Open Mon–Sun 10am–5pm
Fairs Shepton Mallet, Exeter Livestock Market, Great Dorset Steam Fair
Services Restoration

The Curiosity Shop on the Quay
Contact David Pinches
✉ **13 Trinity Road, Weymouth, Dorset, DT4 8TJ** P
☎ 01305 769988 F 01305 769988
Est. 1990 *Stock size* Large
Stock General collectors' shop, Victoriana, collectables, Moorcroft, Poole pottery and Pendelfin
Open Mon–Sun 10am–5pm
Fairs Shepton Mallet, Exeter West Point

Hy Duke & Son (SOFAA)
Contact Chris Copson
✉ **The Weymouth Auction Rooms, St Nicholas Street, Weymouth, Dorset, DT4 8AA** P
☎ 01305 761499
Est. 1823
Open By appointment
Sales Twice monthly sales on Tues at 10.30am of general antiques. Viewing Mon prior 9am–5.30pm
Catalogues No

Nautical Antique Centre
Contact Mr D C Warwick
✉ **3a Cove Passage, off Hope Square, near Brewers Quay, Weymouth, Dorset, DT4 8TR** P
☎ 01305 777838/783180
M 07833 707247
E nauticalantiques@tinyworld.co.uk
W www.nauticalantiques weymouth.co.uk
Est. 1988 *Stock size* Large
Stock Original maritime items, telescopes, sextants, clocks, barometers, logs, bells, lights, ships models, nautical collectables and memorabilia for collectors or commercial and domestic interior decor
Open Tues–Fri 10am–1pm 2–5pm (please ring in case shop is closed for fairs) evenings and weekends by appointment
Services Historical documentation on purchases

The Shrubbery
Contact Mrs Sally Dench
✉ **15 Westham Road, Weymouth, Dorset, DT4 8NS** P
☎ 01305 768240
Est. 1997 *Stock size* Large
Stock Collectable dolls, dolls' houses, teddy bears, miniatures
Open Mon–Sat 10am–4pm
Fairs Weymouth

The Treasure Chest
Contact Mr P Barrett
✉ **29 East Street, Weymouth, Dorset, DT4 8BN** P
☎ 01305 772757
Est. 1969 *Stock size* Medium
Stock Curios, coins, medals, local prints, brass, copper, china, army badges
Open Mon–Sat 10am–5pm closed 1–2.30pm Wed 10am–1pm
Services Medal mounting, full size or miniature medals

WIMBORNE

Minster Books
Contact Mr or Mrs Child
✉ **12 Cornmarket, Wimborne, Dorset, BH21 1JL**
☎ 01202 883355
Est. 1991 *Stock size* Large
Stock Antiquarian and second-hand books
Open Mon–Sat 10am–5pm
Services Valuations, restoration

Rectory Rocking Horses
Contact Geoff Boyd
✉ **The Barn, Pamphill Dairy, Pamphill, Wimborne, Dorset, BH21 4ED** P
☎ 01202 881100 F 01202 881100
W www.antiquerockinghorses.co.uk
Est. 1997 *Stock size* Medium
Stock Antique rocking horses
Open Tues–Fri 10am–5pm Sat Sun 11am–3pm
Services Restoration

The Wimborne Emporium
Contact Trisha Gurney
✉ **9 West Borough, Wimborne, Dorset, BH21 1LT** P
☎ 01202 882980
Est. 1999 *Stock size* Large
Stock Antiques and collectables
Open Mon–Sat 9am–5pm closed Tues Wed

SOMERSET

BATH

Abbey Galleries (NAG, NPA)
Contact Richard Dickson
✉ **9 Abbey Church Yard, Bath, Somerset, BA1 1LY**
☎ 01225 460565 F 01225 484192
Est. 1950 *Stock size* Large
Stock Jewellery, Oriental porcelain, silver
Open Mon–Sat 10.30am–5pm
Services Restoration

Aldridges of Bath
Contact Mr I Street
✉ **Newark House, 26–45 Cheltenham Street, Bath, Somerset, BA2 3EX** P
☎ 01225 462830 F 01225 311319
W www.invaluable.com/aldridges
Est. 1740
Open Mon–Fri 9am–5pm Sat 9am–noon
Sales All sales on Tues 10am,

Victorian and general sales fortnightly, specialist antiques sales 6–8 weeks, collectors' sales 6–8 weeks
Catalogues Yes

Antique Glass (BABAADA)
Contact Margaret Hopkins
33 Belvedere, Lansdown Road, Bath, Somerset, BA1 5HR
01225 312367 01225 312367
m.hopkins@antique-glass.co.uk
antique-glass.co.uk
Est. 1988 *Stock size* Medium
Stock Georgian glass, collectors' drinking glasses, rummers, ales, friggers, decanters, other curiosities
Open Tues–Sat 10am–6pm
Services Search

Antique Textiles and Lighting (BABAADA, BACA Award Winner 2002)
Contact Joanna Proops
34 Belvedere, Lansdown Road, Bath, Somerset, BA1 5HR
01225 310795 01225 443884
Est. 1970 *Stock size* Large
Stock Antique textiles, tapestries, samplers, Paisleys, fans, beadwork, linen, lace, wall and ceiling lighting, chandeliers
Open Tues–Sat 10am–5pm Sat 9am–1pm
Fairs Bath Decorative Fair
Services Valuations

Assembly Antiques Centre (BABAADA)
Contact Linda Brine
5–8 Saville Row, Bath, Somerset, BA1 SPF
01225 448488 01225 426288
www.assemblyantiques.co.uk
Est. 1969 *Stock size* Large
No. of dealers 5
Stock 18th–19thC furniture, lighting, chess sets, tea caddies, jewellery, scent bottles, porcelain
Open Tues–Sat 10am–5pm Wed 8am–5pm
Services Valuations, restoration, gemologist

Bartlett Street Antiques Centre (BABAADA)
5–10 Bartlett Street, Bath, Somerset, BA1 2QZ
01225 469998 01225 444146
Est. 1983 *Stock size* Large
No. of dealers 50 dealers + 70 show cases
Stock Antiques and collectables
Open Mon–Sat 9.30am–5pm Wed 8am–5pm
Services Restaurant

Bath Antiques Online
Contact Sue Turner
Unit 3, 14 Fountain Buildings, Lansdown Mews, Bath, Somerset, BA1 5DX
01225 311061 0117 9608 309
info@bathantiquesonline.com
www.bathantiquesonline.com
Est. 1998 *Stock size* Large
Stock Antiques and collectables
Open Mon–Sat 10am–4pm

Bath Antiquities Centre
Contact Antonia Kent
4 Bladud Buildings, Bath, Somerset, BA1 5LS
01225 316889 01225 316889
Est. 1998 *Stock size* Medium
No. of dealers 9
Stock Prehistoric, neolithic, medieval, Chinese, Greek, Egyptian antiques
Open Mon–Sat 9.30am–5pm

Bath Old Books (PBFA)
Contact Steven Ferdinando
9c Margaret's Buildings, Bath, Somerset, BA1 2LP
01225 422244
bathbooks@hotmail.com
Est. 1991 *Stock size* Medium
Stock Antiquarian and second-hand books
Open Mon–Sat 10am–5pm
Fairs PBFA
Services Valuations, book binding, book searches

George Bayntun (ABA)
Contact Mr Edward Bayntun-Coward
Manvers Street, Bath, Somerset, BA1 1JW
01225 466000 01225 482122
ebc@georgebayntun.com
www.georgebayntun.com
Est. 1894 *Stock size* Large
Stock Antiquarian and rare books, English literature first editions, fine bindings
Open Mon–Fri 9am–1pm 2–5.30pm Sat 9.30am–1pm
Services Valuations, binding service

Bedsteads (BABAADA)
Contact Nicola Ashton
2 Walcot Buildings, London Road, Bath, Somerset, BA1 6AD
01225 339182
www.bedsteads-uk.com
Est. 1990 *Stock size* Medium
Stock Antique bedsteads in iron, brass and exotic woods
Open Mon–Sat 10am–5.30pm Sun by appointment
Services Restoration

Bonhams
1 Old King Street, Bath, Somerset, BA1 2JT
01225 788988 01225 446675
bath@bonhams.com
www.bonhams.com
Open Mon–Fri 9am–5.30pm
Sales Regional Saleroom. Frequent sales. Regular house and attic sales across the country; contact London offices for further details. Free auction valuations; insurance and probate valuations
Catalogues Yes

Bonstow and Crawshay Antiques
Contact Simon Crawshay
46 Palace Avenue, Paignton, Devon, TQ3 3HF
01803 390850 01803 390850
07989 418592
bonstowandcrawshayantiques@talk21.com
Est. 1996 *Stock size* Medium
Stock Pre-1830 period English furniture, decorative items, marble, stonework, mirrors, sculpture
Open By appointment
Fairs West Point
Services Valuations, restoration

Le Boudoir
Contact Sue Turner
The Basement, George Street Antiques Centre, George Street, Bath, Somerset, BA1 2EE
01225 311061 0117 9608 309

WEST COUNTRY

suemarie@blueyonder.co.uk
www.le-boudoir-online.com
Est. 1988 *Stock size* Large
Stock Perfume bottles, dolls, decorative interior items, jewellery, Art Deco ceramics, Bakelite, petit point and beaded purses, decoupage materials and paper
Open Mon–Sat 9am–5pm
Wed 8am–5pm
Services Valuations, restoration of ceramics

Lawrence Brass
Apple Studio, Bath, Somerset, BA1 5YX
☎ 01225 852222
www.lawrencebrass.com
Est. 1973 *Stock size* Medium
Stock Furniture
Open Mon–Sat 9am–5pm
Services Valuations, restoration

Lynda Brine Antiques
Contact Lynda Brine
Assembly Antiques, 5–8 Saville Row, Bath, Somerset, BA1 2QP
☎ 01225 448488 Ⓕ 01225 429661
Ⓜ 07715 673716
lyndabrine@yahoo.com
www.scentbottlesandsmells.co.uk
Est. 1986 *Stock size* Large
Stock Perfume bottles, vinaigrettes, pomanders, objects of virtue, jewellery, silver
Open Tues–Sat 10am–5pm
Fairs NEC, USA
Services Valuations

Camden Books (PBFA)
Contact Victor or Elizabeth Suchar
146 Walcot Street, Bath, Somerset, BA1 5BL
☎ 01225 461606 Ⓕ 01225 461606
suchcam@msn.com
www.camdenbooks.com
Est. 1984 *Stock size* Large
Stock Antiquarian books, architecture, philosophy and science
Open Mon–Sat 10am–5pm
Fairs PBFA

Brian and Caroline Craik Ltd
Contact Mrs C Craik
8 Margarets Buildings, Bath, Somerset, BA1 2LP
☎ 01225 337161
Est. 1962 *Stock size* Medium
Stock General portable items, china and metalwork
Open Mon–Sat 10am–4pm (resident on premises)

Mary Cruz Antiques (LAPADA, CINOA, BABAADA)
Contact Ms M Cruz
5 Broad Street, Bath, Somerset, BA1 5LJ
☎ 01225 334174 Ⓕ 01225 423300
Est. 1974 *Stock size* Large
Stock 18th–19thC English and French furniture, 18th–20thC paintings, bronze and marble statues
Open Mon–Sat 10am–7pm
Services Valuations, restoration

D & B Dickinson (BADA, BABAADA)
Contact Mr Dickinson
22 New Bond Street, Bath, Somerset, BA1 1BA
☎ 01225 466502
www.dickinsonsilver.co.uk
Est. 1917 *Stock size* Large
Stock Silver, jewellery, silver plate
Open Mon–Sat 9.30am–1pm 2–5pm

Frank Dux Antiques (BABAADA)
Contact Mr F Dux
33 Belvedere, Lansdown Road, Bath, Somerset, BA1 5HR
☎ 01225 312367 Ⓕ 01225 312367
m.hopkins@antique-glass.co.uk
www.antique-glass.co.uk
Est. 1988 *Stock size* Medium
Stock 18th–19thC glass
Open Tues–Sat 10am–6pm
Services Search

Frogmore House Antiques
Contact Andrew Tinson
Bartlett Street Antique Centre, Bartlett Street, Bath, Somerset, BA1 2QZ
☎ 01225 445054 Ⓕ 01225 445054
Ⓜ 07976 225988
Est. 1976 *Stock size* Large
Stock Novelties, objects of virtue, silver, good smalls
Open Mon–Sat 9.30am–5pm
Wed trade day 8am–5pm
Fairs NEC, Newark

George Street Antique Centre
Contact Paul Kembery
8 Edgar Buildings, George Street, Bath, Somerset, BA1 2QZ
☎ 01225 422322
Ⓜ 07850 623237
kembery@kdclocks.co.uk
www.kdclocks.co.uk
Est. 2004 *Stock size* Small
No. of dealers 4
Stock Clocks, barometers, jewellery, music boxes, pocket watches, silver, porcelain
Open Mon–Sat 9.30am–5pm

Christina Grant
Contact Mr P Scott
Bartlett Street Antiques Centre, Bath, Somerset, BA1 2QZ
☎ 01225 310457 Ⓕ 01225 319821
Ⓜ 07850 639770
Est. 1981 *Stock size* Medium
Stock Antique prints, decorative items
Open Mon–Sat 9.30am–5pm

Jadis Antiques Ltd (BABAADA)
Contact Ms M Taylor
14 & 15 Walcot Buildings, London Road, Bath, Somerset, BA1 6AD
☎ 01225 333130 Ⓕ 01225 333130
Ⓜ 07768 232133
jadpalad@aol.com
www.jadis-ltd.com
Est. 1970 *Stock size* Large
Stock French furniture and decorative items
Open Mon–Sat 9.30am–6pm or by appointment
Fairs Bath Decorative and Antiques Fair
Services Design service, mural painting

Kembery Antique Clocks Ltd (BABAADA)
Contact Mr Paul Kembery
George Street Antique Centre, 8 Edgar Buildings, Bath, Somerset, BA1 2EE
☎ 0117 9565281 Ⓕ 0117 9565281
Ⓜ 07850 623237
kembery@kdclocks.co.uk
www.kdclocks.co.uk
Est. 1993 *Stock size* Medium
Stock Longcase, wall, mantel, bracket, carriage clocks and

barometers
Open Mon–Sat 9.30am–5pm
Fairs NEC
Services Valuations, restoration, shipping

⊞ Ann King Antique Clothes
Contact Mrs Ann King
✉ **38 Belvedere, Lansdown Road, Bath, Somerset, BA1 5HR** 🅿
☎ 01225 336245
Est. 1980 ***Stock size*** Medium
Stock Antique clothes, quilts, lace
Open Tues–Sat 10am–5pm
Services Valuations

⊞ Looking Glass of Bath
Contact Anthony Reed
✉ **94 Walcot Street, Bath, Somerset, BA1 5BG** 🅿
☎ 01225 461969 Ⓕ 01225 316191
Ⓜ 07831 323878
Ⓔ info@lookinglassofbath.co.uk
Ⓦ www.lookinglassofbath.co.uk
Est. 1968 ***Stock size*** Medium
Stock Antique and replica period mirrors, picture frames
Open Mon–Sat 9am–6pm
Fairs House & Garden Olympia
Services Valuations, restoration, shipping, manufacturers of mercury mirror plates

⊞ E P Mallory and Son Ltd (BADA)
Contact N Hall or P Mallory
✉ **1–4 Bridge Street, Bath, Somerset, BA2 4AP** 🅿
☎ 01225 788800 Ⓕ 01225 442210
Ⓔ mail@mallory-jewellers.com
Ⓦ www.mallory-jewellers.com
Est. 1898 ***Stock size*** Large
Stock Silver, jewellery
Open Mon–Sat 9.30am–5pm
Services Valuations

⊞ S Millard Antiques (BABAADA)
Contact Simon Millard
✉ **Bartlett Street Antiques Centre, 5–10 Bartlett Street, Bath, Somerset, BA1 2QZ** 🅿
☎ 01225 469785
Ⓔ tmillard@dircon.co.uk
Est. 1987 ***Stock size*** Medium
Stock Jewellery
Open Mon–Sun 10am–5pm Wed 8am–5pm

🏛 Old Bank Antiques Centre (BABAADA)
Contact David Moore
✉ **16, 17 & 20 Walcot Buildings, London Road, Bath, Somerset, BA1 6AD** 🅿
☎ 01225 469282/338813
Ⓔ alexatmontague@aol.com
Ⓦ www.oldbankantiquescentre.com
Est. 2002 ***Stock size*** Large
No. of dealers 9
Stock 17th–early 20thC English and Continental furniture, glass, ceramics, lighting, rugs, textiles, metalwork, paintings including English portraits
Open Mon–Sat 10am–6pm Wed 8am–6pm closed Thur Sun 11am–4pm
Services Valuations, shipping

⊞ The Orientalist
Contact Steve Lee
✉ **10 Argyle Street, Bath, Somerset, BA2 4BQ** 🅿
☎ 01225 469848 Ⓕ 01225 469849
Ⓜ 07932 189824
Ⓔ enquiries@theorientalist.com
Ⓦ www.theorientalist.com
Est. 2002 ***Stock size*** Large
Stock Oriental antiques
Open Mon–Sat 10am–4.30pm
Services Restoration

⊞ Patterson Liddle (ABA, PBFA)
Contact John Patterson or Steve Liddle
✉ **10 Margarets Buildings, Brock Street, Bath, Somerset, BA1 2LP** 🅿
☎ 01225 426722 Ⓕ 01225 426722
Ⓔ mail@pattersonliddle.com
Ⓦ www.pattersonliddle.com
Est. 1982 ***Stock size*** Medium
Stock Antiquarian and second-hand books
Open Mon–Sat 10am–5.30pm

⊞ Piccadilly Antiques (BABAADA)
Contact John Davies
✉ **280 High Street, Batheaston, Bath, Somerset, BA1 2QZ** 🅿
☎ 01225 851494 Ⓕ 01225 851120
Ⓜ 07785 966132
Ⓔ piccadillyantiques@ukonline.co.uk
Est. 2001 ***Stock size*** Medium
Stock English and French furniture, decorative accessories aimed at the US market
Open Mon–Sat 9.30am–5.30pm or by appointment
Fairs Bath Decorative and Antiques Fair

⊞ Quiet Street Antiques (BABAADA)
Contact Mr Kerry Hastings-Spital
✉ **14–15 John Street, Bath, Somerset, BA1 2JG** 🅿
☎ 01225 483003
Ⓜ 07860 818212
Ⓔ kerry@quietstreetantiques.co.uk
Ⓦ www.quietstreetantiques.co.uk
Est. 1985 ***Stock size*** Large
Stock 18th–19thC furniture, clocks, tea caddies, boxes, mirrors, Royal Worcester, works of art
Open Mon–Sat 10am–6pm
Services Valuations, free delivery within 100 miles, export services

⊞ Quiet Street Antiques (BABAADA)
Contact Mr Kerry Hastings-Spital
✉ **3 Quiet Street, Bath, Somerset, BA1 2JS** 🅿
☎ 01225 315727 Ⓕ 01225 448300
Ⓜ 07860 818212
Ⓔ kerry@quietstreetantiques.co.uk
Ⓦ www.quietstreetantiques.co.uk
Est. 1985 ***Stock size*** Large
Stock 18th–19thC furniture, clocks, tea caddies, boxes, mirrors, Royal Worcester, works of art
Open Mon–Sat 10am–6pm
Services Valuations, free delivery within 100 miles, export services

⊞ Roland Gallery (BABAADA)
Contact Mike Pettitt
✉ **33 Monmouth Street, Bath, BA1 2AN** 🅿
☎ 01225 312330/319464
Ⓕ 01225 312330
Ⓜ 07889 723272
Ⓔ therolandgallery@aol.com
Est. 2000 ***Stock size*** Large
Stock Eclectic mix of 20thC design including silver, ivory, decorative items, paintings
Open Wed–Sat 11am–4pm or by appointment
Fairs NEC Birmingham, Newark, Sandown Park

⊞ Michael Saffell Antiques (BABAADA)
Contact Mr M Saffell
✉ **3 Walcot Buildings, London Road, Bath, Somerset,**

BA1 6AD 🅿
☎ 01225 315857 ⓕ 01225 315857
Ⓜ 07941 158049
ⓔ michael.saffell@virgin.net
Est. 1975 *Stock size* Medium
Stock Advertising items, British tins (biscuit, tobacco, confectionery, mustard etc), decorative items
Open Mon–Fri 9am–5pm (telephone in advance) or by appointment
Fairs Newark, Bath Antiques & Decorative Fair
Services Valuations

⊞ Tim Snell Antiques (BABAADA)
Contact Tim Snell
✉ **5–6 Cleveland Terrace, Bath, Somerset, BA1 5DF**
☎ 01225 423045 ⓕ 01225 423045
Est. 1979 *Stock size* Large
Stock 19th–20thC oak furniture, Arts and Crafts
Open Fri–Sat 10am–5pm
Services Valuations, restoration, house clearances

⊞ Source (BABAADA)
Contact Mr R Donaldson
✉ **11 Claverton Buildings, High Street, Widcombe, Bath, Somerset, BA2 4LD** 🅿
☎ 01225 469200
ⓦ www.source-antiques.co.uk
Est. 1978 *Stock size* Medium
Stock Architectural antiques and lights including 1950s aluminium kitchens
Open Tues–Sat 10am–5pm
Fairs Bath Decorative and Antiques Fair
Services Valuations

⊞ Susannah (BABAADA, The Textiles Society)
Contact Mrs S Holley
✉ **25 Broad Street, Bath, Somerset, BA1 5LW** 🅿
☎ 01225 445069 ⓕ 01225 339004
Est. 1989 *Stock size* Medium
Stock General, decorative items, textiles
Open Mon–Sat 10am–5pm please telephone in advance
Fairs Bath Decorative and Antiques Fair, Kensington Brocante, The Textiles Society Fair in Manchester

⊞ James Townshend Antiques (BABAADA)
Contact Mr Townshend
✉ **1 Saville Row, Bath, Somerset, BA1 2QP** 🅿
☎ 01225 332290 ⓕ 01225 332290
Ⓜ 01225 332290
ⓔ sales@jtownshendantiques.co.uk
ⓦ www.jtownshendantiques.co.uk
Stock size Large
Stock 19thC furniture, decorative items, mirrors
Open Mon–Sat 10am–5pm
Fairs Kempton
Services Valuations, restoration

⊞ Vintage to Vogue (BABAADA)
Contact Teresa Langton
✉ **28 Milsom Street (entry in the passage off Broad Street car park), Bath, Somerset, BA1 1DG** 🅿
☎ 01225 337323
ⓦ www.vintagetovogue.com
Est. 1994 *Stock size* Large
Stock 1850s–1950s period clothing and accessories, costume lace, white linens
Open Tues–Sat 10.30am–5pm

⊞ Walcot Reclamation Ltd (BABAADA)
Contact Rick Knapp
✉ **108 Walcot Street, Bath, Somerset, BA1 5BG** 🅿
☎ 01225 444404 ⓕ 01225 448163
ⓔ rick@walcot.com
ⓦ www.walcot.com
Est. 1975 *Stock size* Large
Stock Architectural antiques including bathrooms, radiators, fireplaces, garden furniture and reproductions of hard-to-find items
Open Mon–Fri 9am–5.30pm Sat 9am–5pm
Fairs The Country Living Fairs, Business Design Centre Islington (spring)
Services Restoration of marble, stone and old radiators

⊞ Waterfall Antiques (BABAADA)
Contact Mr or Mrs R D Waterfall
✉ **57 Walcot Street, Bath, Somerset, BA1 5BN** 🅿
☎ 01225 444201
Ⓜ 07990 690240
Est. 1991 *Stock size* Medium
Stock Georgian, Victorian and early 20thC furniture and collectables
Open Mon–Sat 10.30am–5.30pm
Services Deliveries

BITTON

⊞ Barrow Lodge Antiques
Contact Derek Wookey
✉ **Kings Square, Bitton, Bristol, BS30 6HR** 🅿
☎ 0117 9324205
Ⓜ 07836 293993
Est. 1975 *Stock size* Large
Stock Furniture
Open By appointment
Fairs Newark, Ardingly
Services Restoration, stripping

BLACKFORD

⊞ L D Watts
Contact L D Watts
✉ **Blackford County Old Primary School, Sexey's Road, Blackford, Wedmore, Somerset, BS28 4NX** 🅿
☎ 01934 712372
Est. 1970 *Stock size* Medium
Stock 18th–19thC furniture
Open By appointment
Services Valuations

BRIDGWATER

Tamlyn and Son
Contact Julie Howard
✉ **56 High Street, Bridgwater, Somerset, TA6 3BN** 🅿
☎ 01278 445251/458241 ⓕ 01278 458242
Ⓜ 07850 335928
ⓔ saleroom@tamlynandson.co.uk
ⓦ www.tamlynandson.co.uk
Est. 1893
Open Mon–Fri 9am–5.30pm
Sales Antiques and general sales monthly, 2 catalogue sales per annum May and Nov, viewing day before sale
Catalogues Yes

BRISTOL

⊞ A & C Antique Clocks (BWCG)
Contact Mr David Andrews
✉ **The Clock Shop, 86 Bryants Hill, Hanham, Bristol, BS5 8QT** 🅿
☎ 0117 947 6141

Ⓔ info@antiquecorner.org.uk
Ⓦ www.antiquecorner.org.uk
Est. 1992 *Stock size* Large
Stock Clocks, barometers
Open Tues Thur Fri Sat please telephone for hours
Services Clock repair service, valuations, restoration, shipping

The Antiques Warehouse Ltd (RADS)
Contact Chris Winsor
430 Gloucester Road, Horfield, Bristol, BS7 8TX Ⓟ
☎ 0117 942 4500 Ⓕ 0117 942 4140
Ⓔ chriswinsor@theantiqueswarehouseltd.co.uk
Ⓦ www.theantiqueswarehouseltd.co.uk
Est. 1994 *Stock size* Large
Stock Georgian–Edwardian and post-Edwardian furniture, carpets, mirrors
Open Tues–Sun 11am–5pm
Services Valuations, restoration and upholstery

Arcadia Antiques & Interiors
Contact Julia Irish
4 Boyces Avenue, Clifton, Bristol, BS8 4AA
☎ 0117 914 4479 Ⓕ 0117 923 9308
Ⓔ r.irish@phoenix-net.co.uk
Est. 1994 *Stock size* Small
Stock Furniture, collectables, upholstery, prints, paintings
Open Mon–Sat 10am–5.30pm

Aristocratz
Contact Mr Zaid
115 Coldharbour Road, Redlands, Bristol, BS6 7SD Ⓟ
☎ 0117 904 0091
Ⓜ 07770 393020
Ⓦ www.aristocratz.co.uk
Est. 1980 *Stock size* Medium
Stock General antiques
Open Mon–Sat 10am–5pm
Fairs Newark, Ardingly
Services Valuations, shipping

Au Temps Perdu (SALVO)
Contact Mr or Mrs Chapman
28-30 Midland Road, St Phillips, Bristol, BS2 0JY Ⓟ
☎ 0117 929 9143
Ⓔ autempsperdu@autempsperdu.com
Ⓦ www.autempsperdu.com
Est. 1980 *Stock size* Medium
Stock Architectural antiques
Open Tues–Sat 10am–5pm

Gloria Barnes of Clifton Antiques Centre
Contact Gloria Barnes
The Clifton Antiques Centre, 18 The Mall, Clifton, Bristol, BS8 4DR Ⓟ
☎ 0117 973 7843
Est. 1979 *Stock size* Medium
Stock Russell Flint prints, paintings, Indian art, stone jewellery
Open Tues–Sat 10am–6pm
Services Valuations

The Bed Workshop
Contact Dr Scott Jones
The Old Pickle Factory, Braunton Road, Bristol, BS3 3AA Ⓟ
☎ 0117 963 6659
Ⓔ thebedworkshop@aol.com
Est. 1981 *Stock size* Large
Stock French antique furniture
Open Mon–Sat 9.30am–6pm

Bedsteads (BABAADA)
Contact Nicola Ashton
15 Regent Street, Clifton, Bristol, BS8 4HW Ⓟ
☎ 0117 923 9181 Ⓕ 0117 923 9181
Ⓦ www.bedsteads-uk.com
Est. 1990 *Stock size* Medium
Stock Antique bedsteads in iron, brass and exotic woods
Open Mon 11.30am–5.30pm Tues–Sat 10am–6pm
Services Restoration

Bishopston Books
Contact Bill Singleton
259 Gloucester Road, Bishopston, Bristol, BS7 8NY Ⓟ
☎ 0117 944 5303
Ⓔ bishopstonbook@btinternet.com
Est. 1993 *Stock size* Small
Stock Antiquarian and second-hand books
Open Thurs Fri 10am–5.30pm Sat 9.30am–4.30pm
Services Book search

Bristol Bookbarn
Contact Mr Belton
Central Trading Estate, (A4 at Amos Vale, Brislington), Bristol, Somerset, BS4 3EH Ⓟ
☎ 01173 005400
Ⓔ bookbarn@bookbarn.co.uk
Ⓦ www.bookbarn.co.uk
Est. 1997 *Stock size* Large
Stock Antiquarian and second-hand books
Open Mon–Sun 10am–6pm

Bristol Brocante
Contact David or Elizabeth Durant
123 St Georges Road, College Green, Hotwells, Bristol, BS1 5UW Ⓟ
☎ 0117 909 6688
Est. 1970 *Stock size* Large
Stock French antiques
Open Mon–Sat 11am–6pm
Fairs Newark, Kensington Brocante (Sep), Sandown Park Fair (Oct)

Bristol Trade Antiques
Contact Mr L Dyke
192 Cheltenham Road, Bristol, BS6 5RB Ⓟ
☎ 0117 942 2790
Est. 1969 *Stock size* Medium
Stock Victorian and Edwardian furniture
Open Mon–Sat 9am–5.30pm
Services Valuations, exports to the USA

Caledonia Antiques
Contact Mrs M T Kerridge
6 The Mall, Clifton, Bristol, BS8 4DR Ⓟ
☎ 0117 974 3582 Ⓕ 0117 946 7997
Ⓜ 07810 401261
Est. 1981 *Stock size* Medium
Stock Jewellery and silver
Open Mon–Sat 10am–5.30pm

Circle Books
Contact Mr Mike Piddock
65 North Street, Bedminster, Bristol, BS3 1ES Ⓟ
☎ 0117 966 2622
Est. 1999 *Stock size* Medium
Stock Antiquarian, second-hand, rare and out-of-print books
Open Mon–Sat 10am–5.30pm
Services Valuations, café in shop

Clifton Antique Centre
Contact Mrs Barnes or Marlene Risdale
18 The Mall, Clifton, Bristol, BS8 4DR Ⓟ
☎ 0117 973 7843

Est. 1965 *Stock size* Large
No. of dealers 6
Stock Silver, silver plate, paintings, clocks, ceramics, Moorcroft
Open Tues–Sat 10am–6pm
Services Valuations

Clifton Hill Textiles
Contact Mrs Hodder
4 Lower Clifton Hill, Clifton, Bristol, BS8 1BT
0117 929 0644
cliftex@yahoo.com
www.cliftext.freeserve.co.uk
Est. 1984 *Stock size* Large
Stock Textiles, buttons, buckles
Open Mon–Sat 10am–5pm
Services Valuations

Cotham Antiques
Contact Susan Miller
39a Cotham Hill, Cotham, Bristol, BS6 6JZ
0117 973 3326
Est. 1983 *Stock size* Medium
Stock General
Open Tues–Sat 10.30am–5.30pm
Services Friendly advice

Cotham Galleries
Contact Mr D Jury
22 Cotham Hill, Bristol, BS6 6LF
0117 973 6026
07885 166811
Est. 1969 *Stock size* Medium
Stock General
Open Mon–Fri 9am–5.30pm
Sat 10am–noon
Services Valuations, restoration

Dreweatt Neate Bristol Salerooms (SOFAA)
Contact Edward Chetwynd
St John's Place, Apsley Road, Clifton, Bristol, BS8 2ST
0117 973 7201 0117 973 5671
bristol@dnfa.com
www.dnfa.com
Est. 1759
Open Mon–Fri 8.45am–6pm
Sales Antiques and decorative items. Monthly sale Tues 10.30am, viewing Sat 9.30am–1pm Mon 9.30am–7pm day of sale from 9am. General sale alternate Thurs at Baynton Road, Ashton, Bristol. Collectors sale bi-monthly at Baynton Road. Catalogues available on website
Catalogues Yes

Dreweatt Neate Bristol Salerooms (SOFAA)
Contact Edward Chetwynd
Saleroom 2, Baynton Road, Ashton, Bristol, BS3 2EB
0117 953 1603 0117 953 1598
bristol@dnfa.com
www.dnfa.com
Est. 1759
Open Mon–Fri 8.45am–6pm
Sales Victorian and modern furniture and effects sale, Thurs 10.30am, viewing Wed 11am–6pm day of sale from 9am
Frequency Fortnightly
Catalogues Yes

K Faulkner
Contact Kenneth Faulkner
The Club Shop, Gloucestershire County Cricket Club, Neville Road, Bristol, BS9 EJ
0117 910 8020
kfaulkner@bowmore.demon.co.uk
www.bowmore.demon.co.uk
Est. 1995 *Stock size* Medium
Stock Sporting memorabilia, specializing in cricket
Open Mon–Fri 9am–5pm
Sat 9am–1pm
Services Valuations, mail order

Focus on the Past
Contact Mrs Alison Roylance
25 Waterloo Street, Clifton, Bristol, BS8 4BT
0117 973 8080
Est. 1978 *Stock size* Large
Stock Furniture, pine, kitchenware, china, glass and books, jewellery, 20thC collectables
Open Mon–Sat 9.30am–5.30pm
Sun 11am–5.30pm
Fairs Ardingly, Newark

Grey-Harris & Co
Contact Mr Grey-Harris
12 Princess Victoria Street, Clifton, Bristol, BS8 4BP
0117 973 7365
Est. 1969 *Stock size* Large
Stock Antique jewellery, silver
Open Mon–Sat 9am–6pm
Services Valuations, restoration

Grimes Militaria
Contact Christopher or Hazel Grimes
13–14 Lower Park Row, Bristol, BS1 5BN
0117 929 8205
Est. 1967 *Stock size* Medium
Stock Scientific instruments, nautical memorabilia, militaria
Open Mon–Sat 11am–6pm
Fairs Exeter (Marsh Barton), Shepton Mallet, Newark
Services Valuations

Margaret R Jubb
Contact Mrs Jubb
6 The Clifton Arcade, Boyces Avenue, Clifton, Bristol, BS8 4AA
0117 973 3105
07974 095554
maggs@kenmoor.demon.co.uk
www.kenmoor.demon.co.uk/antiques
Est. 1974 *Stock size* Medium
Stock General antiques
Open Mon–Fri 11am–5pm
Sat 11.30am–5pm
Services Valuations

David & Sally March Antiques (LAPADA, CINOA)
Contact David March
Oak Wood Lodge, Stoke Leigh Woods, Abbots Leigh, Bristol, BS8 3QB
01275 372422 01275 372422
07774 838376
david.march@lineone.net
Est. 1973 *Stock size* Medium
Stock 18thC English porcelain figures, Plymouth and Bristol a speciality
Open By appointment only
Fairs LAPADA, NEC, Olympia
Services Valuations

Marlenes
Contact Marlene Risdale
Clifton Antiques Centre, 23 The Mall, Clifton, Bristol, BS8 4DR
0117 973 7645
Est. 1958 *Stock size* Medium
Stock Silver, jewellery
Open Tues–Sat 10am–6pm
Fairs Sandown, Stafford
Services Valuations

Robert Mills Architectural Antiques (SALVO)
Contact Colin Scull
Narroways Road, Eastville, Bristol, BS2 9XB

☎ 0117 955 6542 Ⓕ 0117 955 8146
Ⓔ sales@rmills.co.uk
Ⓦ www.rmills.co.uk
Est. 1970 *Stock size* Large
Stock Architectural antiques including Gothic church fittings, stained glass, pub interiors, fittings
Open Mon–Fri 9am–5pm

Jan Morrison
Contact Jan Morrison
✉ **3 Clifton Arcade, Boyces Avenue, Clifton, Bristol, BS8 4AA** Ⓟ
☎ 0117 970 6822 Ⓕ 0117 970 6822
Ⓜ 07789 094428
Est. 1979 *Stock size* Medium
Stock 18th–19thC glass and silver, modern jewellery
Open Tues–Sat 10am–5.30pm
Services Valuations

Oldwoods
Contact Sid Duck
✉ **4 Colston Yard, Bristol, BS1 5BD** Ⓟ
☎ 0117 929 9023
Est. 1982 *Stock size* Small
Stock Victorian and pine furniture, decorative items
Open Mon–Fri 10am-5pm or by appointment
Services Restoration

Olliff's Architectural Antiques (SALVO)
Contact Marcus Olliff
✉ **19–21 Lower Redland Road, Redland, Bristol, BS6 6TB** Ⓟ
☎ 0117 923 9232 Ⓕ 0117 923 9880
Ⓜ 07850 235793
Ⓔ marcus@olliffs.com
Ⓦ www.olliffs.com
Est. 1993 *Stock size* Large
Stock Georgian–Edwardian marble, stone and timber fireplaces, garden statuary, garden decorative items, doors, door furniture, stone doorways and windows, gates, lighting, mirrors, oak flooring
Open Fri–Sat 10am–5pm or by appointment
Services Valuations, restoration, shipping

Pastimes (OMRS)
Contact Mr A H Stevens
✉ **22 Lower Park Row, Bristol, BS1 5BN** Ⓟ
☎ 0117 929 9330
Est. 1974 *Stock size* Large
Stock Militaria
Open Mon–Sat 10.30am–1.45pm 2.45–5pm Wed 11am–5pm
Fairs Mark Carter Fairs
Services Medal mounting

Period Fireplaces
Contact John Ashton
✉ **The Old Station Building, Station Road, Montpelier, Bristol, BS6 5EE** Ⓟ
☎ 0117 944 4449 Ⓕ 0117 942 4091
Ⓔ enquiries@periodfireplaces.co.uk
Ⓦ www.periodfireplaces.co.uk
Est. 1984 *Stock size* Large
Stock Fireplaces
Open Mon–Fri 9am–5pm Sat 10am–4pm
Services Restoration

Piano Export
Contact Mr T W Smallridge
✉ **Bridge Road, Kingswood, Bristol, BS15 4FW** Ⓟ
☎ 0117 956 8300
Est. 1982 *Stock size* Medium
Stock Grand pianos – Steinway, Bechstein and decorative pianos
Open Mon–Fri 8am–5pm or by appointment

Porchester Antiques
Contact Mrs Devonia Andrews
✉ **58 The Mall, Clifton, Bristol, BS8 4JG** Ⓟ
☎ 0117 373 0256 Ⓕ 01275 810629
Ⓜ 07970 970449
Ⓔ devonia@porchester-collectables.co.uk
Ⓦ www.porchester-collectables.co.uk
Est. 1978 *Stock size* Medium
Stock Moorcroft, enamels and pottery, Sally Tuffin pottery, fine jewellery
Open Tues–Sat 10am–6pm
Services Valuations

Pride & Joy Antiques
Contact Martin Williams
✉ **25 North View, Westbury Park, Bristol, BS6 7SD** Ⓟ
☎ 0117 973 5806
Est. 1994 *Stock size* Medium
Stock Victorian–Edwardian furniture
Open Mon–Sat 10.30am–1pm 2–5pm
Services Upholstery

Raw Deluxe
Contact Mr J Stewart
✉ **148 Gloucester Road, Bishopston, Bristol, BS7 8NT** Ⓟ
☎ 0117 942 6998
Est. 1998 *Stock size* Medium
Stock General antiques, collectables
Open Thurs–Sat 10am–5pm
Services Restoration

Vincents of Clifton
Contact Paul Risdale
✉ **Clifton Antique Centre, 18 The Mall, Clifton, Bristol, BS8 4DR** Ⓟ
☎ 0117 973 7645
Est. 1984 *Stock size* Medium
Stock Jewellery, silver and gold
Open Tues–Sat 10am–6pm
Fairs Cheltenham, Sandown and Stafford

Whiteladies Antiques & Collectables
Contact Sylvia Skerritt
✉ **49c Whiteladies Road, Clifton, Bristol, BS8 2LS** Ⓟ
☎ 0117 973 5766
Est. 2001 *Stock size* Large
No. of dealers 25
Stock Antiques and collectables, small furniture
Open Mon–Sat 10.30am–5pm

BRUTON

The Antiques Shop Bruton
Contact David Gwilliam
✉ **5 High Street, Bruton, Somerset, BA10 0AB** Ⓟ
☎ 01749 813264
Est. 1976 *Stock size* Medium
Stock Furniture, brass, copper, jewellery, silver, china and collectables
Open Thurs–Sat 10am–5.30pm
Services Jewellery repairs, restringing, watch, clock repairs

European Accent
Contact Steve Green
✉ **Station Road, Bruton, Somerset, BA10 0EH** Ⓟ
☎ 01749 814961 Ⓕ 01749 814962
Ⓜ 07977 496762
Ⓔ enquiries@europeanaccent.co.uk
Ⓦ www.europeanaccent.co.uk

Est. 1998 *Stock size* Medium
Stock Country decorative, painted, pine and fruitwood furniture, smalls
Open Mon–Fri 8.30am–5.30pm or by appointment
Fairs Newark, Shepton Mallet
Services Valuations

Michael Lewis Gallery
Contact Mrs J L Lewis
17 High Street, Bruton, Somerset, BA10 0AB
01749 813557
Est. 1980 *Stock size* Large
Stock Antiquarian maps and prints
Open Mon–Sat 9.30am–5.30pm closed Thurs 1pm

M G R Exports
Contact Mr M Read
Station Road, Bruton, Somerset, BA10 0EH
01749 812460 F 01749 812882
E enquiries@mgrexports.co.uk
W www.mgrexports.co.uk
Est. 1979 *Stock size* Large
Stock General
Open Mon–Fri 8.30am–5.30pm Sat 9am–1pm for trade
Services Packing, shipping and containers packed

BURNHAM-ON-SEA

Adams Auctions
Contact Mrs R Combes
28 Adam Street, Burnham-on-Sea, Somerset, TA8 1PQ
01278 793709 F 01278 793709
Est. 1993
Open Mon–Sat 10am–1pm
Sales Antique and general sales monthly Wed 6pm, viewing Tues 2–6pm Wed 10am–6pm
Catalogues Yes

The Burnham Model & Collectors Shop
Contact W Loudon
3 College Court, College Street, Burnham-on-Sea, Somerset, TA8 1AR
01278 780066 F 01278 780066
Est. 1994 *Stock size* Large
Stock Ephemera, postcards, banknotes, coins, medals, die-cast models, cigarette cards
Open Mon–Sat 9.30am–5pm
Services Valuations

Heape's
Contact Mrs M Heap
39 Victoria Street, Burnham-on-Sea, Somerset, TA8 1AN
01278 782131 F 01278 782131
Est. 1988 *Stock size* Large
Stock Porcelain, silverware, fine art, glass, collectables
Open Tues Thurs–Sat 10am–4.30pm Wed 10am–1pm
Services Bespoke framing, hand-made lampshades, specialist table lamps

CASTLE CARY

Antiquus
Contact Gerald Davison
West Country House, Woodcock Street, Castle Cary, Somerset, BA7 7BJ
01963 351246
M 07968 810092
W www.chinesemarks.com
Est. 2002 *Stock size* Medium
Stock English and Oriental antiques
Open Tues Fri Sat 10am–5pm
Services Lectures on Chinese ceramics

Johnsons Antiques
Contact Nicholas Johnson
7 Pithers Yard, Castle Cary, Somerset, BA7 7AN
01963 351530 F 01963 351030
Est. 1865 *Stock size* Medium
Stock Interesting and wacky objects
Open Tues–Sun 9.30am–4pm

Pandora's Box
Contact Mrs Liz Thring
Fore Street, Castle Cary, Somerset, BA7 7BG
01963 350926
Est. 1988 *Stock size* Medium
Stock Furniture, quilts, textiles and decorative items
Open Tues–Sat 10am–5pm

CHARD

Chard Antiques Centre
Contact Julie Hills or Alistair Smith
23 High Street, Chard, Somerset, TA20 1QF
01460 63517
E julie@chardantiques.fsnet.co.uk
Est. 1997 *Stock size* Medium
No. of dealers 7
Stock General antiques, furniture, ceramics and decorative items
Open Mon–Sat 10am–5pm or by appointment

CHEDDAR

Matthew Bayly Antiques
Contact Matthew Bayly
Mark Hole Cottage, The Cliffs, Cheddar, Somerset, BS27 3QH
01934 743990
Est. 1972 *Stock size* Small
Stock General small antiques
Open By appointment
Services Valuations, restoration

Cheddar Antiques & Upholstery
Contact Joy Maloney
Barrows House, Tweentown, Cheddar, Somerset, BS27 3HU
01934 744816 F 01934 744816
Est. 1976 *Stock size* Medium
Stock Antique upholstered chairs, chaises longues, Victorian furniture, Art Deco, ceramics, china, glass
Open Tues–Sat 10am–6.30pm

CHILCOMPTON

Billiard Room Antiques (LAPADA, BABAADA, CINOA)
Contact Mrs J Mckeivor
The Old School, Church Lane, Chilcompton, Bath, Somerset, BA3 4HP
01761 232839 F 01761 232839
E info@billiardroom.co.uk
W www.billiardroom.co.uk
Est. 1990 *Stock size* Medium
Stock Billiard room furnishings
Open By appointment only
Fairs Olympia
Services Valuations, restoration and shipping

CHIPPING SODBURY

Sodbury Antiques
Contact Millicent Brown
70 Broad Street,

Chipping Sodbury, Bristol,
BS37 6AG P
☎ 01454 273369 F 01454 273369
Est. 1989 *Stock size* Medium
Stock China, jewellery and bric-a-brac
Open Mon–Sat 9.30am–5.30pm closed Wed

CLEVEDON

Clevedon Books (PBFA)
Contact Mr or Mrs Douthwaite
✉ **The Gallery, 29 Copse Road, Clevedon, Somerset, BS21 7QN** P
☎ 01275 790579/872304
F 01275 342817
E clevedonbooks@globalnet.co.uk
Est. 1970 *Stock size* Medium
Stock Antiquarian books, maps and prints, second-hand books, history, science and technology a speciality
Open Thurs–Sat 11am–4.30pm
Fairs PBFA
Services Print and map colouring

Clevedon Salerooms
Contact Marc Burridge
✉ **The Auction Centre, Kenn Road, Kenn, Clevedon, Somerset, BS21 6TT** P
☎ 01275 876699 F 01275 343765
E clevedon-salerooms@blueyonder.co.uk
W www.clevedon-salerooms.com
Est. 1880
Open Mon–Fri 9am–5.30pm
Sales Fine art and antiques sales, Thurs 10.30am, viewing Tues 2–5.30pm Wed 10am–6.30pm 9am morning of sale. Fortnightly sales of Victorian and later household furniture, effects, Thurs 10am, viewing Wed 10am–7.30pm morning of sale 9am
Catalogues Yes

The Collector
Contact Malcolm or Tina Simmonds
✉ **14 The Beach, Clevedon, Somerset, BS21 7QU** P
☎ 01275 875066
Est. 1992 *Stock size* Small
Stock Smalls and collectables including Beatrix Potter figures
Open Mon–Sat 10am–5pm Sun noon–5pm closed Thurs
Fairs Malvern Three Counties, Brunel Temple Meads, Bristol
Services Valuations

Nostalgia
Contact Wendy Moore
✉ **65a Hill Road, Clevedon, Somerset, BS21 7PD** P
☎ 01275 342587
Est. 1984 *Stock size* Medium
Stock General antiques including linen, furniture, china
Open Tues–Sat 10am–4.30pm
Services House calls to buy

COXLEY

Mrs Mitchell
Contact Mrs Mitchell
✉ **Clover Close House, Main Road, Coxley, Somerset, BA5 1QZ** P
☎ 01749 679533
Est. 1984 *Stock size* Medium
Stock General antiques
Open Mon–Sat 9am–5pm
Services Valuations, caning and upholstery

CREWKERNE

Antiques and Country Pine
Contact Mrs Wheeler
✉ **14 East Street, Crewkerne, Somerset, TA18 7AG** P
☎ 01460 75623
Est. 1979 *Stock size* Medium
Stock Antique and country pine furniture
Open Tues–Sat 10am–5pm

Books Galore
Contact Mrs Hall
✉ **The Old Warehouse, North Street, Crewkerne, Somerset, TA18 7AJ** P
☎ 01460 74465 F 01460 74465
M 07957 986053
E hallbook@aol.com
Est. 1969 *Stock size* Large
Stock Second-hand books, countryside topics a speciality
Open Mon–Sat 10am–1pm 2.30–5pm
Services Book search

Crewkerne Antiques
Contact Eddie Blewden
✉ **16 Market Street, Crewkerne, Somerset, TA18 7LA** P
☎ 01460 77111 F 01460 77111
Est. 1991 *Stock size* Large
No. of dealers 50
Stock General antiques, garden section
Open Mon–Sat 9.30am–4.30pm
Services Valuations

Gresham Books (PBFA, ABA)
Contact James Hine
✉ **31 Market Street, Crewkerne, Somerset, TA18 7JU** P
☎ 01460 77726 F 01460 52479
E jameshine@gresham-books.demon.co.uk
Est. 1972 *Stock size* Large
Stock Antiquarian and second-hand books including early cookery and architectural
Open Mon–Sat 10am–5pm
Fairs London Bookfair (monthly), most major book fairs (phone for details)
Services Valuations

Lawrence Fine Art Auctioneers Ltd (ARVA, SOFAA)
Contact Leah Ferguson
✉ **4 Linen Yard, South Street, Crewkerne, Somerset, TA18 8AB** P
☎ 01460 73041 F 01460 270799
E enquiries@lawrences.co.uk
W www.lawrences.co.uk
Est. 1900
Open Mon–Fri 9am–5pm
Sales 5 fine art sales a year. General household sale every Wed 9.30am, viewing Tues 9.30am–7pm
Catalogues Yes

Noah's
Contact Mrs Edmonds
✉ **41 Market Square, Crewkerne, Somerset, TA18 7LP** P
☎ 01460 77786
Est. 2001 *Stock size* Medium
Stock Fine art and antiques, silver, jewellery
Open Mon–Sat 10am–4.30pm
Services Valuations

Phoenix Books
Contact Dennis Hann
✉ **5 The George Precinct, Crewkerne, Somerset,**

TA18 7LU 🅿
☎ 01460 76579
Est. 1990 *Stock size* Medium
Stock Antiquarian and second-hand books, crime, modern first editions
Open Mon–Sat 10am–5pm

CROWCOMBE

Newmans (BAFRA)
Contact Tony Newman
Tithe Barn, Crowcombe, Somerset, TA4 4AQ 🅿
Ⓜ 07970 252518
Ⓔ tony@cheddon.fsnet.co.uk
Est. 1991 *Stock size* Small
Stock 18th–19thC furniture
Open Sun–Mon 9am–5pm or by appointment
Services Valuations, restoration

DULVERTON

Acorn Antiques
Contact Peter Hounslow
39 High Street, Dulverton, Somerset, TA22 9DW 🅿
☎ 01398 323286
Ⓔ Peter@exmoorantiques.co.uk
Ⓦ www.exmoorantiques.co.uk
Est. 1988 *Stock size* Medium
Stock 18th–19thC furniture, decorative items and general antiques
Trade only Yes
Open Mon–Sat 9.30am–5.30pm or Sun by appointment
Services Interior design

Guy Dennler Antiques
Contact Mr G Dennler
The White Hart, 23 High Street, Dulverton, Somerset, TA22 9HB
☎ 01398 324300 Ⓕ 01398 324301
Ⓔ guydennler@btconnect.com
Est. 1979 *Stock size* Medium
Stock 18th–19thC English furniture, decorative items
Open Mon–Fri 10am–5pm or by appointment
Fairs Battersea Decorative Fair
Services Restoration, interior design

Out Of The Blue
Contact Finny or Nigel Muers-Raby
4 Fore Street, Dulverton, Somerset, PA22 9EX 🅿
☎ 01398 324155
Est. 2001 *Stock size* Medium
Stock Decorative items
Open Tues–Sat 10.30am–4pm

Anthony Sampson
Contact Mr A Sampson
Holland House, Bridge Street, Dulverton, Somerset, TA22 9HJ 🅿
☎ 01398 324247
Ⓜ 07767 842409
Est. 1968 *Stock size* Medium
Stock Furniture, general antiques
Open Mon–Sat 9.30am–5.30pm Sun by appointment
Services Valuations

DUNSTER

The Crooked Window
Contact Robert Ricketts
7 High Street, Dunster, Somerset, TA24 6SF 🅿
☎ 01643 821606
Ⓜ 07787 722606
Ⓔ thecrookedwindow@supanet.com
Est. 1987 *Stock size* Medium
Stock 17th–18thC English furniture, Chinese and European ceramics and works of art, including jade
Open Mon–Sat 10am–5.30pm
Fairs Wilton House
Services Valuations

The Linen Press
Contact Anne Fisher
22 Church Street, Dunster, Somerset, TA24 6SH 🅿
☎ 01643 821802
Est. 1986 *Stock size* Large
Stock Antique and new English and French linen and textiles
Open Mon–Sun 10.30am–5pm
Services Mail order

EAST PENNARD

Cottage Collectibles
Contact Mrs S Kettle
2 Pennard House, East Pennard, Somerset, BA4 6TP 🅿
☎ 01749 860266 Ⓕ 01749 860732
Ⓜ 07967 713512
Ⓔ sheila@cottagecollectibles.co.uk
Ⓦ www.cottagecollectibles.co.uk
Est. 1995 *Stock size* Medium
Stock English and Continental country antiques, kitchenware, pine furniture, garden and dairy tools
Open Mon–Sat 10am–5pm
Services Restoration

Pennard House Antiques (BABAADA, LAPADA)
Contact Martin Dearden
East Pennard, Shepton Mallet, Somerset, BA4 6TP 🅿
☎ 01749 860731 Ⓕ 01749 860732
Ⓜ 07802 243569
Ⓔ pennardantiques@ukonline.co.uk
Est. 1979 *Stock size* Large
Stock French and English country furniture and decorative items
Open Mon–Sat 9.30am–5.30pm or by appointment
Fairs Bath Decorative and Antiques Fair
Services Restoration, shipping and deliveries

FRESHFORD

Freshfords (LAPADA, CINOA, BABAADA)
Contact Mr Simon Powell
High Street, Freshford, Bath, Somerset, BA2 7WF 🅿
☎ 01225 722111 Ⓕ 01225 722991
Ⓜ 07970 517332 or 07720 838877
Ⓔ antiques@freshfords.com
Ⓦ www.freshfords.com
Est. 1973 *Stock size* Large
Stock Regency period furniture
Open Mon–Fri 10am–5pm Sat by appointment 10am–1pm
Fairs Olympia, Chelsea
Services Valuations, restoration, shipping, book search

FROME

Antiques and Country Living
Contact Mrs D M Williams
43–44 Vallis Way, Frome, Somerset, BA11 3BA 🅿
☎ 01373 463015
Ⓜ 07808 933076
Est. 1994 *Stock size* Large
No. of dealers 4
Stock 18th–19thC pottery and porcelain, Georgian–Edwardian furniture, books
Open Mon–Sun 9.30am–5.30pm

Steve Vee Bransgrove Collectables
Contact Steve
6 Catherine Hill, Frome, Somerset, BA11 1BY
01373 453225
0797 769 4537
Est. 1995 *Stock size* Medium
Stock Collectables, advertising, vintage magazines, ephemera and nostalgia
Open Mon–Sat 10am–5pm Thurs closed in winter 10am–2pm in summer
Services Valuations

Cooper and Tanner Chartered Surveyors
Contact Dennis Barnard
The Agricultural Centre, Standerwick, Frome, Somerset, BA11 2QB
01373 831010 01373 831103
agricultural@cooperandtanner.co.uk
Est. 1900
Open Mon 2.30–5pm Tues 9am–4pm Wed 8.30am–5.30pm Thurs 9am–12.30pm
Sales Furniture, fine art and antiques sale Wed 10.30am, viewing Tues 9am–4pm Wed 8.30am prior to sale
Frequency Weekly
Catalogues No

Frome Reclamation (SALVO)
Contact Steve Horler
Station Approach, Frome, Somerset, BA11 1RE
01373 463919 01373 453122
07836 277507
info@fromerec.co.uk
www.fromerec.co.uk
Est. 1987 *Stock size* Large
Stock Architectural antiques, including roofing, flooring, period fireplaces, doors, bathrooms, etc
Open Mon–Fri 8am–5.30pm Sat 8am–4.30pm

GLASTONBURY

Courtyard Books
Contact Mr Mills
2–4 High Street, Glastonbury, Somerset, BA6 9DU
01458 831800 08717 172155
courtyard@speakingtree.co.uk
Est. 1995 *Stock size* Large
Stock Antiquarian, esoteric, New Age and magic books
Open Mon–Sun 9.30am–5.30pm

HINTON ST GEORGE

David Carstairs
Hinton St George, Somerset, TA18
01460 54489 01460 55407
Est. 1986 *Stock size* Small
Stock 18th–19thC furniture and works of art
Open By appointment
Fairs NEC
Services Valuations for probate and insurance

ILCHESTER

Gilbert and Dale
Contact Roy Gilbert or Joan Dale
The Old Chapel, Church Street, Ilchester, Yeovil, Somerset, BA22 8LN
01935 840464 01935 841599
roygilbertantiques.freeserve.co.uk
Est. 1969 *Stock size* Medium
Stock English and French country furniture and accessories
Trade only Mainly trade
Open Mon–Fri 9am–5.30pm

ILMINSTER

Stuart Interiors Antiques Ltd (LAPADA)
Contact Peter Russell
Barrington Court, Barrington, Ilminster, Somerset, TA19 0NG
01460 240349 01460 242069
design@studiointeriors.com
www.studiointeriors.com
Est. 1976 *Stock size* Large
Stock Early English oak and decorative pieces
Open Mon–Fri 9am–5.30pm Sat 10am–1pm

KNOLE

Knole Barometers
Contact David Crawshaw
Lower Knole Farm, Knole, Long Sutton, Longport, Somerset, TA10 9HZ
01458 241015 01458 241706
07785 364567
dccops@btconnect.com
Est. 1997 *Stock size* Medium
Stock Barometers, scientific instruments
Open Mon–Fri 9am–5pm
Services Valuations, restoration

LANGPORT

Myrtle Antiques
Contact David or Chris Knight
Staceys Court, Bow Street, Langport, Somerset, TA10 9PQ
01458 252666 01458 252666
07967 355490
www.myrtleantiques.co.uk
Est. 1992 *Stock size* Medium
Stock English and European furniture, reproduction pine and elm
Open Mon–Fri 9am–5.30pm
Services Restoration and furniture makers

Oldnautibits
Contact Geoff Pringle
PO Box 67, Langport, Somerset, TA10 9WJ
01458 241816
07947 277833
geoff.pringle@oldnautibits.com
www.oldnautibits.com
Est. 2002 *Stock size* Medium
Stock Aeronautical, maritime collectables
Open Mon–Fri 9am–5pm
Fairs DNG Bath and West Showground

LYDEARD ST LAWRENCE

The Coach House
Contact Clare Roberts
Handycross Farmhouse, Handycross, Lydeard St Lawrence, Taunton, Somerset, TA4 3PL
01984 667568
Est. 1996 *Stock size* Large
No. of dealers 11
Stock A wide range of furniture, collectables, silver, ceramics
Open Thurs–Sun Bank Holidays 11am–5pm

Castle Reclamation (SALVO)
Contact Mr A Wills
Parrett Works, Martock, Somerset, TA12 6AE
01935 826483 01935 826791
info@castlereclamation.com

Ⓦ www.castlereclamation.com
Est. 1989 *Stock size* Medium
Stock Architectural antiques, stone masonry, hand-carved natural stone fireplaces, oak flooring, 16th–17thC-style oak furniture, pannelling
Open Mon–Fri 8.30am–5pm Sat 10am–1pm
Fairs Bath and West, Dyrham Park, Kingston Lacy

MIDSOMER NORTON

Somervale Antiques (BADA, LAPADA, CINOA, BABAADA)
Contact Wing Commander Ron Thomas
The Poplars, 6 Radstock Road, Midsomer Norton, Radstock, Somerset, BA3 2AJ P
☎ 01761 412686 Ⓕ 01761 412686
Ⓜ 07885 088022
Ⓔ ronthomas@somervaleantiquesglass.co.uk
Ⓦ www.somervaleantiquesglass.co.uk
Est. 1972 *Stock size* Large
Stock English 18th–19thC drinking glasses, decanters, cut and coloured, Bristol and Nailsea glass, scent bottles
Open By appointment. Trains to Bath met by arrangement
Services Valuations

MINEHEAD

Chris's Crackers
Contact Peter Marshall
Townsend Garage, Main Road, Carhampton, Minehead, Somerset, BA24 6LH P
☎ 01643 821873
Ⓦ www.chriscrackers.net
Est. 1995 *Stock size* Large
Stock Reclamation, agricultural antiques, pine furniture, collectables
Open Mon–Sun 10.30am–5.30pm

NORTH CHERITON

Paper Pleasures (PBFA)
Contact Lesley Tyson
Holt Farm, North Cheriton, Somerset, BA8 0AQ P
☎ 01963 33718
Ⓔ books@paperpleasures.bchip.com
Ⓦ www.paperpleasures.com
Stock size Small
Stock Antiquarian and second-hand books
Open By appointment
Services Book search

NORTH PETHERTON

Hallidays (LAPADA)
Contact James Halliday
35 Fore Street, North Petherton, Somerset, TA6 6PY P
☎ 01278 662397 Ⓕ 01823 324073
Est. 1987 *Stock size* Medium
Stock 18th–19thC furniture, upholstery, ceramics
Open Mon–Sat 9.30am–5.30pm
Services Valuations, upholstery, furniture renovation

Jays Antiques and Collectables
Contact Mrs J Alba
121a Fore Street, North Petherton, Bridgwater, Somerset, TA6 6SA P
☎ 01278 662688
Est. 1994 *Stock size* Medium
Stock China, glass, clocks
Open Mon 10am–1pm Tues–Sat 10am–4.30pm closed Wed
Fairs Talisman Fairs, Bristol

PORLOCK

Magpie Antiques & Jewellery
Contact Glenys Battams
High Street, Porlock, Somerset, TA24 8PT P
☎ 01271 850669
Ⓜ 07721 679020
Est. 1980 *Stock size* Medium
Stock Antique jewellery, silver, scent bottles, objects of virtue
Open Telephone call advisable
Fairs Westpoint, Newark, Shepton Mallet
Services Valuations, restoration

Porlock Antiques and Gallery Ltd
Contact Sara Goodson
High Street, Porlock, Somerset, TA24 8AL P
☎ 01643 862226 Ⓕ 01643 863461
Ⓔ porlockantiques@aol.com
Est. 2002 *Stock size* Medium
Stock Furniture, paintings
Open Mon–Sat 9.30am–5pm

Rare Books & Berry
Contact Michael Berry
Lowerbourne House, High Street, Porlock, Somerset, TA24 8PT P
☎ 01643 863255 Ⓕ 01643 863092
Ⓔ info@rarebooksandberry.co.uk
Ⓦ www.rarebooksandberry.co.uk
Est. 1982 *Stock size* Medium
Stock Antiquarian and second-hand books
Open Mon–Sat 9.30am–5pm
Services Book search

QUEEN CAMEL

Steven Ferdinando (PBFA)
Contact Mr Steven Ferdinando
The Old Vicarage, Queen Camel, Yeovil, Somerset, BA22 7NG P
☎ 01935 850210
Est. 1978 *Stock size* Medium
Stock Antiquarian and second-hand books
Open Visitors welcome by appointment
Fairs PBFA
Services Valuations, book search

RADSTOCK

Notts Pine
Contact Jeff Nott
Old Redhouse Farm, Stratton-on-the-Fosse, Radstock, Bath, Somerset, BA3 4QE P
☎ 01761 419911
Est. 1986 *Stock size* Medium
Stock Antique pine furniture
Open Mon–Fri 9am–6pm

SHEPTON MALLET

Edward Marnier Antiques (BABAADA)
Contact Mr E Marnier
Old Bowlish House, Forum Lane, Bowlish, Shepton Mallet, Somerset, BA4 5JA P
☎ 01749 343340
Ⓜ 07785 110122
Ⓔ emarnier@ukonline.co.uk
Est. 1989 *Stock size* Medium
Stock 17th–20thC furniture, pictures, mirrors, interesting items, antique rugs, carpets
Open Mon–Sun 9am–6pm or by appointment
Fairs Olympia, Bath, Battersea
Services Valuations

Parkways Antiques
Contact Pauline Brereton
31 High Street, Shepton Mallet, Somerset, BA4 5AQ
01749 345065
Est. 1972 *Stock size* Small
Stock Period and Victorian furniture and reproduction pine
Open Mon–Fri 10am–4pm closed Wed
Services Reproduction pine made to order

SOMERTON

John Gardiner
Contact Mr John Gardiner
Monteclefe House, Kirkham Street, Somerton, Somerset, TA11 7NL
01458 272238 01458 274329
07831 274427
Est. 1968 *Stock size* Medium
Stock General antiques, decorative items
Open Appointment advisable
Services Workshop facilities

London Cigarette Card Company Ltd
Contact Mr Laker
West Street, Somerton, Somerset, TA11 6QP
01458 273452 01458 273515
cards@londoncigcard.co.uk
www.londoncigcard.co.uk
Est. 1927 *Stock size* Large
Stock Cigarette cards, trade cards
Open Mon–Sat 9.30am–5pm closed Wed Sat pm
Services Direct sales, public/postal auctions. Publishes catalogues, card collectors' magazines, trade cards

Simon's Books
Contact Mr B Ives
Broad Street, Somerton, Somerset, TA11 7NH
01458 272313
Est. 1979 *Stock size* Medium
Stock General antiquarian and second-hand books
Open Mon–Sat 10am–4.30pm

Somerton Antique Centre
Contact Maurice Waite
Market Place, Somerton, Somerset, TA11 7NB
01458 274423 01458 274423
Est. 1997 *Stock size* Large
No. of dealers 50
Stock General antiques including paintings, linen, militaria, pine and oak
Open Mon–Sat 10am–5pm
Services Restoration

Westville House Antiques
Contact Derek or Margaret Stacey
Westville House, Littleton, Somerton, Somerset, TA11 6NP
01458 273376 01458 273376
antique@westville.co.uk
www.westville.co.uk
Est. 1986 *Stock size* Large
Stock Antique country, pine, oak and mahogany furniture
Open Mon–Sat 9am–5.30pm or by appointment

STOKE SUB HAMDON

R G Watkins (PBFA)
Contact Mr R G Watkins
9 North Street Workshops, Stoke sub Hamdon, Somerset, TA14 6QR
01935 822891 01935 822891
rgw@eurobell.co.uk
www.rgw.eurobell.co.uk
Est. 1985 *Stock size* Small
Stock Antiquarian books, prints, portraits, books on art and antiques a speciality
Open Fri 10am–5pm or by appointment
Fairs PBFA
Services Valuations

TAUNTON

Aarons Antiques
27–29 Silver Street, Taunton, Somerset, TA1 3DH
01823 698295
Est. 1982 *Stock size* Large
Stock Small antiques, collectables
Open Mon 9am–4pm

Aarons Coins
27–29 Silver Street, Taunton, Somerset, TA1 3DH
01823 698295
Est. 1982 *Stock size* Large
Stock Coins and banknotes, ancient and modern
Open Mon 9am–4pm

The Bookshop
Contact Sarah Allen
13a Paul Street, Taunton, Somerset, TA1 3PF
01823 326963 01458 241007
07971 245301
Est. 1997 *Stock size* Medium
Stock Rare and second-hand books
Open Mon Tues Fri Sat 10am–4.30pm Thurs noon–4.30pm
Services Book search

Cider Press Antiques Centre
Contact Norman Clarke or Mark Blake
58 Bridge Street, Taunton, Somerset, TA1 1UD
01823 283050 01823 283050
Est. 2000 *Stock size* Large
No. of dealers 12
Stock Period furniture, ceramics, jewellery, stamps, collectables
Open Mon–Sat 10am–5pm Sun 11am–4pm
Services Valuations

Greenslade Taylor Hunt (SOFAA)
Contact Keith Amor
Magdalene House, Church Square, Taunton, Somerset, TA1 1SB
01823 332525 01823 353120
fine.art@gth.net
www.gth.net
Est. 1843
Open Mon–Fri 9am–5pm
Sales Bi-monthly fine art sales last Thurs 10am, viewing Tues 9.30am–4.30pm Wed 9.30am–7.30pm. Fortnightly household sale Wed 10am, viewing Tues 2.30–5pm. Also collectors' sales. Telephone for details
Catalogues Yes

Hallidays (LAPADA)
Contact James Halliday
6 St James Street, Taunton, Somerset, TA1 1JH
01823 324073 01823 324073
Est. 1987 *Stock size* Medium
Stock 18th–19thC furniture, upholstery, ceramics
Open Mon–Sat 9.30am–5.30pm
Services Valuations, upholstery, furniture renovation

Selwoods Antiques
Contact Mr J R Selwood
Queen Anne Cottage, Mary Street, Taunton, Somerset, TA1 3PE
01823 272780
Est. 1927 *Stock size* Large
Stock Furniture
Open Mon–Sat 9.30am–5pm

Taunton Antiques Market
Contact Mike Spooner
25–29 Silver Street, Taunton, Somerset, TA1 3DH
01823 289327 F 01823 286555
Est. 1978 *Stock size* Large
No. of dealers 100
Stock General antiques and collectables including specialists in most fields
Open Mon 9am–4pm including Bank Holidays

TEMPLE CLOUD

Bookbarn Ltd
Contact Mr Belton
White Cross, (10 miles south of Bristol Junction of A37 and A39), Temple Cloud, Somerset, BS39 6EX
01761 451777
E bookbarn@bookbarn.co.uk
W www.bookbarn.co.uk
Est. 1997 *Stock size* Large
Stock Antiquarian and second-hand books
Open Mon–Sun 10am–6pm

TIMSBURY

Ministry of Pine
Contact Tony or Susan Lawrence
Timsbury Village Workshop, Unit 2, Timsbury Industrial Estate, Hayeswood Road, Timsbury, Bath, Somerset, BA2 OHQ
01761 472297/434938
F 01761 479685
M 07770 588536
E ministryofpine.uk@virgin.net
W www.ministryofpine.co.uk
Est. 1980 *Stock size* Large
Stock Antique pine furniture both painted and stripped
Open Mon–Fri 9am–6pm Sat Sun 10am–4pm
Services Valuations, restoration and stripping

WATCHET

Clarence House Antiques
Contact Mr or Mrs Cotton
41 Swain Street, Watchet, Somerset, TA23 0AE
01984 631389
Est. 1972 *Stock size* Medium
Stock Antiques, curios, collectables
Open Mon–Sat 11am–5.30pm

WELLINGTON

Michael & Amanda Lewis Oriental Carpets and Rugs (LAPADA)
Contact Amanda Lewis
8 North Street, Wellington, Somerset, TA21 8LT
01823 667430
E rugmike@btopenworld.com
Est. 1981 *Stock size* Medium
Stock Antique and old Oriental rugs
Open Tues–Fri 10.30am–1pm 2–5.30pm Sat by appointment
Services Valuations, restoration, cleaning

Graham Sparks Restoration
Contact Mr Graham Sparks
Unit 63, Tone Mill, Tonedale, Wellington, Somerset, TA21 0AB
01823 663636 F 01823 667393
Est. 1979
Stock Desks, cabinets
Open Mon–Fri 8am–6pm Sat 8am–1pm
Services Restoration

WELLS

Alcove Antiques
Contact Nancy Alcock
1 Priest Row, Wells, Somerset, BA5 2PY
01749 672164 F 01749 678925
Est. 1979 *Stock size* Medium
Stock China, brass, copper, pine, Victorian and Edwardian mahogany
Open Tues Thurs–Sat 10.30am–5pm Wed 10.30am–1pm
Services Restoration

Country Brocante (BABAADA)
Contact Tim Ovel
Fir Tree Farm, Lower Godney, Wells, Somerset, BA5 1RZ
01458 833052 F 01458 835611
M 07970 719708
E ovel@compuserve.com
Est. 1993 *Stock size* Large
Stock French furniture, chandeliers, early mirrors
Open By appointment
Fairs Newark, Shepton Mallet

Bernard G House Longcase Clocks
Contact Mr B G House
13 Market Place, Wells, Somerset, BA5 2RF
01749 672607 F 01749 672607
W www.antiqueclocksand barometers.co.uk
Est. 1971 *Stock size* Medium
Stock Longcase clocks, barographs, barometers, clocks, telescopes, scientific instruments
Open Mon–Sat 10am–5.30pm or by appointment
Services Repair and restoration of clocks and barometers

Wells Auction Rooms
Contact Nick Ewing or Cynthia Peak
66–68 Southover, Wells, Somerset, BA5 1UH
01749 678094/0117 973 7201
Est. 1845
Sales Sale monthly Wed 1.30pm, viewing Tues noon–5pm day of sale from 9am
Catalogues Yes

Wells Reclamation Company
Coxley, Wells, Somerset, BA5 1RQ
01749 677087 F 01749 671098
E enquiries@wellsreclamation.com
W www.wellsreclaimation.com
Est. 1984 *Stock size* Large
Stock Architectural antiques, bricks, tiles, slates, fireplaces, doors, finials, pews, etc
Open Mon–Fri 8.30am–5.30pm Sat 9am–4pm
Services Oak studded doors made to order

WESTBURY-ON-TRYM

⊞ Kemps
Contact Michael Kemp
✉ **9 Carlton Court, Westbury-on-Trym, Somerset, BS9 3DF** Ⓟ
☎ 0117 950 5090
Est. 1881 *Stock size* Medium
Stock Jewellery
Open Mon–Fri 9am–5.15pm Sat 9am–1pm

WESTON-SUPER-MARE

⊞ David Hughes Antiques
Contact Mr Hughes
✉ **37 Baker Street, Weston-super-Mare, Somerset, BS23 3AD** Ⓟ
☎ 01934 628007
Ⓜ 07860 964100
Est. 1974 *Stock size* Medium
Stock General antiques, Arts and Crafts, Art Nouveau
Open Mon–Sat 9am–1pm Fri 9am–1pm 2–4pm closed Thurs
Fairs Newark, Ardingly
Services House clearances

⊞ Sterling Books (ABA, PBFA)
Contact Mr Nisbet
✉ **43a Locking Road, Weston-super-Mare, Somerset, BS23 3DG** Ⓟ
☎ 01934 625056
Ⓔ sterling.books@talk21.com
Est. 1966 *Stock size* Large
Stock Antiquarian and second-hand books on every subject
Open Tues–Sat 10am–5.30pm Thurs 10am–1pm
Services Valuations, book binding and picture framing

⊞ Richard Twort
Contact Richard Twort
✉ **12 Sand Road, Sand Bay, Weston Super Mare, Somerset, BS22 9UH** Ⓟ
☎ 01934 612439 Ⓕ 01934 641900
Ⓜ 07711 939789
Ⓔ walls@mirage-interiors.com
Est. 1962 *Stock size* Medium
Stock Barographs, thermographs, rain gauges, all types of meteorological instruments
Open By appointment

WINCANTON

⊞ Green Dragon Antiques and Crafts Centre
Contact Sally Denning
✉ **24 High Street, Wincanton, Somerset, BA9 9JF** Ⓟ
☎ 01963 34111
Ⓦ www.greendragonantiques.com
Est. 1991 *Stock size* Large
Stock General antiques, jewellery, crafts
Open Mon–Sun 9am–5pm
Services Valuations, free gift wrap, jewellery repairs

⊞ The Old School Rooms Antiques
Contact Philip Broomfield
✉ **16 Mill Street, Wincanton, Somerset, BA9 9AP** Ⓟ
☎ 01963 824259
Ⓜ 07768 726276
Ⓔ oldschoolantiques@aol.com
Est. 1987 *Stock size* Large
Stock Furniture
Open Tues Wed Fri Sat 10am–4pm
Services Restoration

⊞ Ottery Antique Restorers Ltd (BABAADA)
Contact Mr C James
✉ **Wessex Way, Wincanton Business Park, Wincanton, Somerset, BA9 9RR** Ⓟ
☎ 01963 34572 Ⓕ 01963 34572
Ⓜ 07770 923955
Ⓔ charles@otteryantiques.co.uk
Ⓦ www.otteryantiques.co.uk
Est. 1986 *Stock size* Medium
Stock Antique furniture
Open Mon–Fri 8am–5.30pm
Services Restoration

⊞ Wincanton Antiques
Contact Tony or Clare
✉ **London House, 12 High Street, Wincanton, Somerset, BA9 9JL** Ⓟ
☎ 01963 32223
Est. 1997 *Stock size* Large
Stock Georgian–Edwardian furniture, beds, French antiques
Open Mon–Sat 9.30am–5pm
Services Upholstery

WIVELISCOMBE

⊞ Yew Tree Antiques Warehouse
Contact N Nation
✉ **Old Brewery, Wiveliscombe, Taunton, Somerset, TA4 2NT** Ⓟ
☎ 01984 623950/623914
Est. 1997 *Stock size* Large
Stock Victorian, Edwardian and French furniture, Lloyd Loom
Open Tue–Fri 11am–4.30pm Sat 10am–5pm

YEOVIL

⊞ Yeovil Collectors Centre
Contact Barry Scott
✉ **16 Hendford, Yeovil, Somerset, BA20 1TE** Ⓟ
☎ 01935 433739 Ⓕ 01935 433739
Est. 1969 *Stock size* Small
Stock Militaria, postcards, general collectables, animals, blue and white, Toby jugs
Open Mon Wed–Sat 9am–5pm

WILTSHIRE

AVEBURY

⊞ Avebury Antiques
Contact Brian Sumbler
✉ **High Street, Avebury, Wiltshire, SN8 1RF** Ⓟ
☎ 01672 539436
Est. 1984 *Stock size* Small
Stock Antiques and collectables
Open Mon–Sun 10am–6pm

BRADFORD-ON-AVON

⊞ Avon Antiques (BADA)
Contact Andrew Jenkins
✉ **25, 26 & 27 Market Street, Bradford-on-Avon, Wiltshire, BA15 1LL**
☎ 01225 862052 Ⓕ 01225 868763
Ⓔ avonantiques@aol.com
Ⓦ www.avon-antiques.co.uk
Est. 1963 *Stock size* Large
Stock 17th–mid 19thC furniture, clocks, barometers, metalwork, needlework, treen, English furniture, folk art pictures
Open Mon–Sat 9.30am–5.30pm
Fairs Grosvenor House Antiques Fair

⊞ Andrew Dando (BADA, BACA Award Winner 2002)
Contact Andrew Dando
✉ **34 Market Street, Bradford-on-Avon, Wiltshire, BA15 1LL** Ⓟ
☎ 01225 865444
Ⓔ andrew@andrewdando.co.uk
Ⓦ www.andrewdando.co.uk
Est. 1915 *Stock size* Large
Stock Pottery and porcelain 1750–1870
Open Tues–Sat 10am–5pm
Fairs Olympia (June)

⊞ Granary Pine (BABAADA)
Contact Julia or Tony Chowles
✉ **The Granary, Pound Lane, Bradford-on-Avon, Wiltshire, BA15 1LF** Ⓟ
☎ 01225 867781 Ⓕ 01225 867781
Ⓔ tony@granarypine.co.uk
Ⓦ www.granarypine.co.uk
Est. 1987 *Stock size* Large
Stock Country pine furniture, collectables
Open Mon–Sun 10am–5pm

⊞ Mac Humble Antiques (BADA)
Contact Mr Humble
✉ **7–9 Woolley Street, Bradford-on-Avon, Wiltshire, BA15 1AD** Ⓟ
☎ 01225 866329 Ⓕ 01225 866329
Ⓜ 07702 501888
Ⓔ mac.humble@virgin.net
Ⓦ www.machumbleantiques.co.uk
Est. 1979 *Stock size* Small
Stock 18th–19thC furniture, needlework, samplers, metalware and decorative items
Open Mon–Fri 9am–6pm Sat 9am–1pm
Fairs Olympia (Nov), BADA (March)
Services Valuations, restoration

⊞ Moxhams Antiques (LAPADA, BABAADA)
Contact Roger, Jill or Nick Bichard
✉ **17 Silver Street, Bradford-on-Avon, Wiltshire, BA15 1JZ** Ⓟ
☎ 01225 862789 Ⓕ 01225 867844
Ⓜ 07768 960295
Ⓔ info@moxhams-antiques.demon.co.uk
Ⓦ www.moxhams-antiques.demon.co.uk
Est. 1967 *Stock size* Large
Stock Good 17th–early 19thC mahogany and oak furniture, ceramics, tapestries and objects
Open Mon–Sat 9am–5.30pm
Fairs Olympia (June and Nov)
Services Furniture restoration

⊞ Revival
Contact Douglas Vallance
✉ **Unit 8, Tythebarn Workshops, Pound Lane, Bradford-on-Avon, Wiltshire, BA15 1LF** Ⓟ
☎ 01225 864780
Est. 1967 *Stock size* Medium
Stock Georgian–Edwardian furniture
Open Tues–Sun 10am–5pm
Services Restoration

BRINKWORTH

⊞ North Wilts Exporters
Contact Caroline Thornbury
✉ **Farm Hill House, The Street, Brinkworth, Swindon, Wiltshire, SN5 5AJ** Ⓟ
☎ 01666 510876
Ⓔ mike@northwilts.demon.co.uk
Ⓦ www.northwiltsantiqueexporters.com
Est. 1974 *Stock size* Large
Stock Eastern European pine, oak, and mahogany furniture
Open Mon–Sat 9am–5pm or by appointment
Fairs Newark
Services Packers and shippers

BROAD HINTON

⊞ Bookmark Children's Books (PBFA)
Contact Leonora Excell or Anne Excell
✉ **Fortnight, Wick Down, Broad Hinton, Swindon, Wiltshire, SN4 9NR** Ⓟ
☎ 01793 731693 Ⓕ 01793 731782
Ⓜ 07788 841305
Ⓔ leonora.excell@btinternet.com
Est. 1972 *Stock size* Medium
Stock Children's and illustrated antiquarian books, nursery china, toys, games
Open By appointment
Fairs PBFA
Services Book search

CALNE

⊞ Calne Antiques
Contact Malcolm Blackford
✉ **2a London Road, Calne, Wiltshire, SN11 0AB** Ⓟ
☎ 01249 816311
Est. 1981 *Stock size* Large
Stock English and Continental pine furniture
Open Mon–Sun 9.30am–5pm

CHERHILL

⊞ P A Oxley Antique Clocks & Barometers (LAPADA)
Contact Mr M Oxley
✉ **The Old Rectory, Cherhill, Calne, Wiltshire, SN11 8UX** Ⓟ
☎ 01249 816227 Ⓕ 01249 821285
Ⓔ info@paoxley.com
Ⓦ www.british-antiqueclocks.com
Est. 1971 *Stock size* Large
Stock Antique clocks and barometers, longcase clocks a speciality
Open Mon–Sat 9.30am–5pm closed Wed Sun or by appointment
Services Delivery and shipping

CHIPPENHAM

⊞ Ancient & Modern
Contact Ken Charles
✉ **3 Club Building, Park Lane, Chippenham, Wiltshire, SN15 1LP** Ⓟ
☎ 01249 656477
Est. 2002 *Stock size* Medium
Stock General antiques, collectables, bric-a-brac
Open Mon–Sat 10am–4pm closed Wed
Services Valuations

Chippenham Auction Rooms
Contact Richard Edmonds
✉ **St Mary's Street, Chippenham, Wiltshire, SN15 3JM** Ⓟ
☎ 01249 462222 Ⓕ 01249 4654970
Ⓜ 07980 745441
Ⓔ richard@chippenhamauctionrooms.co.uk
Est. 2001
Open Mon–Fri 9am–1pm 2–6pm
Sales General antiques monthly Sat 10am, viewing Thurs 4–9pm Fri 10am–5pm Sat 8.30–10am. Five fine art sales a year at Lackham College, Lackham Tues 10am, viewing Sun noon–6pm Mon 10am–5pm. Also garden and farm machinery sales
Catalogues Yes

Collectors Corner
Contact Karen Groves
36 The Causeway, Chippenham, Wiltshire, SN15 3DB
01249 461617
Est. 1990 *Stock size* Large
Stock Antiques, collectables, musical instruments
Open Mon–Sat 9am–5pm

Cross Hayes Antiques (LAPADA)
Contact David Brooks
Unit 6 Westbrook Farm, Draycot Cerne, Chippenham, Wiltshire, SN15 5LH
01249 720033 F 01249 720033
david@crosshayes.co.uk
www.crosshayes.co.uk
Est. 1976 *Stock size* Large
Stock Furniture
Open Mon–Fri 9am–5pm or by appointment
Services Container packing service

CHRISTIAN MALFORD

Harley Antiques
Contact Mr Harley
The Comedy, Main Road, Christian Malford, Chippenham, Wiltshire, SN15 4BS
01249 720112 F 01249 720553
thecomedy.wilts@ukonline.co.uk
Est. 1959 *Stock size* Large
Stock General antiques including decorative and unusual items, conservatory furniture and objects
Open Mon–Sun 9am–6pm

CODFORD

Tina's Antiques
Contact Tina Alder
The High Street, Codford, Warminster, Wiltshire, BA12 0ND
01985 850828
Est. 1989 *Stock size* Medium
Stock General antiques
Open Mon–Sat 9am–5pm
Services Valuations

CORSHAM

Automattic Comics
Contact Matthew Booker
Unit 1, 17 Pickwick Road, Corsham, Wiltshire, SN13 9BQ
01249 701647
automattic.comics@bigfoot.com
Est. 1995 *Stock size* Large
Stock American import comics, old and new action figures, *Star Wars* figures
Open Mon Tues noon–5pm Thurs–Sat 10am–5pm
Fairs NEC Memorabilia (March, Nov)

Matthew Eden
Contact Mrs M Eden or Matthew Eden
Pickwick End, Corsham, Wiltshire, SN13 0JB
01249 713335 F 01249 713644
M 07899 926076
mail@mattheweden.co.uk
www.mattheweden.com
Est. 1952 *Stock size* Large
Stock General including garden furniture
Open Mon–Sat 9am–6pm
Fairs Chelsea Flower Show

Gardiner Houlgate
Contact Nicholas Houlgate
9 Leafield Way, Corsham, Wiltshire, SN13 9SW
01225 812912 F 01225 811777
auctions@gardiner-houlgate.co.uk
www.invaluable.com
Est. 1987
Open Mon–Fri 9am–5.30pm
Sales Quarterly antiques and works of art sales, 8 Victoriana and later furnishings sales, Thurs 10.30am, viewing Tues Wed 9am–5.30pm morning of sale 9–11am. Also specialist sales of clocks, musical instruments, decorative art and silver
Catalogues Yes

CRUDWELL

Philip A Ruttleigh Antiques incorporating Crudwell Furniture
Contact Philip Ruttleigh
Odd Penny Farm, Crudwell, Wiltshire, SN16 9SJ
01285 770970
M 07989 250077
enquiries@crudwellfurniture.co.uk
www.crudwellfurniture.co.uk
Est. 1987 *Stock size* Small
Stock General antique furniture
Open Mon–Fri 9am–5pm or by appointment
Services Restoration, paint removal from all wood types

DEVIZES

Henry Aldridge & Son
Contact Alan Aldridge
Unit 1, Bath Road Business Centre, Devizes, Wiltshire, SN10 1XA
01380 720199
andrew.aldridge@virgin.net
www.henry-aldridge.co.uk
Est. 1989
Open Mon–Fri 10am–4pm
Sales Fortnightly Victorian and later effects sales, bi-monthly antiques sales, bi-annual maritime and Titanic sales held on Sat
Catalogues Yes

Frantiques of Devizes
Contact Molly Hopkins
14A Bridewell Street, Devizes, Wiltshire, SN10 1NQ
01380 729901
molly@frantiques.co.uk
www.frantiques.co.uk
Est. 1999 *Stock size* Medium
Stock Georgian–Victorian English furniture, vintage clothing, silver, jewellery, collectables
Open Mon–Sat 10am–5pm closed Wed or by appointment
Services Valuations, restoration

Margaret Mead Antiques
Contact Mrs M Mead
19 Northgate Street, Devizes, Wiltshire, SN10 1JT
01380 721060 or 01793 533085
M 07740 536560
Est. 1982 *Stock size* Medium
Stock General antiques, Georgian–Edwardian furniture, clocks, china, brass
Open Tues–Sat 10am–5pm closed Wed
Services Restoration

St Mary's Chapel Antiques (BABAADA)
Contact Richard Sankey
St Mary's Chapel, Northgate Street, Devizes, Wiltshire, SN10 1DE
01380 721399 F 01380 721399
richard@rsankey.freeserve.co.uk

Est. 1971 *Stock size* Large
Stock Original painted and country furniture, garden antiques and accessories
Open Mon–Sat 10am–6pm closed Wed
Fairs Bath Decorative and Antiques Fair
Services Selective restoration

Upstairs Downstairs
Contact Judy Coom
40 Market Place, Devizes, Wiltshire, SN10 1JG P
☎ 01380 730266 Ⓕ 01380 730266
Ⓜ 07974 074220
Ⓔ judith.coom@btopenworld.com
Est. 2002 *Stock size* Large
No. of dealers 32
Stock Antiques and collectables, furniture, postcards, pictures, toys, dolls, china
Open Mon–Sat 9.30am–4.30pm Sun 9.30am–3pm closed Wed
Services Doll repair

DURRINGTON

Cannon Militaria
Contact Mr L Webb
21 Bulford Road, Durrington, Salisbury, Wiltshire, SP4 8DL P
☎ 01980 655099
Est. 1995 *Stock size* Large
Stock Military collectables
Open Wed 1–5pm Thurs Fri 10am–5pm Sat 9am–1pm
Services Valuations

LYNEHAM

Pillars Antiques
Contact Mr K Clifford
10 The Banks, Lyneham, Chippenham, Wiltshire, SN15 4NS P
☎ 01249 890632
Ⓔ enquiries@pillarsantiques.com
Ⓦ www.pillarsantiques.com
Est. 1986 *Stock size* Large
Stock Old pine, 1940s shipping oak, mahogany furniture, bric-a-brac
Open Mon–Sat 10am–5pm Sun 11am–5pm Wed by appointment closed Thurs

MALMESBURY

Athelstan's Attic
Contact Tim Harvey
The Cross Hayes, Malmesbury, Wiltshire, SN16 9AU P
☎ 01666 825544/822678
Ⓔ tharvey@freeserve.co.uk
Est. 1997 *Stock size* Large
Stock General house clearance items, antique and garden effects
Open Mon Tue Wed Fri Sat 10am–4.30pm
Services House clearance

Hilditch Auction (NAVA)
Contact Mr Hilditch
Gloucester Road Trading Estate, Malmesbury, Wiltshire, SN16 9JT P
☎ 01666 822577 Ⓕ 01666 825597
Ⓔ sales@hilditchauctions.co.uk
Ⓦ www.hilditchauctions.co.uk
Est. 1990
Open Mon–Fri 8.30am–5pm
Sales General household sale fourth Sat of month 10am, viewing Fri 10am–7pm, call for alternate dates
Frequency Monthly
Catalogues Yes

Rene Nicholls
Contact Mrs I Nicholls
56 High Street, Malmesbury, Wiltshire, SN16 9AT
☎ 01666 823089
Est. 1979 *Stock size* Medium
Stock English pottery and porcelain
Open Mon–Sat 9.30am–6pm or by appointment
Services Valuations, restoration

MANINGFORD BRUCE

Indigo
Contact Marion Bender or Richard Lightbown
Dairy Barn, Maningford Bruce, Wiltshire, SN9 6JW P
☎ 01672 564722 Ⓕ 01672 564733
Ⓜ 07867 982233
Ⓔ antique@indigo-uk.com
Ⓦ www.indigo-uk.com
Est. 1982 *Stock size* Large
Stock Antique Indian, Chinese, Japanese and Tibetan furniture
Trade only Yes
Open Mon–Fri 9am–5pm Sat 10am–4pm
Fairs House and Garden fair
Services Restoration

MARLBOROUGH

Blanchard Ltd (LAPADA)
Contact Orlando Harris
Froxfield, Marlborough, Wiltshire, SN8 3LD P
☎ 01488 680666 Ⓕ 01488 680668
Ⓔ orlando@jwblanchard.com
Est. 1950 *Stock size* Large
Stock English and Continental furniture, decorative items, works of art, lighting
Open Mon–Fri 9.30am–5.30pm Sat 10am–5pm
Fairs June Olympia

Brocante Antiques Centre
Contact Robert Stenhouse
6 London Road, Marlborough, Wiltshire, SN8 1PH P
☎ 01672 516512 Ⓕ 01672 516512
Est. 1995 *Stock size* Medium
Stock Furniture, ceramics, decorative items, books, taxidermy
Open Wed–Sat 10am–5pm
Services Valuations, pine stripping

The Cats Whiskers Antiques
Contact Sue Rumbold
44a Kingsbury Street, Marlborough, Wiltshire, SN8 1JE P
☎ 01672 511577 or 01264 850801
Ⓜ 07712 018543
Est. 2002 *Stock size* Medium
Stock Antiques, collectables, blue and white china, quilts, gardening items
Open Mon–Sat 10am–5.30pm telephone call advisable

Eureka Antiques
Contact Mr Newman
5 London Road, Marlborough, Wiltshire, SN8 1PH
☎ 01672 512072
Est. 1979 *Stock size* Medium
Stock Antique pots and furniture
Open Mon–Sun 9am–6pm

Graylings Antiques
Contact Gail Young
Brocante Antiques Centre, 6 London Road, Marlborough, Wiltshire, SN8 1PH P

☎ 01264 710077 Ⓕ 01264 710077
Ⓜ 07732 293302
Ⓔ tremorfa1@onetel.com
Ⓦ www.staffordshire-figures.com
Est. 1995 *Stock size* Medium
Stock Staffordshire pottery
Open By appointment
Fairs Newark
Services Valuations

Hamptons International Auctioneers and Valuers
Contact Sheldon Cameron
✉ **The Marlborough Auction Rooms, Hilliers Yard, High Street, Marlborough, Wiltshire, SN8 1AA** Ⓟ
☎ 01672 516161 Ⓕ 01672 515882
Ⓔ marlboroughauctions@hamptons-int.com
Ⓦ www.hamptons.co.uk/fineart
Open Mon–Fri 9.30am–5.30pm
Sales An eclectic mix of antique, collectable and household items. Valuations Fri 10am–2pm. Telephone for auction and viewing times
Catalogues Yes

Katharine House Gallery
Contact Christopher Gange
✉ **Katharine House, The Parade, Marlborough, Wiltshire, SN8 1NE** Ⓟ
☎ 01672 514040
Est. 1983 *Stock size* Medium
Stock Antiquarian and second-hand books, 20thC British pictures, general antiques and antiquities
Open Mon–Sat 10am–5.30pm

The Long Room
Contact Mr Newman
✉ **Rope Works, 20 Kennett Place, Marlborough, Wiltshire, SN8 1NG** Ⓟ
☎ 01672 512111
Est. 1979 *Stock size* Medium
Stock Antique and later furniture
Open Mon–Sun 10am–5pm

The Marlborough Parade Antique Centre
Contact Gary Wilkinson or Penny Morgan
✉ **The Parade, Marlborough, Wiltshire, SN8 1NE** Ⓟ
☎ 01672 515331
Est. 1985 *Stock size* Large
No. of dealers 50
Stock Small items, general antiques, very good quality
Open Mon–Sun 10am–5pm closed Christmas, Boxing and New Year's Days

The Old Rope Works
Contact The Manager
✉ **20 Kennet Place, Marlborough, Wiltshire, SN8 1NG** Ⓟ
☎ 01672 512111
Est. 1995 *Stock size* Large
Stock Furniture 1780–1950
Open Mon–Sat 10.30am–4.30pm
Services Restoration

Anthony Outred Antiques Ltd (BADA)
Contact Anthony Outred
✉ **Blanchard, Froxfield, Marlborough, Wiltshire, SN8 3LD** Ⓟ
☎ 01488 680666 Ⓕ 020 7371 9869
Ⓜ 07767 848132
Ⓔ antiques@outred.co.uk
Ⓦ www.outred.co.uk
Est. 1977 *Stock size* Medium
Stock 18th–19thC English, Irish and Continental furniture, sculptures, lighting, oil paintings
Open By appointment
Fairs Olympia (June)

MELKSHAM

Peter Campbell Antiques
Contact Mr P Campbell
✉ **59 Bath Road, Atworth, Melksham, Wiltshire, SN12 8JY** Ⓟ
☎ 01225 709742
Est. 1976 *Stock size* Medium
Stock Country furniture and decorative items
Open Mon–Sat 10am–5pm Thurs and Sun by appointment

Dann Antiques Ltd (BABAADA)
Contact Gary Low
✉ **Unit S1, New Broughton Road, Melksham, Wiltshire, SN12 8BS** Ⓟ
☎ 01225 707329 Ⓕ 01225 790120
Ⓔ sales@dannantiques.com
Ⓦ www.dannantiques.com
Est. 1984 *Stock size* Large
Stock English mahogany furniture, furniture accessories
Open Mon–Fri 8.30am–5.30pm Sat 9.30am–3.30pm or by appointment
Services Restoration

Jaffray Antiques (BABAADA)
Contact Mrs J Carter
✉ **16 The Market Place, Melksham, Wiltshire, SN12 6EX** Ⓟ
☎ 01225 702269 Ⓕ 01225 790413
Ⓔ jaffray.antiques@fsmail.net
Est. 1955 *Stock size* Large
Stock 18th–19thC furniture, tallboys, desks, linen presses, bamboo, dining tables, chests-of-drawers, Staffordshire, metalware
Open Mon–Fri 9am–5pm or by appointment

King Street Curios
Contact Lizzie Board
✉ **8–10 King Street, Melksham, Wiltshire, SN12 6HD** Ⓟ
☎ 01225 790623
Est. 1987 *Stock size* Large
Stock General antiques, collectables
Open Mon–Sat 10am–5pm
Fairs Shepton Mallet, Royal Fairs

Polly's Parlour
Contact Pauline Hart
✉ **4 King Street, Melksham, Wiltshire, SN12 6HD** Ⓟ
☎ 01225 706418
Est. 1999 *Stock size* Large
Stock General antiques, collectables, decorative items
Open Mon–Sat 10am–4.30pm or by appointment

MERE

Finan and Co
Contact Robert Finan
✉ **The Square, Mere, Wiltshire, BA12 6DJ** Ⓟ
☎ 01747 861411 Ⓕ 01747 861944
Ⓔ enquiries@finanandco.co.uk
Ⓦ www.finanandco.co.uk
Est. 1997
Open Tues Thurs Sat 10am–6pm or by appointment
Sales Two antiques sales April and October Sat, viewing Thurs Fri 10am–7pm Sat 9–11am prior to sale. 2 collectables sales January and July
Catalogues Yes

NETHERHAMPTON

Edward Hurst Antiques
Contact Edward Hurst
✉ **The Battery, Rockbourne Road,**

Coombe Bissett, Salisbury, Wiltshire,
SP5 4LP 🅿
☎ 01722 718859
Ⓜ 07768 255557
Est. 1985 *Stock size* Medium
Stock 17th–18thC British furniture and associated works of art
Open Open regularly please telephone

⊞ Victor Mahy (BADA)
Contact John H Parnaby
✉ **Netherhampton House, Netherhampton, Salisbury, Wiltshire,**
SP2 8PU 🅿
☎ 01722 743131
ⓔ johnparnaby@netherhampton house.co.uk
Ⓦ www.netherhamptonhouse.co.uk
Est. 1918 *Stock size* Large
Stock 17th–18thC furniture
Open Mon–Sat 9.30am–5.30pm

NORTH WRAXALL

⊞ Delomosne & Son Ltd (BADA, BABAADA)
Contact Mr T N M Osborne
✉ **Court Close, North Wraxall, Chippenham, Wiltshire,**
SN14 7AD 🅿
☎ 01225 891505 ⓕ 01225 891907
ⓔ timosborne@delomosne.co.uk
Ⓦ www.delomosne.co.uk
Est. 1905 *Stock size* Large
Stock Glass, porcelain, pottery, enamels, needlework pictures, treen, bygones, period glass lighting
Open Mon–Fri 9.30am–5.30pm or by appointment
Fairs The Grosvenor House Art & Antiques, Winter Olympia
Services Valuations, restoration, commission buying

PEWSEY

⊞ Rupert Gentle Antiques (BADA)
Contact Mrs Belinda Gentle
✉ **The Manor House, Milton Lilbourne, Pewsey, Wiltshire,**
SN9 5LQ 🅿
☎ 01672 563344 ⓕ 01672 563563
Ⓜ 07748 696203
ⓔ belindagentle@tiscali.co.uk
Est. 1976 *Stock size* Small
Stock 17th–19thC English and Continental domestic metalwork, treen, needlework
Open Mon–Sat 9am–6pm or by appointment
Fairs Grosvenor House (June), Olympia, BADA (March, Chelsea)
Services Valuations

⊞ Time Restored Ltd
Contact J H Bowler-Reed
✉ **20 High Street, Pewsey, Wiltshire,**
SN9 5AQ 🅿
☎ 01672 563544
ⓔ time.restored@btopenworld.com
Est. 1978 *Stock size* Small
Stock Antique clocks, musical boxes, barometers
Open Mon–Fri 10am–6pm
Services Restoration

RAMSBURY

⊞ Heraldry Today (ABA)
Contact Mrs Henry
✉ **Parliament Piece, Ramsbury, Wiltshire,**
SN8 2QH 🅿
☎ 01672 520617 ⓕ 01672 520183
ⓔ heraldry@heraldrytoday.co.uk
Ⓦ www.heraldrytoday.co.uk
Est. 1954 *Stock size* Large
Stock Antiquarian books on heraldry, geneaology and peerage
Open Mon–Fri 9.30am–4.30pm

⊞ Inglenook Antiques
Contact Dennis White
✉ **59 High Street, Ramsbury, Wiltshire,**
SN8 2QN 🅿
☎ 01672 520261
Est. 1969 *Stock size* Large
Stock Victorian oil lamps, long case clocks
Open Tues Thur Fri Sat 10am–5pm or by appointment
Services Long case clock restoration

⊞ D P White
Contact Mr White
✉ **59 High Street, Ramsbury, Marlborough, Wiltshire,**
SN8 2QN 🅿
☎ 01672 520261
Est. 1969 *Stock size* Large
Stock Victorian oil lamps, oil lamp spares (old and new stocked), 50 oil lamps always in stock, brass, copper, furniture, clocks
Open Tues–Sat 10am–1pm 2–5pm closed Wed or by appointment
Services Longcase clock mechanism restoration

SALISBURY

⊞ 21st Century Antics
Contact Ben Scott
✉ **13 Brown Street, Salisbury, Wiltshire,**
SP1 1HE 🅿
☎ 01722 337421 ⓕ 01722 337421
Est. 1998 *Stock size* Large
Stock General furniture, antiques
Open Mon–Thurs Sat 9am–5.30pm Fri 9am–5pm
Services House clearance

⊞ The Barn Book Supply
Contact John Head
✉ **88 Crane Street, Salisbury, Wiltshire,**
SP1 2QD 🅿
☎ 01722 327767
Est. 1958 *Stock size* Large
Stock Antiquarian books, specializing in all field sports
Open By appointment
Services Book search

⊞ Robert Bradley Antiques
Contact Mr R Bradley
✉ **71 Brown Street, Salisbury, Wiltshire,**
SP1 2BA
☎ 01722 333677 ⓕ 01722 339922
Est. 1970 *Stock size* Medium
Stock 17th–18thC furniture
Open Mon–Fri 9.30am–5.30pm

⊞ Castle Galleries (OMRS)
Contact John Lodge
✉ **81 Castle Street, Salisbury, Wiltshire,**
SP1 3SP 🅿
☎ 01722 333734 ⓕ 01722 333734
Ⓜ 07709 203745
ⓔ john.lodge1@tesco.net
Est. 1971 *Stock size* Medium
Stock Coins, medals, small items and jewellery
Open Tues Thurs Fri 9am–4.30pm Sat 9am–1pm
Services Valuations

⊞ Fisherton Antiques Market
Contact Nigel Roberts
✉ **53 Fisherton Street, Salisbury, Wiltshire,**

SP2 7SU 🅿
☎ 01722 422147
Est. 1997 *Stock size* Small
Stock Victorian and Edwardian furniture, jewellery, modern and collectables
Open Mon–Sat 9.30am–5pm

Jonathan Green Antiques
Contact Jonathan Green
✉ **The Antiques Market, 37 Catherine Street, Salisbury, Wiltshire, SP1 2DH** 🅿
☎ 01722 332635 Ⓕ 01722 332635
Est. 1979 *Stock size* Medium
Stock Silver, silver plate and decorative items
Open Mon–Sat 10am–5pm

Myriad
Contact Karen Montlake
✉ **48–54 Milford Street, Salisbury, Wiltshire, SP1 2BP** 🅿
☎ 01722 413595/718203
Ⓕ 01722 416395
Ⓔ enquiries@myriad-antiques.co.uk
Ⓦ www.myriad-antiques.co.uk
Est. 1994 *Stock size* Large
Stock Georgian–Victorian furniture in pine, mahogany, oak. Lamps, clocks, mirrors, rugs
Open Mon–Sat 9.30am–5pm Sun by appointment
Services Stripping, collection and delivery within 80 miles, antique search

Salisbury Antiques Market
Contact Peter Beck
✉ **37 Catherine Street, Salisbury, Wiltshire, SP1 2DH** 🅿
☎ 01722 326033
Est. 1988 *Stock size* Large
No. of dealers 70
Stock Antiques, collectables
Open Mon–Sat 10am–5pm

Salisbury Antiques Warehouse Ltd
Contact Kevin Chase
✉ **94 Wilton Road, Salisbury, Wiltshire, SP2 7JJ** 🅿
☎ 01722 410634 Ⓕ 01722 410635
Ⓔ kevin@salisbury-antiques.co.uk
Est. 1965 *Stock size* Large
No. of dealers 12
Stock 18th–19thC furniture, paintings, clocks, bronzes, barometers
Open Mon–Fri 9.15am–5.30pm Sat 10am–4pm

Chris Wadge Clocks
Contact Patrick Wadge
✉ **83 Fisherton Street, Salisbury, Wiltshire, SP2 7ST** 🅿
☎ 01722 334467
Est. 1985 *Stock size* Small
Stock Carriage clocks, Vienna regulators, dial and mantel clocks, 1890–1900
Open Tues–Sat 9am–4pm closed 1–2pm
Services Restoration

Woolley and Wallis Salisbury Salerooms Ltd (SOFAA, BACA Award Winner 2002, 2003)
Contact Sarah Bennie
✉ **51–61 Castle Street, Salisbury, Wiltshire, SP1 3SU** 🅿
☎ 01722 424500 Ⓕ 01722 424508
Ⓔ enquiries@woolleyandwallis.co.uk
Ⓦ www.woolleyandwallis.co.uk
Est. 1884
Open Mon–Fri 9am–5.30pm Sat 9am–noon
Sales Household sales generally fortnightly on Fri at 10am, viewing Thurs 10am–7pm. 30 specialist sales a year including furniture, ceramics, silver and jewellery, books and maps, paintings, 20thC Decorative Arts, Art Deco, clocks and barometers
Catalogues Yes

SWINDON

Penny Farthing Antiques
Contact Ann Farthing
✉ **Victoria Centre, 138–139 Victoria Road, Swindon, Wiltshire, SN1 3BU** 🅿
☎ 01793 536668
Est. 1999 *Stock size* Large
No. of dealers 9
Stock Antiques and collectables
Open Mon–Sat 10am–5pm
Services Valuations

Sambourne House Antique Pine Ltd
Contact Tim or Kim Cove
✉ **Units 49–51, Brunel Shopping Centre, Swindon, Wiltshire, SN1 1LF** 🅿
☎ 01793 610855
Ⓔ tkcove34@globalnet.co.uk
Ⓦ www.sambourne-antiques.co.uk
Est. 1986 *Stock size* Large
Stock Antique and reproduction pine furniture, smalls, decorative items
Open Mon–Sun 9am–5pm
Services Hand-built kitchens

Allan Smith
Contact Mr A Smith
✉ **Amity Cottage, 162 Beechcroft Road, Upper Stratton, Swindon, Wiltshire, SN2 7QE** 🅿
☎ 01793 822977 Ⓕ 01793 822977
Ⓜ 07778 834342
Ⓔ allansmithclocks@lineone.net
Ⓦ www.allansmithantiqueclocks.co.uk
Est. 1988 *Stock size* Large
Stock 50–60 Fully restored longcase clocks including Moonphase, automata, painted dial, brass dial, 30-hour, 8-day etc in mahogany, lacquer, walnut and marquetry plus a selection of other antique clocks
Open By appointment any time
Services Valuations and clockfinder service

John Williams (PBFA)
Contact Mr Williams
✉ **93 Goddard Avenue, Swindon, Wiltshire, SN1 4HT** 🅿
☎ 01793 533313
Ⓔ john.williams24@virgin.net
Est. 1994 *Stock size* Small
Stock Antiquarian and second-hand children's and illustrated books. Three catalogues a year
Open By appointment
Fairs PBFA

Dominic Winter Book Auctions
Contact Admin Office
✉ **The Old School, Maxwell Street, Swindon, Wiltshire, SN1 5DR** 🅿
☎ 01793 611340 Ⓕ 01793 491727
Ⓔ info@dominicwinter.co.uk
Ⓦ www.dominicwinter.co.uk
Est. 1988
Open Mon–Fri 9.30am–5.30pm
Sales General book sale Wed 11am, viewing day prior to sale

10am–7pm. Specialist single category sale Thurs 11am, viewing day prior to sale 10am–7pm
Frequency Every 5 weeks
Catalogues Yes

WARMINSTER

Cassidy Antiques and Restorations (BABAADA)
Contact Matthew Cassidy
7 Silver Street, Warminster, Wiltshire, BA12 8PS
01985 213313 01985 213313
07050 206806
mat_cassidy@yahoo.com
www.cassidyantiques.com
Est. 1994 *Stock size* Medium
Stock Georgian and Victorian furniture
Open Mon–Fri 9am–5pm Sat 10am–5pm
Services Restoration

Choice Antiques
Contact Avril Bailey
4 Silver Street, Warminster, Wiltshire, BA12 8PS
01985 218924
Est. 1987 *Stock size* Medium
Stock Small, the unusual, furniture, decorative objects
Open Mon–Sat 10am–5pm
Services Valuations, shipping

Collectable Interiors
Contact David Swanton
33 Silver Street, Warminster, Wiltshire, BA12 8PT
01985 217177
Est. 1967 *Stock size* Medium
Stock Furniture and accessories
Open Mon–Sat 10am–5pm

Annabelle Giltsoff
Contact Anabelle Giltsoff
3 Silver Street, Warminster, Wiltshire, BA12 8PS
01985 218933
Est. 1984 *Stock size* Medium
Stock Paintings and frames
Open Mon–Sat 9.30am–1pm 2–5pm
Services Picture restoration and gilding

Isabella Antiques (BABAADA)
Contact Mr B W Semke
3 Silver Street, Warminster, Wiltshire, BA12 8PS
01985 218933
Est. 1990 *Stock size* Medium
Stock 18th–19thC mahogany furniture, 19thC gilt mirrors
Open Mon–Sat 10am–5pm

Lewis Antiques & Interiors
Contact Sandie Lewis
9 Silver Street, Warminster, Wiltshire, BA12 8PS
01985 846222
07764 576106
Est. 2004 *Stock size* Medium
Stock General antiques, furniture, textiles, rugs, silver, glass, ceramics
Open Wed–Sat 10am–5pm
Fairs Bath Decorative
Services Valuations, restoration, shipping, antiques search

Obelisk Antiques (LAPADA, BABAADA)
Contact Mr P Tanswell
2 Silver Street, Warminster, Wiltshire, BA12 8PS
01985 846646 01985 219901
07718 630673
all@obelisk-antiques.freeserve.co.uk
Est. 1979 *Stock size* Large
Stock 18th–19thC French, English and Continental furniture
Open Mon–Sat 10am–1pm 2–5.30pm

Warminster Antique Centre (BABAADA)
Contact Mr P Walton
6 Silver Street, Warminster, Wiltshire, BA12 8PT
01985 847269 01985 211778
07860 584193
Est. 1993 *Stock size* Large
No. of dealers 15
Stock Wide range of antiques and collectable items, furniture, clocks, paintings, models, linens, fabrics, etc
Open Mon–Sat 10am–5pm
Services Valuations

WEST YATTON

Heirloom & Howard Ltd (BABAADA)
Contact David or Angela Howard
Manor Farm, West Yatton, Chippenham, Wiltshire, SN14 7EU
01249 783038 01249 783039
Est. 1973 *Stock size* Medium
Stock Chinese armorial and other export porcelain, armorial paintings, coach panels, hall chairs, portrait engravings
Open Mon–Fri 10am–6pm Sat 10am–6pm or by appointment
Services Bidding at auction

WESTBURY

Ray Coggins Antiques
Contact Mr R Coggins
1 Fore Street, Westbury, Wiltshire, BA13 3AU
01373 826574 01373 827996
Est. 1974 *Stock size* Large
Stock Antique, country and decorative furniture, architectural antiques
Open Mon–Thurs 9am–5pm Fri 9am–2pm

WILTON

Bay Tree Antiques
Contact Mrs J D Waymouth
26 North Street, Wilton, Wiltshire, SP2 0HJ
01722 743392 01722 743392
Est. 1997 *Stock size* Medium
Stock Period furniture, decorative furniture and items
Open Mon–Sat 9am–5.30pm
Fairs Battersea Decorative, Arundel Castle

Hingstons of Wilton
Contact Nick Hingston
36 North Street, Wilton, Wiltshire, SP2 0HJ
01722 742263
nick@hingston-antiques.freeserve.co.uk
hingston-antiques.freeserve.co.uk
Est. 1976 *Stock size* Large
Stock 18th–early 20thC furniture, clocks, pictures
Open Mon–Fri 9am–5pm Sat 10am–4pm
Services Valuations

EAST

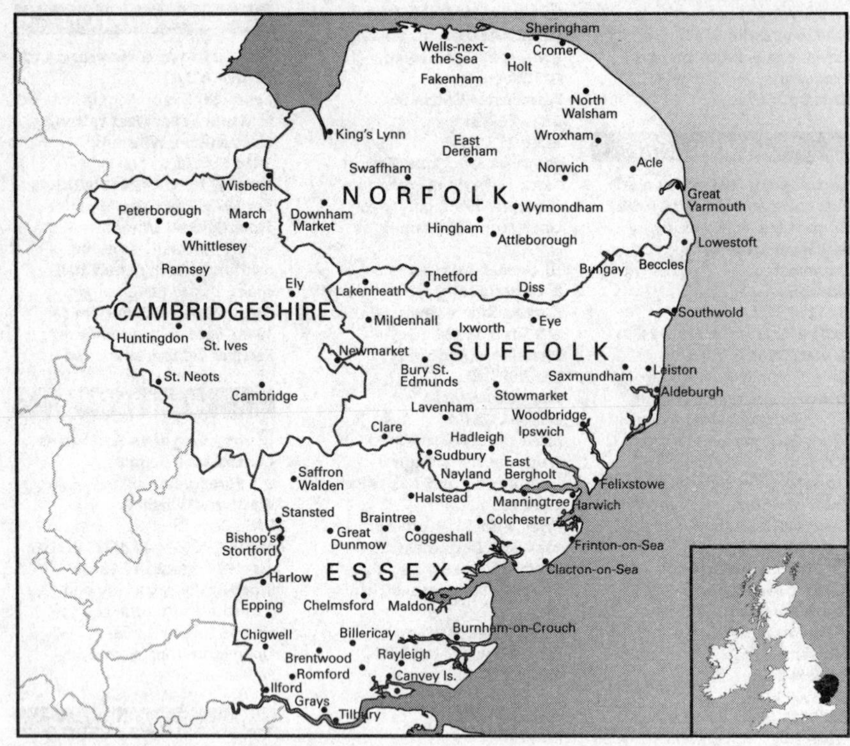

CAMBRIDGESHIRE

BALSHAM

⊞ Ward-Thomas Antiques
Contact Mr C R F Ward-Thomas
✉ **7 High Street, Balsham, Cambridge, Cambridgeshire, CB1 6DJ** 🅿
☎ 01223 892431 Ⓕ 01223 892367
Ⓔ wtantiques@onetel.com
Est. 1997 *Stock size* Large
Stock Continental pine furniture, furniture accessories
Open Mon–Fri 9am–5pm
Sat 10am–5pm Sun 10am–4pm
Fairs Newark, Kempton Park
Services Restoration, mail orders

BURWELL

⊞ Peter Norman Antiques
Contact Mr Peter Norman
✉ **55 North Street, Burwell, Cambridge, Cambridgeshire, CB5 0BA** 🅿
☎ 01638 616914
Ⓦ www.peternormanantiques.co.uk
Est. 1979 *Stock size* Medium
Stock 18th–19thC furniture, Oriental rugs, clocks, pictures, prints
Open Mon–Sat 9am–5.30pm
Fairs Stafford, Newmarket
Services Restoration

CAMBRIDGE

⊞ Jess Applin (BADA)
Contact Mr J Applin
✉ **8 Lensfield Road, Cambridge, Cambridgeshire, CB2 1EG** 🅿
☎ 01223 315168
Est. 1975 *Stock size* Medium
Stock 17th–19thC furniture, works of art
Open Mon–Sat 9.30am–5.30pm

⊞ John Beazor & Sons Ltd (BADA)
Contact Mr M Beazor
✉ **78–80 Regent Street, Cambridge, Cambridgeshire, CB2 1DP**
☎ 01223 355178 Ⓕ 01223 355183
Ⓜ 07774 123379
Ⓔ martin@johnbeazorantiques.co.uk
Ⓦ www.johnbeazorantiques.co.uk
Est. 1875 *Stock size* Large
Stock English furniture late 17th–early 19thC furniture, clocks, barometers, decorative items
Open Mon–Fri 9.15am–5pm
Sat 10am–4pm
Fairs Open weekend exhibitions held on the premises in May, November
Services Valuations

⊞ La Belle Epoque
Contact Mrs C Keverne
✉ **55a Hills Road, Cambridge, Cambridgeshire, CB2 1NT** 🅿
☎ 01223 506688
Est. 1986 *Stock size* Medium
Stock Period lighting, small items
Open Tues–Sat 11am–5pm

Bonhams
17 Emmanuel Road, Cambridge, Cambridgeshire, CB1 1JW
01223 366523 012223 300208
cambridge@bonhams.com
www.bonhams.com
Open Mon–Fri 8.30am–5pm
Sales Regional office. Regular house and attic sales across the country; contact London offices for further details. Free auction valuations; insurance and probate valuations

The Book Shop
Contact Mr P Bright or Mr H Hardinge
24 Magdalene Street, Cambridge, Cambridgeshire, CB3 0AF
01223 362457
Est. 1996 *Stock size* Medium
Stock Antiquarian, second-hand, out-of-print books
Open Mon–Sat 10.30am–5.30pm

Books & Collectables Ltd
Contact Mr A Doyle
Unit 7–8, Railway Arches, Coldhams Road, Cambridge, Cambridgeshire, CB1 3EW P
01223 412845 01223 412845
07703 795206
ask@booksandcollectables.com
www.booksandcollectables.com
Est. 1996 *Stock size* Large
Stock 16thC–modern books, comics, toys, postcards, cigarette cards, records, pop memorabilia, magazines, china, furniture
Open Mon–Sat 9.30am–5pm Sun 10am–4pm
Services Valuations, shipping

Buckies (NAG, LAPADA)
Contact Robin Wilson
31 Trinity Street, Cambridge, Cambridgeshire, CB2 1TB
01223 357910 01233 357920
Est. 1953 *Stock size* Medium
Stock Jewellery, silver
Open Tues–Sat 9.45am–5pm
Services Valuations

Cheffins
Contact J G Law, C B Ashton or R Haywood
2 Clifton Road, Cambridge, Cambridgeshire, CB1 4BW P
01223 213343 01223 413396
fine.art@cheffins.co.uk
www.cheffins.co.uk
Est. 1824
Open Mon–Fri 9am–5pm
Sales 45 sales a year of antiques and later furnishings, specialist fine art and furniture sales. Catalogues and information available on website
Frequency Fortnightly
Catalogues Yes

Peter Crabbe Antiques
Contact Mr P Crabbe
3 Pembroke Street, Cambridge, Cambridgeshire, CB2 3QY
01223 357117
Est. 1988 *Stock size* Large
Stock English furniture, Oriental porcelain, works of art
Open Mon–Sat 9.30am–5pm
Services Valuations

G David (ABA, PBFA, BA)
Contact David Asplin, N T Adams or B L Collings
16 St Edward's Passage, Cambridge, Cambridgeshire, CB2 3PJ
01223 354619 01223 324663
Est. 1896 *Stock size* Large
Stock Antiquarian books, prints, publishers' remainders, fine antiquarian books a speciality
Open Mon–Sat 9am–5pm
Fairs PBFA Oxford, London (June), ABA (Nov)

Gabor Cossa Antiques
Contact David Theobald
34 Trumpington Street, Cambridge, Cambridgeshire, CB2 1QY P
01223 356049
Est. 1947 *Stock size* Large
Stock 18th–19thC ceramics, small items
Open Mon–Sat 10am–5.30pm

Gannochy Coins and Medals
Contact Mr A Hawk
46 Burleigh Street, Cambridge, Cambridgeshire, CB1 1DJ P
01223 361662
coingranta@aol.com
Est. 1978 *Stock size* Large
Stock Coins and medals, bank notes
Open Mon–Sat 9am–5pm Sun 11am–4pm
Services Valuations, appraisals, probate

Gwydir Street Antiques
Contact Mrs P Gibb
Units 1 & 2, Dales Brewery, Gwydir Street, Cambridge, Cambridgeshire, CB1 2LJ P
01223 356391
Est. 1987 *Stock size* Medium
No. of dealers 10
Stock Furniture, bric-a-brac, collectables, decorative items
Open Mon–Sat 10am–5pm Sun 11am–5pm

The Haunted Bookshop (PBFA)
Contact Mrs Sarah Key
9 St Edward's Passage, Cambridge, Cambridgeshire, CB2 3PJ
01223 312913 08700 0569392
sarahkey@hauntedbooks.demon.co.uk
Est. 1987 *Stock size* Medium
Stock Antiquarian, second-hand, children's books, particularly girls' school stories
Open Mon–Sat 10am–5pm
Fairs PBFA
Services Mail order worldwide, book search for children's titles, catalogues, valuations

The Hive
Contact Brenda Blakemore
Unit 3, Dales Brewery, Gwydir Street, Cambridge, Cambridgeshire, CB1 2LG P
01223 300269
Est. 1987 *Stock size* Medium
No. of dealers 10
Stock Antique pine, kitchenware, collectables, period lighting, pictures, Victorian–Edwardian furniture, bric-a-brac, tiles
Open Mon–Sat 9.30am–5.30pm Sun 11am–5pm
Services Commissions undertaken

The Old Chemist Shop Antique Centre
Contact Mrs J Tucker
206 Mill Road, Cambridge, Cambridgeshire, CB1 3NF P
01223 247324
Est. 1996 *Stock size* Large

No. of dealers 5
Stock General antiques, collectables
Open Mon–Fri 10am–5pm Sat 10am–5.30pm
Services Clock repair, house clearance

Those Were The Days
Contact Julia or Richard Henderson
91 & 93 Mill Road, Cambridge, Cambridgeshire, CB1 2AW P
01223 300440
Est. 1991 *Stock size* Large
No. of dealers 12
Stock Furniture, lighting, fireplaces
Open Mon–Fri 10am–5pm Sat 9.30am–5.30pm Sun 11am–5pm

Willroy Antiques Centre
Contact Mr Roy Williams
Unit 5, Dales Brewery, Gwydir Street, Cambridge, Cambridgeshire, CB1 2LJ P
01223 311687 F 01480 352853
M 07793 0193830
E rwilliams4@ntl.com
Est. 1985 *Stock size* Large
No. of dealers 6
Stock General antiques
Open Mon–Sat 10am–5pm Sun noon–4pm
Services Restoration

CHATTERIS

James Fuller and Son
Contact Steven Fuller
51 Huntingdon Road, Chatteris, Cambridgeshire, PE16 6JE P
01354 692740
Est. 1919 *Stock size* Large
Stock Telephone and letter boxes
Open Mon–Fri 8am–12.30pm 1.30–5pm

CHITTERING

Simon & Penny Rumble Antiques
Contact Mrs P Rumble
Causeway End Farmhouse, School Lane, Chittering, Cambridge, Cambridgeshire, CB5 9PW P
01223 861831
M 07778 917300
E prumble@beeb.net
Est. 1980 *Stock size* Small
Stock Early oak, country furniture, woodcarving
Open By appointment
Fairs NEC

COMBERTON

Comberton Antiques & Interiors
Contact Mrs Tunstall
5 Green End, Comberton, Cambridgeshire, CB3 7DY
01223 262674
E enquiries@combertonantiques.co.uk
W www.combertonantiques.co.uk
Est. 1984 *Stock size* Large
Stock General furniture including Continental pine, soft furnishings
Open Mon Thurs–Sat 10am–5pm Sun 2–5pm
Fairs Newark, Ardingly
Services Shipping

DUXFORD

Riro D Mooney
Contact Mr R Mooney
Mill Lane, Duxford, Cambridgeshire, CB2 4PS
01223 832252
Est. 1946 *Stock size* Large
Stock Victorian–Edwardian furniture
Open Mon–Sat 9am–6.30pm Sun 10am–noon 2.30–5pm
Services Restoration

ELY

Cloisters Antiques (PBFA)
Contact Barry Lonsdale
1a Lynn Road, Ely, Cambridgeshire, CB7 4EG P
01353 668558
M 07767 881677
E info@cloistersantiques.co.uk
W www.cloistersantiques.co.uk
Est. 1997 *Stock size* Medium
Stock General clocks, china, second-hand and antiquarian books, mainly smalls
Open Mon–Sat 10.30am–4.30pm Sun 12.30–4.30pm closed Tues
Services Valuations

Griffin Antiques
Contact E Griffin
13 Fore Hill, Ely, Cambridgeshire, CB7 4AA
01353 666672
E egriffinantiques@btconnect.com
Est. 2000 *Stock size* Medium
Stock General antiques
Open Mon–Sat 10am–5.30pm
Services Valuations, restoration

Mrs Mills' Antiques Etc.
Contact Mrs M Mills
1a St Mary's Street, Ely, Cambridgeshire, CB7 4ER P
01353 664268
Est. 1968 *Stock size* Large
Stock Porcelain, silver, jewellery
Open Mon–Sat 10am–5pm closed Tues

Rowley Fine Art
Contact Diane White
8 Downham Road, Ely, Cambridgeshire, CB6 1AH P
01353 653020 F 01353 653022
W www.rowleyfineart.com
Est. 1994
Open Mon–Fri 9am–5pm
Sales Fine art and antique sales, specialist sales of film posters, taxidermy, toys
Frequency 6 per annum
Catalogues Yes

Valued History
Contact Mr Paul Murawski
9 Market Place, Ely, Cambridgeshire, CB7 4NP
01353 654080 F 01353 654080
E murawski@pmurawski.fsnet.co.uk
W www.historyforsale.co.uk
Est. 1996 *Stock size* Medium
Stock Coins, antiquities
Open Tues–Sat 10am–5pm
Services Valuations

Waterside Antiques
Contact Mr G Peters
The Wharf, Waterside, Ely, Cambridgeshire, CB7 4AU P
01353 667066
Est. 1985 *Stock size* Large
No. of dealers 68
Stock Furniture, collectables
Open Mon–Sat 9.30am–5.30pm Sun 11.30am–5.30pm
Services Valuations, clearances

FORDHAM

Phoenix Antiques
Contact Mr K Bycroft
Homelands, 1 Carter Street, Fordham, Ely, Cambridgeshire, CB7 5NG
01638 720363
Est. 1966 *Stock size* Medium
Stock Everything for a European interior prior to 1750
Open By appointment
Services Valuations

HADDENHAM

Hereward Books (PBFA)
Contact Mr R Pratt
17 High Street, Haddenham, Ely, Cambridgeshire, CB6 3XA
01353 740821 01353 741721
sales@herewardbooks.co.uk
www.herewardbooks.co.uk
Est. 1984 *Stock size* Medium
Stock Rare and collectable books, specializing in field sports and fishing
Open Mon Tues Thurs 10am–4pm Fri Sat 10am–1pm
Fairs PBFA Russell Hotel, CLA Game Fair

Ludovic Potts Antiques (BAFRA)
Contact Mr Ludovic Potts
Unit 1–1a, Station Road, Haddenham, Ely, Cambridgeshire, CB6 3XD
01353 741537 01353 741822
07889 341671
mail@restorers.co.uk
www.restorers.co.uk
Est. 2001 *Stock size* Small
Stock Polished wood furniture, upholstered chairs, sofas, soft furnishings, porcelain, gilt mirrors
Open By appointment
Services Restoration

HUNTINGDON

Houghton Antiques
Contact Jean Stevens
Thicket Road, Houghton, Huntingdon, Cambridgeshire, PE28 2BQ
01480 461887
07803 716842
Est. 2000 *Stock size* Medium
Stock General antiques, small items of furniture, pottery, porcelain, silver, sporting items, prints
Open Mon–Sun 1–5.30pm
Fairs Alexandra Palace

Huntingdon Trading Post
Contact Mr John De'Ath
1 St Mary's Street, Huntingdon, Cambridgeshire, PE29 3PE
01480 450998 01480 431142
j.death@ntlworld.com
www.huntingdontradingpost.co.uk
Est. 2001 *Stock size* Large
No. of dealers 42
Stock General antiques, including furniture, clocks, collectables, brassware, pictures
Open Mon–Sat 9am–5pm Sun 10am–2pm

IMPINGTON

Woodcock House Antiques
Contact Mr A M Peat
83–85 Station Road, Impington, Cambridge, Cambridgeshire, CB4 9NP
01223 232858
Est. 1978 *Stock size* Large
Stock Late 19thC decorative furniture, Aesthetic items, smalls, furniture
Open Mon–Fri 10am–5pm or by appointment
Services Valuations

KIMBOLTON

Mark Seabrook Antiques (LAPADA)
Contact Mr M Seabrook
PO Box 396, Kimbolton, Huntingdon, Cambridgeshire, PE28 0ZA
01480 861935
07770 721931
enquiries@markseabrook.com
www.markseabrook.com
Est. 1996 *Stock size* Medium
Stock Early English oak, country furniture, metalware, treen, ceramics
Open By appointment 7 days
Fairs NEC, Kensington, Chelsea
Services Restoration

LANDBEACH

Cambridge Pianola Company and J V Pianos
Contact Tom Poole
The Limes, High Street, Landbeach, Cambridgeshire, CB4 8DR
01223 861348 01223 441276
ftpoole@talk21.com
www.cambridgepianolacompany.co.uk
Est. 1972 *Stock size* Medium
Stock Pianos, pianolas and player pianos
Open Appointment preferred
Services Restoration

MARCH

Fagins
Contact Mrs P Humby
9 Station Road, March, Cambridgeshire, PE15 0JL
01354 656445
Est. 1998 *Stock size* Medium
Stock General antiques, furniture, collectables
Open Mon–Sat 10am–5pm closed Tues

PEAKIRK

Peakirk Bookshop
Contact Jeffrey Lawrence
St Pegas Road, Peakirk, Peterborough, Cambridgeshire, PE6 7NF
01733 253182
peakirkbooks@btinternet.com
www.peakirkbooks.com
Est. 1997 *Stock size* Medium
Stock Collectable and out-of-print books
Open Thurs Fri Sat 9.30am–5pm Sun noon–4pm or by appointment
Services Catalogue on request

PETERBOROUGH

Antiques & Curios Shop
Contact Mr M Mason
249 Lincoln Road, Millfield, Peterborough, Cambridgeshire, PE1 2PL
01733 314948
07749 876456
Est. 1989 *Stock size* Medium
Stock Mahogany, oak, pine, country furniture, fireplaces

Open Mon–Sat 10am–5pm
Fairs Newark, RAF Swinderby
Services Restoration

T V Coles
Contact Mr T V Coles
981 Lincoln Road, Peterborough, Cambridgeshire, PE4 6AH
01733 577268
Est. 1980 *Stock size* Medium
Stock Antiquarian, out-of-print, second-hand books, militaria, ephemera, postcards etc
Open Mon–Sat 9am–4.30pm

Fitzwilliam Antiques Centre
Contact Mr Paul Stafford
20–22 Fitzwilliam Street, Peterborough, Cambridgeshire, PE1 2RX
01733 566346 01733 565415
Est. 1990 *Stock size* Large
No. of dealers 20
Stock General antiques, collectables
Open Mon–Sat 10am–5pm
Services Valuations, restoration, repairs

RAMSEY

Abbey Antiques
Contact Mr J Smith
63 Great Whyte, Ramsey, Cambridgeshire, PE26 1HL
01487 814753
Est. 1979 *Stock size* Medium
Stock General antiques, collectables
Open Tues–Sun 10am–5pm
Fairs Alexandra Palace
Services Valuations, Mabel Lucie Attwell Museum and Collectors' Club

Antique Barometers
Contact William Rae
Wingfield, 26 Biggin Lane, Ramsey, Cambridgeshire, PE26 1NB
01487 814060 01487 814060
antiquebarometers@talk21.com
Est. 1996 *Stock size* Medium
Stock Early stick and wheel barometers, barographs
Open By appointment
Fairs Hinchingbrook House, Putteridge Bury House
Services Valuations, restoration

SOHAM

Burwell Auctions
Contact Mr N Reed-Herbert
The Church Hall, High Street, Soham, Ely, Cambridgeshire, CB7 5HD
01353 727100 01353 727101
Est. 1984
Open By appointment
Sales General antique sales, viewing day prior to sale 9am–5pm and day of sale 9am–10.30am or by appointment
Catalogues Yes

ST IVES

Hyperion Auction Centre (ICOM)
Contact Mrs Pat Bernard
Station Road, St Ives, Huntingdon, Cambridgeshire, PE27 5BH
01480 464140 01480 497552
enquiries@hyperion-auctions.co.uk
www.hyperion-auctions.co.uk
Est. 1995
Open Mon–Sat 9.30am–5pm
Sales General antiques sale 2nd Mon monthly 10.30am, viewing Sat prior 9.30am–5pm Mon 9.30–10.30am
Catalogues Yes

Quay Court Antiques
Contact Mr M Knight
Bull Lane, Bridge Street, St Ives, Huntingdon, Cambridgeshire, PE17 4AZ
01480 468295
michaelknight@compuserve.com
Est. 1972 *Stock size* Medium
Stock Pottery, porcelain, pictures, jewellery
Open Mon 11am–2pm
Wed 10.30am–4pm
Fri 11am–2pm Sat 11am–4pm
Services Valuations, talks to antiques clubs

ST NEOTS

Brentside Programmes
Contact Mr Chris Ward
1 Dial Close, Little Paxton, St Neots, Huntingdon, Cambridgeshire, PE19 4QN
01480 474682 01480 370650
sales@brentside.co.uk
www.brentside.co.uk
Est. 1974 *Stock size* Medium
Stock Football memorabilia, mostly mail order
Open Mon–Fri 9am–5pm

Peggy's Pandora
Contact Mr B George
10 Crosskeys Mews, Market Square, St Neots, Huntingdon, Cambridgeshire, PE19 2AR
01480 403580
Est. 1991 *Stock size* Medium
Stock Postcards, medals, coins, toys, small items
Open Mon–Sat 9am–5pm

WHITTLESEY

The Old Pine Shop
Contact Kent or Adele Griffin
96 Norfolk Street, Wisbech, Cambridgeshire, PE13 2LS
01945 464555
Est. 1992 *Stock size* Medium
Stock Antique English and Continental pine furniture
Open Mon–Sat 9am–5pm

WISBECH

Steve Carpenter
Contact Mr S Carpenter
95 Norfolk Street, Wisbech, Cambridgeshire, PE13 2LF
01945 588441 01945 588441
Est. 1997 *Stock size* Medium
Stock 18th–19thC country furniture, longcase clocks, quality smalls
Open Mon–Sat 9am–5pm

Peter A Crofts
Contact Mrs Crofts
117 High Road, Wisbech, Cambridgeshire, PE14 0DN
01945 584614
Est. 1949 *Stock size* Large
Stock General antiques, furniture, silver, china, jewellery
Open By appointment
Services Valuations

Granny's Cupboard Antiques
Contact Mr R J Robbs
34 Old Market, Wisbech, Cambridgeshire, PE13 1NF
01945 589606/870730

Ⓜ 07721 616154
Est. 1985 *Stock size* Medium
Stock Victorian–Edwardian china, glass and furniture to 1950s
Open Tues Thurs 10.30am–4pm Sat 10.30am–3pm
Fairs The Maltings, Ely

Grounds & Co
Contact Mr R Barnwell
✉ **2 Nene Quay, Wisbech, Cambridgeshire, PE13 1AQ** Ⓟ
☎ 01945 580713 Ⓕ 01945 580713
Ⓜ 07885 431520
Ⓔ antiques@grounds-wisbech.co.uk
Ⓦ www.grounds.co.uk
Est. 1792
Open Mon–Fri 9am–5pm Sat 9am–4pm
Sales Antiques and collectors' sales 3 times a year. Telephone for details
Catalogues Yes

Maxey & Son
Contact John Maxey
✉ **Auction Hall, Cattle Market Chase, Wisbech, Cambridgeshire, PE13 1RD** Ⓟ
☎ 01945 584609 Ⓕ 01945 589440
Ⓔ mail@maxeyandson.co.uk
Ⓦ www.maxeyandson.co.uk
Est. 1856
Open Mon–Fri 9am–5pm Sat 9am–noon
Sales General sales with some antiques and collectables twice weekly on Wed and Sat 10am, viewing any day. Occasional special antiques sales
Catalogues No

ESSEX

BASILDON

Bear Essentials
Contact Kim Brown
✉ **64a Eastgate Shopping Centre, Basildon, Essex, SS14 1AF** Ⓟ
☎ 01268 270154 Ⓕ 01268 270154
Ⓔ hugs@companyofbears.com
Ⓦ www.companyofbears.com
Est. 2000 *Stock size* Large
Stock Collectable bears, Steiff, Dean's and Hermann Club store
Open Mon–Sat 10am–5.30pm

Sport and Star Autographs (UACC, IADA)
Contact Toni McLennan
✉ **64 East Gate Shopping Centre, Southernhay, Basildon, Essex, SS14 1AF**
☎ 01268 524500
Ⓦ www.autographs.me.uk
Est. 2000 *Stock size* Large
Stock Autographs, sport, film, music, signed memorabilia
Open Mon–Sat 9.30am–5.30pm
Services Valuations

BATTLESBRIDGE

Battlesbridge Antiques Centre
Contact Jim Gallie
✉ **Hawk Hill, Battlesbridge, Wickford, Essex, SS11 7RE** Ⓟ
☎ 01268 575000 Ⓕ 01268 575001
Ⓔ jim.gallie@virgin.net
Ⓦ www.battlesbridge.com
Est. 1969 *Stock size* Large
No. of dealers 80
Stock General antiques, collectables
Open Mon–Sun 10am–5.30pm
Services Valuations

The Bones Lane Antiques Centre
Contact Mr Pettitt
✉ **The Green, Chelmsford Road, Battlesbridge, Wickford, Essex, SS11 7RJ** Ⓟ
☎ 01268 763500 Ⓕ 01268 763500
Est. 1969 *Stock size* Medium
No. of dealers 12
Stock Gas, oil and early electric lighting, gramophones
Open Tues–Sun 10am–4.30pm closed Thurs
Services Restoration of lighting and gramophones

Bridgebarn Antiques (EADA)
Contact Mr Pettitt
✉ **The Bones Lane Antiques Centre, The Green, Chelmsford Road, Battlesbridge, Wickford, Essex, SS11 7RJ** Ⓟ
☎ 01268 763500 Ⓕ 01268 763500
Est. 1969 *Stock size* Medium
Stock Gas, oil and early electric lighting, gramophones
Open Tues–Sun 10am–4.30pm closed Thurs
Services Restoration of lighting and gramophones

Jim Gallie Antiques
Contact Paul Elliott
✉ **Muggeridge Farm, Maltings Road, Battlesbridge, Essex, SS11 7RF** Ⓟ
☎ 01268 769000 Ⓕ 01268 769006
Ⓔ jim@jimgallieantiques.com
Ⓦ www.jimgallieantiques.com
Est. 1969 *Stock size* Large
Stock General antiques
Open Mon–Sun 10am–5pm
Services Valuations

Phoenix Fireplaces
Contact John or Cris
✉ **Hawk Hill, Battlesbridge, Essex, SS11 7RE** Ⓟ
☎ 01268 768844 Ⓕ 01268 768844
Ⓜ 07956 556442
Ⓦ www.phoenix-fireplaces.co.uk
Est. 1991 *Stock size* Large
Stock Fireplaces
Open Mon–Sun 10am–5.30pm

Trails End Collectables Ltd
Contact Pat Stoneham
✉ **3rd Floor, The Old Granary, Battlesbridge Antique Centre, Battlesbridge, Wickford, Essex, SS11 7RE** Ⓟ
☎ 01277 656750 Ⓕ 01268 764138
Ⓜ 07941 179031
Ⓔ vintage@collectibles99.freeserve.co.uk
Est. 1991 *Stock size* Small
Stock 20thC US collectables
Open Mon–Sun 10am–5.30pm

BENFLEET

E J & C A Brooks (BNTA, IBNS)
Contact Mr E J Brooks
✉ **44 Kiln Road, Thundersley, Benfleet, Essex, SS7 1TB** Ⓟ
☎ 01268 753835
Ⓜ 07850 262629
Est. 1974 *Stock size* Large
Stock Coins, English and foreign bank notes
Open By appointment
Fairs York, Birmingham, Cumberland Hotel
Services Free valuations

BRENTWOOD

Le-Potier
Contact Mr S Hall
✉ **42 King's Road,**

Brentwood, Essex,
CM14 4DW
☎ 01277 216310
Est. 1985 *Stock size* Small
Stock Collectables
Open Tues Wed Fri Sat
10am–5pm
Services China restoration

BRIGHTLINGSEA

Shipwreck Centre
Contact Mr M K Kettle
22e Marshes Yard, Victoria Place, Brightlingsea, Colchester, Essex, CO7 0BX P
☎ 01206 307307
Est. 1995 *Stock size* Large
No. of dealers 15
Stock Collectables, furniture, books, arts, crafts
Open Mon–Sun 10am–5pm
Services House clearance

BROOMFIELD

Ruegavarret Ltd
Contact Mr I Honeywood
93 Main Road, Broomfield, Chelmsford, Essex, CM1 7DQ P
☎ 01245 442013/363977
Est. 1994 *Stock size* Medium
Stock Antique pine furniture, ceramics, brass, pictures
Open Wed–Sun 10am–3pm
Services Free delivery

BURSTALL

Lion House Antiques Ltd (EADA)
Contact Mr P Young
Fen Farm, Hadleigh Road, Burstall, Ipswich, Essex, IP8 3EG P
☎ 01473 652084
M 07802 955829 or 07884 266901
E lionpy@aol.com
Est. 1991 *Stock size* Large
Stock 17th–19thC English furniture, chairs, oak farmhouse tables, hand-made replica furniture
Open By appointment
Fairs Newark, DMG fairs, Arthur Swallow fairs, High Point Furniture Market, North Carolina
Services Valuations, restoration, house clearance

CHELMSFIELD

Yesterdays Components Ltd
Contact Harry Edwards
Wellwood Farm, Lowestock Road, Chelmsfield, Essex, CM8 8UY
☎ 01277 840697 F 01277 841185
Est. 1986 *Stock size* Large
Stock Spare parts for pre-war design Morris vehicles
Open Mail order only
Services Item search

CHELMSFORD

Garners at The Maltings Antiques, Clocks & Collectables Centre
Contact Nick Garner
Chelmsford Road, Norton Heath, Chelmsford, Essex, CM4 0LN P
☎ 01277 823975
M 07970 206682
E nickgarner@btinternet.com
W www.ngarners.co.uk
Est. 1998 *Stock size* Large
Stock Studio and art pottery, Sally Tuffin (Dennis chinaworks), Roger Cockram, Highland stoneware, Dartington pottery, Malcolm Sutcliffe glass, clocks, barometers, furniture
Open Mon–Sat 10am–5pm
Sun 10am–4pm
Services Valuations

The Maltings Antiques Centre
Contact Nick Garner
Chelmsford Road, Norton Heath, Chelmsford, Essex, CM4 0LN P
☎ 01277 823975
M 07970 206682
E themaltings@themaltingsantiques.co.uk
W www.themaltingsantiques.co.uk
Est. 1998 *Stock size* Medium
No. of dealers 20
Stock Clocks, barometers, furniture, jewellery, china, glass, porcelain, collectables, silver, silver plate, art pottery
Open Mon–Sat 10am–5pm
Sun 10am–4pm

S H Rowland
Contact Mr S H Rowland
42 Mildmay Road, Chelmsford, Essex, CM2 0DZ P
☎ 01245 354251 F 01245 344466
Est. 1946
Open Mon–Fri 9am–5.30pm
Sales Lesser-quality goods alternate weeks, antiques 2–3 a year on Wed, viewing Tues 9am–4.30pm Wed 9–10am
Catalogues Yes

COGGESHALL

English Rose Antiques
Contact Mr M Barrett
7 Church Street, Coggeshall, Essex, CO6 1TU P
☎ 01376 562683 F 01376 563450
M 07770 880790
E englishroseantiques@hotmail.com
Est. 1983 *Stock size* Large
Stock Antiques and country pine furniture
Open Mon–Sun 10am–5.30pm
Fairs Ardingly, Newark
Services Stripping, finishing

Partners in Pine
Contact Mr W T Newton
63–65 West Street, Coggeshall, Colchester, Essex, CO6 1NS P
☎ 01376 561972
Est. 1983 *Stock size* Medium
Stock Victorian pine furniture
Open Mon–Sun 10am–6pm
closed Wed

COLCHESTER

Elizabeth Cannon Antiques
Contact Mrs E Cannon
85 Crouch Street, Colchester, Essex, CO3 3EZ P
☎ 01206 575817
Est. 1978 *Stock size* Large
Stock Antique glass, jewellery, silver, porcelain, furniture
Open Mon–Sat 9.30am–5.30pm

The Castle Book Shop (PBFA)
Contact Mr R Green
40 Osborne Street, Colchester, Essex, CO2 7DB
☎ 01206 577520 F 01206 577520
Est. 1947 *Stock size* Large
Stock Antiquarian and second-

hand books, East Anglia, archaeology, modern first editions, maps, prints
Open Mon–Sat 9am–5pm
Fairs PBFA
Services Book search

Katamaras Collectors Centre
Contact Roger Steward
6 Church Walk, Off Head Street, Colchester, Essex, CO1 1NS
01206 769224
Est. 1989 *Stock size* Medium
Stock Stamps
Open Tues Wed Fri Sat 10am–3pm
Services Valuations

Mill Antiques
Contact J Wingfield
10 East Street, Colchester, Essex, CO1 2TX P
01206 500996
Est. 1960 *Stock size* Large
Stock Victorian, Edwardian mahogany furniture
Open Mon–Sat 10am–5pm

Reeman, Dansie, Howe & Son
Contact Mr J Grinter
12 Headgate, Colchester, Essex, CO3 3BT
01206 574271 F 01206 578213
E auctions@reemans.com
Est. 1881
Open Mon–Fri 9am–5.30pm
Sales Antiques and general sales Wed 10am, viewing Tues 9am–7pm Wed 9am–10pm. Also weekly household goods sales
Frequency Every 6–8 weeks
Catalogues Yes

Stanfords
Contact Mr David Lord
11 East Hill, Colchester, Essex, CO1 2QX P
01206 868070 F 01206 869590
E info@stanfords-colchester.co.uk
Est. 1995
Open Mon–Fri 9am–5.30pm
Sales Quarterly general goods Sat 10.30am, antique furniture, collectables, viewing Fri 2–6pm Sat 8.30–10.30am
Frequency Weekly
Catalogues Yes

Trinity Antiques Centre
Contact Janet Last
7 Trinity Street, Colchester, Essex, CO1 1JN
01206 577775
Est. 1976 *Stock size* Medium
No. of dealers 12
Stock Silver, jewellery, military, glass, collectables
Open Mon–Sat 9.30am–5pm

DANBURY

Danbury Antiques (EADA)
Contact Mrs Southgate
Eves Corner, Danbury, Chelmsford, Essex, CM3 4QF P
01245 223035
M 07711 704652
Est. 1979 *Stock size* Large
Stock Jewellery, silver, ceramics, porcelain, furniture
Open Tues–Sat 10am–5pm Wed 10am–1pm
Fairs Furze Hill
Services Restoration

DEBDEN

Debden Antiques (EADA)
Contact Mr Edward Norman
Elder Street, Debden, Saffron Walden, Essex, CB11 3JY P
01799 543007 F 01799 542482
E info@debden-antiques.co.uk
W www.debden-antiques.co.uk
Est. 1999 *Stock size* Large
No. of dealers 30
Stock 17th–19thC furniture, paintings, jewellery, silver, glass, rugs, garden ornaments, furniture
Open Mon–Sat 10am–5.30pm Sun 11am–4pm
Services Valuations, restoration, shipping

FINCHINGFIELD

Finchingfield Antiques Centre
Contact Mr Peter Curry
The Green, Finchingfield, Braintree, Essex, CM7 4JX P
01371 810258
Est. 1996 *Stock size* Large
No. of dealers 30
Stock Furniture, silver, porcelain, antiquarian books, jewellery, collectables
Open Mon–Sun 10am–5pm

FRINTON-ON-SEA

Dickens Curios
Contact Miss M Wilsher
151 Connaught Avenue, Frinton-on-Sea, Essex, CO13 9AH P
01255 674134
Est. 1970 *Stock size* Large
Stock Antiques, china, glass, pewter, copper, jewellery
Open Mon Fri 11am–1pm 2.15–5.30pm Tues–Thurs 10am–1pm 2.15–5.30pm Sat 9.45am–5pm closed Wed pm
Services Buying from public

No 24 of Frinton
Contact Mr C Pereira
24 Connaught Avenue, Frinton-on-Sea, Essex, CO13 9PR P
01255 670505
W www.artdecoclassics.co.uk
Est. 1993 *Stock size* Large
Stock Art Deco, general antiques, original prints
Open Mon–Sat 10am–5pm Sun 2–4pm closed Wed

Phoenix Trading
Contact Mr Tom Sheldon
130 Connaught Avenue, Frinton-on-Sea, Essex, CO13 9AD P
01255 851094 F 01255 851094
Est. 1996 *Stock size* Large
Stock Antique pine
Open Tues–Sat 10am–4pm
Services Restoration, stripping, cabinet makers

GRAYS

Atticus Books
Contact Mr R Drake
8 London Road, Grays, Essex, RM17 5XY P
01375 371200
Est. 1983 *Stock size* Large
Stock Antiquarian, out-of-print, second-hand books
Open Thurs–Sat 9am–4pm
Services Book search

GREAT BADDOW

The Antique Brass Bedstead Co Ltd
Contact Mr I Rabin
Baddow Antiques Centre, Church Street, Great Baddow, Chelmsford, Essex, CM2 7JW
01245 471137
www.llph.co.uk/bedsteads.htm
Est. 1978 *Stock size* Large
Stock Victorian brass and iron bedsteads
Open Mon–Sat 10am–5pm Sun 11am–5pm
Services Restoration

Baddow Antique Centre (EADA)
The Bringey, Church Street, Great Baddow, Chelmsford, Essex, CM2 7JW
01245 476159
Est. 1974 *Stock size* Large
No. of dealers 20+
Stock 18th–20thC furniture, silver, glass, porcelain, paintings, Victorian brass and iron bedsteads
Open Mon–Sat 10am–5pm Sun 11am–5pm
Services Valuations, restoration

GREAT DUNMOW

Mullocks Wells (NAVA)
Contact Lloyd Rust
The Old Town Hall, Great Dunmow, Essex, CM6 1AU
01371 873014 01371 878239
trembathwelsh@ic24.net
www.trembathwelchauctions.co.uk
Est. 1886
Open Mon–Fri 9am–5.30pm Sat 10am–noon
Sales Chequers Lane, Great Dunmow, fine art and antiques sales quarterly, general sales every 2 weeks. Telephone for details
Catalogues Yes

F B Neill
Contact Mr F B Neill
Ivydene, Chelmsford Road, White Roding, Great Dunmow, Essex, CM6 1RG
01279 876376
Est. 1975 *Stock size* Medium
Stock Antique furniture
Open By appointment

Clive Smith
Contact Mr C Smith
Brick House, North Street, Great Dunmow, Essex, CM6 1BA
01371 873171 01371 873171
clivesmith@route56.co.uk
Est. 1975 *Stock size* Small
Stock Antiquarian books, British Isles, topography, military, natural history
Trade only Yes
Open Mail order or by appointment

GREAT WALTHAM

The Stores
Contact Scott Saunders
The Stores, Great Waltham, Chelmsford, Essex, CM3 1DE
01245 360277
Est. 1975 *Stock size* Large
Stock English antique pine and country furniture
Open Wed–Sat 10am–5pm Sun 11am–4pm
Services Deliveries

HAINAULT

Gallerie Antiques (EADA)
Contact Mrs Gregory
62–70 Fowler Road, Hainault, Essex, IG6 3UT
020 8501 2229 020 8501 2209
Est. 1998 *Stock size* Large
No. of dealers 80
Stock Absolutely everything
Open Mon–Sat 10am–5.30pm Sun 11am–5pm
Services Valuations, restoration, shipping

HALSTEAD

The Antique Bed Shop
Contact Mrs V McGregor
Napier House, Head Street, Halstead, Essex, CO9 2BT
01787 477346 01787 478757
07801 626047
Est. 1976 *Stock size* Large
Stock Antique wooden beds
Open Thurs–Sat 9am–5pm or by appointment
Services Free delivery

Appleton's Allsorts
Contact Barry Appleton
9 Head Street, Halstead, Essex, CO9 2AT
01787 476273
07715 035934
Est. 1997 *Stock size* Large
Stock General antiques, second-hand and household items
Open Mon–Sat 9am–5pm closed Wed
Services Stripping, house clearance

Townsford Mill Antiques Centre
Contact Rosemary Bennett
The Causeway, Halstead, Essex, CO9 1ET
01787 474451
Est. 1987 *Stock size* Large
No. of dealers 80
Stock Antiques, collectables, furniture, silver, porcelain, lace, copper, Beswick, Royal Doulton, kitchenware
Open Mon–Sat 10am–5pm Sun Bank Holidays 11am–5pm

HARLOW

West Essex Antiques
Contact Mr C Dovaston
Stone Hall, Down Hall Road, Matching Green, Harlow, Essex, CM17 0RA
01279 730609 01279 730609
chris@essexantiques.co.uk
www.essexantiques.co.uk
Est. 1975 *Stock size* Large
Stock Furniture
Open Mon–Fri 9am–5pm or by appointment

HARWICH

Harwich International Antiques Centre
Contact Mr Hans Scholz
19 Kings Quay Street, Harwich, Essex, CO12 3ER
01255 554719 01255 554719
info@antiques-access-agency.com
www.antiques-access-agency.com
Est. 1996 *Stock size* Large
No. of dealers 45

Stock A wide range of antiques, collectables and decorative items
Open Tues–Sat 10am–5pm
Sun 1–5pm

HOLLAND-ON-SEA

Bookworm
Contact Mr A Durrant
100 Kings Avenue, Holland-on-Sea, Essex, CO15 5EP
☎ 01255 815984 Ⓕ 01255 815984
Ⓔ andy@adr-comms.demon.co.uk
Ⓦ www.bookwormshop.com
Est. 1995 *Stock size* Medium
Stock Antiquarian and general second-hand books, fiction, modern first editions
Open Mon–Sat 9am–5pm
Bank Holidays 10am–4pm
Services Free book search

ILFORD

Goodwins
Contact Mr C E Goodwin
773 Becontree Avenue, Dagenham, Essex, RM8 3HH
☎ 020 8590 4560/8595 7118
Est. 1964 *Stock size* Small
Stock General antiques
Open Mon–Sat 9am–6pm

INGATESTONE

Hutchison Antiques and Interiors (EADA)
Contact Mr Gavin Hutchison
60 High Street, Ingatestone, Essex, CM4 9DW
☎ 01277 353361 Ⓕ 01277 353361
Est. 1984 *Stock size* Large
Stock Furniture, paintings, antique and contemporary lamps
Open Mon–Sat 10am–5pm
Fairs NEC
Services Valuations, interior design service

Megarry's Antiques (EADA, BACA Award Winner 2002)
Contact Judy Wood
Jericho Cottage, The Duckpond Green, Blackmore, Ingatestone, Essex, CM4 0RR
☎ 01277 821031
Est. 1994 *Stock size* Large
Stock General antiques, small furniture, collectables, ceramics, blue and white china, prints, mirrors, small silver plate
Open Wed–Sun 11am–5pm
Services Valuations, restoration advice

KELVEDON

Colton Antiques
Contact Mr G Colton
Station Road, Kelvedon, Colchester, Essex, CO5 9NP
☎ 01376 571504
Est. 1992 *Stock size* Small
Stock 18th–19thC furniture, Georgian, decorative furniture
Open Mon–Sat 8am–5pm
Services Restoration

LEIGH-ON-SEA

Astoria Art Deco
Contact Mr or Mrs R Taylor
80 Rectory Grove, Leigh-on-Sea, Essex, SS9 2HJ
☎ 01702 471800
Ⓜ 07711 332148
Ⓔ astoriaartdeco@aol.com
Est. 1987 *Stock size* Large
Stock Furniture, mirrors, lighting, accessories
Open Tues–Sat 10.30am–5pm
closed Mon Wed
Fairs Battersea, Hove
Services Polishing, upholstery

Castle Antiques
Contact Mrs Barbara Gair
PO Box 1911, Leigh-on-Sea, Essex, SS9 1JG
☎ 01702 711390 Ⓕ 01702 475732
Ⓜ 07973 674355
Ⓔ castle@enterprise.net
Ⓦ www.castle-antiques.com
Est. 1979 *Stock size* Large
Stock 19thC Staffordshire figures, Ironstone wares, tribal artefacts, good taxidermy
Trade only Yes
Open By appointment
Fairs NEC, Newark
Services Valuations

Chalkwell Auctions Ltd (EADA)
Contact Trevor or David
The Arlington Rooms, Leigh-on-Sea, Essex, SS0 8NU
☎ 01702 710383 Ⓕ 01702 710383
Est. 1990
Sales Antiques and collectables sale monthly, normally 2nd Wed 6.30pm, viewing 4.30pm
Frequency Monthly
Catalogues Yes

Collectors Paradise
Contact Pearl Smith
993 London Road, Leigh-on-Sea, Essex, SS9 3LB
☎ 01702 473077
Est. 1963 *Stock size* Medium
Stock Clocks, postcards, cigarette cards, 1930s lighters, stamps
Open Mon–Thurs Sat 10am–5pm

Deja Vu Antiques
Contact Mr S Lewis
876 London Road, Leigh-on-Sea, Essex, SS9 3NQ
☎ 01702 470829
Ⓔ info@deja-vu-antiques.co.uk
Ⓦ www.deja-vu-antiques.co.uk
Est. 1994 *Stock size* Large
Stock 18th–19thC French furniture
Open Mon–Sat 9.30am–5.30pm
Services Restoration

Drizen Coins
Contact Mr Harry Drizen
1 Hawthorns, Leigh-on-Sea, Essex, SS9 4JT
☎ 01702 521094
Est. 1961 *Stock size* Medium
Stock Coins, tokens, medallions, medals
Open Mon–Sat 9am–9pm

Othellos
Contact Mr F Bush or Mrs M Layzell
1376 London Road, Leigh-on-Sea, Essex, SS9 2UH
☎ 01702 473334
Ⓜ 07710 764175
Ⓔ othellos@hotmail.com
Est. 1999 *Stock size* Large
Stock Out-of-print and second-hand books
Open Tues–Sat 9.30am–5pm

Paris Antiques (EADA)
Contact N Rodgers
193 Leigh Road, Leigh-on-Sea, Essex, SS9 1JE

☎ 01702 712832 Ⓕ 01702 712832
Ⓔ parisantiques@btconnect.com
Est. 1983 *Stock size* Large
Stock 18th–early 20thC furniture, Art Nouveau
Open Mon–Fri 9.30am–5pm Sat 9.30am–6pm closed Wed
Services Valuations

John Stacey & Sons
Contact Mr P J Stacey
✉ **86–90 Pall Mall, Leigh-on-Sea, Essex, SS9 1RG** Ⓟ
☎ 01702 477051 Ⓕ 01702 470141
Ⓔ jstacey@easynet.co.uk
Ⓦ www.jstacey.com
Est. 1946
Open Mon–Fri 9am–5.30pm Sat 9am–1pm
Sales Antiques and collectables sales every 3 weeks Tues 10.30am, viewing Sat 10am–4pm Sun 10am–2pm Mon 10am–4pm
Fairs Newark, Ardingly
Catalogues Yes

John Stacey & Sons
Contact Mr P J Stacey
✉ **86–90 Pall Mall, Leigh-on-Sea, Essex, SS9 1RG** Ⓟ
☎ 01702 477051 Ⓕ 01702 470141
Ⓔ jstacey@easynet.co.uk
Ⓦ www.jstacey.com
Est. 1946 *Stock size* Medium
Stock Victorian–Edwardian furniture, clocks, ceramics
Open Mon–Fri 9am–5.30pm Sat 9am–1pm
Fairs Newark, Ardingly
Services Adult education courses, valuations, house clearance

J Streamer
Contact Mrs J Streamer
✉ **86 Broadway, Leigh-on-Sea, Essex, SS9 1AE**
☎ 01702 472895
Est. 1963 *Stock size* Medium
Stock Jewellery, silver, small furniture, art items
Open Mon–Sat 9am–5pm closed Wed
Services Jewellery repair

J Streamer
Contact Mrs J Streamer
✉ **212 Leigh Road, Leigh-on-Sea, Essex, SS9 1BS** Ⓟ
☎ 01702 472895
Est. 1963 *Stock size* Medium
Stock Objets d'art, small furniture
Open Mon–Sat 9am–5pm closed Wed

Tillys Antiques
Contact Mr S T Austen or Mr R J Austen
✉ **1801 London Road, Leigh-on-Sea, Essex, SS9 2ST** Ⓟ
☎ 01702 557170
Ⓜ 07803 866318
Est. 1972 *Stock size* Large
Stock General antiques, furniture, antique dolls
Open Mon–Sat 9am–4.30pm closed Wed
Services Valuations, restoration

LITTLE WALTHAM

Collectors' Corner
Contact Peter Workman or Alasdair MacInnes
✉ **100 The Street, Little Waltham, Chelmsford, Essex, CM3 3NT** Ⓟ
☎ 01245 361166 Ⓕ 01245 361166
Est. 1987 *Stock size* Large
Stock Paper-type collectables, postcards, cigarette cards, ephemera, books
Open Mon–Sat 9am–5pm
Services Picture framing

LOUGHTON

Ambrose Auctioneers & Valuers
Contact Chrina Jarvis
✉ **Ambrose House, Old Station Road, Loughton, Essex, IG10 4PE** Ⓟ
☎ 020 8502 3951 Ⓕ 020 8532 0833
Ⓔ info@ambroseauction.co.uk
Ⓦ www.ambroseauction.co.uk
Est. 1900
Open Mon–Fri 9am–1pm 2–5.30pm
Sales General antiques
Frequency Monthly
Catalogues Yes

MALDON

All Books
Contact Mr K Peggs
✉ **2 Mill Road, Maldon, Essex, CM9 5HZ** Ⓟ
☎ 01621 856214
Ⓔ kevin@allbooks.demon.co.uk
Ⓦ www.allbooks.demon.co.uk
Est. 1975 *Stock size* Large
Stock Antiquarian and second-hand books, especially sailing and maritime history
Open Mon–Sat 10am–5pm Sun 1.30–5pm
Services Valuations

The Antique Rooms (RADS)
Contact Mrs Ellen Hedley
✉ **104a High Street, Maldon, Essex, CM9 5EG** Ⓟ
☎ 01621 856985
Est. 1977 *Stock size* Large
Stock 19th–20thC general antiques
Open Mon–Sat 10am–4pm closed Wed
Services Scandinavian spoken

Clive Beardall (BAFRA, EADA)
Contact Mr Clive Beardall
✉ **104b High Street, Maldon, Essex, CM9 5ET** Ⓟ
☎ 01621 857890 Ⓕ 01621 850753
Ⓔ info@clivebeardall.co.uk
Ⓦ www.clivebeardall.co.uk
Est. 1982 *Stock size* Small
Stock 18th–20thC furniture
Open Mon–Fri 8am–5.30pm Sat 9am–4pm
Services Valuations, restoration

MANNINGTREE

Out In The Sticks
Contact Paul Matthews
✉ **2 The Lanes, Manningtree, Essex, CO11 1AW** Ⓟ
☎ 01206 391555
Est. 1999 *Stock size* Large
Stock General antiques, reclamation kitchens
Open Mon–Sat 10am–5pm

NEWPORT

Brown House Antiques
Contact Brian Hodgkinson
✉ **The Brown House, High Street, Newport, Essex, CB11 3QY** Ⓟ
☎ 01799 540238
Est. 1966 *Stock size* Medium

Stock Mainly 19thC pine and country furniture
Open Mon–Sat 10am–5.30pm

Omega Decorative Arts
Contact Mr Tony Phillips or Mrs Sybil Hooper
High Street, Newport, Saffron Walden, Essex, CB11 3PF P
01799 540720
Est. 1985 *Stock size* Medium
Stock 1860–1960, Art Deco, Arts and Crafts
Open Mon–Sat 10am–6pm closed Thurs
Services Restoration

RAYLEIGH

F G Bruschweiler Antiques Ltd (LAPADA)
Contact Mr F Bruschweiler
41–67 Lower Lambricks, Rayleigh, Essex, SS6 8DA P
01268 773761/773932
F 01268 773318
E info@fgbantiques.com
W www.fgbantiques.com
Est. 1960 *Stock size* Large
Stock General antique furniture, public house bars
Open Mon–Fri 8.30am–5pm
Services Restoration

ROMFORD

Carey's Bookshop
Contact Mr Robert Carey
91 High Road, Chadwell Heath, Romford, Essex, RM6 6PB P
020 8597 4165
Est. 1985 *Stock size* Medium
Stock Antiquarian and second-hand books, especially sci-fi and crime
Open Mon–Sat 10am–5pm

Collectors Forum (BNTA, PTS, BCCA)
Contact Mr Renoize
30 Victoria Road, Romford, Essex, RM1 2JH P
01708 723357 F 020 8590 0926
Est. 1970 *Stock size* Large
Stock Medals, coins, banknotes, stamps
Open By appointment only
Services Valuations

SAFFRON WALDEN

Arts Decoratifs (EADA)
Contact Ann Miller
The Cockpit, Off Market Hill, Saffron Walden, Essex, CB10 1HQ P
01799 513666 F 0870 900 7997
M 07774 003851
E contactus@artsdecoratifs.co.uk
W www.artsdecoratifs.co.uk
Est. 2002 *Stock size* Medium
Stock Small furniture, silver, metalware, jewellery, ceramics, glass, costume bags
Open Tues Wed 10am–4pm Fri Sat 10am–5pm
Fairs Alexandra Palace

Bush Antiques (EADA)
Contact Mrs J M Hosford
26–28 Church Street, Saffron Walden, Essex, CB10 1JQ
01799 523277
Est. 1960 *Stock size* Medium
Stock Country furniture, copper, brass, treen, ceramics, glass
Open Mon–Sat 11am–4.30pm closed Thurs

Ickleton Antiques
Contact Mr B Arbury
4 Gold Street, Saffron Walden, Essex, CB10 1EJ
01799 513114
Est. 1995 *Stock size* Medium
Stock Militaria, postcards, collectables WWI, WWII
Open Mon–Fri 10am–4pm Sat 10am–5pm

Lankester Antiques & Books
Contact Mr P Lankester
The Old Sun Inn, Church Street, Saffron Walden, Essex, CB10 1JW
01799 522685
Est. 1967 *Stock size* Large
Stock General antiques, antiquarian and second-hand books
Open Tues–Sat 10am–5pm

Market Row Antiques & Collectables
Contact Mr P Bowyer or Mr D Miller
14 Market Row, Saffron Waldon, Essex, CB10 1HB
01799 516131
M 07759 493613
Est. 1994 *Stock size* Small
Stock General antiques, clocks, barometers, porcelain,
Open Mon–Wed Fri Sat 10am–5pm Thurs 2–5pm
Fairs London and Birmingham clock fairs
Services Clock and watch repairs

Maureen Morris (BADA, LAPADA)
Contact Maureen Morris
Saffron Walden, Essex
01799 521338 F 01799 522802
E mm@antiqueembroidery.com
W www.antiqueembroidery.com
Est. 1979 *Stock size* Medium
Stock Samplers, embroidery, quilts
Open By appointment
Fairs Olympia
Services Shipping, book search

T. Reed & Son
Contact Meg Reed
22 Castle Street, Saffron Walden, Essex, CB10 1BJ P
01799 522363
Est. 1881 *Stock size* Small
Stock Country antiques
Open Tues Sat 10am–1pm 2–5pm

Saffron Walden Antiques Centre
Contact Mr P Rowell or Mrs J Rowell
1 Market Row, Saffron Walden, Essex, CB10 1HA P
01799 524534
W www.saffronantique.sco.uk
Est. 1997 *Stock size* Large
No. of dealers 50
Stock Huge range of antiques, collectables, bygones, furniture, silver, jewellery, porcelain, lighting, pictures, sporting memorabilia
Open Mon–Sat 10am–5.30pm Sun 11am–4pm

Saffron Walden Auctions
Contact Mr C Peeke-Voute
1 Market Street, Saffron Walden, Essex, CB10 1JB
01799 513281 F 01799 513334
E info@saffronwaldenauctions.com
W www.saffronwaldenauctions.com

Est. 1905
Open Tues Thurs Fri 10am–4pm
Sales Antiques sales Saturday 10am every 6 weeks, viewing Fri 10am–5pm
Catalogues Yes

SIBLE HEDINGHAM

Hedingham Antiques
Contact Mrs P Patterson
100 Swan Street, Sible Hedingham, Halstead, Essex, CO9 3HP P
01787 460360 F 01787 469109
M 07802 265702
E patriciapatterson@totalise.co.uk
W www.silberausengland.co.uk
Est. 1980 *Stock size* Medium
Stock Antique and early 20thC silver, silver plate, glass
Open By appointment
Services Silver and furniture restoration

Lennard Antiques (LAPADA)
Contact G Pinn
124 Swan Street, Sible Hedingham, Halstead, Essex, CO9 3HP P
01787 461127
Est. 1969 *Stock size* Medium
Stock Oak and country furniture, Delftware
Open Mon–Sat 9.30am–6pm
Fairs Olympia, Chelsea Spring and Autumn, Kensington

W A Pinn & Sons (LAPADA, BADA)
Contact Mr J Pinn or Mr K Pinn
124 Swan Street, Sible Hedingham, Halstead, Essex, CO9 3HP P
01787 461127
Est. 1969 *Stock size* Medium
Stock 17th–early 19thC furniture, accessories
Open Mon–Sat 9.30am–6pm
Fairs Olympia, Chelsea Spring and Autumn, Kensington

SOUTH BENFLEET

Classique Antiques (EADA)
Contact Chris Elliott
356 High Road, South Benfleet, Essex, SS7 5HP P
01268 566695 F 01268 566695
Est. 1999 *Stock size* Large
Stock General antiques, furniture, decorative arts, Clarice Cliff, Moorcroft, Staffordshire, Toby jugs
Open Mon–Sat 9am–4pm

SOUTHEND-ON-SEA

CurioCity
Contact Sheila or Matt
333–335 Chartwell Square, Victoria Plaza, Southend-on-Sea, Essex, SS2 5SP P
01702 611350
W www.curio-city.co.uk
Est. 1998 *Stock size* Large
Stock Wide range of antiques, collectables
Open Mon–Fri 10am–5pm Sat 9am–5pm
Services Café

David Morton
Contact Mr D Morton
Rear of 61–69 Princes Street, Southend-on-Sea, Essex, SS1 1PT P
01702 354144
Est. 1967 *Stock size* Large
Stock 19thC furniture, general antiques
Trade only Yes
Open By appointment

R & J Coins (BNTA)
Contact Mr R Harvey
21b Alexandra Street, Market Place, Southend-on-Sea, Essex, SS1 1BX P
01702 345995
Est. 1967 *Stock size* Medium
Stock Coins, medals, bank notes, cap badges
Open Mon–Fri 10am–4pm Wed 10am–2pm Sat 10am–3pm

STANFORD-LE-HOPE

Stanford Antique Centre
Contact Jaqueline Rourke
The Old Bank, The Green, Stanford-le-Hope, Essex, SS17 0ET P
01375 671771 F 01375 400008
M 0795 774 5997
Est. 2001 *Stock size* Medium
No. of dealers 60 cabinets
Stock Collectables, china, bric-a-brac
Open Mon Thurs–Sat 9.30am–5pm

STANSTED MOUNTFITCHET

Linden House Antiques
Contact Mr A W Sargeant
3 Silver Street, Stansted Mountfitchet, Essex, CM24 8HA P
01279 812372
Est. 1962 *Stock size* Large
Stock 18th–19thC furniture, pictures
Open Mon–Sat 10am–5pm
Services Valuations

G E Sworder & Sons
Contact Mr Guy Schooling RICS
14 Cambridge Road, Stansted Mountfitchet, Essex, CM24 8BZ P
01279 817778 F 01279 817779
E auctions@sworder.co.uk
W www.sworder.co.uk
Est. 1782
Open Mon–Fri 9am–5pm
Sales Weekly sales of Victoriana Wed 11am, viewing Tues 2–5pm. Bi-monthly Fine Art sales Tues 10am, viewing Fri previous 10am–5pm Sat Sun 10am–1pm Mon 10am–5pm
Catalogues Yes

Valmar Antiques (BADA, LAPADA, CINOA)
Contact J A or M R Orpin
Croft House Cottage, High Lane, Stansted Mountfitchet, Essex, CM24 8LQ P
01279 813201 F 01279 816962
M 07831 093701
E valmar-antiques@cwcom.net
Est. 1967 *Stock size* Large
Stock 18th–19thC furniture and accesssories, Arts and Crafts
Open By appointment only
Fairs Olympia BADA

THAXTED

Harris Antiques (BAFRA, EADA)
Contact Brian Harris
24 Town Street, Thaxted, Essex, CM6 2LA P
01371 832832
Est. 1956 *Stock size* Large
Stock 16th–20thC furniture,

clocks, barometers
Open Mon–Sat 9am–5pm
Fairs NEC
Services Valuations, restoration

UPMINSTER

Collectors Fair
Contact Sally Reynolds
59 Station Road, Upminster, Essex, RM14 2SU
☎ 01708 224410
Est. 2000 *Stock size* Medium
No. of dealers 15
Stock Antiques, collectables
Open Tues–Sat 10am–5pm
Services Valuations

WESTCLIFF-ON-SEA

Dealers
Contact Gary Bell
659 London Road, Westcliff-on-Sea, Essex, SS0 9PD
☎ 01702 300052 Ⓕ 01702 300050
Ⓦ www.les-and-gary.co.uk
Est. 1977 *Stock size* Large
Stock General antiques
Open Mon–Sun 9am–5pm

Hamlet Antiques & Collectables
Contact Carol Short
31 Hamlet Court Road, Westcliff-on-Sea, Essex, SS0 7EY
☎ 01702 434326 Ⓕ 01702 338230
Ⓔ hamletandcc@ad.com
Est. 2002 *Stock size* Large
No. of dealers 40
Stock Collectables
Open Mon–Sat 9.30am–5.30pm Sun 10am–4pm closed Wed

It's About Time (EADA)
Contact Mr Paul Williams
863 London Road, Westcliff-on-Sea, Essex, SS0 9SZ
☎ 01702 472574 Ⓕ 01702 472574
Ⓔ iat@clocking-in.demon.co.uk
Ⓦ www.clocking-in.demon.co.uk
Est. 1979 *Stock size* Medium
Stock Clocks, furniture
Open Tues–Sat 9am–5.30pm or by appointment
Services Restoration

Prust & Sons Antique Furniture
Contact Mr Prust
9 West Road, Westcliff-on-Sea, Essex, SS0 9AU
☎ 01702 391093 Ⓕ 01702 391093
Ⓔ sales@prust.co.uk
Ⓦ www.prust.co.uk
Est. 1987 *Stock size* Large
Stock General antiques
Open Mon–Sat 8.30am–5.30pm Sun 10am–3pm
Services Restoration

Ridgeway Antiques (EADA)
Contact Trevor or Simon
66 The Ridgeway, Westcliff-on-Sea, Essex, SS0 8NU
☎ 01702 710383 Ⓕ 01702 710383
Ⓦ www.ridgeweb.co.uk
Est. 1987 *Stock size* Medium
Stock 18thC–pre-war furniture, general antiques
Open Mon–Sat 10.30am–5pm
Fairs Hallmark, Ridgeway Fairs
Services Valuations

WOODFORD GREEN

Mill Lane Antiques
Contact Mr N McArtney
29 Mill Lane, Woodford Green, Essex, IG8 0UG
☎ 020 8502 9930
Est. 1987 *Stock size* Large
Stock Georgian–Victorian furniture, lighting, ironwork, collectables
Open Tues Thurs–Sat 10am–4.30pm
Fairs Kempton Park
Services House clearance

WRITTLE

Whichcraft Jewellery (EADA)
Contact Alan Turner
54–56 The Green, Writtle, Chelmsford, Essex, CM1 3DU
☎ 01245 420183
Est. 1978 *Stock size* Large
Stock Antique and modern jewellery, small silver items
Open Tues–Sat 9.30am–5.30pm
Services Jewellery repairs and restoration

NORFOLK

ACLE

Horners Auctioneers (ISVA)
Contact Mr N Horner-Glister FRICS
Acle Salerooms, Norwich Road, Acle, Norwich, Norfolk, NR13 3BY
☎ 01493 750225 Ⓕ 01493 750506
Ⓔ auction@horners.co.uk
Ⓦ www.horners.co.uk
Est. 1900
Open Mon–Fri 9am–1pm 2–5pm
Sales General antiques sale Thurs 10am, viewing Wed 2–4pm, bi-monthly antiques and collectables sale Sat 10am
Frequency Weekly
Catalogues Yes

AYLSHAM

Keys
Contact Mr D J Lines
Aylsham Salerooms, Off Palmers Lane, Aylsham, Norfolk, NR11 6JA
☎ 01263 733195 Ⓕ 01263 732140
Ⓔ info@gakey.co.uk
Ⓦ www.aylshamsalerooms.co.uk
Est. 1953
Open Mon–Fri 9am–5pm closed 1–2pm Sat 9am–noon
Sales Weekly general sale, antique sale every 3 weeks Tues Wed. Every 2 months book sale Fri, collectors' sale Thurs, picture sales Fri. Telephone for details
Catalogues Yes

Pearse Lukies Ltd
Contact The Manager
The Old Vicarage, Aylsham, Norfolk, NR11 6HE
☎ 01263 734137
Ⓜ 01263 734502
Est. 1974 *Stock size* Medium
Stock Pre-1800 antiques
Open By appointment

BRANCASTER STAITHE

Staithe Antiques
Contact Martin Allen
Main Road, Brancaster Staithe, Norfolk, PE31 8BJ
☎ 01485 210600

EAST

Est. 2003 ***Stock size*** Medium
Stock Period oak and country, walnut, mahogany furniture, gardening antiques
Open Mon–Sun 10.30am–5pm
Services Collection, delivery

BROOKE

⊞ Country House Antiques
Contact Mr G Searle
✉ **Green Acre, Seething, Nr Brooke, Norwich, Norfolk, NR15 1AL** 🅿
☎ 01508 558144 Ⓕ 01508 558144
Ⓔ geoffatcountryhouse@btopenworld.com
Est. 1980 ***Stock size*** Medium
Stock 17th–19thC furniture
Trade only Yes
Open By appointment
Services Valuations, restoration, shipping

BURNHAM MARKET

⊞ Brazenhead Ltd
Contact David Kenyon
✉ **Greenside, Market Place, Burnham Market, King's Lynn, Norfolk, PE31 8HD** 🅿
☎ 01328 730700 Ⓕ 01328 730929
Ⓔ brazenheadbook@aol.com
Est. 1979 ***Stock size*** Large
Stock Antiquarian, second-hand, out-of-print books, specializing in children's books, also books concerning Nelson
Open Mon–Sat 9.30am–5pm
Services Valuations, book search

⊞ M & A Cringle
Contact Mr or Mrs Cringle
✉ **The Old Black Horse, Market Place, Burnham Market, Norfolk, PE31 8HD** 🅿
☎ 01328 738456
Est. 1965 ***Stock size*** Small
Stock Late 18thC furniture, prints, maps, china, pottery
Open Mon–Sat 9am–1pm 2–5pm closed Wed
Services Valuations

⊞ Market House Antiques (BADA)
Contact Mr or Mrs D Maufe
✉ **Market House, Burnham Market, Norfolk, PE31 8HF** 🅿
☎ 01328 738475 Ⓕ 01328 730750
Est. 1976 ***Stock size*** Medium
Stock 18th–early 19thC furniture and works of art, mirrors, bronzes
Open By appointment or by chance
Fairs BADA March, Summer and Winter Olympias

COLTISHALL

⊞ Roger Bradbury Antiques
Contact Roger Bradbury
✉ **Church Street, Coltishall, Norfolk, NR12 7DJ** 🅿
☎ 01603 737444 Ⓕ 01603 737018
Ⓜ 07860 372528
Est. 1967 ***Stock size*** Medium
Stock Chinese porcelain cargoes, 18th–19thC furniture, pictures, objets d'art
Open Mon–Sat 9am–5pm Sun 10am–4pm

⌂ Coltishall Antique Centre
Contact Isabel Ford
✉ **7 High Street, Coltishall, Norwich, Norfolk, NR12 7AA** 🅿
☎ 01603 738306
Est. 1977 ***Stock size*** Medium
No. of dealers 6
Stock Glass, ceramics, militaria, jewellery, silver, fishing, golfing items, collectables
Open Mon–Sat 10am–4.30pm

CROMER

⊞ Bond Street Antiques (NAG, GAGTL)
Contact Mr M R T Jones
✉ **6 Bond Street, Cromer, Norfolk, NR27 9DA** 🅿
☎ 01263 513134
Est. 1970 ***Stock size*** Medium
Stock Silver, jewellery
Open Mon–Sat 9am–5pm
Services Valuations

⊞ Books Etc.
Contact Mr Kevin Reynor
✉ **15a Church Street, Cromer, Norfolk, NR27 9ES**
☎ 01263 515501
Ⓔ bookskcr@aol.com
Est. 1997 ***Stock size*** Large
Stock Antiquarian and second-hand books
Open Easter–Sept Sun–Mon 11am–4pm winter Wed–Sat 11am–4pm

⊞ Collectors' Cabin
Contact Diana Hazell Bennington
✉ **The Kiosk, North Lodge Park Promenade, Cromer, Norfolk, NR27 9HE** 🅿
☎ 01263 512195 Ⓕ 01263 515961
Est. 1997 ***Stock size*** Large
Stock All ceramics, glass, Crown Derby
Open Tues–Sun 10am–5pm
Services Restoration

⊞ Collectors' World
Contact Mrs Irene Nockels
✉ **6 New Parade, Church Street, Cromer, Norfolk, NR27 9EP** 🅿
☎ 01263 515330/514174
Ⓔ nockels@25nr.fsnet.co.uk
Est. 1994 ***Stock size*** Large
Stock Furniture, general antiques, collectables
Open Tues–Sat 10am–5pm
Fairs Norwich, Newark
Services Valuations, house clearance

DEREHAM

Case & Dewing
Contact John Dewing
✉ **Church Street, Dereham, Norfolk, NR19 1DJ** 🅿
☎ 01362 692004 Ⓕ 01362 693103
Ⓔ info@case-dewing.co.uk
Ⓦ www.case-dewing.co.uk
Est. 1900
Open Mon–Fri 9am–5.30pm Sat 9am–3.30pm
Sales General antiques and effects Tues, viewing morning of sale
Frequency 2 weeks
Catalogues No

Tyrone R Roberts
Contact T R Roberts
✉ **10 Brunswick Close, Toftwood, Dereham, Norfolk, NR19 1XW** 🅿
☎ 01362 691267 Ⓕ 01362 691267
Ⓜ 07702 642362
Ⓔ tyroneroberts@yahoo.co.uk
Ⓦ www.tyroneroberts.com
Est. 1970
Open Mon–Sun 9am–5pm or by appointment

Sales General antiques
Frequency Monthly
Catalogues Yes

Village Books
Contact Mr Jack James
20a High Street, Dereham, Norfolk, NR19 1DR P
01362 853066
villagebkdereham@aol.com
Est. 1996 *Stock size* Large
Stock General books, maps, ephemera
Open Mon Tues Thurs Fri 9.30am–4.30pm Wed 9.30am–3pm Sat 9.30am–5pm
Services Free book search, Readers' Club, postal sales

DISS

Antique and Collectors' Centre Diss
Contact Mr D Cockaday
The Works, 3 Cobbs Yard, St Nicholas Street, Diss, Norfolk, IP22 4LB P
01379 644472
Est. 1999 *Stock size* Large
No. of dealers 28
Stock General antiques, 1850–1970, Art Deco china and glass, commemoratives
Open Mon–Thurs 10am–4.30pm Fri 9am–4.30pm Sat 10am–4.30pm
Services Valuations

Diss Antiques & Interiors (LAPADA)
Contact Mr Brian Wimshurst
2–3 Market Place, Diss, Norfolk, IP22 34T
01379 642213 F 01379 642213
M 07770 477368
Est. 1971 *Stock size* Medium
Stock Tudor–Edwardian furniture, ceramics, silver
Open Mon–Sat 9am–5pm
Fairs Snape
Services Valuations, restoration

Thos Wm Gaze & Son
Contact Alan M Smith FRICS
Diss Auction Rooms, Roydon Road, Diss, Norfolk, IP22 4LN P
01379 650306 F 01379 644313
sales@dissauctionrooms.co.uk
www.twgaze.com
Est. 1857
Open Mon–Fri 9am–5pm Sat 9am–noon
Sales Weekly Fri sales of antiques and collectables, Victorian pine and shipping furniture, modern furniture and effects. Periodic Fri sales of decorative arts, modern furniture and decor, 19th–20thC paintings, books, ephemera. Periodic Sat sales decorative arts, modern furniture, decor, toys, nostalgia, architectural salvage, statuary, rural and domestic bygones. Auction calendars available, viewing Thurs 2–8pm Fri Sat from 8.30am
Catalogues Yes

DOWNHAM MARKET

Antiques and Gifts
Contact Mrs Addrison
47 Bridge Street, Downham Market, Norfolk, PE38 9DW P
01366 387700
Est. 1998 *Stock size* Medium
Stock Victorian–Edwardian furniture, second-hand books, china, glass, smalls, general antiques
Open Mon–Sat 9am–5pm

Barry L Hawkins
Contact Mr B Hawkins FRICS
15 Lynn Road, Downham Market, Norfolk, PE38 9NL P
01366 387180 F 01366 386626
M 07860 451721
Barry@barryhawkins.co.uk
www.barryhawkins.co.uk
Est. 1840
Open Mon–Fri 9am–5pm
Sales Monthly antiques and general sale of goods first Wed, viewing morning of sale 8–11am. Wine sales and Oriental carpet sales, catalogued
Catalogues No

FAKENHAM

James Beck Auctions
Contact Mr James Beck
The Cornhall, Cattle Market Street, Fakenham, Norfolk, NR21 9AW P
01328 851557 F 01328 851044
jamesbeck@auctions18.fsnet.co.uk
www.jamesbeckauctions.co.uk
Est. 1840
Open Tues 10am–1pm Thurs 10am–5pm Fri 10am–2pm
Sales General antiques sales on Thurs at 11am, specialist sales occasionally, viewing Wed 2–5pm Thurs 9–11am
Frequency Weekly
Catalogues No

Fakenham Antiques Centre
Contact Mandy Allen or Julie Hunt
The Old Congregational Church, 14 Norwich Road, Fakenham, Norfolk, NR21 8AZ P
01328 862941
norfolkantiques@tiscali.co.uk
Est. 1984 *Stock size* Large
No. of dealers 20
Stock Period furniture, antiques, curios, collectables
Open Mon–Sat 10am–4.30pm
Services Restoration

Sue Rivett Antiques
Contact Sue Rivett
6 Norwich Road, Fakenham, Norfolk, NR21 8AX P
01328 862924
Est. 1969 *Stock size* Small
Stock General antiques, Victorian and pre-Victorian items
Open Mon–Sat 10am–1pm closed Wed

GREAT YARMOUTH

Barry's Antiques
Contact Mr Barry Nichols
35 King Street, Great Yarmouth, Norfolk, NR30 2PN P
01493 842713 F 01493 745312
M 07802 619579
Est. 1979 *Stock size* Large
Stock Jewellery, porcelain, silver
Open Mon–Sat 9.30am–4.30pm closed Thurs
Services Jewellery repair, insurance valuer and agent

Curiosity Too
Contact Mr or Mrs R Moore
163 Northgate Street, Great Yarmouth, Norfolk, NR30 1BY P
01493 859690
Est. 1983 *Stock size* Medium
Stock China, glass, pictures,

general antiques, small furniture
Open Mon–Fri 10am–4.30pm Sat 10.30am–3.30pm closed Thurs
Services House clearance

Garry M Emms and Co Ltd
Contact Garry Emms
Great Yarmouth Salerooms, Beevor Road, Great Yarmouth, Norfolk, NR30 3PS
01493 332668 01493 728290
g_emms@great-yarmouth-auctions.com
www.great-yarmouth-auctions.com
Est. 1994
Open Thurs–Fri 10am–4pm accept goods for sale
Sales Weekly sales of antiques Wed 10am, viewing Tues 2–8pm Wed 9–10am, quarterly special sales
Catalogues No

David Ferrow (ABA, PBFA)
Contact David Ferrow
77 Howard Street South, Great Yarmouth, Norfolk, NR30 1LN
01493 843800
Est. 1940 *Stock size* Large
Stock General antiquarian books, local topography
Open Mon–Wed Fri Sat 10am–4.30pm closed Bank Holidays
Services Valuations

Readers' Dream
Contact Miss T Kemp
12 Market Gate Shopping Centre, Great Yarmouth, Norfolk, NR30 2AX
01493 330705
Est. 1998 *Stock size* Large
Stock Antiquarian books, first editions
Open Mon–Sat 10am–5.30pm
Services Book search

HARLESTON

The Old Coach House
Contact David Burrough
Church Hill, Starston, Harleston, Norfolk, IP2 9PT
01379 852123
Est. 1990 *Stock size* Small
Stock Restored Georgian–Victorian walnut and mahogany furniture,
Open Mon–Sat 9am–5pm
Services Restoration

HINGHAM

Mongers Architectural Salvage (SALVO)
Contact Mrs Sam Coster
15 Market Place, Hingham, Norwich, Norfolk, NR9 4AF
01953 851868 01953 851870
sam@mongersofhingham.co.uk
www.mongersofhingham.co.uk
Est. 1997 *Stock size* Large
Stock Architectural salvage
Open Mon–Sat 9.30am–5.30pm
Services Stripping, fireplace restoration

Past & Present
Contact Christine George
16a Fairland, Hingham, Norwich, Norfolk, NR9 4HN
01953 851471 01953 851471
Est. 1999 *Stock size* Large
Stock Fine art and antiques, lighting
Open Tues–Sun 10am–5pm

HOLT

Baron Art
Contact Mr A Baron
9 Chapel Yard, Albert Street, Holt, Norfolk, NR25 6HJ
01263 713906 01263 711670
baronholt@aol.com
Est. 1990 *Stock size* Large
Stock Antiquarian books
Open Mon–Sat 9am–5pm
Services Framing

Baron Art
Contact Mr A Baron
17 Chapel Yard, Albert Street, Holt, Norfolk, NR25 6HG
01263 713430 01263 711670
baronholt@aol.com
Est. 1990 *Stock size* Large
Stock Art Deco, paintings
Open Mon–Sat 9am–5pm

Cobwebs
Contact Ann Buchanan
2 Fish Hill, Holt, Norfolk, NR25 6BD
01263 711955 01328 829592
0798 00 87889
Est. 1996 *Stock size* Large
Stock Bygones, collectables, woodworking and agricultural tools
Open Mon–Fri 10.30am–5pm Sat 10.30am–6pm

Cottage Collectables
Contact Philip or Linda Morris
Fish Hill, Holt, Norfolk, NR25 6BD
01263 711707
Est. 1984 *Stock size* Large
Stock General antiques, jewellery
Open Mon–Sun 10am–5pm
Fairs Newark, The International Antique and Collectables Fair, RAF Swinderby, Peterborough and Norwich showgrounds
Services Restoration, house clearance

Anthony Fell Antiques & Works of Art (BADA, LAPADA)
Contact Anthony Fell
Chester House, 47 Bull Street, Holt, Norfolk, NR25 6HP
01263 712912
afellantiques@tiscali.co.uk
Est. 1996 *Stock size* Medium
Stock 17th–18thC English furniture and works of art
Open Mon–Sat 10am–5pm telephone call advisable
Services Valuations, restoration

Heathfield Antiques
Contact Stephen Heathfield
Candlestick Lane, Thornage Road, Holt, Norfolk, NR25 6SU
01263 711609 01263 711609
info@antique-pine.net
www.antique-pine.net
Est. 1991 *Stock size* Large
Stock Antique pine, country items
Open Mon–Sat 8.30am–5pm
Services Restoration

Holt Antique Centre
Contact Mr D Attfield
Albert Street, Holt, Norfolk, NR25 6HX
01263 712097
Est. 1982 *Stock size* Large
No. of dealers 15
Stock Antiques, collectables
Open Mon–Sun 10am–5pm

Holt Antique Gallery
Contact Mrs J Holliday
2 Shire Hall Plain, Holt, Norfolk, NR25 6HT
☎ 01263 711991 Ⓕ 01263 711991
Est. 1997 *Stock size* Large
Stock Antique furniture, china, brass, silver
Open Mon–Sun 10am–5pm
Fairs Newark, The International Antique and Collectables Fair, RAF Swinderby

Mews Antique Emporium
Contact Mr Howard Heathfield
17 High Street, Holt, Norfolk, NR25 6BN
☎ 01263 713224
Est. 1998 *Stock size* Large
No. of dealers 14
Stock Furniture, pictures, pottery, china
Open Mon–Sat 10am–5pm Sun 11am–4pm
Services Valuations, restoration

Past Caring
Contact Mrs Lynda Mossman
6 Chapel Yard, Albert Street, Holt, Norfolk, NR25 6HG Ⓟ
☎ 01263 713771 Ⓕ 01362 680078
Ⓔ pstcaring@aol.com
Est. 1987 *Stock size* Large
Stock Linen, lace, vintage clothing, accessories, costume jewellery 1800s–1950
Open Mon–Sat 11am–5pm
Fairs Alexandra Palace

Richard Scott Antiques
Contact Mr Richard Scott
30 High Street, Holt, Norfolk, NR25 6BH Ⓟ
☎ 01263 712479
Est. 1972 *Stock size* Large
Stock Ceramics, studio pottery, oil lamps
Open Tues–Fri 10am–5pm Sat 10am–5pm closed Thurs
Fairs Newark
Services Advice on valuation, restoration

Simon Finch Norfolk
Contact Mr Tristram Hull
3–5 Fish Hill, Holt, Norfolk, NR25 6BD Ⓟ
☎ 01263 712650 Ⓕ 01263 711153
Est. 1974 *Stock size* Large
Stock General stock, antiquarian books
Open Mon–Sat 10am–5pm

KING'S LYNN

Farm House Antiques
Contact P Philpot
Whites Farm House, Barkers Drove, Stoke Ferry, King's Lynn, Norfolk, PE33 9TA Ⓟ
☎ 01366 500588 Ⓕ 01366 500588
Ⓜ 07971 859151
Est. 1969 *Stock size* Small
Stock Antique furniture
Open By appointment
Services Restoration

The Old Curiosity Shop
Contact Mrs Wright
25 St James Street, King's Lynn, Norfolk, PE30 5DA Ⓟ
☎ 01553 766591
Ⓜ 07802 348635
Est. 1984 *Stock size* Small
Stock General antiques, collectables, furniture
Open Mon–Sat 11am–5pm
Fairs Alexandra Palace, Lee Valley Park
Services Teddy bear restoration, clock, watch repairs, bead restringing

The Old Granary Antique Centre
Contact Mrs J L Waymouth
Kings Staithe Lane, King's Lynn, Norfolk, PE30 1LZ Ⓟ
☎ 01553 775509
Est. 1979 *Stock size* Medium
No. of dealers 18
Stock General antiques, collectables, coins, medals, stamps, books
Open Mon–Sat 10am–5pm (4.30pm in winter)
Services Valuations

Roderick Richardson (BNTA)
Contact Mr Roderick Richardson
The Old Granary Antique Centre, Kings Staithe Lane, King's Lynn, Norfolk, PE30 1LZ Ⓟ
☎ 01553 670833 for coins only
Ⓕ 01553 670833
Ⓜ 0778 637 2444
Ⓔ roderickrichardson@yahoo.co.uk
Ⓦ www.roderickrichardson.com
Est. 1995 *Stock size* Large
Stock English hammered and early milled gold and silver
Open By appointment
Fairs Midland Coin Fair, London Coin Fair, Coinex
Services Valuations, buy on commission, illustrated circular

MARSHAM

Euro Antiques
Contact Mr Case Van Woerkom
1–6 Outbuildings, Grove Farm, Norwich Road, Marsham, Norwich, Norfolk, NR10 5SR Ⓟ
☎ 01263 731377 Ⓕ 01263 731377
Ⓜ 07771 727420
Est. 1979 *Stock size* Medium
Stock Pine, general furniture
Open Mon–Fri 9am–5pm Sat by appointment
Services Leathering, polishing, restoration

Brian Watson Antique Glass (LAPADA)
Contact Brian Watson
Foxwarren Cottage, High Street, Marsham, Norwich, Norfolk, NR10 5QA Ⓟ
☎ 01263 732519 Ⓕ 01263 732519
Ⓜ 07718 860535
Ⓔ brian.h.watson@talk21.com
Est. 1991 *Stock size* Medium
Stock Georgian–Victorian drinking glasses, decanters and other glass of the period
Open By appointment
Fairs NEC, Penman fairs, Olympia
Services Valuations

MULBARTON

Junk and Disorderly
Contact Colin Whiting
The Dell, Birchfield Lane, Mulbarton, Norfolk, NR14 8AA Ⓟ
☎ 01603 470495
Ⓜ 07903 323527
Est. 1976 *Stock size* Large
Stock General antiques
Open Sat 8am–4pm
Services House clearance, removals

NORTH WALSHAM

The Angel Bookshop (PBFA)
Contact Mr E Green
4 Aylsham Road, North Walsham, Norfolk, NR28 0BH
01692 404054
angelbooks@onetel.net.uk
Est. 1989 *Stock size* Medium
Stock General antiquarian books, cycling, bicycles, Norfolk and natural history topics a speciality
Open Thurs Fri 9.30am–5pm Sat 9.30am–3.30pm
Fairs PBFA
Services Book search

Horners Auctioneers (ISVA)
Contact Mr N Horner-Glister FRICS
North Walsham Sales Rooms, Midland Road, North Walsham, Norfolk, NR28 9JR P
01692 500603 F 01692 500480
auction@horners.co.uk
www.horners.co.uk
Est. 1993
Open Mon–Fri 9am–1pm 2–5pm
Sales Monthly antiques and collectables sale Sat 10am, viewing Fri 10am–8pm
Catalogues Yes

Park Lane Antiques
Contact Philip Sneddon
2 Park Lane, North Walsham, Norfolk, NR28 9JZ
01692 409775
www.parklaneantique.com
Est. 2002 *Stock size* Medium
Stock Antique furniture pre 1900
Open Wed–Sat 10.30am–4.30pm
Services Valuations, restoration

NORWICH

Antique Chair Shop
Contact Simon Hunt
Kirstead Green, Norwich, Norfolk, NR15 1EB P
01508 550051
info@antiquechairshop.co.uk
www.antiquechairshop.co.uk
Est. 1985 *Stock size* Small
Stock Chairs
Open Mon–Sat 9am–5pm Thur 9am–12.30pm
Services Restoration

Antiques & Interiors
31–35 Elm Hill, Norwich, Norfolk, NR3 1HG P
01603 622695 F 01603 632446
Est. 1996 *Stock size* Large
Stock Art Deco and other furniture, porcelain
Open Mon Wed Fri Sat 10am–5pm

James Brett Ltd (BADA)
Contact Mrs T Lotis
42 St Giles Street, Norwich, Norfolk, NR2 1LW P
01603 628171 F 01603 630245
Est. 1870 *Stock size* Large
Stock 17th–18thC furniture, fine art
Open Mon–Fri 9.30am–1pm 2–5pm
Fairs Olympia

The Collectors' Shop
Contact Mr L Downham
2 Angel Road, Norwich, Norfolk, NR3 3HP P
01603 765672
Est. 1975 *Stock size* Large
Stock Stamps, postcards, coins, models, small items, collectables
Open Tues–Sat 9.30am–5.30pm closed Thurs
Fairs Bloomsbury

Clive Dennett (BNTA, IBNS)
Contact Mr C Dennett
66 St Benedict's Street, Norwich, Norfolk, NR2 4AR P
01603 624315 F 01603 624315
Est. 1970 *Stock size* Large
Stock Coins, medals, banknotes, currency
Open Mon–Sat 9am–5pm closed Thurs
Fairs The Cumberland Coin Fairs

Elm Hill Antiques
Contact Mr Guyner
28 Elm Hill, Norwich, Norfolk, NR3 1HG P
01603 667414
Est. 1993 *Stock size* Small
Stock Victorian furniture, china, linen
Open Mon–Sat 10am–4.30pm closed Thurs

Nicholas Fowle Antiques (BADA)
Contact Mr N Fowle
Websdales Court, Bedford Street, Norwich, Norfolk, NR2 1AR
01603 219964 F 01692 630378
M 07831 218808
Est. 1995 *Stock size* Medium
Stock 18th–19thC furniture
Open Mon–Fri 9am–5.30pm Sat by appointment
Fairs BADA
Services Restoration

Philip Hodge Antiques
Contact Philip Hodge
Hall Farm Cottage, Easthill Lane, Kirby Bedon, Norwich, Norfolk, NR14 7DZ P
01508 493136 F 01508 493136
philip@philiphodgeantiques.co.uk
www.philiphodgeantiques.co.uk
Est. 1992 *Stock size* Medium
Stock Furniture
Open By appointment
Fairs Lomax Fairs

Knights Sporting Auctions
Contact Tim Knight
Cuckoo Cottage, Town Green, Alby, Norwich, Norfolk, NR11 7PR
01263 768488 F 01263 768788
tim@knights.co.uk
www.knights.co.uk
Est. 1993
Open Mon–Fri 9am–5pm
Sales Sporting memorabilia, especially cricket, football, at varied venues and dates, see website or call for details, viewing day prior to sale
Frequency Quarterly
Catalogues Yes

Leona Levine Silver Specialist (BADA)
Contact Leona Levine
2 Fishers Lane (off St Giles Street), Norwich, Norfolk, NR2 1ET P
01603 628709 F 01603 628709
Est. 1865 *Stock size* Large
Stock Silver, old Sheffield plate
Open Tues Wed Fri 9.30am–4.30pm or by appointment
Services Valuations, restoration

Maddermarket Antiques (NAG)
Contact Mr T Earl
18c Lower Goat Lane, Norwich, Norfolk, NR2 1EL
01603 620610 01603 620610
Est. 1984 *Stock size* Large
Stock Antique, second-hand, modern jewellery, silverware
Open Mon–Sat 9am–5pm

The Movie Shop
Contact Mr P Cossey
11 St Gregory's Alley, Norwich, Norfolk, NR2 1ER
01603 615239
petecossey@ntlworld.com
www.thenorwichmovieshop.com
Est. 1985 *Stock size* Large
Stock General antiquarian books, movie, TV, theatre and vinyl
Open Mon–Sat 11am–5.30pm
Services Valuations

Norfolk Antiques
Contact Kevin Matthews
Leopold Road, Norwich, Norfolk, NR4 7PG
01603 506348
Est. 1970 *Stock size* Small
Stock General antiques
Open Mon–Sat 10am–2pm

Norwich Auction Rooms
Contact Mr J Sutton
The Auction Centre, Bessemer Road, Norwich, Norfolk, NR4 6DQ
01603 666502 01603 666502
Est. 1991
Open Mon–Fri 9am–5pm
Sales Monthly antiques and collectables Sun 2pm, viewing day of sale 10am. Special sales occasionally
Catalogues Yes

Timgems Jewellers
Contact Tim Snelling
30 Elm Hill, Norwich, Norfolk, NR3 1HG
01603 623296 01603 666183
tim.snelling@btinternet.com
Est. 1969 *Stock size* Medium
Stock Antique jewellery, silverware
Open Tues–Sat 11am–4.30am
Services Valuations, restoration

Tombland Antiques Centre
Contact Nick Barker
Augustine Stewart House, 14 Tombland, Norwich, Norfolk, NR3 1HF
01603 619129
Est. 1999 *Stock size* Large
No. of dealers 53
Stock A wide range of antiques and collectables
Open Mon–Sat 10am–5pm Sun by appointment
Services Valuations

Tombland Bookshop
Contact Mr J Freeman
8 Tombland, Norwich, Norfolk, NR3 1HF
01603 490000 01603 760610
tombland.bookshop@virgin.net
Est. 1973 *Stock size* Large
Stock Antiquarian, second-hand books
Open Mon–Fri 9.30am–5pm Sat 9.30am–4.30pm

Malcolm Turner
Contact Mr M Turner
15 St Giles Street, Norwich, Norfolk, NR2 1JL
01603 627007 01603 627007
Est. 1971 *Stock size* Large
Stock Mixed porcelain, bronze figures, silver, jewellery
Open Tues–Sat 10am–5pm
Services Valuations

RAVENINGHAM

M D Cannell
Contact Mr M Cannell
Castell Farm, Beccles Road, Raveningham, Norfolk, NR14 6NU
01508 548406 01508 548406
07801 416355
mal@raveningham.demon.co.uk
Est. 1984 *Stock size* Large
Stock European decorative furniture, carpets, Oriental rugs
Open Fri–Mon 10am–6pm or by appointment
Fairs Newark, Bath Decorative

REEPHAM

Bonhams
The Market Place, Reepham, Norwich, Norfolk, NR10 4JJ
01603 871443 01603 872973
norfolk@bonhams.com
www.bonhams.com
Est. 1793
Open Mon–Fri 9am–1pm 2–5pm
Sales Regional office. Regular house and attic sales across the country; contact London offices for further details. Free auction valuations; insurance and probate valuations
Catalogues Yes

Echo Antiques
Contact Marion Stiefel
Church Hill, Reepham, Norwich, Norfolk, NR10 4JW
01603 873291
Est. 1997 *Stock size* Large
Stock General antiques, English and French furniture
Open Mon–Sat 10am–5pm closed Thurs
Services Valuations

RINGSTEAD

Ringstead Village Antique & Collectors Centre
Contact Mr or Mrs Roberts
41 High Street, Ringstead, Hunstanton, Norfolk, PE36 5JU
01485 525270
Est. 1998 *Stock size* Large
No. of dealers 30
Stock Antiques and collectables, corkscrews, china, pottery, glass
Open Mon Thurs Fri Sun 8am–5.30pm Tues Wed Sat 8am–1pm

SCRATBY

Keith Lawson Antique Clocks (BHI)
Contact Keith Lawson
Scratby Garden Centre, Beach Road, Scratby, Great Yarmouth, Norfolk, NR29 3AJ
01493 730950 01493 730658
Est. 1979
Stock Antique clocks
Open Mon–Sun 2–6pm
Services Valuations, restoration

SHERINGHAM

Dorothy's Antiques
Contact Mrs D E Collier
23 Waterbank Road,

Sheringham, Norfolk,
NR26 8RB
01263 822319
Est. 1975 *Stock size* Medium
Stock Royal Worcester, Royal Doulton, small furniture, collectables
Open Mon–Sun 11.15am–3.30pm

STALHAM

Stalham Antique Gallery (LAPADA)
Contact Mr Mike Hicks
29 High Street, Stalham, Norwich, Norfolk, NR12 9AH
01692 580636 01692 580636
mbhickslink@talk21.com
Est. 1970 *Stock size* Large
Stock Period furniture, associated items
Open Mon–Fri 9am–5pm Sat 9am–1pm or by appointment
Services Valuations, restoration

STIFFKEY

Stiffkey Lamp Shop
Contact David Mann
Stiffkey, Norfolk, NR23 1AJ
01328 830460 01328 830005
enquiries@stiffkeylampshop.co.uk
www.stiffkeylampshop.co.uk
Est. 1976 *Stock size* Medium
Stock Antique lighting
Open Mon–Sun 10am–5pm Oct–Easter closed Wed Thur
Services Shipping

SWAFFHAM

Cranglegate Antiques
Contact Mrs R D Buckie
59 Market Place, Swaffham, Norfolk, PE37 7LE
01760 721052
www.buckie-antiques.com
Est. 1973 *Stock size* Medium
Stock Furniture, decorative, small items
Open Tues Thurs Sat 10am–1pm 2–5.30pm
Fairs Newark

TACOLNESTON

Freya Books and Antiques
Contact Colin Lewsey
St Marys Farm, Cheneys Lane, Tacolneston, Norwich, Norfolk, NR16 1DB
01508 489252
07799 401067
freyaantiques@ic24.net
www.freyaantiques.co.uk
Est. 1971 *Stock size* Medium
Stock Furniture, books
Open By appointment
Fairs Long Melford, Sudbury, Bob Evans Norwich
Services Valuations, restoration, book search, shipping, Freya Fair Organizer

TOTTENHILL

Jubilee Antiques
Contact A J Lee
Coach House, Whincommon Road, Tottenhill, King's Lynn, Norfolk, PE33 0RS
01553 810681 01553 760128
07899 753222
Est. 1971 *Stock size* Medium
Stock 18th–19thC furniture
Open Mon–Sun 9am–6pm or by appointment
Services Restoration

WATTON

J C Books (PBFA)
Contact Mr J A Ball
55 High Street, Watton, Thetford, Norfolk, IP25 6AB
01953 883488 01953 883488
j_c_books@lineone.net
Est. 1990 *Stock size* Medium
Stock General antiquarian books, ephemera, Victorian and Edwardian theatre a speciality
Open Mon–Wed Fri Sat 10am–4.30pm Thurs 10am–1pm
Fairs PBFA
Services Book search

Watton Salerooms
Contact Mr S Roberts
Breckland House, Newgreen Business Park, Norwich Road, Watton, Thetford, Norfolk, IP25 6DU
01953 885676 01953 885676
watton.salerooms@eidosnet.co.uk
www.thesalerooms.co.uk
Est. 1989
Open Mon 8am–8pm Tues 8am–6pm Wed–Fri 10am–3pm Sat 10am–1pm
Sales 7 or 8 antiques sales yearly on Bank Holidays, viewing day before the sale 3–6pm day of sale from 9am. Also antiques and general household Tues, viewing Mon 4–8pm and day of sale
Frequency Weekly
Catalogues No

WELLS-NEXT-THE-SEA

Wells Antique Centre
Contact Mr Vallance
The Old Mill, Maryland, Wells-next-the-Sea, Norfolk, NR23 1LY
01328 711433
Est. 1989 *Stock size* Medium
No. of dealers 15
Stock General antiques, copper, brass, porcelain, glass, rugs, furniture, jewellery, linen, collectables
Open Mon–Sun 10am–5pm

WOLFERTON

Holt's (GTA)
Contact Mr N Holt
Church Farm Barns, Wolferton, Norfolk, PE31 6HA
01485 542822 01485 544463
enquiries@holtandcompany.co.uk
www.holtandcompany.co.uk
Est. 1993
Open Mon–Fri 9am–5pm
Sales Fine modern and antique gun sales at the Duke of York's Barracks, Chelsea, London, Thurs 2pm, viewing Tues 10am–8pm Wed 9am–6pm morning of sale
Frequency 4 per annum
Catalogues Yes

WROXHAM

Eric Bates & Sons Ltd
Contact Graham or Eric Bates
Horning Road West, Hoveton, Wroxham, Norfolk, NR12 8QJ
01692 403221 01692 404388
07887 776149
furniture@bates.fsnet.co.uk
www.batesfurniture.co.uk
Est. 1982 *Stock size* Large
Stock General 19thC antiques, Victorian chairs
Open Mon–Fri 9am–5pm Sat 9am–4.30pm
Fairs Newark

T C S Brooke (BADA)
Contact Mr S T Brooke
The Grange, Norwich Road, Wroxham, Norfolk, NR12 8RX
01603 782644 01603 782644
Est. 1936 *Stock size* Large
Stock General antiques, 18thC furniture, Georgian items, 18thC porcelain
Open Tues–Sat 9.15am–1pm 2.15–5.30pm
Services Valuations of complete house contents

Bradley Hatch Jewellers
Contact Mr Bradley Hatch
Tunstead Road, Wroxham, Norwich, Norfolk, NR12 8QG
01603 782233 01603 784679
sales@bradleyhatch.com
www.bradleyhatch.com
Est. 1994 *Stock size* Medium
Stock Jewellery, watches, silver, clocks, gifts, pocket watches
Open Mon–Sat 9am–5pm
Services Valuations, restoration, shipping

WYMONDHAM

Margaret King
Contact Margaret King
16 Market Place, Wymondham, Norfolk, NR18 0AX
01953 604758
Est. 1975 *Stock size* Large
Stock General antiques, furniture, porcelain, glass, silver
Open Thurs–Sat 9am–1pm 2–4pm
Fairs Langley, Woolverstone, all Lomax Fairs

M and A C Thompson
Contact Mr A C Thompson
The Bookshop, 1 Town Green, Wymondham, Norfolk, NR18 0PN
01953 602244
Est. 1981 *Stock size* Medium
Stock Antiquarian, general second-hand books
Open Mon–Fri 10.30am–4.45pm closed Wed

Wymondham Antique Centre
Contact Kay Hipperson
3 Town Green, Wymondham, Norfolk, NR18 0PN
01953 604817 01603 811112
Est. 1987 *Stock size* Large
Stock General antiques, china, furniture, books, pictures
Open Mon–Sun 10am–5pm
Services Valuations

SUFFOLK

ALDEBURGH

Mole Hall Antiques
Contact Mr P Weaver
102 High Street, Aldeburgh, Suffolk, IP15 5AB
01728 452361
Est. 1981 *Stock size* Large
Stock General antiques
Open Mon–Sat 10am–5pm

BECCLES

Besley's Books (PBFA, ABA)
Contact Piers or Gaby Besley
4 Blyburgate, Beccles, Suffolk, NR34 9TA
01502 715762 01502 675649
piers@besleysbooks.demon.co.uk
www.besleysbooks.demon.co.uk
Est. 1970 *Stock size* Medium
Stock Antiquarian books, gardening, natural history, art, private press a speciality
Open Mon–Sat 9.30am–5pm closed Wed
Fairs PBFA, ABA
Services Valuations, restoration, booksearch, 2 catalogues a year

Blyburgate Antiques
Contact Mrs Kate Lee
27–29 Blyburgate, Beccles, Suffolk, NR34 9TB
01502 711174
katherine.lee@lineone.net
Est. 1997 *Stock size* Medium
Stock General antiques, furniture
Open Tues–Sat 10am–4.30pm closed Wed
Fairs Alexandra Palace
Services Valuations

Durrants Auction Rooms
Contact Mr Miles Lamdin
Gresham Road, Beccles, Suffolk, NR34 9QN
01502 713490 01502 711039
info@durrantsauctionrooms.com
www.durrantsauctionrooms.com
Est. 1853
Open Mon–Fri 9am–4pm Sat 9am–noon
Sales General antiques sales every Fri. Special sale once every 6 weeks, viewing every Thurs and sale day
Catalogues No

Fauconberges
Contact Mr R D Howard or Mr R J Crozier
8 Smallgate, Beccles, Suffolk, NR34 9AD
01502 716147
Est. 1980 *Stock size* Medium
Stock 17th–19thC furniture, pictures, glass
Open Mon–Sat 10am–5pm
Fairs Lomax, Graham Turner (Long Melford)
Services Valuations for insurance and probate, sales on commission, decanter cleaning and renovation

BUNGAY

Black Dog Antiques
Contact Mr M Button
51 Earsham Street, Bungay, Suffolk, NR35 1AF
01986 895554
Est. 1985 *Stock size* Medium
Stock General, collectables, pine furniture
Open Mon–Sat 10am–5pm Sun 11am–4.30pm

Cork Brick Antiques & Gallery
Contact Ken Skipper
6 Earsham Street, Bungay, Suffolk, NR35 1AG
01986 892875
corkbrick2@tiscali.co.uk
Est. 1990 *Stock size* Medium
Stock Decorative antiques, country furnishings, contemporary art
Open Tues–Sat 10.30am–5pm

Friend or Faux
Contact Jane Cudlipp or Kim Sisson
28 Earsham Street, Bungay, Suffolk, NR35 1AQ
01502 714246 01502 714246
Est. 1989 *Stock size* Medium

Stock Antiques, decorative objects, murals, paintings, hand-painted furniture
Open Fri–Sat 10am–5pm
Services Restoration, faux finishes

One Step Back
Contact Mrs Diane Wells
4a Earsham Street, Bungay, Suffolk, NR35 1AG P
☎ 01986 896626
Est. 1998 **Stock size** Medium
Stock General antiques, furniture
Open Tues–Sat 10am–5pm closed Wed
Services Restoration

BURES

Major Iain Grahame (ABA)
Contact Major Iain Grahame
Daws Hall, Lamarsh, Bures, Suffolk, CO8 5EX P
☎ 01787 269213 F 01787 269634
E majorbooks@compuserve.com
W www.iaingrahamerarebooks.com
Est. 1979 **Stock size** Medium
Stock Antiquarian books, especially sporting, natural history, Africana
Open By appointment

BURROUGH GREEN

R E and G B Way (ABA, PBFA)
Contact Mr G Way
Brettons, Church Lane, Burrough Green, Newmarket, Suffolk, CB8 9NA P
☎ 01638 507217 F 01638 508058
E waybks@msn.com
Est. 1950 **Stock size** Large
Stock Antiquarian, out-of-print, horse, hunting, racing, field-sport books
Open Mon–Sat 9am–5pm telephone to check
Fairs Russell Book Fair

BURY ST EDMUNDS

Chimney Mill Galleries
Contact Hilary Murfitt
West Stow, Bury St Edmunds, Suffolk, IP28 6ER P
☎ 01284 728234 F 01284 728234
Est. 1976 **Stock size** Medium
Stock Antique stipped pine furniture
Open Wed–Sat 11am–5pm or by appointment
Services Restoration

Lacy Scott & Knight (SOFAA)
Contact Edward Crichton
10 Risbygate Street, Bury St Edmunds, Suffolk, IP33 3AA P
☎ 01284 748600 F 01284 748620
E fineart@lsk.co.uk
W www.lsk.co.uk
Est. 1869
Open Mon–Fri 9am–1pm 2–5.30pm
Sales Quarterly fine art sale and model and collectors' sales. Victoriana sales every 3–4 weeks, viewing Fri 3–7pm
Frequency Monthly
Catalogues Yes

Marshall Buck and Casson
Contact Mr B Moss
The Auction Rooms, Eastgate Street, Bury St Edmunds, Suffolk, IP33 1YQ P
☎ 01284 756081/753361
F 01284 756081
M 07768 324102
Est. 1999
Open Wed 8am–8pm
Sales Mixed antiques and general sales Sat, viewing Fri 2.30–8pm and Sat 8–9am. Periodic special antiques sales
Frequency Every 3 weeks
Catalogues Yes

Thrift Cottage Antiques (BADA)
Contact Diane Oddy
PO Box 113, Bury St Edmunds, Suffolk, IP33 2RQ P
☎ 01284 702470
E thriftcottageantiques@britishporcelain.com
W www.britishporcelain.com
Est. 1984 **Stock size** Medium
Stock 18th–19thC British porcelain
Open By appointment
Fairs Olympia

CAMPSIE ASH

Abbotts Auction Rooms
Contact Mrs Linda Coates
Campsie Ashe, Woodbridge, Suffolk, IP13 0PS P
☎ 01728 746323 F 01728 748173
E auction.rooms@abbottscountrywide.co.uk
W www.abbottsauctionrooms.co.uk
Est. 1920
Open Mon–Fri 9am–5.30pm Sat 9–11am
Sales General auction every Mon 11am, viewing Sat 9–11am day of sale 8.30–11am. Special antiques auctions (6 per annum) Wed 10am, viewing Sat Mon prior to sale 2–8pm Tues 10am–4pm morning of sale from 8.30am
Catalogues Yes

Ashe Antiques Warehouse
Contact Mr G Laffling
Station Road, Campsie Ash, Woodbridge, Suffolk, IP13 0PT P
☎ 01728 747255 F 01728 747255
Est. 1987 **Stock size** Large
Stock 18thC oak furniture, Victorian smalls, mirrors etc
Open Mon–Sun 10.30am–5pm
Fairs The International Antique and Collectables Fair, RAF Swinderby, Newark
Services French polishing, upholstery, ceramic restoration

CAVENDISH

Cavendish Rose Antiques
Contact Toby Patterson
1 Clarks Yard, High Street, Cavendish, Sudbury, Suffolk, CO10 8AT P
☎ 01787 282133 F 01787 280332
Est. 1974 **Stock size** Large
Stock 18thC–Edwardian furniture, dining tables, chairs, desks, chests-of-drawers, bookcases
Open Mon–Sat 10.30am–5pm

CLARE

Robin Butler
Contact Robin Butler
The Old Bank House, Market Hill, Clare, Suffolk, CU10 8NN P

☎ 01787 279111
ⓔ robin.butler@btconnect.com
Est. 1963 *Stock size* Large
Stock Fine 18th–19thC furniture, silver, wine-related objects
Open By appointment
Services Valuations, lectures
Fairs Olympia, Bury St Edmunds

Clare Antique Warehouse
Contact Leonard Edwards
✉ **The Mill, Malting Lane, Clare, Sudbury, Suffolk, CO10 8NW** Ⓟ
☎ 01787 278449 ⓕ 01787 278449
Est. 1988 *Stock size* Large
No. of dealers 85
Stock General, pine, oak furniture
Open Mon–Sat 9.30am–5pm Sun 1–5pm
Services Restoration, shipping, valuations

Dyson & Son
Contact Mr M Dyson
✉ **The Auction Rooms, Church Street, Clare, Sudbury, Suffolk, CO10 8PD** Ⓟ
☎ 01787 277993 ⓕ 01787 277996
ⓔ info@dyson-auctioneers.co.uk
ⓦ www.dyson-auctioneers.co.uk
Est. 1977
Open Mon–Fri 9am–5pm closed 1–2pm Sat 9am–1pm
Sales General antiques sales every 3 weeks Sat, 600–700 lots, viewing Fri 9am–9pm day of sale 9–11am. A yearly calendar is available on request
Catalogues Yes

Christina Parker Antiques
Contact Christina Parker
✉ **Church Street, Clare, Sudbury, Suffolk, CO10 8PD** Ⓟ
☎ 01787 278570 or 0207 628 4545
ⓕ 0207 428 5942
ⓔ chrismparker@hotmail.com
ⓦ www.jewelspast.com
Est. 1999 *Stock size* Small
Stock Vintage clothing, textiles, accessories, jewellery
Open Fri–Sat 10am–5pm
Fairs Newmarket

F D Salter
Contact Mr F D Salter
✉ **1–2 Church Street, Clare, Sudbury, Suffolk, CO10 8PD** Ⓟ
☎ 01787 277693
Est. 1960 *Stock size* Medium
Stock 18th–19thC furniture, porcelain, glass
Open Mon–Sat 9am–5pm closed Wed
Fairs West London
Services Furniture restoration

Sarah Smith Scent Bottles and Collectables
Contact Sarah Smith
✉ **2 Mortimer Place, Clare, Sudbury, Suffolk, CO10 8QP**
☎ 01787 277609
Ⓜ 07939 950251
Est. 2001 *Stock size* Small
Stock Scent bottles, handbags, compacts, jewellery
Open By appointment

Trinder's Fine Tools (PBFA)
Contact Mr P D Trinder
✉ **Malting Lane, Clare, Sudbury, Suffolk, CO10 8NW** Ⓟ
☎ 01787 277130 ⓕ 01787 277677
ⓔ peter@trindersfinetools.co.uk
ⓦ www.trindersfinetools.co.uk
Est. 1974 *Stock size* Medium
Stock Woodworking tools including British infill planes by Norris, Spiers, Mathieson, Preston, second-hand, new books on furniture and woodworking, horology, architecture, art reference, collecting, metalworking, model engineering
Open Mon–Fri 10am–1pm 2–5pm Wed Sat 10am–1pm advisable to telephone to check times

DEBENHAM

Edward Bigden Fine Art
Contact Edward Bigden
✉ **48 High Street, Debenham, Suffolk, IP14 6QW** Ⓟ
☎ 01728 862065
ⓔ eb@edwardbigden.com
ⓦ www.edwardbigden.com
Est. 2001 *Stock size* Medium
Stock Medieval to modern fine art
Open By appointment

Debenham Antiques
Contact Simon Sodeaux or Chris Bigden
✉ **73 High Street, Debenham, Suffolk, IP14 6QS** Ⓟ
☎ 01728 860707 ⓕ 01728 860333
Ⓜ 07836 260650
ⓔ info@debenhamantiques.com
Est. 1974 *Stock size* Large
Stock 17th–19thC furniture, paintings
Open Mon–Sat 9.30am–5.30pm

DRINKSTONE

Denzil Grant (BADA, LAPADA)
Contact Mr D Grant
✉ **Drinkstone House, Gedding Rd, Drinkstone, Bury St Edmunds, Suffolk, IP30 9TG** Ⓟ
☎ 01449 736576 ⓕ 01449 737679
Ⓜ 07836 223312
ⓔ denzil@denzilgrant.com
ⓦ www.denzilgrant.com
Est. 1979 *Stock size* Medium
Stock 17th–19thC country furniture
Open By appointment
Fairs LAPADA, BADA, Olympias

EASTON

Marilyn Garrow Fine Textile Art (LAPADA, BADA, CINOA)
Contact Marilyn Garrow
✉ **Reckford Farmhouse, Middleton, Saxmundham, Suffolk, IP17 3NS** Ⓟ
☎ 01728 648671 ⓕ 01728 648671
Ⓜ 07774 842074
ⓔ marogarrow@aol.com
Est. 1977 *Stock size* Large
Stock Textiles
Open By appointment
Services Valuations

EXNING

Exning Antiques & Interiors
Contact Mrs M Tabbron
✉ **14–16 Oxford Street, Exning, Newmarket, Suffolk, CB8 7EW** Ⓟ
☎ 01638 600015 ⓕ 01638 600073
Est. 1993 *Stock size* Small
Stock Beds, canopies, covers, drapes, mirrors, original lighting
Open Mon–Sat 10am–5pm
Fairs Newark
Services Restoring and cleaning lighting

EYE

English and Continental Antiques
Contact Mr Steven Harmer
1 Broad Street, Eye, Suffolk, IP23 7AF
01379 871199 F 01379 871199
englishantiques@onetel.com
www.englishandcontinentalantiques.com
Est. 1975 *Stock size* Medium
Stock 17th–19thC furniture
Open Wed–Sat 11am–5pm
Services Restoration, upholstery

FELIXSTOWE

Diamond Mills & Company (FSVA)
Contact Mr N J Papworth, FRICS
117 Hamilton Road, Felixstowe, Suffolk, P11 7BL
01394 282281 F 01394 671791
diamondmills@btconnect.com
www.diamondmills.co.uk
Est. 1908
Open Mon–Fri 9am–6pm Sat 9am–3pm
Sales Antiques sales monthly, usually Wed, telephone for details, 3 special sales annually
Catalogues Yes

Poor Richard's Books (PBFA)
Contact Dick Moffat
17 Orwell Road, Felixstowe, Suffolk, IP11 7EP
01394 283138
moffatsfx@aol.com
Est. 1997 *Stock size* Large
Stock General and antiquarian books, modern first editions
Open Mon–Sat 9am–5pm
Fairs Norwich, Woodbridge, Aldeburgh, Dedham, Oxford, Cambridge
Services Valuations, restoration, book search

Tea and Antiques
Contact David George
109 High Road East, Old Felixstowe, Suffolk, IP11 9PS
01394 277789
Est. 2000 *Stock size* Medium
Stock Antiques, collectables, furniture
Open Thurs–Sun Bank Holidays 10am–5pm
Services Tea shop

The Treasure Chest Books (PBFA)
Contact Mr Robert Green
61 Cobbold Road, Felixstowe, Suffolk, IP11 7BH
01394 270717
Est. 1981 *Stock size* Large
Stock Antiquarian and second-hand books
Open Mon–Sat 9.30am–5.30pm

FINNINGHAM

Abington Books
Contact Mr J Haldane
Primrose Cottage, Westhorpe Road, Finningham, Stowmarket, Suffolk, IP14 4TW
01449 780303 F 01449 780202
Est. 1971 *Stock size* Medium
Stock Antiquarian books on Oriental and other carpets, classical tapestries
Open By appointment
Services Valuations, restoration, book search

FRAMLINGHAM

Richard Goodbrey Antiques
Contact Mrs M Goodbrey
29 Double Street, Framlingham, Woodbridge, Suffolk, IP13 9BN
01728 621191 F 01728 724626
M 07802 868622
merlin@zetnet.co.uk
Est. 1965 *Stock size* Large
Stock 18th–19thC Continental antiques, some English furniture, sleigh beds, painted furniture, pottery, glass
Open Sat 9am–1pm 2–5.30pm or by appointment
Fairs Newark

The Green Room
Contact Mrs J Shand Kydd
2 Church Street, Framlingham, Woodbridge, Suffolk, IP13 9BE
01728 723009
Est. 1986 *Stock size* Medium
Stock Textiles, quilts, curtains, bed covers
Open Fri Sat 11am–4.45pm

Honeycombe Antiques
Contact Keith Honeycombe
8 Market Hill, Framlingham, Suffolk, IP13 9AN
01728 622011
kfh@honeycombeantiques.co.uk
Stock size Medium
No. of dealers 7
Stock Silver, furniture, sewing accessories
Open Mon–Sat 9.30am–5pm
Services Valuations

The Theatre Antiques Centre
Contact Wig Darby
10 Church Street, Framlingham, Suffolk, IP13 9BH
01728 621069
wig@darbyw.freeserve.co.uk
www.darbyw.freeserve.co.uk
Est. 2002 *Stock size* Large
No. of dealers 8
Stock Country and fine furniture, smalls
Open Mon–Sat 9.30–5.30pm

HACHESTON

Hardy's Antiques
Contact Mrs Joyce Hardy
Wisteria Cottage, The Street, Hacheston, Woodbridge, Suffolk, IP3 0DS
01728 746485
Est. 1962 *Stock size* Medium
Stock Antique pine furniture, wardrobes, dressers, chests of drawers
Open Mon–Sat 9.30am–5.30pm Sun 10am–noon
Fairs Ardingly, Ipswich

HADLEIGH

Randolph Antiques (BADA)
Contact Mr Baden F Marston
97–99 High Street, Hadleigh, Ipswich, Suffolk, IP7 5EJ
01473 823789 F 01473 823867
Est. 1929 *Stock size* Medium
Stock English furniture up to 1830, accessories
Open By appointment only

HALESWORTH

P & R Antiques Ltd
Contact Pauline Lewis
Fairstead Farm Buildings,

Wash Lane, Spexhall, Halesworth, Suffolk, IP19 0RF 🅿
☎ 01986 873232 Ⓕ 01896 874682
Ⓔ pauline@prantiques.com
Ⓦ www.prantiques.com
Est. 1996 *Stock size* Large
Stock 17th–19thC furniture
Open By appointment

IPSWICH

A Abbott Antiques
Contact Mr A Abbott
✉ **757 Woodbridge Road, Ipswich, Suffolk, IP4 4NE** 🅿
☎ 01473 728900 Ⓕ 01473 728900
Ⓜ 07771 533413
Ⓔ abbott_antiques@hotmail.com
Est. 1974 *Stock size* Medium
Stock General antiques, furniture, smalls, clocks
Open Mon–Sat 9.30am–5pm closed Wed
Fairs Newark, Ardingly

Antiques and Restoration
Contact Mr R Rush
✉ **Unit 5, Penny Corner, Farthing Road, Ipswich, Suffolk, IP1 5AP** 🅿
☎ 01473 464609 Ⓕ 01473 464609
Ⓜ 07939 220041
Ⓔ info@antiquesandrestoration.co.uk
Ⓦ www.antiquesandrestoration.co.uk
Est. 1997 *Stock size* Medium
Stock 18th–19thC furniture
Open Mon–Fri 8am–6pm Sat 8am–1.30pm
Services Restoration

Bonhams
✉ **32 Boss Hall Road, Ipswich, Suffolk, IP1 5DJ**
☎ 01473 740494 Ⓕ 01473 741091
Ⓔ ipswich@bonhams.com
Ⓦ www.bonhams.com
Open Mon 9am–7pm Sat 9am–noon
Sales Regional Saleroom. Frequent sales. Regular house and attic sales across the country; contact London offices for further details. Free auction valuations; insurance and probate valuations
Catalogues Yes

Claude Cox Books (ABA, PBFA)
Contact Anthony Brian Cox
✉ **3–5 Silent Street, Ipswich, Suffolk, IP1 1TF** 🅿
☎ 01473 254776 Ⓕ 01473 254776
Ⓔ books@claudecox.co.uk
Ⓦ www.claudecox.co.uk
Est. 1974 *Stock size* Large
Stock Antiquarian and second-hand books, fine printing, private press, catalogues issued, Suffolk maps and prints a speciality
Open Wed–Sat 10am–5pm or by appointment
Services Book binding, repairs

Hubbard's Antiques
Contact Mr Max Hubbard
✉ **16 St Margaret's Green, Ipswich, Suffolk, IP4 2BS** 🅿
☎ 01473 233034 Ⓕ 01473 253639
Ⓔ sales@hubbard-antiques.com
Ⓦ www.hubbard-antiques.com
Est. 1965 *Stock size* Large
Stock 18th–19thC antique furniture, decorative items, works of art
Open Mon–Sat 9am–6pm or by appointment
Services Valuations by Internet

Lockdale Coins Ltd (BNTA)
Contact Dan Daley
✉ **37 Upper Orwell Street, Ipswich, Suffolk, IP4 1HP** 🅿
☎ 01473 218588 Ⓕ 01473 218588
Ⓔ lockdales@shop1.freeserve.co.uk
Ⓦ lockdales.co.uk
Est. 1994 *Stock size* Medium
Stock British and foreign coins, banknotes, metal detectors and accessories
Open Mon–Sat 9.30am–4.30pm
Fairs Cumberland Hotel Show, Olympia
Services Valuations, auctioneering

Lockdale Coins Ltd
Contact Dan Daley
✉ **37 Upper Orwell Street, Ipswich, Suffolk, IP4 1HP** 🅿
☎ 01473 218588 Ⓕ 01473 218588
Ⓔ lockdales@shop1.freeserve.co.uk
Ⓦ www.lockdales.com
Est. 1996
Open Mon–Sat 9.30am–5pm
Sales Telephone for details of sales. Coins, jewellery, medals, militaria, ephemera, autographs
Frequency Bi-monthly
Catalogues Yes

Maud's Attic
Contact Mrs W Childs
✉ **25 St Peter's Street, Ipswich, Suffolk, IP1 1XF** 🅿
☎ 01473 221057 Ⓕ 01473 221056
Ⓔ maudsattic@hotmail.com
Ⓦ www.maudsatticantiques.com
Est. 1996 *Stock size* Large
Stock Antiques, collectables
Open Tues–Sat 10am–5pm

Merchant House Antiques
Contact Mr G Childs
✉ **27–29 St Peter's Street, Ipswich, Suffolk, IP1 1XF** 🅿
☎ 01473 221054 Ⓕ 01473 221056
Ⓜ 07768 068575
Ⓔ merchanthouse@hotmail.com
Ⓦ www.merchanthouseantiques.com
Est. 2000 *Stock size* Medium
Stock Antiques and reclamation
Open Tues–Sat 10am–5pm

The Suffolk Antique Bed Centre
Contact Mr A Sandham
✉ **273 Norwich Road, Ipswich, Suffolk, IP1 4BP** 🅿
☎ 01473 252444
Est. 1985 *Stock size* Large
Stock Brass and iron bedsteads
Open Mon–Sat 9am–5.30pm
Services Hand-made mattresses

Suffolk Sci-fi Fantasy
Contact Mr M Milliard
✉ **17 Norwich Road, Ipswich, Suffolk, IP1 2ET** 🅿
☎ 01473 400655 Ⓕ 01473 400656
Est. 1992 *Stock size* Large
Stock Sci-fi collectables, ephemera, collectable card games, trade cards
Open Mon–Sat 9am–6pm

IXWORTH

E W Cousins & Son (LAPADA)
Contact Mr Robert Cousins
✉ **Old School, Thetford Road, Ixworth, Bury St Edmunds, Suffolk, IP31 2HJ** 🅿

☎ 01359 230254 Ⓕ 01359 232370
Ⓔ john@ewcousins.co.uk
Ⓦ www.ewcousins.co.uk
Est. 1920 *Stock size* Large
Stock 18th–19thC furniture
Open Mon–Fri 8.30am–5pm
Sat 8.30am–1pm
Services Restoration, containers packed

LAVENHAM

J & J Baker
Contact Mrs Joy Baker
✉ **12–14 Water Street, Lavenham, Sudbury, Suffolk, CO10 9RW** Ⓟ
☎ 01787 247610
Est. 1970 *Stock size* Large
Stock General English antiques, furniture, porcelain
Open Mon–Sat 10am–5.30pm
Sun by appointment

Timbers Antiques & Collectables
Contact Tom or Jenny White
✉ **High Street, Lavenham, Sudbury, Suffolk, CO10 9PT** Ⓟ
☎ 01787 247218
Ⓦ www.timbersantiques.com
Est. 1996 *Stock size* Large
No. of dealers 48
Stock Antique furniture, silver, glass, china, jewellery, clocks,
Open Mon–Sat 9.30am–5pm
Sun 10am–5pm

LEISTON

Leiston Trading Post
Contact Mrs L Smith
✉ **17 High Street, Leiston, Suffolk, IP16 4EL** Ⓟ
☎ 01728 830081
Ⓜ 0771 259 6005
Est. 1967 *Stock size* Large
Stock Shipping goods, general antiques, china, bric-a-brac
Open Mon–Sat 9.30am–1pm
2–4.30pm half day Wed
Services Valuations

Warren Antiques
Contact Mr J Warren
✉ **31 High Street, Leiston, Suffolk, IP16 4EL** Ⓟ
☎ 01728 831414 Ⓕ 01728 831414
Ⓜ 07989 865598
Ⓔ jrwantiques@aol.com
Ⓦ www.warrenantiques.co.uk
Est. 1970 *Stock size* Medium
Stock Late 18thC–1930s furniture
Open Mon–Tues 9am–1pm
2–5pm Thurs–Sat 9am–12.30pm
Fairs Newark, Ardingly (DMG)
Services Restoration

LONG MELFORD

Sandy Cooke Antiques
Contact Mr Sandy Cooke
✉ **Hall Street, Long Melford, Sudbury, Suffolk, CO10 9JQ** Ⓟ
☎ 01787 378265 Ⓕ 01284 830935
Ⓔ sandycooke@englishfurniture.co.uk
Ⓦ www.englishfurniture.co.uk
Est. 1974 *Stock size* Large
Stock 1700–1830 English furniture
Open Mon Fri Sat 10am–5pm

Cottage Antiques
Contact Mr R Jarman
✉ **Melford Antiques Warehouse, Hall Street, Long Melford, Sudbury, Suffolk, CO10 9JB** Ⓟ
☎ 01268 764138 Ⓕ 01268 764138
Ⓜ 07958 618629
Ⓔ bob@cottageantiquefurniture.com
Ⓦ www.cottageantiquefurniture.com
Est. 1986 *Stock size* Large
Stock Georgian–Edwardian items, mainly furniture, collectables
Open Mon–Sun 10am–5.30pm
Services Furniture restoration, French polishing, furniture search

Long Melford Antiques Centre
Contact Mr Groves
✉ **Chapel Maltings, Little St Mary's, Long Melford, Sudbury, Suffolk, CO10 9HX** Ⓟ
☎ 01787 379287 Ⓕ 01787 379287
Est. 1983 *Stock size* Medium
No. of dealers 43
Stock Antiques, collectables, decorative items, glass, china
Open Mon–Sat 9.30am–5.30pm

Alexander Lyall Antiques
Contact Mr A J Lyall
✉ **Belmont House, Hall Street, Long Melford, Sudbury, Suffolk, CO10 9JF** Ⓟ
☎ 01787 375434 Ⓕ 01787 311115
Ⓔ alex@lyallantiques.com
Ⓦ www.lyallantiques.com
Est. 1977 *Stock size* Medium
Stock Georgian–Victorian furniture
Open Mon–Sat 10am–5.30pm
closed Bank Holidays

Magpie Antiques
Contact Pat Coll
✉ **Hall Street, Long Melford, Sudbury, Suffolk, CO10 9JT** Ⓟ
☎ 01787 310581 Ⓕ 01787 310581
Ⓔ collterry@hotmail.com
Est. 1984 *Stock size* Large
Stock Stripped old pine, country collectables
Open Tues Thurs Fri
10.30am–1pm 2.15–4.30pm
Sat 11am–5pm

Melford Antiques Warehouse
Contact Patrick
✉ **Hall Street, Long Melford, Sudbury, Suffolk, CO10 9JB** Ⓟ
☎ 01787 379638
Ⓔ patrick@worldwideantiques.co.uk
Ⓦ www.antiques-access-agency.com
Est. 1979 *Stock size* Large
Stock 17th–20thC furniture, decorative items, large variety of dining tables, book cases, chairs, clocks etc
Open Mon–Sat 9.30am–5pm
Sun 1–5pm
Services Valuations, restoration, shipping

Noel Mercer Antiques
Contact Mr Noel Mercer
✉ **Aurora House, Hall Street, Long Melford, Sudbury, Suffolk, CO10 9JR** Ⓟ
☎ 01787 311882
Est. 1991 *Stock size* Large
Stock Early English oak, walnut furniture
Open Mon–Sat 10am–5pm

Seabrook Antiques
Contact Mr John Tanner
✉ **Melford Gallery, Hall Street, Long Melford, Sudbury, Suffolk, CO10 9JF** Ⓟ
☎ 01787 375787
Est. 1978 *Stock size* Large
Stock 17th–19thC oak and decorative furniture
Open Mon–Sat 9.30am–5.30pm
Services Interior design

The Stables
Contact Mrs P Gee
Hall Street, Long Melford, Sudbury, Suffolk, CO10 9JB P
☎ 01787 310754
Est. 1980 *Stock size* Medium
Stock Interiors, antiques, collectables
Open Mon–Sat 10am–4.30pm Sun 11am–4.30pm closed Thurs

Trident Antiques (LAPADA)
Contact Mr Tom McGlynn
2 Foundry House, Hall Street, Long Melford, Sudbury, Suffolk, CO10 9JR P
☎ 01787 883388 F 01787 378850
M 07860 221402
E tridentoak@aol.com
Est. 1994 *Stock size* Large
Stock Early oak, English furniture, related objects, barometers
Open Mon–Sat 10am–5.30pm
Fairs LAPADA (Jan NEC)
Services Valuations, restoration, security implanting

Matthew Tyler Antiques
Contact Matthew Tyler
Hall Street, Long Melford, Suffolk, CO10 9JL P
☎ 01787 377523 F 01799 599978
M 07770 496350
E m.tyler1@btopenworld.com
Stock size Medium
Stock 17th–19thC English furniture and works of art
Open Mon Fri Sat 10am–5pm or by appointment
Fairs Snape, Lomax
Services Valuations, restoration, shipping

Village Clocks
Contact Mr J Massey
Little St Mary's, Long Melford, Sudbury, Suffolk, CO10 0LQ P
☎ 01787 375896
Est. 1989 *Stock size* Large
Stock Antique clocks
Open Mon–Sat 10am–4pm closed Wed
Services Restoration

LOWESTOFT

Lockdale Coins Ltd (BNTA)
Contact Dan Daley
168 London Road South, Lowestoft, Suffolk, NR33 0BB P
☎ 01502 568468 F 01502 568468
E ddaley@lockdales.freeserve.co.uk
W www.lockdales.co.uk
Est. 1998 *Stock size* Medium
Stock Gold, silver jewellery, British and world coins, banknotes, metal detectors, accessories
Open Mon–Sat 9.30am–4.30pm
Fairs Cumberland Hotel, Olympia
Services Valuations, jewellery, watch, clock repairs, auctioneering

Lockdale Coins Ltd
Contact Jean Daley
168 London Road South, Lowestoft, Suffolk, NR33 0BB P
☎ 01502 568468 F 01502 568468
E ddaley@lockdales.freeserve.co.uk
W www.lockdales.co.uk
Est. 1996
Open Mon–Sat 9.30am–4.30pm
Sales Telephone for details of sales in Ipswich. Coins, jewellery, medals, militaria, ephemera, autographs
Frequency Bi-monthly
Catalogues Yes

Lowestoft Auction Rooms
Contact Mr J Peyto
Pinbush Road, South Lowestoft Industrial Estate, Lowestoft, Suffolk, NR33 7NL P
☎ 01502 531532 F 01502 531241
E lowestoft@auctioneer.net
Est. 1985
Open Mon–Fri 8am–5.30pm
Sales Large house sales on site
Frequency Twice monthly
Catalogues Yes

Odds and Ends
Contact Mr B Smith
127 High Street, Lowestoft, Suffolk, NR32 1HP P
☎ 01502 568569 F 01502 568569
Stock All smalls, jewellery, collectables
Open Mon–Sat 10am–5pm
Services Valuations, restoration of jewellery and watches

M G Osborne
Contact Mr M G Osborne
140 High Street, Lowestoft, Suffolk, NR33 1HR P
☎ 01502 508988
Est. 1988 *Stock size* Large
Stock General antiques
Open Mon–Sat 9.30am–4pm closed Thurs
Fairs The International Antique and Collectables Fair, RAF Swinderby

John Rolph
Contact Mr John Rolph
Manor House, Pakefield Street, Lowestoft, Suffolk, NR33 0JT P
☎ 01502 572039
Est. 1948 *Stock size* Medium
Stock 17thC–1950, second-hand books
Open Tues–Sat 11am–1pm 2.30–5pm closed Thurs

MARLESFORD

The Antiques Warehouse
Contact John or Lesley Ball
The Old Mill, Main Road, Marlesford, Suffolk, IP13 0AG P
☎ 01728 747438 F 01728 747627
E omtc@antiqueswarehouse.fsnet.co.uk
Est. 1989 *Stock size* Large
Stock Country furniture, mirrors, lighting, general antiques
Open Mon–Fri 7.30am–4.30pm Sat 10am–4.30pm Sun 11am–4.30pm

MARTLESHAM

Martlesham Antiques
Contact Mr R Frost
Thatched Roadhouse, Main Road, Martlesham, Woodbridge, Suffolk, IP12 4RJ P
☎ 01394 386732 F 01394 382959
E bob@martleshamantiques.com
Est. 1983 *Stock size* Large
Stock 18th–20thC furniture
Open Mon–Fri 9am–5pm Sat 10am–4pm

NAYLAND

Town Prints
Contact Mr P Betts
Longwood Cottage, Nayland, Colchester, Suffolk, CO6 4HT
01206 262483
jonesnayland@tiscali.co.uk
Est. 1976 *Stock size* Medium
Stock Woodblock, copper and steel engravings of Colchester and district
Open By appointment
Services Framing

NEEDHAM MARKET

Old Town Hall Antique & Collectors Centre
Contact Mr R Harrison
Old Town Hall, High Street, Needham Market, Suffolk, IP6 8AL
01449 720773
Est. 1979 *Stock size* Large
No. of dealers 30
Stock Antiques, collectables
Open Mon–Sat 10am–5pm

The Tool Shop (LAPADA)
Contact Mr Tony Murland
78 High Street, Needham Market, Ipswich, Suffolk, IP6 8AW
01449 722992 01449 722683
tony@antiquetools.co.uk
www.antiquetools.co.uk
Est. 1991 *Stock size* Large
Stock Antique woodworking tools, new quality French, Japanese, American
Open Mon–Sat 10am–5pm
Fairs All major national woodworking exhibitions

NEWMARKET

Jemima Godfrey Antiques
Contact Mrs A Lanham
5 Rous Road, Newmarket, Suffolk, CB8 8DH
01638 663584
Est. 1964 *Stock size* Small
Stock Small silver, linen, jewellery, Victorian china fairings
Open Thurs Fri 10am–1pm 2pm–4.30pm

ORFORD

Castle Antiques
Contact Ms S Simpkin
Market Hill, Orford, Woodbridge, Suffolk, IP12 2LH
01394 450100 01394 450536
stephanie@castle-estates.uk.com
Est. 1959 *Stock size* Small
Stock Furniture, lamps, pictures, glass, bric-a-brac
Open Mon–Sun 11am–4pm

PEASENHALL

Peasenhall Art & Antiques Gallery
Contact Mr M Wickens
The Street, Peasenhall, Saxmundham, Suffolk, IP17 2HJ
01728 660224
Est. 1972 *Stock size* Large
Stock 18th–early 20thC watercolours, oil paintings, country furniture in all woods
Open Mon–Sun 9am–6pm
Services Restoration

RISBY

Past and Present
Contact Joe Aldridge
The Risby Barn Complex, South Street, Risby, Bury St Edmunds, Suffolk, IP28 6QU
01284 811480
Est. 1996 *Stock size* Large
No. of dealers 30
Stock Furniture, antique to present day china, silver, jewellery, bric-a-brac, pictures, books, glass, pine, Victorian-Edwardian furniture, European furniture, collectable toys
Open Mon–Sat 10am–5pm Sun 10.30am–4.30pm
Services Restoration, coffee shop, garden centre

The Risby Barn Antique Centre
Contact Mr R Martin
Risby Barn, South Street, Risby, Bury St Edmunds, Suffolk, IP28 6QU
01284 811126 01284 810783
r.martin@lineone.net
Est. 1980 *Stock size* Large
No. of dealers 30
Stock Victorian furniture, china, silver, clocks, rural bygones
Open Mon–Sat 9am–5.30pm Sun Bank Holidays 10am–5pm
Services Coffee shop, restoration

SAXMUNDHAM

Original Vintage Costume Jewellery
Contact Judy Portway
Snape Antiques and Collectors Centre, Saxmundham, Suffolk, IP17 1SR
01449 775060
Est. 1989 *Stock size* Large
Stock Original vintage costume jewellery, compacts, handbags
Open Mon–Sun 10am–5pm

Keith A Savage
Contact Mr K A Savage
35 High Street, Saxmundham, Suffolk, IP17 IAJ
01728 604538 or 01986 872231
Est. 1992 *Stock size* Medium
Stock Second-hand, collectors' books, second-hand ephemera, children's books a speciality
Open Mon Sat 10.30am–1pm Tues Wed Fri 10.30am–5pm

SOUTHWOLD

Architectural Artefacts
Contact Mr B Howard or Mrs J Twist
The Rope House, Station Road, Southwold, Suffolk, IP18 6AX
01502 723075 01502 724346
aa@ropehouse.easynet.co.uk
Est. 1996 *Stock size* Small
Stock Stained glass, architectural antiques, taps, sinks, chimney pots
Open Mon–Fri 9am–5pm
Services Stained glass design

Cannonbury Antiques Southwold
Contact Mr David Brinsmead
Bridgefoot Corner, Reydon, Southwold, Suffolk, IP18 6NF
01502 722133
Est. 1998 *Stock size* Medium
Stock General, furniture, decorative antiques
Open Tues–Fri 11am–4pm Sat 10am–5pm Sun noon–4pm
Services Valuations

Puritan Values at the Dome
Contact Anthony Geering
St Edmunds Business Park, St Edmunds Road, Southwold, Suffolk, IP18 6BZ
01502 722211 F 01502 722734
M 07966 371676
E sales@puritanvalues.com
W www.puritanvalues.com
Est. 1985 *Stock size* Medium
Stock Arts and Crafts movement, aesthetic movement, gothic revival, important furniture
Open Mon–Sat 10am–6pm Sun 11am–5pm
Fairs NEC, SEC, Olympia
Services Valuations, restoration

T Schotte Antiques
Contact Mrs Schotte
Old Bakehouse, Blackmill Road, Southwold, Suffolk, IP18 6AQ
01502 722083
Est. 1989 *Stock size* Small
Stock Antiques, decorative items
Open Mon–Sat 10am–4pm closed Wed

S J Webster-Speakman (BADA)
Contact Mrs S J Webster-Speakman
Southwold, Suffolk
01502 722252
Est. 1968 *Stock size* Medium
Stock 18th–19thC furniture, clocks, Staffordshire animals
Open By appointment
Services Restoration of clocks

SPROUGHTON

Heritage Reclamations
Contact Mr Richard Howells
1a High Street, Sproughton, Ipswich, Suffolk, IP8 3AF
01473 748519 F 01473 748519
E heritage@reclamations.fsnet.co.uk
W www.heritage-reclamations.co.uk
Est. 1985 *Stock size* Large
Stock Ironmongery, stoves, ranges, fireplaces, garden ornaments, stained glass, radiators, pews
Open Mon–Fri 9am–5pm Sat 9.30am–5pm Sun 10am–4pm
Fairs Newark, Ardingly, Swinderby, Kempton Park
Services Restoration

STOWMARKET

What-Not-Shop Antiques
Contact Mr F J Smith
28 Bury Street, Stowmarket, Suffolk, IP14 1HH
01449 613126
Est. 1979 *Stock size* Medium
Stock Jewellery, china, glass, clocks
Open Mon–Sat 9am–4.30pm Tues closed
Services Repairs

SUDBURY

Beckham Books (PBFA)
Contact Mrs Jenny Beckham
Chilton Mount, Newton Road, Sudbury, Suffolk, CO10 2RS
01787 373683 F 01787 375441
E sales@beckhambooks.com
W www.beckhambooks.com
Est. 1996 *Stock size* Small
Stock Antiquarian, theological books, bibles
Open By appointment
Fairs PBFA Fairs
Services Book search

Napier House Antiques
Contact Mrs Veronica McGregor
3 Church Street, Sudbury, Suffolk, CO10 2BJ
01787 375280 F 01787 478757
M 07768 703406
Est. 1976 *Stock size* Large
Stock 18th–19thC mahogany furniture
Open Mon–Sat 10am–4.30pm closed Wed
Services Free delivery UK mainland

Neate Militaria & Antiques (OMRS)
Contact Gary Neate
PO Box 3794, Preston St Mary, Sudbury, Suffolk, CO10 9PX
01787 248168 F 01787 248363
E gary@neatemedals.co.uk
W www.neatemedals.co.uk
Est. 1984 *Stock size* Medium
Stock Worldwide orders, decorations, medals, with an emphasis on British material
Open Mon–Fri 9am–6pm
Fairs Brittania Medal Fair, Aldershot Medal Fair
Services Valuations, restoration, mail order catalogue

Olivers (SOFAA)
Contact Mr J Fletcher
The Sale Room, Burkitts Lane, Sudbury, Suffolk, CO10 1HB
01787 880305 F 01787 880305
Est. 1766
Open Mon–Fri 9am–1pm 2–5pm
Sales Regular sales of antiques and works of art. Victorian, later furniture, household effects fortnightly Thurs 1pm, viewing day of sale from 9am
Catalogues Yes

Sasha
Contact Susan Bailey
79 Melford Road, Sudbury, Suffolk, CO10 1JT
01787 375582
M 07781 453250
Est. 1986 *Stock size* Medium
Stock Small furniture, ceramics, collectables, books
Open Mon–Sat 10.30am–5pm
Services Book search

Sitting Pretty Antiques
Contact Mr Darren Barrs
16 Friars Street, Sudbury, Suffolk, CO10 2AA
01787 880908
M 07974 689044
Est. 1987 *Stock size* Large
Stock Re-upholstered period furniture, 18thC–1930s
Open Mon–Sat 9.30am–5pm
Services Upholstery, interior design consultations

Suffolk Rare Books
Contact Mr T Cawthorne
7 New Street, Sudbury, Suffolk, CO10 1JB
01787 372075
E morrisbooks@hotmail.com
Est. 1975 *Stock size* Medium
Stock Antiquarian books, topography, military, history
Open Tues–Sat 10.30am–4.30pm closed Wed

WOODBRIDGE

Blake's Books (PBFA)
Contact Mr R Green
88 The Thoroughfare,

Woodbridge, Suffolk,
IP12 1AL
☎ 01394 380302
Stock Antiquarian and second-hand books, Suffolk and sailing books a speciality
Open Mon–Sat 9.30am–5pm
Fairs Woodbridge Book Fair

Church Street Centre
Contact Miss M Brown
✉ 6e Church Street, Woodbridge, Suffolk, IP12 1DH
☎ 01394 388887
Est. 1994 *Stock size* Large
No. of dealers 10
Stock Wide range of items including small furniture, jewellery, china, glass, silver, ephemera, textiles, pictures, bygones, clocks, collectables
Open Mon-Sat 10am–5pm
Services Free local delivery

Dix-Sept Antiques
Contact Miss Sophie Goodbrey
✉ 17 Station Road, Woodbridge, Suffolk, IP13 9EA
☎ 01728 621505 F 01728 724884
Est. 1985 *Stock size* Medium
Stock French antiques, furniture, glass, pottery, textiles
Open Sat 10am–1pm 2–5.30pm or by appointment
Fairs Newark

David Gibbins (BADA)
Contact Mr David Gibbins
✉ The White House, 14 Market Hill, Woodbridge, Suffolk, IP12 4LU
☎ 01394 383531 F 01394 383531
M 07702 306914
E david@gibbinsantiques.co.uk
Est. 1966 *Stock size* Medium
Stock 18thC furniture, Lowestoft porcelain
Open By appointment
Fairs The West London Antiques and Fine Art Fair, Louise Walker Harrogate Fair, BADA Fair
Services Valuations, restoration

Hamilton Antiques (LAPADA)
Contact Hamilton or Rosemary Ferguson
✉ 5 Church Street, Woodbridge, Suffolk, IP12 1DH
☎ 01394 387222 F 01394 383832
M 07747 033437
E enquiries@hamiltonantiques.co.uk
W www.hamiltonantiques.co.uk
Est. 1976 *Stock size* Large
Stock 18th–20thC furniture
Trade only Yes
Open Mon–Fri 8.30am–5pm Sat 10am–5pm
Services Restoration, polishing

Anthony Hurst
Contact Mr Christopher Hurst
✉ 13 Church Street, Woodbridge, Suffolk, IP12 1DS
☎ 01394 382500 F 01394 382500
Est. 1968 *Stock size* Large
Stock 18th–19thC furniture, mahogany, oak
Open Mon–Fri 9.30am–1pm 2–5.30pm closed Wed pm Sat 10am–1pm

Raymond Lambert
Contact Mr Raymond Lambert
✉ The Bull Ride, 70a New Street, Woodbridge, Suffolk, IP12 1DX
☎ 01394 382380
E mary@lamberts667.fsnet.co.uk
Est. 1963 *Stock size* Medium
Stock 19th–20thC furniture
Open Mon–Sat 9.30am–1pm 2–5pm closed Wed

Sarah Meysey-Thompson Antiques
Contact Sarah Meysey-Thompson
✉ 10 Church Street, Woodbridge, Suffolk, IP12 1DH
☎ 01394 382144
Est. 1961 *Stock size* Medium
Stock Georgian–Victorian furniture, curios, decorative pieces, textiles
Open Mon–Sat 10am–5pm
Fairs Battersea Park Decorative Antique and Textile Fair

Neal Sons & Fletcher
Contact Mr Edward Fletcher FRICS
✉ 26 Church Street, Woodbridge, Suffolk, IP12 1DP
☎ 01394 382263 F 01394 383030
E enquiries@nsf.co.uk
W www.nsf.co.uk
Est. 1951
Open Mon–Fri 9am–5.30pm Sat 9am–4pm
Sales General monthly antiques sales, viewing day prior to sale 2.15–4.30pm 6.30–8pm sale day 9.30–10.30am. Bi- or tri-annual specialist sales of period English and Continental furniture, pictures, books, carpets etc at The Theatre Street Sale Room, viewing Sat prior to sale 10am–1pm day preceding sale 11am–4.30pm 6.30–8pm sale day 9.30–10.30am
Catalogues Yes

The Old Brewery Antiques
Contact Maurice Finch
✉ Melton Road, Melton, Woodbridge, Suffolk, IP12 1PD
☎ 01394 388836 F 01394 388836
Est. 2003 *Stock size* Large
Stock General antiques, collectables
Open Mon–Sat 9am–5pm closed Wed

Isobel Rhodes
Contact Mrs I Rhodes
✉ 10 & 12 Market Hill, Woodbridge, Suffolk, IP12 4LS
☎ 01394 382763
Est. 1964 *Stock size* Medium
Stock Oak, country furniture, pewter, pottery, brass
Open Mon–Sat 10am–1pm 2–5pm

E F Wall Antiques
Contact Libby Wall
✉ 32 Church Street, Woodbridge, Suffolk, IP12 1DH
☎ 01394 610511
E libbyswall@ukonline.co.uk
Est. 1979 *Stock size* Large
Stock Reproduction French polished furniture
Trade only Yes
Open Mon–Sat 10am–5pm
Services Restoration

Woodbridge Gallery
Contact Mr David Bethell
✉ 23 Market Hill, Woodbridge, Suffolk, IP12 4LX
☎ 01394 386500 F 01394 386500
Est. 1998 *Stock size* Large
No. of dealers 20
Stock General antiques, fine art gallery
Open Mon–Sat 10am–5.30pm Wed 10am–1pm

WOOLPIT

John Heather
Contact John Heather
Old Crown, The Street, Woolpit, Bury St Edmunds, Suffolk, IP30 9SA P
☎ 01359 240297
Ⓜ 07715 282600
Ⓔ john@johnheather.co.uk
Est. 1946 *Stock size* Medium
Stock Late 18thC furniture
Open Mon–Sun 9am–6pm
Services Restoration

WRENTHAM

Bly Valley Antiques
Contact Mr Eric Ward
Old Reading Rooms, 7 High Street, Wrentham, Beccles, Suffolk, NR34 7HD P
☎ 01502 675376 or 01728 454508
Ⓕ 01502 675376
Ⓦ www.bly-valley-antiques.com
Est. 1971 *Stock size* Large
Stock China, glass, pictures, furniture, antiquarian books
Open Tues–Sat 10.30am–5pm

Wren House Antiques
Contact Ms V Kemp
1 High Street, Wrentham, Beccles, Suffolk, NR34 7HD P
☎ 01502 675276
Ⓜ 07900 552216
Ⓔ tony.kemp1@btopenworld.com
Est. 1984 *Stock size* Medium
Stock Small antique furniture, collectables
Open Thurs–Sun 10.30am–5pm

YOXFORD

The Garden House
Contact Ann Gray or Janet Hyde-Smith
High Street, Yoxford, Saxmundham, Suffolk, IP17 3ER P
☎ 01728 668044
Est. 1969 *Stock size* Large
Stock Antiques, vintage, decorative and pretty things, books
Open Mon Thurs–Sun 10am–4.30pm closed Tues

Suffolk House Antiques (BADA)
Contact Mr A Singleton
High Street, Yoxford, Saxmundham, Suffolk, IP17 3EP P
☎ 01728 668122 Ⓕ 01728 668122
Ⓜ 07860 521583
Ⓔ andrew.singleton@suffolk-house-antiques.co.uk
Ⓦ www.suffolk-house-antiques.co.uk
Est. 1991 *Stock size* Large
Stock Early English furniture, ceramics, associated works of art
Open Mon–Sat 10am–1pm 2.15–5.15pm closed Wed
Fairs BADA, Snape

HEART OF ENGLAND

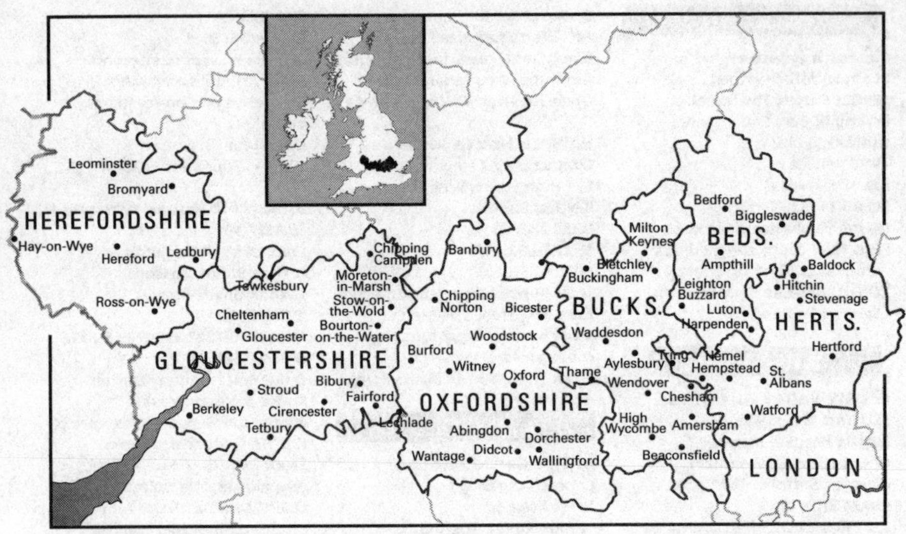

BEDFORDSHIRE

AMPTHILL

Ampthill Antiques
Contact Mr Shayler
Market Square, Church Street, Ampthill, Bedfordshire, MK45 2EH
01525 403344
Est. 1980 *Stock size* Large
Stock General antiques
Open Mon–Sun 11am–6pm

Ampthill Antiques Emporium
Contact Marc Legg
6 Bedford Street, Ampthill, Bedfordshire, MK45 2NB P
01525 402131 F 01582 737527
M 07831 374919
E info@ampthillantiquesemporium.co.uk
W www.ampthillantiquesemporium.co.uk
Est. 1979 *Stock size* Large
No. of dealers 40
Stock Georgian–Edwardian furniture, smalls, shipping goods
Open Mon–Sun 10am–5pm closed Tues
Services Upholstery, valuations, shipping, furniture restoration, pine stripping, picture framing

Antiquarius
Contact Mr P Caldwell
107 Dunstable Street, Ampthill, Bedfordshire, MK45 2NG P
01525 841799
M 07776 216907
E peter.caldwell@tesco.net
W www.antiquariusofampthill.com
Est. 1996 *Stock size* Medium
Stock Georgian–Edwardian sitting and dining room furniture
Open Mon–Sat 10.30am–5pm Sun 1–5pm
Services Restoration, upholstery

House of Clocks (BHI)
Contact Mrs H Proud
102–104 Dunstable Street, Ampthill, Bedfordshire, MK45 2JP P
01525 403136
E helgaginty@aol.com
W www.houseofclocks.co.uk
Est. 1984 *Stock size* Large
Stock Fine-quality antiques, reproduction clocks
Open Mon–Sat 9am–5pm
Fairs Motorcycle Museum, NEC, Brunel University
Services Restoration

David Litt Antiques
Contact Mr D Litt
The Old Telephone Exchange, Claridges Lane, Ampthill, Bedfordshire, MK45 2HU P
01525 404825 F 01525 404563
M 07802 449027
E litt@ntlworld.com
W www.davidlittantiques.co.uk
Est. 1967 *Stock size* Large
Stock French provincial, 19thC furniture
Open Mon–Fri 7am–5pm
Fairs Battersea, Olympia
Services Restoration

Paris Antiques
Contact Mr Paul Northwood
97b Dunstable Street, Ampthill, Bedfordshire, MK45 2NG P
01525 840488 F 01525 840488
M 07802 535059
Est. 1984 *Stock size* Medium
Stock 18th–early 20thC furniture and effects
Open Tues–Sun 9.30am–5.30pm
Services Valuations, restoration

Pilgrim Antiques
Contact Mr G Lester
111 Dunstable Street, Ampthill, Bedfordshire, MK45 2NG P
01525 633023
Est. 1996 *Stock size* Large
Stock General antiques, Georgian–Edwardian furniture, glass, china, jewellery
Open Tues–Sun 10am–5pm

Pilgrim Antiques Centre
Contact Gary Lester
111 Dunstable Street, Ampthill, Bedfordshire, MK45 2NE P
01525 633023
Est. 1996 *Stock size* Large
No. of dealers 6
Stock Antique furniture
Open Tues–Sat 10am–5pm Sun 11am–4.30pm

The Pine Parlour
Contact Mrs J Barker
1 Chandos Road, Ampthill, Bedfordshire, MK45 2LF P
01525 403030
Est. 1987 *Stock size* Medium
Stock Victorian–Edwardian original pine, wardrobes, dressers, chests, kitchenware, sleigh beds
Open Mon–Sun 10am–5pm

BEDFORD

The Eagle Bookshop
Contact Mr Peter Budek
103 Castle Road, Bedford, Bedfordshire, MK40 3QP P
01234 269295
customers@eaglebookshop.co.uk
www.eaglebookshop.co.uk
Est. 1991 *Stock size* Medium
Stock General second-hand and antiquarian books, special section on science and mathematics
Open Mon–Sat 10am–5.30pm closed Wed
Services Stock displayed on website

W & H Peacock
Contact Mark Baker or Simon Rowell
26 Newnham Street, Bedford, Bedfordshire, MK40 3JR P
01234 266366 F 01234 269082
info@peacockauction.co.uk
www.peacockauction.co.uk
Est. 1901
Open Mon–Thurs 9am–5.30pm Fri 9am–8.30pm Sat 8.30am–5pm
Sales General and antiques sale Sat 9.30am, viewing Fri 9am–8pm Sat 8.30am prior to sale, also Thurs 11am, viewing Wed 9am–8pm Thurs 8.30am prior to sale. Monthly antiques and collectables sale first Fri 10.45am, viewing Fri 5–8pm in week before Thurs 9am–6pm in week of sale and Fri 8.30–10.45am prior to sale
Frequency Weekly
Catalogues Yes

Victoria House
Contact Helen Felts
70a Tavistock Street, Bedford, Bedfordshire, MK40 2RP P
01234 320000
Est. 1998 *Stock size* Large
Stock Victorian–Edwardian furniture, antiques, reproduction and decorative pieces
Open Mon–Fri 11.30am–5pm Sat 11am–5pm Sun 12.30am–4.30pm closed Wed
Services Interior design

BIGGLESWADE

Shortmead Antiques
Contact Mr S E Sinfield
46 Shortmead Street, Biggleswade, Bedfordshire, SG18 0AP P
01767 601780
Est. 1989 *Stock size* Medium
Stock Victorian–Edwardian furniture, china, silver, glass, general antiques
Open Tues Wed Fri Sat 10am–4.30pm

Simply Oak
Contact Anna Kilgarriff or Dick Sturman
Oak Tree Farm, Potton Road, Biggleswade, Bedfordshire, SG18 0EP P
01767 601559 F 01767 312855
antiques@simplyoak.freeserve.co.uk
Est. 1997 *Stock size* Large
Stock Late Victorian–1930s restored oak furniture
Open Mon–Sat 10am–5pm Sun 11am–4pm
Services Restoration

BROMHAM

Paperchase
Contact Brian Moakes
77 Wingfield Road, Bromham, Bedford, Bedfordshire, MK43 8JY
01234 825942
brianmoakes@aol.com
Est. 1991
Open Mon–Fri 9am–5pm
Sales Postal auction of transport-related paper memorabilia
Frequency 6 per annum
Catalogues Yes

CHOWSTON

John Moore Antiques
Contact John Moore
College Farm Workshops, Chowston, Bedfordshire, MK44 3BH P
01480 214165
www.johnmooreantiques.co.uk
Est. 2004 *Stock size* Medium
Stock 17th–early 19thC furniture, gifts, period possessions
Open Fri Sat 9.30am–5.30pm

DUNSTABLE

Bernard Gulley Antiques (BADA, CINOA)
Contact Bernard Gulley
Lancotbury Manor, Totternhoe, Dunstable, Bedfordshire, LU6 1RG P
01582 606435
Est. 1969 *Stock size* Large
Stock Oak and country furniture, rural, naïve and decorative period accessories
Open By appointment only
Fairs Olympia

EGGINGTON

Robert Kirkman Ltd (ABA, PBFA)
Contact Robert Kirkman
Kings Cottage, Eggington, Leighton Buzzard, Bedfordshire, LU7 9PG P
01525 210647 F 01525 211184
robertkirkmanltd@btinternet.com
www.robertkirkman.co.uk
Est. 1988 *Stock size* Small
Stock Antiquarian books, specializing in English literature, Churchill, English Bibles, sets of standard authors
Open By appointment only
Fairs ABA, PBFA
Services Restoration, book binding, shipping

HENLOW

Hanworth House Antiques & Interiors
Contact Rose Jarvis

92 High Street,
Henlow, Bedfordshire,
SG16 6AB P
☎ 01462 814361 F 01462 814361
E hanworthhouse@aol.com
Est. 2000 *Stock size* Large
Stock Antique furniture and decorative smalls
Open Tues–Sat 11am–5.30pm Sun noon–5.30pm
Services Antique search, framing

LEIGHTON BUZZARD

David Ball Antiques
Contact David Ball
59 North Street,
Leighton Buzzard, Bedfordshire,
LU7 1EQ P
☎ 01525 210753
M 07831 111661
Est. 1970 *Stock size* Medium
Stock Furniture, clocks, barometers, 18th–early 20thC porcelain
Open Mon 10am–5pm or by appointment
Fairs Luton Antiques Fair, Mid Beds Antiques Fair
Services Restoration

LOWER STONDON

Memory Lane Antiques
Contact Mrs Liz Henry
14 Bedford Road,
Lower Stondon,
Henlow, Bedfordshire,
SG16 6EA P
☎ 01462 812716
M 07702 715477
Est. 1998 *Stock size* Medium
Stock Furniture, silver, porcelain, crystal, collectables
Open Mon–Sun 10.30am–5pm closed Wed Thurs
Services Appraisals

LUTON

Bargain Box
Contact Dean Dickinson
4 & 6a Adelaide Street,
Luton, Bedfordshire,
LU1 5BB P
☎ 01582 423809
Est. 1962 *Stock size* Medium
Stock Collectables
Open Mon–Sat 9.30am–5pm

Off World
Contact Mr J Woollard
141a–143a Market Hall,
The Luton Arndale Centre,
Luton, Bedfordshire,
LU1 2TP P
☎ 01582 736256
Est. 1995 *Stock size* Large
Stock Collectable toys, *Star Wars*, Transformers, comics, cards etc
Open Mon–Sat 9.30am–5.30pm Wed 9.30am–2pm

POTTON

Wesley J West & Son
Contact Mr A West
58 King Street,
Potton, Sandy,
Bedfordshire,
SG19 2QZ P
☎ 01767 260589
Est. 1931 *Stock size* Medium
Stock Georgian–Edwardian furniture
Open Mon–Fri 9am–5pm Sat 9am–noon
Services Restoration, upholstery

SHEFFORD

S and S Timms Antiques Ltd (LAPADA)
Contact Sue Timms
2–4 High Street,
Shefford, Bedfordshire,
SG17 5DG P
☎ 01462 851051 F 01462 817047
M 07885 458541
E info@timmsantiques.com
W www.timmsantiques.com
Est. 1976 *Stock size* Large
Stock 18th–19thC town and country furniture
Open Mon–Fri 9.30am–5.30pm Sat Sun 11am–5pm or by appointment
Fairs Chelsea, LAPADA

SLAPTON

Nick & Janet's Antiques
Contact Janet Griffin
Bury Farm,
Mill Road, Slapton,
Leighton Buzzard,
Bedfordshire,
LU7 9BT P
☎ 01525 220256
E nick@buffallogold.com
W www.nickandjanets.co.uk
Est. 1991 *Stock size* Large
Stock Devon, Torquay, Brannam pottery, Martin Brothers, modern Moorcroft
Open By appointment

STANFORD

Ayuka Ltd
Contact Mune Ota
Village Farm,
Stanford, Bedfordshire,
SG18 9JQ P
☎ 01438 362494 F 01438 228494
M 07796 804032
E sales@ayuka.co.uk
W www.ayuka.co.uk
Est. 1998 *Stock size* Medium
Stock Antique furniture, furnishings
Trade only Yes
Open Mon–Sun 9am–8pm
Services Accompanied antique buying service

WILSTEAD

Manor Antiques and Interiors
Contact Mrs S Bowen
The Manor House,
Cotton End Road, Wilstead,
Bedford, Bedfordshire,
MK45 3BT P
☎ 01234 740262 F 01234 740262
M 07831 419729
E brianmottram16@hotmail.com
Est. 1979 *Stock size* Large
Stock 19thC and Edwardian furniture, antique and replica mirrors, lighting
Open Mon–Sat 10am–5pm
Fairs House & Garden, Olympia

WOBURN

Geoffrey Hugall
Contact Mr G Hugall
Woburn Abbey Antique Centre, Woburn Abbey,
Bedfordshire,
MK17 9WA P
☎ 020 7838 0457 or 01525 290350
M 07973 273485
Est. 1971 *Stock size* Medium
Stock General antiques, mirrors, period furniture
Open Mon–Sun 10am–5.30pm
Services Valuations

Charles Ross Fine Art Auctioneers
Contact Charles Ross
The Old Town Hall,
Woburn, Bedfordshire,
MK17 9PZ P
☎ 01525 290502 F 01525 290864
E info@charles-ross.co.uk
W www.charles-ross.co.uk

Est. 1975
Open Mon–Fri 9am–5pm
Sales General antiques and fine art
Frequency Monthly
Catalogues Yes

Christopher Sykes
Contact Mr C Sykes or Mrs Sally Lloyd
The Old Parsonage, Bedford Street, Woburn, Bedfordshire, MK17 9QL
01525 290259 F 01525 290061
sykes.corkscrews@sykes-corkscrews.co.uk
www.sykes-corkscrews.co.uk
Est. 1960 *Stock size* Large
Stock Items associated with wine, speciality corkscrews, scientific instruments
Open Mon–Sat 9am–5pm

Town Hall Antiques
Contact Mr or Mrs Groves
Market Place, Woburn, Bedfordshire, MK17 9PZ
01525 290950 F 01525 292501
info@townhallantiques.co.uk
Est. 1993 *Stock size* Large
Stock Varied
Open Mon–Sat 10am–5.30pm Sun 11am–5.30pm
Services Valuations

Woburn Abbey Antiques Centre
Contact Ian Osborn
Woburn, Bedfordshire, MK17 9WA
01525 290350 F 01525 292102
antiques@woburnabbey.co.uk
Est. 1967 *Stock size* Large
No. of dealers 40
Stock Furniture (dateline 1910), porcelain, silver, paintings (dateline 1940)
Open 363 days a year 10am–5.30pm

Yew Tree
Contact Anna Maggs
Woburn Abbey Antiques Centre, Shop 7, Woburn, Bedfordshire, MK17 9WA
01582 872514 F 01582 873816
Est. 1983 *Stock size* Medium
Stock Farm and garden tools, related rural items, 18th–20thC decorative prints
Open 363 days a year 10am–5.30pm
Fairs NEC, Decorative Antiques & Textiles Fair, Battersea

BUCKINGHAMSHIRE

AMERSHAM

The Amersham Auction Rooms (RICS)
Contact Pippa Ellis
125 Station Road, Amersham, Buckinghamshire, HP7 0AH
01494 729292 F 01494 722337
info@amershamauctionrooms.co.uk
www.amershamauctionrooms.co.uk
Est. 1877
Open Mon–Fri 9am–5.30pm Sat 9–11.30am
Sales Antiques and collectors' first Thurs of month. Victorian and general furniture other Thurs weekly 10.30am, viewing Tues 2–5pm Wed 9.30am–8pm Thurs 9–10.15am
Catalogues Yes

Old Amersham Auctions
Contact Mr M King
2 School Lane, Amersham, Buckinghamshire, HP7 0EL
01494 722758 F 01494 722758
Est. 1979
Open Mon–Sat 9am–5pm
Sales General and antiques sale Sat noon, viewing Sat 9am prior to sale. Occasional house sales, telephone for details
Frequency Fortnightly
Catalogues Yes

Pop Antiques
12 The Broadway, Amersham, Buckinghamshire, HP7 0HP
01494 434443 F 01494 434443
M 07768 366606
www.popantiques.com
Est. 2001 *Stock size* Large
Stock Late 19thC French painted furniture, mirrors
Open Mon–Sat 10am–5pm
Services Shipping

Liz Quilter
Contact Liz or Jackie Quilter
38 High Street, Amersham, Buckinghamshire, HP7 0DJ
01494 433723 F 01494 433723
jackie@quilters-antiques.fsnet.co.uk
Est. 1969 *Stock size* Large
Stock Old pine collectables, copper, brass, rustic furniture
Open Mon–Fri 10am–5pm Sat 10am–5.30pm

Sundial Antiques
Contact Mr A Macdonald
19 Whielden Street, Amersham, Buckinghamshire, HP7 0HU
01494 727955
M 07866 819314
Est. 1970 *Stock size* Medium
Stock 19thC copper and brass, small furniture, ceramics
Open Mon–Sat 9.30am–5.30pm closed Thurs

ASTON CLINTON

Dismantle & Deal Direct
Contact Mr T Pattison
108 London Road, Aston Clinton, Buckinghamshire, HP22 5HS
01296 632300 F 01296 631346
info@ddd-uk.com
www.ddd-uk.com
Est. 1992 *Stock size* Large
Stock Doors, entrance ways, chimney pieces, lighting, stained glass, mirrors, garden statuary, other architecturally unusual items
Open Mon–Sat 10am–5pm
Services Architectural salvage brokers

AYLESBURY

Gillian Neale Antiques (BADA)
Contact Gillian Neale
PO Box 247, Aylesbury, Buckinghamshire, HP20 1JZ
01296 423754 F 01296 334601
gillianneale@aol.com
www.gilliannealeantiques.co.uk
Est. 1980 *Stock size* Large
Stock English blue printed pottery 1780–1900
Open By appointment
Fairs Olympia, BADA, NEC
Services Valuations, restoration, export, search

BEACONSFIELD

Buck House Antique Centre
Contact Mrs B Whitby

✉ **47 Wycombe End, Beaconsfield, Buckinghamshire, HP9 1LZ** P
☎ 01494 670714 Ⓕ 01494 670714
Ⓔ bachantiques@supanet.com
Est. 1982 *Stock size* Medium
Stock Clocks, furniture, metalware, ceramics, general antiques
Open Mon–Sat 10am–5pm closed Wed

Grosvenor House Interiors
Contact Mr T Marriott
✉ **51 Wycombe End, Beaconsfield, Buckinghamshire, HP9 1LX** P
☎ 01494 677498 Ⓕ 01494 677498
Ⓜ 07747 014098
Est. 1978 *Stock size* Large
Stock 18th–19thC furniture, pictures, mirrors, clocks, fireplaces
Open Mon–Sat 10am–1pm 2–5pm closed Wed

Claudia Hill (BADA)
Contact Claudia Hill
✉ **Beaconsfield, Buckinghamshire, HP9 2DJ** P
☎ 01494 678880
Ⓜ 07720 317899
Ⓔ claudia.hill@ellisonfineart.co.uk
Ⓦ www.ellisonfineart.com
Est. 2000 *Stock size* Large
Stock Portrait miniatures
Open By appointment
Fairs Olympia, Harrogate Antiques and Fine Art fairs

Period Furniture Showrooms (TVADA)
Contact Mr R E W Hearne
✉ **49 London End, Beaconsfield, Buckinghamshire, HP9 2HW** P
☎ 01494 674112 Ⓕ 01494 681046
Ⓔ sales@periodfurniture.net
Ⓦ www.periodfurniture.net
Est. 1966 *Stock size* Large
Stock Victorian–Edwardian furniture
Open Mon–Sat 9am–5.30pm
Fairs TVADA Spring
Services Restoration of furniture

BOURNE END

Bourne End Antiques Centre
Contact Mr Simon Shepheard
✉ **67 The Parade, Bourne End, Buckinghamshire, SL8 5SB** P
☎ 01628 533298
Ⓜ 07776 176876
Est. 1996 *Stock size* Large
No. of dealers 45
Stock General antiques, oak, pine, mahogany, silver, jewellery
Open Mon–Sat 10am–5.30pm Sun Bank Holidays noon–4pm

Bourne End Auction Rooms
Contact Mr S Brown
✉ **Station Approach, Bourne End, Buckinghamshire, SL8 5QH** P
☎ 01628 531500 Ⓕ 01628 522158
Ⓔ be.auctions@lineone.net
Ⓦ www.bournendauctionroom.com
Est. 1992
Open Mon–Fri 9am–5pm Sat 9am–noon
Sales Weekly general sale Wed 10.30am, antiques sale 1st Wed monthly 10.30am, viewing Tues 9.30am–7pm Wed 9–10.30am
Catalogues Yes

La Maison (TVADA)
Contact Mr J Pratt
✉ **The Crossings, Cores End Road, Bourne End, Buckinghamshire, SL8 5AL** P
☎ 01628 525858 Ⓕ 01494 670363
Ⓜ 07885 209001
Ⓔ jeremy@la-maison.co.uk
Ⓦ www.la-maison.co.uk
Est. 1994 *Stock size* Medium
Stock French mirrors, beds, tables, gifts, garden furniture and statuary, painted armoires
Open Mon 1–5.30pm Tues–Sat 10am–5.30pm Sun 11am–5pm
Fairs Ardingly
Services Upholstery, restoration

BUCKINGHAM

Buckingham Antiques Centre Ltd
Contact Mr P Walton
✉ **5 West Street, Buckingham, Buckinghamshire, MK18 1HL** P
☎ 01280 824464
Ⓜ 07904 242877
Ⓔ peterwalton@whsmithnet.co.uk
Est. 1992 *Stock size* Small
Stock General antiques, furniture, clocks, silver, china
Open Mon–Sat 9am–5pm closed Wed or by appointment
Services Valuations

Dickins Auctions
Contact Louise Gostelow
✉ **1 Claydon Sale Room, Calvert Road, Buckingham, Buckinghamshire, MK18 2EZ** P
☎ 01296 714436 Ⓕ 01296 714492
Ⓔ info@dickins-auctions.com
Ⓦ www.dickins-auctions.co.uk
Est. 1999
Open Mon–Fri 9.30am–5.30pm
Sales County, sporting, fine art and general monthly antique sales
Catalogues Yes

Flappers Antiques
Contact Mr or Mrs N Goodwin
✉ **2 High Street, Buckingham, Buckinghamshire, MK18 1NT** P
☎ 01280 813115
Est. 1980 *Stock size* Large
Stock Country pine furniture, accessories
Open Mon–Sat 9.30am–5.30pm closed Thurs

CHALFONT ST GILES

Gallery 23 Antiques
Contact Mr F Vollaro
✉ **5 High Street, Chalfont St Giles, Buckinghamshire, HP8 4QH** P
☎ 01494 871512 Ⓕ 01494 871512
Est. 1989 *Stock size* Large
Stock China, silver, furniture, glass, pictures, prints, clocks
Open Mon–Sat 10am–5pm
Services Valuations

St Giles Old Pine Company
Contact Toby Smith
✉ **The Furniture Village, London Road, Chalfont St Giles, Buckinghamshire, HP8 4RD** P
☎ 01494 873031
Ⓜ 07860 265130
Ⓔ tobysmith@stgilesfurniture.com
Est. 1968 *Stock size* Large
Stock Antique, English and Continental oak and pine furniture
Open Mon–Sat 9am–5pm Sun noon–4pm

CHESHAM

The Attic
Contact Karen Page
3 High Street, Chesham, Buckinghamshire, HP5 1BG
01494 794114
Est. 1998 *Stock size* Large
Stock Collectables, furniture, jewellery, paintings, pictures, china, pottery, clocks, brass, commemoratives
Open Mon–Sat 9.30am–5.30pm Sun 11am–5pm

Chess Antiques (LAPADA)
Contact Mr Wilder
85 Broad Street, Chesham, Buckinghamshire, HP5 3EF
01494 783043 01494 791302
07831 212454
mike_wilder44@hotmail.com
Est. 1971 *Stock size* Medium
Stock Clocks
Open Mon–Fri 9am–5pm Sat 10am–5pm
Services Valuations

A E Jackson
Contact Ann Jackson
Queen Anne House, 57 Church Street, Chesham, Buckinghamshire, HP5 1HY
01494 783811
Est. 1910 *Stock size* Medium
Stock Home antiques
Open Wed Fri Sat 10am–12.30pm 1.30–5pm

Stuff & Nonsense
Contact Helen or Elaine Robb
70 Broad Street, Chesham, Buckinghamshire, HP5 3DX
01494 775988/782877
Est. 1998 *Stock size* Large
No. of dealers 20
Stock Collectables, books, antiques, furniture
Open Mon–Sat 9.30am–5.30pm Sun 11am–5.30pm closed Wed

DENHAM

Hobday Toys (Dolls Club of Great Britain)
Contact Wendy Hobday
Denham, Buckinghamshire, UB9 5AD
01895 834348
wendyhobday@freenet.co.uk
Est. 1985 *Stock size* Large
Stock Dolls houses and furniture, tin-plate toys
Open By appointment
Fairs Sandown, Lyndhurst, Pudsey, Stafford
Services Valuations

HIGH WYCOMBE

Glade Antiques (BADA, CINOA)
Contact Sonia Vaughan
PO Box 873, High Wycombe, Buckinghamshire, HP14 3ZQ
01494 882818
07771 552328
sonia@gladeantiques.com
Stock Oriental porcelain, bronzes, jades, antiquities
Open By appointment
Fairs BADA, Olympia, LAPADA
Services Valuations

IVER

Yester-Year
Contact Mr P J Frost
12 High Street, Iver, Buckinghamshire, SL0 9NG
01753 652072
Est. 1968 *Stock size* Medium
Stock General antiques, furniture, pictures, china, glass, metalwork
Open Mon–Sat 10am–6pm
Services Valuations, restoration, picture framing, clock repairs

MARLOW

Bosley's Military Auctioneers (BACA Award Winner 2004)
Contact Mr S Bosley
The White House, Marlow, Buckinghamshire, SL7 1AH
01628 488188 01628 488111
www.bosleys.co.uk
Est. 1994
Open By appointment only
Sales Militaria sales Wed noon at Court Gardens, viewing Wed 8am–noon prior to sale
Frequency Quarterly
Catalogues Yes

Coldstream Military Antiques (LAPADA)
Contact Mr S Bosley
The White House, Marlow, Buckinghamshire, SL7 1AH
01628 488188 01628 488111
Est. 1978 *Stock size* Large
Stock Militaria including swords, medals, pictures, campaign furniture
Open By appointment only

Marlow Antiques Centre (TVADA)
Contact Marilyn Short
35 Station Road, Marlow, Buckinghamshire, SL7 1NW
01628 473223 01628 478989
07802 188345
Est. 1995 *Stock size* Large
No. of dealers 30
Stock 18th–20thC furniture, collectors' china, Staffordshire figures, chandeliers, silver, decorative glass, writing slopes, tea caddies, postcards, pens, cuff links, equestrian items
Open Mon–Sat 10.30am–5pm Sun 11am–4pm
Services Restoration, shipping

MILTON KEYNES

Grange Antiques Ltd
Contact Shuna Spencer
The Market, Bell Walk, Winslow, Milton Keynes, Buckinghamshire
01296 713011
07734 218935
shuna@postmaster.co.uk
www.grangeantiques.com
Est. 1991 *Stock size* Large
Stock Victorian and earlier furniture, smalls
Open Tues–Sun 10am–4pm
Fairs Gemsco, Bowman's
Services Upholstery

NEWPORT PAGNELL

Ken's Paper Collectables (UACC, Ephemera Society)
Contact Ken Graham
29 High Street, Newport Pagnell, Buckinghamshire, MK16 8AR
01908 210683/610003
01908 610003
ken@kens.co.uk

Ⓦ www.kens.co.uk
Est. 1983 ***Stock size*** Large
Stock Autographs, vintage magazines, posters, historic newspapers, British comics, documents, printed, written ephemera, show business memorabilia
Open Mon–Wed Fri 9.30am–5pm Sat 9.30am–4pm
Fairs Bloomsbury Postcard Fair, Ephemera fairs, Film fairs

OLNEY

The Antique Centre at Olney
Contact Robert Sklar
✉ **13 Osborns Court, Off High Street South, Olney, Buckinghamshire, MK46 4LA** Ⓟ
☎ 01234 710942 Ⓕ 01234 710947
Ⓜ 07710 057750
Ⓔ webmaster@antiques-of-britain.co.uk
Ⓦ www.antiques-of-britain.co.uk
Est. 2001 ***Stock size*** Large
No. of dealers 80
Stock Furniture, jewellery, silver china
Open Tues–Sat 10am–5pm Sun noon–5pm

Olney Antiques
Contact Andrea Wood
✉ **No 1 Market Place, Olney, Buckinghamshire, NK46 4EA** Ⓟ
☎ 01234 714141
Est. 2001 ***Stock size*** Medium
Stock Period furniture, silver, jewellery
Open Tues–Sun 9am–5pm

Pine Antiques
Contact Linda Wilkinson
✉ **10 Market Place, Olney, Buckinghamshire, MK46 4EA** Ⓟ
☎ 01234 711065 Ⓕ 01234 711065
Ⓜ 07711 917049
Est. 1990 ***Stock size*** Medium
Stock Pine furniture
Open Mon Tues Thurs Fri 10am–5pm Wed 10am–4pm Sat 9.30am–5pm

Robin Unsworth Antiques
Contact Robin Unsworth
✉ **1a Weston Road, Olney, Buckinghamshire, MK46 5BD** Ⓟ
☎ 01234 711210
Ⓜ 07860 809584
Est. 1972 ***Stock size*** Large
Stock 18th–19thC furniture, clocks
Open Mon–Sun 10am–4pm or by appointment

PENN

Penn Barn
Contact Paul Hunnings
✉ **By the Pond, Elm Road, Penn, Buckinghamshire, HP10 8LB** Ⓟ
☎ 01494 815691
Est. 1968 ***Stock size*** Medium
Stock Antiquarian books, maps, prints, watercolours, oil paintings
Open Tues–Sat 10.30am–1pm 2–4pm

Penn Village Centre for Antiques and Interiors
Contact Steve Thame
✉ **3 Hazlemere Road, Penn, High Wycombe, Buckinghamshire, HP10 8AA** Ⓟ
☎ 01494 812244 Ⓕ 01494 812244
Ⓔ info@pennvillage.co.uk
Ⓦ www.pennvillage.co.uk
Est. 2003 ***Stock size*** Large
No. of dealers 20
Stock Antiques, collectables and interior design, furniture and furnishings up to the present day
Open Mon–Sat 10am–5pm Sun 11am–4pm

STONY STRATFORD

CIRCA Antiques & Art
Contact Victoria Holton
✉ **6 Church Street, Stony Stratford, Buckinghamshire, MK11 1BD** Ⓟ
☎ 01908 567100
Ⓔ info@circa-antiques.co.uk
Ⓦ www.circa-antiques.co.uk
Est. 2000 ***Stock size*** Medium
Stock Victorian–Edwardian furniture, interesting pre-1939 pieces
Open Tues–Sat 10am–5pm
Fairs NEC
Services House clearance

Daeron's Books (FSB, SSBA)
Contact Mrs A Gardner
✉ **13 Market Square, Stony Stratford, Milton Keynes, Buckinghamshire, MK11 1BE** Ⓟ
☎ 01908 568989 Ⓕ 01908 266092
Ⓔ books@daerons.co.uk
Ⓦ www.daerons.co.uk
Est. 1993 ***Stock size*** Medium
Stock Fantasy, science fiction books, Tolkien and C S Lewis a speciality
Open Mon–Fri 9.30am–5.30pm Sat 9am–5pm Sun by appointment
Fairs Stony Stratford
Services Valuations, book search, book fair organiser, suppliers of English designed and made portable bookcases

Periplus Books
Contact Mr J Phillips
✉ **2 Timor Court, High Street, Stony Stratford, Milton Keynes, Buckinghamshire, MK11 1EJ** Ⓟ
☎ 01908 263300
Ⓔ periplus@btconnect.com
Est. 1997 ***Stock size*** Small
Stock General second-hand, antiquarian books
Open Tues–Sat 10.30am–5pm Thurs by appointment

Stony Stratford Antiques
Contact M K Millen
✉ **1 Timor Court, Stony Stratford, Milton Keynes, Buckinghamshire, MK11 1ES** Ⓟ
☎ 01908 568886
Est. 1998 ***Stock size*** Medium
Stock Furniture
Open Mon–Fri 10.30am–5pm Sat 9.30am–5pm closed Thurs

WAVENDON

Jeanne Temple Antiques
Contact Mrs Temple
✉ **Stockwell House, 1 Stockwell Lane, Wavendon, Milton Keynes, Buckinghamshire, MK17 8LS** Ⓟ
☎ 01908 583597 Ⓕ 01908 281149
Est. 1960 ***Stock size*** Medium
Stock Furniture, collectable items, lighting
Open Tues–Sat 10am–5pm Sun by appointment
Fairs Luton, Silsoe, Kempton Park, Alexander Palace

WENDOVER

Antiques at Wendover
Contact Mrs N Gregory
The Old Post Office, 25 High Street, Wendover, Buckinghamshire, HP22 6DU P
☎ 01296 625335 F 01296 620401
M 07712 032565
E antiques@antiqueswendover.co.uk
W www.antiqueswendover.co.uk
Est. 1987 *Stock size* Large
No. of dealers Over 30
Stock Town and country antiques, furniture, silver, glass, rugs, English garden tools and statuary, kitchenware, architectural antiques, barometers, antiquities, guns, pocket watches, Art Deco (dateline 1940)
Open Mon–Sat 10am–5.30pm Sun Bank Holidays 11am–5pm
Services Restoration of caning, ceramics, metals, jewellery, furniture

Sally Turner Antiques (LAPADA)
Contact Sally Turner
Hogarth House, High Street, Wendover, Buckinghamshire, HP22 6DU P
☎ 01296 624402 F 01296 624402
M 07860 201718
E majorsally@hotmail.com
Est. 1979 *Stock size* Large
Stock 18th–19thC furniture, decorative items, jewellery, works of art
Open Mon–Sat 10am–5pm closed Wed (before Christmas open every day)
Services Repairs

WHITCHURCH

Deerstalker Antiques
Contact Mrs. L. Eichler
28 High Street, Whitchurch, Buckinghamshire, HP22 4JT P
☎ 01296 641505
Est. 1978 *Stock size* Small
Stock General country antiques
Open Tues–Thurs Sat 10am–6pm or by appointment
Fairs Milton Keynes
Services Restoration of period furniture only

WINSLOW

Winslow Antique Centre
Contact Mr Taylor
15 Market Square, Winslow, Buckinghamshire, MK18 3AB P
☎ 01296 714540 F 01296 714556
Est. 1990 *Stock size* Large
No. of dealers 20
Stock Country antiques, Staffordshire, pottery
Open Mon–Sat 10am–5pm Sun 1–5pm closed Wed

GLOUCESTERSHIRE

ALMONDSBURY

Tower House Decorative Antiques (LAPADA)
Contact Graham Pendrill or Tony Yoe Smith
Tower House, Almondsbury, Gloucestershire, BS32 4HA P
☎ 01454 626233 F 01454 619203
Est. 2003 *Stock size* Large
Stock 19thC decorative antiques
Open By appointment
Services Valuations

ASTON SUBEDGE

Cottage Farm Antiques
Contact Tony or Ann Willmore
Cottage Farm, Aston Subedge, Chipping Campden, Gloucestershire, GL55 6PZ P
☎ 01386 438263 F 01386 438263
E info@cottagefarmantiques.co.uk
W www.cottagefarmantiques.co.uk
Est. 1986 *Stock size* Large
Stock Original Victorian–Edwardian furniture, mostly pine, unfitted kitchens
Open Mon–Sun 9am–5pm
Services Shipping

BERKELEY

Berkeley Market
Contact Mr Keith Gardener
11 The Market Place, Berkeley, Gloucestershire, GL13 9BD P
☎ 01453 511032
M 07802 304534
Est. 1988 *Stock size* Large
No. of dealers 5
Stock Bric-a-brac, period furniture, general antiques
Open Tues–Sat 9.30am–5pm or by appointment
Services Free tea or coffee

Proudfoot Antiques (FATG)
Contact Peter or Penny Proudfoot
16–18 High Street, Berkeley, Gloucestershire, GL13 9BJ P
☎ 01453 811513 F 01453 511616
M 07802 911894
E berkeley.framing@tesco.net
Est. 1956 *Stock size* Medium
Stock General antiques
Open Mon–Sun 9.30am–5.30pm
Services Valuations, picture framing

BIBURY

Mill Antiques Etc
Contact Mr B Goodall
Arlington Mill, Arlington, Bibury, Cirencester, Gloucestershire, GL7 5NL P
☎ 01285 740199
M 07788 681998
Est. 1999 *Stock size* Large
Stock General antiques, gifts, souvenir collectables, exclusive tea towels
Open Mon–Sun 9am–6pm

BISLEY

High Street Antiques
Contact Heather Ross
Bisley, Stroud, Gloucestershire, GL6 7BA P
☎ 01452 770153
M 07703 755841
Est. 1975 *Stock size* Small
Stock Oriental rugs, small furniture, collectables
Open Mon–Sat 2–6pm
Fairs Malvern

BOURTON-ON-THE-WATER

Humberts Incorporating Tayler & Fletcher
Contact Mr Martin Lambert
London House, High Street, Bourton-on-the-Water, Gloucestershire, GL54 2AP P
☎ 01451 821666 F 01451 820818
M 07074 821666
E bourton@humberts.co.uk

Ⓦ www.taylerfletcher.com
Est. 1790
Open Mon–Fri 9am–5.30pm
Sat 9am–12.30pm
Sales Monthly furniture sales held at The Royal British Legion Hall, Bourton-on-the-Water Sat 10am, viewing Fri 1–6pm morning of sale from 7.30am. Three fine art and antiques sales per annum held at The Frog Mill Hotel, Andoversford Tues 10.30am, viewing Mon 1–7pm morning of sale from 8am
Catalogues Yes

Hungry Ghost
Contact Mrs V Kern
2 Bourton Link, Bourton Industrial Park, Bourton-on-the-Water, Gloucestershire, GL54 2HQ P
☎ 01451 822988 Ⓕ 01451 822220
Ⓔ interiors@hungry-ghost.co.uk
Ⓦ www.hungry-ghost.co.uk
Est. 1998 *Stock size* Large
Stock Chinese furniture, Oriental china, gifts
Open Mon–Fri 9am–5pm
Sat by appointment

The Looking Glass
Contact Mrs A P Jones
Portland House, Victoria Street, Bourton-on-the-Water, Gloucestershire, GL54 2BX
☎ 01451 810818
Est. 2001 *Stock size* Small
Stock Glass, small furniture, collectables, silver, pottery, china, studio pottery
Open Mon–Sun 10am–5pm

CHALFORD

Minchinhampton Architectural Salvage Co (SALVO)
Contact Jemma Colborne
Cirencester Road, Aston Down, Chalford, Stroud, Gloucestershire, GL6 8PE P
☎ 01285 760886 Ⓕ 01285 760838
Ⓔ masco@catbrain.com
Ⓦ www.catbrain.com
Est. 1983 *Stock size* Large
Stock Architectural antiques, statuary, garden ornaments, reclaimed materials, metalwork, gates, staddle stones, window frames, chimney pieces
Open Mon–Fri 9am–5pm
Sat 9am–3pm Sun 11am–2pm
Fairs Gatcombe Horse Trials
Services Valuations, garden design

CHARLTON KINGS

Latchford Antiques
Contact Mrs R Latchford
203 London Road, Charlton Kings, Cheltenham, Gloucestershire, GL52 6HX P
☎ 01242 226263 Ⓕ 01242 226263
Est. 1985 *Stock size* Medium
Stock Victorian and pine, period furniture, jewellery, gifts
Open Mon–Sat 10am–5.30pm
Sun 11am–4pm

CHELTENHAM

Antique Fireplaces
Contact Martin Canning
41–43 Great Norwood Street, Cheltenham, Gloucestershire, GL50 2BQ P
☎ 01242 255235 Ⓕ 01242 255235
Est. 1996 *Stock size* Large
Stock Fireplaces
Open Mon–Sat 10am–5pm
Fairs Newark, Olympia

Bicks Jewellers & Antiques
Contact Mr Morris
5 Montpellier Walk, Cheltenham, Gloucestershire, GL50 1SD P
☎ 01242 524738 Ⓕ 01242 524738
Est. 1895 *Stock size* Medium
Stock Antique jewellery and silver, occasional smalls, glass and paintings
Open Tues–Sat 10am–4pm
Services Valuations, restoration

Cheltenham Antique Market
Contact Mr K Shave
54 Suffolk Road, Cheltenham, Gloucestershire, GL50 2AQ P
☎ 01242 529812
Est. 1979 *Stock size* Large
No. of dealers 9
Stock Victorian–20thC furniture, chandeliers
Open Mon–Sat 10am–5pm

The Cotswold Auction Co Ltd
Contact Mrs Elizabeth Poole
Chapel Walk Sale Room, Chapel Walk, Cheltenham, Gloucestershire, GL50 3DS
☎ 01242 256363 Ⓕ 01242 571734
Ⓔ info@cotswoldauction.co.uk
Ⓦ www.cotswoldauction.co.uk
Est. 1890
Open Mon–Fri 9am–5.30pm
Sales General and specialist sale Tues 11am, viewing day prior 10am–5pm day of sale 9–11am
Frequency Monthly
Catalogues Yes

Giltwood Gallery
Contact Mr Jeff Butt or Mrs Gill Butt
30 Suffolk Parade, Cheltenham, Gloucestershire, GL50 2AE
☎ 01242 512482 Ⓕ 01242 512482
Est. 1994 *Stock size* Medium
Stock Eclectic furniture, mirrors, chandeliers, pictures
Open Mon–Sat 9am–5.30pm
Services Restoration, upholstery

Greens of Cheltenham Ltd (GAGTL)
Contact Mr S Reynolds
15 Montpellier Walk, Cheltenham, Gloucestershire, GL50 1SD P
☎ 01242 512088 Ⓕ 01242 512088
Ⓔ steve@greensofcheltenham.co.uk
Ⓦ www.greensofcheltenham.co.uk
Est. 1947 *Stock size* Large
Stock Jewellery, Oriental works of art
Open Mon–Sat 9am–1pm 2–5pm
Fairs Olympia (June), Miami Beach (Jan)
Services Jewellery restoration, repairs

Catherine Hunt Oriental Antiques (TADA)
Contact Catherine Hunt
PO Box 743, Cheltenham, Gloucestershire, GL52 5ZB P
☎ 01242 227794 Ⓕ 01242 227794
Ⓜ 07976 319344
Ⓔ cathyhunt@btinternet.com
Est. 1986 *Stock size* Large
Stock Chinese ceramics, Ming, Qing etc, furniture, textiles from Ming onwards

Open By appointment
Fairs Wilton House, Penman Fair Petersfield

Mallams
Contact Robin Fisher
Grosvenor Galleries, 26 Grosvenor Street, Cheltenham, Gloucestershire, GL52 2SG P
☎ 01242 235712 Ⓕ 01242 241943
Ⓔ cheltenham@mallams.co.uk
Ⓦ www.mallams.co.uk/fineart
Est. 1788
Open Mon–Fri 9am–5.30pm Sat 9am–noon
Sales Antiques and general sale Thurs 11am, viewing Tues 9am–7pm Wed prior 9am–5pm. Ceramics sales, 2 per annum Thurs 11am, viewing Tues 9am–7pm Wed 9am–5pm
Frequency Monthly
Catalogues Yes

Montpellier Clocks (BADA, CINOA)
Contact Toby Birch
13 Rotunda Terrace, Cheltenham, Gloucestershire, GL50 1SW P
☎ 01242 242178 Ⓕ 01242 242178
Ⓔ montpellier.clocks@virgin.net
Ⓦ www.montpellierclocks.com
Est. 1959 ***Stock size*** Medium
Stock Longcase clocks, bracket clocks, chronometers, barometers, carriage clocks
Open Mon–Sat 9am–5pm
Services Restoration, conservation (BADA qualified)

Patrick Oliver Antiques
Contact Michael Oliver
4 Tivoli Street, Cheltenham, Gloucestershire, GL50 2UW P
☎ 01242 519538
Est. 1902 ***Stock size*** Medium
Stock General antiques
Open Mon–Fri 9am–1pm
Services Valuations

Promenade Antiques
Contact Mr B Mann
18 Promenade, Cheltenham, Gloucestershire, GL50 1LR
☎ 01242 524519
Est. 1980 ***Stock size*** Large
Stock Antique and second-hand jewellery, clocks, watches, silver, plated items
Open Mon–Sat 9am–5pm
Services Valuations, repairs

Q & C Militaria (OMRS)
Contact Mr John Wright
22 Suffolk Road, Cheltenham, Gloucestershire, GL50 2AQ P
☎ 01242 519815 Ⓕ 01242 519815
Ⓜ 07778 613977
Ⓔ john@qc-militaria.freeserve.co.uk
Est. 1994 ***Stock size*** Large
Stock Militaria
Open Tues–Sat 10am–5pm
Fairs Brittania Medal Fairs
Services Medal mounting

Michael Rayner Bookseller
Contact Michael Rayner
11 St Lukes Road, Cheltenham, Gloucestershire, GL53 7JQ P
☎ 01242 512806
Est. 1988 ***Stock size*** Medium
Stock Antiquarian and second-hand books
Open Wed–Sat 10am–6pm or by appointment
Services Valuations, restoration

Catherine Shinn Decorative Textiles
Contact Catherine Shinn
5–6 Well Walk, Cheltenham, Gloucestershire, GL50 3JX P
☎ 01242 574546 Ⓕ 01242 578495
Ⓦ www.catherineshinn.com
Est. 1988 ***Stock size*** Large
Stock Decorative textiles, antique cushions, furnishings, accessories
Open Mon–Sat 10am–5pm
Services Advice

Tapestry Antiques
Contact Mrs G Hall
33 Suffolk Parade, Cheltenham, Gloucestershire, GL50 2AE P
☎ 01242 512191
Est. 1984 ***Stock size*** Large
Stock Decorative antiques, pine, beds, garden furniture, mirrors
Open Mon–Sat 10am–5.30pm

Triton Gallery
Contact Mr L Bianco
27 Suffolk Parade, Cheltenham, Gloucestershire, GL50 2AE P
☎ 01242 510477
Est. 1984 ***Stock size*** Large
Stock Antique mirrors, chandeliers, paintings, Continental and decorative furniture
Open Mon–Sat 9am–5pm

CHIPPING CAMDEN

Draycott Books
Contact Mr R H McClement
2 Sheep Street, Chipping Campden, Gloucestershire, GL55 6DX
☎ 01386 841392
Ⓔ draycottbooks@hotmail.com
Est. 1981 ***Stock size*** Medium
Stock Second-hand and antiquarian books
Open Mon–Fri 10am–1pm 2–5pm Sat 10am–5.30pm
Services Valuations, book search

Schoolhouse Antiques
Contact Mr Hammond
The Headmaster's House, The Old School, High Street, Chipping Camden, Gloucestershire, GL55 6HB P
☎ 01386 841474
Ⓔ hamatschoolhouse@aol.com
Ⓦ www.schoolhouseantiques.co.uk
Est. 1969 ***Stock size*** Large
Stock 17th–19thC furniture, pictures, clocks, Victorian oils, musical boxes
Open Mon–Sun 10am–5pm closed Thurs Oct–Mar
Services Valuations

CIRENCESTER

Cirencester Arcade
Contact Mr P Bird
25 Market Place, Cirencester, Gloucestershire, GL7 2NX P
☎ 01285 644214
Est. 1995 ***Stock size*** Large
No. of dealers 70
Stock Furniture, china, glass, jewellery, coins, stamps, postcards
Open Mon–Sun 9.30am–5pm
Services Shipping, book search, clock repair

Corinium Auctions (PTA)
Contact Mr K Lawson
25 Gloucester Street,

Cirencester, Gloucestershire,
GL7 2DJ 🅿
☎ 01285 659057 Ⓕ 01285 652047
Est. 1990
Open Mon–Fri 10am–1pm 3–7pm
Sales 3 sales in Jan June Oct selling printed ephemera, cigarette cards, books, postcards
Catalogues Yes

Corner Cupboard Curios
Contact P. Larner
✉ **2 Church Street, Cirencester, Gloucestershire, GL7 1LE** 🅿
☎ 01285 655476
Est. 1975 *Stock size* Medium
Stock General antiques and collectables
Open By appointment

The Cotswold Auction Co Ltd (RICS)
Contact Elizabeth Poole
✉ **Swan Yard, West Market Place, Cirencester, Gloucestershire, GL7 2NH** 🅿
☎ 01285 642420 Ⓕ 01285 642400
Ⓔ info@cotswoldauction.co.uk
Ⓦ www.cotswoldauction.co.uk
Est. 1890
Open Mon–Fri 9am–5.30pm
Sales Held at The Bingham Hall, King Street, Cirencester. General antiques and specialist sales Fri 10am, viewing Thurs prior 10am–8pm day of sale 9–10am
Frequency Monthly
Catalogues Yes

Forum Antiques
Contact Mr Weston Mitchell
✉ **Springfield Farm, Perrott's Brook, Cirencester, Gloucestershire, GL7 7DT** 🅿
☎ 01285 831821
Ⓔ enquiries@westonmitchell.com
Ⓦ www.westonmitchell.com
Est. 1985 *Stock size* Small
Stock 18thC and earlier veneered walnut, early oak, Empire furniture
Open By appointment only

Hare's Antiques Ltd
Contact Allan Hare
✉ **4 Blackjack Street, Cirencester, Gloucestershire, GL7 2AA** 🅿
☎ 01285 640077 Ⓕ 01285 653513
Ⓜ 07860 350097/6
Ⓔ hares@hares-antiques.com
Ⓦ www.hares-antiques.com
Est. 1972 *Stock size* Large
Stock 18th–19thC English furniture, Howard upholstery
Open Mon–Sat 10am–5.30pm or by appointment
Fairs Olympia
Services Restoration, upholstery

Moore, Allen & Innocent (FNAVA)
Contact Mrs Marjorie Williams
✉ **Norcote, Cirencester, Gloucestershire, GL7 5RH** 🅿
☎ 01285 646050 Ⓕ 01285 652862
Ⓔ fineart@mooreallen.co.uk
Ⓦ www.mooreallen.co.uk
Est. 1852
Open Mon–Fri 9am–5.30pm Sat 9am–noon
Sales Selective antiques sale quarterly Fri 10am. Sporting 6 monthly Fri 10am. Picture sale 6 monthly Fri 10am. General sale every 2 weeks Fri 9.30am, viewing day prior 10.30am–8.00pm sale day 9am–3pm
Frequency Twice monthly
Catalogues Yes

Original Architectural Antiques Co Ltd (SALVO)
Contact John Rawlinson
✉ **Ermin Farm, Cricklade Road, Cirencester, Gloucestershire, GL7 5PN** 🅿
☎ 01285 869222 Ⓕ 01285 862221
Ⓜ 07774 979735
Ⓔ info@originaluk.com
Ⓦ www.originaluk.com
Est. 1980 *Stock size* Large
Stock Architectural antiques, fireplaces, columns, limestone troughs, oak doors
Open Mon–Sat 9am–5pm Sun 10am–4pm
Services Valuations, restoration

Parlour Farm Antiques
Contact Mr N Grunfeld
✉ **Unit 12b, Wilkinson Road, Love Lane Industrial Estate, Cirencester, Gloucestershire, GL7 1YT** 🅿
☎ 01285 885336 Ⓕ 01285 885338
Ⓔ info@parlourfarm.com
Ⓦ www.parlourfarm.com
Est. 1994 *Stock size* Large
Stock Reclaimed pine furniture, kitchens, garden furniture
Open Mon–Sun 10am–5pm
Services Furniture made to order

Silver Street Antiques
Contact Mr S Tarrant
✉ **9 Silver Street, Cirencester, Gloucestershire, GL7 2BJ**
☎ 01285 641600 Ⓕ 01285 641600
Est. 1994 *Stock size* Medium
Stock General antiques, kitchenware
Open Mon Tues Thurs–Sat 10am–5pm Wed Sun noon–5pm
Services House clearance

Specialised Postcard Auctions (PTA)
Contact Mr K Lawson
✉ **25 Gloucester Street, Cirencester, Gloucestershire, GL7 2DJ** 🅿
☎ 01285 659057 Ⓕ 01285 652047
Est. 1976
Open As per viewing
Sales Auctions in Feb, Apr, May, July, Sept, Nov Mon 2pm, viewing Mon–Fri prior 10am–1pm 3–7pm day of sale 10am–2pm
Frequency Every 5 weeks
Catalogues Yes

William H Stokes (BADA, CADA)
Contact Mr Peter Bontoft
✉ **The Cloisters, 6–8 Dollar Street, Cirencester, Gloucestershire, GL7 2AJ**
☎ 01285 653907 Ⓕ 01285 653907
Est. 1968 *Stock size* Medium
Stock Early oak furniture, associated items
Open Mon–Fri 9.30am–5.30pm Sat 9.30am–4.30pm

Patrick Waldron Antiques
Contact Patrick Waldron
✉ **18 Dollar Street, Cirencester, Gloucestershire, GL7 2AN** 🅿
☎ 01285 652880
Est. 1994 *Stock size* Medium
Stock 18th–early 19thC English furniture
Open Mon–Sat 9.30am–6pm
Services Restoration

COLEFORD

Simon Lewis Transport Books
Contact Mr S Lewis
✉ **PO Box 9, Coleford, Gloucestershire,**

GL16 8YF P
☎ 01594 839369 ⓕ 01594 839369
ⓔ simon@simonlewis.com
ⓦ www.simonlewis.com
Est. 1985 *Stock size* Medium
Stock 1910–present transport-related books
Open By appointment

CUTSDEAN

Architectural Heritage (CADA)
Contact Alex Puddy
✉ **Taddington Manor, Taddington, Cutsdean, Gloucestershire, GL54 5RY** P
☎ 01386 584414 ⓕ 01386 584236
ⓔ puddy@architectural-heritage.co.uk
ⓦ www.architectural-heritage.co.uk
Est. 1973 *Stock size* Large
Stock Garden ornaments, chimneypieces, wood wall panelling
Open Mon–Fri 9.30am–5.30pm Sat 10.30am–4.30pm
Fairs Chelsea
Services Valuations, bespoke and replica garden ornaments, chimney pieces, panelling

FAIRFORD

Blenheim Antiques (CADA)
Contact Mr Neil Hurdle
✉ **Acacia House, Market Place, Fairford, Gloucestershire, GL7 4AB** P
☎ 01285 712094
Est. 1973 *Stock size* Medium
Stock 18th–19thC town and country furniture, clocks, accessories
Open Mon–Sat 9am–6pm

Mark Carter Antiques (CADA)
Contact Mrs Chester-Master
✉ **Market Place, Fairford, Gloucestershire, GL7 4AB** P
☎ 01285 712790 ⓕ 01285 712790
ⓜ 07836 260567
ⓔ markcarterantiques@hotmail.com
Est. 1972 *Stock size* Large
Stock 18th–19thC English mahogany, fruitwood, oak, country furniture
Open Mon–Sat 10am–5.30pm or by appointment

Anthony Hazledine Oriental Carpets
Contact Anthony Hazeldine
✉ **High Street, Fairford, Gloucestershire, GL7 4AD** P
☎ 01285 713400 ⓕ 01285 713400
ⓔ tonyhazrugs@aol.com
Est. 1982 *Stock size* Medium
Stock Antique Oriental rugs and carpets
Open Mon–Sat 9.30am–5pm
Services Valuations, restoration, cleaning

FILKINS

Corner House Antiques
Contact Mr John Downes-Hall
✉ **Gardener's Cottage, Broughton Poggs, Filkins, Lechlade, Gloucestershire, GL7 3JH** P
☎ 01367 860078
ⓔ jdhis007@btopenworld.com
ⓦ www.cornerhouseantiques.co.uk
Est. 1995 *Stock size* Medium
Stock Antique silver, jewellery, country furniture, porcelain, objets d'art
Open By appointment
Services Designer and silversmith, restoration of old silver

GLOUCESTER

The Cotswold Auction Co Ltd
Contact Robert Short FRICS
✉ **4–6 Clarence Street, Gloucester, Gloucestershire, GL1 1DX**
☎ 01452 521177 ⓕ 01452 305883
ⓔ info@cotswoldauction.co.uk
ⓦ www.cotswoldauction.co.uk
Est. 1890
Open Mon–Fri 9am–5.30pm
Sales Antiques, collectables and general sale at St Barnabas Church Hall Tues 10am, viewing Mon 9am–9pm
Frequency Every 2 months
Catalogues Yes

The Cottage
Contact Mrs Helen Webb
✉ **55 Southgate Street, Gloucester, Gloucestershire, GL1 1TX**
☎ 01452 526027
Est. 1998 *Stock size* Large
Stock Antiques, collectables, gifts of distinction
Open Mon–Sat 9.30am–4.30pm Wed 12.30–4.30pm
Services Repairs

Gloucester Antique Centre
Contact Mrs Wright
✉ **The Historic Docks, 1 Severn Road, Gloucester, Gloucestershire, GL1 2LE** P
☎ 01452 529716 ⓕ 01452 307161
ⓔ mail@antiques-center.com
ⓦ www.antiques-center.com
Est. 1990 *Stock size* Large
No. of dealers 140
Stock General antiques, collectables
Open Mon–Sat 10am–5pm Sun 1–5pm
Services Valuations, shipping, book search

M & C Cards
Contact Mr M W Cant
✉ **Shop 30, The Antiques Centre, Severn Road, Gloucester, Gloucestershire, GL1 2LE** P
☎ 01452 506361 ⓕ 01452 307161
ⓔ mick@mandccards.co.uk
Est. 1991 *Stock size* Medium
Stock Postcards, cigarette cards, advertising collectables
Open Thurs–Mon 10am–5pm Sun 1–5pm
Fairs Cheltenham Race Course Card Fair

M & C Stamps
Contact Mr M W Cant
✉ **Shop 30, The Antiques Centre, Severn Road, Gloucester, Gloucestershire, GL1 2LE** P
☎ 01452 506361 ⓕ 01452 307161
ⓔ mick@mandcstamps.co.uk
Est. 1984 *Stock size* Medium
Stock Stamps, first day covers, accessories
Open Thurs–Mon 10am–5pm Sun 1–5pm
Fairs Stamp Fair Cheltenham Town Hall
Services Valuations, new issue service

Ronson's Architectural Effects
Contact Ron Jones
✉ **Sandhurst Quay, Upper Parting, Sandhurst Lane, Gloucester, Gloucestershire,**

GL2 9NQ
☎ 01452 731236 ℱ 01452 731888
Ⓜ 07714 266414
ℯ info@ronsonsreclamation.co.uk
Ⓦ www.ronsonsreclamation.com
Est. 1982 *Stock size* Large
Stock Architectural antiques
Open Mon–Sat 8am–5pm
Services Shipping

Upstairs Downstairs
Contact Vic or Shirley Foster
✉ **2 The Cottage, Severn Road, Gloucester, Gloucestershire, GL1 2LE**
☎ 01452 421170
Ⓜ 07786 316060
Est. 1990 *Stock size* Large
No. of dealers 5
Stock General antiques, clocks, 18th–19thC English and French furniture
Open Mon–Sun 10am–5pm

W H Webber Antique Clocks
Contact W H Webber
✉ **First Floor, Gloucester Antique Centre, Historic Docks, Gloucester, Gloucestershire, GL1 2LE**
☎ 029 2070 2313 ℱ 029 2071 2141
Ⓜ 07909 745155
ℯ whwebber@talk21.com
Est. 1994 *Stock size* Medium
Stock Antique clocks, especially longcase, wall clocks
Open Mon–Sat 10am–5pm
Sun 1–5pm
Services Valuations, repairs, restoration

KEMPSFORD

Ximenes Rare Books Inc (ABA, PBFA)
Contact Mr Stephen Weissman
✉ **Kempsford House, Kempsford, Fairford, Gloucestershire, GL7 4ET**
☎ 01285 810640 ℱ 01285 810650
ℯ steve@ximenes.com
Est. 1965 *Stock size* Medium
Stock Rare books
Open By appointment only
Fairs Olympia (June)
Services Catalogues

LECHLADE

Jubilee Hall Antiques Centre
Contact Mr John Calgie
✉ **Oak Street, Lechlade, Gloucestershire, GL7 3AY**
☎ 01367 253777
ℯ sales@jubileehall.co.uk
Est. 1997 *Stock size* Large
No. of dealers 25
Stock Furniture, objets d'art, metalware, pottery, porcelain
Open Mon–Sat 10am–5pm
Sun 11am–5pm
Services Shipping, delivery arranged

Lechlade Arcade
Contact Mr J Dickson
✉ **5–7 High Street, Lechlade, Gloucestershire, GL7 3AD**
☎ 01367 252832
Ⓜ 07949 130875
Est. 1990 *Stock size* Large
No. of dealers 25
Stock 40 rooms of china, smalls, small furniture, cast-iron, farm tools and implements, antique pistols, guns, medals, Roman artefacts
Open Mon–Sun 9am–5pm
Services House clearance

The Old Ironmongers Antiques Centre
Contact Mark Serle or Geoff Allen
✉ **5 Burford Street, Lechlade, Gloucestershire, GL7 3AP**
☎ 01367 252397
Est. 2000 *Stock size* Large
No. of dealers 40
Stock Tools, town and country furniture, gramophones, iron, copperware, architectural, books, gardening bygones, pot lids
Open Mon–Sun 10am–5pm
Services Restoration, shipping, book search

MINCHINHAMPTON

Mick & Fanny Wright
Contact Mr M Wright
✉ **The Trumpet, West End, Minchinhampton, Stroud, Gloucestershire, GL6 9JA**
☎ 01453 883027
Est. 1979 *Stock size* Medium
Stock General antiques, more smalls than furniture, second-hand books, watches, clocks
Open Wed–Sat 10.30am–5.30pm
Fairs Kempton

MORETON-IN-MARSH

Benton Fine Art and Antiques (LAPADA)
Contact Melanie Benton
✉ **Regent House, High Street, Moreton-in-Marsh, Gloucestershire, GL56 0AX**
☎ 01608 652153 ℱ 01608 652153
ℯ bentonfineart@excite.com
Est. 1972 *Stock size* Medium
Stock 19th–20thC oils and watercolours, 19th–20thC fine furniture
Open Mon–Sat 10am–5.30pm
Sun 11am–5.30pm closed Tues
Fairs LAPADA Birmingham, NEC

Berry Antiques (LAPADA)
Contact Mr C Berry
✉ **3 High Street, Moreton-in-Marsh, Gloucestershire, GL56 0AH**
☎ 01608 652929 ℱ 01608 652929
ℯ chris@berryantiques.co.uk
Ⓦ www.berryantiques.co.uk
Est. 1984 *Stock size* Medium
Stock 18th–19thC furniture, 19thC oil paintings
Open Mon–Sat 10am–5.30pm
Sun 11am–5pm closed Tues

Paula Biggs (Silver Society)
Contact Paula Biggs
✉ **Windsor House Antiques Centre, High Street, Moreton-in-Marsh, Gloucestershire, GL56 0AD**
☎ 01993 869245 ℱ 01993 869247
ℯ john@thebiggs.co.uk
Est. 1978 *Stock size* Large
Stock Antiques, collectable silver items, objects of virtue
Open Mon–Sat 10am–5pm
Tues Sun noon–5pm

Chandlers Antiques
Contact Ian Kellam
✉ **Chandlers Cottage, High Street, Moreton-in-Marsh, Gloucestershire, GL56 OAD**
☎ 01608 651347 ℱ 01608 651347
Est. 1984 *Stock size* Large
Stock All small porcelain, glass, jewellery, silver
Open By appointment
Services Valuations

Cox's Architectural Salvage Yard Ltd (SALVO)
Contact Mr P Watson
10 Fosse Way Industrial Estate, Stratford Road, Moreton-in-Marsh, Gloucestershire, GL56 9NQ P
☎ 01608 652505 F 01608 652881
E info@coxsarchitectural.co.uk
W www.coxsarchitectural.co.uk
Est. 1991 *Stock size* Large
Stock Architectural antiques, doors, fireplaces, Gothic-style windows, floorboards, flagstones, radiators
Open Mon–Fri 9am–5pm Sat 9am–4pm
Services Valuations, shipping

Dale House
Contact Nicholas Allen
High Street, Moreton-in-Marsh, Gloucestershire, GL56 0AD P
☎ 01608 652950 F 01608 652424
Est. 1973 *Stock size* Large
Stock 18th–early 20thC furniture, works of art
Open Mon–Sat 10am–5.30pm Sun 11am–5pm

Jeffrey Formby Antiques (BADA)
Contact Mr J Formby
Orchard Cottage, East Street, Moreton-in-Marsh, Gloucestershire, GL56 0LQ P
☎ 01608 650558
M 07770 755546
E jeff@formby-clocks.co.uk
W www.formby-clocks.co.uk
Est. 1994 *Stock size* Small
Stock English clocks, horological books, longcase, bracket, skeleton, lantern clocks
Open By appointment
Fairs Olympia, BADA

Jon Fox Antiques (CADA)
Contact Mr Jon Fox
High Street, Moreton-in-Marsh, Gloucestershire, GL56 0AD P
☎ 01608 650325
Est. 1983 *Stock size* Large
Stock Garden antiques, furniture, country bygones
Open Mon–Sat 9.30am–5.30pm closed Tues

Grimes House Antiques & Fine Art
Contact Stephen or Val Farnsworth
High Street, Moreton-in-Marsh, Gloucestershire, GL56 0AT P
☎ 01608 651029
E grimes_house@cix.co.uk
W www.cranberryglass.co.uk or www.grimeshome.co.uk
Est. 1977 *Stock size* Large
Stock Victorian and later coloured glass, Royal Worcester
Open Mon–Sat 9.30am–5.30pm closed 1–2pm
Services Valuations

London House Antique Centre
Contact Mr Dudley Thompson
London House, High Street, Moreton-in-Marsh, Gloucestershire, GL56 0AH P
☎ 01608 651084
Est. 1979 *Stock size* Large
No. of dealers 11
Stock General antiques, Chinese porcelain, furniture, silver, porcelain, pictures
Open Mon–Sun 10am–5pm

Seaford House Antiques (LAPADA)
Contact Mr or Mrs D Young
Seaford House, High Street, Moreton-in-Marsh, Gloucestershire, GL56 0AD P
☎ 01608 652423 F 01608 652423
M 07714 485632
Est. 1988 *Stock size* Medium
Stock 18th–early 20thC small furniture, porcelain, pictures, objets d'art
Open Wed–Sat 10am–5pm Sun 1am–4pm

Geoffrey Stead (BADA)
Contact Geoffrey Roberts
Wyatts Farm, Todenham, Moreton-in-Marsh, Gloucestershire, GL56 9NY P
☎ 01608 650997 F 01608 650597
M 07768 460450
E geoffrey@geoffreystead.com
Est. 1963 *Stock size* Medium
Stock 19th–early 19thC European furniture, decorative objects
Trade only Yes
Open By appointment only
Fairs Olympia, BADA
Services Valuations

Windsor House Antiques Centre
Contact Mr T Sutton
High Street, Moreton-in-Marsh, Gloucestershire, GL56 0AD P
☎ 01608 650993 F 01858 565438
E windsorhouse@btinternet.com
W www.windsorhouse.co.uk
Est. 1992 *Stock size* Large
No. of dealers 48
Stock High-quality general antiques, porcelain, glass, silver, clocks, paintings, furniture
Open Mon–Sat 10am–5pm Tues Sun noon–5pm
Services Shipping, delivery

Gary Wright Antiques Ltd
Contact Gary or Gill Wright
5 Fosseway Business Park, Stratford Road, Moreton-in-Marsh, Gloucestershire, GL56 9NQ P
☎ 01608 652007 F 01608 652007
M 07831 653843
E garywrightantiques@fsbdial.co.uk
W www.garywrightantiques.co.uk
Est. 1972 *Stock size* Large
Stock Georgian mahogany, walnut, marquetry, unusual, decorative objects, 17th–19thC good-quality furniture from £500 to £20,000
Open Mon–Sat 9.30am–5.30pm
Services Valuations, buys at auction

NAILSWORTH

Copper Kettle Antiques Centre
Contact Susan Blackwell
51 George Street, Nailsworth, Gloucestershire, GL6 0AG P
☎ 01453 832233
Est. 2000 *Stock size* Large
No. of dealers 15
Stock General antiques, collectables
Open Mon–Sat 10am–5pm

Old Mother Hubbard
Contact Anne Russell
Doys Mill, Old Market, Nailsworth, Gloucestershire,

GL6 0BL Ⓟ
☎ 01453 835679 Ⓕ 01453 833590
Est. 1998 *Stock size* Large
Stock General antiques, furniture, pine, mirrors, lighting
Open Mon–Sat 9.30am–5.30pm Sun 11am–5pm
Fairs Swinderby, Ardingly
Services Restoration, shipping

NEWENT

⊞ Jillings (LAPADA, CINOA, BADA)
Contact John or Doro Jillings
✉ **Croft House, 17 Church Street, Newent, Gloucestershire, GL18 1PU** Ⓟ
☎ 01531 822100 Ⓕ 01531 822666
Ⓜ 07973 830110
Ⓔ clocks@jillings.com
Ⓦ www.jillings.com
Est. 1987 *Stock size* Medium
Stock 18th–early 19thC English and Continental clocks
Open Fri Sat 9.30am–5.30pm or by appointment
Fairs BADA, LAPADA, Olympia, Harrogate
Services Valuations, repair and restoration to all fine antique clocks

NEWNHAM

⊞ The Antique Shop
Contact Mrs Berry
✉ **11 High Street, Newnham, Gloucestershire, GL14 1AD** Ⓟ
☎ 01594 516460
Est. 2000 *Stock size* Large
Stock China, silver, brass, copper, furniture
Open Mon–Sat 10am–1pm 2–5pm closed Wed

⊞ Christopher Saunders (PBFA, ABA)
Contact Mr C Saunders
✉ **Kingston House, High Street, Newnham, Gloucestershire, GL14 1BB** Ⓟ
☎ 01594 516030 Ⓕ 01594 517273
Ⓔ chrisbooks@aol.com
Est. 1980 *Stock size* Large
Stock Antiquarian cricket books, memorabilia
Open By appointment only
Fairs PBFA

NORTHLEACH

⊞ Keith Harding's World of Mechanical Music
Contact Keith Harding
✉ **The Oak House, High Street, Northleach, Gloucestershire, GL54 3ET** Ⓟ
☎ 01451 860181 Ⓕ 10451 861133
Ⓔ keith@mechanicalmusic.co.uk
Ⓦ www.mechanicalmusic.co.uk
Est. 1961 *Stock size* Medium
Stock Mechanical musical antiques, clocks
Open Mon–Sun 10am–6pm closed Christmas Day Boxing Day
Services Restoration, museum

SOUTHAM

BK Art & Antiques (SOFAA)
Contact Mr Simon Chorley
✉ **The Tithe Barn Sale Room, Southam Lane, Southam, Cheltenham, Gloucestershire, GL52 3NY** Ⓟ
☎ 01452 880030 Ⓕ 01452 880088
Ⓔ artantiques@bkonline.co.uk
Ⓦ www.bkonline.co.uk
Est. 1862
Open Mon–Fri 8.30am–5.30pm
Sales Art and antiques sales, telephone for details
Frequency Every 6 weeks
Catalogues Yes

STOW-ON-THE-WOLD

⊞ Yvonne Adams Antiques (BADA)
Contact Yvonne Adams
✉ **The Coffee House, 3–4 Church Street, Stow-on-the-Wold, Gloucestershire, GL54 1BB** Ⓟ
☎ 01451 832015 Ⓕ 01451 833826
Ⓜ 07973 961101
Ⓔ antiques@adames.demon.co.uk
Ⓦ www.antiquemeissen.com
Est. 1955 *Stock size* Large
Stock 18thC Meissen porcelain
Open By appointment
Fairs Olympia June
Services Valuations

⊞ Ashton Gower Antiques (LAPADA)
Contact Chris Gower or Barry Ashton
✉ **9 Talbot Court, Market Square, Stow-on-the-Wold, Gloucestershire, GL54 1BQ** Ⓟ
☎ 01451 870699 Ⓕ 01451 870699
Ⓔ ashtongower@aol.com
Est. 1987 *Stock size* Large
Stock Gilded mirrors, French decorative furniture, 20thC Lucite
Open Mon–Sat 10am–5pm
Services Valuations

⊞ Baggott Church Street Ltd (BADA, CADA)
Contact Mrs C Baggott
✉ **Church Street, Stow-on-the-Wold, Gloucestershire, GL54 1BB**
☎ 01451 830370 Ⓕ 01451 832174
Est. 1976 *Stock size* Large
Stock English 17th–19thC furniture, paintings, objects
Open Mon–Sat 9.30am–5.30pm
Services Annual exhibition in October

⊞ Duncan J Baggott (LAPADA, CADA)
Contact Mrs C Baggott
✉ **Woolcomber House, Sheep Street, Stow-on-the-Wold, Gloucestershire, GL54 1AA**
☎ 01451 830662 Ⓕ 01451 832174
Est. 1967 *Stock size* Large
Stock English furniture, portraits, landscape paintings, domestic metalware, fireplace accoutrements, pottery, glass, garden statuary, ornaments
Open Mon–Sat 9.30am–5.30pm
Services Annual exhibition in October

⊞ Paula Biggs (Silver Society)
Contact Paula Biggs
✉ **Durham House, Sheep Street, Stow-on-the Wold, Gloucestershire, GL54 1AA** Ⓟ
☎ 01993 869245 Ⓕ 01993 869247
Ⓔ john@thebiggs.co.uk
Est. 1978 *Stock size* Large
Stock Antiques, collectable silver items, objects of virtue
Open Mon–Sat 10am–5pm Sun 11am–5pm

⊞ Bookbox (PBFA)
Contact Mrs C Fisher
✉ **Chantry House, Sheep Street, Stow-on-the-Wold, Gloucestershire,**

GL54 1AA 🅿
☎ 01451 831214
Est. 1977 *Stock size* Medium
Stock Antiquarian, second-hand books, 19th–20thC good literature, art, topography
Open Mon–Sat 11am–1pm 2.30–5pm closed Wed winter only Thurs–Sat

La Chaise Antiques
Contact Roger Clark
✉ **Beauport Sheep Street, Stow-on-the-Wold, Gloucestershire, GL54 1AA** 🅿
☎ 01451 830582
ⓔ lachaise@tiscali.co.uk
Est. 1963 *Stock size* Medium
Stock Furniture
Open Mon–Sat 9am–6pm Sun 10am–4pm

Christopher Clarke Antiques (LAPADA, CADA, BACA Award Winner 2004)
Contact Mr Simon Clarke
✉ **The Fosseway, Stow-on-the-Wold, Gloucestershire, GL54 1JS** 🅿
☎ 01451 830476 ⓕ 01451 830300
ⓜ 07971 287733
ⓔ cclarkeantiques@aol.com
ⓦ www.campaignfurniture.com
Est. 1961 *Stock size* Large
Stock Campaign, military and English furniture, travel items
Open Mon–Sat 9.30am–5.30pm or by appointment
Fairs Olympia (June November), CADA (October)

Country Life Antiques
Contact Ann or David Rosa
✉ **Grey House, The Square, Stow-on-the-Wold, Gloucestershire, GL54 1AF** 🅿
☎ 01451 831564 ⓕ 01451 831564
ⓔ grey.house@ukonline.co.uk
Est. 1974 *Stock size* Large
Stock Scientific instruments, decorative accessories, metalware, furniture, paintings
Open Mon–Sat 10am–5pm

Durham House
Contact Mr Alan Smith
✉ **Sheep Street, Stow-on-the-Wold, Gloucestershire, GL54 1AA** 🅿
☎ 01451 870404
ⓔ durhamhousegb@aol.com
Est. 1994 *Stock size* Large
No. of dealers 36
Stock General antiques, silver, clocks, oak, mahogany, porcelain, Derby, Worcester, Staffordshire, Mason's, linens, prints, paintings, samplers, sewing accessories
Open Mon–Sat 10am–5pm Sun 11am–5pm

Fox Cottage Antiques
Contact Miss Sue London
✉ **Digbeth Street, Stow-on-the-Wold, Gloucestershire, GL54 1BN** 🅿
☎ 01451 870307
Est. 1995 *Stock size* Medium
No. of dealers 10
Stock Pottery, porcelain, glassware, silver, plated ware, small furniture, decorative items, country goods, mainly pre-1910
Open Mon–Sat 10am–5pm

Grandfather Clock Shop
Contact Mr W J Styles
✉ **The Little House, Sheep Street, Stow-on-the-Wold, Gloucestershire, GL54 1JS** 🅿
☎ 01451 830455 ⓕ 01451 830455
ⓔ info@stylesofstow.co.uk
ⓦ www.stylesofstow.co.uk
Est. 1996 *Stock size* Large
Stock Clocks including longcase clocks, 18th–19thC furniture, 19th–20thC oil paintings and watercolours
Open Mon–Sat 10am–5pm or by appointment
Services Valuations, restoration

Keith Hockin Antiques (BADA, CADA)
Contact Mr K Hockin
✉ **The Elms, The Square, Stow-on-the-Wold, Gloucestershire, GL54 1AF** 🅿
☎ 01451 831058 ⓕ 01451 831058
ⓔ keith.hockin@talk21.com
Est. 1973 *Stock size* Medium
Stock 17th–early 18thC English oak furniture, pewter, early brass, 16th–17thC wood carvings
Open Thurs–Sat 10am–5pm closed 1–2pm or by appointment

Huntington Antiques Ltd (LAPADA, CADA, BACA Award Winner 2002)
✉ **Church Street, Stow-on-the-Wold, Gloucestershire, GL54 1BE** 🅿
☎ 01451 830842 ⓕ 01451 832211
ⓔ info@huntington-antiques.com
ⓦ www.huntington-antiques.com
Est. 1975 *Stock size* Large
Stock Early furniture and works of art, tapestries, English and Continental metalwork
Open Mon–Sat 9.30am–5.30pm
Fairs LAPADA London and Birmingham
Services Valuations, restoration, interior decoration

Roger Lamb Antiques and Works of Art (LAPADA, CADA)
Contact Roger Lamb
✉ **The Square, Stow-on-the-Wold, Gloucestershire, GL54 1AB** 🅿
☎ 01451 831371 ⓕ 01451 832485
ⓜ 07860 391959
Est. 1993 *Stock size* Medium
Stock 18th–early 19thC period furniture, decorative oils, watercolours, antique lighting, accessories
Open Mon–Sat 10am–5pm
Fairs LAPADA

Malthouse Antiques
Contact Chris Mortimer
✉ **The Malthouse, Digbeth Street, Stow-on-the-Wold, Gloucestershire, GL54 1BN** 🅿
☎ 01451 830592
ⓔ malthousestow@aol.com
ⓦ www.malthouseantiques.co.uk
Est. 2003 *Stock size* Large
Stock Furniture, paintings, specialist books, dental, medical items, wine-related material, ceramics, boxes and other interesting collectables
Open Mon–Sat 10am–5.30pm Sun in summer 11am–5pm closed Tues
Fairs NEC
Services Valuations, restoration, shipping, book search, coffee lounge

Simon Nutter and Thomas King-Smith
Contact Mr T M King-Smith or Mr S W Nutter
✉ **Wraggs Row, Fosseway,**

Stow-on-the-Wold, Gloucestershire, GL54 1JT
☎ 01451 830658
Ⓜ 07775 864394
Est. 1975 ***Stock size*** Medium
Stock 18th–19thC furniture, silver, porcelain
Open Mon–Sat 9.30am–5.30pm
Fairs Westonbirt
Services Valuations

Park House Antiques
Contact Mr George Sutton
✉ **8 Park Street, Stow-on-the-Wold, Gloucestershire, GL54 1AQ** P
☎ 01451 830159
Ⓔ teamsutton@btinternet.com
Ⓦ www.thetoymuseum.co.uk
Est. 1987 ***Stock size*** Large
Stock Old toys, textiles, small furniture, porcelain, pottery
Open Wed–Sat 10am–1pm 2–4.30pm Feb–Apr June–Oct other times by appointment
Services Repairs, toy museum, teddy bear repair

John Pearman
Contact John Pearman
✉ **Tudor House Antiques, Sheep Street, Stow-on-the-Wold, Gloucestershire, GL54 1AA** P
☎ 01451 830021 Ⓕ 01451 830021
Ⓔ john.pearman@talk21.com
Est. 1983 ***Stock size*** Medium
Stock 19thC glass, ceramics
Open Mon–Sat 10am–5pm Sun 11am–4pm

Antony Preston Antiques (BADA)
Contact Antony Preston
✉ **The Square, Stow-on-the-Wold, Gloucestershire, GL54 1AB** P
☎ 01451 831586
Est. 1977 ***Stock size*** Large
Stock Early 18th–19thC English furniture and objets d'art
Open Mon–Sat 9.30am–5.30pm
Fairs Grosvenor House, BADA

Michael Rowland Antiques
Contact Michael Rowland
✉ **Little Elms, The Square, Stow-on-the-Wold, Gloucestershire, GL54 1AF** P
☎ 01451 870089
Ⓜ 07779 509753
Est. 1991 ***Stock size*** Medium
Stock 17th–18thC oak and fruitwood country furniture
Open Mon–Sat 10am–5pm

Ruskin Decorative Arts (CADA)
Contact Mr or Mrs T W Morris
✉ **5 Talbot Court, Stow-on-the-Wold, Gloucestershire, GL54 1DP** P
☎ 01451 832254 Ⓕ 01451 832167
Ⓔ william.anne@ruskindecarts.co.uk
Est. 1989 ***Stock size*** Small
Stock Decorative Arts 1880–1960, Arts and Crafts, Art Nouveau, Art Deco, the Cotswold Movement including the Guild of Handicraft, Gordon Russell, Gimson and the Barnsleys, Heals furniture, Scandinavian glass
Open Mon–Sat 10am–5.30pm
Fairs NEC, Antiques for Everyone
Services Valuations for insurance and probate

Samarkand Galleries (LAPADA, CADA, CINOA)
Contact Brian MacDonald
✉ **7–8 Brewery Yard, Sheep Street, Stow-on-the-Wold, Gloucestershire, GL54 1AA** P
☎ 01451 832322 Ⓕ 01451 832322
Ⓔ mac@samarkand.co.uk
Ⓦ www.samarkand.co.uk
Est. 1979 ***Stock size*** Large
Stock Antique and contemporary rugs from Near East and central Asia, decorative carpets, nomadic weavings
Open Mon–Sat 10am–5.30pm
Fairs HALI Antique Textile Art Fair
Services Valuations, restoration, search

Arthur Seager Antiques
Contact Mr A Seager
✉ **50 Sheep Street, Stow-on-the-Wold, Gloucestershire, GL54 1AA** P
☎ 01451 831605
Ⓔ arthur.seager@btconnect.com
Ⓦ www.arthurseager.co.uk or www.arthurseager.moonfruit.com
Est. 1979 ***Stock size*** Medium
Stock 16th–17thC objects, oak furniture, carvings
Open Thurs–Sat 10am–4pm

Stow Antiques (CADA, LAPADA, CINOA)
Contact Mrs H Hutton-Clarke
✉ **The Square, Stow-on-the-Wold, Gloucestershire, GL54 1AF** P
☎ 01451 830377 Ⓕ 01451 870018
Ⓔ hazel@stowantiques.demon.co.uk
Est. 1969 ***Stock size*** Large
Stock 18th–19thC mahogany furniture, large tables, sets of chairs, sideboards, bookcases
Open Mon–Sat 10am–5.30pm or by appointment
Services Shipping

Tudor House
Contact Mr Peter Collingridge
✉ **Sheep Street, Stow-on-the-Wold, Gloucestershire, GL54 1AA** P
☎ 01451 830021 Ⓕ 01451 830021
Est. 2001 ***Stock size*** Large
No. of dealers 18
Stock 18th–early 20thC furniture, clocks, watercolours, porcelain, metalware, fountain pens, garden furniture, lighting, Arts and Crafts
Open Mon–Sat 10am–5pm Sun 11am–4pm
Services Valuations

Twyford Antiques Centre
Contact Rob Pierce
✉ **Wick Hill, Stow-on-the-Wold, Gloucestershire, GL54 1HY** P
☎ 01451 870003
Est. 1986 ***Stock size*** Large
No. of dealers 15
Stock General antiques, collectables
Open Mon–Sat 9am–5pm Sun 10am–4pm
Services Coffee shop

Vanbrugh House Antiques
Contact John or Monica Sands
✉ **Vanbrugh House, Park Street, Stow-on-the-Wold, Gloucestershire, GL54 1AQ** P
☎ 01451 830797
Est. 1978 ***Stock size*** Medium
Stock Early fine furniture, musical boxes, early maps
Open Mon–Sat 10am–5.30pm
Services Valuations

STROUD

Ian Hodgkins & Co Ltd (ABA)
Contact Mr Simon Weager
Upper Vatch Mill, The Vatch, Stroud, Gloucestershire, GL6 7JY P
☎ 01453 764270 F 01453 755233
E i.hodgkins@dial.pipex.com
W www.ianhodgkins.com
Est. 1974 *Stock size* Medium
Stock Antiquarian, 19thC art, literature, children's books
Open By appointment
Fairs Chelsea (November)

Inprint
Contact Mr Mike Goodenough
31 High Street, Stroud, Gloucestershire, GL5 1AJ P
☎ 01453 759731 F 01453 759731
E enquiries@inprint.co.uk
W www.inprint.co.uk
Est. 1979 *Stock size* Medium
Stock Antiquarian, second-hand, out-of-print books on fine, applied and performing arts
Open Mon–Sat 10am–5pm
Services Book search

TETBURY

Philip Adler Antiques (CADA)
Contact Mr P Adler
35 Long Street, Tetbury, Gloucestershire, GL8 8AA P
☎ 01666 505759 F 01452 770525
M 07710 477891
E philipadlerantiques@hotmail.com
Est. 1979 *Stock size* Large
Stock Eclectic, general stock of decorative and period antiques
Open Mon–Sat 10am–6pm or by appointment
Fairs Bath Fair
Services Valuations, restoration

Alchemy Antiques
Contact Debbie Sayers
The Old Chapel, Long Street, Tetbury, Gloucestershire, GL8 8AA
☎ 01666 505281
Est. 2004 *Stock size* Large
Stock Treen, metalware, English, French furniture, oak, fruitwoods, mahogany furniture, antiquities, silver, porcelain, glass, lighting, garden antiques
Open Mon–Sat 10am–5pm
Services Shipping

Alderson (BADA, CINOA)
Contact Mr C J Alderson
58 Long Street, Tetbury, Gloucestershire, GL8 8AQ P
☎ 01666 500888
Est. 1976 *Stock size* Medium
Stock 18th–19thC furniture and works of art
Open Mon–Sat 10am–5pm or by appointment
Fairs Olympia

The Ark Angel
Contact Arthur Smith
33 Long Street, Tetbury, Gloucestershire, GL8 8AA P
☎ 01666 505820
Est. 2001 *Stock size* Large
Stock Decorative antiques, garden furniture
Open Mon–Sat 10am–5pm

Art Nouveau Lighting
Contact Jennie Horrocks
Top Banana Antique Mall, 1 New Church Street, Tetbury, Gloucestershire, GL8 8DS P
M 07836 264896
E info@jenniehorrocks.plus.com
W www.artnouveaulighting.co.uk
Est. 1978 *Stock size* Medium
Stock Art Nouveau and Edwardian lighting
Open Mon–Sat 10am–5.30pm Sun 1–5pm
Fairs NEC, Newark

Artique (TADA)
Contact George Bristow
Talboys House, 17 Church Street, Tetbury, Gloucestershire, GL8 8JG
☎ 01666 503597 F 01666 503597
M 07836 337038
E george@artique.demon.co.uk
W www.artique.uk.com
Est. 1990 *Stock size* Large
Stock Central Asian artefacts, rugs, jewellery, furniture, textiles, architectural items
Open Mon–Wed 10am–6pm Thurs Fri 10am–8pm Sun noon–4pm

Ball & Claw Antiques (TADA)
Contact Mr Chris Kirkland
45 Long Street, Tetbury, Gloucestershire, GL8 8AA P
☎ 01666 502440
M 07957 870423
W www.ballandclaw.co.uk
Est. 1994 *Stock size* Medium
Stock 17th–19thC furniture, Arts and Crafts, engravings, pictures, prints, ceramics, smalls
Open Mon–Sat 10am–5pm
Services Valuations

Biggs, Paula (Silver Society)
Contact Paula Biggs
Long Street Antiques, Stamford House, 14 Long Street, Tetbury, Gloucestershire, GL8 8AQ P
☎ 01993 869245 F 01993 869247
E john@thebiggs.co.uk
Est. 1978 *Stock size* Large
Stock Antiques, collectable silver items, objects of virtue
Open Mon–Sat 10am–5pm Sun noon–5pm

The Black Sheep
Contact Mr Oliver Mcerlain
51 Long Street, Tetbury, Gloucestershire, GL8 8AA P
☎ 01666 505026
Est. 2000 *Stock size* Medium
Stock 18th–19thC decorative country furniture, 19thC pictures
Open Mon–Sat 10am–5pm or Sun noon–4pm

Bonhams
22a Long Street, Tetbury, Gloucestershire, GL8 8AQ
☎ 01666 502200 F 01666 505107
E tetbury@bonhams.com
W www.bonhams.com
Open Mon–Fri 9am–5.30pm
Sales Regional office. Regular house and attic sales across the country; contact London offices for further details. Free auction valuations; insurance and probate valuations

Bread & Roses
Contact Rose Smith
The Ark Angel, Long Street, Tetbury, Gloucestershire, GL8 8AA P

☎ 01666 505820
Ⓜ 07810 508804
Est. 1995 *Stock size* Large
Stock Kitchenware
Open Mon–Sat 10am–5pm
Fairs NEC, Newark

Breakspeare Antiques (LAPADA, CADA)
Contact Michael or Sylvia Breakspeare
✉ **36 Long Street, Tetbury, Gloucestershire, GL8 8AQ** Ⓟ
☎ 01666 503122
Ⓔ mark.breakspeare@hemscott.net
Ⓦ www.breakspeare-antiques.com
Est. 1962 *Stock size* Medium
Stock English period furniture, mahogany, 1750–1835, early veneered walnut, 1690–1740
Open Mon–Sat 10am–5pm

Geoffrey Breeze (BABAADA)
Contact Mr Breeze
✉ **Top Banana Antiques Mall, 1 New Church Street, Tetbury, Gloucestershire, GL8 8DS** Ⓟ
Ⓔ geoffrey@geoffreybreeze.co.uk
Ⓦ www.antiquecanes.co.uk
Est. 1972 *Stock size* Medium
Stock Canes, walking sticks
Open Mon–Sat 10am–5.30pm Sun (summer only) 11am–5pm
Fairs Bath Decorative and Antiques Fair, Antiques for Everyone, South Cotswolds Antiques Fair, Westonbirt School

The Chest of Drawers (TADA)
Contact Mrs P Bristow
✉ **24 Long Street, Tetbury, Gloucestershire, GL8 8AQ** Ⓟ
☎ 01666 502105
Ⓜ 07710 292064
Est. 1969 *Stock size* Medium
Stock English furniture, 17thC onwards
Open Mon–Fri 9.30am–5.30pm

Cottage Collectibles
Contact Mrs S Kettle
✉ **Long Street Antiques, 14 Long Street, Tetbury, Gloucestershire, G18 8AQ** Ⓟ
☎ 01666 500850
Ⓜ 07967 713512
Ⓔ sheila@cottagecollectibles.co.uk
Ⓦ www.cottagecollectibles.co.uk
Est. 1995 *Stock size* Medium
Stock English and Continental country antiques, kitchenware, pine furniture, garden and dairy tools
Open Mon–Sat 10am–5pm Sun noon–4pm
Fairs NEC, SECC
Services Restoration

Day Antiques (BADA, CADA)
Contact Mrs A or Roger Day
✉ **5 New Church Street, Tetbury, Gloucestershire, GL8 8DS** Ⓟ
☎ 01666 502413 Ⓕ 01666 505894
Ⓜ 07836 565763
Ⓔ dayantiques@lineone.net
Ⓦ www.dayantiques.com
Est. 1975 *Stock size* Medium
Stock Early oak, country furniture, related items
Open Mon–Sat 10am–5pm

The Decorator Source (TADA)
Contact Mr Colin Gee
✉ **39a Long Street, Tetbury, Gloucestershire, GL8 8AA** Ⓟ
☎ 01666 505358 Ⓕ 01666 505358
Est. 1979 *Stock size* Large
Stock French and Italian provincial furniture, accessories, English country house furniture and objects
Open Mon–Sat 10am–5.30pm or by appointment
Services Shipping

Anne Fowler (TADA)
Contact Anne Fowler
✉ **59 Long Street, Tetbury, Gloucestershire, GL8 8AA** Ⓟ
☎ 01666 505044/504043
Ⓜ 07968 945715
Est. 1995 *Stock size* Medium
Stock Mirrors, lustres, oil paintings, prints, linen, early garden and painted furniture, faïence, pottery, French items a speciality
Open Mon–Sat 10am–5.30pm
Fairs Bath (Mar)
Services Interior design

Jan Hicks Antiques (TVADA, LAPADA)
Contact Jan Hicks
✉ **Top Banana, 32 Long Street, Tetbury, Gloucestershire, GL8 8AQ** Ⓟ
☎ 01488 683986 Ⓕ 01488 681222
Ⓜ 07770 230686
Ⓔ antiques@janhicks.com
Est. 1987 *Stock size* Large
Stock French and English country furniture, 18thC and earlier, oil paintings
Open Mon–Sat 10am–5.30pm Sun (summer only) 11am–5pm
Fairs TVADA, Antiques & Audacity (Arundel Castle)

Jester Antiques (TADA)
Contact Mr Peter Bairsto
✉ **10 Church Street, Tetbury, Gloucestershire, GL8 8JG** Ⓟ
☎ 01666 505125 Ⓕ 01666 505125
Ⓜ 07974 232783
Ⓔ sales@jesterantiques.co.uk
Ⓦ www.jesterantiques.co.uk
Est. 1995 *Stock size* Medium
Stock Exciting, colourful stock of furniture, decorative items, lamps, mirrors, garden and architectural antiques
Open Mon–Sun 10am–5.30pm
Services Shipping

Lansdown Antiques (BABAADA)
Contact Chris or Ann Kemp
✉ **1 New Church Street, Tetbury, Gloucestershire, GL8 8DS** Ⓟ
☎ 07801 013663
Ⓜ 07947 668279
Ⓔ lansdown-antiques@lineone.net
Est. 1983 *Stock size* Medium
Stock Painted pine and country furniture, metalware and decorative items
Open Mon–Sat 10am–5.30pm Sun 1–5pm
Fairs Bath Decorative and Antiques Fair

Long Street Antiques
Contact Ray or Samantha White
✉ **Stamford House, 14 Long Street, Tetbury, Gloucestershire, GL8 8AQ** Ⓟ
☎ 01666 500850 Ⓕ 01666 500950
Ⓜ 07876 793248
Ⓔ longstantiques@aol.com
Ⓦ www.longstreetantiques.co.uk
Est. 2004 *Stock size* Large
No. of dealers 45–50
Stock Antiques, collectables,

works of art, kitchenware, textiles, glass, silver, country and antique furniture
Open Mon–Sat 10am–5pm
Sun Bank Holidays noon–4pm
Services Over 45 specialist dealers displaying on two floors

Merlin Antiques
Contact Mr Brian Smith
Shops 4 & 5, Chippingcourt Shopping Mall, Chipping Street, Tetbury, Gloucestershire, GL8 8ES
☎ 01666 505008
Est. 1994 *Stock size* Large
Stock Mixed, china, pictures, Victorian–Edwardian furniture, costume jewellery, reproduction furniture, garden stoneware
Open Mon–Sat 9.30am–5pm
Sun by appointment
Services Valuations, repairs, items purchased, single or house clearance

Bobbie Middleton (TADA, CADA)
Contact Bobbie Middleton, **Tetbury, Gloucestershire, GL9**
Ⓜ 07774 192660
Ⓔ bobbiemiddleton@lineone.net
Ⓦ www.bobbiemiddleton.com
Est. 1986 *Stock size* Medium
Stock Classic country house furniture including painted pieces, mirrors, decorative accessories, upholstered furniture
Open By appointment
Services Antique search service, interior design

Peter Norden Antiques (LAPADA, TADA)
Contact Mr P Norden
61 Long Street, Tetbury, Gloucestershire, GL8 8AA
☎ 01666 503854 Ⓕ 01666 505595
Ⓜ 07778 013108
Ⓔ peternorden_antiques@lineone.net
Ⓦ www.peter-norden-antiques.co.uk
Est. 1960 *Stock size* Medium
Stock Early oak and country furniture, early wood carvings, pewter, brass, treen
Open Mon–Sat 10am–5.30pm or by appointment
Services Valuations

Porch House Antiques (TADA)
Contact Mrs L A Woodburn
42 Long Street, Tetbury, Gloucestershire, GL8 8AQ
☎ 01666 502687
Ⓜ 07715 32793
Est. 1976 *Stock size* Large
Stock 17th–20thC furniture, decorative items
Open Mon–Sat 10am–5pm most Sundays

Sieff (TADA)
Contact Kirsty Sylvester
49 Long Street, Tetbury, Gloucestershire, GL8 8AA
☎ 01666 504477 Ⓕ 01666 504478
Ⓔ sieff@sieff.co.uk
Ⓦ www.sieff.co.uk
Est. 1984 *Stock size* Large
Stock 18th–19thC French provincial fruitwood, 20thC furniture
Open Mon–Sat 10am–5.30pm
Fairs Decorative Antique & Textile Fair

Tetbury Old Books
Contact Mr P M Gibbons
4 The Chipping, Tetbury, Gloucestershire, GL8 8ET
☎ 01666 504330 Ⓕ 01666 504458
Ⓔ oldbooks@tetbury.co.uk
Est. 1994 *Stock size* Medium
Stock Antiquarian and second-hand books, prints and maps, specialized collection of Black's colourbooks
Open Mon–Sat 10am–6pm
Sun 11am–5pm

Top Banana Antiques Mall
Contact Sarah Townsend
1 New Church Street, Tetbury, Gloucestershire, GL8 8DS
☎ 0871 288 1102 Ⓕ 0871 288 1103
Ⓔ info@topbananaantiques.com
Ⓦ www.topbananaantiques.com
Est. 2002 *Stock size* Large
No. of dealers 60
Stock A group shop of decorative antiques and interior inspiration
Open Mon–Sat 10am–5.30pm
Sun (summer only) 11am–5pm
Services Packing, shipping

Top Banana Antiques Mall
Contact Peter Bartholomew
32 Long Street, Tetbury, Gloucestershire, GL8 8AQ
☎ 0871 288 1110 Ⓕ 0871 288 1103
Ⓔ info@topbananaantiques.com
Ⓦ www.topbananaantiques.com
Est. 2002 *Stock size* Large
No. of dealers 15
Stock A group shop of decorative antiques and interior inspiration
Open Mon–Sat 10am–5.30pm
Sun (summer only) 11am–5pm
Services Packing, shipping

Townsend Bateson (TADA)
Contact Lynda Townsend-Bateson
Unit 1, 51 Long Street, Tetbury, Gloucestershire, GL8 8AA
☎ 01666 505083 Ⓕ 01666 505083
Ⓜ 07865 513856
Ⓔ townendbateson@btopenworld.com
Ⓦ www.townsendbatesonantiques.com
Est. 1995 *Stock size* Medium
Stock French, painted, fruitwood furniture, mirrors, lighting, etc
Open Mon–Sat 10am–5pm
Sun most Bank Holidays 1–5pm

Westwood House Antiques (TADA)
Contact R Griffiths
29 Long Street, Tetbury, Gloucestershire, GL8 8AA
☎ 01666 502328 Ⓕ 01666 502328
Ⓔ westwoodhouseantiques@tinyworld.co.uk
Ⓦ www.westwoodhouseantiques.com
Est. 1993 *Stock size* Large
Stock 17th–19thC oak, elm and ash country furniture, some French fruitwood, decorative pottery, pewter, treen
Open Mon–Sat 10am–5.30pm

TEWKESBURY

Cornell Books Ltd
Contact Mr G Cornell
93 Church Street, Tewkesbury, Gloucestershire, GL20 5RS
☎ 01684 293337 Ⓕ 01684 273959
Ⓔ gtcornell@aol.com
Est. 1996 *Stock size* Medium
Stock Antiquarian and second-hand books
Open Mon–Sat 10.30am–5pm

Gainsborough House
Contact A or B Hillson
81 Church Street, Tewkesbury, Gloucestershire, GL20 5RX P
01684 293072
Est. 1962 *Stock size* Large
Stock Period furniture, porcelain, silver
Open Mon–Sat 10am–5pm closed Thurs

Tewkesbury Antiques Centre
Contact Mrs Patricia Rose
Tolsey Hall, Tolsey Lane, Tewkesbury, Gloucestershire, GL20 5AE P
01684 294091 or 01531 822211
F 01531 822211
Est. 1991 *Stock size* Medium
No. of dealers 13
Stock Antiques, bric-a-brac, collectables, books, records, jewellery, furniture, radios, old tools
Open Mon–Sat 10am–5pm Sun 11am–5pm

WICKWAR

Bell Passage Antiques (LAPADA)
Contact Mrs D Brand
36–38 High Street, Wickwar, Wotton-under-Edge, Gloucestershire, GL12 8NP P
01454 294251
Est. 1966 *Stock size* Medium
Stock General antiques, furniture, glass, porcelain
Open Mon–Fri 9am–5pm Sat 9am–3pm closed Wed or by appointment
Services Restoration, upholstery, caning

WINCHCOMBE

Berkeley Antiques
Contact Peter or Susan Dennis
3 Hailes Street, Winchcombe, Gloucestershire, GL54 5HU P
01684 292034 F 01684 292034
M 07836 243397
Est. 1974 *Stock size* Medium
Stock 17th–19thC brass, copper, china
Open Mon–Sat 10am–5.30pm closed Thurs pm
Services Valuations, restoration

Government House Quality Antique Lighting
Contact Mr M Bailey
St George's House, High Street, Winchcombe, Cheltenham, Gloucestershire, GL54 5LJ P
01242 604562
M 07970 430684
Est. 1980 *Stock size* Large
Stock Antique pre-1939 lighting
Open By appointment
Services Restoration

In Period Antiques
Contact John Edgeler
Queen Anne House, High Street, Winchcombe, Gloucestershire, GL54 5LJ P
01242 602319
M 07816 193027
E john@cotswolds.uk.com
W www.cotswolds.uk.com
Est. 1999 *Stock size* Medium
Stock 17th–19thC furniture, metalwork, glass, porcelain, decorative items
Open Thurs–Sat 9.30am–5pm or by appointment
Services Valuations

Newsum Antiques (CADA)
Contact Mark Newsum
2 High Street, Winchcombe, Gloucestershire, GL54 5HT
01242 603446
M 07968 196668
E mark@newsumantiques.co.uk
W www.newsumantiques.co.uk
Est. 1985 *Stock size* Medium
Stock Oak and country furniture, treen, Swedish metalware, Scandinavian folk art
Open Tues–Sat 10.30am–5pm
Fairs NEC, Penman Fairs Kensington, Chelsea, Petersfield

Prichard Antiques (CADA)
Contact Keith and Debbie Prichard
16 High Street, Winchcombe, Gloucestershire, GL54 5LJ P
01242 603566
Est. 1979 *Stock size* Large
Stock 17th–19thC formal and country furniture, clocks, treen, boxes, metalware, decorative items, garden furniture
Open Mon–Sat 9am–5.30pm

WOTTON-UNDER-EDGE

Wotton Auction Rooms Ltd
Contact Mr Philip Taubenheim
Tabernacle Road, Wotton-under-Edge, Gloucestershire, GL12 7EB P
01453 844733 F 01453 845448
E info@wottonauctionrooms.co.uk
W www.wottonauctionrooms.co.uk
Est. 1991
Open Mon–Fri 9am–5pm
Sales Tues smalls, Wed furniture, viewing Mon 10am–7pm Tues 9–10.30am
Frequency Monthly
Catalogues Yes

HEREFORDSHIRE

ABBEY DORE

Ernest Howes
Contact Ernest Howes
The Old Rectory, Abbey Dore, Herefordshire, HR20AA P
01981 240311
E howesdore@btopenworld.com
Est. 1975 *Stock size* Small
Stock Georgian country furniture, mainly oak
Open Mon–Sat 9am–5pm appointment advisable

HAY-ON-WYE

Addyman Annexe
Contact Mr Addyman
27 Castle Street, Hay-on-Wye, Herefordshire, HR3 5DF
01497 821600
E madness@hay-on-wyebooks.com
W www.addyman-books.co.uk
Est. 1987 *Stock size* Medium
Stock Antiquarian books on all subjects, modern first editions, occult, myths and legends, leather-bound sets
Open Mon–Sun 10.30am–5.30pm

Addyman Books
Contact Anne Brichto
39 Lion Street, Hay-on-Wye, Herefordshire, HR3 5AA
01497 821136 F 01497 821732
E madness@hay-on-wyebooks.com
W www.addyman-books.co.uk
Est. 1987 *Stock size* Medium

Stock Antiquarian and second-hand books specializing in English literature, modern first editions
Open Mon–Sat 10am–6pm
Sun 10.30am–5.30pm

C Arden Bookseller (PBFA)
Contact Mrs C Arden
Radnor House, Church Street, Hay-on-Wye, Herefordshire, HR3 5DQ
01497 820471 F 01497 820498
c.arden@virgin.net
www.ardenbooks.co.uk
Est. 1992 *Stock size* Large
Stock Antiquarian books on natural history, gardening, botany
Open Fri–Mon 10.30am–5.30pm telephone call advisable
Fairs PBFA

Richard Booth's Bookshop Ltd
Contact Mr R G W Booth
44 Lion Street, Hay-on-Wye, Herefordshire, HR3 5AJ
01497 820322 F 01497 821150
postmaster@richardbooth.demon.co.uk
www.richardbooth.demon.co.uk
Est. 1969 *Stock size* Large
Stock Antiquarian, second-hand and illustrated books, literature, military, topography, natural history, children's fantasy and science fiction, languages, law, paperbacks, sport, science and technology
Open Mon–Sat 9am–7pm
Sun 11.30am–5.30pm
Services Mail order

Richard Booth's Bookshop Ltd
Contact Hope Booth
Hay Castle, Hay-on-Wye, Herefordshire, HR3 5DL
01497 820503 F 01497 821314
books@haycastle.co.uk
www.richardbooth.demon.co.uk
Est. 1961 *Stock size* Large
Stock Antiquarian, second-hand and illustrated books, American Indians, art and architecture, cinema, crafts, humour, photography and images, transport, maps and prints
Open Mon–Sun 9.30am–5pm
Fairs Photography Book Fair, London
Services Valuations

Boz Books (ABA)
Contact Peter Harries
13a Castle Street, Hay-on-Wye, Herefordshire, HR3 5DF
01497 821277 F 01497 821277
peter@bozbooks.demon.co.uk
www.bozbooks.co.uk
Est. 1989 *Stock size* Medium
Stock Antiquarian, rare, second-hand books, 19thC English literature
Open Mon–Sat 10am–5pm closed 1–2pm variable in winter
Services Book search

Bullring Antiques
Contact Mrs S Spencer or Marjorie Abel
Bear Street, Hay-on-Wye, Herefordshire, HR3 5AN
01497 820467
Est. 1994 *Stock size* Medium
No. of dealers 4
Stock Wide general stock of good-quality antiques, furniture, ceramics, pictures, glass, silver
Open Mon–Sat 10am–5pm
Sun 11am–5pm

The Children's Bookshop
Contact Judith Gardener
Toll Cottage, Pontvaen, Hay-on-Wye, Herefordshire, HR3 5EW
01497 821083 F 01497 821083
bob@childrensbookshop.com
www.childrensbookshop.com
Est. 1981 *Stock size* Medium
Stock 18th–20thC children's books
Open Mon–Sat 9.30am–5.30pm
Sun 10am–5pm
Services Book search, catalogue on website

davidleesbooks.com
Contact Julie Freeman
Marches Gallery, 2 Lion Street, Hay-on-Wye, Herefordshire, HR3 5AA
01497 822969 F 01568 780468
enquiries@davidleesbooks.com
www.davidleesbooks.com
Est. 1986 *Stock size* Medium
Stock Antiquarian books
Open Mon–Sun 11am–5pm winter times may vary
Fairs Kinver Book Fair

Marijana Dworski Books
Contact Marijana Dworski
Travel and Language Bookshop, 21 Broad Street, Hay-on-Wye, Herefordshire, HR3 5DB
01497 820200 F 01497 820200
sam@dworskibooks.com
www.dworskibooks.com
Est. 1991 *Stock size* Medium
Stock Antiquarian books, specializing in Russia, Eastern Europe and minority languages
Open Mon–Sun 10.30am–5.30pm and mail order
Services 3 catalogues per year

Hancock & Monks
Contact Jerry Monks
6 Broad Street, Hay-on-Wye, Herefordshire, HR3 5DB
01497 821784 F 01591 610778
jerry@hancockandmonks.co.uk
www.hancockandmonks.co.uk
Est. 1974 *Stock size* Medium
Stock Antiquarian books on music, antiquarian sheet music
Open Mon–Sun 10am–5pm
Services Book search

Hay Antique Market
Contact Jenny Price
6 Market Street, Hay-on-Wye, Herefordshire, HR3 5AF
01497 820175
Est. 1989 *Stock size* Large
No. of dealers 17
Stock China, glass, jewellery, linen, country furniture, period furniture, rural and rustic items, period clothing, lighting, pictures, brass
Open Mon–Sat 10am–5pm
Sun 11am–5pm

Hay Cinema Bookshop (PBFA, ABA)
Contact Mr Greg Coombes
The Old Cinema, Castle Street, Hay-on-Wye, Herefordshire, HR3 5DF
01497 820071 F 01497 821900
sales@haycinemabookshop.co.uk
www.haycinemabookshop.co.uk
Est. 1855 *Stock size* Large
Stock Antiquarian and second-

hand books, leather-bound books, art, antiques topics a speciality, voyages, travel, naval, military, social sciences
Open Mon–Sat 9am–7pm Sun 11.30am–5.30pm
Fairs PBFA, ABA

Hay on Wye Booksellers
Contact Mrs J Jordan
14 High Town, Hay-on-Wye, Herefordshire, HR3 5AE P
01497 820875 F 01497 847129
M 07866 420741
E sales@hayonwyebooksellers.com
W www.hayonwyebooksellers.com
Est. 1969 *Stock size* Large
Stock Antiquarian, second-hand, cut-price new books, publishers' returns
Open Mon–Sat 9am–6pm Sun 9.30am–6pm

Lion Fine Arts & Books
Contact Mr Charles Spencer
19 Lion Street, Hay-on-Wye, Herefordshire, HR3 5AD P
01497 821726
W www.hay-on-wye.co.uk/LionFine
Est. 1995 *Stock size* Medium
Stock Small antique furniture, porcelain, pottery, Georgian–early 19thC glass, old prints, treen, interesting collectables, antiquarian books
Open Mon Thurs Sat 10am–5pm other days variable, open most afternoons, telephone first

Lion Street Books
Contact Mr Mark Williams
1 St John's Place, Hay-on-Wye, Herefordshire, HR3 5BN P
01497 820121 F 01497 820121
M 07967 604732
E mark@boxingstuff.com
W www.boxingstuff.com
Est. 1993 *Stock size* Large
Stock Boxing memorabilia, books, programmes, magazines, photos
Open Mon–Sat 10am–5pm
Services Mail order catalogue

Murder & Mayhem
Contact Mr Addyman
5 Lion Street, Hay-on-Wye, Herefordshire, HR3 5AA
01497 821613 F 01497 821732
E madness@hay-on-wyebooks.com
W www.hay-on-wyebooks.com
Est. 1997 *Stock size* Medium
Stock Antiquarian and second-hand books, specializing in detective fiction, crime, horror
Open Mon–Sat Sun in season 10.30am–5.30

Rose's Books
Contact Mrs M Goddard
14 Broad Street, Hay-on-Wye, Herefordshire, HR3 5DB P
01497 820013 F 01497 820031
E enquiry@rosesbooks.com
W www.rosesbooks.com
Est. 1984 *Stock size* Medium
Stock Rare, out-of-print, children's, illustrated books
Open Mon–Sun 9.30am–5pm
Services Regular e-mail or paper lists sent out for authors, illustrators or subjects of interest

Mark Westwood Books (ABA, PBFA)
Contact Evelyn Westwood
Grove House, High Town, Hay-on-Wye, Herefordshire, HR3 5AE P
01497 820068 F 01497 821641
E books@markwestwood.co.uk
Est. 1976 *Stock size* Medium
Stock Antiquarian, scholarly second-hand books on most subjects
Open Mon–Sun 10.30am–6pm
Fairs Oxford

HEREFORD

The Antique Tea Shop
Contact Miss J Cockin
5a St Peters Street, Hereford, Herefordshire, HR1 2LA
01432 342172
Est. 1990 *Stock size* Small
Stock Small items, pastry forks, afternoon tea knives, 1920s–1930s jewellery, French furniture, mirrors, ceramics
Open Tues–Sat 9.45am–5pm
Services Tea shop

I and J L Brown Ltd
Contact Mr Simon Hilton
Whitestone Park, Whitestone, Hereford, Herefordshire, HR1 3SE P
01432 851991 F 01432 851994
E enquiries@brownantiques.com
W www.brownantiques.com
Est. 1978 *Stock size* Large
Stock English country, French provincial furniture, largest source in UK
Open Mon–Sat 9am–5.30pm or by appointment
Services Re-rushing, restoration, makes reproduction furniture especially Windsor chairs

Hereford Antique Centre
Contact Georgina Smith
128 Widemarsh Street, Hereford, Herefordshire, HR4 9HN P
01432 266242
Est. 1989 *Stock size* Large
No. of dealers 35
Stock Furniture, pictures, fireplaces, china etc
Open Mon–Sat 10am–5pm Sun noon–5pm
Services Delivery

Hereford Map Centre (IMTA)
Contact Mr J Davey
24–25 Church Street, Hereford, Herefordshire, HR1 2LR
01432 266322 F 01432 341874
E info@themapcentre.com
W www.themapcentre.com
Est. 1984 *Stock size* Large
Stock Old maps of varying scales, 1:10,000, 1:2,500, 1:500, tythe maps, hand-painted, County Series maps
Open Mon–Sat 9am–5.30pm
Services Laminating, mounting

Sunderlands Sale Rooms
Contact Mr Graham Baker
Newmarket Street, Hereford, Herefordshire, HR4 9HX P
01432 266894 F 01432 266901
E sunderlandsfinearts.co.uk
W www.sunderlandshereford.co.uk
Est. 1868
Open Mon–Fri 9am–5pm
Sales General furniture sale Mon 5pm. Antiques sale every 2 months Tues 11am, viewing Mon Tues prior to sale (telephone Head Office on 01432 356161 for further details)
Frequency Fortnightly
Catalogues No

⊞ Waring's Antiques
Contact Mrs E Sullivan
✉ **45–47 St Owen Street, Hereford, Herefordshire, HR1 2JB**
☎ 01432 276241
Est. 1959 *Stock size* Large
Stock General antiques, collectables, pine, both new and old
Open Mon–Sat 9am–5pm

KINGTON

⊞ Castle Hill Books
Contact Mr P Newman
✉ **12 Church Street, Kington, Herefordshire, HR5 3AZ** P
☎ 01544 231195 F 01544 231161
E sales@castlehill.books.co.uk
W www.castlehillbooks.co.uk
Est. 1989 *Stock size* Medium
Stock New, antiquarian, out-of-print, second-hand books, general stock, most subjects covered, some specialist subjects including archaeology, British and Welsh topography
Open Mon–Fri 10.30am–1pm Sat 10.30am–1pm 2–4pm
Services Book search, valuations, restoration

⊞ Kington Antiques
Contact Paul Sheppard
✉ **15 High Street, Kington, Herefordshire, HR5 3AX** P
☎ 01544 340528
M 07773 216041
E office@kington-antiques.co.uk
W www.kington-antiques.co.uk
Est. 1976 *Stock size* Medium
Stock Collectables, memorabilia, art, antiques of Eastern European interest
Open Tues–Sat 11am–4pm closed Wed or by appointment
Services Valuations, shipping

LEDBURY

⊞ John Nash Antiques and Interiors (LAPADA, IDDA)
Contact John Nash
✉ **17c High Street, Ledbury, Herefordshire, HR8 1DS** P
☎ 01531 635714 F 01531 635050
M 07831 382970
W www.johnnash.co.uk
Est. 1973 *Stock size* Medium
Stock 18th–19thC fine mahogany and walnut furniture
Open Mon–Sat 9am–5.30pm Sun by appointment
Services Valuations, restoration, interior design

H J Pugh and Co
Contact Mr Howard Pugh
✉ **Ledbury Sale Rooms, Market Street, Ledbury, Herefordshire, HR8 2AQ** P
☎ 01531 631122 F 01531 631818
E auctions@hjpugh.com
W www.hjpugh.com
Est. 1990
Open Mon–Fri 9am–5.30pm
Sales General antiques sale Tues 6pm, viewing Tues 10am–6pm prior to sale
Frequency Monthly
Catalogues Yes

⊞ Serendipity
Contact Mrs R Ford
✉ **The Tythings, Preston Court, Ledbury, Herefordshire, HR8 2LL** P
☎ 01531 660245 F 01531 660421
E sales@serendipity-antiques.co.uk
W www.serendipity-antiques.co.uk
Est. 1969 *Stock size* Large
Stock 18thC furniture, long dining tables, four-poster beds, Regency period furniture
Open Mon–Sat 9am–5.30pm
Fairs Olympia, Battersea, Penman Antique Fairs Chelsea
Services Restoration

⊞ Keith Smith Books (PBFA)
Contact Mr K Smith
✉ **78b The Homend, Ledbury, Herefordshire, HR8 1BX** P
☎ 01531 635336 F 0870 0529986
E keith@ksbooks.demon.co.uk
Est. 1989 *Stock size* Medium
Stock Antiquarian, general, second-hand books, WWI poetry, needlecrafts
Open Mon–Sat 10am–5pm
Fairs Churchdown

LEOMINSTER

⊞ 22 Broad Street
Contact Daphne Sturley
✉ **22 Broad Street, Leominster, Herefordshire, HR6 8BS** P
☎ 01568 620426
M 07811 359473
Est. 1999 *Stock size* Medium
Stock French furniture, textiles, decorative items, curtains, mirrors
Open Mon–Sat 10.30am–5pm

⊞ The Barometer Shop
Contact Verity or Colin Jones
✉ **New Street, Leominster, Herefordshire, HR6 8BT** P
☎ 01568 610200
W www.thebarometershop.co.uk
Stock size Medium
Stock Antiques, collectables, barometers, clocks
Open Mon–Fri 9am–5pm Sat 10am–4pm
Services Restoration

Brightwells
Contact Roger Williams
✉ **The Fine Art Sale Room, Easters Court, Leominster, Herefordshire, HR6 0DE** P
☎ 01568 611122 F 01568 610519
E fineart@brightwells.com
W www.catalogs.icollector.com/brightwells
Est. 1846
Open Mon–Fri 9am–5pm
Sales Antiques sale Wed Thurs 10am, viewing Tues 9am–5pm. 5–6 ceramics sales per year Wed 11am, viewing Tues 9am–5pm
Frequency 3–4 sales per month
Catalogues Yes

⊞ Courts Miscellany
Contact Mr G Court
✉ **48a Bridge Street, Leominster, Herefordshire, HR6 8DZ** P
☎ 01568 612995
Est. 1983 *Stock size* Medium
Stock Selection of collectables and antiques relating to social history, sporting, militaria, brewery, political
Open Mon–Sat 10.30am–5pm or by appointment

⊞ Jeffery Hammond Antiques (LAPADA)
Contact Mr J Hammond
✉ **Shaftesbury House, 38 Broad Street, Leominster, Herefordshire, HR6 8BS** P
☎ 01568 614876 F 01568 614876

Ⓜ 07971 289367
Ⓔ enquiries@jefferyhammondantiques.co.uk
Ⓦ www.jefferyhammondantiques.co.uk
Est. 1970 *Stock size* Medium
Stock Good quality 18th–early 19thC walnut, mahogany, rosewood furniture, some clocks, paintings, mirrors
Open Mon–Sat 9am–5.30pm or by appointment
Services Valuations for insurance, probate

Leominster Antique Centre
Contact Mr J Weston
✉ **34 Broad Street, Leominster, Herefordshire, HR6 8BS** Ⓟ
☎ 01568 615505
Est. 1998 *Stock size* Large
No. of dealers 35
Stock Period furniture, early porcelain, pottery, objets d'art, antiquarian books, garden furniture
Open Mon–Sat 10am–5pm Sun 11am–4pm
Services Tea rooms, gardens

Leominster Antique Market
Contact Mrs O G Dyke
✉ **14 Broad Street, Leominster, Herefordshire, HR6 8BS** Ⓟ
☎ 01568 612189
Est. 1975 *Stock size* Large
No. of dealers 16
Stock Glass, china, silver, pine, furniture
Open Mon–Sat 10am–5pm April–Sept Sun 11am–3pm

Leominster Clock Repairs
Contact Ashley Prosser
✉ **Unit 2, The Railway Station, Worcester Road, Leominster, Herefordshire, HR6 8AR** Ⓟ
☎ 01568 612298
Est. 2000 *Stock size* Small
Stock Georgian–Victorian longcase and dial clocks
Open Mon–Sat 9am–6pm
Services Repairs, specialist in longcase and early British domestic clocks

Linden House Antiques
Contact Michael Clayton or Caroline Scott Mayfield
✉ **1 Drapers Lane, Leominster, Herefordshire, HR6 8ND** Ⓟ
☎ 01568 620350
Ⓜ 07790 671722
Est. 1972 *Stock size* Large
No. of dealers 10
Stock Furniture, lighting, glass, silver, porcelain, paintings, early country pewter etc, collectables
Open Mon–Sat 10am–1pm 2–5pm Sun by appointment
Services Valuations (free if brought to shop on Sat)

Old Merchant's House Antiques Centre
Contact Elaine Griffin
✉ **10 Corn Square, Leominster, Herefordshire, HR6 8LR** Ⓟ
☎ 01568 616141 Ⓕ 01568 616141
Est. 1997 *Stock size* Large
No. of dealers 26
Stock General antiques, collectables
Open Mon–Sat 10am–5pm
Services Upholstery

The Old Shoe Box
Contact Stacey Williams or Eric Titchmarsh
✉ **2 Church Street, Leominster, Herefordshire, HR6 8NE** Ⓟ
☎ 01568 611414
Ⓜ 07980 286414
Ⓔ staceycharleswilliams@yahoo.com
Est. 1997 *Stock size* Small
Stock Collectables, furniture, soft furnishings, pictures, books, antique lighting
Open Tues–Sat 10am–5pm
Services Book search, picture valuation, restoration

Tea Gowns & Textiles
Contact Annie Townsend
✉ **28 & 30 Broad Street, Leominster, Herefordshire, HR6 8BS** Ⓟ
☎ 01568 612999 or 01982 560422
Ⓜ 07900 375410
Est. 2002 *Stock size* Medium
Stock Vintage clothing and accessories
Open Mon–Sat 10am–5pm

Utter Clutter
Contact Mrs L M Mackenzie
✉ **16 West Street, Leominster, Herefordshire, HR6 8ES** Ⓟ
☎ 01568 611277
Est. 1995 *Stock size* Medium
Stock General antiques, collectables, early toys
Open Mon–Sat 10am–5pm

LONGTOWN

Abergavenny Reclamation
Contact Mr Simon Thomas
✉ **Lower Ponthendre, Longtown, Herefordshire, HR2 0NY** Ⓟ
☎ 01873 860633
Ⓜ 07970 318399
Est. 1993 *Stock size* Varies
Stock Architectural salvage, reclaimed building materials
Open By appointment

PONTRILAS

Nigel Ward & Co
Contact Mr Nigel Ward
✉ **The Border Property Centre, Pontrilas, Herefordshire, HR2 0EH** Ⓟ
☎ 01981 240140 Ⓕ 01981 240857
Ⓔ office@nigel-ward.co.uk
Ⓦ www.nigel-ward.co.uk
Est. 1988
Open Mon–Fri 9am–5.30pm
Sales Monthly sales of antique and country furniture, porcelain and collectables at Pontrilas Sale Room
Catalogues Yes

ROSS-ON-WYE

Fritz Fryer Antique Lighting
Contact Simon, Karen, or Margaret
✉ **23 Station Street, Ross-on-Wye, Herefordshire, HR9 7AG** Ⓟ
☎ 01989 567416 Ⓕ 01989 566742
Ⓔ enquiries@fritzfryer.co.uk
Ⓦ www.fritzfryer.co.uk
Est. 1982 *Stock size* Large
Stock Antique lighting 1820–1950, crystal chandeliers, gasoliers, wall lights, table lights, nickel and silver fittings, industrial and post-modern lights
Open Mon–Sat 10am–5.30pm
Services Lighting design, restoration, conversion, shipping, removals and delivery

⊞ Andy Gibbs
✉ **29 Brookend Street, Ross-on-Wye, Herefordshire, HR9 7EE** P
☎ 01989 566833
Ⓜ 07850 354480
Est. 1993 *Stock size* Large
Stock Furniture including dining tables, chairs, reformed Gothic and Gothic revival
Open Tues–Sat 10am–1pm 2–5.30pm
Services Valuations, restoration

⊞ W John Griffiths Antiques
Contact Mr Griffiths
✉ **30a Brookend Street, Ross-on-Wye, Herefordshire, HR9 7EE** P
☎ 01989 763682
Ⓜ 07768 606507
Est. 1997 *Stock size* Medium
Stock 18th–early 20thC oak and mahogany furniture, decorative objects, pictures, paintings, prints
Open Mon–Sat 10am–1pm 2–5.30pm

⊞ Robin Lloyd Antiques
Contact Mr R R Knightley
✉ **23–24 Brookend Street, Ross-on-Wye, Herefordshire, HR9 7EE** P
☎ 01989 562123 Ⓕ 01989 562123
Ⓔ rrknightley@aol.com
Ⓦ www.robinlloydantiques.com
Est. 1972 *Stock size* Large
Stock Welsh country furniture, longcase clocks, farmhouse tables
Open Mon–Sat 10am–5.30pm
Services Valuations

Morris Bricknell
Contact Mr Nigel Morris
✉ **Stroud House, 30 Gloucester Road, Ross-on-Wye, Herefordshire, HR9 5LE** P
☎ 01989 768320 Ⓕ 01989 768345
Ⓔ morrisbricknell@lineone.net
Ⓦ www.morrisbricknell.com
Est. 1989
Open Mon–Fri 9am–5.30pm
Sales General antiques sale Sat 10.30am at V H Whitchurch and Goodrich, viewing Sat 8.30am prior to sale. Occasional special and marquee sales (telephone for details)
Frequency Monthly
Catalogues No

⊞ Ross Old Books and Print Shop (PBFA)
Contact Mr P Thredder
✉ **51–52 High Street, Ross-on-Wye, Herefordshire, HR9 5HH** P
☎ 01989 567458
Ⓔ enquiries@rossoldbooks.co.uk
Ⓦ www.rossoldbooks.com
Est. 1987 *Stock size* Medium
Stock Antique, second-hand, rare books selling for £1–£1,000, British county maps
Open Mon–Sat 10am–5pm closed mid-Jan to mid-Feb
Fairs PBFA
Services Post inland and overseas

Ross-on-Wye Antique Gallery
Contact Mr Michael Aslanian
✉ **Gloucester Road, Ross-on-Wye, Herefordshire, HR9 5BU** P
☎ 01989 762290 Ⓕ 01989 762291
Ⓔ michael.aslanian@btinternet.com
Ⓦ www.rossantiquesgallery.com
Est. 1996 *Stock size* Large
No. of dealers 50
Stock Gothic-style church, period furniture, oak, mahogany, country furniture, oil paintings, antiquarian books, silver, gold, jewellery, English and Continental porcelain, English and French glass, Oriental antiques, rugs, Art Deco, spoons, other cutlery, longcase clocks
Open Mon–Sat noon–5pm Sun Bank Holidays by appointment
Services Valuations

⊞ Waterfall Antiques
Contact Mr O McCarthy
✉ **2 High Street, Ross-on-Wye, Herefordshire, HR9 5HL** P
☎ 01989 563103
Est. 1991 *Stock size* Large
Stock Pine and country furniture
Open Mon–Sat 9.30am–4.30pm closed Wed Fri pm
Fairs Newark

Williams & Watkins Auctioneers Ltd
Contact Roger Garlick
✉ **Ross-on-Wye Auction Centre, Overcross, Ross-on-Wye, Herefordshire, HR9 7QF** P
☎ 01989 762225 Ⓕ 01989 566082
Ⓔ willwat@auctionmarts.com
Est. 1866
Open Mon–Fri 9am–5pm
Sales Wed 10am. General antiques sales, viewing Tues 1–7pm and day of sale 9–10am
Frequency monthly
Catalogues Yes

HERTFORDSHIRE

BARNET

⊞ Antiques Little Shop
Contact Mrs F O'Gorman
✉ **2 Bruce Road, Barnet, Hertfordshire, EN5 4LS** P
☎ 020 8449 9282
Est. 1996 *Stock size* Medium
Stock Furniture, collectables, Georgian–1950s
Open Wed–Sat 10am–5pm Fri 11am–5pm
Services House clearance

Barnet Bygones
Contact Mrs M Phillips
✉ **2 Bruce Road, Barnet, Hertfordshire, EN5 4LS** P
☎ 020 8440 7304
Est. 1994 *Stock size* Large
No. of dealers 5
Stock Furniture, smalls, collectables
Open Wed Fri Sat 9am–5pm

⊞ C Bellinger Antiques
Contact Mr C Bellinger
✉ **91 Wood Street, Barnet, Hertfordshire, EN5 4BX** P
☎ 020 8449 3467
Est. 1971 *Stock size* Small
Stock General antiques
Open Thurs–Sat 10am–3pm

BERKHAMSTED

⊞ Country Life Interiors
Contact Mr Peter Myers
✉ **88 High Street, Berkhamsted, Hertfordshire, HP4 2BW** P
☎ 01442 387337 Ⓕ 01442 387338
Ⓔ info@countrylifeinteriors.com
Ⓦ www.countrylifeinteriors.com
Est. 1982 *Stock size* Large
Stock Victorian pine, reproduction pine in old wood, oak furniture, painted furniture, giftware, fitted and free-standing kitchens

Open Mon–Sat 10am–5.30pm
Sun 11am–4pm
Services Worldwide shipping arranged

Heritage Antique Centre
Contact Pauline Beales
24 Castle Street, Berkhamsted, Hertfordshire, HP4 2DW P
01442 873819
Est. 1985 *Stock size* Medium
No. of dealers 25
Stock Bric-a-brac, Georgian furniture, garden furniture
Open Mon–Sun 10am–5.30pm

Home & Colonial Antique Centre
Contact Ali Reid-Davies
134 High Street, Berkhamsted, Hertfordshire, HP4 3AT P
01442 877007
homeandcolonial@btinternet.com
www.homeandcolonial.co.uk
Est. 1996 *Stock size* Large
No. of dealers 50
Stock English, French period furniture, clocks, pine and country furniture, Arts and Crafts, painted furniture, garden antiques, jewellery, collectables
Open Mon–Sat 10am–5.30pm
Sun 11am–5pm closed Wed

BOREHAMWOOD

Barnet-Cattanach Antiques (BADA, LAPADA)
Contact Mr R J Gerry
The Old Marble Works, Glenhaven Avenue, Borehamwood, Hertfordshire, WD6 1BB P
020 8207 6792 F 020 8381 5889
info@barnetcattanach.fsnet.co.uk
Est. 1964 *Stock size* Large
Stock 18thC period furniture, pre-1830 accessories
Open By appointment only
Fairs Olympia (June, Nov)
Services Carriage

The Book Exchange
Contact Mr Brian Berman
120 Shenley Road, Borehamwood, Hertfordshire, WD6 1EF P
020 8236 0966 F 020 8953 6673
books@thebookexchange.info
Est. 1993 *Stock size* Large
Stock General antiquarian, second-hand, some new books
Open Mon–Sat 9.30am–5.30pm
Services Book search

BUNTINGFORD

Times Past
Contact Adrian Piggott
61 High Street, Buntingford, Hertfordshire, SG9 9AE P
01763 274069
timespast61@aol.com
Est. 1999 *Stock size* Large
Stock Continental, Victorian pine, ceramics
Open Mon–Sat 10am–5pm closed Wed or by appointment

BUSHEY

Bushey Antique Centre
Contact Mr G Lindsey
39 High Street, Bushey, Hertfordshire, WO20 1BD
020 8950 5040
Est. 1988 *Stock size* Medium
No. of dealers 8
Stock Furniture
Open Mon–Sat 9.30am–5pm
Sun 10am–2pm
Services Restoration, upholstery

C and B Antiques
Contact Carol Epstein
22 Brooke Way, Bushey Heath, Watford, Hertfordshire, WD23 4LG P
020 8950 1844 F 020 8950 1844
M 07831 647274
Est. 1979 *Stock size* Large
Stock 1790–1930 porcelain and small furniture
Open By appointment or at fairs
Fairs The Moat House, The Bell House, Shepton Mallet
Services Valuations

Country Life Interiors
Contact Mr Peter Myers
33a High Street, Bushey, Watford, Hertfordshire, WD23 1BD P
020 8950 8575 F 020 8950 6982
info@countrylifeinteriors.com
www.countrylifeinteriors.com
Est. 1982 *Stock size* Large
Stock Victorian pine, reproduction pine in old wood, oak furniture, painted furniture, giftware, fitted and free-standing kitchens
Open Mon–Sat 10am–5.30pm
Sun 11am–4pm
Services Worldwide shipping arranged

Marcel Cards (Cartophilic Society)
Contact Marcel Epstein
22 Brooke Way, Bushey Heath, Watford, Hertfordshire, WD23 4LG P
020 8950 1844 F 020 8950 1844
M 07887 648255
Est. 1991 *Stock size* Large
Stock Cigarette cards 1890–1939, new collectors' cards, tea, bubblegum cards
Open By appointment and at Marcel Fairs
Fairs Peterborough, Ardingly, Dunstable
Services Odd cards to complete sets, card search, valuations

CHESHUNT

Cheshunt Antiques
Contact Mr Peter Howard
126–128 Turners Hill, Cheshunt, Waltham Cross, Hertfordshire, EN8 9BN P
01992 637337
Est. 1991 *Stock size* Large
Stock Georgian–early 20thC furniture
Open Tues–Fri 10am–2pm
Sat 10am–4pm
Fairs Newark
Services Restoration, French polishing

CHORLEYWOOD

Douglas Roberts Antiques
Contact Andy Roberts
31 Lower Road, Chorleywood, Hertfordshire, WD3 5LQ P
01923 283111
M 07970 773917
meta.roberts@btinternet.com
Est. 2004 *Stock size* Small
Stock Georgian–1930s furniture, pictures, glass
Open Tues–Sat 10am–5pm

DAGNALL

Ashridge Antique Flooring
Contact Richard Facer

✉ **Mile Barn Farm, Hemel Hempstead Road, Dagnall, Berkhamsted, Hertfordshire, HP4 1QR** P
☎ 01442 843077
M 07774 757200
Est. 1987 *Stock size* Large
Stock Reclaimed oak beams, flooring and furniture
Open Mon–Sat 9am–5pm

HEMEL HEMPSTEAD

Cherry Antiques
Contact Mr R S Cullen
✉ **101 High Street, Hemel Hempstead, Hertfordshire, HP1 3AH** P
☎ 01442 264358
Est. 1981 *Stock size* Medium
Stock General antiques
Open Mon–Sat 9.30am–4.30pm Wed 9.30am–1pm
Services Valuations

Heritage Reclamation
Contact Mr L Leadbetter
✉ **Wood Lane, Paradise Industrial Estate, Hemel Hempstead, Hertfordshire, HP2 4TL** P
☎ 01442 219936 F 01442 219936
W www.heritage-reclamation.co.uk
Est. 1998 *Stock size* Medium
Stock Victorian pews, roll-top baths, internal and external doors, stained glass, French burners, Victorian fireplaces, reclaimed bricks, tiles, floor boarding
Open Mon–Fri 8am–5pm Sat 9am–4.30pm
Services Supply and fit flooring

The House of Elliott
Contact Michele
✉ **11 High Street, Hemel Hempstead, Hertfordshire, HP1 3AA** P
☎ 01442 405325
E michele@house-of-elliott.fsnet.co.uk
W www.houseofelliott.org
Est. 2001 *Stock size* Small
Stock Pine furniture, clocks, fob watches, Victorian silver, jewellery, collectables
Open Mon–Sat 10am–5.30pm Sun 11am–4.30pm

Fairs Great Missenden, Kempton, Ardingly
Services Upholstery, clock repairs

Jordans Antique Centre
Contact Margaret Munn
✉ **63 High Street, Old Town, Hemel Hempstead, Hertfordshire**
☎ 01442 263451
Est. 1988 *Stock size* Medium
No. of dealers 25
Stock China, glass, furniture, jewellery
Open Mon–Sun 10am–5pm

Libritz Stamps
Contact Mr R Hickman
✉ **70 London Road, Apsley, Hemel Hempstead, Hertfordshire, HP3 9SD** P
☎ 01442 242691 F 01442 242691
E info@libritzstampshop.co.uk
W www.libritzstampshop.co.uk
Est. 1967 *Stock size* Large
Stock Banknotes, stamps, coins, cigarette cards, accessories, albums, catalogues
Open Mon–Sat 10am–5pm
Services Want lists serviced

Off the Wall
Contact Michelle Smith
✉ **52 High Street, Hemel Hempstead, Hertfordshire, HP1 3AF** P
☎ 01442 218300
M 07771 724700
E off_thewallantiques@hotmail.com
Est. 2001 *Stock size* Medium
No. of dealers 4
Stock Furniture, decorative items, glassware
Open Mon–Sat 10am–5.30pm Sun 11am–1pm

HERTFORD

Bazaar Boxes (LAPADA)
Contact Andrew Grierson or Mark Brewster
✉ **Hertford, Hertfordshire, SG14** P
☎ 01992 504454 F 01992 504454
M 07970 909204/909206
E bazaarboxes@hotmail.com
W www.bazaarboxes.com
Est. 1998 *Stock size* Medium
Stock Tortoiseshell, ivory and mother-of-pearl tea caddies and boxes, objects of virtue, Oriental items
Open By appointment
Fairs Decorative Antique and Textile Fair, Olympia

Beckwith and Son
Contact Mr G Gray
✉ **St Nicholas Hall, St Andrew Street, Hertford, Hertfordshire, SG14 1HZ** P
☎ 01992 582079
E sales@beckwithandsonantiques.co.uk
W www.beckwithandsonantiques.co.uk
Est. 1903 *Stock size* Large
Stock 17thC–1930s mahogany, pine, oak furniture, silver, glass, pictures, metalware, general antiques, clocks
Open Mon–Sat 9am–5.30pm
Services Restoration, valuations

Gillmark Map Gallery
Contact Mr Mark Pretlove
✉ **25 Parliament Square, Hertford, Hertfordshire, SG14 1EX** P
☎ 01992 534444 F 01992 554734
E gillmark@btinternet.com
W www.gillmark.com
Est. 1997 *Stock size* Large
Stock Antique maps, prints, second-hand books
Open Tues–Sat 10am–5pm half day Thurs
Services Restoration, conservation, framing, hand-colouring

Hertford Antiques
Contact Mr S Garratt
✉ **51 St Andrew Street, Hertford, Hertfordshire, SG14 1HZ** P
☎ 01992 589776
E simon@hertfordantiques.fsnet.co.uk
W www.hertfordantiques.co.uk
Est. 1994 *Stock size* Large
No. of dealers 60
Stock Period furniture, porcelain, silver, prints, pictures, jewellery
Open Mon–Sat 10am–5.30pm Sun 11am–4.30pm

Tapestry Antiques
Contact Mrs P Stokes
✉ **27 St Andrew Street, Hertford, Hertfordshire, SG14 1HZ** P
☎ 01992 587438
E pjstokes27@yahoo.com
Est. 1974 *Stock size* Large
Stock General 18th–19thC

furniture, brass, copper, porcelain, Staffordshire figures, lighting, mirrors
Open Mon–Sat 10am–5pm
Services Valuations for probate

HITCHIN

⊞ The Book Bug
Contact Mrs S Jevon
✉ **1 The Arcade, Hitchin, Hertfordshire, SG5 1ED** Ⓟ
☎ 01462 431309
Est. 1984 *Stock size* Large
Stock General second-hand and antiquarian books
Open Mon–Sat 9am–5pm closed Wed

⊞ Michael Gander
Contact Mr M Gander
✉ **10 & 11 Bridge Street, Hitchin, Hertfordshire, SG5 2DE** Ⓟ
☎ 01462 432678
Ⓜ 07885 728976
Est. 1974 *Stock size* Medium
Stock Period furniture, small items
Open Wed Thurs Sat 9am–5pm or by appointment

⊞ Eric T Moore
Contact John Leeson
✉ **24 Bridge Street, Hitchin, Hertfordshire, SG5 2DF** Ⓟ
☎ 01462 450497
Ⓔ booksales@erictmoore.co.uk
Ⓦ www.erictmoore.co.uk
Est. 1965 *Stock size* Large
Stock General, second-hand, antiquarian books, maps, loose prints
Open Mon–Sat 8.30am–6pm Sun 11am–5pm

⊞ Phillips of Hitchin Antiques Ltd (BADA)
Contact Mr J Phillips
✉ **The Manor House, 26 Bancroft, Hitchin, Hertfordshire, SG5 1JW** Ⓟ
☎ 01462 432067 Ⓕ 01462 441368
Est. 1884 *Stock size* Medium
Stock English furniture, 1730–1830, unusual items such as campaign furniture, new and out-of-print reference books on antique furniture
Open Mon–Fri 9am–5.30pm

LEAVESDEN

⊞ Peter Taylor and Son
Contact Mr P Taylor
✉ **1 Ganders Ash, Leavesden, Watford, Hertfordshire, WD25 7HE** Ⓟ
☎ 01923 663325
Ⓔ taylorbooks@clara.co.uk
Est. 1973 *Stock size* Medium
Stock Tudor and medieval history antique books, documents
Open Catalogue order
Services Valuations

LETCHWORTH GARDEN CITY

⊞ The Barn Antiques
Contact Mr or Mrs Ryde
✉ **27 The Wynd, Letchworth Garden City, Hertfordshire, SG6 3EL** Ⓟ
☎ 01462 678459
Est. 1997 *Stock size* Large
Stock Victorian–1940s hardwood furniture, china, Doulton, Beatrix Potter, Toby jugs, model boats
Open Mon Thurs–Sat 10am–5pm
Services Valuations, house clearance

⊞ Past & Present
Contact Paul Lawrence
✉ **18 Openshore Way, Letchworth Garden City, Hertfordshire, SG6 3ER** Ⓟ
☎ 01462 485117
Ⓜ 07976 426704
Est. 1998 *Stock size* Medium
Stock Antiques, collectables
Open Mon–Sat 9.45am–5pm closed Wed
Fairs Newark, Swinderby
Services Valuations

PUCKERIDGE

⊞ St Ouen Antiques
Contact Jonathan Blake or Timothy Blake
✉ **The Vintage Corner, Old Cambridge Road, Puckeridge, Ware, Hertfordshire, SG11 1SA** Ⓟ
☎ 01920 821336 Ⓕ 01920 822506
Est. 1967 *Stock size* Large
Stock 18thC English furniture
Open Mon–Sat 9.30am–5pm
Services Valuations, restoration

REDBOURN

⊞ Bushwood Antiques (LAPADA, CINOA)
Contact Mr A Bush
✉ **Stags End Equestrian Centre, Gaddesden Lane, Redbourn, Hemel Hempstead, Hertfordshire, HP2 6HN** Ⓟ
☎ 01582 794700
Ⓔ antiques@bushwood.co.uk
Ⓦ www.bushwood.co.uk
Est. 1967 *Stock size* Large
Stock 18th–19thC English and Continental furniture, accessories, objets d'art
Open Mon–Fri 8.30am–4pm Sat 10am–4pm

⊞ J N Antiques
Contact Mrs J Brunning
✉ **86 High Street, Redbourn, St Albans, Hertfordshire, AL3 7BD** Ⓟ
☎ 01582 793603
Est. 1974 *Stock size* Large
Stock General antiques
Open Mon–Sat 9am–6am
Services Valuations

⊞ Tim Wharton (LAPADA)
Contact Mr T Wharton
✉ **24 High Street, Redbourn, St Albans, Hertfordshire, AL3 7LL** Ⓟ
☎ 01582 794371
Ⓜ 07850 622880
Ⓔ tim@timwhartonantiques.co.uk
Est. 1973 *Stock size* Large
Stock 17th–19thC oak, country furniture, some period mahogany, metalware, treen, country pictures
Open Tues Wed Fri 10am–5pm Sat 10am–4pm Thurs by appointment
Fairs LAPADA (Birmingham), Olympia

RICKMANSWORTH

⊞ Country House Antiques
Contact Jane
✉ **251 Uxbridge Road, Rickmansworth, Hertfordshire, WD3 2DP** Ⓟ
☎ 01923 712666 Ⓕ 01923 712666
Ⓔ countryhouse@waitrose.com
Est. 1980 *Stock size* Medium
Stock Country furniture, mainly

pine, cast-iron fireplaces
Open Mon–Sat 10am–5pm
Fairs Newark

ROYSTON

Ronald Gill Antiques
Contact Ronnie Gill
The Grain Barn, Road Farm, Wendy, Royston, Hertfordshire, SG8 0AA
01223 208332
01223 207735
ronald.gill@btinternet.com
Est. 1996 *Stock size* Medium
Stock Country pine and oak furniture
Open Tues–Sun 10am–5pm

Lovers of Blue and White
Contact Andrew Pye
Steeple Morden, Royston, Hertfordshire, SG8 0RN
01763 853800 01763 853700
china@blueandwhite.com
www.blueandwhite.com
Est. 1995 *Stock size* Large
Stock British transfer ware 1780–present
Open By appointment
Services Valuations, identification, mail order

SAWBRIDGE

Acorn Antiques & Collectors Centre
Contact Shirley Rowley
The Maltings, Station Road, Sawbridge, Hertfordshire, CM21 9JX
01279 722012
Est. 1993 *Stock size* Large
No. of dealers 80
Stock Antiques, collectables
Open Mon–Fri 10am–5pm
Sat Sun 10.30am–5.30pm
Services Valuations

SAWBRIDGEWORTH

Arcane Antiques Centre (EADA)
Contact Mr Nigel Hoy or Miss Nicola Smith
The Maltings, Station Road, Sawbridgeworth, Hertfordshire, CM21 9JX
01279 600562
07957 551899
nicola@charnwoodantiques.co.uk
Est. 1999 *Stock size* Large
No. of dealers 25
Stock Oriental and European ceramics, 18thC glasses, silver, oils, watercolours, prints, jewellery, Georgian–Edwardian furniture, longcase and other clocks
Open Tues–Fri 10am–5pm
Sat Sun 11am–5pm
Services Antique furniture restoration, cabinet-making, upholstery, cabinet-lining, French polishing, glass repair, picture framing

The Herts & Essex Antique Centre
Contact Robert Sklar
The Maltings, Station Road, Sawbridgeworth, Hertfordshire, CM21 9JX
01279 722044 01279 725445
07710 057750
webmaster@antiques-of-britain.co.uk
www.antiques-of-britain.co.uk
Est. 1981 *Stock size* Large
No. of dealers 120
Stock Furniture, jewellery, silver china
Open Mon–Fri 10am–5pm
Sat Sun 10.30am–5.30pm
Services Tea room

Riverside Antiques Centre
Contact Mr J Maynard
Unit 1, The Maltings, Station Road, Sawbridgeworth, Hertfordshire, CM21 9JX
01279 600985
Est. 1998 *Stock size* Large
No. of dealers 300
Stock Probably the largest antiques centre in Hertfordshire and Essex. Antiques, collectables, furniture, etc
Open Mon–Sun 10am–5pm
Services Restoration and repair of furniture, glass, ceramics

ST ALBANS

James of St Albans
Contact Stephen James
11 George Street, St Albans, Hertfordshire, AL3 4ER
01727 856996
Est. 1956 *Stock size* Small
Stock Victorian–Edwardian furniture, collectables
Open Mon–Sat 10am–5pm
Thurs 10am–4pm

Magic Lanterns
Contact J A Marsden
By George, 23 George Street, St Albans, Hertfordshire, AL3 4ES
01727 865680
Est. 1987 *Stock size* Large
Stock 1800–1950 antique lighting, mirrors, jewellery
Open Mon–Fri 10am–5pm
Sat 10am–5.30pm Sun 1–5pm
Services Lighting consultancy for period houses

Paton Books
Contact Richard Child
34 Holywell Hill, St Albans, Hertfordshire, AL1 1DE
01727 853984 01727 865764
patonbooks@aol.com
www.patonbooks.co.uk
Est. 1962 *Stock size* Large
Stock General secondhand and antiquarian books, specializing in history, military history, transport, art and craft, travel
Open Mon–Sat 9am–6pm
Sun 10am–6pm

Reg & Philip Remington (ABA)
Contact Mr R Remington
23 Homewood Road, St Albans, Hertfordshire, AL1 4BG
01727 893531 01727 893532
philip@remingtonbooks.com
www.remingtonbooks.com
Est. 1979 *Stock size* Medium
Stock Antiquarian, rare, second-hand books, voyages, travel books a speciality
Open By appointment
Fairs Olympia

TRING

John Bly (BADA)
Contact Mr Perris
The Old Billiards Room, Church Yard, Tring, Hertfordshire, HP23 5AG
01442 890802
Est. 1891 *Stock size* Large
Stock Georgian furniture, porcelain, silver, glass, other quality antiques

Open Tues–Sat 10am–4pm
Fairs Grosvenor House, Florida
Services Valuations, restoration

Country Clocks
Contact Mr Terry Cartmell
3 Pendley Bridge Cottages, Tring Station, Tring, Hertfordshire, HP23 5QU P
☎ 01442 825090
Est. 1976 *Stock size* Medium
Stock 18th–19thC wall, longcase, mantel clocks
Open Mon–Fri by appointment Sat 9am–5pm Sun 2–5pm
Services Valuations, restoration, repairs

Farrelly Antiques
Contact Mr Paul Farrelly
The Long Room, Courtyard, Churchyard, Tring, Hertfordshire, HP23 5AE P
☎ 01442 891905
Est. 1979 *Stock size* Medium
Stock Antique furniture up to 1900
Open Mon–Sat 10am–5pm
Services Restoration

New England House Antiques
Contact Mr S Munjee
50 High Street, Tring, Hertfordshire, HP23 5AG P
☎ 01442 827262 F 01442 827262
M 07711 224422
E enquiries@newenglandhouseantiques.co.uk
W www.newenglandhouseantiques.co.uk
Est. 1992 *Stock size* Large
Stock Georgian–Victorian furniture, silver, glass, paintings, clocks, table lamps
Open Tues–Sat 10.30am–5pm
Services Restoration, free search and find for furniture

TRINGFORD

Piggeries Pine
Contact Paul Brown
Tringford Road, Tringford, Hertfordshire, HP23 4LH P
☎ 01442 827961
Est. 1987 *Stock size* Large
Stock Pine furniture, kitchens
Open Mon–Sun 10am–5pm
Services Stripping

WARE

Amwell Auctions
Contact Marian Haldane
The Function Room, Hertford Rugby Football Club, Ware, Hertfordshire
☎ 01920 871901 F 01920 871901
M 07765 446976
Est. 1999
Open Mon–Fri 9am–7pm Sat 9am–1pm
Sales General antiques
Frequency Monthly
Catalogues Yes

Ware Militaria Auctions
Contact Martin Greenfield
The Function Room, Hertford Rugby Football Club, Ware, Hertfordshire
☎ 01920 871383 F 01920 871901
M 07747 860746
E martin@ware-militaria-auction.com
W www.ware-militaria-auction.com
Est. 1999
Open Mon–Fri 9am–7pm Sat 9am–1pm
Sales Militaria
Frequency Bi-monthly
Catalogues Yes

WATFORD

Cards Inc
Contact Mr P Freedman
Unit 9, Woodshots Meadow, Croxley Business Park, Watford, Hertfordshire, WD1 8YU P
☎ 01923 200138 F 01923 200134
E paul@cardsinc.com
W www.cardsinc.com
Est. 1987 *Stock size* Small
Stock Collectable trading cards
Open By appointment

Collectors Corner
Contact Mr L Dronkes
Charter Place, Watford Market, Watford, Hertfordshire, WD1 2RN P
☎ 01923 248855 or 020 8904 0552
Est. 1968 *Stock size* Small
Stock Coins, medals, bank notes, cigarette cards, small collectables
Open Tues Fri Sat 10am–5pm
Services Valuations, medal mounting

The Pine Furniture Store
Contact Ben
304a High Street, Watford, Hertfordshire, WD12JE P
☎ 01923 441604
Est. 1980 *Stock size* Large
Stock Eastern European, English pine furniture, pine and iron beds, mirrors, cast-iron fireplaces
Open Mon–Sat 10am–5pm or by appointment
Fairs Newark, Ardingly
Services Stripping

Quicktest
Contact Raffi Katz
PO Box 180, Watford, Hertfordshire, WD18 8PH P
☎ 01923 220206
M 07976 831953
E info@quicktest.co.uk
W www.quicktest.co.uk
Est. 1986 *Stock size* Large
Stock Testers, magnifiers, weighing machines, jewellery boxes, hand tools
Open Visitors welcome by appointment, map and directions on web site
Fairs Newark, Alexandra Palace, Ardingly, Kempton, Shepton, Birmingham, Sandown

WHEATHAMPSTEAD

Collins Antiques
Contact Mr Michael Collins
Corner House, Church Street, Wheathampstead, Hertfordshire, AL4 8AP P
☎ 01582 833111
Est. 1907 *Stock size* Medium
Stock 17th–19thC furniture, including oak and mahogany tables, chairs, chests-of-drawers
Open Mon–Sat 9am–1pm 2–5pm
Services Valuations

The Old Bakery Antiques Ltd
Contact Mr Maurice Shifrin
3 Station Road, Wheathampstead, Hertfordshire, AL4 8BU P
☎ 01582 831999 F 01582 831555
Est. 1997 *Stock size* Large
Stock Mainly Victorian–Edwardian furniture, Oriental carpets

Open Mon–Sun 10am–5pm closed Wed
Fairs Newark, Ardingly

Thomas Thorp (ABA, PBFA)
Contact Mr Jim Thorp
64 Lancaster Road, St Albans, Hertfordshire, AL1 4ET P
☎ 01727 864778 F 01727 864778
E thorpbooks@compuserve.com
Est. 1883 *Stock size* Small
Stock General antiquarian books, specializing in early printed English history, literature, modern, private press editions
Open By appointment
Fairs Olympia (Jun), Chelsea (Nov)

OXFORDSHIRE

ASCOTT-UNDER-WYCHWOOD

William Antiques
Contact Mr R Gripper
Manor Barn, Manor Farm, Ascott-under-Wychwood, Chipping Norton, Oxfordshire, OX7 6AL P
☎ 01993 831960 F 01993 830395
E robgripper@aol.com
Est. 1982 *Stock size* Medium
Stock Good-quality decorative antiques, Georgian–Victorian furniture
Open Mon–Fri 9am–5pm Sat pm by appointment
Services Restoration

BANBURY

Banbury Antiques Centre
Contact Veronica Hammond
18 Southam Road, Banbury, Oxfordshire, OX16 2EG P
☎ 01295 267800
M 07968 870019
Est. 2003 *Stock size* Large
No. of dealers 40
Stock Clocks, furniture including pine, collectables, gardening antiques, silver, china, pictures, glass, linen
Open Mon–Sat 10am–5pm Sun 11am–4pm
Services Valuations

Blender Antiques
Contact Patsy Irana
Cotefield Farm, Bodicote, Banbury, Oxfordshire, OX15 4AQ P
☎ 01295 254754
M 07969 922531
E blenderantiques@btopenworld.com
Est. 2003 *Stock size* Medium
Stock 18th–19thC Continental furniture
Open Mon–Sat 10am–5pm

Bonhams
48 North Bar, Banbury, Oxfordshire, OX16 0TH
☎ 01295 272723 F 01295 272726
E banbury@bonhams.com
W www.bonhams.com
Open Mon–Fri 9am–5.30pm
Sales Regional Saleroom. Frequent sales. Regular house and attic sales across the country; contact London offices for further details. Free auction valuations; insurance and probate valuations

Comic Connections
Contact Mr Glyn Smith
4a Parsons Street, Banbury, Oxfordshire, OX16 5LW
☎ 01295 268989 F 01295 268989
Est. 1994 *Stock size* Large
Stock American comic books, graphic novels, action figures, science-fiction items
Open Mon–Fri 10.30am–5pm Sat 9.30am–5pm
Fairs D and J Fair, NEC
Services Standing order for comics, magazines, videos

Holloways (LAPADA)
Contact Mr Tim Holloway
49 Parsons Street, Banbury, Oxfordshire, OX16 5PF P
☎ 01295 817777 F 01295 817701
E enquiries@hollowaysauctioneers.co.uk
W www.hollowaysauctioneers.co.uk
Open Mon–Fri 9am–5.30pm Sat 9am–noon
Sales Fortnightly general sales Tues 11am, viewing Mon 9am–7pm Sat 9am–noon. Every 2 months specialist sales Tues 11am, viewing Fri 9am–5pm Sat 9am–noon Mon 9am–7pm Tues 9am–5pm and day of sale
Catalogues No

BICESTER

R A Barnes Antiques (LAPADA)
Contact John Langin
PO Box 82, Bicester, Oxfordshire, OX25 1RA P
☎ 01844 237388
E AngeloUno2@aol.com
Est. 1970 *Stock size* Medium
Stock Continental glass, English and Continental porcelain, Art Nouveau, paintings, English metalware, 18th–19thC brass, Belleek, Wedgwood
Open By appointment
Fairs NEC, Little Chelsea
Services Valuations

Lisseters Antiques
Contact Mr M Lisseter
3 Kings End, Bicester, Oxfordshire, OX6 7DR P
☎ 01869 252402
M 07801 667848
Est. 1959 *Stock size* Large
Stock Antiques, used furniture
Open Mon–Sat 9am–5pm

Mallams (SOFAA)
Contact C Turner
Pevensey House, 27 Sheep Street, Bicester, Oxfordshire, OX26 6JF P
☎ 01869 252901 F 01869 320283
E bicester@mallams.co.uk
W www.mallams.co.uk/fineart
Est. 1788
Open Mon–Fri 9am–5pm Sat 9am–1pm on viewing days only
Sales General antiques sale Mon 11am, viewing Fri 9am–5pm Sat 9am–1pm morning of sale 9–11am. Valuations service
Frequency 16 per year
Catalogues Yes

Serendepity
Contact Mr A J Slade
22 Wesley Lane, Bicester, Oxfordshire, OX6 7JW P
☎ 01869 322533
Est. 1993 *Stock size* Large
Stock New, old, collectable teddy bears, dolls
Open Mon Thurs–Sat 9am–5pm
Fairs NEC, Donnington Park
Services Bear, doll restoration

BLEWBURY

Blewbury Antiques
Contact E Richardson
London Road, Blewbury,

Didcot, Oxfordshire,
OX11 9NX 🅿
☎ 01235 850366
Est. 1970 *Stock size* Medium
Stock General, furniture, garden ornaments, books, glass, china, clocks
Open Mon–Sun 10am–6pm closed Tues Wed

BLOXHAM

⊞ Antiques of Bloxham
Contact Mr S Robinson
✉ **Church Street, Bloxham, Banbury, Oxfordshire, OX15 4ET** 🅿
☎ 01295 721641
Est. 1996 *Stock size* Large
Stock General antiques
Open Wed–Sat 11am–4.30pm Sun noon–4.30pm
Services Delivery, clock repairs

BODICOTE

J S Auctions
Contact Joseph Smith
✉ **Cotefield Farm Saleroom, Oxford Road, Bodicote, Banbury, Oxfordshire, OX15 4EQ** 🅿
☎ 01295 272488
Ⓜ 07775 848982
Ⓔ joesmith@jsauctions.co.uk
Ⓦ www.jsauctions.co.uk
Est. 1994
Open Mon–Sat 9am–5pm
Sales Fortnightly general antiques sale Sat 10am, viewing Fri 9am–7pm. Two special sales a year
Frequency Fortnightly
Catalogues Yes

BURFORD

Antiques @ The George
Contact Coral Oswald
✉ **104 High Street, Burford, Oxfordshire, OX18 4QJ** 🅿
☎ 01993 823319
Est. 1992 *Stock size* Large
No. of dealers 23
Stock China, glass, furniture, treen, books, pictures, rugs, carpets
Open Mon–Sat 10am–5pm Sun noon–5pm

⊞ Burford Antiques Centre
Contact Mr G Viventi
✉ **The Roundabout, Cheltenham Road, Burford, Oxfordshire, OX18 4JA** 🅿
☎ 01993 823227
Est. 1988 *Stock size* Large
Stock General antiques, 1930s–modern, period reproduction furniture
Open Mon–Sat 10am–6pm Sun noon–5pm

⊞ Bygones
Contact Mrs Jenkins
✉ **29 Lower High Street, Burford, Oxfordshire, OX18 4RN** 🅿
☎ 01993 823588 Ⓕ 01993 704338
Ⓔ sale@bygones-of-burford.co.uk
Ⓦ www.bygones-of-burford.co.uk
Est. 1986 *Stock size* Medium
Stock General collectables, curios
Open Mon–Sat 10am–1pm 2–5pm Sun noon–5pm

⊞ Jonathan Fyson Antiques (CADA)
Contact Mr J Fyson
✉ **50–52 High Street, Burford, Oxfordshire, OX18 4QF**
☎ 01993 823204 Ⓕ 01993 823204
Ⓔ j@fyson.co.uk
Est. 1971 *Stock size* Large
Stock English and Continental furniture, brass, lighting, fireplaces, accessories, club fenders, papier mâché, tôle, treen, porcelain, glass, prints, jewellery
Open Mon–Fri 9.30am–5.30pm closed 1–2pm Sat 10am–5.30pm closed 1–2pm
Services Valuations

⊞ Gateway Antiques (CADA)
Contact Mr Paul Brown or Mr Michael Ford
✉ **Cheltenham Road, Burford Roundabout, Burford, Oxfordshire, OX18 4JA** 🅿
☎ 01993 823678 Ⓕ 01993 823857
Ⓔ enquiries@gatewayantiques.com
Ⓦ www.gatewayantiques.co.uk
Est. 1985 *Stock size* Large
Stock 17th–20thC furniture, farmhouse furniture, Arts and Crafts, decorative objects, accessories
Open Mon–Sat 10am–5.30pm Sun 2–5pm
Services Shipping worldwide, multi-lingual courier service and driver, accommodation, storage, stock on website

⊞ Horseshoe Antiques
Contact Mr B Evans
✉ **97 High Street, Burford, Oxfordshire, OX18 4QA** 🅿
☎ 01993 823244
Ⓜ 07711 525383
Est. 1979 *Stock size* Medium
Stock 17th–18thC furniture, oil paintings, copper, brass, horse brasses, clocks, longcase clocks
Open Mon–Sat 9.30am–5pm

⊞ David Pickup (BADA, CADA)
Contact Mr D Pickup
✉ **115 High Street, Burford, Oxfordshire, OX18 4RG** 🅿
☎ 01993 822555
Est. 1980 *Stock size* Medium
Stock Fine English furniture, emphasis on the Cotswold Arts and Crafts movement early 20thC
Open Mon–Fri 9.30am–5.30pm Sat 10.30am–4.30pm
Fairs Olympia (Spring, Nov)

⊞ Saracen Antiques Ltd
Contact Mr C Mills
✉ **Upton Downs Farm, Burford, Oxfordshire, OX18 4LY** 🅿
☎ 01993 822987
Ⓔ cmills6702@aol.com
Est. 1996 *Stock size* Large
Stock Predominantly 18th–19thC English furniture
Open Mon–Sat 9am–5.30pm
Services Restoration

⊞ Manfred Schotten Antiques (CADA, BACA Award Winner 2002)
✉ **109 High Street, Burford, Oxfordshire, OX18 4RG** 🅿
☎ 01993 822302 Ⓕ 01993 822055
Ⓔ antiques@schotten.com
Ⓦ www.schotten.com
Est. 1976 *Stock size* Large
Stock Sporting antiques, prints, library furniture, leather furniture
Open Mon–Sat 9.30am–5.30pm
Fairs Olympia
Services Exhibition held in Oct every year

Swan Gallery Antiques (CADA)
Contact Mr D Pratt
127 High Street, Burford, Oxfordshire, OX18 4RE P
☎ 01993 822244 Ⓕ 01993 822244
Est. 1977 *Stock size* Large
Stock Early oak and period furniture
Open Mon–Sat 10am–5.30pm

CHALGROVE

Hitchcox's Antiques
Contact Rupert Hitchcox
The Garth, Warpsgrove, Chalgrove, Oxford, Oxfordshire, OX44 7RW P
☎ 01865 890241 Ⓕ 01865 890241
Ⓜ 07710 561505
Ⓔ rupertsantiques@aol.com
Ⓦ www.ruperthitchcoxantiques.co.uk
Est. 1957 *Stock size* Large
Stock 1650–1950 mainly English furniture
Open Tues–Sat 10am–5pm or by appointment
Services Valuations, buys at auction

CHARNEY BASSETT

Brian Davis Antiques
Contact Mr B Davis
Goosey Wick Farm, Goosey Wick, Charney Bassett, Wantage, Oxfordshire, OX12 0EY P
☎ 01367 718933
Est. 1981 *Stock size* Large
Stock English and Continental period pine
Open Tues–Sat 9am–5.30pm

CHILTON

Country Markets Antiques & Collectables
Contact Mr G Vaughan
Wyevale Garden Centre, Newbury Road, Chilton, Didcot, Oxfordshire, OX11 0QN P
☎ 01235 835125 Ⓕ 01235 833068
Ⓔ country.markets.antiques@breathemail.net
Ⓦ www.countrymarkets.co.uk
Est. 1989 *Stock size* Large
No. of dealers 35
Stock Furniture, glass, jewellery, cased fish, porcelain, ceramics etc
Open Mon 10.30am–5pm Tues–Sat 10am–5.30pm Sun Bank Holidays 10.30am–4.30pm
Services Valuations, restoration

CHINNOR

Number 6
Contact Pam Lievesley
6 Thame Road, Chinnor, Oxfordshire, OX9 4QS P
☎ 01844 354344
Est. 1994 *Stock size* Small
Stock Antiques, decorative items
Open Mon–Sun 10am–5pm

CHIPPING NORTON

Antique English Windsor Chairs (BADA, CINOA, CADA)
Contact Michael Harding-Hill
9 Horse Fair, Chipping Norton, Oxfordshire, OX7 5AL P
☎ 01608 643322 Ⓕ 01608 644322
Ⓜ 07798 653134
Ⓔ michael@antique-english-windsor-chairs.com
Ⓦ www.antique-english-windsor-chairs.com
Est. 1971 *Stock size* Large
Stock Antique English Windsor chairs 18th–19thC, sets, singles for collectors and everyday use.
Open 10am–5pm Wed–Sat or by appointment
Fairs Olympia (June, Nov)

Chipping Norton Antique Centre
Contact Michael Mence
Ivy House, Middle Row, Chipping Norton, Oxfordshire, OX7 5NH P
☎ 01608 644212 Ⓕ 01608 641369
Est. 1986 *Stock size* Large
No. of dealers 15
Stock General antiques, collectables, Georgian–Edwardian furniture, china, silver, kitchenware
Open 10am–5.30pm Mon–Sun
Services Tea room

Cotswold Home & Garden
Contact Chris Holroyd
14 New Street, Chipping Norton, Oxfordshire, OX7 5LJ P
☎ 01608 644084
Ⓜ 07770 904036
Ⓦ kate@chippingnorton.fsworld.co.uk
Est. 1999 *Stock size* Medium
Stock Gardening antiques, eclectic taste, benches, arches, urns, gazebos, statuary – designer-led
Open Mon–Sat 10am–5pm most Sun 10am–5pm closed Tues

Georgian House Antiques (LAPADA)
Contact Sheila Wissinger
21 West Street, Chipping Norton, Oxfordshire, OX7 5EU P
☎ 01608 641369 Ⓕ 01608 641369
Stock size Large
Stock Period oak, mahogany, walnut furniture, paintings, chairs, farmhouse furniture
Open Mon–Sun 10am–5pm or by appointment
Services Delivery, shipping arranged

Kellow Books
Contact Mr P Combellack
6 Market Place, Chipping Norton, Oxfordshire, OX7 5NA P
☎ 01608 644293
Est. 1998 *Stock size* Medium
Stock Antiquarian, rare, second-hand collectable books
Open Mon–Sat 10am–4.30pm
Services Book search

Key Antiques
Contact Jane Riley
11 Horsefair, Chipping Norton, Oxfordshire, OX7 5AL P
☎ 01608 643777
Ⓜ 07860 650112
Est. 1972 *Stock size* Medium
Stock Period oak, country furniture, related objects of 17th–18thC
Open Wed–Sat 10am–5.30pm
Services Valuations of period oak and associated items

Manchester House Antique Centre
Contact Mrs Shepherd
Manchester House, 5 Market Place, Chipping Norton, Oxfordshire, OX7 5NA
☎ 01608 646412
Ⓦ www.chippingnorton.net
Est. 1997 *Stock size* Medium
No. of dealers 5

Stock Pine, oak furniture, kitchenware, china, upholstered chairs
Open Mon–Sun 10am–5pm

Number 20
Contact Chris Holroyd
20 New Street, Chipping Norton, Oxfordshire, OX7 5LJ P
☎ 01608 644084
Ⓜ 07770 904036
Ⓦ kate@chippingnorton.fsworld.co.uk
Est. 1999 *Stock size* Medium
Stock Gardening antiques, eclectic taste, chandeliers, benches, lighting – designer-led – painted furniture
Open Mon–Sat 10am–5pm most Sun 10am–5pm closed Tues

The Quiet Woman Antiques Centre
Contact Ann Marriott
Southcombe, Chipping Norton, Oxfordshire, OX7 5QH P
☎ 01608 646262 Ⓕ 01608 646262
Ⓜ 07860 889524
Est. 1998 *Stock size* Medium
No. of dealers 20
Stock Furniture, china, general antiques, gardening antiques, architectural
Open Mon–Fri 10am–6pm Sat 10am–5.30pm Sun 10am–5pm
Services Coffee shop

Station Mill Antiques Centre
Contact Jo Piperakis
Station Road, Chipping Norton, Oxfordshire, OX7 5HX P
☎ 01608 644563 Ⓕ 07092 310632
Ⓔ TL@stationmill.com
Ⓦ www.stationmill.com
Est. 1996 *Stock size* Large
No. of dealers 70
Stock Complete range of antiques, collectables
Open Mon–Sun 10am–5pm
Services Tea room

CHURCHILL

Clive Payne (LAPADA, BAFRA)
Contact Clive Payne
Unit 4, Mount Farm, Junction Road, Churchill, Chipping Norton, Oxfordshire, OX7 6NP P
☎ 01608 658856 Ⓕ 01608 658856
Ⓜ 07764 476776
Ⓔ clive.payne@virgin.net
Ⓦ www.clivepayne.com
Est. 1986 *Stock size* Medium
Stock 17thC–early Victorian furniture, Mason's Ironstone china
Open Mon–Fri 9am–5pm
Services Antique furniture restoration

CLEVELEY

A and E Foster Ltd (BADA, CINOA)
Contact Stephen Foster
The Old Chapel, Cleveley, Oxfordshire, OX7 4DX P
☎ 01608 678731 Ⓕ 01608 678731
Ⓜ 07802 895146
Ⓔ foster436@aol.com
Est. 1970 *Stock size* Medium
Stock European works of art and sculpture
Open By appointment
Fairs Grosvenor House, Spring and Winter Olympia

DEDDINGTON

Castle Antiques Ltd (LAPADA)
Contact John and Judy Vaughan
Manor Farm, Clifton, Deddington, Oxfordshire, OX15 0PA P
☎ 01869 338688
Est. 1972 *Stock size* Large
Stock General antiques, furniture, metalware, silver, reproduction garden furniture
Open By appointment

Deddington Antique Centre (TVADA)
Contact Mrs Brenda Haller
Laurel House, Bullring, Deddington, Banbury, Oxfordshire, OX15 0TT P
☎ 01869 338968 Ⓕ 01869 338916
Ⓔ deddingtonantiquecentre@yahoo.co.uk
Est. 1977 *Stock size* Large
No. of dealers 20
Stock Period furniture, silver, porcelain, oil and watercolours, jewellery, clocks, linen, glass
Open Mon–Sat 10am–5pm Sun 11am–5pm
Services Porcelain, silver and jewellery repairs, glass exports

DORCHESTER

Dorchester Antiques (TVADA, LAPADA)
Contact Mrs S or Jonty Hearnden
The Barn, 3 High Street, Dorchester, Oxfordshire, OX10 7HH P
☎ 01865 341373 Ⓕ 01865 341373
Est. 1992
Stock Georgian furniture, interesting country pieces
Open Tues–Sat 10am–5pm
Fairs TVADA
Services Finding service

Hallidays (Fine Antiques) Ltd (LAPADA, CINOA, TVADA)
Contact Mr E M Reily Collins
High Street, Dorchester, Oxfordshire, OX10 7HL P
☎ 01865 340028 Ⓕ 01865 341149
Ⓔ antiques@hallidays.com
Ⓦ www.hallidays.com
Est. 1942 *Stock size* Large
Stock 17th–19thC English furniture, decorative items, paintings
Open Mon–Fri 9am–5pm Sat 10am–4pm
Fairs Olympia, LAPADA (Jan)
Services Shipping

EAST HAGBOURNE

Craig Barfoot Clocks
Contact Craig Barfoot
Tudor House, East Hagbourne, Oxfordshire, OX11 9LR P
☎ 01235 818968 Ⓕ 01235 818968
Ⓜ 07710 858158
Ⓔ craig.barfoot@tiscali.co.uk
Est. 1991 *Stock size* Medium
Stock Longcase, organ, musical clocks
Open By appointment
Services Restoration, buys at auction

E M Lawson and Co (ABA, ILAB)
Contact Mr J Lawson
Kingsholm, Main Road, East Hagbourne, Didcot, Oxfordshire, OX11 9LN P
☎ 01235 812033
Est. 1919 *Stock size* Small
Stock Rare and antiquarian books, early English literature,

science, medicine, economics, travel
Open Mon–Fri 9am–6pm or by appointment

FARINGDON

Brushwood Antiques (TVADA)
Contact Nathan Sherriff
29 Marlborough Street, Faringdon, Oxfordshire, SN7 7JL
01367 244269
nathan@brushwoodantiques.com
www.brushwoodantiques.com
Est. 1992 *Stock size* Medium
Stock 18th–19thC furniture
Open Tues–Sat 10am–5pm appointment advisable
Fairs TVADA
Services Furniture restoration

HENLEY-ON-THAMES

Bonhams
The Coach House, 66 Northfield End, Henley-on-Thames, Oxfordshire, RG9 2JN
01491 413636 01494 413637
henley@bonhams.com
www.bonhams.com
Open Mon Fri 9am–5pm 1st Sat of month 10am–1pm
Sales Regional office. Regular house and attic sales across the country; contact London offices for further details. Free auction valuations; insurance and probate valuations

The Country Seat (TVADA, LAPADA, BACA Award Winner 2003)
Contact William Clegg
Huntercombe Manor Barn, Henley-on-Thames, Oxfordshire, RG9 5RY
01491 641349 01491 641533
ferryandclegg@thecountryseat.com
www.thecountryseat.com
Est. 1971 *Stock size* Large
Stock Furniture designed by architects 17th–20thC, post-war furniture, art pottery, metalwork, Whitefriars glass
Open Mon–Fri 9am–5pm Sat 10am–5pm
Fairs TVADA

The Ferret (Friday Street Antiques Centre)
Contact Mrs D Etherington
4 Friday Street, Henley-on-Thames, Oxfordshire, RG9 1AH
01491 574104 01491 641039
Est. 1984 *Stock size* Medium
No. of dealers 6
Stock Silver, furniture, china, books, collectables, musical instruments, stylized animals
Open Mon–Sat 10am–5.30pm Sun noon–5.30pm

Henley Antique Centre
Contact Mr D Shepherd
2–4 Reading Road, Henley-on-Thames, Oxfordshire, RG9 1AG
01491 411468
Est. 1999 *Stock size* Large
No. of dealers 54
Stock Furniture, glass, china, silver, coins, scientific instruments, tools
Open Mon–Sat 10am–5.30pm Sun noon–5.30pm

Jonkers (ABA, PBFA)
Contact Sam Jonkers
24 Hart Street, Henley-on-Thames, Oxfordshire, RG9 2AU
01491 576427 01491 573805
info@jonkers.co.uk
www.jonkers.co.uk
Est. 1990 *Stock size* Medium
Stock Antiquarian literature, 19th–20thC first editions, illustrated and children's books
Open Mon–Sat 10am–5.30pm
Fairs Olympia

Simmons & Sons (RICS)
Contact Mr S Jones or Miss M Share
32 Bell Street, Henley-on-Thames, Oxfordshire, RG9 2BH
01491 571111 01491 579833
auctions@simmonsandsons.com
www.simmonsandsons.com
Est. 1802
Open Mon–Fri 9am–5.30pm Sat 9am–noon
Sales 8 sales of general antiques per annum, valuations
Catalogues Yes

Tudor House Antiques and Collectables
Contact Mr D Potter
49 Duke Street, Henley-on-Thames, Oxfordshire, RG9 1UR
01491 573680
07717 132913
Est. 1996 *Stock size* Large
Stock General antiques, collectables
Open Mon–Sun 10am–5pm
Services Valuations, house clearance

Ways Bookshop (ABA)
Contact Diana Cook
54b Friday Street, Henley-on-Thames, Oxfordshire, RG9 1AH
01491 576663 01491 576663
Est. 1977 *Stock size* Medium
Stock Rare and second-hand books bought and sold
Open Mon–Sat 10am–5.30pm
Services Book search, bookbinding, valuations

LONG WITTENHAM

Otter Antiques
Contact Mr P Otter
Greenbank, High Street, Long Wittenham, Oxford, Oxfordshire, OX14 4QD
01865 407396 01865 407396
www.otterantiques.co.uk
Est. 1994 *Stock size* Medium
Stock 18th–19thC boxes
Open By appointment
Services Restoration of boxes

MIDDLE ASTON

Cotswold Pine
Contact Mr Bob Prancks
The Poultry Unit, Middle Aston, Bicester, Oxfordshire, OX25 5QL
01869 340963 01869 340963
Est. 1972 *Stock size* Large
Stock General antique furniture including mahogany, oak, pine
Open Mon–Sat 9am–6pm Sun 10am–4.30pm
Services Restoration, stripping

NETTLEBED

Nettlebed Antique Merchants (TVADA)
Contact Mr W Bicknell
1 High Street, Nettlebed, Henley-on-Thames, Oxfordshire, RG9 5DA
01491 642062 01491 628811
07770 554559
willow@willowantiques.co.uk
www.nettlebedantiques.co.uk
Est. 1980 *Stock size* Large
Stock 1800–1970s from the fine to the funky, architectural, garden items
Open Mon–Sat 10am–5.30pm or by appointment
Fairs TVADA (Spring, Autumn)
Services Upholstery, restoration, finding service, copying and making furniture

NORTH ASTON

Elizabeth Harvey-Lee (BACA Award winner 2003)
Contact Elizabeth Harvey-Lee
1 West Cottages, Middle Aston Road, North Aston, Oxfordshire, OX25 5QB
01869 347164 01869 347956
north.aston@btinternet.com
www.elizabethharvey-lee.com
Est. 1989 *Stock size* Medium
Stock Old master prints, 19th–20thC artists' original etchings, wood engravings, etc
Open By appointment
Fairs London Original Print Fair, Olympia (Jun, Nov)
Services Catalogues by subscription

NORTHMOOR

Soames Country Auctioneers
Contact Gary Martin Soame
Pinnocks Farm, Northmoor, Witney, Oxfordshire, OX29 5AY
01865 300626 01865 300432
soame@msn.com
www.soamesauctioneers.co.uk
Est. 1991
Open By appointment
Sales General monthly antiques sales Sat 10.30am, viewing Thurs noon–6pm Fri 10am–8pm
Catalogues Yes

OXFORD

Antiques on High Ltd (TVADA)
Contact Mr P Lipson or Mrs S Young
85 High Street, Oxford, Oxfordshire, OX1 4BG
01865 251075
Est. 1997 *Stock size* Large
No. of dealers 38
Stock Smalls, collectables
Open Mon–Sat 10am–5pm Sun Bank Holidays 11am–5pm
Services Repairs

Barclay Antiques
Contact Mr Colin Barclay
107 Windmill Road, Headington, Oxford, Oxfordshire, OX3 7BT
01865 769551
Est. 1980 *Stock size* Large
Stock China, glass, silver, bronzes, lighting
Open Mon–Sat 10am–5.30pm closed Wed
Services Repairs to lighting

Blackwell's Rare Books (ABA, PBFA)
Contact Mr P Brown
48–51 Broad Street, Oxford, Oxfordshire, OX1 3BQ
01865 333555 01865 794143
rarebooks@blackwell.co.uk
www.rarebooks.blackwell.co.uk
Est. 1879 *Stock size* Large
Stock Modern first editions, private press books, antiquarian English literature, juvenilia, general antiquarian books
Open Mon Wed–Sat 9am–6pm Tues 9.30am–6pm
Fairs Olympia, 1 American fair per year east or west coast
Services Shipping, book search

Bonhams
39 Park End Street, Oxford, Oxfordshire, OX1 1JD
01865 723524 01865 791064
oxford@bonhams.com
www.bonhams.com
Open Mon–Fri 9am–5.30pm
Sales Regional Saleroom. Frequent sales. Regular house and attic sales across the country; contact London offices for further details. Free auction valuations; insurance and probate valuations
Catalogues Yes

Reginald Davis (Oxford) Ltd (BADA, NAG)
Contact David Marcus
34 High Street, Oxford, Oxfordshire, OX1 4AN
01865 248347
finesilverware@aol.com
Est. 1966 *Stock size* Large
Stock Jewellery, silver, old Sheffield plate
Open Tues–Fri 9am–5pm Sat 10am–6pm
Services Valuations, repairs, restoration

Jericho Books (PBFA)
Contact Mr F Stringer
48 Walton Street, Oxford,

Oxfordshire, OX2 6AD P
☎ 01865 511992
Ⓜ 07968 566591
Ⓔ shop@jerichobooks.com
Ⓦ www.jerichobooks.com
Est. 1996 *Stock size* Medium
Stock Rare, antiquarian, general second-hand books
Open Mon–Sun 10am–6.30pm
Fairs Russell Square, London
Services Valuations, restoration, book search

Liscious Interiors
Contact Fran or Walter
✉ **63 Banbury Road, Oxford, Oxfordshire, OX2 6PG** P
☎ 01865 552232
Ⓜ 07973 479057
Ⓦ www.liscious.co.uk
Est. 1995 *Stock size* Medium
Stock French mirrors, Italian chandeliers, original painted furniture, French country antiques, Art Deco, 1950s lighting, costumes, textiles
Open Mon–Sat 10.30am–6pm or by appointment

Roger Little Antique Pottery (English Ceramic Circle)
Contact Roger Little
✉ **White Lodge, Osler Road, Headington, Oxford, Oxfordshire, OX3 9BJ** P
☎ 01865 762317 Ⓕ 01865 741595
Ⓔ rogerlittle@hotmail.com
Est. 1985 *Stock size* Medium
Stock English and Continental pottery, tiles, 1650–1800
Open By appointment only
Fairs NEC
Services Valuations

Mallams
Contact Mr B Lloyd
✉ **Bocardo House, St Michael's Street, Oxford, Oxfordshire, OX1 2EB** P
☎ 01865 241358 Ⓕ 01865 725483
Ⓔ oxford@mallams.co.uk
Ⓦ www.mallams.co.uk
Est. 1788
Open Mon–Fri 9am–5.30pm Sat 9am–1pm
Sales Sales of antiques, silver, jewellery, books, pictures
Catalogues Yes

Oxford Furniture Warehouse
Contact F & P K Mitchell
✉ **272 Abingdon Road, Oxford, Oxfordshire, OX1 4TA** P
☎ 01865 202221 Ⓕ 01865 202221
Est. 1992 *Stock size* Large
Stock Old pine, oak and general furniture, some Continental furniture
Open Mon–Sat 10am–5.30pm Sun 11am–4.30pm

Payne and Son (Goldsmiths) Ltd (BADA, NAG)
Contact Judy Payne or David Thornton
✉ **131 High Street, Oxford, Oxfordshire, OX1 4DH** P
☎ 01865 243787 Ⓕ 01865 793241
Ⓔ silver@payneandson.co.uk
Ⓦ www.payneandson.co.uk
Est. 1790 *Stock size* Large
Stock 17thC–present day silver including Arts and Crafts and contemporary designs
Open Mon–Fri 9.30am–5.30pm Sat 9am–5.30pm
Fairs BADA Chelsea, Olympia
Services Restoration

Sanders of Oxford (PBFA)
Contact Sarah Boada-Momtahan
✉ **104 High Street, Oxford, Oxfordshire, OX1 4BW** P
☎ 01865 242590 Ⓕ 01865 721748
Ⓔ sox-shop2@btclick.com
Ⓦ www.sandersofoxford.com
Est. 1964 *Stock size* Large
Stock Antique prints, maps especially Oxford related
Open Mon–Sat 10am–6pm
Fairs London and Cork Original Print Fair

St Clements Antiques
Contact Mr G Power
✉ **93 St Clements Street, Oxford, Oxfordshire, OX4 1AR** P
☎ 01865 727010 Ⓕ 01865 864690
Est. 1999 *Stock size* Medium
Stock Town and country pieces from home and abroad
Open Mon–Sat 10am–5pm
Services Valuations

STANDLAKE

Manor Farm Antiques
Contact Charles Gower
✉ **159 Abingdon Road, Standlake, Witney, Oxfordshire, OX29 7RL** P
☎ 01865 300303 Ⓕ 01865 300153
Est. 1964 *Stock size* Large
Stock Brass, iron, wooden bedsteads
Open Mon–Sat 10am–5pm

STEVENTON

Bennett and Kerr Books (PBFA, ABA)
Contact Mr E Bennett
✉ **Millhill Warehouse, Church Lane, Steventon, Abingdon, Oxfordshire, OX13 6SW** P
☎ 01235 820604
Ⓔ bennettkerr@aol.com
Est. 1982 *Stock size* Medium
Stock Antique, scholarly books on Middle Ages, Renaissance, medieval studies
Open By appointment
Fairs PBFA, Oxford
Services Catalogues issued

TETSWORTH

Quillon Antiques of Tetsworth (TVADA)
Contact Peter Magrath
✉ **The Old Stores, 42a High Street, Tetsworth, Nr Thame, Oxfordshire, OX9 7AS** P
☎ 01844 281636
Ⓔ quillona1@aol.com
Est. 1982 *Stock size* Medium
Stock Medieval armour 14th–19thC, period oak and country furniture, French antiques
Open Tues Thurs 10am–6pm Sat Sun 10am–6pm
Services Valuations

The Swan at Tetsworth (TVADA, BACA Award Winner 2004)
Contact Rita Woodman
✉ **High Street, Tetsworth, Nr Thame, Oxfordshire, OX9 7AB** P
☎ 01844 281777
Ⓔ antiques@theswan.co.uk
Ⓦ www.theswan.co.uk
Est. 1994 *Stock size* Large
No. of dealers 80
Stock 80 dealers in historic Elizabethan coaching inn in 40 showrooms. Georgian–Art Deco furniture, silver, mirrors, rugs, glass, ceramics, jewellery, boxes, garden statuary
Open Mon–Sun 10am–6pm
Services Renowned restaurant, delivery arranged, events, shipping

THAME

Rosemary & Time
Contact Mr Tom Fletcher
42 Park Street, Thame, Oxfordshire, OX9 3HR
01844 216923
Est. 1983 *Stock size* Large
Stock Clocks
Open Tues–Sat 9am–5.30pm
Services Restoration, repairs

WALLINGFORD

Alicia Antiques
Contact Mrs A Collins
Lamb Arcade, High Street, Wallingford, Oxfordshire, OX10 0BS
01491 833737
Est. 1979 *Stock size* Medium
Stock Silver, plate, glass, small furniture
Open Mon–Sat 10am–5pm
Services Silver repairs

M & J De Albuquerque
Contact Mrs J De Albuquerque
The Old Bakery, Thames Street (car park), Wallingford, Oxfordshire, OX10 0BP
01491 832322 F 01491 832322
janedealb@tiscali.co.uk
Est. 1982 *Stock size* Medium
Stock 18th–19thC French and English furniture, objects of the period
Open By apointment
Fairs Brocante (Chelsea Town Hall)
Services Restoration, framing, gilding

Toby English Antiquarian & Secondhand Bookshop (PBFA)
Contact Mr T English
10 St Mary's Street, Wallingford, Oxfordshire, OX10 0EL
01491 836389 F 01491 836389
toby@tobyenglish.com
www.tobyenglish.com
Est. 1984 *Stock size* Large
Stock Art, architectural, Renaissance literature, large general stock
Open Mon–Sat 9.30am–5pm
Fairs PBFA
Services Book search, valuations, catalogues issued

The Lamb Arcade (TVADA)
Contact Mrs P Hayward
83 High Street, Wallingford, Oxfordshire, OX10 0BX
01491 835166 F 01491 824247
patriciantiques@aol.com
www.thelambarcade.co.uk
Est. 1979 *Stock size* Large
No. of dealers 45
Stock Everything from period furniture to small items
Open Mon–Fri 10am–5pm Sat 10am–5.30pm

O'Donnell Antiques
Contact Lin or Chris O'Donnell
26 High Street, Wallingford, Oxfordshire, OX10 0BU
01491 839332
Est. 1974 *Stock size* Large
Stock General antiques, Georgian–early 20thC furniture, taxidermy, rugs, English pine, Oriental items, silver, Gaudy Welsh, Staffordshire
Open Mon–Sat 9.30am–5pm

Phoenix Furniture
Contact David Belcher
The Victorian Gallery, 3 Lamb Arcade, High Street, Wallingford, Oxfordshire, OX10 0BY
01491 833555
M 07860 889524
Est. 1985 *Stock size* Large
Stock Antique pine, Georgian–Victorian mahogany furniture
Open Mon–Fri 10am–5pm Sat 10am–5.30pm
Services Bespoke pine furniture, restoration

Summers Davis Antiques Ltd (TVADA, LAPADA)
Contact Mr J Driver-Jones
Calleva House, 6 High Street, Wallingford, Oxfordshire, OX10 0BP
01491 836284 F 01491 833443
antiques@summersdavis.co.uk
www.summersdavisantiques.co.uk
Est. 1915 *Stock size* Large
Stock 11 showrooms of 17th–19thC English and Continental furniture
Open Mon–Fri 9am–5.30pm Sat 9am–5pm Sun 11am–5pm
Fairs TVADA

Tooley, Adams and Co (IMCOS, ABA, IAMA)
Contact Steve Luck
PO Box 174, Wallingford, Oxfordshire, OX10 0YT
01491 838298 F 01491 834616
steve@tooleys.co.uk
www.tooleys.co.uk
Est. 1982 *Stock size* Large
Stock Antiquarian maps by Blaeu, Bowen, Gibson, Fullarton, Porcacchi, Saxton, Speed, Zatta atlases
Open By appointment
Fairs London Map Fair (June Olympia), Bonnington Map Fair (6 months per year), Miami (February)
Services Valuations

WHEATLEY

Country Collections
Contact Mrs A Descenclos
47 High Street, Wheatley, Oxford, Oxfordshire, OX33 1XX
01865 875701
Est. 1992 *Stock size* Medium
Stock Small items, furniture, general antiques
Open Mon–Sat 10am–4.30pm
Fairs Milton Keynes

WITNEY

Church Green Books (PBFA)
Contact Margaret or Roger Barnes
46 Market Square, Witney, Oxfordshire, OX28 6AL
01993 700822
books@churchgreen.co.uk
www.churchgreen.co.uk
Est. 1995 *Stock size* Medium
Stock General second-hand and antiquarian books, books on bellringing a speciality
Open Mon–Fri 10am–4pm
Services Book search

Julian Eade
Witney, Oxon, OX29
M 07973 542971
julian.eade@cbre.com
Est. 1983 *Stock size* Medium
Stock Worcester, Minton, Derby, Artist, Doulton stoneware
Open By appointment
Fairs NEC
Services Valuations

Colin Greenway Antiques (CADA)
Contact Jean Greenway
90 Corn Street, Witney, Oxfordshire, OX28 6BU
01993 705026 01993 705026
07831 585014
jean_greenway@hotmail.com
www.greenwayantiques.viewing.at
Est. 1974 *Stock size* Medium
Stock 17th–early 20thC furniture, general antiques, interesting, unusual items, garden furniture, gilt frames, rocking horses
Open Mon–Fri 9.30am–5.30pm Sat 10am–4pm
Services Valuations

W R Harvey & Co (Antiques) Ltd (LAPADA, CADA)
Contact Mr David Harvey
86 Corn Street, Witney, Oxfordshire, OX28 6BU
01993 706501 01993 706601
antiques@wrharvey.co.uk
www.wrharvey.co.uk
Est. 1950 *Stock size* Large
Stock Important stock of English furniture, clocks, pictures, mirrors, works of art, 1680–1830
Open Mon–Sat 9.30am–5.30pm
Fairs Chelsea Spring & Autumn Fair, Olympia (June)
Services Valuations, restoration, conservation, buying at auction for clients

Teddy Bears of Witney
Contact Ian Pout
99 High Street, Witney, Oxfordshire, OX28 6HY
01993 702616 01993 702344
www.teddybears.co.uk
Est. 1985 *Stock size* Large
Stock Steiff, Merrythought, Deans, Hermann, artists' bears
Open Mon–Fri 9.30am– 5.30pm Sat 9.30am–5pm Sun 10.30am–4.30pm
Services Valuations

Witney Antiques (BADA, LAPADA, CADA)
Contact Mrs C J Jarrett
96–100 Corn Street, Witney, Oxfordshire, OX28 6BU
01993 703902 01993 779852
witneyantiques@community.co.uk
www.witneyantiques.com
Est. 1963 *Stock size* Large
Stock 17th–early 19thC furniture, clocks, works of art, needlework, probably the largest selection of samplers in the UK
Open Wed–Sat 10am–5pm Mon Tues by appointment
Fairs Grosvenor House, BADA
Services Restoration, catalogues

WOODSTOCK

Antiques at Heritage (TVADA)
Contact John Howard
No 6 Market Place, Woodstock, Oxfordshire, OX20 1TA
01993 811332
dealers@heritage.co.uk
www.atheritage.co.uk
Est. 1984 *Stock size* Large
No. of dealers 12
Stock Antiques, pre-1940
Open Mon-Sat 10am–5pm Sun 1–5pm

Chris Baylis Country Chairs (TVADA)
Contact Mr C Baylis
16 Oxford Street, Woodstock, Oxfordshire, OX20 1TS
01993 813887 01993 812379
rcwood@mcmail.com
www.realwoodfurniture.co.uk
Est. 1979 *Stock size* Large
Stock English country chairs 1780–present day, Windsor, rush-seated ladder and spindleback chairs, kitchen chairs etc
Open Tues–Sat 10.30am–5.30pm Sun 11am–5pm

Bees Antiques (TVADA)
Contact Mr or Mrs J Bateman
30 High Street, Woodstock, Oxfordshire, OX20 1TG
01993 811062
Est. 1989 *Stock size* Medium
Stock Fine 18th–19thC British and Continental ceramics, glass, jewellery, decorative furniture, metalware
Open Mon–Sat 10am–1pm 1.30–5pm Sun 11am–5pm closed Tues or by appointment
Services Valuations for ceramics, glass, jewellery

The Chair Set
Contact Allan James
18 Market Place, Woodstock, Oxfordshire, OX20 1TA
01428 707301 01428 707457
07801 754760
allanjames@thechairset.com
www.thechairset.com
Est. 1985 *Stock size* Large
Stock 18th–19thC sets of chairs and dining room antiques
Open Mon–Sun 10.30am–5.30pm
Services Valuations, search

John Howard (BADA, CADA)
Contact John Howard
No 6 Market Place, Woodstock, Oxfordshire, OX20 1TA
0870 444 0678 0870 444 0678
07831 850544
john@johnhoward.co.uk
www.antiquepottery.co.uk
Est. 1975 *Stock size* Large
Stock British 18th–19thC pottery
Open Mon–Sat 10am–5pm Sun 1–5pm
Fairs Olympia, New York Ceramics Fair

The Woodstock Bookshop (PBFA)
Contact Mr Mark Wratten
3 Market Place, Woodstock, Oxfordshire, OX20 1SY
01993 811005
Est. 1989 *Stock size* Small
Stock Antiquarian and second-hand books on literature, travel, topography, art, history of art, prints
Open Mon–Sun 10am–5pm closed 1–2pm
Fairs PBFA

YARNTON

Yarnton Antique Centre
Contact Mr M Dunseath
within Yarnton Nurseries, Sandy Lane, off A44, Yarnton, Kidlington, Oxfordshire, OX5 1PA
01865 379600
Est. 1998 *Stock size* Large
No. of dealers 45 (21 cabinets)
Stock Furniture, silver, china, brass, books, jewellery, lighting, decorative items
Open Mon–Sun 10am–4.30pm

MIDLANDS

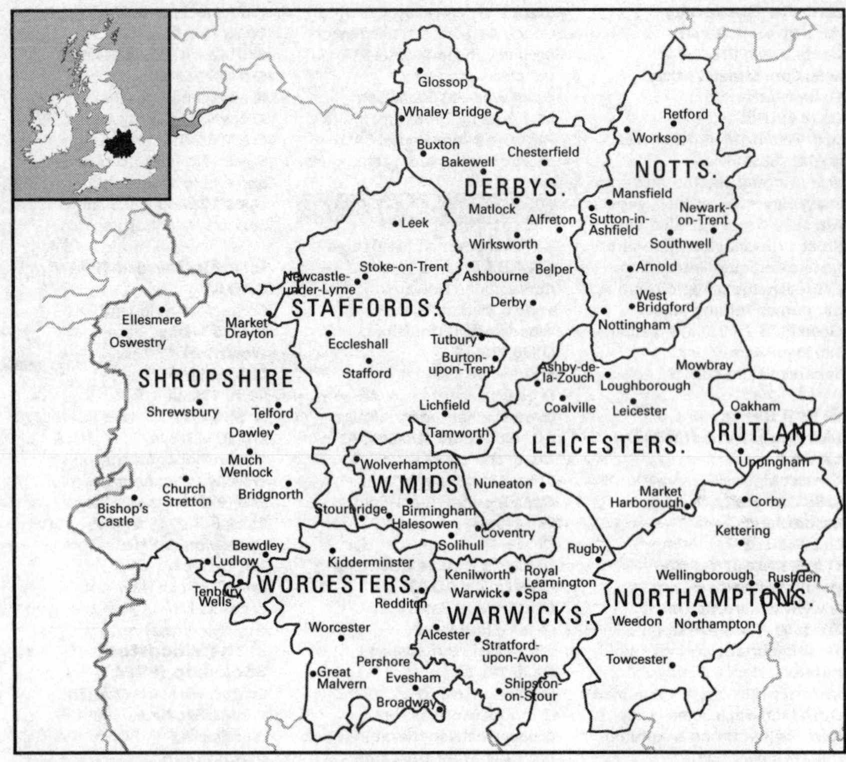

DERBYSHIRE

ALFRETON

Alfreton Antique Centre
Contact Helen Dixon
11 King Street, Alfreton, Derbyshire, DE55 7AF P
☎ 01773 520781
Ⓜ 07970 786968
Ⓔ alfretonantiques@supanet.com
Ⓦ www.alfretonantiquescentre.com
Est. 1996 *Stock size* Large
No. of dealers 35
Stock General antiques, collectables, furniture, clocks, silver, militaria, books, postcards, lighting
Open Mon–Sat 10am–4.30pm Sun 11am–4.30pm
Services Derby replacement service, ceramic restoration

Curiosity Shop
Contact Kenneth Allsop
37 King Street, Alfreton, Derbyshire, DE55 7BY P
☎ 01773 832429
Ⓜ 07932 7674663
Est. 1974 *Stock size* Medium
Stock General antiques
Open Mon–Sat 9.30am–5pm

ALPORT

Peter Bunting (LAPADA, BADA, CINOA)
Contact Mr P Bunting
Harthill Hall, Alport, Bakewell, Derbyshire, DE45 1LH P
☎ 01629 636203 Ⓕ 01629 636101
Ⓜ 07860 540870
Ⓔ peter@peterbunting.com
Ⓦ www.peterbunting.com
Est. 1975 *Stock size* Medium
Stock English oak and country furniture, tapestries, portraits
Open By appointment
Fairs Olympia, NEC, CHELSEA

ASHBOURNE

Antiques in Ashbourne
Contact P J Chapman
41 Church Street, Ashbourne, Derbyshire, DE6 1AJ P
☎ 01335 347199
Ⓔ lemonpierre@aol.com
Est. 2003 *Stock size* Medium
Stock Clocks, furniture
Open Thurs–Sat 10am–5pm
Fairs Birmingham Clock Fair, Brunel Clock Fair

Ashbourne Antiques Ltd
Contact Robert Allsebrook
Blake House Farm, Shirley, Ashbourne, Derbyshire, DE6 3AS P
☎ 01335 361236
Ⓜ 07970 094883
Est. 1975 *Stock size* Large
Stock 18th–20thC furniture
Open By appointment
Services Restoration, shipping, removals, storage

M G Bassett
Contact Mrs G Bassett or Mr M Bassett
38 Church Street,

Ashbourne, Derbyshire,
DE6 1AJ
☎ 01335 300061/347750 (workshop) Ⓕ 01335 300061
Ⓔ mgbassett@aol.com
Est. 1979 *Stock size* Large
Stock General antiques, French, English country pine
Open Mon–Sat 10am–5pm closed Wed

⊞ Daniel Charles Antiques
Contact Keith Phillips-Moul
✉ **33 Church Street, Ashbourne, Derbyshire, DE6 1AE** Ⓟ
☎ 01335 300002 Ⓕ 01335 348200
Ⓔ k3iths@btinternet.com
Ⓦ www.danielcharlesantiques.com
Est. 2000 *Stock size* Medium
Stock 17th–20thC furniture, paintings, chandeliers, decorative items
Open Mon–Sat 10am–5pm
Services Restoration

⊞ Eclectica Interiors
Contact Quinton Heyre
✉ **30 Clifton Road, Ashbourne, Derbyshire, DE6 1DT** Ⓟ
☎ 01335 346113 Ⓕ 01335 346113
Ⓜ 07971 660949
Est. 2003 *Stock size* Medium
Stock Continental and English antiques, interior design
Open Mon–Sat 10.30am–4.30pm closed Wed
Fairs Keddleston Hall

⊞ Pamela Elsom Antiques (LAPADA)
Contact Mrs P Elsom
✉ **5 Church Street, Ashbourne, Derbyshire, DE6 1AE** Ⓟ
☎ 01335 343468/344311
Est. 1965 *Stock size* Medium
Stock General antiques
Open Thurs–Sat 10am–5pm
Services Valuations

⊞ Hotspur & Nimrod
Contact Mrs Jarrett
✉ **14 Church Street, Ashbourne, Derbyshire, DE6 1AE** Ⓟ
☎ 01335 342518
Ⓜ 07792 404336
Ⓦ www.hotspurandnimrod antiques.co.uk
Est. 1997 *Stock size* Medium
Stock General antiques
Open Mon–Sat 10am–5pm Sun noon–4pm
Services Coffee shop

⊞ J H S Antiques Ltd (LAPADA, CINOA, Pewter Society, Metalware Society)
Contact Mr J H Snodin
✉ **45 & 47 Church Street, Ashbourne, Derbyshire, DE6 1AJ** Ⓟ
☎ 01335 347733
Ⓜ 07810 122248
Est. 1970 *Stock size* Medium
Stock Period oak, metalware, carving, treen
Open Tues–Sat 10am–5pm closed Wed

⊞ Prestwood Antiques
Contact Mr Chris Ball
✉ **28b & 39 Church Street, Ashbourne, Derbyshire, DE6 1AJ** Ⓟ
☎ 01335 342198 Ⓕ 01335 342198
Ⓜ 07976 767629
Ⓔ chris@spurrier-smith.fsnet.co.uk
Est. 1989 *Stock size* Large
Stock General antiques
Open Mon–Sat 10am–5pm closed Wed
Services Restoration

⊞ Rose Antiques
Contact Mrs G Rose
✉ **37 Church Street, Ashbourne, Derbyshire, DE6 1AE** Ⓟ
☎ 01335 343822 Ⓕ 01335 343822
Est. 1984 *Stock size* Medium
Stock General antiques
Open Mon–Sat 10am–5pm closed Wed

⊞ Spurrier-Smith Antiques (LAPADA, CINOA)
Contact Mr I Spurrier-Smith
✉ **28b & 39 Church Street, Ashbourne, Derbyshire, DE6 1AE** Ⓟ
☎ 01335 343669 Ⓕ 01335 342198
Ⓜ 07831 454603
Ⓔ ivanspurrier-smith@fsnet.com
Ⓦ www.spurrier-smith.co.uk
Est. 1974 *Stock size* Large
Stock General antiques, large pine warehouse, furniture, decorative items
Open Mon–Sat 10am–5pm closed Wed
Services Valuations

⊞ Top Drawer Antiques
Contact Justin Flint
✉ **30 Church Street, Ashbourne, Derbyshire, DE6 1AE** Ⓟ
☎ 01335 343669
Ⓜ 07970 720133
Ⓔ sarah@topdrawerantiques. freeserve.co.uk
Est. 1990 *Stock size* Large
Stock General antiques, pine, kitchenware, decorative items
Open Mon–Sat 10am–5pm closed Wed or by appointment
Services Restoration

BAKEWELL

⊞ Allens
Contact Mike or Mavis Allen
✉ **Chappells Antiques Centre, Bakewell, 1–4 King Street, Bakewell, Derbyshire, DE45 1DZ** Ⓟ
☎ 01629 812496 Ⓕ 01629 411918
Ⓔ books@allensbooks.co.uk
Ⓦ www.allensbooks.co.uk
Est. 1996 *Stock size* Medium
Stock 20thC ceramics, quality second-hand books
Open Mon–Sat 10am–5pm Sun noon–5pm

⊞ Rex Boyer Antiques
Contact Rex Boyer
✉ **Chappells Antiques Centre, Bakewell, 1–4 King Street, Bakewell, Derbyshire, DE45 1DZ** Ⓟ
☎ 01629 812496 Ⓕ 01629 814531
Ⓔ ask@chappellsantiquescentre.com
Ⓦ www.chappellsantiquescentre.com
Est. 1960 *Stock size* Small
Stock 18th–19thC furniture
Open Mon–Sat 10am–5pm Sun noon–5pm

⊞ Cambridge Fine Art (LAPADA)
Contact Nick Lury
✉ **Chappells Antiques Centre, Bakewell, 1–4 King Street, Bakewell, Derbyshire, DE45 1DZ** Ⓟ
☎ 01629 812496 Ⓕ 01629 814531
Ⓔ ask@chappellsantiquescentre.com
Ⓦ www.chappellsantiquescentre.com
Est. 1973 *Stock size* Large
Stock Fine British and Continental oil paintings 1750–1940
Open Mon–Sat 10am–5pm Sun noon–5pm
Fairs Olympia, Chester, NEC

MIDLANDS

DERBYSHIRE • BAKEWELL

Chappells Antiques Centre, Bakewell
Contact Mrs J Chappell
1–4 King Street, Bakewell, Derbyshire, DE45 1DZ P
☎ 01629 812496 F 01629 814531
E ask@chappellsantiquescentre.com
W www.chappellsantiquescentre.com
Est. 1992 *Stock size* Large
No. of dealers 30
Stock 17th–20thC furniture, decorative and collectors' items
Open Mon–Sat 10am–5pm Sun noon–5pm
Services Restoration, valuation for sale, wedding lists, finance

Clocks in the Peak (BHI)
Contact D Cockayne
Chappells Antiques Centre, Bakewell, 1–4 King Street, Bakewell, Derbyshire, DE45 1DZ P
☎ 01629 812496 F 01629 814531
E dcockayne@virgin.net
W www.chappellsantiquescentre.com
Est. 1989 *Stock size* Medium
Stock 18th–19thC brass and japanned dial longcase clocks
Open Mon–Sat 10am–5pm Sun noon–5pm
Services Restoration, conservation

Cottage Antiques
Contact P Milling
Chappells Antiques Centre, Bakewell, 1–4 King Street, Bakewell, Derbyshire, DE45 1DZ P
☎ 01283 562670 F 01283 562670
E ask@chappellsantiquescentre.com
W www.chappellsantiquescentre.com
Est. 1970 *Stock size* Large
Stock Late 19thC curtain furniture, curtain poles, pelmets, tie-backs, curtain rings, small decorative antiques
Open Mon–Sat 10am–5pm Sun noon–5pm
Fairs NEC, Harrogate, Chester Spirit of Christmas, Daily Telegraph House and Garden Show Olympia

Stephanie Davison Antiques (LAPADA, CINOA)
Contact Stephanie Davison
Chappells Antiques Centre, Bakewell, 1–4 King Street, Bakewell, Derbyshire, DE45 1DZ P
☎ 01629 812496 F 01629 814531
M 07771 564993
E stephanie.davison@btopenworld.com
W www.stephanie.davisonantiques.com
Est. 1999 *Stock size* Large
Stock Oak and country furniture, longcase clocks, treen, metalware and associated items
Open Mon–Sat 10am–5pm Sun noon–5pm
Fairs NEC, Tatton, Buxton, Harrogate
Services Restoration of clocks and furniture

J Dickinson Maps & Prints
Contact J Dickinson
Stand 4, Chappells Antiques Centre, Bakewell, 1–4 King Street, Bakewell, Derbyshire, DE45 1DZ P
☎ 01629 812496 F 01629 814531
M 07885 174890
E ask@chappellsantiquescentre.com
W www.chappellsantiquescentre.com
Est. 1994 *Stock size* Large
Stock Antiquarian maps and engravings, mainly topographical, but also railway, children's and decorative prints, Derbyshire books and related items
Open Mon–Sat 10am–5pm Sun noon–5pm
Fairs Bailey Fairs and other datelined fairs in the north of England
Services Map search, cleaning, restoring, mounting and fixing, valuations, restoration

Elizabeth Ann Antiques (LAPADA)
Contact D Green
Chappells Antiques Centre, Bakewell, 1–4 King Street, Bakewell, Derbyshire, DE45 1DZ P
☎ 01629 812496 F 01629 814531
M 07768 832616
E antiques@dggreen.co.uk
W www.chappellsantiquescentre.com
Est. 1970 *Stock size* Large
Stock 18–19thC furniture, desks, upholstered chairs and settees, dining tables, chests-of-drawers, decorative mirrors, furnishings
Open Mon–Sat 10am–5pm Sun noon–5pm
Fairs Buxton, Newark

Etceteras
Contact B Austin
Chappells Antiques Centre, Bakewell, 1–4 King Street, Bakewell, Derbyshire, DE45 1DZ P
☎ 01629 812496 F 01629 814531
E ask@chappellsantiquescentre.com
W www.chappellsantiquescentre.com
Est. 1970 *Stock size* Small
Stock Vintage handbags, jewellery, bijouterie, compacts, linen
Open Mon–Sat 10am–5pm Sun noon–5pm

G W Ford & Son Ltd (LAPADA)
Contact Ian Thomson
Stands 1 and 2, Chappells Antiques Centre, 1–4 King Street, Bakewell, Derbyshire, DE45 1DZ P
☎ 01246 410512 F 01246 419223
M 07740 025936
E enquiries@gwfordantiques.co.uk
W www.gwfordantiques.co.uk
Est. 1908 *Stock size* Medium
Stock 18th–early 20thC town and country furniture, sculpture, decorative items, treen, silver, old Sheffield plate, metalware
Open Mon–Sat 10am–5pm Sun noon–5pm
Fairs Buxton
Services Restoration, commisioning

Ganymede Antiques
Contact Keith Petts
Stand 9, Chappells Antiques Centre, Bakewell, 1–4 King Street, Bakewell, Derbyshire, DE45 1DZ P
☎ 01629 812496 F 01629 814531
E ganymede@talk21.com
W www.chappellsantiquescentre.com
Est. 1992 *Stock size* Medium
Stock Scientific and medical antiques
Open Mon–Sat 10am–5pm Sun noon–5pm
Fairs International Scientific Instrument Fair

Martin and Dorothy Harper Antiques (LAPADA)
Contact Martin or Dorothy Harper
King Street, Bakewell, Derbyshire,

DE45 1DZ P
☎ 01629 814757
Ⓜ 07885 347134
Est. 1971 *Stock size* Medium
Stock 18th–early 20thC furniture, metalware, decorative items
Open Tues Wed Fri Sat 10am–5pm or by appointment
Services Valuations

Brian L Hills
Contact Brian L Hills
✉ **Stands 5 and 6, Chappells Antiques Centre, Bakewell, 1–4 King Street, Bakewell, Derbyshire, DE45 1DZ** P
☎ 01629 812496 Ⓕ 01629 814531
Ⓜ 07860 453940
Ⓔ ask@chappellsantiquescentre.com
Ⓦ www.chappellsantiquescentre.com
Est. 1978 *Stock size* Medium
Stock 17th–19thC furniture, bronze sculpture, works of art, marble, treen, metalware, paintings, decorative objects, longcase and bracket clocks
Open Mon–Sat 10am–5pm Sun noon–5pm

J Lawrence
Contact J Lawrence
✉ **Chappells Antiques Centre, Bakewell, 1–4 King Street, Bakewell, Derbyshire, DE45 1DZ** P
☎ 01629 812496 Ⓕ 01629 814531
Ⓔ ask@chappellsantiquescentre.com
Ⓦ www.chappellsantiquescentre.com
Est. 1980 *Stock size* Medium
Stock Silver and silver plate, scent bottles, porcelain, tortoiseshell and mother-of-pearl card cases etc, vesta cases, bijouterie
Open Mon–Sat 10am–5pm Sun noon–5pm

Millennium Antiques
Contact Peter or Jennifer Wilcock
✉ **Chappells Antiques Centre, Bakewell, 1–4 King Street, Bakewell, Derbyshire, DE45 1DZ** P
☎ 01629 812496 Ⓕ 01629 814531
Ⓔ pandj@millenniumantiques.co.uk
Ⓦ www.millenniumantiques.co.uk
Est. 1992 *Stock size* Medium
Stock Antique silver and old Sheffield plate, quality costume jewellery
Open Mon–Sat 10am–5pm Sun noon–5pm
Fairs Buxton (May), NEC Antiques for Everyone
Services Valuations, restoration

Walter Moores & Son
Contact Peter Moores
✉ **Chappells Antiques Centre, Bakewell, 1–4 King Street, Bakewell, Derbyshire, DE45 1DZ** P
☎ 07071 226202 Ⓕ 07071 226202
Ⓜ 07710 019045
Ⓔ waltermoores@btinternet.com
Ⓦ www.waltermoores.co.uk
Est. 1925 *Stock size* Medium
Stock Georgian–Victorian furniture, mainly mahogany
Open Mon–Sat 10am–5pm Sun noon–5pm
Fairs Buxton (May), Harrogate Antiques and Fine Art Fairs

M F Morris Antiques
Contact Mike Morris
✉ **Chappells Antiques Centre, Bakewell, 1–4 King Street, Bakewell, Derbyshire, DE45 1DZ** P
☎ 01629 812496 Ⓕ 01629 814531
Ⓜ 07967 196228
Ⓔ mike@mfmorris.freeserve.co.uk
Est. 1982 *Stock size* Large
Stock Derby and Lynton porcelain, watercolours and oils by local artists, Staffordshire figures, toasting forks
Open Mon–Sat 10am–5pm Sun noon–5pm
Fairs NEC, Buxton (May)

Original Vintage Costume Jewellery
Contact Judy Portway
✉ **Chappells Antiques Centre, Bakewell, 1–4 King Street, Bakewell, Derbyshire, DE45 1DZ** P
☎ 01629 812496 Ⓕ 01629 814531
Ⓔ ask@chappellsantiquescentre.com
Ⓦ www.chappellsantiquescentre.com
Est. 1989 *Stock size* Medium
Stock Original vintage costume jewellery, compacts, handbags
Open Mon–Sat 10am–5pm Sun noon–5pm
Fairs Snape

Paraphernalia
Contact Steve or Jo Bentley
✉ **Stand 11, Chappells Antiques Centre, Bakewell, 1–4 King Street, Bakewell, Derbyshire, DE45 1DZ** P
☎ 01629 812496 Ⓕ 01298 71648
Ⓔ stevebentley@btinternet.com
Ⓦ www.chappellsantiquescentre.com
Est. 1992 *Stock size* Large
Stock Period lighting, Arts and Crafts, metalware, small furniture, decorative glass
Open Mon–Sat 10am–5pm Sun noon–5pm
Fairs Buxton
Services Valuations, restoration, fitting, delivery

Michael Pembery Antiques
Contact Michael Pembery
✉ **Peppercorn House, Kings Street, Bakewell, Derbyshire, DE45 1FD** P
☎ 01629 814161
Est. 1967 *Stock size* Medium
Stock 17th–18thC oak and walnut furniture, blue john, Ashford marble
Open Mon–Sat 10am–5pm closed Thurs

Doug Pye
Contact Douglas Pye
✉ **Chappells Antiques Centre, Bakewell, 1–4 King Street, Bakewell, Derbyshire, DE45 1DZ** P
☎ 01629 812496 Ⓕ 01629 814531
Ⓜ 07890 328449
Ⓔ douglas.pye@tesco.net
Ⓦ www.chappellsantiquescentre.com
Est. 1975 *Stock size* Medium
Stock Early blue and white, Ironstone china, copper lustre, Flow blue, clocks and barometers
Open Mon–Sat 10am–5pm Sun noon–5pm
Services Courier service, buying advice

Renaissance Antiques
Contact J Barnicott
✉ **Chappells Antiques Centre, Bakewell, 1–4 King Street, Bakewell, Derbyshire, DE45 1DZ** P
☎ 01629 812496 Ⓕ 01629 814531
Ⓜ 07812 395275
Ⓔ judybarnicott@renaiseants.fsnet.co.uk
Ⓦ www.chappellsantiquescentre.com
Est. 1984 *Stock size* Medium
Stock Staffordshire figures and other pottery, treen, brass and copper ware, glass, silver,

portrait miniatures
Open Mon–Sat 10am–5pm
Sun noon–5pm

Scarlett Antiques
Contact Robert Furmage
Chappells Antiques Centre, Bakewell, 1–4 King Street, Bakewell, Derbyshire, DE45 1DZ P
☎ 01629 812496 F 01629 814531
M 07813 701146
E ask@chappellsantiquescentre.com
W www.chappellsantiquescentre.com
Est. 1900 *Stock size* Medium
Stock Antique gemstone jewellery, bracket clocks
Open Mon–Sat 10am–5pm
Sun noon–5pm
Services Restoration of jewellery and clocks

Shirley May
Contact S M Smith
Chappells Antiques Centre, Bakewell, 1–4 King Street, Bakewell, Derbyshire, DE45 1DZ P
☎ 01629 812496 F 01629 814531
E ask@chappellsantiquescentre.com
W www.chappellsantiquescentre.com
Est. 1985 *Stock size* Medium
Stock Cornish ware, Denby ware, old linen and lace, interesting bygones and kitchenware
Open Mon–Sat 10am–5pm
Sun noon–5pm

Sudbury Antiques
Contact Roger DeVille
Chappells Antiques Centre, Bakewell, 1–4 King Street, Bakewell, Derbyshire, DE45 1DZ P
☎ 01629 812496 F 01629 814531
M 07798 793857
E ask@chappellsantiquescentre.com
W www.chappellsantiquescentre.com
Est. 1980 *Stock size* Medium
Stock 18th–19thC pottery, Mason's Ironstone, Prattware, creamware, Delft, saltglaze, blue and white, printed wares, commemoratives
Open Mon–Sat 10am–5pm
Sun noon–5pm
Fairs Kensington, Chelsea, Earls Court, NEC, Penman Chester
Services Valuations

Sandra Wallhead
Contact Sandra Wallhead
Stand 14, Chappells Antiques Centre, Bakewell, 1–4 King Street, Bakewell, Derbyshire, DE45 1DZ P
☎ 01629 812496 F 01629 814531
M 07748 005954
E ask@chappellsantiquescentre.com
W www.chappellsantiquescentre.com
Est. 1980 *Stock size* Medium
Stock Cranberry glass, music boxes, hatpins, small Victorian furniture, clocks and barometers, silver, dolls, Clarice Cliff, scent bottles
Open Mon–Sat 10am–5pm
Sun noon–5pm
Fairs Newark

N I Wilkinson
Contact Ian Wilkinson
Chappells Antiques Centre, Bakewell, 1–4 King Street, Bakewell, Derbyshire, DE45 1DZ P
☎ 01629 812496 F 01629 814531
E ask@chappellsantiquescentre.com
W www.chappellsantiquescentre.com
Est. 1983 *Stock size* Small
Stock Pottery, metalware, treen, gardening antiques, collectables, textiles
Open Mon–Sat 10am–5pm
Sun noon–5pm

BAMFORD

High Peak Antiques
Contact Denise Shaw or Richard Casey
High Peak Garden Centre, Sickleholme, Bamford, Derbyshire, S33 0AH P
☎ 01433 659595
M 07976 934007
Est. 1998 *Stock size* Large
Stock Sports memorabilia, books, Victoriana, jewellery, Moorcroft, toys, kitchenware, paintings, furniture, linen, glass, china, silver
Open Mon–Sun 10am–5.30pm

BARLOW

Hackney House Antiques
Contact Mrs J M Gorman
Hackney House, Hackney Lane, Barlow, Dronfield, Derbyshire, S18 7TF P
☎ 0114 289 0248
Est. 1981 *Stock size* Medium
Stock Longcase and wall clocks, Georgian–Edwardian furniture, silver, pictures, porcelain, glass
Open Tues–Sun 9am–6pm

BASLOW

Antiques in Baslow
Contact Richard Crabtree
Barbrook House, Nether End, Baslow, Bakewell, Derbyshire, DE45 1SR P
☎ 01246 583659
M 07946 277814
Est. 1993 *Stock size* Medium
Stock General antiques, clocks, barometers, children's toys, rocking horses, pedal cars
Open Fri–Sat 10.30am–4.30pm
Sun 12.30–4.30pm or by appointment
Services Clock restoration

BELPER

Derwentside Antiques
Contact Mr M J Adams
Derwent Street, Belper, Derbyshire, DE56 1WN P
☎ 01773 828008 F 01773 828983
E enquiries@derwentsidehome centre.co.uk
W www.derwentsidehome centre.co.uk
Est. 1994 *Stock size* Large
Stock General antiques
Open Mon–Sun 8.30am–5pm
Fairs Newark, Swinderby
Services Architectural salvage

Sweetings Antiques Belper
Contact Mr or Mrs Sweeting
1 & 1a The Butts, Belper, Derbyshire, DE56 1HX P
☎ 01773 825930
M 07973 658640
Est. 1972 *Stock size* Large
Stock General antiques, country pine furniture, home accessories
Open Mon–Sat 9.30am–5.30pm
Sun 11am–4.30pm
Services Restoration and pine stripping

BRADWELL

Bradwell Antiques Centre
Contact Mr N Cottam
Newburgh Hall, Netherside, Bradwell, Derbyshire,

S33 9JL 🅿
☎ 01433 621000 Ⓕ 01433 621000
Ⓔ info@bradwellantiques.com
Ⓦ www.bradwellantiques.com
Est. 2000 *Stock size* Large
No. of dealers 28
Stock Furniture, paintings, general antiques, collectables
Open Mon–Sat 10am–5pm Sun 11am–5pm
Services Licensed café, book search, restoration

BUXTON

⊞ Antiques Warehouse
Contact Nigel Thompson
✉ **25 Lightwood Road, Buxton, Derbyshire, SK17 7BJ** 🅿
☎ 01298 72967 Ⓕ 01298 22603
Ⓜ 07947 050552
Est. 1979 *Stock size* Large
Stock General antiques
Open Mon–Fri 10am–3pm Sat 10am–4pm Sun by appointment
Services Valuations, restoration

⊞ Back to Front
Contact Miss Simone Jordan-Lomas
✉ **9–11 Market Street, Buxton, Derbyshire, SK17 6JY** 🅿
☎ 01298 23969
Est. 1974 *Stock size* Large
Stock Antique textiles
Open Mon–Sun 10am–8pm
Fairs Newark, The International Antique and Collectables Fair at RAF Swinderby

⊞ A & A Needham
Contact Ann Needham
✉ **8 Cavendish Circus, Buxton, Derbyshire, SK17 6AT** 🅿
☎ 01298 24546
Ⓜ 07941 436931
Est. 1953 *Stock size* Small
Stock French, Dutch, English furniture, paintings, bronzes, works of art
Open Mon–Sat 9am–5pm
Fairs Chester

⊞ What Now Antiques
Contact Mrs L Carruthers
✉ **Unit 8, Cavendish Arcade, The Crescent, Buxton, Derbyshire, SK17 6BQ** 🅿
☎ 01298 27178
Est. 1987 *Stock size* Medium
Stock General 19th–20thC antiques
Open Tues–Sat 10am–5pm Sun 1–4pm
Services Valuations

CASTLE DONINGTON

⊞ Once Removed
Contact Mrs Whiston
✉ **25 Borough Street, Castle Donington, Derbyshire, DE74 2LA** 🅿
Ⓜ 07931 993251
Est. 1998 *Stock size* Small
Stock Furniture, glass, china
Open Mon Fri 9.30am–4pm Thurs 9.30am–3pm Sat 10am–1pm
Services Valuations

⊞ The Gallery Book Shop
Contact Mrs J Ethelston
✉ **17 Borough Street, Castle Donnington, Derbyshire, DE74 2LA** 🅿
☎ 01332 814391
Est. 2000 *Stock size* Medium
Stock Antiquarian and collectable books, prints
Open Mon–Fri 9am–4.30pm Sat 9am–1pm closed Tues Wed
Services Picture framing

CASTLETON

⊞ Hawkridge Books
Contact Irene or Joe Tierney
✉ **Cruck Barn, Cross Street, Castleton, Derbyshire, S33 8WH** 🅿
☎ 01433 621999
Ⓦ www.hawkridge.co.uk
Est. 1995 *Stock size* Large
Stock Antiquarian, rare and second-hand books, ornithology
Open Mon–Fri 10am–5pm Sat 10am–5.30pm Sun noon–5.30pm

CHESTERFIELD

⊞ Ian Morris
Contact Mr I Morris
✉ **479 Chatsworth Road, Chesterfield, Derbyshire, S40 3AD** 🅿
☎ 01246 235120
Est. 1974 *Stock size* Medium
Stock General antiques
Open By appointment

⊞ Marlene Rutherford Antiques
Contact Mrs M Rutherford
✉ **401 Sheffield Road, Whittington Moor, Chesterfield, Derbyshire, S41 8LS** 🅿
☎ 01246 450209
Ⓜ 07885 665440
Est. 1984 *Stock size* Large
Stock General antiques, upholstered furniture, oil lamps, clocks
Open Mon Tues Fri Sat 1–4pm Thurs 10am–4pm

CLOWNE

⊞ Wartime Wardrobe
Contact Mr Barry Draycott
✉ **105 Portland Street, Clowne, Chesterfield, Derbyshire, S43 4SA** 🅿
Ⓜ 07966 450726
Est. 1995 *Stock size* Medium
Stock Military and civilian 1940s vintage clothing, general militaria
Open Any time by appointment
Fairs Most 1940s themed events throughout the UK, some military shows
Services Valuations, advice

CROMFORD

⊞ Antiques Loft
Contact Brendan Rogerson
✉ **Market Place, Cromford, Matlock, Derbyshire, DE4 3QH** 🅿
☎ 01629 826565
Est. 1993 *Stock size* Large
Stock Victorian pine, shipping furniture
Open By appointment
Fairs Swinderby, Newark

DERBY

⊞ Finishing Touches
Contact Lynne Robertson
✉ **224 Uttoxeter Old Road, Derby, Derbyshire, DE1 1NF** 🅿
☎ 01332 721717
Ⓜ 07789 727596
Ⓦ www.derbyantiques.co.uk
Est. 1994 *Stock size* Medium
Stock Georgian–Victorian fireplaces and fire surrounds, pine doors, locks, handles, window catches, pine furniture
Open Thur–Sat 10am–5.30pm or by appointment

⊞ Friargate Antiques Company
Contact Glyn or Daryl Richards

✉ **120 Friargate, Derby, Derbyshire, DE1 1EX** 🅿
☎ 01332 297966 ℗ 01332 297966
Ⓜ 07976 929456
ⓔ daryl@friargateantiques.co.uk
ⓦ www.friargateantiques.co.uk
Est. 1978 *Stock size* Large
Stock General antiques, Royal Crown Derby
Open Mon–Fri 10am–4pm Sat 10am–5pm
Fairs Newark
Services Valuations, restoration

⊞ Friargate Pine Co Ltd
Contact John Marianszi
✉ **Old Pump House, Stafford Street, Derby, Derbyshire, DE1 1JL** 🅿
☎ 01332 341215 ℗ 01332 341215
ⓔ enquiries@friargatepine.co.uk
ⓦ www.friargatepine.co.uk
Est. 1984 *Stock size* Medium
Stock Antique, reproduction pine
Open Mon–Sat 9am–5pm
Services Made to measure

DUFFIELD

⊞ Wayside Antiques
Contact Brian Harding
✉ **62 Town Street, Duffield, Belper, Derbyshire, DE56 4GG** 🅿
☎ 01332 840346
Est. 1976 *Stock size* Large
Stock 18th–19thC furniture
Open Mon–Sat 10am–6pm
Services Valuations, restoration

FURNESS VALE

⊞ Furness Vale Antiques
Contact Mrs K Thomas
✉ **95 Buxton Road, Furness Vale, High Peak, Derbyshire, SK23 7PL** 🅿
☎ 01663 747183
Est. 1980 *Stock size* Small
Stock General antiques
Open Thurs 10am–4pm

GLOSSOP

⊞ Chapel Antiques
Contact Mr Norman Pogsom
✉ **126 Brookfield, Glossop, Derbyshire, SK13 6JE** 🅿
☎ 01457 866711
Est. 1984 *Stock size* Medium
Stock Clocks, barometers, pottery, general antiques
Open Thurs–Sun 10am–5pm

⊞ Cottage Antiques
Contact Mrs J Shapter
✉ **Unit 13, Brookfield, Glossop, Derbyshire, SK13 6JF** 🅿
☎ 01457 860092
Est. 1979 *Stock size* Large
Stock General antiques
Open Thurs–Sun Bank Holidays 10am–5pm
Services Valuations, house clearance

⊞ Derbyshire Clocks
Contact Terry or Judith Lees
✉ **104 High Street West, Glossop, Derbyshire, SK13 8BB** 🅿
☎ 01457 862677
Est. 1971 *Stock size* Medium
Stock Clocks, barometers and other related items, pre-1880 longcase and wall clocks
Open Thurs–Sat 9am–5pm Sun noon–4.30pm
Services Restoration

⌂ Glossop Antique Centre
Contact Mr G Conway
✉ **Brookfield, Glossop, Derbyshire, SK13 6JE** 🅿
☎ 01457 863904
Est. 1990 *Stock size* Medium
No. of dealers 12
Stock General antiques
Open Thurs–Sun 10am–5pm
Services Valuations, restoration, café

⊞ O'Sullivan Antiques Ltd
Contact Michael O'Sullivan
✉ **Unit 3, Glossop Antique Centre, Brookfield, Glossop, Derbyshire, SK13 6JE** 🅿
☎ 01457 864488
Ⓜ 07834 478555
Est. 2003 *Stock size* Medium
Stock Victorian–Edwardian furniture, collectables
Open Thur–Sun 10am–5pm

HAYFIELD

⊞ Paul Pickford Antiques
Contact Paul Pickford
✉ **Top of the Town, Hayfield, High Peak, Derbyshire, SK22 2JE** 🅿
☎ 01663 747276/743356
Ⓜ 07887 585891
ⓔ paul@pickfordantiques.co.uk
ⓦ www.pickfordantiques.co.uk
Est. 1974 *Stock size* Medium
Stock General antiques, furniture, stripped pine, light fittings
Open Tues Thurs Sat 11am–4pm Sun 1–5pm

HEANOR

⌂ Heanor Antiques Centre
Contact Jane Richards
✉ **Church Square, 1–2 Ilkeston Road, Heanor, Derbyshire, DE75 7AE** 🅿
☎ 01773 531181
Est. 1997 *Stock size* Large
No. of dealers 120
Stock General antiques and small collectable items
Open Mon–Sun 10.30am–4.30pm
Services Café

ILKESTON

⊞ Flourish Farm Antiques
Contact Joyce Mumford
✉ **Dale Abbey, Ilkeston, Derbyshire, DE7 4PQ** 🅿
☎ 01332 667820
Ⓜ 07970 055151
Est. 1995 *Stock size* Medium
Stock Original pine furniture, cast-iron fireplaces, doors and door fittings
Open Tues–Sat 10am–5pm closed Wed pm
Services Wood stripping

MATLOCK

⊞ Antique Centre
Contact Margaret O'Reilly or Keith Allsop
✉ **190 South Parade, Matlock Bath, Derbyshire, DE4 3NR** 🅿
☎ 01629 582712
Est. 1970 *Stock size* Large
Stock Victorian–Edwardian furniture, upholstered furniture
Open Mon–Sun 10am–6pm or later

⊞ Archway Antiques
Contact Martin Powys
✉ **4 The Market Place,**

Wirksworth, Matlock, Derbyshire, DE4 4ET P
☎ 01629 825373
Est. 1990 *Stock size* Large
Stock Collectables, bric-a-brac, small items
Open Fri–Sat 11am–1pm 2–5pm or by appointment

R F Barrett Rare Books
Contact Mr R Barrett
87 Dale Road, Matlock, Derbyshire, DE4 3LU P
☎ 01629 57644
Est. 1979 *Stock size* Medium
Stock Antique, rare and second-hand books
Open Mon–Sun 10am–5pm

Matlock Antiques & Collectables
Contact Miss Wendy Shirley
7 Dale Road, Matlock, Derbyshire, DE4 3LT P
☎ 01629 760808 F 01629 760808
W www.matlock-antiques-collectables.cwc.net
Est. 1996 *Stock size* Large
No. of dealers 70+
Stock General antiques, collectables
Open Mon–Sun 10am–5pm
Services Delivery, riverside café

Noel Wheatcroft (FNAVA, FNAEA)
Contact Mrs J Kinnear
Matlock Auction Gallery, The Old Picture Palace, Dale Road, Matlock, Derbyshire, DE4 3LT
☎ 01629 57460 F 01629 57956
E mag@wheatcroft-noel.co.uk
W www.wheatcroft-noel.co.uk
Est. 1923
Open Mon–Fri 10am–4pm closed Thurs
Sales Monthly, see website
Catalogues Yes

NEW MILLS

Michael Allcroft Antiques
Contact Michael Allcroft
203 Buxton Road, Newtown, New Mills, Nr Stockport, SK12 2RA P
☎ 01663 744014 F 01663 744014
M 07798 781642
Est. 1986 *Stock size* Large
Stock General antiques, Victorian–Edwardian and 1930s furniture, ideal for Japanese market
Open Tues–Fri noon–6pm Sat 10.30am–noon
Fairs Newark

Antiques & Pine Shop
Contact Mrs Pickering
2 High Street, New Mills, Derbyshire, SK22 4AL P
☎ 01663 744710
Est. 1979 *Stock size* Medium
Stock Antique and pine furniture, bric-a-brac, giftware, pictures, glass
Open Thurs Fri Sat 9am–5.30pm or by appointment
Services House clearance

OCKBROOK

The Good Olde Days
Contact Mr S Potter
6 Flood Street, Ockbrook, Derby, Derbyshire, DE72 3RF P
☎ 01332 544244
Est. 1995 *Stock size* Large
Stock General antiques
Open Tues–Sat 10am–5pm Wed noon–5pm
Fairs Swinderbury, Kettering, Kedlaston Hall
Services Valuations

RIDDINGS

steam-models.uk.com
Contact Mr R Evison
31 South Street, Riddings, Alfreton, Derbyshire, DE55 4EJ P
☎ 01773 541527 F 01773 541527
M 07713 514320
E raevison@aol.com
W www.steammodels.uk.com
Est. 1990 *Stock size* Large
Stock Old and new live steam models
Open Mon–Fri 9am–5pm

RIPLEY

A A Ambergate Antiques
Contact Mr C Lawrence
8 Derby Road, Ripley, Derbyshire, DE5 3HR P
☎ 01773 745201
M 07885 327753
W www.upstairsdownstairsantiques.co.uk
Est. 1971 *Stock size* Large
Stock Edwardian bedroom furniture
Open Mon–Sat 10am–4.30pm
Services Valuations, restoration

Memory Lane Antiques
Contact Jim Cullen
Nottingham Road, Ripley, Derbyshire, DE5 3AS P
☎ 01773 570184
M 07703 115626
E JamesGC1@aol.com
Est. 1993 *Stock size* Large
No. of dealers 40
Stock General antiques, collectables, shipping goods, kitchenware, Derby
Open Mon–Sun 10.30am–4pm only closed Christmas Day
Services Valuations, talks, house clearance. A permanent display of all 150+ Derby domestic ware patterns produced from 1940

Upstairs Downstairs Antiques
Contact Mr C Lawrence
8 Derby Road, Ripley, Derbyshire, DE5 3HR P
☎ 01773 745201
M 07885 327753
W www.upstairsdownstairsantiques.co.uk
Est. 1974 *Stock size* Large
Stock Edwardian–Victorian bedroom furniture, bookcases, pottery, china, pictures
Open Mon–Sat 10am–4pm
Services Restoration, clock repair

SHARDLOW

Shardlow Antiques
Contact Nina or Nigel
24 The Wharf, Shardlow, Derbyshire, DE72 2GH P
☎ 01332 792899
Est. 1977 *Stock size* Large
Stock Georgian furniture, general antiques
Open Mon–Thurs 10.30am–5pm Sat 10am–5pm Sun noon–5pm
Fairs Newark

MIDLANDS

DERBYSHIRE • SWADLINCOTE

SWADLINCOTE

⊞ Brewery House Antiques & Collectables
Contact Margi or David Morton
✉ **32 High Street, Woodville, Swadlincote, Derbyshire**
☎ 01283 218681
Est. 2004 *Stock size* Medium
Stock Victoriana, Art Deco, wash stands, fireplaces, linen, collectables
Open Fri Sat 10am–6pm Sun 10am–4pm

⊞ Escolme House Antiques
Contact Shirley May Smith
✉ **118 High Street, Woodville, Swadlincote, Derbyshire, DE11 7DU** P
☎ 01283 216699
ⓔ escolmehouse@btopenworld.com
Est. 2003 *Stock size* Small
Stock Pine furniture, ceramics, kitchenalia, Victorian–Edwardian glass
Open Tues Thur Fri Sat 9am–5.30pm
Services Pine stripping service

WHALEY BRIDGE

⊞ Nimbus Antiques
Contact Mr H C Brobbin
✉ **14 Chapel Road, Whaley Bridge, High Peak, Derbyshire, SK23 7JZ** P
☎ 01663 734248 ⓕ 01663 734248
ⓔ nimbusantiques@hotmail.com
ⓦ www.antiques-atlas.com/nimbus.htm
Est. 1979 *Stock size* Large
Stock General antiques, Georgian–Victorian furniture and clocks
Open Mon–Fri 9am–5.30pm Sat 10am–5.30pm Sun 2–5.30pm

LEICESTERSHIRE

ASHBY DE LA ZOUCH

⊞ Affordable Antiques
Contact Mrs J Sidwells
✉ **The Old Forge, North Street, Ashby de la Zouch, Leicestershire, LE65 1HS**
☎ 01530 413744
ⓜ 07966 424861
Est. 1994 *Stock size* Medium
Stock Pre-1950s furniture and effects
Open Mon–Sat 10am–5pm closed Wed
Fairs Newark, Swinderby
Services Pine, oak stripping

COALVILLE

⊞ Coalville Pine & Antiques
Contact Mr Truswell
✉ **115–117 Belvoir Road, Coalville, Leicestershire, LE67 3PN** P
☎ 01530 830099 ⓕ 01530 830099
ⓜ 07812 608654
Est. 2003 *Stock size* Medium
Stock Antique pine furniture, oak furniture
Open Tues–Sat 9am–5pm
Services Restoration

⊞ Keystone Antiques (LAPADA)
Contact Miss H McPherson FGA
✉ **66 London Road, Coalville, Leicestershire, LE67 3JA** P
☎ 01530 835966 ⓕ 01530 817773
ⓔ keystone@heathermcpherson.co.uk
Est. 1980 *Stock size* Medium
Stock General antiques, jewellery, silver, small collectables
Open Mon–Wed by appointment Thurs–Sat 10am–5pm
Fairs NEC
Services Valuations for jewellery, silver

ENDERBY

⊞ The Glory Hole
Contact Mark Crowston
✉ **2 Penn Craig, Harold Lane, Enderby, Leicestershire, LE19 4AF** P
☎ 0116 286 9123
ⓜ 07710 101364
ⓦ www.gloryholeantiques.co.uk
Est. 1994 *Stock size* Large
Stock Victorian–Edwardian furniture, general antiques
Open Mon–Sat 10am–5.30pm Sun 10am–4pm
Fairs Newark, Ardingly
Services Restoration, door and furniture stripping

FINEDON

⌂ 3 Church Street Antiques
Contact Bob Harrison
✉ **3 Church Street, Finedon, Northamptonshire, NN9 5NA** P
☎ 01933 682515 ⓕ 01933 682210
ⓜ 07860 679116
ⓔ sales@frenchbeds.com
ⓦ www.frenchbeds.com
Est. 1985 *Stock size* Large
No. of dealers 4
Stock English, French furniture, decorative items, clocks, French beds, mirrors
Open Mon–Sat 9am–5.30pm Sun 11am–5pm
Services Valuations, restoration, shipping, nationwide delivery

GREAT GLEN

⊞ Sitting Pretty
Contact Mrs J Jones-Fenleigh
✉ **45a Main Street, Great Glen, Leicestershire, LE8 9EH** P
☎ 01162 593711
Est. 1979 *Stock size* Medium
Stock Antiques and period upholstered furniture
Open Thurs–Sat 10am–5.30pm
Services Upholstery restoration

GRIMSTON

⊞ Ancient and Oriental Ltd (ADA)
Contact Mr Alex Szolin
✉ **Park View, Grimston, Melton Mowbray, Leicestershire, LE14 3BZ** P
☎ 01664 812044
ⓔ alex@antiquities.co.uk
ⓦ www.antiquities.co.uk
Est. 1992
Stock Ancient art and items of archaeological interest from major world cultures, ancient–medieval
Open By appointment
Services Mail order, catalogues and website

HINCKLEY

⊞ Bob Harrison Antiques
Contact Bob Harrison
✉ **27 Burbage Road, Burbage, Hinckley, Leicestershire, LE10 2TS** P
☎ 01455 611689
ⓜ 07860 679116
ⓔ bob@bobharrisonantiques.co.uk
Est. 1985 *Stock size* Medium
Stock Decorative, general antiques, furniture, mirrors

Trade only Yes
Open By appointment
Services Valuations, restoration

House Things Antiques
Contact P Robertson
44 Mansion Street, Trinity Lane, Hinckley, Leicestershire, LE10 0AU
01455 618518
Est. 1976 *Stock size* Medium
Stock General antiques
Open Mon–Sat 10am–6pm closed Tues
Services Valuations, restoration

Magpie
Contact Michelle Johnson or David Wassell
126 Castle Street, Hinckley, Leicestershire, LE10 1DD
01455 891819
07713 099744
michelle@magpieantiques.fsnet.co.uk
Est. 1985 *Stock size* Medium
Stock Georgian to pre-1950s household effects, kitchenware, toys
Open Mon–Sat 9am–5pm
Fairs Newark, Swinderby
Services House clearance

HOBY

Withers of Leicester
Contact Simon Frings
The Old Rutland, 6 Regent Road, Hoby, Leicestershire, LE14 3DU
01664 434803
07836 526595
Est. 1860 *Stock size* Medium
Stock 17th–early 20thC furniture
Open Mon–Sat telephone first
Services Valuations, restoration

KIBWORTH

Kibworth Pine Co
Contact Mrs Burdett
16 Harcourt Estate, Kibworth, Leicestershire, LE8 0NE
0116 279 3475
www.kibworthpinecompany.com
Est. 1981 *Stock size* Large
Stock Antique pine furniture
Open Tues–Sat 9.30am–5.30pm Sun noon–4pm

LEICESTER

The Black Cat Bookshop (PBFA)
Contact Mr P Woolley
90 Charles Street, Leicester, Leicestershire, LE1 1GE
0116 251 2756 0116 281 3545
blackcatuk@aol.com
www.blackcatbookshop.com
Est. 1987 *Stock size* Large
Stock Antiquarian, rare and second-hand books, British comics, magazines, printed ephemera
Open Mon–Sat 9.30am–5pm
Fairs Memorabilia Fair (NEC)
Services Worldwide mail order, book search, catalogues

Brass & Wood Still Looking Good
Contact Marcus Adams
PO Box 3046, 20 Deacon Street, Leicester, Leicestershire, LE2 3EF
07973 294622
brassandwood.stilllookinggood@btinternet.com
Est. 2000 *Stock size* Small
Stock Brass and wood, furniture, lighting
Open By appointment
Fairs Chelsea Brocante, Royal Horticultural Hall
Services Restoration

Churchgate Auctions Ltd
Contact Mr D Dearman
66 Churchgate, Leicester, Leicestershire, LE1 4AL
0116 262 1416 0116 251 7711
info@churchgateauctions.co.uk
www.churchgateauctions.co.uk
Est. 1966
Open Mon–Fri 8.30am–6pm Sat 8.30am–noon
Sales General and antiques sales Fri 10am, viewing Thurs 2–6pm
Frequency Weekly
Catalogues Yes

Clarendon Books (PBFA)
Contact Mr J Smith
144 Clarendon Park Road, Leicester, Leicestershire, LE2 3AE
0116 270 1856 0116 270 9020
07710 683996
clarendonbooks@aol.com
Est. 1986 *Stock size* Medium
Stock Antiquarian, rare and second-hand books
Open Mon–Sat 10am–5pm
Fairs PBFA

Corry's Antiques (LAPADA)
Contact Mrs E I Corry
26 Francis Street, Stoneygate, Leicester, Leicestershire, LE2 2BD
0116 270 3794 0116 270 3794
www.corrys-antiques.com
Est. 1964 *Stock size* Large
Stock General antiques, clocks, mirrors, porcelain, silver, furniture

MIDLANDS

LEICESTERSHIRE • LOUGHBOROUGH

Open Mon–Sat 10am–5pm
Fairs NEC
Services Restoration

Glory Hole Antiques
69 High Street, Earl Shilton, Leicester, Leicestershire, LE9 7DH
01455 847922
07710 101364
mark@thegloryhole.co.uk
www.thegloryhole.co.uk
Est. 1994 *Stock size* Large
Stock General antiques, Victorian–Edwardian items
Open Mon–Sat 10am–5.30pm
Fairs Newark, Ardingly
Services Valuations, restoration, stripping, shipping

Leicester Antiques Warehouse
Clarkes Road, Wigston, Leicester, Leicestershire, LE18 2BG
0116 288 1315 0116 281 1742
webmaster@antiques-of-britain.co.uk
www.antiques-of-britain.co.uk
Est. 2002 *Stock size* Large
No. of dealers 60
Stock General antiques, collectables
Open Tues–Sat 10am–5pm Sun noon–5pm

Oxford Street Antique Centre
Contact Mr P Giles
16–26 Oxford Street, Leicester, Leicestershire, LE1 5XU
0116 255 3006 0116 255 5863
Est. 1987 *Stock size* Large
Stock Victorian–present-day furniture
Open Mon–Fri 10am–5.30pm Sat 10am–5pm Sun 2–5pm
Services Export, container packing

Retrobuy
Contact Mr Mark Williamson
62 Silver Arcade, Leicester, Leicestershire, LE1 5FB
0116 242 5949 0116 242 5949
retrobuy@ntlworld.com
www.retrobuy.co.uk
Est. 1997 *Stock size* Large
Stock Retro toys, clothes, arcade, home, music, records
Open Mon–Sat noon–5pm
Fairs NEC, Donnington
Services Valuations, mail order

The Rug Gallery
Contact Mr R Short
50 Montague Road, Leicester, Leicestershire, LE2 1TH
0116 270 0085 0116 270 0113
Est. 1987 *Stock size* Large
Stock Old and new Oriental rugs and kilims, antique Oriental furniture
Open Fri Sat 10am–4pm or by appointment

Treasure Trove Books
Contact Linda Sharman
21 Mayfield Road, Leicester, Leicestershire, LE2 1LR
0116 275 5933
sales@treasuretrove-books.co.uk
Est. 1993 *Stock size* Medium
Stock Second-hand books, pop records, CDs, tapes
Open Mon–Sat 9.30am–5.30pm
Fairs Leicestershire, Missing Book Fair

LOUGHBOROUGH

Malcolm Hornsby
Contact Mr Malcolm Hornsby
41 Church Gate, Loughborough, Leicestershire, LE11 1UE
01509 269860 01509 269860
info@hornsbybooks.co.uk
Est. 1969 *Stock size* Large
Stock Antique, rare and second-hand books, Eastern Mediterranean travel books and maps a speciality
Open Mon–Sat 10am–5.30pm

Loughborough Antiques Centre
Contact Richard or Carol Wesley
50 Market Street, Loughborough, Leicestershire, LE11 3ER
01509 239931
Est. 1979 *Stock size* Medium
Stock General antiques, jewellery, clocks
Open Tues Thurs–Sat 10am–5pm
Services Valuations

Lowe of Loughborough
Contact Richard Lowe
37–40 Church Gate, Loughborough, Leicestershire, LE11 1UE
01509 212554/217876
Est. 1846 *Stock size* Medium
Stock Furniture, clocks, maps
Open Mon–Fri 8am–5.30pm
Services Restoration

LUBENHAM

Oaktree Antiques
Contact Gillian Abraham
The Drapers House, Main Street, Lubenham, Market Harborough, Leicestershire, LE16 9TF
01858 410041
www.oaktreeantiques.co.uk
Stock size Large
Stock Town and country 17th–19thC furniture, longcase clocks, works of art
Open Wed–Sun 10am–6pm

MARKET BOSWORTH

Bosworth Antiques
Contact Mr J H Thorp
12 Main Street, Market Bosworth, Leicestershire, CV13 0JW
01455 292134
Est. 1986 *Stock size* Medium
Stock General antiques and collectables
Open Wed–Sat 10am–5pm
Services Valuations

MARKET HARBOROUGH

Aquarius Books
Contact Mr R Lack
8 St Marys Road, Market Harborough, Leicestershire, LE16 7DU
01858 431060
raylack@btconnect.com
www.aquariusbooks.co.uk
Est. 1989 *Stock size* Medium
Stock Antiquarian, rare and second-hand books
Open Mon–Sat 10am–4pm

Bonhams
34 High Street, Market Harborough, Leicestershire, BN3 2JN
01858 438900 01858 438909
marketharborough@bonhams.com

Ⓦ www.bonhams.com
Est. 1793
Open Mon–Fri 9am–1pm 2–5pm
Sales Regional office. Regular house and attic sales across the country; contact London offices for further details. Free auction valuations; insurance and probate valuations
Catalogues Yes

The Furniture Barn
Contact Richard Kimbell
Rockingham Road, Market Harborough, Leicestershire, LE16 7QE Ⓟ
☎ 01858 433444 Ⓕ 01858 461301
Ⓦ www.thefurniturebarn.com
Est. 1969 *Stock size* Medium
Stock Antique, pine and country furniture, upholstery, end-of-line fabrics
Open Mon–Wed Fri 10am–6pm Thurs 10am–8pm Sat 9am–6pm Sun 10.30am–4.30pm

Gildings
Contact John Gilding
Roman Way, Market Harborough, Leicestershire, LE16 7PQ Ⓟ
☎ 01858 410414 Ⓕ 01858 432956
Ⓔ sales@gildings.co.uk
Ⓦ www.gildings.co.uk
Est. 1980
Open Mon–Fri 9am–5pm
Sales Regular fine art, antiques, specialist sales, weekly Victoriana and collectables sales
Frequency Monthly
Catalogues Yes

Edward Pritchard Antiques & 20thC Furniture
Contact Edward Pritchard
The Courtyard, Bennetts Place, 30–31 High Street, Market Harborough, Leicestershire, LE16 7NL Ⓟ
☎ 01858 439974
Ⓔ edwardpritchard@bennettsplace.fsnet.co.uk
Est. 2002 *Stock size* Medium
Stock Antique and 20thC furniture
Open Mon noon–5.30pm Tues–Sat 10am–5.30pm
Fairs NEC

J Stamp & Sons
Contact Mark Stamp
The Chestnuts, 15 Kettering Road, Market Harborough, Leicestershire, LE16 8AN Ⓟ
☎ 01858 462524 Ⓕ 01858 465643
Ⓔ jstampandsons@btconnect.com
Ⓦ www.jstampandsons.co.uk
Est. 1946 *Stock size* Medium
Stock Georgian–Edwardian furniture
Open Mon–Fri 8.30am–5.30pm Sat 9am–1pm or by appointment
Services Valuations, restoration

MELTON MOWBRAY

Flagstones Pine and Country Furniture
Contact Julie Adcock
24 Burton Street, Melton Mowbray, Leicestershire, LE13 1AF Ⓟ
☎ 01664 566438
Ⓜ 07971 299206
Ⓦ www.flagstonespine.com
Est. 1984 *Stock size* Medium
Stock Pine and country furniture, old and reproduction lighting, accessories
Open Tues Sat 9.30am–5.15pm Sun 10.30am–3.30pm
Services Stripping service, custom-built furniture

NARBOROUGH

Ken Smith Antiques Ltd (LAPADA)
Contact Mr K Smith
215–217 Leicester Road, Enderby, Leicester, Leicestershire, LE19 2BJ Ⓟ
☎ 0116 286 2341
Ⓔ KSL@kensmithltd.co.uk
Ⓦ www.kensmithltd.co.uk
Est. 1888 *Stock size* Medium
Stock General antiques, furniture and collectables
Open Mon–Sat 9.30am–5pm
Fairs Newark

OSGATHORPE

David E Burrows Antiques (LAPADA)
Contact Mr David Burrows
Manor House Farm, Osgathorpe, Loughborough, Leicestershire, LE12 9SY Ⓟ
☎ 01530 222218 Ⓕ 01530 223139
Ⓜ 07702 059030
Ⓔ david.burrows2@virgin.net
Est. 1970 *Stock size* Large
Stock Pine, oak, mahogany and walnut furniture, clocks, pictures
Trade only Yes
Open By appointment
Services Valuations, shipping

David Stanley Auctions
Contact David Stanley
Stordon Grange, Osgathorpe, Loughborough, Leicestershire, LE12 9SR Ⓟ
☎ 01530 222320 Ⓕ 01530 222523
Ⓔ auctions@davidstanley.com
Ⓦ www.davidstanley.com
Est. 1979
Open Mon–Sat 8am–5pm
Sales Antique woodwork tools (telephone for details)
Frequency Bi-monthly
Catalogues Yes

QUENIBOROUGH

J Green & Son
Contact Mr R Green
1 Coppice Lane, Queniborough, Leicestershire, LE7 3DR Ⓟ
☎ 01162 606682 Ⓕ 01162 606682
Ⓜ 07860 513121
Est. 1949 *Stock size* Medium
Stock Georgian and period furniture
Open By appointment

QUORN

Quorn Pine
Contact Steven Yates or Steven Parker
The Mills, Leicester Road, Quorn, Leicestershire, LE12 8ES Ⓟ
☎ 01509 416031 Ⓕ 01509 416051
Ⓦ www.quorn-pine.co.uk
Est. 1983 *Stock size* Large
Stock Mainly antique pine and country furniture, clocks, doors, fireplaces, reproduction furniture
Open Mon–Fri 9am–5.30pm Sat 9.30am–5.30pm Sun 2–5pm
Services Restoration, stripping

SEAGRAVE

Miller Services
Contact Robert Miller
43–45 Swan Street, Seagrave, Leicestershire, LE12 7NL Ⓟ

☎ 01509 812037 Ⓕ 01509 812037
Est. 1986
Open Mon–Fri 9am–5pm
Sat 10am–12.30pm
Sales Monthly antiques and jewellery sales, Seagrave Village Hall Sun 12.30pm, viewing 10am
Catalogues Yes

Miller Services
Contact Robert Miller
43–45 Swan Street, Seagrave, Leicestershire, LE12 7NL Ⓟ
☎ 01509 812037 Ⓕ 01509 812037
Est. 1986
Stock Pottery, glass, silver
Open Mon–Fri 9am–5pm Sat 10am–12.30pm
Fairs Arthur Swallow, DMG
Services Auctions, valuations

THURMASTON

Thurmaston Antiques Centre
Contact Mr Chapman
5 Garden Street, Thurmaston, Leicestershire, LE4 8DS Ⓟ
☎ 0116 269 4477 Ⓕ 0116 269 4477
Ⓦ www.antiques@home.co.uk
Est. 1990 *Stock size* Large
No. of dealers 100
Stock 2 main halls, 5 rooms of cabinets, clocks, furniture, modern art, bronzes, coins, stamps, toys, militaria, telephones, oil lamps
Open Mon–Fri 9.30am–5.30pm Sat 9am–5pm Sun Bank Holidays 10am–5pm

WHITWICK

Charles Antiques
Contact Mr Haydon
Whitwick, Leicestershire, LE67 Ⓟ
☎ 01530 836932
Ⓜ 07831 204406
Ⓔ charles.antiques@btopenworld.com
Est. 1973 *Stock size* Large
Stock Clocks, furniture
Open By appointment
Fairs Birmingham Motorcycle Museum

WIGSTON

The Leicester Antiques Warehouse
Contact Robert Sklar
Clarkes Road, Wigston, Leicestershire, LE18 2BG Ⓟ
☎ 0116 288 1315 Ⓕ 0116 281 1742
Ⓜ 07710 057750
Ⓔ webmaster@antiques-of-britain.co.uk
Ⓦ www.antiques-of-britain.co.uk
Est. 2002 *Stock size* Large
No. of dealers 60
Stock Furniture, jewellery, silver china
Open Tues–Sat 10am–5pm
Sun noon–5pm

WYMESWOLD

N F Bryan-Peach Antiques
Contact Mr N Bryan-Peach
30 Brook Street, Wymeswold, Loughborough, Leicestershire, LE12 6TU Ⓟ
☎ 01509 880425 Ⓕ 01509 880425
Ⓜ 07860 559590
Ⓔ norm@bryanpeach.demon.co.uk
Est. 1974 *Stock size* Medium
Stock 18th–19thC furniture, clocks, barometers
Open By appointment
Services Valuations, restoration

WYMONDHAM

The Old Bakery Antiques
Contact Tina Bryan
The Old Bakery, Main Street, Wymondham, Melton Mowbray, Leicestershire, LE14 2AG Ⓟ
☎ 01572 787472
Est. 1990 *Stock size* Medium
Stock Architectural and reclaimed items, door hardware, stained glass, doors, tiles, fireplaces, chimney pots, pine furniture, kitchenware, advertising items
Open Mon–Sat 10am–5.30pm closed Thur

NORTHAMPTONSHIRE

BRACKLEY

Brackley Antiques
Contact Mrs B H Nutting
69 High Street, Brackley, Northamptonshire, NN13 7BW Ⓟ
☎ 01280 703362 Ⓕ 01280 703362
Ⓜ 07761 443726
Est. 1979 *Stock size* Medium
Stock General antiques
Open Mon–Sat 10am–6pm
Wed by appointment
Services Traditional upholstery

The Brackley Antiques Cellar
Contact Debbe Perry
Drayman's Walk, Brackley, Northamptonshire, NN13 6BE Ⓟ
☎ 01280 841851 Ⓕ 01280 841851
Est. 2000 *Stock size* Large
No. of dealers 102+
Stock General antiques, smalls, collectables, furniture, militaria
Open Mon–Sun 10am–5pm
Services Tea room

The Old Hall Bookshop (ABA, PBFA, ILAB)
Contact Tom Dixon
32 Market Place, Brackley, Northamptonshire, NN13 7DP Ⓟ
☎ 01280 704146 Ⓕ 01280 705131
Ⓔ books@oldhallbooks.com
Ⓦ www.oldhallbooks.com
Est. 1977 *Stock size* Large
Stock A wide range of second-hand and antiquarian books
Open Mon–Fri 9.30am–5.30pm
Sat 9.30am–1pm 2–5.30pm
Fairs ABA, PBFA
Services Book search for out-of-print books

DAVENTRY

Bygone Days
Contact Sue Pratley
16 Sheaf Street, Daventry, Northamptonshire, NN11 4AB Ⓟ
☎ 01327 878617
Ⓔ susanbygonedays@aol.com
Est. 1999 *Stock size* Medium
Stock General antiques, collectables, furniture, glass, Worcester, Crown Derby
Open Mon–Sat 10am–5pm
Fairs Lamport Hall

DESBOROUGH

Old Bus Station Antiques Ltd
Contact Fiona Kimbell
The Old Bus Station, Harborough Road, Desborough,

Northamptonshire,
NN14 2QX P
☎ 01536 762093 F 01536 763263
E enquiries@oldbus-antiques.com
Est. 1980 *Stock size* Large
Stock Decorative pine, painted country furniture
Trade only Yes
Open Mon–Fri 9am–5pm or by appointment
Services Container packing, shipping

EVENLEY

Amors of Evenley
Contact Mr Amor
✉ **Evenley, Brackley, Northamptonshire, NN13 5SB** P
☎ 01869 811342
E amorsofevenley@hotmail.com
Est. 1960 *Stock size* Large
No. of dealers 6
Stock 17th–19thC furniture, porcelain, ceramics, paintings
Open Mon–Sat 9am–5.30pm Sun 10am–4pm
Services Valuations, house clearance

FINEDON

Aspidistra Antiques
Contact Patricia Moss
✉ **51 High Street, Finedon, Wellingborough, Northamptonshire, NN9 5JN** P
☎ 01933 680196
M 07768 071948
E info@aspidistra-antiques.com
W www.aspidistra-antiques.com
Est. 1994 *Stock size* Medium
No. of dealers 6
Stock Specialist in decorative arts, good selection of smalls and furniture
Open Mon–Sat 10am–5pm Sun 11am–5pm
Services Valuations, commission sales, restoration

Simon Banks Antiques
Contact Mr S Banks
✉ **28 Church Street, Finedon, Wellingborough, Northamptonshire, NN9 5NA** P
☎ 01933 680371
M 07976 787539
Est. 1984 *Stock size* Large
Stock General antiques, dining room furniture, clocks, silver, silver plate, pottery, porcelain
Open Mon–Sat 10am–5.30pm Sun 11am–4.30pm
Services Valuations

Michael Chapman Antiques (LAPADA)
Contact Michael Chapman
✉ **3 Church Street, Finedon, Northamptonshire, NN9 5NA** P
☎ 01933 681260
E sales@finedonantiques.com
Est. 1973 *Stock size* Medium
Stock 18th–early 20thC English, Continental furniture, clocks, decorative items, shipping goods, upholstery
Open Mon–Sat 9am–5.30pm Sun 11am–5pm
Services Valuations

Robert Cheney Antiques
Contact Robert Cheney
✉ **11–13 High Street, Finedon, Wellingborough,**

Northamptonshire,
NN9 5JN P
☎ 01933 681048
Est. 1992 *Stock size* Medium
Stock General antiques
Open Mon–Sat 9am–5pm
Sun 11am–4pm
Services Valuations and house clearances

⊞ E K Antiques

Contact E Kubacki
✉ **37 High Street, Finedon, Northamptonshire, NN9 5JN** P
☎ 01933 681882
Ⓜ 07711 245530
Est. 1991 *Stock size* Medium
Stock General antiques
Open Mon–Sat 9.30am–5pm
Sun 11am–4pm
Fairs Hinchingbrooke, Hunts
Services Valuations, restoration, house clearance

⊞ Finedon Antiques Ltd (LAPADA)

Contact Michael Chapman
✉ **3 Church Street, Finedon, Wellingborough, Northamptonshire, NN9 5ND** P
☎ 01933 681260/682210
Ⓕ 01933 682210
Ⓔ sales@finedonantiques.com
Ⓦ www.finedonantiques.com
Est. 1972 *Stock size* Large
Stock 18th–19thC English and French furniture, pottery, porcelain, decorative items
Open Mon–Sat 9am–5.30pm
Sun 11am–5pm
Services Valuations, restoration

FLORE

⊞ Blockheads

Contact Richard Sear
✉ **The Hunter Shields, Flore, Northamptonshire, NN7 4LZ** P
☎ 01327 340718 Ⓕ 01327 349263
Est. 1965 *Stock size* Large
Stock Restored wooden hat blocks, restored, polished and mounted as a decorative item
Open By appointment
Fairs Newark

⊞ Granary Antiques

Contact Richard Sear
✉ **The Hunter Shields, Flore, Northamptonshire, NN7 4LZ** P
☎ 01327 340718 Ⓕ 01327 349263
Est. 1965 *Stock size* Large
Stock Early metalwork, country furniture
Open By appointment
Fairs Newark

⊞ Christopher Jones Antiques

Contact Robert Black
✉ **Flore House, The Avenue, Flore, Northamptonshire, NN7 4LZ** P
☎ 01327 342165 Ⓕ 01327 349230
Ⓔ florehouse@msn.com
Ⓦ www.christopherjones antiques.co.uk
Est. 1993 *Stock size* Large
Stock Decorative objects and furniture 18th–early 20thC
Open Mon–Sat 10am–5pm
Fairs Olympia

HARPOLE

⊞ Inglenook Antiques

Contact Tony or Pamela Havard
✉ **23 High Street, Harpole, Northamptonshire, NN7 4DH** P
☎ 01604 830007
Est. 1971 *Stock size* Small
Stock Small country items, copper, brass, Victoriana, general antiques
Open Mon–Sat 9am–6.30pm
Services Longcase clock restoration

ISLIP

⊞ John Roe Antiques

Contact Mr John Roe
✉ **Furnace Site, Kettering Road, Islip, Kettering, Northamptonshire, NN14 3JW** P
☎ 01832 732937 Ⓕ 01832 732937
Est. 1969 *Stock size* Large
Stock General antique furniture
Open Mon–Fri 9am–6pm Sat 10am–5pm Sun by appointment
Fairs Newark
Services Shipping, packing

KETTERING

⊞ Dragon Antiques

Contact Sandra Hunt
✉ **85 Rockingham Road, Kettering, Northamptonshire, NN16 8LA** P
☎ 01536 517017
Est. 1982 *Stock size* Small
Stock General antiques, paintings
Open Mon–Sat 10am–4pm closed Thurs
Services Picture framing, restoration

NORTHAMPTON

⊞ Cave's

Contact Allan Cave
✉ **111 Kettering Road, Northampton, Northamptonshire, NN1 4BA** P
☎ 01604 638278 Ⓕ 01604 230177
Est. 1879 *Stock size* Large
Stock Georgian furniture
Open Mon–Sat 9am–5.30pm closed Thurs

⊞ Inglenook Antiques

Contact Mrs Hull
✉ **92 St Leonards Road, Northampton, Northamptonshire, NN4 8DW** P
☎ 01604 708754
Ⓔ inglenook98@btopenworld.com
Ⓦ www.inglenook.org.uk
Est. 1998 *Stock size* Medium
Stock Victorian and older furniture
Open Mon–Sun 11am–4pm or by appointment
Services Delivery within 150 mile radius

Merry's Auctions

Contact Mrs Denise Cowling FGA
✉ **Northampton Auction & Sales Centre, Liliput Road, Brackmills, Northampton, Northamptonshire, NN4 7BY** P
☎ 01604 769990 Ⓕ 01604 763155
Ⓜ 07818 003786
Ⓔ denise@northantsauctions.co.uk
Ⓦ www.northantsauctions.com
Est. 1815
Open Mon–Wed 9.30am–1pm or by appointment
Sales Bi-monthly antique, fine art and collectables sale. Victorian, later and general antiques sale twice per month, view Wed 5–8pm Thurs 10am–4pm and morning of sale. Bar and cafeteria
Catalogues Yes

⊞ Giuseppe Miceli (OMRS, BNTA)

Contact Mr Giuseppe Miceli

204 Bants Lane, Northampton, Northamptonshire, NN5 6AH P
01604 581533
Est. 1969 *Stock size* Medium
Stock Coins, medals
Open Mon–Sat 9am–6pm
Services Valuations

The Old Brigade
Contact Mr S Wilson
10a Harborough Road, Kingsthorpe, Northampton, Northamptonshire, NN2 7AZ P
01604 719389 F 01604 712489
theoldbrigade@btconnect.com
www.theoldbrigade.co.uk
Est. 1985 *Stock size* Medium
Stock 1850–1945 militaria, Third Reich
Open Mon–Sat 10.30am–5pm by appointment only
Services Valuations

OUNDLE

Harpurs of Oundle
Contact Nigel Hill
5a West Street, Oundle, Northamptonshire, PE8 4EJ P
01234 344831 F 01234 344831
info@harpurjewellery.com
www.harpurjewellery.com
Est. 1981 *Stock size* Medium
Stock Antique, contemporary and new jewellery, small collectables, watches, silver
Open Mon–Sat 10am–4.30pm closed Wed

Geraldine Waddington Books and Prints (PBFA)
Contact Geraldine Waddington
3 West Street, Oundle, Northamptonshire, PE8 4EJ P
01832 275028 F 01832 275028
g.waddington@dial.pipex.com
Est. 1999 *Stock size* Medium
Stock Books, illustrations, contemporary wood engravings
Open Mon–Sat 10am–5pm closed Wed
Fairs Fine Press Fair Oxford, PBFA

POTTERSPURY

Reindeer Antiques Ltd (LAPADA, BADA)
Contact Nicholas Fuller
43 Watling Street, Potterspury, Northamptonshire, NN12 7QD P
01908 542407/542200
F 01908 542121
M 07711 446221
nicholas.fuller@reindeer-antiques.co.uk
www.reindeerantiques.co.uk
Est. 1969 *Stock size* Large
Stock Early 17th–mid-19thC fine English furniture, 17thC–contemporary works of art
Open Mon–Fri 9am–6pm Sat 10am–5pm
Fairs BADA
Services Valuations, restoration

Tillmans Antiques
Contact Nick Tillman
Wakefield Country Courtyard, Wakefield Farm, Potterspury, Northamptonshire, NN12 7QX P
01327 811882
M 07711 570798
weedonantiques@tiscali.co.uk
Est. 1999 *Stock size* Medium
No. of dealers 17
Stock Porcelain, silver, glass, small range of furniture, pictures
Open Wed–Sat 10am–5pm Sun Bank Holidays 10.30am–4pm

RUSHDEN

Magpies
Contact Mr J E Ward
1 East Grove, Rushden, Northamptonshire, NN10 0AP P
01933 411404
Est. 1994 *Stock size* Medium
Stock General antiques
Open Mon–Sat 10am–5pm Sun noon–4pm

D W Sherwood Ltd
Contact Mrs S Sherwood
59 Little Street, Rushden, Northamptonshire, NN10 0LS P
01933 353265
Est. 1959 *Stock size* Large
Stock General antiques, paintings, clocks, furniture, prints, maps, glass, china, lace bobbins
Open Tues–Sat 11am–5pm closed Thurs
Services Valuations

SILVERSTONE

Collectors Carbooks
Contact Mr C Knapman
2210 Silverstone Technology Park, Silverstone Circuit, Silverstone, Northamptonshire, NN12 8TN P
01327 855888 F 01327 855999
sales@collectorscarbooks.com
www.collectorscarbooks.com
Est. 1991 *Stock size* Large
Stock Rare, out-of-print, motoring and motor-racing books, magazines, posters, autographs, programmes, new car-related books
Open Mon–Sat 9am–5pm Race Saturdays 8.30am–2.30pm
Fairs All major historic race meetings, classic car shows
Services Free book search, international mail order

THRAPSTON

Granary Antiques
Contact Mr A H Cox
The Old Granary, Manor House Farm, Addington Road, Woodford, Thrapston, Northamptonshire, NN14 4ES P
01832 732535
M 07732 169884
Est. 2003 *Stock size* Large
Stock Pine, oak, walnut furniture, clocks, glass, china, general antiques
Open Mon–Sun 10am–5.30pm closed Thurs
Services Valuations, restoration

TOWCESTER

Ron Green
Contact M or N Green
227 & 239 Watling Street West, Towcester, Northamptonshire, NN12 6DD P
01327 350615 F 01327 350387
M 07740 774152
ron@green227.freeserve.co.uk
www.rongreenantiques.com
Est. 1954 *Stock size* Medium
Stock General antiques, furniture, 18th–19thC Continental, English furniture
Open Mon–Sat 8.30am–5.30pm Sun by appointment
Services Valuations for probate and insurance

Lorraine Spooner Antiques Ltd
Contact Lorraine Spooner
211 Watling Street West, Towcester, Northamptonshire,

NN12 6BX P
☎ 01327 358777 F 01327 358777
E lorraine@lsantiques.com
W www.lsantiques.com
Est. 2003 *Stock size* Medium
Stock Furniture, clocks, silver, porcelain, glass, paintings, prints, linens, books
Open Tues–Sat 9.30am–5.30pm closed Wed 1.30pm

WEEDON

Helios and Co
Contact Mr B Walters
25–27 High Street, Weedon, Northamptonshire, NN7 4QD P
☎ 01327 340264 F 01327 342235
Est. 1976 *Stock size* Large
Stock General antiques, reproduction 18thC-style oak furniture
Open Tues–Sat 9.30am–5pm
Sun 10.30am–4pm
Mon by appointment
Services Valuations, restoration

Old Timers (BHI)
Contact Mr M Harris
Village Antique Centre, High Street, Weedon, Northamptonshire, NN7 4QD P
☎ 01327 342015
M 07836 505111
W www.old-timers.co.uk
Est. 1993 *Stock size* Medium
Stock Antique clocks including longcase, furniture
Open Mon–Sun 9.30am–5.30pm
Services Valuations, restoration

Rococo Antiques & Interiors
Contact Neville Griffiths
Bridge Street, Lower Weedon, Northamptonshire, NN7 4PN P
☎ 01327 341288
M 07939 212542
W www.nevillegriffiths.co.uk
Est. 1983 *Stock size* Medium
Stock Antiques and architectural salvage
Open Mon–Sat 10am–5pm
Sun by appointment
Services Restoration, metal polishing, conservation of period property

Shabby Genteel
Contact Mrs N Hesketh
29a High Street, Weedon, Northamptonshire, NN7 4QD
☎ 01327 342139/340218
Est. 1994 *Stock size* Medium
Stock General antiques, collectables
Open Mon–Fri 11am–4pm
Sat Sun 11am–5pm
Services Free local delivery

Streeton Antiques Ltd
Contact Les Streeton
Watling Street, Weedon, Northamptonshire, NN7 4QG P
☎ 01327 340999 F 01327 342234
E les@streeton.com
W www.streeton.com
Est. 1986 *Stock size* Large
Stock Pine furniture
Open Mon–Sat 9am–5pm

The Village Market Antiques
Contact Mrs M Howard
62 High Street, Weedon, Northamptonshire, NN7 4QD P
☎ 01327 342015
Est. 1981 *Stock size* Large
No. of dealers 40
Stock General antiques, collectables
Open Mon–Sun 10.30am–5.15pm including Bank Holidays

Weedon Antiques
Contact Nick Tillman
23 High Street, Weedon, Northamptonshire, NN7 4QD P
☎ 01327 349777
M 07711 570798
E weedonantiques@tiscali.co.uk
Est. 2000 *Stock size* Large
No. of dealers 21
Stock Porcelain, silver, glass, small range of furniture, pictures
Open Wed–Sat 10am–5pm
Sun 10.30am–4.30pm

WELLINGBOROUGH

Wilfords
Contact Mr S Wilford
76 Midland Road, Wellingborough, Northamptonshire, NN8 1NB P
☎ 01933 222760 F 01933 271796
Est. 1934
Open Mon Tues 9am–5pm
Wed 8am–6pm Thur Fri 8am–5pm
Sat 8–11am
Sales General antiques weekly on Thurs 9.30am, viewing Wed 8–6pm
Frequency Weekly
Catalogues No

WEST HADDON

Paul Hopwell Antiques (BADA, LAPADA)
Contact Mr or Mrs P Hopwell
30 High Street, West Haddon, Northampton, Northamptonshire, NN6 7AP P
☎ 01788 510636 F 01788 510044
E paulhopwell@antiqueoak.co.uk
W www.antiqueoak.co.uk
Est. 1969 *Stock size* Large
Stock 17th–18thC English oak furniture, metalware, treen, Delftware
Open Mon–Sat 10am–6pm
Sun by appointment
Fairs Olympia, Chelsea, NEC
Services Valuations, restoration

NOTTINGHAMSHIRE

BEESTON

Turner Violins
Contact Steve Turner
1–5 Lily Grove, Beeston, Nottinghamshire, NG9 1QL P
☎ 0115 943 0333 F 0115 943 0444
E info@turnerviolins.co.uk
W www.turnerviolins.co.uk
Est. 1980 *Stock size* Large
Stock Violins, double basses, violas, cellos, bows
Open Mon–Fri 9am–6pm, Sat 9am–5pm
Services Instrument and bow repairs, valuations, consultations, export

BOBBERSMILL

Philips Traditional Bathrooms
Contact Philip Lucas
418–424 Alfreton Road, Bobbersmill, Nottinghamshire, NG7 5NG P
☎ 0115 970 5552 F 0115 841 3752
E shop@b-b-1.co.uk
W www.b-b-1.co.uk
Est. 1997 *Stock size* Medium
Stock Antique bathrooms
Open Mon–Sat 9am–5pm

BUDBY

Dukeries Antiques Centre
Contact John Coupe
✉ **Thoresby Park, Budby, Nottinghamshire, NG22 9EX** P
☎ 01623 822252 F 01623 822209
M 07836 635312
E dukeriesantiques@aol.com
Est. 2001 *Stock size* Large
No. of dealers 18
Stock Antique furniture, paintings, porcelain, glass, silver
Open Mon–Sun 10am–5pm
Services Valuations, restoration

DUNHAM ON TRENT

R G Antiques
Contact Mr R G Barnett
✉ **Main Street, Dunham on Trent, Newark, Nottinghamshire, NG22 0TY** P
☎ 01777 228312
Est. 1979 *Stock size* Medium
Stock General antiques, arms and armour
Open Mon–Sun 10am–6pm
Fairs Newark
Services Valuations

FARNSFIELD

A B Period Pine
Contact Alan Baker
✉ **The Barn, 38 Main Street, Farnsfield, Newark, Nottinghamshire, NG22 8EA** P
☎ 01623 882288 F 01623 883793
E alan@abperiodpine.fsnet.co.uk
W www.periodpine.co.uk
Est. 1998 *Stock size* Large
Stock Pine
Open Mon–Sat 10am–5pm
Sun 11am–4.30pm
Services Farmhouse and painted pine and oak kitchens

GOTHAM

T Vennett-Smith Auctioneers and Valuers
Contact T or M A Vennett-Smith
✉ **11 Nottingham Road, Gotham, Nottingham, Nottinghamshire, NE11 0HE** P
☎ 0115 983 0541 F 0115 983 0114
E info@vennett-smith.com
W www.vennett-smith.com
Est. 1989
Open Mon–Fri 9am–5.30pm
Sales Autographs, postcards, cigarette cards, 5 sales per year, 2 theatre, cinema memorabilia, 3 postal auctions of postcards and cigarette cards, 2 sports auctions including cricket, football, general sports, 1 postal sports auction
Catalogues Yes

GRINGLEY ON THE HILL

Peter Young Auctioneers
Contact Mr P Young
✉ **Hillside, Beacon Hill Road, Gringley on the Hill, Nottinghamshire, DN10 4RQ** P
☎ 01777 816609
M 07801 079818
Est. 1961
Open Mon–Fri 9.30am–5.30pm
Sales Antiques and collectables Sat 10am, viewing Fri 4–9pm Sat 9–10am.
Frequency Quarterly
Catalogues Yes

KIRKBY IN ASHFIELD

Kyrios Books
Contact Mr K Parr
✉ **11 Kingsway, Kirkby in Ashfield, Nottingham, Nottinghamshire, NG17 7BB** P
☎ 01623 452556
E keith@kyriosbooks.co.uk or kyriosbooks@tiscali.co.uk
W www.kyriosbooks.co.uk
Est. 1989 *Stock size* Large
Stock Rare and second-hand Christian and philosophy books
Open Mon–Sat 9.30am–noon 1–4.30pm or by appointment
Services Mail order. Bi-monthly catalogue available from www.abebooks.com

LANGFORD

T Baker
Contact Mr T Baker
✉ **Langford House Farm, Langford, Newark, Nottinghamshire, NG23 7RR** P
☎ 01636 704026
Est. 1966 *Stock size* Medium
Stock Period and Victorian furniture
Open Mon–Fri 8am–5pm or by appointment

LONG EATON

Miss Elany
Contact Mr D Mottershead
✉ **2 Salisbury Street, Long Eaton, Nottinghamshire, NG10 1BA** P
☎ 0115 973 4835 F 0115 973 4835
W www.misselany.com
Est. 1977 *Stock size* Large

MIDLANDS

NOTTINGHAMSHIRE • MANSFIELD

Stock Antiques and pianos
Open Mon–Sat 9am–5pm
Fairs Newark, Swinderby
Services Valuations

MANSFIELD

Mansfield Antique Centre
Contact Dave Buckinger
185 Yorke Street, Mansfield Woodhouse, Mansfield, Nottinghamshire, NG19 2NJ P
☎ 01623 661122 F 01623 631738
Est. 1992 *Stock size* Medium
Stock General antiques
Open Thurs–Sun 10am–5.30pm

Tom's Clock Shop (BWCG)
Contact Mr Tom Matthews
20 Station Street, Mansfield Woodhouse, Mansfield, Nottinghamshire, NG19 8AB P
☎ 01623 476097
M 07752 735605
E tomclockrepairs@lineone.net
W www.tomclockrepairs.co.uk
Est. 1974 *Stock size* Large
Stock Antique clocks, watches, jewellery
Open Mon–Fri 8.45am–4.45pm Sat 9am–2pm
Fairs Birmingham Clock Fair
Services Valuations, restoration of clocks and jewellery

NEWARK

N F Bryan-Peach Antiques
Contact Mr N Bryan-Peach
No. One Castlegate Antiques, 1–3 Castlegate, Newark, Nottinghamshire, NG24 1AZ P
☎ 01636 701877
E norm@bryanpeach.demon.co.uk
Est. 1974 *Stock size* Medium
Stock 18th–19thC furniture, clocks, barometers
Open Mon–Fri 9.30am–5pm Sat 9.30am–5.30pm
Services Valuations, restoration

Castlegate Antique Centre
Contact John Dench
55 Castle Gate, Newark, Nottinghamshire, NG24 1BE P
☎ 01636 700076 F 01636 700144
Est. 1983 *Stock size* Large
No. of dealers 9
Stock General antiques
Open Mon–Sat 9.30am–5.30pm
Services Valuations, restoration

Galerie
Contact Gillian Jennison
18 Kirkgate, Newark, Nottinghamshire, NG24 1AB P
☎ 01636 705899
M 07951 691487
Est. 2000 *Stock size* Small
Stock French furniture, lights, mirrors, paintings, textiles
Open Mon–Sat 9.30am–5.30pm

Lawrence Books
Contact Mr A Lawrence
Newark Antique Centre, Lombard Street, Newark, Nottinghamshire, NG24 1XP P
☎ 01636 605865/701619
E arthurlawrence@totalise.co.uk
Est. 1987 *Stock size* Small
Stock Antiquarian, rare and second-hand books
Open Mon–Sat 9.30am–4.30pm Sun 11am–4pm
Services Valuations

R R Limb Antiques
Contact Mr R Limb
31–35 North Gate, Newark, Nottinghamshire, NG24 1HD P
☎ 01636 674546
Est. 1955 *Stock size* Large
Stock General antiques, pianos
Open By appointment
Fairs Newark, Swinderby
Services Piano exporters

M B G Antiques (DGA)
Contact Margaret Begley-Gray DGA
41b Castlegate, Newark, Nottinghamshire, NG24 1BE P
☎ 01636 704442 F 01636 679586
M 07702 209808
E margaretbegleygray@aol.com
Est. 1982 *Stock size* Medium
Stock Period jewellery, quality pictures, diamond rings
Open Wed–Sat 11am–4pm closed Thurs
Services Picture search

Newark Antiques Centre
Contact Mr M Tinsley
Regent House, Lombard Street, Newark, Nottinghamshire, NG24 1XP P
☎ 01636 605504 F 01636 605101
W www.newarkantiquescentre.com
Est. 1988 *Stock size* Large
No. of dealers 101
Stock General antiques
Open Mon–Sat 9.30am–4.30pm Sun Bank Holidays 11am–4pm
Services Valuations, upholstery, clock repairs, specialist book service

Newark Antiques Warehouse Ltd
Contact Nick Mellors
Kelham Road, Newark, Nottinghamshire, NG24 1BX P
☎ 01636 674869 F 01636 612933
M 07974 429185
E enquiries@newarkantiques.co.uk
W www.newarkantiques.co.uk
Est. 1984 *Stock size* Large
No. of dealers 80
Stock Good furniture, collectables, smalls
Open Mon–Fri 8.30am–5.30pm Sat 9.30am–4pm Sun at Newark Antiques Fair 9am–7pm
Services Valuations

No. One Castlegate Antiques
1–3 Castlegate, Newark, Nottinghamshire, NG24 1AZ P
☎ 01636 701877
Est. 1974 *Stock size* Large
No. of dealers 10
Stock 18th–19thC antique furniture, clocks, barometers, decorative items
Open Mon–Fri 9.30am–5pm Sat 9.30am–5.30pm
Services Valuations, restoration of clocks and barometers

Pearman Antiques & Interiors
Contact Jan Parnham
9 Castle Gate, Newark, Nottinghamshire, NG24 1AZ P
☎ 01636 679158 or 01949 837693
Est. 2001 *Stock size* Medium
Stock Oak and mahogany furniture
Open Wed–Sat 10am–4pm

Portland Antiques & Curios
Contact Brendan or

Carole Sprakes
✉ **5 Portland Road, West Bridgeford, Nottinghamshire, NG2 6DN** 🅿
☎ 0115 914 2123
Est. 1999 *Stock size* Large
Stock General antiques
Open Wed–Sat 10am–5pm

NOTTINGHAM

⊞ Acanthus Antiques & Collectables
Contact Trak or Sandra Smith
✉ **140 Derby Road (off Canning Circus), Nottingham, Nottinghamshire, NG7 1LR** 🅿
☎ 0115 924 3226
Ⓔ trak.e.smith@ntlworld.com
Ⓦ www.acanthusantiques.co.uk
Est. 1979 *Stock size* Medium
Stock General antiques
Open Mon–Fri 10am–2.30pm Sat 12.30–4pm Sun by appointment
Fairs Newark, Swinderby, Donnington
Services Valuations, lectures and teaching

⊞ Antiques Across the World (LAPADA)
Contact Mr Rimes
✉ **James Alexander Buildings, London Road, Manvers Street, Nottingham, Nottinghamshire, NG2 3AE** 🅿
☎ 0115 979 9199 Ⓕ 0116 239 3134
Ⓜ 07785 777787
Ⓔ tonyrimes@btinternet.com
Est. 1992 *Stock size* Large
Stock Georgian–Edwardian furniture
Open Mon–Fri 9am–5pm Sat 10am–2pm
Fairs Newark
Services Valuations, courier service, antique finder service

⊞ The Autograph Collectors Gallery
Contact Mr or Mrs G Clipson
✉ **7 Jessops Lane, Gedling, Nottingham, Nottinghamshire, NG4 4BQ**
☎ 0115 961 2956/987 6578
Ⓕ 0115 961 2956
Ⓔ graham@autograph-gallery.co.uk
Ⓦ www.autograph-gallery.co.uk
Est. 1990 *Stock size* Large
Stock Signed photographs, documents, letters
Open Telephone 9am–8pm
Services Mail order only

⚒ Bonhams
✉ **57 Mansfield Road, Nottingham, Nottinghamshire, NG1 3PL** 🅿
☎ 0115 947 4414 Ⓕ 0115 947 4885
Ⓔ nottingham@bonhams.com
Ⓦ www.bonhams.com
Open Mon–Fri 10am–5pm
Sales Regional office. Regular house and attic sales across the country; contact London offices for further details. Free auction valuations; insurance and probate valuations

⊞ Castle Antiques
Contact Mr L Adamson
✉ **78 Derby Road, Nottingham, Nottinghamshire, NG1 5FD** 🅿
☎ 0115 947 3913
Est. 1979 *Stock size* Medium
Stock General antiques, pictures, maps, prints, lighting
Open Mon–Sat 9.30am–5pm

⊞ Cathay Antiques
Contact Jenny Bu
✉ **74 Derby Road, Nottingham, Nottinghamshire, NG1 5FD** 🅿
☎ 0115 988 1216
Ⓔ paulshum8@hotmail.com
Est. 2000 *Stock size* Medium
Stock Furniture, porcelain, ceramic, pottery, Chinese folk art
Open Mon–Sat 11am–5pm

⊞ Collectors World
Contact Mr M Ray
✉ **188 Wollaton Road, Wollaton, Nottingham, Nottinghamshire, NG8 1HJ** 🅿
☎ 0115 928 0347 Ⓕ 0115 928 0347
Est. 1991 *Stock size* Large
Stock Coins, banknotes, cigarette cards, postcards
Open Tues–Sat 10.30am–4.30pm
Fairs Specialist fairs
Services Valuations, currency exchange, framing

⊞ Dutton & Smith Medals & Badges
Contact Mr A Dutton or Mr T Smith
✉ **140 Derby Road, Nottingham, Nottinghamshire, NG7 1LR** 🅿
☎ 0115 924 3226
Ⓔ trak.e.smith83@ntlworld.com
Ⓦ www.acanthusantiques.co.uk
Est. 1991 *Stock size* Medium
Stock Campaign medals, gallantry awards, militaria and badges
Open Mon–Fri 10.30am–2pm Sat 12.30–4pm
Fairs Newark, Swinderby, Donnington
Services Valuations

⊞ Fourways Antiques
Contact Mr Peter Key
✉ **38 Owen Avenue, Nottingham, Nottinghamshire, NG10 2FS** 🅿
☎ 0115 972 1830
Ⓜ 07850 973889
Est. 1974 *Stock size* Medium
Stock General antiques
Open By appointment
Fairs Newark, Swinderby

⊞ Gatehouse Workshops
Contact Mr S J Waine
✉ **163 Castle Boulevard, Nottingham, Nottinghamshire, NG7 1FS** 🅿
☎ 0115 948 3954 Ⓕ 0115 948 3954
Ⓦ www.gatehouseworkshops.co.uk
Est. 1979 *Stock size* Medium
Stock Architectural antiques, stained glass
Open Mon–Fri 9.30am–4pm Sat 9am–5pm
Services Pine stripping

⊞ Harlequin Antiques
Contact Peter Hinchley
✉ **79–81 Mansfield Road, Nottingham, Nottinghamshire, NG5 6BH** 🅿
☎ 0115 967 4590
Ⓔ sales@antiquepine.net
Ⓦ www.antiquepine.net
Est. 1993 *Stock size* Large
Stock Antique pine furniture
Open Mon–Sat 9.30am–5pm Sat 9am–5pm
Services Restoration of all period furniture, door and furniture stripping

⊞ Andy Holmes Books (PBFA)
✉ **82 Highbury Avenue, Bulwell, Nottingham, Nottinghamshire, NG6 9DB** 🅿
☎ 0115 979 5603 Ⓕ 0115 979 5616
Ⓔ holmesbook@aol.com
Est. 1996 *Stock size* Large
Stock Antiquarian, rare and

second-hand books, 19thC travel, gypsies, folklore and general topics
Open By appointment only
Fairs London Royal National, Buxton
Services Valuations, book search

D D & A Ingle (OMRS)
Contact Mr D Ingle
380 Carlton Hill, Carlton, Nottingham, Nottinghamshire, NG4 1JA P
☎ 0115 987 3325 Ⓕ 0115 987 3325
Ⓔ ddaingle@talk21.com
Est. 1968 *Stock size* Medium
Stock General antiques
Open Mon–Sat 9am–5pm
Services Valuations

Jeremy & Westerman
Contact Geoff Blore
203 Mansfield Road, Nottingham, Nottinghamshire, NG1 3FF
☎ 0115 947 4522
Est. 1981 *Stock size* Medium
Stock Antique and second-hand books
Open Mon–Sat 11am–5pm
Fairs HD Book fairs

Arthur Johnson & Sons
Contact Mr R Hammersley
Nottingham Auction Centre, Meadow Lane, Nottingham, Nottinghamshire, NG2 3GY P
☎ 0115 986 9128 Ⓕ 0115 986 2139
Ⓔ arthurjohnson@btconnect.com
Est. 1899
Open Mon–Fri 9am–5pm closed lunch
Sales Antique and export furniture and collectables Sat 10am, viewing Fri 2–6.45pm Sat from 9am
Frequency Weekly
Catalogues Yes

Lights, Camera, Action (UACC)
Contact Mr N Straw
6 Western Gardens, Western Boulevard, Nottingham, Nottinghamshire, NG8 5GP P
☎ 0115 913 1116
Ⓜ 0797 034 2363
Est. 1998 *Stock size* Large
Stock Collectors' items, autographs, *Titanic* memorabilia
Open By appointment
Fairs NEC, Olympia, Newark
Services Free valuations

Michael D Long Ltd (GTA, BACA Award Winner 2001)
Contact Mr Robert Hedger
96–98 Derby Road, Nottingham, Nottinghamshire, NG1 5FB P
☎ 0115 941 3307 Ⓕ 0115 941 4199
Ⓔ sales@michaeldlong.com
Ⓦ www.michaeldlong.com
Est. 1964 *Stock size* Large
Stock Fine antique arms and armour
Open Mon–Fri 9.30am–5.15pm Sat 10am–4pm
Fairs London Arms Fair, Birmingham, Nottingham
Services Valuations

Luna
Contact Paul Rose
23 George Street, Nottingham, Nottinghamshire, NG1 3BH P
☎ 0115 924 3267
Ⓔ info@luna-online.co.uk
Ⓦ www.luna-online.co.uk
Est. 1993 *Stock size* Medium
Stock 1950s–1970s objects for the home
Open Mon–Sat 10.30am–5.30pm
Fairs Newark
Services Sourcing items, hire

Mellors & Kirk (RICS)
Contact Nigel Kirk or Martha Parvin
The Auction House, Gregory Street, Nottingham, Nottinghamshire, NG7 2NL P
☎ 0115 979 0000 Ⓕ 0115 978 1111
Ⓔ menquiries@mellorsandkirk.com
Ⓦ www.mellorsandkirk.com
Est. 1993
Open Mon–Fri 8.30am–5pm Sat 9am–noon
Sales Weekly general sale on Tues. Fine art sale every six to eight weeks
Frequency Six weekly
Catalogues yes

N S E Medal Department (OMRS)
Contact Dennis Henson
97 Derby Road, Nottingham, Nottinghamshire, NG1 5BB P
☎ 0115 950 1882
Ⓔ nsemed@totalserve.com
Est. 1974 *Stock size* Large
Stock Antique coins and medals, cap badges
Open Mon–Sat 7.30am–3pm
Services Valuations

Neales Auctioneers (SOFAA, ARVA)
Contact Bruce Fearn, ARICS
192 Mansfield Road, Nottingham, Nottinghamshire, NG1 3HU P
☎ 0115 962 4141 Ⓕ 0115 985 6890
Ⓔ fineart@neales-auctionscom
Ⓦ www.neales-auctions.com
Est. 1840
Open Mon–Fri 9am–5.30pm Sat 9am–12.30pm
Sales Specialist antique and fine art sales every 2–3 months plus general antiques and collectables sales
Frequency Weekly
Catalogues Yes

The Poison Dwarf
Contact Andrew Kulka
111 Alfreton Road, Nottingham, Nottinghamshire, NG7 3JL P
☎ 0115 970 5552 Ⓕ 0115 970 5553
Ⓔ info@thepoisondwarf.com
Ⓦ www.thepoisondwarf.com
Est. 2004 *Stock size* Small
Stock Antique Continental furniture
Open Tues–Sat 11am–6pm Sun 11am–5pm

John Pye & Sons Ltd (NAVA)
Contact Adam Pye FNAVA
James Shipstone House, Radford Road, Nottingham, Nottinghamshire, NG7 7EA
☎ 0115 970 6060 Ⓕ 0115 942 0100
Ⓔ ap@johnpye.co.uk.
Ⓦ www.johnpye.co.uk
Est. 1969
Open Mon–Fri 8am–4.30pm
Sales General
Frequency Weekly
Catalogues No

Top Hat Antiques
Contact Mrs J Wallis
62 Derby Road, Nottingham, Nottinghamshire, NG1 5FD P
☎ 0115 941 9143 Ⓕ 0115 877 4185

Ⓔ info@tophat-antiques.co.uk
Ⓦ www.tophat-antiques.co.uk
Est. 1979 *Stock size* Large
Stock Surprises from the past, furniture, silver, glass, ceramics, jewellery, pictures, metalware, collectables
Open Mon–Sat 10am–5pm

RADFORD

Nottingham Architectural Antiques & Reclamation (SALVO)
Contact Jo Sanders
St Albans Works, 181 Hartley Road, Radford, Nottinghamshire, NG7 3DW Ⓟ
☎ 0115 979 0666 Ⓕ 0115 845 8936
Ⓔ admin.naar@ntlworld.com
Ⓦ www.naar.co.uk
Est. 2003 *Stock size* Medium
Stock Original period fireplaces, architectural salvage, doors, fireplaces, parquet flooring, stained glass
Open Mon–Sat 9am–6pm
Services Restoration

Bonhams
20 Square, Retford, Nottinghamshire, DN22 6XE Ⓟ
☎ 01777 708 633 Ⓕ 01777 706724
Ⓔ retford@bonhams.com
Ⓦ www.bonhams.com
Open Mon–Fri 9am–5pm
Sales Regional office. Regular house and attic sales across the country; contact London offices for further details. Free auction valuations; insurance and probate valuations

Lynn Guest Antiques
Contact Lynn Guest
15 Mill Lane, Rockley, Retford, Nottinghamshire, DN22 0QP Ⓟ
☎ 01777 838498
Est. 1979 *Stock size* Medium
Stock General antiques and collectables
Open Mon–Fri 9am–6pm or by appointment
Fairs Newark
Services Valuations, house clearance

SANDIACRE

The Glory Hole
Contact Mr or Mrs C Reid
14 Station Road, Sandiacre, Nottingham, Nottinghamshire, NG10 5BG Ⓟ
☎ 0115 939 4081 Ⓕ 0115 939 4085
Est. 1984 *Stock size* Medium
Stock Antique furniture, fireplaces
Open Mon–Sat 10am–5.30pm
Services Restoration

SUTTON-IN-ASHFIELD

C B Sheppard & Son
Contact Mr B Sheppard
The Auction Gallery, 87 Chatworth Street, Sutton-in-Ashfield, Nottinghamshire, NG17 4GG
☎ 01623 556310
Ⓜ 07714 798244
Est. 1951
Open Fri (auction weeks Tues–Fri) 10am–4pm
Sales General antiques
Frequency Monthly
Catalogues Yes

Yesterday and Today
Contact Mr J Turner
82 Station Road, Sutton-in-Ashfield, Nottinghamshire, NG17 5HB Ⓟ
☎ 01623 442215
Ⓜ 07957 552753
Est. 1984 *Stock size* Medium
Stock Collectables, 1920s and 1930s oak furniture
Open Tues–Sat 9am–5pm
Fairs Newark, Swinderby

RUTLAND

MANTON

David Smith Antiques
Contact Mr D Smith
20 St Mary's Road, Manton, Oakham, Rutland, LE15 8SY Ⓟ
☎ 01572 737244/737119
Est. 1952 *Stock size* Medium
Stock General antiques
Open Mon–Sat 9am–5pm or by appointment
Fairs Kettering
Services Valuations, restoration

OAKHAM

Antiques & Curios
Contact Bob Smith
30 Northgate, Oakham, Rutland, LE15 6QS Ⓟ
☎ 01572 771436
Ⓔ smithrob31smith@aol.com
Est. 1992 *Stock size* Small
Stock General antiques, collectables
Open By appointment
Fairs Newark, Swinderby

Robert Bingley Antiques (LAPADA)
Contact Robert Bingley
Church Street, Wing, Oakham, Rutland, LE15 8RS Ⓟ
☎ 01572 737725 Ⓕ 01572 737284
Ⓦ www.robertbingley.com
Est. 1980 *Stock size* Large
Stock George II–Victorian furniture
Open Mon–Sat 9am–5pm
Services Valuations, restoration

Swans Antiques and Interiors
Contact Mr Peter Jones
17 Mill Street, Oakham, Rutland, LE15 6EA Ⓟ
☎ 01572 724364 Ⓕ 01572 755094
Ⓜ 07860 304084
Ⓔ info@swansofoakham.co.uk
Ⓦ www.swansofoakham.co.uk
Est. 1986 *Stock size* Large
Stock Antique beds, English and French decorative furniture
Open Mon–Sat 9am–5.30pm Sun by appointment
Fairs Newark
Services Valuations, restoration, retail

Treedale Antiques
Contact Mr G Warren
10b Mill Street, Oakham, Rutland, LE15 6EA Ⓟ
☎ 01572 757521 Ⓕ 01572 757521
Est. 1968 *Stock size* Medium
Stock 17th–18thC furniture, specializing in walnut and oak
Open Mon–Sat 9am–5.30pm Sun 2–5pm
Services Restoration

UPPINGHAM

Garner Fine Art Antiques, John
Contact John or Paul Garner
51 & 53 High Street East, Uppingham,

Rutland,
LE15 9PY 🅿
☎ 01572 823607 Ⓕ 01572 821654
Ⓜ 07850 596556
Ⓔ sales@johngarnerantiques.com
Ⓦ www.johngarnerantiques.com
Est. 1966 *Stock size* Large
Stock Antiques, 17th–18thC furniture and 19thC paintings, garden statuary, clocks, bronzes, sporting prints
Open Mon–Sat 9am–5.30pm Sun by appointment
Fairs Newark, Miami
Services Valuations, restoration, publishes sporting prints

Goldmark Gallery
Contact Ian Broughton
✉ **14 Orange Street, Uppingham, Oakham, Rutland, LE15 9SQ** 🅿
☎ 01572 822694 Ⓕ 01572 821503
Ⓔ Mike@mgoldmark.freeserve.co.uk
Ⓦ www.goldmarkart.com
Est. 1974 *Stock size* Large
Stock 20thC prints
Open Mon–Sat 9.30am–5.30pm Sun 2.30–5.30pm

Tattersalls
Contact Mrs J Tattersall
✉ **14b Orange Street, Uppingham, Oakham, Rutland, LE14 2AG** 🅿
☎ 01572 821171
Ⓔ janice_tattersall@hotmail.com
Est. 1985 *Stock size* Medium
Stock Antique and old Persian rugs
Open Tues–Sat 9.30am–5pm
Services Restoration

Woodmans House Antiques
Contact Mr or Mrs J Collie
✉ **35 High Street East, Uppingham, Oakham, Rutland, LE15 9PY** 🅿
☎ 01572 821799
Ⓔ woodmanshouse@aol.com
Est. 1992 *Stock size* Medium
Stock Georgian furniture, designer fabrics
Open Mon–Sat 9.30am–5pm or Sun by appointment
Fairs NEC, Olympia
Services Valuations, restoration, reference library, complete interior design service

SHROPSHIRE

ATCHAM

Mytton Antiques
Contact M A Nares
✉ **Norton Crossroads, Atcham, Shrewsbury, Shropshire, SY4 4UH** 🅿
☎ 01952 740229 Ⓕ 01952 440229
Ⓜ 07860 575639
Ⓔ nares@myttonantiques.freeserve.co.uk
Ⓦ www.myttonantiques.com
Est. 1979 *Stock size* Medium
Stock 18th–19thC furniture and smalls, longcase clocks, country furniture, restoration materials
Open Mon–Sat 10am–5pm or by appointment
Services Valuations, restoration, shipping, courier service

BISHOPS CASTLE

Autolycus
Contact Mr David Wilkinson
✉ **10 Market Square, Bishops Castle, Shropshire, SY9 5BN** 🅿
☎ 01588 630078 Ⓕ 01588 630078
Ⓔ autolycusbc@aol.com
Ⓦ www.booksonline.uk.com
Est. 1996 *Stock size* Medium
Stock Antiquarian and quality second-hand books, specializing in modern first editions, illustrated, children's, travel, topography, fine sporting prints and pictures, antiques, decorative items
Open Mon–Fri 11am–4.30pm Sat 10.30am–5pm
Services Valuations, book search

Decorative Antiques
Contact Richard Moulson
✉ **47 Church Street, Bishops Castle, Shropshire, SY9 5AD** 🅿
☎ 01588 638851 Ⓕ 01588 638851
Ⓔ enquiries@decorative-antiques.co.uk
Ⓦ www.decorative-antiques.co.uk
Est. 1996 *Stock size* Medium
Stock Art Deco 1860–1960, Arts and Crafts, pottery, glass, jewellery, metalware, evening bags, early plastics
Open Mon–Sat 9.30am–5.30pm closed Wed pm
Services Identification and informal valuations

BRIDGNORTH

The Book Passage
Contact Mr David Lamont
✉ **57a High Street, Bridgnorth, Shropshire, WV16 4DX** 🅿
☎ 01746 768767
Ⓔ bookman@btconnect.com
Est. 1999 *Stock size* Large
Stock Antiquarian and second-hand books
Open Mon–Sat 9am–5.30pm

Bridgnorth Antiques Centre
Contact Mr Richard Lewis
✉ **Whitburn Street, Bridgnorth, Shropshire, WV16 4QP** 🅿
☎ 01746 768055
Est. 1994 *Stock size* Large
No. of dealers 19 (6 rooms)
Stock Late Victorian, Edwardian and 1930s furniture, collectables
Open Mon–Sat 10am–5.30pm Sun 10.30am–4.30pm
Services Clock repairs

English Heritage
Contact Mrs M Wainwright
✉ **2 Whitburn Street, Bridgnorth, Shropshire, WV16 4QN** 🅿
☎ 01746 762097
Est. 1988 *Stock size* Medium
Stock General antiques, giftware, medals, coins and silverware
Open Mon–Sat 10am–5pm closed Thurs

Malthouse Antiques
Contact Mrs Susan Mantle
✉ **6 Underhill Street, Bridgnorth, Shropshire, WV16 4BB** 🅿
☎ 01746 763054 Ⓕ 01746 763054
Est. 1979 *Stock size* Large
Stock Victorian–Edwardian furniture, chandeliers
Open Mon–Sat 10am–6pm Sun 2–5pm closed Wed
Services Restoration

Old Mill Antique Centre
Contact Mr Dennis Ridgeway
✉ **48 Mill Street, Bridgnorth, Shropshire, WV15 5AG** 🅿
☎ 01746 768778 Ⓕ 01746 768944
Est. 1996 *Stock size* Large
No. of dealers 90
Stock Complete range of

antiques and collectables
Open Mon–Sun 10am–5pm
Services Restaurant

Perry & Phillips
Contact Dennis Ridgeway
Old Mill Auction Rooms, Mill Street, Bridgnorth, Shropshire, WV15 5AG P
☎ 01746 762248 F 01746 768944
E sales@perryandphillips.co.uk
W www.perryandphillips.co.uk
Est. 1835
Open Mon–Fri 9am–5pm
Sales General antiques sales Tues 10.30am, viewing Sat 10am–2pm Sun 10am–4pm Mon 10am–5pm. Occasional special sales
Frequency Monthly
Catalogues Yes

BURLTON

North Shropshire Reclamation and Antique Salvage (SALVO)
Contact Mrs J Powell
Wackley Lodge Farm, Wackley, Burlton, Shrewsbury, Shropshire, SY4 5TD P
☎ 01939 270719 F 01939 270895
M 07802 315038
Est. 1997 *Stock size* Large
Stock Garden statuary, bricks, baths, hand basins, tiles, doors, architectural salvage of all types
Open Mon–Fri 9am–6pm Sat Sun 9am–5.30pm
Services Paint stripping

CHURCH STRETTON

Funnye Olde Worlde
Contact Brian Taylor
54 The High Street, Church Stretton, Shropshire, SY2 6AP P
☎ 01743 244626
M 07754 084949
Est. 1991 *Stock size* Small
Stock Antiques, bygones
Open Tues Thurs Fri 10am–4pm Sat 10.30am–4.30pm
Services Valuations

Old Post Office Antiques
Contact Mr A Walker
46 Sandford Avenue, Church Stretton, Shropshire, SY6 6BH P
☎ 01694 724491
M 07971 164083
Est. 1998 *Stock size* Large
Stock Jewellery, Halcyon Days, Steiff bears, Carr's silver
Open Mon–Sat 10am–5pm

The Snooker Room
Contact Mr A Walker
46a Sandford Avenue, Church Stretton, Shropshire, SY6 6BH P
☎ 01694 724491
M 07971 164083
Est. 1939 *Stock size* Large
Stock Snooker tables, lighting, accessories
Open Mon–Sat 10am–5pm
Fairs Olympia

Stretton Antiques Market
Contact Terry or Lisa Elvins
36 Sandford Avenue, Church Stretton, Shropshire, SY6 6BH P
☎ 01694 723718 F 01694 723718
Est. 1985 *Stock size* Large
No. of dealers 60
Stock Wide range of antiques and collectables
Open Mon–Sat 9.30am–5.30pm Sun 10.30am–4.30pm

COSFORD

Martin Quick Antiques (LAPADA)
Contact Mr C Quick
Unit 2, Long Lane, Cosford, Shropshire, TF11 8PJ P
☎ 01902 754703
M 07774 124859
E cqantiques@aol.com
Est. 1970 *Stock size* Large
Stock Georgian–Victorian and later furniture, French furniture
Trade only Yes
Open By appointment or chance
Fairs Newark
Services Valuations

Walker, Barnett & Hill
Contact Christopher Sidebottom
Cosford Auction Rooms, Long Lane, Cosford, Shropshire, TF11 8PJ P
☎ 01902 375555 F 01902 375566
E wbhauctions@lineone.net
W www.walker-barnett-hill.co.uk
Est. 1780
Open Mon–Fri 9.30am–4pm
Sales Fortnightly antique and contemporary furniture sales, fine art sales 6-weekly
Catalogues Yes

CRAVEN ARMS

Marine
Contact Mark Jarrold
Lower House Farm, Middlehope, Craven Arms, Shropshire, SY7 9JT P
☎ 01584 841210
M 07776 193193
E mark@markjarrold.plus.com
Est. 1989
Stock Binoculars, ships' models, navigational instruments, chronometers, clocks, optical equipment
Open By appointment
Fairs Birmingham International Arms Fair
Services Valuations, restoration

DITTON PRIORS

Priors Reclamation (SALVO)
Contact Miss V Bale
Unit 65, Ditton Priors Industrial Estate, Ditton Priors, Bridgnorth, Shropshire, WV16 6SS P
☎ 01746 712450 F 01746 712450
M 07989 302488
E vicki@priorsrec.co.uk
W www.priorsrec.co.uk
Est. 1998 *Stock size* Large
Stock Reclaimed flooring, new oak flooring, reclaimed doors, brass and iron door furniture
Open By appointment at any time
Services Delivery, doors made to order from reclaimed timber

ELLESMERE

Bowen, Son & Watson
Contact Mr Eddie Bowen
Wharf Road, Ellesmere, Shropshire, SY12 0EJ P
☎ 01691 622534 F 01691 623603
E bsw.ellesmere@virgin.net
W www.bowensonandwatson.co.uk
Est. 1869
Open Mon–Fri 9am–5pm Sat 9am–noon
Sales Antique and household goods monthly Tues 11am, viewing Mon 9am–5pm Tues 9–11am
Frequency Monthly
Catalogues No

MIDLANDS

SHROPSHIRE • IRONBRIDGE

⊞ Judith Charles Antiques & Collectables
Contact Judith Charles
⊠ **2c Wharf Road, Ellesmere, Shropshire, SY12 0EL** P
☎ 01691 653524 F 01691 624416
M 07855 253617
Est. 2001 *Stock size* Large
Stock Royal Doulton, china, porcelain, small items, furniture, Beswick, Royal Albert, Sadler, jewellery
Open Mon–Fri 10am–3pm Sat 10am–5pm
Fairs Ellesmere
Services Valuations

IRONBRIDGE

⊞ Bears on the Square
Contact Margaret Phillips
⊠ **2 The Square, Ironbridge, Telford, Shropshire, TF8 7AQ** P
☎ 01952 433924 F 01952 433926
E bernie@bearsonthesquare.com
W www.bearsonthesquare.com
Est. 1991 *Stock size* Large
Stock Steiff, Deans, Hermann, Spielwaren, Artist and second-hand bears, Country Life, Boyds
Open Mon–Sun 10am–5pm
Services Worldwide mail order

⊞ Tudor House Antiques
Contact Mr Peter Whitelaw
⊠ **11 Tontine Hill, Ironbridge, Telford, Shropshire, TF8 7AL** P
☎ 01952 433783
E tudoriron@aol.com
W www.tudorhouse.co.uk
Est. 1964 *Stock size* Large
Stock Coalport, Caughley, general English ceramics
Open Mon–Sat 10am–5pm Sun by appointment
Services Valuations

LUDLOW

⊞ Bayliss Antiques
Contact Mr A B Bayliss
⊠ **22–24 Old Street, Ludlow, Shropshire, SY8 1NP** P
☎ 01584 873634 F 01584 873634
M 07831 672211
Est. 1968 *Stock size* Medium
Stock Oak and mahogany furniture, paintings
Open Mon–Sat 9am–6pm or by appointment
Services Valuations

⊞ Bread & Roses
Contact Rose Smith
⊠ **Corve Street, Ludlow, Shropshire, SY8 1DA** P
☎ 01584 877200
M 07810 508804
Est. 1995 *Stock size* Medium
Stock Kitchenware
Open Mon–Sat 10am–5pm closed Thurs
Fairs NEC, Newark

⊞ R G Cave & Sons Ltd (LAPADA, BADA)
Contact Mr R G Cave or John Cave
⊠ **17 Broad Street, Ludlow, Shropshire, SY8 1NG** P
☎ 01584 873568 F 01584 875050
Est. 1965 *Stock size* Medium
Stock Period furniture, metalwork, works of art
Open Mon–Sat 10am–5.30pm
Services Valuations for probate and insurance, shippers of Bordeaux wine

⊞ Corve Street Antiques
Contact Mr Jones or Mr Mcavoy
⊠ **141a Corve Street, Ludlow, Shropshire, SY8 2PG** P
☎ 01584 879100
Est. 2001 *Stock size* Medium
Stock Longcase clocks, oak, country, mahogany furniture, copper, brass, pictures
Open Mon–Sat 10am–5pm
Services Valuations

⊞ Garrard Antiques
Contact Mrs C Garrard
⊠ **139a Corve Street, Ludlow, Shropshire, SY8 2PG** P
☎ 01584 876727 F 01584 781277
M 07971 588063
Est. 1985 *Stock size* Large
Stock Period pine, oak and country furniture, pottery, porcelain, glass, treen, books, collectables
Open Mon–Fri 10am–1pm 2–5pm Sat 10am–5pm

⊞ Leon Jones
Contact Mr L Jones
⊠ **Mitre House Antiques, Corve Bridge, Ludlow, Shropshire, SY8 1DY** P
☎ 01584 872138
M 07976 549013
Est. 1972 *Stock size* Large
Stock Country furniture, mahogany, clocks
Open Mon–Sat 9am–5pm
Fairs Newark, Ardingly

⊞ Little Paws
Contact Mr Martin Rees-Evans
⊠ **4 Castle Street, Ludlow, Shropshire, SY8 1AT** P
☎ 01584 875286
Est. 1992 *Stock size* Medium
Stock Traditional teddy bears, dolls
Open Mon–Sat 10am–5pm

⊞ Ludlow Antique Beds & Fireplaces
Contact Mr G Jones or Mrs S Small
⊠ **142 Corve Street, Ludlow, Shropshire, SY8 2PG** P
☎ 01584 875506
M 07850 841609
Est. 1987 *Stock size* Medium
Stock Pine country and garden furniture, kitchen units, iron, wooden beds
Open Mon Fri 11am–4pm Sat 11am–5pm

McCartneys
Contact Mr Daniel Fielder or Miss Mary-Jane Hughes
⊠ **The Ox Pasture, Overton Road, Ludlow, Shropshire, SY8 4AA** P
☎ 01584 872251 F 01584 875727
E fineart@mccartneys.co.uk
W www.maccartneys.co.uk
Est. 1874
Open Mon–Fri 9am–5.30pm
Sales Fine art, antiques and household effects Fri 10.30am, viewing Thurs 2–7pm day of sale 9–10.30am
Frequency Monthly
Catalogues No

K W Swift
Contact Mr K W Swift
⊠ **56 Mill Street, Ludlow, Shropshire, SY8 1BB** P
☎ 01584 878571 F 01746 714407
E ken@bookshopbookfair.demon.co.uk
Est. 1989 *Stock size* Medium
No. of dealers 20
Stock Book market, total circa 5,000 volumes (frequently changed), antiquarian maps and prints
Open Mon–Sat 10am–5pm
Services Mounting, framing

⊞ Zany Lady
Contact Sue Humphreys
⊠ **Corve Street, Ludlow,**

Shropshire,
SY8 1DA P
☎ 01584 877200
Est. 2001 *Stock size* Medium
Stock Decorative stock, country furniture, textiles, French garden furniture
Open Mon–Sat 10am–5pm closed Thurs

MARKET DRAYTON

Kev 'n' Di's Antiques
Contact Mr K Williams
✉ **Country Needs, Rosehill Road, Market Drayton, Shropshire, TF9 2JG** P
☎ 01630 638320 F 01630 638658
M 07976 547174
E Kevanddi.williams@btinternet.com
Est. 1980 *Stock size* Large
Stock Edwardian and Victorian shipping furniture, memorabilia, kitchenware, pine, enamel, house clearance, antiques purchased
Open Flexi hours and by appointment
Fairs Swinderby, Newark
Services Valuations, courier service

Richard Midwinter Antiques
Contact Mr R Midwinter
✉ **Market Drayton, Shropshire, TF9 4EF** P
☎ 01630 673901 F 01630 672289
M 07836 617361
E antiques@midwinter.fslife.co.uk
Est. 1972 *Stock size* Medium
Stock Town and country furniture, longcase clocks, samplers, needlework pictures, decorative objects
Open By appointment
Fairs Olympia, NEC, Penman Chester
Services Restoration

MUCH WENLOCK

Cruck House Antiques
Contact Mrs B Roderick Smith
✉ **23 Barrow Street, Much Wenlock, Shropshire, TF13 6EN** P
☎ 01952 727165 F 01952 727165
Est. 1984 *Stock size* Medium
Stock Silver, pictures, small furniture, collectables
Open Mon–Sat 10am–5pm

John King (BADA)
Contact Mr J King
✉ **Raynalds Mansion, Much Wenlock, Shropshire, TF13 6AE** P
☎ 01952 727456 F 01952 727456
E kingj896@aol.com
Est. 1967 *Stock size* Large
Stock Period furniture and associated items
Open By appointment only
Services Advice on furnishing homes

NEWPORT

Corner Farm Antiques
Contact Mr Tim Dams
✉ **102 Kings Street, Weston Heath, Newport, Shropshire, TF11 8RX** P
☎ 01952 691543 F 01952 691543
M 07971 578585
W www.antique-clocks.com
Est. 1995 *Stock size* Large
Stock Georgian–Victorian and dining furniture, clocks, barometers, longcase clocks, collectables
Open Mon–Sun 10am–5pm
Services Restoration, clock repairs, valuations

Davies, White & Perry
Contact Mr J P Davies
✉ **45–47 High Street, Newport, Shropshire, TF10 7AT** P
☎ 01952 811003 F 01952 811439
E newport@davieswhiteperry.co.uk
W www.davieswhiteperry.co.uk
Est. 1806
Open Mon–Fri 8.15am–5pm Sat 9am–4pm closed noon–2pm Sun 11am–4pm
Sales Occasional antiques sales on site
Catalogues Yes

NORBURY

Brook Farm Antiques
Contact Mr Tucker or Mr James
✉ **Brook Farm, Gauntons Bank, Norbury, Shropshire, SY13 4HY** P
☎ 01948 666043
M 07754 418777
Est. 1983 *Stock size* Medium
Stock Victorian–Edwardian dining tables
Open Mon–Sun 9am–5pm
Fairs Stafford Bingley Hall, DMG Shepton Mallet
Services Restoration

OSWESTRY

Bookworld
Contact Mr J Cranwell
✉ **32 Beatrice Street, Oswestry, Shropshire, SY11 1QG** P
☎ 01691 657112 F 01691 657112
E jcbookworld@arrowweb.co.uk
W www.tgal.co.uk/bookworld
Est. 1995 *Stock size* Medium
Stock Antiquarian and second-hand books
Open Mon–Sat 9am–5pm
Services Book search

PREES HEATH

Whitchurch Antique Centre
Contact Mr John Simcox
✉ **Heath Road, Prees Heath, Whitchurch, Shropshire, SY13 2AD** P
☎ 01948 662626 F 01948 662604
W www.whitchurchantiques.co.uk
Est. 1979 *Stock size* Large
Stock French and English furniture and pine
Open Mon–Sun 9am–5pm
Services Packing, shipping

SHIFNAL

Davies, White & Perry
Contact Mr J P Davies
✉ **18 Market Place, Shifnal, Shropshire, TF11 9AZ** P
☎ 01952 460523
W www.davieswhiteperry.co.uk
Est. 1806
Open Mon–Fri 9am–5pm closed 1pm–2pm Sat 9am–noon
Sales Occasional antiques sales on site
Catalogues Yes

SHREWSBURY

Antique Barometer & Clock Shop
Contact Clive Hickman
✉ **21a Castle Street, Shrewsbury, Shropshire, SY1 2AZ**
☎ 01743 360415
E clocks.barometers@virgin.net
W www.thebarometershop.com

MIDLANDS

SHROPSHIRE • SHREWSBURY

Est. 1999 *Stock size* Large
Stock Antique clocks, barometers
Open Tues Thurs Fri Sat 10.30am–5pm
Services Restoration

⊞ Bear Steps Antiques
Contact John or Sally Wyatt
✉ **2 Bear Steps, Fish Street, Shrewsbury, Shropshire, SY1 1UR** 🅿
☎ 01743 344298
Ⓜ 07743 118192
Ⓦ www.bear-steps-antiques.co.uk
Est. 1990 *Stock size* Large
Stock 18th–early 19thC English porcelain
Open Mon–Sat 9am–5pm
Fairs NEC Antiques for Everyone

⊞ Candle Lane Books
Contact Mr J Thornhill
✉ **28 Princess Street, Shrewsbury, Shropshire, SY1 1LW** 🅿
☎ 01743 365301
Est. 1965 *Stock size* Large
Stock Antiquarian and second-hand books
Open Mon–Sat 9.30am–1pm 2–4.45pm

⊞ Collectors Gallery (IBNS, IBSS, ANA, BNTA)
Contact Mr Veissid
✉ **24 The Parade, St Mary's Place, Shrewsbury, Shropshire, SY1 1DL** 🅿
☎ 01743 272140 Ⓕ 01743 366041
Ⓔ m.veissid@btinternet.com
Ⓦ www.collectors-gallery.co.uk
Est. 1976 *Stock size* Medium
Stock Coins, medals, stamps, bank notes, postcards, bonds and shares
Open Mon–Fri 9am–5.30pm Sat 9.30am–5pm
Services Mail order

⊞ Collectors Place
Contact Mr Keith Jones or Mrs June Jones
✉ **29a Princess Street, Shrewsbury, Shropshire, SY1 1LW** 🅿
☎ 01743 246150
Ⓦ www.collectors-place.co.uk
Est. 1996 *Stock size* Large
Stock Antique bottles, pot lids, Wade, Beswick, Carlton ware, Art Deco, collectables
Open Tues–Sat 10am–4pm
Services Valuations on bottles

⊞ Deborah Paul
Contact Debbie or Paul
✉ **23 Belle Vue Road, Shrewsbury, Shropshire, SY3 7LN** 🅿
☎ 01743 357696
Ⓜ 07890 926530
Ⓔ pgurden@aol.com
Est. 2000 *Stock size* Medium
Stock Decorative and period furniture
Open Wed–Fri 10am–5pm Sat 10am–2pm
Services Clock restorer on site

⊞ Deja Vu Antiques
Contact Mr I Jones
✉ **48 High Street, Shrewsbury, Shropshire, SY13 1EU** 🅿
☎ 01743 362251
Ⓜ 07720 691939
Ⓔ dejavuantiques@lineone.net
Ⓦ www.antiquephones.co.uk
Est. 1984 *Stock size* Medium
Stock Antique telephones, Art Deco, pine furniture, jewellery
Open Mon–Sat 9.30am–5pm usually closed Thurs
Fairs Chester, Leeds and Loughborough Art Deco fairs, Warwick
Services Valuations, restoration, repairs, mail order service

⊞ Expressions
Contact Mrs J Griffiths
✉ **17 Princess Street, Shrewsbury, Shropshire, SY1 1LP** 🅿
☎ 01743 351731
Est. 1991 *Stock size* Medium
Stock Art Deco, furniture, pictures, glass, ceramics
Open Mon–Sat 10am–4pm

Halls Fine Art Auctions (ARVA, SOFAA, BACA Award Winner 2004)
Contact Richard Allen or Jeremy Lamond, RICS
✉ **Welsh Bridge, Shrewsbury, Shropshire, SY3 8LA** 🅿
☎ 01743 231212 Ⓕ 01743 246191
Ⓔ fineart@halls-auctioneers.ltd.uk
Ⓦ www.hallsgb.com
Est. 1865
Open 9am–5pm
Sales Antiques sales every 6 weeks, general and collectors sales every Fri 10.30am, viewing Thurs 9.30am–7pm
Catalogues Yes

⊞ Brian James Antiques (FSB)
Contact Brian James
✉ **Unit 9, Rodenhurst Business Park, Rodington, Shrewsbury, Shropshire, SY4 4QU** 🅿
☎ 01952 770856 Ⓕ 01952 770856
Ⓜ 07909 886903
Ⓔ bjames45@hotmail.com
Est. 1986 *Stock size* Medium
Stock Georgian–Edwardian chests of drawers
Open Mon–Fri 9am–6pm Sat 9am–1pm or by appointment
Services Wholesale export, conversion and manufacturing specialist

⊞ The Little Gem (NAG)
Contact Mrs M A Bowdler
✉ **18 St Mary's Street, Shrewsbury, Shropshire, SY1 1ED** 🅿
☎ 01743 352085 Ⓕ 01743 352085
Ⓔ mbowdler@littlegem.freeserve.co.uk
Ⓦ www.thelittlegem.co.uk
Est. 1960 *Stock size* Medium
Stock Antique and second-hand jewellery, modern Waterford crystal, lighting, hand-made jewellery
Open Mon–Sat 9am–5.30pm
Services Jewellery and watch repair

⊞ F C Manser & Son Ltd (LAPADA)
Contact Paul Manser
✉ **Coleham Head, Shrewsbury, Shropshire, SY3 7BJ** 🅿
☎ 01743 351120 Ⓕ 01743 271047
Ⓔ mansers@theantiquedealers.com
Ⓦ www.theantiquedealers.com
Est. 1944 *Stock size* Large
Stock Antiques, furniture, porcelain, glassware
Open Mon–Sat 9am–5pm
Fairs LAPADA NEC
Services Valuations, restoration

Princess Antique Centre
Contact Mr John Langford
✉ **14a The Square, Shrewsbury, Shropshire, SY1 1LH**
☎ 01743 343701
Est. 1984 *Stock size* Large
No. of dealers 100
Stock Complete range of antiques and collectables
Open Mon–Sat 9.30am–5.15pm

Quayside Antiques
Contact Mr Chris Winter
9 Frankwell, Shrewsbury, Shropshire, SY3 8JY P
☎ 01743 360490 or 01948 830363
Ⓜ 07715 748223
Ⓦ www.quaysideantiques shrewsbury.co.uk
Est. 1974 *Stock size* Large
Stock Victorian and Edwardian mahogany furniture, large tables, sets of chairs
Open Tues–Sat 10am–4pm closed Thurs
Fairs NEC
Services Restoration

Remains To Be Seen
Contact Mr Moseley or Ms Roberts
62 Wyle Cop, Shrewsbury, Shropshire, SY1 1UX P
☎ 01743 361560
Ⓜ 07715 597137
Est. 1991 *Stock size* Medium
Stock Arts and Crafts, Art Nouveau, Gothic revival
Open Mon–Fri 10am–5pm Sat 10am–6pm

Shrewsbury Antique Centre
Contact Mr John Langford
15 Princess House, The Square, Shrewsbury, Shropshire, SY1 1JZ P
☎ 01743 247704
Est. 1984 *Stock size* Large
No. of dealers 70
Stock Wide range of stock
Open Mon–Sat 9.30am–5.15pm

Shrewsbury Clock Shop (BHI)
Contact Mr A Donnelly
The Clock Shop, 7 The Parade, St Mary's Place, Shrewsbury, Shropshire, SY1 1DL P
☎ 01743 361388 Ⓕ 01743 361388
Ⓔ clockshopshrewsbury@ btopenworldcom
Ⓦ www.clockshopshrewsbury.co.uk
Est. 1987 *Stock size* Medium
Stock Clocks, especially longcase, and barometers
Open By appointment
Fairs NEC Spring
Services Clock and barometer repairs and restoration

STANTON UPON HINE HEATH

Marcus Moore Antiques
Contact Mr M Moore
Booley House, Booley, Stanton upon Hine Heath, Shrewsbury, Shropshire, SY4 4LY P
☎ 01939 200333 Ⓕ 01939 200333
Ⓜ 07976 228122
Ⓔ mmooreantiques@aol.com
Ⓦ www.marcusmoore-antiques.com
Est. 1980 *Stock size* Large
Stock Georgian–Victorian oak, country and mahogany furniture and associated items
Open By appointment any time
Services Restoration, upholstery, search, courier

WALL UNDER HEYWOOD

Mullock & Madeley (RICS, ISVA)
Contact John Mullock or Paul Madeley
The Old Shippon, Wall under Heywood, Church Stretton, Shropshire, SY6 7DS P
☎ 01694 771771 Ⓕ 01694 771772
Ⓔ info@mullockmadeley.co.uk
Ⓦ www.mullockmadeley.co.uk
Est. 1997
Open Mon–Fri 9am–5pm
Sales Sporting memorabilia, vintage fishing tackle, historical documents, autographs. Regular Internet sales of fishing tackle and sporting memorabilia. Sales venues Ludlow Race Course, Sutton Coldfield Town Hall. Specialist football, golf auctions held in Midlands venues
Frequency Every 3 months
Catalogues Yes

WELLINGTON

Lesley Arrowsmith Antiques & Collectables
Contact Lesley Arrowsmith
Wellington Market, Market Street, Wellington, Telford, Shropshire, SY1 3SF
☎ 01743 361007
Ⓜ 07814 666569
Est. 1993 *Stock size* Medium
No. of dealers 130
Stock 1930's oak furniture, china, glass
Open Tues Thurs–Sat 8am–4.30pm

WEM

Heritage Antiques
Contact M Nelms
Unit 2, Trench Farm, Tilley Green, Wem, Shropshire, SY4 5PJ P
☎ 01939 235463 Ⓕ 01939 235416
Ⓔ heritageantiques@btconnect.co.uk
Ⓦ www.heritageantiques.co.uk
Est. 1988 *Stock size* Medium
Stock Regency–Edwardian furniture and collectables
Open Mon–Fri 9am–5pm Sat by appointment
Services Restoration

STAFFORDSHIRE

BASFORD

The Pottery Buying Centre
Contact Mr P Hume
535 Etruria Road, Basford, Stoke-on-Trent, Staffordshire, ST5 0PN P
☎ 01782 635453
Ⓜ 07971 711612
Est. 1997 *Stock size* Medium
Stock Fine ceramics, collectables, Doulton, Moorcroft, Beswick, small furniture
Open Mon–Sat 10am–4pm
Services Valuations, restoration of ceramics

BREWOOD

Passiflora
Contact David or Paula Whitfield
25 Stafford Street, Brewood, Staffordshire, ST19 9DX P
☎ 01902 851557
Ⓜ 07711 682216
Ⓔ paula.whitfield@ukonline.co.uk
Est. 1988 *Stock size* Large
Stock Antiques and collectables dating back to Victorian times, glass, china, pottery, copper, brass, cast-iron, curios, leather, ephemera, postcards, children's books, bric-a-brac, garden tools, garden statuary, small furniture, decorative items including Mabel Lucie Attwell, small furniture, bric-a-brac, decorative items
Open Mon–Sat 10am–4pm telephone call advisable
Fairs Stafford Bingley Hall, West Midlands Fairs
Services Valuations and house clearance

MIDLANDS

STAFFORDSHIRE • BURTON-ON-TRENT

BURTON-ON-TRENT

Brearley's Antiques Corner Curios
Contact James Brearley
54 New Street, Burton-on-Trent, Staffordshire, DE14 3QY
01283 532600 01283 532600
Est. 1984 *Stock size* Medium
Stock Antiques, collectables
Open Mon–Sat 10am–6pm
Services House clearance

Burton Antiques
Contact Mr M Rodgers
1–2 Horninglow Road, Burton-on-Trent, Staffordshire, DE14 2PR
01283 542331
Est. 1978 *Stock size* Medium
Stock Antique pine and other antique furniture, shipping
Open Mon–Sat 9am–5pm Sun 11am–4pm
Services Valuations and pine stripping

Byrkley Books Ltd
Contact Mrs P Tebbett
159 Station Street, Burton-on-Trent, Staffordshire, DE14 1BE
01283 565900
Est. 1963 *Stock size* Medium
Stock Antiquarian, second-hand and remainder books, horse racing a speciality
Open Mon–Fri 9.30am–5pm Sat 9am–5pm

Roy C Harris (LAPADA)
Contact Roy Harris
Burton-on-Trent, Staffordshire
01283 520355
07718 500961
rchclocks@aol.com
Est. 1983 *Stock size* Medium
Stock Longcase clocks, bracket, mantel and wall clocks
Open By appointment
Fairs NEC
Services Valuations, restoration, shipping

Alan Winson Antiques
Contact Alan Winson
147 Derby Street, Burton-on-Trent, Staffordshire, DE14 2LG
01283 510429
Est. 1987 *Stock size* Medium
Stock Decorative antiques
Open Mon–Fri 9am–5pm Sat 10am–4pm

Richard Winterton Auctioneers and Valuers (NAVA)
Contact Mr A Rathbone or Mr R Winterton
School House Auction Rooms, Hawkins Lane, Burton-on-Trent, Staffordshire, DE14 1PT
01283 511224 01283 568650
adrianrathbone@btconnect.com
www.invaluable.com/richard winterton
Est. 1864
Open Mon–Fri 9am–5pm Tues 9am–6.30pm
Sales Weekly auctions of ceramics, glass, silver, fine art, jewellery, furniture, toys, sporting memorabilia, collectors items, antiquarian books, shipping furniture
Catalogues Yes

CHEADLE

Country Pine Trading Co
Contact Mr S Beard
Unit D, The Green, Cheadle, Staffordshire, ST10 1PH
01538 756894 01538 750244
07959 585133
www.countrypinetrading.co.uk
Est. 1974 *Stock size* Large
Stock Country pine and antique pine furniture
Open Mon–Fri 8am–5pm Sat 8am–1pm or by appointment
Fairs Newark
Services Restoration and pine stripping

ECCLESHALL

Cottage Collectibles
Contact Mrs S Kettle
62 High Street, Eccleshall, Staffordshire, ST21 6BZ
01785 850210 01785 850757
07967 713512
sheila@cottagecollectibles.co.uk
www.cottagecollectibles.co.uk
Est. 1995 *Stock size* Medium
Stock English and Continental country antiques, kitchenware, pine furniture, garden and dairy tools
Open By appointment only
Services Restoration

HARRISEAHEAD

David J Cope
Contact Mr D Cope
Fox Earth, Harriseahead Lane, Harriseahead, Stoke-on-Trent, Staffordshire, ST7 4RF
01782 511926 01782 516931
07712 880695
Est. 1979 *Stock size* Medium
Stock Moorcroft, Royal Worcester, Royal Doulton and porcelain
Open Mon–Sun 10am–5pm
Fairs Newark
Services Valuations

LEEK

The Antique Store
Contact Mrs J Hopwood
1 Clerk Bank, Leek, Staffordshire, ST13 5HE
01538 386555 01782 570119
07775 582058
Est. 1999 *Stock size* Medium
Stock Traditional English decorative items, garden items, architectural antiques
Open Wed Sat 10am–5pm

Antiques Within
Contact Mr R Hicks or Mrs K Hicks
Ground Floor, Compton Mill, Compton, Leek, Staffordshire, ST13 5NJ
01538 387848 01538 387848
antiques.within@virgin.net
www.antiques-within.com
Est. 1994 *Stock size* Large
Stock Pine, oak, mahogany and Continental furniture, brass, copper, mirrors, collectables
Open Mon–Sat 10am–5.30pm Sun 1–5pm
Fairs Newark, Swinderby and Ardingly
Services Container packing

Anvil Antiques
Contact Mrs Lynn Davis
Cross Street Mill, Cross Street, Leek, Staffordshire, ST13 6BL
01538 371657 01538 385118
Est. 1975 *Stock size* Medium
Stock Reproduction and old pine furniture, Old French dark-wood furniture
Open Mon–Fri 9am–5pm Sat noon–5pm Sun by appointment
Services Restoration, stripping

Bury & Hilton
Contact John Hilton
6 Market Street, Leek, Staffordshire, ST13 6HZ
01538 383344 · 01538 371314
info@buryandhilton.co.uk
Est. 1887
Open Mon–Fri 9am–5.30pm
Sales Monthly antiques and general sales 1st Thurs 10am. Special antiques sales April and October
Catalogues No

Compton Mill Antique Emporium
Contact Mrs S K Butler
Compton Mill, Compton, Leek, Staffordshire, ST13 5NJ
01538 373396 · 01538 399092
kelly.butler@ntlbusiness.co.uk
Est. 1996 *Stock size* Large
No. of dealers 20
Stock Wide range of antiques
Open Mon–Sat 10am–5.30pm Sun 1–5pm
Services Pine furniture made from reclaimed timber

K Grosvenor
Contact Mr K Grosvenor
71 St Edward Street, Leek, Staffordshire, ST13 5DH
01538 385669 · 01538 385669
keith.grosvenor@virgin.net
Est. 1970 *Stock size* Large
Stock Clocks, barometers, scientific instruments
Open Mon–Sat 9am–4pm or by appointment
Services Restoration, repair of clocks

Roger Haynes Antique Finder
Contact Mr R Haynes
31 Compton, Leek, Staffordshire, ST13 5NJ
01538 385161 · 01538 385161
info@rogerhaynesantiquefinder.com
Est. 1959 *Stock size* Large
Stock Decorative English and French items, pine and country small items, collectables
Trade only Yes
Open By appointment only
Services Export trade

Johnsons
Contact Mr P Johnson
Chorley Mill, 1 West Street, Leek, Staffordshire, ST13 8AF
01538 386745 · 01538 388375
07714 288765
Est. 1976 *Stock size* Medium
Stock English and French country furniture, decorative accessories, unique objects
Open Mon–Fri 8am–5pm Sat Sun by appointment
Services Suppliers to export market

Jonathan Charles Antiques
Contact Mr J Heath
6 Broad Street, Leek, Staffordshire, ST13 5NS
01538 381883
Est. 1999 *Stock size* Medium
Stock Pine furniture, country furniture
Open Mon–Sat 11am–5pm
Services One-off pieces made to measure

Leek Antiques Centre (Barclay House)
Contact Mr P Lumley
4–6 Brook Street, Leek, Staffordshire, ST13 5JE
01538 398475
07721 413095
Est. 1969 *Stock size* Large
No. of dealers 7–8
Stock Wide range of antiques including dining tables, sets of chairs, bedroom furniture, chests of drawers, pottery, watercolours, oil paintings, pine
Open Mon–Sat 10.30am–5pm
Services Restoration, polishing and upholstery

Molland Antique Mirrors
Contact John Molland
2 Duke Street, Leek, Staffordshire, ST13 5LG
01538 372553 · 01538 372553
07774 226042
sales@mollandmirrors.co.uk
www.mollandmirrors.co.uk
Est. 1988 *Stock size* Large
Stock 19thC French and English mirrors
Open Mon–Fri 8am–5pm
Fairs NEC, Earls Court
Services Export packing, restoration

Odeon Designs Ltd (Lighting Association)
Contact Mr S Ford
76–78 St Edward Street, Leek, Staffordshire, ST13 5DL
01538 387188 · 01538 387188
07973 317961
odeonantiques@hotmail.com
www.odeonantiques.co.uk
Est. 1993 *Stock size* Large
Stock Antique and some reproduction country furniture, lighting, small decorative objects
Open Mon–Sat 11am–5pm
Services Valuations, restoration of lighting

Page Antiques
Contact Denis Page
Antiques Within Ltd, Ground Floor, Compton Mill, Leek, Staffordshire, ST13 5NJ
01663 732358 · 01663 732358
07966 154993
Est. 1979 *Stock size* Medium
Stock General antiques, Georgian–Edwardian furniture
Open Mon–Sat 10am–5pm
Fairs Swinderby, Buxton
Services Valuations, exports

Richardson Antiques Ltd
Contact Mr Richardson
Antiques Within, Compton Mill, Leek, Staffordshire, ST13 5NJ
01270 625963
Est. 1984 *Stock size* Medium
Stock Furniture, china
Open Mon–Sat 10am–5pm Sun 1–5pm

Roberts & Mudd Antiques
Contact Mr C Mudd
Compton Mill, Compton, Leek, Staffordshire, ST13 5NJ
01538 371284 · 01538 371284
07768 845942
robertsmudd@compuserve.com
www.robertsandmudd.com
Est. 1993 *Stock size* Large
Stock French, pine and country furniture, decorative items, French and English furniture
Open Mon–Fri 8am–6pm Sat 9am–noon
Services Restoration

MIDLANDS

STAFFORDSHIRE • LICHFIELD

⊞ Simpsons
Contact Mr M Simpson
✉ **39 St Edward Street, Leek, Staffordshire, ST13 5DN** 🅿
☎ 01538 371515 Ⓕ 01538 371515
Est. 1989 *Stock size* Medium
Stock Original painted furniture and decorative items for the home and garden, antique mirrors
Open Mon–Sat 10am–5pm Thurs 11am–4pm
Services Bespoke items made to customers' requirements

LICHFIELD

⊞ Cathedral Gallery
Contact Mrs R Thompson-Yates
✉ **22 Dam Street, Lichfield, Staffordshire, WS13 6AA**
☎ 01543 253115
Est. 1984 *Stock size* Large
Stock Antique maps, prints
Open Mon–Sat 10am–5pm closed Wed
Services Valuations, restoration, framing, colouring

Curborough Hall Farm Antiques Centre
Contact Mr J Finnemore
✉ **Unit 10, Curborough Hall Farm, Watery Lane, Lichfield, Staffordshire, WS13 7SE** 🅿
☎ 01543 417100
Ⓜ 07885 285053
Est. 1995 *Stock size* Large
No. of dealers 31
Stock Furniture, china, collectables, jewellery, books, linen, pictures
Open Tues–Sun Bank Holidays 10am–4.30pm
Services Restaurant

⊞ The Essence of Time (BHI)
Contact Malcolm Hinton
✉ **Unit 2, Curborough Antiques and Lichfield Craft Centre, Curborough Hall Farm, Watery Lane, Lichfield, Staffordshire, WS13 8ES** 🅿
☎ 01543 418239 or 01902 764900 (evenings)
Ⓜ 07944 245064 (any time)
Est. 1990 *Stock size* Large
Stock Longcase, Vienna, wall, mantel and novelty clocks
Open Wed–Sun 10.45am–5pm

⊞ James A Jordan (BHI Qualified member)
Contact Mr J Jordan
✉ **7 The Corn Exchange, Conduit Street, Lichfield, Staffordshire, WS13 6JR** 🅿
☎ 01543 416221
Est. 1988 *Stock size* Large
Stock Jewellery, watches, clocks, silver, small antique furnishings
Open Mon–Sat 9am–5pm closed Wed
Services Watch, clock and barometer repairs

⊞ Milestone Antiques (LAPADA)
Contact Humphrey or Elsa Crawshaw
✉ **5 Main Street, Whittington, Lichfield, Staffordshire, WS14 9JU** 🅿
☎ 01543 432248
Est. 1988 *Stock size* Medium
Stock Georgian–early Victorian traditional English furniture, 19thC English porcelain, decorative items
Open Thurs–Sat 10am–6pm Sun 11am–3pm or by appointment

⊞ Royden Smith
Contact Mr R Smith
✉ **Church View House, Farewell Lane, Burntwood, Lichfield, Staffordshire, WS7 9DP** 🅿
☎ 01543 682217
Est. 1973 *Stock size* Large
Stock Antiquarian and second-hand books
Open Sat 10am–4.30pm Sun 11am–4.30pm or by appointment
Services Valuations

⊞ The Staffs Bookshop
Contact Miss S Hawkins
✉ **4 & 6 Dam Street, Lichfield, Staffordshire, WS13 6AA** 🅿
☎ 01543 264093
Est. 1930 *Stock size* Large
Stock Children's, antiquarian, second-hand and new books, Samuel Johnson, 18thC literature
Open Mon–Sat 9.30am–5.30pm Sun 1–5pm
Services Valuations

Wintertons Ltd (SOFAA)
Contact Charles Hanson
✉ **Lichfield Auction Centre, Fradley Park, Lichfield, Staffordshire, WS13 8NF** 🅿
☎ 01543 263256 Ⓕ 01543 415348
Ⓔ enquiries@wintertons.co.uk
Ⓦ www.wintertons.co.uk
Est. 1864
Open Mon–Fri 9am–5.30pm
Sales Victorian and general sales, every 2 or 3 weeks Thurs 10.30am, viewing Wed 1–7pm. Bi-monthly 2-day fine art sale, Wed Thurs 10.30am, viewing Tues noon–8pm and day of sale
Catalogues Yes

PENKRIDGE

⊞ Golden Oldies
Contact Mr Knowles
✉ **5 Crown Bridge, Penkridge, Staffordshire, ST19 5AA** 🅿
☎ 01785 714722
Est. 1973 *Stock size* Large
Stock Antique and reproduction stock mainly furniture and general antiques
Open Mon–Sat 9.30am–5.30pm
Fairs Newark

RUGELEY

Rugeley Antique Centre
Contact Mr Thornhill
✉ **161 Main Road, Brereton, Rugeley, Staffordshire, WS15 1DX** 🅿
☎ 01889 577166 Ⓕ 01889 577166
Ⓜ 07980 756602
Est. 1980 *Stock size* Large
No. of dealers 20
Stock Antiques and collectables
Open Sun–Thurs 10am–4.30pm Fri Sat 10am–5pm
Services Small parcel shipping

STAFFORD

⊞ Windmill Antiques
Contact Mr I Kettlewell
✉ **9 Castle Hill, Broad Eye, Stafford, Staffordshire, ST16 2QB** 🅿
☎ 01785 228505 Ⓕ 01785 228505
Est. 1992 *Stock size* Large
Stock Antiques, jewellery, decorative items, woodworking tools
Open Mon–Sat 10am–5pm closed Tues
Services Valuations, ceramic restoration

STOKE-ON-TRENT

Abacus Gallery
Contact Mr D Mycock
56–60 Millrise Road, Milton, Stoke-on-Trent, Staffordshire, ST2 7BW P
☎ 01782 543005
Est. 1980 *Stock size* Medium
Stock Antiquarian and second-hand books, postcards
Open Mon–Fri 9am–5pm Sat 9am–4pm
Fairs Buxton Book Fair

Ann's Antiques
Contact Mrs A Byatte
26 Leek Road, Stockton Brook, Stoke-on-Trent, Staffordshire, ST9 9NN P
☎ 01782 503991
Est. 1969 *Stock size* Large
Stock Victorian–Edwardian furniture, cranberry glass, Victorian oil lamps, jewellery, pottery, porcelain, rocking horses, dolls' houses
Open Fri Sat 10am–5pm or by appointment

Antiquities of Hartshill
Contact Mrs J Brunetti
311 Hartshill Road, Hartshill, Stoke-on-Trent, Staffordshire, ST4 7NR P
☎ 01782 620222
Est. 1996 *Stock size* Large
Stock Wide range of antiques including furniture, china, dolls, porcelain
Open Mon–Sat 10am–4.30pm
Services Valuations, Hummel figures found

Ceramics International
Contact Christine Cope
Unit 1, Top Bridge Works, Trubshaw Cross, Burslem, Stoke-on-Trent, Staffordshire, ST6 4LR P
☎ 01782 575545 F 01782 814447
E emailceramics.int@btconnect.com
Est. 1996 *Stock size* Large
Stock English, imported ceramics, Worcester, Wedgewood, Moorcroft, chintz, Flow blue
Trade only Yes
Open Mon–Fri 9am–5.30pm

Checkley Interiors
Contact Mr S Clegg
493–495 Hartshill Road, Hartshill, Stoke-on-Trent, Staffordshire, ST4 6AA P
☎ 01782 717522 F 01782 717522
Est. 1998 *Stock size* Medium
Stock Victorian and Edwardian upholstered and occasional furniture
Open Mon–Sat 9.30am–5pm closed Thurs
Services Restoration, upholstery, room interior service

H Chesters & Sons
Contact Mr H Chesters
196 Waterloo Road, Burslem, Stoke-on-Trent, Staffordshire, ST6 3HQ P
☎ 01782 822344
Est. 1912
Open Mon–Fri 10am–5pm telephone service 7am–noon
Sales Fine antiques sales, 2 per annum, Feb and Sept, viewing advertised locally
Catalogues Yes

On the Hill Antiques
Contact Ms Sue Bird
450 Hartshill Road, Stoke-on-Trent, Staffordshire, ST4 7PL P
☎ 01782 252249 F 01782 252249
M 07932 726035
Est. 1996 *Stock size* Large
Stock 1930s oak furniture, pottery, collectables
Open Mon–Sat 9am–5pm
Fairs Bingley, Staffordshire
Services Valuations

Potteries Antique Centre
Contact Ms K Ware
271 Waterloo Road, Cobridge, Stoke-on-Trent, Staffordshire, ST6 3HR P
☎ 01782 201455 F 01782 201518
E www@potteriesantiquecentre.com
W www.potteriesantiquecentre.com
Est. 1990 *Stock size* Large
Stock Wedgewood, Doulton, Beswick, Moorcroft, Crown Devon, Coalport, Minton, Clarice Cliff, Crown Derby, Wade, Shelley, Carlton ware
Open Mon–Sat 9am–5.30pm
Fairs Royal Doulton & Beswick Fairs
Services Valuations

Potteries Specialist Auctions
Contact Martyn Bullock
271 Waterloo Road, Cobridge, Stoke-on-Trent, Staffordshire, ST6 3HR P
☎ 01782 286622 F 01782 213777
E enquiries@potteriesauctions.com
W www.potteriesauctions.com
Est. 1986
Open Mon–Fri 9am–5.30pm
Sales Mainly British 20thC pottery, view 10am–4pm day prior morning of sale 9–11am. See website for sale dates
Frequency Monthly
Catalogues Yes

Louis Taylor Fine Art Auctioneers
Contact Mr C Hillier MRICS
Britannia House, 10 Town Road, Hanley, Stoke-on-Trent, Staffordshire, ST1 2QG P
☎ 01782 214111 F 01782 215283
Est. 1877
Open Mon–Fri 9am–5pm closed 1–2pm
Sales Quarterly 2-day fine art sales Mon Tues 10am, viewing Thurs 10am–7pm Fri 10am–4pm day of sale from 9am. Specialist Doulton and Beswick quarterly, viewing as for fine art. General and Victoriana every two weeks Mon 10am, viewing Fri 10am–4pm Sat 9am–noon
Frequency Fortnightly
Catalogues Yes

The Tinder Box
Contact Mrs P Yarwood
61 Lichfield Street, Hanley, Stoke-on-Trent, Staffordshire, ST1 3EA P
☎ 01782 261368 F 01782 261368
M 07946 445659
Est. 1969 *Stock size* Large
Stock Jewellery, pottery, silver, lamps, spares for oil lamps
Open Mon–Fri 10am–6pm
Services Valuations, restoration

Wooden Heart
Contact Mrs Y Quirke
51 Stoke Road, Shelton, Stoke-on-Trent, Staffordshire, ST4 2QN P
☎ 01782 411437
Est. 1995 *Stock size* Large
Stock Edwardian–Victorian mahogany furniture and decorative items
Open Mon–Fri 8.30am–5pm Sat 10.30am–3.30pm
Services Restoration

MIDLANDS

STAFFORDSHIRE • STONE

STONE

Hallahan
Contact Hilary Jeffries
13 Station Road, Stone, Staffordshire, ST15 8JP
01785 815187 F 01785 815187
Est. 1995 *Stock size* Large
Stock 1960s–70s collectables, antiques, upholstered furniture, antiquarian books, jewellery
Open Mon–Sat 9.30am–5pm closed Wed
Services Upholstery

TUTBURY

The Clock Shop (BHI)
Contact Ms A James
1 High Street, Tutbury, Burton-on-Trent, Staffordshire, DE13 9LP
01283 814596 F 01283 814594
M 07710 161949
E sales@antique-clocks-watches.co.uk
W www.antique-clocks-watches.co.uk
Est. 1987 *Stock size* Large
Stock Antique clocks, longcase clocks and watches, barometers
Open Mon–Sat 10am–5pm
Services Valuations, restoration and repair

Old Chapel Antiques & Collectables Centre
Contact Roger Clarke
The Old Chapel, High Street, Tutbury, Burton-on-Trent, Staffordshire, PE13 9LP
01283 815255
Est. 1996 *Stock size* Large
No. of dealers 30
Stock Antiques, collectables
Open Mon–Sun 10am–5pm

UTTOXETER

Lion Antiques Centre
Contact Mrs Vicky Jacques
8 Market Place, Uttoxeter, Staffordshire, ST14 8HP
01889 567717 F 01889 567717
Est. 1999 *Stock size* Large
No. of dealers 28+
Stock Wide range of antiques
Open Mon–Sat 10am–5pm
Services Sourcing service, design

WOODSEAVES

A D Antiques
Contact Alison Davey
PO Box 2407, Woodseaves, Stafford, Staffordshire, ST15 8WY
M 07811 783518
E alison@adantiques.com
W www.adantiques.com
Est. 1997 *Stock size* Medium
Stock Decorative arts, ceramics and metalware, Moorcroft, Doulton Lambeth, William de Morgan, Pilkington's lustre, Wedgwood
Open By appointment
Fairs NEC, Bingley Hall, Penman's Chester

YOXALL

H W Heron & Son Ltd (LAPADA)
Contact Mrs J Heron
The Antique Shop, King Street, Yoxall, Burton-on-Trent, Staffordshire, DE13 8NF
01543 472266 F 01543 473800
M 07773 337809
E shop@hwheronantiques.com
W www.hwheronantiques.com
Est. 1949 *Stock size* Medium
Stock Period furniture, ceramics, objects, paintings
Open Mon–Fri 9am–6pm
Sat 9am–5.30pm
Sun by appointment
Services Valuations

WARWICKSHIRE

ALCESTER

Malthouse Antiques Centre
Contact Pat Alcock
4 Market Place, Alcester, Warwickshire, B49 5AE
01789 764032
Est. 1984 *Stock size* Large
No. of dealers 10
Stock 18th–early 20thC furniture, ceramics, silver, collectables etc
Open Mon–Sat 10am–5pm
Sun 1–4pm

Justin Neales Antiques & Interiors
Contact Mr Justin Neales
3 Evesham Street, Alcester, Warwickshire, B49 5DS
01789 766699
W www.jneales.com
Est. 1987 *Stock size* Large
Stock Georgian, Victorian and Edwardian furniture, painted furniture, tapestry, cushions, mirrors, silver picture frames
Open Mon–Fri 9am–5pm
Sat 10am–5pm
Services Restoration, upholstery

BIDFORD-ON-AVON

Bidford Antiques & Collectables
Contact Thelma Hughes
94 High Street, Bidford-on-Avon, Warwickshire, B50 4AF
01789 773680
Est. 1980 *Stock size* Medium
No. of dealers 5
Stock Furniture, jewellery, paintings, china
Open Mon–Sat 11am–5pm
Sun 1.30–5pm

Steven B Bruce Auctioneers Ltd (NAVA, SOFAA)
Contact Mr S Bruce
Unit 5, Clayhall Farm, Honeybourne Road, Bidford-on-Avon, Warwickshire, B49 5PD
01789 490450
M 07778 595952
E stevenbbruce@hotmail.com
W www.stevenbbruce.co.uk.co.uk
Est. 1995
Open Mon–Sat 9.30am–5.30pm
Sales Regular sales held at Stratford Racecourse and on-site country house sales
Frequency Monthly
Catalogues Yes

BRINKLOW

Annie's Attic
Contact Ann Wilson
19a Broad Street, Brinklow, Warwickshire, CV23 0LS
01788 833094
Est. 1998 *Stock size* Medium
Stock Clocks, small furniture, metalwork, old and interesting objects, period lighting
Open Fri Sat 11am–5pm
Sun 11am–4pm also some Wed
Services Clock restoration

DUNCHURCH

Now & Then
Contact Mike Best
6 The Green, Dunchurch,

Rugby, Warwickshire,
CV22 6NX P
☎ 01788 811211
M 07711 248951
Est. 2001 *Stock size* Large
Stock General antiques
Open Mon–Sun 10am–5pm

HATTON

The Stables Antique Centre
Contact Mr John Colledge
✉ **Hatton Country World, Dark Lane, Hatton, Warwick, Warwickshire, CV35 8XA** P
☎ 01926 842405 F 01926 842023
Est. 1992 *Stock size* Large
No. of dealers 25
Stock Old clocks, furniture, curios, china etc
Open Mon–Sun 10am–5pm
Services Craft centre, café, bar, clock repairs

HENLEY-IN-ARDEN

Henley Antiques & Collectables Centre
Contact Mrs Rosie Montague
✉ **Rear of Henley Bakery, 92 High Street, Henley-in-Arden, Warwickshire, B95 5BY** P
☎ 01564 795979
M 07950 324376
Est. 2000 *Stock size* Large
No. of dealers 15–20
Stock Georgian–Edwardian furniture, wide range of antiques, ceramics, glass, silver, collectables
Open Mon–Sat 10.30am–5pm
Sun Bank Holidays 11am–4pm

ILMINGTON

Peter Finer (BADA)
Contact Peter Finer or Nickki Eden
✉ **The Old Rectory, Ilmington, Shipston-on-Stour, Warwickshire, CV36 4JQ**
☎ 01608 682267 F 01608 682575
E pf@peterfiner.com
W www.peterfiner.com
Est. 1970 *Stock size* Large
Stock Arms, armour and related objects
Open Strictly by appointment
Fairs International Fine Art New York, Palm Beach International Art & Antiques Fair
Services Restoration, displays

LEAMINGTON SPA

Kings Cottage Antiques (LAPADA)
Contact Mr A Jackson
✉ **4 Windsor Street, Leamington Spa, Warwickshire, CV32 5EB** P
☎ 01926 422927
Est. 1993 *Stock size* Medium
Stock Early oak and country furniture
Open Mon–Fri 9am–5pm
Sat by appointment

Locke & England
Contact Claire Hudson
✉ **18 Guy Street, Leamington Spa, Warwickshire, CV32 4RT** P
☎ 01926 889100 F 01926 470608
E info@leauction.co.uk
W www.leauction.co.uk
Est. 1834
Open Mon–Fri 9am–5.30pm
Sales Household and Victoriana auctions weekly, antiques and fine art auctions monthly
Catalogues Yes

Portland Books
Contact Mr Martyn Davies or Gareth Wyatt
✉ **93 Warwick Street, Leamington Spa, Warwickshire, CV32 4RJ** P
☎ 01926 888118 F 01926 885305
E twiceportlandbooks@quicknetuk.com
W www.portlandbooks.com
Est. 1974 *Stock size* Large
Stock Antiquarian, second-hand and new books, Warwickshire history a speciality, modern books at discounted prices
Open Mon–Sat 9.30am–5.30pm
Services Valuations, book search

LONG MARSTON

Barn Antique Centre
Contact Bev or Graham Simpson
✉ **Station Road, Long Marston, Stratford-upon-Avon, Warwickshire, CV37 8RP** P
☎ 01789 721399 F 01789 721390
E info@barnantique.co.uk
W www.barnantique.co.uk
Est. 1978 *Stock size* Large
No. of dealers 40
Stock Huge barn full of antiques and collectables, Georgian–Edwardian furniture, pine, fireplaces, silver, kitchenware, porcelain
Open Mon–Sat 10am–5pm
Sun noon–6pm
Services Licensed restaurant

NUNEATON

The Granary Antiques
Contact Gordon Stockdale
✉ **Hoar Park, Craft Village, Ansley, Nuneaton, Warwickshire, CV10 0QU** P
☎ 024 7639 5551 F 024 7639 4433
E jl@hpcv.freeserve.co.uk
W www.hpcv.freeserve.co.uk
Est. 1996 *Stock size* Large
Stock General antiques, pine, kitchenware, Edwardian furniture, porcelain and Mason's Ironstone in a 17thC converted building
Open Tues–Sun 10am–5pm
Services Restaurant

G Payne Antiques
Contact Mr G Payne
✉ **25 Watling Street, Nuneaton, Warwickshire, CV11 6JJ** P
☎ 024 7632 5178
M 07836 754489
Est. 1991 *Stock size* Medium
Stock Mahogany and oak furniture
Open Mon–Sat 8am–6pm

POLESWORTH

G & J Chesters (PBFA)
Contact Mr G Chesters
✉ **14 Market Street, Polesworth, Warwickshire, B78 1HW** P
☎ 01827 894743
E gandjchesters@bun.com
Est. 1970 *Stock size* Large
Stock Antiquarian and second-hand books, maps, prints
Open Mon–Sat 9.30am–5.30pm
Wed 9.30am–9pm
Fairs NEC Antiques for Everyone

RUGBY

272 Antiques
Contact Sue Walters
✉ **272 Hillmorton Road, Rugby, Warwickshire, CV22 5BW** P
☎ 01788 541818 F 01788 541818
Est. 2001 *Stock size* Small
Stock French country and English

pine furniture
Open Wed–Sat 10.30am–5pm
Services Restoration, pine stripping

M G Seaman & Daughter
Contact Mrs M or Miss L Seaman
16–18 Albert Street, Rugby, Warwickshire, CV21 2RS P
☎ 01788 542367/543445
Est. 1979 *Stock size* Large
Stock 1920s–1960s antiques, glass, china, clothing, accessories, jewellery
Open Mon–Sat 9am–5pm closed Wed

SHENTON

Whitemoors Antique Centre
Contact Mr Colin Wightman
Main Street, Shenton, Warwickshire, CV13 6BZ P
☎ 01455 212250
Est. 1993 *Stock size* Large
No. of dealers 25
Stock Furniture, pottery, clocks, bric-a-brac, paperweights
Open Mon–Sun summer 11am–5pm winter 11am–4pm

SHIPSTON-ON-STOUR

Church Street Gallery
Contact Mr Robert Field
24 Church Street, Shipston-on-Stour, Warwickshire, CV36 4AP P
☎ 01608 662431 F 01608 662431
W www.churchstreetgallery.co.uk
Est. 1979 *Stock size* Large
Stock Antique maps and prints, late 19th–early 20thC watercolours, oils, furniture, bric-a-brac
Open Mon–Fri 9.30am–6pm Thurs 9.30am–1pm Sat 10am–5.30pm
Services Picture framing, restoration

The Richard Harvey Collection Ltd
Contact Mr C Harvey
28 Church Street, Shipston-on-Stour, Warwickshire, CV36 4AP P
☎ 01608 662168 F 01608 662168
Est. 1973 *Stock size* Large
Stock Chinese antiques, painted Gustavian furniture, leather furniture, rugs, contemporary lighting
Open Mon–Sat 9am–5.30pm or by appointment

Pine and Things
Contact Mr R Wood
Portobello Farm, Campden Road, Shipston-on-Stour, Warwickshire, CV36 4PY P
☎ 01608 663849 F 01608 663849
E mailus@pinethings.co.uk
W www.pinethings.co.uk
Est. 1991 *Stock size* Large
Stock Victorian and earlier pine furniture
Open Mon–Sat 9am–5pm

James Wigington
Contact James Wigington
21 High Street, Shipston-on-Stour, Warwickshire, CV36 4AB P
☎ 01608 661661 F 01608 661598
M 07881 528001
E info@jameswigington.com
W www.jameswigington.com
Est. 1979 *Stock size* Medium
Stock Arms and armour
Open Mon–Sat 10am–4pm
Fairs NEC, Park Lane Arms & Armour Fair

SNITTERFIELD

Phillips Brothers (NAVA)
Contact Robin Phillips
The Sale Room, Bearley Road, Snitterfield, Stratford-upon-Avon, Warwickshire, CV37 0EZ P
☎ 01789 731114 F 01789 731114
Est. 1980
Open Mon–Fri 9.30am–5pm
Sales General and antiques sales Sat 10am, viewing from 9am. Occasional antiques sales Sat, viewing 9am
Frequency Fortnightly
Catalogues No

STRATFORD-UPON-AVON

Arbour Antiques Ltd
Contact Mr Colwell
Poets Arbour, Sheep Street, Stratford-upon-Avon, Warwickshire, CV37 6EF
☎ 01789 293453
Est. 1954 *Stock size* Large
Stock 16th–19thC arms and armour
Open Mon–Fri 9am–5pm

Thomas Crapper & Co (SALVO)
Stable Yard, Alscot Park, Stratford-upon-Avon, Warwickshire, CV37 8BL P
☎ 01789 450522 F 01789 450523
E wc@thomas-crapper.com
W www.thomas-crapper.com
Est. 1861 *Stock size* Medium
Stock Victorian–Edwardian and unusual bathroom fittings
Open Mon–Fri 9.30am–5pm or by appointment
Services Restoration, catalogues (£5 refundable on purchase)

Goodbye To All That
Contact Mr Briggs
50 Henley Street, Stratford-upon-Avon, Warwickshire, CV37 6QL P
☎ 01789 262906
M 07867 611923
Est. 1999 *Stock size* Small
Stock Firearms, scientific instruments
Open Mon–Sun 10am–5.30pm

Pickwick Gallery
Contact Mr H D Dankenbring
32 Henley Street, Stratford-upon-Avon, Warwickshire, CV37 6QW P
☎ 01789 294861
E mm@meridienmaps.co.uk
W www.meridenmaps.co.uk
Est. 1986 *Stock size* Medium
Stock Antique maps, sporting prints, 1600–1880
Open Mon–Sat 10am–5pm Sun Bank Holidays 11am–4.30pm

George Pragnell The Jeweller (CNAG)
Contact Mary Machin
5 & 6 Woods Street, Stratford-upon-Avon, Warwickshire, CV37 6JA P
☎ 01789 267072 F 01789 415131
E enquiries@pragnell.co.uk

Ⓦ www.pragnell.co.uk
Est. 1954 *Stock size* Medium
Stock Antique silver, jewellery
Open Mon–Sat 9.15am–5.30pm
Fairs NEC

Riverside Antiques
Contact Mr Richard Monk
60 Ely Street, Stratford-upon-Avon, Warwickshire, CV37 6LN P
☎ 01789 262090
Ⓜ 07931 512325
Est. 1996 *Stock size* Medium
Stock Clarice Cliff, antique and designer jewellery
Open Mon–Sun Oct–Mar 10am–5pm Jun–Sept 10am–5.30pm
Services Rings designed and made

Stratford Antiques and Interiors
Contact Mr or Mrs Kerr
Dodwell Trading Estate, Evesham Road, Stratford-upon-Avon, Warwickshire, CV37 9SY P
☎ 01789 297729 Ⓕ 01789 297710
Ⓔ drewkerr@tiscali.co.uk
Ⓦ www.stratfordantiques.co.uk
Est. 1995 *Stock size* Large
No. of dealers 20
Stock A wide range of antiques and collectables, home furnishings and decorative items
Open Mon–Sun 10am–5pm

Stratford Antiques Centre
Contact Mr Mike Conway
59–60 Ely Street, Stratford-upon-Avon, Warwickshire, CV37 6LN P
☎ 01789 204180
Est. 1981 *Stock size* Large
No. of dealers 50
Stock Wide range of antiques and collectables. One of the largest antiques markets in the Midlands
Open Mon–Sun summer 10am–5.30pm winter 10am–5pm
Services Restaurant

TIDDINGTON

Bigwood Auctioneers Ltd (SOFAA)
Contact Mr C Ironmonger
The Old School, Tiddington, Stratford-upon-Avon, Warwickshire, CV37 7AW P
☎ 01789 269415 Ⓕ 01789 294168
Ⓔ sales@bigwoodauctioneers.co.uk
Ⓦ www.bigwoodauctioneers.co.uk
Est. 1849
Open Mon–Fri 9am–5.30pm closed 12.45–2pm Sat 9am–noon
Sales Quarterly fine furniture and works of art, monthly antiques and collectables, sporting memorabilia (Mar Sept) wine sales (March June Sept Dec) collectables, games, toys (April Oct)
Frequency 50 per annum
Catalogues Yes

WARTON

Afford Decorative Antiques (LAPADA)
Contact Jan Afford
Warton, Warwickshire, B79 P
☎ 01827 330042
Ⓜ 07831 114909
Ⓔ affordantiques@fsmail.net
Ⓦ www.afforddecarts.com
Est. 1980 *Stock size* Medium
Stock All decorative arts 1870–1950
Open By appointment
Fairs Antiques for Everyone, LAPADA
Services Valuations, restoration

WARWICK

Duncan M Allsop (ABA)
Contact Mr D Allsop
68 Smith Street, Warwick, Warwickshire, CV34 4HU P
☎ 01926 493266 Ⓕ 01926 493266
Ⓔ duncan.allsop@btopenworld.com
Ⓦ www.allsop-books.freeserve.co.uk
Est. 1966 *Stock size* Medium
Stock Varied stock of books including antiquarian, fine bindings and modern books
Open Mon–Sat 9.30am–5.30pm
Fairs Royal National

Apollo Antiques Ltd (LAPADA, CINOA)
Contact Roger Mynott
The Saltisford, Warwick, Warwickshire, CV34 4TD P
☎ 01926 494746/494666
Ⓕ 01926 401477
Ⓔ mynott@apolloantiques.com
Ⓦ www.apolloantiques.com
Est. 1968 *Stock size* Large
Stock English 18th–19thC furniture, sculpture, paintings, decorative items, Arts and Crafts, Gothic revival
Open Mon–Fri 9.30am–5.30pm Sat by appointment
Services Free delivery service to London

W J Casey Antiques (LAPADA, CINOA)
Contact Mr Bill Casey
9 High Street, Warwick, Warwickshire, CV34 4AP P
☎ 01926 499199
Ⓜ 07771 920475 *Stock size* Large
Stock 18th–19thC furniture, especially dining room furniture
Open Mon–Sat 10am–5pm or by appointment

Castle Antiques
Contact Julia Reynolds
24 Swan Street, Warwick, Warwickshire, CV34 4BJ P
☎ 01926 401511
Est. 1998 *Stock size* Large
Stock Edwardian–Victorian furniture, small items
Open Mon–Sat 10am–5pm
Services Restoration

Dorridge Antiques
Contact Mrs P Spencer
Warwick Antique Centre, 22–24 High Street, Warwick, Warwickshire, CV34 4AP P
☎ 01926 499857
Est. 1981 *Stock size* Medium
Stock Silver, jewellery
Open Mon–Sat 10am–5pm

Entente Cordiale
Contact Carol Robson
9 High Street, Warwick, Warwickshire, CV34 4AP P
☎ 01926 403733 Ⓕ 01905 754129
Est. 2000 *Stock size* Small
Stock Mixture of English and French generally small furniture
Open Mon–Sat 10am–5pm or by appointment

John Goodwin & Sons
Contact Mr Neil Goodwin
22–24 High Street, Warwick, Warwickshire,

CV34 🅿
☎ 01926 853332
Est. 1969 *Stock size* Large
Stock General antiques, furniture, pictures, collectables
Open Mon–Sat 8.30am–5.30pm

Russell Lane Antiques
Contact Mr Lane
2–4 High Street, Warwick, Warwickshire, CV34 4AP 🅿
☎ 01926 494494 Ⓕ 01926 492972
Ⓔ russell.laneantiques@virgin.net
Est. 1974 *Stock size* Large
Stock Antique jewellery and silver. Official jewellers to the Royal Show
Open Mon–Sat 10am–5pm
Services Replacement insurance claims

Patrick & Gillian Morley (LAPADA)
Contact Mr P Morley
62 West Street, Warwick, Warwickshire, CV34 6AW 🅿
☎ 01926 494464
Ⓜ 07768 835040
Est. 1969 *Stock size* Large
Stock Period decorative and unusual furniture, works of art
Open Tues–Fri 10am–5.30pm appointment advisable

Christopher Peters Antiques
Contact Mr C or Mrs J Peters
28 West Street, Warwick, Warwickshire, CV34 6AN 🅿
☎ 01926 494106 or 02476 303300
Ⓕ 02476 303300
Ⓔ enquiries@christopherpetersantiques.co.uk
Ⓦ www.christopherpetersantiques.co.uk
Est. 1985 *Stock size* Large
Stock 17th–19thC painted fruitwood and country furniture, design and installation of original bespoke kitchens
Open Mon–Sat 10am–5.30pm or by appointment
Fairs NEC (Spring, Summer)

Quinneys of Warwick
Contact James Reeve
9 Church Street, Warwick, Warwickshire, CV34 4AB 🅿
☎ 01926 498113 Ⓕ 01926 498113
Est. 1865 *Stock size* Large
Stock 17th–19thC English furniture
Open Mon–Fri 9.30am–5.30pm Sat 9.30am–1pm
Services Restoration

Andrew Ross Antiques
Contact Mr A Ross
59 Smith Street, Warwick, Warwickshire, CV34 4HU 🅿
☎ 01926 411772
Est. 1964 *Stock size* Medium
Stock Victorian furniture, copper, brass, china, general antiques
Open Mon–Sat 2pm–6pm

Summersons
Contact Mr Peter Lightfoot
172 Emscote Road, Warwick, Warwickshire, CV34 5QN 🅿
☎ 01926 400630 Ⓕ 01926 400630
Ⓔ clocks@summersons.com
Ⓦ www.summersons.com
Est. 1979 *Stock size* Medium
Stock Clocks, barometers
Open Mon–Fri 9am–5pm Sat 10am–1pm
Services Restoration, repair of clocks and barometers, sales of materials for restoration

Tango Art Deco & Antiques
Contact Jenny and Martin Wills
46 Brook Sreet, Warwick, Warwickshire, CV34 4BL 🅿
☎ 01926 496999 Ⓕ 0121 704 4969
Ⓜ 07889 046969
Ⓔ info@tango-artdeco.co.uk
Ⓦ www.tango-artdeco.co.uk
Est. 1987 *Stock size* Large
Stock Decorative arts 1880–1940, ceramics, furniture, accessories
Open Thurs–Sat 10am–5pm

Vintage Antiques Centre (WADA)
Contact Mr Peter Sellors
36 Market Place, Warwick, Warwickshire, CV34 4SH 🅿
☎ 01926 491527
Ⓔ vintage@globalnet.co.uk
Est. 1979 *Stock size* Large
No. of dealers 20
Stock Victorian glass, 19thC ceramics, 20thC collectables, 1950s, smalls, 19th–20thC costume, agate, gemstone jewellery
Open Mon–Sat 10am–5pm Sun 11.30am–4.30pm

Warwick Antique Centre
Contact Mr P Viola
22–24 High Street, Warwick, Warwickshire, CV34 4AP 🅿
☎ 01926 491382
Ⓜ 07770 897707
Est. 1971 *Stock size* Large
No. of dealers Over 30
Stock General antiques, collectables, coins
Open Mon–Sat 10am–5pm
Services Valuations

John Williams Antique & Collectables
Contact Mr John Williams
Warwick Antiques Centre, 22–24 High Street, Warwick, Warwickshire, CV34 4AP 🅿
☎ 01926 419966
Ⓔ johnowilliams@hotmail.com
Ⓦ www.johnowilliams.co.uk
Est. 1981 *Stock size* Medium
Stock Cameras, toys, tools, collectables, militaria, scientific instruments
Open Mon–Sat 10am–4.30pm
Fairs Alexandra Palace, Birmingham Rag Market, NEC, Motorcycle Museum Birmingham
Services Valuations

WOOTTON WAWEN

Le Grenier
Contact Joyce Ellis
Yew Tree Farm, Stratford Road, Wootton Wawen, Stratford-upon-Avon, Warwickshire, B95 6BY 🅿
☎ 01564 795401
Ⓜ 07712 126048
Ⓔ info@legrenierantiques.com
Ⓦ www.legrenierantiques.com
Est. 1989 *Stock size* Large
Stock French beds and country furniture, some English
Open Tues–Sun 9am–5.30pm
Services Restoration

WEST MIDLANDS

BIRMINGHAM

Acme Toy Company
Contact Mr P Hall
17 Station Road, Erdington, Birmingham, West Midlands, B23 6UB 🅿

☎ 0121 384 8835
Ⓦ www.solnet.co.uk/acme
Est. 1995 *Stock size* Medium
Stock Antique and collectable toys – TV, Sci-Fi, Action Man
Open Mon–Thurs 11am–3pm Fri Sat 10.30am–5pm
Fairs D & G Fairs

Biddle & Webb Ltd
Contact Mr Thornton
✉ **Icknield Square, Ladywood, Middleway, Birmingham, West Midlands, B16 0PP** Ⓟ
☎ 0121 455 8042 Ⓕ 0121 454 9615
Ⓔ antiques@biddleandwebb.freeserve.co.uk
Ⓦ www.invaluable.com/biddleandwebb.
Est. 1955
Open Mon–Fri 9am–5pm Thurs 10am–1pm free valuation service
Sales Pictures and prints 11am 1st Fri of month, viewing Sat prior 9am–noon Wed Thur 10am–4pm. Antiques and later furnishings, porcelain, glass sale 2nd Fri, viewing as previously. Toys, juvenalia 3rd Fri alternate months. Jewellery 4th Fri
Catalogues Yes

The Birmingham Antique Centre
Contact Mr Baldock
✉ **1407 Pershore Road, Stirchley, Birmingham, West Midlands, B30 2JR** Ⓟ
☎ 0121 459 4587
Est. 1994 *Stock size* Large
No. of dealers 65+
Stock Antique furniture, lightly used furniture, bric-a-brac
Open Mon–Sat 9am–5.30pm Sun 10am–4pm
Services Valuations, house clearance

Birmingham Coins
Contact Mr D Harris
✉ **30 Shaftmoor Lane, Acocks Green, Birmingham, West Midlands, B27 7RS** Ⓟ
☎ 0121 707 2808 Ⓕ 0121 707 2808
Est. 1996 *Stock size* Large
Stock General, world and British coins and bank notes, collectors' models, medals
Open Tues Thurs Fri 10.30am–5pm

Cambridge House Antiques
Contact Mr T McIntosh
✉ **168 Gravelly Lane, Birmingham, West Midlands, B23 5SN** Ⓟ
☎ 0121 386 1346
Est. 1998 *Stock size* Large
Stock General antiques
Open Mon–Sat 10am–5.30pm
Fairs Newark, Birmingham Rag Market

Chesterfield Antiques
Contact Mrs Mara Cirjanic
✉ **181 Gravelly Lane, Birmingham, West Midlands, B23 5SG** Ⓟ
☎ 0121 373 3876
Est. 1974 *Stock size* Large
Stock Victorian, Edwardian and 1930s furniture and sets of chairs
Open Mon–Sat 9.30am–5.30pm

Peter Clark Antiques (LAPADA)
Contact Peter Clark
✉ **36 St Mary's Row, Moseley, Birmingham, West Midlands, B13 8JG** Ⓟ
☎ 0121 449 8245 Ⓕ 0121 449 7598
Ⓔ peterclarkantiques@btopenworld.com
Est. 1969 *Stock size* Medium
Stock Georgian mahogany furniture, mirrors, decorative items
Open Mon–Sat 9am–5.30pm
Services Valuations, restoration

Fellows & Sons (BJA)
Contact Mr S Whittaker
✉ **Augusta House, 19 Augusta Street, Birmingham, West Midlands, B18 6JA** Ⓟ
☎ 0121 212 2131 Ⓕ 0121 212 1249
Ⓔ info@fellows.co.uk
Ⓦ www.fellows.co.uk
Est. 1876
Open Mon–Thurs 9am–5pm Fri 9am–4pm
Sales 5 antique furniture, porcelain, pictures, clocks and collectables sales per annum. Also general furniture and household contents sales. Fortnightly sales of jewellery and watches from pawnbrokers nationwide. 8 antique and modern jewellery, watch and silver sales per annum
Catalogues Yes

Format Coins (IAPN, BNTA)
Contact Mr D Vice
✉ **18–19 Bennetts Hill, Birmingham, West Midlands, B2 5QJ** Ⓟ
☎ 0121 643 2058 Ⓕ 0121 643 2210
Est. 1970 *Stock size* Medium
Stock Coins, medallions, bank notes.
Open Mon–Fri 9.30am–5pm
Fairs London Coinex

Lindsay Architectural Antiques
Contact Mr G Lindsay
✉ **25 Passfield Road, Stetchford, Birmingham, West Midlands, B33 8EU** Ⓟ
☎ 0121 789 8295
Ⓜ 07966 221632
Ⓔ glindsay@zoom.co.uk
Ⓦ www.authenticfireplaces.co.uk
Est. 1996 *Stock size* Large
Stock Architectural salvage, fireplaces, quarry tiles, wrought-iron gates, stained glass
Open By appointment
Fairs Newark, Swinderby
Services Restoration and fitting service

MDS Ltd
Contact Mr R Wootton
✉ **14–16 Stechford Trading Estate, Lyndon Road, Stechford, Birmingham, West Midlands, B33 8BU** Ⓟ
☎ 0121 783 9274 Ⓕ 0121 783 9274
Ⓜ 07836 649064
Est. 1969 *Stock size* Medium
Stock Architectural antiques
Open Mon–Fri 8am–6pm Sat 8am–1pm

Moseley Emporium
Contact Miss G Dorney
✉ **116 Alcester Road, Moseley, Birmingham, West Midlands, B13 3EF** Ⓟ
☎ 0121 449 3441
Ⓜ 07973 156902
Est. 1993 *Stock size* Large
Stock Victorian, Edwardian and period furniture, architectural antiques
Open Mon–Sat 9.30am–6pm
Services Restoration

Raven Reclaim & Architectural Salvage Ltd
Contact Mr M Coughlan
✉ **453 Stockfield Road, Yardley,**

Birmingham, West Midlands, B25 8JH 🅿
☎ 0121 765 4840
Est. 1979 *Stock size* Medium
Stock Architectural antiques
Open Mon–Sat 8am–5.30pm

Turner Violins
Contact Marcus Coulter
✉ **1 Gibb Street, off Digbeth High Street, Birmingham, West Midlands, B9 4AA** 🅿
☎ 0121 772 7708
Ⓔ birmingham@turnerviolins.co.uk
Ⓦ www.turnerviolins.co.uk
Est. 1980
Stock Violins, double basses, violas, cellos, bows
Open Mon–Sat 9.30am–6pm
Services Instrument and bow repairs, valuations, consultations, export

Weller & Dufty Ltd (GTA)
Contact Mr W Farmer
✉ **141 Bromsgrove Street, Birmingham, West Midlands, B5 6RQ** 🅿
☎ 0121 692 1414 Ⓕ 0121 622 5605
Ⓔ sales@wellerandduFty.co.uk
Ⓦ www.wellerandduFty.co.uk
Est. 1835
Open Mon–Fri 9am–4.30pm
Sales Arms and armour
Frequency 6–8 per annum
Catalogues Yes

Windworld
Contact Marcus Coulter
✉ **1 Gibb Street, off Digbeth High Street, Birmingham, West Midlands, B9 4AA** 🅿
☎ 0121 772 7889
Ⓔ info@wind-world.co.uk
Est. 1980
Stock Wind instruments
Open Mon–Sat 9.30am–6pm
Services Instrument and bow repairs, valuations, consultations, export

Stephen Wycherley (PBFA)
Contact Mr S Wycherley
✉ **508 Bristol Road, Selly Oak, Birmingham, West Midlands, B29 6BD** 🅿
☎ 0121 471 1006
Ⓔ s.wycherley@btopenworld.com
Est. 1971 *Stock size* Large
Stock Traditional general second-hand and antiquarian bookshop
Open Mon–Sat 10am–5pm closed Wed Jul Aug Thurs–Sat 10am–5pm
Fairs PBFA
Services Valuations

BRIERLEY HILL

Cast Offs
Contact Mr Terence Young
✉ **Moor Street Industrial Estate, Moor Street, Brierley Hill, West Midlands, DY5 3EH** 🅿
☎ 01384 486456
Ⓜ 07711 661135
Est. 1996 *Stock size* Medium
Stock Quarry tiles, paviors, cast-iron fireplaces, troughs, baths, radiators, sinks, taps, doors, furniture, chimney pots, gates, fencing, bricks
Open Mon–Fri 9am–5pm Sat 9am–2pm

COVENTRY

Antiques Adventure
Contact Lesley Lawrence
✉ **Rugby Road, Binley Woods, Coventry, West Midlands, CV3 2AW** 🅿
☎ 024 7645 3878 Ⓕ 024 7644 5847
Ⓔ sales@antiquesadventure.com
Ⓦ www.antiquesadventure.com
Est. 2000 *Stock size* Large
No. of dealers 35+
Stock Antiques, collectables
Open Mon–Sun 10am–5pm
Services Shipping, delivery

Armstrong's Books & Collectables
Contact Mr Colin Armstrong
✉ **178 Albany Road, Earlsdon, Coventry, West Midlands, CV5 6NG** 🅿
☎ 024 7671 4344
Est. 1983 *Stock size* Medium
Stock General second-hand books, paperbacks, first editions, special sci-fi comics, annuals, magazines, posters, postcards
Open Tues–Sat 10am–5pm

The Bookshop
Contact Mr A R Price
✉ **173 Walsgrave Road, Coventry, West Midlands, CV2 4HH** 🅿
☎ 024 7645 5669
Est. 1990 *Stock size* Medium
Stock Antiquarian and second-hand books on all subjects
Open Mon–Sat 9am–5pm
Services Valuations

Earlsdon Antiques
Contact Mrs V Kemp
✉ **35 Hearsall Lane, Coventry, West Midlands, CV5 6HF** 🅿
☎ 024 7667 5456
Est. 1984 *Stock size* Medium
Stock General antiques and collectables
Open Fri Sat noon–5pm

Warwick Auctions (NAVA)
Contact Mr R Beaumont
✉ **3 Queen Victoria Road, Coventry, West Midlands, CV1 3JS** 🅿
☎ 024 7622 3377/30992
Ⓕ 024 7622 0044
Ⓔ sales@warwick-auctions.co.uk
Ⓦ www.warwickauctions.com
Est. 1947
Open Mon–Fri 9am–5pm
Sales General household goods Wed 10am, viewing Tues 9am–4.30pm Wed 9–10am. Antiques and collectables sales first Wed of each month, except Jan
Frequency Weekly
Catalogues Yes

CRADLEY HEATH

R & L Furnishings
Contact Mr R Randall
✉ **244 Halesowen Road, Old Hill, Cradley Heath, West Midlands, B64 6NH** 🅿
☎ 01384 410077
Est. 1980 *Stock size* Medium
Stock Antique furniture, bric-a-brac
Open Mon–Sat 10.30am–5.30pm closed Wed
Services House clearance

HAGLEY

Walton & Hipkiss
Contact Mr J Carter
✉ **111 Worcester Street, Hagley, Stourbridge, West Midlands, DY9 0NG** 🅿
☎ 01562 886688 Ⓕ 01562 886655
Ⓔ hagley@waltonandhipkiss.co.uk
Ⓦ www.waltonandhipkiss.co.uk
Est. 1929

Open Mon–Fri 9am–5.30pm
Sat 9am–4pm
Sales 5 auctions per year, general antiques, telephone for details
Catalogues Yes

HALESOWEN

Anvil Books
Contact Mr J K Maddison
52 Summer Hill, Halesowen, West Midlands, B63 3BU
0121 550 0600
jkm@anvilbookshalesowen.co.uk
www.anvilbookshalesowen.co.uk
Est. 1997 *Stock size* Small
Stock General second-hand and antiquarian books, local history, transport and maritime topics specialities
Open Tues Thurs Sat 10am–5pm
Fairs Kinver Book Fair, Waverley Fairs
Services Book search

Tudor House Antiques
Contact Mr D J Taylor
68 Long Lane, Halesowen, West Midlands, B62 9LS
0121 561 5563
Est. 1991 *Stock size* Medium
Stock Architectural antiques, stripped pine furniture
Open Tues–Sat 9.30am–5pm
Services Restoration, stripping

KNOWLE

Bonhams (BACA Award Winner 2003)
The Old House, Station Road, Knowle, Solihull, West Midlands, B93 0HT
01564 776151 F 01564 778069
knowle@bonhams.com
www.bonhams.com
Open Mon–Fri 9am–5pm
Sales Regional Saleroom. Frequent sales. Regular house and attic sales across the country; contact London offices for further details. Free auction valuations; insurance and probate valuations
Catalogues Yes

OLDBURY

S J Wilder Antiques
Contact Mr S Wilder
97 Stourbridge Road, Halesowen, West Midlands, B63 3NA
0121 550 8228 F 0121 585 5611
Est. 1975 *Stock size* Large
Stock General antiques, shipping furniture, silver, china
Open Mon–Sat 9.30am–5.30pm
Fairs Stafford

SOLIHULL

Alscot Bathroom Company (SALVO)
Contact Mr Cockroft
1 Oak Farm, Hampton Lane, Catherine de Barnes, Solihull, West Midlands, B92 0JB
0121 709 1901 F 0121 709 1800
alscotbathrooms@tiscali.co.uk
www.alscotbathrooms.co.uk
Est. 1960 *Stock size* Large
Stock Victorian–Edwardian and Art Deco sanitary ware, roll-top baths
Open By appointment
Services Restoration

Dorridge Antiques & Collectables Centre
Contact Colleen Swift
7 Forest Court, Dorridge, Solihull, West Midlands, B93 8HN
01564 779336 or 01574 779768
Est. 1996 *Stock size* Large
No. of dealers 20
Stock Furniture, ceramics, paintings, prints, glass, jewellery, guns, swords, silver, bric-a-brac
Open Mon–Sat 11am–5.30pm
Services Valuation & restoration advice

Yoxall Antiques & Fine Arts
Contact Mr Paul Burrows
68 Yoxall Road, Solihull, West Midlands, B90 3RP
0121 744 1744
07860 168078
sales@yoxallantiques.co.uk
www.yoxallantiques.co.uk
Est. 1988 *Stock size* Large
Stock Period furniture, quality porcelain, glassware, clocks, barometers
Open Mon–Sat 9.30am–5pm or by appointment
Fairs NEC
Services Restoration

STOURBRIDGE

Lye Antique Furnishings
Contact Paul Smith
206 High Street, Lye, Stourbridge, West Midlands, DY9 8JZ
01384 897513
07976 765142
Est. 1980 *Stock size* Medium
Stock Antiques, collectables
Open Mon–Sat 9am–5pm
Fairs Swinderby Market, Birmingham Rag Market
Services Valuations

Memory Lane Antiques
Contact Mr Paul Jones
129 Brettell Lane, Stourbridge, West Midlands, DY8 4BA
01384 370348
07801 139949
Est. 1989 *Stock size* Large
Stock Country furniture, architectural antiques
Open Mon–Sat 10am–6pm
Fairs Newark, Ardingly

Stourbridge Antiques Centre
Contact Paul Smith
1 Market Street, Stourbridge, West Midlands, DY8 1DW
01384 444148 F 01384 444148
paulsmithruskin@hotmail
Est. 2003 *Stock size* Small
No. of dealers 30
Stock Small collectables
Open Tues–Sat 10am–5pm

SUTTON COLDFIELD

Acres Fine Art Auctioneers & Valuers
Contact Mr I Kettlewell
28 Beeches Walk, Sutton Coldfield, West Midlands, B73 6HN
0121 355 1133 F 0121 354 5251
www.acres.co.uk
Est. 1992
Open Mon–Sat 9am–5.30pm
Sales Antiques sales. Telephone for details
Frequency Quarterly
Catalogues Yes

Thomas Coulborn and Sons (BADA, CINOA)
Contact Jonathan, Peter or

MIDLANDS

WEST MIDLANDS • WALSALL

James Coulborn
✉ **Vesey Manor, 64 Birmingham Road, Sutton Coldfield, West Midlands, B72 1QP** P
☎ 0121 354 3974 F 0121 354 4614
M 07941 252299
E jc@coulborn.com
W www.coulborn.com
Est. 1940 *Stock size* Large
Stock 18thC furniture and works of art, 19th–20thC paintings and watercolours
Open Mon–Sat 9.15am–1pm 2–5.30pm
Services Valuations

S & J Antiques
Contact Mr Steve Dowling
✉ **431 Birmingham Road, Wylde Green, Sutton Coldfield, West Midlands, B72 1AX** P
☎ 0121 384 1595
Est. 1988 *Stock size* Large
Stock Silver, silver plate, oak, period and stripped-pine furniture, coins
Open Mon–Sat 10am–5.30pm
Fairs Birmingham Rag Market, Newark
Services Restoration, re-plating

WALSALL

Collectors Centre
Contact Mr Tom Moran
✉ **79 Bridge Street, Walsall, West Midlands, WS1 1JT** P
☎ 01922 625518
Est. 1979 *Stock size* Large
Stock Coins, medals, militaria, postcards, cigarette cards, toys, antique jewellery
Open Mon–Sat 9am–5pm Thurs 9am–1pm
Services Valuations

WEDNESBURY

Abacus
Contact Mr Lambert
✉ **37 Lower High Street, Wednesbury, West Midlands, WS10 7AQ** P
☎ 0121 502 4622
Est. 1988 *Stock size* Medium
Stock General second-hand and antiquarian books
Open Mon–Sat 9am–2pm closed Wed
Services Book search

WOLVERHAMPTON

Antiquities
Contact Mrs M Konczyk
✉ **75–76 Dudley Road, Wolverhampton, West Midlands, WV2 3BY** P
☎ 01902 459800
Est. 1968 *Stock size* Large
Stock General antiques
Open Mon–Sat 10.30am–5pm

Doveridge House Antiques (BADA, CINOA)
Contact Commander Harry Bain
✉ **PO Box 1856, Wolverhampton, West Midlands, WV3 9XH** P
☎ 01902 312211
Est. 1976 *Stock size* Large
Stock Fine antique furniture, lamps, paintings, silver, decorative objects
Open By appointment
Fairs NEC (Spring Autumn pre-Christmas)
Services Honorary vetting advisors to Antiques for Everyone Fairs

Lamb Antique Fine Arts & Craft Originals (LAPADA)
Contact Beris or Cheryl Lamb
✉ **77 Fancourt Avenue, Penn, Wolverhampton, West Midlands, WV4 4HZ** P
☎ 01902 338150 F 01902 830805
M 07850 406907
E berislamb.artscrafts@blueyonder.co.uk
W www.antiques-originals.com
Est. 1985 *Stock size* Medium
Stock Arts and Crafts, pottery, pewter, prints, silver, glass, jewellery, copper, furniture
Open By appointment only
Fairs Bowman Fairs, NEC

Newhampton Road Antiques
Contact Mr R G Hill
✉ **184–184a Newhampton Road East, Wolverhampton, West Midlands, WV1 4PQ** P
☎ 01902 334363
M 07930 894719
Est. 1985 *Stock size* Large
Stock Antiques and collectables
Open Mon–Sat 9.30am–3.30pm
Fairs Newark, Swinderby
Services House clearance

No. 9 Antiques
Contact Miss C Weaver
✉ **9 Upper Green, Tettenhall, Wolverhampton, West Midlands, WV6 8QQ** P
☎ 01902 755333
Est. 1995 *Stock size* Medium
Stock 19thC furniture, porcelain, silver, watercolours
Open Wed–Fri 10am–6pm Sat 9am–5.30pm

Old Book Shop
Contact Kate Lee
✉ **53 Bath Road, Wolverhampton, West Midlands, WV1 4EL** P
☎ 01902 421055 F 01902 421055
E theoldbookshop@btopenworld.com
Est. 1975 *Stock size* Large
Stock Antiquarian and second-hand books
Open Mon 1–3pm Tues–Fri 10am–4pm Sat 10am–5pm
Services Book search

Martin Taylor Antiques (LAPADA)
Contact Mr Martin Taylor
✉ **140b Tettenhall Road, Wolverhampton, West Midlands, WV6 0BQ** P
☎ 01902 751166 F 01902 746502
M 07836 636524
E enquiries@mtaylor-antiques.co.uk
W www.mtaylor-antiques.co.uk
Est. 1976 *Stock size* Large
Stock Furniture c1800–1930, quality replica furniture, country-made furniture
Open Mon–Fri 8.30am–5.30pm Sat 10am–5pm
Services Search, restoration and delivery

Martin Taylor Antiques (LAPADA)
Contact Mr Martin Taylor
✉ **323 Tettenhall Road, Wolverhampton, West Midlands, WV6 0BQ** P
☎ 01902 751166 F 01902 746502
M 07836 636524
E enquiries@mtaylor-antiques.co.uk
W www.mtaylor-antiques.co.uk
Est. 1976 *Stock size* Small
Stock Antique furniture, gifts
Open Mon–Sat 10am–5.30pm

West Midlands Collectors Centre
Contact Mr S Moran
✉ **9 Heatin House, Salop Street,**

Wolverhampton, West Midlands, WV3 0SQ P
☎ 01902 772570
Est. 1983 *Stock size* Small
Stock Stamps, coins, medals, bank notes, curios, die-cast models
Open Mon–Sat 9.30am–5pm

Wood 'n' Things
Contact Mrs K Carter
388 Penn Road, Wolverhampton, West Midlands, WV4 4DF P
☎ 01902 333324
Ⓜ 07808 444786
Est. 1983 *Stock size* Medium
Stock Antiques, collectables, Victorian, Edwardian and 1920s furniture
Open Mon–Sat 10am–5pm
Wed 10am–1pm
Services Restoration

Woodward Antique Clocks Ltd (LAPADA)
Contact Patricia Woodward
14 High Street, Tettenhall, Wolverhampton, West Midlands, WV6 8QT P
☎ 01902 745608 Ⓕ 01902 743565
Ⓔ woodwardclocks@bun.com
Ⓦ www.antiqnet.co.uk/woodward
Est. 1993 *Stock size* Large
Stock Antique clocks, decorative French mantel clocks, longcase, bracket, carriage and wall clocks
Open Wed–Sat 11am–5.30pm
Fairs NEC
Services Valuations, restoration

WORCESTERSHIRE

BARNT GREEN

Barnt Green Antiques
Contact Neville Slater
93 Hewell Road, Barnt Green, Birmingham, Worcestershire, B45 8NL P
☎ 0121 445 4942 Ⓕ 0121 445 4942
Est. 1977 *Stock size* Medium
Stock Furniture, clocks
Open Mon–Fri 9am–5.30pm
Sat 9am–1pm
Services Valuations, restoration

BEWDLEY

Bewdley Antiques
Contact Mrs A Hamilton
62a Load Street, Bewdley, Worcestershire, DY12 2AP P
☎ 01299 405636 Ⓕ 01299 841568
Est. 1999 *Stock size* Medium
No. of dealers 12
Stock 19th–20thC furniture, collectables, small decorative pieces
Open Mon–Sat 10am–5.30pm
Services Valuations, picture framing, jewellery repairs

BROADWAY

Art Nouveau Originals (LAPADA)
Contact Mrs C Turner
The Bindery Gallery, 69 High Street, Broadway, Worcestershire, WR12 7OP P
☎ 01386 854645 Ⓕ 01386 854645
Ⓜ 07774 718096
Ⓔ cathy@anor1900.com
Ⓦ www.artnouveauoriginals.com
Est. 1980 *Stock size* Medium
Stock An eclectic mix of items from the decorative arts 1860–1930
Open Please telephone or e-mail for opening times
Fairs NEC

Stephen Cook Antiques Ltd (LAPADA)
Contact Stephen Cook
58 High Street, Broadway, Worcestershire, WR12 7DP P
☎ 01386 854716 Ⓕ 01386 859360
Ⓔ stephen@scookantiques.com
Est. 1986 *Stock size* Medium
Stock 17th–18thC oak and walnut furniture
Open Mon–Sat 10am–5.30pm

Fenwick & Fenwick Antiques (CADA)
Contact Mr G Fenwick
88–90 High Street, Broadway, Worcestershire, WR12 7AJ P
☎ 01386 853227/841724
Ⓕ 01386 858504
Est. 1980 *Stock size* Large
Stock 17th–early 19thC oak, mahogany, walnut furniture and works of art, treen, boxes, pewter, lace bobbins, Chinese porcelain, corkscrews, early metalware
Open Mon–Sat 10am–6pm

Gallimaufry
Contact Chris Stone
51a High Street, Broadway, Worcestershire, WR12 7DP P
☎ 01386 852898
Est. 1992 *Stock size* Medium
Stock China, glass, furniture, pictures, collectables
Open Mon–Sat 10am–5pm
Sun 11am–5pm

Howards of Broadway
Contact Robert Light
27a High Street, Broadway, Worcestershire, WR12 7DP P
☎ 01386 858924
Ⓜ 07850 066312
Ⓔ robert.light@talk21.com
Est. 1989 *Stock size* Medium
Stock Antique and modern silver and jewellery
Open Mon–Sat 10am–5.30pm
Services Valuations, restoration

H W Keil Ltd (BADA, CADA)
Contact Mr Keil
Tudor House, Broadway, Worcestershire, WR12 7DP P
☎ 01386 852408 Ⓕ 01386 852069
Ⓔ info@hwkeil.co.uk
Ⓦ www.hwkeil.co.uk
Est. 1932 *Stock size* Large
Stock Early 17th–early 19thC furniture, works of art
Open Mon–Sat 9.15am–1.15pm
2.15–5.30pm
Services Restoration

John Noott Galleries (BADA, LAPADA, CADA)
Contact Kathryn Plume
28 High Street, Broadway, Worcestershire, WR12 7DT P
☎ 01386 854868 Ⓕ 01386 854919
Ⓔ info@john-noott.com
Ⓦ www.john-noott.com
Est. 1972 *Stock size* Large
Stock 19th–early 20thC oils and watercolours
Open Mon–Sat 10am–1pm
2pm–5pm
Fairs NEC, Harrogate, Olympia
Services Valuations, restoration, shipping

BROMSGROVE

Worcester Medal Service Ltd (OMRS)
Contact Mrs K McDermott
56 Broad Street, Sidemoor, Bromsgrove, Worcestershire,

B61 8LL 🅿
☎ 01527 835375 Ⓕ 01527 576798
Ⓔ wms@worcmedals.com
Ⓦ www.worcmedals.com
Est. 1988 *Stock size* Large
Stock Medals and medal mountings
Open Mon–Fri 9am–5pm Sat 8.30–noon
Services Suppliers of specialist cases, medal mounting, valuations

CLEOBURY MORTIMER

M & M Baldwin
Contact Dr M Baldwin
✉ **24 High Street, Cleobury Mortimer, Kidderminster, Worcestershire, DY14 8BY** 🅿
☎ 01299 270110 Ⓕ 01299 270110
Ⓔ mb@mbaldwin.free-online.co.uk
Est. 1978 *Stock size* Medium
Stock Second-hand and antiquarian books, books on transport, industrial history, WWII intelligence and codebreaking a speciality
Open Wed 2–6pm Fri (Easter–October) 10am–1pm 2–6pm Sat 10am–1pm 2–6pm or by appointment
Services Book search, valuations

DROITWICH SPA

Robert Belcher Antiques
Contact Mr R Belcher
✉ **128 Worcester Road, Droitwich Spa, Worcestershire, WR9 8AN** 🅿
☎ 01905 772320
Est. 1984 *Stock size* Large
Stock Georgian–Victorian furniture, paintings, fine art, decorative items
Open Tues–Sat 9.30am–5.30pm
Fairs NEC
Services Furniture restoration, picture framing

EVESHAM

Bookworms of Evesham (PBFA)
Contact Mr T Sims
✉ **81 Port Street, Evesham, Worcestershire, WR11 3LF** 🅿
☎ 01386 45509
Est. 1971 *Stock size* Medium
Stock Second-hand and antiquarian books on most subjects, Gloucestershire and Worcestershire topics specialities
Open Tues–Sat 10am–5pm
Fairs Churchdown, Gloucestershire Book Fair (1st Sunday of each month)

FLADBURY

The Hayloft Antiques
Contact Mrs S Pryse-Jones
✉ **Craycombe Farm, Old Worcester Road, Fladbury, Evesham, Worcestershire, WR10 2QS** 🅿
☎ 01386 861166
Est. 1994 *Stock size* Medium
No. of dealers 9
Stock Antique furniture, stripped pine, collectables, china, glass, paintings, prints, books, linen, textiles
Open Mon–Sun summer 10.30am–5pm winter 10.30am–4pm
Services Pine stripping, French polishing, furniture restoration

HALLOW

Antique Map & Print Gallery
Contact Margaret Nichols, **Hallow, Worcestershire, WR2 6LS** 🅿
☎ 01905 641300
Ⓔ antiquemap@aol.com
Est. 1983 *Stock size* Large
Stock Maps, illustrated books, Vanity Fair prints
Open By appointment

KIDDERMINSTER

BBM Jewellery, Coins & Antiques (BJA)
Contact Mr W V Crook
✉ **9 Lion Street, Kidderminster, Worcestershire, DY10 1PT** 🅿
☎ 01562 744118 Ⓕ 01562 829444
Ⓔ williamvcrook@btinternet.com
Est. 1980 *Stock size* Large
Stock Antique and second-hand jewellery, coins, medals, porcelain, silver
Open Wed–Sat 10am–5pm
Services Restoration and repair

Kidderminster Antique Centre
Contact Mrs V Bentley
✉ **5–8 Lion Street, Kidderminster, Worcestershire, DY10 1PT** 🅿
☎ 01562 740389 Ⓕ 01562 740389
Est. 1980 *Stock size* Large
No. of dealers 10
Stock Furniture, china, glass, silver, jewellery, architectural salvage, cast-iron fireplaces, surrounds, tiles, books
Open Mon–Sat 10am–5pm
Services Jewellery and clock repairs, furniture and door stripping, furniture restoration

Kidderminster Market Auctions
Contact Mr B Cooke
✉ **Wholesale Market, Comberton Hill, Kidderminster, Worcestershire, DY10 1QH** 🅿
☎ 01562 741303 Ⓕ 01562 865495
Est. 1957
Open Mon–Fri 9am–5pm Sat 9am–1pm
Sales General antiques sale Thurs 10.30am furniture 2.30pm, viewing Wed 4–8pm Thurs from 7am
Frequency Weekly

Phipps & Pritchard
Contact Mr A Mayall
✉ **31 Worcester Street, Kidderminster, Worcestershire, DY10 1EQ** 🅿
☎ 01562 822244 Ⓕ 01562 825401
Ⓜ 07970 218140
Ⓔ amayall@phippspritchard.demon.co.uk
Est. 1848
Open Mon–Fri 9am–5.15pm Sat 9am–3.30pm
Sales General antiques and collectables Sat 10.30am, viewing Fri 3–6.30pm Sat from 8.30am. Sale held at Hartlebury Village Hall
Frequency Every 7–8 weeks
Catalogues Yes

MALVERN

Carlton Antiques
Contact Mr D W Roberts
✉ **43 Worcester Road, Malvern, Worcestershire, WR14 4RB** 🅿
☎ 01684 573092
Ⓔ dave@carlton-antiques.com
Ⓦ www.carlton-antiques.com
Est. 1991 *Stock size* Medium
Stock Furniture, ephemera,

postcards, bottles, die-cast toys, second-hand books etc
Open Mon–Sun 10am–5pm

Foley Furniture
Contact Mr D W Roberts
Foley Bank, Malvern, Worcestershire, WR14 4QW
01684 573092
dave@carlton-antiques.com
www.carlton-antiques.com
Est. 1991 *Stock size* Medium
Stock Furniture of all periods, postcards, bottles, die-cast toys, books etc
Open Wed–Sun 10am–5pm

Foley House Antiques
Contact Roger Hales
28 Worcester Road, Great Malvern, Worcestershire, WR14 4QW
01684 575750
07773 421143
Est. 2003 *Stock size* Large
No. of dealers 12
Stock Victorian–Edwardian furniture
Open Mon–Sat 10am–5.30pm Sun Bank Holidays 11am–5pm
Services Restoration, shipping

Great Malvern Antiques
Contact Mr R Rice or Mr L Sutton
Salisbury House, 6 Abbey Road, Malvern, Worcestershire, WR14 3HG
01684 575490 gma@dsl.pipex.com
gmantiques@dial.pipex.com
Est. 1984 *Stock size* Medium
Stock Decorative furniture and furnishings, paintings
Trade only Yes
Open By appointment
Fairs Bath Decorative Antiques Fair, Decorative Antiques and Textiles Fair

Kimber & Son
Contact Mr E M Kimber
6 Lower Howsell Road, Malvern, Worcestershire, WR14 1EF
01684 574339
Est. 1950 *Stock size* Medium
Stock 18th–early 20thC furniture, English, European and American markets
Open Mon–Fri 9am–5.30pm Sat 9am–1pm

Philip Laney
Contact Mr P Laney
Malvern Auction Centre, Portland Road, off Victoria Road, Malvern, Worcestershire, WR14 2TA
01684 893933 01684 577948
philiplaney@aol.com
Est. 1969
Open Mon–Fri 9am–1pm 2–4.30pm
Sales General antiques and collectables sales
Frequency Monthly (14–15 a year)
Catalogues Yes

Lechmere Antiquarian Books
Contact Mr R Lechmere
Primswell, Evandrine, Colwall, Malvern, Worcestershire, WR13 6DT
01684 540340
Est. 1945 *Stock size* Small
Stock Antiquarian, rare and second-hand books on Hereford, Worcester, Australia
Open Mail order only
Services Mail order

The Malvern Bookshop
Contact Howard Hudson
7 Abbey Road, Malvern, Worcestershire, WR14 3ES
01684 575915 01684 575915
browse@malvern-bookshop.co.uk
Est. 1954 *Stock size* Medium
Stock Antiquarian, rare and second-hand books, books on music and sheet music a speciality
Open Mon–Sat 10am–5pm
Services Book search

Malvern Studios (BAFRA, UKIC, NCCR)
Contact Jeff Hall
56 Cowleigh Road, Malvern, Worcestershire, WR14 1QD
01684 574913 01684 569475
Est. 1961
Stock 18th–20thC furniture
Open Mon Tues Thurs 9am–5.15pm Fri Sat 9am–4.45pm
Services Restoration

Miscellany Antiques
Contact R S or E A Hunaban
20 Cowleigh Road, Malvern, Worcestershire, WR14 1QD
01684 566671 01684 560562
liz.hunaban@virgin.net
www.freespace.virgin.net/lizhunaban
Est. 1974 *Stock size* Medium
Stock Georgian–Edwardian furniture, some country oak, bronzes, ivories, silver, jewellery, decorative items
Open Mon–Sat 9am–5pm
Services Valuations, restoration

Priory Books
Contact Mr L P Kelly
Church Walk, Malvern, Worcestershire, WR14 2XH
01684 560258
Est. 1985 *Stock size* Medium
Stock Wide range of antiquarian and second-hand books
Open Mon–Sat 9.30am–5.25pm
Services Valuations, book search

Promenade Antiques & Books
Contact Mr M Seldester
41 Worcester Road, Malvern, Worcestershire, WR14 4RB
01684 566876 01684 566876
promant@bigfoot.com
Est. 1990 *Stock size* Medium
Stock Victorian–Edwardian furniture, collectables, decorative items, reproduction lamps, books
Open Mon–Sat 10am–5pm Sun noon–5pm

Philip Serrell Auctioneers & Valuers
Contact P Serrell FRICS
Barnards Green Road, Malvern, Worcestershire, WR14 3LW
01905 26200 01905 21202
serrell.auctions@virgin.net
www.serrell.com
Open Mon–Fri 9am–5pm closed 1–2pm
Sales General and fine art sales at the Malvern Sale Room, Malvern. Special sales of Worcester porcelain
Frequency Fortnightly
Catalogues Yes

St James Antiques
Contact Mr Hans Van Wyngaarden
De Lys, Wells Road, Malvern, Worcestershire, WR14 4JL
01684 563404
Est. 1992 *Stock size* Large

Stock Pine furniture, lighting, decorative items
Open Mon–Sat 9am–5.30pm

PERSHORE

Coach House Books
Contact Mr P Ellingworth
17a Bridge Street, Pershore, Worcestershire, WR10 1AJ
01386 552801/554633
01386 554633
sue.chb@virgin.net
Est. 1982 *Stock size* Large
Stock Antiquarian, rare, new and second-hand books, prints
Open Mon–Sat 9am–5pm
Services Book search, picture framing

Hansen Chard Antiques (BHI)
Contact Mr P Ridler
126 High Street, Pershore, Worcestershire, WR10 1EA P
01386 553423
Est. 1984 *Stock size* Large
Stock Clocks, barometers, old and antique model steam engines, scientific instruments
Open Tues–Sat 10am–4pm closed Thurs or by appointment
Fairs Bracknell Clock Fair, Birmingham Clock Fair, Brunel
Services Valuations, restoration

Ian K Pugh Books
Contact Mr I Pugh
40 Bridge Street, Pershore, Worcestershire, WR10 1AT P
01386 552681
Est. 1974 *Stock size* Medium
Stock Antiquarian, rare and second-hand books on most subjects. Antiques, fine art, horticulture and military topics specialities
Open Mon–Fri 10.30am–5pm Sat 9.30am–5pm closed Thur
Services Valuations, book search

S W Antiques
Contact Mr Adrian Whiteside
Abbey Showrooms, Newlands, Pershore, Worcestershire, WR10 1BP P
01386 555580 01386 556205
catchall@sw-antiques.co.uk
www.sw-antiques.co.uk
Est. 1978 *Stock size* Large
Stock 19th–early 20thC furniture, antique beds
Open Mon–Sat 9am–5pm
Services Valuations, restoration

REDDITCH

Angel Antiques
Contact Mrs C Manners
211 Mount Pleasant, Redditch, Worcestershire, B97 4JG P
01527 545844
Est. 1989 *Stock size* Medium
Stock Georgian–Edwardian antique furniture, decorative items
Open Mon Tues Thurs Fri 10am–3.30pm Wed 10am–2pm Sat 10am–5pm
Services Restoration

Arrow Auctions (NAVA)
Contact Mr A Reeves
Bartleet Road, Washford, Redditch, Worcestershire, B98 0DG P
01527 517707 01527 510924
enquiries@arrowauctions.co.uk
www.arrowauctions.co.uk
Est. 1982
Open Mon–Fri 8.30am–5pm
Sales General household sale every Tues 6pm, viewing from 9am. Specialist bi-annual fine art sales Tues 11am. Free valuations. Removal, collection and storage facilities available. On-site restaurant
Catalogues Yes

UPTON-UPON-SEVERN

Boar's Nest Trading
Contact Mr G Smith
37a–37b Old Street, Upton-upon-Severn, Worcester, Worcestershire, WR8 0HN P
01684 592540
Est. 1992 *Stock size* Large
Stock Second-hand and antiquarian books, non-fiction a speciality
Open Mon–Sun 10am–5pm
Services Valuations

WHITBOURNE

Juro Farm and Garden Antiques
Contact Mr R Hughes
Whitbourne, Worcester, Worcestershire, WR6 5SF P
01886 821261 01886 821261
roy@juro.co.uk
www.juro.co.uk
Est. 1991 *Stock size* Large
Stock Garden antiques, staddle stones, troughs, cider mills, statuary, farming and garden implements
Open Mon–Sat 9am–5pm
Fairs Newark, Hampton Court, Malvern Spring Garden Show
Services Valuations

WORCESTER

Antiques & Curios
Contact Mr B Inett
50 Upper Tything, Worcester, Worcestershire, WR1 1JY P
01905 25412 01905 25412
Est. 1980 *Stock size* Large
Stock Victorian–Edwardian furniture, mirrors, clocks, porcelain, glass, decorative items
Open Mon–Sat 9.30am–5.30pm
Services Valuations, restoration

The Antiques Warehouse
Contact Mr D Venn
74 Droitwich Road (rear), Worcester, Worcestershire, WR1 8BW P
01905 27493
Est. 1979 *Stock size* Large
Stock Pine furniture, Victorian interior doors, antique and reproduction fireplaces
Open Mon–Fri 8am–6pm Sat 10am–5pm
Services Restoration, stripping

The Barbers Clock
Contact Graham Gopsill
37 Droitwich Road, Worcester, Worcestershire, WR3 7LG P
01905 29022
07710 486598
Graham@barbersclock37@fsnet.co.uk
Est. 1993 *Stock size* Medium
Stock Clocks from 1840–1930, wind-up gramophones, Art Deco, WWII uniforms, badges
Open Mon–Sat 9am–5pm
Services Valuations, gramophone and clock repairs

Box Bush Antiques
Contact Mrs P Difford
43 Upper Tything, Worcester,

Worcestershire,
WR1 1JZ 🅿
☎ 01905 28617
Est. 1995 *Stock size* Medium
Stock 18th–19thC pine, mahogany and walnut furniture, decorative items, silver
Open Mon–Sat 9am–5.30pm
Services Valuations, restoration, wood turning

B Browning & Son
Contact Mr A Browning
✉ **35a Wylds Lane, Worcester, Worcestershire, WR5 1DA** 🅿
☎ 01905 355646
Est. 1904 *Stock size* Medium
Stock Modern and antique general household furniture
Open Mon–Sat 9am–5pm closed Thurs
Services House clearance

Bygones by the Cathedral (LAPADA, FGA)
Contact Gabrielle Bullock
✉ **Cathedral Square, Worcester, Worcestershire, WR1 2JD** 🅿
☎ 01905 25388 ℻ 01905 23132
Est. 1946 *Stock size* Medium
Stock Decorative antiques, silver, jewellery, porcelain, furniture, paintings, glass, metalwork
Open Mon–Fri 9.30am–5.30pm Sat 9.30am–1pm 2–5.30pm

Bygones of Worcester (LAPADA, FGA)
Contact Gabrielle Bullock
✉ **55 Sidbury, Worcester, Worcestershire, WR1 2HU** 🅿
☎ 01905 23132 ℻ 01905 23132
Est. 1946 *Stock size* Medium
Stock 17th–20thC furniture, paintings, bronzes, silver, porcelain
Open Mon–Sat 9.30am–1pm 2–5.30pm

Andrew Grant Fine Art Auctioneers (RICS)
Contact Christopher Jarrey
✉ **St Marks House, St Marks Close, Worcester, Worcestershire, WR5 3DJ** 🅿
☎ 01905 357547 ℻ 01905 763942
Ⓔ fine.arts@andrew-grant.co.uk
Ⓦ www.andrew-grant.co.uk
Est. 1980
Open Mon–Fri 9am–5.30pm
Sales Quarterly antiques and fine art sale Thurs, viewing day prior 10am–7pm. Monthly Victoriana and collectables sale Wed, viewing day prior 10am–7pm
Catalogues Yes

Grays Antiques
Contact Mr D Gray
✉ **29 The Tiding, Worcester, Worcestershire, WR1 1JL**
☎ 01905 724456 ℻ 01905 723433
Ⓔ enquiries@grays-antiques.com
Ⓦ www.grays-antiques.com
Est. 1984 *Stock size* Large
Stock Early 19th–early 20thC furniture and furnishings and decorative items including chandeliers
Open Mon–Sat 8.30am–5.30pm
Services Restoration

Heirlooms
Contact Mrs L Rumford
✉ **46 Upper Tything, Worcester, Worcestershire, WR1 1JZ** 🅿
☎ 01905 23332
Est. 1988 *Stock size* Large
Stock Antique and old reproduction furniture, china, glass, decorative items
Open Mon–Sat 9.30am–4.30pm

P J Hughes Antiques
Contact Mr P J Hughes
✉ **3 Barbourne Road, Worcester, Worcestershire, WR1 1RS** 🅿
☎ 01905 610695
Ⓜ 07774 204127
Est. 1972 *Stock size* Large
Stock Jewellery, collectables, china, silver, small furniture
Open Tues–Sat 9.30am–5pm
Fairs St Martin's Market, Birmingham
Services Valuations

M Lees & Son (LAPADA)
Contact Mr M Lees
✉ **Tower House, 1 Castle Place, Severn Street, Worcester, Worcestershire, WR1 2NB** 🅿
☎ 01905 26620 ℻ 01905 26620
Ⓜ 07860 826218
Est. 1974 *Stock size* Medium
Stock Period furniture, china, pictures, decorative items, mirrors
Open Mon–Fri 9.30am–4.45pm Thurs 9.30am–12.45pm Sat 10.30am–4pm and by appointment
Services Valuations

The Old Toll House
Contact Mr D Askew
✉ **1 Droitwich Road, Worcester, Worcestershire, WR3 7LG** 🅿
☎ 01905 20608
Ⓔ merylasken@aol.com
Est. 1980 *Stock size* Medium
Stock Pine furniture, reclaimed wooden doors, pottery, porcelain, glass
Open Mon–Sat 10am–6pm
Services Restoration, stripping

Philip Serrell Auctioneers & Valuers
Contact P Serrell FRICS
✉ **Field House, 6 Sansome Walk, Worcester, Worcestershire, WR1 1NU** 🅿
☎ 01905 26200 ℻ 01905 21202
Ⓔ serrell.auctions@virgin.net
Ⓦ www.serrell.com
Open Mon–Fri 9am–5pm closed 1–2pm
Sales General and fine art sales at the Malvern Sale Room, Malvern. Special sales of Worcester porcelain
Frequency Fortnightly
Catalogues Yes

Tything Antiques Centre
Contact Mr or Mrs Shuckburgh
✉ **39 The Tything, Worcester, Worcestershire, WR1 1JL** 🅿
☎ 01905 723322
Est. 1994 *Stock size* Large
No. of dealers 12
Stock General antiques
Open Mon–Sat 10am–5.30pm

Worcester Antiques Centre
Contact Mr S Zacaroli
✉ **Unit 15, Reindeer Court, Mealcheapen Street, Worcester, Worcestershire, WR1 4DS** 🅿
☎ 01905 610680
Ⓔ worcsantiques@aol.com
Est. 1991 *Stock size* Large
No. of dealers 45
Stock Porcelain, early Worcester, furniture, silver, jewellery, Art Nouveau, Arts and Crafts, militaria, scientific instruments
Open Mon–Sat 9am–5pm

YORKS & LINCS

EAST RIDING OF YORKSHIRE

BEVERLEY

⊞ David Hakeney Antiques
Contact David Hakeney
✉ **PO Box 171, Beverley, East Riding of Yorkshire, HU17 8GX** Ⓟ
☎ 01482 677006
Ⓜ 07860 507774
Est. 1970 ***Stock size*** Medium
Stock General antiques, quality items
Open By appointment
Fairs NEC, Newark
Services Restoration

⊞ Hawley Antiques (LAPADA)
Contact John Hawley
✉ **5 North Bar Within, Beverley, East Riding of Yorkshire, HU17 8AP** Ⓟ
☎ 01430 470654
Ⓜ 07850 225805
Ⓔ info@hawleys.info
Ⓦ www.hawleys.info
Est. 1966 ***Stock size*** Medium
Stock General antiques, mainly Georgian–Victorian
Open By appointment
Services Valuations, restoration

St Crispin Antiques & Collectors Centre
Contact Chris Fowler
✉ **11 Butcher Row, Beverley, East Riding of Yorkshire, HU17 0AA** Ⓟ
☎ 01482 869583
Ⓜ 07951 252101
Est. 1997 ***Stock size*** Large
No. of dealers 70
Stock Antiques, collectables, furniture, books

Open Mon–Sat 10am–5pm
Sun 10.30–4.30pm
Services Valuations, restoration

Time and Motion (BHI, BWCG)
Contact Mr Peter Lancaster
1 Beckside, Beverley, East Riding of Yorkshire, HU17 0PB P
01482 881574
Est. 1984 *Stock size* Large
Stock Antique clocks and barometers
Open Mon–Sat 10am–5pm closed Thurs
Services Valuations, restoration

Vicar Lane Antique Centre
Contact Chris Fowler
The Old Granary, Vicar Lane, North Bar Within, Beverley, East Riding of Yorkshire, HU17 8DF P
01482 888088
07951 252101
Est. 2002 *Stock size* Medium
No. of dealers 20
Stock Pre-1910 furniture, small antiques
Open Mon–Sat 10am–5pm
Sun 10.30am–4pm
Services Valuations, restoration

BRIDLINGTON

Dixons Medals (OMRS)
Contact Mr C J Dixon
23 Prospect Street, Bridlington, East Riding of Yorkshire, YO15 2AE P
01262 603348 F 01262 606600
chris@dixonsmedals.co.uk
www.dixonsmedals.co.uk
Est. 1969 *Stock size* Large
Stock Medals from Peninsular war, Victorian campaigns to present day
Open Mon–Fri 9.30am–5pm
Fairs OMRS convention
Services Restoration of medals, catalogue, mail order worldwide, Dixons Gazette

The Emporium
Contact Mr Burdall
59 St John Street, Bridlington, East Riding of Yorkshire, YO16 7NN P
01262 677560
07779 200335
Est. 1979 *Stock size* Large
Stock Sanitary ware, doors, radiators, pine furniture, cast-iron fires, French stoves, brass ware, reclaimed timber etc
Open Tues–Sat 10am–5.30pm or by appointment
Services Valuations, restoration, stripping

The Georgian Rooms
Contact David Rothwell
56 High Street, Bridlington, East Riding of Yorkshire, YO16 4QA P
01262 608600
Est. 2000 *Stock size* Large
No. of dealers 15
Stock General antiques, silver, jewellery, furniture, paintings
Open Mon–Sat 10am–5pm

The Magpie's Nest
Contact Ms R Szpakowski
92 St John Street, Bridlington, East Riding of Yorkshire, YO16 7JS P
01262 4604517
07721 090414
Est. 1994 *Stock size* Medium
Stock Antiques, bric-a-brac, collectables
Open Variable Mon–Fri 10am–5pm
Fairs Wetherby, Harrogate, Swinderby, Doncaster

BROUGH

Lincoln House Antiques (LAPADA)
Contact Mr J Daggett
51 Market Place, South Cave, Brough, East Riding of Yorkshire, HU15 2BS P
01430 424623
07764 273695
Est. 1993 *Stock size* Medium
Stock Georgian–Edwardian furniture, porcelain, pictures, clocks
Open Mon–Sat 10am–5pm closed Wed or by appointment
Fairs Burley, Harrogate
Services Valuations

DRIFFIELD

The Crested China Co
Contact Mr David Taylor
Station House, Railway Station, Driffield, East Riding of Yorkshire, YO25 6PX P
01377 255002/257042
dt@thecrestedchinacompany.com
www.thecrestedchinacompany.com
Est. 1978 *Stock size* Large
Stock Goss and crested china
Open By appointment
Fairs Goss Collectors Club Fairs
Services Mail order, bi-monthly illustrated catalogue

Dee, Atkinson and Harrison
Contact Owen Nisbet or Helen Pickering
The Exchange, Driffield, East Riding of Yorkshire, YO25 6LD P
01377 253151 F 01377 241041
driffield@dee.atkinson.harrison.co.uk
www.dee.atkinson.harrison.co.uk
Est. 1880
Open 9am–5.30pm
Sales 6 Antique and collectors' sales per annum, 2 collectors' sports and toy sales per annum, fortnightly 19thC and modern sales
Catalogues Yes

Smith & Smith Designs (Driffield) Ltd
Contact Mr D Smith
58a Middle Street North, Driffield, East Riding of Yorkshire, YO25 6SU P
01377 256321 F 01377 256070
07941 034446
shop@pine-on-line.co.uk
www.pine-on-line.co.uk
Est. 1976 *Stock size* Medium
Stock Antique, replica antique and reproduction pine furniture, period furniture, clocks, decorative items, lighting, water features
Open Mon–Sat 9.30am–5.30pm or by appointment
Services Restoration

GOOLE

Arcadia Antiques Centre
Contact Mr Martin Spavin
10–14 The Arcade, Goole, East Riding of Yorkshire, DN14 5QT P
01405 720549 F 01405 750549
07775 557499
Est. 1991 *Stock size* Medium
No. of dealers 20
Stock Collectables, costume jewellery, pictures, furniture etc

Open Mon–Sat 10am–5pm
Sun by appointment
Services Valuations, clock and watch repairs

Clegg & Son
Contact Mr C Clegg
68 Aire Street, Goole, East Riding of Yorkshire, DN14 5QE
☎ 01405 763140 Ⓕ 01405 764235
Ⓔ gooleoffice@cleggandson.co.uk
Ⓦ www.cleggandson.co.uk
Est. 1895
Open Mon–Fri 9am–5pm
Sales Antiques and household sale Sat am, viewing day of sale 9am–sale. Held at St Mary's Church Hall, Goole
Catalogues Yes

HORNSEA

Second Time Around
Contact Mr T Brown
61–61a Southgate, Hornsea, East Riding of Yorkshire, HU18 1AL
☎ 01964 532037
Est. 1981 *Stock size* Large
Stock General antiques, furniture, pottery, collectables, china
Open Mon–Sat 10am–4.30pm closed Wed
Fairs Newark, Birmingham
Services Restoration, upholstery

HOWDEN

Kemp Booksellers (ABA, PBFA, BA)
Contact Mike Kemp
5–7 Vicar Lane, Howden, East Riding of Yorkshire, DN14 7BP
☎ 01430 432071 Ⓕ 01430 431666
Ⓔ kemp.books@dial.pipex.com
Ⓦ www.kempbooksellers.co.uk
Est. 1979 *Stock size* Medium
Stock Mervyn Peake, modern first editions, Yorkshire and Lincolnshire topography
Open Mon–Sat 9am–5pm
Fairs ABA, PBFA, BA

HULL

City of Hull Antiques Centre
Contact Mr R Craft
21a Baker Street, Hull, East Riding of Yorkshire, HU2 8HE
☎ 01482 620606 Ⓕ 01482 327904
Ⓔ info@cityofhullantiquescentre.com
Ⓦ www.cityofhullantiquescentre.com
Est. 2003 *Stock size* Large
No. of dealers 30
Stock Antique furniture of all periods, clocks, jewellery, collectables, memorabilia, pianos
Open Mon–Sat 10am–5pm
Sun 11am–4pm

Hull Antiques Centre
Contact Melvin Anderson
Andersons Wharf, Wincolm Lee, Hull, East Riding of Yorkshire, HU2 8AH
☎ 01482 609958
Ⓜ 07966 282060
Est. 2000 *Stock size* Medium
No. of dealers 8
Stock Furniture and general antiques
Open Mon–Fri 9am–5pm
Sat Sun 10am–4pm
Services Valuations, restoration

Imperial Antiques
Contact M Langton
397 Hessle Road, Hull, East Riding of Yorkshire, HU3 4EH
☎ 01482 327439
Est. 1980 *Stock size* Medium
Stock Pine furniture
Open Mon–Sat 9am–5pm

Kilnsea Antiques
Contact Tony Smith
The Old Barn, Kilnsea Road, Hull, East Riding of Yorkshire, HU12 0UB
☎ 01964 650311
Ⓔ tsantiques@hotmail.com
Est. 1981 *Stock size* Medium
Stock Furniture and collectables from the late 1800s
Open Tues–Sun 10am–5pm

Mill Antiques
Contact John Mills
388–390 Beverley Road, Hull, East Riding of Yorkshire, HU5 1LN
☎ 01482 342248
Ⓔ john@millantiques.co.uk
Est. 1971 *Stock size* Medium
Stock Antique pine, brass beds, cast-iron fireplaces, architectural
Open Mon–Sat 9am–5pm
Services Valuations, pine stripping

Pine-Apple Antiques
Contact Diane Todd
321–327 Beverley Road, Hull, East Riding of Yorkshire, HU5 1LD
☎ 01482 441384 Ⓕ 01482 441073
Ⓜ 07860 874480
Ⓔ diane@pine-apple.co.uk
Ⓦ www.pine-apple.co.uk
Est. 1981 *Stock size* Large
Stock Architectural antiques, pine, oak, beech furniture, lighting, clocks, pottery, curios, fireplaces, bathrooms, bespoke kitchens
Open Mon–Sat 9am–5.30pm
Sun 11am–4pm

MARKET WEIGHTON

R Hornsey & Sons
Contact Mr M Swann
33 High Street, Market Weighton, East Riding of Yorkshire, YO43 3AQ
☎ 01430 872551 Ⓕ 01430 871387
Ⓜ 07711 200854
Ⓔ sales@hornseys.uk.com
Ⓦ www.hornseys.uk.com
Est. 1884
Open Mon–Fri 9am–5pm
Sat 9am–noon
Sales General antiques
Frequency Periodic
Catalogues No

Mount Pleasant Antiques Centre
Contact Linda Sirrs
46 Cliffe Road, Market Weighton, East Riding of Yorkshire, YO43 3BP
☎ 01430 872872
Est. 1999 *Stock size* Large
No. of dealers 20
Stock Good-quality furniture, collectables, 4,000 sq ft showroom
Open Mon–Sun 9.30am–5pm
Services Restoration

PATRINGTON

Clyde Antiques
Contact Ms S Nettleton
12a Market Place, Patrington, Hull, East Riding of Yorkshire, HU12 0RB
☎ 01964 630650
Est. 1980 *Stock size* Medium
Stock Wide range of antique

stock from collectables to period furniture
Open Tues–Sat 10am–5pm closed Wed
Services Valuations

Frank Hill & Son
Contact Mr R E Ward
18 Market Place, Patrington, Hull, East Yorkshire, HU12 0RB
01964 630531 01964 631203
07980 864909
Est. 1926
Open Mon–Fri 9am–5pm Sat 9am–noon
Sales Antique and modern household furniture and effects quarterly, telephone for details, viewing morning of sale. Held at Church Hall, Ottringham
Frequency Quarterly
Catalogues Yes

THORNTON

Abacus Fireplaces
Contact Mr J White
Common End Farm, Thornton, Melbourne, East Riding of Yorkshire, YO42 4RZ
01759 318575 01759 318136
07703 517544
abacus03@globalnet.co.uk
Est. 1969 *Stock size* Large
Stock Architectural antiques, fireplaces, fireplace furnishings
Open Mon–Sat 9am–4.30pm
Services Restoration of all antiques, custom-made castings

WITHERNSEA

Mathy's Emporium
Contact Mr M Quinn
2 Pier Road, Withernsea, East Riding of Yorkshire, HU19 2JS
01964 615739
Est. 1994 *Stock size* Large
Stock Brass, furniture, pottery, Wade, collectables
Open Mon–Sun 10am–5pm closed Wed
Services Valuations

NORTH YORKSHIRE

ALLERTON MAULEVERER

Mauleverer Antiques
Contact Ms Caroline Louise Forster
Allerton Park Castle, Allerton Mauleverer, Knaresborough, North Yorkshire, HG5 0SE
01423 340170 01423 340170
07974 255087
mauleverer@tiscali.co.uk
www.earlyenglishoak.co.uk
Est. 1984 *Stock size* Medium
Stock 1650–1850 early English oak and provincial furniture
Open By appointment only
Fairs Tatton Park, NEC, The Northern Antique Fair, Harrogate

Mauleverer Antiques
Contact Ms Caroline Louise Forster
The Old Cottage, Shaw Lane, Farnham, Knaresborough, North Yorkshire, HG5 9JE
01423 340170 01423 340170
07974 255087
mauleverer@tiscali.co.uk
www.earlyenglishoak.co.uk
Est. 1984 *Stock size* Medium
Stock 1650–1850 early English oak and provincial furniture
Open By appointment only
Fairs Tatton Park, NEC, The Northern Antique Fair, Harrogate

ASKRIGG

J R Hopper & Co
Contact Mr D Lambert
Wood End Countersett, Askrigg, North Yorkshire, DL8 3DE
01969 650776 01969 650893
brian.carlisle@easynet.co.uk
Est. 1886
Open Possible to contact at all times
Sales General antiques, household furnishings
Frequency Monthly
Catalogues Yes

AUSTWICK

Austwick Hall Books
Contact Michael Pearson
Townhead Lane, Austwick, Nr Settle, North Yorkshire, LA2 8BS
01524 251794
austwickhall@btinternet.com
Est. 2000 *Stock size* Medium
Stock Antiquarian, rare and second-hand books, including natural history and science
Open By appointment only
Services Book search

BEDALE

Bedale Antiques
Contact Mr or Mrs R C Stubley
2a Sussex Street, Bedale, North Yorkshire, DL8 2AJ
01677 427765
Est. 1998 *Stock size* Medium
Stock Period furniture, pottery
Open Mon–Sat 10am–4.30pm closed Thurs

Bennetts Antiques & Collectables Ltd
Contact Paul Bennett
7 Market Place, Bedale, North Yorkshire, DL8 1ED
01677 427900 01677 426858
info@bennetts.uk.com
www.bennetts.uk.com
Est. 1997 *Stock size* Large
Stock Furniture, clocks, works of art, 19thC Yorkshire paintings, collectables
Open Mon–Sat 9am–5pm Sun by appointment
Services Restoration, clock repair

Bonhams
14 Market Place, Bedale, North Yorkshire, DL8 1EQ
01667 424 114 01677 424 115
bedale@bonhams.com
www.bonhams.com
Open Mon–Fri 9am–1pm 2–5pm
Sales Regional office. Regular house and attic sales across the country; contact London offices for further details. Free auction valuations; insurance and probate valuations

M W Darwin & Son
Contact Mr M W Darwin
The Dales Furniture Hall, Bridge Street, Bedale, North Yorkshire, DL8 2AD
01677 422846 01609 779072
mwdarwin1@estategazette.net
Est. 1959
Open Mon–Fri 9am–4.30pm Thurs 9am–noon
Sales General antiques sales held on Fri
Frequency Every 3 weeks
Catalogues No

Dovetail Interiors of Bedale
Contact Brian Jutsum

Bridge Street, Bedale, North Yorkshire, DL8 2AD P
☎ 01677 426464 F 01677 426464
W www.dovetailinteriors.com
Est. 1997 *Stock size* Medium
Stock Antiques, bespoke furniture, ethnic artefacts
Open Mon–Sun 10am–5pm

BILLINGHAM

Margaret Bedi Antiques and Fine Art
Contact Mrs Margaret Bedi
5 Station Road, Billingham, Stockton-on-Tees, TS23 1AG P
☎ 01642 782346
M 07860 577637
Est. 1976 *Stock size* Large
Stock Fine furniture 1660–1920, watercolours, oils
Open By appointment only
Fairs Northern Antiques Fair, Harrogate
Services Valuations, restoration

BOLTON ABBEY

Grove Rare Books
Contact Mr A Sharpe
The Old Post Office, Bolton Abbey, Skipton, North Yorkshire, BD23 6EX P
☎ 01756 710717
W www.groverarebooks.co.uk
Est. 1997 *Stock size* Medium
Stock Antique, rare, and second-hand books, local topography a speciality
Open Tues–Sat 10.30am–4pm variable during winter
Services Restoration, book search

BOROUGHBRIDGE

Lister Haigh
Contact Mr Paul Johnston
5 St James Square, Boroughbridge, North Yorkshire, YO51 9AS
☎ 01423 322382 F 01423 324735
E boroughbridge@listerhaigh.co.uk
W www.listerhaigh.co.uk
Est. 1919
Open Mon–Fri 9am–5.30pm Sat 9–11.30am
Sales General antiques and periodic catalogue sales
Frequency Monthly
Catalogues Yes

J Wilson
Contact Mr John Wilson or Mr P Wilson
St James Square, Boroughbridge, North Yorkshire, YO5 9AR P
☎ 01423 322508 F 01423 326690
Est. 1989 *Stock size* Small
Stock General antiques, 18th–19thC furniture
Open Mon–Sat by appointment
Services Valuations, restoration

R S Wilson & Son
Contact Mr R Wilson
PO Box 41, Boroughbridge, North Yorkshire, YO51 9WY P
☎ 01423 322417 F 01423 322417
M 07711 794801
E richard.wilsonantiques@virgin.net
Est. 1917 *Stock size* Small
Stock 17th–19thC furniture
Open By appointment

EASINGWOLD

Easingwold Antiques
Contact Jane Fish
108 Long Street, Easingwold, North Yorkshire, YO61 3HX P
☎ 01347 822977
M 07968 088705 or 07977 108907
Est. 2003 *Stock size* Large
Stock Glass, silver, ceramics, linen, pre-20thC furniture
Open Tues–Sat 10am–5pm
Fairs Harrogate
Services Restoration

Milestone Antiques
Contact Mr A Streetley
Farnley House, 101 Long Street, Easingwold, York, North Yorkshire, YO61 3HY P
☎ 01347 821608
E milestoneantiques-easingwold@fsmail.net
Est. 1982 *Stock size* Medium
Stock Furniture, clocks
Open Mon–Sat 9am–5.30pm Sun by appointment
Services Valuations

Vale Antiques (GADAR)
Contact J M Leach
Mooracres, North Moor, Easingwold, York, North Yorkshire, YO61 3NB P
☎ 01347 821298 F 01347 821298
E chris.leach@ukonline.co.uk
Est. 1990 *Stock size* Medium
Stock Georgian, Victorian and later furniture, collectables
Open Mon–Sun 9am–5.30pm
Services Furniture restoration

FLAXTON

Flaxton Antique Gardens (SALVO)
Contact Tim Richardson
Glebe Farm, Flaxton, North Yorkshire, YO60 7RU P
☎ 01904 468468 F 01904 468468
W www.salvo.co.uk/dealers/flaxton
Est. 1990 *Stock size* Large
Stock Garden antiques, terracotta urns, seats, Victorian edging, bird baths, troughs, sundials
Open Mon–Sun 10am–4pm closed Tues (winter times telephone call advisable)
Services Valuations

GARGRAVE

Dickinson Antiques Ltd
Contact H H or A E Mardall
Estate Yard, West Street, Gargrave, Skipton, North Yorkshire, BD23 3PH P
☎ 01756 748257
Est. 1959 *Stock size* Medium
Stock Early antique furniture
Open Mon–Sat 9am–5.30pm or by appointment

Gargrave Gallery
Contact Mr B Herington
48 High Street, Gargrave, Skipton, North Yorkshire, BD23 1JP P
☎ 01756 749641
Est. 1974 *Stock size* Medium
Stock General antiques, Georgian–Victorian furniture
Open Mon–Sat 10am–4pm

R N Myers & Son (BADA)
Contact Simon Myers
Endsleigh House, High Street, Gargrave, Skipton, North Yorkshire, BD23 3LX P
☎ 01756 749587 F 01756 749322
M 07801 310126
E rnmyersson@aol.com
Est. 1890 *Stock size* Medium

Stock 17th–early 19thC furniture, ceramics, works of art
Open Mon–Sat 9am–5pm or by appointment
Services Valuations

GUISBOROUGH

Curiosity Corner
Contact Mr B Wilson
47 Church Street, Guisborough, Cleveland, North Yorkshire, TS14 6HG
01287 636660
Est. 1987 *Stock size* Medium
Stock General antiques, longcase clocks
Open Mon–Sat 9am–4.30pm

HARROGATE

Armstrong Antiques (BADA)
Contact M A Armstrong
10–11 Montpellier Parade, Harrogate, North Yorkshire, HG1 2TJ
01423 506843 01423 506843
07802 721815
Est. 1983 *Stock size* Medium
Stock Fine18th–early 19thC English furniture
Open Mon–Sat 10am–5.30pm
Fairs Olympia
Services Valuations

Richard Axe Books
Contact Mr R Axe
12 Cheltenham Crescent, Harrogate, North Yorkshire, HG1 1DH
01423 561867 01423 561837
rja@axebooks.com
Est. 1980 *Stock size* Large
Stock Antiquarian, rare, second-hand books, Yorkshire topics a speciality
Open Tues–Sat 10am–5.30pm

Margaret Bedi's Antiques and Fine Art
Contact Mrs Margaret Bedi
Corn Exchange Building, The Ginnel, Harrogate, North Yorkshire, HG1 2RB
01642 782346
07860 577637
Est. 1976 *Stock size* Large
Stock Fine furniture 1660–1920, watercolours, oils
Open Mon–Sat 9.30–5pm
Fairs Northern Antiques Fair, Harrogate
Services Valuations, restoration

Carlton Hollis Ltd
Contact Paul Hollis
10 Montpellier Mews, Montpellier Street, Harrogate, North Yorkshire, HG1 2TQ
01423 500216 01423 500283
07711 188565
Est. 2000 *Stock size* Medium
Stock Antique silver and jewellery
Open Mon–Sat 10am–5pm
Services Valuations, restoration

Crown Jewellers of Harrogate
Contact Steve Kramer, FGA, DGA
23 Commercial Street, Harrogate, North Yorkshire, HG1 1UB
01423 502000 01423 502000
sask@crownjewellers.freeserve.co.uk
Est. 2000 *Stock size* Medium
Stock Second-hand gold jewellery, new silver jewellery, porcelain, glass, silver
Open Mon–Sat 10am–5pm closed Wed
Services Valuations, jewellery repairs

John Daffern Antiques
Contact John Daffern
38 Forest Lane Head, Harrogate, North Yorkshire, HG2 7TS
01423 889832
Est. 1968 *Stock size* Medium
Stock Fine 17th–18thC furniture, clocks
Open Mon Wed Fri Sat 10.30am–5.30pm

Derbyshire Antiques Ltd
Contact Mr R Derbyshire
27 Montpellier Parade, Harrogate, North Yorkshire, HG1 2TG
01423 503115
07860 580836
Est. 1962 *Stock size* Medium
Stock Early oak pieces, associated items, Georgian furniture to 1820
Open Mon–Sat 10am–5.30pm

Dragon Antiques
Contact Mr Peter Broadbelt
10 Dragon Road, Harrogate, North Yorkshire, HG1 5DF
01423 562037
Est. 1964 *Stock size* Medium
Stock General antiques, ephemera, postcards
Open Mon–Sat 11am–6pm

Garth Antiques (LAPADA)
Contact Mr or Mrs J Chapman
16 Montpellier Parade, Harrogate, North Yorkshire, HG1 2TG
01423 530573 01423 564084
Est. 1978 *Stock size* Medium
Stock General antiques
Open Mon–Sat 10am–5.30pm
Services Restoration

The Ginnel Antique Center
Contact David Cook
Corn Exchange Building, The Ginnel, Harrogate, North Yorkshire, HG1 2RB
01423 508857 01423 508857
enquiries@theginnel.com
www.theginnel.co.uk
Est. 1986 *Stock size* Large
No. of dealers 50
Stock Quality datelined antiques
Open Mon–Sat 9.30am–5.30pm
Services Courier service, café, licensed restaurant

Grandad's Attic
Contact Miss B F Dawson
2 Granville Road, Harrogate, North Yorkshire, HG1 1BY
01423 503003
Est. 1984 *Stock size* Medium
Stock Antique usable tools, garden tools, kitchenware
Open Thurs Fri Sat 10.30am–4.30pm or by appointment
Fairs David Stanley Tools Auction

Havelocks Pine and Antiques
Contact Philip Adam
13–17 Westmoreland Street, Harrogate, North Yorkshire, HG1 5AY
01423 506721 01423 506721
07802 914419
Est. 1986 *Stock size* Large
Stock General antiques
Open Mon–Sat 10am–5pm Sun 11am–4pm
Fairs Newark
Services Restoration, pine stripping, valuations

⊞ Charles Lumb & Sons Ltd (BADA)
Contact Mr A Lumb
✉ **2 Montpellier Gardens, Harrogate, North Yorkshire, HG1 2TF** P
☎ 01423 503776 F 01423 530074
E info@harrogateantiques.com
W www.harrogateantiques.com
Est. 1910 *Stock size* Medium
Stock 18th–19thC English furniture, works of art, metalware
Open Mon–Fri 9.30am–6pm closed 1–2pm Sat 9.30am–1pm

Christopher Matthews
Contact Christopher Matthews
✉ **23 Mount Street, Harrogate, North Yorkshire, HG2 8DQ** P
☎ 01423 871756 F 01423 879700
Est. 1989
Open Mon–Fri 9am–5pm
Sales Quarterly antiques auctions, telephone for details
Catalogues Yes

Montpellier Mews Antique Market
✉ **Montpellier Street, Harrogate, North Yorkshire, HG1 2TQ** P
☎ 01423 530484
Est. 1987 *Stock size* Medium
No. of dealers 10
Stock General antiques, collectables, golf antiques, silver, china
Open Mon–Sat 10am–5pm

Morphets of Harrogate (SOFAA)
Contact Elizabeth Pepper-Darling
✉ **6 Albert Street, Harrogate, North Yorkshire, HG1 1JL**
☎ 01423 530030 F 01423 500717
W www.morphets.co.uk
Est. 1895
Open Mon–Fri 9am–5.30pm Wed 9am–6pm Sat 9am–noon
Sales Fine art and antiques sale quarterly Thurs 10am, viewing Tues 2–7pm Wed 10am–5pm Thurs 8.30–10am. Victorian and later furniture and effects Thurs 10am, viewing Wed 10am–7pm Thurs 8.30–10am
Catalogues Yes

⊞ Paul M Peters (LAPADA)
Contact Mr Paul Peters
✉ **15a Bower Road, Harrogate, North Yorkshire, HG1 1BE** P
☎ 01423 560118 F 01423 560118
M 07803 082378
Est. 1964 *Stock size* Large
Stock Chinese, Japanese, European ceramics, Oriental works of art
Open Mon–Fri 10am–5pm
Fairs Olympia

⊞ Elaine Phillips Antiques Ltd (BADA)
Contact Elaine, Colin or Louise Phillips
✉ **1–2 Royal Parade, Harrogate, North Yorkshire, HG1 2SZ** P
☎ 01423 569745
M 07710 793753
E elainephillips@heliscott.co.uk
Est. 1965 *Stock size* Medium
Stock 17th–18thC oak furniture, metalware, treen, some mahogany
Open Mon–Sat 9.30am–5.30pm or by appointment
Fairs Harrogate (Apr Sept)
Services Interior design

⊞ Shieling Antiques
Contact Mrs Irene Meyler
✉ **5 Montpellier Mews, Montpellier Street, Harrogate, North Yorkshire, HG1 2TQ** P
☎ 01423 521884
Est. 1994 *Stock size* Small
Stock Pine and country furniture, brass and copper, decorative items for the country kitchen
Open Mon–Sat 10am–5pm

⊞ Smiths the Rink Ltd
Contact R T Smith
✉ **Dragon Road, Harrogate, North Yorkshire, HG1 5DR** P
☎ 01423 557890 F 01423 520416
W www.smithstherink.co.uk
Est. 1906 *Stock size* Medium
Stock General antiques
Open Mon–Sat 9am–5.30pm Sun 11am–4.30pm

⊞ St Julien
Contact Mr J White
✉ **4 Royal Parade, Harrogate, North Yorkshire, HG1 2SZ** P
☎ 01423 526569 F 01423 524999
M 07703 517544
E abacus03@globalnet.co.uk
Est. 1998 *Stock size* Large
Stock Antique and period lighting, door furniture, fireplaces
Open Mon–Sat 10am–5.30pm
Fairs Newark
Services Restoration, light fittings, custom-made brass castings

Tennants Auctioneers
Contact Mr N Smith
✉ **34 Montpellier Parade, Harrogate, North Yorkshire, HG1 2TG** P
☎ 01423 531661 F 01423 530990
E harrogate@tennants-ltd.co.uk
W www.tennants.co.uk
Est. 1899
Open Mon–Fri 9am–5pm Sat 9.30am–3.30pm
Sales Almost weekly general sales of antiques, Victorian and later estate and house contents. International Fine Art Catalogue sales in spring, summer and autumn. Specialist catalogue sales of books, stamps, postcards and coins are held regularly. Special sections of decorative arts, textiles, dolls, toys, militaria, railwayana, general collectables, cameras etc
Catalogues Yes

⊞ Thorntons of Harrogate (LAPADA)
Contact Jason or Hugh Thornton
✉ **1 Montpellier Gardens, Harrogate, North Yorkshire, HG1 2TF** P
☎ 01423 504118 F 01423 528400
E tofh@harrogateantiques.com
W www.harrogateantiques.com
Est. 1973 *Stock size* Medium
Stock 18th–19thC furniture, clocks, barometers, decorative items
Open Mon–Sat 9.30am–5.30pm or by appointment
Fairs Harrogate (Apr May)
Services Restoration, valuations

⊞ Walker Galleries (BADA, LAPADA, CINOA)
Contact Ian Walker
✉ **1 Crown Place, Harrogate, North Yorkshire, HG1 2RY** P
☎ 01423 520599 F 01423 536664
E walkermodern@aol.com
W www.walkerfineart.co.uk
Est. 1972 *Stock size* Large
Stock 20thC British paintings, French impressionist paintings
Open Tues–Sat 9.30am–5.30pm

Fairs Olympia, BADA, Harrogate Fine Art and Antique Fair
Services Valuations, restoration

Walker Galleries (BADA, LAPADA, CINOA)
Contact Ian Walker
6 Montpellier Gardens, Harrogate, North Yorkshire, HG1 2TF
01423 567933 01423 536664
wgltd@aol.com
www.walkerfineart.co.uk
Est. 1972 *Stock size* Large
Stock 18th–20thC British and Continental watercolours and oil paintings, small furniture, bronzes
Open Mon–Sat 9.30am–5.30pm
Fairs Olympia, BADA, Harrogate Fine Art and Antique Fair
Services Valuations, restoration

Weatherell's Antiques (LAPADA)
Contact Mr J Weatherell
29–30 Montpellier Parade, Harrogate, North Yorkshire, HG1 2TG
01423 507810 01423 520005
Est. 1964 *Stock size* Large
Stock 18th–early 20thC English and Continental furniture, paintings, objets d'art
Open Mon–Sat 9am–5.30pm

Chris Wilde Antiques (LAPADA)
Contact Mr C Wilde
134 Kings Road, Harrogate, North Yorkshire, HG1 5HY
01423 525855 01423 552301
07831 543268
chris@harrogate.com
www.antiques.harrogate.com
Est. 1995 *Stock size* Large
Stock Georgian–Victorian furniture, longcase clocks, pictures
Open Mon–Sat 10am–5pm
Fairs NEC Antiques for Everyone, Bailey fair Harrogate
Services Valuations, restoration

HAWES

Cellar Antiques
Contact Mr Ian Iveson
Bridge Street, Hawes, North Yorkshire, DL8 3QL
01969 667224
Est. 1987 *Stock size* Medium
Stock General antiques, country oak period furniture, clocks, longcase clocks
Open Mon–Sun 10am–5pm
Services Valuations, house clearance

Sturmans Antiques (LAPADA)
Contact Mr Peter Sturman
Main Street, Hawes, North Yorkshire, DL8 3QW
01969 667742
enquiries@sturmansantiques.co.uk
www.sturmansantiques.co.uk
Est. 1984 *Stock size* Medium
Stock 18th–19thC furniture, clocks, porcelain
Open Mon–Sat 10am–5.30pm Sun 11am–5pm
Services Valuations, restoration, nationwide delivery, overseas shipping arranged

HELMSLEY

Buckingham Antiques
Contact Mrs H Wilson
17 Bridge Street, Helmsley, York, North Yorkshire
01439 771642
Est. 1997 *Stock size* Large
Stock General antiques, jewellery
Open Tues–Sat 10am–5pm

Castle Gate Antiques
Contact Mr D Hartshorne
14 Castle Gate, Helmsley, York, North Yorkshire, YO62 5AB
01439 770370 01439 770370
Est. 1999 *Stock size* Large
Stock General antiques
Open Mon–Sun 10.30am–5pm
Services Valuations

Helmsley Antiquarian & Secondhand Books
Contact Mr M Moorby
Old Fire Station, Borogate, Helmsley, North Yorkshire, YO62 5BN
01439 770014
Est. 1985 *Stock size* Medium
Stock Antique, rare, and second-hand books, Yorkshire topography a speciality
Open Mon–Sat 10am–5pm Sun noon–5pm

Westway Pine
Contact Mr J Dzierzek
Carlton Lane, Helmsley, North Yorkshire, YO62 5HB
01439 771399 01439 771401
westway-pine@btopenworld.com
Est. 1987 *Stock size* Large
Stock Antique pine, French oak furniture
Open Mon–Fri 9am–5pm Sat 10am–5pm Sun 1–5pm closed Tues
Services Valuations, restoration

York Cottage Antiques (LAPADA)
Contact G or E M Thornley
7 Church Street, Helmsley, North Yorkshire, YO62 5AD
01439 770833
Est. 1965 *Stock size* Medium
Stock Early oak and country furniture, metalware, pewter, blue and white pottery, maps, prints
Open Fri Sat 10am–4pm or by appointment

KILLINGHALL

Thompson Auctioneers
Contact Mr B D Thompson
The Dales Salesroom, Levens Hall Park, Lund Lane, Killinghall, Harrogate, North Yorkshire, HG3 2BG
01423 709086 01423 709085
bryan@thompsonsauctions.co.uk
thompsonsauctioneers.co.uk
Est. 1989
Open Mon–Fri 9am–5pm Sat 9.30am–noon closed Thurs pm
Sales General antiques Fri 1pm quarterly antiques and collectables sale
Frequency Weekly
Catalogues No

KNARESBOROUGH

Early Oak
Contact Mr André Gora
Knaresborough, North Yorkshire, HG5
01904 627823
info@earlyoak.co.uk
www.earlyoak.co.uk
Est. 1985 *Stock size* Large
Stock Oak and country furniture, samplers, rugs, Delft and other ceramics, pewter, metalware
Open By appointment
Fairs Newark

Frantique
Contact Mr I Hughes
20 The High Street, Knaresborough, North Yorkshire, HG5 0EQ P
☎ 01423 797799 F 01943 463380
M 07802 740012
E ivor@frantique.fsnet.co.uk
W www.frantique.co.uk
Est. 1998 *Stock size* Medium
Stock Continental decorative arts, including faïence, kitchen antiques, clocks, bronzes, glass, metalware, enamelware
Open Mon–Sat 11am–4pm Sun noon–4pm
Services Anglo-French antiques press relations and translation

John Thompson Antiques (LAPADA)
Contact Mr John Thompson
Swadforth House, Gracious Street, Knaresborough, North Yorkshire, HG5 8DT P
☎ 01423 864698 F 01423 864698
M 07831 899948
Est. 1967 *Stock size* Medium
Stock Fine 18th–19thC furniture, related decorative objects
Open Mon–Sat 9am–5.30pm or by appointment
Fairs Olympia

Thornton & Linley
Contact Mr I A Thornton
2–4 Jockey Lane, High Street, Knaresborough, North Yorkshire, HG5 0HG P
☎ 01423 862271 F 01423 862271
E thornton.linley@virgin.net
Est. 1909
Open Tues–Fri 9am–5pm closed 1–2pm
Sales General antiques
Frequency Periodic
Catalogues Yes

LEALHOLM

Stepping Stones
Contact Mrs J Davies
Lealholm, Whitby, North Yorkshire, YO21 2AJ P
☎ 01947 897382
Est. 1974 *Stock size* Medium
Stock General antiques, books
Open Daily 10am–5pm
Services Bed and breakfast

LEYBURN

Leyburn Antiques Centre
Contact Paul Ashford
Harnby Road, Leyburn, North Yorkshire, DL8 5NF P
☎ 01969 625555 F 01969 625507
Est. 2001 *Stock size* Large
No. of dealers 36
Stock General antiques, collectables
Open Mon–Sun 10.30am–4.30pm

LEYBURN

Tennants Auctioneers (BACA Award Winner 2000, 2001)
Contact Mr Rodney Tennant
The Auction Centre, Leyburn, North Yorkshire, DL8 5SG P
☎ 01969 623780 F 01969 624281
E enquiry@tennants-ltd.co.uk
W www.tennants.co.uk
Open Mon–Fri 9am–5pm
Sales Frequent general antiques sales. 3 fine art sales per annum, 3 book sales and collectors' sales per annum
Catalogues Yes

MALTON

Boulton & Cooper Fine Art (SOFAA)
Contact Mr A McMillan
Forsyth House, Market Place, Malton, North Yorkshire, YO17 7LR P
☎ 01653 696151 F 01653 600311
E antiques@boultoncooper.co.uk
Est. 1801
Open Mon–Fri 9am–5.30pm Sat by appointment
Sales General antiques
Frequency Alternate months
Catalogues Yes

Cundalls
Contact Mr F H Dimmey
15 Market Place, Malton, North Yorkshire, YO17 7LP
☎ 01653 697820 F 01653 698305
W www.cundalls.co.uk
Est. 1860
Open Mon–Fri 9am–5.30pm
Sales General antiques sales, telephone for details
Catalogues Yes

Matthew Maw
Contact Mr M Maw
18 Castlegate, Malton, North Yorkshire, YO17 7DT
☎ 01653 694638 F 01653 694638
Est. 1974 *Stock size* Medium
Stock General antiques
Open Mon–Sat 9am–5pm

Old Talbot Gallery
Contact Mrs C Bull
Old Talbot Gallery, 9 Market Street, Malton, North Yorkshire, YO17 7LY P
☎ 01653 696142
Est. 1981 *Stock size* Medium
Stock Books, prints, pictures, maps
Open Please telephone
Services Valuations, restoration

MASHAM

Aura Antiques
Silver Street, Masham, North Yorkshire, HE4 4DX P
☎ 01765 689315
E robert@aura-antiques.co.uk
W www.aura-antiques.co.uk
Est. 1986 *Stock size* Medium
Stock Georgian, Regency, mahogany and oak furniture
Open Mon–Sat 10am–4.30pm
Services Delivery throughout UK

MIDDLEHAM

Castle Antiques
Contact Mr D Jarvill or Mrs J Jarvill
34 Market Place, Middleham, North Yorkshire, DL8 4QW P
☎ 01969 624655
Est. 1992 *Stock size* Large
No. of dealers 13
Stock Furniture, art pottery, porcelain, glassware, blue and white, pictures, prints, clocks, scientific instruments, lamps, jewellery, books, general antiques, collectors' items
Open Wed–Mon 10am–5.30pm Tues by appointment

Middleham Antiques
Contact Mr Mike Pitman
The Corner Shop, Kirkgate, Middleham, North Yorkshire, DL8 4PF P
☎ 01969 622982 F 01969 622982

Ⓜ 07729 921140
Ⓔ middlehamantique@aol.com
Ⓦ www.antiques.middlehamonline.com
Est. 1986 *Stock size* Small
Stock Pre-1830 oak and country furniture, longcase clocks, pewter, pearlware, Delft, curios
Open Most days 10am–5.30pm Wed by appointment, telephone call before visiting recommended

NORTHALLERTON

Northallerton Auctions Ltd
Contact Brian Weighell
Applegarth Sales Rooms, Romanby Road, Northallerton, North Yorkshire, DL7 8LZ Ⓟ
☎ 01609 772034 Ⓕ 01609 778786
Ⓜ 07789 373095
Est. 1920
Open Mon–Sat 9am–5pm
Sales General antiques fortnightly, watercolours by Yorkshire artists, Border Fine Arts and Beswick
Catalogues Yes

NORTON

Northern Antiques Co
Contact Mrs Ashby-Arnold
2 Parliament Street, Scarborough Road, Norton, Malton, North Yorkshire, YO17 9HE Ⓟ
☎ 01653 697520 Ⓕ 01653 690056
Est. 1990 *Stock size* Medium
Stock Georgian–Victorian furniture, decorative accessories
Open Mon–Fri 9am–5pm closed 1–2pm Sat 9.30am–12.30pm

PATELEY BRIDGE

H S C Fine Arts Ltd
Contact David Hinchliffe
45 High Street, Pateley Bridge, North Yorkshire, HG3 5LB Ⓟ
☎ 01423 712218
Ⓔ rhinch4426@aol.com
Ⓦ www.earlyantique-glass.co.uk
Est. 1997 *Stock size* Medium
Stock Small furniture, porcelain, Royal Worcester, pictures, 18thC wine glasses
Open By appointment

Brian Loomes (BACA Award Winner 2001)
Contact Brian Loomes
Calf Haugh Farm, Pateley Bridge, Harrogate, North Yorkshire, HG3 5HW Ⓟ
☎ 01423 711163
Ⓔ clocks@brianloomes.com
Ⓦ www.brianloomes.com
Est. 1966 *Stock size* Large
Stock British clocks
Open By appointment
Services Restoration, valuation, author of several books on British clocks

Needfull Things Ltd
Contact Rebecca Hinchliffe
32 High Street, Pateley Bridge, North Yorkshire, HG3 5JZ Ⓟ
☎ 01423 712851 Ⓕ 01423 712851
Ⓔ rhinch4426@aol.com
Est. 1999 *Stock size* Medium
Stock Jewellery, glassware, ceramics
Open Fri–Sun 10am–4pm or by appointment

David South (HADA)
Contact James South or David South
15 High Street, Pateley Bridge, North Yorkshire, HG3 5AP Ⓟ
☎ 01423 712022 Ⓕ 01423 712412
Ⓔ sales@davidsouth.co.uk
Ⓦ www.davidsouth.co.uk
Est. 1985 *Stock size* Medium
Stock Upholstered furniture
Open Mon–Sat 9am–5.30pm
Services Restoration

PICKERING

Country Collector
Contact Grahame Berney
11–12 Birdgate, Pickering, North Yorkshire, YO18 7AL Ⓟ
☎ 01751 477481
Ⓔ enquiries@country-collector.co.uk
Ⓦ www.country-collector.co.uk
Est. 1992 *Stock size* Small
Stock Art Deco, ceramics, blue and white china, glass, silver, metalware, collectables
Open Mon–Sat 10am–5pm closed Wed
Services Valuations

Inch's Books (PBFA, ABA)
Contact Mr P Inch
6 Westgate, Pickering, North Yorkshire, YO18 8BA Ⓟ
☎ 01751 474928 Ⓕ 01751 475939
Ⓔ inchs.books@dial.pipex.com
Ⓦ www.inchsbooks.co.uk
Est. 1982 *Stock size* Medium
Stock Antique and second-hand books
Open By appointment
Fairs ABA Chelsea, PBFA June fair
Services Mail order, catalogues (8 per year)

Pickering Antique Centre
Contact Mrs C Vance
Southgate, Pickering, North Yorkshire, YO18 8BN
01751 477210 01751 477210
sales@pickantiques.freeserve.co.uk
Est. 1998 *Stock size* Large
No. of dealers 40
Stock General antiques, bedsteads, furniture, glass, books, postcards, pictures, collectables
Open Mon–Sun 10am–5pm
Services Valuations, metal restoration service, pine stripping, delivery

C H & D M Reynolds
Contact Mr Colin Reynolds
The Curiosity Shop, 122 Eastgate, Pickering, North Yorkshire, YO18 7DW
01751 472785
07714 355676
Est. 1949 *Stock size* Large
Stock General antiques, furniture, curios
Open Mon–Sat 9.30am–5.30pm Sun by appointment
Services Valuations

Stable Antiques
Contact Mrs Yvonne Kitching-Walker
Pickering Antique Centre, Southgate, Pickering, North Yorkshire, YO18 8BN
01751 477210
Est. 1998 *Stock size* Medium
Stock General antiques
Open Mon–Sun 10am–5pm

RICHMOND

York House (Antiques)
Contact Mrs Christine Swift
60 Market Place, Richmond, North Yorkshire, DL10 4JQ
01748 850338
07711 307045
christina.swift@tiscali.co.uk
Est. 1997 *Stock size* Medium
Stock Oak, mahogany, pine furniture, general antiques, furnishings, chandeliers, fireplaces
Open Mon–Sat 9.30am–5.30pm Sun noon–4pm
Services Restoration, pine stripping

RIPON

Hornsey's of Ripon
Contact Bruce, Susan or Daniel Hornsey
3 Kirkgate, Ripon, North Yorkshire, HG4 1PA
01765 602878 01765 601692
hornseys@ripon-internet.co.uk
Est. 1974 *Stock size* Large
Stock Antiques, collectables, rare books, fine linen, lace, maps, prints
Open Mon–Sat 9am–5.30pm or by appointment
Services Valuations

Sigma Antiques
Contact Mr David Thomson
The Old Opera House, Water Skellgate, Ripon, North Yorkshire, HG4 1BH
01765 603163 01765 603163
Est. 1964 *Stock size* Large
Stock General antiques
Open Mon–Sat 9am–5.30pm

Skellgate Curios
Contact Mrs J Wayne
2 Low Skellgate, Ripon, North Yorkshire, HG4 1BE
01765 601290
Est. 1975 *Stock size* Medium
Stock General antiques
Open Mon–Sat 11am–5pm closed Wed

ROBIN HOOD'S BAY

John Gilbert Antiques
Contact John Gilbert
King Street, Robin Hood's Bay, Whitby, North Yorkshire, YO22 4SY
01947 880528
Est. 1990 *Stock size* Medium
Stock 18th–19thC oak, country furniture, treen
Open Mon Tues Thurs 2–4pm telephone call advisable Sat 10am–1pm Sun 10am–4pm or by appointment
Services Valuations, restoration

SALTBURN-BY-THE-SEA

Anderson Antiques
Contact Mrs K Anderson
20 Milton Street, Saltburn-by-the-Sea, Cleveland, North Yorkshire, TS12 1DG
01287 624810 01287 625349
07798 587622
andersak@fsbdial.co.uk
Est. 1996 *Stock size* Medium
Stock Furniture, pictures, porcelain, jewellery, clocks, linen
Open Mon–Sat 10am–5pm closed Wed
Services Valuations

J C Simmons & Son
Contact Mr G Aked
Saltburn Salerooms, Diamond Street, Saltburn-by-the Sea, North Yorkshire, TS12 1EB
01287 622366
www.saltburnsalerooms.com
Est. 1949
Open Viewing Mon–Sat 10am–4pm
Sales General antiques
Frequency Periodic
Catalogues Yes

Jösef Thompson
Contact Jösef Thompson
Saltburn Bookshop, 3 Amber Street, Saltburn-by-the-Sea, Cleveland, North Yorkshire, TS12 1DT
01287 623335
joseftthompson@freeuk.com
Est. 1977 *Stock size* Large
Stock Second-hand books
Open March–Oct Mon–Sat 11am–1pm 2–5pm Nov–Feb Mon–Sat 11am–1pm 2–4pm
Services Book search

SCARBOROUGH

Antique and Collector's Centre (PTA)
Contact Colin Spink
35 St Nicholas Cliff, Scarborough, North Yorkshire, YO11 2ES
01723 365221
07730 202405
spink@collectors.demon.co.uk
www.collectors.demon.co.uk
Est. 1965 *Stock size* Medium
Stock General antique jewellery, ephemera, cigarette cards, coins, postcards, antiques, commemorative ware, etc
Open Mon–Sat 10am–4.30pm
Services Valuations

Bar Bookstore (The Antiquary Ltd) (PBFA)
Contact Mr M Chaddock
4 Swan Hill Road, Scarborough, North Yorkshire, YO11 1BW P
01723 500141
antiquary@btinternet.com
Est. 1976 *Stock size* Medium
Stock Antiquarian, rare and second-hand books
Open Tues–Sat 10.30am–5pm
Fairs York, Harrogate, Darlington
Services Valuations, book search

David Duggleby Fine Art
Contact Jane Duggleby
The Vine Street Salerooms, Scarborough, North Yorkshire, YO11 1XN P
01723 507111 F 01723 507222
auctions@davidduggleby.com
www.davidduggleby.com
Est. 1996
Open Mon–Fri 8.30am–5pm
Sales Fortnightly 500-lot house contents and Victoriana sales, 700 lots of fine art and antiques every 8 weeks. Picture sales Sept and March at the Paddock Salerooms, Whitby
Catalogues Yes

Allen Reed
Contact Mr A Reed
109 Fallsgrave Road, Scarborough, North Yorkshire, YO12 5EG P
01723 360251
Est. 1999 *Stock size* Large
Stock General antiques
Open Mon–Sat 11am–4pm

Ward Price Ltd (ASVA)
Contact Mr I Smith, ARICS
Royal Auction Rooms, 14–15 Queen Street, Scarborough, North Yorkshire, YO11 1HA
01723 353581 F 01723 369926
www.wardprice.co.uk
Est. 1901
Open Mon–Fri 9am–5pm
Sat 10am–2pm
Sales General antiques
Frequency Alternate months
Catalogues Yes

SESSAY

Potterton Books
Contact Mrs Clare Jameson
The Old Rectory, Sessay, Nr Thirsk, North Yorkshire, YO7 3LZ P
01845 501218 F 01845 501439
enquiries@pottertonbooks.co.uk
www.pottertonbooks.co.uk
Est. 1980
Stock Fine and decorative arts books
Open Mon–Fri 9am–5pm
Fairs Fine Art Olympia, Decorex International
Services Book search

SETTLE

Anderson Slater
Contact K C Slater
Duke Street, Settle, North Yorkshire, BD24 9DW P
01729 822051
Est. 1959 *Stock size* Large
Stock 18th–19thC oak, mahogany furniture
Open Mon–Sat 10am–5pm
Services Valuations, restoration, interior designs

Mary Milnthorpe & Daughters
Contact Miss Judith Milnthorpe
Market Place, Settle, North Yorkshire, BD24 9DX P
01729 822331 F 01729 823062
Est. 1959 *Stock size* Medium
Stock Antique jewellery, silver
Open Mon–Sat 9.30am–5pm closed Wed
Services Valuations, repairs

Nanbooks
Contact Mr or Mrs J L Midgley
Roundabout, 41 Duke Street, Settle, North Yorkshire, BD24 9DJ P
01729 823324
midglui@aol.com
Est. 1955 *Stock size* Medium
Stock English and Continental ceramics, some 18th–19thC glass
Open Tues Fri Sat 11am–5pm closed 12.30–2pm or by appointment

Thistlethwaite Antiques
Contact Mr E C Thistlethwaite
Market Square, Settle, North Yorkshire, BD24 9EF P
01729 822460
Est. 1978 *Stock size* Medium
Stock 18th–19thC country furniture, metalware
Open Mon–Sat 9am–5pm closed Wed

SHERBURN-IN-ELMET

The Glass-House
Contact Sara Qualter
Low Street Farm, Sherburn-in-Elmet, North Yorkshire, LS25 6BB P
01977 689119 F 01977 682673
M 07890 134063
theglasshouse@ic24.net
Est. 2001 *Stock size* Medium
Stock Antiques and collectables, oak and country furniture, pine, 20thC design
Open Tues–Sun 9am–5pm
Fairs Swinderby, Newark
Services Shipping

Malcolms No 1 Auctioneers & Valuers
Contact Mr Malcolm Dowson
The Chestnuts, 16 Park Avenue, Sherburn-in-Elmet, North Yorkshire, LS25 6EF P
01977 684971 F 01977 681046
M 07774 130784
info@malcolmsno1auctions.co.uk
www.malcolmsno1auctions.co.uk
Est. 1980
Open Mon–Fri 9am–5pm
Sales Antiques and collectables, named ceramics (all periods), viewing Mon 10am–6.15pm Sun 1–6pm. Held at Trustees Hall, High Street, Boston Spa, Wetherby, North Yorkshire
Frequency Monthly
Catalogues Yes

SKIPTON

Skipton Antiques & Collectors Centre
Contact Ann Hall
The Old Foundry, Cavendish Street, Skipton, North Yorkshire, BD23 2AB P
01756 797667
Est. 1995 *Stock size* Large
No. of dealers 30
Stock General antiques and collectables, Art Deco, clocks, books, ceramics, pine, etc
Open Mon–Sat 10.30am–4.30pm Sun 11am–4pm

YORKS & LINCS

SLEIGHTS

Eskdale Antiques
Contact Mr P Smith
164 Coach Road, Sleights, Whitby, North Yorkshire, YO22 5EQ P
☎ 01947 810297
M 07813 589117
Est. 1979 *Stock size* Medium
Stock Antique stripped pine, garden ornaments
Open Tues–Sun 9.30am–5pm
Services Valuations

SLINGSBY

Tony Popek Antiques
Contact Mr E Popek
West View, Railway Street, Slingsby, York, North Yorkshire, YO62 24A P
☎ 01653 628533
M 07752 796335
Est. 1989 *Stock size* Medium
Stock General antiques
Open Tues Fri Sat 10am–5pm or by appointment
Fairs Harrogate, Swinderby, Newark

STAITHES

Staithes Antiques
Contact Mrs Sweeting
28 High Street, Staithes, North Yorkshire, TS13 5BH P
☎ 01947 840313
Est. 1998 *Stock size* Medium
Stock Small furniture, general antiques
Open Easter–October Tues–Sun 11am–5pm or by appointment

STOKESLEY

Lithgow Sons & Partners
Contact Richard Storry
The Auction Houses, Station Road, Stokesley, North Yorkshire, TS9 7AB P
☎ 01642 710158 F 01642 712641
E info@lithgowsauctions.com
W www.lithgowsauctions.com
Est. 1868
Open Mon–Fri 9am–5pm
Sales Weekly sale Wed 10.30am viewing Tues noon–4pm
Catalogues Yes

Mantle Antiques
Contact Mr Derek Bushby
23 College Square, Stokesley, North Yorkshire, TS9 5DN P
☎ 01642 714313
M 07713 155772
Est. 1973 *Stock size* Medium
Stock Victorian furniture, architectural antiques
Open Tues Thurs Fri Sat 10am–4pm

Alan Ramsey Antiques (LAPADA)
Contact Mr Alan Ramsey
7 Wainstones Court, Stokesley Industrial Estate, Stokesley, North Yorkshire, TS9 5JY P
☎ 01642 713008
M 07702 523246 or 07762 049848
E a.ramseyantiques@btinternet.com
W www.alanramseyantiques.co.uk
Est. 1970 *Stock size* Large
Stock Georgian–Edwardian furniture, clocks
Open By appointment

TADCASTER

Scarthingwell Antiques
Contact Mr B Brier
Scarthingwell Centre, Scarthingwell Farm, Tadcaster, North Yorkshire, LS24 9PG P
☎ 01937 557877 F 01937 558084
Est. 1989 *Stock size* Large
Stock General antiques
Open Mon–Sun 10am–5pm closed Sat

Scarthingwell Auction Centre
Contact John Griffiths or Christine Bridge
Scarthingwell, Tadcaster, North Yorkshire, LS24 9PG P
☎ 01937 557955 F 01937 557955
M 07778 520463
W www.scarthingwellauctions.co.uk
Est. 1990
Open Mon–Fri 10am–5pm
Sales Antiques and general sales Tues 5pm every 2–3 weeks, viewing Sun prior to sale noon–5pm Tues 2pm or by appointment
Catalogues Yes

THIRSK

Hambleton Books
Contact Mr T F Parr
43 Market Place, Thirsk, North Yorkshire, YO7 1HA P
☎ 01845 522343
E hambooks@btinternet.com
Est. 1979 *Stock size* Medium
Stock Antique, rare and second-hand books, books on cricket a speciality
Open Mon–Sat 9am–5.30pm Sun 10am–4pm

Millgate Antiques
Contact Tim Parvin
Abel Grange, Newsham Road, Thirsk, North Yorkshire, YO7 4DB P
☎ 01845 523878 F 01845 523878
M 07966 251609
E babs.jenkins@btinternet.com
Est. 1991 *Stock size* Large
Stock Pine furniture, panelled doors
Open Mon–Sat 8.30am–5pm
Fairs Newark, Swinderbury
Services Stripping, restoration

Millgate Pine & Antiques
Contact Tim Parvin
12 Millgate, Thirsk, North Yorkshire, YO7 1AA P
☎ 01845 523878 F 01845 523878
M 07966 251609
E babs.jenkins@btinternet.com
Est. 1991 *Stock size* Large
Stock Pine furniture, panelled doors
Open Mon–Sat 8.30am–5pm
Fairs Newark, Swinderbury
Services Stripping

THORNTON-LE-DALE

Cobweb Books
Contact Mr Robin Buckler
Ye Olde Corner Shoppe, 1 Pickering Road, Thornton-le-Dale, North Yorkshire, YO19 7LG P
☎ 01751 476638
E sales@cobwebbooks.co.uk
W www.cobwebbooks.co.uk
Est. 1991 *Stock size* Medium
Stock Antiquarian, rare and second-hand books
Open Tues–Sun 10am–5pm
Fairs Royal National Hotel Book Fair, London
Services Book search

TOCKWITH

Tomlinson Antiques (LAPADA, CINOA)

Contact Sarah Worrall
Moorside, Tockwith, York, North Yorkshire, YO26 7QG
01423 358833 01423 358188
info@antique-furniture.co.uk
antique-furniture.co.uk
Est. 1977 *Stock size* Large
Stock Quality Georgian–pre-war furniture, china, silver, silver plate, longcase clocks, rugs, Art Deco, reproduction furniture
Trade only Mon–Fri; retail club at weekends
Open Mon–Fri 9am–5pm Sun 10am–4pm
Services Restoration, shipping, bespoke manufacturing service

UPPER POPPLETON

D Wombell & Son

Contact Mr W Rice
Northminster Business Park, Upper Poppleton, York, North Yorkshire, YO41 4AR
01904 790777 01904 798018
www.invaluable.com/wombell
Est. 1984
Open Mon–Fri 10am–5pm
Sales General antiques monthly
Frequency Monthly
Catalogues Yes

WHITBY

Abbey Antiques

Contact Mr A L Barsby
4 & 5 Grape Lane, Whitby, North Yorkshire, YO22 4DD
01947 821424
Est. 1996 *Stock size* Large
Stock General antiques, collectables
Open Flexible, please telephone

Clewlow Antiques (PBFA)

Contact Mr A Clewlow
Sandringham House, 6–8 Skinner Street, Whitby, North Yorkshire, YO21 3AJ
01947 825508
fiona.clewlow@ntlworld.com
Est. 1977 *Stock size* Large
Stock General antiques
Open Summer Mon–Sat 10am–5pm winter Fri Sat only

Curio Corner

Contact Mr A L Barsby
7 Market Place, Whitby, North Yorkshire, YO22 4DD
01947 821424
Est. 1969 *Stock size* Small
Stock General antiques, collectables
Open Flexible hours or by appointment

Endeavour Books

Contact Mrs L Allison
1 Grape Lane, Whitby, North Yorkshire, YO22 4BA
01947 821331
linda@enbooks.co.uk
www.enbooks.co.uk
Est. 1989 *Stock size* Medium
Stock Rare and second-hand books
Open Mon–Sun summer 10am–8pm winter 10.30am–5pm

Eskdale Antiques

Contact Mr P Smith
85 Church Street, Whitby, North Yorkshire, YO22 4BH
01947 600512
Est. 1982 *Stock size* Medium
Stock Ceramics, pictures, bottles, advertisements
Open Easter–Oct Mon–Sun 10.30am–5pm or by appointment

Picfair Antiques

Contact Mr J Robertson
67 Haggersgate, Whitby, North Yorkshire, YO21 3PP
01947 602483
picfair@amserve.net
picfair.com
Est. 1987 *Stock size* Medium
Stock General antiques including glass, costume jewellery, porcelain
Open Mon–Sun noon–6pm
Services Valuations, advice to collectors

The Staffordshire Knot

Contact Ricky Clarke
The Shambles Market, Market Place, Whitby, North Yorkshire, YO22 4TY
07796 595465
Est. 2004 *Stock size* Medium
Stock Ceramics, glass, Art Deco
Open Mon–Sun 10am–5.30pm

YARM

Farthing

Contact Shirley Smith or Sybil Watson
57a High Street, Yarm, Cleveland, North Yorkshire, TS15 9BH
01642 785881
Est. 1977 *Stock size* Medium
Stock General antiques, prints, gifts
Open Mon–Sat 9.30am–5.30pm
Services Picture framing

YORK

Advena Antiques & Fairs

Contact Alan White
Cavendish Antique Centre, 44 Stonegate, York, North Yorkshire, YO1 8AS
01904 668785
07713 150510
advena.antiques@ntlworld.com
Est. 1992 *Stock size* Medium
Stock Antique silver, jewellery
Open Mon–Sat 9am–6pm Sun 10am–4pm
Services Valuations, repairs

Ancient World (ADA)

Contact John Moor
16 High Petergate, York, North Yorkshire, YO1 7EH
01904 624062
lindsay@ancientworldyork.co.uk
Est. 1975 *Stock size* Medium
Stock Ancient coins, antiquities
Open Mon–Sun 10am–5pm
Fairs ADA

The Antiques Centre York

Contact Liz Robson
41 Stonegate, York, North Yorkshire, YO1 8AW
01904 635888 01904 676342
Est. 1996 *Stock size* Large
No. of dealers 100
Stock General antiques
Open Mon–Sun 9am–6pm
Services Café

Margaret Bedi Antiques and Fine Art

Contact Mrs Margaret Bedi
The Red House Antique Centre, Duncombe Place, York, North Yorkshire,

YO1 2EF 🅿
☎ 01642 782346
Ⓜ 07860 577637
Est. 1976 *Stock size* Large
Stock Fine furniture 1660–1920, watercolours, oils
Open Mon–Sun 9.30am–5pm
Fairs Northern Antiques Fair, Harrogate
Services Valuations, restoration

Bishopgate Antiques
Contact Mr R Weatherill
✉ **23–24 Bishopgate, York, North Yorkshire, YO23 1JH** 🅿
☎ 01904 623893 Ⓕ 01904 626511
Est. 1965 *Stock size* Medium
Stock General antiques
Open Tues–Sat 9.15am–6pm

Barbara Cattle (BADA)
Contact Mr Richard Pool
✉ **45 Stonegate, York, North Yorkshire, YO1 8AW**
☎ 01904 623862
Ⓔ info@barbaracattle.co.uk
Ⓦ www.barbaracattle.co.uk
Stock Jewellery, silver, old Sheffield plate
Open Mon–Sat 9am–5.30pm
Services Valuations, repairs, restoration

Cavendish Antiques & Collectors Centre
Contact Debbie or Mark Smith
✉ **44 Stonegate, York, North Yorkshire, YO1 8AS**
☎ 01904 621666 Ⓕ 01904 675747
Est. 1999 *Stock size* Large
No. of dealers 60
Stock General antiques
Open Mon–Sun 9am–6pm

Jack Duncan
Contact Mr Alex Helstrip
✉ **36 Fossgate, York, North Yorkshire, YO1 9TF** 🅿
☎ 08704 204372 Ⓕ 01904 672184
Est. 1984 *Stock size* Medium
Stock Antique, scholarly and second-hand books, English literature a speciality
Open Mon–Sat 10am–5.30pm

Mike Fineron Cigarette Cards & Postcards
Contact Mike Fineron
✉ **28 The Pastures, Dringhouses, York, North Yorkshire, YO24 2JE** 🅿
☎ 01904 703911
Ⓔ fineronmikef@yahoo.co.uk
Est. 1997 *Stock size* Medium
Stock Cigarette cards, postcards, Yorkshire postcards a speciality
Open By appointment
Fairs Pudsey, Chester le Street, Sheffield
Services Valuations, postal service

French House Antiques
Contact Steve
✉ **74 Micklegate, York, North Yorkshire, YO1 6LF** 🅿
☎ 01904 624465 Ⓕ 01904 629965
Ⓔ info@thefrenchhouse.co.uk
Ⓦ www.thefrenchhouse.co.uk
Est. 1995 *Stock size* Large
Stock Antique French furniture
Open Mon–Sat 9.30am–5.30pm
Services Restoration

Harpers Jewellers Ltd
Contact Nicholas Wiseman
✉ **2–6 Minster Gates, York, Yorkshire, YO1 7HL**
☎ 01904 632634 Ⓕ 01904 673370
Ⓔ info@vintage-watches.co.uk
Ⓦ www.vintage-watches.co.uk
Est. 1990 *Stock size* Large
Stock Jewellery, watches
Open Mon–Sat 9am–5.30pm
Services Valuations

Hunts Pine (GADAR)
Contact Mr W Dougherty
✉ **Unit 6a, Victoria Farm, Water Lane, York, North Yorkshire, YO30 6PQ** 🅿
☎ 01904 690561 Ⓕ 01904 690561
Est. 1995 *Stock size* Medium
Stock Antique pine furniture
Open Mon–Fri 9am–5.30pm Sat 9am–2pm
Fairs Newark
Services Stripping

Laurel Bank Antiques
Contact Mr K Lamb
✉ **52 Clarence Street, York, North Yorkshire, YO31 7EW** 🅿
☎ 01904 676030
Ⓔ sales@laurelbankantiques.co.uk
Ⓦ www.laurelbankantiques.co.uk
Est. 1997 *Stock size* Medium
Stock General antiques, collectables, Georgian–Edwardian furniture, longcase, wall and mantel clocks
Open Mon–Sat 10am–5pm closed Tues
Services Restoration, French polishing

Minstergate Bookshop (PBFA)
Contact Mr N Wallace
✉ **8 Minster Gates, York, North Yorkshire, YO1 7HL**
☎ 01904 621812 Ⓕ 01904 622960
Ⓔ rarebooks@minstergatebooks.co.uk
Ⓦ www.minstergatebooks.co.uk
Est. 1977 *Stock size* Medium
Stock Books, children's and illustrated books a speciality
Open Mon–Sun 10am–5.30pm
Services Valuations, book search

Robert Morrison & Son (BADA)
Contact Charles or Pauline Morrison
✉ **Trentholme House, 131 The Mount, York, North Yorkshire, YO24 1DU** 🅿
☎ 01904 655394
Ⓔ info@york-antiques.com
Ⓦ www.york-antiques.com
Est. 1865 *Stock size* Large
Stock 17th–19thC English furniture
Open Mon–Sat 9.30am–5pm

The Mulberry Bush Antique Shop
Contact Mr P A Young
✉ **36 Goodramgate, York, North Yorkshire, YO1 7LF**
☎ 01904 638842 Ⓕ 01904 468665
Ⓔ mulberryan@aol.com
Est. 1994 *Stock size* Medium
Stock General antiques, watercolours, oils, clocks
Open Mon–Sat 9.30am–5pm Sun 11–3pm
Services Clock and furniture restoration, valuations

Janette Ray Rare Books (PBFA, ABA)
Contact Miss J Ray
✉ **8 Bootham, York, North Yorkshire, YO30 7BL** 🅿
☎ 01904 623088 Ⓕ 01904 625528
Ⓔ books@janetteray.co.uk
Ⓦ www.janetteray.co.uk

Est. 1995 *Stock size* Medium
Stock Architectural and decorative arts, rare and second-hand books, landscape design, gardens, specializing in 19thC Arts and Crafts, Art Deco, Modernism
Open Fri–Sat 10am–5.30pm other times by appointment
Fairs York PBFA, London PBFA
Services Book search, valuations

The Red House Antique Centre
Contact Mrs P Stephenson
Duncombe Place, York, North Yorkshire, YO1 2EF P
☎ 01904 637000 F 01904 637000
W www.redhouseyork.co.uk
Est. 1999
No. of dealers 60
Stock Datelined stock
Open Mon–Fri 9.30am–5.30pm Sat 9.30am–6pm Sun 10.30am–5.30pm July–Sep Mon–Fri 9.30am–7pm
Services Antiques and arts lecture programmes, café and restaurant, antiques parties, courier service

John Simpson
Contact Mr John Simpson
4 Forest Grove, Stockton Lane, York, North Yorkshire, YO3 0BL P
☎ 01904 424797
Est. 1984
Open By appointment
Sales General antiques
Frequency Quarterly
Catalogues Yes

J Smith (BNTA)
Contact Mr J Smith
47 Shambles, York, North Yorkshire, YO1 7LX
☎ 01904 654769 F 01904 677988
Est. 1963 *Stock size* Large
Stock Coins, stamps, medals
Open Mon–Sat 9am–4pm
Services Valuations

Ken Spelman (ABA, PBFA, ILAB)
Contact P Miller or A Fothergill
70 Micklegate, York, North Yorkshire, YO1 6LF P
☎ 01904 624414 F 01904 626276
E rarebooks@kenspelman.com
W www.kenspelman.com
Est. 1948 *Stock size* Large
Stock Antique, rare, second-hand books
Open Mon–Sat 9am–5.30pm
Fairs Olympia
Services Valuations, restoration, catalogues

Taikoo Books Ltd
Contact Mr David Chilton
46 Bootham, York, North Yorkshire, YO30 7BZ P
☎ 01904 641213
Est. 1978 *Stock size* Medium
Stock Books on Africa and the Orient
Open Mon–Fri 10am–5pm or by appointment

York Antiques Centre
Contact Mr S Revere
2a Lendal, York, North Yorkshire, YO1 8AA
☎ 01904 641445
Est. 1984 *Stock size* Large
No. of dealers 15
Stock General antiques
Open Mon–Sat 10am–5pm

York Vale Antiques (GADAR)
Contact Mr W Dougherty
Unit 6a, Victoria Farm, Water Lane, York, North Yorkshire, YO30 6PQ P
☎ 01904 690561 F 01904 690561
Est. 1995 *Stock size* Medium
Stock General antique furniture
Open Mon–Fri 9am–5.30pm Sat 9am–2pm
Fairs Newark
Services Restoration, repairs

SOUTH YORKSHIRE

BARLOW

Byethorpe Antiques
Contact John Gelsthorpe
Shippen Rural Business Centre, Church Farm, Barlow, South Yorkshire, S18 7TR P
☎ 0114 289 9111
W www.byethorpe.com
Est. 1977 *Stock size* Medium
Stock Traditional oak and mahogany furniture
Open Mon–Sat 9am–5.30pm

BARNSLEY

BBR Auctions
Contact Mr Alan Blakeman
Elsecar Heritage Centre, Barnsley, South Yorkshire, S74 8HJ P
☎ 01226 745156 F 01226 361561
E sales@bbrauctions.co.uk
W www.bbrauction.co.uk
Est. 1979
Open Mon–Fri 9am–4pm
Sales Antique bottles and pot lids 3 per annum. Antique advertising every 6 months. Doulton, Beswick and 20thC pottery 2 per annum. Kitchenware 2 per annum. Breweriana and pub jugs 2 per annum. All sales Sun 11am, viewing full week prior 9am–5pm
Catalogues Yes

Elsecar Antiques Centre
Contact Graham Wilson
The Elsecar Heritage Centre, Wath Road, Elsecar, Barnsley, South Yorkshire, S74 8HJ P
☎ 01226 744425 F 01226 361561
M 07712 834895
E sales@elsecarantiques.co.uk
W www.elsecarantiques.co.uk
Est. 2003 *Stock size* Large
No. of dealers 100
Stock Antiques, collectables, jewellery, dolls, furniture, pottery, glass, Chinese antiquities, collectors' books
Open Mon–Sun 10am–5pm

BENTLEY

Past & Present
Contact Mrs C Wiggett
224 Aston Road, Bentley, Doncaster, South Yorkshire, DN5 0EU P
☎ 01302 873557
Est. 2002 *Stock size* Large
Stock Furniture, bureaux, desks, pottery, pictures, lamps, light fittings, mirrors
Open Tues–Sun 10am–5pm

Phoenix Trading Company – South Yorkshire
Contact John A Hallam
127–129 Askern Road, Bentley, Doncaster, South Yorkshire, DN5 0JH P
☎ 01302 872547
M 07801 631072
Est. 1995 *Stock size* Large

YORKS & LINCS

Stock Georgian–Victorian furniture, shipping items, brass, copper, ceramics, silver, curios
Open Mon–Sat 9am–5pm
Fairs Newark, Harrogate
Services Restoration, repairs, valuations

CAWTHORNE

Cawthorne Antiques Centre
Contact Mr P Gates
2 Church Street, Cawthorne Village, Barnsley, South Yorkshire, S75 4HP P
☎ 01226 792237
Est. 1997 *Stock size* Large
No. of dealers 50
Stock Wide range of antique stock, collectables
Open Mon–Sat 10am–4pm Sun 10.30am–4.30pm closed Wed
Services Tea room

DONCASTER

Harrison Sales
Contact Mr F Harrison
3 Carr Hill, Balby, Doncaster, South Yorkshire, DN4 8BS P
☎ 01302 769400 F 01302 812958
Est. 1995
Open Mon–Sat 9.30am–5pm
Sales Antiques sale last Sat of the month 10am, vewing day prior noon–7pm Sat 8.30am–10am. Weekly general sale Sat 11am, viewing Fri 4–7pm Sat 9–11am
Catalogues Yes

FISHLAKE

Fishlake Antiques
Contact Fiona Trimingham
Vine Cottage, Hay Green Corner, Fishlake, South Yorkshire, DN7 5LA P
☎ 01302 841411
Est. 1979 *Stock size* Medium
Stock Country furniture, clocks
Open Sun 1–4pm or by appointment
Services Restoration

KILLAMARSH

Havenplan Ltd
Contact Mrs M Buckle
The Old Station, Station Road, Killamarsh, Sheffield, South Yorkshire, S21 1EN P
☎ 0114 248 9972
Ⓜ 07720 635889
Est. 1972 *Stock size* Large
Stock Mainly Victorian pine furniture, architectural items, panelling, doors, fireplaces, troughs, gates, lighting
Open Tues–Thurs Sat 10am–2pm
Services Prop hire

MALTBY

A J's Antiques
Contact Mr H Hall
14 Abbey Glen, Carr, Maltby, Rotherham, South Yorkshire, S66 8PS P
☎ 01709 816312
Ⓦ www.internet-antiques.com
Est. 1993 *Stock size* Large
Stock Furniture
Open By appointment
Fairs Swinderby, Newark

PENISTONE

Penistone Pine & Antiques
Contact Mr P W Lucas
Unit 2–3, Sheffield Road, Penistone, Sheffield, South Yorkshire, S36 6HG P
☎ 01226 370018
Est. 1985 *Stock size* Large
Stock Antique, original Victorian pine furniture
Open Mon–Sat 9am–5pm
Services Restoration, stripping

ROTHERHAM

Roger Appleyard Ltd (LAPADA)
Contact Roger Appleyard
Fitzwilliam Road, Eastwood Trading Estate, Rotherham, South Yorkshire, S65 1SL P
☎ 01709 367670 F 01709 829395
Ⓔ apple.antiques@dial.pipex.com
Est. 1971 *Stock size* Large
Stock Turn-of-the-century and shipping furniture
Trade only Yes
Open Mon–Fri 8am–5pm
Services Shipping

Foster Antiques Centre
Contact Sally Foster
Doncaster Road, Thrybergh, Rotherham, South Yorkshire, S65 4BE P
☎ 01709 850337
Est. 1997 *Stock size* Medium
No. of dealers 20
Stock General antiques
Open Mon–Sat 10am–4.30pm Sun 11am–5pm
Services Coffee shop, garden centre, craft shop

John Shaw Antiques Ltd
Contact Ms D Ellis
The Old Methodist Chapel, Broad Street, Parkgate, Rotherham, South Yorkshire, S62 6DL P
☎ 01709 522340 F 01709 528593
Est. 1969 *Stock size* Large
Stock Wide range of Victorian–Edwardian furniture, clocks, pictures, mirrors etc
Open Mon–Fri 9am–5pm Sat 9.30am–5pm
Services Valuations Sat 10am–noon

Wentworth Arts, Crafts & Antiques
Contact Jan Sweeting
The Old Builders Yard, Cortworth Lane, Wentworth, Rotherham, South Yorkshire, S62 7SB P
☎ 01729 822051
Ⓦ www.wentworthartscraftsandantiques.co.uk
Est. 1999 *Stock size* Large
No. of dealers 53
Stock General antiques, collectables
Open Mon–Sun 10am–5pm
Services Wheelchair access, coffee shop

SHEFFIELD

Abbeydale Antiques
Contact Mr D Barks
639 Abbeydale Road, Sheffield, South Yorkshire, S7 1TB P
☎ 0114 255 5646 F 0114 255 2555
Est. 1974 *Stock size* Large
Stock 1950s furniture
Open By appointment

Acorn Antiques
Contact Mr B Priest
298 Abbeydale Road, Sheffield, South Yorkshire, S7 1FL P
☎ 0114 255 5348 F 0114 225 5348
Ⓔ info@acornantique.co.uk

Est. 1988 *Stock size* Large
Stock General antiques, small furniture, collectables
Open Mon–Sat 10am–6pm

Antics
Contact Bronwen Stone
224 Abbeydale Road, Sheffield, South Yorkshire, S7 1FL
0114 255 1664
07957 861151
ja.fp@virgin.net
Est. 1997 *Stock size* Large
Stock Furniture, fireplaces, dressers, oil paintings, old French enamelled fires, soft furnishings, contemporary design
Open Mon–Sat 10am–5pm
Sun by appointment
Fairs Newark
Services Advice on furniture renovation, upholstery

Any Old Iron
Contact Miss Leigh Bell
10 Town End Road, Ecclesfield, Sheffield, South Yorkshire, S35 9YY
0114 257 7117
07971 522448
Est. 1996 *Stock size* Large
Stock Victorian cast-iron fireplaces
Open Thurs–Sun 10am–5pm
Fairs Swinderby, Newark
Services Restoration

Banners Collectors & Antiques Centre
Contact Miss S Bates
Banners Business Centre, Attercliffe Road, Sheffield, South Yorkshire, S9 3QS
0114 244 0742
Est. 1997 *Stock size* Large
No. of dealers 40
Stock Wide range of antiques, collectables, Wade, Beanies, McDonald's, clocks etc
Open Mon–Sat 10am–4.30pm
Sun 11am–4.30pm
Services Lists of goods wanted, deliveries, all collectables bought

Barmouth Court Antique Centre (LAPADA)
Contact Annette or Norman Salt
Barmouth Court, Barmouth Road, Sheffield, South Yorkshire, S7 2DH
0114 255 2711 0114 258 2672
07801 101363
Est. 1999 *Stock size* Large
No. of dealers 60
Stock Complete range of antiques, Art Deco, collectables
Open Mon–Sat 10am–5pm
Sun 11am–4pm
Services Valuations

Beech House
Contact Mr M Beech
361 Abbeydale Road, Sheffield, South Yorkshire, S7 1FS
0114 250 1004 0114 250 1004
beech.house@lineone.net
Est. 1996 *Stock size* Medium
Stock Rustic country pine furniture, cupboards, tables, dressers, chairs, fine art, kitchens
Open Mon–Sat 10am–5pm
closed Thurs or by appointment
Fairs Newark, Swinderby, Chatsworth

Chapel Antiques Centre
Contact Mrs Kate Bonshall
99 Broadfield Road, Sheffield, South Yorkshire, S8 0XH
0114 258 8288 0114 258 8288
info@antiquesinsheffield.com
www.antiquesinsheffield.com
Est. 1997 *Stock size* Medium
No. of dealers 20
Stock English and French antique furniture, mirrors, chandeliers, garden antiques, discounted upholstery fabrics
Open Mon–Sat 10am–5pm
Sun Bank Holidays 11am–5pm
Services Restoration, upholstery, French polishing, custom-made furniture from reclaimed wood, paint effecting, finding service, picture framing

Courthouse Antiques Centre
Contact Mrs S M Grayson
2–6 Town End Road, Ecclesfield, Sheffield, South Yorkshire, S35 9YY
0114 257 0641
thecourthouse@email.com
www.courthouseantiques.co.uk
Est. 1994 *Stock size* Large
No. of dealers 35
Stock Town and country furniture, jewellery, kitchenware, clocks, textiles, decorative items, French furniture, mirrors, lighting
Open Mon–Sat 10.30am–5pm
Sun 11.30am–5pm

The Door Stripping Company Ltd
Contact Mr B Findley
32 Main Road, Renishaw, Sheffield, South Yorkshire, S21 3UT
01246 435521
Est. 1984 *Stock size* Medium
Stock Pine furniture
Open Mon–Fri 9am–5pm
Sat–Sun 11am–2pm
Services Stripping

A E Dowse & Son (NAVA)
Contact Michael Dowse ANAVA
Cornwall Galleries, Scotland Street, Sheffield, South Yorkshire, S3 7DE
0114 272 5858 0114 249 0550
aedowse@aol.com
www.aedowseandson.com
Est. 1915
Open Mon–Fri 9.30am–4pm
Sales Antiques and collectables monthly. Fine art and antiques quarterly Wed 11am. Die-cast, tinplate and collectors' toys quarterly Sat 11am, viewing for Wed sales Mon 4–7pm Tues 10am–7pm Wed 9–11am, viewing for Sat sales Fri 2.30–7.30pm Sat 9.30–11am
Catalogues Yes

Earnshaw Antiques
Contact Mr Earnshaw
58 Abbeydale Road, Sheffield, South Yorkshire, S7 1FD
0114 258 1220
Est. 1990 *Stock size* Medium
Stock Furniture, chairs, wardrobes, fireplaces
Open Mon–Sat 10am–4pm
or by appointment

ELR Auctions Ltd
Contact Liz Dashper
The Nichols Building, Shalesmoor, Sheffield, South Yorkshire, S3 8UJ
0114 281 6161 0114 281 6162
elauctions@btconnect.com
www.elrauctions.com
Est. 1840
Open Mon–Fri 9am–5pm
Sales Specialist sales of coins, stamps, medals, postcards, cigarette cards, sporting memorabilia, football

programmes. Quarterly antique and fine art sales. Please see website for details
Frequency Frequent
Catalogues Yes

Filibuster & Booth Ltd
Contact Mr A Booth
158 Devonshire Street, Sheffield, South Yorkshire, S3 7SG
0114 275 2311
Stock Unusual, eclectic mixture of genuine things
Open Please telephone, times irregular
Services Valuations

Just Military Ltd
Contact Mr T Smith
701 Abbeydale Road, Sheffield, South Yorkshire, S7 2BE
0114 255 0536
Est. 1994 *Stock size* Large
Stock Militaria, WWI–Falklands, 1940s clothing, memorabilia, uniforms etc
Open Mon–Fri 10am–4pm
Sat 10am–5pm
Services Medal mounting, uniform hire

Langton's Antiques & Collectables
Contact Jill Mitchell
443 London Road, Sheffield, South Yorkshire, S2 4HJ
0114 258 1791
07815 754880
Est. 1998 *Stock size* Large
No. of dealers 70
Stock General antiques, specializing in the 1950s–70s
Open Mon–Sat 10am–5pm
Sun 10.30am–4.30pm
Services Café, disabled parking

Nichols Antique Centre
Contact Mr T Vickers
Nichols Building, Shalesmoor, Sheffield, South Yorkshire, S3 8UJ
0114 281 2811 0114 278 7578
Est. 1994 *Stock size* Large
No. of dealers 65
Stock Wide range of antique stock, specializing in Victorian furniture
Open Mon–Sun 10.30am–5pm
Services In-house auctioneers

Paraphernalia
Contact W K Keller
66–68 Abbeydale Road, Sheffield, South Yorkshire, S7 1FD
0114 255 0203
Est. 1969 *Stock size* Large
Stock Large range of antique stock including porcelain, glass, light fittings, brass, iron beds, chimney pots, kitchenware
Open Mon–Sat 9.30am–5pm closed Thurs

Renishaw Antique & Pine Centre
Contact Mr B Findley
32 Main Road, Sheffield, South Yorkshire, S21 3UT
01246 435521
Est. 1988 *Stock size* Medium
Stock Victorian–Edwardian and 1930s furniture, pine, architectural items
Open Mon–Fri 8am–1pm
Sun 11am–2pm

N P and A Salt Antiques (LAPADA)
Contact Mrs Annette Salt
Barmouth Court Antiques Centre, Barmouth Road, Sheffield, South Yorkshire, S7 2DH
0114 255 2711 0114 258 2672
07801 101363
Est. 2000 *Stock size* Large
Stock General antiques, collectables, furniture, jewellery, toys
Open Mon–Sat 10am–5pm
Sun 11am–4pm
Services Restoration

Sarah Scott Antiques (LAPADA)
Contact Sarah Scott
6 Hutcliffe Wood Road, Sheffield, South Yorkshire, S8 0EX
0114 236 3100
sarahscottantiques@tiscali.co.uk
www.antiquefurnishings.co.uk
Est. 1998 *Stock size* Medium
Stock Mirrors, lighting, Georgian–Edwardian town furniture
Open Tues–Sat 10am–5pm
Fairs Antiques for Everyone, Buxton Pavilions

Michael J Taylor Antiques
Contact Michael Taylor
Barmouth Court Antiques Centre, Barmouth Road, Sheffield, South Yorkshire, S7 2DH
01226 340595
07970 437248
Est. 1995 *Stock size* Large
Stock Georgian–Edwardian furniture, porcelain
Open Mon–Sat 10am–5pm
Sun 11am–4pm
Services Valuations

Tilleys Vintage Magazine Shop
Contact Mr A Tilley
281 Shoreham Street, Sheffield, South Yorkshire, S1 4SS
0114 275 2442 0114 275 2442
07939 066872
tilleys281@aol.com
www.tilleysmagazines.com
Est. 1978 *Stock size* Large
Stock Antique, rare, second-hand books, magazines
Open Mon 1.30–4.30pm
Tues–Fri 10am–4.30pm
Sat 10am–1.30pm 3.15–4.30pm

Paul Ward Antiques
Contact Paul or Christine Ward
Owl House, 8 Burnell Road, Sheffield, South Yorkshire, S6 2AX
0114 233 5980 0114 233 5980
07702 309000
Est. 1977 *Stock size* Large
Stock Country chairs
Trade only Yes
Open By appointment only

Y S F Books Ltd
Contact Mr R Eldridge or Mrs J Eldridge
365 Sharrowvale Road, Sheffield, South Yorkshire, S11 8ZG
0114 268 0687
ysfbooks@ysfbooks.com
www.ysfbooks.com
Est. 1986 *Stock size* Large
Stock General range of antiquarian, rare and second-hand books
Open Mon–Sat 9am–5pm

THURCROFT

Paul Beighton Auctioneers Ltd
Contact Miss S Lally
Woodhouse Green, Thurcroft,

Rotherham, South Yorkshire,
S66 9AQ P
☎ 01709 700005 F 01709 700244
E paul.beighton@btconnect.com
W www.paulbeightonauctioneers.co.uk
Est. 1987
Open Mon–Fri 9am–5pm
Sales Antiques, furniture and fine art Sun 11am, viewing Fri prior 11am–4pm Sun 9–11am. Quarterly fine art sales Sun 11am, see website
Frequency Fortnightly
Catalogues Yes

WENTWORTH

Holly Farm Antiques
Contact Mrs Linda Hardwick
✉ **Holly Farm, Harley, Wentworth, Rotherham, South Yorkshire, S62 7UD** P
☎ 01226 744077
Est. 1989 *Stock size* Medium
Stock Porcelain, Coalport, Worcester, Rockingham, silver, silver plate, jewellery, mirrors, furniture, lamps
Open Sat Sun 10am–5pm weekdays by appointment
Services Valuations

WEST YORKSHIRE

ABERFORD

Aberford Country Furniture
Contact J W H Long
✉ **Hicklam House, Aberford, Leeds, West Yorkshire, LS25 3DP** P
☎ 0113 281 3209 F 0113 281 3121
M 07712 657867
E johnwhlong@aol.com
W www.aberfordpine.co.uk
Est. 1973 *Stock size* Medium
Stock Oak and pine country furniture
Open Tues–Sat 9am–5.30pm Sun 10am–5.30pm

BAILDON

The Baildon Furniture Co Ltd
Contact Mr R Parker
✉ **Spring Mills, Otley Road, Baildon, Bradford, West Yorkshire, BD17 6AD** P
☎ 01274 414345 F 01274 414345
E baildonfurniture@aol.com
Est. 1974 *Stock size* Large
Stock General antique furniture
Open Mon–Fri 9.30am–5pm Sat 10.30am–5pm
Services Valuations, restoration

Browgate Antiques
Contact Mrs D Shaw
✉ **13 Browgate, Baildon, Shipley, West Yorkshire, BD17 6BP** P
☎ 01274 597494
Est. 1995 *Stock size* Medium
Stock Georgian–Victorian furniture, clocks, porcelain
Open Mon–Sun 10.30am–5pm closed Thurs
Services Valuations

BATLEY

Tansu
Contact Mr N Hall or Mr C Battye
✉ **Red Brick Mill, 218 Bradford Road, Batley Carr, Batley, West Yorkshire, WF17 6JF** P
☎ 01924 460044/459441
F 01924 462844
E tansu@tansu.co.uk
W www.tansu.co.uk
Est. 1992 *Stock size* Large
Stock Chinese, Japanese antique furniture, silk kimonos, dolls, scrolls, prints
Open Mon–Sat 9.30am–5.30pm Sun 11am–5pm
Fairs Ideal Homes
Services Storage, restoration, valuations, customer pick-up service, airports and train stations

Tansu
Contact Mr N Hall or Mr C Battye
✉ **211 Bradford Road, Batley Carr, Batley, West Yorkshire, WF17 6JF** P
☎ 01924 459441 F 01924 462844
E tansu@tansu.co.uk
W www.tansu.co.uk
Est. 1992 *Stock size* Large
Stock Chinese, Japanese antique furniture, silk kimonos, dolls, scrolls, prints
Open By appointment please telephone
Fairs Ideal Homes
Services Storage, restoration, valuations, customer pick-up service, airports and train stations

Village Antiques
Contact Mr W Brown
✉ **Jessops Mill Complex, 10 Station Road, Bottom Soothill Lane, Batley, West Yorkshire, WF17 5SU** P
☎ 01924 478002
E angie@jessops10.freeserve.co.uk
Est. 1996 *Stock size* Large
No. of dealers 28
Stock General antiques, collectables, music memorabilia
Open Mon–Sun 10am–4pm

Dale Wood & Co
Contact Mr Dale Wood
✉ **20 Station Road, Batley, West Yorkshire, WF17 5SU** P
☎ 01924 479439 F 01924 472291
M 07711 645236
E dalewoodandco@hotmail.com
Est. 1989
Open Mon–Thurs 9am–5pm Fri 9am–4pm
Sales General antiques and general furnishings
Frequency Fortnightly
Catalogues Yes

BRADFORD

Cottingly Antiques
Contact Mr P Nobbs
✉ **286 Keighley Road, Bradford, West Yorkshire, BD9 4LH** P
☎ 01274 545829
Est. 1979 *Stock size* Medium
Stock General antiques, pine furniture
Open Tues–Sat 9am–4.30pm
Services Restoration

de Rome
Contact Mr S Le Blancq
✉ **12 New John Street, Bradford, West Yorkshire, BD1 2QY**
☎ 01274 734116 F 01274 729970
Est. 1948
Open Mon–Fri 9am–5.15pm
Sales General antiques
Frequency Periodic
Catalogues Yes

Windle & Co
Contact Mr A Windle
✉ **535 Great Horton Road, Bradford, West Yorkshire, BD7 4EG** P
☎ 01274 572998 F 01274 572998

YORKS & LINCS

Est. 1971
Open Mon–Thurs 9.15am–5.30pm Fri 9.15am–noon
Sales General antiques Wed 6.30pm, viewing Wed from 10am
Frequency Weekly

BRAMHAM

⊞ Priory Furnishing
Contact Mr or Mrs J Furniss
✉ **The Biggin', Bramham Park, Bramham, West Yorkshire, LS2 3 6LR** 🅿
☎ 01937 843259 Ⓕ 01937 843259
Ⓔ john_furniss100@hotmail.com
Est. 1992 *Stock size* Large
Stock 17th–18thC oak, mahogany and walnut furniture
Open Tues–Sun 10am–5pm
Services Valuations

BURLEY IN WHARFEDALE

⊞ Beacon Antiques
Contact L Cousins
✉ **128 Main Street, Burley in Wharfedale, West Yorkshire, LS29 7JP** 🅿
☎ 01943 864772
Ⓜ 07887 812858
Ⓔ les@beacon-antiques.co.uk
Ⓦ beacon-antiques.co.uk
Est. 1994 *Stock size* Medium
Stock Porcelain, silver, small Georgian–Edwardian furniture
Open Wed–Fri 10.30am–4.30pm Sat 9.30am–12.30pm
Fairs Harrogate, Stafford

BURTON SALMON

⊞ Old Hall Antiques
Contact Mr J Fenteman
✉ **21 Main Street, Burton Salmon, Leeds, West Yorkshire, LS25 5JS** 🅿
☎ 01977 607778
Ⓔ jfenteman@aol.com
Est. 1998 *Stock size* Large
Stock Antique oak and country furniture
Open Tues–Sun 10am–5pm

CROSS HILLS

⊞ Heathcote Antiques (BACA Award Winner 2004)
Contact Mr Michael Webster
✉ **Skipton Road Junction Crossroads, Cross Hills, Keighley, West Yorkshire, BD20 7DS** 🅿
☎ 01535 635250 Ⓕ 01535 637205
Ⓜ 07836 259640
Ⓔ heathcote1@btopenworld.com
Est. 1974 *Stock size* Large
Stock General antiques, original English unstripped pine, pottery, porcelain
Open Wed–Sat 10am–5.30pm Sun 12.30–4.30pm
Services Most

DENBY DALE

⊞ Worlds Apart
Contact Mrs Sharon Dawson
✉ **Unit 6a, Springfield Mill, Norman Road, Denby Dale, Huddersfield, West Yorkshire, HD8 8TH** 🅿
☎ 01484 866713
Ⓜ 07801 349960
Ⓔ shaz@chris216.fsnet.co.uk
Est. 1995 *Stock size* Large
Stock Antiques, collectables
Open Tues–Sat 10am–5pm Sun noon–5pm

DEWSBURY

⊞ Collectors Corner
Contact Mr Tranter
✉ **246 Lees Hall Road, Dewsbury, West Yorkshire, WF12 9HF** 🅿
☎ 01924 464111 Ⓕ 01924 464111
Est. 1995 *Stock size* Medium
Stock General collectables
Open Mon–Fri 9.30am–3.30pm Sat 9am–noon
Fairs Newark, Leeds
Services Valuations

FEATHERSTONE

⊞ A645 Trading Post
Contact Mr G Thomas
✉ **Chapel Works, Wakefield Road, Featherstone, Pontefract, West Yorkshire, WF7 5HL** 🅿
☎ 01977 695255
Est. 1982 *Stock size* Large
Stock Furniture, collectables, books, die-cast toys, ceramics
Open Mon–Sat 10am–5pm Sun 11am–5pm closed Wed

GREETLAND

⊞ West Vale Trading Post
Contact Mr T Gresty
✉ **61–63 Saddleworth Road, Greetland, West Vale, Halifax, West Yorkshire, HX4 8AG** 🅿
☎ 01422 311630 Ⓕ 01422 311630
Est. 1989 *Stock size* Large
Stock General antiques, second-hand items
Open Wed–Sat 9am–5pm
Fairs Newark

HALIFAX

⊞ Art Deco Originals/Muir Hewitt
Contact Mr M Hewitt
✉ **Halifax Antique Centre, Queens Road Mills, Gibbet Street, Halifax, West Yorkshire, HX1 4LR** 🅿
☎ 01422 347377 Ⓕ 01422 347377
Ⓔ muir.hewitt@virgin.net
Ⓦ www.muirhewitt.com
Est. 1982 *Stock size* Large
Stock Art Deco ceramics, decorative arts, furniture, lighting, mirrors, chrome
Open Tues–Fri 10.30am–4.30pm Sat 10.30am–5pm closed Bank Holidays please telephone for seasonal time changes
Fairs Chester, Leeds Art Deco fairs
Services Valuations

⊞ Collectors Old Toy Shop
Contact Simon Haley
✉ **89 Northgate, Halifax, West Yorkshire, HX1 1XF** 🅿
☎ 01422 822148/360434
Ⓔ collectorsoldtoy@aol.com
Est. 1983 *Stock size* Medium
Stock Dinky, Corgi, die-casts, tin-plate toys, railways, money boxes
Open Tues Wed Fri Sat 10.30am–4.30pm
Fairs Sandown Park, Harrogate International
Services Insurance valuations

⌂ Halifax Antique Centre
Contact Mr M Carroll
✉ **Queens Road, Halifax, West Yorkshire, HX1 4LR** 🅿
☎ 01422 366657 Ⓕ 01422 369293
Ⓦ www.halifaxantiques.co.uk
Est. 1981 *Stock size* Large
No. of dealers 30
Stock French and English furniture, Art Deco, costume, kitchenware, collectables, Italian chandeliers
Open Tues–Sat 10am–4.30pm
Services Valuations, restoration, café

⊞ Holmfirth Antiques
Contact Ken Priestley
✉ **Halifax,
West Yorkshire,
HX1** P
☎ 01484 686854
Ⓜ 07973 533478
ⓔ ken@fonograf.com
Ⓦ www.fonograf.com
Est. 1988 *Stock size* Medium
Stock Mechanical music, gramophones, phonographs
Open By appointment
Services Valuations, restoration, mail order

HAWORTH

⊞ Bingley Antiques
Contact J B or J Poole
✉ **Springfield Farm Estate, Flappit, Haworth, Keighley, West Yorkshire, BD21 5PT** P
☎ 01535 646666 ⓕ 01535 646666
ⓔ john@bingleyantiques.com
Ⓦ www.bingleyantiques.com
Est. 1969 *Stock size* Large
Stock General antiques, see website
Open Thurs Fri Sat 9am–5pm
Services Valuations

⊞ Yorkshire Relics
Contact Colin Ruff
✉ **11 Main Street, Haworth, West Yorkshire, BD22 8DA** P
☎ 01535 642218/662093
ⓕ 01535 642218
Ⓜ 07808 757851
Est. 1987 *Stock size* Large
Stock Antiquarian and collectable books, records, general collectables
Open Mon–Fri noon–5pm
Sat Sun 11am–5pm

HEBDEN BRIDGE

⊞ Cornucopia
Contact Mrs C Nassor
✉ **13 West End, Hebden Bridge, West Yorkshire, HX7 8JP** P
☎ 01422 844497
Est. 1974 *Stock size* Medium
Stock General antiques
Open Thurs–Fri Sun noon–5pm
Sat 11am–5pm
Fairs Newark, Nottinghamshire

⊞ G J Saville (BADA)
Contact Graham Saville
✉ **Foster Clough, Hebden Bridge, West Yorkshire, HX7 5QZ** P
☎ 01422 882808 ⓕ 01422 882808
Ⓜ 07801 071710
ⓔ g.j.saville@btinternet.com
Est. 1968 *Stock size* Large
Stock 1750–1830 caricatures, caricature reference books
Open By appointment
Fairs Olympia, BADA
Services Valuations

HOLMFIRTH

⊞ Old Friendship Antiques
Contact Mr C J Dobson
✉ **77 Dunford Road, Holmfirth, Huddersfield, West Yorkshire, HD7 1DT** P
☎ 01484 682129
Est. 1984 *Stock size* Large
Stock Antique furniture, old pine, clocks
Open Mon–Fri 9.30am–5.30pm
Sat 9am–4pm Sun 2–4pm
Fairs Newark
Services Pine stripping

William Sykes & Son
Contact Mr R Dixon
✉ **Sude Hill, New Mill, Holmfirth, Huddersfield, West Yorkshire, HD9 3JH** P
☎ 01484 683543 ⓕ 01484 683543
Ⓜ 07799 507898
ⓔ info@wmsykes.co.uk
Ⓦ www.wmsykes.com
Est. 1866
Open Mon–Fri 9am–5.15pm
Sat 9am–2pm Sun 11am–2pm
Sales General antiques every 3rd Friday

⊞ Upperbridge Antiques
Contact Mr I Ridings
✉ **9 Huddersfield Road, Holmfirth, Huddersfield, West Yorkshire, HD7 1JR**
☎ 01484 687200
Est. 1987 *Stock size* Medium
Stock General antiques
Open Wed-Sat 1–5pm
Sun 2–5pm
Fairs Newark, Swinderby

HONLEY

⊞ Holme Valley Warehouse
Contact Paula Moss or Michael Silkstone
✉ **11 Westgate, Honley, Holmfirth, Huddersfield, West Yorkshire, HD9 1AA** P
☎ 01484 667915 ⓕ 01484 667915
Est. 1995 *Stock size* Large
Stock Pine furniture, quirky items, artwork
Open Mon–Sun 10am–5pm
Services Restoration, stripping

⊞ Honley Antiques & Pine
Contact Mr P Brown
✉ **2 Woodhead Road, Honley, Holmfirth, West Yorkshire, HD9 6PX** P
☎ 01484 660806
ⓔ honleyantiques@onetel.net.uk
Est. 1997 *Stock size* Large
Stock Georgian–modern furniture, silver, longcase clocks, paintings, pine, collectables, jewellery
Open Tues–Sat 10am–5pm
Sun 11am–4pm
Services Valuations

HUDDERSFIELD

⊞ Christopher J L Dawes
Contact Mr C Dawes
✉ **26 Lidget Street, Lindley, Huddersfield, West Yorkshire, HD3 3JP** P
☎ 01484 649515
Est. 1999 *Stock size* Small
Stock General antiques, porcelain, glass, silver
Open Tues–Sat 10am–5pm
closed Wed
Fairs Mytholmroyd, West Yorkshire, Newark

⊞ Huddersfield Picture Framing Co.
Contact Miss P Ward
✉ **Cloth Hall Street, Huddersfield, West Yorkshire, HD1 2EG** P
☎ 01484 546075
Est. 1979 *Stock size* Medium
Stock Paintings, swept frames, ovals, circles, mouldings etc
Open Mon Tues Thurs Fri
9am–5pm Wed 9am–1pm Sat
9am–4pm
Services Restoration, framing

Serendipity Antiques
Contact Mr Franco
1 Bridge Street, Huddersfield, West Yorkshire, HD4 6EL
01484 428223
07967 919292
samfranco59@hotmail.com
Est. 1988 *Stock size* Medium
Stock Situated in a Georgian coach house, selling general antiques, pine, porcelain, Victorian–Edwardian furniture
Open Wed–Sat 10.30am–5pm
Services Valuations, restoration

ILKLEY

Coopers of Ilkley (LAPADA)
Contact Charles Cooper
46–50 Leeds Road, Ilkley, West Yorkshire, LS29 8EQ
01943 608020 F 01943 604321
enquiries@coopersantiques ilkley.co.uk
www.coopersantiquesilkley.co.uk
Stock size Medium
Stock Period and Victorian furniture
Open Mon–Fri 9am–1pm 2–5.30pm Sat 9am–5.30pm
Services Restoration

Andrew Hartley Fine Arts (ISVA, SOFAA)
Contact Mr A D Hartley, ARICS
Victoria Hall, Little Lane, Ilkley, West Yorkshire, LS29 8EA
01943 816363 F 01943 817610
info@andrewhartleyfinearts.co.uk
www.andrewhartleyfinearts.co.uk
Est. 1906
Open Mon–Fri 9am–5.30pm Sat 9am–12.30pm
Sales Victorian and later every Wed 10am, viewing Tues prior 9am–7pm. Antique and fine art sale every two months Wed Thurs 10am, viewing Sat prior 9.30am–12.30pm Mon Tues prior 9.30am–4.30pm day of sale 9–10am
Catalogues Yes

KEIGHLEY

Revival
Contact Peter Pryimuk
104–106 South Street, Keighley, West Yorkshire, BD21 1EH
01535 606837
Est. 1987 *Stock size* Medium
Stock General antiques, architectural items, pine, bric-a-brac
Open Mon–Sat 10am–5pm telephone call advisable

LEEDS

Abbey Auctions
Contact John Midgely
11 Morris Lane, Kirkstall, Leeds, West Yorkshire, LS5 3JT
0113 275 8787
Open Mon–Fri 8am–5pm Sat 8am–noon
Sales General antiques sales Tues 10am
Frequency Weekly
Catalogues No

Aladdin's Cave
Contact Roberta Spencer
19 Queen's Arcade, Leeds, West Yorkshire, LS1 6LF
0113 245 70903
robertajspencer@hotmail.com
Est. 1985 *Stock size* Large
Stock Antique jewellery
Open Mon–Sat 10am–5pm
Services Valuations, repairs

Antique Boutique
Contact E Viol
56–59 Merrion Centre Superstore, Merrion Centre, Leeds, West Yorkshire, LS2 8LY
0113 244 4174
Est. 1981 *Stock size* Large
Stock Fancy dress, retro clothes, wigs, theatrical accessories for sale and hire
Open Mon–Sat 10am–5pm Wed 10am–2pm

Aquarius Antiques
Contact Peter McGlade
Abbey Mills, Abbey Road, Leeds, West Yorkshire, LS5 3HP
0113 278 9216
Est. 1979 *Stock size* Medium
Stock General antiques, Georgian–Victorian furniture
Open Mon–Sat 9am–5pm
Services Repairs, restoration

Bonhams (BACA Award Winner 2003)
17a East Parade, Leeds, West Yorkshire, LS1 2BH
0113 244 8011 F 0113 242 9875
leeds@bonhams.com
www.bonhams.com
Sales Regional Saleroom. Frequent sales. Regular house and attic sales across the country; contact London offices for further details. Free auction valuations; insurance and probate valuations

Headrow Antiques
Contact Sally Hurrell
Level 3, The Headrow Shopping Centre, The Headrow, Leeds, West Yorkshire, LS1 6JE
0113 245 5344
www.headrowantiques.com
Est. 1992 *Stock size* Large
No. of dealers 17
Stock General antiques
Open Mon–Sat 10am–5pm Nov Dec Sun 11am–4pm

Swiss Cottage Furniture
Contact Mr J Howorth
85 Westfield Crescent, Burley, Leeds, West Yorkshire, LS3 1DJ
0113 242 9994
www.swisscottageantiques.com
Est. 1987 *Stock size* Large
Stock General antiques, salvage yard
Open Mon–Sat 10am–5pm closed Tues
Fairs Newark

Toot-Sweet
Contact Lily Bennett
1st Floor, 39 Call Lane, Leeds, West Yorkshire, LS1 7BT
0113 244 6133
leeds@toot-sweet.co.uk
Est. 1980 *Stock size* Medium
Stock Wind instruments
Open Mon–Sat 9.30am–6pm
Services Instrument and bow repairs, valuations, consultations, export

Turner Violins
Contact Lily Bennett
1st Floor, 39 Call Lane, Leeds, West Yorkshire,

LS1 7BT P
☎ 0113 244 6133
E leeds@turnerviolins.co.uk
W www.turnerviolins.co.uk
Est. 1980
Stock Violins, double basses, violas, cellos, bows
Open Mon–Sat 10am–6pm
Services Instrument and bow repairs, valuations, consultations, export

Woodstock Antiques
Contact Mr R J Link
✉ **134 Woodhouse Street, Leeds, West Yorkshire, LS6 2JN**
☎ 0113 246 1296
Est. 1990 *Stock size* Medium
Stock General antiques
Open Mon–Sat 10am–5pm
Fairs Newark

Works of Iron
Contact Mr G Higgins
✉ **Beaver Works, 36 Whitehouse Street, Leeds, West Yorkshire, LS10 1AD** P
☎ 0113 234 0555 F 0113 234 2555
Est. 1985 *Stock size* Large
Stock Antique beds
Open Wed–Sat 11am–5pm
Services Valuations, restoration

Year Dot
Contact Mr Adrian Glithro
✉ **41 The Headrow, Leeds, West Yorkshire, LS1 6PU** P
☎ 0113 246 0860
Est. 1977 *Stock size* Medium
Stock General antiques, jewellery
Open Mon–Sat 9.30am–5pm

LEPTON

K L M & Co
Contact Mr K L Millington
✉ **Wakefield Road, Lepton, West Yorkshire, HD8 0EL** P
☎ 01484 607763 F 01484 607763
M 07860 671547
Est. 1981 *Stock size* Large
Stock Antiques, 1940s furniture
Open Mon–Sat 10.30am–5pm

MENSTON

J Hanlon Antiques
Contact Mrs J Hanlon
✉ **101 Bradford Road, Menston, Ilkley, West Yorkshire, LS29 6BU** P
☎ 01943 877634
Est. 1974 *Stock size* Medium
Stock Small collectables, textiles, jewellery, silver
Open Thurs–Sat 2.30–5pm
Fairs Newark

Park Antiques
Contact Brian O'Connell
✉ **2 North View, Menston, Ilkley, West Yorkshire, LS29 6JU** P
☎ 01943 872392
M 07811 034123
W www.parkantiques.com
Est. 1980 *Stock size* Medium
Stock Early Georgian–Edwardian paintings, ceramics, clocks, furniture
Open Wed–Fri 10.30am–4.30pm Sat 9.30am–5.30pm Sun noon–5pm
Services Restoration

OSSETT

John Walsh & Co. (NAVA)
Contact Mr J Walsh
✉ **Ashfield House Auction Rooms, Illingworth Street, Ossett, West Yorkshire, WF5 8AI** P
☎ 01924 264030 F 01924 267758
M 07976 241587
E auctions@john-walsh.co.uk
W www.john-walsh.co.uk
Est. 1989
Open Mon–Fri 9am–5.30pm
Sales General antiques
Frequency 8 per annum
Catalogues Yes

OTLEY

Otley Antiques Centre
Contact Andrew Monkman
✉ **6 Bondgate, Otley, West Yorkshire, LS21 3AB** P
☎ 01943 850342
Est. 1988 *Stock size* Small
No. of dealers 15
Stock General antiques
Open Mon–Sat 10am–5pm closed Wed

PUDSEY

Geary Antiques
Contact Mr J A Geary
✉ **114 Richardshaw Lane, Pudsey, Leeds, West Yorkshire, LS28 6BN** P
☎ 0113 256 4122
M 07802 441245
E jag@t-nlbi.demon.co.uk
Est. 1933 *Stock size* Large
Stock General antique English furniture
Open Mon–Sat 10am–5.30pm Sun noon–4pm
Services Restoration, interior design, furnishing fabrics, wallpapers

SALTAIRE

Mick Burt (Antique Pine)
Contact Andrew Draper
✉ **The Victoria Centre, 3–4 Victoria Road, Saltaire, Shipley, West Yorkshire, BD18 3LA** P
☎ 01274 530611 F 01274 533722
Est. 1994 *Stock size* Medium
Stock Restored antique pine furniture
Open Mon–Sun 10.30am–5pm
Services Restoration

Harwood Antiques
Contact Mr R Harwood
✉ **The Victoria Centre, 3–4 Victoria Road, Saltaire, Shipley, West Yorkshire, BD18 3LA** P
☎ 01274 874138
M 07885 137573
Est. 1974 *Stock size* Medium
Stock Antique furniture, clocks
Open Wed–Sun 10.30am–5.30pm
Services Valuations

John Lewis
✉ **The Victoria Centre, 3–4 Victoria Road, Saltaire, Shipley, West Yorkshire, BD18 3LA** P
☎ 01274 533722 F 01274 533722
Est. 1988 *Stock size* Large
Stock Burmantoft's art pottery
Open Mon–Sun 10.30am–5.30pm
Fairs NEC, Alexandra Palace

Swan Antiques
Contact Mrs B Harwood
✉ **The Victoria Centre, 3–4 Victoria Road, Saltaire, Shipley, West Yorkshire, BD18 3LA** P
☎ 01274 533722
Est. 1998 *Stock size* Small
Stock General antiques, country furniture
Open Wed–Sun 10.30am–5.30pm

The Victoria Centre
Contact Mr Andrew Draper
3–4 Victoria Road, Saltaire, Shipley, West Yorkshire, BD18 3LA P
☎ 01274 533722/530611
F 01274 533722
E info@victoriacentre.co.uk
W www.victoriacentre.co.uk
Est. 1994 *Stock size* Large
No. of dealers 40
Stock General antiques, furniture, fine art and collectables, oil paintings, clocks
Open Mon–Sun 10.30am–5pm
Services Valuations, restoration

SOWERBY BRIDGE

Talking Point Antiques
Contact Mr Paul Austwick
66 West Street, Sowerby Bridge, West Yorkshire, HX6 3AP P
☎ 01422 834126
E tpagrams@aol.com
Est. 1985
Stock Gramophones, other mechanical antiques
Open Thurs–Sat 10.30am–5.30pm or by appointment
Fairs NEC Vintage Communications Fair, Blackpool Vintage Technology Fair

WAKEFIELD

The Old Vicarage Bookshop
Contact Mr J Longfellow
24 Zetland Street, Wakefield, West Yorkshire, WF1 1QT
☎ 01924 200400/366444
M 07976 737684
E oldvic@dsl.pipex.co
Est. 1987 *Stock size* Large
Stock Antiquarian, rare and second-hand books
Open Daily 10.30am–5pm closed Wed Sun
Services Valuations

WOODLESFORD

ABC Antiques
Contact Colin McCarthy
Trafalgar Works, Bowers Row, Leeds Road, Woodlesford, Leeds, West Yorkshire, LS26 8AN P
☎ 0113 287 5955 F 0113 287 5966
Est. 1995 *Stock size* Large
No. of dealers 30
Stock General antiques
Open Mon–Fri 9am–5pm Sat Sun 11am–5pm
Services Valuations, restoration

LINCOLNSHIRE

ALFORD

Town and Country Antiques Centres
Contact Louise Chatterton
7–8 West Street, Alford, Lincolnshire, LN13 9DG P
☎ 01507 466953
M 07771 718514
Est. 1999 *Stock size* Large
No. of dealers 24
Stock Antiques both small and large
Open Mon–Sun 10am–4.30pm

ALLINGTON

Garth Vincent Antique Arms and Armour (LAPADA)
Contact Garth Vincent
The Old Manor House, Allington, Nr Grantham, Lincolnshire, NG32 2DH P
☎ 01400 281358 F 01400 282658
M 077835 352151
E garthvincent@aolcom
W www.guns.uk.com
Est. 1980 *Stock size* Large
Stock International guns, swords, helmets, reproduction arms and armour
Open By appointment only
Fairs Birmingham and London Arms Fairs
Services Valuations

AYLESBY

Robin Fowler Period Clocks (LAPADA)
Contact Mr R Fowler
Washingdales, Washingdales Lane, Aylesby, Grimsby, Lincolnshire, DN37 7LH P
☎ 01472 751335 F 01472 751335
M 07949 141891
E periodclocks@washingdales.fsnet.co.uk
Est. 1968 *Stock size* Large
Stock Antique clocks, barometers, scientific instruments
Open By appointment
Fairs LAPADA, Bailey, Galloway
Services Valuations, restoration

BELTON

Richard Ellory Furniture
Contact Richard Ellory
Unit 5, Sandtoft Industrial Estate, Sandtoft Road, Belton, Lincolnshire, DN9 1PN P
☎ 01427 874064 F 01427 875055
E richard@ellory.fsnet.co.uk
Est. 1981 *Stock size* Medium
Stock English pine
Open Mon–Sat 9am–5pm Sun 10am–4pm

BOSTON

Antique Workshop Ltd
Contact Mr Murphy
4a Pulvertoft Lane, Boston, Lincolnshire, PE21 8TA P
☎ 01205 368692 F 01205 368692
Est. 1967 *Stock size* Large
Stock General antique furniture
Open Mon–Sat 8am–5pm
Services Restoration

Junktion Antiques
Contact Mr Jack Rundle
The Old Railway Station, Main Road, New Bolingbroke, Boston, Lincolnshire, PE22 7LN P
☎ 01205 480068 F 01205 480132
M 07836 345491
Est. 1983 *Stock size* Large
Stock Early toys, advertising, bygones, architectural and mechanical antiques 1880–1960
Open Wed Thurs Sat 10am–5pm
Fairs Newark, Swinderby

Pennyfarthing Antiques
Contact Mr Hale
1 Red Lion Street, Boston, Lincolnshire, PE21 6NY P
☎ 01205 362988
W www.pennyfarthingantiques.net
Est. 2000 *Stock size* Medium
Stock General antiques
Open Tues Wed Fri Sat 10am–4.30pm

BOURNE

Antique and Second Hand Traders
Contact Mr Alan Thompson

✉ **39 West Street, Bourne, Lincolnshire, PE10 9N3** 🅿
☎ 01778 394700 Ⓕ 01778 394700
Ⓜ 07885 694299
Est. 1969 ***Stock size*** Large
Stock Antique and second-hand furniture
Open Mon–Sat 10am–5pm closed Wed Thurs
Fairs Newark, Ardingly
Services House clearance, removals

BRIGG

DDM Auction Rooms
Contact Robert Horner
✉ **Old Courts Road, Brigg, North Lincolnshire, DN20 8JD** 🅿
☎ 0845 230 4202 Ⓕ 01652 650085
Ⓜ 07970 126311
Ⓔ auctions@ddmauctionrooms.co.uk
Ⓦ www.ddmauctionrooms.co.uk
Est. 1889
Open Mon–Fri 9am–5.30pm auction Sat
Sales Antiques and fine art sale every 6 weeks Tues Wed 9.30am. Fortnightly auction of contemporary and antique Sat 9.30am, ring for details, viewing day prior 2–7pm, day of auction from 8.30am
Catalogues Yes

CLEETHORPES

Cleethorpes Collectables
Contact Mr A Dalton
✉ **34 Alexandra Road, Cleethorpes, Lincolnshire, DN35 8LF** 🅿
☎ 01472 291952 Ⓕ 01472 291952
Est. 1999 ***Stock size*** Large
Stock General antiques, collectables, curios
Open Mon–Sun 10am–5pm
Services Valuations

Yesterdays Antiques
Contact Mr N Bishop
✉ **86 Grimsby Road, Cleethorpes, Lincolnshire, DN35 7DP** 🅿
☎ 01472 343020
Ⓔ n.bishop2@ntlworld.com
Ⓦ yesterdaysantiques.org.uk
Est. 1987 ***Stock size*** Large
Stock General antiques, fireplaces a speciality
Open Mon–Sat 9am–5pm or by appointment
Services Valuations, restoration, polishing

GAINSBOROUGH

Drewery and Wheeldon
Contact Mr M G Tomson
✉ **124 Trinity Street, Gainsborough, Lincolnshire, DN21 1JD** 🅿
☎ 01427 616118 Ⓕ 01427 811070
Ⓔ drewery.wheeldon@btconnect.com
Ⓦ www.dreweryandwheeldon.co.uk
Est. 1879
Open Mon–Fri 9am–5.30pm Sat 9am–12.30pm
Sales General antiques sales, telephone for details
Catalogues Yes

Pilgrims Antiques Centre
Contact Mr M Wallis
✉ **66a Church Street, Gainsborough, Lincolnshire, DN21 2JR** 🅿
☎ 01427 810897 Ⓕ 01427 810897
Est. 1985 ***Stock size*** Large
No. of dealers 8
Stock General antiques
Open Tues–Sat 10am–4.30pm closed Wed

R M Antiques
Contact Mr R Maclennan
✉ **4a Tennyson Street, Gainsborough, Lincolnshire, DN21 2GJ** 🅿
☎ 01427 810624 Ⓕ 01427 810624
Est. 1984 ***Stock size*** Large
Stock General antiques
Trade only Yes
Open Mon–Sat 9am–3pm
Services Export

GRANTHAM

Golding Young (NAVA)
Contact Mr Colin Young RICS
✉ **The Grantham Auction Rooms, Old Wharf Road, Grantham, Lincolnshire, NG31 7AA** 🅿
☎ 01476 565118 Ⓕ 01476 561475
Ⓔ enquiries@goldingyoung.com
Ⓦ www.goldingyoung.com
Est. 1900
Open Mon–Fri 9am–5pm closed 1–2pm
Sales Fortnightly general antiques sale, bi-monthly antique and fine art sale
Catalogues Yes

Grantham Clocks
Contact M R Conder
✉ **30 Lodge Way, Grantham, Lincolnshire, NE31 8DD** 🅿
☎ 01476 561784
Est. 1987 ***Stock size*** Medium
Stock Clocks
Open By appointment
Services Valuations

Grantham Furniture Emporium
Contact K or J E Hamilton
✉ **4–6 Wharf Road, Grantham, Lincolnshire, NG31 6BA** 🅿
☎ 01476 562967
Ⓜ 07710 483865
Est. 1976 ***Stock size*** Large
Stock Victorian–Edwardian and 1920s shipping furniture,
Open Tues–Sun 11am–4pm closed Wed

Harlequin Antiques
Contact Tony or Sandra Marshall
✉ **46 Swinegate, Grantham, Lincolnshire, NG31 6RL**
☎ 01476 563346
Est. 1995 ***Stock size*** Medium
Stock General antiques
Open Mon–Sat 9am–5pm
Services Valuations

Notions Antiques Centre
Contact Mr or Mrs L Checkley
✉ **1–2a Market Place, Grantham, Lincolnshire, NG31 6LQ** 🅿
☎ 01476 563603
Ⓜ 07736 677978
Ⓔ scheckley@fsbdial.co.uk
Est. 1984 ***Stock size*** Large
No. of dealers 70
Stock General antiques
Open Mon–Fri 10am–5pm Sat 9.30am–5pm Sun 11am–4pm

Marilyn Swain Auctions (SOFAA)
Contact John Munroe
✉ **The Old Barracks, Sandon Road, Grantham, Lincolnshire, NG31 9AS** 🅿
☎ 01476 568861 Ⓕ 01476 576100
Est. 1991
Open Mon–Fri 9am–5.30pm
Sales General antiques
Frequency Fortnightly
Catalogues Yes

Marcus Wilkinson Jewellers & Antiques (BHI, AHS, NAWCC)
Contact Mr Marcus Wilkinson
The Time House, 1 Blue Court, Guildhall Street, Grantham, Lincolnshire, NG31 6NJ P
☎ 01476 560400 F 01476 568791
M 07966 154590
E info@thetimehouse.com
W www.thetimehouse.com
Est. 1935 *Stock size* Small
Stock Clocks, watches, jewellery
Open Mon–Sat 9.30am–4.30pm
Fairs San Francisco Fall Antique Show, Los Angeles Spring Antique Show, London House and Garden
Services Valuations, restoration, repairs

GRIMSBY

Bell Antiques
Contact Mr Victor Hawkey
68 Harold Street, Grimsby, Lincolnshire, DN32 7NQ P
☎ 01472 695110
Est. 1964 *Stock size* Large
Stock Clocks, music boxes, barometers
Open By appointment
Services Valuations

Jackson Green & Preston
Contact Mr D Arliss
New Cartergate, Grimsby, Lincolnshire, DN31 1RB P
☎ 01472 311115 F 01472 311114
E auction@jacksongreenpreston.co.uk
W www.jacksongreenpreston.co.uk
Est. 1920
Open By appointment
Sales General household and antiques sale Fri 10.30am, viewing Thurs 2.30–7pm at 41–45 Duncombe Street, Grimsby, DN32 7SG
Frequency Weekly
Catalogues No

HEMSWELL

Advena Antiques & Fairs
Contact Alan White
Building II, Hemswell Antique Centre, Caenby Corner Estate, Hemswell Cliff, Gainsborough, Lincolnshire, DN21 5TJ P
☎ 01427 668389 F 01427 668935
M 07713 150510
E advena.antiques@ntlworld.com
Est. 1992 *Stock size* Large
Stock Antique silver, jewellery, silver plate
Open Mon–Sun 10am–5pm
Services Valuations, repairs

Astra House Antique Centre
Contact Mr M J Frith
Old RAF Hemswell, Nr Caenby Corner, Hemswell Cliff, Gainsborough, Lincolnshire, DN21 5TL P
☎ 01427 668312 F 01427 668312
E astraantiqueshemswell@btinternet.com
Est. 1992 *Stock size* Large
No. of dealers 50+
Stock General antiques and collectables including second-hand items
Open Mon–Sun 10am–5pm
Services Shipping

Barleycorn Antiques
Contact Shirley or John Wheat
Hemswell Antiques Centre, Caenby Corner Estate, Hemswell Cliff, Gainsborough, Lincolnshire, DN21 5TW P
☎ 01427 668789
M 07850 673965
W www.barleycorn-antiques.co.uk
Est. 1982
Stock Furniture, brass, lighting, ceramics, clocks,
Open Mon–Sun 10am–5pm

Guardroom Antiques
Contact Mr C Lambert
RAF Station Hemswell, Gainsborough, Lincolnshire, DN21 5TU P
☎ 01427 667113
Est. 1993 *Stock size* Large
No. of dealers 50
Stock General antiques including Victorian and Georgian furniture
Open Mon–Sun 10am–5pm

Hemswell Antique Centres
Contact Robert Miller
Caenby Corner Estate, Hemswell Cliff, Gainsborough, Lincolnshire, DN21 5TJ P
☎ 01427 668389 F 01427 668935
E info@hemswell-antiques.com
W www.hemswell-antiques.com
Est. 1989 *Stock size* Large
No. of dealers 300
Stock General antiques
Open Daily 10am–5pm
Services Furniture restoration

Trevor Moss Antiques
Contact Mr T Moss
Building 1, Hemswell Antique Centre, Caenby Corner Estate, Hemswell, Gainsborough, Lincolnshire, DN21 5TW P
☎ 01427 668389 F 01427 668935
Est. 1985 *Stock size* Large
Stock General antiques
Open Mon–Sun 10am–5pm
Fairs Newark, Swinderby
Services Restoration

Second Time Around
Contact Mr Geoff Powis
Hemswell Antique Centre, Caenby Corner Estate, Hemswell Cliff, Gainsborough, Lincolnshire, DN21 5TJ P
☎ 01522 543167 or 01427 668389
M 07860 679495
Est. 1984 *Stock size* Large
Stock Period longcase and bracket clocks, other clocks 17th–19thC and up to 1940s
Open Mon–Sun 10am–5pm
Services Valuations, restoration

Smithson Antiques
Contact Skip or Janie Smithson
Hemswell Antique Centre, Caenby Corner Estate, Hemswell Cliff, Lincolnshire, DN21 5TJ P
☎ 01754 810265
M 07831 399180
Est. 1984 *Stock size* Medium
Stock Victorian kitchen and dairy antiques
Open Daily 10am–5pm

HOLBEACH

P J Cassidy
Contact Mr P Cassidy
1 Boston Road, Holbeach, Spalding, Lincolnshire, PE12 7LR P
☎ 01406 426322
E bookscass@aol.com
Est. 1974 *Stock size* Large
Stock Antiquarian books, maps, prints, Lincolnshire topography
Open Mon–Sat 10am–6pm
Services Framing

HOLTON LE CLAY

C A Johnson
Contact Mr C A Johnson
32 Pinfold Lane, Holton Le Clay, Grimsby, Lincolnshire, DN36 5DH
01472 822406 F 01472 822406
Est. 1979 *Stock size* Medium
Stock General antiques
Open By appointment
Fairs Newark
Services Valuations

HORNCASTLE

G Baker Antiques
Contact Geoffrey or Christine Baker
16 South Street, Horncastle, Lincolnshire, LN9 6DX
01507 526553
M 07767 216264
Est. 1973 *Stock size* Medium
Stock Period and general furniture
Open Mon–Sat 9am–5pm or by appointment
Fairs Newark, Swinderby
Services Restoration

Clare Boam
Contact Clare Boam
22–38 North Street, Horncastle, Lincolnshire, LN9 5DX
01507 522381 F 01507 524202
E clareboam@btconnect.com
W www.greatexpectations horncastle.co.uk
Est. 1976 *Stock size* Large
Stock General antiques and collectables
Open Mon–Sat 9am–5pm Sun 2–4.30pm

Drill Hall Antiques Centre
Contact Mrs V Ginn
The Old Drill Hall, South Street, Horncastle, Lincolnshire, LN9 6EF
01507 525370
Est. 2004 *Stock size* Large
No. of dealers 30
Stock High quality antiques pre 1949, furniture, pictures, porcelain, silver, jewellery, lighting
Open Mon–Sat 10am–4.30pm Sun 1–4pm Bank Holidays 11am–4pm

Great Expectations
Contact Miss M C Boam
37–43 East Street, Horncastle, Lincolnshire, LN9 6AZ
01507 524202 F 01507 524202
E clareboam@btconnect.com
W www.greatexpectations horncastle.co.uk
Est. 1996 *Stock size* Large
No. of dealers 80
Stock General antiques
Open Mon–Sat 9am–5pm Sun 1–4.30pm and Bank Holidays

Horncastle Antiques Centre
Contact Mrs P Sims or Mr D Sims
26 Bridge Street, Horncastle, Lincolnshire, LN9 5HZ
01507 527777 F 01507 527777
E horncastleantiques@hotmail.com
W www.horncastleantiquescentre.com
Est. 1976 *Stock size* Large
No. of dealers over 60
Stock General antiques and collectables
Open Mon–Sat 10am–5pm Sun 1–5pm
Services Valuations, restoration, shipping

Lindsay Court Architectural
Contact Mr Lindsay White
Lindsay Court, Horncastle, Lincolnshire, LN9 5DH
01507 527794
M 07768 396117
E horncastlestone@aol.com
Est. 1987 *Stock size* Large
Stock Architectural antiques, stoneware, garden statuary, salvage, reclaims
Open Tues Thurs–Sat 9.30am–5pm or by appointment
Fairs Newark
Services Export, container packing

Alan Read
Contact Mr A Read, Liveryman of The Worshipful Company of Furniture Makers
60 & 62 West Street, Horncastle, Lincolnshire, LN9 5AD
01507 524324/525548
F 01507 525548
M 07778 873838
Est. 1981 *Stock size* Large
Stock 17th–18thC English furniture and decorative items
Open Tues–Sat 10am–4.30pm closed Wed or by appointment 7 days a week
Services Valuations, bespoke replicas made

Seaview Antiques
Contact Mr M Chalk
Stanhope Road, Horncastle, Lincolnshire, LN9 5DG
01507 524524
E tracey@seaviewantiques.co.uk
W www.seaviewantiques.co.uk
Est. 1972 *Stock size* Large
Stock General antiques
Open Mon–Sat 9am–5pm
Fairs Newark

Laurence Shaw Antiques
Contact Laurence Shaw
77 East Street, Horncastle, Lincolnshire, LN9 6AA
01507 527638
Est. 1971 *Stock size* Medium
Stock A complete range of general antiques
Open By appointment

KIRTON

Kirton Antiques (LAPADA)
Contact Alan Marshall
3 High Street, Kirton, Boston, Lincolnshire, PE20 1DR
01205 722595 F 01205 722895
M 07860 531600
E alan.marshall@modcomp.net
Est. 1973 *Stock size* Large
Stock Wholesale and retailers of antiques and related items
Open Mon–Fri 8.30am–5pm Sat 8.30am–noon or by appointment
Services Valuations, property hire

LINCOLN

Eric A Bird Jewellers (BHI)
Contact Mr S Thompson
1 St Mary's Street, Lincoln, Lincolnshire, LN5 7EQ
01522 520977 F 01522 560586
W www.eric-a-bird.co.uk
Est. 1959 *Stock size* Medium
Stock Antique and modern

clocks, pocket watches
Open Tues–Sat 9am–5pm
Services Valuations, restoration and repairs

C & K Dring
Contact Mr C Dring
111 High Street, Lincoln, Lincolnshire, LN5 7PY P
01522 540733
Est. 1977 *Stock size* Medium
Stock Victorian and Edwardian inlaid furniture, clocks, music boxes, tinplate toys
Open Mon–Sat 10am–5pm closed Wed
Fairs Newark, Swinderby
Services Valuations, restoration

David J Hansord and Son (BADA, BACA Award Winner 2001)
Contact John Hansord
6–7 Castle Hill, Lincoln, Lincolnshire, LN1 3AA P
01522 530044 F 01522 530044
M 07831 183511
Est. 1972 *Stock size* Large
Stock 18thC English furniture, works of art and objects
Open Mon–Sat 10am–5pm
Fairs Olympia
Services Valuations, restoration

Harlequin Gallery (PBFA)
Contact Mrs Anna Cockram
20–22 Steep Hill, Lincoln, Lincolnshire, LN2 1LT P
01522 522589
E harlequin@acockram.fsbusiness.co.uk
Est. 1964 *Stock size* Large
Stock Antiquarian and second-hand books, maps, prints
Open Mon–Sat 10.30am–5.45pm Wed 11am–4.30pm
Services Valuations, antique globe restoration

Dorrian Lamberts
Contact Mr R Lambert
64 & 65 Steep Hill, Lincoln, Lincolnshire, LN2 1LR P
01522 545916
Est. 1984 *Stock size* Medium
Stock General antiques
Open Mon–Sat 10am–5pm
Fairs Newark, Swinderby
Services Valuations

Thomas Mawer & Son Ltd
Contact Mr J C Slingsby
Dunston House, Portland Street, Lincoln, Lincolnshire, LN5 7NN P
01522 524984
E auctions@thos-mawer.co.uk
W www.thos-mawer.co.uk
Est. 1864
Open Mon–Thurs 9am–5.30pm Fri 9am–4pm Sat 9am–noon
Sales Victorian and later first Sat of every month, quarterly antiques, regular specialist sales
Catalogues Yes

LONG SUTTON

Chapel Emporium
Contact Miss B Hill
London Road, Long Sutton, Spalding, Lincolnshire, PE12 9EA P
01406 364808
E barbara.hill4@btopenworld.com
Est. 1983 *Stock size* Large
Stock General antiques
Open Tues Sun 10am–5pm
Services Restoration

Long Sutton Antique and Craft Centre
Contact Ms G Shergold
72–74 London Road, Long Sutton, Spalding, Lincolnshire, PE12 9EB P
01406 362991
Est. 1998 *Stock size* Large
No. of dealers 64
Stock General antiques, collectables and craft centre
Open Mon–Sat 10.30am–5.30pm Sun 11am–4pm

LOUTH

The Old Maltings Antique Centre
Contact Mr Norman Coffey
Aswell Street, Louth, Lincolnshire, LN11 9HP P
01507 600366
M 07885 536607
E margaret@eastcoast88.freeserve.co.uk
Est. 1979 *Stock size* Large
No. of dealers 20
Stock General antiques, collectables, Victorian–Edwardian furniture
Open Mon–Sat 10am–4.30pm
Services Valuations, restoration

John Taylor's
Contact Mrs A Laverack
The Wool Mart, Kidgate, Louth, Lincolnshire, LN11 9EZ
01507 611107 F 01507 601280
E enquiries@johntaylors.com
W www.johntaylors.com
Est. 1869
Open Mon–Fri 9am–5.15pm Sat 9am–2pm
Sales General antiques
Frequency Monthly
Catalogues Yes

MARKET DEEPING

Market Deeping Antiques & Craft Centre
Contact John Strutt
50–56 High Street, Market Deeping, Lincolnshire, PE6 8EB P
01778 380238
Est. 1995 *Stock size* Large
No. of dealers 70
Stock General antiques, collectables, crafts
Open Mon–Sat 10am–5pm Sun 11am–5pm

Portland House Antiques
Contact Mr Cree
23 Church Street, Market Deeping, Lincolnshire, PE6 8AN P
01778 347129
Est. 1971 *Stock size* Large
Stock 18thC–early 19thC furniture, pictures and clocks
Open Sat 10am–4pm or by appointment
Services Valuations

MARKET RASEN

M H Beeforth (LAPADA)
Contact Michael or Megan Beeforth
Market Rasen, Lincolnshire, LN8 P
01673 858229 F 01673 858279
E info@antique-silverware.com
W www.antique-silverware.com
Est. 1980 *Stock size* Medium
Stock 18th–20thC silver
Open By appointment
Fairs NEC, Galloway Fairs, Cooper Fairs

NETTLEHAM

Autumn Leaves
Contact Mrs Susan Young
Unit 2 Co-op Building, 19 The Green, Nettleham, Lincoln, Lincolnshire, LN2 2NR P
☎ 01522 750779
Ⓔ leaves@onetel.net.uk
Ⓦ www.abebooks.com/home/autumn_leaves
Est. 1997 *Stock size* Medium
Stock Second-hand books on all subjects
Open Tues–Thurs 9.15am–4.30pm Fri 9.15am–5pm Sat 9.15am–12.30pm
Services Book search

Homme de Quimper
Contact Mr S Toogood
Hillstead, 11 Church Street, Nettleham, Lincoln, Lincolnshire, LN2 2PD P
☎ 01522 753753
Ⓜ 07831 773622
Ⓔ steve.toogood@ntlworld.com
Ⓦ www.hommedequimper.co.uk
Est. 1996 *Stock size* Large
Stock Antique French faïence pottery, 19thC Quimper, Malicome, Desevres, 18thC La Rochelle, Nevers, Rouen, Moustiers, etc
Open Mon–Sun 9am–6pm
Services Valuations, restoration

Juke Box World
Contact Mr S Toogood
Hillstead, 11 Church Street, Nettleham, Lincoln, Lincolnshire, LN2 2PD P
☎ 01522 753753
Ⓔ steve.toogood@ntlworld.com
Est. 1985 *Stock size* Medium
Stock 20thC juke boxes
Open Mon–Sun 9am–6pm
Fairs Ascot Racecourse, Copthorne
Services Valuations, restoration

SCUNTHORPE

Canter & Francis (NAEA)
Contact Mr S J Francis, NAEA
41 Oswald Road, Scunthorpe, Lincolnshire, DN15 7PN P
☎ 01724 858855 Ⓕ 01724 858855
Est. 1947
Open Mon–Fri 9am–5pm
Sales General antiques
Frequency 2–3 a year
Catalogues No

SPALDING

R Longstaff & Co
Contact Mr J A Smith
5 New Road, Spalding, Lincolnshire, PE11 1BS P
☎ 01775 766766 Ⓕ 01775 762289
Ⓔ admin@longstaff.com
Ⓦ www.longstaff.com
Est. 1770
Open Mon–Fri 9am–6pm Sat 9am–3pm Sun 11am–3pm
Sales General antiques, house clearance
Frequency Bi-monthly
Catalogues No

M & M Antiques
Contact M Dawson
17a The Crescent, Spalding, Lincolnshire, PE11 1AF P
☎ 01775 766125
Ⓜ 07904 157657
Est. 1990 *Stock size* Large
Stock General antiques 1850–1950
Open Mon–Sat 10am–5pm
Fairs Loughborough Art Deco

Munton & Russell (ISVA)
Contact Mr James Smith
16 Sheep Market, Spalding, Lincolnshire, PE11 1BE P
☎ 01775 722475 Ⓕ 01775 769958
Ⓦ www.muntonandrussell.co.uk
Est. 1964
Open Mon–Fri 9am–6pm
Sales General antiques
Frequency Periodic
Catalogues No

Penman Clockcare (BWCMG)
Contact Mr M Strutt
Unit 4–5, Pied Calf Yard, Sheepmarket, Spalding, Lincolnshire, PE11 1BE P
☎ 01775 714900
Ⓜ 07940 911167
Ⓔ strutt@clara.net
Ⓦ www.antique-clockrepairs.co.uk
Est. 1997 *Stock size* Medium
Stock Antique clocks, watches and jewellery
Open Mon–Fri 9am–5pm Sat 9am–4pm
Services Restoration, full repair service, home calls

Spalding Antiques
Contact Mr John Mumford
1 Abbey Path, Spalding, Lincolnshire, PE11 1AY
☎ 01775 713185
Est. 1987 *Stock size* Medium
Stock General antiques, clocks, watches
Open Mon–Sat 10am–5pm

STAMFORD

Batemans Auctioneers & Valuers
Contact Miss Kate Bateman
Broad Street, Stamford, Lincolnshire, PE9 1PX P
☎ 01780 766466 Ⓕ 01780 765071
Ⓔ info@batemans-auctions.co.uk
Ⓦ www.batemans-auctions.co.uk
Open Mon–Fri 10am–5pm
Sales Fine arts, antiques, collectables and general household sales Sat 10.30am, viewing Thurs 10am–5pm Fri 10am–7pm
Frequency Monthly
Catalogues Yes

The Forge Antiques & Collectables
Contact Tessa Easton
5 St Mary Street, Stamford, Lincolnshire, PE9 2DE P
☎ 01780 767874
Ⓜ 07763 334703
Ⓔ theforgeantiques@fsmail.net
Est. 2000 *Stock size* Large
Stock Furniture, clocks, silver, jewellery, china, glass, textiles
Open Mon–Sat 9.30am–5pm Sun and Bank Holidays 10am–4pm
Fairs Swinderby
Services Search service

Hunters Interiors (Stamford) Ltd
Contact Jill Hunter
9a St Mary's Hill, Stamford, Lincolnshire, PE9 2DP P
☎ 01780 757946 Ⓕ 01780 757946
Ⓜ 07976 796969
Ⓔ huntersinteriors@btopenworld.com
Ⓦ www.huntersinteriorsofstamford.co.uk
Est. 2000 *Stock size* Small
Stock Furniture, glass, china, ornaments, tapestries, other soft furnishings, 18thC mirrors,
Open Mon–Sat 9am–5.30pm
Services Restoration

Robert Johnson Coin Co
Contact Mr R Johnson
PO Box 181, Stamford, Lincolnshire, PE9 4XA
01778 561529
Est. 1971 *Stock size* Medium
Stock Greek, Roman, English, hammered and milled coins
Open By appointment only
Services Valuations

Robert Loomes Clock Restoration (BWCG MBHI)
Contact Mr R Loomes
3 St Leonards Street, Stamford, Lincolnshire, PE9 2HU
01780 481319
www.dialrestorer.co.uk
Est. 1987 *Stock size* Small
Stock Clocks
Open Mon–Fri 9am–5pm or by appointment Sat 10am–4pm
Services Restoration

Graham Pickett Antiques
Contact Mrs H Pickett
7 High Steet, St Martins, Stamford, Lincolnshire, PE9 2LF
01780 481064
07710 936948
graham@pickettantiques.demon.co.uk
www.pickettantiques.demon.co.uk
Est. 1987 *Stock size* Medium
Stock English and French provincial furniture, beds, silver
Open Mon–Sat 10am–5.30pm Sun by appointment
Fairs Newark

St Georges Antiques
Contact Mr G Burns
1 St Georges Square, Stamford, Lincolnshire, PE9 2BN
01780 754117
07779 528713
Est. 1974 *Stock size* Large
Stock General antiques, furniture
Trade only Yes
Open Mon–Fri 9am–1pm 2–4.30pm

St Martins Antiques Centre
Contact Peter Light or Tina Higgins
23a High Street, Stamford, Lincolnshire, PE9 2LF
01780 481158 01780 481158
Est. 1993 *Stock size* Large
No. of dealers 65+
Stock General antiques, furniture, porcelain, clocks, jewellery, silver, prints, books, textiles, lighting, fireplaces, copper, brass, ephemera
Open Mon–Sat 10am–5pm Sun 10.30am–5pm
Services Shipping, wheelchairs provided

St Mary's Books & Prints
Contact Mr Tyers
9 St Mary's Hill, Stamford, Lincolnshire, PE9 2DP
01780 763033 01780 763033
info@stmarysbookscom
www.stmarysbooks.com
Est. 1971 *Stock size* Large
Stock Antiquarian, rare and second-hand books, Wisden's *Cricketers Almanac* a speciality, literature, modern first editions, field sports, leather bindings
Open Mon–Sun 8am–6.30pm
Services Book binding, free valuations, restoration and book search

St Paul's Street Bookshop (PBFA)
Contact Mr J Blessett
7 St Paul's Street, Stamford, Lincolnshire, PE9 2BE
01780 482748 01778 38053
jimblessett@aol.com
Est. 1978 *Stock size* Medium
Stock Antiquarian, rare and second-hand books, specializing in motoring books
Open Mon–Sat 10am–5pm closed Wed
Services Valuations

Staniland Booksellers (PBFA)
Contact Mr B J Valentine-Ketchum
4–5 St Georges Street, Stamford, Lincolnshire, PE9 2BJ
01780 755800 01780 755800
stanilandbooksellers@btinternet.com
Est. 1972 *Stock size* Large
Stock Antiquarian, library sets and bindings, rare and second-hand scholarly books, architecture, applied art, art, philosophy, music history, literature, natural history
Open Mon–Sat 10am–1pm 2–5pm
Fairs London Book Fairs
Services Valuations, probate and insurance valuations

Andrew Thomas
Contact Mr A Thomas
Old Granary, 10 North Street, Stamford, Lincolnshire, PE9 1EH
01780 762236 01780 762236
Est. 1969 *Stock size* Large
Stock General antiques and antique painted furniture
Open Mon–Sat 9am–6pm

Undercover Books
Contact Mr T Dobson
30 Scotgate, Stamford, Lincolnshire, PE9 2YQ
01780 480989 01780 763963
undercoverbooks@btinternet.com
www.ukbookworld.com/members/undercover
Est. 1989 *Stock size* Large
Stock Antiquarian, rare and second-hand books, law enforcement a speciality
Open Tues–Sat 10am–5pm

Vaughan Antiques (LAPADA)
Contact Mr Barry Vaughan
45 Broad Street, Stamford, Lincolnshire, PE9 1PX
01780 765888 01778 342053
07712 657414
vaughanantiques@aol.com
Est. 1994 *Stock size* Large
Stock English furniture, clocks, decorative items, 17th–19thC furniture a speciality
Open Mon–Sat 10am–5pm
Fairs NEC, LAPADA

STICKNEY

B & B Antiques
Main Road, Stickney, Boston, Lincolnshire, PE22 8AD
01205 480204
Stock General antiques
Open By appointment

SUTTON BRIDGE

Old Barn Antiques
Contact Mr Steve Jackson
48–50 Bridge Road,

Sutton Bridge, Spalding, Lincolnshire, PE12 9UA 🅿
☎ 01406 359123/350435 (warehouse) Ⓕ 01406 359158
Ⓜ 07956 677228
Ⓔ oldbarnants@aol.com
Est. 1984 ***Stock size*** Large
Stock Victorian, Edwardian and 1920s furniture
Trade only Yes
Open Mon–Fri 9am–5pm Sat 10am–5pm Sun 11am–4pm
Fairs Newark
Services Containers packed

SWINDERBY

Graham the Hat
Contact Graham Rodwell
✉ **Newark Road, Swinderby, Lincolnshire, LN6 9HN**
☎ 01493 650217 Ⓕ 01493 650217
Ⓜ 07899 892337
Ⓔ graham@grahamthehat.com
Ⓦ www.grahamthehat.com
Est. 1997 ***Stock size*** Large
Stock Collectables
Open By appointment
Fairs Swinderby, Ardingly
Services Trade prices on request

TATTERSHALL

Wayside Antiques
Contact Mr G Ball
✉ **10 Market Place, Tattershall, Lincolnshire, LN4 4LQ** 🅿
☎ 01526 342436
Est. 1972 ***Stock size*** Medium
Stock General antiques
Open By appointment any time

WAINFLEET

Ann-Tiques
Contact Mrs M Bark
✉ **40 High Street, Wainfleet, Lincolnshire, PE24 43H** 🅿
☎ 01754 880770
Est. 1981 ***Stock size*** Medium
Stock General antiques
Open Tues–Sat 10am–12.30pm 1.30–4pm closed Thurs
Fairs Swinderby
Services Repair of clocks and jewellery

Naylor's Auctions
Contact Ian Naylor
✉ **20 St John's Street, Wainfleet, Skegness, Lincolnshire, PE24 4DJ** 🅿
☎ 01754 881210 Ⓕ 01522 6980006
Ⓜ 07932 749334
Est. 1979
Open By appointment
Sales General antiques held weekly Bargate Green, Boston, last Sat every month Butterwick Village Hall 10am, viewing day prior 4–7pm and from 8am day of sale
Catalogues No

WALESBY

Lincolnshire Antiques and Fine Art
Contact Mr N J Rhodes
✉ **White House Farm, Walesby, Market Rasen, Lincolnshire, LN8 3UW** 🅿
☎ 01673 838278
Ⓜ 07950 271898
Est. 1979 ***Stock size*** Medium
Stock Quality 17th–19thC oil paintings and furniture
Open By appointment only

WOODHALL SPA

M & J Antiques
Contact Mr J Goodyear
✉ **Tattershall Road, Woodhall Spa, Lincolnshire, LN10 6QJ** 🅿
☎ 01526 352140
Est. 1990 ***Stock size*** Medium
Stock General antiques
Open Flexible

Underwood Hall Antiques
Contact G Underwood
✉ **5 The Broadway, Woodhall Spa, Lincolnshire, LN10 6ST** 🅿
☎ 01526 353815
Est. 1974 ***Stock size*** Medium
Stock Small furniture, 19th–20thC pottery, porcelain, silver, jewellery, postcards
Open Mon–Sat 10.30am–4.30pm Sun 1–4pm or by appointment
Fairs Newark
Services Valuations

VOC Antiques (LAPADA)
Contact David Leyland
✉ **27 Witham Road, Woodhall Spa, Lincolnshire, LN10 6RW** 🅿
☎ 01526 352753 Ⓕ 01526 352753
Ⓔ djleyland@tinyworld.co.uk
Est. 1975 ***Stock size*** Medium
Stock Georgian–Victorian furniture, brass, copper, general antiques
Open Mon–Sat 9.30am–5.30pm Sun 2–5pm
Services Valuations, restoration

NORTH EAST

CO DURHAM

BARNARD CASTLE

⊞ Edward Barrington-Doulby
Contact Mike or Fiona
✉ **23 The Bank,**
Barnard Castle, Co Durham,
DL12 8PH 🅿
☎ 01833 630500
Ⓜ 07817 287204
Ⓔ m.venus@ntlworld.com
Est. 1994 *Stock size* Medium
Stock Furniture, smalls, hardware, door furniture, ironmongery, kitchenware
Open Tues–Sat 11am–5pm Sun 1–5pm

⊞ James Hardy Antiques Ltd
Contact Alan or Amanda Hardy
✉ **12 The Bank,**
Barnard Castle, Co Durham,
DL12 8PQ 🅿
☎ 01833 695135 Ⓕ 01833 695135
Ⓜ 07710 162003
Ⓔ alan@jameshardyantiques.co.uk
Ⓦ www.jameshardyantiques.co.uk
Est. 1993
Stock 17th–19thC oak, mahogany period furniture, silver both for the serious collector and for special occasion gifts
Open 10am–5pm closed Thurs Sun
Fairs Harrogate
Services Restoration of silver and furniture

⊞ Kingsley & Co
Contact David Harper
✉ **Springwood Cottage,**
Barnard Castle, Co Durham,
DL12 9DD 🅿
☎ 01833 650551 Ⓕ 01833 650551
Ⓜ 07711 639035
Ⓔ sales@kingsleysofas.co.uk
Ⓦ www.kingsleysofas.co.uk
Est. 2000 *Stock size* Medium
Stock Furniture, smalls, Asian works of art, restored antique upholstery, hand-made sofas
Open Mon–Sat 10.30am–5.30pm
Services Valuations, restoration, upholstery, renovation

⊞ Robson's Antiques
Contact Mr or Mrs Robson
✉ **36 The Bank,**
Barnard Castle,
Co Durham,
DL12 8PN 🅿
☎ 01833 690157 Ⓕ 01833 638700
Ⓜ 07977 146584
Ⓔ dale.hunter.robson@virgin.net
Ⓦ www.robsonsantiques.co.uk
Est. 1975 *Stock size* Large
Stock Fireplaces, Durham quilts, glass, silver, cutlery, general antiques
Open Mon–Fri 10am–5.30pm Sat 10am–6pm Sun 1.30–5pm
Fairs Birmingham Glass Fair, Newark, Manchester Textile Fair, NEC
Services Fireplace restoration and fitting

BISHOP AUCKLAND

⊞ Eden House Antiques
Contact Chris Metcalfe
✉ **10 Staindrop Road,**
West Auckland,
Bishop Auckland,
Co Durham,
DL14 9JX 🅿
☎ 01388 833013
Ⓔ chrismetcalfe@aol.com
Ⓦ www.antiques.co.uk
Est. 1977 *Stock size* Medium
Stock Furniture, clocks, china, pottery
Open Mon–Sun 10am–6pm
Services Valuations, restoration

G H Edkins and Son
Contact Denis Edkins
✉ **Auckland Auction Rooms,**
58 Kingsway,
Bishop Auckland,
Co Durham,
DL14 7JF 🅿
☎ 01388 603095 Ⓕ 01388 661239
Ⓜ 07860 321312
Est. 1907
Open Mon–Thurs 9.30am–4.30pm Fri 9.30am–4pm
Sales General antiques household sale every Thurs, viewing Wed 9.30am–noon 2–5pm
Catalogues No

CONSETT

⊞ Harry Raine
Contact Mr N C Raine
✉ **Kelvinside House,**
91 Villa Real Road,
Consett, Co Durham,
DH8 6BL 🅿
☎ 01207 503935
Ⓜ 07758 838328
Est. 1965 *Stock size* Medium
Stock General antiques
Trade only Yes
Open By appointment only

Rutherford Interiors
Contact Karen Rutherford
80 Medomsley Road, Consett, Co Durham, DH8 5HS
01207 500200 01207 500220
Est. 2004 *Stock size* Medium
Stock English and European furniture, antiques, decorative items
Open Mon–Sat 9am–5pm closed Wed

Westend Antiques & Jewellery
Contact L Newman
63 Middle Street, Consett, Co Durham, DH8 5QG
01207 582228 01207 582228
westendantiques@consett.btopenworld.com
Est. 1996 *Stock size* Large
Stock General antiques, jewellery, Roman, medieval artefacts, bric-a-brac
Open Mon–Sat 9am–5pm
Fairs Newark
Services Valuations, restoration, clock, watch and pottery repairs

DARLINGTON

The Quest Antiques
Contact Stephen King
417 North Road, Darlington, Co Durham, DL1 3BN
01325 286156
steveatquest@aol.com
Est. 1981 *Stock size* Medium
Stock Antiques, collectables 1950s–60s
Open Mon–Sat 1–4pm
Services Valuations

Tango Curios
3a Houndgate, Darlington, Co Durham, DL1 5RL
01325 465768
07977 979770
Est. 1986 *Stock size* Large
Stock 20thC decorative arts, glass, ceramics, metalware, pictures
Open Fri Sat 5pm 10am–5pm
Fairs Antiques for Everyone, Loughborough Art Deco Antiques Fair
Services Valuations

DURHAM

Capercaillie Antiques
Contact David Rogers
25–27 High Street North, Langley Moor, Durham, Co Durham, DH7 8JG
0191 378015
07930 251116
Est. 1964 *Stock size* Large
Stock Antique furniture
Open Fri 1–4pm Sat 10am–4pm or by appointment

Finley's Finds
Contact Mr B Finley
23 Flambard Road, Durham, Co Durham, DH1 5HY
0191 384 1643
Est. 1995
Stock Furniture, china, jewellery
Open Mon–Fri 9am–5pm
Fairs Newark, Swinderby
Services Valuations, house clearance

Old & Gold
Contact Pam Tracey
87b Elvet Bridge, Durham, Co Durham, DH1 3AG
0191 386 0728
07831 362252
Est. 1989 *Stock size* Medium
Stock General antiques
Open Mon–Sun 10am–5pm
Fairs Newark
Services Jewellery repairs

HARTLEPOOL

Spring Garden Furniture & Antiques
Contact Deborah Herring
124 Stockton Road, Hartlepool, Co Durham, TS25 5AB
01429 266716 01429 266716
Est. 1998 *Stock size* Small
Stock Victorian–Edwardian furniture, collectables
Open Mon–Sat 10am–5pm Wed 1.30–5pm
Services Stripping

PETERLEE

Emeralds Antiques
Contact Alan Brown
1a Seaside Lane, Easington Colliery, Peterlee, Co Durham, SR8 1PF
0191 523 7320
Est. 1998 *Stock size* Large
Stock General antiques
Open Mon–Sat 9.30am–5pm
Services Valuations, restoration, house clearance

ST HELEN AUCKLAND

Something Different
Contact Mr Peter Reeves or Mr Melvin Holmes
34a Maude Terrace, St Helen Auckland, Bishop Auckland, Co Durham, DL14 9BD
01388 664366
07718 391880
melh@bishopauck.freeserve.co.uk
Est. 1980 *Stock size* Large
Stock Memorabilia, militaria, furniture, clocks, collectables, silver, lights, decorative items, carpets, rugs, Continental antiques
Open Mon–Sat 9.30am–5.30pm Sun 10am–5pm
Services Valuations, clock restoration, delivery

WOLSINGHAM

Rams Head Antiques
Contact Keith Thompson
17 Front Street, Wolsingham, Bishop Auckland, Co Durham, DL13 3DF
01388 526834
Est. 1998 *Stock size* Small
Stock Antique furniture
Open Mon–Sat 11am–5pm

NORTHUMBERLAND

ALNWICK

Barter Books
Contact Stuart Manley
Alnwick Station, Alnwick, Northumberland, NE66 2NP
01665 604888 01665 604444
bb@barterbooks.co.uk
www.barterbooks.co.uk
Est. 1991 *Stock size* Large
Stock Antiquarian and second-hand books, records, CDs, videos
Open Summer Mon–Sun 9am–7pm winter Mon–Sun 9am–5pm Thurs 9am–7pm
Services Book search, valuations

John Smith of Alnwick Ltd
Contact Mr P Smith
West Cawledge Park Gallery, Alnwick, Northumberland,

NE66 2HJ 🅿
☎ 01665 604363
Est. 1972 *Stock size* Medium
Stock Country and general antiques, rugs, pictures, furniture
Open Mon–Sun 9am–5pm

Tamblyn Antiques
Contact Professor Hirst
✉ **12 Bondgate Without, Alnwick, Northumberland, NE66 1PP** 🅿
☎ 01665 603024
ⓔ profbehirst@tamblynant.freeserve.co.uk
Est. 1981 *Stock size* Medium
Stock Small period furniture, ceramics, Finnish, Swedish and Dutch glass
Open Mon–Sat 9.30am–4.30pm
Services Valuations

ASHINGTON

The Miner's Lamp
Contact Dorothy Kindley
✉ **10a Milburn Road, Ashington, Northumberland, NE63 0HD** 🅿
☎ 01670 815327
Est. 1972 *Stock size* Small
Stock General antiques, smalls
Open Mon–Sat 10am–4pm closed Wed

BERWICK-UPON-TWEED

Dillons Antiques
Contact Tom Dillon
✉ **12–14 Bridge Street, Berwick-upon-Tweed, Northumberland, TD15 1AQ** 🅿
☎ 01289 303917
Est. 1999 *Stock size* Small
Stock General antiques
Open Mon–Sat 9am–4pm
Services Valuations, removal service

Leslies Mount Road Auction Galleries
Contact Miss A Watson
✉ **Berwick-upon-Tweed, Northumberland, TD15 2BA** 🅿
☎ 01289 304635 ⓕ 01289 304635
ⓔ leslies@auctionhouse.freeserve.co.uk
ⓦ www.auctionhouse.freeserve.co.uk
Est. 1995
Open Mon–Fri 10am–5pm
Sales Antiques and fine art sales at Marshall Meadows Country House Hotel
Frequency Quarterly
Catalogues Yes

James E McDougall
Contact James E McDougall MRICS
✉ **St Duthus, 6 Palace Street East, Berwick-upon-Tweed, Northumberland, TD15 1HT** 🅿
☎ 01289 330791
ⓔ james.mcdougall@caucasian-rugs.co.uk
ⓦ www.caucasian-rugs.co.uk
Est. 1989 *Stock size* Small
Stock Antique carpets, rugs
Open By appointment
Services Valuations

CHATTON

Jim Railton
Contact Jim Railton
✉ **Nursery House, Chatton, Alnwick, Northumberland, NE66 5PY** 🅿
☎ 01668 215323 ⓕ 01668 215400
Ⓜ 07774 241111
ⓔ jim@jimrailton.com
ⓦ www.jimrailton.com
Est. 1993
Open Mon–Sat 9am–5pm or by appointment
Sales General antiques sale, specializing in country house sales at historic properties
Frequency 4 per annum
Catalogues Yes

CORBRIDGE

Judith Michael
Contact Gillian Anderson or Judith Troldahl
✉ **20a Watling Street, Corbridge, Northumberland, NE45 5AH** 🅿
☎ 01434 633165 ⓕ 01434 633165
ⓔ jma@supanet.com
ⓦ www.judithmichael.co.uk
Est. 1989 *Stock size* Medium
Stock General antiques, decorative items, jewellery, small furniture, glass, china, gardening section
Open Tues–Sat 10am–5pm
Services Interior design

CRAMLINGTON

Granny's Attic
Contact Elizabeth Buhagier
✉ **33 Arlington Grove, Cramlington, Northumberland, NE23 3G2** 🅿
☎ 01670 731868 ⓕ 01670 731868
ⓔ joe,buh@virgin.net
Est. 1987 *Stock size* Large
Stock Antiques, collectables
Open Mon–Sat 10am–5pm
Services Valuations, house clearance

HEXHAM

Hedley's of Hexham
Contact Mrs P Torday
✉ **3 St Mary's Chare, Hexham, Northumberland, NE46 1NQ** 🅿
☎ 01434 602317
ⓔ hedley@torday96.fsnet.co.uk
Est. 1819 *Stock size* Medium
Stock General antiques, furniture, collectables, china, clocks, Moorcroft
Open Tues–Sat 9.30am–5pm
Services Restoration

Hencotes Books and Prints (PBFA)
Contact Mrs Penny Pearce
✉ **8 Hencotes, Hexham, Northumberland, NE46 2EJ** 🅿
☎ 01434 605971
ⓔ enquiries@hencotesbooks.onyx.net.co.uk
Est. 1992 *Stock size* Medium
Stock Antiquarian and second-hand books, specializing in local history, literature, children's books, gardening, cookery
Open Mon–Sat 10.30am–5pm closed Thurs
Fairs Local PBFA, Durham, Newcastle
Services Booksearch

Hexham and Northern Mart
Contact Mr Brian Rogerson
✉ **Mart Office, Tyne Green, Hexham, Northumberland, NE46 3SG** 🅿
☎ 01434 605444 or 01669 620392 (Rothbury)
ⓔ furniture@hexhammart.co.uk
ⓦ www.hexhammart.co.uk
Est. 1850
Open Mon–Fri 9am–5pm
Sales House clearances, antiques sales (held at Rothbury), viewing 2 days prior to sale
Frequency Every 2 or 3 months
Catalogues No

Hexham Antiques
Contact John and Dorothy Latham
Unit 10, Acomb Industrial Estate, Acomb, Hexham, Northumberland, NE46 4SA
01434 603851
Est. 1978 *Stock size* Large
Stock General antiques, collectables, pictures, bric-a-brac
Open Mon Tues Sat 10.30am–4pm or by appointment
Fairs Hexham, Carlisle
Services Picture framing, valuations, house clearance

Pine Workshop (ADA)
Contact John Askell
28 Priestpopple, Hexham, Northumberland, NE46 1PQ P
01434 601121
Est. 1987 *Stock size* Medium
Stock Antique pine and oak
Open Mon–Sat 9am–5pm

Priestpopple Books
Contact Mr J B Patterson
9b Priestpopple, Hexham, Northumberland, NE46 1PF
01434 607773
priestpopple.books@tinyworld.co.uk
Est. 1998 *Stock size* Large
Stock Antiquarian books, general antiques, militaria, music, entertainment, art
Open Mon–Sat 9am–5pm
Services Valuations, restoration

MORPETH

Louis Johnson
Contact John Hayes
63 Bridge Street, Morpeth, Northumberland, NE61 1PQ P
01670 513025 F 01670 503267
lj@lj-fsbusiness.co.uk
www.louis-johnson.co.uk
Est. 1955
Open Mon–Fri 9am–5pm
Sales Antiques, fine art and collectables, cars, motorcycles, general household. Sale dates upon application
Catalogues Yes

Pottery Bank Antiques
Contact Mr Michael Everitt
43 Bullers Green, Morpeth, Northumberland, NE61 1DF P
01670 516160
apope@morpethnet.co.uk
www.morpethnet.co.uk
Est. 1977 *Stock size* Medium
Stock General antiques, furniture, silver
Open Mon–Sat 11.30am–5.30pm or by appointment

Ruperts of Rothbury
Contact Linda Thompson
Townfoot, Rothbury, Morpeth, Northumberland, NE65 7SN P
01669 620350
Est. 2001 *Stock size* Medium
Stock General antiques
Open Sat Sun by appointment
Fairs Newark, Swinderby
Services Picture restoration

ROTHBURY

Golfark International
Contact Michael Arkle
5 Tollgate Crescent, Rothbury, Northumberland, NE65 7RE P
01669 620487 F 01669 620487
M 07710 693860
michael@golfark.freeserve.co.uk
Est. 1997 *Stock size* Small
Stock Old golf clubs, bags and balls, sporting antiques, golfing memorabilia
Open By appointment

SCREMERSTON

Woodside Reclamation (SALVO)
Contact Keith Allan
Woodside, Scremerston, Berwick-upon-Tweed, Northumberland, TD15 2SY P
01289 331211/302658
F 01289 330274
info@redbaths.co.uk
www.redbaths.co.uk
Est. 1990 *Stock size* Medium
Stock Fireplaces, antique baths, bathroom ware, doors, timber, beams, flooring
Open Tues–Sat 9am–5pm
Services Furniture and door stripping, restoration

WOOLER

Hamish Dunn Antiques
Contact Mr Dunn
17 High Street, Wooler, Northumberland, NE71 6BU P
01668 281341 F 01668 281341
M 07940 530123
Est. 1986 *Stock size* Medium
Stock General antiques, second-hand and antiquarian books
Open Mon–Sat 9am–4.30pm

Millers Antiques of Wooler (LAPADA)
Contact James Miller
1–5 Church Street, Wooler, Northumberland, NE71 6BZ P
01668 281500 F 01668 282383
M 07714 332441
jmiller.antiques@virgin.net
www.millersantiquesofwooler.com
Est. 1947 *Stock size* Large
Stock Georgian and Victorian furniture
Open Mon–Fri 9.30am–5pm Sat Sun by appointment
Fairs DMG Newark

TYNE AND WEAR

EAST BOLDON

Boldon Auction Galleries
Contact Mr Hodges
Front Street, East Boldon, Tyne and Wear, NE36 0SJ P
0191 537 2630 F 0191 536 3875
boldon@btconnect.com
www.boldonauctions.co.uk
Est. 1981
Open Mon–Fri 9am–5pm
Sales General household and Victorian sales Wed 10am, viewing Tues 2–6pm, 4 antiques sales annually, 2 collectors toy and 20thC modern design sales annually, 2 antiquarian and first edition book sales annually
Catalogues Yes

GATESHEAD

Mulroys Antiques
Contact Miss J Mulroy
24 The Boulevard, Metro Centre, Gateshead, Tyne and Wear, NE11 9YL P
0191 461 1211 F 0191 461 1211
Est. 1959 *Stock size* Large
Stock General antiques and period jewellery
Open Mon–Fri 10am–8pm

Thurs 10am–9pm Sat 9am–7pm
Sun 11am–5pm
Services Valuations, restoration

GOSFORTH

Anna Harrison Antiques (LAPADA)
Contact Mr or Mrs Harrison
Harewood House, 49 Great North Road, Gosforth, Newcastle-upon-Tyne, Tyne and Wear, NE3 2DG
☎ 0191 284 3202 Fax 0191 284 3202
Email annaharrisonantiques@ukgateway.net
Est. 1976 *Stock size* Large
Stock Early porcelain, Georgian–Edwardian furniture, dining and lounge furniture
Open Mon–Fri 8am–5pm Sat 10am–5pm or by appointment
Fairs Galloway Fairs, Bailey Fairs
Services Restoration

Jane Kirsopp-Reed Antiques
Contact Jane Kirsopp-Reed
49 Great North Road, Gosforth, Tyne & Wear, NE3 2DQ
☎ 0191 284 3202 Fax 0191 284 3202
Est. 1984 *Stock size* Medium
Stock Furniture, porcelain
Open Mon–Fri 9am–5pm Sat 10am–5pm
Services Restoration

The Wooden Betty
Contact Susan Markall
Gosforth, Tyne and Wear, NE3
Mobile 07796 531477
Est. 2000 *Stock size* Small
Stock Period furniture
Open By appointment
Services Restoration

NEWCASTLE-UPON-TYNE

Aladdins Architectural Antiques (SALVO)
Contact Mr D Crowley
626 Welbeck Road, Walker, Newcastle-upon-Tyne, Tyne and Wear, NE6 1DJ
☎ 0191 262 7373
Mobile 07762 527640
Est. 1976 *Stock size* Large
Stock General antiques
Open Mon–Sat 10am–6pm
Services Valuations, restoration

Anderson & Garland (SOFAA)
Contact Mr A McCoull
Marlborough House, Marlborough Crescent, Newcastle-upon-Tyne, Tyne and Wear, NE1 4EE
☎ 0191 232 6278 Fax 0191 261 8665
Email andersongarland@aol.com
Web www.auction-net.co.uk
Est. 1840
Open Mon–Fri 9am–5.30pm
Sales Fine art sales every 3 months, general antiques sales fortnightly
Catalogues Yes

Antiques Centre
Contact Chris Parkin
142 Northumberland Street, Newcastle-upon-Tyne, Tyne and Wear, NE1 7DQ
☎ 0191 232 9832
Email timeantiques@zoom.co.uk
Est. 1983 *Stock size* Large
No. of dealers 13
Stock General antiques, Art Nouveau, decorative arts, Arts and Crafts, clocks, watches, jewellery
Open Mon–Sat 10am–5pm
Services Valuations, restoration, tea room

Attica
Contact Stephen Pierce
2 Old George Yard, Off Highbridge, Newcastle-upon-Tyne, Tyne and Wear, NE1 1EZ
☎ 0191 261 4062
Est. 1983 *Stock size* Medium
Stock Vintage clothing, 1950s–1970s, furniture, decor
Open Mon–Sat 10.30am–5.30pm

Bonhams
30–32 Grey Street, Newcastle-upon-Tyne, Tyne and Wear, NE1 6AE
☎ 0191 233 9930 Fax 0191 233 9933
Web www.bonhams.com
Open Mon–Fri 9am–5pm
Sales Regional office. Regular house and attic sales across the country; contact London offices for further details. Free auction valuations; insurance and probate valuations

B J Coltman Antiques
Contact Barry Coltman
80 Meldon Terrace, Heaton, Newcastle-upon-Tyne, Tyne & Wear, NE6 5XP
☎ 0191 224 5209
Mobile 077867 077539
Est. 1994 *Stock size* Large
Stock 18th–19thC furniture
Open Mon–Fri 9am–5pm
Services Restoration

Corbitt's (ASDA, APS, BNTA, PTS)
Contact Mr D McMonagle
5 Mosley Street, Newcastle-upon-Tyne, Tyne and Wear, NE1 1YE
☎ 0191 232 7268 Fax 0191 261 4130
Email info@corbitts.com
Web www.corbitts.com
Est. 1964 *Stock size* Medium
Stock Stamps, postal history, coins, medals
Open Tues–Fri 9am–5pm
Services Valuations

Corbitt's
Contact Mr D McMonagle
5 Mosley Street, Newcastle-upon-Tyne, Tyne and Wear, NE1 1YE
☎ 0191 232 7268 Fax 0191 261 4130
Email info@corbitts.com
Web www.corbitts.com
Est. 1964
Open Mon–Fri 9am–5pm Sat 9.30am–4pm
Sales Antique coins, medals, 3 per year. Stamps, history 4 per year. Cigarette cards, ephemera 2 per year
Catalogues Yes

Dog Leap Antiques
Contact Mr N MacDonald
61 The Side, Newcastle-upon-Tyne, Tyne and Wear, NE1 3JE
☎ 0191 232 7269
Est. 1969 *Stock size* Medium
Stock Antiquarian prints and reproductions
Open Mon–Fri 9.15am–5pm Sat 9am–1pm

Owen Humble Antiques (LAPADA)
Contact Mr M Humble
Clayton House, Walbottle Road, Lemington, Newcastle-upon-Tyne, Tyne and Wear, NE15 9RU
0191 267 7220 Ⓕ 0191 267 3377
Ⓔ antiques@owenhumble.com
Ⓦ www.owenhumbleantiques.com
Est. 1959 *Stock size* Large
Stock General antiques
Open Mon–Fri by appointment Sat 10am–1pm
Fairs LAPADA
Services Valuations, restoration, trade warehouse

Intercoin
Contact Mr Brian
103 Clayton Street, Newcastle-upon-Tyne, Tyne and Wear, NE1 5PZ
0191 232 2064
Est. 1964 *Stock size* Large
Stock Coins, medals, bank notes
Open Mon–Sat 9.30am–4.30pm
Services Valuations

Little Theatre Antiques Centre
Contact Mr J Bell
Fern Avenue, Jesmond, Newcastle-upon-Tyne, Tyne and Wear, NE2 2RA
0191 2094321
Ⓔ john@bennettbell.demon.co.uk
Ⓦ www.bennett-bell.demon.co.uk
Est. 1993 *Stock size* Large
No. of dealers 13
Stock General antiques, pine furniture, porcelain, glass, Arts and Crafts
Open Mon–Sat 10am–5.30pm

Thomas N Miller Auctioneers
Contact Mr A Scott
Algernon Road, Byker, Newcastle-upon-Tyne, Tyne and Wear, NE6 2UZ
0191 265 8080 Ⓕ 0191 265 5050
Ⓔ tnmiller@btinternet.com
Ⓦ www.millersauctioneers.co.uk
Est. 1902
Open Mon–Fri 8.30am–5pm
Sales General antiques, later furniture, viewing Sun 10am–noon Mon Tues 9.30am–4pm
Frequency Weekly
Catalogues Yes

Phoenix Design & Antiques
Contact Mrs M Ryle
The Old Monastery, Blackfriars, Newcastle-upon-Tyne, Tyne and Wear, NE1 4XN
0191 230 3804
Est. 1984 *Stock size* Small
Stock General antiques
Open Mon–Fri 11.30am–4.30pm Sat 10.30am–5pm

Shiners of Jesmond (SALVO)
Contact Mike Nolan or Brian Gibbons
81 Fern Avenue, Jesmond, Newcastle-upon-Tyne, Tyne and Wear, NE2 2RA
0191 281 6474 Ⓕ 0191 281 9041
Ⓜ 07708 099722
Ⓔ contactus@shinersofjesmond.com
Ⓦ www.shinersofjesmond.com
Est. 1983 *Stock size* Large
Stock Internal fittings, antique doors and door furniture, antique marble and slate surrounds, Victorian cast fireplaces, inserts
Open Mon–Sat 10am–5pm Sun 11am–2pm
Services Polishing

Frank Smith Maritime Aviation Books (PBFA)
Contact Alan Parker
92 Heaton Road, Newcastle-upon-Tyne, Tyne and Wear, NE6 5HL
0191 265 6333 Ⓕ 0191 224 2620
Ⓔ books@franksmith.freeserve.co.uk
Est. 1981 *Stock size* Medium
Stock Antiquarian, rare and out-of-print books, maritime and aviation
Open Mon–Fri 10am–4pm
Fairs PBFA
Services Free monthly catalogues on maritime and aviation

Graham Smith Antiques (LAPADA)
Contact Mr Graham Smith
83 Fern Avenue, Jesmond, Newcastle-upon-Tyne, Tyne and Wear, NE2 2RA
0191 281 5065 Ⓕ 0191 281 5072
Ⓔ gsmithantiques@aol.com
Est. 1973 *Stock size* Medium
Stock Furniture, clocks, smalls
Open Mon–Sat 10am–5pm

Robert D Steedman (ABA)
Contact Mr David Steedman
9 Grey Street, Newcastle-upon-Tyne, Tyne and Wear, NE1 6EE
0191 232 6561
Est. 1907 *Stock size* Medium
Stock Second-hand and antiquarian books
Open Mon–Fri 9am–5pm Sat 9am–12.30pm
Fairs Olympia, Edinburgh

Turnburrys Ltd (SALVO)
257 Jesmond Road, Newcastle-upon-Tyne, Tyne and Wear, NE2 1LB
0191 281 1770 Ⓕ 0191 240 2569
Ⓔ info@turnburrys.co.uk
Ⓦ www.turnburrys.co.uk
Est. 1996 *Stock size* Medium
Stock Hardwood flooring, fireplaces, doors, radiators, mirrors, bespoke doors, etched and stained glass
Open Mon–Sat 9am–6pm Sun 11am–3pm
Services Valuations

NORTH SHIELDS

Chimney Pieces
Contact Mr T Chester
98a Howard Street, North Shields, Tyne and Wear, NE30 1NA
0191 2572118
Ⓦ www.chimneypieces.com
Est. 1985 *Stock size* Medium
Stock Antique chimney pieces, architectural antiques, fireplaces in marble and wood
Open Mon–Sat 10am–5pm
Fairs Newark
Services Restoration

The Clock Shop
Contact Mr G Ball
1a John Street, Cullercoates, North Shields, Tyne and Wear, NE30 4PL
0191 290 1212
Est. 1997 *Stock size* Medium
Stock General antiques
Open Mon–Sat 10am–5pm
Fairs Swinderby, Newark
Services Valuations, restoration, clock repairs

Keel Row Books
Contact Bob and Brenda Cook
11 Fenwick Terrace,

Preston Road, North Shields, Tyne and Wear, NE29 0LU 🅿
☎ 0191 296 0664/287 3914
Est. 1980 *Stock size* Large
Stock General antiquarian books, children's, military, mountaineering, local history, cinema a speciality
Open Mon–Sat 10.30am–5pm Sun 11am–4pm closed Wed

⊞ Tynemouth Architectural Salvage (SALVO)
Contact Mr Robin Archer
✉ **28 Tynemouth Road, North Shields, Tyne and Wear, NE30 4AA** 🅿
☎ 0191 296 6070 Ⓕ 0191 296 6097
Ⓔ robin@tynemoutharchitecturalsalvage.com
Ⓦ www.antiquebathsco.co.uk
Stock size Large
Stock Architectural antiques
Open Mon–Fri 9am–5pm Sat 10am–5pm
Fairs Newark
Services Door stripping

SOUTH SHIELDS

⊞ The Curiosity Shop
Contact Mr G Davies
✉ **16 Frederick Street, South Shields, Tyne and Wear, NE33 5EA** 🅿
☎ 0191 456 5560 Ⓕ 0191 427 7597
Ⓜ 07860 219949
Ⓔ glenda47@yahoo.co.uk
Est. 1969 *Stock size* Medium
Stock General antiques, Royal Doulton
Open Mon–Sat 9am–5pm closed Wed
Fairs Newark
Services Valuations

⊞ De-Ja-Vu
Contact Mr J Atkinson
✉ **2 Imeary Street, South Shields, Tyne and Wear, NE33 4EG** 🅿
☎ 0191 425 0031
Est. 1998 *Stock size* Small
Stock General antiques
Open Mon–Sat 10am–5pm

⊞ Dolly Domain
Contact Liz Bonner
✉ **45 Henderson Road, Simonside, South Shields, Tyne and Wear, NE34 9QW** 🅿
☎ 0191 424 0400
Ⓔ shop@dollydomain.com
Ⓦ www.dollydomain.com
Est. 1991 *Stock size* Large
Stock Dolls and bears
Open Tues–Sat 10am–5pm
Fairs Dolly Domain Fairs

SUNDERLAND

⊞ Decades
Contact Judith Richardson
✉ **5b Villette Road, Sunderland, Tyne & Wear, SR2 8RH** 🅿
☎ 0191 565 5142
Est. 1994 *Stock size* Large
Stock General antiques, furniture, collectables, pottery
Open Mon–Sat 10.30am–4.30pm closed Wed
Fairs Swinderby, Newark

⊞ Peter Smith Antiques (LAPADA)
Contact Mrs Smith
✉ **12–14 Borough Road, Sunderland, Tyne and Wear, SR1 1EP** 🅿
☎ 0191 567 3537/514 0008
Ⓕ 0191 514 2286
Ⓜ 07802 273372
Ⓔ petersmithantiques@btinternet.com
Ⓦ www.petersmithantiques.co.uk
Est. 1968 *Stock size* Large
Stock General antiques
Open Mon–Fri 9.30am–4.30pm Sat 10am–1pm or by appointment
Services Valuations

TYNEMOUTH

⊞ Coast Antiques
Contact Mrs Dorothy Wadge or Mr Alex Beacham
✉ **10 Front Street, Tynemouth, Tyne and Wear, NE30 4RG** 🅿
☎ 0191 296 0700 Ⓕ 0191 296 0700
Ⓜ 07977 780248
Est. 1989 *Stock size* Medium
Stock Victorian, Edwardian furniture and associated items
Open Sat 10.30am–4.30pm Sun noon–4pm or by appointment
Services Interest-free credit, free local delivery

⊞ Curio Corner
Contact Mrs S Welton
✉ **Units 5 & 6, Land of Green Ginger, Front Street, Tynemouth, North Shields, Tyne and Wear, NE30 4BP** 🅿
☎ 0191 296 3316 Ⓕ 0191 296 3319
Ⓜ 07831 339906
Ⓦ www.curiocorner.com.uk
Est. 1988 *Stock size* Large
Stock General antique furniture
Open Mon–Sat 11am–4.30pm
Fairs Newark
Services Restoration

⊞ Ian Sharp Antiques (LAPADA, CINOA)
Contact Mr Ian Sharp
✉ **23 Front Street, Tynemouth, North Shields, Tyne and Wear, NE30 4DX** 🅿
☎ 0191 296 0656 Ⓕ 0191 296 0656
Ⓜ 07850 023689
Ⓔ iansharp@sharpantiques.com
Ⓦ www.sharpantiques.com
Est. 1988 *Stock size* Medium
Stock Georgian–Edwardian furniture, pottery
Open Mon–Sat 10am–1pm 1.30–5.30pm or by appointment
Fairs Newark

WASHINGTON

⊞ Harold J Carr Antiques
Contact Margaret Carr
✉ **Field House, Eastlands, High Rickleton, Washington, Tyne & Wear, NE38 9HQ** 🅿
☎ 0191 388 6442 Ⓕ 0191 388 6442
Est. 1971 *Stock size* Medium
Stock Georgian, Victorian and later furniture
Open By appointment
Services Shipping

WHITLEY BAY

⊞ Olivers Bookshop
Contact Mr John Oliver
✉ **48a Whitley Road, Whitley Bay, Tyne and Wear, NE26 2NF** 🅿
☎ 0191 251 3552
Est. 1986 *Stock size* Medium
Stock Antiquarian, rare and second-hand books
Open Mon Thurs Fri Sat 11am–5pm
Fairs Tynemouth Book Fair

⊞ Treasure Chest Antiques
Contact Mr J Rain
✉ **2a–4 Norham Road, Whitley Bay, Tyne and Wear, NE26 2SB** 🅿
☎ 0191 251 2052
Ⓜ 07808 966611
Est. 1969 *Stock size* Medium
Stock General antiques
Open Mon–Sat 10.30am–4pm closed 1–2pm

CHESHIRE

ALSAGER

⊞ Trash 'n' Treasure
Contact George G Ogden
✉ 48 Sandbach Road South, Alsager, Cheshire, ST7 2LP 🅿
☎ 01270 873246/872972
Est. 1962 *Stock size* Medium
Stock Furniture, ceramics, pictures
Open Tues–Sat 10am–4pm closed Wed
Services Valuations

ALTRINCHAM

⊞ Abacus Books
Contact Mr C Lawton
✉ 24 Regent Road, Altrincham, Cheshire, WA14 1RP 🅿
☎ 0161 928 5108
Est. 1979 *Stock size* Medium
Stock Antiquarian and second-hand books, arts, gardening and crafts specialities
Open Tue–Sat 10am–5pm
Services Valuations

Patrick Cheyne Auctions
Contact Mr P Cheyne, RICS
✉ 38 Hale Road, Altrincham, Cheshire, WA14 2EX 🅿
☎ 0161 941 4879 Ⓕ 0161 941 4879
Est. 1982
Open Mon–Fri 10am–5.30pm
Sales Every 2 months Sat 10.30am, viewing Fri 2–4.30pm 6–8pm Sat 9–10.30am. Held at St Peter's Assembly Rooms, Hale
Catalogues Yes

⊞ Church Street Antiques Ltd (LAPADA)
Contact Mr A Smalley
✉ 4–4a Old Market Place, Altrincham, Cheshire, WA14 4NP 🅿
☎ 0161 929 5196 Ⓕ 0161 929 5196
Ⓜ 07768 318661
Ⓔ sales@churchstreetantiques.com
Ⓦ www.churchstreetantiques.com
Est. 1992 *Stock size* Large
Stock Fine Georgian and Victorian furniture, art, objets d'art, carpets, decorative items
Open Mon–Sat 10am–5pm Sun noon–4pm closed Tues
Fairs Baileys, Coopers, Louise Walker (Harrogate), Penman (Chester)
Services Valuations, restoration

⊞ Squires Antiques
Contact Mrs V Phillips
✉ 25 Regent Road, Altrincham, Cheshire, WA14 1RX 🅿
☎ 0161 928 0749
Est. 1977 *Stock size* Large
Stock Silver, jewellery, porcelain, brass, copper, lighting, small fine furniture
Open Tues–Sat 10am–5pm closed Wed
Services Valuations

⊞ Village Farm Antiques
Contact Mr C Thomason
✉ Village Farm, Station Road, Dunham Massey, Altrincham, Cheshire, WA14 5SA 🅿
☎ 0161 929 4468
Ⓜ 07977 139708
Ⓦ www.villagefarmantiques.co.uk
Est. 1987 *Stock size* Large
Stock Wide range of stock including pine furniture, architectural antiques, fireplaces,

NORTH WEST

chaise longues etc
Open Mon–Sun 9am–5pm
Fairs Newark, Swinderby
Services Wood stripping, upholstery

BARTON

Derek & Tina Rayment Antiques (BADA, CINOA)
Contact Derek or Tina Rayment
Orchard House, Barton, Farndon, Cheshire, SY14 7HT P
☎ 01829 270429 F 01829 270893
M 07702 922410 or 07860 666629
E raymentantiques@aol.com
W www.antique-barometers.com
Est. 1960 *Stock size* Large
Stock Antique barometers
Open By appointment
Fairs Olympia, Chelsea, BADA, NEC (Jan)
Services Restoration, repairs

BEESTON

Beeston Reclamations
Contact Trevor Jones
The Old Coal Yard, Whitchurch Road, Beeston, Tarporley, Cheshire, CW6 9NW P
☎ 01829 260299
M 07903 949480
Est. 1998 *Stock size* Large
Stock Garden statuary, bricks, slates, oak beams, pine beams, floorboards, York stone, fireplaces, block flooring
Open Mon–Sat 8am–5pm Sun 10am–3pm
Services Valuations, restoration

Wright-Manley
Contact Mr W T Witter
Beeston Castle Salerooms, Beeston Castle, Tarporley, Cheshire, CW6 9NZ P
☎ 01829 262150 F 01829 261829
E wendymiller@wrightmanley.co.uk
W www.wrightmanley.co.uk
Est. 1861
Open Mon–Fri 8.30am–5pm
Sales Victoriana 1st and 3rd Thurs of month 10.30am, viewing Wed 10am–6pm. Quarterly Fine Art sale (telephone for details)
Frequency Fortnightly
Catalogues Yes

BELGRAVE

Antique Garden
Contact Maria Hopwood
Grosvenor Garden Centre, Wrexham Road, Belgrave, Chester, Cheshire, CH4 9EB P
☎ 01244 629191
M 07976 539990
Est. 1991 *Stock size* Medium
Stock Garden items
Open Mon–Sun 10am–4.30pm
Services Valuations, shipping

CHESTER

Adams Antiques of Chester (LAPADA)
Contact Mr B Adams
65 Watergate Row, Chester, Cheshire, CH1 2LE P
☎ 01244 319421
Est. 1975 *Stock size* Medium
Stock 18th–19thC furniture, clocks, glass, 19th–early 20thC small silver, mechanical devices, lighting
Open Mon–Sat 10am–5pm
Services Valuations, restoration, export service

Aldersey Hall Ltd
Contact Anthony Wilding
Aldersey Hall, 47 Northgate Street, Chester, Cheshire, CH1 2HQ P
☎ 01244 324885
Est. 1990 *Stock size* Medium
Stock General antiques
Open Mon–Sat 8.30am–5.30pm
Fairs Deco Fair Chester

Antique Scientific Instruments
Contact Charles Tomlinson, Chester, Cheshire, CH1 P
☎ 01244 318395 F 01244 318395
E charlestomlinson@tiscali.co.uk
Est. 1980
Stock Slide rules, calculators, early scientific instruments and drawing equipment, microscopes, microscope slides
Open By appointment
Services Valuations

The Antique Shop
Contact Peter Thornber
40 Watergate Street, Chester, Cheshire, CH1 2LA
☎ 01244 316286
Est. 1987 *Stock size* Medium
Stock Small items, mainly brass, copper, pewter
Open Mon–Sat Sun from Easter to Christmas 10am–5.30pm
Services Metal repair, restoration, polishing

Ask Simon
Contact Mr S Cleveland
25 Christleton Road, Chester, Cheshire, CH3 5UF P
☎ 01244 320704
M 07815 559431 *Stock size* Large
Stock Decorative antiques, domestic paraphernalia, sporting and farming items, pictures, collectables, furniture
Open Mon–Sat 10am–5pm
Fairs Newark, Ardingly

Bonhams
New House, 150 Christleton Road, Chester, Cheshire, CH3 5TD
☎ 01244 313936 F 01244 340028
E chester@bonhams.com
W www.bonhams.com
Sales Regional Saleroom. Frequent sales. Regular house and attic sales across the country; contact London offices for further details. Free auction valuations; insurance and probate valuations
Catalogues Yes

Borg's Antiques
Contact Mr R Borg
26 Christleton Road, Chester, Cheshire, CH3 5UG P
☎ 01244 400023
M 07939 227165
Est. 1991 *Stock size* Medium
Stock Silver, furniture, porcelain, Royal Doulton, small decorative items etc
Open Mon–Sat 10am–5.30pm Sun 11am–4pm
Fairs Swinderby, Newark

Bowstead Antiques (LAPADA)
Contact Olwyn Bowstead
Chester, Cheshire, CH1 P
☎ 01244 671797

Est. 1981 *Stock size* Medium
Stock 18th–19thC town and country furniture, oil paintings, metalware
Open Mon–Sat 10am–6pm by appointment
Fairs NEC
Services Valuations

Byrne's Auctioneers
Contact Mr A Byrne MRICS
Booth Mansion, 30 Watergate Street, Chester, Cheshire, CH1 2LA
01244 312300 01244 312112
auctions@byrnesauctioneers.co.uk
www.byrnesauctioneers.co.uk
Est. 1999
Open Mon–Fri 9am–5pm
Sales General sales every 3 weeks Wed 10am, viewing Mon Tues prior 10am–pm. Quarterly antiques sales Wed 11am, viewing Mon Tues 10am–5pm
Frequency Monthly
Catalogues Yes

Cameo Antiques
Contact The Manager
19 Watergate Street, Chester, Cheshire, CH1 2LB
01244 311467 01244 311467
Est. 1994 *Stock size* Medium
Stock Silver, jewellery, porcelain, Moorcroft, Sally Tufton
Open Mon–Sat 9am–5pm
Services Valuations, shipping

Cestrian Antiques
Contact Mr Malcolm Tice
28 Watergate Street, Chester, Cheshire, CH1 2LA
01244 400444
Est. 1993 *Stock size* Large
Stock Small items of furniture, oak coffers, boxes, silver, glass, ceramics, longcase clocks, mantel clocks, wall clocks, pictures, lighting
Open Mon–Sat 10am–5.30pm or by appointment Sun evenings
Services Valuations

D K R Refurbishers
Contact Mr D Wisinger
26b High Street, Saltney, Chester, Cheshire, CH4 8SE
01244 680290
Est. 1984 *Stock size* Large
Stock Original pine and oak furniture
Open Mon–Sat 10am–4.30pm Sun noon–4pm
Services Valuations, restoration

Dollectable
Contact Mo Harding
53 Lower Bridge Street, Chester, Cheshire, CH1 1RS
01244 344888/679195
01244 679469
Est. 1972 *Stock size* Large
Stock Antique dolls
Open Fri noon–5pm Sat 10am–5pm or by appointment
Fairs Kensington, Chelsea, Newark
Services Valuations, restoration

Farmhouse Antiques
Contact Mrs K Appleby
23 Christleton Road, Boughton, Chester, Cheshire, CH3 5UF
01244 322478 01244 322478
07768 645818
progsunited@aol.com
Est. 1973 *Stock size* Large
Stock Wide range of antiques, country furniture, collectables, clocks
Open Mon–Sat 10am–5pm

Grosvenor Antiques & Interiors
Contact John Martin
61 Watergate Row, Chester, Cheshire, CH1 2LE
01244 401185 01244 401695
Est. 2002 *Stock size* Medium
Stock Antique French furniture, decorative objects
Open Mon–Sat 10.30am–5.30pm
Services Restoration

Uri Jacobi Oriental Carpet Gallery (LAPADA)
Contact Uri Jacobi
55–57 Watergate Row, Chester, Cheshire, CH1 2LE
01244 311300 01244 311300
07973 760722
urijacobi@aol.com
www.urijacobi.co.uk
Est. 1994 *Stock size* Medium
Stock Contemporary and antique carpets, rugs and tapestries
Open Mon–Sat 9am–5pm
Fairs NEC, LAPADA
Services Valuations, restoration, cleaning

Jamandic Ltd
Contact Dominic McParland
22 Bridge Street Row, Chester, Cheshire, CH1 1NN
01244 312822
Est. 1975 *Stock size* Small
Stock General antiques
Open Mon–Fri 9.30am–5.30pm Sat 9.30am–1pm
Services Interior design

K D Antiques
Contact Mrs D Gillett
11 City Walls, Chester, Cheshire, CH1 1LD
01244 314208
Est. 1997 *Stock size* Medium
Stock Boxes, Staffordshire figures, prints, collectables, glass
Open Mon–Sat 10am–5pm
Fairs Welsh circuit, Manchester G-Mex

Kayes (LAPADA, NAG)
Contact Mr Nick Kaye
9 St Michaels Row, Chester, Cheshire, CH1 1EF
01244 327149/343638
01244 318404
kayesgem@globalnet.co.uk
www.kayeschester.com
Est. 1949 *Stock size* Large
Stock Second-hand, antique and new jewellery and silver
Open Mon–Sat 9.30am–5pm
Services Valuations, restoration

Lowe and Sons (NAG, BACA Award Winner 2002)
Contact Kevin Parry
11 Bridge Street Row, Chester, Cheshire, CH1 1PD
01244 325850 01244 345536
lowes.chester@virgin.net
Est. 1770 *Stock size* Large
Stock Antiques, silver, jewellery, decorative arts, Lalique
Open Mon–Sat 9am–5.30pm
Services Restoration

Made of Honour
Contact Mr Eric Jones
11 City Walls, Chester, Cheshire, CH1 1LD
01244 314208
eric.antiques@virginnet.co.uk
Est. 1969 *Stock size* Medium
Stock 18th–19thC British pottery

and porcelain, decorative items, boxes, caddies, Staffordshire figures
Open Mon–Sat 10am–5pm
Fairs Welsh circuit, Anglesey
Services Talks, lectures

McLarens Antiques & Interiors
Contact Jude Leach
Boughton House, 38 Christleton Road, Chester, Cheshire, CH3 5UE
01244 320774 F 01244 314774
Est. 1983 *Stock size* Large
Stock French and Italian furniture, European and reclaimed pine
Open Tues–Sat 10am–6pm Sun 11am–5pm

Moor Hall Antiques
Contact John Murphy
27 Watergate Row, Chester, Cheshire, CH1 2LE
01244 340095
Est. 1993 *Stock size* Medium
Stock 18th–19thC British furniture
Open Mon–Sat 10am–5.30pm

O'Keeffe Antiques
Contact Mr D O'Keeffe
2 Christleton Road, Chester, Cheshire, CH3 5UG
01244 311279
okeefeantiques@ireland.com
Est. 1998 *Stock size* Large
Stock Antique lighting, architectural antiques
Open Tues–Sat 10am–5pm

Objets d'Art
Contact Martin De Rooy
67–71 Watergate Row, Chester, Cheshire, CH1 2LE
01244 312211 F 01244 400880
Est. 1998 *Stock size* Large
Stock Clocks, furniture, quality decorative items
Open Mon–Sat 10am–5pm
Services Restoration

The Old Warehouse Antiques
Contact Mrs U O'Donnell
7–9 Delamere Street, Chester, Cheshire, CH1 4DS
01244 383942
M 07790 533850
modonnell@xln.co.uk
Est. 1991 *Stock size* Large
Stock Victorian–Edwardian furniture, beds, soft furnishings
Open Mon–Sat 10am–5.30pm
Services Valuations

Richmond Galleries
Contact Mrs M Armitage
Watergate Buildings, New Crane Street, Chester, Cheshire, CH1 4JE
01244 317602 F 01244 317602
Est. 1974 *Stock size* Large
Stock New and old country pine furniture, decorative items
Open Mon–Sat 9.30am–5pm

Saltney Restoration Services
Contact Mr J Moore
50 St Marks Road, Chester, Cheshire, CH4 8DQ
01244 671110 F 01244 679722
M 07713 823383
Est. 1967 *Stock size* Small
Stock Lighting, sanitary ware, furniture, ironware
Open By appointment
Services Restoration

Second Time Around
Contact Graham Shacklady
6 Christleton Road, Boughton, Chester, Cheshire, CH3 5UG
01244 316394 F 01244 322042
Est. 1979 *Stock size* Large
Stock Georgian–Edwardian furniture, Victorian burr walnut
Open Mon–Sat 9am–5pm
Fairs Newark
Services Packing, courier, export

Second Time Around
Contact Graham Shacklady
Staff Yard, 34 Spital Walk, Boughton, Cheshire, CH3 5DB
01244 316394 F 01244 322042
Est. 1979 *Stock size* Large
Stock Georgian–Edwardian furniture
Services Packing, courier, export

Stothert Old Books (PBFA)
Contact Mr A Checkley
4 Nicholas Street, Chester, Cheshire, CH1 2NX
01244 340756
M 07778 137461
Est. 1970 *Stock size* Large
Stock Wide range of antiquarian and second-hand books including local history, topography, natural history, good illustrated books etc
Open Mon–Sat 10am–5pm
Fairs PBFA, North West Book Fairs
Services Valuations, book search

Watergate Antiques
Contact Mr A Shindler
56 Watergate Street, Chester, Cheshire, CH1 2LD
01244 344516 F 01244 320350
watergate.antiques@themail.co.uk
Est. 1968 *Stock size* Large
Stock Silver, silver plate, ceramics
Open Mon–Sat 9.30am–5pm
Fairs Newark
Services Restoration, repairs

Wheatsheaf Antiques Centre
Contact Jeremy Marks
57 Christleton Road, Boughton, Chester, Cheshire, CH3 5UF
01244 403743 F 01244 351713
info@antiquesonlineuk.com
www.antiquesonlineuk.com
Stock size Large
No. of dealers 7
Stock General antiques 17thC–1930s, books, china, prints, clocks, silver plate, vintage clothing
Open Mon–Sat 11am–4pm Sun noon–4pm or by appointment
Services Shipping

CONGLETON

Whittaker & Biggs (RICS)
Contact Mr J W Robinson
The Auction Room, Macclesfield Road, Congleton, Cheshire, CW12 1NS
01260 279858 F 01260 271629
www.whittakerandbiggs.co.uk
Est. 1931
Open Mon–Fri 9am–5pm
Sales General household furniture and effects 1st Sat of month and 2nd and 4th Fri 10am. Antiques, reproduction and collectables auction 3rd Fri 4pm,

viewing evening prior 5–7pm
Frequency Weekly
Catalogues Yes

CREWE

Antique & Country Pine
Contact Mr S Blackhurst
102 Edleston Road, Crewe, Cheshire, CW2 7HD
01270 258617
Est. 1990 *Stock size* Small
Stock English and Continental original and stripped pine, hand-made reproductions
Open Mon–Sat 9.30am–5.30pm closed Wed
Services Restoration

Copnal Books
Contact Ruth Ollerhead
18 Meredith Street, Crewe, Cheshire, CW1 2PW
01270 580470
Est. 1982 *Stock size* Medium
Stock Wide variety of second-hand, antiquarian and religious books
Open Mon–Sat 9.30am–4.30pm
Services Valuations

DISLEY

Coopers Auctioneers
Contact Geoff Cooper
7 Buxton Road, Disley, Cheshire, SK12 2DX
01663 765630
Est. 1999
Open Mon–Sat 10am–5.30pm
Sales Antiques, collectables
Frequency Every 4–6 weeks
Catalogues Yes

Crescent Antiques
Contact Mr J Cooper
7 Buxton Road, Disley, Stockport, Cheshire, SK12 2DZ
01663 765677
Est. 1972 *Stock size* Medium
Stock Wide range of furniture, silver, porcelain
Open Mon–Sun 10am–5.30pm
Services Valuations

Mill Farm Antiques
Contact Mr F Berry
50–54 Market Street, Disley, Stockport, Cheshire, SK12 2DT
01663 764045 F 01663 762690
E mfa@millfarmantiques.fsbusiness.co.uk
Est. 1971 *Stock size* Medium
Stock Longcase and other clocks, general antiques, mechanical music
Open Mon–Sat 9am–6pm Sun noon–6pm or by appointment
Services Valuations, restoration of clocks, mechanical music, barometers

FRODSHAM

Eddisbury Antiques
Contact Sheila Lloyd
35 Church Street, Frodsham, Cheshire, WA6 6PN
01928 734477
M 07787 557584
E sheila.lloyd@btopenworld.com
Est. 2003 *Stock size* Medium
No. of dealers 8
Stock Georgian–Edwardian furniture, silver, clocks, jewellery, pictures, ceramics, glass
Open Tues–Sat 10am–5pm Sun noon–4pm
Services Restoration

Sweetbriar Gallery (Paperweights) Ltd (Paperweight Collectors Association)
Contact Ray Metcalfe
3 Collinson Court, Off Church Street, Frodsham, Cheshire, WA6 6PN
01928 730064 F 01928 730066
M 07860 907532
E sales@sweetbriar.co.uk
W www.sweetbriar.co.uk
Est. 1988 *Stock size* Large
Stock Paperweights
Open Mon–Fri 9am–5pm
Fairs Glass Fairs, DMG Fairs
Services Valuations

HALE

Bonhams
The Stables, 213 Ashley Road, Hale, Cheshire, WA15 9TB
0161 927 3822 F 0161 927 3824
E manchester@bonhams.com
W www.bonhams.com
Open Mon–Fri 9am–5pm
Sales Regional office. Regular house and attic sales across the country; contact London offices for further details. Free auction valuations; insurance and probate valuations

Porcupine
Contact Ms V Martin
110 Ashley Road, Hale, Altrincham, Cheshire, WA14 2UN
0161 928 4421
Est. 1982 *Stock size* Medium
Stock Antique pine, pottery
Open Tues–Sat 9.30am–5.30pm Sun noon–4pm closed Wed 1pm

HATTON

H & H Classic Auctions Ltd
Contact Simon Hope or Mark Hamilton
Whitegate Farm, Hatton Lane, Hatton, Cheshire, WA4 4BZ
01925 730630 F 01925 730830
E info@classic-auctions.co.uk
W www.classic-auctions.co.uk
Est. 1993
Open Mon–Fri 9am–5pm
Sales Veteran, vintage, pre-war, classic and collectors car, motorcycles and automobilia sales. Held at the Pavilion Gardens, Buxton, Derbyshire and other venues around the UK. Automobilia sales Tues noon, viewing from 10am. Car and motorcycle sales Wed 1pm, viewing day before 2–7pm morning of sale from 9am
Catalogues Yes

HUNTINGTON

Huntington Antiques
Contact Mrs Gregson
53 Chester Road, Huntington, Cheshire, CH3 6BS
01244 324162
Est. 1994 *Stock size* Small
Stock Furniture, clocks, paintings
Open Mon–Fri 9am–5.30pm
Services Restoration

KNUTSFORD

Forest Books of Cheshire
Contact Mrs E Mann
Hartford, Cheshire, CW8

☎ 01606 882388
ⓔ info@forest-books.co.uk
Est. 1996 *Stock size* Small
Stock Antiquarian, rare, second-hand, new books, pictures, prints
Open By appointment
Fairs Buxton Book Fair

King Street Antiques
Contact Mrs E L MacDougal
✉ **1 King Street, Knutsford, Cheshire, WA16 6DW** Ⓟ
☎ 01565 750387
Est. 1993 *Stock size* Small
Stock Furniture, porcelain, silver
Open Tues–Fri 10.30am–5pm Sat 10am–5pm closed Wed
Services Valuations

Knutsford Antique Centre
Contact David McLeod
✉ **113 King Street, Knutsford, Cheshire, WA16 6EH**
☎ 01565 654092
Est. 1996 *Stock size* Large
No. of dealers 15
Stock General antiques, collectables
Open Tues–Sat 10am–5pm

The Lemon Tree
Contact Mr S Nelson
✉ **103 King Street, Knutsford, Cheshire, WA16 6EQ** Ⓟ
☎ 01565 751101 ⓕ 01565 751101
Est. 1997 *Stock size* Medium
Stock English country furniture in satin walnut, stripped pine
Open Mon–Sat 10am–5.30pm Sun noon–5pm

Frank R Marshall & Co
Contact Mr A Partridge
✉ **Marshall House, Church Hill, Knutsford, Cheshire, WA16 6DH** Ⓟ
☎ 01565 653284 ⓕ 01565 652341
ⓜ 07808 483435
ⓔ antiques@frankmarshall.co.uk
ⓦ www.antiques@frankmarshall.co.uk
Est. 1969
Open Mon–Fri 9am–5.30pm closed noon–1pm
Sales General antiques and collectors' sales, 5 per annum, Tues 10am. Fortnightly household sales Tues 10am, viewing Mon 9am-6.30pm
Catalogues Yes

LYMM

Baron Antiques (LAPADA)
Contact Mrs Roberts
✉ **Port of Willow Pool, Burford Lane, Lymm, Cheshire, WA13 0SH** Ⓟ
☎ 01925 757827 ⓕ 01925 758101
Est. 1964 *Stock size* Medium
Stock Architectural antiques, decorative arts, salvage and general antiques
Open Mon–Sun 9am–6pm
Fairs Newark, Ardingly
Services Tea shop

MACCLESFIELD

Gatehouse Antiques
Contact Mr W Livesley
✉ **5–7 Chester Road, Macclesfield, Cheshire, SK11 8DG** Ⓟ
☎ 01625 426476 ⓕ 01625 426476
ⓦ www.gatehouseantiques.co.uk
Est. 1974 *Stock size* Large
Stock Wide range of antiques including 18th–20thC furniture, jewellery, silver, glass
Open Mon–Fri 9am–5pm Wed 9am–1pm Sat 10am–5pm
Services Valuations, restoration, repairs

Derek Hill Antiques
Contact Mr D Hill
✉ **Unit 47, Market Hall, Grosvenor Centre, Macclesfield, Cheshire, SK11 6AR** Ⓟ
☎ 01625 420777
ⓜ 07711 855937
ⓔ hillsantiques@tinyworld.co.uk
ⓦ www.hillsantiques.co.uk
Est. 1969 *Stock size* Large
Stock Collectables, brass, copper, militaria, jewellery, stamps, cigarette cards etc
Open Mon–Sat 9am–5.30pm
Services Valuations, jewellery repairs

Mereside Books (PBFA)
Contact Ms S Laithwaite
✉ **75 Chestergate, Macclesfield, Cheshire, SK11 6DG**
☎ 01625 425352
Est. 1996 *Stock size* Small
Stock Antiquarian and second-hand books, local history and illustrated books a speciality
Open Wed–Sat 10am–5pm
Fairs Cheshire, Buxton

MOBBERLEY

Limited Editions
Contact Charles Fogg
✉ **The Barn, Oak Tree Farm, Knutsford Road, Mobberley, Cheshire, WA16 7PU** Ⓟ
☎ 0161 480 1239
ⓔ info@ltd-editions.co.uk
ⓦ www.antique-co.com
Est. 1974 *Stock size* Large
Stock Mostly furniture, especially dining tables and chairs
Open Thurs–Sat 10am–5.30pm Sun noon–4pm
Services Restoration, joinery, polishing, upholstery

NANTWICH

Adams Antiques (BADA, LAPADA, BACA Award Winner 2003)
Contact Mrs Sandy Summers
✉ **Churche's Mansion, 150 Hospital Street, Nantwich, Cheshire, CW5 5RY** Ⓟ
☎ 01270 625643 ⓕ 01270 625643
ⓜ 07901 855200
ⓔ sandy@adams-antiques.net
ⓦ www.adams-antiques.net
Est. 1970 *Stock size* Large
Stock Early oak, walnut and country furniture, Welsh dressers, Mason's Ironstone, longcase clocks
Open Tues–Sat 10am–5pm
Fairs NEC, BADA
Services Valuations, restoration, vetting

Barn Antiques
Contact Mr Brian Lee
✉ **8 The Cocoa Yard, Pillory Street, Nantwich, Cheshire, CW5 5BL** Ⓟ
☎ 01270 627770
ⓔ j.lee2@btinternet.com
Est. 1993 *Stock size* Medium
Stock Wide range of china, small furniture, copper, brass, collectables including Carlton ware, Beswick
Open Mon Tues 10am–4pm Thurs Fri 9.30am–4.30pm Sat 9.30am–5pm closed 12.30–1.30pm

Chapel Antiques
Contact Mrs D Atkin
✉ **47 Hospital Street,**

Nantwich, Cheshire,
CW5 5RL Ⓟ
☎ 01270 629508
Est. 1983 *Stock size* Medium
Stock Georgian–Victorian furniture, decorative items, mirrors
Open Tues–Sat 9.30am–5.30pm
Services Furniture restoration

Clock Corner (BHI)
Contact Mr M Green
✉ **176 Audlem Road, Nantwich, Cheshire, CW5 7QJ** Ⓟ
☎ 01270 624481
ⓔ clock.corner@virgin.net
ⓦ www.clockcorner.co.uk
Est. 1975 *Stock size* Large
Stock Antique clocks of all types, bracket, Vienna, longcase, mantel
Open By appointment
Services Valuations

Dagfields Crafts & Antiques Centre
Contact Mr I Bennion
✉ **Dagfields Farm, Walgherton, Nantwich, Cheshire, CW5 7LG** Ⓟ
☎ 01270 841336 ⓕ 01270 842604
ⓔ ian@dagfields.co.uk
ⓦ www.dagfields.co.uk
Est. 1989 *Stock size* Large
No. of dealers 150
Stock Collectables and furniture of all periods
Open Mon–Sun 10am–5pm
Services 2 restaurants

Roderick Gibson
Contact Mrs R Gibson
✉ **70–72 Hospital Street, Nantwich, Cheshire, CW5 5RP** Ⓟ
☎ 01270 625301 ⓕ 01270 629603
ⓔ antiques@sfc.co.uk
ⓦ www.sfc.co.uk/antiques
Est. 1975 *Stock size* Medium
Stock Antique and reproduction furniture, small collectables
Open Mon–Sat 9am–5pm
Services Valuations, probate service

Love Lane Antiques
Contact Mary Simon
✉ **Love Lane, Nantwich, Cheshire, CW5 5BH** Ⓟ
☎ 01270 626239
Est. 1979 *Stock size* Medium
Stock General antiques
Open Mon–Sat 10am–5pm closed Wed

Peter Wilson (SOFAA)
Contact Mr R Stones
✉ **Victoria Gallery, Market Street, Nantwich, Cheshire, CW5 5DG** Ⓟ
☎ 01270 623878 ⓕ 01270 610508
ⓔ auctions@peterwilson.co.uk
ⓦ www.peterwilson.co.uk
Est. 1955
Open Mon–Fri 9am–5.30pm Sat 9.30am–noon
Sales 2-day sales, 5 per annum, Wed Thurs 10.30am, viewing Sun prior 2–4pm Mon Tues 10am–4pm. Uncatalogued fast weekly sale Thurs 11am, viewing Wed 10am–7pm
Frequency 40 per annum
Catalogues Yes

NORTHWICH

Northwich Antiques Centre
Contact Freddie Cockburn
✉ **132 Witton Street, Northwich, Cheshire, CW9 5NP** Ⓟ
☎ 01606 47540
ⓜ 07980 645738
ⓦ www.northwichantiques.com
Est. 1999
No. of dealers 7
Stock Period furniture, collectables, china, Moorcroft, Beswick, Doulton
Open Mon–Sun 10am–5pm

POYNTON

Recollections
Contact Angela Smith
✉ **69 Park Lane, Poynton, Stockport, Cheshire, SK12 1RD** Ⓟ
☎ 01625 859373
ⓜ 07778 993307
Est. 1984 *Stock size* Medium
Stock Furniture, costume jewellery, decorative china, glass
Open Mon–Sat 10am–5pm
Services House clearance

SANDBACH

Andrew Hilditch & Son Ltd
Contact Mr T Spencer Andrew
✉ **Hanover House, 1a The Square, Sandbach, Cheshire, CW11 1AP** Ⓟ
☎ 01270 767246 ⓕ 01270 767246
Est. 1866
Open Mon–Fri 9am–5pm closed 12.30–2pm
Sales Quarterly general antiques Wed 10.30am, viewing Mon 10.30am–3pm Tues 10am–3.30pm 7–8.30pm. General sale weekly, Wed 10am, viewing Tues 10.30am–3.30pm
Catalogues Yes

Saxon Cross Antiques Emporium
Contact John Jones
✉ **Town Mill, High Street, Sandbach, Cheshire, CW11 1AH** Ⓟ
☎ 01270 753005 ⓕ 01270 753005
ⓦ www.saxonantique.co.uk
Est. 1993 *Stock size* Large
No. of dealers 32
Stock Fine antiques from 17th–20thC, porcelain, silver, collectables
Open Tues–Sat 10am–5pm Sun 11am–4pm

STRETTON

Harlequin Antiques
Contact Bernard Snagg
✉ **Roadside Farm, London Road, Stretton, Cheshire, WA4 5PG** Ⓟ
☎ 01925 730031 ⓕ 01925 730781
Est. 1997 *Stock size* Large
Stock Victorian pine, oak, mahogany furniture
Open Tues–Sun 10am–6pm

TARPORLEY

Tarporley Antique Centre
Contact Peter Wright
✉ **76 High Street, Tarporley, Cheshire, CW6 0AT** Ⓟ
☎ 01829 733919
Est. 1991 *Stock size* Large
No. of dealers 10
Stock Pictures, brass, copper, glass, books, furniture
Open Mon–Sat 10am–5pm Sun 11am–4pm

TATTENHALL

Great Northern Architectural Antiques Co Ltd
Contact Mrs J Devoy

✉ **New Russia Hall, Chester Road, Tattenhall, Chester, Cheshire, CH3 9AH** 🅿
☎ 01829 770796 Ⓕ 01829 770971
Ⓔ gnaacoltd@enterprise.net
Est. 1990 *Stock size* Large
Stock Stone, church exteriors, fireplaces, doors, brass ware, sanitary ware, pews, statuary etc
Open Mon–Sun 9.30am–5pm or by appointment
Services Valuations, restoration

WARRINGTON

Rocking Chair Antiques
Contact Michael Barratt
✉ **Unit 3, St Peters Way, Warrington, Cheshire, WA2 7BL** 🅿
☎ 01925 652409 Ⓕ 01925 652409
Est. 1976 *Stock size* Large
Stock Victorian–Edwardian bedroom and dining room furniture
Open Mon–Fri 8am–5pm Sat 10am–4pm
Fairs Swinderby
Services Valuations

WAVERTON

Antique Exporters of Chester
Contact Mike Kilgannon
✉ **Guy Lane Farm, Guy Lane, Waverton, Chester, Cheshire, CH3 7RZ** 🅿
☎ 01829 741001 Ⓕ 01829 749204
Est. 1969 *Stock size* Large
Stock 18thC–1930s furniture
Open Mon–Sun 9am–7pm
Services Restoration, shipping

J Alan Hulme (IMCOS)
Contact Alan Hulme
✉ **52 Mount Way, Waverton, Cheshire, CH3 7QF** 🅿
☎ 01244 336472
Ⓜ 07774 280871
Ⓔ alanhulme@pssa.freeserve.co.uk
Est. 1956 *Stock size* Medium
Stock Maps of British Isles 1540–1860, prints of fashion, humour, ornithology, butterflies, flowers 1750–1890, some topographical 1770–1890
Open By appointment
Fairs NEC, Robert Bailey fairs
Services Valuations

White House Antiques & Stripped Pine
Contact Mrs E Rideal
✉ **The White House, Whitchurch Road, Waverton, Chester, Cheshire, CH3 7PB** 🅿
☎ 01244 335063 Ⓕ 01244 335098
Ⓔ rideal@whitehousescientifics.com
Est. 1979 *Stock size* Large
Stock German and English stripped-pine furniture of all types
Open Mon–Sat 10am–5pm

WOODFORD

Maxwells of Wilmslow incorporating Dockrees
Contact Mr M Blackmore FRICS
✉ **133a Woodford Road, Woodford, Cheshire, SK7 1QD** 🅿
☎ 0161 439 5182 Ⓕ 0161 439 5182
Ⓦ www.maxwell-auctioneers.co.uk
Est. 1989
Open Mon–Fri 9am–5pm
Sales 2 general chattels sales per month, quarterly antiques sales
Frequency 2 per month
Catalogues Yes

CUMBRIA

ALSTON

Alston Antiques
Contact Mrs J Bell
✉ **10 Front Street, Alston, Cumbria, CA9 3HU** 🅿
☎ 01434 382129
Ⓜ 07778 624021
Est. 1974 *Stock size* Large
Stock Wide range of antiques, furniture, clocks, barometers, china, textiles etc
Open Mon–Sat 10am–5pm Sun 1–5pm closed Tues
Fairs Newark

APPLEBY IN WESTMORLAND

Barry McKay Rare Books (PBFA)
Contact Mr B McKay
✉ **Kingstone House, Battlebarrow, Appleby in Westmorland, Cumbria, CA16 6XT** 🅿
☎ 017683 52282 Ⓕ 017683 52706
Ⓔ barry.mckay@britishlibrary.net
Est. 1986 *Stock size* Medium
Stock Antiquarian, second-hand and new books, specializing in all aspects of book production and distribution, some books on Cumbria and the North
Open Mon–Sat 10am–4pm preferably by appointment
Services Book search, catalogue

BOWNESS-ON-WINDERMERE

The White Elephant
Contact Mrs J Moore
✉ **66 Quarry Rigg, Bowness-on-Windermere, Windermere, Cumbria, LA23 3DO** 🅿
☎ 01539 446962 Ⓕ 01539 446962
Est. 1989 *Stock size* Large
Stock General range of antiques, furniture, porcelain, pewter, mahogany furniture
Open Mon–Sun 10am–5pm closed Wed

BRAMPTON

The Cumbrian Antiques Centre
Contact Steve Summerson-Wright
✉ **St Martins Hall, Front Street, Brampton, Cumbria, CA8 1NT** 🅿
☎ 01697 742515 Ⓕ 01697 742515
Ⓔ cumbrianantiques@hotmail.com
Est. 2000 *Stock size* Large
No. of dealers 40
Stock General antiques, collectables
Open Mon–Sat 10am–5pm Sun noon–5pm
Services Valuations, house clearance

Moat Antiques
Contact Carol Irving
✉ **32–34 Main Street, Brampton, Cumbria, CA8 1RF** 🅿
☎ 01697 741176
Est. 1987 *Stock size* Medium
Stock General antiques
Open Tues–Sat 10am–4.30pm or by appointment

Something Old, Something New
Contact Mrs J Potts
✉ **46 Main Street, Brampton, Cumbria, CA8 1SB** 🅿
☎ 0169 774 1740
Est. 1979 *Stock size* Large

Stock Victorian pine furniture, country items, French decorative furniture
Open Mon–Sat 10am–4.30pm

CANONBIE

John R Mann Fine Antique Clocks (MBWCG)
Contact John Mann
✉ **The Clock Showrooms, Canonbie, Carlisle, Cumbria, DG14 0SY** P
☎ 01387 371337 F 01387 371337
M 07850 606147
E jmannclock@aol.com
W www.johnmannantiqueclocks.co.uk
Est. 1987 **Stock size** Large
Stock Fine antique clocks
Open By appointment
Services Restoration, delivery, shipping, valuations

CARLISLE

Bonhams
✉ **48 Cecil Street, Carlisle, Cumbria, CA1 1NT**
☎ 01228 542422 F 01228 590106
E carlisle@bonhams.com
W www.bonhams.com
Open Mon Tues Thurs Fri 8.30am–1pm 2–5pm
Sales Regional office. Regular house and attic sales across the country; contact London offices for further details. Free auction valuations; insurance and probate valuations

Bookcase
Contact Mr S Matthews
✉ **17–19 Castle Street, Carlisle, Cumbria, CA3 8SY** P
☎ 01228 544560 F 01228 544775
E bookcasecarlisle@aol.com
W www.bookscumbria.com
Est. 1978 **Stock size** Large
Stock Antiquarian, rare and second-hand books, maps, prints, classical CDs and LPs, art gallery
Open Mon–Sat 10am–5pm
Services Book search, repairs, valuations

Carlisle Antique Centre
Contact Mrs W Mitton
✉ **Cecil Hall, 46a Cecil Street, Carlisle, Cumbria, CA1 1NT** P
☎ 01228 536910 F 01228 536910
E wendymitton@aol.com
Est. 1986 **Stock size** Large
No. of dealers 3
Stock Wide range of antiques, clocks, watches, jewellery, silver, porcelain
Open Mon–Sat 9am–5pm
Services Restaurant

The Eddie Stobart Fan Club Shop
Contact Linda Shore
✉ **Brunthill Road, Kingstown Industrial Estate, Carlisle, Cumbria, CA3 0EH** P
☎ 01228 517800 F 01228 517808
W www.eddiestobart.co.uk
Est. 1996 **Stock size** Medium
Stock Eddie Stobart collection, die-cast models, clothing, ceramics, pens, mugs, limited editions
Open Mon–Fri 9am–5pm
Sat 10am–2pm

Eddie Stobart Promotions Ltd
Contact Ms Debbie Rodgers
✉ **Brunthill Road, Kingstown Industrial Estate, Carlisle, Cumbria, CA3 0EH** P
☎ 01228 514151 F 01228 515158
E promotions@eddiestobart.co.uk
W www.eddiestobart.co.uk
Est. 1993 **Stock size** Large
Stock Eddie Stobart collection, die-cast models, clothing, ceramics, pens, limited editions
Open Mon–Fri 8.30am–5.30pm
Services Mail-order service with catalogue

H & H King (NAVA)
Contact Howard Naylor
✉ **Cumbria Auction Rooms, 12 Lowther Street, Carlisle, Cumbria, CA3 8DA** P
☎ 01228 525259 F 01228 597183
E cumbriaauctions@aol.com
W www.cumbriaauctions.com
Est. 1890
Open Mon–Fri 9am–5pm
Sat 9am–noon
Sales Weekly sale of Victorian and later furniture and effects Mon. Quarterly antiques and works-of-art sales Mon 9.30am, viewing Fri 9am–5pm
Sat 9am–noon
Catalogues Yes

Valerie Main Ltd (BADA)
Contact Valerie or David Main
✉ **PO Box 92, Carlisle, Cumbria, CA5 7GD** P
☎ 01228 711342 F 01228 711341
M 07860 679307
E valerie.main@btinternet.com
W www.royalworcester.co.uk
Est. 1986 **Stock size** Large
Stock 20thC English porcelain
Open By appointment
Fairs NEC, Harrogate
Services Shipping

St Nicholas Galleries Ltd
Contact Mr C Carruthers
✉ **39 Bank Street, Carlisle, Cumbria, CA3 8HJ** P
☎ 01228 544459 F 01228 511015
Est. 1975 **Stock size** Medium
Stock Late Victorian–Edwardian furniture, watercolours, silver, silver plate, Doulton figures, Rolex and Omega watches, diamond and other jewellery
Open Tues–Sat 10am–5pm
Services Jewellery repairs

Thomson, Roddick & Medcalf Auctioneers
Contact John Thomson
✉ **Coleridge House, Shaddongate, Carlisle, Cumbria, CA2 5TU** P
☎ 01228 528939 F 01228 592128
E auctions@thomsonroddick.com
Est. 1880
Sales 10 Antiques and collectors' sales per annum plus specialist sales of pictures, books, medals, coins, militaria
Frequency 20 per annum
Catalogues Yes

COCKERMOUTH

CG's Curiosity Shop
Contact Corrine Ritchie or Colin Graham
✉ **Cocker Bridge, 43 Market Place, Cockermouth, Cumbria, CA13 9LT** P
☎ 01900 824418 or 016973 21108
M 07712 206786
E cgcuriosity@hotmail.com
Est. 1987 **Stock size** Large
Stock Unusual items, pictures, militaria, furniture, porcelain, glass, books, records

Open Mon–Sat 10am–12.45pm 1.45–5pm
Fairs Newark, Swinderby
Services Restoration, house clearance

Cockermouth Antiques
Contact Ms E Bell
5 Station Street, Cockermouth, Cumbria, CA13 9QW P
☎ 01900 826746
e elainebell@aol.com
Est. 1984 *Stock size* Large
Stock Large range of antiques, ceramics, glass, metalware, silver, jewellery, books, pictures, fireplaces
Open Mon–Sat 10am–5pm closed 1–2pm

Cockermouth Antiques & Craft Market
Contact Mrs P Gilbert
The Old Courthouse, Main Street, Cockermouth, Cumbria, CA13 9LU P
☎ 01900 824346
Est. 1978 *Stock size* Large
No. of dealers 3
Stock Wide range of antiques including jewellery, china, glass, postcards, books, ephemera
Open Mon–Sat 10am–5pm
Services Pine stripping and French polishing

Mitchell's Auction Company (ISVA)
Contact Mr M Wise or Mr K Scott
The Furniture Hall, 47 Station Road, Cockermouth, Cumbria, CA13 9PZ P
☎ 01900 827800 f 01900 828073
e info@mitchellsfineart.com
w www.mitchellsfineart.com
Est. 1873
Open Mon–Fri 9am–5pm
Sales 5 Fine Art and antiques sales per annum Thurs Fri 10am, weekly general sale Thurs 9.30am
Catalogues Yes

GRANGE-OVER-SANDS

Anthemion (BADA, LAPADA)
Contact Jonathan Wood
Cartmel, Grange-over-Sands, Cumbria, LA11 6QD P
☎ 015395 36295 f 015395 38881
m 07768 443757
Est. 1989 *Stock size* Large
Stock Georgian furniture, decorative items
Open Mon–Sun 10am–5pm
Fairs BADA, LAPADA, Olympia (June), Harrogate

Gedyes Auctioneers & Estate Agents (NAEA)
Contact Mr N Gedyes
The Auction Centre, Albert Road, Grange-over-Sands, Cumbria, LA11 7EZ P
☎ 015395 33366 f 015395 33366
m 07740 174537
e gedyes@aol.com
Est. 1968
Open Mon–Fri 9am–noon
Sales General and antiques sales Fri 10am, viewing Thurs 1–6pm
Frequency Monthly
Catalogues No

Norman Kerr (PBFA)
Contact Mrs H Kerr
Priory Barn, Priest Lane, Cartmel, Grange-over-Sands, Cumbria, LA11 6PX P
☎ 015395 36247
Est. 1933 *Stock size* Medium
Stock Second-hand and antiquarian books concerning art, architecture, travel, natural history, sport, transport, engineering
Open By appointment only
Services Valuations

Utopia Antiques Ltd
Contact Mrs J Wilkinson
Yew Tree Barn, High Newton, Grange-over-Sands, Cumbria, LA11 6JP P
☎ 01539 530065 f 01539 530676
e utopia@utopiaantique.com
w www.utopiaantique.com
Est. 1993 *Stock size* Large
Stock Indian and Asian antique furniture, handicrafts
Open Mon–Sat 10am–5pm Sun 11am–5pm
Fairs NEC Furniture Show (Jan)

GRASMERE

Lakes Craft & Antiques Gallery
Contact Joe or Sandra Arthy
3 Oakbank, Broadgate, Grasmere, Ambleside, Cumbria, LA22 9TA P
☎ 015394 35037 f 015394 44271
e allbooks@globalnet.co.uk
Est. 1991 *Stock size* Medium
Stock Antiques, craft and gift items, china, silver, jewellery, small furniture, antiquarian books, postcards, cameras etc
Open Mon–Sun March–Nov 9.30am–6pm winter 10am–4pm

GREAT SALKELD

G K Hadfield (BHI)
Contact G K Hadfield
Beck Bank, Great Salkeld, Penrith, Cumbria, CA11 9LN P
☎ 01768 870111 f 01768 870111
m 07968 775694
e gkhadfield@dial.pipex.com
Est. 1966 *Stock size* Large
Stock Clocks, horological books, clock restoration materials
Open Mon–Sat 9am–5pm or by appointment
Fairs Specialist clock fairs
Services Gilding, dial restoration, silvering, book restoration, hand-cut hands, frets in wood or brass

GREYSTOKE

Roadside Antiques
Contact Mrs K Sealby
Watsons Farm, Greystoke Gill, Greystoke, Penrith, Cumbria, CA11 0UQ P
☎ 017684 83279
Est. 1988 *Stock size* Large
Stock Antique ceramics, glass, Staffordshire figures, longcase clocks, Victorian–Edwardian furniture, silver, jewellery, paintings
Open Mon–Sun 10am–6pm
Services Porcelain restoration

KENDAL

Dower House Antiques
Contact Mrs J H Blakemore
40 Kirkland, Kendal, Cumbria, LA9 5AD P
☎ 01539 722778
Est. 1959 *Stock size* Small
Stock 18th–19thC pottery, porcelain, furniture, pictures
Open By appointment
Services Valuations

⊞ Granary Collectables
Contact Mr B Cross
✉ **29 Allhallows Lane, Kendal, Cumbria, LA9 4JH** 🅿
☎ 01539 740770
Est. 1998 *Stock size* Medium
Stock Kitchenware, advertising, stoneware, pottery, collectables, pictures
Open Tues–Sat 10am–4.30pm

Kendal Auction Rooms
Contact Kevin Kendal
✉ **Sandylands Road, Kendal, Cumbria, LA9 6ES** 🅿
☎ 01539 720603 Ⓕ 01539 740037
Ⓜ 07713 787509
Ⓔ kevkendal@btconnect.com
Ⓦ www.kendalauction.co.uk/furniture
Est. 1818
Open Mon–Fri 9am–5.30pm
Sales Monthly antique furniture sales Sat, view Fri 2–6pm
Frequency Monthly
Catalogues Yes

⊞ Kendal Studio Pottery Antiques
Contact Mr R Aindow
✉ **2–3 Wildman Street, Kendal, Cumbria, LA9 6EN** 🅿
☎ 01539 723291
Est. 1953 *Stock size* Medium
Stock Oak furniture, art pottery, maps, prints
Open 10.30am–4.30pm usually or by appointment

⊞ Lakeland Architectural Antiques
Contact Mr G Fairclough
✉ **146 Highgate, Kendal, Cumbria, LA9 4HW** 🅿
☎ 01539 737147 Ⓕ 01539 737147
Ⓔ gordonfairclough@cs.com
Ⓦ www.architecturalantiques.co.uk
Est. 1987 *Stock size* Medium
Stock Fireplaces, mirrors, lighting
Open Mon–Sat 10am–5pm
Services Valuations

⊞ The Lion's Den
Contact Mrs L Marwood
✉ **28c Finkle Street, Kendal, Cumbria, LA9 4AB** 🅿
☎ 01539 720660
Est. 1998 *Stock size* Large
Stock Antique and reproduction jewellery, clocks, pottery etc
Open Mon–Sat 10am–5pm closed Wed
Services Hand-made gold jewellery

⊞ Shambles Antiques
Contact Mr John or Mrs Janet Smyth
✉ **17–19 New Shambles, Off Market Place, Kendal, Cumbria, LA9 4TS** 🅿
☎ 01539 729947
Ⓜ 07710 245059
Ⓔ jansmyth@btinternet.com
Est. 1991 *Stock size* Medium
Stock Arts and Crafts, ceramics, glass, objects of virtue
Open Tues–Sat 10am–4pm
Services Valuations

⊞ John Smyth Antiques
Contact J Smyth
✉ **16 New Shambles, Off Market Place, Kendal, Cumbria, LA9 4TS** 🅿
☎ 01539 729947
Ⓔ jansmyth@btinternet.co.uk
Est. 1992 *Stock size* Small
Stock Furniture, paintings, works of art
Open Tues–Sat 10am–5pm
Services Valuations

⊞ Thomond Antiques
Contact Mr D Masters
✉ **33 Allhallows Lane, Kendal, Cumbria, LA9 4JH** 🅿
☎ 01539 736720
Ⓔ thomondantiques@aol.com
Est. 1998 *Stock size* Medium
Stock China, glass, silver plate, 18th–20thC ceramics
Open Mon–Sat 10am–4.30pm
Services Valuations

⊞ Utopia Antiques Ltd
Contact Mrs J Wilkinson
✉ **40 The Market Place, Kendal, Cumbria, LA9 4TN** 🅿
☎ 01539 722862 Ⓕ 01539 530676
Ⓔ utopia@utopiaantique.com
Ⓦ www.utopiaantique.com
Est. 1993 *Stock size* Large
Stock Indian and Asian antique furniture, handicrafts
Open Mon–Sat 10am–5pm Sun 11am–5pm
Fairs NEC Furniture Show (Jan)

KESWICK

⊞ Keswick Bookshop (PBFA)
Contact Ms J Kinnaird
✉ **4 Station Street, Keswick, Cumbria, CA12 5HT** 🅿
☎ 017687 75535
Est. 1994 *Stock size* Medium
Stock Antiquarian and second-hand books, maps, prints
Open Easter–Oct Mon–Sat 10.30am–5pm winter Sat only advisable to telephone

⊞ Keswick Collectables
Contact Mr M Stainton or David Lomas
✉ **18 St Johns Street, Keswick, Cumbria, CA12 5AS** 🅿
☎ 01768 774928
Est. 1997 *Stock size* Medium
Stock Collectables, stamps, books, records, Victoriana, Beatles memorabilia
Open Mon–Sun 10am–6pm
Services Postal service

⊞ Lakes Antiques & Collectables
Contact Mrs B Wren
✉ **5 St Johns Street, Keswick, Cumbria, CA12 5AP** 🅿
☎ 01768 775855
Est. 1992 *Stock size* Medium
Stock Collectables, china, glass, jewellery, hat pins etc
Open Mon–Sat 10.30am–4.30pm
Fairs Newark
Services Valuations

⊞ John Young & Son Antiques (LAPADA)
Contact Mr J Young
✉ **12–14 Main Street, Keswick, Cumbria, CA12 5JD** 🅿
☎ 017687 73434 Ⓕ 017687 73306
Est. 1890 *Stock size* Large
Stock Fine selection of 17th–19thC oak and mahogany furniture, longcase clocks
Open Mon–Sat 9.30am–5pm advisable to ring Wed

KIRKBY STEPHEN

⊞ The Book House (PBFA)
Contact Mr C Irwin
✉ **Ravenstonedale, Kirkby Stephen, Cumbria, CA17 4NG** 🅿
☎ 015396 23634 Ⓕ 015396 23634

Ⓔ mail@thebookhouse.co.uk
Ⓦ www.thebookhouse.co.uk
Est. 1984 *Stock size* Medium
Stock Wide range of general books, history of technology, gardening literature, children's and language
Open Mon–Sat 9am–5pm closed Tues
Fairs PBFA
Services Catalogues issued

Haughey Antiques (LAPADA, BACA Award Winner 2003)
Contact D M Haughey
28–30 Market Street, Kirkby Stephen, Cumbria, CA17 4QW Ⓟ
☎ 017683 71302 Ⓕ 017683 72423
Ⓔ hagheyantiques@aol.com
Est. 1969 *Stock size* Large
Stock 17th–19thC furniture, decorative items
Open Mon–Fri 10am–5.30pm Sat 11am–6pm or by appointment
Fairs Olympia (June, Nov), LAPADA Birmingham (Jan)
Services Valuations, restoration

David Hill
Contact Mr D Hill
36 Market Square, Kirkby Stephen, Cumbria, CA17 4QT Ⓟ
☎ 01768 371598
Est. 1966 *Stock size* Medium
Stock Small antiques, kitchenware, collectables, metalware
Open Thurs–Sat 9.30am–4pm

LONG MARTON

Ben Eggleston Antiques Ltd
Contact Ben Eggleston
The Dovecote, Long Marton, Nr Appleby, Cumbria, CA16 6BJ Ⓟ
☎ 01768 361849 Ⓕ 01768 361849
Ⓔ ben@benegglestonantiques.co.uk
Ⓦ www.benegglestonantiques.co.uk
Est. 1974 *Stock size* Large
Stock Restored and unrestored antique pine furniture
Open By appointment
Fairs Newark

LONGTOWN

T Potts
Contact Mr T Potts
Scaurbank House, Netherby Road, Longtown, Carlisle, Cumbria, CA6 5NX Ⓟ
☎ 01228 791513
Ⓜ 07702 449770
Est. 1974 *Stock size* Large
Stock Period furniture
Open By appointment
Services Valuations

NEWBY BRIDGE

Townhead Antiques (LAPADA)
Contact Mr C P Townley
Townhead, Newby Bridge, Cumbria, LA12 8NP Ⓟ
☎ 01539 531321 Ⓕ 01539 530019
Ⓔ townhead@aol.com
Ⓦ www.townhead.com
Est. 1960 *Stock size* Large
Stock Wide variety of antiques, including oak, mahogany, walnut, rosewood furniture, porcelain, glass, brass, silver etc
Open Mon–Sat 10am–5pm evenings and Sun by appointment
Services Valuations

PENRITH

Antiques of Penrith
Contact Mrs S Tiffin
4 Corney Square, Penrith, Cumbria, CA11 7PX Ⓟ
☎ 01768 862801
Est. 1953 *Stock size* Large
Stock Varied stock of furniture, decorative items, collectables
Open Mon–Fri 10am–5pm closed noon–1.30pm Sat 10am–1pm closed Wed

Brunswick Antiques
Contact Mr Martin Hodgson
8 Brunswick Road, Penrith, Cumbria, CA11 7LU Ⓟ
☎ 01768 899338
Ⓜ 07971 295991
Est. 1987 *Stock size* Medium
Stock 18th–19thC clocks, furniture, glass, ceramics, collectables
Open Mon–Sat 10am–4pm closed Wed
Services Clock repairs

Penrith Farmers' & Kidd's PLC
Contact Mr M Huddleston
Skirsgill Saleroom, Skirsgill, Penrith, Cumbria, CA11 0DN Ⓟ
☎ 01768 890781 Ⓕ 01768 895058
Ⓔ info@pfkauctions.co.uk
Ⓦ www.antiquestradegazette.com/penrithfarmers
Est. 1876
Open Mon–Fri 9am–5pm Tues 9am–6pm
Sales General sales of Victoriana and later furnishings and effects fortnightly Wed 9.30am, viewing Tues noon–6pm
Frequency Fortnightly
Catalogues Yes

RAUGHTON HEAD

Cumbria Architectural Salvage (SALVO)
Contact Mr R Temple
Birkshill, Raughton Head, Carlisle, Cumbria, CA5 7DH Ⓟ
☎ 016974 76420 Ⓕ 016974 76420
Ⓜ 07703 881170
Est. 1986 *Stock size* Small
Stock Fireplaces, sanitary ware, oak beams, sandstone flags, doors, radiators, kitchen ranges
Open Mon–Fri 9am–5pm Sat 9am–noon
Services Fireplace restoration

SEDBERGH

R F G Hollett & Son (ABA)
Contact Mr C G Hollett
6 Finkle Street, Sedbergh, Cumbria, LA10 5BZ Ⓟ
☎ 01539 620298 Ⓕ 01539 621396
Ⓔ hollett@sedbergh.demon.co.uk
Ⓦ www.holletts-rarebooks.co.uk
Est. 1960 *Stock size* Large
Stock Wide selection of antiquarian books including natural history, travel, northern topography
Open By appointment
Services Valuations, catalogues

Sleepy Elephant Books & Artefacts
Contact Mrs A Whittle
16 Back Lane, Sedbergh, Cumbria, LA10 5AQ Ⓟ
Ⓜ 07967 638503
Ⓔ avrilsbooks@aol.com
Est. 2003 *Stock size* Small
No. of dealers 8 book dealers and 2 antiques deaalers
Stock Second-hand and antiquarian books, general antiques
Open Mon–Sat 10am–5pm Sun noon–5pm (winter open Fri–Mon)
Services Valuations

Avril Whittle, Bookseller
Contact Mrs A Whittle
Whittle's Warehouse, 7–9 (Rear) Bainbridge Road, Sedbergh, Cumbria, LA10 5AU
☎ 01539 621770 Ⓕ 01539 621770
Ⓜ 07967 638503
Ⓔ avrilsbooks@aol.com
Est. 1980 *Stock size* Medium
Stock Scarce, out-of-print and antiquarian books on art, craft and design
Open By appointment
Services Book search, valuations

SHAP

David A H Grayling (PBFA)
Verdun House, Shap, Penrith, Cumbria, CA10 3NG
☎ 01931 716746 Ⓕ 01931 716746
Ⓔ graylingbook@fsbdial.co.uk
Ⓦ www.davidgraylingbooks.com
Est. 1972 *Stock size* Medium
Stock Rare, out-of-print and new books on big game, deer, shooting, angling, hunting and natural history
Open By appointment only
Fairs Game fairs
Services Book search, catalogue, mail order, valuations, fine binding

SKELTON

The Pen & Pencil Gallery
Contact Mrs J Marshall
Church House, Skelton, Penrith, Cumbria, CA11 9TE
☎ 01768 484300
Ⓜ 07720 708181
Ⓔ ppgallery@aol.com
Est. 1995 *Stock size* Large
Stock Vintage and modern fountain pens, writing equipment, pencils, dip pens, inkwells
Open By appointment
Fairs London, Northern, USA pen shows
Services Valuations, repairs

STAVELEY

Staveley Antiques
Contact Mr J Corry
27 Main Street, Staveley, Kendal, Cumbria, LA8 9LU
☎ 01539 821393
Est. 1990 *Stock size* Large
Stock Brass and iron beds, French wooden beds, lighting, metalware
Open Mon–Sat 10am–5pm
Services Metalware restoration

ULVERSTON

Brogden Books
Contact Mr I Chapman
11 Brogden Street, Ulverston, Cumbria, LA12 7AH
☎ 01229 588222
Ⓦ www.brogdenbooks.co.uk
Est. 1998 *Stock size* Medium
Stock Antiquarian and second-hand books
Open Mon–Sat 10am–5pm closed Wed
Services Valuations

Elizabeth & Son
Contact Mr J Bevins
Market Hall, New Market Street, Ulverston, Cumbria, LA12 7LJ
☎ 01229 582763
Est. 1961 *Stock size* Small
Stock Late 1800–1900s china, glass, jewellery, books
Open Mon–Sat 9am–5pm closed Wed
Services Valuations

WHITEHAVEN

Michael Moon (PBFA)
Contact Mr M Moon
19 Lowther Street, Whitehaven, Cumbria, CA28 7AL
☎ 01946 599010 Ⓕ 01946 599010
Est. 1970 *Stock size* Large
Stock Rare, second-hand and antiquarian books on cinema, history, local history
Open Mon–Sat 9am–5pm closed Wed Jan–Easter
Services Valuations, book search, catalogues (2–3 a year)

WINDERMERE

Serpentine Antiques
Contact Mrs M Worsley
30 Main Road, Windermere, Cumbria, LA23 1DY
☎ 01539 442189
Ⓔ mworsley@nascr.net
Est. 1974 *Stock size* Medium
Stock Furniture, collectables, china, glass, pictures, jewellery
Open Mon–Sat 9.30am–5.30pm Sun by appointment

WORKINGTON

Castle Antiques
Contact Mr K Wallace
18 Pow Street, Workington, Cumbria, CA14 3AG
☎ 01900 607499
Est. 1997 *Stock size* Medium
Stock Collectors' items, curios, furniture, pictures. Publisher of local history books
Open Mon–Sat 9am–5pm
Fairs Charnock Richard, Newark
Services Valuations

GREATER MANCHESTER

ATHERTON

The Emporium
Contact Mr G Wilson
486 Blackburn Road, Atherton, Bolton, Lancashire, BL1 8PE
☎ 01204 303090 Ⓕ 01204 302299
Est. 1989 *Stock size* Large
Stock Wide variety of second-hand Victorian–Edwardian furniture, china, collectables, glass
Open Mon–Sat 9am–5pm Sun 11am–4pm
Services Valuations

BOLTON

Bolton Pianos & Antique Export
Contact Frank Sotgiu
Victoria Buildings, Hanover Street, Bolton, Lancashire, BL1 4TG
☎ 01204 362036 Ⓕ 01204 380355
Ⓦ www.antica.co.uk
Est. 1983 *Stock size* Large
Stock Georgian–Edwardian furniture for export
Open Mon–Sat 9am–5pm
Services Shipping

B J Dawson (BNTA)
Contact Mr P Dawson
52 St Helens Road, Bolton, Lancashire, BL3 3NN
☎ 01204 63732 Ⓕ 01204 63732
Ⓜ 07801 537412
Ⓔ dawsoncoins@btconnect.com
Ⓦ historycoin.com
Est. 1966 *Stock size* Large
Stock Ancient coins – Greek, Roman, Byzantine, medallions, old English coins
Open Mon–Fri 9am–5pm

Sat 9am–noon
Fairs London Coin Fair
Services Valuations, lists, medal mounting

Ironchurch Antique Centre
Contact Mr P Wilkinson
Iron Church, Blackburn Road, Bolton, Lancashire, BL1 8DR
01204 383616
Est. 1993 *Stock size* Large
No. of dealers 20
Stock Antiques, furniture, pottery, porcelain, clocks, paintings
Open Mon–Sun 10am–5pm

G Oakes & Son
Contact Mr S Hughes
The Warehouse, 30 Blackbank Street, Bolton, Lancashire, BL1 8JA
01204 526587
07774 284609
ycs12@dial.pipex.com
www.Antique-DealerUK.com
Est. 1959 *Stock size* Large
Stock Antiques, Georgian–1920s furniture, shipping furniture
Open Mon–Fri noon–5pm or by appointment
Services Shipping

Olde Mill Antiques
Contact Paul Morris
Grecian Mill, Fletcher Street, Bolton, Lancashire, BL3 6NN
0800 542 5756 or 01204 528678
Est. 1980 *Stock size* Large
Stock Georgian–Victorian and shipping furniture
Open Mon–Fri 9am–5.30pm
Sat Sun 9.30am–4pm

BOWDON

English Garden Antiques
Contact Bill Seddon
The White Cottage, Church Brow, Bowdon, Altrincham, Cheshire, WA14 2SF
0161 928 0854 0161 929 8081
bill@english-garden-antiques.co.uk
www.english-garden-antiques.co.uk
Est. 1996 *Stock size* Large
Stock English garden antiques including stone troughs, sundials, bird baths, cast-iron urns, staddle stones, gargoyles
Open 10am–5pm confirm by telephone
Services Valuations, restoration, repair

French Country Style
Contact Margaret Ernstone
The Old Forge, 7a Church Brow, Bowdon, Cheshire, WA14 2SF
0161 927 9041 0161 927 9041
Est. 2000 *Stock size* medium
Stock French decorative items, furniture, lighting, mirrors
Open Wed–Sat 10am–5pm or by appointment
Services Restoration

Richmond Antiques
Contact Mr J Freeman
The Hollies, Richmond Road, Bowdon, Altrincham, Cheshire, WA14 2TT
0161 928 1229 0161 233 0431
07720 416055
info@richmondantiques.com
www.richmondantiques.com
Est. 1993 *Stock size* Large
Stock Decorative furniture, chandeliers, mirrors including 19thC French and English
Open Tues–Sat noon–6pm or by appointment
Services Valuations, restoration

BREDBURY

The Old Curiosity Shop
Contact Mrs S Crook
123 Stockport Road West, Bredbury, Stockport, Greater Manchester, SK6 2AN
0161 494 9469
Est. 1983 *Stock size* Large
Stock 1920s furniture, barley-twist a speciality, brass, clocks, pottery
Open Mon–Sat 10am–6pm
Sun noon–5pm closed Wed
Services Hand stripping service

BROMLEY CROSS

Drop Dial Antiques
Contact Irene Roberts
Last Drop Village, Hospital Road, Bromley Cross, Bolton, Lancashire, BL7 9PZ
01204 307186 or 01257 480995
Est. 1974 *Stock size* Medium
Stock Clocks, barometers, boxes, small items of furniture
Open Tues–Sun 12.30–4.30pm closed Mon
Fairs Ripley Castle, Stoneyhurst (Galloway Fairs), Naworth Castle, Duncombe Park
Services Clock and barometer restoration

Siri Ellis Books (PBFA)
Contact Siri Ellis
Last Drop Village, Hospital Road, Bromley Cross, Bolton, Lancashire, BL7 9PZ
01204 597511
mail@siriellisbooks.co.uk
www.siriellisbooks.co.uk
Est. 1998 *Stock size* Medium
Stock Antiquarian and second-hand illustrated and children's books
Open Mon–Fri noon–5pm
Sat Sun 10am–5pm
Fairs Buxton, Pudsey, PBFA
Services Free book search

BURY

Newtons of Bury
Contact Mr Glen Wild
151 The Rock, Bury, Lancashire, BL9 0ND
0161 764 1863 0161 761 7129
Est. 1989 *Stock size* Medium
Stock Antiques, furniture, china
Open Mon–Sat 9am–5pm
Sun noon–4pm
Services House clearance

CHEADLE HULME

John Arnold & Co
Contact Mr W Bradshaw
Central Salerooms, 15 Station Road, Cheadle Hulme, Cheshire, SK8 5AF
0161 485 2777 0161 485 3777
Est. 1865
Open Mon–Fri 10am–4pm
Sales Antiques and general sale Wed 11am, viewing day prior 11am–4pm day of sale 10–11am
Frequency Weekly
Catalogues No

Andrew Foott Antiques
Contact Andrew Foott
4 Claremont Road, Cheadle Hulme, Cheshire, SK8 6EG
0161 485 3559
Est. 1986 *Stock size* Small
Stock Georgian furniture, barometers

Open Mon–Fri 9am–5pm
Fairs NEC
Services Restoration

David Lloyd
Contact David Lloyd
10 Ravenoak Road, Cheadle Hulme, Cheshire, SK8 7DL
0161 486 6368
07711 948403
dloyd@onetel.net.uk
Est. 1991 *Stock size* Medium
Stock 18th–20thC silver, silver plate, flatware
Open By appointment only
Fairs Newark, Staffordshire, NEC
Services Matching flatware for canteens

FAILSWORTH

Failsworth Mill Antiques
Contact Mr I Macdonald
Failsworth Mill, Ashton Road West, Failsworth, Manchester, Lancashire, M35 0SD
0161 684 7440 F 0161 681 7111
Est. 1993 *Stock size* Large
Stock Furniture, small collectables etc in large warehouse
Open Mon–Fri 9am–5pm Sun 10am–4pm closed Bank Holidays
Services Restoration, export

The New Cavern Antiques & Collectors' Centre
Contact Mr Peter Stanley
Failsworth Mill, Ashton Road West, Failsworth, Manchester, Lancashire, M35 0FD
0161 684 7802
akg21353@aol.com
Est. 1997 *Stock size* Large
No. of dealers 40+
Stock Antiques, collectables, furniture
Open Mon–Sun 10am–4.30pm closed Sat
Services Shipping, valuations

R J O'Brien & Son Antiques Ltd
Contact Mr R O'Brien
Failsworth Mill, Ashton Road West, Failsworth, Manchester, Lancashire, M35 0FD
0161 688 4414 F 0161 688 4414
obantiques@btinternet.com
www.antique-exports.com
Est. 1972 *Stock size* Large
Stock Antique furniture
Open Mon–Fri 9am–5pm or by appointment
Services Container and courier service

T L H & Company
Contact Mr Thomas Higham
Unit 5, Victory Industrial Estate, Mill Street, Failsworth, Manchester, Lancashire, M35 0BJ
0161 688 9099 F 0161 688 9050
tlh@auctions1.freeserve.co.uk
Est. 1994
Open Mon–Sat 9am–5.30pm
Sales Sales weekly, Tues 11am, viewing Tues 9–11am, Thurs 11am, viewing 9–11am
Catalogues Yes

HALEBARNS

Cottage Antiques
Contact John Gholam
Hasty Lane, Halebarns, Altrincham, Cheshire, WA15 8UT
0161 980 7961
Est. 1975 *Stock size* Medium
Stock General antiques including oak, mahogany furniture, brass, copper, paintings, ceramics
Open Mon–Sat 9am–5pm or by appointment
Services Valuations

HAZEL GROVE

A F Brock & Co Ltd
Contact Mr A F Brock or Mrs W Jensen
269 London Road, Hazel Grove, Stockport, Cheshire, SK7 4PL
0161 456 5050 F 0161 456 5112
info@afbrock.co.uk
www.afbrock.co.uk
Est. 1969
Open Mon–Fri 9am–5pm Sat 9am–4pm closed Wed
Sales 6 coins, jewellery and antiques sales per year, telephone for details of sale. Specialist coin and banknote sales periodically. Held at the Acton Court Hotel, Stockport
Catalogues Yes

HEYWOOD

Heywood Antiques
Contact Mr Norman Marsh
5 Manchester Road, Heywood, Lancashire, OL10 2DZ
01706 621281
Est. 1989 *Stock size* Medium
Stock Late Victorian, Edwardian furniture, clocks
Open Mon–Sat 9.30am–5pm closed Tues
Services Clock repair and restoration

HOLLINGWORTH

Annatique
Contact Mr G MacKay
3 Woolley Lane, Hollingworth, Hyde, Cheshire, SK14 8NW
01457 852960
Est. 1977 *Stock size* Large
Stock Small furniture, clocks, lighting, mirrors, collectables
Open Thurs–Sat noon–6pm
Services Clock repairs

LEVENSHULME

Aaron Antiques
Contact Geoffrey Parkinson
The Antique Village, Stockport Road, Levenshulme, Manchester, M19 L1
01706 366413
Est. 1975 *Stock size* Medium
Stock General antiques
Open Mon–Sat 10.30am–5pm

Levenshulme Antiques Village
Contact Mr Tony Warburton
965 Stockport Road, Levenshulme, Manchester, M19 3NP
0161 256 4644
Est. 1979
No. of dealers 20 in Old Town Hall
Stock Furniture
Open Mon–Sat 10am–5.30pm Sun 11am–4pm
Services Restoration, wood stripping

G Long Antiques
Contact Gladys Long
811 Stockport Road, Levenshulme, Manchester, M19 3BF

☎ 0161 224 0845
Est. 1932 *Stock size* Large
Stock General antiques, 18th–19thC furniture
Open Mon–Sat 9am–5pm
Services Valuations, delivery

Ross Fireplaces
Contact Carl Ross
1026–1028 Stockport Road, Levenshulme, Manchester, M19 3WX P
☎ 0161 224 2550
rossfireplaces@aol.com
Est. 1988 *Stock size* Large
Stock Fireplaces
Open Mon–Sun 10am–4pm
Services Restoration

LITTLEBOROUGH

George Kelsall (PBFA)
Contact Mr B Kelsall
22 Church Street, Littleborough, Lancashire, OL15 9AA P
☎ 01706 370244
kelsall@bookshop22.fsnet.co.uk
Est. 1979 *Stock size* Large
Stock Mainly second-hand, modern and antiquarian books on art, history, reference, topography of Northern England, industrial history, transport, social history
Open Mon 11am–5pm Tues 1–5pm Wed–Sat 10am–5pm
Fairs PBFA (Lancashire, Yorkshire)

Nostalgia
Contact Mr Philip Sunderland
24 Church Street, Littleborough, Lancashire, OL15 9AA P
☎ 01706 377325
M 07711 503755
Est. 1994 *Stock size* Medium
Stock General antiques, furniture, lighting, Victorian fireplaces
Open Mon–Sat 10.30am–5pm closed Tues

MANCHESTER

Capes, Dunn & Co (ISVA)
Contact Alison Lakin
38 Charles Street, Manchester, M1 7DB P
☎ 0161 273 1911 F 0161 273 3474
capesdunn@compuserve.com
www.ukauctioneers.com
Est. 1826
Open Mon–Fri 9am–5pm
Sales Victorian and later period furniture and effects Mon noon, viewing from 10am day of sale. Specialist sales most Tues noon, viewing Mon 10am–4pm Tues 10–noon
Frequency Fortnightly
Catalogues Yes

Dollies Bear-Gere Ltd
Contact Susan Cottrill
113 Regents Crescent, The Trafford Centre, Manchester, M17 8AR P
☎ 0161 749 9898 F 0161 486 9400
www.dolliesbear-gere.com
Est. 1998 *Stock size* Large
Stock New and second-hand Steiff and collectable bears, dolls
Open Mon–Fri 10am–10pm Sat 10am–8pm Sun noon–6pm

Empire Exchange
Contact Mr David Ireland
1 Newton Street, Manchester, M1 1HW P
☎ 0161 236 4445 F 0161 273 5007
enquiries@empire-uk.com
www.empire-uk.com
Est. 1986 *Stock size* Large
Stock Collectors' items, old and new books, toys, football memorabilia, dolls, teddy bears, jewellery, military
Open Mon–Sun 9am–7.30pm
Services Publishing company, valuations

Phoenix Antiques
Contact Dave Brock
Unit L7, Royal Exchange Antique Centre, Cross Street, Manchester, M2 7DB
☎ 0161 834 6777
Est. 1986 *Stock size* Medium
Stock Jewellery, silverware
Open Mon–Sat 10.30am–5pm Sun by appointment

Secondhand & Rare Books
Contact Mr E Hopkinson
1 Church Street, Manchester, M4 1PN P
☎ 0161 834 5964 or 01625 861608
Est. 1972 *Stock size* Medium
Stock Antiquarian and second-hand books, some topography and special interest
Open Mon–Sat noon–4pm

Select
Contact Mr Abushal
274 Claremont Road, Manchester, M14 4TS P
☎ 0161 226 1152 F 0161 226 1152
Est. 1994 *Stock size* Medium
Stock General antiques, mostly furniture
Open Mon–Sat 10am–5pm

MARPLE BRIDGE

Townhouse Antiques
Contact Mr Paul Buxcey
21 Town Street, Marple Bridge, Stockport, Cheshire, SK6 5AA P
☎ 0161 427 2228
Est. 1985 *Stock size* Medium
Stock Stripped pine furniture, carved wood, brass, iron beds, decorative antiques
Open Mon–Sat 10am–6pm

OLDHAM

The Collectors Centre
Contact Mr I Thorogood
12a Waterloo Street, Oldham, Lancashire, OL1 1SQ P
☎ 0161 624 1365
Est. 1991 *Stock size* Large
No. of dealers 4
Stock Broad range of collectables – records, pop memorabilia, brass, pressed and old English glass, china, pottery, silver, videos, toys, etc
Open Mon–Sat 10am–5pm closed Tues
Services Valuations

Bob Lees
Contact Mr Bob Lees
65 George Street, Oldham, Lancashire, OL1 1LX P
☎ 0161 628 4693
Est. 1994 *Stock size* Large
Stock General bookshop, second-hand, some antiquarian, local history
Open Mon–Sat 10.30am–6pm
Fairs Pudsey Book Fair, Buxton

Marks Antiques, Jewellers/Pawnbrokers
Contact Mrs Marks
16 Waterloo Street, Oldham, Lancashire, OL1 1SQ P
☎ 0161 624 5975 F 0161 624 5975
M 07979 508495

Est. 1970 *Stock size* Medium
Stock Jewellery, pottery, good-quality furniture
Open Mon–Sat 9.30am–5pm closed Tues
Fairs Newark
Services Pawnbroker, valuations

PRESTWICH

Family Antiques
Contact Jean Ditondo
405–407 Bury New Road, Prestwich, Manchester, M25 1AA
☎ 0161 798 0036 Ⓕ 0161 798 0036
Est. 1984 *Stock size* Large
Stock Antique furniture
Open Mon–Sat 10am–5pm
Fairs Newark, Swinderby
Services Valuations

Village Antiques
Contact Ruth Weidenbaum
416 Bury New Road, Prestwich, Manchester, M25 1BD
☎ 0161 773 3612
Est. 1981 *Stock size* Medium
Stock Porcelain, pottery, glass, pewter, small furniture
Open Mon–Sat 10am–5pm closed Wed

RADCLIFFE

Partners Antiques
Contact Mr L Ditondo
Walker Street, Radcliffe, Manchester, M26 1FH
☎ 0161 796 7095 Ⓕ 0161 796 7095
Ⓔ luigi.ditondo@btinternet.com
Ⓦ www.luigi.ditondo@btinternet.com
Est. 1991 *Stock size* Large
Stock Victorian and shipping furniture
Open Mon–Sun 9am–6pm
Fairs Newark, Ardingly
Services Container service

ROCHDALE

Antiques & Bygones
Contact Mr K Bonn
100 Drake Street, Rochdale, Lancashire, OL16 1PQ
☎ 01706 648114
Ⓔ ken.bonn@btopenworld.com
Est. 1983 *Stock size* Medium
Stock Small antique items including pottery, silver, coins, medals, jewellery, militaria, collectables
Open Wed–Sat 10am–3pm

Central Auction Rooms
Contact Terry Pickering
4 Baron Street, Rochdale, Lancashire, OL16 1SJ
☎ 01706 646298 Ⓕ 01706 646298
Est. 1919
Open Mon–Fri 9.30am–4.30pm
Sales General household sales Tues 2pm, viewing Mon 9.30am–4.30pm. Occasional antiques and small items Tues 1pm, viewing Mon 9.30am–4pm
Frequency Fortnightly
Catalogues Yes

ROMILEY

Romiley Antiques & Jewellery
Contact Mr Peter Green
42 Stockport Road, Romiley, Stockport, Cheshire, SK6 3AA
☎ 0161 494 6920
Ⓜ 07939 668819
Est. 1984 *Stock size* Medium
Stock Antique and second-hand jewellery, Georgian and Victorian furniture, pottery, general antiques, clocks, barometers
Open Thurs Sat 9am–5pm or by appointment
Services Valuations, house clearance

SALFORD

A S Antique Galleries
Contact Audrey Sternshine
26 Broad Street, Pendleton, Salford, Greater Manchester, M6 5BY
☎ 0161 737 5938
Ⓔ as@sternshine.demon.co.uk
Est. 1973 *Stock size* Large
Stock Art Nouveau and Art Deco, bronze and bronze and ivory figures, lighting, cameo glass, pewter, ceramics, furniture, jewellery, silver and general antiques
Open Thurs–Sat 10am–5.30pm or by appointment
Services Valuations, restoration, purchase on commission

STALYBRIDGE

Highams Auctions (NAVA)
Contact Mr M McLaughlin
Waterloo House, Waterloo Road, Stalybridge, Cheshire, SK15 2AU
☎ 0161 338 8698 Ⓕ 0161 338 4183
Ⓔ info@highamsauctions.com
Ⓦ www.highamsauctions.com
Est. 1941
Open Mon–Fri 9am–5pm
Sales General antiques sales Sat 10am, viewing Fri 1–4.30pm Sat 9–10am
Frequency Fortnightly
Catalogues Yes

STOCKPORT

Antique Furniture Warehouse
Contact Mr M Shields
Unit 3–4, Royal Oak Buildings, Cooper Street, Stockport, Cheshire, SK1 3QJ
☎ 0161 429 8590 Ⓕ 0161 480 5375
Est. 1981 *Stock size* Large
Stock Wide range of antiques Georgian–1940s including porcelain, English inlay furniture, decorative items, architectural antiques, credenzas, walnut and mahogany bookcases
Open Mon–Sat 9am–5pm

Flintlock Antiques
Contact Mr F Tomlinson
28–30 Bramhall Lane, Stockport, Cheshire, SK2 6HR
☎ 0161 480 9973
Est. 1968 *Stock size* Medium
Stock Scientific instruments, telescopes, military items, paintings, marine models, furniture
Open Mon–Fri 10am–6pm

Hole in the Wall Antiques
Contact Mr A Ledger
20 Buxton Road, Heaviley, Stockport, Cheshire, SK2 6NU
☎ 0161 476 4013 Ⓕ 0161 285 2860
Ⓔ paul@antiquesimportexport.freeserve.co.uk.
Est. 1963 *Stock size* Large
Stock 1850–1920 American,

Georgian–Edwardian furniture
Open Mon–Sat 9.30am–5.30pm or by appointment
Fairs Newark
Services Courier

Imperial Antiques (LAPADA)
Contact Alfred Todd
295 Buxton Road, Great Moor, Stockport, Cheshire, SK2 7NR P
☎ 0161 483 3322 F 0161 483 3376
E alfred@imperialantiques.com
W www.imperialantiques.com
Est. 1975 *Stock size* Medium
Stock Oriental antiques, ceramics, carpets, lighting, silver, silver plate
Open Mon–Fri 9am–5pm
Fairs NEC
Services Valuations

Manchester Antique Company
Contact Mr J Long
Mac House, St Thomas Place, Stockport, Cheshire, SK1 3TZ P
☎ 0161 355 5566 F 0161 355 5588
E sales@manchester-antique.co.uk
W www.manchester-antique.co.uk
Est. 1969 *Stock size* Large
Stock General antiques, second-hand and European furniture
Trade only Mainly trade
Open Mon–Fri 8am–5pm Sat 10am–4pm

Nostalgia (LAPADA)
Contact Mrs E Durrant
Holland's Mill, Shaw Heath, Stockport, Cheshire, SK3 8BH P
☎ 0161 477 7706 F 0161 477 2267
E info@nostalgia-uk.com
W www.nostalgia-uk.com
Est. 1977 *Stock size* Large
Stock Antique fireplaces 1780–1900, sanitary ware
Open Tues–Fri 10am–6pm Sat 10am–5pm

Strippadoor
Contact Danny Russell
Victoria Works, Units 2 and 3, Hempshaw Lane, Stockport, Cheshire, SK1 4LG P
☎ 0161 477 8980 F 0161 477 6302
Est. 1979
Stock Antique pine, original doors and fireplaces
Open Mon–Fri 9am–5.30pm Sat 10.30am–2.30pm
Services Stripping

STRETFORD

Insitu (SALVO)
Contact Mr F Newsham
4 Longford Road, Stretford, Manchester, Lancashire, M32 0HQ P
☎ 0161 865 2110
E insitu-@btconnect.com
W www.insituarchitectural.com
Est. 1984 *Stock size* Large
Stock Complete range of antiques, fixtures and fittings
Open Mon–Sat 9am–5.30pm

WIGAN

Avaroot
Contact Mr P Prescott
53a Mesnes Street (rear), Wigan, Lancashire, WN1 1QX P
☎ 01942 241500
Est. 1994 *Stock size* Large
Stock Collectables including Doulton, Beswick, books, cigarette cards, records, coins, badges, railwayana, lamps
Open Mon–Sat 10am–5pm

Beech Hill Antiques
Contact Mr Breheny
90 Beech Hill Avenue, Beech Hill, Wigan, Lancashire, WN6 8NY P
☎ 01942 495585
Est. 2001 *Stock size* Medium
Stock Furniture, pottery
Open Mon Thurs–Sat 10.30am–5pm Sun 11am–3.30pm

J W Antiques
Contact William Kenny
127 Bolton Road, Wigan, Greater Manchester, WN4 8AE P
☎ 01942 271212
Est. 1996 *Stock size* Large
Stock Leaded windows, shipping furniture
Open Mon–Sat 9am–5pm

John Robinson Antiques
Contact Mrs E Halliwell
172–176 Manchester Road, Higher Ince, Wigan, Lancashire, WN2 2EA P
☎ 01942 247773 F 01942 824964
Est. 1963 *Stock size* Large
Stock Wholesale exporters, mostly shipping furniture
Trade only Yes
Open By appointment only

Colin de Rouffignac (BNTA)
Contact Mr C de Rouffignac
57 Wigan Lane, Wigan, Lancashire, WN1 2LF P
☎ 01942 237927
Est. 1970 *Stock size* Medium
Stock 18th–early 20thC furniture, early coins, medals, general antiques, paintings
Open Mon–Sat 10am–4.30pm closed Wed
Fairs Tatton
Services Valuations

Steve's World Famous Movie Store
Contact Mr S Ellison
45 Cadogan Drive, Winstanley, Wigan, Lancashire, WN3 6JH P
☎ 01942 213541 F 01942 213541
E movie.store@virgin.net
W www.worldfamousmovie.com
Est. 1973 *Stock size* Large
Stock Stills, posters, vinyl and CD soundtracks, books and movie magazines from 1916 onwards, other memorabilia, autographs
Open By appointment
Services Free search, mail order, valuations

Wiend Books & Collectables (PBFA)
Contact Mr P G Morris
8–10 & 12 The Wiend, Wigan, Lancashire, WN1 1PF P
☎ 01942 820500 F 01942 820500
M 07976 604203
E wiendbooks@lycos.co.uk
W www.wiendbooks.co.uk
Est. 1997 *Stock size* Large
Stock General stock of antiquarian and second-hand books, printed collectables, comics, stamps, programmes, badges, Wade
Open Mon–Sat 9.30am–5pm closed Tues
Fairs PBFA
Services Valuations

WORSLEY

Northern Clocks (LAPADA)
Contact Robert or Mary Anne

✉ Boothsbank Farm, Worsley, Manchester, M28 1LL P
☎ 0161 790 8414
Ⓜ 07970 820258
Ⓔ info@northernclocks.co.uk
Ⓦ www.northernclocks.co.uk
Est. 1997 *Stock size* Medium
Stock Longcase, bracket, wall clocks
Open Thurs–Sat 10am–5pm or by appointment
Fairs Antiques for Everyone, Chester, Buxton
Services Valuations, restoration

LANCASHIRE

ACCRINGTON

Alpha Coins & Medals
Contact Mr P Darlington
✉ **20 Abbey Street, Accrington, Lancashire, BB5 1EB** P
☎ 01254 395540
Est. 1994 *Stock size* Medium
Stock Post-1800 British coins and medals
Open Mon–Sat 9.30am–5pm
Services Medal mounting

Revival
Contact Mr Ian Smith
✉ **6 Warner Street, Accrington, Lancashire, BB5 1HN** P
☎ 01254 382316
Est. 1989 *Stock size* Large
Stock Costume, textiles, jewellery from 1900–1970s
Open Mon–Sat 10.30am–5pm closed Wed or by appointment
Fairs Hammersmith Textiles
Services Costume hire

BARTON

Kopper Kettle Furniture
Contact Mr Steve Round
✉ **639 Garstang Road, Barton, Preston, Lancashire, PR3 5DQ** P
☎ 01772 861064
Est. 1998 *Stock size* Medium
Stock Edwardian–Victorian furniture, some reproduction
Open Mon–Sun 10.30am–5.30pm
Services Valuations, metal polishing

BLACKBURN

Ancient and Modern (NAG, OMRS)
Contact Zac Coles
✉ **17 Newmarket Street, Blackburn, Lancashire, BB1 7DR** P
☎ 01254 677866 Ⓕ 01254 677866
Est. 1943 *Stock size* Large
Stock Georgian–modern jewellery, watches, silver, coins, medals
Open Mon–Sat 9am–5.30pm
Fairs Miami, Bangkok
Services Valuations, restoration

Decades (Textile Society)
Contact Janet Conroy
✉ **20 Lord Street West, Blackburn, Lancashire, BB2 1JX** P
☎ 01254 693320
Est. 1989 *Stock size* Large
Stock Costumes, textiles, accessories, pottery, small furniture, pictures, glass, curios, collectables
Open Tues–Sat 10.30am–5pm or by appointment
Fairs Margaret Bulger Art Fairs, Hammersmith

Fieldings Antiques & Clocks
Contact Mr Andrew Fielding
✉ **149 Blackmoor Road, Blackburn, Lancashire, BB1 2LG** P
☎ 01254 263358
Ⓜ 07973 698961
Est. 1964 *Stock size* Large
Stock Longcase and other clocks, period oak furniture, steam engines, vintage motorcycles
Open Mon–Fri 9am–5pm

Mitchells Lock Antiques
Contact Mr S Mitchell
✉ **76 Bolton Road, Blackburn, Lancashire, BB2 3PZ** P
☎ 01254 664663
Ⓜ 07977 856725
Est. 1973 *Stock size* Large
Stock General antiques
Open Mon–Sat 9am–5pm
Fairs Newark, Swinderby

BLACKPOOL

Ascot Antiques
Contact Mr C Winwood
✉ **106 Holmefield Road, Blackpool, Lancashire, FY2 9RF** P
☎ 01253 356383
Est. 1987 *Stock size* Medium
Stock Georgian–Victorian furniture and oil paintings
Trade only Yes
Open By appointment
Services Valuations

Peter Christian
Contact Mrs Ann Christian
✉ **400–402 Waterloo Road, South Shore, Blackpool, Lancashire, FY4 4BL** P
☎ 01253 763268 Ⓕ 01253 763268
Est. 1978 *Stock size* Medium
Stock 1860s–1920s decorative arts
Open Tues–Sat 10am–5.30pm closed Wed

Robinsons Timber Building Supplies Ltd
Contact Mr A Robinson
✉ **3–7 Boothley Road, Blackpool, Lancashire, FY1 3RS** P
☎ 01253 628826
Est. 1938 *Stock size* Large
Stock Architectural antiques, doors, floors etc, garden items
Open Mon–Fri 8am–5.30pm Sat 8am–2pm
Services Timber flooring restoration

B Scott-Spencer
Contact Mr J Neiman
✉ **228 Church Street, Blackpool, Lancashire, FY1 3PX** P
☎ 01253 294489 Ⓕ 01253 626977
Stock Wide range of general antiques, jewellery, stamps, collectables etc
Open Mon–Fri 10am–4pm telephone for appointment
Services Valuations, repairs, buying large diamonds

BRETHERTON

The Old Corn Mill Antique Centre
Contact Mr M Fellows
✉ **64 South Road, Bretherton, Lancashire, PR5 7AG** P
☎ 01772 601371 Ⓕ 01772 601932
Est. 1999 *Stock size* Large
No. of dealers 50

Stock Antiques and collectables
Open Mon–Sat 10.30am–5.30pm
Sun 11am–5pm

BURNLEY

Brun-Lea Antiques
Contact Mr John Waite
Unit 1, Elm Street Business Park, Burnley, Lancashire, BB10 1DG
01282 413513 (F) 01282 832769
(E) jwaite@freenetname.co.uk
(W) www.antiques-atlas.com
Est. 1973 *Stock size* Large
Stock Period furniture to 1930s
Open Mon–Thurs 8.30am–5.30pm Fri Sat 8.30am–4pm Sun noon–4pm

Brun-Lea Antiques
Contact Mr John Waite
3 & 5 Standish Street, Burnley, Lancashire, BB11 1AP
01282 432396
(E) jwaite@freenetname.co.uk
(W) www.antiques-atlas.com
Est. 1973 *Stock size* Large
Stock Edwardian–Victorian furniture
Open Mon–Sat 9am–5pm

Lonesome Pine Antiques
Contact Mr P Berry
19 Bank Parade, Burnley, Lancashire, BB11 1UH
01282 428415
Est. 1987 *Stock size* Medium
Stock Antique pine furniture, period furniture, reclaimed pine furniture
Open Mon–Sat 9am–5pm
Services Bespoke furniture

BURSCOUGH

West Lancashire Antiques Export (LAPADA)
Contact Brett Griffiths
Victoria Mill, Victoria Street, Burscough, Lancashire, LN40 0SN
01704 894634
Est. 1969 *Stock size* Large
Stock Antique furniture
Open Mon–Fri 9am–5.30pm Sat Sun 10am–5.30pm
Fairs Swinderby, Newark
Services Shipping

CHARNOCK RICHARD

Park Hall
Contact Mr David Fletcher
Exhibition Halls, Charnock Richard, Lancashire, PR7 5LP
07800 508178 (F) 01989 730339
Stock size Medium
No. of dealers 100
Stock General antiques, collectables. General antiques fair held every Sunday. £2 entrance fee
Open Sun 8am–3pm

CLEVELEYS

Smythe's
Contact Mr P Smythe
174 Victoria Road West, Cleveleys, Lancashire, FY5 3NE
01253 852184 (F) 01253 854084
(E) smythe@btinternet.com
(W) www.smythes.net
Est. 1929
Open Mon–Fri 9am–5.30pm Sat 9am–noon
Sales General sales every 2 weeks, antiques sales every 6 weeks
Catalogues Yes

CLITHEROE

Clitheroe Collectables
Contact Mrs J Spensley
13 Duck Street, Clitheroe, Lancashire, BB7 1LP
01200 422222 (F) 01200 422223
(E) sales@clicollect.fsnet.co.uk
(W) www.clitheroecollectables.co.uk
Est. 1989 *Stock size* Medium
Stock Pottery, Victorian pine furniture
Open Mon–Sat 9am–5pm
Fairs Harrogate
Services Restoration of antique pine

Past and Present Fireplaces
Contact Mr David Hollings
22 Whalley Road, Clitheroe, Lancashire, BB7 1AW
01200 428678/445373
Est. 1987 *Stock size* Large
Stock Architectural antiques, general antiques, fireplaces a speciality
Open Mon–Sat 10.30am–5pm Sun by appointment closed Wed
Fairs Newark
Services Fitting service, fire accessories

Roundstone Books
Contact Mr J Harding
29 Moor Lane, Clitheroe, Lancashire, BB7 1BE
01200 444242
(E) joharbooks@aol.com
(W) www.roundstonebooks.co.uk
Est. 1995 *Stock size* Medium
Stock Antiquarian and second-hand books, general stock including alternative medicine, poetry, literature, children's books
Open Tues–Sat 10am–5pm closed Wed
Services Book search

DARWEN

Belgrave Antiques Centre
Contact Mr M Cooney
Brittania Mill, 136 Bolton Road, Darwen, Lancashire, BB3 1BZ
01254 777714
(E) belgraveantiques@aol.com
Est. 1997 *Stock size* Large
No. of dealers 40
Stock Furniture, pottery, Victorian stripped pine, architectural antiques, collectables
Open Tue–Sat 9.30am–5pm Sun 11am–4.30pm
Services Stripping, shipping

K C Antiques (LAPADA)
Contact Mr C Davies
538 Bolton Road, Darwen, Lancashire, BB3 2JR
01254 772252
(E) mickdavies@breathe.mail.net.
Est. 1970 *Stock size* Medium
Stock 18th–19thC furniture and decorative items
Open Mon–Sat 9am–5.30pm Sun 10am–4pm and by appointment
Fairs NEC LAPADA

ECCLESTON

Bygone Times
Contact Ged Wood
Grove Mill, The Green, Eccleston, Chorley, Lancashire, PR7 5PD

☎ 01257 451889 ⓕ 01257 451090
ⓔ ged.wood@virgin.net
ⓦ www.bygonetimes.co.uk
Est. 1988 *Stock size* Large
No. of dealers 250 stalls
Stock Antiques, furniture, small items, collectables, memorabilia
Open Mon–Sun 10am–6pm Wed 10am–8pm

GREAT HARWOOD

Benny Charlsworth's Snuff Box
Contact Naomi Walsh
✉ **51 Blackburn Road, Great Harwood, Blackburn, Lancashire, BB6 7DF** Ⓟ
☎ 01254 888550
Est. 1983 *Stock size* Large
Stock Antique furniture, paintings, pottery, costume jewellery, linen etc
Open Mon–Fri 10am–1pm 2pm–5pm Sat 10am–noon closed Tues
Fairs Newark

Jeans Military Memories
Contact Mrs J South
✉ **32 Queen Street, Great Harwood, Blackburn, Lancashire, BB6 7QQ** Ⓟ
☎ 01254 877825 ⓕ 01254 877825
Ⓜ 07710 636069
Est. 1996 *Stock size* Large
Stock Militaria, guns of all types, edge weaponry 1800–2002
Open Mon–Fri 9am–5pm Sat 9am–4pm or by appointment

HAPTON

Pipkins Antiques
Contact Maurice Bradley
✉ **5 The Stables, Hapton, Nr Burnley, Lancashire, BB12 7LL** Ⓟ
☎ 07778 265909 ⓕ 01282 770548
ⓔ maurice@pipkins.fsbusiness.co.uk
Est. 1996 *Stock size* Large
Stock Doors, door furniture, Belfast sinks, general architectural salvage
Open By appointment

HARLE SYKE

Kings Mill Antique Centre
Contact Linda Heuer
✉ **Unit 6, Kings Mill, Queen Street, Harle Syke, Burnley, Lancashire, BB10 2HX** Ⓟ
☎ 01282 431953 ⓕ 01282 839470
Ⓜ 07803 153752
ⓔ antiques@kingsmill.demon.co.uk
ⓦ www.kingsmill.demon.co.uk
Est. 1996 *Stock size* Large
No. of dealers 30
Stock Antique furniture, European collectables
Open Mon–Sat 10am–5pm Thurs 10am–7pm Sun 11am–5pm
Services Container service, courier service, export

HASLINGDEN

P J Brown Antiques
Contact Mrs K Brown
✉ **8 Church Street, Haslingden, Rossendale, Lancashire, BB4 5QU** Ⓟ
☎ 01706 224888 ⓕ 01706 224888
Est. 1979 *Stock size* Medium
Stock Georgian–Edwardian furniture, small antiques, advertising items, shop fittings, old bottles, pot lids
Open Mon–Fri 10am–5.30pm Sat 10am–4pm or by appointment
Fairs Newark
Services Containers

Holden Wood Antiques Centre
Contact John Ainslough
✉ **St Stephens, Grane Road, Haslingden, Rossendale, Lancashire, BB4 4AT** Ⓟ
☎ 01706 830803
ⓔ john@holdenwood.co.uk
ⓦ www.holdenwood.co.uk
Est. 1996 *Stock size* Large
No. of dealers 30+
Stock Ceramics, clocks, watches, paintings, period and country furniture
Open Mon–Sun 10am–5.30pm
Services Valuations, restoration, tea rooms

HESKIN GREEN

Heskin Hall Antiques
Contact Mr Dennis Harrison
✉ **Wood Lane, Heskin, Chorley, Lancashire, PR7 5PA** Ⓟ
☎ 01257 452044 ⓕ 01257 450690
ⓔ heskinhall@aol.com
Est. 1995 *Stock size* Large
No. of dealers 65
Stock A complete range of antiques and collectables
Open Mon–Sun 10am–5.30pm
Services Restoration

HORWICH

The Toy Shop
Contact Mr D Brandwood
✉ **138a Wright Street, Horwich, Bolton, Lancashire, BL6 7HU** Ⓟ
☎ 01204 669782 ⓕ 01204 669782
Est. 1972 *Stock size* Large
Stock Collectable toys, Dinky, Corgi, Hornby, Triang, Matchbox
Open Mon Thurs Fri 9.30am–5pm Sat 9.30am–2pm
Services Valuations

KIRKBY LONSDALE

Architus Antiques & Collectables
Contact Mrs J Pearson
✉ **14 Main Street, Kirkby Lonsdale, Carnforth, Lancashire, LA6 2AE** Ⓟ
☎ 01524 272409
Est. 1994 *Stock size* Medium
Stock Wide range of antiques and collectables
Open Mon–Sat 10am–5pm
Services Valuations

LANCASTER

Anything Old & Military Collectables
Contact Mr G H Chambers
✉ **55 Scotforth Road, Lancaster, Lancashire, LA1 4SA** Ⓟ
☎ 01524 69933
Est. 1984 *Stock size* Medium
Stock Militaria including medals, cap badges, edged weapons, uniforms, helmets, Third Reich militaria
Open Wed Sat 1.30–6pm other times by appointment
Services Valuations, medal mounting

Atticus Bookshop
Contact Miss Tracey Mansell
✉ **26 King Street, Lancaster, Lancashire, LA1 1JY** Ⓟ
☎ 01524 381413

trace@atticusbooks.demon.co.uk
Est. 1974 *Stock size* Medium
Stock General second-hand stock of books
Open Mon–Sat 10am–5pm
Services Book search

G B Antiques Centre
Contact Mr Alan Blackburn
Lancaster Leisure Park, Wyresdale Road, Lancaster, Lancashire, LA1 3LA
01524 844734 01524 844735
Est. 1990 *Stock size* Large
No. of dealers 140
Stock Wide range of antiques, collectables
Open Mon–Sun 10am–5pm
Services Café, factory shop

Lancastrian Antiques & Co
Contact Mr S Wilkinson
70–72 Penny Street, Lancaster, Lancashire, LA1 1XF
01524 847004
info@rectorylancs.co.uk
Est. 1981 *Stock size* Medium
Stock General, period furniture, porcelain, pottery, paintings
Open Mon–Sat 10am–4.30pm closed Wed
Services Valuations

LONGRIDGE

Berry Antiques & Interiors
Contact Kerry Barnett or Eloise Halsall
61 Berry Lane, Longridge, Preston, Lancashire, PR3 3NH
01772 780476
Est. 2001 *Stock size* Medium
Stock General antiques, collectables
Open Mon–Sat 10am–4pm

Henry Holden & Son Ltd
Contact Mrs S MacCarthy or Mrs E Harvey
Central Salerooms, Towneley Road, Longridge, Preston, Lancashire, PR3 3EA
01772 783274 01772 783274
info@holmesandsons.co.uk
www.holmesandsons.co.uk
Est. 1890
Open Mon–Fri 9.30am–4.30pm
Sales Fortnightly on Sat, household 10am, antiques noon, viewing Fri 10am–8pm day of sale 9–10am

LYTHAM ST ANNE'S

Mike Mallinson
Contact Mr M Mallinson
Lot 3 Auction Hall, 3 Kingsway, Lytham St Anne's, Lancashire, FY8 1AB
01253 731600 01253 731614
Est. 1993
Open Mon–Fri 9am–5pm
Sales Antiques, reproductions and collectables every 3rd Wed 9.30am–2.30pm, viewing Sat 10am–noon Mon 10am–6pm Tues 10am–5pm

Windmill Bookshop
Contact Gail Welsh
62a Preston Road, Lytham St Anne's, Lancashire, FY8 5AE
01253 732485 01253 732485
07743 989532
Est. 1993 *Stock size* Medium
Stock General stock of antiquarian and second-hand books
Open Mon–Sun 9.30am–5.30pm
Fairs Buxton, Pudsey

MORECAMBE

Clocktower Antiques
Contact John Hawthorn
9 & 11 Queen Street, Morecambe, Lancashire, LA4 5EQ
01524 833331
sales@clocktowerantiques.com
www.clocktowerantiques.com
Est. 1986 *Stock size* Large
Stock Antique clocks, mixed period furniture
Open Mon–Sun 9am–5pm closed Wed
Services Restoration and repair of clocks, polishing

NELSON

Brittons Watches (NAG)
Contact Mr P Walden or Glen Britton
4 King Street, Clitheroe, Lancashire, BB7 2EP
01200 425555 or 01282 697659
0870 136 1597
info@brittons-watches.co.uk
www.brittons-watches.co.uk
Est. 1969 *Stock size* Large
Stock Quality pre-owned wrist watches from 1920s to present day, antique and quality second-hand jewellery
Open Mon–Sat 10am–5pm
Services Watch and jewellery repairs, valuations

ORMSKIRK

Browzaround
Contact Mrs P Graham
16 Derby Street West, Ormskirk, Lancashire, L39 3NH
01695 576999
Est. 1975 *Stock size* Medium
Stock Pre-war furniture, collectables and antique agricultural tools
Open Tues–Sat 10am–4pm closed Wed

Collectors Corner
Contact Mr B Jermyn
117 Aughton Street, Ormskirk, Lancashire, L39 3BN
01695 577455
07710 741250
beaniebob@btinternet.com
Est. 1997 *Stock size* Large
Stock Cigarette cards, Beanie Babies, dolls' houses
Open Thur–Sat 10.30am–5pm Wed 10.30am–4pm
Services Valuations

Green Lane Antiques
Contact Mr J Swift
Unit B20, Malthouse Business Centre, 48 Southport Road, Ormskirk, Lancashire, L39 1QR
01695 580731
www.greenlaneantiques.co.uk
Est. 1998 *Stock size* Large
Stock Architectural antiques, period furniture, clocks, pine etc
Open Mon–Sun 10am–4pm
Services Restoration

A Grice
Contact Mr A Grice
106 Aughton Street, Ormskirk, Lancashire, L39 3BS
01695 572007
Est. 1946 *Stock size* Small
Stock Furniture
Open Mon–Sat 10am–5pm closed Wed
Services Valuations, antique furniture restoration

PADIHAM

Discretion Antiques Ltd
Contact Iris Owen
37 Burnley Road, Padiham, Burnley, Lancashire, BB12 8BY P
01282 775693
Est. 1992 *Stock size* Medium
Stock Small modest-cost antiques and collectables
Open Mon–Fri 10.30am–4.45pm Sat 10.30am–12.30pm closed Tues

PRESTON

The Antique Centre
Contact Louise Allison
56 Garstang Road, Preston, Lancashire, PR1 1NA P
01772 882078 F 01772 252842
M 01772 882078
E info@paulallisonantiques.co.uk
W www.paulallinsonantiques.co.uk
Est. 1991 *Stock size* Large
No. of dealers 20
Stock Furniture
Open Mon–Fri 9am–5.30pm Sat 9.30am–5.30pm Sun 10.30am–4.30pm
Services Valuations, restoration, book search, shipping

European Fine Arts & Antiques
Contact Mr Brian Beck
10 Cannon Street, Preston, Lancashire, PR1 3NR P
01772 883886 F 01772 823888
E info@european-fine-arts.co.uk
W www.european-fine-arts.co.uk
Est. 1969 *Stock size* Large
Stock Victorian gallery, furniture, Louis XIV-style furniture
Open Mon–Sat 9.30am–5.30pm or by appointment

Fine Art Antiques
Contact Mr Mark Pedler
109 New Hall Lane, Preston, Lancashire, PR1 5PB P
01772 794010
Est. 1987 *Stock size* Medium
Stock Georgian oak furniture, bracket and longcase clocks, barometers, general antiques
Open Mon–Fri 10am–4pm
Fairs Newark
Services Restoration, chandelier re-wiring

David Greenhalgh Antiques
Contact David Greenhalgh
Preston Antique Centre, Horrock's Mill, New Hall Lane, Preston, Lancashire, PL1 5NX P
01229 462001
M 07768 582337
Est. 1960 *Stock size* Medium
Stock General antiques, shipping goods
Open Mon–Fri 8.30am–5.30pm Sat 10am–4pm Sun 10am–5pm

K C Antiques & K D Interiors at Samlesbury Hall
Contact Julie Robinson
The Long Gallery, Samlesbury Hall, Preston New Road, Preston, Lancashire, PR5 0UP P
01254 813883
W www.antique-interiors.co.uk
Est. 1990 *Stock size* Medium
Stock 18th–19thC furniture and decorative items
Open Mon–Fri 11am–4.30pm Sun 10am–4pm

Nelson Antiques
Contact Mr W Nelson
113 New Hall Lane, Preston, Lancashire, PR1 5PB P
01772 794896
Est. 1969 *Stock size* Medium
Stock General antiques, small items, silver, jewellery, copper, miners' lamps, collectables
Open Mon–Sat 9.30am–5pm
Fairs Newark

The Odd Chair Company
Contact Sue Cook
The Studio, Eaves Cottage Farm, Eaves, Preston, Lancashire, PR4 0BH P
01772 691777 F 01772 691888
E info@theoddchaircompany.com
W www.theoddchaircompany.com
Est. 1969 *Stock size* Large
Stock 19thC antique chairs, sofas and decorative furniture
Open Mon–Fri 9am–5pm Sat by prior arrangement
Fairs Newark, Ardingly
Services Interior design

Preston Antiques Centre
Contact Sue Shalloe
The Mill, New Hall Lane, Preston, Lancashire, PL1 5NX P
01772 794498 F 01772 651694
E prestonantiques@talk21.com
W www.prestonantiquescentre.com
Est. 1978 *Stock size* Large
No. of dealers 50
Stock General antiques, clocks, fine arts, porcelain
Open Mon–Fri 8.30am–5pm Sat 10am–4pm Sun 10am–5pm

Ribble Reclamation (SALVO)
Contact Mr Joe Hindle
Ducie Place, Off New Hall Lane, Preston, Lancashire, PR1 4UJ P
01772 794534 F 01772 794604
E joe@ribble-reclamation.com
W www.ribble-reclamation.com
Est. 1977 *Stock size* Large
Stock Garden statuary, arches, stone flags, lamp posts, fountains, architectural antiques, reclaimed building materials
Open Mon–Fri 8am–5pm Sat 8am–1pm
Fairs Holker Hall Country Garden Festival, Harrogate Spring Flower Show

ROSSENDALE

Fieldings Antiques & Clocks
Contact Mr Andrew Fielding
176–180 Blackburn Road, Haslingden, Rossendale, Lancashire, BB4 5HW P
01706 214254
M 07973 698961
Est. 1964 *Stock size* Large
Stock Longcase and other clocks, period oak furniture, steam engines, vintage motorcycles
Open Mon–Fri 9am–5pm

SABDEN

Walter Aspinall Antiques
Contact Mr W Aspinall
Pendle Antiques Centre, Union Mill, Watt Street, Sabden, Clitheroe, Lancashire, BB7 9ED P
01282 778642 F 01282 778643
E walter.aspinall@btinternet.com

Est. 1986 *Stock size* Large
Stock General antiques Victorian–1940s, shipping furniture, collectables, leaded windows etc
Open Mon–Thurs 9am–6pm Fri 9am–5pm Sat 10am–5pm Sun 11am–5pm or by appointment
Services Shipping, restoration, café

Pendle Antiques Centre Ltd
Contact Mr Jason Billington
Union Mill, Watt Street, Sabden, Clitheroe, Lancashire, BB7 9ED
01282 776311 F 01282 777642
sales@pendleantiquescentre.co.uk
www.pendleantiquescentre.co.uk
Est. 1984 *Stock size* Large
No. of dealers 15
Stock Wide range of antiques including architectural and shipping wares, bric-a-brac
Open Mon–Sat 10am–5pm Sun 11am–5pm
Services Shipping

TODMORDEN

The Border Bookshop (PBFA, BA)
Contact Mr V H Collinge
61a Halifax Road, Todmorden, Lancashire, OL14 5BB
01706 814721
collinge@borderbookshop.fsnet.co.uk
www.borderbookshop.co.uk
Est. 1979 *Stock size* Large
Stock Second-hand books (large sports section), comics, story papers 1880–1970
Open Mon–Fri 10am–1pm 2–5pm Sat 9am–5pm closed Tues
Fairs PBFA
Services Book tokens

Cottage Antiques
Contact Angelica Slater
788 Rochdale Road, Walsden, Todmorden, Lancashire, OL14 7UA
01706 813612 F 01706 813612
M 07773 798032
www.ukcottageantiques.co.uk
Est. 1984 *Stock size* Medium
Stock Country furniture (particularly with original paint finishes), European antiques, country collectables, kitchenware
Open Wed–Sun 11am–5.30pm
Services Stripping, polishing, paint finishes, renovations, custom-built furniture

Echoes
Contact Mrs P Oldman
650a Halifax Road, Eastwood, Todmorden, Lancashire, OL14 6DW
01706 817505
Est. 1986 *Stock size* Large
Stock Clothing, textiles, pre-Victorian to late 1950s
Open Wed–Sat 11am–6pm Sun noon–5pm
Fairs Manchester Textile Fairs
Services Valuations

Fagin & Co
Contact Mr John Ratcliff
54 Burnley Road, Todmorden, Lancashire, OL14 5EY
01706 819499/814773
M 07899 774257
mrhillside@aol.com
Est. 1994 *Stock size* Medium
Stock General antiques, collectables, advertising
Open Mon–Sat 10.30am–5pm closed Tues
Services Valuations

Todmorden Antique Centre
Contact Mr E Hoogeveen
Sutcliffe House, Halifax Road, Todmorden, Lancashire, OL14 5BG
01706 818040 F 01706 814344
mr.ed@freenet.co.uk
Est. 1994 *Stock size* Large
No. of dealers 30
Stock Wide range of antiques, collectables and collectors' cars
Open Mon–Fri 10am–5pm Sat 10am–4pm Sun noon–4pm

WHALLEY

As Time Goes By
Contact Mrs J Bland
3 Accrington Road, Whalley, Clitheroe, Lancashire, BB7 9TD
01254 822199 F 01254 822199
M 07989 063395
Est. 1989 *Stock size* Medium
Stock Antique and new furniture, decorative items, lighting, textiles etc
Open Tues–Sat 12.30–4.30pm by appointment
Services Upholstery

Brindle Fine Arts Ltd (LAPADA)
Contact Julian Brindle
King Street, Whalley, Lancashire, BB7 9SP
01254 825200 F 01200 440090
www.antiqueweb.co.uk/tbrindle
Est. 1961 *Stock size* Large
Stock Good quality antiques
Open Mon–Fri 9am–5pm or by appointment
Fairs Olympia

Edmund Davies & Son Antiques
Contact Philip Davies
32 King Street, Whalley, Clitheroe, Lancashire, BB7 9SL
01254 823764 F 01254 823764
M 07879 877306
Est. 1960 *Stock size* Medium
Stock Longcase clocks, country furniture
Open Mon–Sat 10am–5pm
Services Clock and furniture restoration

MERSEYSIDE

BEBINGTON

UK Toy & Model Auctions Ltd
Contact Tony Oakes or Barry Stockton
46 Wirral Gardens, Bebington, Wirral, Merseyside, CH63 3BH
01270 841558 F 01270 841558
M 07771 396459
Open By appointment
Sales Sales of toys and models held at the Queen Hotel, City Road, Chester
Frequency 3–4 per year
Catalogues Yes

BIRKENHEAD

D & T Architectural Salvage
Contact Mr Dave Lyons
106 Church Road, Birkenhead, Merseyside, CH42 0LJ
0151 670 0058
M 07970 698518
Est. 1990 *Stock size* Large
Stock Original interior doors, fireplaces, all salvage material
Open Wed–Sat 9am–5pm

Mistermicawber.Co.Ltd
Contact Mr Barrington
100 Woodchurch Lane, Birkenhead, Merseyside, CH42 9PD
0151 608 5445
mistermicawber.co@btinternet.com
Est. 1974 *Stock size* Medium
Stock Pre-1930s furniture
Open Mon–Sat 9am–5pm closed Thurs

BROMBOROUGH

Full of Beans
Contact Kris Richards
Unit 34, Croft Retail Park, Dinsdale Road, Bromborough, Wirral, Merseyside, CH62 3PY
0151 334 6999
www.fullofbeanies.com
Est. 1999 *Stock size* Large
Stock Beanie Babies and accessories
Open Mon–Sat 10am–5pm Sun Bank Holidays 10.30am–4pm

HESWALL

The Antique Shop
Contact Mr C Rosenberg
120–122 Telegraph Road, Heswall, Wirral, Merseyside, CH60 0AQ
0151 342 1053 0151 342 1053
Est. 1961 *Stock size* Medium
Stock Victorian jewellery, silver, bric-a-brac
Open Fri Sat 10am–5pm
Services Jewellery repairs, silver repairs, valuations

HOYLAKE

Kingsleys Auctions Ltd
Contact Mr I McKellar
3–4 The Quadrant, Hoylake, Wirral, Merseyside, CH47 2EE
0151 632 5821
kingsleyauctions@msn.com
Est. 1972
Open Mon–Fri 9am–5pm closed 1–2pm
Sales General auction sale Tues 10am, viewing Sat 9am–12.30pm Mon 9am–5pm day of sale 9–10am
Frequency Weekly
Catalogues Yes

Mansell Antiques & Collectables
Contact Mr Gary Challinor
Mulberry House, 128–130 Market Street, Hoylake, Wirral, Merseyside, CH47 3BH
0151 632 0892 0151 632 6137
www.antiquesatlas.com
Est. 1998 *Stock size* Large
Stock 20thC collectables, Art Deco, Carlton ware, Shelley etc
Open Mon–Sat 9am–5pm closed Wed
Fairs Birmingham Rag Market, Chester Racecourse

LIVERPOOL

Abram & Mitchell
Contact Mr Crane
6 Stanhope Street, Liverpool, Merseyside, L8 5RF
0151 708 5180 0151 707 2454
johncrane@cato-crane.co.uk
www.cato-crane.co.uk
Est. 1880
Open Mon–Fri 9am–5pm Sat by appointment
Sales Antique, general and household furnishings sales every Thursday
Catalogues No

Antique Cottage
Contact Thomas or Rita Smith
64 Moss Lane, Liverpool, Merseyside, L9 8AN
0151 524 0805
07932 495888
rita@doll96.fsnet.co.uk
Est. 2003 *Stock size* Large
Stock General antiques, bisque dolls
Open Mon–Sat 9am–6pm
Fairs Swinderby, Newark
Services Valuations

Cato Crane & Co
Contact Mr J Crane AMATA
6 and 33–39 Stanhope Street, Liverpool, Merseyside, L8 5RF
0151 709 5559 0151 707 2454
info@cato-crane.co.uk
www.cato-crane.co.uk
Est. 1986
Open Mon–Fri 9am–5pm Sat 9am–1pm or by appointment
Sales Auctions every Tuesday Thursday including antique Victorian and 20thC furniture, collectables and decorative objects. Quality antiques and fine art auction every month
Catalogues Yes

Circa 1900
Contact Mr W Colquhoun
11–13 Holts Arcade, India Buildings, Water Street, Liverpool, Merseyside, L2 0RR
0151 236 1282 0151 236 1282
www.merseyworld.com/circa1900
Est. 1996 *Stock size* Large
Stock Art Nouveau, classic Art Deco, applied arts
Open Mon–Fri 10am–6pm or by appointment

Hartley & Co
Contact Mr J Brown
12–14 Moss Street, Low Hill, Liverpool, Merseyside, L6 1HF
0151 263 6472/1865
0151 260 3417
Est. 1849
Open Mon–Fri 9am–4.30pm
Sales General household, antique and reproduction sales Fri 10.15am, viewing Thurs 9am–4.30pm Fri 9–10.15am. Merseyside Police lost property
Frequency Fortnightly
Catalogues No

Liverpool Militaria
Contact Mr Bill Tagg
17 Cheapside, Liverpool, Merseyside, L2 2DY
0151 236 4404
liverpoolmilitaria@hotmail.com
Est. 1977 *Stock size* Medium
Stock General military antiques
Open Mon–Sat 10.30am–5pm closed Wed
Fairs Northern Arms & Armour, International – Birmingham

Maggs Shipping Ltd
Contact Mr R Webster
66–68 St Anne Street, Liverpool, Merseyside, L3 3DY
0151 207 2555 0151 207 2555
maggsantiques@compuserve.com
Est. 1971 *Stock size* Large
Stock Restored Georgian-style, country and pine furniture, French decorative furniture
Trade only Yes
Open Mon–Fri 9am–5pm
Services Restoration, packing, shipping

Mersey Collectables
Contact Mr J Foy
81 Renshaw Street, Liverpool, Merseyside, L1 2SJ
0151 708 9012
jfoy71160@aol.com
Est. 1995 *Stock size* Large
Stock Collectable toys
Open Mon–Sat 10am–5pm

Outhwaite & Litherland (SOFAA)
Contact Mr Kevin Whay
Kingsway Galleries, Fontenoy Street, Liverpool, Merseyside, L3 2BE
0151 236 6561 0151 236 1070
auction@lots.uk.com
www.lots.uk.com
Est. 1907
Open Mon–Fri 9am–5pm
Sales Antiques sales 4–5 per annum Wed. Weekly general household sales Tues 10.30am, viewing Mon 9am–5pm Tues 9–10.30am. Monthly cavalcade collectors' sales 1st Tues of month or day prior to major fine art and antiques sale
Catalogues Yes

Pilgrim's Progress
Contact Selwyn Hyams
1a–3a Bridgewater Street, Liverpool, Merseyside, L1 0AR
0151 708 7515 0151 708 7515
www.pilgrimsprogress.co.uk
Est. 1979 *Stock size* Large
Stock Five floors of mainly 19th and early 20thC furniture
Open Mon–Fri 9am–5pm Sat 10.30am–1.30pm
Services Valuations, restoration

Seventeen Antiques
Contact Mr J Brake
306 Aigburth Road, Liverpool, Merseyside, L17 9PW
0151 727 1717
07712 189604
annebrake@btconnect.com
Est. 1997 *Stock size* Large
Stock Antique pine furniture, cast-iron fireplaces
Open Mon–Sat 10am–5.30pm closed Wed
Services Restoration, stripping

Stefani Antiques
Contact Mrs T Stefani
497 Smithdown Road, Liverpool, Merseyside, L15 5AE
0151 734 1933/733 4836
07946 646395
Est. 1987 *Stock size* Large
Stock General antiques
Open Mon–Sat 10am–5pm closed Wed
Services Valuations, restoration

Turner & Sons (1787) (NAVA)
Contact Mr Kevin Davies
Century Salerooms, 28–36 Roscoe Street, Liverpool, Merseyside, L1 9DW
0151 709 4005 0151 709 4005
07831 445816
turnersauctions@aol.com
Est. 1787
Open Mon–Fri 9.15am–4.45pm
Sales General household, antique and commercial sales Thurs 11am, viewing Wed 9am–4.45pm Thurs 9–11am
Frequency Weekly
Catalogues No

SOUTHPORT

Birkdale Antiques
Contact John Napp
119a Upper Aughton Road, Southport, Merseyside, PR8 5NH
01704 550117
07973 303105
johnnapp@tiscali.co.uk
Est. 1990 *Stock size* Small
Stock French bedroom suites 1820–1900s, chandeliers
Open Tues–Wed 10.30am–5.30pm or by appointment
Fairs Bingley Hall, Stafford
Services Valuations, restoration

Bonhams
Churchtown, Southport, Merseyside, PR9 7NE
01704 507875 01704 507877
southport@bonhams.com
www.bonhams.com
Open Mon–Fri 9am–1pm 2–5pm
Sales Regional office. Regular house and attic sales across the country; contact London offices for further details. Free auction valuations; insurance and probate valuations

Broadhursts of Southport Ltd (ABA, PBFA)
Contact Laurens Hardman
5–7 Market Street, Southport, Merseyside, PR8 1HD
01704 532064 01704 542009
litereria@aol.com
Est. 1926
Stock Wide range of scarce and collectable books
Open Mon–Sat 9am–5.30pm
Fairs Chelsea, Olympia
Services Valuations, restoration, book search

King Street Antiques
Contact Mr John Nolan
27–29 King Street, Southport, Merseyside, PR8 1LH
01704 540808
07714 088388
Est. 1969 *Stock size* Large
Stock Antique furniture, interior design service
Open Mon–Sat 10am–5pm or by appointment
Services Packing, courier

Molloy's Furnishers Ltd
Contact Mr S Molloy
6–8 St James Street, Southport, Merseyside, PR8 5AE
01704 535204 01704 548101
sales@molloysfurnishers.co.uk
www.molloysfurnishers.co.uk
Est. 1976 *Stock size* Medium
Stock Antique shipping, reproduction furniture
Open Mon–Sat 9am–5.30pm

Osiris
Contact Mr Paul Wood
The Royal Arcade, 131a Lord Street, Southport, Merseyside, PR8 1PU
01704 500991/560418
07802 818500
Est. 1979 *Stock size* Medium
Stock Art Nouveau, Art Deco ceramics, Arts and Crafts, glass, metalware, lighting
Open Mon–Sun 11am–5pm
Fairs Newark
Services Lectures, talks, valuations

K A Parkinson Books
Contact K A or J Parkinson
359–363 Lord Street, Southport, Merseyside, PR8 1NH
01704 547016 01704 386416
tony@parki.co.uk

Ⓦ www.parki.com
Est. 1972 *Stock size* Large
Stock Antiquarian and second-hand books, sheet music, maps, prints, prehistoric, ancient and medieval antiquities, natural history items, vinyl records, autographs, manuscripts
Open Mon–Sat 10am–5pm Sun 1–5pm
Services Book search

⊞ David M Regan
Contact Mr David Regan
✉ **25 Hoghton Street, Southport, Merseyside, PR9 0NS** Ⓟ
☎ 01704 531266
Est. 1983 *Stock size* Medium
Stock Coins, postcards, medals
Open Mon Wed Fri Sat 10am–5pm
Services Valuations

Royal Arcade
Contact Ray Parkinson
✉ **127–131 Lord Street, Southport, Merseyside, PR8 1PU** Ⓟ
☎ 01704 542087
Ⓦ www.theroyalarcade.com
Est. 2002 *Stock size* Large
No. of dealers 70
Stock Antiques, collectables, clocks, mirrors, chandeliers, jewellery, militaria, Art Deco, Art Nouveau
Open Mon–Sat 9.30am–5.30pm Sun 11am–5pm
Services Valuations

⊞ Southport Antiques
Contact Steven Ross
✉ **19 Market Street, Southport, Merseyside, PR8 1HJ** Ⓟ
☎ 01704 533122
Ⓜ 07790 551117
Ⓔ stephrs7@aol.com
Est. 1997 *Stock size* Large
Stock Victorian–Edwardian furniture
Open Mon–Sat 9am–5pm
Services Restoration

⊞ Southport Antiques
Contact Steven Ross
✉ **119a Portland Street, Southport, Merseyside, PR8 6RA** Ⓟ
☎ 01704 533122
Ⓜ 07790 551117
Est. 1997 *Stock size* Large
Stock Victorian–Edwardian furniture
Open Mon–Sat 9am–5pm
Services Restoration

⊞ Southport Antiques
Contact Steven Ross
✉ **4 Wesley Street, Southport, Merseyside, PR8 1BN** Ⓟ
☎ 07790 551117
Ⓜ 07790 551117
Ⓔ stephrs7@aol.com
Est. 1997 *Stock size* Large
Stock Victorian–Edwardian furniture
Open Mon–Sat 9am–5pm
Services Restoration

⊞ The Spinning Wheel Antiques (IBNS, TPCS)
Contact Roy or Pat Bell
✉ **Royal Arcade Antique Centre, 127–131 Lord Street, Southport, Merseyside, PR8 1PU** Ⓟ
☎ 01704 542087
Ⓜ 07833 314932
Ⓔ roybell@value-on-line.co.uk
Ⓦ www.value-on-line.co.uk
Est. 1974 *Stock size* Medium
Stock General collectables, coins, medals, porcelain, small fine furniture, clocks, violins, barometers, dolls, golf memorabilia etc
Open Mon–Sat 9.30am–5.30pm Sun 11am–5pm
Fairs Newark, Swinderby

WALLASEY

⊞ Arbiter
Contact Mr P Ferrett
✉ **10 Atherton Street, New Brighton, Wallasey, Merseyside, CH45 2NY** Ⓟ
☎ 0151 639 1159
Est. 1983 *Stock size* Medium
Stock Small objects, 1850–1970 decorative arts, Asian, tribal, base metal, treen, 20thC prints, Oriental, Islamic
Open By appointment
Services Valuations

⊞ Decade Antiques & Interiors
Contact A Duffy
✉ **Wallasey, Merseyside, CH45** Ⓟ
☎ 0151 639 6905
Ⓜ 07967 431184
Est. 1974 *Stock size* Medium
Stock Decorative antiques, textiles, contemporary furniture, fine art
Open By appointment
Fairs Manchester Textile Fairs

⊞ Victoria Antiques
Contact Mr J Collier
✉ **155–157 Brighton Street, Wallasey, Merseyside, CH44 8DU** Ⓟ
☎ 0151 639 0080
Ⓦ www.victoriaantiques.com
Est. 1990 *Stock size* Large
Stock Victorian–Edwardian furniture, grandfather clocks
Open Mon–Sat 9.30am–5.30pm closed Wed
Services Restoration

WALES

CARMARTHENSHIRE

CARMARTHEN

Audrey Bull Antiques
Contact Jane Bull
2a Jacksons Lane, Carmarthen, Carmarthenshire, SA31 1WD
☎ 01267 222655
Est. 1949 *Stock size* Medium
Stock General Antiques, Georgian—Edwardian furniture, antique jewellery
Open Mon–Sat 10am–5pm
Services Valuations, restoration, repairs

Bonhams
Napier House, Spilman Street, Carmarthen, Carmarthenshire, SA31 1JY
☎ 01267 238231 Ⓕ 02920 727989
Ⓔ carmarthen@bonhams.com
Ⓦ www.bonhams.com
Open By appointment only
Sales Regional office. Regular house and attic sales across the country; contact London offices for further details. Free auction valuations; insurance and probate valuations

Eynon Hughes
Contact Eynon Hughes
Mount Antiques Centre, 1 & 2 The Mount, Castle Hill, Carmarthen, Carmarthenshire, SA31 1JW Ⓟ
☎ 01994 427253
Est. 1984 *Stock size* Medium
Stock 18th–20thC furniture, collectables
Open Mon–Sat 10am–5pm
Services Valuations, restoration

The Mount Antique Centre
Contact Robert Lickley

⊠ **1 & 2 The Mount, Castle Hill, Carmarthen, Carmarthenshire, SA31 1JW** P
☎ 01267 220005 Ⓕ 01267 231286
Est. 1999 *Stock size* Large
No. of dealers 20
Stock Furniture, china, reclamation
Open Mon–Sat 10am–5pm Sun 10am–4pm in summer only
Services Upholstery

CROSS HANDS

⊞ C J C Antiques
Contact John or Caroline Carpenter
⊠ **Llanllyan Foelgastell, Cross Hands, Carmarthenshire, SA14 7HA** P
☎ 01269 831094 Ⓕ 01269 831094
Ⓔ sales@cjcantiques.co.uk
Ⓦ www.cjcantiques.co.uk
Est. 1979 *Stock size* Large
Stock Various Victorian items, musical instruments
Trade only Yes
Open By appointment
Services Shipping, valuations

Welsh Country Auctions
Contact Andrew or Bethan Williams
⊠ **2 Carmarthen Road, Cross Hands, Llanelli, Carmarthenshire, SA14 6JP** P
☎ 01269 844428 Ⓕ 01269 844428
Ⓦ www.welshcountryauctions.com
Est. 1995
Open Mon–Fri 9am–5pm Sat 9am–12.30pm
Sales General antiques
Frequency Every 2–3 weeks
Catalogues Yes

KIDWELLY

⊞ Country Antiques (Wales) (BADA, CINOA)
Contact R Bebb
⊠ **Castle Mill, Kidwelly, Carmarthenshire, SA17 4UU** P
☎ 01554 890534 Ⓕ 01554 891705
Ⓔ info@welshantiques.com
Ⓦ www.welshantiques.com
Est. 1969 *Stock size* Large
Stock Welsh oak furniture, pottery, folk art, metalware
Open Tues–Sat 10am–5pm or by appointment
Services Valuations

⊞ Kidwelly Antiques (BADA, CINOA)
Contact Mr R Bebb
⊠ **31 Bridge Street, Kidwelly, Carmarthenshire, SA17 4UU** P
☎ 01554 890328 Ⓕ 01554 891705
Ⓔ info@welshantiques.com
Ⓦ www.welshantiques.com
Est. 1969 *Stock size* Large
Stock Georgian–Victorian furniture and accessories
Open Tues–Sat 10am–5pm telephone call advisable

LLANDEILO

⊞ James Ash Antiques
Contact James Ash
⊠ **The Warehouse, Station Road, Llandeilo, Carmarthenshire, SA19 6NG** P
☎ 01558 823726/822130
Ⓕ 01558 822130
Ⓔ james@ashantiques.freeserve.co.uk
Est. 1976 *Stock size* Large
Stock Victorian and Welsh country furniture
Open Mon–Fri 10.30am–5pm or by appointment
Fairs Newark
Services Valuations

Jones & Llewelyn (NAEA)
Contact Mrs Ann Rees or Mr Hefin Jones
⊠ **Llandeilo Auction Rooms, 21 New Road, Llandeilo, Carmarthenshire, SA19 6DE** P
☎ 01558 823430 Ⓕ 01558 822004
Ⓔ enquiries@jonesllewelyn.freeserve.co.uk
Ⓦ www.jonesllewelyn.freeserve.co.uk
Est. 1948
Open Mon–Fri 9am–5.30pm
Sales General antiques and collectables once a quarter, antiques and effects 2 weekly
Catalogues Yes

Bob Jones Prytherch & Co Ltd
Contact Jonathon Morgan
⊠ **50 Rhosmaen Street, Llandeilo, Carmarthenshire, SA19 6HA** P
☎ 01558 822468 Ⓕ 01558 823712
Ⓔ property@bjpandco.s9.co.uk
Ⓦ www.bjpproperty.co.uk
Est. 1996
Open Mon–Fri 9am–5.30pm
Sales General antiques
Frequency Infrequent
Catalogues No

The Works Antiques Centre
Contact Steve Watts or Jon Storey
⊠ **Station Road, Llandeilo, Carmarthenshire, SA19 6NH** P
☎ 01558 823964
Ⓔ theworks@storeyj.clara.co.uk
Ⓦ www.works-antiques.co.uk
Est. 2001 *Stock size* Large
No. of dealers 60
Stock General antiques and collectables
Open Tues–Sat 10am–6pm Sun 10am–5pm
Services Restoration

LLANDOVERY

Clee Tompkinson & Francis
Contact Nick Jones
⊠ **Ty Ocsiwn Tywi Auction House, Llandovery, Carmarthenshire, SA18 2LY** P
☎ 01269 591884 or 01550 720440
Ⓕ 01269 595482
Ⓔ ammanford@ctf-uk.com
Est. 1996
Open Mon–Fri 9am–5.30pm Sat 9am–1pm
Sales General antiques
Frequency Monthly
Catalogues No

⊞ Phillips Antiques and French Polishing (BWCG)
Contact Philip Wyvill-Bell
⊠ **11 Market Square, Llandovery, Carmarthenshire, SA20 0AB** P
☎ 01550 721355 Ⓕ 01550 721355
Ⓔ wyvillbell@aol.com
Ⓦ www.phillips-antiques.com
Est. 1970 *Stock size* Large
Stock Period to Victorian furniture, clocks, porcelain
Open Mon–Sat 10am–5pm
Services French polishing, valuations, restoration, repairs

LLANELLI

⊞ Llanelli Antiques
Contact W Knapp
⊠ **12 Great Western Crescent, Llanelli, Carmarthenshire, SA15 2RL** P

☎ 01554 759448
ⓔ diane.knapp@btclick.com
Est. 1962 *Stock size* Medium
Stock General antiques, Victorian–Edwardian furniture
Open Mon–Sat 10am–1pm
Fairs Newark, Ardingly
Services Valuations, restoration

⊞ Radnedge Architectural Antiques
Contact Julian Cooper
✉ **Dafen Inn Row, Llanelli, Carmarthenshire, SA14 8LX** Ⓟ
☎ 01554 755790 ⓕ 01554 755790
ⓔ rantiques@radnedge.fsworld.co.uk
ⓦ www.radnedge-arch-antiques.co.uk
Est. 1980 *Stock size* Large
Stock Architectural antiques, fireplaces, timber, stone
Open Mon–Sat 9am–5pm

LLANWRDA

⊞ Mark Rowan Antiques
Contact Mark Rowan
✉ **Garreg Fawr, Porthyrhyd, Llanwrda, Carmarthenshire, SA19 8NY** Ⓟ
☎ 01558 650478 ⓕ 01558 650712
ⓔ sales@markrowan.co.uk
ⓦ www.markrowan.co.uk
Est. 1975 *Stock size* Medium
Stock Country furniture and antiques
Open By appointment only

LLANYBYDDER

⊞ Jen Jones Antiques
Contact Jen Jones
✉ **Pontbrendu, Llanybydder, Carmarthenshire, SA40 9UJ** Ⓟ
☎ 01570 480610 ⓕ 01570 480112
ⓔ quilts@jen-jones.com
ⓦ www.jen-jones.com
Est. 1971 *Stock size* Large
Stock Welsh quilts and blankets, small Welsh country antiques
Open Mon–Sat 10am–6pm
Sun by appointment
Fairs BABAADA (March)

NEWCASTLE EMLYN

⊞ The Old Saddler's Antiques
Contact Mr or Mrs Coomber
✉ **Bridge Street, Newcastle Emlyn, Carmarthenshire, SA38 9DU** Ⓟ
☎ 01239 711615 (shop hours only)
Ⓜ 07971 625113
ⓔ Dotcoomb@aol.com
Est. 1995 *Stock size* Large
Stock General antiques, country-style furniture, horse-orientated antiques
Open Mon–Sat 10am–5pm
closed Wed in winter
Fairs Carmarthen

CEREDIGION

ABERYSTWYTH

⊞ The Furniture Cave
Contact P David
✉ **33 Cambrian Street, Aberystwyth, Ceredigion, SY23 1NZ** Ⓟ
☎ 01970 611234 ⓕ 01970 611234
Ⓜ 07816 408871
ⓔ thecave@btconnect.com
ⓦ www.furniture-cave.co.uk
Est. 1979 *Stock size* Medium
Stock General antiques and pine
Open Mon–Fri 9am–5pm
Sat 10am–5pm
Fairs Birmingham Antiques Fair
Services Valuations, restoration, repairs

Lloyd Herbert & Jones
Contact J A Griffiths FRICS
✉ **10 Chalybeate Street, Aberystwyth, Ceredigion, SY23 1HS** Ⓟ
☎ 01970 624328/612559
ⓕ 01970 617934
ⓔ sales@lhj-property.co.uk
ⓦ www.lhj-property.co.uk
Est. 1904
Open Mon–Sat 9am–5.30pm
Sales Quarterly general antiques Wed 11am, viewing 9–11am
Catalogues No

Jim Raw-Rees & Co (ISVA)
Contact Charles
✉ **1–3 Chalybeate Street, Aberystwyth, Ceredigion, SY23 1HJ** Ⓟ
☎ 01970 617179 ⓕ 01970 6627262
Ⓜ 07970 605040
ⓔ propertysales@raw-rees.co.uk
ⓦ www.raw-rees.co.uk
Est. 1948
Open Mon–Fri 9am–5.30pm
Sat 9.30am–4pm
Sales General antiques
Frequency Periodically
Catalogues No

⊞ Julian Shelley Books
Contact Julian Shelley
✉ **16 Northgate Street, Aberystwyth, Ceredigion, SY23 2JS** Ⓟ
☎ 01970 627926
ⓔ julianshelley@hotmail.com
Est. 1996 *Stock size* Medium
Stock Rare and second-hand books, jewellery, collectables, items on Welsh topography
Open Mon–Sat 10am–5pm
Services Book search

⊞ Ystwyth Books (BA)
Contact Mrs H M Hinde
✉ **7 Princess Street, Aberystwyth, Ceredigion, SY23 1DX**
☎ 01970 639479
Est. 1976 *Stock size* Medium
Stock Rare and second-hand books, specializing in Welsh interest
Open Mon–Sat 9.30am–5.15pm

CARDIGAN

J J Morris
Contact Mr Mal Evans
✉ **5 High Street, Cardigan, Ceredigion, SA43 1HJ** Ⓟ
☎ 01239 612343 ⓕ 01239 615237
ⓔ cardigan@jjmestateagents.co.uk
ⓦ www.jjmestateagents.co.uk
Est. 1969
Open Mon–Fri 9am–5.30pm
Sat 9am–noon
Sales General antiques
Frequency Periodic
Catalogues No

LAMPETER

The Tarrystone
Contact Jennipha Denning
✉ **Bristol House, Station Terrace, North Road, Lampeter, Ceredigion, SA48 7HZ** Ⓟ
☎ 01545 570864
Ⓜ 07977 938277
ⓔ jennipha@thetarrystone.co.uk
Est. 2000 *Stock size* Medium
No. of dealers 7
Stock Country furniture, tools, lace, linen, period clothing, textiles, stoneware
Open Mon–Sat 9.30am–5pm

LLANDYSUL

Fred Davies & Co (FNAVA)
Contact Fred Davies
The Square Synod Inn, Llandysul, Ceredigion, SA44 6JA
01545 580005 01545 580006
07831 852511
Est. 1992
Open Mon–Fri 9am–5pm
Sat 10am–2pm
Sales General antiques, modern furniture
Frequency Monthly
Catalogues No

CONWY

COLWYN BAY

Colwyn Books
Contact John Beagan
66 Abergele Road, Colwyn Bay, Conwy, LL29 7PP
01492 530683
lindaandjohn@davies-beagan.freeserve.co.uk
Est. 1989 *Stock size* Medium
Stock General stock of antiquarian and second-hand books
Open Mon–Sat 9.30am–5pm
Wed 9.30am–1pm
Services Book search

Cryers Antiques
Contact Mr Chris Cryer
24 Abergele Road, Colwyn Bay, Conwy, LL29 7PA
01492 532457
Est. 1974 *Stock size* Large
Stock General antiques and collectables
Open Mon–Sat 11am–4.30pm
Fairs Newark, Ardingly, Swinderby
Services Valuations

North Wales Antiques
Contact Mr F Robinson
58 Abergele Road, Colwyn Bay, Conwy, LL29 7PP
01492 530521 or 01352 720253 (after 6pm)
Est. 1959 *Stock size* Large
Stock Furniture
Open Mon–Sat 10am–4pm
Fairs Newark
Services House clearance, probate valuations, valuations

Rogers Jones & Co
Contact Mr David Rogers Jones
33 Abergele Road, Colwyn Bay, Conwy, LL29 7RU
01492 532176 01492 533308
rogersjones@btconnect.com
www.rogersjones.co.uk
Est. 1991
Open Mon–Thurs 9am–5pm
Fri 9am–noon
Sales Furniture, ceramics, silver, paintings, collectables last Tues in month, general and collectables bi-monthly
Catalogues Yes

CONWY

The Bookshop
Contact Mr D Crewe
21 High Street, Conwy, LL32 8DE
01492 592137
bookshopconwy.co.uk
Est. 1985 *Stock size* Medium
Stock Rare and second-hand books
Open Mon–Sat 9.30am–5pm

Castle Antiques
Contact John Nickson
71 Station Road, Deganwy, Conwy, LL31 9DF
01492 583021
Est. 1980 *Stock size* Medium
Stock Georgian–Victorian furniture, oak, mahogany, jewellery, china, silver, paintings, ornaments
Open Mon–Sat 10am–5pm
Services Valuations, shipping

Paul Gibbs Antiques & Decorative Arts
Contact Paul Gibbs
25 Castle Street, Conwy, LL32 8AY
01492 593429 01492 593429
paul@teapotworld.co.uk
Est. 1959 *Stock size* Medium
Stock Ceramics, glass, decorative arts, focus on teapot design with reference collection open to the public exhibiting 1200 rare and early teapots
Open Mon–Sat 10am–5pm
Fairs Newark
Services Valuations, restoration, repairs

Knights Gone By
Contact Mr B Tunstall
Castle Square, Conwy, LL32 8AY
01492 596119 01492 596119
knightsgoneby2@aol.com
www.knightsgoneby.com
Est. 1998 *Stock size* Medium
Stock Collectable weaponry
Open Mon–Sun 11am–5pm

DEGANWY

Castle Antiques
Contact John Nickson
Victoria Building, 71 Station Road, Deganwy, Conwy, LL31 9DF
01492 583021
Est. 1980 *Stock size* Large
Stock General antiques
Open Mon–Sat 10am–5pm
Services Valuations

LLANDUDNO

20th Century China & Pottery
Contact Julia Jackson
18 Mostyn Avenue, Craig-y-Don, Llandudno, Conwy, LL30 1BJ
01492 650611
juliajackson@artlovers.co.uk
Est. 2004 *Stock size* Small
Stock China, pottery, porcelain, ornamental ware 1900–1999
Open By appointment
Services Shipping

Drew Pritchard Ltd (SALVO, BSMGP)
Contact Drew Pritchard or Clive Holland
St George's Church, Church Walks, Llandudno, Conwy, LL30 2HL
01492 874004 01492 874003
enquiries@drewpritchard.co.uk
www.drewpritchard.co.uk
Est. 1987 *Stock size* Large
Stock Antique stained glass, architectural antiques
Open Mon–Fri 9am–5pm
Sat 10am–4pm
Fairs Newark, SALVO
Services Restoration, commissions

LLANDUDNO JUNCTION

Collinge Antiques
Contact Nicky Collinge
Old Fyffes Warehouse, Conwy Road,

Llandudno Junction, Conwy, LL31 9LU P
☎ 01492 580022 F 01492 580022
E sales@collinge-antiques.co.uk
W www.collinge-antiques.co.uk
Est. 1980 ***Stock size*** Large
Stock General antiques, Georgian–Edwardian furniture
Open Mon–Sat 9am–5.30pm Sun 10.30am–4.30pm
Services Restoration, valuations, shipping, upholstery

LLANRWST

Carrington House Antiques
Contact Richard Newstead
✉ **Ancaster Square, Llanrwst, Conwy, LL26 0LD** P
☎ 01492 642500 F 01492 642500
E richard@carringtonhouse.co.uk
W www.carringtonhouse.co.uk
Est. 1975 ***Stock size*** Medium
Stock Antiques, pine, mahogany and oak furniture
Open Wed–Sun 10.30am–5pm
Services Valuations

Prospect Books
Contact Mike Dingle
✉ **10 Trem Arfon, Llanrwst, Conwy, LL26 0BT** P
☎ 01492 640111 F 01492 640111
E prospectbooks@aol.com
W www.gunbooks.co.uk
Est. 1977 ***Stock size*** Small
Stock Rare and second-hand books on weapons
Open By appointment
Fairs Arms Fairs
Services Catalogues

Snowdonia Antiques
Contact Jeffery Collins
✉ **Bank Building, Station Road, Llanrwst, Conwy, LL26 0EP** P
☎ 01492 640789 F 01492 640789
M 07802 503552
Est. 1965
Stock Antiques, Welsh dressers, longcase clocks
Open Mon–Sat 9am–5pm Sun by appointment
Services Restoration

RHOS-ON-SEA

Rhos Point Books
Contact Gwyn Morris
✉ **85 The Promenade, Rhos-on-Sea, Conwy, LL28 4PR** P
☎ 01492 545236 F 01492 540862
E rhos.point@btinternet.com
W www.rhos.point.btinternet.com
Est. 1984 ***Stock size*** Medium
Stock 20,000 antiquarian and second-hand titles, North Wales topography a speciality
Open Mon–Sun 10am–5.30pm July Aug 10am–9pm
Fairs Ludlow
Services Book search

DENBIGHSHIRE

CHIRK

Seventh Heaven
✉ **Chirk Mill, Chirk, Wrexham, Denbighshire, LL14 5BU** P
☎ 01691 777622 F 01691 777313
E requests@seventh-heaven.co.uk
W www.seventh-heaven.co.uk
Est. 1971 ***Stock size*** Large
Stock Antique beds, mattresses, bases, bed linen
Open Mon–Sat 9am–5pm Sun 10am–4pm

DOWNSBY GARRATT

Downsby Antiques & Collectables
Contact Philip Garratt
✉ **6 High Street, Rhuddlan, Downsby Garratt, Denbighshire, LL18 2UB** P
☎ 01745 590666
M 07879 845478
E downsbyantiques@tiscali.co.uk
Est. 2002 ***Stock size*** Small
Stock General antiques
Open Tues–Sat 10.30am–5.30pm
Fairs Newark, Swinderby
Services Picture framing

ERBISTOCK

Simon Wingett Ltd (LAPADA)
Contact Mr Simon Wingett
✉ **The Garden House, Erbistock, Wrexham, Denbighshire, LL13 0DL** P
☎ 01978 781144 F 01978 781144
M 07774 410889
Est. 1972 ***Stock size*** Medium
Stock 18th–19thC English furniture, paintings, objets d'art, garden sculpture
Open By appointment
Fairs LAPADA, Chelsea
Services Valuations

LLANGOLLEN

Aquaduct Auctions
Contact Mr Knight
✉ **Bryn Seion Chapel, Station Road, Trevor, Llangollen, Denbighshire, LL20 7TP** P
☎ 01691 774567
M 07778 279614
E satkin1057@aol.com
W www.romantiques.co.uk
Est. 2004
Open Mon–Fri 9am–5pm
Sales Monthly sales of antiques and collectables
Catalogues Yes

J & R Langford
Contact Mr P C Silverston
✉ **10 Bridge Street, Llangollen, Denbighshire, LL20 8PF** P
☎ 01978 860182
Est. 1952 ***Stock size*** Medium
Stock 18th–19thC Welsh dressers, 18thC–early 20thC furniture, china, pictures
Open Tues Fri Sat 9.30am–5pm or by appointment
Services Valuations, probate, insurance

Passers Buy
Contact Marie Evans
✉ **Oak Street/Chapel Street, Llangollen, Denbighshire, LL20 8NN** P
☎ 01978 860861
Est. 1978 ***Stock size*** Medium
Stock Range of furniture, china, brass, ceramics
Open Tues Fri Sat 11.30am–5pm or by appointment
Fairs Anglesea, Gwyn Davis Fair

MARCHWEIL

Bryn-y-Grog Emporium
Contact Tony David
✉ **Bryn-y-Grog Hall, Marchweil, Wrexham, Denbighshire, LL13 0SR** P
☎ 01978 355555
Est. 2002 ***Stock size*** Medium
No. of dealers 30
Stock Antiques, collectables
Open Mon–Sun 10am–5pm

RHYL

The Aquarius
Contact Mrs Gaynor Williams
2 Market Street Street, Rhyl, Denbighshire, LL18 1RL
01745 332436
Est. 1980 *Stock size* Medium
Stock Period clothing, accessories, costume jewelley, lace, collectables
Open Mon–Sat 10.30am–5pm winter closed Tues am

RUTHIN

Grandpa's Collectables
Contact Yvonne Jones
40 Well Street, Ruthin, Denbighshire, LL15 1AE
01824 705601 01824 705601
Est. 1998 *Stock size* Large
Stock Antiques, collectables, some French furniture
Open Tues–Sat 10am–5pm

TREVOR

Romantiques Antique Centre
Contact Mr Knight
The Methodist Chapel, Holyhead Road, Froncysyllte, Llangollen, Denbighshire, LL20 7RA
019691 774567
07778 279614 (day)
satkin1057@aol.com
www.romantiques.co.uk
Est. 1993 *Stock size* Large
Stock Antiques, collectables
Open Mon–Fri 9am–5pm Sat Sun 11am–4pm
Services Upholstery, restoration of clocks, furniture, barometers

WREXHAM

Wingett's
Contact Mr J Lloyd or Mr R Hughes
29 Holt Street, Wrexham, Denbighshire, LL13 8DH
01978 353553 01978 353264
auctions@wingetts.co.uk
www.wingetts.co.uk
Est. 1942
Open Mon–Fri 9am–5pm
Sales Monthly fine art auctions and specialist sales
Catalogues Yes

DYFED

CARDIGAN

Joyce Williams
Contact Joyce Williams
Hurstlands House, Aberporth, Cardigan, Dyfed, SA43 2EN
01239 810330
07974 387004
joyceantiques@btinternet.com
Est. 1972 *Stock size* Small
Stock Small antiques
Open Mon–Sat 9am–5pm or by appointment

FLINTSHIRE

CONNAH'S QUAY

Whitehead & Sons
Contact Mr T Whitehead
264 High Street, Connah's Quay, Deeside, Flintshire, CH5 4DJ
01244 818414
Est. 1995
Open Mon–Sat 9am–6pm
Sales General sales including antique china, furniture, household goods, pawnbrokers' jewellery and regular bailiff's sales, Tues 6.20pm summer, Tues 1.30pm winter
Frequency Every Tuesday

HAWARDEN

Capricorn Antiques
Contact Mr K Roberts
Ashfield Farm, Gladstone Way, Hawarden, Deeside, Flintshire, CH5 3HE
01244 535344
Est. 1987 *Stock size* Large
Stock Early pine and Edwardian furniture, 1920s stripped oak
Open Mon–Sat 9am–5pm Sun 11am–4pm
Services Restoration, wood stripping

On The Air Ltd (British Vintage Wireless Society)
Contact Steve Harris
The Vintage Technology Centre, The Highway, Hawarden, Deeside, Flintshire, CH5 3DN
01244 530300 01244 530300
07778 767734
info@vintageradio.co.uk
www.vintageradio.co.uk
Est. 1990 *Stock size* Large
Stock Vintage radios, gramophones
Open Variable
Fairs NVCF (NEC)
Services Valuations, restoration, shipping

Village Pine Antiques
Contact Ray Stewart
32 Glynne Way, Hawarden, Flintshire, CH5 3NL
01244 532211
07889 548952
Est. 1980 *Stock size* Medium
Stock Antique pine, smalls
Open Tues–Sat 11am–5pm
Services Valuations, restoration

MOLD

J Bradburne-Price & Co
Contact Mr Roger Griffiths
16 Chester Street, Mold, Flintshire, CH7 1EG
01352 753873 01352 700071
Est. 1904
Open Mon–Fri 9am–5pm Sat 9am–noon
Sales Periodic sales of antiques and modern furniture in Mold Market
Frequency Infrequent
Catalogues No

NORTHOP

Parkview Antiques
Contact Nic Eastwood
High Street, Northop, Flintshire, CH7 6BQ
01352 840627
Est. 1984 *Stock size* Medium
Stock Pine, oak country furniture
Open Mon–Sat 10am–5pm
Services Restoration, upholstery

GWYNEDD

BANGOR

David Windsor Gallery (IPC, FATG)
Contact Mrs E Kendrick
173 High Street, Bangor, Gwynedd, LL57 1NU
01248 364639 01248 364639

davidwindsorgallery@aol.com
Est. 1970 *Stock size* Medium
Stock 1580–1850 old maps, prints, lithographs, oil paintings, watercolours
Open Mon–Sat 10am–5pm closed Wed
Services Valuations, restoration, framing

BARMOUTH

Chapel Antiques Centre
Contact Danny Jones or Brenda Evans
High Street, Barmouth, Gwynedd, LL42 IDS
01341 281377 01341 281377
jonestheantique@supanet.com
www.chapelantiqueswales.co.uk
Est. 1993 *Stock size* Medium
No. of dealers 24
Stock General antiques, country furniture, collectables, decorative items
Open Mon–Sun 10.30am–5pm closed Wed out of season
Services Delivery within UK, shipping can be arranged

Fron House Antiques Decorative Items
Contact Mrs B Howard
Fron House, Jubilee Road, Barmouth, Gwynedd, LL42 1EE
01341 280649 01341 280649
07881 471875
Est. 1969 *Stock size* Medium
Stock General antiques, collectables, militaria, nautical antiques
Open Mon–Sun 10am–5pm closed Wed Oct–April
Fairs Swinderby, Newark
Services Credit and debit cards accepted

Walter Lloyd Jones
Contact V West
High Street, Barmouth, Gwynedd, LL42 1DW
01341 281527 01341 280577
staff@w-lloydjones.com
www.w-lloydjones.com
Est. 1905 *Stock size* Medium
Stock Furniture, china, Gaudy Welsh, cranberry, books
Open Mon–Fri 10am–5pm Sat 10am–4.30pm winter closed Tues Wed
Services Sales on commission

Walter Lloyd Jones Saleroom
Contact V West
High Street, Barmouth, Gwynedd, LL42 1DW
01341 281 527 01341 280577
staff@w-lloydjones.com
www.w-lloydjones.com
Est. 1905
Open Mon–Fri 10am–5.30pm Sat 10am–4.30pm winter closed Tues Wed
Sales Irregular sales of antique furniture, smalls, job lots held 3 times a year. Sales on commission at all times

BEAUMARIS

M Jones A'i Fab Antiques
Contact Merfyn Jones
42a Castle Street, Beaumaris, Gwynedd, LL58 8BB
01248 810624
07778 489496
Est. 1984 *Stock size* Medium
Stock Welsh country furniture, related decorative antiques
Open Mon–Sat 10am–5pm
Services Valuations, restoration

BETHESDA

A E Morris Books (WBA)
Contact A E Morris
40 High Street, Bethesda, Bangor, Gwynedd, LL57 3AN
01248 602533
Est. 1986 *Stock size* Medium
Stock Rare and second-hand books, antiquarian prints
Open Mon–Sat 10am–5pm

CAERNARFON

Days Gone By
Contact Sue
6 Palace Street, Caernarfon, Gwynedd, LL55 1RR
01286 678010 01286 678554
sue@daysgonebyantiques.co.uk
www.daysgonebyantiques.co.uk
Est. 1994 *Stock size* Medium
Stock General antiques, period furniture, collectables, jewellery
Open Mon–Sat 9.30am–5.30pm

CRICCIETH

Capel Mawr Collectors' Centre
Contact Alun Turner
21 High Street, Criccieth, Gwynedd, LL52 OBS
01766 523600
capelmawr@aol.com
Est. 1998 *Stock size* Large
Stock Rare and second-hand books, old postcards, cigarette cards, antiques
Trade only Yes
Open Mid-May–end Sept Mon–Sun winter Tues Thurs–Sat 10am–5pm
Services Mail order

Criccieth Gallery Antiques
Contact Anita Evens
London House, High Street, Criccieth, Gwynedd, LL52 ORN
01766 522836
Est. 1971 *Stock size* Medium
Stock General antiques
Open Mon–Sun 9am–5.30pm
Fairs Newark, Mona, Towy
Services Restoration of pottery and porcelain

DOLGELLAU

Cader Idris Bookshop (PBFA, WBA)
Contact Barbara or Neil Beeby
2 Maldwyn House, Finsbury Square, Dolgellau, Gwynedd, LL40 1RF
01341 421288 or 01341 423779
Est. 1987 *Stock size* Medium
Stock Antiquarian and second-hand books including Welsh topography
Open Mon–Sat 9.30am–5pm Wed 9.30am–1pm
Services Book search

Cecil Williams Antiques
Contact Cecil Williams
Mervinian House, Meyrick Street, Dolgellau, Gwynedd, LL40 1LN
01341 421404
Est. 2000 *Stock size* Large
Stock 17th–18thC furniture, paintings
Open Mon–Sun 9am–5pm
Fairs Chester Race Course

PONTLYFNI

Sea View Antiques
Contact Mr D Ramsell
Sea View, Pontlyfni, Caernarfon, Gwynedd,

LL54 5EF 🅿
☎ 01286 660436
Ⓜ 07990 976562
Est. 1997 *Stock size* Medium
Stock General antiques, collectables
Open Mon–Sun noon–6pm

PORTHMADOG

Huw Williams Antiques
Contact Huw Williams
✉ **The Antique Shop, Madoc Street, Porthmadog, Gwynedd, LL49 9NL** 🅿
☎ 01766 514741 Ⓕ 01766 762673
Ⓜ 07785 747561
Ⓔ huwantiques@aol.com
Ⓦ www.antiquegunswales.co.uk
Est. 1996 *Stock size* Medium
Stock 19th–19thC antique weaponry, country furniture, 19th–early 20thC pottery
Open Mon–Sat 10am–5pm closed Wed
Fairs London Arms Fairs, Birmingham International Arms Fair

PWLLDEFAID

T Evans Antiques
Contact T Evans
✉ **Pwlldefaid, Aberdafon, Pwllheli, Gwynedd, LL53 8BT** 🅿
☎ 01758 760215
Est. 1984 *Stock size* Medium
Stock General antiques especially Welsh country furniture
Open Mon–Sun 9am–5pm
Fairs Carmarthen, Cardiff
Services House clearance

PWLLHELI

Rodney Adams Antiques
Contact Rodney Adams
✉ **Hall Place, 10 Penlan Street, Pwllheli, Gwynedd, LL53 5DU** 🅿
☎ 01758 613173 Ⓕ 01758 613173
Stock size Large
Stock General antiques, longcase clocks, early oak furniture
Open Mon–Sat 9am–5pm
Services Valuations, repairs, restoration

Penlan Pine
Contact Michael Adams
✉ **7 Penlan Street, Pwllheli, Gwynedd, LL53 7DH** 🅿
☎ 01758 613173 Ⓕ 01758 613173
Ⓜ 07785 313553 *Stock size* Small
Stock Reproduction and antique pine furniture
Open Mon–Sat 9am–5pm Thurs 9am–1pm
Services Valuations, restoration and repair

Period Pine
Contact Allan Stanley
✉ **Units 1–3, Bron-y-Berth, Penrhos, Pwllheli, Gwynedd, LL53 7UL** 🅿
☎ 01758 614343 Ⓕ 01758 614100
Ⓜ 07768 875875
Ⓔ diame@periodpine.freeserve.co.uk
Ⓦ www.periodpine.com
Est. 1987 *Stock size* Large
Stock General antiques, complete house furnishings and interiors, brass beds, lamps
Open Mon–Fri 9am–5pm Sat Sun 10am–4.30pm
Services Restoration of antiques

ISLE OF ANGLESEY

BEAUMARIS

The Museum of Childhood Memories
Contact Robert Brown
✉ **1 Castle Street, Beaumaris, Isle of Anglesey, LL58 8AP** 🅿
☎ 01248 712498
Ⓦ www.aboutbritain.com/museumofchildhoodmemories.htm
Est. 1973 *Stock size* Medium
Stock Childhood memorabilia, tinplate, childhood money boxes, pottery and glass, gift items based on museum exhibits
Open Mon–Sat 10.30am–5pm March–Oct Sun noon–5pm
Services Valuations

HOLYHEAD

Gwynfair Antiques
Contact Mrs A McCann
✉ **74 Market Street, Holyhead, Isle of Anglesey, LL65 1UW** 🅿
☎ 01407 763740
Ⓜ 079709 68484
Ⓔ anwenholyhead@aol.com
Est. 1986 *Stock size* Medium
Stock Furniture, jewellery, ornaments
Open 10.30am–4.30pm closed Tues Thurs Sun
Services Valuations

LLANERCHYMEDD

Two Dragons Oriental Antiques
Contact Tony Andrew
✉ **8 High Streeet, Llanerchymedd, Isle of Anglesey, LL71 8EA** 🅿
☎ 01248 470204/470100
Ⓕ 01248 470040
Ⓜ 07811 101290
Est. 1979 *Stock size* Large
Stock Antique Chinese country furniture, signed limited edition prints by Charles Tunnicliffe
Open By appointment only
Fairs Newark

MENAI BRIDGE

41a Antiques
Contact Jack and Jean Harrison
✉ **High Street, Menai Bridge, Gwynedd, LL59 5EF** 🅿
☎ 01248 713300 Ⓕ 01248 852804
Ⓜ 07710 348892
Ⓔ sales@42a.co.uk
Ⓦ www.42a.co.uk
Est. 2002 *Stock size* Medium
Stock Period and reproduction furniture, Chinese, Indian furniture, prints, paintings
Open Mon–Sat 10.30am–5pm Wed 10am–1.30pm
Services Restoration

Better Days
Contact Mr or Mrs Rutter
✉ **The Basement, 31 High Street, Menai Bridge, Gwynedd, LL59 5EF** 🅿
☎ 01248 716657
Ⓔ rosy@betterdaysantiques.co.uk
Est. 1988 *Stock size* Medium
Stock General antiques
Open Mon–Sat 10.30am–4.30pm Wed 11am–1pm
Fairs Anglesey
Services House clearance

VALLEY

Ann Evans (LAPADA)
Contact Mrs Ann Evans
✉ **Carna Shop, Station Road, Valley, Isle of Anglesey, LL65 3EB** 🅿
☎ 01407 741733 Ⓕ 01407 740109

Ⓜ 07753 650376
Ⓦ www.annevansantiques.com
Est. 1989 *Stock size* Medium
Stock Welsh dressers, Staffordshire figures, cranberry glass, silver, country items, jewellery
Open Thurs Fri Sat 10am–4.30pm
Fairs Portmeirion, Gwyn Davies
Services Valuations

MID GLAMORGAN

ABERDARE

Market Antiques
Contact Mr Toms Glanville
15 Duke Street, Aberdare, Mid Glamorgan, CF44 7ED P
☎ 01685 870242 Ⓕ 01685 872453
Ⓔ toms@toms.worldonline.co.uk
Est. 1979 *Stock size* Large
Stock Second-hand and antique furniture, collectables, china, glass, pictures etc
Open Mon–Sat 9.30am–5pm
Fairs Abergavenny
Services House clearances

BRIDGEND

Nolton Antiques & Fine Art
Contact Mr J Gittings
66 Nolton Street, Bridgend, Mid Glamorgan, CF31 3BP P
☎ 01656 667774
Ⓔ gip@welsh-antiques.com
Ⓦ www.welsh-antiques.com
Est. 1999 *Stock size* Large
Stock Antique furniture, ceramics, paintings, clocks, ephemera, books, stamps, decorative reproductions
Open Mon–Sat 9.30–4pm closed Wed
Services Valuations, house clearance

CAERPHILLY

G J Gittins & Sons
Contact Mr John Gittins
10 Clive Street, Caerphilly, Mid Glamorgan, CF83 1GE P
☎ 029 2086 8835
Ⓜ 07941 213771
Ⓔ gittinsantiques@supanet.com
Est. 1928 *Stock size* Medium
Stock General antiques
Open Mon–Sat 10am–4pm closed Wed
Services House clearance

EWENNY

Harvard Antiques
Contact Mrs E Budd
4 Wick Road, Ewenny, Bridgend, Mid Glamorgan, CF35 5BL P
☎ 01656 766113
Est. 1989 *Stock size* Large
Stock Good-quality furniture, porcelain, clocks, longcase clocks
Open Sat 10am–5.30 Sun noon–5.30pm or by appointment
Services Valuations

FLEUR-DE-LIS

Fleur-de-Lis Antiques
Contact Mr Barber
32 High Street, Fleur-de-Lis, Blackwood, Gwent, UP12 3UE P
☎ 01443 835325
Ⓜ 07814 554672
Est. 1978 *Stock size* Large
Stock China, furniture, paintings
Open Mon–Sat 10am–1pm 2–5pm

KENFIG HILL

J & A Antiques
Contact Mrs J Lawson
1 Prince Road, Kenfig Hill, Bridgend, Mid Glamorgan, CF33 6ED P
☎ 01656 746681
Est. 1991 *Stock size* Medium
Stock Victorian–Edwardian china, glass, furniture
Open Mon–Fri 10am–4.30pm closed Wed Sat 10am–1pm

MERTHYR TYDFIL

Halfway Trading
Contact Mr J McCarthy
38 Portmorlais, Merthyr Tydfil, Mid Glamorgan, CF47 8UN P
☎ 01685 350967
Est. 1995 *Stock size* Medium
Stock General range of antiques and new stock
Open Mon–Sat 9am–5pm
Services House clearances

PONTYPRIDD

Pontypridd Auctions Ltd
Contact Mr K Hobbs ARICS
39a Cefn Lane, Glyncoch, Pontypridd, Mid Glamorgan, CF37 3BP P
☎ 01443 403764 Ⓕ 01443 400734
Ⓔ enquiries@pontypriddauctions.com
Ⓦ www.pontypriddauctions.com
Est. 1919
Open Mon–Fri 9am–5pm
Sales Auction Wed 10am, viewing Tues 2–7pm
Frequency Fortnightly
Catalogues Yes

PORTHCAWL

Harlequin Antiques
Contact John or Ann Ball
Dock Street, Porthcawl, Mid Glamorgan, CF36 3BL P
☎ 01656 785910
Ⓜ 07980 837844
Est. 1974 *Stock size* Medium
Stock General antiques, antiquarian books, textiles
Open Mon–Sat 10am–4pm
Services Valuations

TONYPANDY

Jeff's Antiques
Contact Mrs J Howells
88 Dunraven Street, Tonypandy, Mid Glamorgan, CF40 1AP P
☎ 01443 434963
Est. 1976 *Stock size* Large
Stock Shipping furniture, glass, porcelain, collectables
Open Mon–Sat 9.30am–5pm closed Thurs

TREHARRIS

Treharris Antiques
Contact Mr C Barker or Mrs Janet Barker
18 Perrott Street, Treharris, Mid Glamorgan, CF46 5ER P
☎ 01443 413081
Est. 1971 *Stock size* Large
Stock Militaria, china, mining memorabilia, collectable records, Welsh collectables
Open Always open, ring first at weekends
Services Valuations

MONMOUTHSHIRE

ABERGAVENNY

Gingers Trade Antiques
Contact D Edmunds
Park Road, Abergavenny, Monmouthshire, NP7 5TR
01873 855073
07980 170982
Est. 1983 *Stock size* Large
Stock Furniture
Open Mon–Sat 10am–5pm
Sat 1–4pm

J Straker Chadwick & Sons
Contact Mr L H Trumper
Market Street Chambers, Market Street, Abergavenny, Monmouthshire, NP7 5SD
01873 852624 01873 857311
enquiries@strakerchadwick.co.uk
www.strakerchadwick.co.uk
Est. 1872
Open Mon–Fri 9am–5pm
Sat 9.30am–12.30pm
Sales General antiques
Frequency Monthly
Catalogues Yes

ABERSYCHAN

Emlyn Antiques
Contact Emlyn Edmonds
Ffrwd Road, Abersychan, Pontypool, Monmouthshire, NP4 8PP
01495 774982
Est. 1985 *Stock size* Medium
Stock General antiques
Open Mon–Sat 9.30am–6pm
Services Valuations

CHEPSTOW

Foxglove Antiques
Contact Lesley Brain
20 St Mary Street, Chepstow, Monmouthshire, NP16 5EW
01291 622386
07949 244611
foxglovesants@foxglovesants.free-online.co.uk
Est. 1995 *Stock size* Medium
Stock Antiques and collectables
Open Mon–Sat 10am–5pm
closed Wed
Services Valuations, restoration

Plough House Interiors
Contact Peter Jones
Plough House, Upper Church Street, Chepstow, Monmouthshire, NP16 5HU
01291 625200
ploughhouse@amserve.net
Est. 1979 *Stock size* Medium
Stock General antiques, furniture including tables and chairs
Open Mon–Sat 10am–5pm
Services Valuations, upholstery and polishing

MONMOUTH

Blestium Antique Centre
Contact Brent Watkins
The Malthouse, 10–14 St Mary Street, Monmouth, Monmouthshire, NP25 3DB
01600 713999 01600 713999
brent@blestium.co.uk
www.blestium.co.uk
Est. 1999 *Stock size* Large
Stock Furniture, china, collectables, clocks, silver and architectural
Open Mon–Sat 10am–6pm

Frost Antiques & Pine
Contact Nick Frost
8 Priory Street, Monmouth, Monmouthshire, NP25 3BR
01600 716687
nickfrost@frostantiques.com
www.frostantiques.com
Est. 1956 *Stock size* Medium
Stock Pine and country furniture, Staffordshire figures
Open Mon–Sat 9am–5pm
or by appointment
Services Valuations, restoration

The House 1860–1925
Contact Nick Wheatley
6–8 St James Street, Monmouth, Monmouthshire, NP25 3DL
01600 772721
nick@thehouse1860-1925.com
www.thehouse1860-1925.com
Est. 1999 *Stock size* Large
Stock Furniture of the Arts and Crafts Movement
Open Tues–Sat 10am–6pm or by appointment
Services Valuations, restoration, interior design and furnishing

NEWPORT

Beechwood Antiques
Contact William Samuel
418 Chepstow Road, Newport, Monmouthshire, NP19 8JU
01633 279192 01633 279192
07712 1447913
Est. 1979 *Stock size* Medium
Stock General antiques
Open Mon–Sat 10.30am–5.30pm
Fairs Newark, Chepstow
Services Restoration and china repairs

Casnewydd Antiques & Restoration
Contact B J Bartlett
74b Walford Street, Newport, Monmouthshire, NP20 5PG
01633 855552
07855 978773
Est. 2000 *Stock size* Medium
Stock Georgian–Edwardian furniture, ceramics, paintings, clocks
Open Mon–Sat 9.15am–5pm
Fairs Newark, Ardingly
Services Valuations, restoration, shipping

Welsh Salvage Co (SALVO)
Contact Mr S. Lewis
Isca Yard, Milman Street, Newport, Monmouthshire, NP20 2JL
01633 212945 01633 213458
stewartlewis@btconnect.com
www.welshsalvage.co.uk
Est. 1986 *Stock size* Large
Stock Fireplaces, flooring, flagstones, stained glass, reclaimed building materials
Open Mon–Fri 8.30am–5.30pm
Sat 8.30am–4pm Sun 11am–2pm
Services Restoration, repairs

TINTERN

Stella Books (PBFA)
Contact Mrs Chris Tomaszewski
Monmouth Road, Tintern, Monmouthshire, NP16 6SE
01291 689755 01291 689998
enquiry@stellabooks.com
www.stellabooks.com
Est. 1990 *Stock size* Large
Stock Rare and out-of-print

books, specializing in children's books and UK topography
Open Mon–Sun 9.30am–5.30pm

Tintern Antiques
Contact Dawn Floyd
The Old Bakehouse, Tintern, Monmouthshire, NP16 6SE
01291 689705 F 01291 689705
Est. 1979 *Stock size* Medium
Stock General antiques including china, furniture, jewellery
Open Mon–Sun 10am–5pm

TREDEGAR

Circle Antiques
Contact Peter Thomas
6 The Circle, Tredegar, Monmouthshire, NP22 3PS
01495 724428
M 07951 536244
Est. 1979 *Stock size* Small
Stock Small antiques, furniture
Open Mon–Fri 10am–4.30pm Sat 10am–2pm closed Thurs

USK

Brindley John Ayers Antique Fishing Tackle
Contact Mr B J Ayres
Rivermill House, 1 Woodside Court, Usk, Monmouthshire, NP15 1SY
01291 672710 F 01291 673464
E bjayers@vintagefishingtackle.com
W vintagefishingtackle.com
Est. 1988 *Stock size* Large
Stock Antique fishing tackle
Open By appointment
Fairs Newark, Canterbury
Services Catalogues, B & B (for customers)

The Georgian Barn
Contact Sylvia Knee
2 Bridge Street, Usk, Monmouthshire, NP15 1PG
01291 672810
Est. 1986 *Stock size* Medium
Stock General antiques
Open Mon–Sun 10am–4pm
Services House clearance

PEMBROKESHIRE

CRESSELLY

RWG Auctions
Contact Russell Weblin-Grimsley
The Old Manse, Lawrenny Road, Cresselly, Pembrokeshire, SA68 0TB
01646 651427 F 01646 651427
M 07836 774461
Est. 2003
Open Mon–Sat 9am–5pm
Sales General antiques and collectables sales 2nd Sat of month at Carew Airfield, Carew, Nr Tenby, Pembrokeshire.
Catalogues Yes

FISHGUARD

J J Morris
Contact Mr D A Thomas
21 West Street, Fishguard, Pembrokeshire, SA65 9AL
01348 873836 F 01348 874166
E mail@jjmestateagents.co.uk
W www.jjmestateagents.co.uk
Est. 1949
Open Mon–Fri 9am–5.30pm Sat 9am–4pm
Sales General antiques
Frequency Every 4–8 weeks
Catalogues No

HAVERFORDWEST

Sylvia & John Davies Antiques
Contact Sylvia Davies
2b Dark Street, Haverfordwest, Pembrokeshire, SA61 2DS
01437 768550
Est. 1973 *Stock size* Medium
Stock General antiques, lighting
Open Tues–Sat 10.15am–1pm 2–5pm
Fairs Towy

Dyfed Antiques
Contact Giles Chaplin
The Wesleyan Chapel, Perrotts Road, Haverfordwest, Pembrokeshire, SA61 2JD
01437 760496 F 01437 760496
W www.dyfedantiques.com
Est. 1969 *Stock size* Large
Stock General antiques, architectural salvage, bespoke furniture
Open Mon–Sat 10am–5pm
Services Advisory and refurbishment service

Humphries Antiques
Contact Gary Humphries
10b Bank Row, Dew Street, Haverfordwest, Pembrokeshire, SA61 1NJ
01437 779208
M 07814 583998
E ghumphries@talk21.com
Est. 1993 *Stock size* Large
Stock Mainly ceramics, with a wide range of antiques and collectables
Open Mon–Fri 10am–4.30pm Sat 10am–1pm closed Thurs or by appointment
Fairs Carmarthen, Anglesey
Services Valuations, house clearance and collecting advice

Kent House Antiques
Contact Mr Graham Fanstone
Kent House, 15 Market Street, Haverfordwest, Pembrokeshire, SA61 1NF
01437 768175
Est. 1988 *Stock size* Medium
Stock General antiques
Open Tues–Sat 10am–4pm closed Thurs
Services Restoration

Gerald Oliver
Contact Mrs Dawn Williams
14 Albany Terrace, St Thomas Green, Haverfordwest, Pembrokeshire, SA61 1RH
01437 762794
M 07790 565034
E gerald.oliver@zoom.co.uk
Est. 1959 *Stock size* Medium
Stock General antiques
Open Mon–Sat 10am–5pm Thurs 10am–1pm

NARBERTH

The Malthouse
Contact P Griffiths or J Williams
Back Lane, High Street, Narberth, Pembrokeshire, SA67 7AR
01834 860303
Est. 1998 *Stock size* Medium
Stock General antiques, Welsh country furniture, collectables
Open Mon–Sat 10am–5.30pm
Services Pine stripping

NEWPORT

Carningli Centre
Contact Mrs Ann Gent
East Street, Newport, Pembrokeshire, SA42 0SY

☎ 01239 820724
Ⓔ info@carningli.co.uk
Ⓦ www.carningli.co.uk
Est. 1997 *Stock size* Medium
Stock General antiques, second-hand books, art gallery
Open Mon–Sat 10am–5.30pm
Services Furniture restoration and polishing

PEMBROKE

Pembroke Antiques Centre
Contact Michael Blake
✉ **Wesley Chapel, Main Street, Pembroke, Pembrokeshire, SA71 4DE** Ⓟ
☎ 01646 687017
Est. 1979 *Stock size* Large
Stock General antiques, Victorian–Edwardian furniture, china, paintings, ephemera, postcards
Open Mon–Sat 10am–5pm
Services Repairs, restoration and valuations

Pembroke Market Emporium
Contact Russell Weblin-Grimsley or Peter Thorpe
✉ **Main Street, Pembroke, Pembrokeshire, SA71 4DB** Ⓟ
☎ 01646 686894 Ⓕ 01646 651427
Ⓜ 07836 774461
Est. 2003 *Stock size* Medium
No. of dealers 23
Stock Antiques, collectables
Open Mon–Fri 10.30am–5.30pm Sat 10.30am–5pm

Picton Collectables
Contact Mr A L Cuft
✉ **59 Main Street, Pembroke, Pembrokeshire, SA71 4DA** Ⓟ
☎ 01646 621734
Est. 1992 *Stock size* Medium
Stock Collectables
Open Mon–Sat 10am–4pm
Fairs Towy
Services Valuations

PEMBROKE DOCK

Treen Box Antiques
Contact Mr M D Morris
✉ **61 Bush Street, Pembroke Dock, Pembrokeshire, SA72 6AN** Ⓟ
☎ 01646 621800 Ⓕ 01646 621800
Ⓜ 07971 636148
Ⓔ admin@treenbox.fsnet.co.uk
Est. 1990 *Stock size* Large
Stock General antiques, small upholstered chairs
Open Mon–Sat 9am–5pm or by appointment
Fairs Ardingly, Stoneleigh
Services Restoration and repair, upholstery

Victoria Antiques
Contact Mr D Peter
✉ **49 Bush Street, Pembroke Dock, Pembrokeshire, SA72 6AN** Ⓟ
☎ 01646 682652
Est. 1990 *Stock size* Medium
Stock General antiques, maritime artefacts
Open Tues Fri 10am–5pm Wed 10am–1pm Sat 10am–3pm

SAUNDERSFOOT

The Strand Antiques & Collectable
Contact Paul Lewis
✉ **The Strand, Saundersfoot, Pembrokeshire, SA68 9EX** Ⓟ
☎ 01834 814545
Est. 2003 *Stock size* Medium
Stock China, glass, jewellery
Open Mon–Sun 9am–6pm
Fairs Saundersfoot Antiques Fair

TEMPLETON

Barn Court Antiques
Contact David Evans
✉ **Barn Court, Templeton, Narberth, Pembrokeshire, SA67 8SL** Ⓟ
☎ 01834 861224
Ⓔ info@barncourtantiques.com
Ⓦ www.barncourtantiques.com
Est. 1976 *Stock size* Medium
Stock 18th–19thC fine quality furniture, china, glass
Open Mon–Sun 10am–5pm winter closed Mon
Services Valuations, restoration

TENBY

Cofion Books & Postcards (PTA)
Contact A Smosarski
✉ **Bridge Street, Tenby, Pembrokeshire, SA70 7BU** Ⓟ
☎ 01834 845741 Ⓕ 01834 843864
Ⓔ albie@cofin.com
Est. 1987 *Stock size* Large
Stock Second-hand books, Edwardian postcards, varied collectables, specializing in Augustus and Gwen John publications
Open Mon–Sun 10.30am–5.30pm
Fairs Cardiff Postcard Club Annual Fair
Services Valuations, book search, postal approval on postcards

Tenby Antiques Centre
Contact Mrs Thomas
✉ **10 The Green, Tenby, Pembrokeshire, SA70 8EY** Ⓟ
☎ 01834 849058
Est. 1980 *Stock size* Medium
No. of dealers 8
Stock Period oak, small antiques
Open Mon–Sun 10am–6pm

POWYS

BRECON

Books, Maps & Prints
Contact Andrew Wakley
✉ **7 The Struet, Brecon, Powys, LD3 7LL** Ⓟ
☎ 01874 622714 Ⓕ 01874 622714
Est. 1973 *Stock size* Medium
Stock Books, maps and prints
Open Mon–Sat 9am–5pm Wed 9am–1pm
Services Framing

The Brecon Antiques Centre
Contact Lynton Phillips
✉ **22a High Street, Brecon, Powys, LD3 7LA** Ⓟ
☎ 01874 623355
Ⓔ pheulwen@aol.com
Est. 1999 *Stock size* Large
No. of dealers 32
Stock All small antiques
Open Mon–Fri 10am–5pm Sun 11am–4pm

Montague Harris & Co
Contact John Lewis
✉ **16 Ship Street, Brecon, Powys, LD3 9AD** Ⓟ
☎ 01874 623200 Ⓕ 01874 623131
Ⓔ jal@montague-harris.co.uk
Ⓦ www.montague-harris.co.uk
Est. 1900
Open Mon–Fri 9am–5pm Sat 9am–1pm

Sales General antiques
Frequency Periodically
Catalogues Yes

Pritchard & Partners (RICS, ISVA)
Contact David Pritchard
2 The Struet, Brecon, Powys, LD3 7LH
01874 622261 01874 623020
Est. 1959
Open Mon–Fri 9am–5pm
Sat 9am–noon
Sales Antiques and general effects
Frequency Monthly
Catalogues Yes

BUILTH WELLS

McCartneys
Contact Mrs Diana Samuel
46 High Street, Builth Wells, Powys, LD2 3AB
01982 552259 01982 552193
builth@mccartneys.co.uk
www.mccartneys.co.uk
Est. 1949
Open Mon–Fri 9am–5pm
Sat 9.30am–12.30pm
Sales General antiques, furniture and effects
Frequency Periodically
Catalogues No

Smithfield Antiques
Contact Suzanne Price
Smithfield Road, Builth Wells, Powys, LD2 3AN
01982 553022 01982 553022
07879 025577
suzanne@smithfieldjoinery.fsnet.co.uk
www.smithfield-joinery.com
Est. 2000 *Stock size* Medium
Stock General antiques, fireplaces, oak Welsh dressers
Open Mon–Sat 10am–5pm closed Wed

CILMERY

V Nejus
Contact Mr V Nejus
Comyn Cottage, Cilmery, Builth Wells, Powys, LD2 3LH
01982 553792
Est. 1972 *Stock size* Medium
Stock General antiques
Open By appointment only

CRICKHOWELL

Gallop–Rivers Architectural Antiques
Contact Mr Gallop
Tyrash, Brecon Road, Crickhowell, Powys, NP8 1SF
01873 811084 01873 811084
enquiries@gallopandrivers.co.uk
www.gallopandrivers.co.uk
Est. 1985 *Stock size* Large
Stock Architectural, furniture
Open Mon–Sat 9.30am–5pm

FOUR CROSSES

Malthouse Antiques
Contact Neville Foulkes
The Old Malthouse, Pool Road, Four Crosses, Llanymynech, Powys, SY22 6PS
01691 830015 01691 839099
Est. 1983 *Stock size* Medium
Stock Pine and country furniture
Open Mon–Sat 9am–6pm or by appointment
Services Valuations, restoration and repairs

KNIGHTON

Offa's Dyke Antique Centre
Contact Mr I Watkins or Mrs H Hood
4 High Street, Knighton, Powys, LD7 1AT
01547 528635
Est. 1987 *Stock size* Medium
No. of dealers 10
Stock General antiques, ceramics
Open Mon–Sat 10am–1pm and 2–5pm
Services House clearance

Islwyn Watkins Antiques
Contact Mr I Watkins
4 High Street, Knighton, Powys, LD7 1AT
01547 520145
Est. 1977 *Stock size* Large
Stock Ceramics and small country antiques
Open Mon–Sat 10am–1pm 2–5pm
Services Valuations

LLANFAIR CAEREINION

Heritage Restorations
Contact Jonathan Gluck
Llanfair Caereinion, Welshpool, Powys, SY21 0HD
01938 810384 01938 810900
info@heritagerestorations.co.uk
www.heritagerestorations.co.uk
Est. 1970 *Stock size* Large
Stock 18th–19thC pine furniture
Open Mon–Sat 9am–5pm
Services Restoration

LLANFYLLIN

Galata Coins
Contact Paul Withers
Old White Lion, Market Street, Llanfyllin, Powys, SY22 5BX
01691 648765 01691 648765
Paul@galata.co.uk
www.galata.co.uk
Est. 1974 *Stock size* Small
Stock Coins and medals
Open By appointment
Services Valuations

LLANIDLOES

The Great Oak Bookshop
Contact Ross Bozwell or Karin Reiter
35 Great Oak Street, Llanidloes, Powys, SY18 6BW
01686 412959 01686 412959
greatoak@europe.com
www.midwales.com/gob
Est. 1992 *Stock size* Large
Stock Books, antiquarian, new and second-hand
Open Mon–Fri 9.30am–5.30pm
Sat 9.30am–4.30pm
Services Book search

Now & Then
Contact Mrs J Parker
2 Long Bridge Street, Llanidloes, Powys, ST18 6EE
01686 411186
jacqueline@parker7598.freeserve.co.uk
Est. 2003 *Stock size* Medium
Stock Antique Persian rugs, carpets, cranberry glass, collectable ceramics, fine furniture, clocks
Open Mon–Sat 10am–4.30pm
Fairs Swinderby
Services Restoration, delivery

MACHYNLLETH

Dyfi Valley Bookshop (PBFA, WBA)
Contact Mr N Beeby
6 Heol y Doll, Machynlleth, Powys, SY20 8BQ
☎ 01654 703849
beeb@dvbookshop.fsnet.co.uk
www.abebooks.com/home/dvbookshop
Est. 1988 *Stock size* Medium
Stock Rare and second-hand books, specializing in archery, the Old West, firearms
Open Mon–Sat 9.30am–5pm
Fairs Imperial, Bisley, Trafalgar Meeting, Bisley
Services Book search, catalogues

MONTGOMERY

Portcullis Furniture
Contact Mr John Cox or Mrs Sally Allen
Snead Farm, Snead, Montgomery, Powys, SY15 6EB
☎ 01588 638077
Ⓜ 07966 188364
Est. 1995 *Stock size* Large
Stock Antique, reproduction and new furniture, copper, brass, silver, china, clocks
Open Mon–Sat 10am–5.30pm Sun 10.30am–4.30pm
Fairs Newark
Services Shipping

NEWBRIDGE ON WYE

Newbridge Antiques
Contact P Allan
The Old Village Hall, Newbridge on Wye, Llandrindod Wells, Powys, LD1 6LA
☎ 01597 860654 Ⓕ 01597 860655
Est. 1986 *Stock size* Large
Stock General antiques, furniture, architectural
Open Sat 10am–5pm
Services Valuations, stripping and restoration

NEWTOWN

Morris Marshall & Poole
Contact Alun Davies
10 Broad Street, Newtown, Powys, SY16 2LZ
☎ 01686 625900 Ⓕ 01686 623783
mmp@newtown.ereal.net
www.morrismarshall.co.uk
Est. 1862
Open Mon–Fri 9am–5pm Sat 9.30am–2pm
Sales General antiques
Frequency Quarterly
Catalogues Yes

TRECASTLE

The Fire & Stove Shop
Contact Andy Annear or Jim Portsmouth
Vicarage Row (on A40), Trecastle, Brecon, Powys, LD3 8UW
☎ 01874 636888 Ⓕ 02920 614615
Ⓜ 07973 916774
jim@solidfuelstoves.com
www.solidfuelstoves.com
Est. 1998
Stock Multi-fuel stoves, fires, fireplaces, tiles, inserts, surrounds, hearths, dog grates, radiators
Open Mon–Sun 10am–6pm

Trecastle Antique Centre
Contact Ro Williams
Trecastle, Brecon, Powys, LD3 8UN
☎ 01874 638007
Ⓜ 07811 032248
Est. 1996 *Stock size* Large
No. of dealers 10
Stock General antiques
Open Mon–Sun 10am–5pm

WELSHPOOL

F E Anderson & Son (LAPADA)
Contact Ian Anderson
5 High Street, Welshpool, Powys, SY21 7JF
☎ 01938 553340 Ⓕ 01938 590545
Ⓜ 07889 896832
Est. 1842 *Stock size* Large
Stock General antiques, 17th–19thC furniture
Open Mon–Fri 9am–5pm Sat 9am–2pm
Fairs Olympia, Harrogate, Birmingham NEC, Kingston
Services Valuations

Lamplite Antiques
Contact Mrs Parks
2 Boot Street, Welshpool, Powys, SY21 7SA
☎ 01938 555036
Ⓜ 07817 204398
Est. 2000 *Stock size* Large
Stock Country oak furniture, oil lamps, clocks, general collectables
Open Mon–Sat 8.30am–5pm

SOUTH GLAMORGAN

BARRY

Ray Hawkins Antiques
Contact Ray Hawkins
Priory Buildings, Broad Street, Barry, South Glamorgan, CF62 7AD
☎ 01446 744750 Ⓕ 12920 711778
Ⓜ 07971 575044
ray@hawkins.wholesalers.co.uk
www.hawkins-wholesales.co.uk
Est. 1975 *Stock size* Medium
Stock Antique shipping furniture and statues
Open Mon–Fri 9am–5pm Sat 9am–1pm
Fairs Ardingly, Newark
Services Exports furniture to USA, packing facilities

Hawkins Brothers Antiques
Contact Jeff or Terence Hawkins
21–23 Romilly Buildings, Woodham Road, Barry Docks, South Glamorgan, CF63 4JE
☎ 01446 746561 Ⓕ 01446 744271
hawkinsbrosantiques@compuserve.com
Est. 1975 *Stock size* Large
Stock Antique furniture
Open Mon–Sat 9am–5pm
Fairs Newark
Services Restoration

CARDIFF

Anchor Antiques (Wales) Ltd
Contact B A Brownhill
The Pumping Station, Penarth Road, Cardiff, South Glamorgan, CF11 8TT
☎ 029 2023 1308 Ⓕ 029 2023 2588
Ⓜ 07967 264325
Est. 1989 *Stock size* Large
Stock General antiques, clocks and ceramics
Open Mon–Sun 9.30am–5.30pm

Bonhams
7–8 Park Place, Cardiff, South Glamorgan, CF10 3DP
☎ 02920 727980 Ⓕ 02920 727989
Ⓔ cardiff@bonhams.com
Ⓦ www.bonhams.com
Open Mon–Fri 9am–5.30pm
Sales Regional office. Regular house and attic sales across the country; contact London offices for further details. Free auction valuations; insurance and probate valuations

Capital Bookshop
Contact Andrew Mitchell
27 Morgan Arcade, Cardiff, South Glamorgan, CF10 1AF
☎ 029 2038 8423
Est. 1977 *Stock size* Medium
Stock Books, rare and second-hand including Welsh interest
Open Mon–Sat 10am–5.30pm
Fairs Book fairs, Oxford

Cardiff Antique Centre
Contact Jane Rowls
10–12 Royal Arcade, Cardiff, South Glamorgan, CF10 1AE
☎ 029 2039 8891
Est. 1975 *Stock size* Large
No. of dealers 14
Stock General antiques and collectables including Welsh china, jewellery
Open Mon–Sat 10am–5.30pm
Services Valuations

Cardiff Reclamation
Contact Jeff Evans
Unit 7, Tremorfa Industrial Estate, Martin Road, Tremorfa, Cardiff, South Glamorgan, CF24 5SD Ⓟ
☎ 029 2045 8995
Est. 1987 *Stock size* Medium
Stock Architectural antiques, specializing in fireplaces and bathrooms
Open Mon–Fri 9am–5pm Sat 9am–1pm Sun 10am–1pm
Services Bath refinishing, pine stripping, sandblasting

Charleston Antiques
Contact Steve McDonald
129 Woodville Road, Cathays, Cardiff, South Glamorgan, CF24 4DZ Ⓟ
☎ 029 2023 1123
Est. 1970 *Stock size* Large
Stock General antiques
Open Mon–Sat 8am–6pm
Services Valuations

Crwys Antiques
Contact Mr Elfed Caradog
51 Crwys Road, Cardiff, South Glamorgan, CF24 4ND Ⓟ
☎ 029 2022 5318
Est. 1985 *Stock size* Small
Stock General antiques
Open Mon–Sat noon–6pm

Decorative Heating
Contact Jim Portsmouth
Unit 2, Victoria Arcade, The Pumping Station, Cardiff, South Glamorgan, CF11 8TT Ⓟ
☎ 029 2052 2000
Ⓜ 07973 916774
Ⓔ jim@solidfuelstoves.com
Ⓦ www.solidfuelstoves.com
Est. 1998 *Stock size* Medium
Stock Multi-fuel stoves, fires, fireplaces, tiles, inserts, surrounds, hearths, dog grates, radiators
Open Mon–Sun 9am–5.30pm

Hera Antiques
Contact Neil Richards
140 Whitchurch Road, Cardiff, South Glamorgan, CF14 3LZ Ⓟ
☎ 029 2061 9472
Est. 1987 *Stock size* Large
Stock High-quality furniture, porcelain and pictures
Open Mon–Sat 10am–5pm closed Wed
Fairs The Orangery, Margam Abbey, Port Talbot
Services Restoration, valuations

Jacobs Antique Centre
Contact Mr Cooling
West Canal Wharf, Cardiff, South Glamorgan, CF10 5DB Ⓟ
☎ 029 2039 0939 Ⓕ 029 2037 3587
Est. 1982 *Stock size* Medium
No. of dealers 40
Stock General antiques
Open Thurs–Sat 9.30am–5pm

Keepence Antiques
Contact Mr Clive Keepence
34 Clare Road, Cardiff, South Glamorgan, CF11 6RS Ⓟ
☎ 029 2025 5348
Est. 1969 *Stock size* Medium
Stock Victorian, Edwardian furniture, shipping goods
Open Mon–Fri 10am–4pm Sat 10am–2pm

Llanishen Antiques
Contact Mrs J Boalch
26 Crwys Road, Cardiff, South Glamorgan, CF24 4NL Ⓟ
☎ 029 2039 7244
Est. 1974 *Stock size* Medium
Stock General antiques including 19th–20thC furniture
Open Mon–Sat 10am–4pm
Fairs Carmarthen, Shepton Mallet
Services Restoration

Now & Then
Contact Mr A Williams
54 Crwys Road, Cardiff, South Glamorgan, CF24 4NN Ⓟ
☎ 029 2038 3268 Ⓕ 029 2065 7629
Ⓔ frongaled50@hotmail.com
Est. 1989 *Stock size* Medium
Stock General antiques
Open Mon–Sat 9am–5pm

The Pumping Station
Contact Mr M A Brownhill
Penarth Road, Cardiff, South Glamorgan, CF11 8TT Ⓟ
☎ 029 2022 1085 Ⓕ 029 2023 2588
Ⓜ 07774 449443
Est. 1989 *Stock size* Large
No. of dealers 35
Stock General antiques, militaria, model cars, railways
Open Mon–Sun 9.30am–5.30pm
Services Valuations

Roberts Emporium
Contact Ian Roberts
58–60 Salisbury Road, Cardiff, South Glamorgan, CF24 4AD Ⓟ
☎ 029 2023 5630 Ⓕ 029 2039 5935
Ⓜ 07813 283885
Ⓔ info@cheapaschips.cc
Ⓦ worldwideweb.cheapaschips.cc
Est. 1997 *Stock size* Large
Stock General antiques, collectables, props for TV and theatre
Open Mon–Sat 11am–5.30pm
Fairs Newark, Cardiff, Ardingly
Services Valuations

Sambourne House Antique Pine Ltd
Contact Tim or Kim Cove

✉ **145 Colchester Avenue, Cardiff, South Glamorgan, CF23 9AN** P
☎ 02920 487823
ⓔ tkcove34@globalnet.co.uk
ⓦ www.sambourne-antiques.co.uk
Est. 1986 *Stock size* Large
Stock Antique and reproduction pine furniture, smalls, decorative items
Open Mon–Sun 9am–5pm
Services Hand-built kitchens

Tails & The Unexpected Ltd
Contact Mark Williams
✉ **Jacobs Antique Centre, West Canal Wharf, Cardiff, South Glamorgan, CF10 5DB** P
☎ 029 2034 0046 ⓕ 029 2034 0046
ⓜ 07974 344639
ⓔ tailsandtheunexpected@hotmail.com
Est. 1980 *Stock size* Medium
Stock Antique clothing and accessories
Open Wed–Sat 9.30am–5pm

Ty-Llwyd Antiques
Contact Mr Graham Rousell
✉ **Ty-Llwyd, Lisvane Road, Lisvane, Cardiff, South Glamorgan, CF14 0SF** P
☎ 029 2075 4109
Est. 1988 *Stock size* Large
Stock General antiques, clocks
Open By appointment
Services House clearance

Whitchurch Books Ltd (WBA)
Contact Gale Canvin
✉ **67 Merthyr Road, Whitchurch, Cardiff, South Glamorgan, CF14 1DD** P
☎ 029 2052 1956 ⓕ 029 2062 3599
ⓦ www.whitchurchbooks@barclays.net
Est. 1994 *Stock size* Medium
Stock Books, rare and second-hand, specializing in archaeology and history
Open Tues–Sat 10am–5.30pm
Fairs Cardiff
Services Mail order catalogues on archaeology and history

COWBRIDGE

Bookstores Wales
Contact Rob Thomas
✉ **48a Eastgate, Cowbridge, South Glamorgan, CF71 7AB** P
☎ 01446 772929
ⓜ 07887 605706
Est. 2001 *Stock size* Medium
Stock General antiquarian books, history, literature, art
Open Mon–Sat 10am–5pm

Castle Antique Clocks
Contact Mr William Webber
✉ **Vale of Glamorgan Antique Centre, 48 Eastgate, Cowbridge, South Glamorgan, CF71 7AB** P
☎ 029 2070 2313 ⓕ 029 2071 2141
ⓔ whwebber@talk21.com
Est. 1995 *Stock size* Medium
Stock Longcase clocks
Open Mon–Sat 10am–5pm
Services Valuations, restoration

Eastgate Antiques
Contact Liz Herbert
✉ **6 High Street, Cowbridge, South Glamorgan, CF71 7AG** P
☎ 01446 775111
Est. 1984 *Stock size* Medium
Stock Furniture, silver, jewellery
Open Tues–Sat 10am–1pm 2–5.30pm

The Vale of Glamorgan Antique Centre
Contact Mike Haxley
✉ **Ebenezer Chapel, 48 Eastgate, Cowbridge, South Glamorgan, CF71 7AB** P
☎ 01446 771190
ⓜ 07977 091665
ⓔ collectorscorner1@hotmail.com
Est. 1996 *Stock size* Medium
No. of dealers 30
Stock Furniture, china, porcelain, collectables, jewellery, autographs
Open Mon–Sat 10am–5pm
Services Valuations, picture restoration, repairs

WEST GLAMORGAN

CLYDACH

Celtic Antique Fireplaces
Contact Mr R Walker
✉ **Unit 13, John Player Industrial Estate, Clydach, Swansea, West Glamorgan, SA6 5BQ** P
☎ 01792 476047 ⓕ 01792 476047
ⓜ 07973 253655
ⓔ robin-walker@celticfireplaces.co.uk
ⓦ www.celticfireplaces.co.uk
Est. 1992 *Stock size* Large
Stock Antique fireplaces
Open Wed Sat 10am–2pm or by appointment
Services Renovation

Clydach Antiques
Contact Mr R T Pulman
✉ **83 High Street, Clydach, Swansea, West Glamorgan, SA6 5LJ** P
☎ 01792 843209
Est. 1981 *Stock size* Small
Stock General antiques
Open Mon–Fri 10am–5pm
Fairs Swansea
Services Clock repair

MUMBLES

Elizabeth Antiques
Contact Elizabeth Wickstead
✉ **504 Mumbles Road, Oystermouth, Swansea, West Glamorgan, SA3 4BU** P
☎ 01792 361909 ⓕ 01792 361909
ⓜ 07831 554351
ⓔ info@elizabethantiques.com
ⓦ www.elizabethantiques.com
Est. 1978
Stock Furniture, porcelain, glass, jewellery
Open By appointment

Gower House Antiques
Contact Mrs E S Dodds
✉ **28–30 Dunns Lane, Mumbles, Swansea, West Glamorgan, SA3 4AA** P
☎ 01792 369844
Est. 1999 *Stock size* Medium
Stock General antiques, mirrors, lighting, chandeliers
Open Tues–Sat 10am–5.30pm
Services Valuations

NEATH

Neath Market Curios (OMRS)
Contact Mr P D Owen
✉ **General Market, Green Street, Neath, West Glamorgan, SA11 1DP** P
☎ 01639 641775
Est. 1989 *Stock size* Medium
Stock General collectables
Open Tues–Sat 9am–5pm

PONTARDULAIS

The Emporium
Contact Ms Laura Jeremy
112 St Teilo Street, Pontardulais, Swansea, West Glamorgan, SA4 1SR P
01792 885185
07811 758896
laura@the-emporium.freeserve.co.uk
Est. 1990 *Stock size* Medium
Stock Small furniture, collectables, metalware
Open Mon–Fri 10am–5.30pm Sat 10am–1pm

SKETTY

Sketty Antiques & Gifts
Contact Mrs Karen Debenedictis
87 Eversley Road, Sketty, Swansea, West Glamorgan, SA2 9DE P
01792 201616
www.skettyantiques.com
Est. 1995 *Stock size* Medium
Stock General antiques
Open Mon–Fri 11am–3.30pm Sat 11am–2.30pm

SWANSEA

Booth Antiques
Contact Jeff Booth
798 Brynymor Road, Swansea, West Glamorgan, SA1 4JE P
01792 648152
Est. 1985 *Stock size* Medium
Stock Jewellery, fireplaces
Open Mon–Sat 2–5pm

City Antiques
Contact Mr G Aston
14 Ticton Arcade, Swansea, West Glamorgan, SA1 3BE P
01792 413300 F 01792 477551
Est. 1970 *Stock size* Large
Stock Victorian–Edwardian Art Deco and amber marquetry jewellery
Open Tues–Sat 10am–4pm

Stripped Pine Workshop
Contact Mr John Wood
Rear of 28 Catherine Street, Swansea, West Glamorgan, SA1 4JS P
01792 461236
Est. 1970 *Stock size* Medium
Stock Furniture, doors, stripped pine
Open Mon–Sun 11.30am–6pm
Services Pine stripping

Swansea Antique Centre
Contact Mr W Wright or Mr R Sparks
1 King Edward Road, Swansea, West Glamorgan, SA1 4LH P
01792 475194
Est. 1999 *Stock size* Large
No. of dealers 2
Stock General antiques, good furniture
Open Mon–Sat 10am–5.30pm
Services Valuations, restoration, house clearance

YSTRADGYNLAIS

Penybont Farm Antiques
Contact Mrs S Yankovic
Penybont Farm, Penycae, Ystradgynlais, Swansea, West Glamorgan, SA9 1SH P
01639 730620
Est. 1990 *Stock size* Large
Stock General antiques, pine, china
Open Sat Sun 10am–5pm or by appointment
Services Restoration, hand stripping

SCOTLAND

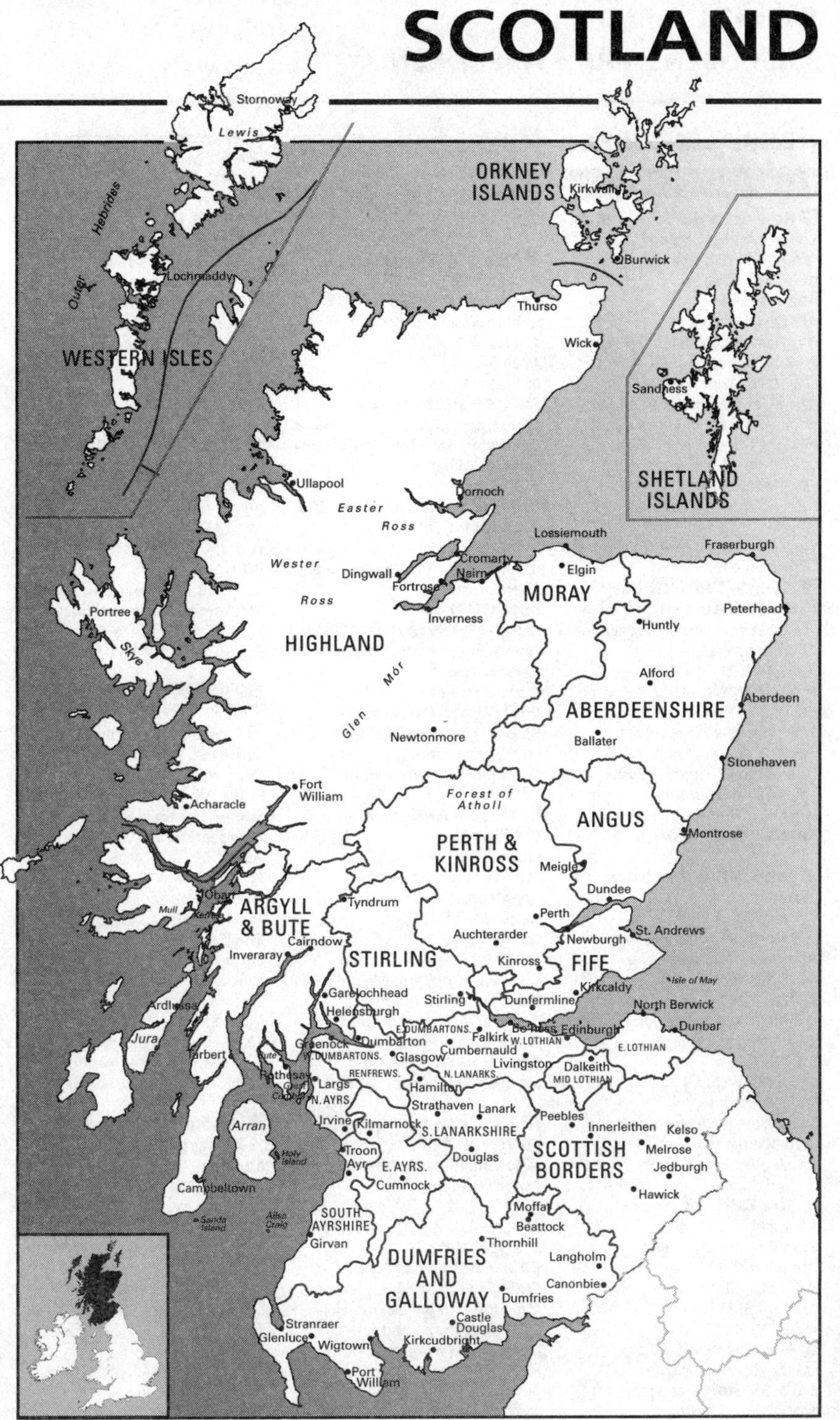

SCOTLAND

ABERDEENSHIRE

ABERDEEN

Bon-Accord Books (PBFA)
Contact Andrew Milne
69–75 Spital, Aberdeen, Aberdeenshire, AB24 3HX P
01224 643209
bonaccordbooks@btinternet.com
www.bon-accordbooks.co.uk
Est. 1998 *Stock size* Medium
Stock General and antiquarian books, Scottish, children's and modern topics, first editions
Open Mon–Fri 10.30am–5.30pm Sat 11am–4.30pm closed Wed
Fairs Aberdeen, Glasgow, York, London
Services Postcards, prints, pictures

Candle Close Gallery
Contact Mrs B Brown
123 Gallowgate, Aberdeen, Aberdeenshire, AB25 1BU P
01224 624940 F 01224 620548
Est. 1994 *Stock size* Medium
Stock Antique pine, collectors' items, curios
Open Mon–Fri 10am–5.30pm Thurs 10am–7pm Sat 9am–5pm Sun noon–4pm
Fairs Newark

John Milne Auctioneers (SAA)
Contact Robert Milne
9 North Silver Street, Aberdeen, Aberdeenshire, AB10 1RJ P
01224 639336 F 01224 645857
info@johnmilne-auctioneers.com
www.johnmilne-auctioneers.com
Est. 1867
Open Mon–Thur 8.30am–5pm Fri 8.30am–4pm
Sales Weekly general sales Wed 10am, view Tues 10am–7pm
Catalogues Yes

The Odd Lot
Contact Mr G Mudie
18 Adelphi, Aberdeen, Aberdeenshire, AB11 5BL P
01224 592551 F 01224 574404
M 07771 926736
George@theoddlot.com
www.theoddlot.com
Est. 1997 *Stock size* Medium
Stock General antiques, furniture, jewellery, Scottish antiques, books
Open Tues–Sat 11am–5pm
Fairs The Academy, Aberdeen
Services House clearance

The Old Aberdeen Bookshop
Contact Mr C Scott-Paul
140 Spital, Aberdeen, Aberdeenshire, AB24 3JU
01224 658355
Est. 1998 *Stock size* Small
Stock Rare and second-hand books
Open Mon–Sat 11am–5.30pm
Services Valuations

Rendezvous Gallery Ltd
Contact Mr C D Mead or Mr Andrew Allan
100 Forest Avenue, Aberdeen, Aberdeenshire, AB15 4TL P
01224 323247 F 01224 323247
info@rendezvousgallery.freeserve.uk
www.rendezvouz-gallery.co.uk
Est. 1975 *Stock size* Medium
Stock Art Nouveau, Art Deco, Scottish paintings
Open Mon–Sat 10am–6pm

Thistle Antiques (LAPADA)
Contact Mr P Bursill
28 Esslemont Avenue, Aberdeen, Aberdeenshire, AB25 1SN P
01224 634692
M 07759 429685
Est. 1969 *Stock size* Medium
Stock General antiques, Georgian–Victorian furniture, Art Nouveau lighting
Open Mon–Fri 10am–5pm Sat 10am–1pm closed Wed

J R Webb Antiques
Contact J R Webb
30 Carden Place, Aberdeen, Aberdeenshire, AB10 1UP P
01224 631222
M 07720 771302
Est. 1908 *Stock size* Large
Stock General antiques, jewellery, arms and armour, especially Scottish artefacts and art
Open Mon–Fri 10am–6pm Sat 10am–1pm closed Wed
Services Valuations and probate service, restoration

Winram's Bookshop
Contact Mrs Margaret Davidson
32–36 Rosemount Place, Aberdeen, Aberdeenshire, AB25 2XB P
01224 630673 F 01224 630673
Est. 1975 *Stock size* Medium
Stock Rare and second-hand books, especially Scottish topics, postcards, local photographs
Open Mon–Sat 10am–5.30pm Wed 10am–1pm
Fairs Aberdeen
Services Valuations

Colin Wood Antiques Ltd
Contact Mr C Wood
25 Rose Street, Aberdeen, Aberdeenshire, AB10 1TX P
01224 643019/644786
F 01224 644786
Est. 1969 *Stock size* Medium
Stock General and antique Scottish maps, prints
Open Mon–Sat 10am–5pm

BALLATER

Deeside Books (PBFA Ballater, Aberdeen)
Contact Mr B Wayte
The Albert Memorial Hall, Station Square, Ballater, Aberdeenshire, AB35 5QB P
01339 754080 F 01339 754080
deesidebk@aol.com
Est. 1998 *Stock size* Large
Stock Out-of-print and antiquarian books, specializing in Scottish, military, topography and travel, field sports
Open March–Oct Mon–Sat 10am–5pm Sun noon–5pm Nov–March please telephone
Services Valuations, book search

Rowan Antiques & Collectables
Contact Nikki Henderson
Tulchan House, 5–7 Victoria Road, Ballater, Aberdeenshire, AB35 5QQ P
013397 56035 F 013397 56035
nikki.rowan@lineone.net
Est. 1986 *Stock size* Medium
Stock Victorian–1930s furniture, fine and country, jewellery, porcelain, prints
Open Mon–Sat 10am–5.30pm
Fairs Aberdeen Tree Tops
Services Valuations, shipping

⊞ Treasures of Ballater
Contact Nikki Henderson
✉ **1 Victoria Road, Ballater, Aberdeenshire, AB35 5QQ** 🅿
☎ 013397 55122 ⓕ 013397 56035
ⓔ nikki.rowan@lineone.net
Est. 1986 *Stock size* Medium
Stock Victorian–1930s furniture, fine and country, jewellery, porcelain, prints
Open Mon–Sat 10am–5.30pm
Fairs Aberdeen Tree Tops
Services Valuations, shipping

CLOLA

Clola Antiques Centre
Contact David Blackburn
✉ **Shannas School, Clola, Peterhead, Aberdeenshire, AB42 5AB** 🅿
☎ 01771 624584
ⓜ 07836 537188
ⓦ www.clolaantiquescentre@aol.com
Est. 1989 *Stock size* Large
No. of dealers 6
Stock Furniture, jewellery, china, glass
Open Mon–Sat 10am–5pm Sun 11am–5pm
Services Restoration, upholstery

DUNECHT

⊞ Magic Lantern
Contact Mrs J White
✉ **Nether Corskie, Dunecht, Aberdeenshire, AB32 7EL** 🅿
☎ 01330 860678
Est. 1978 *Stock size* Medium
Stock General antiques
Open Telephone call advisable
Services Restoration to china, furniture

HUNTLY

⊞ Huntly Antiques
Contact Jean Barker
✉ **43 Duke Street, Huntly, Aberdeenshire, AB54 8DT** 🅿
☎ 01466 793307
Est. 1984 *Stock size* Medium
Stock General antiques
Open Mon–Sat 10am–4pm or by appointment

G G & H R Lumsden
Contact G G Lumsden
✉ **Affleck, Huntly, Aberdeenshire, AB54 6XW** 🅿
☎ 01466 792686
Est. 1948
Open By appointment only
Sales General antiques
Frequency Monthly
Catalogues No

INVERURIE

Thainstone Specialist Auctions
Contact Mark Barrack or L Howie
✉ **Thainstone Centre, Inverurie, Aberdeen, Aberdeenshire, AB51 5XZ** 🅿
☎ 01467 623770 ⓕ 01467 623771
ⓔ tsa@goanm.co.uk
ⓦ www.goanm.co.uk
Est. 1942
Open Mon–Fri 9am–5pm
Sales General antiques Tues 6pm
Frequency Monthly
Catalogues Yes

LAURENCEKIRK

James S T Liddle
Contact Mr B Liddle
✉ **Malvern, 65 Johnstone Street, Laurencekirk, Aberdeenshire, AB30 1AN** 🅿
☎ 01561 377420 ⓕ 01561 377420
ⓜ 07831 475095
Est. 1989
Open Mon–Sat 8am–5pm
Sales General furniture
Frequency Monthly
Catalogues No

LONGHAVEN

⊞ Grannie Used To Have One
Contact Jacqui Harvey
✉ **Sanderling, Longhaven, Nr Peterhead, Aberdeenshire, AB42 0NX** 🅿
☎ 01779 813223 ⓕ 01779 813223
ⓜ 07850 912364
ⓔ jacqui@grannieusedto.co.uk
ⓦ www.grannieusedto.co.uk
Est. 1991 *Stock size* Large
Stock Pottery, including Scottish pottery, porcelain, furniture, glass, metalware
Open Thurs Fri 1–5pm Sat Sun 11am–5pm or by appointment
Fairs Scone Palace, Perthshire, Hopetoun House, Edinburgh
Services Valuations

TARLAND

⊞ The Tower Workshops
Contact George Pirie
✉ **Aberdeen Road, Tarland, Aboyne, Aberdeenshire, AB34 4TB** 🅿
☎ 013398 811544
Est. 1989 *Stock size* Large
Stock Edwardian mahogany and Georgian furniture, soft furnishings, small items, decorative objects
Open Mon–Sun 11am–5pm
Services Valuations, restoration, complete house commissions

ANGUS

DUNDEE

⊞ Angus Antiques
Contact John Czerek or Stanley Paget
✉ **4 St Andrew Street, Dundee, Angus, DD1 2EX** 🅿
☎ 01382 322128
Est. 1972 *Stock size* Medium
Stock General antiques, militaria, jewellery
Open Mon–Fri 10am–4pm
Services Valuations

Curr & Dewar
Contact S Dewar
✉ **Unit E, 6 North Isla Street, Dundee, Angus, DD3 7JQ** 🅿
☎ 01382 833974 ⓕ 01382 835740
ⓔ enquiries@curranddewar.com
ⓦ www.curranddewar.com
Est. 1862
Open See sale times or by appointment
Sales Antiques and quality furnishings Tues 10am, viewing Sun 10am–noon, Mon 9am–5pm Tues 9–10am
Frequency Fortnightly
Catalogues Yes

Dundee Philatelic Auctions (SPTA, PTS, PTA)
Contact Frank Tonelli
✉ **15 King Street, Dundee, Angus, DD1 2JD** 🅿
☎ 01382 224946 ⓕ 01382 224946
ⓔ dundeephilatelicauctions@btconnect.com
Est. 1975
Open Mon–Fri 10am–1pm 2–5pm

closed Wed
Sales Stamps, cigarette cards, coins, banknotes. Public auctions held at Renfield Centre, 260 Bath Street, Glasgow
Frequency 4 per annum
Catalogues Yes

B L Fenton & Son
Contact Richard Fenton
84 Victoria Road, Dundee, Angus, DD1 2NY
01382 226227
Est. 1919
Open Mon–Fri 9am–4.45pm
Sales Antique furniture, general auctioneers
Frequency Every Thurs
Catalogues No

Neil Livingstone (LAPADA)
Contact Neil Livingstone
3 Old Hawkhill, Dundee, Angus, DD1 5EU
01382 907788 F 01382 566332
M 07775 877715
E npl@hemscott.net
Est. 1971 ***Stock size*** Small
Stock Continental works of art and antiques
Open By appointment only

Taymouth Architectural Antiques
Contact Graham Ellis
49–51 Magdalen Yard Road, Dundee, Angus, DD1 4NF
01382 666833 F 01382 666833
Est. 1991 ***Stock size*** Medium
Stock Antique fireplaces, Victorian fixtures and fittings, garden ornaments, antique bathrooms, doors, leaded glass
Open Tues–Sat 9.30am–5.30pm
Fairs Newark, Ardingly
Services Restoration of fireplaces

FORFAR

Gow Antiques and Restoration (BAFRA)
Contact Jeremy Gow
Pitscandly Farm, Forfar, Angus, DD8 3NZ
01307 465342 F 01307 468973
M 07711 416786
E jeremy@knowyourantiques.com
W www.knowyourantiques.com
Est. 1991 ***Stock size*** Medium
Stock Furniture
Open Mon–Fri 9am–5pm or by appointment
Fairs SECC Glasgow
Services Restoration, organizes 3-day antique courses

MONTROSE

Harper–James
Contact John Philp
27 Baltic Street, Montrose, Angus, DD10 8EX
01674 671307 F 01674 671307
M 07970 3055457
E antiques@telco4u.net
W www.harperjamesantiques.com
Est. 1989 ***Stock size*** Large
Stock 18th–19thC quality furniture, porcelain, silver
Open Mon–Fri 10am–5pm Sat 10am–4pm or by appointment
Fairs NEC, Aberdeen
Services Restoration, French polishing, modern polishing, upholstery

ARGYLL & BUTE

COVE

Cove Curios
Contact Mrs Katherine Young
Shore Road, Clifton Place, Cove, Argyll & Bute, G84 8LR
01436 842222 F 01436 850261
Est. 1971 ***Stock size*** Medium
Stock General antiques including second-hand jewellery
Open Seasonal
Services Valuations, repairs

HELENSBURGH

McLaren Books (ABA, PBFA)
Contact George Newlands
91 West Clyde Street, Helensburgh, Argyll & Bute, G84 8BB
01436 676453 F 01436 673747
E mclarenbooks@breathe.co.uk
W www.mclarenbooks.co.uk
Est. 1976 ***Stock size*** Medium
Stock Rare and second-hand books, especially maritime topics
Open Mon–Sat 9.30am–5pm closed 1–2pm closed Wed
Services Valuations, books purchased, book search for maritime titles

Willow Antiques
Contact D J or Mrs C Weatherstone
93 West Clyde Street, Helensburgh, Argyll & Bute, G84 8BB
01436 671174
Est. 1974 ***Stock size*** Medium
Stock General antiques
Open Tues Thurs Fri Sat noon–5pm

ROTHESAY

Craig Alexander Victorian Shop
Contact Rachel Hughes
35 East Princes Street, Rothesay, Isle of Bute, Argyll & Bute, PA20 9DN
01700 505750
W www.isleofbute.com
Est. 1979 ***Stock size*** Medium
Stock General antiques, jewellery
Open Mon–Sat 9am–5.30pm
Services Jewellery repairs

DUMFRIES & GALLOWAY

CASTLE DOUGLAS

Hazel's
Contact Mrs H Hall
St Andrew Street, Castle Douglas, Dumfries & Galloway, DG7 1EL
01556 504573 F 01556 504573
W www.castledouglas.net
Est. 1989 ***Stock size*** Large
Stock General antiques
Open Mon–Sat 9.30am–5pm
Services Valuations

DUMFRIES

Cargenbank Antiques & Tearooms
Contact Laurence Hird
Cargen Bank, Dumfries, Dumfries & Galloway, DG2 8PZ
01387 730303
Est. 1999 ***Stock size*** Medium
Stock 19thC furniture
Open Mon–Sun winter Thurs–Sun 1am–5pm closed Wed

Quarrelwood Art & Antiques
Contact Oscar van Nieuwenhuizen
Quarrelwood,

Kirkmahoe, (Kirton), Dumfries, Dumfries & Galloway, DG1 1TE P
☎ 01387 740654 F 01387 740000
M 07713 643434
E oscar@quarrelwoodantiques.com
W www.quarrelwoodantiques.com
Est. 1999 *Stock size* Medium
Stock Georgian–Victorian furniture, period jewellery, ceramics, glass, objets d'art
Open Wed–Sat 10am–5pm Sun 1–5pm
Services Valuations, restoration, shipping, advisory service, wedding lists

Thomson, Roddick & Medcalf
Contact Sybelle Medcalf
✉ **60 Whitesands, Dumfries, Dumfries & Galloway, DG1 2RS** P
☎ 01387 279879 F 01387 266236
E trmdumfries@btconnect.com
Est. 1899
Open Mon–Fri 9am–5pm
Sales Antiques, fine art, general furnishings
Frequency Weekly
Catalogues Yes

LOCHFOOT

Classic Pen Engineering (Writing Equipment Society)
Contact Mr D Purser
✉ **Auchenfranco Farm, Lochfoot, Dumfries, Dumfries & Galloway, DG2 8NZ** P
☎ 01387 730208 F 01387 730208
M 0770 3690843
E cpe@auchenfranco.freeserve.co.uk
W www.auchenfranco.freeserve.co.uk
Est. 1994
Stock Fountain pens, dip pens, pencils
Open By appointment
Fairs Glasgow Antiques for Everyone, Edinburgh
Services Valuations, restoration

LOCKERBIE

Cobwebs of Lockerbie Ltd
Contact Irene Beck
✉ **30 Townhead Street, Lockerbie, Dumfries & Galloway, DG11 2AE** P
☎ 01576 202554 F 01576 203737
E sales@cobwebsoflockerbie.com
W www.cobwebs-antiques.co.uk
Est. 1993 *Stock size* Large
Stock General antiques and collectables, porcelain, china, mostly Victorian–Edwardian
Open Mon–Sat 9am–5pm

STRANRAER

Lochyran Furniture Stores
Contact A Patterson
✉ **1 Cairnryan Road, Stranraer, Dumfries & Galloway, DG9 8QJ** P
☎ 01776 704442
W www.lochyran.co.uk
Est. 1994 *Stock size* Large
Stock Antiques, second-hand furniture
Open Mon–Sun 10am–5pm
Services Valuations, restoration

THORNHILL

The Hen Hoose
Contact Jo McGregor
✉ **Tynron, Thornhill, Dumfries & Galloway, DG3 4LA** P
☎ 01848 200418
E info@henhoose.co.uk
W www.henhoose.co.uk
Est. 1994 *Stock size* Large
Stock Collectable items from 50p to £5,000, furniture, books, bric-a-brac
Open Tues–Sun 11am–5pm
Services Valuations, restoration, tea room

WHITHORN

Priory Antiques
Contact Mary Arnott
✉ **29 George Street, Whithorn, Dumfries & Galloway, DG8 8NS** P
☎ 01988 500517
Est. 1988 *Stock size* Medium
Stock General antiques
Open Usually Mon–Sun 10.30am–5pm telephone call advisable
Services Valuations

WIGTOWN

The Bookshop
Contact Shaun Bythel
✉ **17 North Main Street, Wigtown, Dumfries & Galloway, DG8 9HL** P
☎ 01988 402499 F 01988 402499
E the-bookshop@freeuk.com
W www.the-bookshop.com
Est. 1987 *Stock size* Large
Stock Antiquarian to modern books, specializing in Scottish topics and history
Open Mon–Sat 9am–5pm
Services Publishing

The Old Bank Bookshop (PBFA)
Contact John Carter
✉ **7 South Main Street, Wigtown, Newton Stewart, Dumfries & Galloway, DG8 9DU** P
☎ 01988 402688
Est. 1987 *Stock size* Large
Stock Rare and second-hand books, specializing in archaeology and art topics
Open Mon–Sat 9am–5pm
Services Framing

EAST AYRSHIRE

KILMARNOCK

D & D Programmes
Contact Mr D Stevenson
✉ **49 Titchfield Street, Kilmarnock, Ayrshire, KA1 1QS** P
☎ 01563 573316
E d-d-programmes@ukf.net
W www.d-d-programmes.ukf.net
Est. 1998 *Stock size* Medium
Stock Football memorabilia
Open Tues–Sat 10am–5pm Fri 10am–8pm
Fairs Glasgow, Alloway
Services Mail-order catalogue available

Q S Antiques and Cabinetmakers
Contact John Cunningham
✉ **Moorfield Industrial Estate, Kilmarnock, Ayrshire, KA2 0DP** P
☎ 01563 571071 F 01563 571055
E qsascotland@aol.com
Est. 1982 *Stock size* Large
Stock Victorian–Edwardian furniture
Open Mon–Fri 9am–5.30pm Sat 9am–5pm
Services Pine stripping, paint and varnish removal, Victorian-style solid wood kitchens

EAST LOTHIAN

GULLANE

⊞ Gullane Antiques
Contact Elizabeth Lindsey
✉ **5 Rosebery Place, Gullane, East Lothian, EH31 2AN** P
☎ 01620 842994
Est. 1980 *Stock size* Large
Stock General antiques, mixed porcelain, glass
Open Mon Tues Fri Sat 10.30am–1pm 2.30–5pm

HADDINGTON

⊞ Yester-Days
Contact Betty Logan
✉ **79 High Street, Haddington, East Lothian, EH41 3ET** P
☎ 01620 824543
Est. 1992 *Stock size* Small
Stock Antiques, collectables
Open Tues Wed Fri Sat 11am–4.30pm

MUSSELBURGH

⊞ Early Technology
Contact Michael Bennett-Levy
✉ **Monkton House, Old Craighall, Musselburgh, East Lothian, EH21 8SF** P
☎ 0131 665 5753 F 0131 665 2839
M 07831 106768
E levy@virgin.net
W www.earlytech.com
Est. 1971 *Stock size* Large
Stock Early electrical and mechanical antiques, clocks, mechanical music
Open By appointment
Services Valuations, restoration, consultancy on collection building

NORTH BERWICK

⊞ Lindsey Antiques
Contact Stephen Lindsey
✉ **49a Kirk Ports, North Berwick, East Lothian, EH39 4HL** P
☎ 01620 894114
Est. 1995 *Stock size* Medium
Stock Furniture, ceramics, glass, pictures, etc
Open Mon–Sat 10.30am–5pm closed Thurs

EDINBURGH

EDINBURGH

⊞ Adam Antiques & Restoration
Contact Charles Bergius
✉ **23c Dundas Street, Edinburgh, EH3 6QQ** P
☎ 0131 556 7555 F 0131 556 7555
Est. 1983 *Stock size* Medium
Stock 18th–19thC mahogany furniture and associated furnishings
Open Tues–Sat 10.30am–6pm Mon by appointment
Services Restoration

⊞ Armchair Books
Contact Mr D Govan
✉ **72–74 West Port, Edinburgh, EH1 2LE**
☎ 0131 229 5927
E davidgovan@hotmail.com
Stock size Medium
Stock Books, especially Victorian illustrated books
Open Mon–Sun 10am–6pm

⊞ Auckinleck
Contact William Stewart
✉ **86 Grassmarket, Edinburgh, EH1 9JR**
☎ 0131 220 0505
Est. 1979 *Stock size* Medium
Stock General antiques, Georgian–Victorian
Open Tues–Sat 10.15am–5.15pm

⊞ Belford Antiques
Contact John Belford
✉ **16 Morningside, Edinburgh, EH10 5LY**
☎ 0131 445 4368
M 07947 671963
Est. 1993 *Stock size* Small
Stock Furniture, collectables
Open Tues–Sat 2–6pm

Bonhams
✉ **65 George Street, Edinburgh, EH2 2JL**
☎ 0131 225 2266 F 0131 220 2547
E edinburgh@bonhams.com
W www.bonhams.com
Sales Regional Saleroom. Frequent sales. Regular house and attic sales across the country; contact London offices for further details. Free auction valuations; insurance and probate valuations
Catalogues Yes

⊞ The Bookworm
Contact Peter Ritchie
✉ **210 Dalkeith Road, Edinburgh, EH16 5DT** P
☎ 0131 662 4357
Est. 1987 *Stock size* Medium
Stock Second-hand and antiquarian books
Open Mon–Sat 9.30am–5.30pm
Services Valuations, book search

⊞ Bow-Well Antiques
Contact Murdo McLeod
✉ **103 West Bow, Edinburgh, EH1 2JP** P
☎ 0131 225 3335 F 0131 226 1259
M 07710 600431
E murdoch.mcleod@virgin.net
Est. 1979 *Stock size* Large
Stock General and Scottish antiquities
Open Mon–Sat 10am–5pm
Services Shipping

⊞ Broughton Books
Contact Peter Galinsky
✉ **2a Broughton Place, Edinburgh, EH1 3RX** P
☎ 0131 557 8010
Est. 1971 *Stock size* Medium
Stock Rare and second-hand books
Open Tues–Fri noon–5pm Sat 10.30am–5.30pm

⊞ Cabaret Antiques
Contact Terry Cavers
✉ **37 Grassmarket, Edinburgh, EH1 2HS** P
☎ 0131 225 8618
Est. 1990 *Stock size* Large
Stock Art Deco, Scottish paperweights, compacts, glass, costume jewellery, ceramics
Open Mon–Sun 10.30am–5.30pm
Fairs Mammoth Fairs

⊞ Calton Gallery (BADA)
Contact Andrew Whitfield
✉ **6a Regent Terrace, Edinburgh, EH7 5BM** P
☎ 0131 556 1010 F 0131 558 1150
M 07887 793781
E mail@caltongallery.co.uk
W www.caltongallery.co.uk
Est. 1980 *Stock size* Large
Stock Fine art, Scottish, marine 19th–early 20thC paintings and watercolours
Open By appointment
Services Valuations, restoration

The Carson Clark Gallery – Scotland's Map Heritage Centre (BCS, IMCOS, SOC)
Contact Paul Clark
181–183 Canongate, Edinburgh, EH18 8BN
0131 556 4710 0131 556 4710
scotmap@aol.com
www.carson-clark-gallery.co.uk
Est. 1972 *Stock size* Large
Stock Maps and charts, engravings, lithographs
Open Mon–Sat 10.30am–6pm
Services Valuations, appraisals, restoration, repairs, framing, shipping

D L Cavanagh Antiques
Contact Simon Cavanagh
49 Cockburn Street, Edinburgh, EH1 1BS
0131 226 3391
Est. 1972 *Stock size* Large
Stock Coins, medals, silver, jewellery, collectors' items
Open Mon–Sat 11am–5.30pm
Services Valuations

Chit Chat Antiques
Contact Victoria Reid
134 St Stephen Street, Edinburgh, EH3 5AA
0131 225 9660
Est. 1984 *Stock size* Small
Stock Flatware, silver plate, ceramics, books, prints
Open Tues–Sat 11am–5.30pm

Bobby Clyde Antiques
Contact Bobby Clyde
5a Grange Road, Edinburgh, EH9 1UH
0131 667 6718
Est. 1976 *Stock size* Medium
Stock General antiques, furniture
Open Mon Thurs Fri Sat 10.30am–5.30pm Sun 1pm–4pm
Services Stripping, delivery

Craiglea Clocks (BWCG)
Contact Mr Rafter
88 Corniston Road, Edinburgh, EH10 5QJ
0131 452 8568
Est. 1977 *Stock size* Medium
Stock Clocks and barometers
Open Mon–Fri 10am–4pm Sat 10am–1pm
Services Restoration

Crawford Walk Showrooms
Contact George Duff
250–252 Leith Walk, Edinburgh, EH6 5EL
0131 554 6407 0131 337 1422
Est. 1876 *Stock size* Large
Stock Export, Edwardian, Victorian furniture
Open Mon–Sun 9am–6pm

Da Capo Antiques
Contact Nick Carter
68 Henderson Row, Edinburgh, EH3 5BJ
0131 557 1918
Est. 1977 *Stock size* Medium
Stock 18th–early 20thC furniture, brass bedsteads, light fittings
Open Wed–Sun 10.30am–5.30pm
Services Valuations, restoration

Alan Day Antiques (LAPADA)
Contact Mr A Day
25a Moray Place, Edinburgh, EH3 6DA
0131 225 2590
07860 533922
doodah.day@virgin.net
Est. 1973 *Stock size* Medium
Stock General antiques
Trade only Yes
Open By appointment

Duncan & Reid
Contact Mrs Reid
5 Tanfield, Canon Mills, Edinburgh, EH3 5DA
0131 556 4591
msduncan@ecosse.net
Est. 1979 *Stock size* Medium
Stock 18th–19thC English, Chinese, Continental ceramics, glass, decorative objects, second-hand and antiquarian books
Open Tues–Sat 11am–5pm

EASY Edinburgh & Glasgow Architectural Salvage Yard (SALVO)
Contact E Barrass
31 West Bowling Green Street, Edinburgh, EH6 5NX
0131 554 7077 0131 554 3070
enquiries@easy-arch-salv.co.uk
www.easy-arch-salv.co.uk
Est. 1987 *Stock size* Medium
Stock Architectural antiques, fireplaces, doors, ranges, pews,
Open Mon–Fri 9am–5pm Sat noon–5pm

ECS (ANA)
Contact Mr T D Brown
11 West Cross Causeway, Edinburgh, EH8 9JW
0131 667 9095/668 2928
0131 668 2926
Est. 1977 *Stock size* Large
Stock Antique coins and medals, stamps, ephemera, cigarette cards, medals
Open Mon–Sat 9am–5pm
Fairs Edinburgh
Services Valuations, auctions of coins and banknotes

Donald Ellis Antiques
Contact Donald Ellis
7 Bruntsfield Place, Edinburgh, EH10 4HN
0131 229 4720
Est. 1969 *Stock size* Medium
Stock General antiques, clocks
Open Mon–Fri 10am–5pm closed Wed pm
Fairs Buxton
Services Clock restoration

Georgian Antiques (LAPADA, CINOA)
Contact John Dixon or Karen Gray
10 Pattison Street, Leith, Edinburgh, EH6 7HF
0131 553 7286 0131 553 6299
info@georgianantiques.net
www.georgianantiques.net
Est. 1987 *Stock size* Large
Stock Furniture
Open Mon–Fri 8.30am–5.30pm Sat 10am–2pm
Services Valuations, restoration, shipping

Gladrags
Contact Kate Cameron
17 Henderson Row, Edinburgh, EH3 5DH
0131 557 1916
Est. 1974 *Stock size* Large
Stock Exquisite vintage clothes, accessories, costume jewellery, linen
Open Tues–Sat 10.30am–6pm

Goodwin's Antiques Ltd
Contact Mr B Goodwin
15–16 Queensferry Street, Edinburgh, EH2 4QW
0131 225 4717 0131 220 1412
bengoodwin@compuserve.com

Est. 1959 *Stock size* Large
Stock General antiques
Open Mon–Fri 9am–5.30pm
Sat 9am–5pm
Services Valuations, repairs

Harlequin Antiques
Contact Charles Harkness
30 Bruntsfield Place, Edinburgh, EH10 4HJ
0131 228 9446
Est. 1996 *Stock size* Medium
Stock Clocks
Open Mon–Sat 10am–5pm
Services Clock restoration

Hawkins & Hawkins (BADA)
Contact Miss Emma Hawkins
9 Atholl Crescent, Edinburgh, EH3 8HA
0131 229 2828 F 0131 229 2128
M 07831 093198
E emma@emmahawkins.co.uk
W www.emmahawkins.demon.co.uk
Est. 1993 *Stock size* Large
Stock Victorian taxidermy, furniture
Open By appointment
Fairs Olympia
Services Valuations, shipping, book search

Holyrood Architectural Salvage
Contact Mr K Fowler
Holyrood Business Park, 146 Duddingston Road West, Edinburgh, EH16 4AP
0131 661 9305 F 0131 656 9404
E Ken@has.abel.co.uk
W www.holyroodarchitecturalsalvage.com
Est. 1993 *Stock size* Large
Stock Period fireplaces, baths, radiators, panelled doors, brassware, stained glass
Open Mon–Sat 9am–5pm
Services Restoration of baths

E D Humphrey
Contact Elizabeth Humphrey
48 Thistle Street, Edinburgh, EH2 1EN
0131 226 3625
Est. 1948 *Stock size* Medium
Stock China, glass, watercolours, etchings
Open Mon–Fri noon–4pm

Allan K L Jackson
67 Causewayside, Edinburgh, EH9 1QF
0131 668 4532
M 07989 236443
Est. 1974 *Stock size* Medium
Stock General antiques
Open Mon–Sat 10am–5pm
Services House clearance

Kaimes Smithy Antiques
Contact John Lynch
79 Howden Hall Road, Edinburgh, Scotland, EH16 6PW
0131 441 2076
M 07973 377198
E john@jlynch.freeserve.co.uk
Est. 1974 *Stock size* Large
Stock 18th–19thC furniture, oriental ceramics, glass, clocks, paintings, curios
Open Tues Wed Fri Sat 1.30–5pm or by appointment

Alan Lawson & Son
Contact Mr A Lawson
181 Causewayside, Edinburgh, EH9 1PH
0131 662 1991
Est. 1974 *Stock size* Medium
Stock General antiques and reproduction items
Open Mon–Sat 11.30am–5.30pm
Services Valuations, house clearance

London Road Antiques
Contact Mr R S Forrest
15 Earlston Place, Edinburgh, EH7 5SU
0131 652 2790
E info@19thC.com
W www.19thC.com
Est. 1979 *Stock size* Large
Stock 19thC furniture, Victorian and Georgian wares, stripped pine
Open Mon–Sat 10am–5pm
Sun 1–5pm

J D Love
Contact Mr J D Love
15–17 Jane Street, Edinburgh, EH6 5HE
0131 554 7609 F 0131 554 7609
M 07774 678423
Est. 1967 *Stock size* Medium
Stock General antiques
Open Mon–Fri 8.30am–4.30pm
Services Valuations, reproduction furniture

Lyon & Turnbull (BACA Award Winner 2004)
Contact John Mackie
33 Broughton Place, Edinburgh, EH1 3RR F 0131 557 8668
E info@lyonandturnbull.com
W www.lyonandturnbull.com
Est. 1826
Open Mon–Fri 8.30am–5.30pm
Sales Regular sales of fine antiques, silver and jewellery, pictures, decorative arts, books, maps and manuscripts. See website for details
Catalogues Yes

J Martinez Antiques
Contact Mr J Martinez
17 Brandon Terrace, Edinburgh, EH3 5DZ
0131 558 8720 F 0131 558 8720
M 07836 608090
Est. 1979 *Stock size* Medium
Stock General antiques, jewellery, clocks
Open Mon–Sat 11am–5pm
Fairs NEC, Ingliston
Services Valuations

McNaughtan's Bookshop (ABA)
Contact Elizabeth Strong
3a & 4a Haddington Place, Edinburgh, EH7 4AE
0131 556 5897 F 0131 556 8220
E mcnbooks@btconnect.com
Est. 1957
Stock General antiquarian and second-hand books including architecture, children's and Scottish topics
Open Tues–Sat 9.30am–5.30pm
Fairs ABA
Services Valuations

Meadow Lamps Gallery
Contact Mr Robertson
48 Warrender Park Road, Edinburgh, EH9 1HH
0131 221 1212
E s4sarok@aol.com
Est. 1900 *Stock size* Medium
Stock Antique lighting
Open Tues Thurs Sat 10am–6pm
Fairs NEC Birmingham, Glasgow
Services Restoration

Millers Antiques
Contact Mrs S Miller
187–191 Causewayside, Edinburgh, EH9 1PH

☎ 0131 662 1429 Ⓕ 0131 662 4187
Est. 1995 *Stock size* Large
Stock General antiques, Georgian–Edwardian furniture, mahogany, oak and pine, unusual collectables
Open Mon–Sat 10am–5.30pm
Fairs Newark, Swinderby
Services Delivery

Neilsons Ltd (National Fireplace Association)
Contact Mr & Mrs Neilson
✉ **56 Bankhead Crossway South, Edinburgh, EH11 4EP** Ⓟ
☎ 0131 453 5820 Ⓕ 0131 453 5820
Ⓔ info@chimneypiece.co.uk
Ⓦ www.chimneypiece.co.uk
Est. 2003 *Stock size* Large
Stock Antique chimney pieces, register grates, hob grates, fenders, fire irons, reproduction grates, mantels, accessories
Open Tues–Fri 9.30am–5pm Sat noon–5pm

Now & Then
Contact Mr D Gordon
✉ **7 & 9 West Cross Causeway, Edinburgh, EH8 9JW** Ⓟ
☎ 0131 668 2927 Ⓕ 0131 668 2926
Ⓜ 07976 360283
Ⓔ mill@oldtoysandantiques.co.uk
Ⓦ oldtoysandantiques.co.uk
Est. 1976 *Stock size* Medium
Stock Old toys, antiques, telephones, old clocks, cameras, bicycles, automobilia, railwayana, pre-WW1 office and domestic equipment, small items of furniture
Open Tues–Sat 1–5.30pm
Fairs Edinburgh, London
Services Tin toy restoration

The Old Children's Bookshelf (PBFA)
Contact Shirley Neilson
✉ **175 Canongate, Royal Mile, Edinburgh, EH8 8BN** Ⓟ
☎ 0131 558 3411
Ⓔ shirleyocb@aol.com
Est. 1998 *Stock size* Medium
Stock Children's novels, annuals, prints, comics
Open Mon–Fri 10.30am–5pm Sat 10am–5pm April–Oct Sun 11am–4.30pm
Fairs PBFA

The Old Town Bookshop (PBFA)
Contact Ron Wilson
✉ **8 Victoria Street, Edinburgh, EH1 2HG** Ⓟ
☎ 0131 225 9237 Ⓕ 0131 229 1503
Ⓜ 07740 625172
Ⓔ sales@oldtownbookshop.co.uk
Ⓦ www.oldtownbookshop.co.uk
Est. 1978 *Stock size* Medium
Stock Antiquarian and second-hand books, maps, prints, specializing in antiquarian art books
Open Mon–Sat 10.30am–6pm
Fairs Dublin, London, Edinburgh
Services Valuations, catalogues

Past & Present (PBFA)
Contact Gary Watt
✉ **54a Clerk Street, Edinburgh, EH8 9JR**
☎ 0131 667 2004 Ⓕ 0131 667 2004
Est. 1994 *Stock size* Medium
Stock General antiques, antiquarian children's books, Art Deco
Open Mon–Fri 10am–5pm Sat 10am–6pm Sun 2–6pm
Fairs Ingliston
Services Valuations, china repair

Reid & Reid
Contact Willie Reid
✉ **134 St Stephen Street, Edinburgh, EH3 5AA** Ⓟ
☎ 0131 225 9660
Est. 1981 *Stock size* Small
Stock Antiquarian books and prints
Open Tues–Sat 11am–5.30pm

Royal Mile Curios
Contact Mr Martin
✉ **363 High Street, Edinburgh, EH1 1PW** Ⓟ
☎ 0131 226 4050
Ⓔ info@antique-jewelry.cc
Ⓦ www.antique-jewelry.cc
Est. 1875 *Stock size* Large
Stock Antique and Scottish jewellery
Open Mon–Sun 10.30am–5.30pm

Royal Mile Gallery
Contact J A Smith
✉ **272 Canongate, Edinburgh, EH8 8AA** Ⓟ
☎ 0131 558 1702
Ⓔ james@royalmilegallery.co.uk
Ⓦ www.royalmilegallery.co.uk
Est. 1994 *Stock size* Large
Stock Antiquarian maps, prints
Open Mon–Sat 11.30am–5pm
Services Valuations, framing service

Samarkand Galleries (LAPADA, CADA, CINOA)
Contact Brian MacDonald
✉ **16 Howe Street, Edinburgh, EH3 6TD** Ⓟ
☎ 0131 225 2010 Ⓕ 0131 225 2010
Ⓔ howe@samarkand.co.uk
Ⓦ www.samarkand.co.uk
Est. 1979 *Stock size* Large
Stock Antique and contemporary rugs from Near East and Central Asia, decorative carpets, nomadic weavings
Open Mon–Sat 10am–6pm Sun 11am–4pm
Fairs HALI Antique Textile Art Fair
Services Search

James Scott
Contact James Scott
✉ **43 Dundas Street, Edinburgh, EH3 6JN**
☎ 0131 556 8260
Est. 1964 *Stock size* Medium
Stock General antiques
Open Mon–Sat 11.30am–5.30pm closed 1–2pm closed Thurs 12.30pm
Services Valuations

Second Edition
Contact W A Smith
✉ **9 Howard Street, Edinburgh, EH3 5JP** Ⓟ
☎ 0131 556 9403
Ⓔ secondedition@tiscali.co.uk
Ⓦ www.secondeditionbookshop.co.uk
Est. 1979 *Stock size* Large
Stock Quality books, militaria, arts, Scottish books
Open Mon–Fri 10.30am–5.30pm Sat 9.30am–5.30pm
Services Valuations, binding

Shapes Fine Art Auctioneers & Valuers
Contact Richard Longwill BA, MRICS
✉ **Bankhead Avenue, Sighthill, Edinburgh, EH11 4BY** Ⓟ
☎ 0131 453 3222 Ⓕ 0131 453 6444
Ⓔ auctionsadmin@shapes auctioneers.co.uk
Ⓦ www.shapesauctioneers.co.uk
Est. 1992
Open Mon–Fri 9am–5pm

Sales Fine art and antiques sale 1st Sat of every month 10am, viewing Thur 10am–7pm Fri 10am–4pm
Catalogues Yes

Still Life
Contact Ewan Lamont
54 Candlemaker Row, Edinburgh, EH1 2QE
0131 225 8524
ewanlamont@mac.com
homepage.mac.com/ewanlamont/PhotoAlbum.html
Est. 1984 *Stock size* Large
Stock General antiques, china, glass, pictures
Open Mon–Sat noon–5pm

The Talish Gallery
Contact John Martin
168 Canongate, Edinburgh, EH8 8DF P
0131 557 8435
Est. 1969 *Stock size* Large
Stock Small general antiques, Oriental wares, silver
Open Mon–Sat 10am–4pm
Fairs Newark

Thomson, Roddick & Medcalf
Contact Sybelle Medcalf
The Edinburgh and Lothian Sale Room, 44/3 Hardengreen Business Park, Eskbank, Edinburgh, EH22 3NX P
0131 454 9090 F 0131 454 9191
t.rm@virgin.net
Est. 1999
Open Mon–Fri 9am–5pm
Sales Antiques, fine art, general furnishings, special quarterly sales
Frequency Weekly
Catalogues Yes

The Thrie Estaits
Contact Peter Powell
49 Dundas Street, Edinburgh, EH3 6RS
0131 556 7084
thethrieestaits@aol.com
Est. 1971 *Stock size* Medium
Stock Unusual antiques, decorative items
Open Tues–Sat 11am–5pm

Till's Bookshop
Contact Mr R Till
1 Hope Park Crescent, Edinburgh, EH8 9NA P
0131 667 0895
tillsbookshop@hotmail.com
Est. 1985 *Stock size* Medium
Stock Literature, fantasy, mystery, humanities, poetry, drama, cinema, general, first editions
Open Mon–Fri noon–7.30pm Sat 11am–6pm Sun noon–5.30pm
Services Valuations

Trinity Curios
Contact Alan Ferguson
4–6 Stanley Road, Edinburgh, EH6 4SG P
0131 552 8481
07715 500719
adfer@btinternet.com
Est. 1987 *Stock size* Large
Stock Quality furniture, porcelain, silver, linen, collectables
Open Tues–Fri 10am–5pm Wed Sat noon–6pm Sun 2–5pm

Unicorn Antiques
Contact N Duncan
65 Dundas Street, Edinburgh, EH3 6RS
0131 556 7176
unicorn@ecosse.net
www.transcotland.com/unicorn
Est. 1969 *Stock size* Small
Stock General antiques, bric-a-brac
Open Mon–Sat 10.30am–6.30pm

West Port Books
Contact Mr H N Barrott
145–147 West Port, Edinburgh, EH3 9DD P
0131 229 4431
west@portbooks.freeserve.co.uk
www.westport.freeserve.co.uk
Est. 1979 *Stock size* Large
Stock Second-hand and antiquarian books, especially fine art books and Indian imports
Open Mon–Tues 10.30am–5.30pm Wed–Sat noon–6pm

Whytock & Reid
Contact Mr Reid
Sunbury House, Belford Mews, Edinburgh, EH4 3DN P
0131 226 4911 F 0131 226 4595
whytockandreid.com
www.whytockandreid.com
Est. 1807 *Stock size* Large
Stock Whytock & Reid 19thC furniture, 18thC furniture, rugs, carpets
Open Mon–Fri 9am–5.30pm Sat 10am–2pm
Services Cabinet-making, French polishing

Wild Rose Antiques
Contact E or Kate Cameron
15 Henderson Row, Edinburgh, EH3 5DH P
0131 557 1916
Est. 1974 *Stock size* Large
Stock Select decorative table silver, ladies' and gentlemen's jewellery, porcelain, pottery, glass, metalware
Open Tues–Sat 10.30am–6pm

Richard Wood Antiques
Contact Richard Wood
66 West Port, Edinburgh, EH1 2LD P
0131 229 6344
Est. 1971 *Stock size* Large
Stock Small silver and Oriental items, collectables
Open Mon–Sat 10am–5pm
Fairs Ingliston Mammoth Fair

FIFE

ABERDOUR

Antiques & Gifts
Contact Jennifer Graham
26 High Street, Aberdour, Fife, KY3 0SW P
01383 860523
Est. 1969 *Stock size* Small
Stock General antiques
Open Tues 2–5pm Wed 11am–2.30pm Thurs–Sat 10am–5pm closed 12.30–2pm

CERES

Ceres Antiques
Contact Evelyn Norrie
1 The Butts, Ceres, Cupar, Fife, KY15 5NF P
01334 828384
Est. 1969 *Stock size* Medium
Stock General antiques, specializing in linen and lace
Open Mon–Sun 10am–6pm or by appointment
Fairs Newark, Birmingham and Harrogate

CUPAR

Oliver & Son
Contact Dorothy Wang
11 East Road, Cupar, Fife,

KY15 4HQ P
☎ 01334 657002 F 01334 653807
M 07850 013191
Est. 1998
Open Mon–Fri 9am–5pm
Sat 10am–5pm Sun noon–5pm
Sales Fortnightly general antiques and household furniture sales
Catalogues Yes

DUNFERMLINE

A K Campbell & Son
Contact Mr A K Campbell
✉ **39 High Street, Dunfermline, Fife, KY12 7DL** P
☎ 01383 724783
Est. 1977 *Stock size* Medium
Stock Watches
Open Mon–Sat 10am–5pm
Services Valuations, repairs

DYSART

Second Notions Antiques
Contact Jim Sinclair
✉ **2 Normand Road, Dysart, Kirkcaldy, Fife, KY1 2XJ** P
☎ 01592 650505 F 01592 573341
M 07977 119787
E james@sinclair1155.freeserve.co.uk
W www.secondnotions.co.uk
Est. 1994 *Stock size* Medium
Stock General antiques
Open Mon–Fri noon–4pm
Sat 10am–4pm
Fairs Swinderby, Newark
Services Exporting of containers

INVERKEITHING

Bargain Centre
Contact Hilda Fleming
✉ **3 Boreland Road, Inverkeithing, Fife, KY11 1NK** P
☎ 01383 416727 F 01383 418054
W www.bargaincentre.com
Est. 1982 *Stock size* Large
Stock General antiques, bric-a-brac, office furniture
Open Mon–Sat 9am–5pm

KIRKCALDY

A K Campbell & Son
Contact Mr A K Campbell
✉ **262 High Street, Kirkcaldy, Fife, KY1 1LA** P
☎ 01592 597022
Est. 1977 *Stock size* Medium
Stock General antiques, militaria, furniture, bric-a-brac, postcards, banknotes
Open Mon–Sat 10am–5pm
Services Valuations, house and estate clearance

A K Campbell & Son
Contact Mr A K Campbell
✉ **277 High Street, Kirkcaldy, Fife, KY1 1JH** P
☎ 01592 264305/597161
Est. 1977 *Stock size* Medium
Stock Family jewellery including antique jewellery, silver
Open Mon–Sat 10am–5pm
Services Valuations, repairs, goods purchased

The Golden Past
Contact Fiona Campbell
✉ **90 Rosslyn Street, Kirkcaldy, Fife, KY1 3AD** P
☎ 01592 653185
Est. 1983 *Stock size* Small
Stock General antiques, pine furniture
Open Tues–Sun 10am–5pm
Services Pine stripping

M D's Auction Ltd
Contact Tommy Stowe or Vicky Cunningham
✉ **Unit 15–16, Smeaton Industrial Estate, Hayfield Road, Kirkcaldy, Fife, KY1 2HE** P
☎ 01592 599969 F 01592 640969
M 07970 737401
E navatmds@aol.com
W www.mdsauction.co.uk
Est. 1989
Open Mon–Fri 9am–5pm
Sat 10am–1pm
Sales 500 lots, Thurs 6.30pm
Frequency Weekly
Catalogues Yes

MARKINCH

Squirrel Antiques
Contact Sheila Green
✉ **13 Commercial Street, Markinch, Fife, KY7 6DE** P
☎ 01592 754386 F 01592 754386
M 07850 912801
Est. 1984 *Stock size* Medium
Stock General antiques, restored pine, Scottish pottery
Open Mon–Sat 9am–5pm closed Wed or by appointment
Services Valuations

NEWBURGH

Henderson-Dark Antiques Ltd
Contact Dawn Dark
✉ **241 High Street, Newburgh, Fife, KY14 6DY** P
☎ 01337 842000
Est. 1990 *Stock size* Medium
Stock Good quality 18th–19thC small items, furniture
Open Mon–Sat 10am–5.30pm
Sun by appointment
Fairs NEC
Services Valuations, restoration and shipping

Newburgh Antiques
Contact Miss D J Fraser
✉ **222 High Street, Newburgh, Cupar, Fife, KY14 9HH** P
☎ 01337 841026
Est. 1989 *Stock size* Small
Stock General antiques
Open Tues–Sat 10am–5pm

NEWPORT-ON-TAY

Mair Wilkes Books (PBFA)
Contact James Mair
✉ **3 St Marys Lane, Newport-on-Tay, Fife, DD6 8AH** P
☎ 01382 542260 F 01382 542260
E mairwilkes.books@zoom.co.uk
Est. 1969 *Stock size* Large
Stock Large selection of rare, second-hand, antiquarian and out-of-print books, specializing in Scottish topics and psychology
Open Tues–Fri 10am–5pm closed 12.30–2pm Sat 10am–5.30pm
Services Valuations, book search

PITTENWEEM

High Street Antiques
Contact R Clark
✉ **39 High Street, Pittenweem, Fife, KY10 2LA** P
☎ 01333 312870
M 07711 300136
Est. 1984 *Stock size* Medium

Stock General antiques, Wemyss ware
Open Mon–Sun 10.30am–5pm
Services Valuations, goods purchased

ST ANDREWS

Bouquiniste
Contact Mrs E A Anderson
31 Market Street, St Andrews, Fife, KY16 9NS
01334 476724
Est. 1981 *Stock size* Medium
Stock Rare and second-hand books
Open Mon–Sat 10am–5pm

A K Campbell & Son
Contact Mr A K Campbell
84c Market Street, St Andrews, Fife, KY16 9PA
01334 474214
Est. 1977 *Stock size* Medium
Stock Antique jewellery
Open Mon–Sat 10am–5pm
Services Valuations, repairs

David Brown Gallery
Contact David Brown
9 Albany Place, St Andrews, Fife, KY16 9HH
01334 477840
Est. 1969 *Stock size* Medium
Stock General antiques, Scottish jewellery, silver, golf memorabilia
Open Mon–Sat 10am–5pm
Services Valuations, restoration

Macgregor Auctions
Contact Mrs Graham
56 Largo Road, St Andrews, Fife, KY16 8RP
01334 472431 F 01334 479606
Est. 1857
Open Viewing and sale days only
Sales Sale Thurs Fri 10.30am, viewing day prior 9am–7pm
Frequency Fortnightly
Catalogues Yes

UPPER LARGO

Waverley Antiques
Contact Dudley StClair
13 Main Street, Upper Largo, Fife, KY8 6EL
01333 360437
Est. 1968 *Stock size* Small
Stock General antiques, furniture, china, etc
Open Mon–Sun 11am–5.30pm

GLASGOW

GLASGOW

Albert Antiques
Contact Ivor Lovatt
338–350 Pollokshaws Road, Glasgow, G41 1QS
0141 423 6497 F 0141 423 6497
Est. 1963 *Stock size* Large
Stock General antiques
Open Mon–Fri 9.30am–4pm

All Our Yesterdays
Contact Susie Robinson
6 Park Road, Kelvinbridge, Glasgow, G4 9JG
0141 334 7788
E antiques@allouryesterdays.fsnet.co.uk
W www.healingroom.org
Est. 1989 *Stock size* Large
Stock General antiques, mineral and crystal specimens
Open Flexible Mon–Fri 11am–6pm Sat noon–5.30pm or by appointment
Services Valuations, search service

Antiques Centre
Contact Alan Abspure
188 Woodlands Road, Charing Cross, Glasgow, G36 1LL
0141 332 5757
Est. 1993 *Stock size* Medium
Stock General antiques, Victorian–Edwardian
Open Mon–Sun 10am–6pm
Services Valuations, restoration

The Antiques Warehouse
Contact Philip Mangan
Unit 3b, Yorkhill Quay Estate, Glasgow, G3 8QE
0141 334 4924 F 0141 334 4924
Est. 1979 *Stock size* Large
Stock General antiques
Open Mon–Fri 9am–5pm Sat 10am–5pm Sun noon–5pm
Services Valuations, restoration and repairs

Bonhams
176 St Vincent Street, Glasgow, G2 5SG
0141 223 8860 F 0141 223 8868
E glasgow@bonhams.com
W www.bonhams.com
Open Mon–Fri 8.30am–5pm
Sales Regional office. Regular house and attic sales across the country; contact London offices for further details. Free auction valuations; insurance and probate valuations

Broadsword Antiques
Contact Robert Corlett
Studio 6, 99 King Street, Kings Court, Glasgow, G1 5RB
07967 826362 F 07967 826362
E broadswordantiques@tinyworld.com
W www.militarymaze.com
Est. 1994 *Stock size* Medium
Stock Militaria
Open By appointment

Browns Clocks
Contact Jim Cairns
13 Radnor Street, Glasgow, G3 7UA
0141 334 6308 F 0141 334 6308
E james@jcairns.greatxscape.net
Est. 1933 *Stock size* Medium
Stock Longcase clocks
Open Mon–Fri 10am–5pm Sat 10am–1pm
Services Restoration of all antique clocks

Butler's Furniture Galleries
Contact Laurence Butler
39 Camelon Street, Carntyne Industrial Estate, Glasgow, G32 6JS
0141 778 5720
M 07950 312355
E butlersantiques@lineone.net
W www.butlersfurnituregalleries.co.uk
Est. 1981 *Stock size* Large
Stock Georgian–Edwardian furniture
Open Mon–Fri 10am–5pm Sun by appointment
Services Valuations, restoration

Caledonian Books
Contact Martin or Maureen Smiley
483 Great Western Road, Glasgow, G12 8HJ
0141 334 9663 F 0141 334 9663
E caledonianbooks@aol.com

ⓦ www.caledonianbooks.co.uk
Est. 1986 *Stock size* Large
Stock Antiquarian and second-hand books
Open Mon–Sat 10.30am–6pm
Services Valuations

Canning Antiques
Contact Kate
✉ **24–26 Millbrae Road, Langside, Glasgow, G42 9UT** P
☎ 0141 632 9853 ⓕ 0141 632 9853
ⓔ kate@canning-antiques.com
ⓦ www.canning-antiques.com
Est. 1997 *Stock size* Medium
Stock Wide range of fine Georgian–Edwardian furniture
Open Mon–Sat 10am–5pm or by appointment
Fairs Antiques for Everyone
Services Restoration

Carpet Auctioneers Ltd (SAA)
Contact Mr T Severn
✉ **32 Washington Street, Glasgow, G3 8ZA** P
☎ 0141 221 9329
Est. 1959
Open Mon–Fri 10am–4pm Sat 9am–1.30pm
Sales Telephone for details

Circa
Contact Sheila Murdoch
✉ **6 Kersland Street, Glasgow, G12 9BG**
☎ 0141 581 3307
Est. 2000 *Stock size* Large
Stock Vintage clothing, handbags, accessories, jewellery
Open Mon–Sat 11.30am–5.30pm

Arthur E Collins & Son (SAA)
Contact Leonard Kerr
✉ **141 West Regent Street, Glasgow, G2 2ST**
☎ 0141 229 1326 ⓕ 0141 248 1591
Est. 1899
Open Mon–Fri 9am–5pm
Sales Pawnbroker sales
Frequency 2 per week
Catalogues Yes

Cooper Hay Rare Books (ABA)
Contact Mr C Hay
✉ **182 Bath Street, Glasgow, G2 4HG** P
☎ 0141 333 1992 ⓕ 0141 333 1992
ⓔ chayrbooks@aol.com
ⓦ www.abebooks.com/home/haybooks
Est. 1984 *Stock size* Medium
Stock Books, prints, specializing in Scottish art and juvenile books
Open Mon–Fri 10am–5.30pm Sat 10am–1pm
Fairs Chelsea, Edinburgh
Services Valuations, book search

Finnie Antiques
Contact Bruce Finnie
✉ **The Renaissance Furniture Store, 103 Niddrie Road, Glasgow, G42 8PR** P
☎ 0141 423 8515 ⓕ 0141 423 8515
ⓜ 07973 315460
ⓔ bruce@finnieantiques.co.uk
ⓦ www.finnieantiques.co.uk
Est. 1992 *Stock size* Medium
Stock Furniture, silver, Arts and Crafts, fireplaces
Open Mon–Fri 10.30am–5pm Sat Sun noon–5pm
Services Valuations

Flying Dutchman Antiques
Contact Hannie Van Riel
✉ **Unit 3b, Yorkhill Quay Estate, Glasgow Harbour, G3 8QE** P
☎ 0141 338 6834 ⓕ 0141 338 6834
ⓔ info@fdantiques.com
Est. 1994 *Stock size* Large
Stock General antiques including Continental European furniture
Open Mon–Fri 9am–5pm Sat 10am–5pm Sun noon–5pm

Great Western Auctions
Contact Mrs A Manning
✉ **29–37 Otago Street, Glasgow, G12 8JJ** P
☎ 0141 339 3290
ⓔ info@greatwesternauctions.com
ⓦ www.greatwesternauctions.com
Est. 1988
Open Mon–Fri 9am–5pm
Sales General antiques
Frequency Fortnightly
Catalogues Yes

A D Hamilton Antiques
Contact Jeff Fineman
✉ **7 St Vincent Place, Glasgow, G1 2DW** P
☎ 0141 221 5423
ⓔ jefffineman@hotmail.com
ⓦ www.adhamilton.com
Est. 1890 *Stock size* Small
Stock General antiques
Open Mon–Sat 9.30am–5pm

Kerr & McAlister (SAA)
Contact Mr Thomas McAlister
✉ **140 Niddrie Road, Glasgow, G20 7XL** P
☎ 0141 423 4271 ⓕ 0141 423 7265
ⓦ kerr-mcalister-auctions.co.uk
Est. 1969
Open Mon–Fri 9am–5pm
Sales Household goods, antique furniture
Frequency Every Thurs evening
Catalogues No

Lovejoy Antiques
Contact Julie Gallagher
✉ **Unit 3b, Yorkhill Quay, Glasgow, G3 8QE** P
☎ 0141 357 3559 ⓕ 0141 357 3559
ⓜ 07949 651897
ⓔ julielovejoy@yahoo.co.uk
Est. 1995 *Stock size* Medium
Stock General antiques
Open Mon–Fri 9am–5pm Sat 10am–5pm Sun noon–5pm
Services Polishing, shipping

Robert McTear & Co (IAA)
Contact Miss Janet Stewart
✉ **Sky Park, 8 Elliot Place, Glasgow, G3 8EP** P
☎ 0141 221 4456 ⓕ 0141 204 5035
ⓔ enquiries@mctears.co.uk
ⓦ www.mctears.co.uk
Est. 1842
Open Mon–Fri 9am–5pm
Sales Weekly auction of general antiques on Fri
Catalogues Yes

Pastimes Vintage Toys
Contact Anne or Gordon Brown
✉ **126 Maryhill Road, St George's Cross, Glasgow, G27 7QS** P
☎ 0141 331 1008
ⓔ anne@dinkydoll.com
ⓦ www.dinkydoll.com
Est. 1976 *Stock size* Medium
Stock Vintage toys, Dinky, Hornby, dolls' houses, medals, militaria, small collectables
Open Tues–Sat 9.30am–5.30pm
Services Mail order, valuations

Patersons Auctioneers & Valuers
Contact Robert Paterson

✉ **8 Orchard Street, Paisley, Glasgow, PA1 1UZ** 🅿
☎ 0141 889 2435 Ⓕ 0141 887 5535
Est. 1848
Open Mon–Fri 9am–5pm
Sales General antiques
Frequency Fortnightly
Catalogues Yes

⊞ Relics
Contact Steven Currie
✉ **Dowanside Lane, Glasgow, G12 9BZ** 🅿
☎ 0141 341 0007
Est. 1989 *Stock size* Medium
Stock General antiques, collectables including 1960s
Open Mon–Sat 10.30am–6pm Sun 12.30–6pm
Services Valuations

⊞ Restore-It
Contact Jean Eddy Devion
✉ **30 Otago Lane, Glasgow, G12 8PB** 🅿
☎ 0141 339 7776 Ⓕ 0141 339 7776
Ⓜ 07770 825555
Ⓦ www.restore-it.co.uk
Est. 1992 *Stock size* Medium
Stock General antiques, architectural salvage
Open Mon–Sun 10am–5pm
Services Restoration

⊞ Rusty Grates
Contact Tom Pearson
✉ **103 Niddrie Road, Queens Park, Glasgow, G42 8PR** 🅿
☎ 0141 423 0022
Ⓜ 07966 362521
Est. 1994 *Stock size* Medium
Stock Georgian, Victorian and Art Nouveau fireplaces
Open Mon–Fri 10am–5pm Sat Sun noon–5pm

⊞ R Rutherford
Contact Mrs R Rutherford
✉ **The Victorian Village, 93 West Regent Street, Glasgow, G2 2BA** 🅿
☎ 0141 332 9808 Ⓕ 0141 332 9808
Est. 1979 *Stock size* Medium
Stock General antiques, Scottish agates
Open Mon–Sat 10am–5pm
Services Valuations

⊞ Samson's Joinery & Antiques (Scottish Furniture Makers Association)
Contact Ross Samson
✉ **Antiques Warehouse, Yorkhill Quay, Clydeside Expressway, Glasgow, G3 8QE**
☎ 0141 632 8681 Ⓕ 0141 649 6089
Ⓜ 07985 046827
Ⓔ samsons.joinery@virgin.net
Ⓦ www.samsonsjoinery.co.uk
Est. 1998 *Stock size* Small
Stock Furniture
Open By appointment
Services Restoration

⊞ Saratoga Trunk Yesteryear Costume & Textiles
Contact David McLay
✉ **Fourth Floor, 61 Hyde Park Street, Glasgow, G3 8BW** 🅿
☎ 0141 221 4433 Ⓕ 0141 221 4433
Est. 1976 *Stock size* Large
Stock Vintage clothing, Victorian–1990s, linens, lace, costume jewellery, etc
Open Mon–Fri 10.30am–5pm
Fairs Manchester, Birmingham, Glasgow
Services Valuations, hire to film, television, theatre productions

⊞ Jeremy Sniders Antiques
Contact Jeremy Sniders
✉ **158 Bath Street, Glasgow, G2 4TB** 🅿
☎ 0141 332 0043 Ⓕ 0141 332 5505
Ⓔ jeremysniders@aol.com
Ⓦ www.jeremysnidersantiques.com
Est. 1981 *Stock size* Medium
Stock General antiques, Scandinavian antiques, silverware, jewellery, Georg Jensen specialist
Open Mon–Sat 9am–5pm
Services Valuations

⊞ St Lucy Wayside Antiques
Contact Joseph Higgins
✉ **7 Overdale Gardens, Lengside, Battlefield, Glasgow, G42 9QG**
☎ 0141 632 3683 Ⓕ 0141 632 3683
Est. 2000 *Stock size* Medium
Stock General antiques
Open Mon–Fri 10am–5pm

⊞ Strachan Antiques
Contact Alex Strachan
✉ **40 Darnley Street, Pollokshields, Glasgow, G41 2SE** 🅿
☎ 0141 429 4411
Ⓜ 07950 262346
Ⓔ alex@strachan-antiques.freeserve.co.uk
Ⓦ www.strachan-antiques.freeserve.co.uk
Est. 1990 *Stock size* Large
Stock Arts and Crafts, Art Nouveau furniture, small decorative items
Open Mon–Sat 10am–5pm Sun noon–5pm
Fairs SECC Glasgow

⊞ Strachan Antiques
Contact Tom Pearson
✉ **Darnley Street, Glasgow, G42 8PR** 🅿
☎ 0141 423 0022
Ⓜ 07966 362521
Est. 1994 *Stock size* Medium
Stock Georgian, Victorian and Art Nouveau fireplaces
Open Mon–Fri 10am–5pm Sat Sun noon–5pm

⊞ The Studio
Contact Liz McKelvie
✉ **DeCourcy's Arcade, 5–21 Cresswell Lane, Glasgow, G12 8AA** 🅿
☎ 0141 334 8211
Ⓜ 07909 742862
Ⓔ lizthestudio@aol.com
Ⓦ www.decourcys.co.uk
Est. 1998 *Stock size* Small
Stock Books, small furniture, ceramics, pictures, glass, textiles, Glasgow-style Arts and Crafts and Art Nouveau, Talwin Morris book bindings
Open Tues–Sat 10am–5.30pm Sun noon–5pm
Services Shipping, booksearch

⊞ The Treasure Bunker Militaria Shop
Contact Mr K J Andrew
✉ **21 King Street, Merchant City, Glasgow, G1 5Q2**
☎ 0141 552 8164 Ⓕ 0141 552 4651
Ⓔ info@treasurebunker.com
Ⓦ www.treasurebunker.com
Est. 1985 *Stock size* Large
Stock Military antiques, Battle of Waterloo–WWII
Open Tues–Sat 11am–5pm
Services Worldwide mail order catalogue

⊞ Victoria Antiques
Contact Jeff Lovatt
✉ **338–350 Pollokshaws Road,**

Glasgow,
G41 1QS 🅿
☎ 0141 423 6497 Ⓕ 0141 423 6497
Est. 1983 *Stock size* Large
Stock General antiques
Open Mon–Fri 9.30am–4pm

⊞ Voltaire & Rousseau
Contact Mr J McGonagle
✉ **18 Otago Lane, Glasgow, G12 8PD** 🅿
☎ 0141 339 1811
Est. 1972 *Stock size* Large
Stock Rare and second-hand books, specializing in Scotland and foreign languages
Open Mon–Sat 10am–6pm
Services Valuations

⊞ Tim Wright Antiques (LAPADA)
Contact Judy or Tim Wright
✉ **147 Bath Street, Glasgow, G2 4SQ** 🅿
☎ 0141 221 0364 Ⓕ 0141 221 0364
Ⓔ tim@timwright-antiques.com
Ⓦ www.timwright-antiques.com
Est. 1972 *Stock size* Large
Stock Quality antiques, furniture, porcelain, glass, bronze, silver, textiles, samplers
Open Mon–Fri 10am–5pm
Sat 10am–4pm
Services Valuations

HIGHLAND

AULDEARN

⊞ Auldearn Antiques
Contact Roger Milton
✉ **Dalmore Manse, Lethen Road, Auldearn, Nairn, Inverness-shire, IV12 5HZ** 🅿
☎ 01667 453087
Ⓜ 07763 350747
Est. 1984 *Stock size* Large
Stock General antiques
Open Mon–Sun 9.30am–5.30pm
Services Valuations, restoration and repairs

BEAULY

⊞ Iain Marr (LAPADA, HADA, Silver Society)
Contact Iain Marr
✉ **3 Mid Street, Beauly, Inverness-shire, IV4 7DP** 🅿
☎ 01463 782372 Ⓕ 01463 783263
Ⓜ 07860 914191
Ⓔ info@iain-marr-antiques.com
Ⓦ www.iain-marr-antiques.com
Est. 1974 *Stock size* Medium
Stock General antiques
Open Mon–Sat 10.30am–5.30pm closed 1–2pm closed Thurs
Services Valuations

DINGWALL

⚒ Dingwall & Highland Marts Ltd (IAA)
Contact Kenneth MacKay
✉ **15 Tulloch Street, Dingwall, Ross-shire, IV15 9JZ** 🅿
☎ 01349 863252 Ⓕ 01349 865062
Ⓔ dingwallmart@cqm.co.uk
Open Mon–Fri 8am–5pm
Sales General antiques
Frequency Weekly
Catalogues No

DORNOCH

⊞ Castle Close Antiques
Contact George or Joyce McLean
✉ **Castle Street, Dornoch, Highland, IV25 3SN** 🅿
☎ 01862 810405 Ⓕ 01862 810405
Ⓔ enquiries@castle-close-antiques.com
Ⓦ www.castle-close-antiques.com
Est. 1983 *Stock size* Medium
Stock General antiques, jewellery, china
Open Mon–Sat 10am–1pm 2–5pm closed Thurs pm

⊞ Little Treasures
Contact Mrs A Taylor
✉ **Shore Road, Dornoch, Highland, IV25 3LS** 🅿
☎ 01862 811175
Ⓔ alliandtrev@aol.com
Ⓦ www.littletreasuresdornoch.co.uk
Est. 1993 *Stock size* Medium
Stock General antiques, small items, curios, costume jewellery
Open Mon–Sat 10am–5pm
Services Valuations

⊞ Cathedral Antiques
Contact Mrs Patricia MacColl
✉ **45 High Street, Fortrose, Ross-shire, IV10 8SU** 🅿
☎ 01381 620161
Ⓜ 07778 817074
Ⓔ cathant@hotmail.com
Est. 1996 *Stock size* Medium
Stock General antiques, 1780–1920 furniture, ceramics, silver, glass, decorative objects
Open Fri Sat 10am–5pm or by appointment
Fairs All Galloway fairs from Newcastle north
Services Valuations

INVERNESS

⊞ Caledonian Antiques
Contact Claire Watson
✉ **3 Lombard Street, Inverness, Inverness-shire, IV1 1QQ**
☎ 01463 711100 Ⓕ 01320 351346
Est. 1998 *Stock size* Large
Stock Antiques, collectables
Open Mon–Sat 10am–5.30pm
Services Valuations, restoration, jewellery repairs

⚒ Frasers Auctioneers
Contact Mrs A Henderson
✉ **8a Harbour Road, Inverness, Inverness-shire, IV1 1SY** 🅿
☎ 01463 232395 Ⓕ 01463 233634
Est. 1900
Open Mon–Thurs 9am–5pm
Fri 9am–4pm
Sales General antiques Wed 6pm, viewing 9am–6pm
Frequency Weekly
Catalogues Yes

⊞ Gallery Persia
Contact Gordon MacDonald
✉ **Upper Myrtlesfield, Nairnside, Inverness, Inverness-shire, IV2 5BX** 🅿
☎ 01463 798500 Ⓕ 01463 798500
Ⓔ mac@gallerypersia.co.uk
Ⓦ www.gallerypersia.co.uk
Est. 1989 *Stock size* Medium
Stock Old and antique rugs from Persia, Caucasus, Afghanistan, exemplary modern rugs
Open Mon–Sun by appointment
Sat 11am–4pm
Fairs Scottish Game Fair July
Services Restoration, repair, search service. Exhibition held in Spring and Autumn

⊞ Oakwood Antique Shop
Contact Gaby Monkhouse
✉ **Dochgarroch, Inverness, Inverness-shire, IV3 8JG** 🅿
☎ 01463 861481 Ⓕ 01463 861481
Ⓔ oakwood@scotland1st40.fsbusiness.co.uk
Est. 1995 *Stock size* Medium

Stock General antiques, collectables
Open Mon–Sun 10am–6pm
Services Restaurant, tea room

NAIRN

Sun-City Indoor Market
Contact S Morris
100 Harbour Street, Nairn, Inverness-shire, IV12 4PH P
☎ 01667 456300
Est. 1989 *Stock size* Large
Stock General antiques, second-hand furniture
Open Mon–Sat 10am–5pm Sun noon–5pm
Services Valuations and house clearance

NEWTONMORE

The Antique Shop
Contact John Harrison
Main Street, Newtonmore, Inverness-shire, PH20 1DD P
☎ 01540 673272
M 07713 093801
Est. 1990 *Stock size* Medium
Stock General antiques, scientific instruments, second-hand books
Open Mon–Sat 10am–5pm

LANARKSHIRE

LANARK

Auld Things
Contact Elizabeth Williamson
14 Broomgate, Lanark, Lanarkshire, ML11 9EE P
☎ 01555 665822
Est. 1999 *Stock size* Large
Stock Antique furniture, ceramics, glass, jewellery
Open Jan–April Mon–Sat 11am–4pm May–Dec Mon–Sat 10am–5pm
Services Valuations

MORAY

ELGIN

Barwood Dochgarroch Antiques
Contact Gaby Monkhouse
Forres Road, Elgin, Moray, IV30 8UU P
☎ 01343 543200 F 01343 545028
Est. 1996 *Stock size* Large
Stock General antiques
Open Mon–Sun 10am–6pm
Services Restaurant, tea rooms

The Oakwood
Contact Gaby Monkhouse
Forres Road, Elgin, Moray, IV30 8UN P
☎ 01343 543200 F 01343 545028
E oakwood@scotland1st40.fsbusiness.co.uk
Est. 1995 *Stock size* Medium
Stock General antiques, collectables
Open Mon–Sun 10am–9pm
Services Restaurant, tea room

FORRES

Forres Saleroom
Contact Alexander Morris
Tytler Street, Forres, Moray, IV36 1EL P
☎ 01309 672422 F 01309 673339
Est. 1895
Open Mon–Fri 9am–5pm Sat 9am–noon
Sales General antiques
Frequency Weekly
Catalogues Yes

NORTH AYRSHIRE

FAIRLIE

E A Alvarino Fairlie Antique Shop
Contact E A Alvarino
86 Main Road, Fairlie, Largs, North Ayrshire, KA29 0AD P
☎ 01475 568613
E oldfairlie@aol.com
Est. 1976 *Stock size* Small
Stock General antiques
Open Sat 1–5 or by appointment
Services Valuations

ISLE OF ARRAN

The Stable Antiques
Contact Alistair Linton
Balmichael Visitors Centre, Shiskine Brodick, Isle of Arran, North Ayrshire, KA27 8DT
☎ 01770 860468
W www.stableantiques-arran.co.uk
Est. 1984 *Stock size* Medium
Stock General antiques
Open Summer Mon–Sat 10am–5pm Sun noon–5pm winter Wed–Sat 10am–5pm Sun noon–5pm
Services Furniture restoration

LARGS

Narducci Antiques
Contact Mr G Narducci
11 Waterside Street, Largs, North Ayrshire, KA30 9LW P
☎ 01475 672612 or 01294 461687
F 01294 470002
M 07771 577777
Est. 1969 *Stock size* Large
Stock General antiques, shipping goods
Open Tues Thur Sat 2.30–5.30pm or by appointment
Services Packing, shipping, European haulage

Nicolson Maps
Contact Malcolm Nicolson
3 Frazer Street, Largs, North Ayrshire, KA30 9HP P
☎ 01475 689242 F 01475 689242
E nicolsonmaps.@btconnect.com
W www.nicolsonmaps.com
Est. 1979 *Stock size* Medium
Stock General maps and charts
Open Mon–Fri 9am–5pm
Fairs International Map Association
Services Free postal service

PERTH & KINROSS

ABERNYTE

The Old Church Antiques
Contact George Whitla
The Old Church Scottish Antique and Art Centre, Abernyte, Perth, Perthshire, PH14 9SJ P
☎ 01828 686642 or 01250 886381
E enquiries@oldchurchantiques.com
W www.oldchurchantiques.com
Est. 1999 *Stock size* Medium
Stock Clocks, general antiques, books
Open Mon–Sun 11am–5pm
Services Valuations, clock repairs

Scottish Antique and Art Centre
Contact Tracy Walsh
Abernyte, Perthshire, PH14 9SJ P
☎ 01828 686401 F 01828 686199
E elaine@scottish-antiques.com
W www.scottish-antiques.com

Est. 1999 *Stock size* Large
No. of dealers 130
Stock Georgian, Victorian, general antiques and collectables
Open Mon–Sun 10am–5pm
Services Valuations, restoration and repairs, shipping, coffee shop, food hall

AUCHTERARDER

Ian Burton Antique Clocks (NAWCC, AHS)
Contact Ian Burton
The Antiques Gallery, 125 High Street, Auchterarder, Perthshire, PH3 1AA P
Ⓜ 07785 114800
Ⓔ ian@ianburton.com
Ⓦ www.ianburton.com
Est. 1974 *Stock size* Large
Stock Antique clocks
Open Mon–Sat 9am–5pm

K Stanley & Son
Contact Chris Stanley
20b Townhead, Auchterarder, Perthshire, PH3 1AH P
☎ 01764 662252 Ⓕ 01764 662252
Ⓜ 07958 777828
Ⓔ ksantique@aol.com
Est. 1956 *Stock size* Medium
Stock General antiques
Open Mon–Sat 10am–5pm
Sun noon–5pm

Times Past Antiques
Contact Andrew or Neil Brown
Broadfold Farm, Auchterarder, Perthshire, PH3 1DR P
☎ 01764 663166 Ⓕ 01764 663166
Est. 1974 *Stock size* Large
Stock Stripped antique pine
Open Mon–Fri 8am–4.30pm
Sat Sun 10am–3pm
Services Restoration, stripping, exporting

Ian Whitelaw Antiques (LAPADA)
Contact Ian Whitelaw
The Loft & Craigrossie Store, Fews, Auchterarder, Perthshire, PH3 1DG P
☎ 01764 664781 Ⓕ 01764 664781
Ⓔ ian@ianwhitelawantiques.co.uk
Ⓦ www.ianwhitelawantiques.co.uk
Est. 1974 *Stock size* Medium
Stock 18th–19thC furniture
Open Mon–Fri 9am–5pm Sat 10am–5pm or by appointment
Services Valuations, restoration

John Whitelaw & Sons (LAPADA)
Contact Alan Whitelaw
125 High Street, Auchterarder, Perthshire, PH3 1AA P
☎ 01764 662482 Ⓕ 01764 663577
Ⓜ 07836 725558
Ⓔ jwsantique@aol.com
Ⓦ www.whitelawantiques.com
Est. 1959 *Stock size* Large
Stock General antiques, Georgian furniture
Open Mon–Sat 9am–5pm
Fairs NEC, LAPADA
Services Repairs, restoration

BLAIRGOWRIE

Roy Sim Antiques
Contact Roy Sim
The Granary Warehouse, Lower Mill Street, Blairgowrie, Perthshire, PH10 6AQ P
☎ 01250 873860 Ⓕ 01250 873860
Ⓔ roy.sim@lineone.net
Est. 1977 *Stock size* Large
Stock Antique furniture, decorative and collectable items, longcase clocks, wall and mantel clocks, copper, brassware
Open Mon–Sat 9am–5.30pm
Sun 12.30–5pm

BRIDGE OF EARN

Imrie Antiques & Interiors (LAPADA)
Contact Ian Imrie
Imrie House, Back Street, Bridge of Earn, Perth, Perthshire, PH2 9AE P
☎ 01738 812784
Est. 1966 *Stock size* Large
Stock General antiques
Open Mon–Sat 9am–5pm
Services Valuations, restoration and repairs

COMRIE

Comrie Antiques
Contact Sylvia Anderson
2 Commercial Lane, Comrie, Crieff, Perthshire, PH6 2DP P
☎ 01764 679899/679015
Est. 1999 *Stock size* Small
Stock Period furniture
Open Mon–Sat 10am–5pm
Services Restoration

DUNKELD

Dunkeld Antiques (LAPADA)
Contact David Dytch
Tay Terrace, Dunkeld, Perthshire, PH8 0AQ P
☎ 01350 728832 Ⓕ 01350 727008
Ⓜ 07713 074932
Ⓔ sales@dunkeldantiques.com
Ⓦ www.dunkeldantiques.com
Est. 1986 *Stock size* Large
Stock General antiques, specializing in 18thC–19thC furniture
Open Mon–Sat 10am–5pm
Sun noon–5pm

GLENDOICK

Becca Gauldie Antiques & Scribe Books
Contact Becca Gauldie
The Old School, Glendoick, Perth, Perthshire, PH2 7NR P
☎ 01738 860870
Ⓔ becca@gauldie.freeserve.co.uk
Est. 1995 *Stock size* Medium
Stock Scottish country antiques, large selection of Mauchlineware, antiquarian and second-hand books
Open Mon–Sat 10am–5pm
Fairs NEC, Earls Court, Caroline Penman

INCHTURE

Inchmartine Fine Art
Contact Paul Stephens
Inchmartine House, Inchture, Perth, Perthshire, PH14 9QQ P
☎ 01828 686412 Ⓕ 01828 686748
Ⓜ 07702 190128
Ⓔ fineart@inchmartine.freeserve.co.uk
Est. 1997 *Stock size* Medium
Stock 19th–early 20thC Scottish paintings
Open Mon–Sat 9am–5.30pm
Fairs Buxton, Chester, Narworth, Scone
Services Valuations, cleaning and framing

Inchmartine Restorations
Contact Andrew Stephens
Inchmartine House, Inchture, Perth, Perthshire, PH14 9QQ P

☎ 01828 686412 ℱ 01828 686748
ⓔ ir@toolbazaar.freeserve.co.uk
ⓦ www.toolbazaar.co.uk
Est. 1989 *Stock size* Medium
Stock 18th–19thC furniture
Open Mon–Sat 9am–5.30pm
Fairs Buxton, Gleneagles
Services Valuations and cabinet-making

⊞ Inchmartine Tool Bazaar
Contact Andrew Stephens
✉ **Inchmartine House, Inchture, Perth, Perthshire, PH14 9QQ** Ⓟ
☎ 01828 686096 ℱ 01828 686748
ⓔ andrew@toolbazaar.freeserve.co.uk
ⓦ www.toolbazaar.co.uk
Est. 1991 *Stock size* Large
Stock Old cabinet-making and woodworking tools
Open Mon–Sat 9am–5.30pm
Fairs Buxton, Scone Palace, SECC Glasgow

⊞ C S Moreton Antiques
Contact Paul Stephens
✉ **Inchmartine House, Inchture, Perth, Perthshire, PH14 9QQ** Ⓟ
☎ 01828 686412 ℱ 01828 686748
Ⓜ 07702 190128
ⓔ moreton@inchmartine.freeserve.co.uk
Est. 1854 *Stock size* Medium
Stock Period furniture, Oriental rugs, paintings, objets d'art, old hand tools
Open Mon–Sat 9am–5.30pm
Fairs Buxton, Chester, Narworth, Scone
Services Valuations, restoration and shipping

KILLIN

⊞ Maureen H Gauld
Contact Maureen Gauld
✉ **Craiglee Main Street, Killin, Perthshire, FK21 8UN** Ⓟ
☎ 01567 820475 ℱ 01567 820605
ⓔ killingallery@btopenworld.com
ⓦ www.killingallery,com
Est. 1973 *Stock size* Medium
Stock Silver, china, glass antiques
Open Mon–Sat 10am–5pm or by appointment

⊞ Killin Gallery
Contact J Gauld
✉ **Craiglea Main Street, Killin, Perthshire, FK21 8UN** Ⓟ
☎ 01567 820475 ℱ 01567 820605
ⓔ killingallery@btopenworld.com
ⓦ www.killingallery.com
Est. 1994 *Stock size* Medium
Stock Furniture, paintings, etchings
Open Mon–Sat 10am–5pm or by appointment

KINROSS

⊞ Miles Antiques (LAPADA)
Contact Ken and Sue Miles
✉ **Mill Street, Kinross, Perth & Kinross, KY13 8DR** Ⓟ
☎ 01577 864858 ℱ 01577 863881
Ⓜ 07836 315589
Est. 1978 *Stock size* Large
Stock Georgian–Victorian furniture, clocks, porcelain, decorative objects
Open Mon–Fri noon–5pm or by appointment

MEIGLE

⊞ Airlie Antiques
Contact J W McGill
✉ **Alyth Road, Meigle, Blairgowrie, Perthshire, PH12 8RS** Ⓟ
☎ 01828 640617 ℱ 01828 640617
ⓔ shop@airlieantiques.co.uk
ⓦ www.airlieantiques.co.uk
Est. 1981 *Stock size* Small
Stock General small antiques, linens
Open Mon–Sun noon–5pm or by appointment
Fairs Newark, Edinburgh
Services Valuations

MUTHILL

⊞ Upstairs-Downstairs
Contact Elizabeth Richardson
✉ **18 Drummond Street, Muthill, Crieff, Perthshire, PH5 2AN** Ⓟ
☎ 01764 681737
Ⓜ 07803 461465
Est. 1996 *Stock size* Small
Stock General antiques, Victorian, Edwardian, Arts and Crafts, Art Nouveau, small furniture items, Continental glass, golf paraphernalia
Open Mon–Sun 2–5.30pm or by appointment

PERTH

⊞ Ainslie's Antiques
Contact Robert Ainslie
✉ **Unit 3, Gray Street, Perth, Perthshire, PH2 0JH** Ⓟ
☎ 01738 636825
Est. 1959 *Stock size* Large
Stock General antiques including Victorian and Edwardian furniture
Open Mon–Fri 9am–5pm or by appointment
Fairs Newark

Lindsay Burns & Co (SAA)
Contact Mr L Burns
✉ **6 King Street, Perth, Perthshire, PH2 8JA** Ⓟ
☎ 01738 633888 ℱ 01738 441322
ⓔ lindsayburns@btconnect.com
ⓦ www.lburns.co.uk
Est. 1982
Open Mon–Fri 9am–5pm Sat 9am–noon
Sales General antiques, household effects bi-weekly Thurs 10.30am, viewing day prior to sale
Frequency Bi-weekly
Catalogues Yes

⊞ Design Interiors
Contact Margaret Blane
✉ **46 South Street, Perth, Perthshire, PH2 8PD** Ⓟ
☎ 01738 635360
ⓔ robert.blane@btconnect.com
Est. 1989 *Stock size* Medium
Stock General antiques and collectables
Open Mon–Sat 10am–5.30pm
Services China restoration, picture cleaning, framing

⊞ Alexander S Deuchar & Son
Contact A S Deuchar
✉ **12 South Street, Perth, Perthshire, PH2 8PG** Ⓟ
☎ 01738 626297
Est. 1911 *Stock size* Medium
Stock General antiques
Open Mon–Fri 10am–5pm

⊞ Maurice Dodd Books (PBFA)
Contact Mr R McRoberts
✉ **1 Burnside Park,**

Pitcairnreen, Perth, Perth & Kinross, PH1 3BF
☎ 01738 583100
doddrarebooks@btconnect.com
Est. 1946 *Stock size* Medium
Stock Antiquarian books including topography, poetry, the Lake District
Open By appointment only
Fairs Russell Hotel
Services Valuations

Loves Auction Rooms (SAA, SOFAA)
Contact Mrs E Reid
52–54 Canal Street, Perth, Perthshire, PH2 8LF
☎ 01738 633337 Fax 01738 629830
enquiries@lovesauctions.co.uk
Est. 1869
Open Mon–Fri 9am–5pm Sat 9am–noon
Sales Antiques quarterly, household effects weekly
Catalogues Yes (quarterly sales only)

Perth Antiques
Contact Robert Blane
50 South Street, Perth, Perthshire, PH2 8PD
☎ 01738 440888
07939 196750
robert.blane@btconnect.com
Est. 1998 *Stock size* Large
Stock General antiques, porcelain, Clarice Cliff, Belleek, Morecroft, Art Deco pottery, Monart glass, chintz
Open Mon–Sat 10am–5pm

Whisper of the Past
Contact Laura Wilson
15 George Street, Perth, Perthshire, PH1 5JY
☎ 01738 635472
Est. 1981 *Stock size* Medium
Stock Country antiques
Open Mon–Sat 9.30am–5pm Jan–Mar closed Wed

Yesterdays Today
Contact W MacGregor
267 Old High Street, Perth, Perthshire, PH1 5QN
☎ 01738 443534
07713 897793
yesterdaystoday@talk21.com
Est. 1995 *Stock size* Medium
Stock General collectables, coins, medals, glass, jewellery, silver, Royal Doulton, Beswick
Open Mon–Sat 9am–5pm
Services Valuations

PITLOCHRY

Blair Antiques
Contact Duncan Huie
by Bruar Falls, Perthshire, PH18 5TW
☎ 01796 483264
07711 669644
adhuie@aol.com
Est. 1976 *Stock size* Medium
Stock General antiques, art
Open Mon–Fri 9am–5pm closed 12.30–2pm
Services Valuations

RAIT

Edward Bowry
Contact Edward Bowry
Rait Village Antique Centre, Rait, Perth, Perthshire, PH2 7RT
☎ 01821 670318
Est. 1990 *Stock size* Medium
Stock Furniture, old woodworking tools, sporting items
Open Mon–Sat 10.30am–5pm
Services Valuations, restoration and repairs

Fair Finds Antiques
Contact Lynda Templeman
Rait Village Antiques Centre, Rait, Perth, Perthshire, PH2 7RT
☎ 01821 670379 Fax 01821 670379
07720 394750
lynda.templeman@btopenworld.com
Est. 1969 *Stock size* Large
Stock Furniture, Wemyss ware, general antiques
Open Mon–Sat 10am–5pm Sun noon–4.30pm

Gordon Loraine Antiques
Contact Liane or Gordon Loraine
The Sawmill, Rait Village Antiques Centre, Rait, Perth, Perthshire, PH2 7RT
☎ 01821 670760 Fax 01821 670760
07798 550017
gordonloraine@supanet.com
Est. 1991 *Stock size* Medium
Stock Good-quality Georgian–Victorian furniture, decorative items, collectables, treen, mauchline
Open Mon–Sat 10am–5pm Sun Sept–Mar noon–4pm

Rait Village Antiques Centre
Contact Lynda Templeman
Rait, Perth, Perthshire, PH2 7RT
☎ 01821 670379 Fax 01821 670379
07720 394750
lynda.templeman@btopenworld.com
Est. 1985 *Stock size* Large
No. of dealers 15
Stock Furniture, silver, pottery, porcelain, Wemyss ware, rugs, paintings, jewellery, garden statuary, collectables
Open Mon–Sat 10am–5pm Sun noon–4.30pm
Services Valuations, restoration, coffee shop

SCONE

Iain M Smith Auctioneers & Valuers
Contact Iain Smith
Unit 18, Perth Airport Business Park, Scone, Perth, Perthshire, PH2 6NP
☎ 01738 551110 Fax 01738 551110
07836 770664
imsauctions@beeb.net
www.iainmsmith.co.uk
Est. 1994
Open Mon–Fri 9am–5pm Sat 10am–1pm
Sales General antiques, modern furniture
Frequency Weekly
Catalogues No

STANLEY

Coach House Antiques Ltd (PADA)
Contact John Walker
Charleston, Stanley, Perthshire, PN1 4PN
☎ 01738 828627
07710 122244
www.goodtradecall.com
Est. 1970 *Stock size* Medium
Stock Period furniture, decorative items, garden items
Open By appointment
Services Valuations, restoration, shipping

RENFREWSHIRE

GREENOCK

McTear's (SAA, IAA)
Contact Brian Clements
22 Forsyth Street, Greenock, Renfrewshire, PA16 8DX P
01475 730343 F 01475 726436
M 07767 376642
E enquiries@mctears.co.uk
W www.mctears.co.uk
Est. 1842
Open Mon–Fri 9am–5pm
Sales Monthly sale of antiques, art, weekly sale Victoriana, 3 annual sales of rare whisky
Catalogues Yes

KILBARCHAN

Gardners 'The Antique Shop' (LAPADA)
Contact George, Robert or David Gardner
Wardend House, Kibbleston Road, Kilbarchan, Johnstone, Renfrewshire, PA10 2PN P
01505 702292 F 01505 702292
E gardantiques@colloquium.co.uk
Est. 1950 *Stock size* Large
Stock General antiques, Georgian–1930s, furniture, porcelain, silver, pictures
Open Mon–Fri 9am–6pm Sat 10am–5pm
Services Valuations

McQuade Antiques
Contact Walter McQuade
7 Shuttle Street, Kilbarchan, Johnstone, Renfrewshire, PA10 2JN P
01505 704249
M 07860 729598
Est. 1967 *Stock size* Medium
Stock General antiques
Open Mon–Fri 10am–5.30pm Sun 2–5.30pm
Fairs Newark

KILMALCOLM

Kilmalcolm Antiques
Contact Hilary McLean
Stewart Place, Bridge of Weir Road, Kilmalcolm, Renfrewshire, PA13 4AF P
01505 873149 F 01505 873149
M 07850 126150
Est. 1974 *Stock size* Large
Stock General antiques, Scottish paintings, pottery, Georgian–Victorian furniture
Open Mon–Sat 10am–1pm 2.30–5.30pm
Fairs Hopeton House, Margam

PAISLEY

Corrigan Antiques
Contact Mr John Corrigan
23 High Calside, Paisley, Renfrewshire, PA2 6BY P
0141 889 6653 F 0141 848 9700
M 07802 631110
E corriganantiques@talk21.com
Est. 1939 *Stock size* Small
Stock Decorative antiques
Open By appointment only

SCOTTISH BORDERS

COLDSTREAM

Fraser Antiques
Contact R Fleming
65 High Street, Coldstream, Scottish Borders, TD12 4DL P
01890 882450 F 01890 882451
E m13border@aol.com
Est. 1968 *Stock size* Medium
Stock General antiques
Open Tues–Sat 10am–1pm 2–5pm
Services Valuations, restoration

GALASHIELS

Crystal's Auctions
Contact Stuart Cameron
36 Melrose Road, Galashiels, Scottish Borders, TD1 2BZ P
01896 751703 F 01896 668967
M 07736 397373
E crystals@hotdisc.net
W www.hotdisc.net/crystals.html
Est. 2003
Open Mon–Fri 9am–9pm
Sales General auctioneers. Monthly auctions at various venues in the Scottish Borders. Please see website for details
Catalogues Yes

Hall's Auctioneers
Contact Michael Hall
Ladhope Vale House, Ladhope Vale, Galashiels, Scottish Borders, TD1 1BT P
01896 754477 F 01896 754477
Est. 1995
Open Mon–Fri 9am–5pm Sat 9am–noon or by appointment
Sales General antiques and collectables
Frequency Monthly
Catalogues Yes

INNERLEITHEN

The Glory Hole
Contact Paul MacNaughton
29 High Street, Innerleithen, Scottish Borders, EH44 6HA P
01896 831306
M 07710 771055
Est. 1996 *Stock size* Medium
Stock General antiques, specializing in old printing items, coins
Open Mon–Fri 11am–5pm closed Tues
Fairs Border fairs

Keepsakes
Contact Mrs M Maxwell
96 High Street, Innerleithen, Scottish Borders, EH44 6HF P
01896 831369
M 07773 477291
E rmaxwells@keepsakes.freeserve.co.uk
W www.website.lineone.net/~rmaxwell
Est. 1979 *Stock size* Medium
Stock General antiques, dolls, toys, Art Deco
Open Mon Thurs–Sat 11am–4.30pm
Fairs Ingliston

The Last Century Antiques
Contact Keith or Gill Miller
34 High Street, Innerleithen, Scottish Borders, EH44 6HF P
01896 831759
E last.century@btinternet.com
Est. 1989 *Stock size* Medium
Stock General antiques including glass, cutlery, antiquarian and out-of-print books
Open Mon–Sat 11am–5pm
Fairs Inglestone
Services Valuations

JEDBURGH

R & M Turner (Antiques & Fine Art) Ltd (LAPADA)
Contact Mr R J Turner
34–36 High Street, Jedburgh, Roxburghshire, TD8 6AG P
01835 863445 F 01835 863349
Est. 1966 *Stock size* Large
Stock Fine art, clocks, furniture, jewellery, bric-a-brac, porcelain, reproductions
Open Mon–Fri 9.30am–5.30pm Sat 10am–5pm
Services Valuations, restoration, shipping

MELROSE

Birch House Antiques at Michael Vee Design
Contact Michael Vee
Birch House, High Street, Melrose, Scottish Borders, TD6 9PA P
01896 822116 F 01896 682320
M 07761 913349
E michael.vee@btinternet.com
W www.michaelveedesign.com
Est. 1990 *Stock size* Medium
Stock French decorative antiques, mirrors, garden statuary, urns, English furniture, lighting
Open Mon–Fri 9am–5pm Sat 9am–3pm

Border Country Furniture
Contact Denni or Christine Reid
2 Palma Place, Melrose, Scottish Borders, TD6 9PR P
01896 823700 F 01896 823700
Est. 1974 *Stock size* Large
Stock General antiques, hand-made furniture
Open Mon–Sat 10am–5pm
Services Made-to-measure tables and fireplaces

John Swan Ltd
Contact Frank Forrest
Newtown St Boswells, Melrose, Scottish Borders, TD6 0PD P
01835 822214 F 01835 823860
E stboswells@johnswan.demon.co.uk
Est. 1899
Open Mon–Fri 9am–5pm
Sales General antiques and house clearance
Catalogues Yes

SHETLAND

LUNNANESS

Antiques & Collectables
Contact Frank Watt
Outrabister House, Lunnaness, Vidlin, Shetland, ZE2 9QF P
01806 577206 F 01806 577206
M 07884 250336
E frank.watt@ntlworld.com
Est. 1994 *Stock size* Large
Stock General antiques and collectables
Open By appointment
Services Valuations, book search

SOUTH AYRSHIRE

GIRVAN

Ainslie Books
Contact Mr G Clark
1 Glendoune Street, Girvan, South Ayrshire, KA26 0AA P
01465 715453 F 01465 715453
E sales@ainsliebooks.co.uk
W www.ainsliebooks.co.uk
Est. 1996 *Stock size* Medium
Stock Rare and second-hand books, specializing in Scottish and Ayrshire topics
Open Mon–Sat 10am–5pm
Services Book search

Clamjamfrey
Contact Ingrid Powell
26 Hamilton Street, Girvan, South Ayrshire, KA26 9EY P
01465 715621
E clamjam@tiscali.co.uk
W www.clamjamfrey.com
Est. 1997 *Stock size* Medium
Stock General antiques, Denby and Poole pottery, 20thC ceramics, metalware
Open Mon–Sat 10am–5pm
Fairs Edinburgh, Swinderby
Services Valuations

PRESTWICK

Crossroads Antiques
Contact Mr T O'Keeffe
7 The Cross, Prestwick, South Ayrshire, KA9 1AJ P
01292 474004
Est. 1989 *Stock size* Medium
Stock General antiques, furniture, china
Open Mon–Sat 10.30am–5pm

TROON

Tantalus Antiques (BWCG)
Contact Iain Sutherland
79 Templehill, Troon, South Ayrshire, KA10 6BQ P
01292 315999
E idsantique@aol.com
W www.tantalusantiques.com
Est. 1997 *Stock size* Medium
Stock General antiques, furniture, jewellery, clocks, watches, pictures, paintings, silverware, ornaments, curios
Open Mon–Sat 10am–5pm or by appointment
Fairs Ayr
Services Full consultation and restoration service

SOUTH LANARKSHIRE

HAMILTON

L S Smellie & Sons Ltd (SAA)
Contact Mr A Smellie
Lower Auchingramont Road, Hamilton, South Lanarkshire, ML3 6HW P
01698 282007 F 01698 207473
E hamiltonauction@btconnect.com
W www.hamiltonauctionmarket.co.uk
Est. 1874
Open Mon–Fri 8am–5pm
Sales Weekly general antiques sale Mon
Frequency Weekly
Catalogues Yes

STRATHAVEN

Avondale Antique Jewellers
Contact Mrs M Hardie
11a Green Street, Strathaven, South Lanarkshire, ML10 6LT P
01357 529854
Est. 1997 *Stock size* Large
Stock Antique jewellery
Open Mon–Sat 10.30am–5pm closed Wed
Services Valuations, repairs

WISTON

Sunnyside Antiques
Contact Mark Attwood
Castledykes, Wiston, Biggar, South Lanarkshire,

ML12 6HT P
☎ 01899 850552 F 01899 850551
M 07798 640629
E info@periodantiques.net
W www.periodantiques.net
Est. 1995 *Stock size* Medium
Stock 17th–19thC period furniture, longcase clocks
Open Mon–Sun 9am–5pm
Fairs Newark
Services Restoration, shipping

STIRLING

BALFRON

Amphora Galleries Antiques
Contact Laurie Ruglen
✉ **16–18 Buchanan Street, Balfron, Stirling, G63 0TT** P
☎ 01360 440329
Est. 1968 *Stock size* Medium
Stock Georgian, Victorian furniture, porcelain, general antiques
Open Mon–Fri 10am–5pm or by appointment

BRIDGE OF ALLAN

Bridge of Allan Books (PBFA)
Contact Andrew Jennings
✉ **2 Henderson Street, Bridge of Allan, Stirling, FK9 4HT** P
☎ 01786 834483 F 01786 834483
E books@bridgeofallenbooks.com
W www.bridgeofallenbooks.com
Est. 1985 *Stock size* Medium
Stock Antiquarian, rare and second-hand books, prints, specializing in Scottish and field sports
Open Mon–Sat 10am–5.30pm
Services Free book search

DOUNE

Scottish Antique and Arts Centre
Contact Victoria Templeman
✉ **Doune, Stirling, FK16 6HG** P
☎ 01786 841203 F 01786 842561
E victempleman@aol.com
W www.scottish-antiques.com
Est. 1974 *Stock size* Large
No. of dealers 100
Stock Georgian–Victorian, general antiques and collectables
Open Mon–Sun 10am–5pm
Services Shipping, coffee shop

FALKIRK

Auction Rooms (NAVA)
Contact Robert Penman
✉ **Central Auction Hall, Bankside, Falkirk, Stirling, FK2 7XF** P
☎ 01324 623000 F 01324 630343
E robert@auctionroomsfalkirk.co.uk
W www.auctionroomsfalkirk.co.uk
Est. 1989
Open Mon Thurs Fri 9am–5pm Tues 8am–8pm Wed 8am–6pm Sat 9am–noon
Sales General antiques sales every Wed evening
Catalogues Yes

GARGUNNOCK

Country Home Antiques
Contact P Christie
✉ **Mains Farm, Gargunnock, Stirling, FK8 3AY** P
☎ 01786 860509 F 01786 860509
E gargunnock@aol.com or antiquestrader@aol.com
W www.scotlandroom.com
Est. 1979 *Stock size* Large
Stock General antiques
Open Mon–Fri 9am–5pm Sat 10am–5pm Sun 12.30–5pm
Services Stripping, waxing, upholstery, French polishing, full restoration, shipping

STIRLING

Abbey Antiques
Contact Stuart Campbell
✉ **4 Friars Street, Stirling, FK8 1HA** P
☎ 01786 447840
M 07801 692126
Est. 1979 *Stock size* Small
Stock Jewellery, silver, militaria, paintings, furniture, bric-a-brac
Open Mon–Sat 9am–5pm
Services Valuations

Stewart Sales Rooms
Contact Mrs Watson-Fargie
✉ **14 Dumbarton Road, Stirling, FK8 2LG** P
☎ 01786 473414
Est. 1969 *Stock size* Large
Stock General antiques
Open Mon–Sat 10am–4pm closed Wed
Services Valuations

STRATHBLANE

What Nots Antiques
Contact Frank Bruce
✉ **16 Milngavie Road, Strathblane, Stirling, G63 9EH** P
☎ 01360 770310
Est. 1969 *Stock size* Medium
Stock General antiques, clocks, selection of horse-drawn vehicles
Open Mon–Sun 9.30am–5pm

WEST LOTHIAN

BO'NESS

D J Manning Auctioneers, Valuers & Appraisers (NAVA)
Contact Andrew Morgan
✉ **Bridgeness Road, Carriden, Bo'Ness, West Lothian, EH51 9SF** P
☎ 01506 827693 F 01506 826495
E info@djmanning.co.uk
W www.djmanning.co.uk
Est. 1969
Open Mon–Fri 9am–5pm
Sales Books, general antiques, collectables
Frequency Quarterly
Catalogues Yes

LINLITHGOW

County Antiques
Contact Mrs Flynn
✉ **30 High Street, Linlithgow, West Lothian, EH49 7AE** P
☎ 01506 671201
Est. 1992 *Stock size* Medium
Stock General antiques, jewellery
Open Mon–Sat 10am–5pm
Fairs Edinburgh
Services Valuations and jewellery repairs

CHANNEL ISLANDS

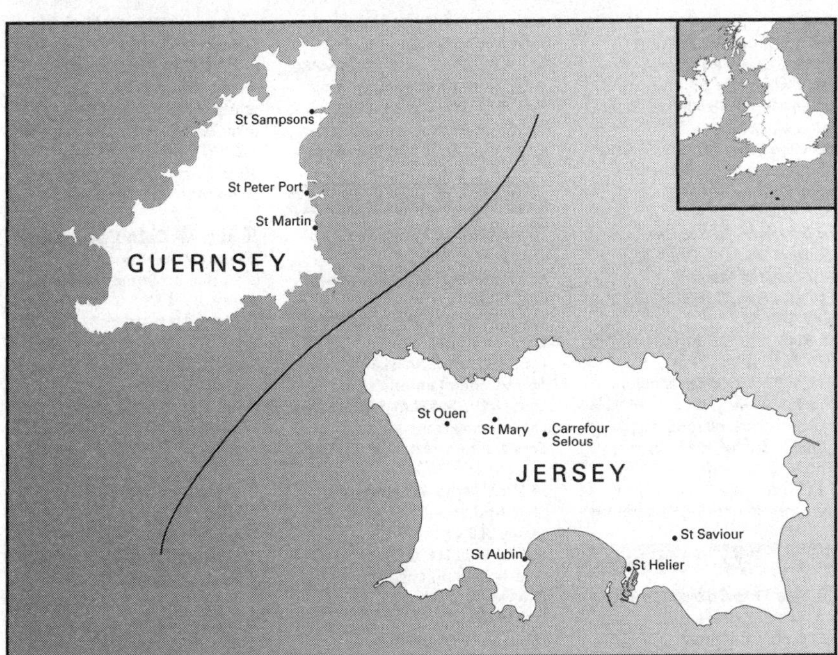

GUERNSEY

ST PETER PORT

田 Stephen Andrews Gallery
Contact Stephen Andrews
✉ **5 College Terrace, The Grange, St Peter Port, Guernsey, GY1 2PX** P
☎ 01481 710380
Est. 1984 *Stock size* Large
Stock Pottery, porcelain, furniture, silver
Open Mon–Sat 9.30am–5pm
Fairs Guernsey Antiques Fair

田 Channel Islands Galleries Ltd
Contact Geoffrey Gavey
✉ **Trinity Square Centre, Trinity Square, St Peter Port, Guernsey, GY1 ILX** P
☎ 01481 723247/247337
Ⓕ 01481 714669
Ⓔ geoff.gavey@cigalleries.f9.co.uk
Ⓦ www.cigalleries.f9.co.uk
Est. 1970 *Stock size* Medium
Stock Channel Island antique maps, prints, watercolours, oil paintings, out-of-print books, bank notes, coins
Open Mon–Fri 10am–5pm
Sat 10am–1pm
Services Valuations, restoration, conservation, picture framing

田 The Collectors Centre
Contact Andrew Rundle
✉ **1 Sausmarez Street, St Peter Port, Guernsey, GY1 2PT** P
☎ 01481 725209
Est. 1985 *Stock size* Medium
Stock Antique prints, engravings, old postcards, coins, bank notes, memorabilia, stamps
Open Mon–Sat 10.30am–6pm
Services Valuations for collectables, mail-order, postal auctions, free catalogue

田 W De La Rue Antiques
Contact William de La Rue
✉ **29 Mill Street, St Peter Port, Guernsey, GY1 1HG**
☎ 01481 723177
Est. 1975 *Stock size* Medium
Stock General antiques, collectors' items
Open Mon–Sat 10am–12.30pm
2–4pm closed Thurs pm
Services Valuations, buying

田 Ann Drury Antiques
Contact Ann Drury
✉ **1 Mansell Street, St Peter Port, Guernsey, GY1 1HP**
☎ 01481 716193
Ⓜ 07781 104304
Est. 1969 *Stock size* Large
Stock 18th–20thC furniture and decorative antiques
Open Mon–Sat 10am–noon
2–4pm closed Thurs
Fairs Guernsey Antiques Fair
Services Valuations

田 Mahogany
Contact Angela Edwards
✉ **7 Mansell Street, St Peter Port, Guernsey, GY1 1HP**
☎ 01481 727574 Ⓕ 01481 727574
Est. 1980 *Stock size* Large
Stock General antiques, collectables
Open Mon–Sat 10am–12.30pm
2–4pm Thurs closed pm
Fairs Guernsey Antiques Fair

田 N St J Paint and Sons Ltd (NAG)
Contact Michael or Paul Paint
✉ **26 Le Pollet, St Peter Port, Guernsey, GY1 1WQ**
☎ 01481 722229 Ⓕ 01481 710241

CHANNEL ISLANDS
GUERNSEY • ST SAMPSONS

Ⓔ paint@guernsey.net
Est. 1947 *Stock size* Large
Stock General antiques, jewellery, silver, objets d'art
Open Mon–Fri 8.45am–5.30pm Sat 8.45am–5pm
Services Valuations, restoration and repairs (goldsmiths and silversmiths)

Parasol Antiques
Contact Marianne Barwick
2 Contree Mansell, St Peter Port, Guernsey, GY1 1HR P
☎ 01481 710780 Ⓕ 01481 710780
Ⓜ 07781 118715
Est. 1993 *Stock size* Medium
Stock Jewellery, silver, furniture, copper, brass, pictures
Open Mon–Sat 10am–5pm Thurs 10am–1pm
Fairs Guernsey Antiques Fair
Services Valuations, restoration

ST SAMPSONS

The Old Curiosity Shop
Contact Mrs Stevens-Cox
Commercial Road, St Sampsons, Guernsey, GY2 4QP P
☎ 01481 245324
Est. 1978 *Stock size* Medium
Stock General small antiques, collectables, second-hand books
Open Tues Wed Fri Sat 10.30am–2pm
Fairs Guernsey Antiques Fair
Services Framing

Ray & Scott Ltd (NAG)
Contact M Search
The Bridge, St Sampsons, Guernsey, GY2 4QN P
☎ 01481 244610 Ⓕ 01481 247843
Est. 1962 *Stock size* Large
Stock Fine jewellery, clocks, silver, second-hand watches
Open Mon–Sat 9am–5pm
Fairs Guernsey Antiques Fair, Beau Sejours Fair
Services Valuations, restoration of jewellery, antique clocks, gold and silversmiths

JERSEY

CARREFOUR SELOUS

David Hick Antiques
Contact David Hick
Alexandra House, Carrefour Selous, St Lawrence, Jersey, JE3 1GL P
☎ 01534 865965 Ⓕ 01534 865448
Ⓔ hickantiques@localdial.com
Est. 1974 *Stock size* Large
Stock Furniture, silver, porcelain
Open Wed Fri Sat 9.30am–5pm

ST HELIER

Antiques Warehouse
Contact Tim Morley
Robin Place, St Helier, Jersey, JE2 4LT P
☎ 01534 873932 Ⓕ 01534 506833
Ⓜ 07797 720234
Est. 1988 *Stock size* Large
Stock General antiques
Open Mon–Sat 8am–5.30pm
Fairs Mainly French fairs
Services Restoration, shipping

Bonhams & Langlois
39 Don Street, St Helier, Jersey, JE2 4TR
☎ 01534 722441 Ⓕ 01534 759354
Ⓔ jersey@bonhams.com
Ⓦ www.bonhams.com
Est. 1940
Open Mon–Fri 9am–5pm
Sales Regional Saleroom. Frequent sales. Regular house and attic sales across the country; contact London offices for further details. Free auction valuations; insurance and probate valuations
Catalogues Yes

Brown's Times Past Antiques
Contact Mick Brown
28 Burrard Street, St Helier, Jersey, JE2 4WS P
☎ 01534 737090/735264
Est. 1984 *Stock size* Medium
Stock Georgian–Edwardian furniture, ceramics, 19thC pottery and glass
Open Mon–Sat 9am–5pm or by appointment
Services Valuations

John Cooper Antiques
Contact John Cooper
16 Central Market, St Helier, Jersey, JE2 4WL
☎ 01534 723600
Est. 1982 *Stock size* Medium
Stock General, mostly small items including jewellery
Open Mon–Sat 9am–5.30pm Thurs half day

David Hick Antiques
Contact David Hick
45 Halkett Place, St Helier, Jersey, JE2 4WQ P
☎ 01534 721162 Ⓕ 01534 721162
Ⓔ hickantiques@localdial.com
Est. 1974 *Stock size* Large
Stock Furniture, silver, porcelain
Open Mon–Sat 10am–5pm

Jersey Coin Company
Contact V or S Dougan
26 Halkett Street, St Helier, Jersey, JE2 4WJ
☎ 01534 725743 Ⓕ 01534 509094
Est. 1965 *Stock size* Medium
Stock Antique coins, bank notes, medals, weapons
Open Mon–Sat 9am–5pm
Services Valuations, jewellery repairs

Peter Le Vesconte Collectables
Contact Peter Le Vesconte
62 Stopford Road, St Helier, Jersey, JE2 4LZ P
☎ 01534 732481 Ⓕ 01534 732481
Ⓜ 07797 826292
Ⓔ plvcollectables@jerseymail.co.uk
Est. 1981 *Stock size* Large
Stock Dinky and Corgi toys, mint and boxed toys, militaria (especially WWII), new collectors' toys
Open Mon–Sat 10am–1pm closed Thurs
Fairs Jersey Toy and Phone Card Collectors Fair
Services Toy valuations

Park Antiques
Contact P Cowan
16 Burrard Street, St Helier, Jersey, JE2 4WF
☎ 01534 280784
Ⓔ park@itl.net
Est. 1969 *Stock size* Large
Stock English and Continental furniture
Open By appointment

A & R Ritchie
Contact A or R Ritchie
7 Duhamel Place, St Helier, Jersey, JE2 4TP P
☎ 01534 873805
Est. 1973 *Stock size* Medium
Stock Collectables, brass, china, glass, toys, silver, jewellery, scent bottles, militaria
Open Mon–Sat 10am–5pm
Services Restoration – militaria and ivory, jewellery

Robert's Antiques
Contact Robert Michieli
14 York Street, St Helier, Jersey, JE2 3RQ
☎ 01534 509071
Ⓜ 07798 876553
Est. 1979 *Stock size* Medium
Stock English silver, porcelain, jewellery, glass
Open Mon–Sat 9am–5.30pm or by appointment
Services Valuations

Thomson's Antiques
Contact Ray or Chris Thomson
60 Kensington Place, St Helier, Jersey, JE2 3PA
☎ 01534 723673 Ⓕ 01534 723673
Ⓜ 07797 766806
Est. 1967 *Stock size* Large
Stock General antiques, furniture
Open Mon–Sat 10am–5pm

Thomson's Antiques
Contact Ray or Chris Thomson
10 Waterloo Street, St Helier, Jersey, JE2 4WT P
☎ 01534 618673
Ⓜ 07797 826414
Est. 1967 *Stock size* Large
Stock Collectors' items, furniture, clocks, silver, barometers
Open Mon–Sat 10am–5pm

ST MARY

Country House and Cottage Antiques
Contact Sarah Johnson
Rue Esboeufs, St Mary, Jersey, JE3 3EQ P
☎ 01534 862547
Est. 1984 *Stock size* Large
Stock Georgian–Edwardian, oak, pine and mahogany furniture, china, glass, ceramics, silver
Open Mon–Fri 10am–4pm
Sat 9am–1pm
Fairs St Mary's Fair
Services Valuations

ST SAVIOUR

Pine for Pine Antiques
Contact Mrs Brenda Clyde Smith
Chateau Clairval, St Saviour, Jersey, JE2 7HN P
☎ 01534 737173/724748
Ⓕ 01534 618384
Est. 1974 *Stock size* Medium
Stock Georgian–Edwardian pine furniture
Open Mon–Fri 10am–4pm
Sat 10am–2pm

NORTHERN IRELAND

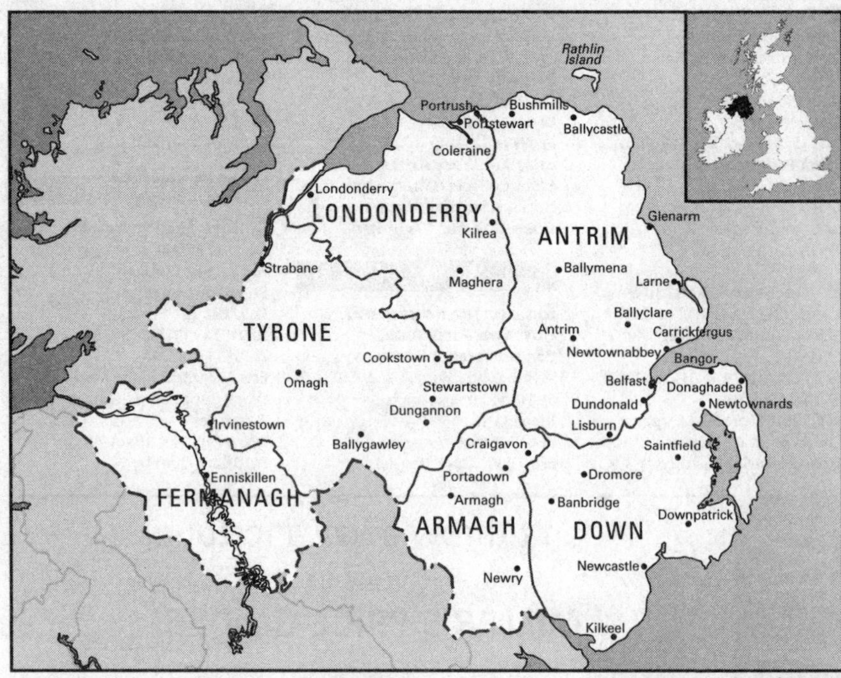

CO ANTRIM

AHOGHILL

⊞ Once Upon a Time Antiques
Contact Sean or Ronan McLaughlin
✉ **The Old Mill, 2 Parkfield Road, Ahoghill, Co Antrim, BT42 2QF** 🅿
☎ 028 2587 1244 ⓕ 028 2587 1244
Est. 1973 *Stock size* Large
Stock Jewellery, furniture, general antiques
Open Mon–Sat 10am–5.30pm
Services Valuations, restoration, coffee shop, craft centre

ANTRIM

⊞ Country Antiques (LAPADA, IADA)
Contact David Wolfenden
✉ **219 Lisnevenagh Road, Antrim, BT41 2JT** 🅿
☎ 028 9442 9498 ⓕ 028 9442 9498
Ⓜ 07768 128800
ⓔ antiquewolfirl@aol.com
Ⓦ www.country-antiques-wolfenden.co.uk
Est. 1984 *Stock size* Large
Stock Furniture, jewellery, general antiques
Open Mon–Sat 10am–6pm
Services Valuations, restoration

⊞ Village Antiques
Contact Mr W J Baird
✉ **99 Main Street, Randalstown, Antrim, BT41 3BB** 🅿
☎ 028 9447 8686
Ⓜ 07703 594522
Est. 1998 *Stock size* Medium
Stock General antiques, furniture
Open Mon–Sat 10am–6pm
Services Restoration, clock repairs

BALLINDERRY

⊞ Ballinderry Antiques
Contact Mr W Mills
✉ **2 Ballinderry Road, Ballinderry, Upper Lisburn, Co Antrim, BT28 2EP** 🅿
☎ 028 9265 1046 ⓕ 028 9265 1580
Est. 1959 *Stock size* Large
Stock Antique furniture, silver
Open Mon–Sat 10am–5.30pm
Fairs Newark
Services Valuations

BALLYCASTLE

P J Mcilroy & Son
Contact Mr Sean Mcilroy FNAEA
✉ **13 Ann Street, Ballycastle, Co Antrim, BT54 6AA** 🅿
☎ 028 2076 2353 ⓕ 028 2076 2126
ⓔ leo@pjmcilroy.freeserve.co.uk
Ⓦ www.pjmcilroy.com
Est. 1967
Open Mon–Fri 9am–5.30pm Sat 10am–12.30pm
Sales General antiques, paintings
Frequency Quarterly
Catalogues Yes

BALLYMENA

⊞ Angela's Antiques
Contact Angela McClelland
✉ **75 Wellington Street, Ballymena, Co Antrim, BT43 6AD**
☎ 028 2564 1999
Est. 1993 *Stock size* Large
Stock Porcelain, jewellery, furniture, general antiques
Open Mon–Sat 9.30am–5pm

Lorraine's Antiques
Contact Ms Lorraine Wylie
84 Galgorm Road, Ballymena, Co Antrim, BT42 1AA P
☎ 028 2564 5359
Est. 1983 *Stock size* Medium
Stock Porcelain, jewellery
Open By appointment
Fairs Ulster Antique and Fine Art Fair, Temple Patrick (Mar)

BALLYMONEY

McAfee Auctions (MIAVI)
Contact Mr Gerry McAfee
51 Main Street, Ballymoney, Co Antrim, BT53 6AN P
☎ 028 2766 7676 F 028 2766 7666
Est. 1992
Open Mon–Fri 9am–5.30pm
Sat 9.30am–12.30pm
Sales Monthly sales of general antiques. Quarterly specialist Irish art sales
Catalogues Yes

BELFAST

Antiquarian
Contact Mr Eric Lauro
67 Royal Avenue, Belfast, Co Antrim, BT1 1FE P
☎ 028 9032 7301
Stock Guns, swords, wartime memorabilia, watches, clocks, stamps, coins
Open Mon–Sat 9am–5.30pm
Thurs 10am–9pm
Services Valuations, repairs

Archives Antique Centre
Contact Laurence Johnston
88 Donegal Passage, Belfast, Co Antrim, BT1 1BX P
☎ 028 9023 2383
Est. 1999 *Stock size* Large
No. of dealers 4
Stock General antiques, collectables, lighting, silver, pub memorabilia
Open Mon–Sat 10.30am–5pm
Services Valuations, brass, and copper restoration

The Bell Gallery
Contact Nelson Bell
13 Adelaide Park, Belfast, Co Antrim, BT9 6FX P
☎ 028 9066 2998 F 028 9038 1524
E bellgallery@btinternet.com
W www.bellgallery.com
Est. 1964 *Stock size* Small
Stock Irish art and contemporary Irish artists, prints, silver, bog oak jewellery, Irish books
Open Mon–Fri 9am–5pm
Services Valuations

Bloomfield Auctions
Contact Mr George Gribben
288 Deersbridge Road, Belfast, Co Antrim, BT5 1DX P
☎ 028 9045 6404
Est. 1991
Open Mon–Fri 10am–5pm
Sales Antiques, fine art
Frequency Every Tues at 6.30pm
Catalogues No

Bookfinders
Contact Miss Mary Denver
47 University Road, Belfast, Co Antrim, BT7 1ND
☎ 028 9032 8269
Est. 1985 *Stock size* Large
Stock Antiquarian, rare and second-hand books
Open Mon–Sat 10am–5.30pm
Services Book search

Cellar Antiques
Contact Jonathan Megaw
Belfast Castle, Antrim Road, Belfast, Co Antrim, BT15 5GR P
☎ 028 9077 6925 ext 31
Est. 1984 *Stock size* Medium
Stock Jewellery, general antiques, collectables
Open Mon–Sat 12.30–10pm
Sun 12.30–5pm
Services Valuations, restoration and repairs

The Collector
Contact William Seawright
42 Rosscoole Park, Belfast, Co Antrim, BT14 8JX
☎ 028 9071 0115
Est. 1964 *Stock size* Large
Stock Antique coins, medals, cigarette cards, postcards
Open Trades through fairs only
Fairs All major fairs in Dublin and Belfast

Harry Hall's Bookshop
Contact Mr Bernard Hope
39 Gresham Street, Belfast, Co Antrim, BT1 1JL
☎ 028 9024 1923
Est. 1970 *Stock size* Large
Stock Antiquarian and second-hand books
Open Mon–Sat 10am–5pm
Fairs Belfast Book Fair

Morgan's Auctions
Contact Mr Haliday or Mr Morgan
6 Duncrue Crescent, Duncrue Road, Belfast, Co Antrim, BT3 9BW P
☎ 028 9077 1552 F 028 9077 4503
Est. 1985
Open Mon 9am–6pm
Tues–Fri 9am–5pm
Sales General and antiques
Frequency Every Tues 11am
Catalogues No

Oakland Antiques
Contact Donald McCluskey
135 Donegal Pass, Belfast, Co Antrim, BT7 1DS P
☎ 028 9023 0176 F 028 9024 8144
M 07831 176438
E sales@oaklandni.com
W www.oaklandni.com
Est. 1975 *Stock size* Large
Stock Georgian–Edwardian furniture, silver, clocks, glass, bronze, spelter, marble, English and Oriental porcelain, oil paintings, watercolours, longcase clocks
Open Mon–Sat 10am–5.30pm
Fairs Ulster Antique and Fine Art Fair
Services Deliveries to anywhere in Northern Ireland

Past & Present
Contact Trevor or Frances McNally
58–60 Donegal Pass, Belfast, Co Antrim, BT7 1BU P
☎ 028 9033 3137 F 028 9033 3137
Est. 1985 *Stock size* Medium
Stock Edwardian–Victorian furniture, collectables
Open Tues–Sat 10.30am–5pm

Petite Antiques
Contact Charlie Tosh
24 Brereton Crescent, Belfast, Co Antrim, BT8 6QD P
☎ 028 9064 4632
M 07850 280777
E enquiries@petiteantiques.com

Ⓦ www.petiteantiques.com
Est. 1973 *Stock size* Small
Stock Clocks, porcelain, jewellery
Open Mon–Fri 9am–5pm
Sat 9.30am–12.30pm
Services Valuations

Phoenix Gallery
Contact Vivienne Jackson
✉ **82 Donegal Pass, Belfast, Co Antrim, BT7 1BX** Ⓟ
☎ 028 9023 8246
Ⓦ www.johncarollantiques.com
Est. 2000 *Stock size* Large
Stock General antiques, art
Open Mon–Fri 10am–5pm
Sat 10am–1pm

John Ross & Company (NIAVI)
Contact Mr Daniel Clarke
✉ **37 Montgomery Street, Belfast, Co Antrim, BT1 4NX** Ⓟ
☎ 028 9032 5448 Ⓕ 028 9033 3642
Ⓔ info@rossbelfast.com
Ⓦ www.rossbelfast.com
Est. 1919
Open Mon–Fri 9am–5pm
Sales Quarterly sales of Irish paintings, weekly sales of antiques
Catalogues Yes

P & B Rowan (IADA)
Contact Peter or Briad Rowan
✉ **Carleton House, 92 Malone Road, Belfast, Co Antrim, BT9 5HP** Ⓟ
☎ 028 9066 6448 Ⓕ 028 9066 3725
Ⓔ peter@pbrowan.thegap.com
Est. 1973 *Stock size* Large
Stock Antiquarian books
Open By appointment
Fairs Irish Antiques Dealers Fair, PBFA (May/June)
Services Valuations

Stormont Antiques
Contact Mrs Ann McMurray
✉ **2a Sandown Road, Upper Newtownards Road, Belfast, Co Antrim, BT5 6GY** Ⓟ
☎ 028 9047 2586
Est. 1979 *Stock size* Large
Stock Jewellery, silver
Open Mon–Fri 11.30am–5pm
Sat 11.30am–4pm
Services Valuations, restoration

The Wake Table
Contact Mr P Rosenberg
✉ **40 Donegal Pass, Belfast, Co Antrim, BT7 1BS** Ⓟ
☎ 028 9032 2147
Est. 1996 *Stock size* Medium
Stock General antiques
Open Mon–Sat 9am–5pm
Fairs Ulster Antique and Fine Art Fair

BUSHMILLS

Brian R Bolt Antiques
Contact Brian or Helen Bolt
✉ **88 Ballaghmore Road, Portballintrae, Bushmills, Co Antrim, BT57 8RL** Ⓟ
☎ 028 2073 1129 Ⓕ 028 2073 1129
Ⓜ 07712 579802
Ⓔ brianbolt@antiques88.freeserve.co.uk
Est. 1979 *Stock size* Medium
Stock Antique and 20thC silver and objects of virtue, decorative arts, antique and 20thC glass, treen, general small items
Open By appointment
Services Valuations, search, worldwide postal service

Causeway Books
Contact Mr D Speers
✉ **110 Main Street, Bushmills, Co Antrim, BT57 8QD**
☎ 028 2073 2596
Est. 1989 *Stock size* Medium
Stock General antiquarian books
Open Mon–Sat 10am–5.30pm

Dunluce Antiques and Crafts
Contact Mrs Clare Ross
✉ **33 Ballytober Road, Bushmills, Co Antrim, BT57 8UU** Ⓟ
☎ 028 207 31140
Ⓔ dunluceantiques@btinternet.com
Ⓦ www.dunlucegallery.com
Est. 1978 *Stock size* Small
Stock General antiques, collectables, Irish art gallery
Open Mon–Thurs 10am–6pm
Sat 2–6pm
Services Valuations and porcelain restoration

CARRICKFERGUS

Robert Christie Antiques (IADA)
Contact Robert Christie
✉ **20 Calhame Road, Ballyclare, Co Antrim, BT39 9NA** Ⓟ
☎ 028 9334 1149 Ⓕ 028 9334 1149
Ⓜ 07802 968846
Est. 1976 *Stock size* Medium
Stock 18th–19thC furniture, clocks, silver and plate, pottery, porcelain
Open Mon–Sat noon–5pm or by appointment
Fairs RDS Fairs, Dublin, Kings Hall, Belfast
Services Valuations

Lennox Auctions and Valuers
Contact Mr A Lennox
✉ **The Basement, 41b Ellis Street, Carrickfergus, Co Antrim, BT38 8AY** Ⓟ
☎ 028 9335 1522 or 028 9337 8527 (pm) Ⓕ 028 9335 1522
Est. 1987
Open Mon–Fri 9.30am–5pm
Sales Weekly sales Thurs 7pm, viewing Mon–Thur 10am–5pm Telephone for details. Periodic house clearance sales
Catalogues No

CARRYDUFF

Carryduff Group Ltd
Contact Mr Robert Jenkins
✉ **10 Comber Road, Carryduff, Co Antrim, BT8 8AM** Ⓟ
☎ 028 9081 3775 Ⓕ 028 9081 4518
Est. 1996
Open Mon–Fri 9am–6pm
Sales General antiques
Frequency Monthly
Catalogues Yes

GLARRYFORD

Antique Builders Suppliers
Contact Mr Hastings White
✉ **94 Duneoin Road, Drumminning, Glarryford, Co Antrim, BT44 9HH** Ⓟ
☎ 028 2568 5444
Ⓜ 07860 675908
Ⓔ sales@whites-architectural salvage.com
Ⓦ www.whites-architectural salvage.com
Est. 1983 *Stock size* Large
Stock Architectural salvage, Bangor blue slates, beams, tiles,

stained glass windows, chimney pots, weathervanes, hardwood flooring, baths
Open Mon–Sat 7am–11pm
Services Delivery

GLENGORMLEY

⊞ Acorns
Contact Mr P McComb
✉ **4 Portland Avenue, Glengormley, Co Antrim, BT36 5EY** P
☎ 028 9080 4100
Est. 1999 *Stock size* Medium
Stock Furniture, general antiques, dolls' houses
Open Mon–Sat 9.30am–5.30pm
Services Local delivery

KELLS

⊞ Cottage Antiques
Contact Rachael Hiles
✉ **2 Greenfield Road, Kells, Co Antrim, BT42 3JL** P
☎ 028 2589 2169
Ⓜ 07808 161052
Est. 1969 *Stock size* Large
Stock General antiques
Open Fri–Sat 1–5.30pm

LARNE

⊞ Bric-A-Brac
Contact Mr J McIlwaine
✉ **4 Riverdale, Larne, Co Antrim, BT40 1LB** P
☎ 028 2827 5657
Est. 1974 *Stock size* Large
Stock General antiques including clocks, furniture, oil lamps, jewellery, paintings
Open Mon–Sat 9am–5.30pm Tues 9am–2pm

⊞ Cobwebs
Contact Mrs D Knox
✉ **94c Agnew Street, Larne, Co Antrim, BT40 1RE** P
☎ 028 2826 7127
Stock General antiques, clocks, antique fireplaces, antique pine
Open Wed–Sat 11.00am–4.30pm

⚒ Colin Wilkinson and Co (IRRV)
Contact Mr Colin Wilkinson
✉ **The Auction Mart, 7 Point Street, Larne, Co Antrim, BT40 1HY** P
☎ 028 2826 0037 Ⓕ 028 2826 0497
Est. 1900
Open Mon–Fri 9.30am–5pm
Sales General antiques, paintings, silver, porcelain
Frequency Monthly
Catalogues No

LISBURN

⊞ Trevor Falconer Antiques
Contact Trevor Falconer
✉ **51 Bridge Street, Lisburn, Co Antrim, BT28 1BZ** P
☎ 028 9260 5879
Ⓦ www.falconerantiques.co.uk
Est. 1984 *Stock size* Medium
Stock Antique country furniture, militaria, clocks, Irish pine
Open Mon–Sat 10am–5pm
Services Restoration and pine stripping

⊞ Jiri Books
Contact Jim and Rita Swindall
✉ **11 Mill Road, Lisburn, Co Antrim, BT27 5TT** P
☎ 028 9082 6443 Ⓕ 028 9082 6443
Ⓔ jiri.books@dnet.co.uk
Est. 1978 *Stock size* Medium
Stock Largely Irish interest, second-hand and antiquarian books
Open By appointment only
Fairs Organizes the Second-hand and Antiquarian Bookfair (part of the Belfast Festival)
Services Book searches

⊞ Parvis (IADA)
Contact Parvis or Meriel Sigaroudinia
✉ **Mountain View House, 40 Sandy Lane, Ballyskeagh, Lisburn, Co Antrim, BT27 5TL** P
☎ 028 9062 1824 Ⓕ 028 9062 3311
Ⓜ 07801 347358
Ⓔ parvissig@aol.com
Ⓦ www.parvis.co.uk
Est. 1973 *Stock size* Large
Stock General antiques and fine art
Open By appointment at any time
Fairs IADA Exhibition, Northern Ireland Antiques Fair
Services Valuations, restoration, consultancy, own exhibitions

⊞ Van-Lyn Antiques
Contact V or W Hastings
✉ **300 Comber Road, Lisburn, Co Antrim, BT27 6TA** P
☎ 028 9263 8358
Ⓜ 07899 935990
Ⓔ vanlunantiques@aol.com
Est. 1979 *Stock size* Medium
Stock General, antique furniture, porcelain, brass, glass, books, clocks
Open Mon–Sat 9am–9pm
Fairs Kings Hall, Belfast

NEWTOWNABBEY

⊞ MacHenry Antiques (IADA)
Contact Rupert or Anne MacHenry
✉ **1–7 Glen Road, Jordanstown, Newtownabbey, Co Antrim, BT37 0RY** P
☎ 028 9086 2036 Ⓕ 028 9085 3281
Ⓜ 07831 135226
Ⓔ rupertmachenry@ntlworld.com
Est. 1964 *Stock size* Medium
Stock 18th–19thC furniture, paintings
Open Fri–Sat 2–7pm or by appointment
Fairs IADA
Services Valuation for insurance, probate and family division, restoration

⚒ Wilson's Auctions (NAVA, IAVI)
Contact Mr Richard Bell
✉ **22 Mallusk Road, Newtownabbey, Co Antrim, BT36 8PP** P
☎ 028 9034 2626 Ⓕ 028 9034 2528
Ⓔ richardbell@wilsonsauctions.com
Ⓦ www.wilsonsauctions.com
Est. 1964
Open Mon–Fri 9am–6pm, viewing Sun noon–5pm
Sales Quarterly sales of Irish art. Other specialist sales throughout the year
Catalogues Yes

PORTRUSH

⊞ Alexander Antiques
Contact Mr David Alexander
✉ **108 Dunluce Road, Portrush, Co Antrim, BT56 8NB** P
☎ 028 7082 2783 Ⓕ 028 7082 2364
Ⓔ sales@alexanderantiques.com
Ⓦ www.alexanderantiques.com
Est. 1973 *Stock size* Large

Stock Georgian–Edwardian furniture
Open Mon–Sat 10am–5.30pm
Services Valuations, restoration

Atlantic Antiques
Contact Mr Samuel Dickie
22 Portstewart Road, Portrush, Co Antrim, BT56 8EQ
028 7082 5988
Est. 1997 *Stock size* Medium
Stock General antiques
Open Mon–Sat 11am–6pm Sun 2–6pm

Kennedy Wolfenden
Contact Miss Eleanor Wolfenden
86 Main Street, Portrush, Co Antrim, BT56 8BN
028 7082 2995 F 028 7082 5587
M 07831 453038
E eleanorwolfenden@hotmail.com
W www.kwauctionsni.co.uk
Est. 1974 *Stock size* Large
Stock Antique furniture, porcelain, jewellery, silver and paintings
Open Mon–Sat 11am–5.30pm Jul–Aug later
Services Valuations

TOOMEBRIDGE

Past & Present Antiques
Contact Colin Paul
21 Hillhead Road, Toomebridge, Co Antrim, BT41 3SF P
028 7965 9603
M 07802 657692
Est. 1998 *Stock size* Large
Stock General antiques
Open Tues–Sat 10.30am–5pm
Services Valuations, restoration

CO ARMAGH

ARMAGH

Craobh Rua Books (PBFA)
Contact Mr James Vallely
12 Woodford Gardens, Armagh, Co Armagh, BT60 2AZ
028 3752 6938
E Craobh@btinternet.com
Est. 1990 *Stock size* Medium
Stock Books, prints, selection of newspaper prints relating to 19thC Ireland
Open By appointment only
Fairs The Rare Book Fair, Dublin
Services Catalogue, mail order

CRAIGAVON

Craigavon Marble Products
Contact Pat McIlduff
9 Ulster Street Industrial Estate, Lurgan, Craigavon, Co Armagh, BT67 9AN P
028 3832 6736 F 028 3832 7764
E craigavonmarble@btopenworld.com
W www.craigavonmarble.co.uk
Est. 2000 *Stock size* Medium
Stock Antique marble, cast iron, wooden fireplaces,
Open By appointment
Services Valuations, restoration

LOUGHGALL

Huey's Antique Shop
Contact Bill Huey
45–47 Main Street, Loughgall, Co Armagh, BT61 8HZ P
028 3889 1248
M 07721 844153
E billhuey@loughgallantiques.freeserve.co.uk
Est. 1973 *Stock size* Medium
Stock General antiques
Open Mon–Fri 2–6pm Sat 10.30am–6pm

MOIRA

Four Winds Antiques
Contact Mr John Cairns
96 Main Street, Moira, Co Armagh, BT67 0LH P
028 9261 2226
M 07768 292369 (John) or 07713 081748 (Tina)
Est. 1994 *Stock size* Large
Stock Georgian–Edwardian furniture, porcelain, longcase and bracket clocks
Open Mon–Sat 10am–5.30pm or by appointment

PORTADOWN

Wilson's Auctions Ltd (Portadown) (NAVA, IAVI)
Contact Michael Tomalin
65 Seagoe Industrial Estate, Portadown, Craigavon, Co Armagh, T63 5QE P
028 3833 6433 F 028 3833 6618
E mtomalin@virgin.net
W www.wilsons-auctions.com
Est. 1964
Open Mon–Fri 9am–6pm and on auction nights
Sales Antiques, fine art and disposal auctions Wed 7pm. Advisable to telephone ahead for sale details
Catalogues Yes

CO DOWN

BALLYNAHINCH

Davidson Books
Contact Mr Arthur Davidson
34 Broomhill Road, Spa, Ballynahinch, Co Down, BT24 8QD P
028 9756 2502 F 028 9756 2502
Est. 1959 *Stock size* Large
Stock Antiquarian books, especially Irish
Open By appointment only
Fairs Annual Belfast Second-hand and Antiquarian Bookfair
Services Valuations

The French Warehouse
Contact Heather Cowdy
72 Dunmore Road, Spa, Ballynahinch, Co Down, BT24 8PR P
028 975 61774
E frenchwarehouse@nireland.com
W www.french-warehouse.com
Est. 1988 *Stock size* Large
Stock Antique French beds, 19thC French furniture
Open By appointment
Services Shipping

BANGOR

Annville Antiques
Contact A Chambers
28 Grays Hill, Bangor, Co Down, BT20 3BB P
028 9145 2522
Est. 1984 *Stock size* Small
Stock General antiques
Open Mon–Sat 10.30am–4.30pm

Balloo Moon Antiques
Contact Marie Erwin
Unit 30, Balloo Drive, Bangor, Co Down, BT19 7QY P
028 9145 6886 F 028 9145 3183

Est. 1979 *Stock size* Large
Stock General antiques
Open Mon–Sat 10am–5.30pm

Todd Antiques
Contact Mrs E Heyes
30 Gray's Hill, Bangor, Co Down, BT20 3BB P
028 9145 5850
Est. 1988 *Stock size* Medium
Stock Silver jewellery, clocks, small furniture items
Open Tues–Sat 9.30am–4.30pm closed Thurs
Services Clock and jewellery repairs

DONAGHADEE

Antiquarian Booksellers
Contact M C McAlister
Prospect House, 4 Millisle Road, Donaghadee, Co Down, BT21 0HY P
028 9188 2990 F 028 9188 2990
rarebooks.phb@btopenworld.com
www.antiquarianbookslellers.co.uk
Est. 1981 *Stock size* Medium
Stock Antiquarian and out-of-print books, Ireland, travel, fine buildings and natural history specialities
Open Strictly by appointment only
Fairs Wellington Park (Nov)

Phyllis Arnold Gallery Antiques
Contact Ms Phyllis Arnold
4a Shore Street, Donaghadee, Co Down, BT21 0DG P
028 9188 8199/9185 3122
F 028 9185 3322
marnold@lowryhill.freeserve.co.uk
www.antiquesni.com
Est. 1973 *Stock size* Medium
Stock Maps, prints, furniture, silver, general
Open Wed–Sat 11am–5pm
Services Framing, conservation

Blue Dot Antiques
Contact Sam Parkinson or Peter Bailie
4 Parade, Donaghadee, Co Down, BT21 0AE P
028 9188 3436
M 07775 805362
sam.parkinson@tiscali.co.uk
www.bluedotantiques.com
Est. 2002 *Stock size* Medium
Stock General antiques, collectables
Open Mon–Sat 11am–6pm Sun 2–6pm
Services Valuations

DUNDONALD

Stacks Bookshop
Contact Mr Jim Tollerton
67 Comber Road, Dundonald, Co Down, BT16 OAE P
028 9048 6880
Est. 1992 *Stock size* Medium
Stock Antiquarian Irish, religious, military and poetry books
Open Mon–Sat 10am–6pm
Fairs Belfast Second-hand and Antiquarian Bookfair

GREYABBEY

Archway Antiques
Contact Mrs Boo Hughes
Hoops Courtyard, Main Street, Greyabbey, Newtownards, Co Down, BT22 2NE P
028 4278 8889
M 07703 330900
Est. 1989 *Stock size* Large
Stock 18th–19thC porcelain, 19thC glass, jewellery, furniture, silver, kitchenware, linen, pictures
Open Wed Fri Sat 11am–5pm or by appointment
Fairs Ulster Antique and Fine Art Fair, Culloden
Services Valuations, house clearances

HOLYWOOD

Jacquart Antiques
Contact Mr Dan Uprichard
10–12 Hibernia Street, Holywood, Co Down, BT18 9JE P
028 9042 6642 F 028 9752 1109
M 07831 548803
jacquart@nireland.com
www.jacquart.co.uk
Est. 1992 *Stock size* Large
Stock Imported French antiques, mainly 19th century furniture (walnut, oak), mirrors, rare items
Open Mon–Sat 10am–5.30pm or by appointment
Fairs Ulster Antique and Fine Art Fair
Services Interior-design item search

KILLYLEAGH

Tout Le Monde
Contact Mr Tony Forsyth
12–14 Shore Street, Killyleagh, Co Down, BT30 9QJ P
028 4482 8509 F 028 4482 8509
aforsyth@mac.com
wwwtoutlemonde.co.uk
Est. 1998 *Stock size* Medium
Stock Old country furniture, French, Chinese, Irish antiques
Open Mon–Sat 9am–5pm or by appointment

NEWTOWNARDS

Ballyalton House Architectural Antiques (SALVO)
Contact Leonard Cave
Ballyalton House, 39 Ballyrainey Road, Newtownards, Co Down, BT23 5AD P
028 9181 3235 F 028 9181 3235
andrew@ballyalton.freeserve.co.uk
www.ballyalton.freeserve.co.uk
Est. 1993 *Stock size* Large
Stock General architectural antiques, largest stock of bathrooms in Ireland. Newly quarried stone, granite
Open Mon–Sat 8am–6pm

Bangor Auctions
Contact Mr G Holden-Downes
11 Greenway Industrial Estate, Conlig, Newtownards, Co Down, BT23 7SU P
028 9145 0494 F 028 9127 5993
info@bangorauctions.co.uk
www.bangorauctions.co.uk
Est. 1991
Open Mon Tues Fri 9am–5pm
Sales General antiques sales every Thurs 6pm
Catalogues Yes

Castle Antiques
Contact Peter Moore
6 Regency Manor, Newtownards, Co Down, BT23 8ZD P
028 9181 5710
M 07989 501666
info@castleantiques.co.uk
www.castleantiques.co.uk
Est. 1989 *Stock size* Medium
Stock Art Deco ceramics, enamel signs
Open By appointment only

⊞ Old Forge Collectables
Contact David Eynon
✉ **17 Old Forge Crescent, Newtownards, Co Down, BT23 8GQ** Ⓟ
☎ 028 91 810422
Ⓜ 07743 261487
ⓔ david.eynon1@btopenworld.com
Est. 1987 *Stock size* Medium
Stock Royal Doulton
Open By appointment
Services Valuations

PORTAFERRY

⊞ Time & Tide Antiques (IADA, MAPH)
Contact Mr David Dunlop
✉ **36 Shore Road, Portaferry, Co Down, BT22 1JZ** Ⓟ
☎ 028 4272 8935 Ⓕ 028 4272 9825
Ⓜ 07732 323635
ⓔ david@timeandtideantiques.net
ⓦ www.timeandtideantiques.net
Est. 1990 *Stock size* Large
Stock Clocks, barometers, nautical items, marine instruments, fine small furniture
Open Wed Fri Sat Sun noon–5.30pm or by appointment
Fairs Ulster Antique and Fine Art Fair
Services Restoration

SAINTFIELD

⊞ Agar Antiques
Contact Rosie Agar
✉ **92 Main Street, Saintfield, Co Down, BT24 7AB** Ⓟ
☎ 028 9751 1214
Est. 1991 *Stock size* Medium
Stock Victorian furniture, ceramics, jewellery, Oriental antiques, Delftware, lighting
Open Tues–Sat 11am–5pm
Services Valuations

⊞ Antiques at the Stile
Contact Mr Graham Hancock
✉ **52 Main Street, Saintfield, Co Down, BT24 7AB** Ⓟ
☎ 028 9751 0844
Ⓜ 07831 587078
Est. 1989 *Stock size* Large
Stock Georgian–Edwardian furniture, clocks, porcelain
Open Tues–Sat 10am–5.30pm or by appointment
Services Valuations

⊞ Attic Antiques
Contact Mr Reuben Doyle
✉ **90 Main Street, Saintfield, Co Down, BT24 7AB** Ⓟ
☎ 028 9751 1057
Ⓜ 07803 169799
Est. 1980 *Stock size* Large
Stock General antiques, jewellery, bric-a-brac, large selection of stripped pine
Open Mon–Fri 10am–5pm Sat 10am–5.30pm
Fairs Swinderby
Services Export worldwide, house clearance

⊞ Attic Pine
Contact Mr Reuben Doyle
✉ **88 Main Street, Saintfield, Co Down, BT24 7AB** Ⓟ
☎ 028 9751 1057
Est. 1996 *Stock size* Large
Stock Irish and Continental pine, reclaimed furniture
Open Mon–Sat 10am–5pm
Services Stripping

⊞ Christine Deane Antiques
Contact Christine Deane
✉ **90 Main Street, Saintfield, Co Down, BT24 7AB** Ⓟ
☎ 028 9751 1334
Stock size Medium
Stock Victorian–Edwardian small pieces of furniture, jewellery, silver, porcelain
Open Thurs–Sat 10.30am–4.30pm

⊞ Peter Francis Antiques
Contact Mr Peter Francis
✉ **92 Main Street, Saintfield, Co Down, BT24 7AD** Ⓟ
☎ 028 9751 1214
Est. 1997 *Stock size* Small
Stock Irish glass, pottery and Oriental antiques
Open Mon–Sat 11am–5pm
Services Valuations

⊞ Saintfield Antiques & Fine Books
Contact Mr Joseph Leckey
✉ **68 Main Street, Saintfield, Co Down, BT24 7AB** Ⓟ
☎ 028 9752 8428 Ⓕ 028 9752 8428
ⓔ home@antiquesireland.com
ⓦ www.antiquesireland.com
Est. 1982 *Stock size* Medium
Stock Porcelain 1750–1850, silver (especially Georgian), British and European glass, fine, antiquarian books
Open Thurs–Sat 11.30–5pm or by appointment
Fairs All fairs organised by L&M Fairs Ltd

SEAPATRICK

⊞ Mill Court Antiques
Contact Ms Gillian Close
✉ **99 Lurgan Road, Seapatrick, Banbridge, Co Down, BT32 4NE** Ⓟ
☎ 028 4066 2909
Est. 1979 *Stock size* Medium
Stock Furniture, ceramics, collectables, jewellery
Open Mon–Sat 11.30am–5.30pm closed Thurs
Services Valuations, restoration

CO FERMANAGH

BALLINAMALLARD

⊞ Ballindullagh Barn
Contact Mr Roy Armstrong
✉ **Ballindullagh, Ballinamallard, Co Fermanagh, BT94 2NY**
☎ 028 6862 1802
ⓔ diana@ballindullaghbarn.com
ⓦ www.ballindullaghbarn.com
Est. 1988 *Stock size* Large
Stock Pine country furniture
Open Mon–Sat 8am–6pm
Services Valuations, restoration

ENNISKILLEN

⊞ Cloughcor House Antiques
Contact Mr Ian Black
✉ **22 Shore Road, Enniskillen, Co Fermanagh, BT74 7EF** Ⓟ
☎ 028 6632 4805 Ⓕ 028 6632 8828
Ⓜ 07774 758827
Est. 1964 *Stock size* Large
Stock Victorian–Edwardian furniture, European pine, small silver wares
Open Mon–Sat 9.30am–5.30pm
Services Valuations, restoration and delivery

TEMPO

⊞ Marion Langham
Contact Marion Langham
✉ **Claranagh, Tempo,**

Co Fermanagh,
BT94 3FJ
☎ 028 8954 1247
ⓔ marion@ladymarion.co.uk
Ⓦ www.ladymarion.co.uk
Est. 1982 *Stock size* Large
Stock Belleek, paperweights
Open By appointment
Services Valuations, advice

CO LONDONDERRY

AGHADOWEY

Sarah Rose Antiques
Contact Mr Jim McCaughey
✉ **51 Ardreagh Road, Aghadowey, Coleraine, Co Londonderry, BT51 4DN** Ⓟ
☎ 028 7086 8722
Ⓦ www.srantiques.co.uk
Est. 1989 *Stock size* Medium
Stock General antiques, pine
Open Sat 10.30am–5.30pm

COLERAINE

The Forge Antiques
Contact Margaret or Graham Walker
✉ **24–26 Long Commons, Coleraine, Co Londonderry, BT52 1LH** Ⓟ
☎ 028 7035 1339
Est. 1966 *Stock size* Large
Stock Jewellery, silver, porcelain, furniture, clocks.
Open Mon–Sat 10am–5.30pm closed Thurs

Fountain Antique Studios & Workshop
Contact Ms Anne Morton
✉ **Fountain Villas, 31 Millburn Road, Coleraine, Co Londonderry, BT52 1QT** Ⓟ
☎ 028 703 52260 Ⓕ 028 703 54268
Ⓜ 07771 525650
ⓔ info@fountainantiques.co.uk
Est. 1989 *Stock size* Medium
Stock Kitchenware, furniture, stripped pine, porcelain
Open Mon–Sat 2–5.30pm or by appointment

KILREA

Beeswax Antiques
Contact Pat McNeill
✉ **6 Church Street, Kilrea, Co Londonderry, BT51 5QU**
☎ 028 2954 1104
Est. 1987 *Stock size* Large
Stock Mahogany and pine furniture, general smalls
Open Mon–Sat 10.30am–5.30pm
Fairs Newark
Services Valuations, restoration

LONDONDERRY

Foyle Antiques
Contact Mr John Helfery
✉ **The Old Farmhouse, 16 Whitehouse Road, Londonderry, BT48 0NE** Ⓟ
☎ 028 7126 7626 Ⓕ 028 7126 7626
ⓔ john@foyleantiques.com
Ⓦ foyleantiques.com
Est. 1984 *Stock size* Large
Stock Antiques and reproduction furniture. Showhouse with 16 furnished period rooms
Open Mon–Sat 10am–6pm Sun 2–6pm
Services Restoration, upholstery

Foyle Books
Contact Ken Thatcher or A Byrne
✉ **12 Magazine Street, Londonderry, BT48 6HH** Ⓟ
☎ 028 7137 2530
ⓔ ken@thatcher30.freeserve.uk
Est. 1989 *Stock size* Medium
Stock Antiquarian books, general, books on Derry and Donegal a speciality
Open Mon–Fri 11am–5pm Sat 10am–5pm
Services Valuations

Marcus Griffin Specialists in Silver Jewellery
Contact Ms Marcus Griffin
✉ **2 London Street, Londonderry, BT48 6RQ** Ⓟ
☎ 028 7130 9495
Est. 1974 *Stock size* Large
Stock General antiques, furniture, silver, fossils, objets d'art
Open Mon–Sat 10am–5pm
Fairs Newark

The Whatnot
Contact Ms Margot O'Dowd
✉ **22 Bishop Street, Londonderry, BT48 6TP**
☎ 028 7128 8333
Est. 1984 *Stock size* Medium
Stock General antiques
Open Mon–Sat 11am–5pm

PORTSTEWART

Irish Art Group (PTA)
Contact Michael Hughes
✉ **49 The Promenade, Portstewart, Co Londonderry, BT55 7AE** Ⓟ
☎ 028 7083 4600 Ⓕ 028 7083 4600
ⓔ michael@irishartgroup.com
Ⓦ www.irishartgroup.com
Est. 1982 *Stock size* Large
Stock Irish art, prints, collectables, maps, postcards, cigarette cards, fountain pens
Open Mon–Sat 9.30am–1pm 2–5pm
Fairs NEC Spring & Autumn
Services Catalogue (6 times a year)

CO TYRONE

AUGHNACLOY

Lucy Forsythe Antiques
Contact Mr Michael McNamee
✉ **The Old Rectory, 24 Carnteel Road, Aughnacloy, Co Tyrone, BT69 6DU** Ⓟ
☎ 028 7138 2223
Est. 1992 *Stock size* Small
Stock General antiques
Open Mon–Fri 10am–5.30pm Thurs 9.30am–1pm

BALLYCOLMAN

Melmount Auctions
Contact Mr Michael McNamee
✉ **Unit C, Ballycolman Industrial Estate, Ballycolman, Co Tyrone, BT82 9PH** Ⓟ
☎ 028 7138 2223
Est. 1992
Open Mon–Fri 10am–5.30pm Thurs 9.30am–1pm
Sales General antiques
Frequency Weekly
Catalogues Yes

BALLYGAWLEY

Keepers Cottage Antique Irish Pine
Contact Ann Ross
✉ **101 Kiloleeshill Road, Ballygawley, Co Tyrone, BT70 2HX** Ⓟ
☎ 028 8556 8765
Est. 1987 *Stock size* Medium
Stock Antique Irish pine and country furniture
Open Mon–Sat 9am–5pm
Services Valuations

Old Mill Antiques
Contact Michael and Rose Lippett
The Old Mill, Tulnavern Road, Ballygawley, Co Tyrone, BT70 2HH P
☎ 028 855 67470 F 028 855 67466
M 07831 866235
W www.oldmillantiques.ulsterguide.com
Est. 1970 *Stock size* Large
Stock General antiques
Open Mon–Sat 10am–5.30pm
Fairs Royal Dublin Society Show, King's Hall, Balmoral
Services Valuations

COOKSTOWN

Stamp Shop
Contact Peter McBride
Drumconvis House, Drumconvis Road, Coagh, Cookstown, Co Tyrone, BT8U 0HF P
☎ 028 8673 7804
M 0780 106 3379
E britishstamp@btinternet.com
Est. 1951 *Stock size* Large
Stock Stamps, medals, postcards, letters
Open By appointment
Services Valuations

MOY

Moy Antique Pine
Contact Mr Barry MacNeice
15 Charlemont Street, Moy, Dungannon, Co Tyrone, BT71 7SG P
☎ 028 8778 9909 F 028 8778 4895
M 07909 538784
E macneice@fsnet.co.uk
Est. 1974 *Stock size* Large
Stock General antiques
Open Mon–Sat 9am–6pm
Services Freestanding kitchens made with antique wood

Moy Antiques
Contact Mr Lawrence MacNeice
12 The Square, Moy, Dungannon, Co Tyrone, BT71 7SG P
☎ 028 8778 4895/4755
F 028 8778 4895
E sales@moyantiques.freeserve.co.uk
Est. 1979 *Stock size* Large
Stock General antique furniture, garden statues, original marble fireplaces
Open Mon–Sat 9.30am–6pm
Fairs Newark, Ardingly
Services Valuations

OMAGH

Dromore Road Auction Rooms
Contact Mr Oliver Gormley
Unit 3, Dromore Road Industrial Estate, Omagh, Co Tyrone, BT78 1QZ P
☎ 028 8224 7738 F 028 8225 2797
E info@gormleys.ie
W www.gormleys.ie
Est. 1989
Open Mon–Sat 9am–6pm
Sales Regular sales of antiques and paintings
Catalogues Yes

Gormley's Fine Art & Antiques
Contact Mr Oliver Gormley
Unit 4, Dromore Road, Omagh, Co Tyrone, BT78 IRE P
☎ 028 8224 7738 F 028 8225 2797
E oliver@gormleys.ie
W www.gormleys.ie
Est. 1989 *Stock size* Large
Stock Paintings, general antiques
Open Mon Tues Fri Sat 9am–6pm Wed Thurs 9am–8.30pm
Fairs Newark
Services Valuations, restoration

Kelly Antiques
Contact Mr Louis Kelly
Mullaghmore House, Old Mountfield Road, Omagh, Co Tyrone, BT79 7EX P
☎ 028 8224 2314 F 028 8225 0262
E sales@kellyantiques.com
W www.kellyantiques.com/mullaghmorehouse.com
Est. 1936 *Stock size* Large
Stock Period fireplaces, hardwood furniture, bedroom suites, tables, chairs, lighting
Open Mon–Fri 10am–7pm Sat 10am–5pm
Services Restoration, private auctions. Full-time course in antique furniture restoration

Viewback Auctions
Contact Mr G Simpson
8–10 Castle Place, Omagh, Co Tyrone, BT78 5ER P
☎ 028 8224 6271 F 028 8224 6271
M 07760 275247
E viewback@talk21.com
W www.viewbackantiqueauctions.com
Est. 1979 *Stock size* Large
Stock General antiques
Open Mon–Sat 10am–6pm
Fairs Newark

Viewback Auctions
Contact Mr G Simpson
8–10 Castle Place, Omagh, Co Tyrone, BT78 5ER P
☎ 028 8224 6271 F 028 8224 6271
M 07760 275247
E viewback@talk21.com
W www.viewbackantiqueauctions.com
Est. 1979
Open Mon–Sat 10am–6pm
Sales Auctions of household effects and antiques once a month or more often. See website for details

STEWARTSTOWN

Silversaddle Antiques
Contact Vivian Smith
1 West Street, Stewartstown, Co Tyrone, BT71 5HT P
☎ 028 8773 8088
Est. 1900 *Stock size* Large
Stock Georgian–Edwardian furniture, clocks, Victorian chandeliers
Open Mon–Sat noon–6pm
Services Valuations, restoration

P J Smith (Fair Trades)
Contact Patrick Smith
1 North Street, Stewartstown, Co Tyrone, BT71 5JE P
☎ 028 8773 8071
W ww.pjsmith-antique-fireplace.co.uk
Est. 1979 *Stock size* Large
Stock Antique fireplaces, stained glass, beds
Open Mon–Fri 10.30am–1pm 1.40–6pm Thurs until 9pm Sat 10.30am–6pm
Services Restoration

REPUBLIC OF IRELAND

DONEGAL
Carndonagh
Donegal
Bundoran
NORTHERN IRELAND
Sligo
Manorhamilton
SLIGO
MAYO
Castlebar
Westport
Monaghan
MONAGHAN
Castleblayney
Fenagh
Boyle
LEITRIM
Cavan
Carrickmacross
Dundalk
CAVAN
ROSCOMMON
Virginia
LOUTH
Longford
LONGFORD
Ceanannus Mor (Kells)
Drogheda
Tuam
Balbriggan
WESTMEATH
MEATH
GALWAY
Athlone
Kinnegad
Galway
Ballinasloe
Maynooth
DUBLIN
Dublin
Black Rock
OFFALY
Aran Islands
Loughrea
Portumna
KILDARE
Gort
Birr
Bray
CLARE
LAOIS
WICKLOW
Ennis
Wicklow
Rathdrum
Carlow
Freshford
CARLOW
Limerick
Foynes
Kilkenny
TIPPERARY
Gorey
LIMERICK
KILKENNY
Tipperary
Tralee
Cahir
Clonmel
WEXFORD
Dingle
Mallow
Fermoy
Wexford
KERRY
WATERFORD
Waterford
Cahirciveen
CORK
Saltee Islands
Cork
Bantry
Skibbereen
Fastnet Rock
The international dialling code for the Republic of Ireland is 00353

CO CARLOW

BORRIS

Joe Dunne Auctioneers & Valuers (IAVI)
Contact Joe Dunne
Borris, Co Carlow, Ireland
050 373191 050 373536
movehome@dunnesofborris.ie
www.dunnesofborris.ie
Est. 1984
Open Tues–Sat 9.30am–5pm
Sales Antiques and general household, antiques sales twice yearly
Frequency Every 6 weeks
Catalogues Yes

CO CAVAN

BALLINEA

F J McAvenues & Son
Contact Dennis McAvenues
7 Lower Bridge Street, Ballinea, Co Cavan, Ireland
04995 22204
deninc@eircom.net
Est. 1964 *Stock size* Large
Stock General antiques, furniture, jewellery, silver, clocks
Open Mon–Fri 2–6pm Sat Sun 11am–5pm
Services Valuations

CO CLARE

CLARECASTLE

The Antique Loft
Contact Paul Walsh
Barrack Street, Clarecastle, Co Clare, Ireland
065 6841969 065 6841969
Est. 1991 *Stock size* Large
Stock Victorian–Edwardian furniture, collectables, Persian rugs, carpets
Open Mon–Sat 9am–6.30pm
Services Valuations, restoration

ENNIS

Tony Honan
Contact Mr Tony Honan
14 Abbey Street, Ennis, Co Clare, Ireland
065 682 8137
Est. 1974 *Stock size* Large
Stock Clocks, oil lamps, jewellery
Open Mon–Sat 10am–6pm

CO CORK

BALLYDEHOB

Schull Books
Contact Barbara or Jack O'Connell
Ballydehob, Co Cork, Ireland
028 37317 028 37317
schullbooks@eircom.net
www.schullbooks.com
Est. 1981 *Stock size* Medium
Stock Antiquarian books, second-hand books, military history a speciality
Open June–Sept Mon–Sat 11am–6pm other times by appointment
Fairs All major Irish book fairs
Services Valuations

BANDON

Galvins Antiques
Contact Maisie Galvin
Clonakilty Road, Bandon, Co Cork, Ireland
023 20983 023 20555
Est. 1991 *Stock size* Medium
Stock Antiques and collectables
Open Tues–Sat 10am–5pm closed 1–2pm

CHARLEVILLE

Fortlands Antiques (IADA)
Contact Mary or Carol O'Connor
Fortlands, Charleville, Co Cork, Ireland
063 81295 063 81295
Est. 1974 *Stock size* Large
Stock Georgian–Victorian furniture, silver, brass, china, objets d'art
Open Mon–Sat 11am–5pm Sun 2–5pm
Fairs Irish Antique Dealers' Fair
Services Valuations, restoration

P J O'Gorman MIPAV Auctioneers (IPAV)
Contact P J O'Gorman
Chapel Street, Charleville, Co Cork, Ireland
063 81407 063 81604
ogormanpj@eirecom.net
Est. 1968
Open Mon–Fri 10am–5.30pm Sat Sun by appointment
Sales Furniture sales
Frequency Quarterly
Catalogues Yes

CLONAKILTY

Boyle's Antiques
Contact Joyce Boyle
35 Ashe Street, Clonakilty, Co Cork, Ireland
02334 222
Est. 1993 *Stock size* Small
Stock Jewellery, silver
Open Mon–Sat 10am–6pm closed Wed Jan–Mar Thurs–Sat only
Services Valuations

CORK

Antiques & Curios Centre
Contact Liam Hurley
Upper Johns Street, Cork, Ireland
021 427 9995
Est. 1987 *Stock size* Large
Stock Country furniture, general antiques
Open Mon–Sat 10am–5pm

Georgian Antiques (LAPADA, CINOA, IADA)
Contact Patrick Jones
21 Lavitts Quay, Cork, Ireland
021 427 8153 021 427 9365
0872 563721
info@georgianantiquesltd.com
www.georgianantiquesltd.com
Est. 1998 *Stock size* Large
Stock 18th–19thC Irish, English and continental European furniture, decorations
Open Mon–Fri 2–5pm Sat 10am–5pm
Fairs Irish Antique Dealers' Fair, The Annual Cork Antiques Fair

Helga's Antiques
Contact Helga McCarthy Cleary or John McCarthy
7 Cross Street, Cork, Ireland
021 427 0034 021 487 8954
0868 727075
helgasantiques@eircom.net
Est. 1994 *Stock size* Large
Stock General antiques, jewellery, furniture

Open Mon–Sat 10am–5pm or by appointment
Services Valuations, restoration, French polishing

Ann McCarthy
Contact Ann McCarthy
2 Paul's Lane, Huguenot Quarter, Cork, Ireland
021 427 3755
Est. 1985 *Stock size* Large
Stock Silver, linen, china, glass, lace
Open Mon–Sat 10am–6pm
Services Valuations

Mills Antiques
Contact David Coon or Orla Clarke
3 Paul's Lane, Huguenot Centre, Cork, Ireland
021 427 3528
davidcoon@eircom.net
Est. 1981 *Stock size* Large
Stock General small items, small furniture, paintings, prints, objets d'art
Open Mon–Sat 10.30am–6pm
Services Painting and frame restoration

Monas Antiques
Contact Monica Noonan
79 Oliver Plunkett Street, Cork, Ireland
021 427 8171
Est. 1988 *Stock size* Large
Stock Antique jewellery
Open Mon–Sat 11am–6pm

Moylurg Antiques
Contact T MacDermot-Roe
The Mall, Castletownshend, Cork, Ireland
028 36396
moylurgantiques@eircom.net
Est. 1993 *Stock size* Small
Stock General antiques, picture frames
Open June–Sept Thurs–Sun 11am–7pm
Services Valuations, picture framing

Noble Antique Fireplaces
Contact James O'Driscoll
Unit 1C, Southside Industrial Estate, Pouladuff Road, Cork, Ireland
021 432 3477 F 021 432 3477
Est. 1983 *Stock size* Large
Stock Antiques
Open Mon–Sat 9.30am–5.30pm Sun by appointment
Services Valuations, restoration

Diana O'Mahony Antiques & Jewellery (IADA, BGA)
Contact Diana or Niamh O'Mahony
8 Winthrop Street, Cork, Ireland
021 427 6599
Est. 1970 *Stock size* Large
Stock Victorian jewellery, diamond pieces, Georgian–Victorian silver, Cork and Dublin silver, small furniture
Open Mon–Sat 9.30am–5.30pm
Services Valuations, pearl restringing, remounting

The People's Gallery
Contact Donal O'Regan
2 Fenns Quay, Shares Street, Cork, Ireland
021 422 3577
Est. 1973 *Stock size* Large
Stock English and Irish art
Open Tues–Sun 9am–5pm
Services Valuations

Royal Carberry Books
Contact Gerald Feehan
36 Beechwood Park, Ballinlough, Cork, Ireland
021 429 4191 F 021 429 4191
mgfeehan@eircom.net
Est. 1976 *Stock size* Medium
Stock Antiquarian and out-of-print books, books of Irish interest, postcards
Open By appointment only
Fairs All major Irish book fairs
Services Valuations and book search facility

Stokes Clocks and Watches Ltd
Contact Philip Stokes
48 MacCurtain Street, Cork, Ireland
021 455 1195 F 021 450 9125
stokesclocks@eircom.net
Est. 1969 *Stock size* Large
Stock Clocks, watches, barometers
Open Mon–Fri 9.15am–6pm Sat 10am–5pm
Services Valuations, restoration, repairs

Victoria's Antiques
Contact Ms Frances Lynch
2 Oliver Plunkett Street, Cork, Ireland
021 427 2752 F 021 427 8814
Est. 1987 *Stock size* Large
Stock Jewellery, silver gifts, small items of furniture
Open Mon–Sat 10.30am–6pm
Services Valuations, restoration

Joseph Woodward & Sons Ltd (IAVI)
Contact Tom Woodward
26 Cook Street, Cork, Ireland
021 427 3327 F 021 427 2891
auctions@woodward.ie
www.woodward.ie
Est. 1883
Open Mon–Fri 9am–5.30pm
Sales Antiques, paintings, silver, porcelain. Twice-yearly specialist Irish silver auctions. Internet catalogues available
Frequency Monthly
Catalogues Yes

FERMOY

Country Furniture
Contact Seamus Kirby
Johnstown, Fermoy, Co Cork, Ireland
025 38244 F 025 38244
M 0868 126883
mkirby@aol.ie
Est. 1990 *Stock size* Large
Stock Antique fireplaces, pine, salvage
Open Mon–Sat 9am–6pm Sun 2–6pm other times by appointment only
Services Pine stripping, house renovation, kitchens

KINSALE

Linda's Antiques
Contact Linda or Laura Walsh
Main Street, Kinsale, Co Cork, Ireland
021 477 4754 F 021 477 7582
M 0872 502467
lindasjewellery@eircom.net
Est. 1992
Stock Jewellery, silver, books, prints, oil paintings, watercolours, porcelain, objets d'art
Open Mon–Sat 10.30am–5.30pm Sun 2–6pm
Fairs Cork Antiques Fair

Trading House
Contact Katarina Runske, Olivier Bouche or Carole Norman
54 Main Street, Kinsale, Co Cork, Ireland P
☎ 021 477 7497 F 021 477 3517
M 08724 94722
E katarinarunske@eircom.net
Est. 2000 *Stock size* Medium
Stock Furniture
Open Mon–Sat 10am–6pm Sun 2–6pm

LEAP

Ovne Antique Stoves
Contact Tom Keane or Claire Graham
Main Street, Leap, Co Cork, Ireland P
☎ 028 34917
M 0868 555635
E info@ovnestoves.com
W www.ovnestoves.com
Est. 1990 *Stock size* Medium
Stock Antique stoves from all around the world 1840–1950
Open Mon–Sat 10am–6pm

MALLOW

Aidan Foley Antiques
Contact Aidan Foley
Munster House, Doneraile, Mallow, Co Cork, Ireland P
☎ 022 24557 F 022 829 0680
E sales@irishcountryhome.com
W www.irishcountryhome.com
Est. 1995 *Stock size* Large
Stock Georgian–Victorian mahogany furniture
Open Mon–Fri 9am–5pm
Services Shipping

Lee Hindharsh Antiques
Contact Lee Hindharsh
Main Street, Doneraile, Mallow, Co Cork, Ireland P
☎ 022 24862 F 0876 160036
Est. 2001 *Stock size* Large
Stock Furniture
Open Mon–Sat 9am–6pm
Services Restoration

McMahon's Antiques
Contact Mr McMahon
Dromagh, Mallow, Co Cork, Ireland P
☎ 029 78119
Est. 1977 *Stock size* Large
Stock Pre-1940 general antiques
Open Mon–Sat 10am–9pm Sun noon–9pm

O'Shaughnessy Antiques
Contact Vincent Michiels
Main Street, Doneraile, Mallow, Co Cork, Ireland P
☎ 022 24859 F 086 880 7574
Est. 1993 *Stock size* Medium
Stock Mahogany furniture
Open By appointment

Old Schoolhouse Auction Rooms
Contact Aidan Foley
Main Street, Doneraile, Mallow, Co Cork, Ireland P
☎ 086 829 0680
W www.irishcountryhome.com
Est. 1990
Open Mon–Fri 9am–5pm
Sales Regular general and antiques auctions
Frequency Monthly
Catalogues Yes

Schoolhouse Antiques
Contact John Murphy
Main Street, Doneraile, Mallow, Co Cork
☎ 022 24972 F 087 214 4389
Est. 1990 *Stock size* Large
Stock Antiques, collectables
Open By appointment

MIDLETON

Rostellan Antiques Ltd
Contact Fran Philpott
Rostellan, Midleton, Co Cork, Ireland P
☎ 021 466 1100
E fran6@eirecom.net
Est. 1996 *Stock size* Large
Stock General antiques
Open Sat Sun 2–6pm and by appointment

SCHULL

Fuschia Books
Contact Ms Mary Mackey
Main Street, Schull, Co Cork, Ireland P
☎ 028 28016 F 028 28016
E fuschiabooks@eircom.net
W www.fuschiabooks.com
Est. 1984 *Stock size* Small
Stock Antiquarian stock, especially Irish books, prints
Open Mon–Sat summer 10am–6pm winter 11am–4pm
Services Valuations and book searches

CO DONEGAL

BUNDORAN

Vincent McGowan Antiques
Contact Mr Vincent McGowan
2–3 Main Street, Bundoran, Co Donegal, Ireland P
☎ 072 41536
Est. 1981 *Stock size* Medium
Stock Georgian–Edwardian furniture, small items, clocks, jewellery, Belleek
Open By appointment
Services Valuations, restoration

CARNDONAGH

The Bookshop
Contact Mr Michael Herron
Court Place, Pound Street, Carndonagh, Co Donegal, Ireland P
☎ 074 93 74389 F 074 93 74313
Est. 1987 *Stock size* Large
Stock Irish interest, science, 19thC antiquarian section, general books
Open Mon–Fri 2–6pm Sat 11am–6pm Sun 2–6pm
Fairs Annual Belfast Second-hand and Antiquarian Bookfair
Services Catalogues 4 or 5 a year

DONEGAL

Millcourt Antiques
Contact Tom Dooley
The Craft Village, Donegal, Ireland P
☎ 073 23222 F 073 23274
Est. 1995 *Stock size* Medium
Stock Georgian–Victorian furniture
Open Mon–Sat 9.30am–5.30pm
Services Valuations

Sean Thomas Antiques (IADA)
Contact Sean or Noreen Thomas
Killymard House, Donegal, Ireland P
☎ 073 35024
E killymard@esatclear.ie
Est. 1961 *Stock size* Small

Stock Interesting small items
Open Mon–Sat 10am–6pm
Services Valuations

DUNFANAGHY

The Gallery
Contact Alan and Moira Harley
Dunfanaghy, Co Donegal, Ireland P
☎ 074 913 6224
Est. 1968 *Stock size* Medium
Stock Silver, brass, Asian antiques, pottery, porcelain, jewellery, clocks, old prints, maps
Open Mon–Sat 10am–7pm

CO DUBLIN

BLACKROCK

Adams Blackrock (IAVI)
Contact Ms Martina Noonan
38 Main Street, Blackrock, Co Dublin, Ireland
☎ 01 288 5146 F 01 288 7820
E info@adamsblackrock.com
Est. 1947
Open Mon–Fri 9.30am–5.30pm
Sales 20 furniture fine art auctions per annum, 4 Irish and continental European paintings auctions per annum, 4 jewellery and silver sales per annum, regular house contents sales
Catalogues Yes

De Burca Rare Books (IADA, ABA)
Contact Mr Eamon de Burca
Cloonagashel, 27 Priory Drive, Blackrock, Co Dublin, Ireland P
☎ 01 288 2159 F 01 283 4080
E deburca@indigo.ie
W www.deburcararebooks.com
Stock Irish antiquarian fine books, maps, prints, manuscripts
Open Mon–Fri 9am–5.30pm Sat 10am–1pm
Fairs London and New York book fairs
Services Mail-order service, book search, valuations, book binding

HOK Fine Art (IAVI)
Contact Ms Sarah Kenny or Rory Guthrie
4 Main Street, Blackrock, Co Dublin, Ireland P
☎ 01 288 1000 F 01 288 0838
E fineart@hok.ie
W www.hokres.com
Est. 1944
Open Mon–Fri 9am–5pm
Sales Biannual fine art and furniture sales held at Royal Dublin Society. Blackrock fine art and furniture sales Wed every 6 weeks. House contents sales countrywide. Auctions of Irish art. Telephone for details
Catalogues Yes

Peter Linden Oriental Rugs and Carpets (IADA)
Contact Mr Peter Linden
15 George's Avenue, Blackrock, Co Dublin, Ireland P
☎ 01 288 5875 F 01 283 5616
E lindorient@hotmail.com
W www.peterlinden.com
Est. 1980 *Stock size* Large
Stock Oriental rugs, carpets, kilims, tapestries
Open Tues–Sat 10am–5.30pm
Fairs Irish Antique Dealers' Fair
Services Valuations, restoration

Treasure Chest Antiques
Contact Mr Norman Ludgate
49 Main Street, Blackrock, Co Dublin, Ireland P
☎ 01 288 9961
M 0872 831027
E treasurechest@iol.ie
Est. 1992
Stock Lighting, small furniture, silver, jewellery, clocks, watches, general antiques
Open Mon–Fri 11.30am–6.30pm Sat noon–6pm closed Thurs

DUBLIN

James Adam
26 St Stephen's Green, Dublin 2, Ireland P
☎ 01 676 0261 F 01 662 4725
E info@jamesadam.ie
W www.jamesadam.ie
Est. 1887
Open Mon–Fri 9am–5.30pm closed 1–2pm
Sales Specialist sales throughout the year of Irish art, vintage wine, militaria, toys and ceramics, modern and contemporary art, telephone for details
Catalogues Yes

Anthony Antiques Ltd (IADA, CINOA)
Contact Jeffrey or Roger Dell
7 Molesworth Street, Dublin 2, Ireland P
☎ 01 677 7222 F 01 677 7222
E anthonyantiques@oceanfree.net
W www.irelandantiques.com/anthony
Est. 1963 *Stock size* Large
Stock Decorative antique furniture, mirrors, brass, chandeliers
Open Mon–Sat 9am–6pm
Fairs Irish Antique Dealers' Fair

Antique Prints (IADA, CINOA)
Contact Hugh or Anne Iremonger
16 South Anne Street, Dublin 2, Ireland P
☎ 01 671 9523 or 01 269 8373
E antiqueprints_irl@yahoo.ie
Est. 1969
Stock 17th–20thC prints, maps, books, incunabulae, classical moderne original lithograhs
Open Mon–Sat 11am–5pm

Antique Time
Contact Martin Hennessey
1 The Hill, Mulhuddart Wood, Dublin 15, Ireland
☎ 01 820 7185
E mhenness@hotmail.com
Est. 2001 *Stock size* Medium
Stock Clocks, barometers
Open Tues–Sat 10am–5.30pm
Services Restoration, repair

Architectural Antiques and Salvage
Contact Mr S Bird or Mr S Flanagan
31 South Richmond Street, Dublin, Ireland P
☎ 01 478 4245 F 01 478 4245
W www.arcantiques.ie
Est. 1996 *Stock size* Medium
Stock Architectural salvage, fonts, statues, fireplaces, ecclesiastical items
Open Mon–Sat 10am–6pm

Architectural Classics
Contact Mr Niall McDonagh
South Gloucester Street, Dublin 2, Ireland P F 01 677 3318
M 086 8207700
E info@architecturalclassics.com

ⓦ www.architecturalclassics.com
Est. 1986 ***Stock size*** Large
Stock Antique lighting, door furniture, period fireplaces, garden statuary
Open Mon–Fri 9am–5.30pm Sat 10am–3pm
Fairs IADA Fairs, Dublin
Services Valuations, restoration

⊞ Christy Bird
Contact Christy Bird or Annette Mulkern
✉ **32 South Richmond Street, Portobello, Dublin 2, Ireland** 🅿
☎ 01 475 4049 ⓕ 01 475 8708
ⓔ paul@christybird.com
ⓦ www.christybird.com
Est. 1945 ***Stock size*** Medium
Stock Antiques, collectables
Open Mon–Sat 10am–6pm

⊞ Lorcan Brereton (IADA)
Contact Mr Diarmuid Brereton
✉ **29 South Anne Street, Dublin 2, Ireland**
☎ 01 677 1462 ⓕ 01 677 1125
Est. 1912
Stock Antique and modern jewellery, silver
Open Mon–Sat 9.15am–5.30pm
Fairs IADA
Services Valuations, restoration

⊞ Edward Butler (IADA)
Contact Peter or Elizabeth Bateman
✉ **14 Bachelor's Walk, Dublin 1, Ireland**
☎ 01 873 0296 ⓕ 01 873 0296
ⓜ 0872 486916
ⓔ bateman@iol.ie
ⓦ www.edwardbutlerantiques.com
Est. 1850 ***Stock size*** Medium
Stock Nautical and scientific instruments, 18th–19thC furniture, paintings, clocks
Open Mon–Fri 11am–4pm or by appointment
Fairs Irish Antique Dealers' Fair

⊞ Cathach Books Ltd (ABA, ILAB)
Contact Mr Enda Cunningham
✉ **10 Duke Street, Dublin 2, Ireland** 🅿
☎ 01 671 8676 ⓕ 01 671 5120
ⓔ cathach@rarebooks.ie
ⓦ www.rarebooks.ie
Est. 1964 ***Stock size*** Medium
Stock Specialists in antiquarian and rare books of Irish interest
Open Mon–Sat 9.30am–5.45pm
Services Valuations

⊞ Caxton Prints (IADA CINOA)
Contact Ronan Teevan or Liam Fitzpatrick
✉ **63 Patrick Street, Dublin 8, Ireland** 🅿
☎ 01 453 0060 ⓕ 01 453 0060
ⓜ 0872 429799
ⓔ caxton@vodaphone.ie
Est. 1989 ***Stock size*** Small
Stock Old Masters, 17th–18thC decorative prints
Open Mon–Sat 10.30am–5.30pm
Fairs Irish Antique Dealers' Fair
Services Valuations

⊞ Chapters Book and Music Store (BA)
Contact Mr William Kinsella
✉ **108–109 Middle Abbey Street, Dublin 1, Ireland** 🅿
☎ 01 872 3297 (books) 01 873 0484 (music) ⓕ 01 872 3044
ⓔ chaptersbookandmusicstore@eircom.net
Est. 1983 ***Stock size*** Large
Stock Antiquarian books, new, bargain, second-hand CDs, Irish music, DVDs, games
Open Mon–Sat 9.30am–6.30pm Thurs 9.30am–8pm Sun noon–6.30pm

⊞ Courtville Antiques (IADA, CINOA)
Contact Ms Grainne Pierse
✉ **Powerscourt Townhouse Centre, South William Street, Dublin 2, Ireland** 🅿
☎ 01 679 4042 ⓕ 01 679 4042
Est. 1964 ***Stock size*** Large
Stock Victorian and Art Deco jewellery, silver, paintings, decorative items
Open Mon–Sat 10am–6pm
Fairs Irish Antique Dealers' Fair
Services Commission purchasing

⊞ Delphi Antiques
Contact Mr Declan Corrigan
✉ **Powerscourt Townhouse Centre, South William Street, Dublin 2, Ireland** 🅿
☎ 01 679 0331
Est. 1987 ***Stock size*** Large
Stock Georgian–Edwardian jewellery, Continental and European ceramics, Irish Belleek
Open Mon–Sat 10.30am–5.30pm
Services Porcelain restoration

⊞ Michael Duffy Antiques
Contact Mr Michael Duffy
✉ **9–10 Parnell Street, Dublin 1, Ireland** 🅿
☎ 01 872 6928 ⓕ 01 872 6928
ⓜ 0872 562326
Est. 1949 ***Stock size*** Medium
Stock General Victorian antiques
Open Mon–Sat 10am–5pm

⊞ Samuel Elliot
Contact Mr Samuel Elliot
✉ **12 Fade Street, Dublin 2, Ireland** 🅿
☎ 01 671 1174
Est. 1961 ***Stock size*** Small
Stock Pocket watches, wrist watches, Rolex
Open Mon–Fri 9.30am–6pm Sat by appointment
Services Restoration

⊞ Euricka Antiques
Contact Alexandra Papadakis
✉ **2–7 The Coombe, Francis Street, Dublin 8, Ireland**
☎ 01 454 9779
Est. 1990 ***Stock size*** Small
Stock Furniture and general antiques
Open Mon–Sat 10am–6pm
Services Restoration

⊞ John Farrington Antiques (IADA)
Contact Mr John Farrington
✉ **32 Drury Street, Dublin 2, Ireland** 🅿
☎ 01 679 1899
ⓔ johnfarringtonantiques@eircom.net
Est. 1979 ***Stock size*** Large
Stock Fine-quality jewellery, silver, gilt mirrors
Open Tues–Sat 10.30am–5pm
Fairs Dublin Horse Show, Irish Antique Dealers' Fair

⊞ Flanagans Ltd
Contact Brian or Peter Flanagan
✉ **Deerpark Road, Mount Merrion, Dublin, Ireland** 🅿
☎ 01 288 0218 ⓕ 01 288 1336
ⓔ flan@iol.ie
ⓦ www.theflanagan.com
Est. 1974 ***Stock size*** Large

Stock Antique pianos, 19thC furniture
Open Mon–Sat 10am–6pm Thurs 10am–9pm
Services Restoration

Fleury Antiques (IADA)
Contact C or D Fleury
57 Francis Street, Dublin 8, Ireland
01 473 0878 01 473 0371
fleuryantiques@eircom.net
www.fleuryantiques.com
Est. 1979 *Stock size* Large
Stock 18th–19thC furniture, sculptures, paintings, decorative objects, porcelain, silver
Open Mon–Sat 9am–6pm

Herman & Wilkinson (IAVI)
Contact Mr David Herman or Mr Ray Wilkinson
161 Lower Rathmines Road, Dublin 6, Ireland
01 497 2245 01 496 2245
info@hermanwhite.ie
Est. 1970
Open Mon–Fri 9.30am–5.30pm
Sales Monthly antiques and fine art sales, Thurs 10am, viewing Wed 10am–9pm
Catalogues Yes

Patrick Howard Antiques (IADA)
Contact Patrick Howard
60 Francis Street, Dublin 8, Ireland
01 473 1126 01 473 1126
0872 331870
antiques@dublin.ie
www.patrickhowardantiques.com
Stock size Large
Stock Decorative Arts, furniture, paintings, prints and lighting
Open Mon–Sat 9.30am–6pm

The Jewel Casket (IADA)
Contact Mr Keith Cusack
17 South Anne Street, Dublin 2, Ireland
01 671 1262
Est. 1989 *Stock size* Large
Stock Antique jewellery, silver, curios
Open Tues–Sat 9.30am–6pm

Kevin Jones Antiques (IADA)
Contact Mr Kevin Jones
65–66 Francis Street, Dublin 8, Ireland
01 454 6626
0876 29790
jonesantiques@eircom.net
Est. 1989 *Stock size* Large
Stock 18th–19thC furniture, paintings, objets d'art
Open Mon–Sat 10am–5.30pm

Gerald Kenyon Antiques (IADA, CINOA)
Contact Mr Gerald A Kenyon
6 Great Strand Street, Dublin 1, Ireland
01 873 0625 01 873 0882
mark@kenyon-antiques.com
www.kenyon-antiques.com
Est. 1740 *Stock size* Medium
Stock Fine Georgian furniture, works of art, collectors' items
Open Mon–Fri 9am–6pm
Fairs Irish Antique Dealers' Fair, Dublin Antiques Fair
Services Interior decoration

Mitofsky Antiques (IADA)
Contact Anne Citron
8 Rathfarnham Road, Terenure, Dublin 6, Ireland
01 492 0033 01 492 0188
info@mintofskyartdeco.com
www.mintofskyartdeco.com
Est. 1994 *Stock size* Large
Stock Art Deco, Art Nouveau, Arts and Crafts
Open Mon–Sat 10am–5.30pm
Fairs The Kings Hall (Belfast), IADA

Neptune Gallery (IADA, FATG)
Contact Mr Andrew Bonar Law
41 South William Street, Dublin 2, Ireland
01 671 5021 01 671 5021
abl@nep.ie
Est. 1963 *Stock size* Medium
Stock Irish maps, prints, watercolours, books
Open Mon–Fri 10am–5.30pm Sat 10am–1pm
Fairs Irish Antique Dealers' Fair
Services Valuations, framing, restoration

Gordon Nichol Antiques (IADA CINOA)
Contact Mr Gordon Nichol
67–68 Francis Street, Dublin 8, Ireland
01 454 3322 01 473 5020
Est. 1985 *Stock size* Large
Stock 18th–19thC Irish, English and Continental furniture, chimney pieces, decorative objects
Open Mon–Sat 10.30am–4pm

O'Reillys (IAVI)
Contact Mr Michael Jordan
126 Francis Street, Dublin 8, Ireland
01 453 0311 01 453 0226
info@oreillysfineart.com
www.oreillysfineart.com
Est. 1952
Open Mon–Fri 9.30am–5pm
Sales Fine jewellery and silverware monthly sale Wed 1pm, viewing Sun noon–4pm Mon Tues 11am–6pm Wed 10am–12.30pm prior to sale
Catalogues Yes

O'Sullivan Antiques (IADA)
Contact Ms Chantal O'Sullivan
43–44 Francis Street, Dublin 8, Ireland
01 454 1143 01 454 1156
0862 543399
info@osullivanantiques.com
www.osullivanantiques.com
Est. 1991 *Stock size* Large
Stock 18th–19thC furniture, paintings, mirrors, chandeliers, mantelpieces, garden furniture
Open Mon–Fri 9am–6pm Sat 10am–6pm
Fairs Irish Antique Dealers' Fair
Services Restoration and upholstery

Rathmines Bookshop (BABI)
Contact Mr James Kinsella
201 Lower Rathmines Road, Dublin 6, Ireland
01 496 1064 01 496 1064
Est. 1986 *Stock size* Large
Stock Irish books, first editions
Open Mon–Sat 10am–7pm

Esther Sexton Antiques (IADA)
Contact Ms Esther Sexton
51 Francis Street, Dublin 8, Ireland
01 473 0909 *Stock size* Large
Stock Victorian and Edwardian

furniture, decorative items
Open Mon–Sat 10.30am–5.30pm
Fairs Irish Antique Dealers' Fair

The Silver Shop (IADA)
Contact Mr Ian Haslam
Powerscourt Townhouse Centre, South William Street, Dublin 2, Ireland
☎ 01 679 4147 Ⓕ 01 679 4147
Ⓔ ianhaslam@eircom.net
Est. 1979 *Stock size* Large
Stock 18th–19thC silver, porcelain, portrait miniatures
Open Mon–Sat 11am–6pm Thurs 11am–8pm
Fairs Irish Antique Dealers' Fair
Services Valuations

Stokes Books
Contact Mr Stephen Stokes
19 Market Arcade, South Great George's Street, Dublin 2, Ireland
☎ 01 671 3584 Ⓕ 01 671 3181
Ⓔ stokesbooks@oceanfree.net
Est. 1982 *Stock size* Small
Stock General antiquarian. Catalogues available, books on Irish history and literature a speciality
Open Mon–Sat 10.30am–5.30pm
Services Valuations for probate and insurance

Timepiece Antique Clocks (IADA)
Contact Kevin Chellar
57–58 Patrick Street, Dublin 8, Ireland
☎ 01 454 0774 Ⓕ 01 454 0744
Ⓜ 0872 260212
Ⓔ timepieceireland@eircom.net
Est. 1983 *Stock size* Large
Stock 18th–19thC clocks
Open Tues–Sat 10am–5pm
Fairs Irish Antique Dealers' Fair, Burlington Antiques Fair
Services Valuations, restoration

Jenny Vander
Contact Aidan or Gail Kinsella
50 Drury Street, Dublin 2, Ireland
☎ 01 677 0406
Est. 1964 *Stock size* Large
Stock Clothing (including evening dress), lace, 1930s–1950s, jewellery, Victorian–1960s
Open Mon–Sat 10am–5.30pm

The Victorian Salvage and Joinery Co Ltd (SALVO)
Contact Mark McDonagh
46–47 Townsend Street, Dublin 2, Ireland
☎ 01 672 7000 Ⓕ 01 672 7435
Ⓜ 0872 551299
Ⓔ vicsalv@indigo.ie
Ⓦ www.victorian-salvage.com
Est. 1999 *Stock size* Large
Stock Reclaimed building materials
Open Mon–Fri 8.30am–5.30 Sat 9am–2pm
Services Valuations, restoration, shipping

Weir and Sons Ltd
Contact Allan Kilpatrick
96–99 Grafton Street, Dublin 2, Ireland
☎ 01 677 9678 Ⓕ 01 677 7739
Ⓔ weirs@indigo.ie
Ⓦ www.weirandsons.com
Est. 1869 *Stock size* Large
Stock Silverware (especially Irish), jewellery, pocket and wrist watches
Open Mon–Sat 9.30am–6pm Thurs 9.30am–8pm
Services Valuations, restoration

J W Weldon (IADA)
Contact James or Martin Weldon
55 Clarendon Street, Dublin 2, Ireland
☎ 01 677 1638 Ⓕ 01 670 7958
Ⓔ antiques@weldonsofdublin.com
Ⓦ www.weldonsofdublin.com
Est. 1900 *Stock size* Large
Stock Irish and diamond jewellery, antique and provincial Irish silver
Open Mon–Sat 10am–5.30pm
Fairs IADA

Whyte's
Contact Ian Whyte
38 Molesworth Street, Dublin 1, Ireland
☎ 01 676 2888 Ⓕ 01 676 2880
Ⓔ info@whytes.ie
Ⓦ www.whytes.ie
Est. 1783
Open Mon–Fri 10am–1pm 2–5.30pm
Sales 4 sales annually of Irish art and collectables
Frequency 4 per year
Catalogues Yes

The Winding Stair Bookshop
Contact Mr Kevin Connolly
40 Lower Ormond Quay, Dublin 1, Ireland
☎ 01 873 3292 Ⓕ 01 873 3292
Ⓔ windingstairbooks@tinet.ie
Ⓦ www.windingstair.ie
Est. 1982 *Stock size* Large
Stock New, second-hand and antiquarian books, Irish-interest books a speciality
Open Mon–Sat 9.30am–6pm Sun 1–6pm

DUN LAOGHAIRE

James Fenning, Old and Rare Books (ABA)
Contact Mr James Fenning
12 Glenview, Rochestown Avenue, Dun Laoghaire, Co Dublin, Ireland
☎ 01 285 7855 Ⓕ 01 285 7919
Ⓔ fenning@indigo.ie
Est. 1969 *Stock size* Small
Stock Antiquarian books
Open By appointment
Services Valuations

Naughton's Booksellers
Contact Ms Susan Naughton
8 Marine Terrace, Dun Laoghaire, Co Dublin, Ireland
☎ 01 280 4392
Ⓔ sales@naughtonsbooks.com
Ⓦ www.naughtonsbooks.com
Est. 1978 *Stock size* Medium
Stock Second-hand and antiquarian books
Open By appointment

The Old Shop
Contact Ms Siobhan Nugent
St Michael's Mall, Dun Laoghaire Shopping Centre, Co Dublin, Ireland
☎ 01 280 9915
Est. 1976 *Stock size* Large
Stock Jewellery, silver, porcelain
Open Mon–Sat 9.30am–6pm

Through the Looking Glass
Contact Ms Anna Connolly
2 Salthill Place, Dun Laoghaire, Co Dublin, Ireland
☎ 01 280 6577

Est. 1989 *Stock size* Large
Stock Mirrors, general
Open Tues–Sat 10.30am–5.30pm
Services Restoration of mirrors

MALAHIDE

Drums Malahide
Contact Dennis Drum
New Street, Malahide, Co Dublin, Ireland P
☎ 01 845 2819 F 01 845 3356
E drumsauc@gofree.indigo.ie
Est. 1974
Open Mon–Fri 9am–5pm closed 1–2pm
Sales Fine art sales monthly on Thurs at 7pm, regular fortnightly mixed household sales Thurs
Catalogues Yes

Malahide Antique Shop
Contact Mr Frank Donellan
14 New Street, Malahide, Co Dublin, Ireland P
☎ 01 845 2900
Est. 1974 *Stock size* Large
Stock Jewellery, silver, Georgian furniture, pictures, porcelain
Open Mon–Sat 10am–5.30pm closed 1–2pm
Services Valuations, restoration

SANDYCOVE

Sandycove Fine Arts (IADA)
Contact Ms Fiona O'Reilly
55 Glasthule Road, Sandycove, Co Dublin, Ireland P
☎ 01 280 5956
Est. 1993 *Stock size* Medium
Stock Antique furniture, paintings, china, glass, silver, silver plate
Open Mon–Sat 10.30am–1pm 2–6pm

STILLORGAN

Beaufield Mews Antiques (IADA)
Contact Ms Jill Cox
Woodlands Avenue, Stillorgan, Co Dublin, Ireland P
☎ 01 288 0375 F 01 288 6945
M 0872 427360
E beaumews@iol.ie
W www.antiquesireland.ie
Est. 1948 *Stock size* Large
Stock Early Irish glass and porcelain, 18th–19thC small items of furniture, pictures
Open Tues–Sat 3–9pm Sun 1–5pm
Fairs Irish Antique Dealers' Fair
Services Valuations, award-winning restaurant on site

CO GALWAY

ATHLONE

Arcadia Antiques & Fine Art (IADA)
Contact Ms Imelda O'Flynn
Church Street, Athlone, Co Galway, Ireland P
☎ 0902 74671
Est. 1971 *Stock size* Large
Stock Fine Victorian jewellery, silver, objets d'art, prints, dolls
Open Mon–Sat 9.30am–6pm
Services Jewellery restoration

CLARENBRIDGE

Clarenbridge Antiques
Contact Mr Martin Griffin
Limerick Road (N18), Clarenbridge, Co Galway, Ireland P
☎ 091 796522 F 091 796547
E clarenbridgeantiques@tinet.ie
W www.clarenbridgeantiques.com
Est. 1981 *Stock size* Large
Stock Irish pine furniture, country antiques, mahogany and collectables
Open Summer Mon–Sun winter Mon–Sat 9am–6pm
Services Pine stripping

CLIFDEN

Clifden Antiques
Contact Noreen Allen
Station House, Clifden, Co Galway, Ireland P
☎ 095 22230
M 0876 649845
Est. 1999 *Stock size* Medium
Stock 17th–19thC furniture, contemporary Irish art, general antiques
Open Mon–Sat 10.30am–6pm or by appointment

GALWAY

Cobwebs (IADA)
Contact Mrs Phyllis MacNamara
7 Quay Lane, Galway, Ireland P
☎ 091 564388 F 091 564235
M 0872 375745
E cobwebs@tinet.ie
W www.cobwebsgalway.com
Est. 1972 *Stock size* Large
Stock Antique and fine jewellery
Open Mon–Sat 9.30am–5.30pm
Fairs Irish Antique Dealers Fair

Tempo Antiques
Contact Frank or Phil Greeley
9 Cross Street, Galway, Ireland P
☎ 091 562282
E info@tempoantiques.com
W www.tempoantiques.com
Est. 1995 *Stock size* Large
Stock Victorian–Edwardian, Art Deco antique jewellery, silver, porcelain, collectables
Open Mon–Sat 9.30am–6.30pm
Fairs Galway Bay Hotel

Tolco Antiques
Contact Tom or Breda O'Loughlin
Headford Road, Galway, Ireland P
☎ 091 751146
Est. 1971 *Stock size* Large
Stock General antiques, collectables
Open Mon–Fri 10am–5pm Sat 10am–4pm
Services Valuations

Twice As Nice
Contact Ms Deirdre Grandee
5 Quay Street, Galway, Ireland
☎ 091 566332
E grandideirdre@hotmail.com
Est. 1987 *Stock size* Medium
Stock Period clothes, lace, linen, jewellery
Open Mon–Sat 10am–6pm

The Winding Stair
Contact Mr Val Tyrell
4 Mainguard Street, Galway, Ireland P
☎ 091 561682
E tyrell@eircom.net
Est. 1991 *Stock size* Medium
Stock Prints, lighting, furniture, jewellery, collectables, general antiques
Open Mon–Sat 10am–6pm
Services Shipping – small items only

GORT

Honan's Antiques
Contact Brian or Margaret Honan
Crowe Street, Gort, Co Galway, Ireland
091 631407 F 091 631816
honansantique@eircom.net
www.honansantiques.com
Est. 1976 *Stock size* Large
Stock Antique pine, clocks, lamps, Victorian fireplaces, advertising signs, mirrors, pub fittings etc
Open Mon–Sat 10am–6pm
Services Pine stripping

MOYCULLEN

Moycullen Village Antiques (IADA)
Contact Ms Maura Duffy
Main Street, Moycullen, Co Galway, Ireland
091 555303 F 091 555303
M 0868 235976
Est. 1989 *Stock size* Large
Stock Fine Regency–Edwardian furniture, paintings, prints, fine china, silver
Open Mon–Sat 9.45am–5.30pm Sun 2–5.30pm
Fairs Dublin Horse Show, IADA (Mar, Dec)
Services Valuations, restoration

CO KERRY

ABBEYDORNEY

Abbey Antiques
Contact Jerry O'Donovan
Main Street, Abbeydorney, Co Kerry, Ireland
066 7135460
Est. 1989 *Stock size* Large
Stock Victorian fireplaces, Georgian–Edwardian furniture
Open Sun or by appointment

KILLARNEY

Frameworks (IADA, CINOA)
Contact Katie O'Connell
37 New Street, Killarney, Co Kerry, Ireland
064 35791 F 064 35791
frameworks@eirecom.net
www.frameworks.ie
Est. 1994 *Stock size* Medium
Stock 19th–20thC furniture, 17th–19thC prints, maps, glass gardenware
Open Mon–Sat 10am–6pm
Services Framing
Fairs Dublin (Mar, Sep)

TRALEE

Lots Furniture, Gifts and Antiques
Contact Margaret Brosnan
Dingle Road, Tralee, Co Kerry, Ireland
066 712 7117 F 066 712 7424
lots@eirecom.net
www.lotsworldwide.com
Est. 1990 *Stock size* Medium
Stock Victorian furniture, interesting pieces
Open Mon–Fri 9am–6pm Sat 10am–6pm Sun 2–6pm
Services Restoration

O'Keeffe's Antiques and Heritage
Contact Maurice or Jane O'Keeffe
15 Princes Street, Tralee, Co Kerry, Ireland
06 671 80613 or 06 671 25635
F 066 712 5635
M 08729 98167
okeeffeantiques2@eircom.net
www.irishlifeandlore.com
Est. 1860 *Stock size* Large
Stock Irish antiquarian books, oral history recordings on CD, Irish silver, paintings, prints, watercolours, Irish history, maps, charts, manuscripts, small pieces of 19thC Irish furniture
Open Tues–Sat 9.30am–6pm
Services Valuations

CO KILDARE

MAYNOOTH

Hugh Cash Antiques
Contact Hugh Cash
Main Street, Maynooth, Co Kildare, Ireland
01 628 5946
M 0872 434510
Est. 1969 *Stock size* Large
Stock Georgian–Edwardian furniture
Open By appointment only
Services Valuations

CO KILKENNY

BALLYCALLAN

Edward Comerford Antiques
Contact Edward Comerford
Ballevan, Ballycallan, Co Kilkenny, Ireland
056 776 9384
Est. 2000 *Stock size* Large
Stock General antiques, collectables
Open By appointment

CASTLECOMER

Mealy's Ltd (IAVI)
Contact Fonsie or George Mealy
Chatsworth Street, Castlecomer, Co Kilkenny, Ireland
056 444 1229/1413
F 056 444 1627
info@mealys.com
www.mealys.com
Est. 1934
Open Mon–Fri 9am–1pm 2–6pm
Sales 2 antiquarian book auctions per year, viewing days prior to auction. Also fine art sales
Frequency 8 per year
Catalogues Yes

FRESHFORD

Cass Freshford Antiques
Contact Michael Cass
Bohercrussia Street, Freshford, Co Kilkenny, Ireland
056 32240
cassantiques@dol.ie
Est. 1966 *Stock size* Medium
Stock Antique furniture
Open Mon–Sat 9am–5pm
Services Restoration

GORESBRIDGE

Michael Donohoe & Sons
Contact Martin Donohoe
Goresbridge, Co Kilkenny, Ireland
059 977 5145
Est. 1974
Open Mon–Fri 9am–5.30pm
Sales General antiques sales in Feb, April, Aug, Nov
Catalogues Yes

THOMASTOWN

Tara Antiques
Contact Tom Higginson
Grennan Water Mill, Thomastown, Co Kilkenny, Ireland
05 677 54077 F 05 677 54077
Est. 2000 *Stock size* Medium
Stock Georgian–Edwardian furniture, clocks, mirrors
Open Mon–Sat 10.30am–5pm
Services Restoration

CO LAOIS

ABBEYLEIX

Ireland's Own Antiques
Contact Daniel or Peter Meaney
Main Street, Abbeyleix, Co Laois, Ireland
050 231348
M 07717 676131
Est. 1963 *Stock size* Large
Stock General antiques and furniture
Open By appointment

BALLACOLLA

Glebe Hall Collectables
Contact Carmel Corrigan-Griffin
Old Killernogh Rectory, Rathmakelly Glebe, Ballacolla, Co Laois, Ireland
0502 34105 F 0502 34105
M 0868 784956
Est. 1980 *Stock size* Large
Stock Pine country furniture, porcelain, linen, paintings, kitchenware, silver plate, books, jewellery
Open Weekends and Bank Holidays by appointment
Services Restoration, tuition

DURROW

C Sheppard and Sons (IAVI)
Contact Michael Sheppard
The Square, Durrow, Co Laois, Ireland
050 236123 F 050 236546
E info@sheppards.ie
Est. 1949
Open Mon–Sat 10am–1pm 2–6pm
Sales General antiques, porcelain, furniture, fine arts
Frequency Every 2–3 months
Catalogues Yes

PORTARLINGTON

McDonnell's Antique Furniture
Contact Ray McDonnell
Cloneyhurke, Portarlington, Co Laois, Ireland
05024 3304
Est. 1981 *Stock size* Large
Stock Religious furniture, pulpits, pews, statuary, pine and farmhouse furniture
Open Mon–Sat 8am–8pm

CO LEITRIM

CARRICK ON SHANNON

Trinity Rare Books
Contact Nick or Joanna Kaszuk
Bridge Street, Carrick on Shannon, Co Leitrim
078 22144
E nickk@indigo.ie
W www.indigo.ie/~nickk
Est. 1999 *Stock size* Medium
Stock Antiquarian fine bindings, books, modern first editions
Open Mon–Sat 9.30am–6pm
Services Book search

CO LIMERICK

ADARE

Carol's Antiques (IADA, CINOA)
Contact Ms Carol O'Connor
Rose Cottage, Main Street, Adare, Co Limerick, Ireland
061 453 8948 F 061 439 6991
M 0862 478827
E coconnor@indigo.ie
W www.carolsantiquesadare.com
Est. 1979 *Stock size* Large
Stock Georgian–Victorian furniture, silver, brass, porcelain, objets d'art, jewellery, contemporary Irish art
Open Mon–Sat 9.30am–5.30pm
Fairs Irish Antique Dealers' Fair, Annual Cork Antiques Fair
Services Interior decoration

Manor Antiques
Contact Mr Simon Quilligan
Main Street, Adare, Co Limerick, Ireland
061 396515 or 069 64869
M 0868 365196
Est. 1914 *Stock size* Large
Stock Georgian–Victorian furniture, general antiques
Open Fri Sat 10am–5.30pm or by appointment
Services Shipping

George Stacpoole (IADA)
Contact Mr George Stacpoole
Main Street, Adare, Co Limerick, Ireland
061 396409 F 061 396733
E stacpool@iol.ie
W www.georgestacpooleantiques.com
Est. 1962 *Stock size* Medium
Stock Furniture, silver, books, pictures, china, prints
Open Mon–Sat 10am–5.30pm
Fairs IADA
Services Valuations and interior decoration

LIMERICK

Ann's Antiques
Contact Ann O'Doherty
32 Mallow Street, Limerick, Ireland
061 302492 F 061 413035
Est. 1984 *Stock size* Medium
Stock Mid-late Victorian furniture
Open Tues–Fri 11am–5pm or by appointment
Services Valuations, search

Bygones Antiques
Contact Mr John Costello
16 Nicholas Street, Limerick, Ireland
061 417339
Est. 1979 *Stock size* Medium
Stock Antique pine furniture and beds
Open Mon–Fri 9am–5.30pm half day Sat
Services Pine stripping

John Gunning Antiques
Contact Mr John Gunning
2 Castle Street, Limerick, Ireland
061 410535
Est. 1970 *Stock size* Large
Stock General antiques
Open Mon–Sat 10am–5pm

Noonan Antiques
Contact Jim Noonan
16–17 Ellen Street, Limerick, Ireland
061 413861 061 413861
0872 539165
jandanoonan@eircom.net
Est. 1985 *Stock size* Medium
Stock Antique jewellery, furniture
Open Mon–Sat 10am–5pm

O'Toole Antiques & Decorative Galleries (IADA)
Contact Noel O'Toole
Upper William Street, Limerick, Ireland
061 414490 061 411378
0872 550985
noel.o.toole.antiques@oceanfree.net
Est. 1979 *Stock size* Large
Stock 18th–19thC furniture, pictures, fireplaces, mirrors and porcelain
Open Mon–Sat 9.30am–6pm
Fairs IADA
Services Valuations, restoration

Tess Antiques
Contact Ms Tess Costello
5 Roches Street, Limerick, Ireland
061 416643/399736
Est. 1980 *Stock size* Small
Stock Jewellery, silver, porcelain
Open Tues–Sat 10am–5pm

CO LOUTH

DROGHEDA

Greene's Antiques Galleries (IADA)
Contact Austin Greene
The Mall, Drogheda, Co Louth, Ireland
041 984 5656 041 980 0755
Est. 1886 *Stock size* Large
Stock 18th–20thC furniture
Open Mon–Sat 10am–1pm 2–5.30pm

DUNDALK

Hall's Curio Shop
Contact Margaret or Rory Hall
9–10 Jocelyn Street, Dundalk, Co Louth, Ireland
042 933 4902
Est. 1971 *Stock size* Large
Stock Jewellery, paintings, silver, general
Open Mon–Sat 10am–1pm 2–6pm closed Thurs or by appointment
Services Valuations

CO MAYO

ACHILL SOUND

Roger Grimes (IADA)
Contact Roger Grimes
Old Rectory, Achill Sound, Co Mayo, Ireland 098 27823
rogergrimes@eircom.net
Est. 1977
Stock 17th–19thC provincial furniture, metalware, china, pictures, prints, eccentricities
Open Daily in the summer or by appointment
Fairs IADA
Services Valuations

Vanessa Parker Rare Books (IADA)
Contact Vanessa Parker
Old Rectory, Achill Sound, Co Mayo, Ireland
098 27823 098 27823
vanessaparker@eircom.net
Est. 1977
Stock Antiquarian books, folklore, literature, Irish, 19th–20thC children's books, fine bindings
Open Daily in the summer or by appointment
Fairs IADA
Services Valuations, books bought

DUNSHOUGHLIN

John Duffy Antiques
Contact John Duffy
Raynestown, Dunshoughlin, Co Mayo, Ireland
01 8250335
Est. 1986 *Stock size* Large
Stock General antiques, fireplaces
Open Mon–Sat 10am–6pm
Services Valuations, restoration

WESTPORT

Jonathan Beech Antique Clocks (IADA)
Contact Mr Jonathan Beech
Killeenacoff House, Cloona, Westport, Co Mayo, Ireland
098 28688 098 28688
0872 226247
info@antiqueclocks-ireland.com
www.antiques-ireland.com
Est. 1984 *Stock size* Medium
Stock Clocks
Open By appointment
Fairs Irish Antique Dealers' Fair, Dublin, Galway, Limerick
Services Valuations, restoration

Satch Kiely (IADA, LAPADA, CINOA)
Contact Karen Kiely
Westport Quay, Westport, Co Mayo, Ireland
098 25775 098 25957
08624 81431
satchkielyantiques@eircom.net
Est. 1985 *Stock size* Large
Stock 18th–19thC furniture, Irish and English silver, colonial lamps, fossil bog oak, Killarney furniture, objects
Open Mon–Sat 2–6pm or by appointment (summer noon–5.20pm)
Fairs Irish Antique Dealers' Fair, Annual Cork Antiques Fair, Galway and Hunt Museum, Limerick
Services Valuations

Westport House Antique Shop (IADA)
Contact Earl of Altamont
Westport, Co Mayo, Ireland
098 25430/25404 098 25206
info@westporthouse.ie
www.westporthouse.ie
Est. 1969 *Stock size* Medium
Stock General antiques, prints, postcards, silver, silver plate, jewellery
Open Daily April–June 2–5pm Jul Aug 11.30am–5.30pm or by appointment

CO MEATH

GORMANSTOWN

Delvin Farm Antiques
Contact J or B McCrane
Gormanstown, Co Meath, Ireland
01 841 2285 01 841 3730
08624 65615

e info@delvinfarmpine.com
w www.delvinfarmpine.com
Est. 1974 *Stock size* Large
Stock Antique country furniture
Open Mon–Sat 9am–5pm

KELLS

Oliver Usher (IAVI)
Contact Mr Oliver Usher
John Street,
Kells, Co Meath,
Ireland P
☎ 046 92 41097 f 046 92 41097
e oliverusher@ireland.com
Est. 1978
Open Mon–Fri 9.30am–5.30pm
Sales Antique and high-class furniture sale Tues 5pm mid month at Kells, viewing Sun 2–6pm Mon 11am–7pm Tues 11am–5pm. Spring and Autumn sale at The Conyngham Arms Hotel, Slane
Frequency Monthly
Catalogues Yes

George Williams Antiques (IADA)
Contact George Williams
The Annexe,
Newcastle House,
Kilmainhamwood,
Kells, Co Meath,
Ireland P
☎ 04690 52740
m 0872 529959
e gwilliams@eircom.net
w www.georgian-antiques.com
Est. 1987 *Stock size* Medium
Stock 18th–19thC furniture, paintings
Open By appointment only
Fairs IADA Exhibition, Dublin (Sept)
Services Purchasing on commission, valuations

OLDCASTLE

Mullen Bros Auctions
Contact Michael Mullen
Oldcastle,
Co Meath,
Ireland P
☎ 049 854 1107 f 049 854 1107
Est. 1962
Open Tues–Fri 10am–6pm
Sales General antiques and household goods 1st Tues of every month 6.30pm, viewing 3 days prior
Catalogues No

CO OFFALY

BIRR

Ivy Hall Antiques (IADA, CINOA)
Contact Mrs Ena Hoctor
Carrig, Birr, Co Offaly,
Ireland P
☎ 0509 20148
Est. 1967 *Stock size* Large
Stock 18th–19thC silver, porcelain, furniture, pictures
Open By appointment

EDENDERRY

Edenderry Architectural Salvage Ltd
Contact Brian Murphy
Monasteroris Industrial Estate,
Edenderry, Co Offaly,
Ireland P
☎ 046 97 33156
e bpmurphy@iol.ie
Est. 1995 *Stock size* Large
Stock Reclaimed flooring, bricks, radiators, doors, baths, sinks, beams, railway sleepers, cobblestones, fireplaces
Open Mon–Fri 9am–5pm
Services Cutting and planing of reclaimed timber beams and flooring

CO SLIGO

SLIGO

Louis J Doherty & Sons
Contact Louis
Teeling House,
Teeling Street, Sligo,
Ireland P
☎ 071 916 9494 f 071 915 3877
e ljdoherty@eirecom.net
w www.irish-antiques.com
Est. 1975 *Stock size* Large
Stock General antiques, Victorian–Edwardian furniture
Open Mon–Sat 9.30am–1pm 2–6pm
Services Valuations

Georgian Village Antiques
Contact Louis and John Doherty
Johnstons Court, Sligo,
Ireland P
☎ 071 62421 f 071 69494
e ljdoherty@tinet.ie
Est. 1976 *Stock size* Medium
Stock Small furniture items, jewellery, porcelain, glass
Open Mon–Sat 10am–6pm
Services Valuations

CO TIPPERARY

BALLINDERRY

Kilgarvan Antique Centre
Contact Denise Shaw
Kilgarvan Quay, Ballinderry,
Nenagh, Co Tipperary,
Ireland P
☎ 067 22047
e deniseshaw27@hotmail.com
Est. 1947 *Stock size* Medium
Stock Georgian antiques, mirrors, general china
Open Mon–Sat 10am–7pm Sun after 3pm Apr–Oct by appointment
Services Restoration of giltwood mirrors and antique furniture, restoration and polishing of wooden and carved furniture

CAHIR

Abbey Antiques (IADA)
Contact Mr Michael Kennedy
Abbey Street, Cahir,
Co Tipperary,
Ireland P
☎ 052 41187 f 052 41187
m 0872 728844
e celine@antiquesireland.ie
w www.antiquesireland.ie
Est. 1992 *Stock size* Large
Stock Georgian–Edwardian furniture, French country furniture, lighting, objets d'art
Open Mon–Sat 10.30am–5.30pm
Services Shipping

Fleury Antiques (IADA)
Contact C or D Fleury or P Reidy
The Square, Cahir,
Co Tipperary, Ireland P
☎ 052 41226 f 052 41819
e fleuryantiques@eircom.net
w www.fleuryantiques.com
Est. 1978 *Stock size* Medium
Stock 18th–19thC furniture, sculptures, paintings, decorative objects, jewellery, porcelain, silver
Open Mon–Sat 9am–6pm
Fairs No

CASHEL

Cashel Antiques
Contact Norah or Joe Barry
Bank Place, Cashel,

Co Tipperary,
Ireland
☎ 062 61319
Est. 1979 *Stock size* Medium
Stock Antique furniture, jewellery
Open By appointment

Ladyswell Antiques & Jewellery
Contact Fiona Bourke
✉ **5 Ladyswell Street, Cashel, Co Tipperary, Ireland** P
☎ 062 61267
Est. 1965 *Stock size* Small
Stock General antiques
Open Mon–Sat 2–6pm
Services Valuations, restoration

CO WATERFORD

WATERFORD

An Siopa
Contact Maria Halligan
✉ **60 John Street, Waterford, Ireland** P
☎ 051 877549 F 051 877549
Est. 1972 *Stock size* Large
Stock Antique jewellery, silver
Open Mon–Sat 9am–6pm
Services Valuations

City Auction Rooms (IPAV)
Contact Rody or Ann Keighery
✉ **Georges Quay, Waterford, Ireland** P
☎ 051 873692 F 051 873692
Est. 1948
Open Mon–Sat 9am–5.30pm
Sales Six weekly antiques and general furniture sale Mon 2pm, viewing Fri Sat Sun noon–6pm
Catalogues Yes

R J Keighery (IPAV)
Contact Rody or Ann Keighery
✉ **27a William Street, Waterford, Ireland** P
☎ 051 873692 F 051 873692
Est. 1948 *Stock size* Large
Stock Antiques, furniture, china, silver, collectables
Open Mon–Sat 9am–5.30pm
Services Valuations

The Salvage Shop
Contact Sean Corcoran
✉ **Airport Road, Waterford City, Ireland** P
☎ 051 873260 F 051 858323
M 0872 524657
E salvage@iol.ie
W www.bang2000.com
Est. 1991 *Stock size* Large
Stock Architectural salvage and reclaimed wood furniture
Open Mon–Fri 8am–5.30pm Sat 10am–3pm
Fairs Beyond the Hall Door
Services Restoration, interior design

CO WEXFORD

ROSSLARE

Selskar Antiques
Contact Irene Walker
✉ **Poulrankin, Rosslare, Co Wexford, Ireland** P
☎ 053 73967 F 053 73967
M 0876 791095
E selskarantiques@eircom.net
W www.selskarantiques.biz
Est. 1984 *Stock size* Medium
Stock Antique jewellery, pictures, fine china, small furniture items, glass, collectables
Open Mon–Sat noon–6pm Sun noon–4pm
Fairs O'Donnell Fairs, Wexford Opera Festival
Services Valuations

WEXFORD

Forum Antiques
Contact Nora Liddy
✉ **Selskar, Wexford, Ireland** P
☎ 053 21055 F 053 23630
E info@selskarantiques.com
W www.selskarantiques.com
Est. 1996 *Stock size* Medium
Stock Antiquarian books, maps, prints, china, collectables
Open Mon–Sat 11am–5.30pm winter telephone first
Fairs National Book Fairs
Services Book valuations

CO WICKLOW

BRAY

Clancy Chandeliers (IADA)
Contact Ger, Derek or Tommy Clancy
✉ **Villanova, Ballywaltrim, Bray, Co Wicklow, Ireland** P
☎ 0128 63460 F 0128 63460
M 08724 228838
E info@clancychandeliers.com
W www.clancychandeliers.com
Est. 1989 *Stock size* Large
Stock Period and reproduction chandeliers, wall lights, hall lanterns
Open Strictly by appointment
Fairs IADA Exhibition, Dublin (Sept), IAFAF (Mar)
Services Professional cleaning, restoration, hanging service

RADHDRUM

Cathair Books
Contact Mr Eugene Mallon
✉ **Pound Brook Lane, Radhdrum, Co Wicklow, Ireland** P
☎ 040 446939 F 040 446939
E cathairbks@eircom.net
W www.abebooks.com/home/cathair_books
Est. 1974 *Stock size* Medium
Stock Irish-interest books, prints, maps, postcards
Open Mail order
Fairs Dublin Book Fair and provincial fairs in Limerick and Belfast
Services Valuations

Associated Services

ARCHITECTURAL

Zygmunt Chelminski (UKIC)
Contact Mr Z Chelminski
✉ **Studio GE1, 2 Michael Road, London, SW6 2AD** Ⓟ
☎ 020 7610 9731 Ⓕ 020 7610 9731
Ⓜ 07770 585130
Est. 1993
Services Restoration and conservation of architectural monuments, statues and special effects in marble, granite, stone, terracotta, alabaster, coldstone, iron, bronze, zinc, lead, ormolu, wood, ivory, pietra dura, scagliola, plaster, mother-of-pearl, tortoiseshell, shagreen, amber, onyx, papier-mâché, blue john and semi-precious stones
Open Mon–Fri 10am–5pm appointment advisable

Iron Wright
Contact Mr F Sporik
✉ **5 Cranleigh Mews, Cabul Road, London, SW11 2QL** Ⓟ
☎ 020 7228 2727 Ⓕ 020 7652 4089
Ⓦ www.ironwright.co.uk
Est. 1994
Services Repair and restoration of cast-iron fireplaces
Open Mon–Fri 8am–6pm Sat by appointment

Melluish & Davis
Contact Mr J Davis
✉ **11 Hampton Lane, Hanworth, Middlesex, TW13 6NN** Ⓟ
☎ 020 7622 5731 Ⓕ 020 8893 4178
Ⓜ 07966 247549
Ⓔ johndavis@johndavis.evesham.net
Est. 1972
Services Restoration and research of marble chimneypieces, sculpture and garden ornaments
Open By appointment only

Saltney Restoration Services
Contact Mr J Moore
✉ **50 St Mark's Road, Chester, Cheshire, CH4 8DQ** Ⓟ
☎ 01244 67110
Ⓜ 07713 823383
Est. 1967
Services Brick, metal, steel, glass, furniture, stone, lighting and sanitary ware restoration
Open By appointment only

Salvo
Contact Ruby Kay
✉ **PO Box 28080, London, SE27 0YZ**
☎ 0208 761 2316 Ⓕ 0208 761 2424
Ⓔ admin@salvoweb.com
Ⓦ www.salvoweb.com
Est. 1992
Services Salvo networks information on architectural salvage, garden antiques, reclaimed building materials and reproductions. Salvo publishes SalvoEMAILS several times a week, printed *SalvoNEWS* every 3 weeks, *SALVO* magazine intermittently and *The Salvo Guide*

BOOKS

Antiquarian Bookcrafts
Contact Des Breen
✉ **Craft Centre, Marlay Park, Dublin 16, Ireland** Ⓟ
☎ 01 494 2834 Ⓕ 01 494 2811
Ⓔ desbreen@eirecom.net
Est. 1962
Services Book binding, restoration
Open Mon–Fri 7.45am–4.30pm

C & A J Barmby
Contact C Barmby
✉ **140 Lavender Hill, Tonbridge, Kent, TN9 2AY**
☎ 01732 771590 Ⓕ 01732 771590
Ⓔ bookpilot@aol.com
Est. 1970
Services Reference books on antiques, display stands, accessories, packaging material
Trade only Yes
Open By appointment

The Book Depot
Contact Conrad Wiberg
✉ **111 Woodcote Avenue, London, NW7 2PD**
☎ 020 8906 3708 Ⓕ 020 8906 3708
Est. 1980
Services Free book search for any book
Open Mon–Sun 9am–5pm postal business

Brignell Bookbinders
Contact Barry Brignell
✉ **25 Gwydir Street, Cambridge, Cambridgeshire, CB1 2LG** Ⓟ
☎ 01223 321280 Ⓕ 01223 321280
Est. 1982
Services Book binding, repair, presentation of volumes
Open Mon–Thurs 8.30am–4.45pm Fri 8.30am–4pm

Fullertons Booksearch
Contact Mr Humphrey Boon
✉ **The Duke's House, Moorgate Road, Hindringham, Fakenham, Norfolk, NR21 0PT** Ⓟ
☎ 01420 544088 Ⓕ 01420 542445
Ⓔ fullertons.books@virgin.net
Est. 1991
Services Out-of-print book searching facility. Mail order sales
Open Mon–Fri 9am–5pm

H P Book Finders
Contact Mr Martin Earl
✉ **Mosslaird, Brig O'Turk, Callander, Scotland, FK17 8HT** Ⓟ
☎ 01877 376377 Ⓕ 01877 376377
Ⓔ martin@hp-bookfinders.co.uk
Ⓦ www.hp-bookfinders.co.uk
Est. 1984
Services Book search
Open Mon–Fri 8am–6pm Sat 9am–1pm

F Hutton (Bookbinder) (SOB, Designer Binders)
Contact Felicity Hutton
✉ **Langore House, Langore, Launceston, Cornwall, PL15 8LD** Ⓟ
☎ 01566 773831
Est. 1985
Services Bookbinding and restoration
Open By appointment

Blair Jeary
Contact Blair Jeary
✉ **The Stable Courtyard, Burghley House, Stamford, Lincolnshire, PE9 3JY** Ⓟ
☎ 01780 763725
Ⓜ 07929 663592
Est. 1989
Services Restoration and re-binding of antiquarian books
Open By appointment

Meadowcroft Books
Contact Miss Laing
✉ **21 Upper Bognor Road,**

Bognor Regis, West Sussex, PO21 1JA 🅿
☎ 01243 868614 Ⓕ 01243 868714
Ⓔ enquiries@meadowcroftbooks.demon.co.uk
Ⓦ www.meadowcroftbooks.demon.co.uk
Est. 1996
Services Book search
Open By appointment

BOXES

William Heffer Antiques
Contact Mr W Heffer
✉ **37 Victoria Park, Cambridge, Cambridgeshire, CB4 3EJ** 🅿
☎ 01223 362825
Ⓔ hefferw.vicpark@dial.pipex.com
Est. 1972
Services Small restoration work, caddies, jewellery boxes
Open By appointment

BUYING SERVICE

Ayuka Ltd
Contact Mune Ota
✉ **Village Farm, Stanford, Bedfordshire, SG18 9JQ** 🅿
☎ 01438 362494 Ⓕ 01438 228494
Ⓜ 07796 804032
Ⓔ sales@ayuka.co.uk
Ⓦ www.ayuka.co.uk
Services Personal antique buying service
Open Mon–Sun 9am–8pm

CANING

Cane and Rush Works (Basket Makers Association)
Contact Miss J Swan
✉ **6c Sylvan Road, London, E11 1QH** 🅿
☎ 020 8530 7052
Est. 1981
Services Caning and rushing, country chairs, chair seats, bergère suites and sofas
Open By appointment

Cane Chairs Repaired
Contact Paul Boulton
✉ **Dunmayling, High Street, Burwash, East Sussex, TN19 7EP** 🅿
☎ 0800 027 6869 Ⓕ 01435 882299
Ⓜ 07850 943091
Ⓔ chairs@btconnect.com
Ⓦ www.canechairs.co.uk
Est. 1995
Services Repair of all cane and Lloyd Loom chairs
Open Mon–Fri 8am–6pm

Cane Corner (Basket Makers Association, Devon Rural Skills Trust)
Contact Bridgette Graham
✉ **Behind East Budleigh Garage, Lower Budleigh, East Budleigh, Devon, EX9 7DL** 🅿
☎ 01395 446616
Est. 1985
Services Antique and modern chairs professionally reseated with split cane and rush
Open Mon–Fri 9am–5.30pm

The Cane & Rush Chair Repair Service
Contact R D Nolan
✉ **156 Horton Hill, Epsom, Surrey, KT19 8ST** 🅿
☎ 01372 727063
Ⓜ 07961 313933
Est. 1984
Services Cane and rush repair
Open Mon–Fri 7.30am–5pm Sat 8am–noon

Cane Weaving Repairs
✉ **Ely, Cambridgeshire, CB6** 🅿
☎ 01353 862889 Ⓕ 01353 862889
Est. 1989
Services Hand-woven cane repair
Open By appointment

Caners & Upholders
Contact Steve Warrington
✉ **The Old Beef House, Stubhampton Manor Farm, Tarrant Gunville, Blandford Forum, Dorset, DT11 8JS** 🅿
☎ 01258 830300
Ⓔ steven.warrington@virgin.net
Est. 1989
Services Cane and rush repair and restoration
Open Mon–Fri 9am–5pm or by appointment

Former Glory
Contact Tim or Kim Ravenscroft
✉ **Ferndown, Dorset, BH22** 🅿
☎ 01202 895859 Ⓕ 01202 895859
Ⓔ formerglory@btinternet.com
Ⓦ www.formerglory.co.uk
Est. 1994
Services Cane and rush seating, furniture restoration. Cane, rush and restoration material suppliers
Open By appointment only

Peter Maitland
Contact Mr P J Maitland
✉ **27 Berkeley Road, Bishopstone, Bristol, BS7 8HF** 🅿
☎ 0117 942 6870
Est. 1990
Services Chair restoration, caning
Open Mon–Fri 9am–5pm or by appointment

CARPETS & RUGS

Barin Carpets Restoration
Contact H Barin
✉ **57a New King's Road, London, SW6 4SE** 🅿
☎ 020 7731 0546
Est. 1976
Services Cleaning and restoration of Oriental carpets and rugs, European tapestries, Aubussons. Listed by the conservation unit of The Museums and Galleries Commission
Open Mon–Sat 9am–6pm

Lannowe Oriental Textiles
Contact Joanna Titchell
✉ **Near Bath, Wiltshire**
☎ 01225 891487 Ⓕ 01225 891182
Ⓜ 07714 703535
Ⓔ joanna@lannowe.co.uk
Est. 1976
Services Washing, restoration and conservation of Oriental carpets, rugs and tapestries
Open By appointment

Michael & Amanda Lewis Oriental Carpets
Contact Amanda Lewis
✉ **8 North Street, Wellington, Somerset, TA21 8LT** 🅿
☎ 01823 667430
Ⓔ rugmike@btopenworld.com
Est. 1981
Services Restoration, cleaning, repair to carpets, rugs and flat weave
Open Tues–Fri 10.30am–1pm 2–5.30pm Sat by appointment

M & M Restoration
Contact Marina Jezierzanska
✉ **Mantel House, Broomhill Road, London, SW18 4JQ** 🅿
☎ 020 8871 5098 Ⓕ 020 8877 1940
Ⓜ 07949 107611
Est. 1985
Services Restoration and cleaning of antique tapestries, carpets, textiles
Open Mon–Fri 9am–6pm

The Rug Studio
Contact Rachel Bassill
✉ **34 High Street, Hampton Wick, Hampton Wick, Surrey, KT1 4D** 🅿
☎ 020 8977 4403 Ⓕ 020 8977 4408
Ⓔ info@therugstudio.co.uk
Ⓦ www.therugstudio.co.uk
Est. 1994
Services Rug cleaning, restoration, repair, moth-proofing, search
Open Tues–Fri 10am–5.30pm Sat 10am–4pm Sun (excluding Aug) 11am–4pm

CERAMICS

SOUTH EAST

Carol Basing
Contact Carol Basing
✉ **41 Prospect Road, Sevenoaks, Kent, TN13 3UA**
☎ 01732 456695
Est. 1984
Services Ceramic repair and restoration
Open By appointment

Grenville Godfrey
Contact Mr G Godfrey
✉ **60 Watts Lane, Eastbourne, East Sussex, BN21 2LL** 🅿
☎ 01323 735595
Est. 1997
Services Repair and restoration of ceramics
Open By appointment

Sarah Peek
Contact Miss S Peek
✉ **Studio 9, Level 4 South, New England House, New England Street, Brighton, East Sussex, BN1 4GH** 🅿
☎ 01273 670088 Ⓕ 01273 670088
Ⓔ conservation@sarahpeek.co.uk
Ⓦ www.sarahpeek.co.uk
Est. 1995
Services Restoration of ceramics, glass, enamels
Open By appointment

Helen Warren China Restoration
Contact Helen Warren
✉ **The Roundhouse, Angley Park, Cranbrook, Kent, TN17 2PN** 🅿
☎ 01580 713500
Ⓔ chinarestoration@helenwarren.com
Ⓦ www.helenwarren.com
Est. 1990
Services Ceramic repair and restoration
Open By appointment

LONDON

China Repairers
Contact Virginia Baron
✉ **The Coach House, King Street Mews, King Street, London, N2 8DY** 🅿
☎ 020 8444 3030
Ⓦ www.chinarepairers.co.uk
Est. 1953
Services Ceramic and glass repair. Tuition available
Open Mon–Thurs 10am–4pm

The Conservation Studio (ICOM, IIC, UKIC)
Contact Mrs F Hayward
✉ **77 Troutbeck, Albany Street, London, NW1 4EJ** 🅿
☎ 020 7387 4994 Ⓕ 020 7387 4994
Ⓔ flu_flo@yahoo.co.uk
Est. 1993
Services Restoration and conservation of ceramics, glass, metalwork, ivory and soapstone, specializing in gilding, painting on glass and ceramics
Open Mon–Fri 8.30am–4.30pm Sat by appointment

Rosemary Hamilton China Repairs (IDDA)
Contact Mrs R Hamilton
✉ **44 Moreton Street, London, SW1V 2PB** 🅿
☎ 020 7828 5018 Ⓕ 020 7828 1325
Ⓔ rosemary@rosemaryhamilton.co.uk
Est. 1993
Services China repair and restoration
Open Mon–Fri 9.30am–5.30pm

Laurence Mitchell Antiques (LAPADA)
Contact Laurence Mitchell
✉ **20 The Mall, 359 Islington High Street, Islington, London, N1 0PD**
☎ 020 7359 7579
Ⓔ laurence@buymeissen.com
Ⓦ www.buymeissen.com
Est. 1970
Services Restoration of antiques
Open Tues–Fri 10am–5pm Sat 10am–5.30pm

Q W Conservation (OCS)
Contact Ms Gillian Quartly-Watson
✉ **Studio 5 (2nd Floor), Havelock Terrace, London, SW8 4AS** 🅿
☎ 020 7498 5938 Ⓕ 020 7498 5938
Ⓜ 07710 355743
Ⓔ stylish.moves@virgin.net
Est. 1991
Services Conservation of ceramics and related objects
Open Mon–Fri 10am–6pm or by appointment

SOUTH

Brook Studio
Contact Mrs Joanna Holland
✉ **The Granary, 2 Church Road, Pangbourne, Berkshire, RG8 7AA** 🅿
☎ 0118 984 2014/971 3249
Ⓔ joanna@holland.demon.co.uk
Est. 1978
Services China and porcelain restoration
Open Mon–Sat 9am–6pm

Norman Flynn Restorations
Contact Mr N Flynn
✉ **20 Malden Road, Cheam, Surrey, SM3 8QF** 🅿
☎ 020 8661 9505
Est. 1972
Services Porcelain, pottery, enamel restoration
Open Mon–Fri 8.30am–3.30pm

Regency Antiques
Contact R De Santini
✉ **Bognor Regis, West Sussex**
☎ 01243 861643 Ⓕ 01243 861643
Ⓜ 07947 597311
Est. 1978
Services Porcelain and furniture restoration
Open Mon–Fri 9.30am–5.30pm by appointment only

Sheila Southwell Studio (BCPAA, IPAA)
Contact Mrs S Southwell
✉ **7 West Street, Burgess Hill, West Sussex, RH15 8NN** P
☎ 01444 244307
Est. 1969
Services Restoration of ceramics, china, porcelain, earthenware. Commissions accepted for hand-painted, commemorative porcelain for any occasion
Open By appointment

WEST COUNTRY

Addington Studio Ceramic Repairs
Contact Pam Warner
✉ **1 Addington Cottages, Upottery, Honiton, Devon, EX14 9PN** P
☎ 01404 861519 F 01404 861308
E pam@addingtonstudio.co.uk
W www.addingtonstudio.co.uk
Est. 1991
Services Restoration and conservation of ceramics and glass. Tuition given. Regular London (inside M25) delivery and collection. Supplies for ceramic conservators
Open By appointment

Antique China and Porcelain Restoration
Contact Mr Carl Garratt
✉ **6 Enfield Drive, Evercreech, Shepton Mallet, Somerset, BA4 6LL** P
☎ 01749 831116
Est. 1978
Services Restoration of antique china, oil paintings and objets d'art
Open By appointment

Ceramic Restoration
Contact Martina Gray or Emma Organ
✉ **Unit 1, 24 Cheap Street, Sherborne, Dorset, DT9 3PX** P
☎ 01935 813128
Est. 1989
Services Restoration and conservation of ceramics
Open Mon–Fri 10am–12.30pm 1.30pm–4pm or by appointment

China and Glass Restoration
Contact Mrs Susan Birch
✉ **The Shoe, Old Hollow, Mere, Warminster, Wiltshire, BA12 6EG** P
☎ 01747 861703
Est. 1993
Services China and glass restoration
Open By appointment

Peter Martin Ceramic Restoration
Contact Mr P Martin
✉ **11 Eastbourne Terrace, Westward Ho, Bideford, Devon, EX39 1HG** P
☎ 01237 421446
E pmcr@madasafish.com
Est. 1996
Services Modern and antique ceramic restoration, specializing in decorative pottery and porcelain antiques
Open Strictly by appointment

Reference Works Ltd
Contact Joy or Barry Lamb
✉ **9 Commercial Road, Swanage, Dorset, BH19 1DF** P
☎ 01929 424423 F 01929 422597
E sales@referenceworks.co.uk
W www.referenceworks.co.uk
Est. 1984
Services Mail order reference books on pottery and porcelain. Consultants and advisers on British ceramics. Monthly illustrated newsletters and book lists, extensive website. Small range of 18th–20thC pottery, porcelain
Open Mon–Fri 10.30am–4pm Sat 10.30am–1pm or by appointment

EAST

Emma Bradshaw Ceramic Restorations (UKIC)
Contact Emma Bradshaw
✉ **24 Town Street, Thaxted, Great Dunmow, Essex, CM6 2LA** P
☎ 01371 830305
Est. 1991
Services Conservation and restoration of bone china, earthenware, porcelain, stoneware, terracotta, early English pottery
Open By appointment

Ceramic Restorations
Contact Miss Syms
✉ **10 Valley Lane, Holt, Norfolk, NR25 6SF** P
M 07748 901093
E victoriasyms@hotmail.com
Est. 1989
Services Ceramics, pottery and porcelain restoration, specializing in English blue and white transfer ware
Open By appointment

HEART OF ENGLAND

The China Repairers
Contact Mrs A Chalmers
✉ **1 Street Farm Workshops, Doughton, Tetbury, Gloucestershire, G18 8TH** P
☎ 01666 503551
Est. 1989
Services China, mirror and picture frame restoration (By Appointment to HRH The Prince of Wales)
Open Mon–Fri 9am–5pm

China Repairs & Restorations (UKIC)
Contact David Battams
✉ **Bletchley, Buckinghamshire, MK2** P
M 07956 832375
E david@chinarepairsandrestorations.com
W www.chinarepairsandrestorations.com
Est. 1998
Services Repair and restoration of china using the latest materials and techniques
Open Mon–Fri 1–5pm

Gray Arts
Contact Mr A Gray
✉ **Unit 21b, The Maltings, School Lane, Amersham, Buckinghamshire, HP7 0ET** P
☎ 01494 726502 F 01494 726502
M 07714 274410
Est. 1979
Services Porcelain restoration, clock and watch dial restoration
Trade only Yes
Open By appointment

Rose Antique Restoration
Contact Nicola Gilbert
✉ **5 Windmill Hill, Princes Risborough, Buckinghamshire, HP27 0EP** P
☎ 01844 273517

Ⓔ roserestore@yahoo.com
Est. 1976
Services Restoration of china, porcelain, ceramics
Trade only Trade has preference
Open Mon–Thur 9am–5.30pm

The Traditional Studio (UKIC)
Contact Viki Green
✉ **Welwyn Equestrian Centre, Potters Heath Road, Welwyn, Hertfordshire, AL6 9SZ** Ⓟ
☎ 01707 332084 Ⓕ 01707 332084
Ⓜ 07748 224287
Ⓔ viki@traditionalstudio.fsnet.co.uk
Est. 1997
Services Ceramics, gilded objects, stone, marble sculpture, furniture, lacquer work
Open By appointment

MIDLANDS

Ashdale China Restoration
Contact Mr R Gregory
✉ **19 Boothby Avenue, Ashbourne, Derbyshire, DE6 1EL** Ⓟ
☎ 01335 345965
Ⓜ 07961 957530
Est. 1984
Services Repair and restoration
Open By appointment

Roger Hawkins Restoration
Contact R Hawkins
✉ **Unit 4, The Old Dairy, Winkburn, Newark, Nottinghamshire, NG22 8PQ**
☎ 01636 636666
Est. 1980
Services Restoration of all types of pottery, porcelain. Tuition given
Open Mon–Fri 9am–5pm

Ravensdale Studios
Contact Mr S Nicholls
✉ **77a Roundwell Street, Tunstall, Stoke-on-Trent, Staffordshire, ST6 5AW** Ⓟ
☎ 01782 836810 Ⓕ 01782 836810
Ⓔ restore@ravensdale69.fsnet.co.uk
Ⓦ www.ravensdalestudios.co.uk
Est. 1988
Services Ceramic restoration
Open Mon–Fri 9am–5pm

Warwick–Wright Restoration
Contact Mr S MacGarvey
✉ **19b Wem Business Park, New Street, Wem, Shrewsbury, Shropshire, SY4 5JX** Ⓟ
☎ 01939 234879
Est. 1992
Services Porcelain restoration
Open Mon–Fri 8.30am–4.30pm

YORKSHIRE & LINCOLNSHIRE

Artisan Stock & Business Centre
Contact Mr C Hobs
✉ **Enterprise Centre, 70 Brunswick Street, Stockton-on-Tees, Cleveland, TS18 1DW** Ⓟ
☎ 01642 801020 Ⓕ 01642 391351
Est. 1991
Services Restoration and repair of china and ceramics
Open Mon–Fri 9am–5pm
Sat by appointment

Kaleidescope Porcelain and Pottery Restorers
Contact Mr F Roberts
✉ **Rose Marie, Main Road, Potterhanworth, Lincoln, Lincolnshire, LN4 2DT** Ⓟ
☎ 01522 793869
Est. 1985
Services Antique repair and restoration, also restoraton of modern pieces on request
Open Mon–Fri 9am–7pm
Sat 9am–noon

The Pottery & Porcelain Restoration Co
Contact Mr Tom Cosens
✉ **30 Wharf Street, Sowerby Bridge, West Yorkshire, HX6 2AE** Ⓟ
☎ 01422 834828
Ⓜ 07817 296381
Ⓔ artrestorers@aol.com
Est. 1990
Services Repair and restoration of all ceramics and spelter, china matching service
Open By appointment only

NORTH WEST

Domino Restorations
Contact Mrs J Hargreaves
✉ **c/o G B Antiques Centre, Lancaster Leisure Park, Wyresdale Road, Lancaster, Lancashire, LA1 3LA** Ⓟ
Ⓜ 07710 223170
Ⓔ r.j.hargreaves@ic24.net
Est. 1979
Services Porcelain and china restoration, jewellery repair. Repair and restoration of metalware, tortoiseshell and ivory, spelter, bronze
Open By appointment

Monogram Studios
Contact Mr David R Adams
✉ **25 Kinsey Street, Congleton, Cheshire, CW12 1ES** Ⓟ
☎ 01260 273957
Est. 1962
Services Pottery and porcelain repair and restoration
Open Mon–Fri 8.30am–5pm

Porcelain Repairs Ltd
Contact Mr I Norman or Mr A Jones
✉ **240 Stockport Road, Cheadle Heath, Stockport, Cheshire, SK3 0LX** Ⓟ
☎ 0161 428 9599 Ⓕ 0161 286 6702
Ⓔ porcelain@repairs999.fsnet.co.uk
Est. 1976
Services Repair and restoration of all antique ceramics. Collection and delivery service to central London
Open By appointment only, during office hours

WALES

Ceramic Restoration (GADAR, UKIC)
Contact Lynette Pierce
✉ **Woodlands Studio, Glanhafren, Abermule, Montgomery, Powys, SY15 6NA** Ⓟ
☎ 01686 630219
Ⓜ 07748 868913
Est. 1995
Services China and pottery repair and restoration, figurines a speciality
Trade only Yes
Open By appointment

SCOTLAND

Ellen L Breheny (Accredited Member UKIC)
Contact Ellen L Breheny

✉ **10 Glenisla Gardens, Edinburgh, EH9 2HR** 🅿
☎ 0131 667 2620
ⓔ ellen@breheny.com
Est. 1988
Services Conservation and restoration of ceramics, glass and related materials
Open Mon–Fri 10am–6pm

Renaissance China Restoration
Contact Miss S Harvey
✉ **30 West Annadale Street, Edinburgh, EH7 4JY** 🅿
☎ 0131 557 2762
Est. 1984
Services Invisible ceramic restoration
Open Mon–Fri 10am–1pm 2.30–5pm

REPUBLIC OF IRELAND

Lorna Barnes Conservation (IPCRA, ICOM)
Contact Lorna Barnes
✉ **158 Rialto Cottages, Rialto, Dublin 8, Ireland** 🅿
☎ 01 473 6205
ⓔ barneslorna@hotmail.com
Est. 2000
Services Conservation of glass, ceramic and stone objects, condition surveys, advice on packaging and storage
Open Mon–Fri 9am–6pm

Glebe Hall Restoration Studios
Contact Carmel Corrigan-Griffin
✉ **Old Killernogh Rectory, Rathnakelly Glebe, Ballacolla, Co Laois, Ireland** 🅿
☎ 0502 34105 ⓕ 0502 34105
ⓜ 0868 784956
Est. 1980
Services Furniture restoration, gilding, porcelain, ivory, jade
Open By appointment Sat 11am–4pm

CLOCKS

A A Clockcraft (BHI)
Contact Mr D R Peveley
✉ **13 High Street, Bridlington, East Yorkshire, YO16 4PR** 🅿
☎ 01262 602802
Est. 1984
Services Clock repair and restoration, all periods and all types
Open Mon–Fri 9am–5pm Sat 10.30am–4.30pm

Albion Clocks (BHI)
Contact Colin Bent
✉ **4 Grove Road, Grove Hill, South Woodford, Essex, E18 2LE** 🅿
☎ 020 8530 5570
ⓔ colin.bent@btinternet.com
ⓦ www.albionclocks.com
Est. 1963
Services Restoration of clocks and fine furniture, antiquarian horologist
Open Mon–Sun 9am–7pm by appointment

Anthony Allen Conservation, Restoration, Furniture and Artefacts (BAFRA, UKIC)
Contact Anthony Allen
✉ **The Old Wharf Workshop, Redmoor Lane, Newtown, High Peak, Derbyshire, SK22 3JL** 🅿
☎ 01663 745274 ⓕ 01663 745274
Est. 1970
Services Restoration of clock cases and movements, gilding, marquetry, boulle, upholstery, metalwork, 17th–19thC furniture
Open Mon–Fri 8am–5pm

David Ansell (BAFRA, BHI)
Contact David Ansell
✉ **48 Dellside, Harefield, Middlesex, UB9 6AX** 🅿
☎ 01895 824648
ⓜ 07976 222610
ⓔ davidansell@btinternet.com
Est. 1990
Services Repair and restoration of clocks
Open Mon–Sun 8.30am–5.30pm or by appointment

Antique Renovations
Contact Stephen or Alan Gartland
✉ **Unit 1, Lavenham Studios, Brent Eleigh Road, Lavenham, Sudbury, Suffolk, CO10 9PE** 🅿
☎ 01787 248511
Est. 1960
Services Repair, cabinet work and French polishing. Recommended by Ercol. Specializing in clock case repair
Open Mon–Fri 8.30am–5pm Sat 9am–1pm

The Barometer Shop (BWCG)
Contact Colin or Verity Jones
✉ **25 New Street, Leominster, Herefordshire, HR6 8DP** 🅿
☎ 01568 613652
Est. 1969
Services Supply and restoration of antique mercurial, aneroid barometers, clocks and watches, furniture, ceramics, French polishing, wood finishing, dial painting
Open Mon–Fri 9am–5pm Sat 10am–4pm

David Bates
Contact Mr David Bates
✉ **Church Cottage, Church Lane, Cawston, Norwich, Norfolk, NR10 4AJ** 🅿
☎ 01603 871687
Est. 1995
Services Restoration of painted and brass clock dials
Open Mon–Fri 9am–5pm

Neill Robinson Blaxill
Contact Neill Blaxill
✉ **21 St Johns Hill, Sevenoaks, Kent, TN13 3NX** 🅿
☎ 01732 454179
ⓦ www.antique-clocks.co.uk
Est. 1980
Services Clock and barometer restoration
Open Mon–Sat 10am–6pm or by appointment

Symon E Boyd Clock Restorer (BHI)
Contact Mr S Boyd
✉ **54 Buxton Road, Disley, Stockport, Cheshire, SK12 2EY** 🅿
☎ 01663 763999
Est. 1984
Services Repair and restoration of clocks, barometers, musical boxes and automata
Open By appointment

J W Carpenter Antique Clock Restorer (BHI)
Contact John Carpenter

✉ **Whitehaven, Sandown Road, Sandwich, Kent, CT13 9NY** 🅿
☎ 01304 619787
ⓔ ticking@onetel.co.uk
Est. 1970
Services Antique clock repair and restoration
Open By appointment

Goodacre Engraving (BHI)
Contact John Skeavington
✉ **The Dial House, 120 Main Street, Sutton Bonington, Leicestershire, LE12 5PF** 🅿
☎ 01509 673082 ⓕ 01509 673082
Est. 1948
Services Dial engraving, restoration and clock parts for English longcase and bracket clocks
Open Mon–Sat 9am–5pm telephone for appointment

Gray Arts
Contact Mr A Gray
✉ **Unit 21b, The Maltings, School Lane, Amersham, Buckinghamshire, HP7 0ET** 🅿
☎ 01494 726502 ⓕ 01494 726502
Ⓜ 07714 274410
Est. 1979
Services Porcelain restoration, clock and watch dial restoration
Trade only Yes
Open By appointment

Nick Hansford
Contact Nick Hansford
✉ **Nyth-fa, Llanwrane, Hereford, Herefordshire, HR2 8JE** 🅿
☎ 01981 540460
Est. 1968
Services Clock and watch repair
Open By appointment

Richard Higgins Conservation (BAFRA, UKIC)
Contact Richard Higgins
✉ **The Old School, Longnor, Nr Shrewsbury, Shropshire, SY5 7PP** 🅿
☎ 01743 718162 ⓕ 01743 718022
ⓔ richardhigginsco@aol.com
Est. 1988
Services Restoration of all fine furniture, clocks, movements, dials and cases, casting, plating, boulle, gilding, lacquerwork, carving, upholstery
Open Mon–Fri 8am–6pm

Horological Workshops (BHI, BADA)
Contact Mr M D Tooke
✉ **204 Worplesdon Road, Guildford, Surrey, GU2 9UY** 🅿
☎ 01483 576496 ⓕ 01483 452212
ⓔ enquiries@horological workshops.com
ⓦ www.horologicalworkshops.com
Est. 1968
Services Full restoration of antique clocks
Open Tues–Fri 8.30am–5.30pm Sat 9am–12.30pm

Gavin Hussey Antique Restoration (BAFRA)
Contact G Hussey
✉ **4 Brook Farm, Clayhill Road, Leigh, Reigate, Surrey, RH2 8PA** 🅿
☎ 01306 611634 ⓕ 01306 611634
Est. 1994
Services Full restoration of furniture and clocks
Open By appointment

Leominster Clock Repairs (BHI)
Contact Ashley Prosser
✉ **Unit 2, The Railway Station, Worcester Road, Leominster, Herefordshire, HR6 8AR** 🅿
☎ 01568 612298
Est. 2000
Services Clock restoration, specializing in longcase clocks
Open Mon–Sat 9am–6pm

Llewellyn Clocks
Contact Mr C Llewellyn
✉ **12 Gibson Crescent, Sandbach, Cheshire, CW11 3HW** 🅿
☎ 01270 768525
Est. 1976
Services Complete antique clock repair and restoration
Open By appointment only

Robert Loomes Clock Restoration (BWCG MBHI)
Contact Mr R Loomes
✉ **3 St Leonards Street, Stamford, Lincolnshire, PE9 2HU** 🅿
☎ 01780 481319
ⓦ www.dialrestorer.co.uk
Est. 1987
Services Antique repair and restoration
Open Mon–Fri 9am–5pm or by appointment

Manor House Clocks (BWCMG)
Contact Ken Whitton
✉ **The Old Manor House, 1 Rectory Lane, Harlaxton, Grantham, Lincolnshire, NG32 1HD** 🅿
☎ 01476 574962
Ⓜ 07973 675720
ⓔ ken@manorhouseclocks.co.uk
Est. 1987
Services Repair of longcase clocks and mercury barometers, valuations
Open By appointment

William Mansell (BHI, NAG, BWCG)
Contact Bill Salisbury
✉ **24 Connaught Street, London, W2 2AF** 🅿
☎ 020 7723 4154 ⓕ 020 7724 2273
ⓔ mail@williammansell.co.uk
ⓦ www.williammansell.co.uk
Est. 1864
Services Repair, restoration and sale of clocks, watches, barometers, barographs
Open Mon–Fri 9am–6pm Sat 10am–1pm

Merim Restoration
Contact Ian Potts
✉ **Bow Street, Langport, Somerset, TA10 9PL** 🅿
☎ 01458 252157 ⓕ 01458 250747
ⓔ merimianpots@hotmail.com
Est. 1979
Services Clock restoration, specializing in English longcase
Open Mon–Fri 8am–5pm Sat 8.30am–noon

C Moss
Contact Mr C Moss
✉ **59 Walcot Street, Bath, Somerset, BA1 5BN** 🅿
☎ 01225 445892 ⓕ 01225 445892
Ⓜ 07779 161731
Est. 1985
Services Clock case restoration, marquetry, parquetry, walnut furniture
Open By appointment

Philip Oliver of Knaresborough
Contact Mr P Oliver
✉ **Finkle Street, Knaresborough, North Yorkshire, HG5 8AA** 🅿
☎ 01423 868438
Est. 1961
Services Clock repair, restoration
Open Mon–Sat 8am–5.30pm

Oxford Longcase Clocks
Contact Mr Paul Carroll
✉ **76 Courtland Road, Rose Hill, Oxford, Oxfordshire, OX4 4JB** 🅿
☎ 01865 779660
Est. 1978
Services Clock and barometer repair
Open Mon–Fri 8am–5pm
Sat 8am–noon

Reeves Restoration at the Coach House Antiques
Contact Paul or Louise Reeves
✉ **The Coach House, 60 Station Road, Gomshall, Guildford, Surrey, GU5 9NP** 🅿
☎ 01483 203838 Ⓕ 01483 202999
Ⓜ 07774 729325
Ⓔ coach_house.antiques@virgin.net
Ⓦ www.coachhouseantiques.com
Est. 1984
Services Antique clock, furniture restoration
Open Wed–Sat 9.30am–5pm
Sun noon–5pm closed Mon Tues

J K Speed Antique Furniture Restoration
Contact Mr J Speed
✉ **The Workshop, Thornton Road, New York, Lincoln, Lincolnshire, LN4 4YL** 🅿
☎ 01205 280313
Ⓜ 07734 708672
Est. 1964
Services Antique repair and restoration, light upholstery, specializing in case repair of longcase clocks, French polishing and all ancillary services
Open Mon–Fri 9am–5.30pm

Sundial Antique Clock Service
Contact Mr Peter Mole
✉ **64 The Parade, Brighton Road, Hooley, Coulsdon, Surrey, CR5 3EE** 🅿
☎ 01737 551991 Ⓕ 01737 551991
Ⓜ 07733 408535
Ⓔ sundialclocks@hooley68.fsnet.co.uk
Est. 1965
Services Barometer and clock restoration, specializing in longcase clock repair
Open By appointment

Surrey Clock Centre
Contact Mr Haw or Mr Ingrams
✉ **3 Lower Street, Haslemere, Surrey, GU27 2NY** 🅿
☎ 01428 651313
Ⓦ www.surreyclockcentre.co.uk
Est. 1968
Services Repair, restoration and sales of clocks and barometers
Open Wed 9am–5pm
Sat 9am–1pm

Robert P Tandy (BAFRA)
Contact Robert P Tandy
✉ **Lake House Barn, Off Colehouse Lane, Kenn, Clevedon, Bristol, BS21 6TQ** 🅿
☎ 01275 875014
Ⓔ robertptandy@hotmail.com
Est. 1987
Services Antique furniture and longcase clock casework restoration
Open Mon–Fri 10am–6pm

Tempus Watches (LAPADA)
Contact John Wingate
✉ **Sunninghill, Ascot, Berkshire, SL5** 🅿
☎ 01344 874007
Ⓔ john@tempus-watches.co.uk
Ⓦ www.tempus-watches.co.uk
Est. 1978
Services Restoration of antique clocks and vintage wristwatches
Open By appointment

Time Restored Ltd (BHI)
Contact J H Bowler-Reed
✉ **20 High Street, Pewsey, Wiltshire, SN9 5AQ** 🅿
☎ 01672 563544
Ⓦ www.timerestored.co.uk
Est. 1978
Services Restoration of antique clocks, musical boxes and barometers
Open Mon–Fri 10am–6pm

Timecraft Clocks (BHI)
Contact Mr G Smith
✉ **Unit 2, 24 Cheap Street, Sherborne, Dorset, DT9 3PX** 🅿
☎ 01935 817771 Ⓕ 01935 817771
Est. 1994
Services Clock restoration and repair
Open Tue–Fri 10.30am–5.30pm
Sat 10.30am–2pm

Chris Wadge Clocks
Contact Patrick Wadge
✉ **83 Fisherton Street, Salisbury, Wiltshire, SP2 7ST** 🅿
☎ 01722 334467
Est. 1985
Services Repair, restoration of antique and modern clocks, 400-day anniversary clocks a speciality
Open Tues–Sat 9am–4pm
closed 1–2pm

Warwick Antique Restorations (UKIC)
Contact Mr R Lawman
✉ **32 Beddington Lane, Croydon, Surrey, CR0 4TB** 🅿
☎ 020 8688 4511
Ⓔ info@warwickantiques.co.uk
Ⓦ www.warwickantiques.co.uk
Est. 1976
Services Antique clock restoration, leathering, rushing, upholstery, caning, brass
Open Tues–Sat 9.30am–5pm

Wheelers (BHI, BWCG)
Contact Mr T P Wheeler
✉ **14–16 Bath Place, Worthing, West Sussex, BN11 3BA**
☎ 01903 207656 Ⓕ 01903 207656
Est. 1991
Services Antique clock repair, restoration, sales
Open Mon–Sat 9am–5pm

Ken Wright (CMBHI)
Contact Keith Wright
✉ **99 Carter Drive, Collier Row, Romford, Essex, RM5 2PJ** 🅿
☎ 01708 767455
Est. 1995
Services Mechanical antique clock repair
Open By appointment

CONSERVATION

Archaeological Conservator (ICHAWI, IIC, IPCRA)
Contact Susannah Kelly

✉ **14 Greenmount Lawns, Terenure, Dublin 6**
☎ 01 492 7695/01 716 8503
Ⓜ 08728 48752
Ⓔ csmchale@gofree.indigo.ie
Est. 1993
Services Conservation of archaeological and historical objects, surveys and environmental reports, studies on conservation facilities
Open Mon–Fri 9am–6pm

Roland Haycraft (GADAR)

Contact Mr R Haycraft
✉ **The Lamb Arcade, High Street, Wallingford, Oxfordshire, OX10 0BS** Ⓟ
☎ 01491 839622
Ⓔ ro@fsbdial.co.uk
Ⓦ www.juststolen.com
Est. 1980
Services Antique furniture conservation
Open Mon–Fri 9am–5.30pm

Heritage Care (Accredited conservator of ICHAWI, IPCRA, IMA)

Contact Adrian Kennedy
✉ **Dublin, Ireland**
☎ 01 459 9745 Ⓕ 01 459 9745
Ⓔ heritagecare@oceanfree.net
Est. 1998
Services Conservation and restoration of museum, folk-life and religious-type objects dating from the archaeological period to 20thC
Open Mon–Fri 7.30am–5.30pm by appointment

London Stone Conservation (SPAB)

Contact Florian Kirchertz
✉ **42 Sekforde Street, Finsbury, London, EC1R 0AH** Ⓟ
☎ 020 7251 0592 Ⓕ 020 7251 0592
Ⓜ 07876 685470
Ⓔ lsc@londonstoneconservation.com
Ⓦ www.londonstoneconservation.com
Est. 2004
Services Conservation and restoration of ancient buildings, monuments, masonry, stone carving, letters
Open By appointment

Plowden and Smith Ltd (MGR)

Contact Sarah Giles
✉ **190 St Ann's Hill, London, SW18 2RT** Ⓟ
☎ 020 8874 4005 Ⓕ 020 8874 7248
Ⓔ info@plowden-smith.com
Ⓦ www.plowden-smith.com
Est. 1966
Services Repair and restoration of paintings, furniture, stone, metalwork, decorative arts, object mounting, exhibitions
Open Mon–Fri 9am–5pm

Gordon Richardson

Contact Gordon Richardson
✉ **36 Silverknowes Road, Edinburgh, EH4 5LG** Ⓟ
☎ 0131 312 7959
Services Conservation and restoration of paintings, pictures, prints, drawings, globes, scientific instruments, silverware, metalware, military artefacts, ships' models, decorative objects
Open By appointment

Textile Conservation (UKIC)

Contact Fiona Hutton
✉ **Ivy House Farm, Wolvershill Road, Banwell, Somerset, BS29 6LB** Ⓟ
☎ 01934 822449
Ⓔ fiona@textileconservation.co.uk
Est. 1989
Services Textile conservation
Open Mon–Fri 9am–5pm

Textile Conservation Services

Contact Miss L Bond
✉ **3–4 West Workshops, Welbeck, Worksop, Nottinghamshire, S80 3LW** Ⓟ
☎ 01909 481655
Ⓔ textile.conservation@tesco.net
Est. 1984
Services The conservation of costume, lace and small textiles. Talks and courses on costume and textiles
Open By appointment

Voitek Conservation of Works of Art (IPC)

Contact Mrs E Sobczynski
✉ **9 Whitehorse Mews, Westminster Bridge Road, London, SE1 7QD** Ⓟ
☎ 020 7928 6094 Ⓕ 020 7928 6094
Ⓔ voitekcwa@btinternet.com
Est. 1972
Services Conservation of prints, drawings, watercolours, maps, conservation mounting and project planning. Conservation of sculpture, marble, terracotta, wood
Open By appointment

CONSULTANCY

A D Antiques

Contact Alison Davey
✉ **PO Box 2407, Woodseaves, Stafford, Staffordshire, ST15 8WY**
Ⓜ 07811 783518
Ⓔ alison@adantiques.com
Ⓦ www.adantiques.com
Est. 1997
Services Advice on interior decoration and private decorative arts collections. Collections purchased. Buys on commission at auction
Open By appointment

Tim Corfield Professional Antiques Consultant

Contact Tim Corfield
✉ **Beechcroft, Buckholt Road, Broughton, Stockbridge, Hampshire, SO20 8DA** Ⓟ
☎ 01794 301141 Ⓕ 01794 301141
Ⓜ 07798 881383
Ⓔ antique@tcp.co.uk
Ⓦ www.corfieldmorris.com
Est. 1992
Services Advising clients on purchases at auction or in the trade
Open By appointment

Craftsman Antiques

Contact Mark Haines
✉ **25 Bridget Drive, Sedbury, Chepstow, Monmouthshire, NP16 7AR** Ⓟ
☎ 01291 625145 Ⓕ 01291 625145
Ⓜ 07836 634712
Ⓔ mark@oakden.co.uk
Ⓦ www.antiquekitchenalia.com
Est. 1968
Services Consultancy for kitchenware, providing information, books, films etc from the Stone Age to the present day
Open Mon–Sun 9am–5pm

IDS Valuation Consultants (BWCG)

Contact Iain Sutherland
✉ **79 Templehill, Troon, Ayrshire, KA10 6BQ** Ⓟ
☎ 01292 315999

Est. 1995
Services Valuations and full consultation service
Open Mon–Sat 9.30am–5.30pm or by appointment

Robert Kleiner and Co Ltd (BADA, CINOA)
Contact Robert Kleiner or Jane de Hurtig
✉ 30 Old Bond Street, London, W1S 4AE P
☎ 020 7629 1814 F 020 7629 1239
e robert.kleiner@virgin.net
w www.cloudband.com/gallery/kleiner/playthings
Est. 1989
Services Advice on purchase and sale of Chinese works of art, jades, porcelain, snuff bottles, valuations of collections. Specialist in Chinese snuff bottles.
Open Mon–Fri 9.30am–5.30pm

David C E Lewry (BAFRA, Woodwork Fellowship)
Contact Mr D Lewry
✉ Wychelms, 66 Gorran Avenue, Peel Common, Gosport, Hampshire, PO13 0NF P
☎ 01329 286901 F 01329 289964
M 07785 766844
Est. 1979
Services Consultancy on furniture restoration
Open By appointment

Michael Lipitch Ltd (BADA)
Contact Mr M Lipitch
✉ Mayfair, PO Box 3146, London, EN4 0BP P
M 07730 954347
e michaellipitch@hotmail.com
Est. 1960
Services Specialist advice on forming collections of 18thC fine furniture and objects
Open By appointment

Magic Lanterns
Contact J A Marsden
✉ By George, 23 George Street, St Albans, Hertfordshire, AL3 4ES P
☎ 01727 865680
Est. 1987
Services Lighting consultancy for period houses
Open Mon–Fri 10am–5pm Sat 10am–5.30pm Sun 1–5pm

DISPLAY EQUIPMENT

Arcade Arts Ltd
Contact Mr K Hewitt or Monika Wengraf-Hewitt
✉ 25 West Hill Road, London, SW18 1LL P
☎ 020 8265 2564 F 020 8874 2982
Est. 1997
Services Repair and renovation of art objects and makers of display stands
Open By appointment

C & A J Barmby
Contact C Barmby
✉ 140 Lavender Hill, Tonbridge, Kent, TN9 2AY
☎ 01732 771590 F 01732 771590
e bookpilot@aol.com
Est. 1970
Services Reference books on antiques, display stands, accessories, packaging material
Trade only Yes
Open By appointment

BJK Sales
Contact Christopher Edwards
✉ Unit 9, Apollo Business Centre, Trundleys Road, London, SE8 5JY P
☎ 020 8692 2325 F 020 8694 2391
Est. 1974
Services New and used showcases, towers, counters and tabletop displays
Open Mon–Fri 10am–5pm

Turn On Lighting
Contact Janet Holdstock
✉ 116–118 Islington High Street, Camden Passage, Islington, London, N1 8EG P
☎ 020 7359 7616 F 020 7359 7616
Est. 1976
Services Display lighting
Open Tues–Fri 10am–6pm Sat 9.30am–4.30pm

DOCUMENTATION AND PROVENANCE

DIVA (Digital Inventory and Visual Archive) (GADAR)
Contact Mr R Haycraft
✉ The Lamb Arcade, High Street, Wallingford, Oxfordshire, OX10 0BS P
☎ 01491 839622
e diva@fsbdial.co.uk
w www.diva-id.com
Est. 1980
Services Museum-quality archive documentation, recorded on CD or printed, for insurance, probate, inheritance division and provenance history, plus, if property is stolen, world-wide publicity on two websites. For collectors of all valuable objects
Open Mon–Fri 9am–5.30pm

ENAMEL

Mark Newland Enamel Restorer
Contact Mr M Newland
✉ 1 Whitehouse Way, Southgate, London, N14 7LX P
☎ 020 8361 0429
Est. 1982
Services Restoration of enamelled jewellery and objets d'art
Open By appointment

ETHNOGRAPHICS

George Monger
Contact Mr G Monger
✉ Unit 6, The Barn, Glebe Farm Industrial Units, Onehouse, Stowmarket, Suffolk, IP14 3HL P
☎ 01449 677900 F 01449 674803
M 07703 441265
e geoMcons@tinyworld.co.uk
Est. 1995
Services Conservation and restoration, including social and industrial history and ethnography of pieces
Open By appointment

FLOORS

Holland & Welsh
Contact Michael Nap
✉ Unit 13, Riverside Park, Treforest Industrial Estate, Pontypridd, Mid Glamorgan, CF37 5TG P
☎ 01443 660255 F 01443 660651
Est. 1997
Services Supply and installation of antique flooring
Open Mon–Fri 9am–5pm Sat Sun 9.30am–1.30pm

FRAMES

Baron Art
Contact Mr A Baron
✉ 9 Chapel Yard, Albert Street,

Holt, Norfolk,
NR25 6HJ P
☎ 01263 713430 F 01263 711670
E baronart@aol.com
Est. 2001
Services Framing
Open Mon–Sat 9am–5pm

Berkeley Framing (FATG)
Contact David Gethyn-Jones
✉ **16–18 High Street, Berkeley, Gloucestershire, GL13 9BJ** P
☎ 01453 811513 F 01453 511616
M 07802 911894
E berkeley.framing@tesco.net
Est. 1956
Services Picture framing
Open Mon–Sun 9.30am–5.30pm

Burghley Fine Art Conservation Ltd
Contact Mike Cowell
✉ **The Stable Courtyard, Burghley House, Stamford, Lincolnshire, PE9 3JY** P
☎ 01780 762155 F 01780 762155
Est. 1977
Services Restoration of oil paintings and picture frames
Open By appointment

Courtyard Restoration
Contact Shaun Butler or Cosi Sarkar
✉ **2 Parkfield Road, Ahoghill, Co Antrim, BT42 2QS** P
☎ 028 2587 8875
Est. 1995
Services Furniture restoration, French polishing, re-carving, veneer repair, picture frame restoration
Open Mon–Sat 10am–5.30pm

Huddersfield Picture Framing Co.
Contact Miss P Ward
✉ **Cloth Hall Street, Huddersfield, West Yorkshire, HD1 2EG** P
☎ 01484 546075
Est. 1979
Services Picture framing
Open Mon Tues Thurs Fri 9am–5pm Wed 9am–1pm Sat 9am–4pm

Inglenook Fine Arts (FATG)
Contact Jill Bagshaw
✉ **Greenend Gallery, Greenend, Woodchurch, Shropshire, SY13 1AA** P
☎ 01948 665422 F 01948 665422
E info@inglenookfineart.co.uk
W www.inglenookfineart.co.uk
Est. 1985
Services Picture restoration, framing
Open Mon–Sat 9.30am–5pm Wed closed 1pm

Inglenook Fine Arts (FATG)
Contact Jill Bagshaw
✉ **31 Pillory Street, Nantwich, Cheshire, CW5 5BQ** P
☎ 01270 611188
E info@inglenookfineart.co.uk
W www.inglenookfineart.co.uk
Est. 1993
Services Picture restoration, framing
Open Mon–Sat 9.30am–5pm Wed closed 1pm

Looking Glass of Bath (IIC)
Contact Anthony Reed
✉ **93–96 Walcot Street, Bath, Somerset, BA1 5BG** P
☎ 01225 461969 F 01225 316191
M 07831 323878
E info@lookingglassofbath.co.uk
W www.lookingglassofbath.co.uk
Est. 1968
Services Restoration of mirrors, picture frames, regilding, carving, manufacturer and supplier of antique mirror glass, paper and oil restoration
Open Mon–Sat 9am–6pm

Douglas McLeod Period Frames
Contact Suzie McLeod
✉ **44 Trinity Street, Salisbury, Wiltshire, SP1 2BD** P
☎ 01722 337565 F 01722 337565
Est. 1982
Services Restoration of old frames, picture restoration, carving, gilding, lacewing framing
Open Mon–Fri 9am–5pm Sat 10am–4pm

Renaissance
Contact Mr Peter Cross
✉ **11 Enterprise Close, Croydon, Surrey, CR0 3RZ** P
☎ 020 8664 9686 F 020 8664 9737
Est. 1996
Services Furniture and frame repair and restoration
Open Mon–Fri 10am–6.30pm

FURNITURE

SOUTH EAST

T M Akers Antique Restoration (BAFRA)
Contact Mr T M Akers
✉ **39 Chancery Lane, Beckenham, Kent, BR3 2NR** P
☎ 020 8650 9179
M 07768 948421
W www.akersofantiques.com
Est. 1979
Services Period antique furniture restoration
Open Mon–Fri 9am–5pm

Antique Restorations (BAFRA)
Contact Raymond Konyn
✉ **The Old Wheelwrights', Brasted Forge, Brasted, Kent, TN16 1JL** P
☎ 01959 563863 F 01959 561262
E antique@antique-restorations.org.uk
W www.antique-restorations.org.uk
Est. 1979
Services Full antique furniture restoration, pre-1900 furniture sourcing and acquisition
Open Mon–Fri 9am–5pm

Ashdown Antiques Restoration
Contact Robert Hale
✉ **Old Forge Farm, Old Forge Lane, Horney Common, Uckfield, East Sussex, TB22 3EL** P
☎ 01825 713003
E roberthale.2@yahoo.com
Est. 1975
Services Furniture restoration, painting, gilding, marquetry, inlay work
Open By appointment

Bespoke Furniture
Contact Mr M McEwan
✉ **Ladwood Farm, Acrise, Folkestone, Kent, CT18 8LL** P
☎ 01303 893635
Est. 1994
Services Restoration of antique furniture. Traditional or contemporary individual pieces

of furniture made to order
Open Mon–Fri 8.30am–5pm Sat 9am–2pm Sun by appointment

Bigwood Restoration
Contact Mr S Bigwood
✉ **Bigwood Antiques, High Street, Brasted, Kent, TN16 1JA** P
☎ 01959 564458
ⓔ sales@bigwoodantiques.com
ⓦ www.bigwoodantiques.com
Est. 1984
Services Complete restoration of all antique furniture
Open Mon–Sat 10am–5pm Sun noon–4pm

Kevin Birch (BAFRA)
Contact Kevin Birch
✉ **Unit 2, Service House, 61–63 Rochester Road, Aylesford, Kent, ME20 7BS** P
☎ 01622 790080 ⓕ 01622 790080
ⓜ 07960 721640
ⓔ kevin@kbirch.fsbusiness.co.uk
ⓦ www.kevinbirch.co.uk
Est. 1993
Services Furniture restoration, French polishing and upholstery
Open Mon–Fri 8.30am–5pm

Brightling Restoration
Contact D White
✉ **Little Worge Farm, Brightling, Robertsbridge, East Sussex, TN32 5HN** P
☎ 01424 838424 ⓕ 01424 838681
ⓔ brtrest@aol.com
Est. 2000
Services Restoration of English and Continental furniture
Open Mon–Fri 8am–4.30pm

Christie Antiques Restoration (Furniture)
Contact Stephen Christie
✉ **The Oast, Hurst Farm, Mountain Street, Chilham, Kent, CT4 8DH** P
☎ 01227 730924 ⓕ 01304 613585
ⓔ steve@christieantiques.co.uk
ⓦ www.christieantiques.co.uk
Est. 1989
Services Restoration of furniture and antiques
Open Mon–Fri 9am–4pm

Benedict Clegg (BAFRA)
Contact Mr Benedict Clegg
✉ **Rear of 20 Camden Road, Tunbridge Wells, Kent, TN1 2PY**
☎ 01892 548095
Est. 1987
Services Antique furniture repair and restoration
Open Mon–Fri 9am–5pm

D & C Antique Restorations
Contact Mr C Voles
✉ **1–4 Upper Gardner Street, Brighton, East Sussex, BN1 4AN** P
☎ 01273 670344
Est. 1993
Services Complete antique furniture restoration
Open Mon–Fri 8am–5.30pm

W H Earles
Contact Mr W H Earles
✉ **60 Castle Road, Tankerton, Whitstable, Kent, CT5 2EA** P
☎ 01227 264346
Est. 1978
Services English, Continental and most period furniture restoration and papier mâché
Open Mon–Fri 8.30am–6pm

Farm Cottage Antiques
Contact Mrs Lynn Winder
✉ **Basement, 6a Claremont Road, Seaford, East Sussex, BN25 2AY** P
☎ 01323 896766 ⓕ 01323 894982
ⓜ 07765 292253
Est. 1995
Services Furniture restoration
Open Mon–Fri 9am–1pm or by appointment

Glassenbury Country Furniture Ltd
Contact Clive Cowell
✉ **Iden Green, Goudhurst, Cranbrook, Kent, TN17 2PA** P
☎ 01580 212022
Est. 1985
Services Repair and restoration, makes on commission
Open Mon–Fri 8.30am–5.30pm Sat by appointment

Heritage Restoration
Contact Mr D R Johnson
✉ **782 Lower Rainham Road, Rainham, Gillingham, Kent, ME8 7UD** P
☎ 01634 374609
Est. 1989
Services Antique furniture restoration
Open Mon–Fri 9am–5pm or by appointment

T C Hinton
Contact T C Hinton
✉ **The Board Stores, Spencer Mews, Rear of 20 Camden Rd, Tunbridge Wells, Kent, TN1 2PY** P
☎ 01892 547515 ⓕ 01892 547515
Est. 1979
Services Restoration and conservation of antique furniture, French polishing, gilding, painted furniture, antique paint effects
Open Mon–Fri 9am–1pm 2–5.30pm

R G Jones
Contact R G Jones
✉ **1 Brickfield Cottage, Bilting, Ashford, Kent, TN25 4ER** P
☎ 01233 812849
Est. 1985
Services Antique restoration, gilding
Open Mon–Fri 9am–4pm

R Lindsell
Contact R Lindsell
✉ **2b Southwood Road, Ramsgate, Kent, CT11 0AA** P
☎ 01843 588845
Est. 1973
Services Furniture repair and restoration, French polishing
Open Mon–Fri 11am–7pm

Timothy Long Restoration (BAFRA, Conservation Register)
Contact Timothy Long
✉ **St John's Church, London Road, Dunton Green, Sevenoaks, Kent, TN13 2TE** P
☎ 01732 743368 ⓕ 01732 742206
ⓔ info@timlong.co.uk
Est. 1978
Services Antique furniture restoration, marquetry, boulle, clock cases, upholstery, cabinet work and polishing
Open Mon–Fri 8am–5pm

The Old Forge
Contact Mr Burgess
✉ **South Street, Rotherfield,**

Crowborough, East Sussex, TN6 3LR P
☎ 01892 852060
Est. 1979
Services Furniture restoration
Open Mon–Fri 8am–6pm Sat 8am–2pm

Park View Antiques
Contact Patrick Leith-Ross
✉ **High Street, Durgates, Wadhurst, East Sussex, TN5 6DE** P
☎ 01892 740264 Ⓕ 01892 740264
Ⓜ 07970 202036
Ⓔ leithross@btconnect.com
Ⓦ www.parkviewantiques
Est. 1985
Services Furniture restoration
Open By appointment

Phillburys
Contact Mr G C Rattenbury
✉ **Unit 2, Udimore Workshop, School Lane, Udimore, Rye, East Sussex, TN31 6AS** P
☎ 01797 222361
Est. 1982
Services Restoration of antique furniture
Open Mon–Sat 8am–6pm

Marco Pitt (BADA)
Contact Mr Marco Pitt
✉ **New England House, New England Street, Brighton, East Sussex, BN1 4GH** P
☎ 01273 685009
Ⓜ 07721 022480
Est. 1978
Services Complete furniture restoration, specializing in Russian, French, European pieces
Open Mon–Fri 9am–6pm Sat 9am–1pm

Potter Antiques (GADAR)
Contact Victor Potter
✉ **1 Lansdown Place, Lewes, East Sussex, BN7 2JT** P
☎ 01273 487671 Ⓕ 01273 330143
Ⓜ 07768 274461
Ⓔ cvpotter@aol.com
Ⓦ www.potterantiques.com
Est. 2001
Services Repair and restoration of furniture, wooden items, architectural woodwork, carving, marquetry, inlay, turning, gilding, caning, upholstery. Specialists in replacement of desk and writing slope leathers, baize surfaces and repolishing of ebonized items
Open Wed–Fri 10am–5.30pm

Paul M Read Antique Furniture Restoration
Contact Paul Read
✉ **12b Gaza Trading Estate, Scabharbour Lane, Sevenpoz, Kent, TN11 8PL** P
☎ 01732 460022
Est. 1986
Services Full furniture restoration, cabinet-making, marquetry, inlaying, carving, turning, gilding, leather work, full clock restoration service, upholstery, cane and rush seating, traditional French polishing, on-site polishing and specialist wood finishes
Open By appointment

Vincent Reed Furniture
Contact Vincent
✉ **103a Keymer Road, Keymer, Hassocks, East Sussex, BN6 8QL** P
☎ 01273 845678
Ⓜ 07815 751005
Ⓔ info@vincentreed.com
Ⓦ www.vincentreed.co.uk
Est. 1992
Services 17th–18thC furniture restoration
Open Mon–Sat 9am–5pm

Restore-It (Folkestone) Ltd
Contact Roger Keeling
✉ **69 Tontine Street, Folkestone, Kent, CT20 1JR**
☎ 01303 223726
Est. 1999
Services Furniture restoration and polishing
Open Mon–Fri 9.30am–5.30pm

T Straw Restoration
Contact Mr T Straw
✉ **Ladwood Farm, Acrise, Folkestone, Kent, CT18 8LL** P
☎ 01303 894001
Est. 1989
Services Antique furniture restoration
Open Mon–Fri 8am–6pm or by appointment

V Stringer
Contact Mr V Stringer
✉ **Unit 5, Acorn House, The Broyle, Ringmer, Lewes, East Sussex, BN8 5NN** P
☎ 01273 814434 Ⓕ 01273 814434
Ⓜ 077622 61149
Ⓔ usp47@hotmail.com
Est. 1989
Services Antique restoration, reproduction polishers, furniture makers
Open Mon–Fri 8am–6pm Sat 8am–noon

Temple Jones Restoration
Contact Mr E or Miss B Temple Jones
✉ **Caspers House, Heathfield Road, Burwash Common, East Sussex, TN19 7LT** P
☎ 01435 883130 Ⓕ 01435 883130
Ⓜ 07802 415138
Ⓔ temple-jones@talk21.com
Est. 1996
Services Restoration and conservation work to period antique furniture
Open Mon–Sat 8am–6pm

Tony's Antique Services Ltd
Contact Tony King
✉ **85 Seaside Road, Eastbourne, East Sussex, BN21 3PL**
☎ 01323 733776 Ⓕ 01323 733776
Ⓜ 07752 201786
Est. 1977
Services Furniture restoration, export, search service
Open Tues–Sat 10am–5pm Mon by appointment

LONDON

Abeam Antiques
Contact Joseph Yousif
✉ **159 Carr Road, Northolt, Middlesex, UB5 4RE** P
☎ 020 8426 8857
Est. 1994
Services Furniture, lighting restoration, repair
Open By appointment

J Abrahart
Contact Mr J Abrahart
✉ **62a Valetta Road, London, W3 7TN** P
☎ 020 8746 7260

Est. 1955
Services Antique furniture repair and restoration, French polishing
Open By appointment

G Albanese
Contact Mr G Albanese
✉ **Unit 3a, 100 Rosebery Avenue, London, E12 6PS** Ⓟ
☎ 020 8471 5417
Est. 1978
Services Antique restoration and cabinet-making
Trade only Yes
Open Mon–Fri 7am–5pm

Antique Restorations (BAFRA)
Contact Mr A Smith
✉ **45 Windmill Road, Brentford, Middlesex, TW8 0QQ** Ⓟ
☎ 020 8568 5249 Ⓕ 020 8568 5249
Est. 1987
Services Restorers of painted and decorated furniture. Specialists in Oriental lacquering, japanning, gilding
Open Mon–Fri 9am–4.30pm or by appointment

Ballantyne Booth Ltd (UKIC)
Contact Miss H Mark or Mr Scott Bowram
✉ **Wendover House, 2a Wendover Road, London, NW10 4RT** Ⓟ
☎ 020 8965 2777 Ⓕ 020 8965 2777
Est. 1983
Services Cabinet work, veneering, glazing, carving, polishing, upholstery, aerial conservation and restoration
Open Mon–Fri 9am–5.30pm

Bell House Restoration Ltd
Contact Mr R Humphrey
✉ **20–22 Beardell Street, London, SE19 1TP** Ⓟ
☎ 020 8761 9002 Ⓕ 020 8761 9012
Ⓜ 07771 801269
Ⓔ bellhouserestore@aol.com
Ⓦ www.antique-restoration-london.co.uk
Est. 1984
Services Antique furniture restoration, gilding, polishing, colouring, turning, veneering, restoration abroad, simulation
Open Mon–Fri 8am–5pm

A J Brett & Co
Contact Shane Webb
✉ **168 Marlborough Road, London, N19 4NP** Ⓟ
☎ 020 7272 8462 Ⓕ 020 7272 5102
Ⓔ ajbrett@aol.com
Ⓦ www.ajbrett.co.uk
Est. 1960
Services Furniture restoration, gilding, upholstery
Open Mon–Fri 7.30am–3.30pm

Carlsson Antique
Contact Mr Fell
✉ **Arch No 28, Popes Grove, Strawberry Hill, Twickenham, Middlesex, TW1 4JZ** Ⓟ
☎ 020 8893 9834
Ⓜ 07941 918277
Est. 2000
Services Furniture restoration, French polishing, cabinet-making, wood turning, carving, bespoke carpentry
Open Mon–Fri 10am–6pm

The Collector's Workshop
Contact Mr B Brannan
✉ **Unit 11, The Peacock Estate, 20/22 White Hart Lane, London, N17 8DT** Ⓟ
☎ 020 8808 1920 Ⓕ 020 8808 1920
Ⓜ 07778 754754
Ⓔ enquiries@collectorsworkshop.co.uk
Ⓦ www.collectorsworkshop.co.uk
Est. 1968
Services Antique furniture repair and restoration, upholstery, carving, gilding, leather desk lining, dummy book spines
Open By appointment

W J Cook (BAFRA)
Contact Mr B Cook
✉ **167 Battersea High Street, London, SW11 3JS** Ⓟ
☎ 020 7736 5329
Ⓔ william.cook@virgin.net
Ⓦ www.antiquerestoration.uk.com
Est. 1963
Services Furniture polishing, restoration, upholstery, gilding
Open By appointment

Crafted Interiors
Contact Mr P Harris
✉ **291 Sydenham Road, London, SE26 5EW** Ⓟ
☎ 020 8659 0333
Est. 1987
Services Antique furniture repair and restoration, upholstery, French polishing, woodwork repair
Open Mon–Sat 8.30am–7.30pm

The Craftsman's Joint
Contact Mrs Jo Hollis
✉ **173 Kingston Road, London, SW19 1LH** Ⓟ
☎ 020 8545 0655 Ⓕ 020 8395 4566
Ⓔ craftsmansjoint@aol.com
Est. 1991
Services Furniture restoration, cabinet-making, French polishing, upholstery, caning, leatherwork
Open Mon–Fri 9.30am–5.30pm Sat 9am–3pm closed Wed or by appointment

Crawford Antiques
✉ **87 Cricklewood Lane, London, NW2 1HR** Ⓟ
☎ 020 8450 3660
Est. 1969
Services Antique repair and French polishing
Open Mon–Sat 9am–6pm

G and D Davis Antique Restorers
Contact Mr G Davis
✉ **135 Bowes Road, London, N13 4SE** Ⓟ
☎ 020 8889 4951
Est. 1982
Services Antique furniture restoration, caning, upholstery
Open Mon–Sat 9am–6pm by appointment

Hannerle Dehn
Contact Hannerle Dehn
✉ **Studio 4, Southam Street, London, W10 5PP** Ⓟ
☎ 020 8964 0599 Ⓕ 020 7602 1192
Ⓜ 07798 623715
Ⓔ robinersligh@freeserve.co.uk
Ⓦ www.hannerledehn.co.uk
Est. 1978
Services Restoration of 18th–19thC lacquered and gilded, painted and decorated furniture
Open Mon–Fri 8am–5pm or by appointment

Dyson Furniture
Contact Nick Dyson
✉ **Eel Pie Boatyard, Eel Pie Island,**

Twickenham, Middlesex, TW1 3DY
☎ 020 8891 5309
Est. 1992
Services Complete furniture repair and restoration, turning, marquetry, inlay work, cabinet-making
Open Mon–Fri 10am–6pm

Elizabeth Street Antiques and Restoration Services
Contact Mr Naik
✉ **35 Elizabeth Street, London, SW1W 9RP** 🅿
☎ 020 7730 6777
Ⓜ 07973 909257
Est. 1993
Services Antique restoration, marquetry, French polishing, upholstery
Open Mon–Sat 8am–7pm

Ellington Place Workshop
Contact B J Orton
✉ **Ellington Place, 10 Ellington Road, Muswell Hill, London, N10 3DG** 🅿
☎ 020 8444 6218
Est. 1947
Services Furniture restoration, upholstery
Open Mon–Fri 10am–6pm
Sat by appointment

Fens Restoration and Sales
Contact Mrs M Saville
✉ **46 Lots Road, London, SW10 0QF** 🅿
☎ 020 7352 9883
Est. 1979
Services Repair and restoration of furniture, stripping
Open Mon–Fri 9am–5pm
Sat by appointment

Ivo Geikie-Cobb
Contact Mr I Geikie-Cobb
✉ **Unit 32, Charterhouse Works, Eltringham Street, London, SW18 1TD** 🅿
☎ 020 8874 3767 Ⓕ 020 8874 3767
Ⓜ 07761 561569
Ⓔ restore@ivogc.com
Ⓦ www.ivogc.com
Est. 1991
Services Antique furniture conservation and restoration, gilding, upholstery, re-leathering, French polishing, veneering, architectural restoration
Open Mon–Fri 9.30am–5.30pm

Greenwich Conservation Workshops
Contact Richard Moy
22 Nelson Road, London, SE10 9JB 🅿
☎ 020 8293 1067
Ⓦ www.spreadeagle.org
Est. 1957
Services Restoration of period furniture, oil, watercolours, picture frames, porcelain, pottery
Open Mon–Sat 10.30am–5.30pm

H J Hatfield and Son
✉ **42 St Michael's Street, London, W2 1QP** 🅿
☎ 020 7723 8265 Ⓕ 020 7706 4562
Ⓔ admin@hjhatfield.com
Est. 1834
Services Restoration of furniture, porcelain, paintings, boulle, upholstery, lacquerwork, metalwork, chandeliers, marble
Open Mon–Fri 8am–1pm

Hens Teeth Antiques (TVADA)
Contact Mr M Murray
✉ **2 Baronsmere Road, East Finchley, London, N2 9QB** 🅿
☎ 020 8883 0755
Ⓜ 07970 625359
Ⓔ hens.teeth@virgin.net
Est. 1997
Services Furniture repair and restoration, polishing, gilding, upholstery
Open By appointment

Hope & Piaget (BAFRA)
Contact Mr B Duffy or Mrs K Keate
✉ **Unit 12–13, Burmarsh Workshops, Marsden Street, London, NW5 3JA** 🅿
☎ 020 7267 6040 Ⓕ 020 7267 6040
Ⓔ mail@hope-piaget.co.uk
Ⓦ www.hope-piaget.co.uk
Est. 1982
Services Conservation and restoration of 18th–21stC furniture, japanning, lacquerwork, gilding, carving, tortoiseshell restoration
Open Mon–Fri 9.30am–6pm

Hornsby Furniture Restoration Ltd
Contact Mr M Gough
✉ **35 Thurloe Place, London, SW7 2HJ** 🅿
☎ 020 7225 2888 Ⓕ 020 7838 0235
Ⓔ sales@antiqueous.com
Ⓦ www.hornsbyfurniture.com
Est. 1890
Services Antique furniture restoration including gilding, cabinet-making, upholstery, bespoke furniture, French polishing, caning
Open Mon–Fri 8am–5.30pm
Sat 9am–12.30pm

B S Howells (Antique Restorers) Ltd
Contact Mr B S Howells
✉ **7a Tynemouth Terrace, Tynemouth Road, Tottenham, London, N15 4AP** 🅿
☎ 020 8808 7965 Ⓕ 020 8801 5313
Ⓜ 07734 008865
Est. 1978
Services 18th–19thC antique furniture restoration, leatherwork, gilding, marquetry and copy brasswork, copy chair making, cabinet-making, replica work
Open Mon–Thurs 6.30am–3.30pm Fri 6am–1.30pm
Sat by appointment

Magical Restorations
Contact Mr F Hussain
✉ **Arch 195, 3 Wilson Walk, off Prebend Gardens, London, W4 1TP** 🅿
☎ 020 8741 3799 Ⓕ 020 8741 3799
Ⓜ 07956 681655
Ⓔ enquiries@magical-restorations.com
Ⓦ www.magical-restorations.com
Est. 1997
Services Furniture repair and restoration, carving, gilding, French polishing
Open Mon–Fri 9am–5pm

M Merritt
Contact Mr M Merritt
✉ **8 Brightfield Road, London, SE12 8QF** 🅿
☎ 020 8852 7577
Est. 1983
Services Antique furniture restoration, cabinet-making, veneering
Open Mon–Fri 9am–5pm
or by appointment

Laurence Mitchell Antiques (LAPADA)
Contact Laurence Mitchell
✉ **20 The Mall, 359 Islington High Street,**

Islington, London,
N1 0PD
☎ 020 7359 7579
Ⓔ laurence@buymeissen.com
Ⓦ www.buymeissen.com
Est. 1970
Services Restoration of antiques
Open Tues–Fri 10am–5pm
Sat 10am–5.30pm

Richard G Phillips Ltd
Contact Mr R G Phillips
✉ **95–99 Shernhall Street, London, E17 9HS** Ⓟ
☎ 020 8509 9075 Ⓕ 020 8509 9077
Est. 1984
Services Antique furniture restoration. Also manufactures classical English furniture and decorative four-poster beds
Open By appointment

Piers Furniture Repair Workshop
Contact Mr P Tarrant-Willis
✉ **The Old Air Raid Shelter, Athlone Street, London, NW5 4LN** Ⓟ
☎ 020 7209 5824
Est. 1990
Services Antique furniture repair and restoration, French polishing
Open By appointment

R M W Restorations
Contact Mr R Mark-Wardlaw
✉ **Unit B08, Acton Business Centre, School Road, London, NW10 6TD** Ⓟ
☎ 020 8965 2938 Ⓕ 020 8965 2938
Est. 1986
Services Antique furniture repair and restoration, traditional and modern finishes, insurance work, cabinet work, French polishing
Open Mon–Fri 10am–6pm

Regency Restoration
Contact Mrs E Ball
✉ **Studio 21, Thames House, 140 Battersea Park Road, London, SW11 4NB** Ⓟ
☎ 020 7622 5275 or 020 782 84268
Ⓕ 020 7498 1803
Est. 1987
Services Restoration of 18th–19thC mirrors, picture frames, English and Continental painted and gilded furniture, architectural gilding, church interiors, polychrome sculpture, lacquerwork, oil paintings, carving
Open Mon–Fri 9.30am–5.30pm

Remstone Contracts
Contact Mr D Louden
✉ **69a Southgate Road, London, N1 3JS** Ⓟ
☎ 020 7359 3536 Ⓕ 020 7359 3536
Est. 1968
Services Furniture restoration and repair, polishing, leather colouring, gilding, carving, table lining
Open Mon–Fri 8am–5.30pm

Sears
Contact Mr D Foster
✉ **79 Ashby Mews, Brockley, London, SE4 1TB** Ⓟ
☎ 020 8694 9911 Ⓕ 020 8694 9911
Est. 1975
Services Furniture restoration
Open Mon–Fri 8am–4pm

Michael Slade
Contact M Slade
✉ **42 Quernmore Road, London, N4 4QP** Ⓟ
☎ 020 8341 3194
Ⓜ 07813 377029
Ⓔ mikeslade@ntl.com
Est. 1984
Services Antique repair and restoration, furniture making, upholstery, French polishing, furniture sales
Open Mon–Fri 10am–6pm please telephone first

H A Smith & Son
Contact Mr A Smith
✉ **36a Nelson Road, Harrow on the Hill, Harrow, Middlesex, HA1 3ET** Ⓟ
☎ 020 8864 2335
Est. 1920
Services Antique and modern furniture restoration, repair and upholstery
Open Mon–Fri 9am–6pm
Sat 10am–2pm

Solomon
Contact Solomon
✉ **49 Park Road, London, N8 8SY** Ⓟ
☎ 020 8341 1817 Ⓕ 020 8341 1817
Ⓔ solomon@solomonantiques.fsnet.co.uk
Est. 1981
Services Restoration, upholstery, polishing
Open Mon–Sat 9am–6pm

Titian Studio (BAFRA, UKIC)
Contact Rodrigo Titian
✉ **32 Warple Way, Acton, London, W3 0DJ** Ⓟ
☎ 020 8222 6600 Ⓕ 020 8749 2220
Ⓔ info@titianstudios.co.uk
Ⓦ www.titianstudios.com
Est. 1965
Services Restoration of gilding and lacquering, French polishing, caning, cabinet-making
Open Mon–Fri 8am–5.30pm

Woodbourne Furniture Ltd
Contact Mr G Evans or Mr H Roberts
✉ **Unit 35 Cromwell Industrial Estate, Staffa Road, London, E10 7QZ** Ⓟ
☎ 020 8539 5575 Ⓕ 020 8539 5575
Est. 1984
Services Furniture makers, chair copying, repair and restoration of antique furniture
Open Mon–Fri 8am–6pm
Sat 8am–1pm

SOUTH

Aggeby's
Contact Andrew Agg
✉ **Charlwood Place, Norwood Hill Road, Charlwood, Surrey, RH6 0EB** Ⓟ
☎ 01293 863700
Est. 2001
Services Furniture restoration
Open Mon–Fri 9am–6pm or by appointment

Allen Avery Interiors
Contact Paul Avery
✉ **No 1 High Street, Haselmere, Surrey, GU27 2AG** Ⓟ
☎ 01428 643883 Ⓕ 01428 656815
Est. 1970
Services Restoration
Open Mon Tues Thurs Fri 9am–1pm 2.15–5pm
Wed Sat 9am–1pm

Antique Restorers
Contact Mr W Barker
✉ **2 Station Approach, Stoneleigh, Epsom, Surrey, KT19 0QZ** Ⓟ
☎ 020 8393 9111
Est. 1980
Services Upholstery, French

polishing, furniture repair, cane and rush seating.
Open Mon–Fri 9.30am–4.30pm

B H Woodfinishes
Contact Mr C Hopkins
✉ **Unit 22, Church Lane Industrial Estate, Church Lane, Horsham, West Sussex, RH13 6LU** P
☎ 01403 891551 F 01403 891551
M 07850 051607
E sales@bhwoodfinishes.co.uk
W www.bhwoodfinishes.co.uk
Est. 1988
Services Stripping and repolishing, wood repair, French polishing, leathering, gilding, on-site work (bannisters, staircases etc)
Open Mon–Fri 9am–5pm

Colin Bell, Ben Norris and Co (BAFRA)
Contact Colin Bell
✉ **Knowl Hill Farm, Knowl Hill, Kingsclere, Newbury, Berkshire, RG20 4NY** P
☎ 01635 297950 F 01635 299851
M 07887 637678
Est. 1980
Services Restoration of antique furniture and gilding, reproduction cabinet-making, furniture made to order
Open Mon–Fri 8.30am–5pm

A E Booth and Son
Contact David or Ann Booth
✉ **300 Hook Road, Hook, Chessington, Surrey, KT9 1NY** P
☎ 020 8397 7675 F 020 8397 7675
Est. 1934
Services Restoration of antique and modern reproduction furniture including polishing and upholstery
Open By appointment

C T Bristow
Contact Mr Bristow
✉ **Lydgate, Seale Lane, Seale, Farnham, Surrey, GU10 1LF** P
☎ 01252 782775
Est. 1971
Services French polishing, fine antique furniture restoration
Open By appointment

The Cabinet Repair Shop
Contact Mrs M H Embling
✉ **Woodlands Farm, Blacknest Road, Blacknest, Alton, Hampshire, GU34 4BQ** P
☎ 01252 794260 F 01252 793084
W www.dsembling.co.uk
Est. 1984
Services Restoration of antique and modern furniture, insurance claim work
Open Mon–Fri 8am–5pm
Sat by appointment

Peter Casebow (BAFRA)
Contact Mr P Casebow
✉ **Pilgrims Mill Lane, Worthing, West Sussex, BN13 3DE** P
☎ 01903 264045
M 07790 339602
E pcasebow@hotmail.com
Est. 1987
Services Restoration of period furniture including square-piano restoration
Open By appointment

B Castle (Exhibitor of the Royal Academy & Mall Gallery)
Contact Mr B Castle
✉ **2 Charmandean Road, Worthing, West Sussex, BN14 9LB** P
☎ 01903 239702
Est. 1982
Services Antique repair and restoration of small furniture, decorative items, woodcarver
Open Mon–Sat by appointment

Alan Cooper Antique Restorations
Contact Alan Cooper
✉ **Unit 7, Park Farm, Hundred Acre Lane, Wivelsfield Green, Haywards Heath, West Sussex, RH17 7RU** P
☎ 01273 890017
Est. 1973
Services Antique repair, French polishing, restoration
Open Mon–Fri 8am–3pm

Copperwheat Restoration (RICS)
Contact Carole Copperwheat
✉ **Rear of Pascall Atkey, 29–30 High Street, Cowes, Isle of Wight, PO31 7RX** P
☎ 01983 281011
M 07720 399670
Est. 1985
Services Antique furniture repair, restoration, commissions
Open Any time by prior telephone call

Corwell
Contact Mr S Corbin
✉ **Unit 6, Amners Farm, Burghfield, Reading, Berkshire, RG30 3UE** P
☎ 0118 983 3404 F 0118 983 3404
E info@corwell.co.uk
W www.corwell.co.uk
Est. 1989
Services Antique restoration, cabinet-making
Open Mon–Fri 9am–5pm
Sat 9am–2pm

Davenports Antiques
Contact Mr C Height
✉ **Unit 5, Woodgate Centre, Oak Tree Lane, Woodgate, Chichester, West Sussex, PO20 6GU** P
☎ 01243 544242
M 07932 690210
E height@btinternet.com
Est. 1980
Services Antique furniture restoration
Open Mon–Fri 8.30am–6pm

Sonia Demetriou
Contact Sonia Demetriou
✉ **2 Elbridge Farm Buildings, Chichester Road, Bognor Regis, West Sussex, PO21 5EG** P
☎ 01243 842235 F 01243 842235
E sondem@intelynx.net
W www.art-scope.co.uk
Est. 1977
Services Restoration of antique painted furniture and objets d'art
Open Mon–Fri 9.30am–6pm
Sat by appointment

R G Dewdney
Contact Mr R G Dewdney
✉ **Norfolk Road, South Holmwood, Dorking, Surrey, RH5 4LA** P
☎ 01306 888174 F 01306 742636
Est. 1968
Services General antique repair and restoration, leatherwork
Open Mon–Fri 9am–6pm

Downland Furniture Restoration
Contact Mr S Macintyre
✉ **Wepham Farmyard, Wepham,**

Arundel, West Sussex,
BN18 9RQ 🅿
☎ 01903 883387
Ⓜ 07713 104818
Est. 1984
Services Furniture restoration and conservation
Open Mon–Fri 9am–5pm or by appointment

Dunn and Wright
Contact Mr A Dunn
✉ **Rear of 128 Sheen Road, Richmond, Surrey, TW9 1UR** 🅿
☎ 020 8948 7032
Est. 1974
Services Furniture repair and restoration
Open Mon–Fri 8am–5.30pm

Richard Elderton
Contact R C Elderton
✉ **Home Farm, Mill Lane, Hawkley, Liss, Hampshire, GU33 6NU** 🅿
☎ 01420 538374
ⓔ woodman@cix.co.uk
ⓦ www.cix.co.uk/~woodman/
Est. 1976
Services Antique furniture restoration, new bespoke solid wood furniture, metalworking repair, woodturning
Open Mon–Fri 9am–5pm or by appointment

G and R Fraser-Sinclair (BAFRA)
Contact Mr G Fraser-Sinclair
✉ **Haysbridge Farm, Brickhouse Lane, South Godstone, Godstone, Surrey, RH9 8JW** 🅿
☎ 01342 844112 ⓕ 01342 844112
Est. 1978
Services General restoration of 18thC furniture
Open Mon–Fri 8am–5.30pm

A D Gardner
Contact Mr Gardner
✉ **2a East Road, Reigate, Surrey, RH2 9EX** 🅿
☎ 01737 222430
Est. 1969
Services Antique repair and restoration, fine French polishing, caning, leathering, upholstery
Open Mon–Fri 8.30am–5.30pm

Simon Gooding
Contact Simon Gooding
✉ **Unit 1B, Dorotay Farm, Haselmere, Surrey, GU27 2DQ** 🅿
☎ 01428 651072
Ⓜ 07770 630068
Est. 1984
Services Furniture restoration, French polishing, leather desk tops
Open Mon–Fri 8am–5pm

Goodwood Furniture Restoration (BAFRA)
Contact Bruce Neville
✉ **21 Richmond Road, Westerton, Chichester, West Sussex, PO18 0PQ** 🅿
☎ 01243 778614
Ⓜ 07719 778079
ⓔ bruce@goodwoodrestoration.co.uk
ⓦ www.goodwoodrestoration.co.uk
Est. 1991
Services Antique furniture restoration, cabinet-making
Open Mon–Sat 8.30am–5.30pm

G J Hall, Antique Furniture Restoration
Contact Mr G J Hall
✉ **Unit 1, Rear of Longreach, Branshill Road, Eversley, Hampshire, RG27 0PS** 🅿
☎ 01189 737001
Ⓜ 07711 846712
ⓔ garyh29@hotmail.com
Est. 1984
Services Restoration and conservation of fine antique furniture, copy chair making, French polishing, insurance work, design commissions
Open Mon–Fri 9.30am–5.30pm

Hedgecoe and Freeland (LAPADA, BAFRA)
Contact Justin Freeland
✉ **Rowan House, 21 Burrow Hill Green, Chobham, Woking, Surrey, GU24 8QP** 🅿
☎ 01276 858206 ⓕ 01276 857352
Ⓜ 07771 953870
Est. 1969
Services Cabinet-making, polishing, upholstery, metalwork, gilding, lacquerwork and paintwork
Open Mon–Fri 8am–5.30pm

Stuart Hobbs Antique Furniture Restoration (BAFRA)
Contact Mr S Hobbs
✉ **Meath Paddock, Meath Green Lane, Horley, Surrey, RH6 8HZ** 🅿
☎ 01293 782349 ⓕ 01293 773467
Est. 1981
Services Furniture, longcase, bracket clock and barometer restoration
Open By appointment

Howard Hunt Antiques
Contact Mr H Hunt
✉ **The White Hut, Thackhams Farm, Bottle Lane, Mattingley, Hook, Hampshire, RG27 8LJ** 🅿
☎ 01256 881111 ⓕ 01256 881111
Est. 1989
Services Repair and restoration of furniture, mirrors, porcelain, upholstery, leathering, gilding
Open Mon–Fri 9am–6pm Sat 9am–4pm

John Lloyd (BAFRA)
✉ **Bankside Farm, Jacobs Post, Ditchling Common, West Sussex, RH15 0SJ** 🅿
☎ 01444 480388 ⓕ 01444 480388
Ⓜ 07941 124772
ⓔ info@lloydjohnfinefurniture.co.uk
ⓦ www.johnlloydfinefurniture.co.uk
Est. 1989
Services Complete repair and restoration of period, reproduction and modern furniture, short courses on care and repair of antiques and gilding
Open Mon–Fri 8.30am–5.30pm

C Lopez
Contact Mr C Lopez
✉ **151 London Road, Burgess Hill, West Sussex, RH15 8LH** 🅿
☎ 01444 243176 ⓕ 01444 254208
Est. 1977
Services Antique furniture restoration and hand-made chair copying
Open Mon–Fri 9am–1pm 2–6pm Sat 9am–1pm

Lush Restoration
Contact Mr M Lush
✉ **64d Old Milton Road, New Milton, Hampshire, BH25 6DX** 🅿
☎ 01425 629680

Est. 1992
Services Repair and restoration, upholstery
Open Mon–Fri 8am–1pm 2–5pm

Lymington Restoration
Contact Mr M Cooper
✉ **Fairlea House, 110–112 Marsh Lane, Lymington, Hampshire, SO41 9EE** P
☎ 01590 677558 F 01590 677558
Est. 1996
Services Restoration of antique furniture, gilding, upholstery
Open Mon–Fri 9am–5pm

Maybury Antique Restoration
Contact Mr B Everitt
✉ **Maybury Rough Cottage, Lytton Road, Woking, Surrey, GU22 7EH** P
☎ 01483 762812
Est. 1989
Services All furniture repairs, gilding, leathering, upholstering, French polishing
Open Mon–Fri 8am–6pm Sat 8am–1pm

Malcolm Morrisen, Antique Furniture Restorer
Contact Malcolm Morrisen
✉ **Old Post Office Cottage, East Ilsley, Newbury, Berkshire, RG20 7LF** P
☎ 01635 281349
M 07990 880717
Est. 2003
Services Antique furniture restoration and conservation
Open Mon–Fri 9am–5pm by appointment

A F Mrozinski
Contact Mr Mrozinski
✉ **44 Elizabeth Road, Farncombe, Godalming, Surrey, GU7 3PZ** P
☎ 01483 415028
M 07866 100057
Est. 1979
Services Antique furniture repair, French polishing
Open Mon–Fri 7.30am–5pm

Timothy Naylor Associates (BAFRA)
Contact T Naylor
✉ **24 Bridge Road, Chertsey, Surrey, KT16 8JN** P
☎ 01932 567129 F 01932 564948
E timothy.naylor@talk21.com
Est. 1988
Services Georgian and Regency furniture restoration
Open Mon–Fri 8.30am–5pm

New Forest Antique Restoration Ltd
Contact Piers Paterson
✉ **23 Bridge Street, Fordingbridge, Hampshire, SP6 1AH** P
☎ 0845 2305123
E info@restorer.net
W www.restorer.net
Est. 1995
Services Furniture restoration, upholstery, bespoke hand-made furniture
Open Mon–Fri 8am–5pm or by appointment

Simon Paterson (BAFRA)
✉ **Whitelands, West Dean, Chichester, West Sussex, PO18 0RL** P
☎ 01243 811900
E hotglue@tiscali.co.uk
Est. 1992
Services Repair and restoration of antique furniture and clocks, boulle work, marquetry
Open By appointment

K S Pawlowski
Contact K S Pawlowski
✉ **Unit 3, Turner Dumbrell Workshops, North End, Ditchling, Hassocks, West Sussex, BN6 8TG** P
☎ 01273 846003 F 01273 846003
E pawlowski@ditchling.fsnet.co.uk
Est. 1983
Services Conservation and restoration of antique furniture
Open Mon–Fri 9am–5.30pm Sat by appointment

Eva-Louise Pepperall (BAFRA)
Contact E Pepperall
✉ **Dairy Lane Cottage, Walberton, Arundel, West Sussex, BN18 0PT** P
☎ 01243 551282
E evalouisepepperall@hotmail.com
W www.pepperall.com
Est. 1977
Services Restoration of antique furniture, gilding, japanning
Open By appointment

Mr Pickett's
Contact Mr M Pickett
✉ **Top Barn, Old Park Lane, Bosham, Nr Chichester, West Sussex, PO18 8EX** P
☎ 01243 574573 F 02392 410009
M 07779 997012
E info@mrpicketts.com
W www.mrpicketts.com
Est. 1991
Services Paint stripping, sanding, waxing, full restoration, bespoke items made to order from reclaimed pine
Open By appointment

Albert Plumb Furniture Co (BAFRA)
Contact Mrs S Plumb
✉ **Itchenor Green, Chichester, West Sussex, PO20 7DA** P
☎ 01243 513700 F 01243 513701
Est. 1977
Services Antique furniture restorers and upholsterers. Bespoke cabinet-makers
Open Mon–Fri 8.30am–6.30pm or by appointment

D Potashnick
Contact Mr D Potashnick
✉ **7 The Parade, 73 Stoats Nest Road, Coulsdon, Surrey, CR5 2JJ** P
☎ 020 8660 8403
Est. 1969
Services Restoration of furniture
Open Mon–Fri 9am–5pm or by appointment

Reeves Restoration at the Coach House Antiques
Contact Paul or Louise Reeves
✉ **The Coach House, 60 Station Approach, Gomshall, Surrey, GU5 9NP** P
☎ 01483 203838 F 01483 202999
E coach_house.antiques@virgin.net
W www.coachhouseantiques.com
Est. 1984
Services Antique clocks, furniture restoration
Open Mon–Sat 9.30am–5pm Sun noon–5pm closed Thurs

Renaissance
Contact Mr Peter Cross
⊠ **11 Enterprise Close, Croydon, Surrey, CR0 3RZ** P
☎ 020 8664 9686 F 020 8664 9737
Est. 1996
Services Furniture and frame repair and restoration
Open Mon–Fri 10am–6.30pm

Restore
Contact Mr G R Fisher or Mrs S Fisher
⊠ **37 Walton Street, Tadworth, Surrey, KT20 7RR** P
☎ 01737 817866 F 01737 819518
M 07970 186769
E info@restoreltd.co.uk
W www.restoreltd.co.uk
Est. 1999
Services Antique furniture restoration, sales of antique and contemporary design furniture
Open Mon–Fri 9am–5pm

Robinson Restorations
Contact Mr Nick Robinson
⊠ **Unit 8, Seven House, 34–38 Town End, Caterham, Surrey, CR3 5UG** P
☎ 01883 330111
M 07970 255053
Est. 1896
Services Antique restoration, French polishing
Open Mon–Fri 8am–6pm
Sat 10am–4pm

David A Sayer Antique Furniture Restorer (BAFRA, Furniture History Society, Regional Furniture Society)
Contact David Sayer
⊠ **Courtlands, Park Road, Banstead, Surrey, SM7 3EF** P
☎ 01737 352429 F 01737 373255
M 07775 636009
Est. 1985
Services Comprehensive repair, restoration and conservation service of English and Continental furniture
Open Mon–Fri 8am–6pm

Michael Schryver Antiques
Contact Mr M Schryver
⊠ **The Granary, 10 North Street, Dorking, Surrey, RH4 1DN** P
☎ 01306 881110 F 01306 876168
E schryvermsa@aol.com
Est. 1971
Services 18thC furniture restoration
Open Mon–Fri 8.30am–5.30pm
Sat 8am–noon or by appointment

Seagers Restorations
Contact Mr M L Cheater
⊠ **Seagers Farm, Stuckton, Fordingbridge, Hampshire, SP6 2HG** P
☎ 01425 652245
Est. 1963
Services Restoration of antique furniture
Open Mon–Fri 9am–5.30pm or by appointment

Andrew Sharp Antique Restoration Ltd
Contact Mr A Sharp
⊠ **Unit 1, Forest Villa Courtyard, Lyndhurst Road, Brockenhurst, Hampshire, SO42 7RL** P
☎ 01590 622577
Est. 1996
Services Sale and restoration of Georgian–Victorian furniture
Open Mon–Sat 9am–5.30pm

Surrey Restoration Ltd (AFRA)
Contact Mark Grady
⊠ **Highway Farm, Horsley Road, Downside, Cobham, Surrey, KT11 3JZ** P
☎ 01932 868883 F 01483 268285
E emcghee@surreyrestoration.freeserve.co.uk
Est. 1994
Services Antique furniture restoration, interior wooden panelling of period houses
Open Mon–Sat 8.30am–6.30pm

Sussex Woodcraft
Contact Mr Waters
⊠ **15 Drayton Cottages, Drayton Lane, Drayton, Chichester, West Sussex, PO20 6BN** P
☎ 01243 788830
Est. 1937
Services Cabinet-making and restoration
Open Mon–Fri 8am–5pm

T S Restorations
Contact T Street
⊠ **13 Blatchford Close, Horsham, West Sussex, RH13 5RG** P
☎ 01403 273766
Est. 1989
Services Antique repair and restoration
Open Mon–Fri 8am–5pm

Roy Temple Polishing
Contact Mr R Temple
⊠ **Unit 15, Sheeplands Farm, Twyford Road, Wargrave, Reading, Berkshire, RG10 8DL** P
☎ 01189 402211 or 01628 660106
F 01189 402211
Est. 1996
Services Furniture repair and restoration, polishing, leathering
Open Mon–Sat 9am–5pm

The Traditional Restoration Company Ltd
Contact Ms Thompson
⊠ **The Coach House, Dorney Court, Dorney, Windsor, Berkshire, SL4 6QL** P
☎ 01628 660708
Est. 1991
Services Restoration of 18th–19thC furniture, carving, upholstery, metalwork
Open Mon–Fri 8am–5.30pm weekends by appointment

T R J Troke
Contact T Troke
⊠ **22 Fairview Road, Hungerford, Berkshire, RG17 0BT** P
☎ 01488 683310
Est. 1975
Services Antique furniture repair and restoration
Open By appointment

Martin Tucker Antique Restoration
Contact M Tucker
⊠ **Springbok Estate, Alfold, Cranleigh, Surrey, GU6 8HR** P
☎ 01403 753090
Est. 1984
Services Furniture restoration, French polishing, cabinet-making
Open Mon–Fri 9am–5pm, Sat Sun by appointment

D G Weston
Contact Mr I L Weston
✉ **33 Rowan Drive, Newbury, Berkshire, RG14 1LY** Ⓟ
☎ 01635 43022
Ⓜ 07813 686074
Est. 1958
Services Antique repair and restoration, French polishing, leather lining, upholstery
Open Mon–Fri 9am–5.30pm

G Williams
Contact Graham Williams
✉ **The Builders Yard, Church Street, Betchworth, Surrey, RH3 7DN** Ⓟ
☎ 01737 843266
Est. 1975
Services General restoration, desk-top leathering, gold tooling, French polishing
Open Mon–Fri 9am–6pm Sat 10am–2pm

Wotruba and Son
Contact Mr F F Wotruba
✉ **Clump Workshops, Bassett Green Road, Chilworth, Southampton, Hampshire, SO16 3NF** Ⓟ
☎ 023 8076 6411
Ⓜ 07887 712401
Ⓔ f.f.wotruba@btinternet.com
Est. 1995
Services Antique restoration, including upholstery, polishing, veneering, boulle work, wood turning
Open Mon–Fri 10am–5pm Sat 10am–noon or by appointment

WEST COUNTRY

4b Antiques and Interiors
Contact Jonathan Plant
✉ **4b Northgate Street, Devizes, Wiltshire, SN10 1JL** Ⓟ
☎ 01380 729275
Est. 1972
Services Furniture restoration
Open Mon–Fri 8am–5pm or by appointment

Antique Restoration (Furniture History Society, NACF)
Contact George Judd
✉ **East Farm, Winterbourne Gunner, Salisbury, Wiltshire, SP4 6EW** Ⓟ
☎ 01980 610576/611828
Est. 1975
Services Antique furniture, porcelain and painting restoration, cabinet-making, upholstery, metalwork, leatherwork, gilding
Open Mon–Fri 9am–7pm Sat by appointment

David Battle Antique Furniture Restoration and Conservation (BAFRA)
Contact David Battle
✉ **Brightley Pound, Umberleigh, Devon, EX37 9AL** Ⓟ
☎ 01769 540483
Ⓔ david@brightley.clara.net
Ⓦ brightley.clara.net
Est. 1984
Services Comprehensive service for English and Continental period furniture
Open By appointment

Peter Binnington (BAFRA, Society of Gilders)
Contact Mr Peter Binnington
✉ **Barn Studio, Botany Farm, East Lulworth, Wareham, Dorset, BH20 5QH** Ⓟ
☎ 01929 400224 Ⓕ 01929 400744
Est. 1979
Services General furniture restoration and gilding, specialist in verre églomisé
Open By appointment

Richard Bolton (BAFRA)
Contact Richard Bolton
✉ **The Old Brewery, Mangerton Mill, Mangerton, Bridport, Dorset, DT6 3SG** Ⓟ
☎ 01308 485000
Est. 1981
Services Restoration of fine antique furniture
Open Mon–Fri 9am–5pm

Boughey Antique Restoration
Contact Dave Boughey
✉ **1 Kniel Cottage, The Quay, Millbrook, Torpoint, Cornwall, PL10 1AN** Ⓟ
☎ 01752 829008 Ⓕ 01752 829008
Ⓜ 07970 540644
Est. 1960
Services Furniture restoration, cabinet-making, porcelain and pottery restoration
Open Mon–Fri 8am–5.30pm or by appointment

Jason Bowen
Contact Mr J Bowen
✉ **Unit 2, Alexandra Court, Yeovil, Somerset, BA21 5AL** Ⓟ
☎ 01935 474446
Est. 1984
Services Furniture restoration, French polishing, gilding, carving, cabinet-making
Open Mon–Sat 8.30am–5pm

M and S Bradbury (BAFRA)
Contact Mr S Bradbury
✉ **The Barn, Hanham Lane, Paulton, Bristol, BS39 7PF** Ⓟ
☎ 01761 418910
Est. 1988
Services Furniture restoration including clock cases
Open Mon–Fri 8am–5pm

Lawrence Brass
Contact Lawrence Brass
✉ **Apple Studio, Bath, Somerset, BA1 5YX** Ⓟ
☎ 01225 852222
Ⓦ www.lawrencebrass.com
Est. 1973
Services Antique furniture restoration
Open Mon–Sat 9am–5pm

J E Cadman
Contact Mr Cadman
✉ **15 Norwich Road, Bournemouth, Dorset, BH2 5QZ** Ⓟ
☎ 01202 290973
Est. 1901
Services Antique restoration, mostly furniture
Open Mon–Fri 9am–5pm

Castle House (BAFRA)
Contact Mr Michael Durkee
✉ **Castle House, Units 1 and 3, Bennetts Field Estate, Wincanton, Somerset, BA9 9DT** Ⓟ
☎ 01963 33884 Ⓕ 01963 31278
Est. 1975
Services Antique furniture restoration and conservation
Open Mon–Fri 8.30am–5pm

Christopher Cole
Contact Mr C Cole
✉ **The Workshop, 36 Claude Avenue, Oldfield Park, Bath, Somerset, BA2 1AG** P
☎ 01225 310298 ⓕ 01225 310298
ⓜ 07890 824042
Est. 1994
Services Antique furniture restoration, carving, turning, French polishing
Open Mon–Fri 8.30am–7pm

David Collyer Antique Restorations
Contact David Collyer
✉ **Tunley Farm, Tunley, Bath, Somerset, BA2 0DL** P
☎ 01761 472727 ⓕ 01761 472727
ⓜ 07889 725508
ⓔ david@davidcollyer.com
Est. 1985
Services Furniture restoration and repair
Open Mon–Fri 9am–5.30pm or by appointment

W J Cook (BAFRA)
Contact Mr B Cook
✉ **High Trees, Savernake Forest, Near Marlborough, Wiltshire, SN8 4NE** P
☎ 01672 513017 ⓕ 01672 514455
ⓔ william.cook@virgin.net
ⓦ www.antiquerestoration.uk.com
Est. 1963
Services Furniture polishing, restoration, upholstery, gilding
Open By appointment

Mark Coray Fine Antique Furniture Restoration (BAFRA)
Contact Mark Coray
✉ **The Coach House Workshops, Ford Street, Wellington, Somerset, TA21 9PG** P
☎ 01823 663766/667284
ⓜ 07979 245524
Est. 1999
Services All antique furniture restoration, gilding, furniture made to order
Open Mon–Fri 9am–5pm

N G and C Coryndon (BAFRA)
Contact N G Coryndon or Simon Butler
✉ **Rainscombe Farm, Oare, Marlborough, Wiltshire, SN8 4HZ** P
☎ 01672 562581 ⓕ 01672 563995
ⓔ simonbutler@coryndon.fsbusiness.co.uk
Est. 1964
Services General restoration of furniture, gilding, paint finishes. Collection and delivery
Open Mon–Fri 8.30am–4.30pm

D M Antique Restoration
Contact Mr D Pike
✉ **Purn Farm, Bridgewater, Bleadon, Weston-super-Mare, Somerset, BS24 0AN** P
☎ 01934 811120
Est. 1983
Services Restoration of furniture and chests of drawers
Open Mon–Fri 8am–5pm

M L Davis
Contact Mr M L Davis
✉ **Rear of 1079 Christchurch Road, Bournemouth, Dorset, BH7 6BQ** P
☎ 01202 434684
Est. 1987
Services Full restoration of furniture, brass cleaning
Open Mon–Fri 8.30am–5.30pm or by appointment

Simon Dodson
Contact Mr Dodson
✉ **The Workshop, Odd Penny Farm, Crudwell, Malmesbury, Wiltshire, SN16 9SJ** P
☎ 01285 770810
Est. 1992
Services Antique furniture restoration
Open Mon–Sat 9am–6pm

Christopher John Douglas
Contact Mr C J Douglas
✉ **Befferlands Farm Workshop, Berne Lane, Charmouth, Bridport, Dorset, DT6 6RD** P
☎ 01297 561120
ⓜ 07989 161019
Est. 1975
Services Restoration of antique furniture, old pine, Art Deco
Open Mon–Fri 9am–5.30pm

Dudley and Spencer
Contact John Spencer or Ray Dudley
✉ **Unit 21, Signal Way, Central Trading Estate, Swindon, Wiltshire, SN3 1PD** P
☎ 01793 535394
Est. 1969
Services Furniture restoration, upholstery
Open Mon–Fri 7am–6pm

A A Eddy and Son
Contact Mr K Eddy or Mr M Eddy
✉ **1a Elphinstone Road, Peverell, Plymouth, Devon, PL2 3QQ** P
☎ 01752 787138 ⓕ 01752 789013
Est. 1889
Services Full repair and restoration, French polishing. Free estimates in the Plymouth area
Open Mon–Fri 7.30am–5pm

Esox Antique Restoration
Contact Mr B Elston
✉ **Unit 8, 1 Henderbarrow Cottages, Holwill, Beaworthy, Devon, EX21 5TW** P
☎ 01409 221873 ⓕ 01409 221873
ⓜ 07967 283602
Est. 1987
Services Full furniture restoration, French polishing
Open Mon–Fri 9am–5pm or by appointment

Former Glory
Contact Tim or Kim Ravenscroft
✉ **Ferndown, Dorset, BH22** P
☎ 01202 895859 ⓕ 01202 895859
ⓔ formerglory@btinternet.com
ⓦ www.formerglory.co.uk
Est. 1994
Services Cane and rush seating, furniture restoration. Cane, rush and restoration material supplies
Open By appointment only

Gilboys
Contact Mr S Gilboys
✉ **Hall Farm, Riverford, Staverton, Totnes, Devon, TQ9 6AH** P
☎ 01803 762763
Est. 1992
Services Restoration, French polishing, modern furniture finishes (dining room table heatproofing). Maker of replacement doors
Open Mon–Fri 9am–5pm

ASSOCIATED SERVICES

FURNITURE

John Hamblin
Contact John or Mark
✉ **Unit 6, 15 Oxford Road, Penmill Trading Estate, Yeovil, Somerset, BA21 5HR** Ⓟ
☎ 01935 471154 Ⓕ 01935 471154
Ⓜ 07889 281659
Est. 1981
Services Antique furniture restoration, French polishing, cabinet-making
Open Mon–Sat 9am–5pm

Hart Antiques
Contact Mr M Hart
✉ **Nanscawen, Prideaux Road, St Blazey, Par, Cornwall, PL24 2SR** Ⓟ
☎ 01726 816389
Ⓜ 07816 122730
Est. 1985
Services Antique furniture restoration including upholstery, gilding and lacquerwork
Open Mon–Sat 9am–6pm

Philip Hawkins Furniture (BAFRA)
Contact Mr P Hawkins
✉ **Glebe Workshop, Semley, Shaftesbury, Dorset, SP7 9AP** Ⓟ
☎ 01747 830830 Ⓕ 01747 830830
Ⓔ hawkinssemley@hotmail.com
Est. 1987
Services Restoration and replication of antique furniture
Open Mon–Fri 9am–5pm or by appointment

Bruce Isaac
Contact Mr Bruce Isaac
✉ **Crown Works, 114a Rodden Road, Frome, Somerset, BA11 2AW** Ⓟ
☎ 01373 453277 Ⓕ 01373 830849
Ⓜ 07711 399165
Est. 1990
Services Furniture restoration
Open Mon–Fri 8am–5pm

Mike Keeley
Contact Mike Keeley
✉ **205 Old Church Road, Clevedon, Somerset, BS21 7UD** Ⓟ
☎ 01275 873418
Ⓔ mikeandsheila@blueyonder.co.uk
Est. 1980
Services General repair to antique furniture, specializing in dining furniture
Open By appointment Mon–Fri 9am–5pm

M & J Lazenby Antique Restoration
Contact Mark Lazenby
✉ **The Old Bakery, Terrace View, Horsecastles, Sherborne, Dorset, DT9 3HE**
☎ 01935 816716
Est. 1987
Services Full furniture restoration service
Open Mon–Fri 8am–5pm

Market Place Antiques Restorations
Contact Martin Bryan Turner
✉ **Nuttaberry Works, Nuttaberry Industrial Estate, Bideford East, Bideford, Devon, EX39 4DU** Ⓟ
☎ 01237 476628
Est. 1984
Services Antique furniture restoration
Open By appointment

Alf McKay
Contact Mr A McKay
✉ **Manor Barn, Hewish, Crewkerne, Somerset, TA18 8QT** Ⓟ
☎ 01460 78916 Ⓕ 01460 78916
Ⓜ 07720 810750
Ⓔ info@cabinet-maker.biz
Ⓦ www.cabinet-maker.biz
Est. 1972
Services Restoration, cabinet-maker of traditional furniture
Open By appointment

Rod Naylor
Contact Angela Naylor
✉ **208 Devizes Road, Hilperton, Trowbridge, Wiltshire, BA14 7QP** Ⓟ
☎ 01225 754497 Ⓕ 01225 754497
Ⓔ rod.naylor@virgin.net
Ⓦ www.rodnaylor.com
Est. 1970
Services Restoration of antique wood carvings, supplies replicas of hard-to-find items and materials for caddies, boxes, desks etc, cabinet-making, supplier of power carving machinery and tools
Open By appointment only

Newmans (BAFRA)
Contact Tony Newman
✉ **Tithe Barn, Crowcombe, Somerset, TA4 4AQ** Ⓟ
Ⓜ 07778 615945
Ⓔ tony@cheddon.fsnet.co.uk
Est. 1991
Services All types of restoration
Open Sun–Mon 9am–5pm or by appointment

Oakfield Cabinet Makers
Contact Mr X Haines
✉ **Unit 8, Mount Pleasant, Offwell, Honiton, Devon, EX14 9RN** Ⓟ
☎ 01404 46858 Ⓕ 01404 46858
Ⓔ enquiries@oak-field.co.uk
Ⓦ www.oak-field.co.uk
Est. 1989
Services Cabinet-making and restoration
Open Mon–Fri 7.30am–6pm Sat 9am–1pm

Ottery Antique Restorers Ltd (BABAADA)
Contact Mr C James
✉ **Wessex Way, Wincanton Business Park, Wincanton, Somerset, BA9 9RR** Ⓟ
☎ 01963 34572 Ⓕ 01963 34572
Ⓜ 07770 923955
Ⓔ charles@otteryantiques.co.uk
Ⓦ www.otteryantiques.co.uk
Est. 1986
Services Furniture restoration
Open Mon–Fri 8am–5.30pm

Park Lane Restoration
Contact Matthew Channell
✉ **Unit 2, Marston Park Lane, St Clement, Truro, Cornwall, TR1 1SX** Ⓟ
☎ 01872 223944
Ⓜ 07765 448594
Est. 1984
Services 18th–19thC furniture restoration, cabinet veneering, stripping and French polishing. Fire, flood, shipping damage insurance work
Open Mon–Fri 8am–6pm

Alexander Paul Restorations
Contact Dave Steele
✉ **Fenny Bridges, Honiton, Devon, EX14 3BG** Ⓟ
☎ 01404 850881 Ⓕ 01404 850881

E alexanderpaulre@aol.com
W www.alexanderpaulantiques.com
Est. 2000
Services Full restoration including French polishing, turning, veneering
Open Mon–Fri 9am–5.30pm Sat 10am–4pm

R L Peploe
Contact Mr Peploe
✉ **18 Hughenden Road, Clifton, Bristol, BS8 2TT** P
☎ 0117 923 9349
Est. 1986
Services Cabinet work, gilding, carving, general finishing
Open Mon–Fri 9am–5pm

J Perrin
Contact Mr Perrin
✉ **Hope Chapel, Pitney, Langport, Somerset, TA10 9AE** P
☎ 01458 251150 **F** 01458 251150
Est. 1971
Services Furniture restoration
Open Mon–Sat 8am–6pm

Piers Pisani Antiques
Contact Mr Piers Pisani
✉ **The Old Chapel, Marston Road, Sherborne, Dorset, DT9 4BL** P
☎ 01935 815209 **F** 01935 815209
M 07973 373753
E pp@pierspisani.com
W www.pierspisani.com
Est. 1987
Services Full furniture restoration, cabinet-making
Open Mon–Sat 10am–5pm

Richard S Powell Antique Restorer & Cabinet Maker
Contact Richard S Powell
✉ **3 Puddles Lane, Coate, Devizes, Wiltshire, SN10 3LF** P
☎ 01380 860892
M 07881 934383
Est. 1982
Services English furniture restoration, cabinet-maker
Open By appointment

Robert Pye Antiques Restoration & Conservation of Fine Period Furniture
Contact Robert Pye
✉ **Tuxwell Farm, Spaxton, Bridgwater, Somerset, TA5 1DF** P
☎ 01278 671833 **F** 01278 671803
E robpyeantiques@breathe.com
W www.pyeantiquerestoration.freewebspace.com
Est. 2001
Services Restoration and conservation
Open Mon–Fri 8.30am–6pm Sat Sun by appointment

Revival
Contact Mr B Gould
✉ **South Road, Timsbury, Bath, Somerset, BA3 1LD** P
☎ 01761 472255 **F** 01761 472255
Est. 1979
Services Antique restoration, upholstery, French polishing
Open Mon–Fri 7am–4.30pm

Philip A Ruttleigh Antiques incorporating Crudwell Furniture
Contact Philip Ruttleigh
✉ **Odd Penny Farm, Crudwell, Wiltshire, SN16 9SJ** P
☎ 01285 770970
M 07989 250077
W www.crudwellfurniture.co.uk
Est. 1989
Services Furniture restoration
Open Mon–Fri 9am–5pm or by appointment

F B Sadowski
Contact Mr Sadowski
✉ **Unit 2, Plot 1a, Rospeath Estate, Crowlas, Penzance, Cornwall, TR20 8DU** P
☎ 01736 741083
Est. 1903
Services Furniture restoration. Repairs including boulle work, marquetry
Open Mon–Fri 10.30am–5pm

Graham Sparks Restoration
Contact Mr Graham Sparks
✉ **Unit 63, Tone Mill, Tonedale, Wellington, Somerset, TA21 0AB** P
☎ 01823 663636 **F** 01823 667393
Est. 1979
Services Furniture restoration, upholstery, cabinet-making
Open Mon–Fri 8am–6pm Sat 8am–1pm

St Thomas Antiques
Contact Ken Holdsworth
✉ **74 St Thomas Street, Wells, Somerset, BA5 2UZ** P
☎ 01749 672520
Est. 1969
Services Repair, repolishing
Open Mon–Fri 10am–4pm closed Wed

Robert P Tandy (BAFRA)
Contact Robert P Tandy
✉ **Lake House Barn, Off Colehouse Lane, Kenn, Clevedon, Bristol, North Somerset, BS21 6TQ** P
☎ 01275 875014
E robertptandy@hotmail.com
Est. 1987
Services Antique furniture and longcase clock casework restoration
Open Mon–Fri 10am–6pm

N S L Thomson
Contact Nick Thompson
✉ **Unit 2c, South Hams Business Park, Churchstow, Devon, TQ7 3QH** P
☎ 01548 854380
Est. 1981
Services French polishing and furniture restoration
Open Mon–Sat 8am–6pm and by appointment

John Thorpe Fine Furniture
Contact Mr John Thorpe-Dixon
✉ **Bruno House, 5a Treburley Industrial Estate, Launceston, Cornwall, PL15 9PU** P
☎ 01579 371175
Est. 1990
Services Antique furniture restoration, cabinetry, refinishing. London and all areas West
Open Mon–Fri 9am–5pm

Edward Venn Antiques Restorations
Contact Edward Venn
✉ **Unit 3, 52 Long Street, Williton, Somerset, TA4 4QU** P
☎ 01984 632631
E edwardvenn@aol.com
Est. 1978
Services Furniture and clocks

restoration, valuations, upholstery, reproductions
Open Mon–Fri 10am–5pm or by appointment

Brian Walker
Contact Mr Walker
✉ **Westwood, Dinton Road, Fovant, Salisbury, Wiltshire, SP3 5JW** 🅿
☎ 01722 714370 Ⓕ 01722 714853
Est. 1972
Services Furniture restoration and maker
Open Mon–Fri 8am–6pm Sat by appointment

Westmoor Furniture
Contact Gary Male
✉ **Units 8–9, Walronds Park, Isle Brewers, Hambridge, Taunton, Somerset, TA3 6QP** 🅿
☎ 01460 281535
Est. 1994
Services Antique restoration and repair, custom-made furniture and kitchens
Open Mon–Fri 9am–6pm

N D Whibley Restorations
Contact Mr Whibley
✉ **1166 Ringwood Road, Bear Cross, Bournemouth, Dorset, BH11 9LG** 🅿
☎ 01202 575167
Est. 1975
Services Polishing and restoration of furniture, Georgian and Victorian clock cases, medical cases, scientific instrument cases
Open By appointment

Wood 'n' Things
Contact Mr William Page
✉ **Cross Lanes Farm, Cross Lanes, Pill, Bristol, BS20 0JJ** 🅿
☎ 01275 371660
Est. 1982
Services Furniture restoration, cabinet-making, French polishing
Open Mon–Fri 9am–6pm advisable to call first

EAST

Abbey Antique Restorers
Contact Mr David Carter
✉ **Coxford Abbey Farmhouse, Coxford, King's Lynn, Norfolk, PE31 6TB** 🅿
☎ 01485 528043
Ⓦ www.abbey-restorations.co.uk
Est. 1969
Services Conservation and restoration of antique furniture
Open Mon–Sun 9am–6pm

Albion Clocks (BHI)
Contact Colin Bent
✉ **4 Grove Road, Grove Hill, South Woodford, Essex, E18 2LE** 🅿
☎ 020 8530 5570
Ⓔ colin.bent@btinternet.com
Ⓦ www.albionclocks.com
Est. 1963
Services Restoration of clocks and fine furniture, antiquarian horologist
Open Mon–Sun 9am–7pm by appointment

Antique Restorations
Contact Terry Wheeler
✉ **Unit 2 & 3, Bench Barn Farm, Clare, Sudbury, Suffolk, CO10 8HQ** 🅿
☎ 01787 277635
Ⓔ telwheeler11@aol.com
Ⓦ www.antique-restorations.net
Est. 1978
Services Furniture restoration, commissions to make one-off pieces

Antiques and Restoration
Contact Mr R Rush
✉ **Unit 5, Penny Corner, Farthing Road, Ipswich, Suffolk, IP1 5AP** 🅿
☎ 01473 464609 Ⓕ 01473 464609
Ⓜ 07939 220041
Ⓔ info@antiquesandrestoration.co.uk
Ⓦ www.antiquesandrestoration.co.uk
Est. 1997
Services Restoration, repair of 18thC furniture, gilding, upholstery
Open Mon–Fri 8am–6pm Sat 8am–1.30pm

M Barrett Restoration
Contact Mr M Barrett
✉ **Unit 7, Warbraham Farm, Heath Road, Burwell, Cambridge, Cambridgeshire, CB5 0AP** 🅿
☎ 01638 741700 Ⓕ 01638 741700
Est. 1987
Services Pre-1940s furniture restoration
Open Mon–Fri 8.30am–5pm

Clive Beardall (BAFRA)
Contact Mr Clive Beardall
✉ **104b High Street, Maldon, Essex, CM9 7ET** 🅿
☎ 01621 857890 Ⓕ 01621 850753
Ⓔ info@clivebeardall.co.uk
Ⓦ www.clivebeardall.co.uk
Est. 1982
Services Specializing in period furniture restoration, traditional hand French polishing, wax polishing, upholstery, marquetry, carving, gilding, leather desk-lining, rush and cane seating, decorative finishes, bespoke cabinet-making, valuations
Open Mon–Fri 8am–5.30pm Sat 9am–4pm

K W Box
Contact Mr K W Box
✉ **The Workshop, Upper Street, Stratford St Mary, Colchester, Essex, CO7 6JN** 🅿
☎ 01206 322673
Est. 1985
Services 17th–early 19thC furniture restoration and one-off cabinet-making to order. 25 years experience
Open Mon–Fri 8am–6pm Sat 8am–1pm

Bradshaw Fine Wood Furniture Ltd
Contact Mr Chris Shaw-Williams
✉ **Unit 12, Clovelly Works, Chelmsford Road, Rawreth, Wickford, Essex, SS11 8SY** 🅿
☎ 01268 571414 Ⓕ 01268 571314
Est. 1988
Services French polishing, furniture restoration and repair work
Open Mon–Fri 8am–6pm

The Cabinet Maker
Contact Gary Fitzjohn
✉ **Unit 23, Boleness Road, Wisbech, Cambridgeshire, PE13 2RB** 🅿
☎ 01945 475635 Ⓕ 01945 475635
Ⓜ 07813 391481
Est. 1997
Services Bespoke furniture manufacturers
Open Mon–Fri 8.30am–5pm

Clare Hall Co
Contact Mr M Moore
✉ **The Barns, Clare Hall, Clare,**

Sudbury, Suffolk,
CO10 8PJ 🅿
☎ 01787 278445 Ⓕ 01787 278803
Est. 1960
Services Restoration of all antiques including polishing and upholstery. Replicas of antique globes and four-poster beds
Open By appointment

Steven J Cotterell
Contact Steven Cotterell
✉ **72 Springfield Road, Somersham, Ipswich, Suffolk, IP8 4PQ** 🅿
☎ 01473 831530
Ⓜ 07733 291705
Ⓔ somersham.flyer@yahoo.co.uk
Est. 1975
Services French polishing, furniture restoration and painting
Open Mon–Sat 7.30am–6pm

Michael Dolling (BAFRA)
Contact Mr Michael Dolling
✉ **Church Farm, Barns, Glandford, Holt, Norfolk, NR25 7JR** 🅿
☎ 01263 741115
Est. 1986
Services General furniture restoration and repair
Open Mon–Fri 9am–5pm

A Dunn and Son
Contact Mr R Dunn
✉ **8 Wharf Road, Chelmsford, Essex, CM2 6LU** 🅿
☎ 01245 354452 Ⓕ 01245 494991
Ⓔ info@adunnandson.co.uk
Ⓦ www.adunnandson.com
Est. 1896
Services Antique furniture restoration
Open Mon–Fri 8am–6pm
Sat by appointment

Essex Reupholstery Services
Contact Mr S T Richardson
✉ **49 Chestnut Grove, Southend on Sea, Essex, SS2 5HG**
☎ 01702 464775 Ⓕ 01702 305684
Est. 1987
Services Restoration of antique furniture, paddings, upholstery
Open Mon–Fri 8am–5pm

Forge Studio Workshops
Contact Mr D Darton
✉ **Stour Street, Manningtree, Essex, CO11 1BE** 🅿
☎ 01206 396222 Ⓕ 01206 396222
Est. 1979
Services Antique furniture restoration
Open Mon–Fri 8.30am–5.30pm
Sat 8.30am–1pm

Furse Restoration
Contact Mr Fred Furse or Mr Andrew Furse
✉ **Unit 15 Beechcroft, Damases Lane, Boreham, Chelmsford, Essex, CM3 3AL** 🅿
☎ 01245 466744 Ⓕ 01245 466744
Ⓔ andrew@furserestoration.co.uk
Ⓦ www.furserestoration.co.uk
Est. 1993
Services Antique restoration, bespoke cabinet-making, French polishing, veneer design and pressing
Open Mon–Fri 8am–6pm
Sat 9am–1pm

Michael Goater Restoration (BAFRA)
Contact Michael Goater
✉ **15 Red Barn Yards, Thornham Magna, Eye, Suffolk, IP23 8HH** 🅿
☎ 01379 788722
Ⓔ michaelgoater@primex.co.uk
Ⓦ www.michaelgoater.co.uk
Est. 1987
Services Full restoration and conservation of 18th–19thC furniture
Open Mon–Sun 9am–6pm

P Godden
Contact Mr P Godden
✉ **32 Darcy Road, Old Heath, Colchester, Essex, CO2 8BB** 🅿
☎ 01206 790349
Est. 1942
Services Antique furniture restoration
Open Mon–Sat 9am–5pm

Haig and Hosford
Contact Mr J Hosford
✉ **The Workshop, Trews Chase, High Street, Kelvedon, Colchester, Essex, CO5 9AQ** 🅿
☎ 01376 571502
Est. 1981
Services French polishing, antique restoration
Open Mon–Fri 8.30am–5pm
Sat 8.30am–1pm

Brian Harris Furniture Restorations (BAFRA, EADA)
Contact Brian Harris
✉ **40 Lower Street, Stansted Mountfitchet, Essex, CM24 8LR** 🅿
☎ 01279 812233
Est. 1956
Services Antique furniture restoration including carving, gilding, French polishing, inlay work. Also restoration of clocks, barometers and ceramics
Open Mon–Sat 9am–5pm

Hyde Antique & Reproduction Furniture
Contact Neil Hyde
✉ **Unit 5, Ashwellthorpe Industrial Estate, Norwich, Norfolk, NR16 1ER** 🅿
☎ 01508 481888 Ⓕ 01508 481888
Ⓜ 07970 526975
Est. 1999
Services Restoration of 18thC oak furniture, manufacture of replica furniture
Open Mon–Sat 8am–5.30pm

Jeff Ingall
Contact Mr J Ingall
✉ **33 Hillside Road, Southminster, Essex, CM0 7AL** 🅿
☎ 01621 772686
Est. 1989
Services Antique furniture restoration, furniture maker
Open Mon–Sun 9am–6pm

S Layt
Contact Mr S Layt
✉ **Unit 5, New Cut, Wellington Street, Newmarket, Suffolk, CB8 0HT** 🅿
☎ 01638 668388
Est. 1999
Services Antique furniture restoration, French polishing
Open Mon–Fri 9am–5.30pm

Lomas Pigeon & Co Ltd (BAFRA, AMU)
Contact Mr W A J Pigeon
✉ **37 Beehive Lane, Chelmsford, Essex,**

CM2 9TQ **P**
☎ 01245 353708 **F** 01245 355211
E wpigeon@compuserve.com
W www.lomas-pigeon.co.uk
Est. 1938
Services Upholstery, antique restoration, French polishing, cabinet-making
Open Mon–Fri 10am–4pm Sat 9am–noon closed Wed

Maisey Restoration
Contact Mr Steve Maisey
✉ **Clark's Yard, High Street, Cavendish, Sudbury, Suffolk, CO10 8AT** **P**
☎ 01787 281331
Est. 1991
Services Repair, restoration and French polishing
Open Mon–Fri 8am–5pm

Andrew A Matthews Restoration (Graduate member of the students section BAFRA)
Contact Mr A A Matthews
✉ **Fox House, Gills Hill, Bourn, Cambridge, Cambridgeshire, CB3 7TX** **P**
M 07808 590370
Est. 1998
Services Antique restoration and conservation, cabinet work, veneering, turning, key-making, lock repair, polishing, upholstery, rushing and caning
Open By appointment

R J McPhee
Contact Mr R J McPhee
✉ **20 Muspole Street, Norwich, Norfolk, NR3 1DJ** **P**
☎ 01603 667701 **F** 01603 667701
E r.mcphee@jrmcabinetmaker.co.uk
Est. 1980
Services 17th–18thC fine antique furniture restoration
Open Mon–Fri 8am–1pm 2–5pm Sat by appointment

Peter Norman Antiques
Contact Mr Tony Marpole
✉ **55 North Street, Burwell, Cambridge, Cambridgeshire, CB5 0BA** **P**
☎ 01638 616914
E amarpole@aol.com
W www.peternormanantiques.co.uk
Est. 1977
Services General antique restoration, woodwork, caning, upholstery, relining and restoring oils
Open Mon–Sat 9am–5.30pm prior warning best

The Old Coach House
Contact David Burrough
✉ **Church Hill, Starston, Harleston, Norfolk, IP2 9PT** **P**
☎ 01379 852123
Est. 1990
Services Furniture restoration, French polishing, carving, stripping
Open Mon–Sat 9am–5pm

Mark Peters Antiques
Contact Mr M Peters
✉ **Green Farm Cottage, Oak Road, Thurston, Bury St Edmunds, Suffolk, IP31 3SN** **P**
☎ 01359 230888
E mark@markpetersantiques.com
Est. 1977
Services Furniture restoration
Open Mon–Fri 8am–5pm Sat 9am–noon

Ludovic Potts Restorations (BAFRA)
Contact Mr Ludovic Potts
✉ **Unit 1–1a, Station Road, Haddenham, Ely, Cambridgeshire, CB6 3XD** **P**
☎ 01353 741537 **F** 01353 741822
M 07889 341671
E mail@restorers.co.uk
W www.restorers.co.uk
Est. 1986
Services Modern and antique furniture restoration
Open By appointment

Prust & Sons Antique Furniture Restoration
Contact Mr Prust
✉ **9 West Road, Westcliff-on-Sea, Essex, SS0 9AU**
☎ 01702 391093 **F** 01702 391093
E sales@prust.co.uk
W www.prust.co.uk
Est. 1987
Services Antique furniture restoration
Open Mon–Sat 8.30am–5.30pm Sun 10am–3pm

Richard's Polishing
Contact Mr R Bufton
✉ **Bentley Road, Weeley Heath, Clacton on Sea, Essex, CO16 9DP** **P**
☎ 01255 831539 **F** 01255 831539
M 07712 873864
E sos@sos.uk.com
W www.sos.uk.com
Est. 1979
Services Antique restoration, all polish finishes
Open Mon–Fri 7.30am–5pm

Robert's Antiques
Contact Graham Bettany
✉ **The Barn, South Street, Risby, Bury St Edmunds, Suffolk, IP28 6QU** **P**
☎ 01284 811440 **F** 01284 811440
E info@robertsantiques.co.uk
W www.robertsantiques.co.uk
Est. 1978
Services French polishing
Open Tues–Fri 8.30am–5pm Sat–Sun noon–4pm

D J Short
Contact Mr D Short
✉ **The Stables, High Street, Horseheath, Cambridge, Cambridgeshire, CB1 6QN** **P**
☎ 01223 891983
Est. 1969
Services Antique furniture restoration, upholstery
Open Mon–Fri 9am–5pm Sat 9am–1pm

R J Smith Restoration
Contact Mr R J Smith
✉ **Unit 11, Rear of Keimar House, Tut Hill, Fornham All Saints, Bury St Edmonds, Suffolk, IP28 6LE** **P**
☎ 01284 704894
M 07759 930678
Est. 1991
Services Repair and restoration of Georgian–Edwardian furniture, French polishing
Open Mon–Sat 8.30am–5.30pm

R A Surridge
Contact Mr R Surridge
✉ **The Barn, Thistledown, Latchingdon Road, Cold Norton, Chelmsford, Essex, CM3 6HR** **P**
☎ 01621 828036 **F** 01621 828036
Est. 1978
Services Antique restoration and cabinet-maker
Open Mon–Fri 8am–5pm

Teywood Ltd
Contact Mr K Cottee
✉ **East Gores Farm, Salmons Lane, Coggeshall, Essex, CO6 1RZ** Ⓟ
☎ 01376 563025 ⓕ 01376 563025
Est. 1984
Services Antique furniture restoration and cabinet-maker
Open Mon–Fri 9am–5pm

R Tidder Antique Furniture Restoration
Contact Richard Tidder
✉ **Unit 22, Grainge Road Industrial Estate, Southend-on-Sea, Essex, SS2 5DD** Ⓟ
☎ 01702 600464
ⓔ richardtidder@aol.com
Est. 1988
Services Furniture restoration
Open Mon–Fri 9am–6pm

Whitfield Restoration
Contact Mr J Palmor
✉ **London Road, Cockford, Colchester, Essex, CO6 1LG** Ⓟ
☎ 01206 213212
Ⓜ 07803 044229
Est. 1990
Services Antique furniture restoration, cabinet-making, French polishing
Open Mon–Sat 9am–5pm

Robert Williams (BAFRA)
Contact Mr Robert Williams
✉ **32 Church Street, Willingham, Cambridge, Cambridgeshire, CB4 5HT** Ⓟ
☎ 01954 260972
Est. 1980
Services Restoration of carving, ivory, mother of pearl, bonework, papier mâché, tortoiseshell, weapons. Also cabinet-maker and locksmith
Open Mon–Fri 9am–5pm
Sat Sun by appointment

Justin Wood Restoration
Contact Justin Wood
✉ **Manor Farm Dairy, Manor Road, Hasketon, Woodbridge, Suffolk, IP13 6HZ** Ⓟ
☎ 01394 387791
Ⓜ 07712 131820
ⓔ justin.wood@antique-restoration.net
Ⓦ www.antique-restoration.net
Est. 1997
Services Quality restoration, French polishing, woodcarving, cabinet-making
Open Mon–Fri 9am–5pm
Sat 9am–noon

HEART OF ENGLAND

A C Restorations
Contact Mr Adrian Clark
✉ **Unit 9d, Quickbury Farm, Hatfield Heath Road, Sawbridgeworth, Hertfordshire, CM21 9HY** Ⓟ
☎ 01279 721583
Ⓜ 07905 156976
ⓔ adrian.clark1@virgin.net
Est. 1993
Services Furniture restoration, polishing, leather lining, carving, general services
Open Mon–Fri 9am–5.30pm

Antique and Modern Restoration by Richard Parsons
Contact Mr R Parsons
✉ **85 Pondcroft Road, Knebworth, Hertfordshire, SG3 6DE** Ⓟ
☎ 01438 812200
Est. 1980
Services Antique and modern furniture restoration, French polishing
Open By appointment

Antique Restoration & Polishing
Contact Mr M P Wallis
✉ **1 The Row, Hawridge, Chesham, Buckinghamshire, HP5 2UH** Ⓟ
☎ 01494 758172 ⓕ 01494 758701
ⓔ mikewallis@hawridge.freeserve.co.uk
Est. 1968
Services General antique furniture restoration and polishing
Open By appointment

Keith Bawden (BAFRA)
Contact Keith Bawden
✉ **Mews Workshops, Montpellier Retreat, Cheltenham, Gloucestershire, GL50 2XG** Ⓟ
☎ 01242 230320
Est. 1975
Services Full antique restoration service of furniture, clocks, watercolours, jewellery, ceramics and Oriental carpets
Open Mon–Fri 7am–4.30pm

R Beesly
Contact Mr R Beesly
✉ **41 High Street, Broom, Biggleswade, Bedfordshire, SG18 9NA** Ⓟ
☎ 01767 314918
Est. 1974
Services Cabinet-making, French polishing, clock repair
Open Mon–Sat 8am–6pm or by appointment

Belmont House Antiques
Contact Michael Mastrolasca
✉ **Belmont House, 77 Bedford Road, Willington, Bedfordshire**
☎ 01234 838750
Ⓜ 07761 829709
ⓔ belmonthouse77@aol.com
Est. 1987
Services Antique furniture restoration
Open Mon–Sat 9am–5pm

Andy Briggs
Contact Andy Briggs
✉ **35 Rack End, Standlake, Oxfordshire, OX29 7FA** Ⓟ
☎ 01865 301705
Ⓜ 07977 936882
Est. 1991
Services Restoration and conservation of town and country furniture, cabinet-making, items bought and sold, copies of stolen items made
Open By appointment

Peter Campion Restorations (BAFRA)
Contact Peter Campion
✉ **The Old Dairy, Rushley Lane, Winchcombe, Nr Cheltenham, Gloucestershire, GL54 5JE** Ⓟ
☎ 01242 604403 ⓕ 01242 604403
ⓔ petercampion@ukonline.co.uk
Ⓦ www.petercampion.co.uk
Est. 1959
Services Restoration and conservation of furniture, barometers, clock cases. Also cabinet work, inlays, brass, veneering, polishing, furniture designed and made to order
Open Mon–Fri 9am–5.30pm

ASSOCIATED SERVICES

FURNITURE

Charnwood Antiques (EADA)
Contact Mr Nigel Hoy
✉ **Unit 2e, The Maltings, Station Road, Sawbridgeworth, Hertfordshire, CM21 9JX** 🅿
☎ 01279 600562
Ⓜ 07957 551899
Est. 1988
Services Cabinet-maker, antique furniture restoration, upholstery, cabinet lining, French polishing
Open Tues–Fri 10am–5pm Sat Sun 11am–5pm

Chess Antique Restorations
Contact Mr T Chapman
✉ **85 Broad Street, Chesham, Buckinghamshire, HP5 3EF** 🅿
☎ 01494 783043 Ⓕ 01494 791302
Ⓔ chessrest@aol.com
Est. 1969
Services All cabinet work, hand finishing, upholstery, ceramics, metalwork, picture restoration, traditional polishing
Open Mon–Fri 9am–5pm

N A Copp
Contact Nigel Copp
✉ **Red Lane, Tewkesbury, Gloucestershire, GL20 5BQ** 🅿
☎ 01684 293935
Est. 1984
Services Restorer of antique furniture, maker of kitchens
Open Mon–Fri 8.30am–5.30pm

Martin Coulborn Restorations Ltd
Contact Mr M Coulborn
✉ **Canterbury House, Bridge Road, Frampton on Severn, Gloucestershire, GL2 7HE** 🅿
☎ 01452 740334
Est. 1978
Services Antique furniture restorer, maker of replica 18thC-style furniture
Open Mon–Fri 9am–1pm 2–5pm, please telephone before visiting

Robert H Crawley (BAFRA)
Contact Mr R Crawley
✉ **The Workshops, Huntsmoor Park Farm, Ford Lane, Iver, Buckinghamshire, SL0 9LL** 🅿
Ⓜ 07710 240956
Ⓔ antique.restorer@virgin.net
Est. 1979
Services Antique furniture restoration
Open Mon–Fri 8.30am–4.30pm

D H R Ltd (BAFRA, UKIC)
Contact Mr David Hordern
✉ **8–10 Lea Lane, Thame Road, Long Crendon, Aylesbury, Buckinghamshire, HP18 9RN** 🅿
☎ 01844 202213 Ⓕ 01844 202214
Est. 1985
Services All antique furniture restoration services
Open Mon–Fri 9am–5.30pm

D M E Restorations Ltd (BAFRA)
Contact Duncan Everitt
✉ **11 Church Street, Ampthill, Bedfordshire, MK45 2PL** 🅿
☎ 01525 405819 Ⓕ 01525 756177
Ⓜ 07778 015121
Ⓔ duncan@dmerestorations.com
Ⓦ www.dmerestorations.com
Est. 1986
Services Restoration and conservation of antique furniture
Open Mon–Fri 8am–5pm or by appointment

Deerstalker Antiques
Contact Mr or Mrs Eichler
✉ **28 High Street, Whitchurch, Buckinghamshire, HP22 4JT** 🅿
☎ 01296 641505
Est. 1978
Services Restoration of furniture pre-1850
Open Tue Wed Thurs Sat 10am–5.30pm or by appointment

Dovetail Restoration
Contact Mr Robert Askham
✉ **Home Farm, Ardington, Wantage, Oxfordshire, OX12 8PD** 🅿
☎ 01235 833614 Ⓕ 01235 833110
Est. 1973
Services Antique and modern furniture restoration
Open Mon–Fri 8.30am–5.30pm or Sat by appointment

P M Dupuy
Contact Mr P Dupuy
✉ **132 Bletchley Road, Newton Longville, Milton Keynes, Buckinghamshire, MK17 0AA** 🅿
☎ 01908 367168
Est. 1978
Services Restoration of antique furniture, all woodwork repairs, French and wax polishing, hand-stripping
Open Mon–Sat 9am–6pm

J W Eaton
Contact Mr J Eaton
✉ **The Barn, Tupsley Court Farm, Hampton Dene Road, Hereford, Herefordshire, HR1 1UX** 🅿
☎ 01432 354344
Est. 1990
Services General antique restoration
Open Mon–Fri 9am–5pm

Forum Antiques
Contact Mr Weston Mitchell
✉ **Springfield Farm, Perrott's Brook, Cirencester, Gloucestershire, GL7 7DT** 🅿
☎ 01285 831821
Ⓔ enquiries@westonmitchell.com
Ⓦ www.westonmitchell.com
Est. 1985
Services Restoration of antique furniture
Open By appointment only

Gloucestershire Furniture Hospital
Contact Mr M Deane
✉ **Commonfields Farm, Lower Boulsdon, Newent, Gloucestershire, GL18 1JH** 🅿
☎ 01531 822881
Est. 1999
Services Antique and modern furniture repair including upholstery, caning and French polishing. Collection service
Open Mon–Sat 8am–6pm

Ian Gray Antique Restoration
Contact Ian Gray
✉ **The Stables, Park Farm, Great Hampden, Great Missenden, Buckinghamshire, HG16 9RD** 🅿
☎ 01494 488560
Ⓦ www.iangrayrestoration.co.uk
Est. 1993

Services Furniture restoration, French polishing
Open Mon–Fri 8am–5.30pm

Robert Gripper Restoration
Contact Mr R Gripper
✉ **Manor Barn, Manor Farm, Ascott-under-Wychwood, Chipping Norton, Oxfordshire, OX7 6AL** 🅿
☎ 01993 831960 Ⓕ 01993 830395
Ⓔ robgripper@aol.com
Est. 1982
Services Antique furniture restoration, modern insurance work
Open Mon–Fri 9am–5pm

Roland Haycraft (GADAR)
Contact Mr R Haycraft
✉ **The Lamb Arcade, High Street, Wallingford, Oxfordshire, OX10 0BS** 🅿
☎ 01491 839622
Ⓔ ro@fsbdial.co.uk
Ⓦ www.juststolen.com
Est. 1980
Services Antique furniture conservation, restoration and bespoke cabinet-making
Open Mon–Fri 9am–5.30pm

Alan Hessel (BAFRA)
Contact Mr A Hessel
✉ **The Old Town Workshop, St George's Close, Moreton-in-Marsh, Gloucestershire, GL56 0LP** 🅿
☎ 01608 650026 Ⓕ 01608 650026
Ⓜ 07860 225608
Est. 1975
Services Restoration of fine 17th–19thC furniture
Open Mon–Fri 8.30am–5pm or by appointment

Stephen Hill (BAFRA)
Contact Stephen Hill
✉ **11 Cirencester Workshops, Brewery Court, Cirencester, Gloucestershire, GL7 1JH** 🅿
☎ 01285 658817
Ⓜ 07976 722028
Est. 1979
Services Restoration of 17th–19thC furniture
Open Mon–Fri 9am–5pm

John Hulme
Contact Mr J Hulme
✉ **11a High Street, Chipping Norton, Oxfordshire, OX7 5AD** 🅿
☎ 01608 641692 Ⓕ 01608 641692
Est. 1980
Services Antique furniture restoration and conservation
Open Mon–Fri 7.30am–6pm

Icknield Restorations
Contact Simon Pallister
✉ **Icknield Farm, Tring Road, Dunstable, Bedfordshire, LU6 2JX** 🅿
☎ 01525 222883
Est. 1994
Services Antique furniture restoration
Open Mon–Fri 9.30am–6pm

Ipsden Woodcraft
Contact Mr M Small
✉ **The Post Office, The Street, Ipsden, Wallingford, Oxfordshire, OX10 6AG** 🅿
☎ 01491 680262
Est. 1981
Services Antique furniture restoration
Open Mon–Fri 8am–6pm

J R Jury & Son
Contact Mr Ken Jury
✉ **Springfields, Cobhall Common, Allensmore, Hereford, Herefordshire, HR2 9BJ** 🅿
☎ 01432 279108
Est. 1974
Services Antique furniture restoration, French polishing
Open Mon–Fri 8am–5pm

Robert Lawrence-Jones
Contact Robert Lawrence-Jones
✉ **Frogmarsh Mill, South Woodchester, Stroud, Gloucestershire, GL5 5ET** 🅿
☎ 01453 872817
Est. 1980
Services Cabinet-making, furniture restoration
Open Mon–Fri 9am–5pm or by appointment

E C Legg and Son
Contact Mr C Legg
✉ **3 College Farm Buildings, Tetbury Road, Cirencester, Gloucestershire, GL7 6PY** 🅿
☎ 01285 650695
Est. 1903
Services Furniture restoration, carving, rushing, leather laying
Open Mon–Fri 9am–5pm Sat 9am–noon

Clive Loader Restorations
Contact Mr C Loader
✉ **Stables Workshop, Lodge Cottage, High Street, Shipton under Wychwood, Oxfordshire, OX7 6DG** 🅿
☎ 01993 832727
Est. 1984
Services Antique furniture restoration
Open Mon–Fri 8am–5pm

M K Restorations
Contact Mr M Knight
✉ **Unit 8e4, Quickbury Farm, Hatfield Heath Road, Sawbridgeworth, Hertfordshire, CM21 9HY** 🅿
☎ 01279 726664
Ⓜ 07939 438587
Ⓔ mk-restorations@talk21.com
Est. 1992
Services Antique furniture restoration, specializing in veneering and inlay work
Open Mon–Sat 9am–6.30pm

Miracle Finishing
Contact Mr C Howes or Mr A Howes
✉ **The Cottage, Woodhall Farm, Hatfield, Hertfordshire, AL9 5NU** 🅿
☎ 01707 270587 Ⓕ 01707 270587
Ⓜ 07803 397133
Est. 1992
Services Furniture restoration, French polishing, upholstery, pine stripping
Open Mon–Fri 8.30am–5pm

J Moore Restorations
Contact Mr J Moore
✉ **College Farm House Workshops, Chawston Lane, Chawston, Bedford, Bedfordshire, MK44 3BH** 🅿
☎ 01480 214165
Est. 1975
Services All aspects of furniture restoration, particularly period furniture
Open Mon–Fri 9am–5pm

ASSOCIATED SERVICES

FURNITURE

Clive Payne (BAFRA, LAPADA)
Contact Clive Payne
✉ **Unit 4, Mount Farm, Junction Road, Churchill, Chipping Norton, Oxfordshire, OX7 6NP** 🅿
☎ 01608 658856 Ⓕ 01608 658856
Ⓜ 07801 088363
Ⓔ clive.payne@virgin.net
Ⓦ www.clivepayne.com
Est. 1986
Services Antique furniture restoration, specializing in country furniture and Georgian mahogany
Open Mon–Fri 9am–5pm

Charles Perry Restorations Ltd (BAFRA)
Contact John Carr
✉ **Praewood Farm, Hemel Hempstead Road, St Albans, Hertfordshire, AL3 6AA** 🅿
☎ 01727 853487 Ⓕ 01727 846668
Ⓔ cperry@praewood.freeserve.co.uk
Est. 1986
Services Anything associated with antique furniture restoration including carving, gilding, caning and upholstery
Open Mon–Fri 8.30am–5.30pm

Ashley Pert
Contact Ashley Pert
✉ **Aylesbury, Buckinghamshire**
☎ 01296 482233 Ⓕ 01296 482233
Ⓜ 07793 741143
Ⓔ ashleypert@frenchpolisher.com
Ⓦ www.frenchpolisher.com
Est. 2001
Services French polishing
Open By appointment

Nathan Polley Antique Restoration (TADA)
Contact Mr N Polley
✉ **The Barn, Upton Grove, Tetbury Upton, Tetbury, Gloucestershire, GL8 8LR** 🅿
☎ 01666 504997
Ⓜ 07977 263236
Ⓔ npolleyrestorations@yahoo.co.uk
Est. 1995
Services Repair and restoration
Open Mon–Fri 8am–6.30pm
Sat 8am–4pm

Alan J Ponsford Antique Restorations
Contact Alan Ponsford
✉ **Decora, Northbrook Road, Gloucester, Gloucestershire, GL4 3DP** 🅿
☎ 01452 307700
Est. 1962
Services Restoration
Open Mon–Fri 8am–5pm

R J Poynter
Contact Mr R Poynter
✉ **Lyndhurst, Westland Green, Little Hadham, Ware, Hertfordshire, SG11 2AF** 🅿
☎ 01279 842395
Est. 1984
Services Antique furniture restoration
Open Mon–Fri 10am–5pm
Sat by appointment only

Romark Specialist Cabinet Makers Ltd
Contact Mark Tracy
✉ **3 Shaftesbury Industrial Centre, Icknield Way, Letchworth, Hertfordshire, SG6 1HE** 🅿
☎ 01462 684855 Ⓕ 01462 684833
Ⓜ 07831 326488
Ⓔ romark@aol.com
Ⓦ www.romarkltd.co.uk
Est. 2003
Services Antique furniture restoration, marquetry, brasswork, tortoiseshell, boulle work, ivory work, wax polishing, upholstery, leather top lining, period panelling restoration, de-infestation. Also specialist cabinet-makers
Open Mon–Thurs 7am–4pm
Fri 7am–3pm

Saracen Restoration
Contact Mr C Mills
✉ **Upton Downs Farm, Burford, Oxfordshire, OX18 4LY** 🅿
☎ 01993 822987
Ⓜ 07958 907255
Ⓔ cmills6702@aol.com
Est. 1992
Services Full restoration service including marquetry, French polishing, gilding, upholstery
Open Mon–Sat 9am–5.30pm

J Smith
Contact Mr J Smith
✉ **Wisteria Studio, Wharf Road, Shillingford, Oxfordshire, OX10 7EW** 🅿
☎ 01491 835185
Ⓜ 07745 406175
Ⓦ www.furniture-restorers.co.uk
Est. 1994
Services Antique furniture restoration, conservation of original finishes
Open Mon–Fri 9am–5.30pm

Starkadder
Contact Mr C Rosser
✉ **Unit 4–13, Ditchford Farm, Stretton on Fosse, Moreton-in-Marsh, Gloucestershire, GL56 9RD** 🅿
☎ 01608 664885
Est. 1998
Services Antique furniture restoration
Open By appointment

Sunningend Joiners and Cabinet Makers Ltd
Contact Mr R J Duester
✉ **Industrial Estate, Station Road, Bourton-on-the-Water, Cheltenham, Gloucestershire, GL54 2EP** 🅿
☎ 01451 820761 Ⓕ 01451 810671
Ⓔ sunningend@aol.com
Est. 1972
Services Joinery, cabinet-making, antique furniture restoration
Open Mon–Thurs 8am–5pm
Fri 8am–4pm

Timber Restorations
Contact Mr S Shannon
✉ **Hyde Hall Barn, Sandon, Buntingford, Hertfordshire, SG9 0RU** 🅿
☎ 01763 274849 Ⓕ 01763 274849
Ⓜ 07973 748644
Est. 1997
Services Spray lacquering, French polishing, furniture repair, caustic and non-caustic stripping, wax polishing, furniture sales, leather top inlay
Open Mon–Sat 9am–5pm

Christopher Tombs
Contact Mr C G Tombs
✉ **Unit 45, Northwick Business Centre, Blockley, Moreton-in-Marsh, Gloucestershire, GL56 9RF** 🅿
☎ 01386 700085
Est. 1994
Services English furniture restoration
Open Mon–Fri 8am–5pm

Truman and Bates
Contact Mr P Truman
✉ **Classic Works, Station Road, Banbury, Oxfordshire, OX15 5LS** Ⓟ
☎ 01608 730433
Est. 1961
Services Restoration of antique furniture, French polishing
Open Mon–Fri 8am–5pm

P M Welch
Contact Zoe Greenhalgh
✉ **Unit 4 Bourton Link, Bourton Industrial Park, Bourton-on-the-Water, Gloucestershire, GL5 2HQ** Ⓟ
☎ 01451 810800 Ⓕ 01451 810666
Ⓔ restoration.antiques@virgin.net
Ⓦ www.antiques-restorers.com
Est. 1969
Services Restoration of English and Continental furniture
Open Mon–Fri 7.45am–5.30pm Sat 7.45am–noon

Richard J Young Antiques Restorer
Contact Richard Young
✉ **5 Macaroni Wood, Eastleach, Cirencester, Gloucestershire, GL7 3NF** Ⓟ
☎ 01367 850587
Ⓔ richardyoung.restorer@virgin.net
Est. 1980
Services Restoration of furniture and in house wood
Open By appointment

MIDLANDS

Abbey Restorations
Contact Allan Standing
✉ **Darley Abbey Mills, Darley Abbey, Derbyshire, DE22 1DZ** Ⓟ
☎ 01332 344547
Est. 1974
Services Restoration of furniture, upholstery
Open Mon–Fri 8.30am–5.30pm Sat 8.30am–noon

Anthony Allen Conservation, Restoration, Furniture and Artefacts (BAFRA, UKIC)
Contact Anthony Allen
✉ **The Old Wharf Workshop, Redmoor Lane, Newtown, High Peak, Derbyshire, SK22 3JL** Ⓟ
☎ 01663 745274 Ⓕ 01663 745274
Est. 1970
Services Restoration of 17th–19thC furniture, gilding, marquetry, boulle, upholstery, metalwork, clock cases and movements
Open Mon–Fri 8am–5pm

The Antiques Workshop
Contact Mr Paul Burrows
✉ **68 Yoxall Road, Solihull, West Midlands, B90 3RP** Ⓟ
☎ 0121 744 1744
Ⓜ 07860 168078
Est. 1988
Services Furniture restoration
Open Mon–Sat 9am–5pm

Barnt Green Antiques (BAFRA)
Contact Phillip Slater
✉ **93 Hewell Road, Barnt Green, Birmingham, West Midlands, B45 8NL** Ⓟ
☎ 0121 445 4942 Ⓕ 0121 445 4942
Ⓦ www.barntgreenantiques.co.uk
Est. 1977
Services Furniture and longcase clock restoration. All aspects of polishing and finishing including wax and French polishing, marquetry, inlay
Open Mon–Fri 9am–5.30pm Sat 9am–1pm

M G Bassett
Contact Mrs G Bassett or Mr M Bassett
✉ **38 Church Street, Ashbourne, Derbyshire, DE6 1AJ** Ⓟ
☎ 01335 347750 (workshop)/ 300061 (shop) Ⓕ 01335 300061
Ⓔ mgbassett@aol.com
Est. 1979
Services Restoration of English and French country furniture and decorative items
Trade only Yes
Open Mon–Fri 9am–5pm closed Wed

Belle Vue Restoration
Contact Mr Peter Grady
✉ **19 Belle Vue Road, Shrewsbury, Shropshire, SY3 7LN** Ⓟ
☎ 01743 272210
Est. 1984
Services Antique furniture restoration
Open Mon–Fri 8am–5.30pm

S C Brown
Contact Mr S C Brown
✉ **53 Melton Road, Birmingham, West Midlands, B14 7ET** Ⓟ
☎ 0121 441 1479
Est. 1981
Services Antique furniture restoration, furniture designed and made
Open Mon–Sat 8am–5.30pm

Jacob Butler – Period Joinery Specialist
Contact Jacob Butler
✉ **The Chapel, Main Street, Matlock, Derbyshire, DE4 4LQ** Ⓟ
☎ 01629 822170/825640
Ⓔ jacob@owdman.co.uk
Ⓦ www.jowdman.co.uk
Est. 1987
Services Repair and restoration of period joinery and furniture
Open By appointment

Comfort Solutions (AMU)
Contact Miss Jo MacDonald or Miss Susan Robinson
✉ **Machins Business Centre, Wood Street, Ashby de la Zouche, Leicestershire, LE65 1EL** Ⓟ
☎ 01530 417510 Ⓕ 01530 417510
Est. 1997
Services Repair, restoration and upholstery
Open Mon–Fri 9am–5pm

Ian Dewar
Contact Mr Ian Dewar
✉ **55 Whateleys Drive, Kenilworth, Warwickshire, CV8 2GY** Ⓟ
☎ 01926 856767
Ⓔ DewarRestoration@aol.com
Est. 1989
Services Antique furniture restoration, French polishing
Open Mon–Fri 8.30am–5.30pm

Joyce Ellis
Contact Joyce Ellis
✉ **Yew Tree Farm, Stratford Road, Wootton Wawen, Solihull, West Midlands, B95 6BY** Ⓟ
☎ 01564 795401
Ⓜ 07712 126048
Ⓔ info@legrenantiques.com
Ⓦ www.legrenantiques.com
Est. 1989

Services General restoration, specializing in French beds and farmhouse tables
Open Tues–Sun 9am–5.30pm

T J Gittins
Contact Mr T J Gittins
✉ **The Old Barn, Nagington Grange, Childs Ercall, Market Drayton, Shropshire, TF9 2TW**
☎ 01952 840409
Services Antique furniture restoration
Open By appointment

Guy Goodwin Restoration
Contact Mr Guy Goodwin
✉ **1a St John's, Warwick, Warwickshire, CV34 4NE** P
☎ 01926 407409 F 01926 407409
Est. 1979
Services Antique furniture restoration
Open Mon–Fri 9am–5.30pm

Grantham Workshops Cabinet Makers
Contact Peter Grantham
✉ **51a–57 Union Street, Kettering, Northamptonshire, NN16 9DA** P
☎ 01536 411461 F 01536 392239
E info@grantham-workshops.co.uk
W www.grantham-workshops.co.uk
Est. 1979
Services Conservation and restoration of antique furniture. Veneer and inlay replacement, French polishing and colouring
Open Mon–Fri 9am–5.30pm

Laila Gray
Contact Laila Gray
✉ **25 Welford Road, Kingsthorpe, Northamptonshire, NN2 8AQ** P
M 07941 263236
Est. 1984
Services Antique furniture restoration, French polishing
Open By appointment

Richard Higgins Conservation (BAFRA, UKIC)
Contact Richard Higgins
✉ **The Old School, Longnor, Nr Shrewsbury, Shropshire, SY5 7PP** P
☎ 01743 718162 F 01743 718022
E richardhigginsco@aol.com
Est. 1988
Services Restoration of all fine furniture, clocks, movements, dials and cases, casting, plating, boulle, gilding, lacquerwork, carving, period upholstery
Open Mon–Fri 8am–6pm

L J Holmes Antique Furniture Restoration
Contact Mr L J Holmes
✉ **The Old Stables Workshop, Cowsden, Upton Snodsbury, Worcestershire, WR7 4NX** P
☎ 01905 381892
Est. 1983
Services Furniture restoration
Open Mon–Fri 9am–5pm

Hope Antiques
Contact Mr D White
✉ **The Coach House, Spring Croft, Hartwell Lane, Rough Close, Stoke-on-Trent, Staffordshire, ST3 7NG** P
☎ 01782 399022 F 01782 399022
M 07762 392712
E hopeantiques@btintenet.com
Est. 1986
Services Repair and restoration of furniture, French polishing, pine stripping, inlay work. Country oak furniture made to order (from wood no less than 150 years old)
Open Mon–Sat 8am–6pm

John Hubbard Antiques Restoration & Conservation (LAPADA, CINOA)
Contact John Hubbard
✉ **Castle Ash, Birmingham Road, Blakedown, Worcestershire, DY10 3JE** P
☎ 01562 701020 F 01562 700001
E jphubbard@aol.com
Est. 1968
Services Furniture restoration, French polishing, desktop leathers, upholstery
Open By appointment Mon–Fri 9am–5.30pm

Kings of Loughborough
Contact Mr A King
✉ **5 Oliver Road, Loughborough, Leicestershire, LE11 2BZ** P
☎ 01509 556162 F 01509 556159
Est. 1971
Services Repair, restoration and cabinet-making
Open Mon–Fri 8am–5pm

Lincoln Restorations
Contact Andrew Lincoln
✉ **54 Mill Road, High Heath, Pelsall, Walsall, West Midlands, WS4 1BS** P
☎ 01922 693999
W www.lincolnrestorations.co.uk
Est. 1986
Services Full antique furniture restoration
Open Mon–Fri 8.30am–6pm

Mackenzie & Smith (UKIC)
Contact Mr Tim Smith
✉ **4 The Bullring, Ludlow, Shropshire, SY8 1AD** P
☎ 01584 877133
Est. 1998
Services Antique furniture 17th–19thC restoration, clock case restoration
Open Mon–Fri 9am–5pm

Malvern Studios (BAFRA, UKIC, NCCR)
Contact Jeff Hall
✉ **56 Cowleigh Road, Malvern, Worcestershire, WR14 1QD** P
☎ 01684 574913 F 01684 569475
Est. 1961
Services Restoration of any form of furniture and panelling, including boulle, gilding, tortoiseshell, black lacquer, chinoiserie, satinwood, hand-painted cameos
Open Mon Tues Thurs 9am–5.15pm Fri Sat 9am–4.45pm

Nigel Mayall
Contact Mr N Mayall
✉ **114 Richmond Road, Bewdley, Worcestershire, DY12 2BQ** P
☎ 01299 401754
E ant.unltd.may.uk@virgin.net
Est. 1989
Services High-class French polishing, repair, minor restoration, re-leathering, veneer repair
Open Mon–Fri 10am–6pm

Melbourne Hall Furniture
Contact Mr N Collumbell
✉ **Old Saw Mill Craft Centre, Melbourne Hall, Melbourne, Derby, Derbyshire,**

DE73 1EA 🅿
☎ 01332 864131
Est. 1982
Services Repair and restoration, French polishing
Open By appointment

Middleton Antiques (BAFRA)
Contact Mr S Herberholz
✉ **Middleton Hall, Middleton, Tamworth, Staffordshire, B78 2AE** 🅿
☎ 01827 282858
Ⓜ 07973 151681
Est. 1997
Services Complete repair and restoration of antique furniture including metalwork, turning, upholstery, carving, caning, gilding, porcelain restoration
Open Wed–Sun 11am–5pm

K Needham Restoration Ltd
Contact Kevin Needham
✉ **Unit 2, Old Hall Workshops, School Road, Beely, Derbyshire, DE4 2NU** 🅿
☎ 01629 735455 Ⓕ 01629 735455
Ⓔ kwg@needhams.fsbusiness.co.uk
Ⓦ www.needhamrestorations.co.uk
Est. 1993
Services Repair and restoration
Open Mon–Sat 9am–5pm

Painswick Antiques
✉ **6 Churchgate, Retford, Nottinghamshire, DN22 6PQ** 🅿
☎ 01777 706278
Est. 1977
Services Repair and restoration
Open Mon–Sat 9am–6pm

Perkins Stockwell and Co Ltd
Contact Mr J Stockwell
✉ **12 Abbey Gate, Leicester, Leicestershire, LE4 0AB** 🅿
☎ 01162 516501 Ⓕ 01162 510697
Ⓔ perkinsstockwell@btconnect.com
Est. 1760
Services Repair and restoration of furniture
Open Mon–Fri 7am–4pm

Regency Furniture Restoration
Contact Mr M Houghton
✉ **29 St Kenelm's Avenue, Halesowen, West Midlands, B63 1DW** 🅿
☎ 0121 550 8356 Ⓕ 0121 550 8356
Ⓜ 07966 434947
Est. 1997
Services Antique furniture restoration and cabinet-making
Open Mon–Fri 8am–5pm or by appointment

Renaissance Antiques
Contact Mr S Macrow
✉ **18 Marshall Lake Road, Shirley, Solihull, West Midlands, B90 4PL** 🅿
☎ 0121 745 5140
Est. 1979
Services Antique furniture restoration
Open Mon–Sat 9am–5pm

Tim Ross-Bain
Contact Mr T Ross-Bain
✉ **Halford Bridge, Fosse Way, Halford, Shipston-on-Stour, Warwickshire, CV36 5BN** 🅿
☎ 01789 740778 Ⓕ 01789 740778
Ⓔ info@rossbain.com
Ⓦ www.rossbain.com
Est. 1979
Services Antique furniture restoration, interior decoration and repair, cabinet-making
Open 24 hours by appointment

Sealcraft
Contact Mr P M Sealey
✉ **107 New Road, Bromsgrove, Worcestershire, B60 2LJ** 🅿
☎ 01527 872677
Est. 1995
Services Antique restoration and repair, French polishing
Open By appointment

Anthony Smith
Contact Mr A Smith
✉ **Perton Court Farm, Jenny Walkers Lane, Wolverhampton, West Midlands, WV6 7HB** 🅿
☎ 01902 380303 Ⓕ 01902 380303
Est. 1969
Services Antique and quality furniture restoration
Open Mon–Fri 8.30am–5pm

J A Snelson
Contact Mr J A Snelson
✉ **Jennett Tree Farm, Jennett Tree Lane, Callow End, Worcestershire, WR2 4UA** 🅿
☎ 01905 831887
Ⓜ 07803 469122
Est. 1984
Services Fine antique restoration, French polishing, cabinet work
Open Mon–Fri 9am–5pm Sat 9am–noon

J W Stevens and Son
Contact Mr M J Stevens
✉ **61 Main Street, Lubenham, Market Harborough, Leicestershire, LE16 9TF** 🅿
☎ 01858 463521
Est. 1947
Services Antique furniture restoration
Open By appointment only

Keith Stimpson Ltd
Contact Mr K Stimpson
✉ **43 Watling Street, Pottersbury, Towcester, Northamptonshire, NN12 7QD** 🅿
☎ 01908 542633
Est. 1984
Services Antique furniture restoration
Open Mon–Fri 8am–4.30pm or by appointment

Treedale Antiques
Contact Mr G Warren
✉ **Pickwell Lane, Little Dalby, Melton Mowbray, Leicestershire, LE14 2XB** 🅿
☎ 01664 454535 Ⓕ 01572 757521
Est. 1968
Services 17th–18thC furniture restoration
Open Mon–Sat 8am–6pm Sun by appointment

Clive Underwood Antiques Restorations
Contact Mr Clive Underwood
✉ **Unit 6, The Windmill, Butt Lane, Wymondham, Leicestershire, LE14 2BU** 🅿
☎ 01572 787774
Ⓜ 07712 894955
Est. 1964
Services Antique furniture restorer and cabinet-maker, specializing in dining and carver chairs
Open Mon–Fri 8am–5pm

Upstairs Downstairs Antiques
Contact Mr C Lawrence

ASSOCIATED SERVICES

FURNITURE

✉ **8 Derby Road, Ripley, Derbyshire, DE5 3HR** P
☎ 01773 745201
Ⓜ 07885 327753
Ⓦ www.upstairsdownstairsantiques.co.uk
Est. 1974
Services Furniture restoration, clock repair, French polishing
Open Mon–Sat 10am–4pm

Richard Walker – Antique Restoration
Contact Mr R Walker
✉ **302 Via Gellia Mills, Via Gellia Road, Bonsall, Matlock, Derbyshire, DE4 2AJ** P
☎ 01629 825791
Est. 1992
Services Furniture repair and restoration
Open By appointment

Wizzards Furniture Restorers
Contact D Hayes
✉ **The Old Stables, Meadow Lane, Nottingham, Nottinghamshire, NG2 3HQ** P
☎ 0115 986 7484 Ⓕ 0115 986 7484
Est. 1994
Services Furniture repair and restoration, stripping, French polishing
Open Mon–Fri 8.30am–5pm or by appointment

Wood Restorations
Contact Mr Peter Wood
✉ **Eastfields Farm, Crick Road, Rugby, Warwickshire, CV23 0AB** P
☎ 01788 822253 Ⓕ 01788 822253
Est. 1969
Services Antique furniture restoration
Open By appointment

YORKSHIRE & LINCOLNSHIRE

Anthony James Beech Furniture Conservation & Restoration (BAFRA, UKIC)
Contact Anthony Beech
✉ **The Stable Courtyard, Burghley House, Stamford, Lincolnshire, PE9 3JY** P
☎ 01780 481199 Ⓕ 01780 481199
Est. 1997
Services Furniture restoration
Open By appointment

Adrian J Black
Contact Mr A J Black
✉ **36a Freeman Street, Grimsby, Lincolnshire, DN32 7AG**
☎ 01472 355668
Est. 1968
Services Antique furniture repair and restoration
Open By apppointment

Byethorpe Furniture
Contact Mr B Yates
✉ **Shippen Rural Business Centre, Church Farm, Barlow, Yorkshire, S18 7TR** P
☎ 0114 289 9111 Ⓕ 0114 289 9111
Ⓦ www.byethorpe.com
Est. 1995
Services Antique restoration, maker of bespoke furniture
Open Mon–Sat 9.30am–5.30pm

Kenneth F Clifford
Contact Mr K Clifford
✉ **29 St Aubyn's Place, York, North Yorkshire, YO24 1EQ** P
☎ 01904 635780
Est. 1982
Services Antique repair and restoration
Open By appointment

D A Copley
Contact Mr D A Copley
✉ **54a New Lane, Siddal, Halifax, West Yorkshire, HX3 9AL** P
☎ 01422 351854
Est. 1949
Services Antique repair and restoration, French polishing
Open Mon–Fri 8am–5pm Sat 8am–noon

Edmund Czajkowski & Son (BAFRA)
Contact Michael Czajkowski
✉ **96 Tor O Moor Road, Woodhall Spa, Lincolnshire, LN10 6SB** P
☎ 01526 352895 Ⓕ 01526 352895
Ⓔ michael.czajkowski@ntlworld.com
Ⓦ www.czajkowskiandson.com
Est. 1951
Services Restoration of antique furniture, clocks, barometers
Open Mon–Sat 8.30am–5pm

R D Dunning
Contact Mr R Dunning
✉ **Scaife Cottage, Gate Helmsley, York, North Yorkshire, YO41 1NE**
☎ 01759 371961
Est. 1972
Services Antique furniture repair and restoration
Open Mon–Fri 9am–6pm or by appointment

Easingwold Antiques
Contact Jane Fish
✉ **108 Long Street, Easingwold, North Yorkshire, YO61 3HX** P
☎ 01347 822977
Ⓜ 07968 088705 or 07977 108907
Est. 2003
Services Restoration of wooden furniture
Open Tues–Sat 10am–5pm

Fishlake Antiques
Contact Fiona Trimingham
✉ **Vine Cottage, Hay Green Corner, Fishlake, South Yorkshire, DN7 5LA** P
☎ 01302 841411
Est. 1979
Services Furniture restoration
Open Sun 1–4pm or by appointment

French House Antiques
Contact Steve
✉ **74 Micklegate, York, YO1 6LF** P
☎ 01904 624465 Ⓕ 01904 629965
Ⓔ info@thefrenchhouse.co.uk
Ⓦ www.thefrenchhouse.co.uk
Est. 1995
Services Restoration of antique French furniture
Open Mon–Sat 9.30am–5.30pm

Furniture Revivals
Contact Michael Edwards
✉ **Yeadon, Leeds, LS19** P
Ⓜ 07831 817845
Ⓔ enquiries@furniturerevivals.co.uk
Ⓦ www.furniturerevivals.co.uk
Est. 1991
Services Furniture restoration, upholstery
Open By appointment

Hunters Interiors (Stamford) Ltd
Contact Jill Hunter

✉ 9a St Mary's Hill, Stamford, Lincolnshire, PE9 2DP 🅿
☎ 01780 757946 Ⓕ 01780 757946
Ⓜ 07976 796969
Ⓔ huntersinteriors@btopenworld.com
Ⓦ www.huntersinteriorsofstamford.co.uk
Est. 2000
Services Antique furniture restoration
Open Mon–Sat 9am–5.30pm

Ogee Restorations
Contact Mr L Jackson
✉ **32a Cambridge Street, Cleethorpes, Lincolnshire, DN35 8HD** 🅿
☎ 01472 601701 Ⓕ 01472 601701
Ⓜ 07977 860823
Est. 1973
Services Repair, restoration, veneering, inlaying, French polishing
Open Mon–Fri 8am–5pm
Sat 8am–noon

Park Antiques
Contact Brian O'Connell
✉ **2 North View, Menston, Ilkley, West Yorkshire, LS29 6JU** 🅿
☎ 01943 872392
Ⓜ 07811 034123
Ⓦ www.parkantiques.com
Est. 1980
Services Furniture restoration
Open Wed–Fri 10.30am–4.30pm
Sat 9.30am–5.30pm
Sun noon–5pm

Period Furniture Ltd (LAPADA)
Contact Mrs S Worrall
✉ **Moorside, Tockwith, York, North Yorkshire, YO26 7QG** 🅿
☎ 01423 358399 Ⓕ 01423 359050
Ⓦ www.antique-furniture.co.uk
Est. 1985
Services Antique repair and restoration, sales of Georgian–Art Deco furniture, bespoke furniture makers
Open Mon–Fri 8am–5pm
Sat 9am–5pm Sun 10am–4pm

A G Podmore & Son
Contact Andrew and David Podmore
✉ **North Minster Business Park, Northfield Lane, Poppleton, York, North Yorkshire, YO26 6QU** 🅿
☎ 01904 799800 Ⓕ 01904 799801
Ⓦ www.agpodmore.co.uk
Est. 1968
Services Conservation and restoration of antique furniture, French polishing, wax finishing, specializing in clock cases, pianos, desks, repolishing and restoration of panelling and staircases
Open Mon–Fri 8.30am–5pm

Rainbow Bridge
Contact Mr P Stokes
✉ **2 Kensington Road, Oxbridge, Stockton-on-Tees, North Yorkshire, TS18 4DQ** 🅿
☎ 01642 643033
Est. 1989
Services Antique repair and restoration
Open Mon–Sat 10am–5pm

John W Saggers
Contact Mr J Saggers
✉ **Chapel Hill, Woolsthorpe by Belvoir, Grantham, Lincolnshire, NG32 1NG** 🅿
☎ 01476 870756 Ⓕ 01476 870756
Est. 1966
Services Antique repair and restoration
Open By appointment

K J Sarginson Fine Furniture (UKIC)
Contact Mr K Sarginson
✉ **The Joinery, Escrick Grange, Stillingfleet Road, Escrick, York, North Yorkshire, YO19 6EB** 🅿
☎ 01904 728202 Ⓕ 01904 728202
Est. 1991
Services Antique restoration and repair of fine furniture. Dining tables a speciality
Open Mon–Fri 8.15am–5.30pm or by appointment

Gerald Shaw
Contact Mr M G Shaw
✉ **Jansville, Quarry Lane, Harrogate, North Yorkshire, HG1 3HR** 🅿
☎ 01423 503590 Ⓕ 01423 503590
Est. 1956
Services Repair and restoration of antique furniture
Open By appointment

Tony Smart Restorations
Contact Tony Smart
✉ **Low Barn, Glebe Farm, Lund, Beverley, East Yorkshire, YO25 9TT** 🅿
☎ 01377 217438
Est. 1971
Services General fine furniture restoration
Open Mon–Fri 9am–5pm

David South (HADA)
Contact James South or David South
✉ **15 High Street, Pateley Bridge, North Yorkshire, HG3 5AP** 🅿
☎ 01423 712022 Ⓕ 01423 712412
Ⓔ sales@davidsouth.co.uk
Ⓦ www.davidsouth.co.uk
Est. 1985
Services Restoration of upholstered furniture, French polishing
Open Mon–Sat 9am–5.30pm

J K Speed Antique Furniture Restoration
Contact Mr J Speed
✉ **The Workshop, Thornton Road, New York, Lincoln, Lincolnshire, LN4 4YL** 🅿
☎ 01205 280313
Ⓜ 07761 242219
Est. 1964
Services Antique repair and restoration, light upholstery, specializing in case repair of longcase clocks
Open Mon–Fri 9am–5.30pm

Spires Restoration
Contact Mr G Bexon
✉ **32 Upgate, Louth, Lincolnshire, LN11 9ET** 🅿
☎ 01507 600707 Ⓕ 01507 602588
Ⓜ 07866 230725
Est. 1994
Services Repair and restoration of furniture
Open Mon–Fri 8am–5pm or by appointment

Tomlinson Antiques (LAPADA)
Contact Sarah Worrall
✉ **Moorside, Tockwith, York, North Yorkshire, YO26 7QG** 🅿
☎ 01423 358833 Ⓕ 01423 358188
Ⓔ info@antique-furniture.co.uk

Ⓦ antique-furniture.co.uk
Est. 1977
Services Repair and restoration of furniture, bespoke manufacturing service
Trade only Mon–Fri; retail club at weekends
Open Mon–Fri 8am–5pm
Sun 10am–4pm

Neil Trinder (BAFRA)
Contact Mr N Trinder
✉ **Burrowlee House, Broughton Road, Sheffield, South Yorkshire, S6 2AS** Ⓟ
☎ 0114 285 2428
Ⓔ neiltrinder@yahoo.co.uk
Est. 1985
Services Furniture restoration including gilding, upholstery, marquetry
Open By appointment

Westway Pine
Contact Mr J Dzierzek
✉ **Carlton Lane, Helmsley, York, YO62 5HB** Ⓟ
☎ 01439 771399 Ⓕ 01439 771401
Ⓜ 07890 319325
Ⓔ westway.pine@bropenworld.com
Est. 1986
Services Antique reproductions and restoration
Open Mon Wed–Fri 9am–5pm
Sat 10am–5pm Sun 1–5pm

B D Whitham
Contact Mr B D Whitham
✉ **1 South View Cottage, Draughton, Skipton, North Yorkshire, BD23 6EF** Ⓟ
☎ 01756 710422
Est. 1984
Services Repair and restoration, upholstery
Open Mon–Fri 9am–6pm
and by appointment

Nigel Wright
Contact Mr N Wright
✉ **Unit 106, JC Albyn Complex, Burton Road, Sheffield, South Yorkshire, S38 BZ** Ⓟ
☎ 0114 272 1127
Est. 1983
Services Complete repair and restoration of antique furniture, veneering, inlays, French polishing, colouring, etc
Open By appointment

NORTH EAST

G M Athey
Contact Mr Athey
✉ **Corner Shop, Narrowgate, Alnwick, Northumberland, NE66 1JQ** Ⓟ
☎ 01665 604229
Ⓜ 07836 718350
Ⓔ mathey@alancom.net
Est. 1982
Services Full restoration, French polishing, upholstery. Deals in Georgian and Victorian furniture and china
Open Mon–Sat 8am–4.30pm

B J Coltman Restoration
Contact Barry
✉ **80 Meldon Terrace, Heaton, Newcastle-upon-Tyne, Tyne & Wear, NE6 5XP** Ⓟ
☎ 0191 224 5209
Ⓜ 07786 7077539
Est. 1994
Services Furniture restoration, French polishing, cabinet work
Open Mon–Fri 8am–5pm

Richard Pattison
Contact Richard Pattison
✉ **Unit 4, New Kennels, Blagdon Estate, Seaton Burn, Newcastle-upon-Tyne, Tyne and Wear, NE13 6DB** Ⓟ
☎ 01670 789888
Est. 1977
Services Traditional antique furniture restoration
Open Mon–Sat 9am–5pm

Richard Zabrocki & Son
Contact Mr I Zabrocki
✉ **Hoults Estate, Walker Road, Newcastle-upon-Tyne, Tyne & Wear, NE6 1AB** Ⓟ
☎ 0191 265 5989
Est. 1949
Services Repair and restoration of antique furniture
Open By appointment

NORTH WEST

Antique Furniture Restoration & Conservation (BAFRA, UKIC)
Contact Eric Smith
✉ **The Old Church, Park Road, Darwen, Lancashire, BB3 2LD** Ⓟ
☎ 01254 776222
Ⓜ 07977 811067
Ⓔ ericsmith@restorations.ndo.co.uk
Ⓦ www.bafra.org.uk
Est. 1965
Services Furniture restoration
Open Mon–Sun 9am–7pm

Arrowsmith Antiques & Restoration
Contact Mr P Arrowsmith
✉ **Unit 7–8, Waterside Mill, Waterside, Macclesfield, Cheshire, SK11 7HG** Ⓟ
☎ 01625 611880
Est. 1977
Services Complete repair and restoration service of high-quality antique furniture, including gilding, carving, marquetry, French polishing, ivory and brass inlay work
Open Mon–Fri 8.30am–5.30pm
Sat 10am–2pm

K Bennett
Contact Mr Keith Bennett
✉ **Oak House Farm, Wycollar, Colne, Lancashire, BB8 8SY** Ⓟ
☎ 01282 866853
Est. 1973
Services Antique furniture restoration
Open By appointment

Steve Blackwell French Polishers
Contact Mr S Blackwell
✉ **Ley Print, Unit 3, Leyland Place, Preston, Lancashire, PR25 1UT** Ⓟ
☎ 01772 459735 Ⓕ 01772 459735
Ⓜ 07929 170114
Est. 1989
Services Full antique furniture restoration service and modern finishes
Open Mon–Thurs 8am–5pm
Fri 8am–4.30pm

M Bradley
Contact Mr M Bradley
✉ **25a Oxford Road, Waterloo, Crosby, Merseyside, L22 8QE** Ⓟ
☎ 0151 920 5511
Est. 1969
Services Antique furniture restoration, French polishing,

repair, upholstery repair
Open Mon–Fri 9am–5pm
Sat 9am–noon

Chester Antiques Restoration Ltd
Contact Mike Green
✉ **Unit 4, White Lane Depot, Christelton, Chester, Cheshire, CH3 6AH** Ⓟ
☎ 01244 332796 Ⓕ 01244 332926
Ⓜ 07830 169671
Est. 1983
Services Restoration of antique furniture, French polishing
Open Mon–Fri 9am–5pm
Sat 9am–1.30pm

Michael Clayton French Polisher
Contact Mr M Clayton
✉ **The Workshop, Lestrange Street, Cleethorpes, Lancashire, BU35 7HS** Ⓟ
☎ 01472 602795
Est. 1979
Services French polishing
Open By appointment

Cottage Antiques
Contact Angelica Slater
✉ **788 Rochdale Road, Walsden, Todmorden, Lancashire, OL14 7UA** Ⓟ
☎ 01706 813612 Ⓕ 01706 813612
Ⓜ 07773 798032
Ⓦ www.ukcottageantiques.co.uk
Services Stripping, polishing, renovations, paint finishes, custom-built furniture
Open Tues–Sun 9.30am–5.30pm

Rory Fraser
Contact Mr R Fraser
✉ **Goyt Mill, Upper Hibbert Lane, Marple, Stockport, Cheshire, SK6 7HX** Ⓟ
☎ 0161 427 2122
Est. 1993
Services Good-quality antique furniture restoration, French polishing, leathers fitted, woodturning, carving
Open Mon–Fri 9am–5pm

A Grice
Contact Mr A Grice
✉ **106 Aughton Street, Ormskirk, Lancashire, L39 3BS** Ⓟ
☎ 01695 572007
Est. 1984
Services Furniture restoration
Open Wed Sat 1.30–6pm
or by appointment

Grosvenor Antique Restorations
Contact Richard Wilbraham
✉ **Workshop 1, Redhill House, Hope Street, Saltney, Cheshire, CH4 8BU** Ⓟ
Ⓜ 07973 623416
Est. 1988
Services Full antique restoration service, traditional hand-finished French polishing
Open By appointment

Hamilton Antique Restoration
Contact Mr C Sayle
✉ **1a Orry Place, Douglas, Isle of Man**
☎ 01624 662483
Est. 1989
Services Complete furniture repair and restoration service, upholstery
Open By appointment

Michael Holroyd Restorations
Contact Mr M Holroyd
✉ **Pendle Antique Centre, Union Mill, Watt Street, Sabden, Clitheroe, Lancashire, BB7 9ED** Ⓟ
☎ 01282 771112
Ⓜ 07711 011465
Est. 1996
Services Complete repair and restoration service including spray finish, wax finish, French polishing, cabinet-making and veneering, traditional upholstery
Open Mon–Fri 8am–5pm
Sat by appointment

Hopkins Antique Restoration
Contact Mr Mark Hopkins
✉ **Unit 1, Excelsior Works, Charles Street, Heywood, Lancashire, OL10 2HW** Ⓟ
☎ 01706 620549
Est. 1987
Services Antique furniture restoration, French polishing, cabinet-making
Open Mon–Sat 9am–5pm

J Kershaw Fine Furniture Restoration
Contact Mr J Kershaw
✉ **Unit 10, Normans Hall Farm, Shrigley Road, Pott Shrigley, Macclesfield, Cheshire, SK10 5SE** Ⓟ
☎ 01625 560808 Ⓕ 01625 560808
Est. 1985
Services Full repair and restoration service including French polishing, inlay work, marquetry, lacquerwork
Open By appointment

Peter Lawrenson
Contact Margaret Lawrenson
✉ **Brook Cottage, Scronkey Pilling, Preston, Lancashire, PR3 6SQ** Ⓟ
☎ 01253 790671
Est. 1984
Services Furniture restoration
Open By appointment

M & M Restoration Work Ltd
Contact Mrs M Bean
✉ **Rock Cottage, Castletown, Isle of Man, IM9 4PJ** Ⓟ
☎ 01624 823620 Ⓕ 01624 822463
Est. 1993
Services Repair and restoration of furniture, upholstery, caning, rushing
Open By appointment

Macdonalds Restoration
Contact Mr A Macdonald
✉ **Unit 203, Jurby Industrial Estate, Ramsey, Isle of Man, IM7 3BB** Ⓟ
☎ 01624 897648
Est. 1980
Services Traditional antique and modern furniture repair and restoration, cabinet-making
Open Mon–Sun 8am–6pm

Mansion House Antiques
Contact Mr Andrew Smith
✉ **11 Hand Lane, Leigh, Lancashire, WN7 3LP** Ⓟ
☎ 01942 605634
Est. 1995
Services Antique furniture restoration
Open By appointment

Pilgrim's Progress
Contact Selwyn Hyams
✉ **1a–3a Bridgewater Street, Liverpool, Merseyside, L1 0AR** Ⓟ

☎ 0151 708 7515 Ⓕ 0151 708 7515
Ⓦ www.pilgrimsprogress.co.uk
Est. 1979
Services Cabinet-making, French polishing, traditional upholstery
Open Mon–Fri 9am–5pm
Sat 10.30am–1.30pm

R S M Antique Restoration
Contact Mr Robin Stone
✉ **The Stables, Back Eaves Street, Blackpool, Lancashire, FY1 2HW** Ⓟ
☎ 01253 623839 Ⓕ 01253 623839
Est. 1972
Services Antique furniture, clocks, barometer, restoration, marquetry cutting
Open Mon–Fri 9am–6pm

T N Richards
Contact Mr D Richards
✉ **Hamilton Place, Chester, Cheshire, CH1 2BH** Ⓟ
☎ 01244 320241
Est. 1975
Services Complete repair and restoration service
Open By appointment

R J H Rimmel
Contact Mr R J H Rimmel
✉ **3 Newton Bank Cottages, Newton Hall Lane, Mobberley, Cheshire, WA16 7LB** Ⓟ
☎ 01565 873847
Est. 1974
Services Full furniture restoration service, special commissions and church work undertaken
Open By appointment

Seventeen Antiques
Contact Mr J Brake
✉ **306 Aigburth Road, Liverpool, Merseyside, L17 9PW** Ⓟ
☎ 0151 727 1717
Ⓜ 07712 189604
Ⓦ www.seventeenantiques.gbr.cc
Est. 1997
Services Furniture restoration, stripping
Open Mon–Sat 10am–5.30pm closed Wed

Treen Antiques (GADAR)
Contact Simon Feingold
✉ **Treen House, 72 Parker Road, Prestwich, Greater Manchester, M25 0FA** Ⓟ
☎ 0161 720 7244 Ⓕ 0161 720 7244
Ⓜ 07973 471185
Ⓔ simonfeingold@hotmail.com
Est. 1990
Services Furniture conservation
Open By appointment

J D Worrall (Conservation)
Contact Mr J Worrall
✉ **Unit 4a, The Old Brickworks, Pott Shrigley, Stockport, Cheshire, SK6 7HX** Ⓟ
☎ 01663 733817
Ⓜ 07776 077225
Ⓦ www.jdworrall.co.uk
Est. 1997
Services Complete antique repair and restoration including upholstery, carving, gilding, veneer, inlay, cabinet work and French polishing
Open By appointment

WALES

Iain Ashcroft Furniture
Contact Mr Iain Ashcroft
✉ **Ty Canol Farm, Sunbank, Llangollen, Denbighshire, LL20 7UL** Ⓟ
☎ 01978 860392 Ⓕ 01978 860392
Est. 1987
Services Antique furniture, restoration, carving, inlaying
Open Mon–Fri 9am–5pm

D J Gravell
Contact D J Gravell
✉ **Unit 5, Aber Court, Ferryboat Close Enterprise Park, Morrison, Swansea, West Glamorgan, SA6 8QN** Ⓟ
☎ 01792 310202 Ⓕ 01792 795471
Ⓔ jgravell@universalwoodfinishers.co.uk
Ⓦ www.universalwoodfinishers.co.uk
Est. 1989
Services Antique furniture repair and restoration
Open Mon–Fri 8.30am–5.30pm
Sat 9–11am

Hera Restorations
Contact Neil Richards
✉ **Cardiff, South Glamorgan**
☎ 029 2075 5379 Ⓕ 029 2076 1660
Est. 1987
Services Full French polishing, veneering, carving
Open By appointment only

B G Jones
Contact B G Jones
✉ **Cwmburry Honey Farm, Ferryside, Carmarthenshire, SA17 5TW** Ⓟ
☎ 01267 267318
Ⓔ bgjones@cwmburry.freeserve.co.uk
Est. 1986
Services Antique repair and restoration of furniture
Open Mon–Fri 9am–5pm

G A Parkinson
Contact Mr G A Parkinson
✉ **Glanrapon, Secontmill Road, Caernarfon, Gwynedd, LL55 2YL** Ⓟ
☎ 01286 672865
Est. 1949
Services French polishing, repair, restoration
Open Mon–Sat 9am–5pm

Parkview Antiques
Contact Nic Eastwood
✉ **High Street, Northop, Flintshire, CH7 6BQ** Ⓟ
☎ 01352 840627
Est. 1984
Services Furniture restoration
Open Mon–Sat 10am–5pm

Pastiche
Contact Mr S Pesticcio
✉ **15 Duxford Close, Llandaff, Cardiff, South Glamorgan, CF5 2PR** Ⓟ
☎ 02920 566759
Est. 1975
Services Period and traditional restoration and redecoration of Victorian furniture and property
Open By appointment

Phillips Antiques and French Polishing (BWCG)
Contact Philip Wyvill-Bell
✉ **11 Market Square, Llandovery, Carmarthenshire, SA20 0AB** Ⓟ
☎ 01550 721355 Ⓕ 01550 721355
Ⓔ wyvillbell@aol.com
Est. 1970
Services Restoration, polishing
Open Mon–Sat 10am–5pm

Phoenix Conservation.com (BAFRA, UKIC)
Contact Hugh Haley
✉ **Selwyn Forge, Tenby Road, St Clears, Carmarthenshire, SA33 4JP** Ⓟ

☎ 01994 232109
ⓔ phoenixconservation@hotmail.com
ⓦ www.phoenixconservation.com
Est. 1992
Services Antique furniture conservation and repair
Open By appointment

T N Richards
Contact Mr D Richards
✉ **Caergynog, Llanbedr, Gwynedd, LL45 2PL** Ⓟ
☎ 01341 241485
Est. 1974
Services Complete repair and restoration service
Open By appointment

Snowdonia Antiques
Contact Jeffery Collins
✉ **Bank Building, Station Road, Llanrwst, Conwy Valley, LL26 0EP** Ⓟ
☎ 01492 640789 ⓕ 01492 640789
ⓜ 07802 503552
Est. 1965
Services Antique repair and restoration
Open Mon–Sat 9am–5pm
Sun by appointment

St Helens Restoration
Contact Jo McCarthy
✉ **87–88 St Helens Avenue, Swansea, West Glamorgan, SA1 4NN** Ⓟ
☎ 01792 465240 ⓕ 01792 467788
ⓔ admin@sthelensrestoration.co.uk
ⓦ www.sthelensrestoration.co.uk
Est. 1979
Services Antique repair and restoration, upholstery, French polishing
Open Mon–Fri 9am–5pm
Sat 9.30am–1pm

SCOTLAND

Adam Antiques & Restoration
Contact Charles Bergius
✉ **23c Dundas Street, Edinburgh, EH3 6QQ** Ⓟ
☎ 0131 556 7555 ⓕ 0131 556 7555
Est. 1983
Services Quality repair to 18th–19thC furniture. Sales of 18th–19thC, mainly mahogany furniture and associated furnishings
Open Tues–Sat 10.30am–6pm
Mon by appointment

Antique Furniture Restoration
Contact David Carson
✉ **108bc Causewayside, Edinburgh, EH9 1PU** Ⓟ
☎ 0131 667 1067
ⓜ 07779 824543
ⓔ carsonantrest@btopenworld.com
Est. 1994
Services Repair and restoration of all old and antique furniture
Open Mon–Fri 10am–6pm
Sat 10am–2pm

Castle Restoration
Contact Peter Nicholson
✉ **Auchtertool House, Auchtertool, Kirkcaldy, Fife, KY2 5XW** Ⓟ
☎ 01592 780371 ⓕ 01592 780371
Est. 1964
Services Repair and restoration of all antiques, French polishing
Open By appointment

The Chairman of Bearsden (Scottish Furniture Preservation Society)
Contact David Shuttleton
✉ **157 Queen Margaret Drive, Glasgow, G20 8XU** Ⓟ
☎ 0141 946 2525 ⓕ 0141 946 7878
ⓔ sales@charlesrennie mackintosh.co.uk
ⓦ www.thechairmanofbearsden.co.uk
Est. 1990
Services Furniture restoration and upholstery, French polishing, cabinet-making, bergère suites, cane and rush seating
Open Mon–Sat 9am–5pm

Chisholme Antiques
Contact Kim Roberts
✉ **5 Orrock Place, Hawick, Scottish Borders, TD9 0HQ** Ⓟ
☎ 01450 376928
Est. 1979
Services Antique repair and restoration of furniture, cabinet-making
Open Mon–Fri 9am–5pm

Chylds Hall Fine Furniture Restoration
Contact Stephen Pickering
✉ **Old Dairy Cottage, Upper Stepford, Dunscore, Dumfries & Galloway, DG2 0JP** Ⓟ
☎ 01387 820558 ⓕ 01387 280558
Est. 1991
Services Fine furniture restoration, period paint finish restoration, French polishing
Open By appointment only

Douglas & Kay
Contact Mr P Kay
✉ **23 McPhail Street, Glasgow, G40 1DU** Ⓟ
☎ 0141 556 5564
ⓜ 07974 494618
Est. 1948
Services Repair and restoration of furniture, French polishing
Open By appointment

Roland Gomm
Contact Roland Gomm
✉ **65 Constitution Street, Edinburgh, EH6 7AF** Ⓟ
☎ 0131 467 5525
ⓜ 07947 179774
Est. 1986
Services French polishing, restoration of fine antique furniture, upholstery
Open Mon–Sat 10am–6pm

Gow Antiques and Restoration (BAFRA)
Contact Jeremy Gow
✉ **Pitscandly Farm, Forfar, Angus, DD8 3NZ** Ⓟ
☎ 01307 465342 ⓕ 01307 468973
ⓜ 07711 416786
ⓔ jeremy@knowyourantiques.com
ⓦ www.knowyourantiques.com
Est. 1991
Services Specialists in restoration of European furniture, 17th–18thC marquetry
Open Mon–Fri 9am–5pm
or by appointment

Inchmartine Restorations (BAFRA)
Contact Andrew Stephens
✉ **Inchmartine House, Inchture, Perth, Perthshire, PH14 9QQ** Ⓟ
☎ 01828 686412 ⓕ 01828 686748
ⓔ ir@toolbazaar.freeserve.co.uk
ⓦ www.toolbazaar.co.uk
Est. 1989
Services Restoration of antique furniture pre-1840
Open Mon–Sat 9am–5.30pm

The Tower Workshops
Contact George Pirie
✉ **Aberdeen Road, Tarland,**

Aboyne, Aberdeenshire, AB34 4TB **P**
☎ 013398 811544
Ⓦ www.antiquesagency.co.uk
Est. 1989
Services Antique restoration and sales
Open Mon–Sun 11am–5pm

Graham Watson
Contact Mr G Watson
✉ **The Workshop, Mill Wynd, Greenlaw, Scottish Borders, TD10 6UA** **P**
☎ 01361 810770/810593
Est. 1996
Services Furniture restoration, French polishing
Open Mon–Sat 8am–5pm

NORTHERN IRELAND

Antique Services
Contact David Hosgood
✉ **288 Beersbridge Road, Belfast, Co Antrim, BT5 5DY** **P**
☎ 028 9020 3933
Est. 1984
Services Restoration, re-polishing
Open Mon–Fri 8am–5pm

Cherryvale Polishing
Contact Samuel J Spratt
✉ **47 Drumbroneth Road, Dromore, Co Down, BT25 1PP** **P**
☎ 028 9269 3147
Est. 1988
Services Furniture restoration and repair, French polishing
Open By appointment

Courtyard Restoration
Contact Cosi Shaker or Shaun Butler
✉ **The Old Mill, 2 Parkfield Road, Ahogill, Ballymena, Co Antrim, BT42 2QS** **P**
☎ 028 2587 8875
Ⓜ 07967 144784
Est. 1996
Services Restoration of furniture, frame repair, re-carving
Open Mon–Sat 10am–5pm

Crozier Antique Furniture Restoration
Contact Mr Peter Crozier
✉ **39 Tassagh Road, Keady, Co Armagh, BT60 3TU** **P**
☎ 028 3753 8242
Est. 1986
Services Restoration
Open Mon–Fri 9am–6pm or by appointment

J Davis Restorations
Contact Jonathan Davis
✉ **Rear of 23 Coleraine Road, Portstewart, Co Londonderry, BT55 7HP** **P**
☎ 028 7083 3851
Est. 1989
Services Furniture restoration
Open Mon–Fri 9am–5pm

Kelly Antiques
Contact Mr Louis Kelly
✉ **Mullaghmore House, Old Mountfield Road, Omagh, Co Tyrone, BT79 7EX** **P**
☎ 028 8224 2314 Ⓕ 028 8225 0262
Ⓔ sales@kellyantiques.com
Ⓦ www.kellyantiques.com
Est. 1936
Services Restoration, private bi-annual auctions. International Centre of Excellence for conservation, heritage and restoration. Full-time course in restoration techniques
Open Mon–Fri 10am–7pm Sat 10am–5pm

Peter Williams
Contact Peter Williams
✉ **25 Ballykeigle Road, Comber, Co Down, BT23 5SD** **P**
☎ 028 9752 8360 Ⓕ 028 9752 8360
Est. 1983
Services Furniture restoration
Open By appointment

REPUBLIC OF IRELAND

Sean Carpenter
Contact Sean Carpenter
✉ **65–66 Francis Street, Dublin 8, Co Dublin, Ireland** **P**
☎ 01 454 1806
Est. 1963
Services French polishing, upholstery
Open Mon–Fri 7am–3.30pm

Conservation Restoration Centre for Furniture and Wooden Artefacts (UKIC, ICHAWI)
Contact Colin Piper
✉ **Letterfrack, Co Galway, Ireland** **P**
☎ 095 41036 Ⓕ 095 41100
Ⓔ conserve@aol.ie
Services Conservation and restoration of all historic furniture and related objects. Museum conservation, cabinet-making, French polishing, veneer work, turning and woodcarving, marquetry, boulle work, metal work repair, pietra dura and marble repair
Open Mon–Fri 9am–5.30pm or by appointment

Donal Daly
Contact Donal Daly
✉ **Ballyard, Tralee, Co Kerry, Ireland** **P**
Ⓜ 0868 074848
Est. 1991
Services Furniture restoration
Open By appointment

Euricka Antiques
Contact Alexandra Papadakis
✉ **2–7 The Coombe, Francis Street, Dublin 8, Co Dublin, Ireland**
☎ 01 454 9779
Est. 1990
Services Furniture restoration
Open Mon–Sat 10am–6pm

E Fitzpatrick (GADAR)
Contact E Fitzpatrick
✉ **17 Sidney Park, Wellington Road, Cork, Ireland** **P**
☎ 021 450 3084
Est. 1989
Services Repair and restoration of antique furniture
Open By appointment

Paul Geoghegan
Contact Paul Geoghegan
✉ **9 Elmcastle Park, Kilmainham, Dublin 24, Co Dublin, Ireland** **P**
☎ 01 451 4362
Est. 1970
Services Furniture restoration
Open By appointment

Glebe Hall Restoration Studios
Contact Carmel Corrigan-Griffin
✉ **Old Killernogh Rectory, Rathnakelly Glebe, Ballacolla, Co Laois, Ireland** **P**
☎ 0502 34105 Ⓕ 0502 34105

Ⓜ 0868 784956
Est. 1980
Services Furniture restoration, gilding, porcelain, ivory, jade
Open By appointment
Sat 11am–4pm

Lee Hindmarsh Antiques
Contact Lee Hindmarsh
✉ **Main Street, Doneraile, Mallow, Co Cork, Ireland** Ⓟ
☎ 022 24862 Ⓕ 087 616 0036
Ⓜ 08761 60036
Est. 2001
Services Restoration of antique furniture, French polishing
Open Mon–Sat 9am–6pm

Val Hughes (IPCRA)
Contact Mr Val Hughes
✉ **132 Arden Vale, Tullamore, Co Offaly, Ireland** Ⓟ
☎ 0506 22600
Ⓔ valhughestull@eircom.net
Est. 1990
Services Conservation and restoration of antique and fine furniture
Open Mon–Sat 8.30am–6pm

J & T Hussey
Contact Paul Hussey
✉ **42 Francis Street, Dublin 8, Co Dublin, Ireland** Ⓟ
☎ 01 454 1453
Ⓜ 0879 477882
Est. 1948
Services Furniture restoration, chair-making, cabinet-making, French polishing
Open Mon–Sat 9am–5pm

Stephen McDonnell (BAFRA)
Contact Mr McDonnell
✉ **2 Anglesea Lane, Dun Laoghaire, Co Dublin, Ireland** Ⓟ
☎ 01 280 7077 Ⓕ 01 284 2268
Ⓜ 0863 363537
Est. 1994
Services Furniture restoration, traditional finishing, French polishing, cabinet repair
Open Tues–Sat 9am–5.30pm

Michael O'Connell
Contact Michael O'Connell
✉ **Clodagh, Crookstown, Cork, Co Cork, Ireland** Ⓟ
☎ 02 173 36450
Est. 1908
Services Furniture restoration, French polishing, cabinet-making
Open By appointment

Des Petrie
Contact Des Petrie
✉ **Rosserk, Killala, Co Mayo, Ireland** Ⓟ
☎ 09 632162 Ⓕ 09 632162
Ⓜ 0866 021730
Est. 1985
Services Furniture restoration
Open Mon–Sat 9am–6pm

A Restoration Centre
Contact Kevin O'Reilly
✉ **6 The Pines, Ballintree Avenue, Dun Laoghaire, Co Dublin, Ireland**
☎ 01280 1635
Ⓜ 08727 06565
Est. 1978
Services Furniture restoration
Open By appointment

Restore Repro Ltd
Contact William Harnett
✉ **Ballyquirke, Newcastle West, Co Limerick, Ireland**
☎ 06 92135
Est. 1963
Services Furniture restoration
Open Mon–Fri 8am–6pm

Sealey Furnishings
Contact Ron
✉ **MG Business Park, Galway Road, Tuam, Co Galway, Ireland** Ⓟ
☎ 09 328661 Ⓕ 09 328661
Ⓔ sealey@eircom.net
Ⓦ www.sealeyfurnishings.com
Est. 1975
Services Furniture restoration, upholstery
Open Mon–Sat 10am–5.30pm

GILDING

A J Brett & Co
Contact Shane Webb
✉ **168 Marlborough Road, London, N19 4NP** Ⓟ
☎ 020 7272 8462 Ⓕ 020 7272 5102
Ⓔ ajbretts@aol.com
Ⓦ www.ajbrett.co.uk
Est. 1960
Services Furniture restoration, gilding, upholstery
Open Mon–Fri 7.30am–3.30pm

Alison Cosserat
Contact Miss Alison Cosserat
✉ **13f Tonedale Mills, Tonedale, Wellington, Somerset, TA21 0AW** Ⓟ
☎ 01823 665279
Ⓜ 07989 465427
Est. 1997
Services Gold leaf specialist
Open Mon–Fri 10am–6pm

Michael Ferris
Contact Mr M Ferris
✉ **Rose Cottage, Chapel Lane, South Cockerington, Louth, Lincolnshire, LN11 7EB** Ⓟ
☎ 01507 327463 Ⓕ 01507 327463
Est. 1979
Services Antique repair, restoration, gilding
Open By appointment

Mark Finamore
Contact Mark Finamore
✉ **63 Orford Road, Walthamstow, London, E17 9NJ** Ⓟ
☎ 020 8521 9407
Est. 1981
Services General antiques service, gilding, furniture restoration and conservation
Open Mon–Fri 10.30am–6pm or Sat by appointment

R G Jones
Contact R G Jones
✉ **1 Brickfield Cottage, Bilting, Ashford, Kent, TN25 4ER** Ⓟ
☎ 01233 812849
Est. 1985
Services Antique restoration, gilding
Open Mon–Fri 9am–4pm

Looking Glass of Bath (IIC)
Contact Anthony Reed
✉ **93–96 Walcot Street, Bath, Somerset, BA1 5BG** Ⓟ
☎ 01225 461969 Ⓕ 01225 316191
Ⓜ 07831 323878
Ⓔ info@lookingglassofbath.co.uk
Ⓦ www.lookingglassofbath.co.uk
Est. 1968
Services Restoration of mirrors, picture frames, gilding, carving,

manufacturers and supplier of antique mirror glass, paper and oil restoration
Open Mon–Sat 9am–6pm

Master Gilder (UKIC, The Gilding Society)
Contact Prakash Brinicombe
✉ **158 Kenmare Road, Knowle, Bristol, BS4 1PH**
☎ 0117 949 5956 Ⓕ 0117 949 5956
Ⓜ 07881 634222
Ⓔ prakash@mastergilder.com
Ⓦ www.mastergilder.com
Est. 1978
Services Gold-leaf restoration, invisible repair and matching existing giltwork, conservation and new work
Open By appointment

Regency Restoration
Contact Mrs E Ball
✉ **Studio 21, Thames House, 140 Battersea Park Road, London, SW11 4NB** Ⓟ
☎ 020 7622 5275 or 020 7828 4268
Ⓕ 020 7498 1803
Est. 1987
Services Restoration of 18th–19thC mirrors, picture frames, English and Continental painted and gilded furniture, architectural gilding, church interiors, polychrome sculpture, lacquerwork, oil paintings, carving
Open Mon–Fri 9.30am–5.30pm

Vigi Sawdon
Contact Vigi Sawdon
✉ **79–81 Ledbury Road, London, W11 2AG** Ⓟ
☎ 020 7229 9321/2033
Ⓕ 020 7229 2033
Ⓜ 07979 477102
Ⓔ sawdon@aol.com
Est. 1994
Services Gilding and restoration of old wooden, gesso and composite mirrors, architectural pieces, frames. Also provides French and Italian paint effects, trompe l'oeil, marble, bamboo
Open By appointment

Sussex Gilding
Contact Mark Cashmen
✉ **59 Rodmell Avenue, Saltdean, Brighton, East Sussex, BN2 8PG** Ⓟ
☎ 01273 304890
Ⓜ 07775 742954
Ⓔ sussesgilding@aol.com
Ⓦ www.sussexgilding.com
Est. 1992
Services Restoration of gilding and carving, overmantels and mirrors commissioned to order
Open By appointment

Titian Studio (BAFRA, UKIC)
Contact Rodrigo Titian
✉ **32 Warple Way, Acton, London, W3 0DJ** Ⓟ
☎ 020 8222 6600 Ⓕ 020 8749 2220
Ⓔ info@titianstudios.co.uk
Ⓦ www.titianstudios.com
Est. 1965
Services Restoration of gilding and lacquering, French polishing, caning, cabinet-making
Open Mon–Fri 8am–5.30pm

GLASS

F W Aldridge Ltd
Contact Miss Angela Garwood
✉ **Unit 3, St Johns Industrial Estate, Dunmow Road, Takeley, Essex, CM22 6SP** Ⓟ
☎ 01279 874000 Ⓕ 01279 874002
Ⓔ angela@fwaldridge.abel.co.uk
Ⓦ www.fwaldridgeglass.com
Est. 1926
Services Repair and restoration of glass, supply of Bristol glass for antique and modern table silverware, all glass and silver restoration
Open Mon–Fri 9am–5.30pm

Lorna Barnes Conservation (IPCRA, ICOM)
Contact Lorna Barnes
✉ **158 Rialto Cottages, Rialto, Dublin 8, Ireland** Ⓟ
☎ 01 473 6205
Ⓔ barneslorna@hotmail.com
Est. 2000
Services Conservation of glass, ceramic and stone objects, condition surveys, advice on packaging and storage
Open Mon–Fri 9am–6pm

Facets Glass Restoration
Contact Mrs K Moore
✉ **107 Boundary Road, London, E17 8NQ** Ⓟ
☎ 020 8520 3392 Ⓕ 020 8520 3392
Ⓜ 07778 758304
Ⓔ repairs@facetsglass.co.uk
Ⓦ www.facetsglass.co.uk
Est. 1996
Services Antique glass restoration including supply of blue glass liners for table silverware, re-bristling hair brushes, cutlery restoration, flute and trumpet stopper suppliers
Open By appointment

Looking Glass of Bath (IIC)
Contact Anthony Reed
✉ **93–96 Walcot Street, Bath, Somerset, BA1 5BG** Ⓟ
☎ 01225 461969 Ⓕ 01225 316191
Ⓜ 07831 323878
Ⓔ info@lookingglassofbath.co.uk
Ⓦ www.lookingglassofbath.co.uk
Est. 1968
Services Restoration of mirrors, picture frames, regilding, carving, manufacturers and supplier of antique mirror glass, paper and oil restoration
Open Mon–Sat 9am–6pm

Martyn Pearson Glass
Contact Martyn Pearson
✉ **The Stables Craft Centre, Halfpenny Green Vineyard, Tom Lane, Bobbington, Staffordshire, DY7 5EP** Ⓟ
☎ 01384 221399
Ⓜ 07951 305617
Est. 1995
Services Glass cutting, engraving and repair
Open Thur–Tues 11am–5pm

Red House Glasscrafts
Contact Mrs J Oakley or B Taylor
✉ **Ruskin Glass Centre, Wollaston Road, Amblecote, Stourbridge, West Midlands, DY8 4HE** Ⓟ
☎ 01384 399460 Ⓕ 01384 399460
Ⓜ 07901 522277
Est. 1987
Services Repair and restoration of antique crystal
Open Mon–Fri 9am–5pm
Sat 10am–4pm

The Traditional Studio (UKIC)
Contact Viki Green
✉ **Welwyn Equestrian Centre, Potters Heath Road, Welwyn, Hertfordshire,**

AL6 9SZ P
☎ 01707 332084 F 01707 332084
M 07748 224287
E viki@traditionalstudio.fsnet.co.uk
Est. 1997
Services Glass restoration
Open By appointment

GRAMOPHONES & RADIOS

Philip Knighton (The Gramophone Man) (RETRA)
Contact Philip Knighton
✉ **Bush House, 17b South Street, Wellington, Somerset, TA21 8NR** P
☎ 01823 661618 F 01823 661618
E gramman@msn.com
Est. 1981
Services Supplies and restores gramophones, early wirelesses and sells 78rpm records
Open Tues–Sat 10am–5pm closed Mon

Talking Point Antiques
Contact Mr Paul Austwick
✉ **66 West Street, Sowerby Bridge, West Yorkshire, HX6 3AP** P
☎ 01422 834126
E tpagrams@aol.com
Est. 1985
Services Repair, refurbishment and restoration of wind-up gramophones
Open Thurs Fri Sat 10.30am–5.30pm and by appointment

The Wireless Works
Contact Rob Rusbridge
✉ **27 Fore Street, Bugle, St Austell, Cornwall, PL26 8PA** P
☎ 01726 852200 F 01726 852200
E rob@wirelessworks.co.uk
W www.wirelessworks.co.uk
Est. 1995
Services Radio, gramophone and antique electronics repair, restoration, rebuilding and trading
Open By appointment

INLAY WORK

Castle House (BAFRA)
Contact Mr Michael Durkee
✉ **Castle House, Units 1 and 3, Bennetts Field Estate, Wincanton, Somerset, BA9 9DT** P
☎ 01963 33884 F 01963 31278
Est. 1975
Services Antique furniture restoration and conservation
Open Mon–Fri 8.30am–5pm

B S Howells (Antique Restorers Ltd)
Contact Mr B S Howells
✉ **7a Tynemouth Terrace, Tynemouth Road, Tottenham, London, N15 4AP** P
☎ 020 8808 7965 F 020 8801 5313
M 07734 008865
Est. 1978
Services 18th–19thC antique furniture restoration, leatherwork, gilding, marquetry and copy brasswork, copy chair making
Open Mon–Fri 6.30am–3.30pm

Paul Waldmann Woodwork (Conservation Unit)
Contact Mr P Waldmann
✉ **41 Norfolk Street, Cambridge, Cambridgeshire, CB1 2LD** P
☎ 01223 314001
M 07740 167055
E pm.waldmann@ntlworld.com
Est. 1982
Services Antique furniture restoration, cabinet-making
Open By appointment

JEWELLERY

Aladdin's Cave
Contact Roberta Spencer
✉ **19 Queen's Arcade, Leeds, West Yorkshire, LS1 6LF** P
☎ 0113 245 70903
E robertajspencer@hotmail.com
Est. 1985
Services Jewellery repair, valuations
Open Mon–Sat 10am–5pm

Berkshire Antiques Co Ltd
Contact Mr Sutton
✉ **42 Thames Street, Windsor, Berkshire, SL4 1PR** P
☎ 01753 830100
E b.antiques@btconnect.com
W www.jewels2go.co.uk
Est. 1981
Services Jewellery repair
Open Mon–Sat 10.30am–5.30pm Sun by appointment

Bicks Jewellers & Antiques
Contact Mr Morris
✉ **5 Montpellier Walk, Cheltenham, Gloucestershire, GL50 1SD** P
☎ 01242 524738 F 01242 524738
Est. 1895
Services Jewellery restoration and repair
Open Tues–Sat 10am–4pm

Barry Papworth (NAG)
Contact Steve Park
✉ **28 St Thomas Street, Lymington, Hampshire, SO41 9NE** P
☎ 01590 676422
Est. 1978
Services Restoration of jewellery and silver. Workshop on site.
Open Mon–Sat 9.15am–5.15pm

LEATHER

Antique Leather Dressing
Contact Val Pringle
✉ **PO Box 67, Langport, Somerset, TA10 9WJ**
☎ 01458 241816
M 07947 277833
E sales@antiqueleatherdressing.co.uk
W www.antiqueleatherdressing.co.uk
Est. 2003
Services Leather dressing products
Open Please telephone or e-mail

Antique Leathers (LAPADA)
Contact Jackie Crisp
✉ **Unit 2, Bennetts Field Trading Estate, Wincanton, Somerset, BA9 9DT** P
☎ 01963 33163 F 01963 33164
E info@antique-leathers.co.uk
W www.antique-leathers.co.uk
Est. 1965
Services Hand-dyed leatherwork on desk tops, gold tooling, traditional upholstery, leather chair repair and restoration, bookshelf edging
Open Mon–Fri 9.30am–5pm

J Crisp
Contact Mr J Crisp
✉ **48 Roderick Road, London, NW3 2NL** P
☎ 020 7485 8566 F 020 7485 8566
Est. 1979
Services Loose leather services,

traditional upholstery, French and leather polishing, table liners, leather gilding
Open Mon–Fri 10am–6pm by appointment

Director Furniture Leathergilders
Contact Mrs M Taylor or Mrs P A Rowe
✉ **39 Severn Stoke, Worcester, Worcestershire, WR8 9JA** 🅿
☎ 01905 371339
Est. 1984
Services Replacement leather desk and table linings, hand-coloured and antiqued, hand-gilded in the traditional method to customer's specifications. Full grainhide or skiver
Open By appointment

B S Howells (Antique Restorers Ltd)
Contact Mr B S Howells
✉ **7a Tynemouth Terrace, Tynemouth Road, Tottenham, London, N15 4AP** 🅿
☎ 020 8808 7965 Ⓕ 020 8801 5313
Ⓜ 07734 008865
Est. 1978
Services 18th–20thC antique furniture restoration, leatherwork, gilding, marquetry and copy brasswork, copy chair making
Open Mon–Fri 6.30am–3.30pm

Leather Conservation Centre (UKIC, SSCR)
Contact Roy Thomson
✉ **University College Campus, Boughton Green Road, Moulton Park, Northampton, Northamptonshire, NN2 7AN** 🅿
☎ 01604 719766 Ⓕ 01604 719649
Ⓔ lcc@northampton.ac.uk
Est. 1978
Services Conservation and restoration of leather objects, research, training and information for leather and leather conservation
Open Mon–Fri 9am–5pm

The Manor Bindery Ltd
Contact Philip Bradburn
✉ **Calshot Road, Fawley, Southampton, Hampshire, SO45 1BB** 🅿
☎ 02380 894488 Ⓕ 02380 899418
Ⓔ manorbindery@btconnect.com
Ⓦ www.manorbindery.co.uk
Est. 1976
Services Desk and table top leathering, edging. Supplier of leather-bound books and false books for display
Open Mon–Fri 8am–5pm

Norwich Antique Restoration
Contact John Harvey
✉ **Unit 2, Half Moon Way, Norwich, Norfolk, NR2 4EB** 🅿
☎ 01603 762504 Ⓕ 01603 762504
Ⓔ tee@leatherdesks.com
Est. 1973
Services Leather and desk tops, French polishing
Open Mon–Sat 9am–5pm

Stanstead Abbotts Leathers
Contact Mrs L Ray
✉ **Hedges, Commonside Road, Harlow, Essex, CM18 7EY** 🅿
☎ 01279 453914 Ⓕ 01279 432295
Est. 1981
Services Table liners
Open Mon–Fri 9am–5.30pm

Stocks and Chairs Antique Restoration
Contact Kevin Beale
✉ **The Old Church Hall, Hardy Road, Parkstone, Poole, Dorset, BH14 9HN** 🅿
☎ 01202 718418 Ⓕ 01202 718918
Ⓔ email@stocksandchairsantiques.com
Ⓦ www.stocksandchairsantiques.com
Est. 1979
Services Full restoration service, specializing in hand-dyed leather
Open Mon–Fri 9am–5pm weekends by appointment

Woolnough (AC) Ltd
Contact Mr A Cullen
✉ **Unit 7, Parmiter Industrial Estate, Parmiter Street, Bethnal Green, London, E2 9HZ** 🅿
☎ 020 8980 9813 Ⓕ 020 8980 9814
Est. 1885
Services Desk top leathering, leather upholstery, bookshelf edging, chairback embossing and distressed hand-stained leather upholstery
Open Mon–Fri 7am–3.30pm

LIGHTING

A B C Restoration Ltd
Contact Chris Christofi
✉ **Unit 23A, Rosebury Industrial Park, Rosebury Avenue, Tottenham Hale, London, N17 9SR** 🅿
☎ 020 8880 9697 Ⓕ 020 8801 4618
Est. 1999
Services Restoration, repair of lighting, chandliers, bronzing on metalwork, clocks
Open Mon–Fri 8.30am–5.30pm or by appointment

Abeam Antiques
Contact Joseph Yousif
✉ **159 Carr Road, Northolt, Middlesex, UB5 4RE** 🅿
☎ 020 8426 8857
Est. 1994
Services Furniture, lighting restoration, repair
Open By appointment

George & Peter Cohn
Contact Peter Cohn
✉ **Unit 21, 21 Wren Street, London, WC1X 0HF** 🅿
☎ 020 7278 3749
Est. 1947
Services Repair, restoration and electrification of antique light fittings. Experts in restoration and cleaning of crystal chandeliers
Open Mon–Fri 9.30am–4pm

Dernier and Hamlyn Ltd
✉ **Unit 5, Croydon Business Centre, 214 Purley Way, Croydon, Surrey, CR0 4XG** 🅿
☎ 020 8760 0900 Ⓕ 020 8760 0955
Ⓔ info@dernier-hamlyn.com
Ⓦ www.dernier-hamlyn.com
Est. 1888
Services Traditional and contemporary bespoke lighting specialists, manufacturing and restoration. Holders of royal warrant for manufacture and restoration to HM Queen
Open Mon–Fri 9am–5pm

Karim Restorations
Contact Mr A Karim
✉ **Studio 6, The Bull Theatre Gallery, Barnet, Hertfordshire, EN5 5SJ** 🅿

☎ 020 8449 928647
ⓔ aminsemail@e.mail.com
Est. 1984
Services Restoration of Art Nouveau, Arts and Crafts, pewter, castings and lighting
Open Mon–Fri 10am–5pm

Magic Lanterns
Contact J A Marsden
✉ **By George, 23 George Street, St Albans, Hertfordshire, AL3 4ES** Ⓟ
☎ 01727 865680
Est. 1987
Services Lighting consultancy for period houses
Open Mon–Fri 10am–5pm Sat 10am–5.30pm Sun 1–5pm

David Malik & Son Ltd
Contact Sara Malik
✉ **5 Metro Centre, Britannia Way, Park Royal, London, NW10 7PA** Ⓟ
☎ 020 8965 4232 ⓕ 020 8965 2401
Est. 1950
Services Chandelier, wall bracket, candelabra restoration, re-wiring, gilding
Open Mon–Fri 9am–5pm

Sargeant Restorations
Contact David and Ann Sargeant
✉ **26 London Road, Sevenoaks, Kent, TN13 1AP** Ⓟ
☎ 01732 457304 ⓕ 01732 457688
ⓜ 07771 553624
Est. 1989
Services Restoration of all light fittings, lustres, candelabra
Open Mon–Sat 9am–5.30pm closed Wed

Turn On Lighting
Contact Janet Holdstock
✉ **116–118 Islington High Street, Camden Passage, Islington, London, N1 8EG** Ⓟ
☎ 020 7359 7616 ⓕ 020 7359 7616
Est. 1976
Services Display lighting
Open Tues–Fri 10am–6pm Sat 9.30am–4.30pm

David Turner Workshops
Contact Mr D Turner
✉ **24 Tottenham Road, London, N1 4BZ** Ⓟ
☎ 020 7241 5400 ⓕ 020 7241 5416
ⓔ mo@davidturner.uk.com
Est. 1987
Services Repair and restoration of metalwork, lighting, decorative antiques
Open Mon–Fri 9.30am–6pm

Woodall & Emery Ltd
Contact Mrs Chinn
✉ **Haywards Heath Road, Balcombe, Haywards Heath, West Sussex, RH17 6PG** Ⓟ
☎ 01444 811608 ⓕ 01444 819365
ⓔ enquiries@woodallandemery.co.uk
ⓦ www.woodallandemery.co.uk
Est. 1860
Services Restoration of antique and period lighting
Open Mon–Sat 10am–5pm

LOCKS AND KEYS

Blackstage
Contact David Benford
✉ **PO Box 6132, Swadlincote, Derbyshire, DE12 8YY**
☎ 0870 220 0494 ⓕ 0870 220 0987
ⓜ 07896 637021
ⓔ mail@blackstage.co.uk
ⓦ www.reprolock.co.uk
Est. 2002
Services Restoration, reproduction of locks and keys for furniture, clocks, doors and windows
Open On call 24 hours, 7 days

Lock & Key Centre
Contact Robert Evans
✉ **16 Wesley Lane, Bicester, Oxfordshire, OX26 6JH** Ⓟ
☎ 0800 559 3995
ⓔ admin.lockandkey@btconnect.com
ⓦ www.lockandkeycentre.co.uk
Est. 2001
Services Key cutting specialists
Open Mon–Fri 8.30am–5pm Sat 9.30am–4pm

MARBLE

Rimmer Restoration
Contact Mr J S Rimmer
✉ **14 Hastings Place, Lytham, Lancashire, FY8 5LZ** Ⓟ
☎ 01253 794521
ⓔ rimmer@tesco.net
Est. 1987
Services Marble restorer
Open By appointment

MARQUETRY

Anita Marquetry Ltd
Contact Anita Lear
✉ **Unit 7, Dole Road Industrial Estate, Llandrindod Wells, Powys, LD1 6DF** Ⓟ
☎ 01597 825505 ⓕ 01597 824484
ⓔ lear@marquetry.co.uk
ⓦ www.marquetry.co.uk
Est. 1990
Services Veneer, marquetry, inlays restored
Open Mon–Fri 9am–5pm

Castle House (BAFRA)
Contact Mr Michael Durkee
✉ **Castle House, Units 1 and 3, Bennetts Field Estate, Wincanton, Somerset, BA9 9DT** Ⓟ
☎ 01963 33884 ⓕ 01963 31278
Est. 1975
Services Antique furniture restoration and conservation
Open Mon–Fri 8.30am–5pm

A Dunn and Son
Contact Mr R Dunn
✉ **8 Wharf Road, Chelmsford, Essex, CM2 6LU** Ⓟ
☎ 01245 354452 ⓕ 01245 494991
ⓔ info@adunnandson.co.uk
ⓦ www.adunnandson.com
Est. 1896
Services Makers of marquetry and boulle
Open Mon–Fri 8am–6pm Sat by appointment

Gow Antiques and Restoration (BAFRA)
Contact Jeremy Gow
✉ **Pitscandly Farm, Forfar, Angus, DD8 3NZ** Ⓟ
☎ 01307 465342 ⓕ 01307 468973
ⓜ 07711 416786
ⓔ jeremy@knowyourantiques.com
ⓦ www.knowyourantiques.com
Est. 1991
Services Specialists in restoration of European furniture, 17th–18thC marquetry
Open Mon–Fri 9am–5pm or by appointment

METAL

Marcus Adams
Contact Marcus Adams
✉ **PO Box 3046,**

20 Deacon Street, Leicester, Leicestershire, LE2 3EF Ⓟ
Ⓜ 07973 294622
Ⓔ marcusadams@btinternet.com
Est. 2000
Services Metalware restoration
Open By appointment

Antique Renovations
Contact Philip Lennon
✉ **43 Brent Street, Cheetham Hill, Greater Manchester, M8 8NW**
☎ 0161 834 8000
Est. 1963
Services Restoration of silver, goldware, brass, copperware, polish, lacquer
Open Mon–Fri 7.30am–4.30pm

Antique Restorations
Contact Mr C Christofi
✉ **Unit 23a Rosebery Industrial Park, Rosebery Avenue, London, N17 9SR** Ⓟ
☎ 020 8880 9697 Ⓕ 020 8880 1461
Est. 1968
Services Repair, restoration and refinishing to all metalwork, re-gilding, repairing and casting
Open Mon–Fri 8am–6pm

John Armistead Restorations
Contact Mr John Armistead
✉ **Malham Cottage, Bellingdon, Chesham, Buckinghamshire, HP5 2UR** Ⓟ
☎ 01494 758209 Ⓕ 01494 758209
Ⓔ j.armistead@ntlworld.com
Ⓦ www.john-armistead-restorations.co.uk
Est. 1979
Services Repair and restoration of all antique metalwork including casting, replacement of missing parts, lighting
Open Mon–Fri 9am–5pm

B W Restorations
Contact Mr B W Harris
✉ **44 Hayling Rise, Worthing, West Sussex, BN13 3AG** Ⓟ
☎ 01903 871562 Ⓕ 01903 603846
Ⓜ 07966 539854
Est. 1984
Services Restoration of bronze sculptures
Open By appointment

Bold as Brass Polishers
Contact Mark Mapley
✉ **Unit 13, Visicks Works, Perranarworthal, Truro, Cornwall, TR3 7NR** Ⓟ
☎ 01872 864207
Est. 1994
Services Brass and copper polishing
Open Mon–Fri 9.15am–4.30pm

Bristol Restoration Workshop
Contact Mr Hall
✉ **8 Devon Road, Bristol, BS5 9AD** Ⓟ
☎ 0117 954 2114 Ⓕ 0117 954 2114
Est. 1979
Services Metalware restoration and repair
Open Mon–Fri 8am–5pm

Michael Brook Antique Metal Restoration (BAFRA)
Contact Mr M Brook
✉ **192 Camberwell Grove, London, SE5 8RJ** Ⓟ
☎ 020 7708 0467 Ⓕ 020 7708 0467
Ⓔ michaelbrook@antiquemetalrestoration.co.uk
Ⓦ www.antiqueconservation.co.uk
Est. 1988
Services Antique metal restoration, specializing in ormolu cleaning and repair, patination of fine bronzes and English and French metalwork, especially Matthew Boulton. Listed in the Conservation Register
Open By appointment

E Hansen
Contact Mr E Hansen
✉ **103 Priory Road, Hungerford, Berkshire, RG17 0AW** Ⓟ
☎ 01488 684772
Ⓜ 07885 511986
Ⓔ epgerdes-hans@amserve.net
Est. 1985
Services Metal restoration
Open Mon–Fri 9am–6pm

Rupert Harris Conservation (IIC, UKIC, NACF, SPAB, ICOM)
Contact Ms Roberts
✉ **Unit 5C, 1 Fawe Street, London, E14 6PD** Ⓟ
☎ 020 7987 6231/7515 2020
Ⓕ 020 7987 7994
Ⓔ enquiries@rupertharris.com
Ⓦ www.rupertharris.com
Est. 1982
Services Conservation and restoration of fine metalwork and sculpture
Trade only Yes
Open By appointment

Karim Restorations
Contact Mr A Karim
✉ **Studio 6, The Bull Theatre Gallery, Barnet, Hertfordshire, EN5 5SJ** Ⓟ
☎ 020 8449 928647
Ⓔ aminsemail@e.mail.com
Est. 1984
Services Restoration of Art Nouveau, Arts and Crafts, pewter, castings and lighting
Open Mon–Fri 10am–5pm

Shawlan Antiques (LAPADA)
Contact Mr Shawn Parmakis
✉ **415a Whitehorse Road, Thornton Heath, Surrey, CR7 8SD** Ⓟ
☎ 020 8684 5082 Ⓕ 020 8684 5082
Ⓜ 07889 510253
Est. 1974
Services Metal restoration, foundry work, patination, gilding, chasing
Open Mon–Sat 9am–8pm

David Turner Workshops
Contact Mr D Turner
✉ **24 Tottenham Road, London, N1 4BZ** Ⓟ
☎ 020 7241 5400 Ⓕ 020 7241 5416
Ⓔ mo@davidturner.uk.com
Est. 1987
Services Repair and restoration of metalwork, lighting, decorative antiques
Open Mon–Fri 9.30am–6pm

MILITARIA

Bailiff Forge Manufacturing
Contact Mr John Denbigh or Mr Tom Kay
✉ **Unit 53, Colne Valley Workshops, Linthwaite, Huddersfield, West Yorkshire, HD7 5QG** Ⓟ
☎ 01484 846973 Ⓕ 01484 846973
Ⓔ info@bailiff-forge.co.uk
Ⓦ www.baliff-forge.co.uk
Est. 1984

Services Repair and restoration of swords and armour
Open Mon–Fri 10am–6pm
Sat 2–6pm

The Queen's Shilling
Contact Mrs A Wolf
✉ **87 Commercial Road, Poole, Dorset, BH14 0JD** 🅿
☎ 01202 723335
Est. 1986
Services Medal mounting, sew-on blazer badges for uniforms, sells memorabilia
Open Mon–Fri 9am–5pm
Wed Sat 9am–1pm

Chris Rollason Home Counties Medal Services
Contact Mr C Rollason
✉ **53 Bodiam Crescent, Hampden Park, Eastbourne, East Sussex, BN22 9HQ** 🅿
☎ 01323 506012
Est. 1979
Services Full-size medals restored and mounted to wear or in frame or case. Miniature dress medals supplied and mounted. Regimental ties, blazer badges, buttons, medal accessories also supplied
Open Mon–Fri 9am–5pm

Ian Whitmore
Contact Ian Whitmore
✉ **Hinckley, Leicestershire, LE10**
☎ 01455 444789
ⓔ i.whitmore@ntlworld.com
ⓦ www.beam.to/restorer
Est. 1979
Services Specialist gunmaking, restoration of arms and armour
Open By appointment

MUSICAL INSTRUMENTS

Cambridge Pianola Company and J V Pianos
Contact Tom Poole
✉ **The Limes, High Street, Landbeach, Cambridgeshire, CB4 8DR** 🅿
☎ 01223 861348 ⓕ 01223 441276
ⓔ ftpoole@talk21.com
ⓦ www.cambridgepianola company.co.uk
Est. 1972
Services Restoration, transport and tuning of pianos
Open By appointment

Peter Casebow (BAFRA)
Contact Mr P Casebow
✉ **Pilgrims Mill Lane, Worthing, West Sussex, BN13 3DE** 🅿
☎ 01903 264045
ⓜ 07790 339602
ⓔ pcasebow@hotmail.com
Est. 1987
Services Restoration of period furniture including square-piano restoration
Open By appointment

A Frayling-Cork (BAFRA)
Contact Mr A Frayling-Cork
✉ **2 Mill Lane, Wallingford, Oxfordshire, OX10 0DH** 🅿
☎ 01491 826221
Est. 1979
Services Antique furniture repair, restoration, French polishing, metal fittings, specializing in musical instruments
Open By appointment 24hr answerphone

Peter Goodfellow
Contact Peter Goodfellow
✉ **Ivybank Croft, Lochiepots Road, Miltonduff, Elgin, Moray, IV30 8WL** 🅿
☎ 01343 545045
ⓔ peter@goodfellowviolins.com
ⓦ www.goodfellowviolins.com
Est. 1996
Services Restoration of classic and modern violins, violas, cellos. Provides appraisal, valuation, makes new instruments
Open By appointment

Michael Parfett
Contact Mr M Parfett
✉ **Unit 1E, 9 Queens Yard, White Post Lane, London, E9 5EN** 🅿
☎ 020 8985 5882 ⓕ 020 8985 5882
ⓜ 07811 435221
ⓦ www.michaelparfett.com
Est. 1990
Services Keyboard musical instrument restoration, also harps and stringed instruments, lacquerwork, gilding
Open By appointment

Guinevere Sommers-Hill Violins
Contact Guinevere Sommers-Hill
✉ **The Arbery Centre, Market Place, Wantage, Oxfordshire, OX12 8AB** 🅿
☎ 01235 770094 ⓕ 01235 770094
ⓔ sommershill@yahoo.com
Est. 2001
Services Violin restoration and repair, bow work, also makes new violins
Open Mon–Fri 9.30am–5pm
Sat 9.30am–12.30pm

ORIENTAL

E & C Royall
Contact Mr C Royall
✉ **10 Waterfall Way, Medbourne, Market Harborough, Leicestershire, LE16 8EE** 🅿
☎ 01858 565744
ⓔ royall@telco4u.net
Est. 1981
Services Repair and restoration
Open Mon–Fri 9am–5pm
or by appointment

PACKERS & SHIPPERS

Rolands Antiques
Contact Marion
✉ **Firs Farm, The Square, Thurnby, Leicestershire, LE7 0PX** 🅿
☎ 0116 241 2732 ⓕ 0116 243 1271
ⓔ rolands@wheadon4792. fsbusiness.co.uk
Est. 1973
Services Collection, packing and shipping of antiques
Open Mon–Fri 9am–5pm

Michael Allcroft Antiques
Contact Michael Allcroft
✉ **203 Buxton Road, Newtown, New Mills, Cheshire, SK12 2RA** 🅿
☎ 01663 744014 ⓕ 01663 744014
ⓜ 07798 781642
Est. 1986
Services Packing and export to foreign countries, English oak ideal for the Japanese market
Open Mon–Fri noon–6pm Sat 10am–1pm or by appointment

Anglo Pacific (Fine Art) Ltd (LAPADA)
Contact Malcolm Disson
✉ **Unit 2, Bush Industrial Estate, Standard Road, London, NW10 6DF** 🅿
☎ 020 8838 8008 ⓕ 020 8453 0225

Ⓔ antiques@anglopacific.co.uk
Ⓦ www.anglopacific.co.uk
Est. 1977
Services Packing, shipping and international removals. Also valuations and restoration
Open Mon–Fri 8.30am–5.30pm

Antique Transport Services
Contact Mr Kennedy
✉ **14 Holmfield Avenue, Bournemouth, Dorset, BH7 6SF**
☎ 01202 482265 Ⓕ 01202 482265
Ⓜ 07850 477466
Ⓔ bill-kat@atsremovals.freeserve.co.uk
Est. 1989
Services Removal and transportation of fine antiques and art
Open Mon–Fri 9am–6pm

Robert Boys Shipping
Contact Robert Boys
✉ **North London Freight Centre, York Way, Kings Cross, London, N1 0AU** Ⓟ
☎ 020 7837 4806 Ⓕ 020 7837 4815
Ⓔ info@robertboysshipping.co.uk
Est. 1989
Services Shipping, packing, forwarding
Open Mon–Fri 8am–6pm

Davies Turner Worldwide Movers Ltd
Contact Olivia Ricordini
✉ **49 Wates Way, Mitcham, Surrey, CR4 4HR**
☎ 0207 622 4393 Ⓕ 0207 720 3897
Ⓔ antiques@daviesturner.co.uk
Est. 1870
Services Packing, shipping of antiques and fine art throughout the world
Open Mon–Fri 8am–5pm

Derbyshire Removals
Contact Michael Powell
✉ **Butterley Cottage, Butterley Lane, Ashover, Derbyshire, S45 0JU** Ⓟ
☎ 01629 582762/01246 202289
Ⓜ 07774 422561
Est. 1987
Services Removal service of antique and fine furniture and packing
Open Ring anytime

Alan Franklin Transport Ltd
Contact Alan Franklin
✉ **26 Blackmoor Road, Verwood, Dorset, BH31 6BB**
☎ 01202 826539 Ⓕ 01202 827337
Ⓔ aft@afteurope.co.uk
Ⓦ www.alanfranklintransport.co.uk
Est. 1975
Services Specialist carriers of antiques and fine art world-wide
Open Mon–Fri 8.30am–5.30pm

Gander and White Shipping Ltd (BADA, LAPADA)
Contact O Howell
✉ **21 Lillie Road, London, SW6 1UE** Ⓟ
☎ 020 7381 0571 Ⓕ 020 7381 5428
Ⓔ info@ganderandwhite.com
Ⓦ www.ganderandwhite.com
Est. 1933
Services Packing and shipping
Open Mon–Fri 9am–5.30pm

Hedleys Humpers (LAPADA, BADA, BIFA, BAR, IATA)
✉ **3 St Leonards Road, London, NW10 6SX** Ⓟ
☎ 020 8965 8733 Ⓕ 020 8965 0249
Ⓔ mg@hedleyshumpers.com
Ⓦ www.hedleyshumpers.com
Est. 1973
Services Door-to-door delivery by road, sea and air of single items to full container loads. Arrange collection, export, packing, insurance and all export and customs paperwork on customers' behalf
Open Mon–Fri 8am–6pm

International Furniture Exporters Ltd
Contact Iris Mitchell
✉ **Old Cement Works, South Heighton, Newhaven, East Sussex, BN9 0HS** Ⓟ
☎ 01273 611251 Ⓕ 01273 611574
Ⓦ www.asweb.co.uk/ife
Est. 1990
Services Furniture exporters
Open Mon–Fri 7am–6pm

Kuwahara Ltd (LAPADA, HHGFAA)
Contact Yukio Kuwahara
✉ **6 McNicol Drive, London, NW10 7AW** Ⓟ
☎ 020 8963 1100 Ⓕ 020 8963 0100
Ⓔ yukio@kuwahara.co.uk
Ⓦ www.kuwahara.co.uk
Est. 1983
Services Fine art packing and shipping, door-to-door transport around the world by land, air or sea
Trade only Yes
Open Mon–Fri 9am–5.30pm

C and N Lawrence
Contact Mr N Lawrence
✉ **7 Church Walk, Brighton Road, Horley, Surrey, RH6 7EE** Ⓟ
☎ 01293 783243
Est. 1983
Services Removals, shipping, packing for antiques trade
Trade only Yes
Open Mon–Fri 9am–5pm

Lockson Services Ltd (LAPADA, BIFA)
Contact Bob King
✉ **Unit 1, Heath Park Industrial Estate, Freshwater Road, Chadwell Heath, Essex, RM8 1RX** Ⓟ
☎ 020 8597 2889 Ⓕ 020 8597 5265
Ⓜ 07831 621428
Ⓔ enquiries@lockson.co.uk
Ⓦ www.lockson.co.uk
Est. 1943
Services Packers and shippers
Open Mon–Fri 8am–6pm

John Morgan and Sons (FIDI, OMNI, BAR, BAR Overseas Group, HHGFAA)
Contact Mr William Morgan
✉ **Removal House, 30 Island Street, Belfast, Co Antrim, BT4 1DH** Ⓟ
☎ 028 9073 2333 Ⓕ 028 9045 7402
Ⓔ info@morganremovals.com
Ⓦ www.morganremovals.com
Est. 1915
Services Specialist antique removals and local, worldwide household removals
Open Mon–Fri 9am–5.30pm

PDQ Air Freight/Art Move (LAPADA, CINOA, GTA, BIFA)
✉ **Unit 4, Court 1, Challenge Road, Ashford, Middlesex, TW15 1AX** Ⓟ
☎ 01784 243695 Ⓕ 01784 242237
Ⓔ artmove@pdq.uk.com

Ⓦ www.pdq.uk.com
Est. 1983
Services Packing and shipping, fair logistics, hand-carry couriers, bonded warehouse
Open Mon–Fri 9am–5.30pm

Seabourne Mailpack Worldwide Ltd (LAPADA)
Contact Melanie Lemaire
✉ **Unit 13, Saxon Way, Moor Lane, West Drayton, Middlesex, UB7 0LW** Ⓟ
☎ 020 8897 3888
Ⓜ 07770 612134
Ⓔ info@seabourne-mailpack.com
Ⓦ www.seabourne-mailpack.com
Est. 1962
Services Export packing and world wide delivery of fine art, antiques, furniture
Open Mon–Fri 9am–6pm

The Shipping Company
Contact Matt Walton
✉ **Bourton Industrial Park, Bourton-on-the-Water, Cheltenham, Gloucestershire, GL54 2HQ** Ⓟ
☎ 01451 822451 Ⓕ 01451 810985
Ⓜ 07971 425978
Ⓔ enquiries@theshipping companyltd.com
Ⓦ www.theshippingcompanyltd.com
Est. 1998
Services Packing and shipping of antiques worldwide
Open Mon–Fri 9am–6pm telephone mobile at other times

Sterling Art Services
Contact Oliver Reed
✉ **Unit 5, Cypress Court, Harris Way, Sunbury-on-Thames, Middlesex, TW16 7EL** Ⓟ
☎ 01932 771442 Ⓕ 01932 771443
Ⓔ sales@sterlingartservices.co.uk
Ⓦ www.sterlingartservices.co.uk
Est. 2000
Services Specialists packers and shippers of fine art and antiques
Open Mon–Fri 9am–5pm

Stevens Antiques & Office Removals
Contact Steven McCarrol
✉ **255 Lochburn Road, Glasgow, G20 0QQ**
Ⓜ 07778 742150
Est. 1994
Services Antiques removal service
Open By appointment

A J Williams Shipping (LAPADA)
Contact Jennifer Williams
✉ **607 Sixth Avenue, Central Business Park, Petherton Road, Hengrove, Bristol, BS14 9BZ** Ⓟ
☎ 01275 892166 Ⓕ 01275 891333
Ⓔ aj.williams@btclick.com
Est. 1977
Services Packing and shipping of antiques and fine art worldwide
Open Mon–Fri 9am–5.30pm or by appointment

PAINTED FURNITURE

Steven J Cotterell
Contact Steven Cotterell
✉ **72 Springfield Road, Somersham, Ipswich, Suffolk, IP8 4PQ** Ⓟ
☎ 01473 831530
Ⓜ 07733 291705
Ⓔ somersham.flyer@yahoo.co.uk
Est. 1975
Services French polishing, furniture restoration and painting
Open Mon–Sat 7.30am–6pm

M Tocci
Contact Mr M Tocci
✉ **Unit 4, 81 Southern Row, London, W10 5AL** Ⓟ
☎ 020 8960 4826
Est. 1978
Services Gilding, painted furniture restoration, lacquer on furniture and decorations
Open Mon–Fri 7.30am–4.30pm

PAPER

Cameron Preservation (IPCRA, IPC, SAPCON)
Contact Mr Elgin Cameron
✉ **Flush Business Centre, Flush Place, Lurgan, Co Armagh, BT66 7DT** Ⓟ
☎ 028 3834 3099 Ⓕ 028 3834 3099
Est. 1993
Services Restoration of art on paper, archives, manuscripts, books, also vellum, parchment, globes
Open Mon–Fri 8.30am–5.15 Sat 8.30am–noon

Voitek Conservation of Works of Art (IPC)
Contact Mrs E Sobczynski
✉ **9 Whitehorse Mews, Westminster Bridge Road, London, SE1 7QD** Ⓟ
☎ 020 7928 6094 Ⓕ 020 7928 6094
Ⓔ voitekcwa@btinternet.com
Est. 1972
Services Conservation of prints, drawings, watercolours, maps, conservation mounting and project planning
Open By appointment

PAPIER MACHE

Zygmunt Chelminski (UKIC)
Contact Mr Z Chelminski
✉ **Studio GE1, 2 Michael Road, London, SW6 2AD** Ⓟ
☎ 020 7610 9731 Ⓕ 020 7610 9731
Ⓜ 07770 585130
Est. 1993
Services Restoration and conservation of architectural monuments, statues and special effects in marble, granite, stone, terracotta, alabaster, coldstone, iron, bronze, zinc, lead, ormolu, wood, ivory, pietra dura, scagliola, plaster, mother-of-pearl, tortoiseshell, shagreen, amber, onyx, papier-mâché, blue john and semi-precious stones
Open Mon–Fri 10am–5pm appointment advisable

PICTURE RESTORATION

Roger Allan
Contact Mr R Allan
✉ **The Old Red Lion, Bedingfield, Eye, Suffolk, IP23 7LQ** Ⓟ
☎ 01728 628491
Est. 1973
Services Picture restorer, furniture restorer
Trade only Yes
Open By appointment

Burghley Fine Art Conservation Ltd
Contact Mike Cowell
✉ **The Stable Courtyard, Burghley House, Stamford, Lincolnshire, PE9 3JY** Ⓟ
☎ 01780 762155 Ⓕ 01780 762155
Est. 1977
Services Restoration of oil paintings and picture frames
Open By appointment

The Gallery (LAPADA, CINOA)
Contact Jeffrey S Cohen
✉ **3–5 Church Street, Reigate, Surrey, RH2 0AA** P
☎ 01737 242813 F 01737 362819
M 07711 670676
E the.gallery@virgin.net
W www.thegallery.uk.com
Est. 1990
Services Picture restoration
Open Mon–Sat 10am–5pm

Glebe Hall Restoration Studios
Contact Carmel Corrigan-Griffin
✉ **Old Killernogh Rectory, Rathnakelly Glebe, Ballacolla, Co Laois, Ireland** P
☎ 0502 34105 F 0502 34105
M 0868 784956
Est. 1980
Services Furniture restoration, gilding, porcelain, ivory, jade
Open By appointment, Sat 11am–4pm

Inglenook Fine Arts (FATG)
Contact Jill Bagshaw
✉ **Greenend Gallery, Greenend, Woodchurch, Shropshire, SY13 1AA** P
☎ 01948 665422 F 01948 665422
E info@inglenookfineart.co.uk
W www.inglenookfineart.co.uk
Est. 1985
Services Picture restoration, framing
Open Mon–Sat 9.30am–5pm Wed closed 1pm

Inglenook Fine Arts (FATG)
Contact Jill Bagshaw
✉ **31 Pillory Street, Nantwich, Cheshire, CW5 5BQ** P
☎ 01270 611188 F
E info@inglenookfineart.co.uk
W www.inglenookfineart.co.uk
Est. 1993
Services Picture restoration, framing
Open Mon–Sat 9.30am–5pm Wed closed 1pm

Regency Restoration
Contact Mrs E Ball
✉ **Studio 21, Thames House, 140 Battersea Park Road, London, SW11 4NB** P
☎ 020 7622 5275 or 020 7828 4268
F 020 7498 1803
Est. 1987
Services Restoration of 18th–19thC mirrors, picture frames, English and Continental painted and gilded furniture, architectural gilding, church interiors, polychrome sculpture, lacquerwork, oil paintings, carving
Open Mon–Fri 9.30am–5.30pm

Siracusa Paintings Ltd
Contact Alyson Lawrence
✉ **Lev Antiques Ltd, 97a Kensington Church Street, London, W8 7LN** P
☎ 020 7727 9248 F 020 7727 9248
M 07768 470473
E alyson@richardlawrence.co.uk
Est. 1984
Services Restoration of 17th–20thC oil paintings
Open Tues–Sat 10.30am–5.45pm or by appointment

Andrew Wheeler (IPC)
Contact Andrew Wheeler
✉ **4 Bayswater Avenue, Westbury Park, Bristol, BS6 7NS** P
☎ 0117 942 3003
E andrewwheeler123@yahoo.co.uk
W www.fine-art-on-paper-restoration.co.uk
Est. 1970
Services Restoration of fine prints, watercolours, drawings
Open Mon–Sat 9am–1pm 2.30–6pm

PINE

Heritage Restorations
Contact Jonathan Gluck
✉ **Llanfair Caereinion, Welshpool, Powys, SY21 0HD** P
☎ 01938 810384 F 01938 810900
E info@heritagerestorations.co.uk
W www.heritagerestorations.co.uk
Est. 1970
Services Antique furniture, repair and restoration, specializing in 18th–19thC pine
Open Mon–Sat 9am–5pm

Oldwoods Furniture
Contact Sid Duck
✉ **Unit 4, Colston Yard, Colston Street, Bristol, BS1 5BD** P
☎ 0117 929 9023
Est. 1980
Services Furniture repair and restoration, buying and selling
Open By appointment

The Pine Mine
Contact Mr Caspian Crewe-Read
✉ **100 Wandsworth Bridge Road, London, SW6 2TF** P
☎ 020 7736 1092 F 020 7736 5283
E pinemine@hotmail.com
Est. 1972
Services Country furniture and antique pine repair and restoration, bespoke furniture maker
Open Mon–Sat 9.30am–5.30pm Sun 11am–4pm

Ed Thomas Old Country Pine
Contact Mr E Thomas
✉ **22 Old Hednesford Road, Cannock, Staffordshire, WS11 6LD** P F 01543 506731
M 07966 243477
E edthomasoldcountrypine@altavista.com
Est. 1981
Services Made-to-measure pine furniture using only old original pine.
Open Mon–Sat 9am–5.30pm

Wood Be Good
Contact Mr Dennis Langford
✉ **1 Jarrow Road, London, SE16 3JR** P
☎ 020 7232 2639 F 020 8657 6610
Est. 1984
Services Pine furniture repair and restoration, pine stripping
Open Mon–Sat 7am–5pm

PLASTERWORK

Seamas O'Heocha Teoranta (IPCRA, Irish Georgian Society, An Taisce)
Contact Seamas O'Heocha
✉ **Corbally, Barna, Galway, Ireland** P
☎ 091 590256 F 091 590256
M 0872 581150
E info@seamasoheocha.teo.com
Est. 1987
Services Ornate plasterwork restoration and conservation, contractors and consultants
Open Mon–Fri 9am–6pm

SCIENTIFIC

Osborne Antiques
Contact Mrs L Osborne
✉ **Pentavlon, 9 Hillcrest Close, Wembury, Devon, PL9 0HA** 🅿
☎ 01752 863025 ⓕ 0121 354 7166
ⓔ chris@barometerparts.co.uk
ⓦ www.barometerparts.co.uk
Est. 1975
Services Barometer parts suppliers, scientific glass blowers
Open Tues–Thurs 9am–5pm Fri 9am–5.30pm Sat 9.15am–1pm closed 1–2pm

Russell Scientific Instruments Ltd
Contact Edward Allen
✉ **Rash's Green Industrial Estate, Dereham, Norfolk, NR19 1JG** 🅿
☎ 01362 693481 ⓕ 01362 698548
ⓔ sales@russell-scientific.co.uk
ⓦ www.russell-scientific.co.uk
Est. 1862
Services Restoration of antique barometers, barographs, meteorological equipment, thermometers
Open Mon–Fri 9am–4pm

Weather House Antiques
Contact Kym Walker
✉ **Foster Clough, Hebden Bridge, West Yorkshire, HX7 5QZ** 🅿
☎ 01422 882808/886961 (workshop)
ⓕ 01422 882808
ⓜ 07801 071710
ⓔ kymwalker@btinternet.com
Est. 1986
Services Barometer restoration
Open By appointment only

SCULPTURE

Graciela Ainsworth (SSCR, UKIC)
Contact Graciela
✉ **Unit 4 & 10 Bonnington Mill, 72 Newhaven Road, Edinburgh, EH6 5QG** 🅿
☎ 0131 555 1294 ⓕ 0131 467 7080
ⓔ graciela@graciela-ainsworth.com
Est. 1990
Services Conservation of statues, monuments, stone sculptures. Carving commissions
Open Mon–Fri 9am–6pm

Taylor Pearce Restoration Services Ltd (UKIC)
Contact Mr K Taylor
✉ **Fishers Court, Besson Street, London, SE14 5AF** 🅿
☎ 020 7252 9800 ⓕ 020 7277 8169
ⓔ admin@taylorpearce.co.uk
Est. 1985
Services Sculpture, conservation and restoration of stone, bronze, plaster and terracotta. By appointment to HM Queen
Open By appointment

Voitek Conservation of Works of Art (IPC)
Contact Mrs E Sobczynski
✉ **9 Whitehorse Mews, Westminster Bridge Road, London, SE1 7QD** 🅿
☎ 020 7928 6094 ⓕ 020 7928 6094
ⓔ voitekcwa@btinternet.com
Est. 1972
Services Conservation of sculpture, marble, terracotta, wood
Open By appointment

SEARCH SERVICE

Antique Finder
Contact Linda Chapple
✉ **Boxhurst, Sandhurst, Cranbrook, Kent, TN18 5PE** 🅿
☎ 01580 850219
ⓔ linda.boxhurst@virgin.net
ⓜ 07979 957359
Est. 1995
Services Finds antiques

Jonathan Brearley Antiques
Contact Jonathan Brearley
✉ **17 High Street, Linton, Swadlincote, Derbyshire, DE12 6QL** 🅿
☎ 01283 763233
ⓜ 07973 862040
ⓔ jbrearley@aol.com
Est. 1995
Services Search service for individuals and companies extending to items to create an Edwardian or Regency room
Open Mon–Sat 9am–6pm

Era Vintage Boutique
Contact Donna Kettlewell
✉ **1 Victoria Road, Saltaire, West Yorkshire, BD13 3LA** 🅿
☎ 01274 598777
ⓔ info@eravintage.fsbusiness.co.uk
ⓦ www.cissieandbertha.com
Est. 1991
Services Sourcing 1920s–1970s textiles, home furnishings, jewellery, clothing
Open Mon–Sun noon–5pm

ukauctioneers.com
Contact Eileen McCarthy
✉ **24 Old Wrexham Road, Chester, Cheshire, CH4 7HS**
☎ 01244 679471 ⓕ 01244 680587
ⓜ 07860 123421
ⓔ info@ukauctioneers.com
ⓦ www.ukauctioneers.com
Est. 1998
Services Search facility and on-line commission bidding
Open Mon–Fri 9am–5pm

SILVER

F W Aldridge Ltd
Contact Miss Angela Garwood
✉ **Unit 3, St Johns Industrial Estate, Dunmow Road, Takeley, Essex, CM22 6SP** 🅿
☎ 01279 874000 ⓕ 01279 874002
ⓔ angela@fwaldridge.abel.co.uk
ⓦ www.fwaldridgeglass.com
Est. 1926
Services Repair and restoration of glass, supply of Bristol glass for antique and modern table silverware, all glass and silver restoration
Open Mon–Fri 9am–5.30pm

Antique Renovations
Contact Philip Lennon
✉ **43 Brent Street, Cheetham Hill, Greater Manchester, M8 8NW**
☎ 0161 834 8000
Est. 1963
Services Restoration of silver, goldware, brass, copperware, polish, lacquer
Open Mon–Fri 7.30am–4.30pm

Barry Papworth (NAG)
Contact Steve Park
✉ **28 St Thomas Street, Lymington, Hampshire, SO41 9NE** 🅿
☎ 01590 676422
Est. 1978
Services Restoration of jewellery and silver. Workshop on site
Open Mon–Sat 9.15am–5.15pm

Wellington Gallery (LAPADA)
Contact Mrs M Barclay
⊠ **1 St John's Wood High Street, London, NW8 7NG** 🅿
☎ 020 7586 2620 Ⓕ 020 7483 0716
Est. 1979
Services Restoration of silver and silver plate, gilding, engraving, jewellery, glass, upholstery, paintings, porcelain, furniture, framing, valuations
Open Mon–Fri 10.30am–6pm Sat 10am–6pm

B M Witmond (Freeman of the Goldsmiths Company)
Contact Barry Witmond
⊠ **The Stable Courtyard, Burghley House, Stamford, Lincolnshire, PE9 5JY** 🅿
☎ 01780 480868 Ⓕ 01780 480866
Ⓜ 07774 870513
Ⓦ www.bmwitmond.co.uk
Est. 1976
Services Manufacture and restoration of tortoiseshell, restoration of ivory and English and Continental plate, jewellery manufacture
Open By appointment

STONEWORK

Zygmunt Chelminski (UKIC)
Contact Mr Z Chelminski
⊠ **Studio GE1, 2 Michael Road, London, SW6 2AD** 🅿
☎ 020 7610 9731 Ⓕ 020 7610 9731
Ⓜ 07770 585130
Est. 1993
Services Restoration and conservation of architectural monuments, statues and special effects in marble, granite, stone, terracotta, alabaster, coldstone, iron, bronze, zinc, lead, ormolu, wood, ivory, pietra dura, scagliola, plaster, mother-of-pearl, tortoiseshell, shagreen, amber, onyx, papier-mâché, blue john and semi-precious stones
Open Mon–Fri 10am–5pm appointment advisable

London Stone Conservation (SPAB)
Contact Florian Kirchertz
⊠ **42 Sekforde Street, Finsbury, London, EC1R 0AH** 🅿
☎ 020 7251 0592 Ⓕ 020 7251 0592
Ⓜ 07876 685470
Ⓔ lsc@londonstoneconservation.com
Ⓦ www.londonstoneconservation.com
Est. 2004
Services Conservation and restoration of ancient buildings, monuments, masonry, stone carving, letters
Open By appointment

Voitek Conservation of Works of Art
Contact Mr W Sobczynski
⊠ **9 Whitehorse Mews, Westminster Bridge Road, London, SE1 7QD** 🅿
☎ 020 7928 6094 Ⓕ 020 7928 6094
Ⓔ voitekcwa@btinternet.com
Est. 1972
Services Conservation and restoration of marble, stone, terracotta, wood
Open By appointment

Gwyn Watkins Stonemason and Architectural Stone Carver
Contact Gwyn Watkins
⊠ **Stonemason's Shop, Burghley House, Stamford, Lincolnshire, PE9 3JY** 🅿
☎ 01780 766366
Est. 1988
Services Restoration and repair of garden statuary, stonemason and carver
Open By appointment

STRIPPING

Acorn Antique Interiors
Contact Brian or Margaret
⊠ **Eddystone Road, Wadebridge, Cornwall, PL27 7AL** 🅿
☎ 01208 812815
Est. 1982
Services Paint stripping
Open Mon–Sat 9am–5pm

Back to the Wood
Contact Mr J Davis
⊠ **Riverside Works, Riverside Road, Watford, Hertfordshire, WD1 4HY** 🅿
☎ 01923 222943
Ⓜ 07976 297008
Est. 1981
Services Pine stripping, Victorian–Edwardian fireplaces a speciality
Open Mon–Sat 9am–5pm

Cameo Antiques
Contact Mrs S Hinton
⊠ **3 Liverpool Road East, Church Lawton, Stoke-on-Trent, Staffordshire, ST7 3AQ** 🅿
☎ 01782 772555
Est. 1985
Services Complete repair and restoration of furniture, stripping
Open Mon–Fri 9am–6pm Sat 9am–4pm

E Carty
Contact Mr E Carty
⊠ **51 Trinity Street, Gainsborough, Lincolnshire, DN21 1JF** 🅿
☎ 01427 614452
Ⓜ 07733 474895
Est. 1976
Services Stripping and restoration
Open By appointment

Chiltern Strip & Polish
Contact Mr B Black
⊠ **Kitchener Works, Kitchener Road, High Wycombe, Buckinghamshire, HP11 2SJ** 🅿
☎ 01494 438052
Est. 1986
Services Non-caustic stripping, repair and repolishing. Sale of antique furniture
Open Mon–Fri 9am–5pm Sat 9am–12.30pm

Dip 'n' Strip
Contact Charles Sherry
⊠ **20 Burnham Road, Glasgow, G14 0XA** 🅿
☎ 0141 9529111460
Est. 1980
Services Furniture restoration
Open Mon–Fri 9am–5pm

The Door Stripping Company Ltd
Contact Mr B Findley
⊠ **32 Main Road, Renishaw, Sheffield, South Yorkshire, S21 3UT** 🅿
☎ 01246 435521
Est. 1984
Services Pine stripping, non-caustic restoration of furniture
Open Mon–Fri 9am–5pm Sat–Sun 11am–2pm

Holme Valley Warehouse
Contact Paula Moss or Michael Silkstone
⊠ **11 Westgate, Honley,**

Holmfirth, Huddersfield, West Yorkshire, HD9 1AA 🅿
☎ 01484 667915 ⓕ 01484 667915
Est. 1995
Services Pine stripping and restoration
Open Mon–Sun 10am–5pm

Miracle Stripping
Contact Mr C Howes or Mr A Howes
✉ **The Cottage, Woodhall Farm, Hatfield, Hertfordshire, AL9 5NU** 🅿
☎ 01707 270587 ⓕ 01707 270587
ⓜ 07790 696631
Est. 1992
Services Stripping of doors, cast-iron fireplaces
Open Mon–Fri 8.30am–5pm

Mr Dip
Contact Mr G Broadbridge
✉ **3 Knutsford Road, Alderley Edge, Cheshire, SK9 7SD** 🅿
☎ 01625 584896
Est. 1983
Services Wood stripping, hardwood, softwood and antique items, furniture and fireplaces
Open Mon–Fri 10am–4pm
Sat 10am–2pm closed Wed

Popes Farm Antique Pine & Stripping
Contact Peter Thompson
✉ **Popes Farm, Windmill Hill, Hailsham, East Sussex, BN27 4RS** 🅿
☎ 01323 832159
ⓔ peter@popesfarm.co.uk
ⓦ www.popesfarm.co.uk
Est. 1973
Services Pine stripping
Open Mon–Fri 8.30am–6pm
Sat 8.30am–4pm

Salisbury Stripping Co
Contact Karen Montlake
✉ **48–54 Milford Street, Salisbury, Wiltshire, SP1 2BP**
☎ 01722 413595/718203
ⓕ 01722 416395
ⓔ enquiries@myriad-antiques.co.uk
ⓦ www.myriad-antiques.co.uk
Est. 1994
Services Paint and varnish stripping of furniture and doors, caustic and non-caustic processes, full restoration
Open Mon–Sat 9.30am–5pm
Sun by appointment

Strip Easy Ltd
Contact R Belfield
✉ **Godleton Farm, Silver Street, Sway, Lymington, Hampshire, SO41 6DJ** 🅿
☎ 0203 8033 2293
Est. 1978
Services Restoration pine furniture, paint stripping
Open Mon–Sat 9am–5pm

Strip It Ltd
Contact Mr Panton
✉ **109–111 Pope Street, Birmingham, West Midlands, B1 3AG** 🅿
☎ 0121 243 4000
Est. 1983
Services Stripping furniture
Open Mon–Sat 8am–5.30pm

Strippadoor
Contact Danny Russell
✉ **Victoria Works, Units 2 and 3, Hempshaw Lane, Stockport, Cheshire, SK1 4LG** 🅿
☎ 0161 477 8980 ⓕ 0161 477 6302
Est. 1979
Services Stripping of doors, fireplaces, fire surrounds and furniture
Open Mon–Fri 9am–5.30pm
Sat 10.30am–2.30pm

Stripped Pine Workshop
Contact Mr John Wood
✉ **Rear of 28 Catherine Street, Swansea, West Glamorgan, SA1 4JS** 🅿
☎ 01792 461236
Est. 1970
Services Pine stripping
Open Mon–Sat 11.30am–6pm

The Stripper
Contact Mr K Pinder
✉ **Sneaton Lane, Ruswarp, Whitby, North Yorkshire, YO22 5HL** 🅿
☎ 01947 820035/880966
Est. 1995
Services Stripping of furniture, doors, antique renovation
Open Mon–Fri 8am–6pm
Sat 8am–noon

The Stripping Store
Contact Jeff Low
✉ **10 Backcauseway Street, Parkhead, Glasgow, G32 5HE** 🅿
☎ 0141 550 8195
ⓜ 07796 501633
Est. 1997
Services Hand stripping of period and traditional furniture
Open Mon–Sat 10am–6pm

Windsor Antiques
Contact Mr G Henderson
✉ **Rosemary Farm, Rosemary Lane, Castle Hedingham, Halstead, Essex, CO9 3AJ** 🅿
☎ 01787 461653
Est. 1981
Services Furniture and paint stripping
Open By appointment

York Vale (GADAR)
Contact Mr Evely
✉ **Unit 6a, Victoria Farm, Water Lane, York, North Yorkshire, YO30 6PQ** 🅿
☎ 01904 690561
ⓔ sand@yorkvale.co.uk
Est. 1984
Services Pine stripping, antique repair and restoration, new hand-made kitchens
Open Mon–Fri 9am–5.30pm
Sat 9am–2.30pm

SUPPLIERS

Addington Supplies
Contact Pam Warner
✉ **1 Addington Cottages, Upottery, Honiton, Devon, EX14 9PN** 🅿
☎ 01404 861519 ⓕ 01404 861308
ⓔ pam@addingtonstudio.co.uk
ⓦ www.addingtonstudio.co.uk
Est. 1991
Services Supplies for ceramic conservators
Open By appointment

Antique Leather Dressing
Contact Val Pringle
✉ **PO Box 67, Langport, Somerset, TA10 9WJ**
☎ 01458 241816
ⓜ 07947 277833
ⓔ sales@antiqueleatherdressing.co.uk
ⓦ www.antiqueleatherdressing.co.uk
Est. 2003

Services Leather dressing products, including Pecard
Open Please telephone or e-mail

Antique Restorations (BAFRA)
Contact Raymond Konyn
✉ **The Old Wheelwrights', Brasted Forge, Brasted, Kent, TN16 1JL** Ⓟ
☎ 01959 563863 Ⓕ 01959 561262
Ⓔ info@brasscastings.co.uk
Ⓦ www.brasscastings.co.uk
Est. 1979
Services Cast brass period fittings
Open Mon–Fri 9am–5pm

Richard Barry Southern Marketing Ltd
Contact Mr Richard Fill
✉ **Unit 1–2, Chapel Place, North Street, Portslade, Brighton, East Sussex, BN41 1DR** Ⓟ
☎ 01273 419471 Ⓕ 01273 421925
Ⓦ www.richardbarry.co.uk
Est. 1978
Services Suppliers to the antiques trade of all wood-finishing materials
Open Mon–Fri 8am–5pm

Chemicals Ltd
Contact Sales department
✉ **Unit 2, Ringtail Place, Burscough Industrial Estate, Burscough, Lancashire, L40 7SD** Ⓟ
☎ 01704 897700 Ⓕ 01704 897237
Ⓔ sales@paramose.com
Est. 1982
Services Original and water washable strippers, Paramose stripping machines, restoration materials
Open Mon–Fri 9am–5pm

Classic Finishes
Contact Pat Baker
✉ **40–46 Oak Street, Norwich, Norfolk, NR3 3BP** Ⓟ
☎ 01603 760374 Ⓕ 01603 660477
Est. 1985
Services Restoration materials, advice, specialist paints, French and wax polishes
Open Mon–Fri 8.30am–5.30pm Sat 9am–1pm

Devon Metalcraft Ltd (incorporating Suffolk Brass)
Contact Trevor Ford
✉ **2 Victoria Way, Exmouth, Devon, EX8 1EW**
☎ 01395 272846 Ⓕ 01395 227668
Ⓜ 07860 927177
Ⓔ info@devonmetalcrafts.co.uk
Ⓦ www.devonmetalcrafts.co.uk
Est. 1982
Services Supplies replica cast brass handles from catalogue
Trade only Yes
Open By appointment

Former Glory
Contact Tim or Kim Ravenscroft
✉ **Ferndown, Dorset, BH22** Ⓟ
☎ 01202 895859 Ⓕ 01202 895859
Ⓔ formerglory@btinternet.com
Ⓦ www.formerglory.co.uk
Est. 1994
Services Cane and rush seating, furniture restoration. Cane, rush and restoration material supplies
Open By appointment only

Rod Naylor
Contact Angela Naylor
✉ **208 Devizes Road, Hilperton, Trowbridge, Wiltshire, BA14 7QP** Ⓟ
☎ 01225 754497 Ⓕ 01225 754497
Ⓔ rod.naylor@virgin.net
Ⓦ www.rodnaylor.com
Est. 1970
Services Restoration of antique wood carvings, supplies replicas of hard-to-find items and materials for caddies, boxes, desks etc, cabinet-making, supplier of power carving machinery and tools
Open By appointment only

Pendelfin Studio Ltd
Contact Mrs Morley
✉ **Cameron Mill, Howsin Street, Burnley, Lancashire, BB10 1PP** Ⓟ
☎ 01282 432301 Ⓕ 01282 459464
Ⓔ boswell@pendelfin.co.uk
Ⓦ www.pendelfin.co.uk
Est. 1953
Services Suppliers to retail outlets of collectable stonecraft rabbits and village pieces
Open Mon–Fri 9am–5pm

John Penny Antique Services
Contact Mr J Penny
✉ **Unit 10, City Industrial Park, Southern Road, Southampton, Hampshire, SO15 0HA** Ⓟ
☎ 023 8023 2066 Ⓕ 023 8021 2129
Est. 1981
Services Suppliers of furniture restoration materials
Open Mon–Fri 9am–5pm Sat 9am–12.30pm

Restoration Supplies
Contact Mrs M O'Connell
✉ **The Corn Mill, Claremont, Wyke, Bradford, West Yorkshire, BD12 9JJ**
☎ 01274 691461
Est. 1989
Services Restoration supplies
Open Wed–Sat 10.30am–6pm

TAXIDERMY

Heads 'n' Tails (Guild of Taxidermists)
Contact David McKinley
✉ **Wivelscombe, Somerset, TA4** Ⓟ
☎ 01984 623097 Ⓕ 01984 624445
Ⓔ mac@taxidermyuk.com
Ⓦ www.taxidermyuk.com
Est. 1981
Services Taxidermy, natural history specimens
Open By appointment

TEXTILES

Lannowe Oriental Textiles
Contact Joanna Titchell
✉ **Near Bath, Wiltshire**
☎ 01225 891487 Ⓕ 01225 891182
Ⓜ 0771 470 3535
Ⓔ joanna@lannowe.co.uk
Est. 1976
Services Washing, restoration and conservation of Oriental carpets, rugs and tapestries
Open By appointment

M & M Restoration
Contact Mrs M Druet
✉ **Mantel House, Broomhill Road, London, SW18 4JQ** Ⓟ
☎ 020 8871 5098 Ⓕ 020 8877 1940
Ⓜ 07850 310104
Est. 1985
Services Restoration and cleaning of antique tapestries, carpets and textiles
Open Mon–Fri 9am–6pm

The Restoration Studio
Contact Ela
✉ **63 Jeddo Road, London, W12 9EE** P
☎ 020 8740 4977
Ⓜ 07711 157644
Ⓦ www.restorationstudio.co.uk
Est. 1987
Services Restoration of tapestries, needlework, embroidery, Aubussons
Open Mon–Fri 10am–5pm

The Textile Conservancy Co Ltd (UKIC)
Contact Alexandra Seth-Smith ACR
✉ **Pickhill Business Centre, Smallhythe Road, Tenterden, Kent, TN30 7LZ** P
☎ 01580 761600 Ⓕ 01580 761600
Ⓔ alex@textile-conservation.co.uk
Ⓦ www.textile-conservation.co.uk
Est. 1997
Services Cleaning, repair, condition reports of historic textiles, costumes, tapestries, rugs. Advice on preventative conservation, storage, display, mounting
Open Mon–Fri 9am–6pm by appointment

Textile Conservation (UKIC)
Contact Fiona Hutton
✉ **Ivy House Farm, Wolvershill Road, Banwell, Somerset, BS29 6LB** P
☎ 01934 822449
Ⓔ fiona@textileconservation.co.uk
Est. 1989
Services Textile conservation
Open Mon–Fri 9am–5pm

Textile Conservation Consultancy (FIIC)
Contact Sheila Landi or Liz Clemence
✉ **The Stable Courtyard, Burghley House, Stamford, Lincolnshire, PE9 3JY** P
☎ 01780 480188 Ⓕ 01780 480188
Ⓔ sheilalandi@textileconservation consultancy.co.uk
Ⓦ www.textileconservation consultancy.co.uk
Est. 1992
Services Conservation and repair of all textile objects
Open By appointment

Textile Conservation Services
Contact Miss Lyndall Bond
✉ **3–4 West Workshop, Welbeck, Worksop, Nottinghamshire, S80 3LW** P
☎ 01909 481655 Ⓕ 01909 481655
Ⓔ textile.conservation@tesco.net
Est. 1984
Services The conservation of costume, lace and small textiles. Talks and courses on costume and textiles
Open By appointment

TOYS

Berkshire Antiques Co Ltd
Contact Mr Sutton
✉ **42 Thames Street, Windsor, Berkshire, SL4 1PR** P
☎ 01753 830100
Ⓔ b.antiques@btconnect.com
Ⓦ www.jewels2go.co.uk
Est. 1981
Services Antique dolls' hospital
Open Mon–Sat 10.30am–5.30pm Sun by appointment

Haddon Rocking Horses
Contact Paul Stollery
✉ **5 Telford Road, Clacton-on-Sea, Essex, CO15 4LP** P
☎ 01255 424745 Ⓕ 01255 475505
Ⓔ millers@haddonrockinghorses.co.uk
Ⓦ www.haddonrockinghorses.co.uk
Est. 1971
Services Restorers and manufacturers of rocking horses
Open Mon–Thurs 8am–5pm Fri 8am–1pm

Recollect The Dolls Hospital
Contact Paul Jago
✉ **17 Junction Road, Burgess Hill, West Sussex, RH15 0HR** P
Ⓔ dollshopuk@aol.com
Est. 1973
Services Complete restoration service for all dolls
Open Tues–Fri 10am–4pm Sat 10am–1pm or by appointment

Stevenson Brothers (British Toymakers Guild)
Contact Mark Stevenson or Sue Russell
✉ **The Workshop, Ashford Road, Bethersden, Ashford, Kent, TN26 3AP** P
☎ 01233 820363 Ⓕ 01233 820580
Ⓔ sale@stevensonbros.com
Ⓦ www.stevensonbros.com
Est. 1982
Services Restoration of rocking horses and children's pedal cars
Open Mon–Fri 9am–6pm Sat 10am–1pm

The Toy Works
Contact Paul Commander
✉ **Holly House, Askham, Penrith, Cumbria, CA10 2PG** P
☎ 01931 712077 Ⓕ 01931 712077
Ⓔ info@thetoyworks.co.uk
Ⓦ www.thetoyworks.co.uk
Est. 1985
Services Restoration of old toys, dolls houses, rocking horses, teddy bears
Open Wed–Sat 9am–5pm Sun 11am–4pm

TUITION

AntiquesBreaks.co.uk
Contact Mrs P A Johnson
✉ **PO Box 18, Lydney, Gloucestershire, GL15 4YJ**
☎ 01594 564001 Ⓕ 01594 564001
Ⓜ 07768 922222
Ⓔ info@antiquesbreaks.co.uk
Ⓦ www.antiquesbreaks.co.uk
Services Organizes antiques lectures and holidays in the UK and abroad including Edinburgh (February), London Olympia (June), Cambridge (August) and USA (October)

Richard Bolton (BAFRA)
Contact Richard Bolton
✉ **The Old Brewery, Mangerton Mill, Mangerton, Bridport, Dorset, DT6 3SG** P
☎ 01308 485000
Est. 1981
Services Tuition in antique furniture restoration
Open Mon–Fri 9am–5pm

Buckinghamshire Chilterns University College
Contact Rowena Robertson
✉ **Queen Alexandra Road, High Wycombe, Buckinghamshire, HP11 2JZ** P
☎ 01494 522141 Ⓕ 01494 461196
Ⓔ desenq@bcuc.ac.uk/design
Ⓦ www.bcuc.ac.uk
Est. 1993

Services Courses include furniture conservation and restoration
Open Mon–Fri 9am–5.30pm

The Chippendale International School of Furniture (SSCR)
Contact Mr Anselm Fraser
✉ **Myreside, Gifford, Haddington, East Lothian, EH41 4JA** 🅿
☎ 01620 810680 Ⓕ 01620 810701
Ⓔ info@chippendale.co.uk
Ⓦ www.chippendale.co.uk
Est. 1982
Services International school of furniture, professional training of people to design, make and restore furniture
Open Mon–Fri 7.30am–5pm

Davenports Antiques
Contact Mr C Height
✉ **Unit 5, Woodgate Centre, Oak Tree Lane, Woodgate, Chichester, West Sussex, PO20 6GU** 🅿
☎ 01243 545037
Ⓜ 07932 690210
Ⓔ chris@polishedact.org.uk
Ⓦ www.polishedact.org.uk
Est. 1980
Services Online furniture restoration course
Open Mon–Fri 8.30am–6pm

Glebe Hall Restoration Studios
Contact Camel Corrigan-Griffin
✉ **Old Killernogh Rectory, Rathnakelly Glebe, Ballacolla, Co Laois, Ireland** 🅿
☎ 0502 34105 Ⓕ 0502 34105
Ⓜ 0868 784956
Est. 1980
Services Courses and workshops held on care and conservation of fine and decorative arts and antiquities. Saturday morning clinics by appointment
Open By appointment
Sat 11am–4pm

Gow Antiques and Restoration (BAFRA)
Contact Jeremy Gow
✉ **Pitscandly Farm, Forfar, Angus, DD8 3NZ** 🅿
☎ 01307 465342 Ⓕ 01307 468973
Ⓜ 07711 416786
Ⓔ jeremy@gowantiques.co.uk
Ⓦ www.knowyourantiques.com
Est. 1991
Services Three-day Antique Furniture Recognition Courses. For dates and further information please telephone
Open Mon–Fri 9am–5pm
or by appointment

Roger Hawkins Restoration
Contact R Hawkins
✉ **Unit 4, The Old Dairy, Winkburn, Newark, Nottinghamshire, NG22 8PQ**
☎ 01636 636666
Est. 1980
Services Restoration of all types of pottery, porcelain. Tuition given
Open Mon–Fri 9am–5pm

Leather Conservation Centre (UKIC, SSCR)
Contact Roy Thomson
✉ **University College Campus, Boughton Green Road, Moulton Park, Northampton, Northamptonshire, NN2 7AN** 🅿
☎ 01604 719766 Ⓕ 01604 719649
Ⓔ lcc@northampton.ac.uk
Est. 1978
Services Conservation and restoration of leather objects, research, training and information for leather and leather conservation
Open Mon–Fri 9am–5pm

John Lloyd (BAFRA)
✉ **Bankside Farm, Jacobs Post, Ditchling Common, West Sussex, RH15 0SJ** 🅿
☎ 01444 480388 Ⓕ 01444 480388
Ⓜ 07941 124772
Ⓔ info@lloydjohnfinefurniture.co.uk
Ⓦ www.johnlloydfinefurniture.co.uk
Est. 1989
Services Complete repair and restoration of period, reproduction and modern furniture, short courses on care and repair of antiques and gilding
Open Mon–Fri 8.30am–5.30pm

Mullaghmore House Enterprises
Contact Mr Louis Kelly
✉ **Mullaghmore House, Old Mountfield Road, Omagh, Co Tyrone, BT79 7EX** 🅿
☎ 028 8224 2314 Ⓕ 028 8225 0262
Ⓔ sales@kellyantiques.com
Ⓦ www.kellyantiques.com
Est. 1936
Services International college offering residential courses on restoration techniques
Open Mon–Fri 10am–7pm
Sat 10am–5pm

Simmons & Miles
Contact Stephen Simmons or Helen Miles
✉ **Le Gué Besnard, 61140 Juvigny-sous-Andaine, Orne, France** 🅿
☎ 00 33 2 33 38 40 48
Ⓔ france@simmondsandmiles.co.uk
Ⓦ www.simmonsandmiles.co.uk
Est. 1988
Services One-to-one tuition in antique furniture restoration
Open By appointment

Helen Warren China Restoration
Contact Helen Warren
✉ **Unit 9, Slanley Place Farm, Headcorn Road, Staplehurst, Kent, TN12 0DT** 🅿
☎ 01580 895100
Ⓔ conservation@ifwarren.demon.co.uk
Ⓦ www.ifwarren.demon.co.uk
Est. 1990
Services Restoration courses
Open By appointment

West Dean College
Contact Sheila Walker
✉ **West Dean, Chichester, West Sussex, PO18 0TZ**
☎ 01243 818219 Ⓕ 01243 811343
Ⓔ diplomas@westdean.org.uk
Ⓦ www.westdean.org.uk
Services Courses on the conservation and restoration of books, furniture, fine metalwork, ceramics, buildings, interiors and sites
Open By appointment

The Wiston Project School
Contact Mr N Wears
✉ **The Old School, Wiston, Haverfordwest, Pembrokeshire, SA62 4PS** 🅿
☎ 01437 731579
Est. 1988
Services School of furniture making
Open By appointment

Peter Young Auctioneers
Contact Mr P Young
✉ **Barnby Memorial Hall, Blyth, Worksop, Nottinghamshire, DN10 4RQ** Ⓟ
☎ 01777 816609
Ⓜ 07801 079818
Ⓔ beaconhillside@btopenworld.com
Ⓦ www.peteryoungauctioneers.co.uk
Est. 1961
Services Regular timetable of antiques lectures for local further education groups, plus antiques visits, excursions and holidays
Open Mon–Fri 9.30am–5.30pm

UPHOLSTERY

SOUTH EAST

Kevin Birch (BAFRA)
Contact Kevin Birch
✉ **Unit 2, Service House, 61–63 Rochester Road, Aylesford, Kent, ME20 7BS** Ⓟ
☎ 01622 790080 Ⓕ 01622 790080
Ⓜ 07960 721640
Ⓔ kevin@kbirch.fsbusiness.co.uk
Ⓦ www.kevinbirch.co.uk
Est. 1993
Services Furniture restoration, French polishing and upholstery
Open Mon–Fri 8.30am–5pm

The Chair Repair Workshop
Contact Keith Woodcock or Cecilia Hall
✉ **The Corner Shop, 1–3 North Street, New Romney, Kent, TN28 8DW** Ⓟ
☎ 01797 364374 Ⓕ 01797 364374
Est. 2002
Services Upholstery
Open Mon–Fri 8.30am–5pm Sat 9am–1pm

Deal Upholstery Services
Contact Mr P E Cavanagh
✉ **116 Downs Road, Walmer, Deal, Kent, G14 7TF** Ⓟ
☎ 01304 372297
Est. 1988
Services Antique and modern upholstery, loose covers
Open Mon–Fri 9am–5pm

Norris of Blackheath
Contact Paul Norris
✉ **Dimpleshaven, Pett Road, Pett, East Sussex, TN35 4HE** Ⓟ
☎ 01424 812129
Services Upholstery, free estimates, pick-up and delivery
Open Mon–Fri 8am–6pm

T J Upholstery
Contact Mr Tim Jenner
✉ **Unit One, Hill House Farm, High Street, Wadhurst, East Sussex, TN5 6AA** Ⓟ
☎ 01892 784417
Ⓜ 07867 672707
Est. 1979
Services Traditional upholstery
Open By appointment

The Upholsterers Workshop (Guild of Traditional Upholsterers, Association of Master Upholsterers)
Contact Mr Rodney Henham
✉ **Church Farm Studio, Penhurst, Battle, East Sussex, TN33 9QP** Ⓟ
☎ 01424 893277 Ⓕ 01424 893277
Est. 1996
Services Traditional upholsterers
Open Mon–Fri 8am–4.30pm Sat 8am–1pm or by appointment

LONDON

Ellington Place Workshop
Contact B J Orton
✉ **Ellington Place, 10 Ellington Road, Muswell Hill, London, N10 3DG** Ⓟ
☎ 020 8444 6218
Est. 1947
Services Furniture restoration, upholstery
Open Mon–Fri 10am–6pm Sat by appointment

Kantuta
Contact Mrs N Wright
✉ **1d Gleneagle Road, London, SW16 6AX** Ⓟ
☎ 020 8677 6701
Est. 1986
Services Upholstery and furniture and restoration
Open Mon–Sat 10am–6pm

SOUTH

A and R Upholstery
Contact Matthew Smith
✉ **78 Robin Hood Way, Winnersh, Wokingham, Berkshire, RG41 5JM** Ⓟ
☎ 01491 642167
Est. 1990
Services Upholstery, custom-made headboards
Open Mon–Fri 9am–5pm

Dee Cee Upholstery (AMU)
Contact Mr D A Caplen
✉ **502 Portswood Road, Portswood, Southampton, Hampshire, SO17 3SP** Ⓟ
☎ 023 8055 5888 Ⓕ 023 8067 6761
Ⓔ enquiries@deeceeupholstery.co.uk
Ⓦ www.deeceeupholstery.co.uk
Est. 1978
Services Traditional upholstery specialist, all upholstery and DIY supplies
Open Mon–Thurs 8am–5.30pm Fri 8am–5pm Sat 9am–1pm or by appointment

Hartley Upholstery and Antique Restorations
Contact Paul Bligh
✉ **Unit 2, Priors Farm, Reading Road, Mattingley, Hook, Hampshire, RG27 8JU** Ⓟ
☎ 0118 932 6567 Ⓕ 0118 932 6567
Est. 1984
Services Upholstery, French polishing and cabinet work. Commissions undertaken
Open Mon–Sat 9am–5pm or by appointment

Hythe Furnishings
Contact Mr G Batchelor
✉ **Hythe, Southampton, Hampshire, SO45 3NB** Ⓟ
☎ 02380 845727
Est. 1997
Services Upholstery and reconditioning of furniture
Open Mon–Fri 9am–5.30pm Sat 9am–4pm closed Wed

King & Eastland Upholsterers
Contact Kevin Eastland
✉ **60 Queen Street, Horsham, West Sussex, RH13 5AD** Ⓟ
☎ 01403 275149 Ⓕ 01403 275149
Ⓦ www.kingandeastland.com
Est. 1992
Services Traditional upholstery
Open Mon–Fri 8am–5pm Sat 8am–noon

A H Smith & Son
Contact Mr M Smith
✉ **3, 6–7 The Parade, Old Lodge Lane, Purley, Surrey, CR8 4DG** Ⓟ
☎ 020 8660 1211
Est. 1949
Services Upholstery, French polishing, antique repair
Open Mon–Fri 9am–5pm
Sat 9am–1pm

Suite Dreams Upholstery
Contact Len Double
✉ **Larkwhistle Cottage, Christmas Hill, Sutton Scotney, Winchester, Hampshire, SO21 3ET** Ⓟ
☎ 01962 885630 Ⓕ 01962 885630
Ⓜ 07860 843691
Est. 1991
Services Traditional, modern upholstery, loose covers a speciality
Open Mon–Sat 9am–6pm

WEST COUNTRY

Rocco d'Ambrosio
Contact Mrs R Crees
✉ **94 Benedict Street, Glastonbury, Somerset, BA6 9EZ** Ⓟ
☎ 01458 831541
Est. 1969
Services Upholstery restoration, French polishing, dealer, furniture restoration
Open Mon–Fri 9am–6pm
or by appointment

Daniel Fox Upholstery
Contact Mr D Fox
✉ **Goulds Farm, Nethercott, Braunton, Devon, EX33 1HT** Ⓟ
☎ 01271 815998
Est. 1994
Services Upholstery
Open Mon–Fri 9am–5pm

Russell Hudson Upholsterer
Contact Mr R Hudson
✉ **Unit 2e, Riverside Business Park, Riverside Road, Bath, Somerset, BA2 3DW** Ⓟ
☎ 01225 400003
Ⓔ russell.hudson@virgin.net
Est. 1985
Services Antique upholstery
Open Mon–Fri 8.30am–5.30pm

M J R Upholstery
Contact Mr M J Rowbrey
✉ **Unit 7, Cornishway South, Galmington Trading Estate, Taunton, Somerset, TA1 5NQ** Ⓟ
☎ 01823 338793
Est. 1988
Services Upholstery
Open Mon–Fri 9am–5pm

Wincanton Antiques
Contact Tony or Clare
✉ **London House, 12 High Street, Wincanton, Somerset, BA9 9JL** Ⓟ
☎ 01963 32223
Est. 1997
Services Upholstery
Open Mon–Sat 9.30am–5pm

EAST

Decorcraft Upholsterers (AU)
Contact Mr A Wise
✉ **Sand Acre, Elmham Drive, Nacton, Ipswich, Suffolk, IP10 0DG** Ⓟ
☎ 01473 659396 Ⓕ 01473 659396
Est. 1975
Services Upholstery
Open Mon–Sat 9am–6pm

Ludovic Potts Restorations (BAFRA)
Contact Mr Ludovic Potts
✉ **Unit 1–1a, Station Road, Haddenham, Ely, Cambridgeshire, CB6 3XD** Ⓟ
☎ 01353 741537 Ⓕ 01353 741822
Ⓜ 07889 341671
Ⓔ mail@restorers.co.uk
Ⓦ www.restorers.co.uk
Est. 1986
Services Modern and antique furniture restoration
Open By appointment

Robert's Antiques
Contact Graham Bettany
✉ **The Barn, South Street, Risby, Bury St Edmunds, Suffolk, IP28 6QU** Ⓟ
☎ 01284 811440 Ⓕ 01284 811440
Ⓔ info@robertsantiques.co.uk
Ⓦ www.robertsantiques.co.uk
Est. 1978
Services Restoration of upholstery, French polishing
Open Tues–Fri 8.30am–5pm
Sat–Sun noon–4pm

HEART OF ENGLAND

Camden Re-Upholstery
Contact John Camden
✉ **Askett Works, 51 High Street, Princes Risborough, Buckinghamshire, HP27 0AE** Ⓟ
☎ 01844 344877
Est. 1968
Services Upholstery and upholstery restoration
Open By appointment

Churchill Upholstery
Contact David Matthews
✉ **Unit 1, Mount Farm, Junction Road, Churchill, Chipping Norton, Oxfordshire, OX7 6NP** Ⓟ
☎ 01608 658139 Ⓕ 01608 658139
Ⓜ 07957 355114
Est. 1986
Services Antique upholstery and soft furnishings
Open Mon–Fri 8am–5.30pm

Cottage Upholstery (Guild of Traditional Uphoslterers)
Contact Gregory Cupitt-Jones
✉ **Unit 6, Manor Farm, Nettlebed, Henley-on-Thames, Oxfordshire, RG9 5DA** Ⓟ
☎ 01491 642167
Ⓜ 07885 813558
Ⓔ workshop@cottageupholstery.co.uk
Ⓦ www.cottageupholstery.co.uk
Est. 1994
Services Upholstery of antique and period furniture
Open Mon–Sat 8.30am–5.30pm

Andrew & Philip Leach
Contact Andrew or Philip Leach
✉ **The Railway Station, Worcester Road, Leominster, Herefordshire, HR6 8AR** Ⓟ
☎ 01568 616404
Est. 1982
Services Upholstery, loose covers
Open Mon–Fri 8.30am–5.30pm

MIDLANDS

Abbey Restorations
Contact Allan Standing
✉ **Darley Abbey Mills, Darley Abbey, Derbyshire, DE22 1DZ** Ⓟ
☎ 01332 344547
Est. 1974

Services Restoration of furniture, upholstery
Open Mon–Fri 8.30am–5.30pm
Sat 8.30am–noon

K Davenport
Contact Mr M Davenport
✉ **The Queens Yard, Madac Place, Beatrice Street, Oswestry, Shropshire, SY11 1QJ** P
☎ 01691 652293 F 01691 652293
M 07885 817026
E kdavenportinteriors@theinternetpages.co.uk
W www.kdavenportinteriors.co.uk
Est. 1965
Services Upholstery and restoration of antique furniture
Open Mon–Fri 8.30am–5pm

Heath Upholstery
Contact Mr A Heath
✉ **Marychurch Road, Bucknall, Stoke-on-Trent, Staffordshire, ST2 9BJ** P
☎ 01782 268802 F 01782 268802
M 07974 929221
E a.heath@fsbdial.co.uk
Est. 1973
Services Antique upholstery and contract work
Open Mon–Fri 8.30am–6pm or by appointment

Imperial Upholstery
Contact Mr N Scattergood
✉ **Ferry Street, Stapenhill, Burton-on-Trent, Staffordshire, DE15 9EU** P
☎ 01283 521117
W www.imperialupholstery.co.uk
Est. 1993
Services Upholstery, antique restoration, French polishing
Open Mon–Sat 9am–6pm

John Reed and Son Upholsterers (AMU)
Contact Mr J Reed
✉ **141 Regent Street, Kettering, Northamptonshire, NN16 8QH** P
☎ 01536 510584 F 01536 510584
E johnreed.andson@lineone.net
W www.johnreedandsons.com
Est. 1973
Services Repair, restoration, upholstery, French and spray polishing
Open Mon–Fri 8am–5.30pm

P Woodcock & Co
Contact Mr Paul Day
✉ **56a Salop Road, Oswestry, Shropshire, SY11 2RQ** P
☎ 01691 653317 or 0800 524 0008
F 01691 679724
Est. 1954
Services Upholstery and restoration of antique furniture
Open Mon–Fri 7.15am–5pm
Sat 9am–4pm

YORKSHIRE & LINCOLNSHIRE

Paul Rawcliffe Upholstery Services
Contact Mr P Rawciffe
✉ **Unit 10, New Enterprise Centre, Humber Bank South, South Quay, Grimsby, Lincolnshire, DN31 3SD** P
☎ 01472 251732
M 07714 436710
Est. 1989
Services Repair, restoration of antique furniture, French polishing
Open Mon–Fri 8am–5pm

NORTH WEST

E Callister
Contact Mr E Callister
✉ **24 Lark Lane, Liverpool, Merseyside, L17 8US** P
☎ 0151 727 5679
Est. 1964
Services Upholstery, French polishing
Open Mon–Fri 9am–5pm
Sat 9am–noon

J E Hatcher & Son
Contact Mr C Hatcher
✉ **121a Victoria Road West, Cleveleys, Thornton Cleveleys, Lancashire, FY5 3LA** P
☎ 01253 853162
Est. 1946
Services Traditional upholstery
Open Mon–Fri 8.30am–5.30pm
Sat 8.30am–11am

WALES

Cliff Amey & Son (AMU)
Contact Cliff Amey
✉ **12 Clive Road, Canton, Cardiff, South Glamorgan, CF5 1HJ** P
☎ 02920 233462 F 02920 233462
E dennis.amey@talk21.com
Est. 1951
Services Upholstery
Open Mon–Fri 8am–5pm

Mach Upholstery
Contact Oliver Hubbard
✉ **No 1 Londonderry Terrace, Machynlleth, Powys, SY20 8BG**
☎ 01654 703568 F 01654 703840
Services Upholstery supplies

S M Upholstery Ltd
Contact P Morgan
✉ **212a Whitchurch Road, Cardiff, South Glamorgan, CF14 3NB** P
☎ 029 2061 7579 F 029 2061 7579
E sales@smfoam.co.uk
W www.smfoam.co.uk
Est. 1974
Services Traditional upholstery
Open Mon–Fri 9.30am–1pm 2–5pm Sat 9.30am–1pm

SCOTLAND

Just Chairs
Contact Mr R Kerr
✉ **18/2 Sunnyside Lane, Just off Easter Road, Edinburgh, EH7 5RA** P
☎ 0131 652 0320
Est. 1984
Services Traditional upholstery, antique chairs (restored) bought and sold
Open Mon–Fri 8am–5pm

Sherman Upholstery
Contact Jim Sherman
✉ **Blairdaff Street, Buckie, Morayshire, AB56 1PT** P
☎ 01542 834680 F 01542 834680
M 07703 881903
E linda@sherman73.freeserve.co.uk
Est. 1956
Services Antique repair, restoration, upholstery
Open Mon–Fri 8.30am–4.30pm
Sat 8.30am–noon

W M Stark
Contact William Stark
✉ **88 Peddie Street, Dundee, Tayside, DD1 5LT** P
☎ 01382 660040
Est. 1977
Services Upholstery, re-covering
Open Mon–Fri 8am–4.30pm

REPUBLIC OF IRELAND

Sean Carpenter
Contact Sean Carpenter
✉ **65–66 Francis Street, Dublin 8, Co Dublin, Ireland** 🅿
☎ 01 454 1806
Est. 1963
Services French polishing, upholstery
Open Mon–Fri 7am–3.30pm

The Complete Upholstery Centre
Contact Kevin Meldrum
✉ **Step Lane, Barrack Street, Cork, Co Cork, Ireland** 🅿
☎ 021 496 3186 Ⓕ 021 496 3186
Est. 1976
Services Antique upholstery service
Open Mon–Fri 9am–1pm 2–5.30pm

Sealey Furnishings
Contact Ron
✉ **MG Business Park, Galway Road, Tuam, Co Galway, Ireland** 🅿
☎ 09 328661 Ⓕ 09 328661
Ⓔ sealey@eircom.net
Ⓦ www.sealeyfurnishings.com
Est. 1975
Services Furniture restoration, upholstery
Open Mon–Sat 10am–5.30pm

VACATIONS

AntiquesBreaks.co.uk
Contact Mrs P A Johnson
✉ **PO Box 18, Lydney, Gloucestershire, GL15 4YJ**
☎ 01594 564001 Ⓕ 01594 564001
Ⓜ 07768 922222
Ⓔ info@antiquesbreaks.co.uk
Ⓦ www.antiquesbreaks.co.uk
Services Organizes antiques lectures and holidays in the UK and abroad including Edinburgh (February), London Olympia (June), Cambridge (August) and USA (October)

VALUERS

Alpine Antiques
Contact Mr Carney
✉ **15 Sharples Avenue, Astley Bridge, Bolton, Greater Manchester, BL1 7HB** 🅿
☎ 01204 303364
Services Valuation of antiques
Open By appointment

David Ford & Associates (LAPADA)
Contact David Ford
✉ **Christmas Pie Popse, Green Lane East, Wanborough, Guildford, Surrey, GU32 2JL**
☎ 01483 810230 Ⓕ 01483 810230
Ⓜ 07770 687553
Ⓔ davidnford@hotmail.com
Est. 1965
Services Valuation of antiques and fine art
Open By appointment

IDS Valuation Consultants (BWCG)
Contact Iain Sutherland
✉ **79 Templehill, Troon, Ayrshire, KA10 6BQ** 🅿
☎ 01292 315999
Est. 1995
Services Valuations and full consultation service
Open Mon–Sat 9.30am–5.30pm or by appointment

Lennox Auctions and Valuers
Contact Mr A Lennox
✉ **The Basement, 41b Ellis Street, Carrickfergus, Co Antrim, BT38 8AY** 🅿
☎ 028 9335 1522 or 028 9337 8527 (pm) Ⓕ 028 9335 1522
Est. 1987
Services Valuations on porcelain and glass
Open Mon–Fri 9.30am–5pm

Lovers of Blue and White
Contact Andrew Pye
✉ **Steeple Morden, Royston, Hertfordshire, SG8 0RN** 🅿
☎ 01763 853800 Ⓕ 01763 853700
Ⓔ china@blueandwhite.com
Ⓦ www.blueandwhite.com
Est. 1995
Services Valuation and identification of British transfer ware, 1780–present day
Open By appointment

Nicholas Somers & Company Chartered Arts and Antiques Surveyor
Contact Nicholas Somers, FRICS, FRSA, FIAVI
✉ **45B Lurline Gardens, Battersea, London, SW11 4DD** 🅿
☎ 020 7627 1248 Ⓕ 020 7622 9587
Ⓜ 07836 698889
Est. 1990
Services Insurance valuations and sales advice for antiques, fine art and chattels. Expert witness work. Offices in Bath
Open By appointment

Sotheby's (International Auctioneers)
Contact William Montgomery
✉ **The Estate Office, Grey Abbey, Newtownards, Co Down, BT22 2QA** 🅿
☎ 028 4278 8668 Ⓕ 028 4278 8652
Ⓔ william.montgomery@sothebys.com
Ⓦ www.sothebys.com
Est. 1979
Services Sotheby's Northern Ireland office provides free valuations of antiques for sale by auction. Insurance valuations can be arranged, and advice given on buying, selling and restoration. Free transport of goods for auction is provided to Sotheby's in England
Open By appointment only

Weller King
Contact Alastair Dixon
✉ **36 High Street, Steyning, West Sussex, BN44 3YE** 🅿
☎ 01903 816633 Ⓕ 01903 816644
Ⓜ 07796 174381
Ⓔ enquiries@wellerking.com
Ⓦ www.wellerking.com
Est. 1993
Services Insurance, probate and market valuations, expert witness work
Open Mon–Fri 9am–5.30pm

WEB DESIGN

Sellingantiques.co.uk
Contact David Wilshaw
✉ **PO Box 350, Chichester, West Sussex, PO20 2XN**
☎ 0870 922 0488
Ⓔ contact@sellingantiques.co.uk
Ⓦ www.sellingantiques.co.uk
Est. 2002
Services Professional websites

designed specially for antique dealers
Open Mon–Fri 9am–5.30pm

WOOD & WOOD CARVING

2 K Carving (CGLI)
Contact Saena Ku
✉ **42 Sekforde Street, Finsbury, London, EC1R 0AH** P
☎ 020 7251 0592 F 020 7251 0592
M 07788 143219
Est. 2000
Services Antique restoration, wood carving, gilding and wood conservation
Trade only Yes
Open By appointment

J D P Restorations
Contact Mr Payne
✉ **6 Denbigh Close, Tonteg, Pontypridd, Mid Glamorgan, CF38 1HB** P
☎ 01443 204170
Est. 1980
Services Antique wood restoration
Open Mon–Fri 9am–6pm

Rod Naylor
Contact Angela Naylor
✉ **208 Devizes Road, Hilperton, Trowbridge, Wiltshire, BA14 7QP** P
☎ 01225 754497 F 01225 754497
E rod.naylor@virgin.net
W www.rodnaylor.com
Est. 1970
Services Restoration of antique wood carvings, supplies replicas of hard-to-find items and materials for caddies, boxes, desks, cabinet-making, supplier of power carving machinery and tools
Open By appointment only

WRITING

Classic Pen Engineering (Writing Equipment Society)
Contact Mr D Purser
✉ **Auchenfranco Farm, Lochfoot, Dumfries, Dumfries & Galloway, DG2 8NZ** P
☎ 01387 730208 F 01387 730208
M 07703 690843
E cpe@auchenfranco.freeserve.co.uk
W www.auchenfranco.freeserve.co.uk
Est. 1994
Services Complete refurbishment of writing instruments. Sales and valuations of fountain pens, dip pens and pencils
Open By appointment

Fairs

The Fairs section is divided into two parts. The first part gives an alphabetical list of fair organizers, while the second lists in date order antiques fairs that will take place in the UK and Ireland throughout 2005. Every effort has been made to ensure that this information is correct at the time of going to press. However it is highly recommended that you telephone to confirm the details are still as stated. You may also discover that the event organizer has several additional events, which could not be included at the time of going to press. If you would like your fair(s) to be included in next year's directory, please inform us by October 1st 2005. (FWC = Free with Card).

FAIRS: ORGANIZERS
CONTACT DETAILS

Abbey Fairs
Contact Nick Cox
✉ **PO Box 7482, Nottingham, NG16 2ZQ**
☎ 01773 770422
Ⓔ abbeyfairs@yahoo.co.uk
Ⓦ www.artdeco-fairs-warwick.com
Fairs Art Deco Fairs in Warwick, Twickenham, Battersea, Southampton and Kelam Hall, Newark

Adams Antiques Fairs
Contact Matthew Adams
☎ 020 7254 4054
Ⓦ www.adams-antiques-fairs.co.uk
Fairs Chelsea Brocante and Frock Me! at Chelsea Town Hall. Adams Antiques Fairs at the Royal Horticultural Hall, London and Newbury Showground

Albany Fairs
Contact Robert Davison
☎ 0191 584 2934
Ⓜ 07976 619009
Ⓔ enquiries@albanyfairs.com
Ⓦ www.albanyfairs.com
Fairs Albany Fairs at Pooley Bridge and Howtown, Cumbria, Moffatt, Dumfriesshire and St Andrews, Fife

The Antiquarian Booksellers Association
✉ **Sackville House, 40 Piccadilly, London, W1J 0DR**
☎ 020 7439 3118 Ⓕ 020 7439 3119
Ⓔ info@aba.org.uk
Ⓦ www.aba.org.uk
Fairs The Antiquarian Book Fair (London) and the Chelsea and Edinburgh Book Fairs

Antique Arms Fairs Ltd
Contact Margaret
✉ **PO Box 355, Hereford, Herefordshire, HR1 9XE** Ⓟ
☎ 01432 355416 Ⓕ 01432 371767
Ⓔ info@antiquearmsfairsltd.co.uk
Ⓦ www.antiquearmsfairsltd.co.uk
Fairs London Antiques Arms Fairs, Thistle London Hotel Heathrow

The Antique Dealers Fair Ltd
Contact Ingrid Nilson
✉ **PO Box 119, Cranbrook, Kent, TN18 5WB**
☎ 01797 252030
Fairs The LAPADA Antiques & Fine Art Fair

Antique Forum Group
Contact Carol Baskin
☎ 01782 595805 Ⓕ 01782 596133
Ⓔ info@antiqueforumgroup.com
Ⓦ www.antiqueforumgroup.com
Fairs Big Brum, Birmingham, Antiques Fair, Bristol and Uttoxeter 2-day Antiques Fair. Please phone for details. Also Antiques Market, every Tuesday, and Fleamarket, every Thursday (8am–4pm), Newcastle-under-Lyme

Antiques & Collectors World
✉ **PO Box 129, Tadworth, Surrey, KT20 5YR**
☎ 01737 812989 Ⓕ 01737 813986
Ⓜ 07802 768364
Ⓔ orchard.cottage@clara.co.uk
Fairs Antiques & Collectors Fairs, Lingfield Park and Goodwood Racecourses

Antiques Fairs Ireland
Contact Joan Murray
☎ 00353 167 08295
Ⓔ antiquesfairsireland@esatclear.ie
Ⓦ www.antiquesfairsireland.com
Fairs Antiques Fairs in Dublin. Please phone for details

Artfairs
☎ 0151 639 4920
Ⓔ artfairs@artizania.co.uk
Ⓦ www.artizania.co.uk
Fairs Antique and vintage clothing and textiles fairs across the UK

Arun Fairs
Contact Stephanie Clark
☎ 01903 734112
Ⓜ 07774 852622
Fairs Arun Antiques Fairs at Rustington, West Sussex

BABAADA
☎ 01225 851466 Ⓕ 01225 851120
Ⓔ bathdecorativefair@ukonline.co.uk
Ⓦ www.babaada.com
Fairs Bath Annual Decorative & Antiques Fair

Robert Bailey Fairs Ltd
✉ **PO Box 1110, Brentwood, Essex, CM14 4SE**
☎ 01277 214677 Ⓕ 01277 214550
Ⓔ admin@baileyfairs.co.uk
Ⓦ www.baileyfairs.co.uk
Fairs Cheshire Spring, Summer and Autumn Antiques & Fine Art Fairs, Tatton Park, Knutsford, Harrogate Pavilions Spring Antiques & Fine Art Fair, Claridge's Antiques & Fine Art Fair, London, Buxton Autumn Antiques & Fine Art Fair and Hertfordshire Antiques & Fine Art Fair, Hatfield

The Battersea Pen Home
Contact Simon Gray or Sean Lovell
✉ **PO Box 6128, Epping, CM16 4GG**
☎ 0870 900 1888
Ⓔ info@penhome.co.uk
Fairs The London Pen Show

Beckett Antiques Fairs
Contact Alan Mycock
☎ 0114 289 0656
Fairs Beckett Antiques Fairs at Doncaster and York Racecourses

Bentley Grice Promotions
☎ 01424 845174
Fairs Antiques and Collectors Fairs in Hastings, East Sussex

Best of Fairs
Contact Tom Burt
✉ **Churchgate Barn, Churchgate, Glomsford, Sudbury, Suffolk, CO10 7QE**
☎ 01787 280306
Fairs The Best of Fairs, Copdock, near Ipswich and Long Melford

Biggleswade Antiques Fairs
Contact Mary and Philip Hall
✉ **Field View, Poplar Close, Roxton, Bedfordshire**
☎ 01234 871449 Ⓕ 01234 871449
Ⓜ 07778 789917
Fairs Biggleswade Antiques Fairs at Biggleswade and Kempton, Bedfordshire, Kimbolton, Cambridgeshire and Huntingdon

Blooms A1 Events
Contact A Dowson
☎ 01430 860070
Ⓔ ann@bloomsa1events.fsnet.co.uk
Fairs Antique & Collectors Fairs at The Racecourse, Beverley, East Riding of Yorkshire

Lynne & Richard Bonehill
Contact Richard and Lynne Bonehill
✉ **The Bosuns Nest, Carthew Way, St Ives, Cornwall, TR26 1RJ**
☎ 01736 793213
Ⓔ richard@bonehill3.freeserve.co.uk
Ⓦ www.bonehill3.freeserve.co.uk
Fairs Lostwithiel Antiques & Bygones Fairs

Bowman Antiques Fairs Ltd
Contact Helen Bowman or Ben Wray
✉ **PO Box 64, Shipley, West Yorkshire, BD17 7YA**
☎ 07071 284333 Ⓕ 07071 284334
Ⓜ 07889 828288
Ⓔ info@antiquesfairs.com
Ⓦ www.antiquesfairs.com
Fairs Stafford Bingley Hall Giant 3-Day Antiques Fairs

Boxford Books & Fairs
Contact Ken McLeod
✉ **3 Firs Farm Cottage, Boxford, Colchester, Suffolk, CO10 5NU** Ⓟ
☎ 01787 210810 Ⓕ 01473 823187
Est. 1981
Fairs Suffolk Books Market, Long Melford

British Antique Dealers Association
☎ 020 7589 6108
Fairs The BADA Antiques and Fine Art Fair, London

British Numismatic Trade Association Ltd
Contact General Secretary
✉ **PO Box 2, Rye, East Sussex, TN31 7WE**
☎ 01797 229988 Ⓕ 01797 229988
Ⓔ bnta@lineone.net
Ⓦ www.bnta.net
Est. 1978
Fairs Coinex, London

Margaret Browne Fairs
☎ 0208 874 3622
Fairs Quality Antiques Fairs in Dorking, Surrey

Brunel Clock & Watch Fair
Contact Carol Barnes
✉ **PO Box 273, Uxbridge, Middlesex, UB9 4LP**
☎ 01895 834694 Ⓕ 01895 832904
Fairs Brunel Clock & Watch Fairs, Brunel University, Uxbridge (please phone for details) and Midland Clock & Watch Fairs

Buxton Book Fair
Contact Mrs S Laithwaite
☎ 01625 425352
Fairs Buxton Book Fairs

Mark Carter Militaria & Medal Fairs
Contact Mark Carter
✉ **PO Box 420, Slough, SL3 6RR**
☎ 01753 534777
Ⓔ markgcarter@onetel.com
Fairs Mark Carter Militaria & Medal Fairs, Bristol, Aldershot (please phone for details) and Stratford-upon-Avon

Castle Antique Fairs NI
Contact Peter Moore
✉ **6 Regency Manor, Newtownards, Co Down, BT23 8ZD**
☎ 028 9181 5710 Ⓕ 028 9181 5710
Ⓜ 07989 501666
Ⓔ info@castleantiques.co.uk
Ⓦ www.castleantiques.couk
Fairs Annual St Patrick's Day Antiques & Collectors Fair, Templepatrick, Annual Easter Antique & Fine Art Fair, Coleraine, Annual Charity Antique & Collectors Fairs and August Antique and Fine Art Fair, Newtownards, Northern Ireland

Clarion Events Ltd
Contact Jessica Curtis or Natasha Cubitt
✉ **Earls Court Exhibition Centre, London, SW5 9TA**
☎ 0870 126 1726
Ⓔ info@eco.co.uk
Ⓦ www.halifair.com or www.olympia-antiques.com
Fairs HALI Fair – Carpets, Textiles & Tribal Art (contact Jessica Curtis or Fraser Douglas 0207 970 4600) and Spring, Summer and Winter Fine Art & Antiques Fairs (contact Natasha Cubitt)

Crispin Fairs
Contact Mrs P Wyatt
✉ **43 Tintern Crescent, Coley Park, Reading, Berkshire, RG1 6HB** Ⓟ
☎ 0118 950 2960
Est. 1981
Fairs Crispin Fairs at Wokingham, Berkshire and Hartley Wintney, Hampshire

Cross Country Fairs Ltd
Contact Mr Lionel Parker
☎ 01474 834120
Ⓜ 07860 863300
Fairs Cross Country Fairs Ltd, Effingham Park, West Sussex

Graham Davey
Contact Graham Davey
☎ 01603 758252
Ⓔ graham@v21.me.uk

Don Davidson
Contact Don Davidson
✉ **Burford Terrace, Burford Road, Chipping Norton, Oxfordshire, OX7 5EF**
☎ 01608 641870
Ⓜ 07796 671650
Fairs Chipping Norton Toy Fair

Davidson Monk Fairs
Contact Linda Monk
✉ **PO Box 201, Croydon, Surrey, CR9 7AQ** Ⓟ
☎ 020 865 64583 Ⓕ 020 865 64583
Est. 1987
Fairs Coin fairs at the Drury's Hotel, Great Russell Street, London WC1

Dennis Jewellery
Contact Dennis O'Sullivan
☎ 01202 669061
Ⓜ 07736 42431
Fairs Antique & Collectors Fairs, Poole, Dorset and Avonbridge, Wiltshire. Also Antiques Fair every Tuesday, 8am–2pm at the United Reformed Church, Poole

Devon County Antiques Fairs
✉ **The Glebe House, Bow, Devonshire, EX17 6DB**
☎ 01363 82571 Ⓕ 01363 82312
Ⓔ dcaf@antiques-fairs.com
Ⓦ www.antiques-fairs.com
Fairs Devon County Antiques Fairs at Exeter, Yeovil and Salisbury

DMG Antiques Fairs
✉ **PO Box 100, Newark, Nottinghamshire,**

FAIRS: ORGANIZERS

CONTACT DETAILS

BG24 1DJ 🅿
☎ 01636 702326 Ⓕ 01636 707923
Ⓦ www.dmgantiquefairs.com
Est. 1998
Fairs Newark International Antiques & Collectors Fair, Detling International Antiques & Collectors Fair, Shepton Mallet Antiques & Collectors Fair, Ardingly International Antiques & Collectors Fair, Ardingly Sunday Antiques & Collectors Fair, Newmarket International Antiques & Collectors Fair and Malvern International Antiques & Collectors Fair

Dolly Domain Fairs
Contact Liz and David Bonner
✉ **45 Henderson Road, Simonside, South Shields, Tyne & Wear, NE34 9QW** 🅿
☎ 0191 424 0400 Ⓕ 0771 309 1523
Ⓜ 07713 091523
Ⓔ fairs@dollydomain.com
Ⓦ www.dollydomain.com
Fairs Leeds Doll & Teddy Fair, Tyneside Dolls & Teddy Fair and Tyneside Doll's House & Miniatures Fair

Dualco Promotions
☎ 0161 283 1255 or 0161 766 2012
Fairs Antique and Collectors' Fairs in Bury, Oldham, Preston and Bolton, Lancashire and Leeds, Halifax, Barnsley and Cleckheaton, Yorkshire

Dublin Toy and Train Fair
Contact Brian Kelly or Terry McNally
✉ **24 Albert Road, Glenageary, Co Dublin, Ireland**
☎ 00 353 1 2849199/2803008
Ⓔ brian.kelly@rte.ie
Fairs Dublin Toy and Train Fair

E W Services
Contact David Smith
✉ **PO Box 56, Wellingborough, Northamptonshire, NN8 1SF**
☎ 01933 225674
Ⓔ david.smith34@ntlworld.com
Ⓦ www.ewsfairs.com
Fairs The Milton Keynes Antiques Fair, The St Albans and Southampton Art Deco Fairs

East Preston Festival Fair
☎ 01903 771161
Fairs Antique and Collectables fair in March, June and October at East Preston Village Hall, West Sussex

Bob Evans Fairs
✉ **Ashtrees, Kirby Bellars, Melton Mowbray, Leicestershire, LE14 2DU**
☎ 01664 812627 Ⓕ 01664 813727
Fairs 2-day Peterborough Festival of Antiques. Bob Evans Fairs at Coventry, Hereford, Hinckley, Kettering, Norwich and Peterborough

Fair Antiques
☎ 01548 857588
Ⓜ 07967 631518
Fairs East Berkshire Antiques Fair, near Maidenhead

Fat Cat Fairs
Contact Andy & Sheila Briggs
☎ 01865 301705
Ⓜ 07977 936882
Ⓔ andy@fatcatfairs.co.uk
Ⓦ www.fatcatfairs.co.uk
Fairs Fat Cat Fairs, Burford, Oxfordshire and Lechlade-on-Thames, Gloucestershire and Silhouette Fairs, Abingdon, Oxfordshire

Felix Fairs
Contact Mr Willmers
✉ **16 Beach Road West, Portishead, Bristol, BS20 7HR** 🅿
☎ 01275 842480
Est. 1989
Fairs Monthly antiques fairs in Bristol (please phone for details)

Fleurdelys Antiques Fairs
✉ **PO Box 2313, London, W1N 5GH**
☎ 020 7636 2327
Ⓜ 07798 600437
Ⓔ info@fleurdelysantiques.com
Ⓦ www.fleurdelysantiques.com
Fairs Antiques Fairs in Kensington. Antiques, jewellery and objets d'art

Four In One Promotions
☎ 0116 277 4396 Ⓕ 0121 360 3649
Ⓜ 07902 536636
Ⓔ fourinonepromotions@btinternet.com
Fairs Mammoth Antiques & Collectors Fairs, Castle Donington, Debyshire, Edinburgh and Kelso, Scottish Borders (please phone for details)

Freya Antiques Fairs
☎ 01508 489252
Ⓜ 07799 401067
Ⓔ freyaantiques@btinternet.com
Ⓦ www.freyaantiques.co.uk
Fairs Freya Antiques Fairs at Banham, Haddiscoe, Loddon, Worstead, Swaffham and Norwich, Norfolk and at Brandon, Suffolk (please phone for details)

Galloway Antiques Fairs
✉ **Halston Lodge, 88 Cornwall Road, Harrogate, North Yorkshire, HG1 2NG** 🅿
☎ 01423 522122 Ⓕ 01423 522122
Ⓜ 07966 528725
Ⓔ susan@gallowayfairs.co.uk
Ⓦ www.gallowayfairs.co.uk
Fairs Galloway Antiques Fairs. Please phone for details of venues and dates

Gemsco Promotions
Contact Rodney Weeks
✉ **Wheelwrights Cottage, Harrow Piece, Maulden, Bedford, Bedfordshire, MK45 2DG**
☎ 01525 402596
Ⓜ 07771 570814
Fairs Luton Antiques Fairs, Mid-Beds Antiques Fairs, Silsoe, South Bucks Antiques Fairs, Great Missenden, South Herts Antiques Fairs, Cheshunt and Northamptonshire Antiques Fairs, Towcester Racecourse

Grandma's Attic
☎ 01590 77687 Ⓕ 01590 77687
Fairs Antiques Fairs in Hampshire, Dorset and Wiltshire

Grosvenor Exhibitions Ltd
Contact George Taylor
✉ **21 High Street, Spalding, Lincolnshire, PE11 1TX**
☎ 01775 767400 Ⓕ 01775 713125
Ⓔ house@gxn.co.uk
Fairs The Great Northern International Antiques & Collectors Fair

Harlequin Fairs
Contact Colin Edwards
✉ **PO Box 9, Letchworth, Herts, SG6 3JQ**
☎ 01462 671688 Ⓕ 01462 671688
Fairs Harlequin Fairs, Chalfont St Peter and Mid Anglia Antiques Fair, Saffron Walden

Harrogate Antique & Fine Art Fair Ltd
Contact Louise Walker
✉ **Prioryfield House, 20 Canon street, Taunton, Somerset, TA1 1SW**
☎ 01823 323363 Ⓕ 01823 271072
Ⓔ info@harrogateantique.com
Ⓦ www.harrogateantiquefair.com
Fairs The Harrogate Antique & Fine Art Fair

Harvey Management Services Ltd
Contact Patricia and Ralph Harvey
☎ 020 7624 5173
Ⓔ fairs@decorativefair.com
Ⓦ www.decorativefair.com
Fairs The Decorative Antiques and Textiles Fair, Battersea Park, London

Jan Hicks
Contact Jan Hicks
✉ **1 Leverton Cottages, Chilton Foliat, Hungerford, Berkshire, RG17 0TA**
☎ 01488 683986 Ⓕ 01488 683986
Ⓜ 07770 230686
Fairs Antiques & Audacity, Losely Park, near Guildford, Surrey

Hinchingbrooke Fairs
☎ 01638 662104 Ⓕ 01638 668571
Ⓔ ken@kencharity.com
Ⓦ www.hinchingbrookefairs.co.uk
Fairs Hinchingbrooke House Antiques Fair in the ancestral home of the Cromwell family and the Earls of Sandwich, near Huntingdon

Hoyles Promotions
✉ **PO Box 40, St Annes, Lancashire, FY8 2JR**
☎ 01253 782828 Ⓕ 01253 714715
Ⓔ info@hoylespromotions.co.uk
Ⓦ www.hoylespromotions.co.uk
Est. 1975
Fairs The Antique and Collectors Fair, Southport and The Collector's Market and Boxing Day Antiques and Collector's Fair, Blackpool

Hyson Fairs Ltd
Contact Sheila Hyson
☎ 01647 231459
Fairs Antiques & Collectors' Fairs and Antiques & Fleamarkets, Exmouth, Antiques & Fleamarkets, Holsworthy, Devon and Charity Antiques & Collectors' Fairs, Chagford, Devon. Please phone for details

IMCOS
Contact Jenny Harvey
☎ 020 8789 7358
Ⓔ jeh@harvey27.demon.co.uk
Ⓦ www.imcos-mapcollecting.org
Est. 1980
Fairs IMCOS International Map Fair, Olympia, London

IPM Promotions
✉ **130/132 Brent Street, London, NW4 2DR**
☎ 020 8202 9080 or 020 8203 1500
Ⓕ 020 8203 7031
Ⓔ bloomsbury@memories postcards.co.uk
Ⓦ www.memoriespostcards.co.uk
Fairs Bloomsbury Postcard & Collectors Fairs, Royal National Hotel, London

Ipswich Antiques & Collectables Fair
Contact Vicky Roberts-Barber
☎ 01473 688201
Est. 1977
Fairs Ipswich Antiques & Collectables Fairs, Copdock, near Ipswich

J Fairs
Contact J Gibbons
✉ **23 Kestrel Crescent, Brackley, NN13 6SX**
☎ 01280 703454
Fairs Antique & Collectors Fairs, Berkhamsted

J & K Fairs
Contact K Hasnip
✉ **3 South View, Humberston, Lincolnshire**
☎ 01472 813281
Est. 1981
Fairs J & K Fairs, Lincolnshire Showground

Jaguar Fairs Ltd
✉ **PO Box 158, Derby, DE21 5ZA**
☎ 01332 631404 Ⓕ 01332 631404
Ⓦ www.jaguarfairs.com
Fairs Antiques in the Park at Kedleston Hall, Derbyshire and Sandringham Royal Estate, Norfolk. Also The Giant Wetherby Racecourse and Derby University Antiques Fairs

Janba Fairs
Contact Barry Phillips
✉ **PO Box 1, Wisbech, Cambridgeshire, PE13 4QJ**
☎ 01945 870160 or 07860 517048
Ⓕ 01945 870660
Ⓔ janba@supanet.com
Ⓦ www.janba.supanet.com
Fairs Janba Fairs, King's Lynn, Norfolk and St Ives, Cambridgeshire and Camfairs, Hertford

Jiri Books
Contact Jim or Rita Swindall
☎ 028 9082 6443
Est. 1982
Fairs Annual Belfast Book Fair

Allen Lewis Fairs
Contact Allen Lewis
✉ **64 Lower Blandford Road, Broadstone, Dorset, BH18 8NY**
☎ 01202 604306 Ⓕ 01202 604306
Ⓜ 07768 285970
Ⓔ allen.lewis@btconnect.com
Fairs The Antique Dealers Fair of Wales, Margam Park, West Glamorgan and The Portmeirion Antiques Fair, Portmeirion Village, Gwynedd

Lomax Antiques Fairs
Contact Liz Allport
☎ 01603 737631 Ⓕ 01603 737631
Ⓜ 07747 843074
Ⓔ info@lomaxantiquesfairs.co.uk
Ⓦ www.lomaxantiquesfairs.co.uk
Fairs The North Norfolk Fine Art & Antiques Fair, Burnham Market, The Langley Park Spring Antiques Fair, Loddon, Norfolk and The East Anglian Antiques Dealers Fair, Loddon, Norfolk

London Antiques Fairs
Contact Cliff Woods
19 Maswell Park Road,

Hounslow, Middlesex,
TW3 2DL
☎ 0845 890 1273
Ⓔ info@londonantiquesfairs.co.uk
Ⓦ www.ondonantiquesfairs.co.uk
Fairs Antiques Fairs in Richmond and Hampton Court, Surrey

London Art Deco Fairs
Contact Jean May
✉ **497 Peterbrook Road, Shirley, West Midlands, B90 1HZ**
☎ 0121 430 3767 Ⓕ 0121 436 7912
Ⓦ www.artdecofairs.net
Fairs Chiswick Art Deco Fairs

London Ceramics Fairs
Contact Fred Hynes
☎ 01303 258635 Ⓕ 01303 258635
Fairs London Cermaic Fairs, Lancaster Gate, London

M & S Fairs
Contact Jim Mansfield
☎ 01223 233059
Ⓜ 07960 102889
Fairs M & S Antiques & Collectors Fairs, Meldreth and Cottenham, near Cambridge (Please phone for details)

David Maggs
Contact David Maggs
✉ **Yew Tree Cottage, Whipsnade, Bedfordshire, LU6 2LG**
☎ 01582 872514
Fairs Monthly fairs at Bushey Hall School, Bushey, Hertfordshire

Magna Carta Country Fayres
Contact Diana Ives
☎ 01753 685098
Fairs Magna Carta Fayres, St Leonard's Mansion, Legoland, Windsor, Berkshire (please phone to confirm dates)

Magnum Fairs
Contact Stewart Watt
☎ 01491 681009
Fairs Magnum Antiques Fairs, Midhurst, West Sussex and Winchester

Marcel Fairs
☎ 020 8950 1844
Fairs Marcel Fairs, first Sunday of month at St Paul's Church Hall, The Ridgeway, Mill Hill, London

Midas Fairs
Contact Joy Alder
✉ **PO Box 175, Beaconsfield, Buckinghamshire, HP9 1UL**
☎ 01494 674170
Fairs Midas Fairs, Beaconsfield, Buckinghamshire

Millennium Fairs
✉ **9 Binyon Gardens, Taverham, Norwich, Norfolk, NR8 6SR**
☎ 01603 868575

Monmouthshire County Council
Contact Geoffrey Harris
✉ **Markets Office, Town Hall, Cross Street, Abergavenny, Monmouthshire, NP7 5HD**
☎ 01873 735845
Ⓔ geoffharris@monmouthshire.gov.uk
Ⓦ www.abergavennymarket.co.uk
Fairs Abergavenny Antiques & Collectors Fairs. Also Fleamarket every Wednesday 6am–4pm, Market Hall, Abergavenny

The NEC Group
Contact Fran Foster, **Birmingham, B40 1NT**
☎ 0121 767 2744 Ⓕ 0121 767 3535
Ⓦ www.antiquesforeveryone.co.uk
Fairs The National Fine Art & Antiques Fair, NEC, Birmingham, and Antiques for Everyone, Birmingham, Glasgow and London

Newcomen Fairs Ltd
Contact Graham Wilson
✉ **Elsecar Antique Centre, Elsecar Heritage Centre, Wath Road, Barnsley, South Yorkshire, S74 8HJ** Ⓟ
☎ 01226 744425 Ⓕ 01226 361561
Ⓜ 07712 834895
Ⓔ sales@elsecarantiques.co.uk
Ⓦ www.elsecarantiques.co.uk
Est. 2001
Fairs Newcomen Fairs Ltd, Barnsley, South Yorkshire

Northern Clock & Watch Fairs
☎ 01691 831162 Ⓕ 01691 839203
Ⓔ fairs@oswatch.fsnet.co.uk
Fairs Northern Clock & Watch Fairs, Haydock Park Racecourse, Merseyside. Also a fair at Newark

Louis O'Sullivan
Contact Louis O'Sullivan
☎ 00 353 1 285 9294
Fairs International Irish Antiques and Fine Art Fair, Royal Dublin Society, Dublin, Ireland

Oakleigh Leisure Ltd
Contact John Aitchison
☎ 01279 871110
Fairs Antiques and Collectables Fair Chingford, Essex

The Old Brig
Contact Ann Young
✉ **33 Great King Street, Edinburgh, EG3 6QR**
☎ 0131 556 6728 Ⓕ 0131 556 6728
Fairs The Highland Antiques Fair and The Old Brig Antique & Collectors' Fairs, The Highland Conference Centre, Nairn, Inverness

Pantheon Fairs Ltd
Contact Clare Dorrell
✉ **3a Charlotte Street, Perth, Scotland, PH1 5LW**
☎ 01738 446534 Ⓕ 01738 451388
Ⓜ 07779 297931
Ⓔ antiques@cdorrell.fsworld.com
Fairs The Fine Antiques Fairs of Scotland, Hopetoun House, South Queensferry, near Edinburgh and The Goodwood House Fine Antiques Fairs, Chichester, West Sussex

Paraphernalia Fairs
Contact Jill Robinson
☎ 01305 860012
Fairs Paraphernalia Fairs, Lyndhurst, New Forest, Hampshire (please phone for details)

Pastimes Promotions
☎ 0845 2300 140
Fairs Antiques Fairs and Collectors Markets, Kings Heath, Birmingham

Penman Antiques Fairs
Contact Caroline Penman
✉ **Widdicombe, Bedford Place, Uckfield, East Sussex, TN22 1LW**
☎ 0870 350 2442 Ⓕ 0870 350 2443
Ⓜ 07774 850044
Ⓔ info@penman-fairs.co.uk
Ⓦ www.penman-fairs.co.uk

Fairs West London Antiques & Fine Art Fair, Kensington Town Hall, The Petersfield Antiques Fairs, The Chester Antiques & Fine Art Shows, Morris to Mackintosh, Chelsea Old Town Hall, The Annual Chelsea Art Fair, The Dulwich Art Fair, The Annual Chelsea Antiques Fair, Bury St Edmunds Antiques & Fine Art Fair, The Anglian Art Fair, near Braintree, Essex

Pickwick Promotions
✉ **PO Box 67, Daventry, Northamptonshire, NN11 5EZ**
Ⓜ 07071 203068
Fairs Antiques Fairs in Warwick and Northampton

Pig & Whistle Promotions
Contact Lindy Berkman
☎ 020 8883 7061 Ⓕ 020 8245 8361
Ⓔ info@pigandwhistlepromotions.com
Ⓦ www.allypally-uk.com
Fairs Alexandra Palace Antique & Collectors Fairs, London

Pre-empt Events
Contact Anita Bott
✉ **16 Garden Road, Bromley, Kent, BR1 3LX**
☎ 020 8290 1888 Ⓕ 020 8290 1888
Ⓔ info@vintagefashionfairs.com
Fairs Battersea Vintage Fashion Fairs, Lavender Hill, London

Prospect Promotions
Contact Mrs S Mather
✉ **Primrose Cottage, Howards Lane, Eccleston, St Helens, WA10 5QD**
☎ 01744 750606 Ⓕ 01744 750606
Ⓔ sandracca@aol.com
Ⓦ www.creativecrafts-online.co.uk
Fairs Antique & Collectors Fair, Wilmslow, Cheshire

Provincial Booksellers Fairs Association
✉ **16 Melbourn Street, Royston, Hertfordshire, SG8 7BZ**
☎ 01763 248400 Ⓕ 01763 248921
Ⓔ info@pbfa.org
Ⓦ www.pbfa.org
Fairs Antiquarian book fairs throughout the UK

Scotfairs
Contact R M Torrens
✉ **PO Box 5339, Crieff, Perthshire, PH7 3YL**
☎ 01764 654555 Ⓕ 01764 654340
Fairs Scotfairs Antique and Collectors Fairs, Ayr, Edinburgh, Glasgow (please phone for dates) and Stirling

Simmons Gallery
Contact Frances Simmons
✉ **PO Box 104, Leytonstone, London, E11 1ND**
☎ 020 8989 8097
Ⓔ Lcf@simmonsgallery.co.uk
Ⓦ www.simmonsgallery.co.uk
Fairs London Coin Fair, Bloomsbury, London

Specialist Glass Fairs Ltd
Contact Patricia Hier
☎ 01260 271975
Ⓔ info@glassfairs.co.uk
Ⓦ www.glassfairs.com
Fairs The Original National Glass Collectors Fairs. Please phone for details

Arthur Swallow Fairs
Contact Mr J Ball
☎ 01298 27493/73188
Ⓜ 07860 797200
Fairs The International Antiques & Collectors Fairs at RAF Swinderby

Take Five Fairs
Contact John Slade
✉ **417a Chertsey Road, Whitton, Twickenham, Middlesex, TW2 6LS**
☎ 020 8894 0218
Ⓜ 07904 171137
Ⓦ www.antiquefairs.co.uk
Fairs Antiques & Collectables Fairs, Grand Glass Fairs and Art Nouveau/Deco Fairs, Woking, Surrey and Antiques & Collectables Fairs, Worthing, West Sussex,

Town & Country Markets
✉ **21 Market Street, Wellington, Telford, Shropshire, TF1 1DT**
☎ 01952 242019 Ⓕ 01952 245863
Ⓔ suegoodall@townandcountrymarkets.co.uk
Fairs Fleamarkets and collectors' fairs in Malvern, Worcestershire, Weston-super-Mare, Somerset and Cheltenham, Gloucestershire

Towy Antiques Fairs
Contact Robert and Carol Pugh
✉ **PO Box 24, Carmarthen, SA31 1YS**
☎ 01267 236569 Ⓕ 01267 220444
Ⓜ 027885 333845
Ⓔ towyfairs@btopenworld.com
Ⓦ www.towy-fairs.co.uk
Fairs Carmarthen and Cowbridge Antiques Fairs

Trident Exhibitions
Contact Louise Pridham
✉ **West Devon Business Park, Tavistock, Devon, PL19 9DP**
☎ 01822 614671 Ⓕ 01822 614818
Ⓔ info@trident-exhibitions.co.uk
Ⓦ www.surreyantiquesfair.co.uk
Fairs The Buxton Antiques Fair

TVADA
☎ 01865 341639
Fairs Thames Valley Antiques Fairs; spring at the Bluecoat School, Sonning-on-Thames, Reading and autumn at Radley College, Oxford (please phone for details)

Unicorn Fairs Ltd
Contact David Fletcher
✉ **PO Box 30, Hereford, Herefordshire, HR2 8SW**
☎ 07800 508178
Fairs Buxton Antique & Collectors Fairs

V&A Fairs
✉ **Holly Bank Cottage, Forden, Nr Welshpool, Powys, SY21 8LT**
☎ 01938 580438
Ⓔ vandafairs@talk21.com
Ⓦ www.vandafairs.com
Fairs V&A Antique & Collectors Fairs, Cheadle, Cheshire, Nantwich, Cheshire, Stretton, near Warrington, Cheshire, Whitchurch, Shropshire and Bridgnorth, Shropshire

Virgo Fairs
☎ 01765 620563
Ⓜ 07950 621395
Fairs Antiques and Collectors fairs in Ripley and Harrogate, North Yorkshire

FAIRS: ORGANIZERS
CONTACT DETAILS

Wakefield Ceramics Fairs
☎ 01303 258635 Ⓕ 01303 258635
Fairs Ceramics Fairs at Burford, Oxfordshire and Matlock, Derbyshire

Wessex Antiques Fairs
Contact Jo Wanford
☎ 01278 789568
Ⓔ gerry.wanford@virgin.net
Fairs Wessex Antiques Fairs, Taunton, Churchill and Weston-super-Mare, Somerset

West Country Fairs
Contact Fred Wilcox
✉ **PO Box 2603, Wells, Somerset, BA5 2YL**
☎ 01749 677049 Ⓕ 01749 677049
Fairs Antiques & Collectors Fairs and Annual Wiltshire Fleamarket; Antiques & Collectors Fairs, South Dorset Massive Annual Fleamarket, and Annual Weymouth Fleamarket, Weymouth; The City of Wells Annual Collectors Fleamarket

West Midland Antique Fairs
Contact Nick Fletcher
✉ **PO Box 134, Shrewsbury, Shropshire, SY1 1ZZ** Ⓟ
☎ 01743 271444
Ⓔ mail@staffordantiquesfairs.co.uk
Ⓦ www.staffordantiquesfairs.co.uk
Est. 1973
Fairs Stafford Antiques Fair. Please phone for details

Wilton House
✉ **The Old Riding School, Wilton House, Wilton, Salisbury, Wiltshire**
☎ 01722 746720
Fairs 28th Annual Art Fair at Wilton House

Wonder Whistle Enterprises
Contact Alan and Ludi Kipping
✉ **1 Ritson Road, London, E8 1DE** Ⓟ
☎ 020 7249 4050 Ⓕ 020 7249 5060
Ⓔ alan&ludi@ww-antique-fairs.demon.co.uk
Ⓦ www.ww-antique-fairs.demon.co.uk
Fairs Sandown Park Antique & Collectors Fairs. Please phone to confirm dates

Ann Zierold Fairs
☎ 01824 750500
Ⓔ enquiries@annzieroldfairs.co.uk
Ⓦ www.annzieroldfairs.co.uk
Fairs Antiques, Art Deco, textile and glass fairs in Liverpool, Manchester, Chester, Harrogate and Leeds

JANUARY

1

Bob Evans Fair
Organizer Bob Evans Fairs
Location Leisure Centre, Coventry Road, Hinckley, Leicestershire (tel. 01455 610011) P
Est. 1972
Open 9.30am–4.30pm
Details 120 stalls

V&A Antique & Collectors Fair
Organizer V&A Fairs
Location The Civic Hall, Nantwich, Cheshire P
Est. 2000
Open Trade (FWC) 8.30–10am public 10am–4.30pm
Details 65+ stands, refreshment facilities, disabled facilities

1–2

Janba Fair
Organizer Janba Fairs
Location Burgess Hall, St Ivo Leisure Centre, St Ives, Cambridgeshire P
Est. 1978
Open 10am–4pm
Entrance fee £1.10 seniors 80p accompanied children under 16 free

2

Antiques & Collectables Fair
Organizer Take Five Fairs
Location Canons Leisure Centre, Mitcham, Surrey
Open 8.30am–4pm
Entrance fee £2
Details Antiques and collectables

Cross Country Fairs
Organizer Cross Country Fairs Ltd
Location Effingham Park, West Sussex P
Est. 1990
Open 9am–4.30pm
Entrance fee £2

South Dorset's Collectamania
Organizer West Country Fairs
Location Weymouth Pavilion, The Esplanade, Weymouth, Dorset P
Open Trade 9am public 10am–4pm
Entrance fee Trade FWC public £1
Details Antiques and collectables. Refreshments

V&A Antique & Collectors Fair
Organizer V&A Fairs
Location The Village Hotel & Leisure Club, Cheadle Road, Cheadle, Cheshire P
Est. 2000
Open Trade (FWC) 8.30–10am public 10am–4.30pm
Details 32 stands, refreshment facilities, disabled facilities

Wessex Antiques Fairs
Organizer Wessex Antiques Fairs
Location The Holiday Inn, Taunton, Somerset P
Est. 1988
Open 10am–4.30pm
Entrance fee £1
Details Antiques and collectables

3

Bloomsbury Postcard & Collectors Fair
Organizer IPM Promotions
Location Royal National Hotel, Bedford Way, London WC1 P
Open 10am–4.30pm
Entrance fee £1
Details 120 stands of postcards, printed ephemera, autographs, programmes, photos, cigarette cards, postal history etc

7–9

13th Cheshire Antiques & Fine Art Fair
Organizer Robert Bailey Fairs Ltd
Location Tatton Park, Knutsford, Cheshire P
Open Fri 1–6pm Fri Sat 11am–6pm Sun 11am–5pm
Entrance fee £5
Details 50 dealers, vetted and datelined

8

Antiques and Collectors Fair
Organizer West Country Fairs
Location The Town Hall, Market Square, Wells, Somerset P
Est. 1992
Open Trade 9am public 10am–4pm
Entrance fee Free
Details 25 stands. One of the region's busiest Saturday fairs

9

Antiques & Collectables Fair
Organizer Take Five Fairs
Location Woking Leisure Centre, Kingfield Road, Woking, Surrey P
Open 8.30am–4pm
Entrance fee £2
Details 175 stalls

Bob Evans Fair
Organizer Bob Evans Fairs
Location The Cresset, Bretton Centre, Peterborough (tel. 01733 265705) P
Est. 1974
Open 9.30am–4.30pm
Details 160 stalls

Magna Carta Fayre
Organizer Magna Carta Country Fayres
Location St Leonard's Mansion, Legoland, Windsor, Berkshire P
Est. 2005
Open 10.30am–4.30pm
Entrance fee £2
Details Antiques and collectables (please phone to confirm dates)

Midas Antiques Fair
Organizer Midas Fairs
Location Bellhouse Hotel, Beaconsfield, Buckinghamshire P
Open 10.30am–5pm
Entrance fee £1.50 children (6–16) 50p children under 6 free
Details Quality dateline stands

Scotfairs Antique and Collectors Fairs
Organizer Scotfairs
Location Meadowbank Stadium, London Road, Edinburgh P
Open Trade 8am public 10am–4.30pm
Entrance fee Trade FWC public £1 accompanied children free
Details 150 stands

V&A Antiques & Collectors Fair
Organizer V&A Fairs
Location The Hanover International Hotel, Stretton, Nr Warrington, Cheshire (M56 junction 10) P
Est. 2000
Open Trade (FWC) 8.30–10am public 10am–4.30pm
Details 100 stands, refreshment facilities, disabled facilities

FAIRS: CALENDAR

JANUARY

11–12

Ardingly International Antiques & Collectors Fair
Organizer DMG Antiques Fairs
Location South of England Showground, Ardingly, West Sussex 🅿
Est. 1997
Open Tues10am–6pm Wed 8am–4pm
Entrance fee Tues £20 (includes Wed entry) Wed £5
Details Up to 1700 exhibitors

13–16

West London Antiques & Fine Art Fair
Organizer Penman Antiques Fairs
Location Kensington Town Hall, Hornton Street, London W8
Est. 1976
Open Thurs noon–8pm Fri Sat 10.30am–6pm Sun 10.30am–5pm
Entrance fee £4
Details 70–85 stands, the best of furniture, arts and artefacts from the past 300 years

14–16

The Antique Dealers Fair of Wales
Organizer Allen Lewis Fairs
Location The Orangery, Margam Park, South Wales, West Glamorgan 🅿
Est. 1984
Open 10am–5pm
Entrance fee £3 accompanied children under 16 free
Details Fully stand-fitted quality dateline fair featuring full-time antique dealers

The Great Northern International Antiques & Collectors Fair
Organizer Grosvenor Exhibitions Ltd
Location The Great Yorkshire Showground, Harrogate (A661 Harrogate–Wetherby Road) 🅿
Est. 1985
Open Fri 10.30am–5pm Sat Sun 9.30am–5pm
Entrance fee Fri £4 Sat Sun £5
Details About 400 exhibitors
Trade only Fri 8am (£10)

15

Coin Fair
Organizer Davidson Monk Fairs
Location Drury's Hotel, Great Russell Street, London WC1
Est. 1990
Open 9.30am–2.30pm
Entrance fee £1
Details Coin fair including antiquities and medallions

Scotfairs Antique and Collectors Fairs
Organizer Scotfairs
Location Albert Halls, Dumbarton Road, Stirling 🅿
Open Trade 8am public 10am–4.30pm
Entrance fee Trade FWC public £1 accompanied children free
Details 70 stands

15–16

Detling International Antiques & Collectors Fair
Organizer DMG Antiques Fairs
Location Kent County Showground, Detling, Nr Maidstone, Kent 🅿
Est. 1998
Open Sat 8.30am–5pm Sun 10am–4pm
Entrance fee Sat 8.30am £6 Sat 10am Sun £4.50
Details Up to 500 exhibitors

16

Abergavenny Antiques & Collectors Fairs
Organizer Monmouthshire County Council
Location Abergavenny Market Hall, Abergavenny, Monmouthshire 🅿
Est. 1993
Open 6am–4pm
Entrance fee Free

Alexandra Palace Antique & Collectors Fair
Organizer Pig & Whistle Promotions
Location The Great Hall, Alexandra Palace, Wood Green, London N22 🅿
Est. 1970
Open Trade 10am public 11.30am–5pm
Entrance fee Trade £6 with card public £5
Details London's largest antiques fair with over 700 stands and a substantial amount of furniture

Biggleswade Antiques Fair
Organizer Biggleswade Antiques Fairs
Location Weatherley Centre, Biggleswade, Bedfordshire
Open 9.30am–4.30pm

Bob Evans Fair
Organizer Bob Evans Fairs
Location Leisure Centre, Holmer Road, Hereford (tel. 01432 278178) 🅿
Est. 1974
Open 9.30am–4.30pm
Details 200 stalls

Midland Clock & Watch Fair
Organizer Brunel Clock & Watch Fair
Location National Motorcycle Museum, M42 junction 6, West Midlands 🅿
Est. 1990
Open 9am–3pm
Entrance fee 9am £5 11am £2.50 1pm £1
Details Antique clocks, pocket and mechanical wrist watches, parts and books

Newcomen Fair
Organizer Newcomen Fairs Ltd
Location Elsecar Heritage Centre, Wath Road, Barnsley, South Yorkshire 🅿
Est. 2001
Open Trade 8am public 10am–4pm
Entrance fee Trade £2 public £1

Silhouette Fairs
Organizer Fat Cat Fairs
Location The Guildhall, Abbey Close, Abingdon, Oxfordshire, OX14 3JE
Est. 1972
Open 10am–4pm
Entrance fee £1
Details 70 stalls. Good refreshments available

Wessex Antiques Fairs
Organizer Wessex Antiques Fairs
Location Coombe Lodge, Blagdon, Churchill, Somerset (A368 Churchill to Bath) 🅿
Est. 2001
Open 10am–4.30pm
Entrance fee £1
Details Antiques and collectables

FAIRS: CALENDAR

JANUARY

18–23

The Decorative Antiques and Textiles Fair
Organizer Harvey Management Services Ltd
Location The Marquee, Battersea Park, London
Est. 1985
Open First day noon–8pm then11am–8pm Sat 11am–7pm Sun 11am–6pm
Entrance fee £8 including catalogue
Details Around 100 dealers. Decorative itrems, antiques, modern classics, art and textiles

19

Big Brum
Organizer Antique Forum Group
Location St Martin's Market (The Rag), Edgbaston Street P
Est. 1974
Open 7.30am–12.30pm
Entrance fee Free
Details One of England's busiest fairs

19–23

The National Fine Art Fair
Organizer The NEC Group
Location NEC, Birmingham P
Open Wed 11am–8pm Thurs–Sun 11am–6pm
Entrance fee £10

21–23

35th Harrogate Pavilions Antiques & Fine Art Fair
Organizer Robert Bailey Fairs Ltd
Location Pavilions of Harrogate, Great Yorkshire Showground P
Open Fri 1–6pm Fri Sat 11am–6pm Sun 11am–5pm
Entrance fee £5
Details 80 dealers, vetted and datelined

Shepton Mallet Antiques & Collectors Fair
Organizer DMG Antiques Fairs
Location Royal Bath and West Showground, Shepton Mallet, Somerset P
Est. 1997
Open Sat 8.30am–9.30pm (early entrance 7.30 am) Sun 10am–4pm
Entrance fee Fri £10 Sat 8.30am £7.50 Sat 9.30am Sun £5
Details Up to 600 exhibitors
Trade only Fri 1–5pm

22

Camfair
Organizer Janba Fairs
Location Castle Hall, Hertford P
Est. 1979
Open 10am–4.30pm
Entrance fee £1.10 senior 90p accompanied children under 16 free
Details 1930 dateline

Bloomsbury Postcard & Collectors Fair
Organizer IPM Promotions
Location Royal National Hotel, Bedford Way, London WC1
Details See Bloomsbury Postcard & Collectors Fair 3 Jan

23

Adams Antiques Fair
Organizer Adams Antiques Fairs
Location Lindley Hall, Royal Horticultural Hall, Elverton Street (off Vincent Square) Victoria, London SW1
Est. 1971
Open 10am–4.30pm
Entrance fee £3 accompanied children under 16 free
Details The longest-running Sunday fair in London. All manner of antiques

Biggleswade Antiques Fair
Organizer Biggleswade Antiques Fairs
Location Addison Centre, Kempton, Bedfordshire
Open 9.30am–4.30pm

Fat Cat Fairs
Organizer Fat Cat Fairs
Location Burford School, Burford, Oxfordshire (on A40 to Cheltenham) P
Open 9am–4pm
Entrance fee 75p
Details 46 stalls. Good refreshments available

V&A Antique & Collectors Fair
Organizer V&A Fairs
Location The Community Hall, Low Town (on A442), Bridgnorth, Shropshire P
Est. 2000
Open Trade (FWC) 8.30–10am public 10am–4.30pm
Details 25 stands, refreshment facilities, disabled facilities

Wessex Antiques Fairs
Organizer Wessex Antiques Fairs
Location Winter Gardens Pavilion, Weston-super-Mare
Est. 1988
Open 10am–4.30pm
Entrance fee £1
Details Antiques and collectables

27

V&A Antique & Collectors Fair
Organizer V&A Fairs
Location The Civic Hall, Nantwich, Cheshire
Details See V&A Antique & Collectors Fair 1 Jan

28–30

The International Antiques & Collectors Fair at RAF Swinderby
Organizer Arthur Swallow Fairs
Location RAF Swinderby, A46 between Newark and Lincoln P
Open Fri 7am–5pm Sat Sun 8am–5pm
Entrance fee Fri trade day £10, Sat Sun £4
Details Over 2000 stands

29

Antiques and Collectors Fair
Organizer West Country Fairs
Location The Town Hall, Market Square, Wells, Somerset
Details See Antiques and Collectors Fair 8 Jan

Scotfairs Antique and Collectors Fairs
Organizer Scotfairs
Location Citadel Leisure Centre, Ayr Baths, South Harbour Street, Ayr P
Open Trade 8am public 10am–4.30pm
Entrance fee Trade FWC public £1 accompanied children free
Details 100 stands

29–30

1st South Herts Antiques Fair
Organizer Gemsco Promotions
Location Theobalds Park, Cheshunt, Herts (off Lieutenant Ellis Way) P
Est. 2005
Open Sat 11am–5pm Sun 10am–5pm
Details Datelined event

Buxton Antique & Collectors Fair
Organizer Unicorn Fairs Ltd
Location Pavilion Gardens, Buxton, Derbyshire P
Est. 1977
Open 9am–5pm
Entrance fee £2 Seniors £1.50
Details 100 stalls

30

Bob Evans Fair
Organizer Bob Evans Fairs
Location Sport Village, Drayton High Road, Hellesdon, Norwich (tel. 01603 278178) P
Est. 1974
Open 9.30am–4.30pm
Details 200 stalls

Janba Fair
Organizer Janba Fairs
Location Knights Hill Hotel, King's Lynn, Norfolk, (junction A148/A149) P
Est. 1984
Open 10am–4.30pm
Entrance fee £1.10 concessions 80p accompanied children under 16 free

Northern Clock & Watch Fair
Organizer Northern Clock & Watch Fairs
Location Haydock Park Racecourse, Merseyside P
Est. 1997
Open 9am–3pm
Entrance fee 9am £5 10.30am £2

FEBRUARY

2

Malvern International Antiques & Collectors Fair
Organizer DMG Antiques Fairs
Location Three Counties Showground, Malvern, Worcestershire P
Est. 1997
Open 8.30am–5pm
Entrance fee 8.30am £4 10am £2.50
Details Up to 200 exhibitors

3–5

Newark International Antiques & Collectors Fair
Organizer DMG Antiques Fairs
Location Newark & Notts Showground, Newark P
Est. 1997
Open Thurs noon–6pm Fri 8am–5pm Sat 9am–4pm
Entrance fee Thurs £20 (includes Fri) Fri £10 (includes Sat) Sat £5
Details Up to 4000 exhibitors
Trade only See website for discounts

5

Frock Me!
Organizer Adams Antiques Fairs
Location Chelsea Town Hall, King's Road, Chelsea, London SW3
Est. 2003
Open 10am–5.30pm
Entrance fee £3 accompanied children under 16 free, students with valid card £1.50
Details The fashion and accessories event for Central London. Vintage costume, period fashion, modern design, hats, fans, gloves, shoes, jewellery and accessories

London Coin Fair
Organizer Simmons Gallery
Location Holiday Inn, Coram Street, London WC1 P
Est. 1977
Open 9.30am–5pm
Entrance fee £4.00
Details Largest specialist UK numismatic show, over 70 dealers

Scotfairs Antique and Collectors Fairs
Organizer Scotfairs
Location Albert Halls, Dumbarton Road, Stirling
Details See Scotfairs Antique and Collectors Fairs 15 Jan

6

Antiques & Collectables Fair
Organizer Take Five Fairs
Location Canons Leisure Centre, Mitcham, Surrey
Details See Antiques & Collectables Fair 2 Jan

Art Deco Fair
Organizer Abbey Fairs
Location Twickenham Rugby Ground, Twickenham, Middlesex P
Est. 2001

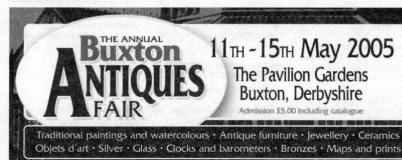

Open 10am–4pm
Entrance fee £2.50
Details Art Deco and early post-war design

Battersea Vintage Fashion Fairs
Organizer Pre-empt Events
Location Battersea Art Centre, Lavender Hill, London SW11 🅿
Est. 2003
Open 9.30am–4.30pm
Entrance fee £4 students £2.50 with card
Details An Aladdin's Cave of beautiful unique pieces. The perfect haunt for individuals looking for one-offs or for research purposes

Bob Evans Fair
Organizer Bob Evans Fairs
Location Sports Connexion, Ryton on Dunsmore, Coventry (tel. 02476 306155) 🅿
Est. 1974
Open 9.30am–4.30pm
Details 300 stalls

Cross Country Fairs
Organizer Cross Country Fairs Ltd
Location Effingham Park, West Sussex
Details See Cross Country Fairs 2 Jan

Dublin Toy and Train Fair
Organizer Dublin Toy and Train Fair
Location Clontarf Castle Hotel, Castle Avenue, Clontarf, Dublin 3
Open 10am–5pm
Details Toy and train fair

Fat Cat Fairs
Organizer Fat Cat Fairs
Location New Memorial Hall, Lechlade-on-Thames, Gloucestershire
Details See Fat Cat Fairs 2 Jan

Malvern International Antiques & Collectors Fair
Organizer DMG Antiques Fairs
Location Three Counties Showground, Malvern, Worcestershire
Details See Malvern International Antiques & Collectors Fair 2 Jan

Mark Carter Militaria & Medal Fair
Organizer Mark Carter Militaria & Medal Fairs
Location Yate Leisure Centre, Kennedy Way, Yate, Bristol 🅿
Est. 1988
Open Trade 9.30am public 10.30am–3pm
Entrance fee £2 trade preview £3.50
Details 100+ tables of quality militaria, medals and military books

Scotfairs Antique and Collectors Fairs
Organizer Scotfairs
Location Meadowbank Stadium, London Road, Edinburgh
Entrance fee
Details See Scotfairs Antique and Collectors Fairs 9 Jan

V&A Antique & Collectors Fair
Organizer V&A Fairs
Location The Village Hotel & Leisure Club, Cheadle Road, Cheadle, Cheshire
Details See V&A Antique & Collectors Fair 2 Jan

Wessex Antiques Fairs
Organizer Wessex Antiques Fairs
Location The Holiday Inn, Taunton, Somerset
Details See Wessex Fairs 2 Jan

8

The Southampton Art Deco Fair
Organizer E W Services/Abbey Fairs
Location West Refectory, Highfield Campus, The University of Southampton, University Road, Southampton 🅿
Est. 2003
Open 9.30am–4.30pm
Entrance fee £2.50
Details 65 dealers specialist Art Deco fair

11–13

The Petersfield Antiques Fair
Organizer Penman Antiques Fairs
Location The Festival Hall, Petersfield, Hampshire 🅿
Est. 1973
Open Fri Sat 10.30am–6pm Sun 10.30am–5pm
Entrance fee £3
Details 43 exhibitors with traditional and affordable vetted antiques.

12

Antiques and Collectors Fair
Organizer West Country Fairs
Location The Town Hall, Market Square, Wells, Somerset
Details See Antiques and Collectors Fair 8 Jan

12–13

59th Luton Antiques Fair
Organizer Gemsco Promotions
Location Putteridge Bury House, Hitchin Road, Luton LU2 8LE (off A505) 🅿
Est. 1975
Open Sat 11am–5pm Sun 10am–5pm
Details Dateline fair, restaurant

12–14

Stafford Bingley Hall Giant 3-Day Antiques Fair
Organizer Bowman Antiques Fairs Ltd
Location Bingley Hall, County Showground, Stafford 🅿
Est. 1978
Open 10am–5pm
Entrance fee £4 seniors £3 children under 16 free
Details Long-established quality antiques fair with 420 stands including 100 furniture stands
Trade only Fri 8.30am Sat 9.30am (£5)

13

Antique & Collectors Fair
Organizer Blooms A1 Events
Location The Racecourse, Beverley, East Riding of Yorkshire 🅿
Est. 2000
Open 9am–4pm
Entrance fee £1
Details 70 stands

Antiques & Collectables Fair
Organizer Take Five Fairs
Location Woking Leisure Centre, Kingfield Road, Woking, Surrey
Details See Antiques & Collectables Fair 9 Jan

FOR FAIR ORGANIZERS SEE PAGE 522

Biggleswade Antiques Fair
Organizer Biggleswade Antiques Fairs
Location Kimbolton Castle, Huntingdon
Open 10am–4.30pm

Magna Carta Fayre
Organizer Magna Carta Country Fayres
Location St Leonard's Mansion, Legoland, Windsor, Berkshire
Details See Magna Carta Country Fayres 9 Jan

Midas Antiques Fair
Organizer Midas Fairs
Location Bellhouse Hotel, Beaconsfield, Buckinghamshire
Details See Midas Antiques Fair 9 Jan

Newcomen Fair
Organizer Newcomen Fairs Ltd
Location Building 21, Elsecar Heritage Centre, Wath Road, Barnsley, South Yorkshire
Details See Newcomen Fair 16 Jan

V&A Antique & Collectors Fair
Organizer V&A Fairs
Location The Hanover International Hotel, Stretton, Nr Warrington, Cheshire (M56 junction 10)
Details See V&A Antique & Collectors Fair 9 Jan

15

Sandown Park Antiques Fairs
Organizer Wonder Whistle Enterprises
Location Sandown Park Racecourse, Portsmouth Road, Esher, Surrey P
Open Trade noon public 2–6pm
Entrance fee Noon £10 2pm £4
Details The largest indoor weekly fair in the South

17–20

The Chester Antiques & Fine Art Show
Organizer Penman Antiques Fairs
Location The County Grandstand, Chester Racecourse, Chester P
Est. 1990
Open Thurs noon–8pm Fri Sat 10.30am–6pm Sun 10.30am–5pm
Entrance fee £4
Details 60 stands, furniture, art & artefacts, mainly pre-1900, a few modern paintings

18–20

Goodwood House Fine Antiques Fairs
Organizer Pantheon Fairs Ltd
Location Goodwood House, Chichester, West Sussex P
Est. 1982
Open 11am–5pm
Entrance fee £4

19–20

Beckett Antiques Fairs
Organizer Beckett Antiques Fairs
Location Doncaster Racecourse, Doncaster, South Yorkshire P
Est. 1973
Open 10am–4.30pm
Entrance fee £2 concessions £1
Details 240 dealers offering antiques and collectables

Cowbridge Antiques Fair
Organizer Towy Antiques Fairs
Location The Leisure Centre, Cowbridge, Vale of Glamorgan P
Est. 2002
Open 10am–5pm
Entrance fee £3
Details Antiques and collectables

Janba Fair
Organizer Janba Fairs
Location Burgess Hall, St Ivo Leisure Centre, St Ives, Cambridgeshire
Details See Janba Fair 1–2 Jan

20

Abergavenny Antiques & Collectors Fairs
Organizer Monmouthshire County Council
Location Abergavenny Market Hall, Abergavenny, Monmouthshire
Details See Abergavenny Antiques & Collectors Fairs 16 Jan

Adams Antiques Fair
Organizer Adams Antiques Fairs
Location Lindley Hall, Royal Horticultural Hall, Elverton Street (off Vincent Square) Victoria, London SW1
Details See Adams Antiques Fair 23 Jan

Biggleswade Antiques Fair
Organizer Biggleswade Antiques Fairs
Location Weatherley Centre, Biggleswade, Bedfordshire
Details See Biggleswade Antique Fair 16 Jan

Bob Evans Fair
Organizer Bob Evans Fairs
Location Leisure Village, Thurston Drive, Kettering, Northamptonshire (tel. 01536 414141) P
Est. 1974
Open 9.30am–4.30pm
Details 300 stalls

Buxton Book Fair
Organizer Buxton Book Fair
Location Pavilion Gardens, Buxton, Derbyshire P
Est. 1982
Open 10am–4.30pm
Entrance fee £1
Details 80 dealers

Chipping Norton Toy Fair
Organizer Don Davidson
Location Chipping Norton School, Burford Road (A361), Chipping Norton, Oxfordshire P
Est. 1990
Open 10.30am–3pm
Details Collectors' toy and train fair. 20 dealers

Newmarket International Antiques & Collectors Fair
Organizer DMG Antiques Fairs
Location Rowley Mile Racecourse, Newmarket, Suffolk P
Est. 1997
Open 8am–4pm
Entrance fee 8am £6 10am £3.50
Details Up to 250 exhibitors

Silhouette Fairs
Organizer Fat Cat Fairs
Location The Guildhall, Abbey Close, Abingdon, Oxfordshire, OX14 3JE
Details See Silhouette Fairs 16 Jan

V&A Antique & Collectors Fair
Organizer V&A Fairs

Location The Civic Centre, High Street, Whitchurch, Shropshire P
Est. 2000
Open Trade (FWC) 8.30–10am public 10am–4.30pm
Details 60 stands, refreshment facilities, disabled facilities

Wessex Antiques Fairs
Organizer Wessex Antiques Fairs
Location Winter Gardens Pavilion, Weston-super-Mare
Details See Wessex Antiques Fair 23 Jan

25–27

The Portmeirion Antiques Fair
Organizer Allen Lewis Fairs
Location Portmeirion Village, Gwynedd, North Wales off A487 P
Est. 1980
Open 10am–5pm
Entrance fee Free please apply for invitation
Details Fully stand-fitted quality dateline fair featuring full-time antique dealers

26

Camfair
Organizer Janba Fairs
Location Castle Hall, Hertford
Details See Camfair 22 Jan

Scotfairs Antique and Collectors Fairs
Organizer Scotfairs
Location Citadel Leisure Centre, Ayr Baths, South Harbour Street, Ayr
Details See Scotfairs Antique and Collectors Fairs 29 Jan

26–27

Detling International Antiques & Collectors Fair
Organizer DMG Antiques Fairs
Location Kent County Showground, Detling, Nr Maidstone, Kent
Details See Detling International Antiques & Collectors Fair 15–16 Jan

27

Art Deco Fair
Organizer Abbey Fairs
Location Hilton Hotel, Junction 15 (M40), A429 Stratford Road, Warwick, CV34 6RE P
Est. 1992
Open 9am–4pm
Entrance fee £2.50
Details Art Deco

Biggleswade Antiques Fair
Organizer Biggleswade Antiques Fairs
Location Addison Centre, Kempton, Bedfordshire
Details See Biggleswade Antique Fair 23 Jan

Bloomsbury Postcard & Collectors Fair
Organizer IPM Promotions
Location Royal National Hotel, Bedford Way, London WC1
Details See Bloomsbury Postcard & Collectors Fair 3 Jan

Bob Evans Fair
Organizer Bob Evans Fairs
Location The Cresset, Bretton Centre, Peterborough (tel. 01733 265705)
Details See Bob Evans Fair 9 Jan

Fat Cat Fairs
Organizer Fat Cat Fairs
Location Burford School, Burford, Oxfordshire (on A40 to Cheltenham)
Details See Fat Cat Fairs 23 Jan

MARCH

1–2

Ardingly International Antiques & Collectors Fair
Organizer DMG Antiques Fairs
Location South of England Showground, Ardingly, West Sussex
Details See Ardingly International Antiques & Collectors Fair 11–12 Jan

1–6

Spring Fine Art & Antiques Fair
Organizer Clarion Events Ltd
Location Olympia Exhibition Centre, London P
Est. 1994
Open Telephone for details
Entrance fee £10 single £16 double
Details The rich variety of specialist stock will appeal to collectors and curators while connoisseurs and private buyers will find something unique. An exceptional choice of antique furniture and fine art is for sale

3–6

The Milton Keynes Antiques Fair
Organizer E W Services
Location Milton Keynes Shopping Centre P
Est. 1999
Open Thurs 10am–8pm Fri 9am–8pm Sat 9am–7pm Sun 11am–5pm
Details 80 dealers, 1939 dateline, stand-fitted and tabletop sections

4–6

28th Annual Art Fair
Organizer Wilton House
Location The Old Riding School, Wilton House, Wilton, Salisbury P
Est. 1977
Open 10am–5pm
Entrance fee £4.50
Details Antiques and collectables

5

Scotfairs Antique and Collectors Fairs
Organizer Scotfairs
Location Albert Halls, Dumbarton Road, Stirling
Details See Scotfairs Antique and Collectors Fairs 15 Jan

5–6

Buxton Antique & Collectors Fair
Organizer Unicorn Fairs Ltd
Location Pavilion Gardens, Buxton, Derbyshire
Details See Buxton Antique & Collectors Fair 29–30 Jan

6

Antiques & Collectables Fair
Organizer Take Five Fairs
Location Canons Leisure Centre, Mitcham, Surrey
Details See Antiques & Collectables Fair 2 Jan

Bob Evans Fair
Organizer Bob Evans Fairs
Location Leisure Centre, Coventry Road, Hinckley, Leicestershire (tel. 01455 610011)
Details See Bob Evans Fair 1 Jan

Cross Country Fairs
Organizer Cross Country Fairs Ltd
Location Effingham Park, West Sussex
Details See Cross Country Fairs 2 Jan

Fat Cat Fairs
Organizer Fat Cat Fairs
Location New Memorial Hall, Lechlade-on-Thames, Gloucestershire
Details See Fat Cat Fairs 2 Jan

Malvern International Antiques & Collectors Fair
Organizer DMG Antiques Fairs
Location Three Counties Showground, Malvern, Worcestershire
Details See Malvern International Antiques & Collectors Fair 2 Jan

Mark Carter Militaria & Medal Fair
Organizer Mark Carter Militaria & Medal Fairs
Location Stratford Leisure & Visitor Centre, Stratford-upon-Avon, Warwickshire P
Est. 1997
Open Trade 9.30am public 10.30am–3pm
Entrance fee £2 trade preview £3 accompanied children free
Details 90 tables of quality militaria, medals and military books

Scotfairs Antique and Collectors Fairs
Organizer Scotfairs
Location Meadowbank Stadium, London Road, Edinburgh
Entrance fee
Details See Scotfairs Antique and Collectors Fairs 9 Jan

The Brocante & Decorative Living Show
Organizer Adams Antiques Fairs
Location Kensington Town Hall, Hornton Street, London SW7 P
Est. 1988
Open 10am–5pm
Entrance fee Preview 10–11am £5 11am £2.50 accompanied children under 16 free
Details Decorative antiques and complementary exhibits

V&A Antique & Collectors Fair
Organizer V&A Fairs
Location The Village Hotel & Leisure Club, Cheadle Road, Cheadle, Cheshire
Details See V&A Antique & Collectors Fair 2 Jan

Wessex Antiques Fairs
Organizer Wessex Antiques Fairs
Location The Holiday Inn, Taunton, Somerset
Details See Wessex Fairs 2 Jan

9–12

Bath Annual Decorative & Antiques Fair
Organizer BABAADA
Location The Pavilion, North Trade Road, Bath
Est. 1989
Open Wed trade day 1–8pm Thurs 1–7pm Fri 11am–7pm Sat 11am–5pm
Entrance fee £2 (phone or email for complementary tickets)
Details BABAADA members and invited guests

9–15

The BADA Antiques and Fine Art Fair
Organizer British Antique Dealers Association
Location The Duke of York Square, Chelsea, London SW3 P
Est. 1993
Open 9th 11am–9pm 10th 11am–5.30pm (6.30–11.30pm Charity Gala) 11th 11am–8pm 12th–13th 11am–6pm 14th 11am–8pm 15th 11am–6pm
Entrance fee Single entry £10 Double entry £15. All tickets include a BADA Annual Handbook and one re-entry pass per person
Details Approximately 100 dealers, members of the British Antique Dealers Association, selling art and antiques

11–13

Morris to Mackintosh
Organizer Penman Antiques Fairs
Location Chelsea Old Town Hall, Kings Road, London SW3
Est. 2005
Open Preview Thurs 6–9pm Fri Sat 11am–7pm Sun 11am–5pm
Entrance fee £5 Preview £10
Details Arts and Crafts to Art Nouveau, 1860–1925. International convention with societies and lectures

The Fine Antiques Fairs of Scotland
Organizer Pantheon Fairs Ltd
Location Hopetoun House, South Queensferry, near Edinburgh P
Est. 1978
Open 11am–5pm
Entrance fee £4

The Great Northern International Antiques & Collectors Fair
Organizer Grosvenor Exhibitions Ltd
Location The Great Yorkshire Showground, Harrogate (A661 Harrogate–Wetherby Road)
Details See The Great Northern International Antiques & Collectors Fair 14–16 Jan

12

Antiques and Collectors Fair
Organizer West Country Fairs
Location The Town Hall, Market Square, Wells, Somerset
Details See Antiques and Collectors Fair 8 Jan

12–13

Carmarthen Antiques Fair
Organizer Towy Antiques Fairs
Location United County Showground, Carmarthen P
Est. 1994
Open 10am–5pm
Details Antiques and collectables

13

Alexandra Palace Antique & Collectors Fair
Organizer Pig & Whistle Promotions
Location The Great Hall,

MARCH

Alexandra Palace,
Wood Green,
London N22
Details See Alexandra Palace Antique & Collectors Fair 16 Jan

Antique & Collectors Fair
Organizer Blooms A1 Events
Location The Racecourse, Beverley, East Riding of Yorkshire
Details See Antique & Collectors Fair 13 Feb

Antiques & Collectables Fair
Organizer Take Five Fairs
Location Woking Leisure Centre, Kingfield Road, Woking, Surrey
Details See Antiques & Collectable Fair 9 Jan

Bob Evans Fair
Organizer Bob Evans Fairs
Location Sport Village, Drayton High Road, Hellesdon, Norwich (tel. 01603 278178)
Details See Bob Evans Fair 30 Jan

Magna Carta Fayre
Organizer Magna Carta Country Fayres
Location St Leonard's Mansion, Legoland, Windsor, Berkshire
Details See Magna Carta Country Fayres 9 Jan

Midas Antiques Fair
Organizer Midas Fairs
Location Bellhouse Hotel, Beaconsfield, Buckinghamshire
Details See Midas Antiques Fair 9 Jan

Midland Clock & Watch Fair
Organizer Brunel Clock & Watch Fair
Location National Motorcycle Museum, M42 junction 6, West Midlands
Details See Midland Clock & Watch Fair 16 Jan

V&A Antique & Collectors Fair
Organizer V&A Fairs
Location The Hanover International Hotel, Stretton, Nr Warrington, Cheshire (M56 junction 10)
Details See V&A Antique & Collectors Fair 9 Jan

Wessex Antiques Fairs
Organizer Wessex Antiques Fairs
Location Coombe Lodge, Blagdon, Churchill, Somerset (A368 Churchill to Bath)
Details See Wessex Antiques Fair 16 Jan

17

15th Annual St Patrick's Day Antiques & Collectors Fair
Organizer Castle Antique Fairs NI
Location Templeton Hotel, Templepatrick, Northern Ireland P
Est. 1989
Open Noon–9pm
Entrance fee £2.50 accompanied children free
Details 35 dealers

18–20

Stafford Bingley Hall Giant 3-Day Antiques Fair
Organizer Bowman Antiques Fairs Ltd
Location Bingley Hall, County Showground, Stafford
Details See Stafford Bingley Hall 12–14 February

19

Coin Fair
Organizer Davidson Monk Fairs
Location Drury's Hotel, Great Russell Street, London WC1
Details See Coin Fair 15 Jan

20

Abergavenny Antiques & Collectors Fairs
Organizer Monmouthshire County Council
Location Abergavenny Market Hall, Abergavenny, Monmouthshire
Details See Abergavenny Antiques & Collectors Fairs 16 Jan

Adams Antiques Fair
Organizer Adams Antiques Fairs
Location Lindley Hall, Royal Horticultural Hall, Elverton Street (off Vincent Square) Victoria, London SW1
Details See Adams Antiques Fair 23 Jan

Biggleswade Antiques Fair
Organizer Biggleswade Antiques Fairs
Location Weatherley Centre, Biggleswade, Bedfordshire
Details See Biggleswade Antique Fair 16 Jan

Bloomsbury Postcard & Collectors Fair
Organizer IPM Promotions
Location Royal National Hotel, Bedford Way, London WC1
Details See Bloomsbury Postcard & Collectors Fair 3 Jan

Bob Evans Fair
Organizer Bob Evans Fairs
Location Leisure Centre, Holmer Road, Hereford (tel. 01432 278178)
Details See Bob Evans Fair 16 Jan

Chiswick Art Deco Fair
Organizer Midland Art Deco Fairs
Location Chiswick Town Hall, Heathfield Terrace, London W4 P
Est. 1988
Open 10am–4.30pm
Entrance fee £2
Details Art Deco Fair plus some 20thC

Grand Glass Fair
Organizer Take Five Fairs
Location Woking Leisure Centre, Kingfield Road, Woking, Surrey P
Open 9.30am–4pm
Entrance fee £3

Janba Fair
Organizer Janba Fairs
Location Knights Hill Hotel, King's Lynn, Norfolk, (junction A148/A149)
Details See Janba Fair 30 Jan

Silhouette Fairs
Organizer Fat Cat Fairs
Location The Guildhall, Abbey Close, Abingdon, Oxfordshire, OX14 3JE
Details See Silhouette Fairs 16 Jan

The Big Weymouth Antiques & Collectors Fair
Organizer West Country Fairs
Location Weymouth Pavilion, The Esplanade, Weymouth,

Dorset P
Est. 1998
Open Trade 9am public 10am–4.30pm
Entrance fee Trade FWC public £1 seniors 80p accompanied children under 12 free
Details 80 stands. Antiques and collectables, small furniture and thousands of postcards. Refreshments

The Old Brig Antique & Collectors' Fair
Organizer The Old Brig
Location Newton Hotel, Nairn, Inverness
Est. 1974
Open 11am–4.30pm
Entrance fee £1

25–26

Albany Fairs
Organizer Albany Fairs
Location Town Hall, Moffat, Dumfriesshire
Est. 1980
Open 10am–4.30pm
Details Antiques and collectables

The Edinburgh Book Fair
Organizer Antiquarian Booksellers Association
Location The Assembly Rooms, George Street, Edinburgh
Est. 2000
Open Fri noon–7pm Sat 11am–5pm
Entrance fee Free
Details Antiquarian Books

25–27

Shepton Mallet Antiques & Collectors Fair
Organizer DMG Antiques Fairs
Location Royal Bath and West Showground, Shepton Mallet, Somerset
Details See Shepton Mallet Antiques & Collectors Fair 21–23 Jan

26

Camfair
Organizer Janba Fairs
Location Castle Hall, Hertford
Details See Camfair 22 Jan

Scotfairs Antique and Collectors Fairs
Organizer Scotfairs
Location Citadel Leisure Centre, Ayr Baths, South Harbour Street, Ayr
Details See Scotfairs Antique and Collectors Fairs 29 Jan

26–28

Ardingly International Antiques & Collectors Fair
Organizer DMG Antiques Fairs
Location South of England Showground, Ardingly, West Sussex
Details See Ardingly International Antiques & Collectors Fair 13–14 Jan

Beckett Antiques Fairs
Organizer Beckett Antiques Fairs
Location Doncaster Racecourse, Doncaster, South Yorkshire
Details See Beckett Antiques Fairs 19–20 Feb

The North Norfolk Fine Art & Antiques Fair
Organizer Lomax Antiques Fairs
Location Sussex Barn, Burnham Market, Norfolk, PE31 8JY P
Est. 2000
Open 26th 11am–6pm 27th 10.30am–6pm 28th 10.30am–5pm
Entrance fee £3.50 including catalogue
Details Fine art and antiques

27

Battersea Vintage Fashion Fairs
Organizer Pre-empt Events
Location Battersea Art Centre, Lavender Hill, London SW11
Details See Battersea Vintage Fashion Fairs 6 Feb

Buxton Book Fair
Organizer Buxton Book Fair
Location Pavilion Gardens, Buxton, Derbyshire
Est. 1982
Details See Buxton Book Fair 20 Feb

Fat Cat Fairs
Organizer Fat Cat Fairs
Location Burford School, Burford, Oxfordshire (on A40 to Cheltenham)
Details See Fat Cat Fairs 23 Jan

V&A Antique & Collectors Fair
Organizer V&A Fairs
Location The Community Hall, Low Town (on A442), Bridgnorth, Shropshire
Details See V&A Antique & Collectors Fair 23 Jan

27–28

Janba Fair
Organizer Janba Fairs
Location Burgess Hall, St Ivo Leisure Centre, St Ives, Cambridgeshire
Details See Janba Fair 1–2 Jan

Wessex Antiques Fairs
Organizer Wessex Antiques Fairs
Location Winter Gardens Pavilion, Weston-super-Mare
Details See Wessex Antiques Fair 23 Jan

28

16th Annual Easter Antique & Fine Art Fair
Organizer Castle Antique Fairs NI
Location Lissanoure Castle, Loughguille, between Ballymena and Ballymoney, Northern Ireland P
Est. 1989
Open 11am–7pm
Entrance fee £2.50 accompanied children free
Details 45 dealers

Art Nouveau/Deco Fair
Organizer Take Five Fairs
Location Woking Leisure Centre, Kingfield Road, Woking, Surrey P
Open 9am–4pm
Entrance fee £2.50
Details 200 stalls

Bob Evans Fair
Organizer Bob Evans Fairs
Location Leisure Village, Thurston Drive, Kettering, Northamptonshire (tel. 01536 414141)
Details See Bob Evans Fair 20 Feb

30–3 APRIL

11th Claridge's Antiques & Fine Art Fair
Organizer Robert Bailey Fairs Ltd
Location Claridge's Hotel, London W1 P

Open Champagne preview Wed 6–9pm Thurs Fri 11am–8pm Sat Sun 11am–6pm
Entrance fee £10 Champagne preview £20
Details A showcase for LAPADA, the association of art and antique dealers. Over 50 dealers, vetted and datelined

31

V&A Antique & Collectors Fair
Organizer V&A Fairs
Location The Civic Hall, Nantwich, Cheshire
Details See V&A Antique & Collectors Fair 1 Jan

APRIL

1–3

International Irish Antiques and Fine Art Fair
Organizer Louis O'Sullivan
Location Royal Dublin Society, Ballsbridge, Dublin 4, Ireland P
Est. 1999
Open Fri 11am–9pm Sat11am–7pm Sun 11am–6pm
Entrance fee €10 (£6.70)
Details Irish Antiques and fine art

The International Antiques & Collectors Fair at RAF Swinderby
Organizer Arthur Swallow Fairs
Location RAF Swinderby, A46 between Newark and Lincoln
Details See The International Antiques & Collectors Fair at RAF Swinderby 28–30 Jan

2

Scotfairs Antique and Collectors Fairs
Organizer Scotfairs
Location Albert Halls, Dumbarton Road, Stirling
Details See Scotfairs Antique and Collectors Fairs 15 Jan

2–3

Buxton Antique & Collectors Fair
Organizer Unicorn Fairs Ltd
Location Pavilion Gardens, Buxton, Derbyshire
Details See Buxton Antique & Collectors Fair 29–30 Jan

3

Antiques & Collectables Fair
Organizer Take Five Fairs
Location Canons Leisure Centre, Mitcham, Surrey
Details See Antiques & Collectables Fair 2 Jan

Cross Country Fairs
Organizer Cross Country Fairs Ltd
Location Effingham Park, West Sussex
Details See Cross Country Fairs 2 Jan

Fat Cat Fairs
Organizer Fat Cat Fairs
Location New Memorial Hall, Lechlade-on-Thames, Gloucestershire
Details See Fat Cat Fairs 2 Jan

Malvern International Antiques & Collectors Fair
Organizer DMG Antiques Fairs
Location Three Counties Showground, Malvern, Worcestershire
Details See Malvern International Antiques & Collectors Fair 2 Jan

Northern Clock & Watch Fair
Organizer Northern Clock & Watch Fairs
Location Haydock Park Racecourse, Merseyside
Details See Northern Clock & Watch Fair 30 Jan

Scotfairs Antique and Collectors Fairs
Organizer Scotfairs
Location Meadowbank Stadium, London Road, Edinburgh
Entrance fee
Details See Scotfairs Antique and Collectors Fairs 9 Jan

The International Art Deco – Art Nouveau – Arts & Crafts Fair
Organizer Abbey Fairs
Location Kelham Hall, Kelham, Newark, Nottinghamshire P
Est. 2004
Open 9.30am–4pm
Entrance fee Early trade £5 public £3.50
Details Art Deco, Arts and Crafts, Art Nouveau, early post-war design
Trade only 9–9.30am

V&A Antique & Collectors Fair
Organizer V&A Fairs
Location The Village Hotel & Leisure Club, Cheadle Road, Cheadle, Cheshire
Details See V&A Antique & Collectors Fair 2 Jan

Wessex Antiques Fairs
Organizer Wessex Antiques Fairs
Location The Holiday Inn, Taunton, Somerset
Details See Wessex Fairs 2 Jan

8–10

Newark International Antiques & Collectors Fair
Organizer DMG Antiques Fairs
Location Newark & Notts Showground, Newark
Details See Newark International Antiques & Collectors Fair 3–5 Feb

8–9

Peterborough Festival of Antiques
Organizer Bob Evans Fairs
Location East of England Showground, Peterborough (tel. 01733 234451)
Details 1700 stalls

9

Antiques and Collectors Fair
Organizer West Country Fairs
Location The Town Hall, Market Square, Wells, Somerset
Details See Antiques and Collectors Fair 8 Jan

10

Antique & Collectors Fair
Organizer Blooms A1 Events
Location The Racecourse, Beverley, East Riding of Yorkshire
Details See Antique & Collectors Fair 13 Feb

Antiques & Collectables Fair
Organizer Take Five Fairs
Location Woking Leisure Centre,

Kingfield Road, Woking, Surrey
Details See Antiques & Collectables Fair 9 Jan

Art Deco Fair
Organizer Abbey Fairs
Location The Grand Hall, Art Centre, Lavender Hill, Battersea, London SW11
Details See Art Deco Fair 13 Feb

Magna Carta Fayre
Organizer Magna Carta Country Fayres
Location St Leonard's Mansion, Legoland, Windsor, Berkshire
Details See Magna Carta Country Fayres 9 Jan

Midas Antiques Fair
Organizer Midas Fairs
Location Bellhouse Hotel, Beaconsfield, Buckinghamshire
Details See Midas Antiques Fair 9 Jan

V&A Antique & Collectors Fair
Organizer V&A Fairs
Location The Hanover International Hotel, Stretton, Nr Warrington, Cheshire (M56 junction 10)
Details See V&A Antique & Collectors Fair 9 Jan

14–17

9th Harrogate Pavilions Antiques & Fine Art & Investment Fair
Organizer Robert Bailey Fairs Ltd
Location Pavilions of Harrogate, Great Yorkshire Showground P
Open Thurs 1–6pm Fri Sat 11am–6pm Sun 11am–5pm
Entrance fee £5

16

Camfair
Organizer Janba Fairs
Location Castle Hall, Hertford
Details See Camfair 22 Jan

16–17

Beckett Antiques Fairs
Organizer Beckett Antiques Fairs
Location Doncaster Racecourse, Doncaster, South Yorkshire
Details See Beckett Antiques Fairs 19–20 Feb

Detling International Antiques & Collectors Fair
Organizer DMG Antiques Fairs
Location Kent County Showground, Detling, Nr Maidstone, Kent
Details See Detling International Antiques & Collectors Fair 15–16 Jan

17

Abergavenny Antiques & Collectors Fairs
Organizer Monmouthshire County Council
Location Abergavenny Market Hall, Abergavenny, Monmouthshire
Details See Abergavenny Antiques & Collectors Fairs 16 Jan

Adams Antiques Fair
Organizer Adams Antiques Fairs
Location Lindley Hall, Royal Horticultural Hall, Elverton Street (off Vincent Square) Victoria, London SW1
Details See Adams Antiques Fair 23 Jan

Biggleswade Antiques Fair
Organizer Biggleswade Antiques Fairs
Location Weatherley Centre, Biggleswade, Bedfordshire
Details See Biggleswade Antique Fair 16 Jan

Chipping Norton Toy Fair
Organizer Don Davidson
Location Chipping Norton School, Burford Road (A361), Chipping Norton, Oxfordshire
Details See Chipping Norton Toy Fair 20 February

Silhouette Fairs
Organizer Fat Cat Fairs
Location The Guildhall, Abbey Close, Abingdon, Oxfordshire, OX14 3JE
Details See Silhouette Fairs 16 Jan

The Old Brig Antique & Collectors' Fair
Organizer The Old Brig
Location The Highland Conference Centre, Nairn, Inverness
Details See The Old Brig Antique & Collectors' Fair 20 Mar

V&A Antique & Collectors Fair
Organizer V&A Fairs
Location The Civic Centre, High Street, Whitchurch, Shropshire
Details See V&A Antique & Collectors Fair 20 Feb

Wessex Antiques Fairs
Organizer Wessex Antiques Fairs
Location Winter Gardens Pavilion, Weston-super-Mare
Details See Wessex Antiques Fair 23 Jan

19–20

Ardingly International Antiques & Collectors Fair
Organizer DMG Antiques Fairs
Location South of England Showground, Ardingly, West Sussex
Details See Ardingly International Antiques & Collectors Fair 11–12 Jan

19–24

The Decorative Antiques and Textiles Fair
Organizer Harvey Management Services Ltd
Location The Marquee, Battersea Park, London
Details See The Decorative Antiques and Textiles Fair 18–23 Jan

21–24

The Annual Chelsea Art Fair
Organizer Penman Antiques Fairs
Location Chelsea Old Town Hall, Kings Road, London SW3
Est. 1996
Open Preview Wed 6–9pm Thurs Fri 11am–9pm Sat 11am–7pm Sun 11am–5pm
Entrance fee £6 Preview £10
Details 45 galleries exhibiting contemporary and modern paintings, prints & sculptures

23–24

The 74th London Antique Arms Fair
Organizer Antique Arms Fairs Ltd
Location Thistle London Hotel

Heathrow, Bath Road, Longford, West Drayton P
Est. 1968
Open Sat 9am–6pm Sun 9am–1pm
Entrance fee Sat 9am £15 (can be prebooked – covers both days) Sat afternoon Sun £7 per day
Details The oldest antique arms fair in the country

24

Biggleswade Antiques Fair
Organizer Biggleswade Antiques Fairs
Location Addison Centre, Kempton, Bedfordshire
Details See Biggleswade Antique Fair 23 Jan

Bloomsbury Postcard & Collectors Fair
Organizer IPM Promotions
Location Royal National Hotel, Bedford Way, London WC1
Details See Bloomsbury Postcard & Collectors Fair 3 Jan

Buxton Book Fair
Organizer Buxton Book Fair
Location Pavilion Gardens, Buxton, Derbyshire
Est. 1982
Details See Buxton Book Fair 20 Feb

Fat Cat Fairs
Organizer Fat Cat Fairs
Location Burford School, Burford, Oxfordshire (on A40 to Cheltenham)
Details See Fat Cat Fairs 23 Jan

Janba Fair
Organizer Janba Fairs
Location Knights Hill Hotel, King's Lynn, Norfolk, (junction A148/A149)
Details See Janba Fair 30 Jan

25

Art Deco Fair
Organizer Abbey Fairs
Location Battersea Town Hall
Details See Art Deco Fair 15 Feb

28

V&A Antique & Collectors Fair
Organizer V&A Fairs
Location The Civic Hall, Nantwich, Cheshire
Details See V&A Antique & Collectors Fair 1 Jan

28–2 MAY

Harrogate Antique & Fine Art Fair
Organizer Harrogate Antique & Fine Art Fair Ltd
Location Harrogate International Centre P
Est. 1974
Open Thurs Fri 11am–8pm Sat Sun 11am–6pm Mon 11am–5pm
Entrance fee £6 including catalogue
Details Antiques and fine art

29–30

Albany Fairs
Organizer Albany Fairs
Location Town Hall, Moffat, Dumfriesshire
Details See Albany Fairs 25–26 Mar

30

Scotfairs Antique and Collectors Fairs
Organizer Scotfairs
Location Citadel Leisure Centre, Ayr Baths, South Harbour Street, Ayr
Details See Scotfairs Antique and Collectors Fairs 29 Jan

30–2 MAY

East Berkshire Antiques Fair
Organizer Fair Antiques
Location Berkshire College of Agriculture, Hall Place, Burchetts Green, Maidenhead P
Open 10am–5pm
Entrance fee £4
Details 50 dealers. Quality event

MAY

1

Antiques & Collectables Fair
Organizer Take Five Fairs
Location Canons Leisure Centre, Mitcham, Surrey
Details See Antiques & Collectables Fair 2 Jan

Art Deco Fair
Organizer Abbey Fairs and E W Services
Location Novotel Hotel, No 1 West Keys, Southampton P
Est. 2003
Open 9.30am–4pm
Entrance fee £2.50
Details Art Deco and early post-war design

Cross Country Fairs
Organizer Cross Country Fairs Ltd
Location Effingham Park, West Sussex
Details See Cross Country Fairs 2 Jan

Fat Cat Fairs
Organizer Fat Cat Fairs
Location New Memorial Hall, Lechlade-on-Thames, Gloucestershire
Details See Fat Cat Fairs 2 Jan

Mark Carter Militaria & Medal Fair
Organizer Mark Carter Militaria & Medal Fairs
Location Yate Leisure Centre, Kennedy Way, Yate, Bristol
Details See Mark Carter Militaria & Medal Fair 6 Feb

Scotfairs Antique and Collectors Fairs
Organizer Scotfairs
Location Meadowbank Stadium, London Road, Edinburgh
Entrance fee
Details See Scotfairs Antique and Collectors Fairs 6 Jan

V&A Antique & Collectors Fair
Organizer V&A Fairs
Location The Village Hotel & Leisure Club, Cheadle Road, Cheadle, Cheshire
Details See V&A Antique & Collectors Fair 2 Jan

1–2

South Dorset Mammoth Annual Fleamarket
Organizer West Country Fairs
Location Weymouth Pavilion, The Esplanade, Weymouth, Dorset P
Open Trade 9am public 10am–5pm
Entrance fee Trade FWC public £1
Details Antiques and collectables. Refreshments

FOR FAIR ORGANIZERS SEE PAGE 522

Wessex Antiques Fairs
Organizer Wessex Antiques Fairs
Location Winter Gardens Pavilion, Weston-super-Mare
Details See Wessex Antiques Fair 23 Jan

2

11th Annual Charity Antique & Collectors Fair
Organizer Castle Antique Fairs NI
Location Queens Hall, Newtownards, Northern Ireland P
Est. 1992
Open 11am–5pm
Entrance fee £2 accompanied children free
Details 34 dealers

Bob Evans Fair
Organizer Bob Evans Fairs
Location The Cresset, Bretton Centre, Peterborough (tel. 01733 265705)
Details See Bob Evans Fair 9 Jan

6–8

Shepton Mallet Antiques & Collectors Fair
Organizer DMG Antiques Fairs
Location Royal Bath and West Showground, Shepton Mallet, Somerset
Details See Shepton Mallet Antiques & Collectors Fair 21–23 Jan

8

Alexandra Palace Antique & Collectors Fair
Organizer Pig & Whistle Promotions
Location The Great Hall, Alexandra Palace, Wood Green, London N22
Details See Alexandra Palace Antique & Collectors Fair 16 Jan

Antiques & Collectables Fair
Organizer Take Five Fairs
Location Woking Leisure Centre, Kingfield Road, Woking, Surrey
Details See Antiques & Collectables Fair 9 Jan

Magna Carta Fayre
Organizer Magna Carta Country Fayres
Location St Leonard's Mansion, Legoland, Windsor, Berkshire
Details See Magna Carta Country Fayres 9 Jan

Malvern International Antiques & Collectors Fair
Organizer DMG Antiques Fairs
Location Three Counties Showground, Malvern, Worcestershire
Details See Malvern International Antiques & Collectors Fair 2 Jan

Midas Antiques Fair
Organizer Midas Fairs
Location Bellhouse Hotel, Beaconsfield, Buckinghamshire
Details See Midas Antiques Fair 9 Jan

V&A Antique & Collectors Fair
Organizer V&A Fairs
Location The Hanover International Hotel, Stretton, Nr Warrington, Cheshire (M56 junction 10)
Details See V&A Antique & Collectors Fair 9 Jan

Wessex Antiques Fairs
Organizer Wessex Antiques Fairs
Location The Holiday Inn, Taunton, Somerset
Details See Wessex Fairs 2 Jan

11–15

The 41st Buxton Antiques Fair
Organizer Trident Exhibitions
Location Pavilion Gardens, Buxton, Derbyshire P
Est. 1964
Open Please telephone for details
Entrance fee £5 (including catalogue)
Details Traditional datelined fair. General antiques and collectables

13–15

Antiques & Audacity
Organizer Jan Hicks
Location Arundel Castle, West Sussex P
Est. 2005
Open Fri 10am–7pm Sat 10am–6.30pm Sun 10am–5.30pm
Entrance fee £5
Details Antiques, contemporary art and design

Antiques for Everyone
Organizer The NEC Group
Location The Scottish Exhibition and Conference Centre, Glasgow P
Open Fri 11am–7pm Sat Sun 11am–6pm
Entrance fee £8

The Great Northern International Antiques & Collectors Fair
Organizer Grosvenor Exhibitions Ltd
Location The Great Yorkshire Showground, Harrogate (A661 Harrogate–Wetherby Road)
Details See The Great Northern International Antiques & Collectors Fair 14–16 Jan

14

Antiques and Collectors Fair
Organizer West Country Fairs
Location The Town Hall, Market Square, Wells, Somerset
Details See Antiques and Collectors Fair 8 Jan

Scotfairs Antique and Collectors Fairs
Organizer Scotfairs
Location Albert Halls, Dumbarton Road, Stirling
Details See Scotfairs Antique and Collectors Fairs 15 Jan

14–15

Carmarthen Antiques Fair
Organizer Towy Antiques Fairs
Location United County Showground, Carmarthen
Details See Carmarthen Antiques Fair 12–13 March

15

Abergavenny Antiques & Collectors Fairs
Organizer Monmouthshire County Council
Location Abergavenny Market Hall, Abergavenny, Monmouthshire
Details See Abergavenny Antiques & Collectors Fairs 16 Jan

Adams Antiques Fair
Organizer Adams Antiques Fairs
Location Lindley Hall, Royal

MAY

Horticultural Hall, Elverton Street (off Vincent Square) Victoria, London SW1
Details See Adams Antiques Fair 23 Jan

Ardingly Sunday Antiques & Collectors Fair
Organizer DMG Antiques Fairs
Location South of England Showground, Ardingly, West Sussex P
Open 8am–10pm
Entrance fee £5
Details Up to 350 stalls of antiques and collectables

Biggleswade Antiques Fair
Organizer Biggleswade Antiques Fairs
Location Weatherley Centre, Biggleswade, Bedfordshire
Details See Biggleswade Antique Fair 16 Jan

Chiswick Art Deco Fair
Organizer London Art Deco Fairs
Location Chiswick Town Hall, Heathfield Terrace, London W4
Details See Chiswick Art Deco Fair 20 Mar

Dublin Toy and Train Fair
Organizer Dublin Toy and Train Fair
Location Clontarf Castle Hotel, Castle Avenue, Clontarf, Dublin 3
Details See Dublin Toy and Train Fair 6 February

Midland Clock & Watch Fair
Organizer Brunel Clock & Watch Fair
Location National Motorcycle Museum, M42 junction 6, West Midlands
Details See Midland Clock & Watch Fair 16 Jan

Newmarket International Antiques & Collectors Fair
Organizer DMG Antiques Fairs
Location Rowley Mile Racecourse, Newmarket, Suffolk
Details See Newmarket Antiques & Collectors Fair 20 Feb

Silhouette Fairs
Organizer Fat Cat Fairs
Location The Guildhall, Abbey Close, Abingdon, Oxfordshire, OX14 3JE
Details See Silhouette Fairs 16 Jan

The Big Weymouth Antiques & Collectors Fair
Organizer West Country Fairs
Location Weymouth Pavilion, The Esplanade, Weymouth, Dorset
Details See Antiques & Collectors Fair 20 Mar

The Old Brig Antique & Collectors' Fair
Organizer The Old Brig
Location The Highland Conference Centre, Nairn, Inverness
Details See The Old Brig Antique & Collectors' Fair 20 Mar

Wessex Antiques Fairs
Organizer Wessex Antiques Fairs
Location Coombe Lodge, Blagdon, Churchill, Somerset (A368 Churchill to Bath)
Details See Wessex Antiques Fair 16 Jan

17

Sandown Park Antiques Fairs
Organizer Wonder Whistle Enterprises
Location Sandown Park Racecourse, Portsmouth Road, Esher, Surrey
Details See Sandown Park Antiques Fairs 15 Feb

21

Camfair
Organizer Janba Fairs
Location Castle Hall, Hertford
Details See Camfair 22 Jan

Coin Fair
Organizer Davidson Monk Fairs
Location Drury's Hotel, Great Russell Street, London WC1
Details See Coin Fair 15 Jan

21–22

9th Mid Beds Antiques Fair
Organizer Gemsco Promotions
Location Silsoe Conference Centre (Cranfield University), Silsoe, Bedfordshire, MK45 4DT (off A6) P
Est. 2001
Open Sat 11am–5pm Sun 10am–5pm
Details Dateline fair, restaurant

22

Art Deco Fair
Organizer Abbey Fairs
Location Twickenham Rugby Ground, Twickenham, Middlesex
Details See Art Deco Fair 27 Feb

Bloomsbury Postcard & Collectors Fair
Organizer IPM Promotions
Location Royal National Hotel, Bedford Way, London WC1
Details See Bloomsbury Postcard & Collectors Fair 3 Jan

Fat Cat Fairs
Organizer Fat Cat Fairs
Location Burford School, Burford, Oxfordshire (on A40 to Cheltenham)
Details See Fat Cat Fairs 23 Jan

Janba Fair
Organizer Janba Fairs
Location Knights Hill Hotel, King's Lynn, Norfolk, (junction A148/A149)
Details See Janba Fair 30 Jan

The Brocante & Decorative Living Show
Organizer Adams Antiques Fairs
Location Kensington Town Hall, Hornton Street, London SW7
Details See The Brocante & Decorative Living Show 6 Mar

V&A Antique & Collectors Fair
Organizer V&A Fairs
Location The Community Hall, Low Town (on A442), Bridgnorth, Shropshire
Details See V&A Antique & Collectors Fair 23 Jan

27–30

The Antique Dealers Fair of Wales
Organizer Allen Lewis Fairs
Location The Orangery, Margam Park, South Wales, West Glamorgan
Details See The Antique Dealers Fair of Wales 14–16 Jan

FOR FAIR ORGANIZERS SEE PAGE 522

28

Scotfairs Antique and Collectors Fairs
Organizer Scotfairs
Location Citadel Leisure Centre, Ayr Baths,
South Harbour Street, Ayr
Details See Scotfairs Antique and Collectors Fairs 29 Jan

28–30

The Langley Park Spring Antiques Fair
Organizer Lomax Antiques Fairs
Location Langley Park School, Loddon, Norfolk, NR14 6BJ P
Est. 1990
Open 28th noon–6pm
29th 10.30am–6pm
30th 10.30am–5pm
Entrance fee £3.50 including catalogue
Details Datelined antiques

29

Art Deco Fair
Organizer Abbey Fairs
Location Warwick Hilton Hotel, Warwick
Details See Art Deco Fair 27 Feb

Battersea Vintage Fashion Fairs
Organizer Pre-empt Events
Location Battersea Art Centre, Lavender Hill,
London SW11
Details See Battersea Vintage Fashion Fairs 6 Feb

Buxton Book Fair
Organizer Buxton Book Fair
Location Pavilion Gardens, Buxton, Derbyshire
Est. 1982
Details See Buxton Book Fair 20 Feb

29–30

Beckett Antiques Fairs
Organizer Beckett Antiques Fairs
Location Doncaster Racecourse, Doncaster, South Yorkshire
Details See Beckett Antiques Fairs 19–20 Feb

Fine Art & Antiques Fair
Organizer Midas Fairs
Location Bellhouse Hotel, Beaconsfield, Buckinghamshire
Open 11am–5pm
Details See Antiques Fair 8 Feb

Janba Fair
Organizer Janba Fairs
Location Burgess Hall, St Ivo Leisure Centre, St Ives, Cambridgeshire
Details See Janba Fair 1–2 Jan

Wessex Antiques Fairs
Organizer Wessex Antiques Fairs
Location Winter Gardens Pavilion, Weston-super-Mare
Details See Wessex Antiques Fair 23 Jan

30

Art Nouveau/Deco Fair
Organizer Take Five Fairs
Location Woking Leisure Centre, Kingfield Road,
Woking, Surrey
Details See Art Nouveau/Deco Fair 28 Mar

Bob Evans Fair
Organizer Bob Evans Fairs
Location Sports Connexion, Ryton on Dunsmore, Coventry (tel. 02476 306155)
Details See Bob Evans Fair 6 Feb

V&A Antique & Collectors Fair
Organizer V&A Fairs
Location The Civic Hall, Nantwich, Cheshire
Details See V&A Antique & Collectors Fair 1 Jan

JUNE

1

Northern Clock & Watch Fair
Organizer Northern Clock & Watch Fairs
Location Haydock Park Racecourse, Merseyside
Details See Northern Clock & Watch Fair 30 Jan

3–5

33rd Bailey Antiques & Fine Art & Investment Fair
Organizer Robert Bailey Fairs Ltd
Location Seaford College, Petworth, West Sussex P
Open Fri 1–6pm Sat 11am–6pm
Sun 11am–5pm
Entrance fee £5

The International Antiques & Collectors Fair at RAF Swinderby
Organizer Arthur Swallow Fairs
Location RAF Swinderby, A46 between Newark and Lincoln
Details See The International Antiques & Collectors Fair at RAF Swinderby 28–30 Jan

4–5

Buxton Antique & Collectors Fair
Organizer Unicorn Fairs Ltd
Location Pavilion Gardens, Buxton, Derbyshire
Details See Buxton Antique & Collectors Fair 29–30 Jan

4–6

The Dulwich Art Fair
Organizer Penman Antiques Fairs
Location Christison Hall, Dulwich College, South Circular Road, Dulwich, London SE21
Est. 2004
Open Preview Thurs 6–9pm
Fri Sat 10.30am–6pm
Sun 10.30am–5pm
Entrance fee £5
Details 40 galleries of paintings, prints and sculptures by famous and emerging artists

5

Antiques & Collectables Fair
Organizer Take Five Fairs
Location Canons Leisure Centre, Mitcham, Surrey
Details See Antiques & Collectables Fair 2 Jan

Cross Country Fairs
Organizer Cross Country Fairs Ltd
Location Effingham Park, West Sussex
Details See Cross Country Fairs 2 Jan

Fat Cat Fairs
Organizer Fat Cat Fairs
Location New Memorial Hall, Lechlade-on-Thames, Gloucestershire
Details See Fat Cat Fairs 2 Jan

FAIRS: CALENDAR

JUNE

Malvern International Antiques & Collectors Fair
Organizer DMG Antiques Fairs
Location Three Counties Showground, Malvern, Worcestershire
Details See Malvern International Antiques & Collectors Fair 2 Jan

Mark Carter Militaria & Medal Fair
Organizer Mark Carter Militaria & Medal Fairs
Location Stratford Leisure & Visitor Centre, Stratford-upon-Avon, Warwickshire
Details See Mark Carter Militaria & Medal Fair 6 Mar

Scotfairs Antique and Collectors Fairs
Organizer Scotfairs
Location Meadowbank Stadium, London Road, Edinburgh
Entrance fee
Details See Scotfairs Antique and Collectors Fairs 9 Jan

V&A Antique & Collectors Fair
Organizer V&A Fairs
Location The Village Hotel & Leisure Club, Cheadle Road, Cheadle, Cheshire
Details See V&A Antique & Collectors Fair 2 Jan

9–11

Newark International Antiques & Collectors Fair
Organizer DMG Antiques Fairs
Location Newark & Notts Showground, Newark
Details See Newark International Antiques & Collectors Fair 3–5 Feb

9–12

The Antiquarian Book Fair
Organizer Antiquarian Booksellers Association
Location Olympia 2, London (parking must be pre-booked) P
Est. 1959
Open Thurs noon–8pm Fri 11am–7pm Sat 11am–6pm Sun 11am–5pm
Entrance fee Thurs £15 (£20 for a double ticket) including Fair Guide Fri–Sun £10 (£15 for a double ticket) Complimentary tickets available on request
Details Antiquarian Books

9–19

HALI Fair - Carpets, Textiles & Tribal Art
Organizer Clarion Events Ltd
Location The National Hall, Olympia, Gallery Level P
Est. 1998
Open First day 6–9pm Private view. Please phone for information on other days
Entrance fee £15 Private view 10–19 Jun £10 for one person £16 for two people
Details The rarest and most precious textile and tribal art from around the world

Summer Fine Art & Antiques Fair
Organizer Clarion Events Ltd
Location Olympia Exhibition Centre, London P
Est. 1973
Open Phone for details
Entrance fee £10 single £16 double
Details The rich variety of specialist stock will appeal to collectors and curators while connoisseurs and private buyers will find something unique. An exceptional choice of antique furniture and fine art is for sale.

11

Antiques and Collectors Fair
Organizer West Country Fairs
Location The Town Hall, Market Square, Wells, Somerset
Details See Antiques and Collectors Fair 8 Jan

Frock Me!
Organizer Adams Antiques Fairs
Location Chelsea Town Hall, King's Road, Chelsea, London SW3
Details See Frock Me! 5 Feb

London Coin Fair
Organizer Simmons Gallery
Location Holiday Inn, Coram Street, London WC1
Details See London Coin Fair 5 Feb

Scotfairs Antique and Collectors Fairs
Organizer Scotfairs
Location Albert Halls, Dumbarton Road, Stirling
Details See Scotfairs Antique and Collectors Fairs 15 Jan

12

Adams Antiques Fair
Organizer Adams Antiques Fairs
Location Lindley Hall, Royal Horticultural Hall, Elverton Street (off Vincent Square) Victoria, London SW1
Details See Adams Antiques Fair 23 Jan

Antiques & Collectables Fair
Organizer Take Five Fairs
Location Woking Leisure Centre, Kingfield Road, Woking, Surrey
Details See Antiques & Collectables Fair 9 Jan

Magna Carta Fayre
Organizer Magna Carta Country Fayres
Location St Leonard's Mansion, Legoland, Windsor, Berkshire
Details See Magna Carta Country Fayres 9 Jan

Midas Antiques Fair
Organizer Midas Fairs
Location Bellhouse Hotel, Beaconsfield, Buckinghamshire
Details See Midas Antiques Fair 9 Jan

V&A Antique & Collectors Fair
Organizer V&A Fairs
Location The Hanover International Hotel, Stretton, Nr Warrington, Cheshire (M56 junction 10)
Details See V&A Antique & Collectors Fair 9 Jan

Wessex Antiques Fairs
Organizer Wessex Antiques Fairs
Location Coombe Lodge, Blagdon, Churchill, Somerset (A368 Churchill to Bath)
Details See Wessex Antiques Fair 16 Jan

13

Art Deco Fair
Organizer Abbey Fairs
Location Battersea Town Hall
Details See Art Deco Fair 15 Feb

17–19

Stafford Bingley Hall Giant 3-Day Antiques Fair
Organizer Bowman Antiques Fairs Ltd
Location Bingley Hall, County Showground, Stafford
Details See Stafford Bingley Hall 12–14 February

18

Camfair
Organizer Janba Fairs
Location Castle Hall, Hertford
Details See Camfair 22 Jan

18–19

The St Albans Art Deco Fair
Organizer E W Services
Location The Alban Arena, Civic Centre, St Albans, Hertfordshire P
Est. 2004
Open Sat 10am–5pm
Sun 10am–4pm
Entrance fee £2.50
Details Specialist Art Deco fair, 100 tables plus furniture

19

Abergavenny Antiques & Collectors Fairs
Organizer Monmouthshire County Council
Location Abergavenny Market Hall, Abergavenny, Monmouthshire
Details See Abergavenny Antiques & Collectors Fairs 16 Jan

Biggleswade Antiques Fair
Organizer Biggleswade Antiques Fairs
Location Weatherley Centre, Biggleswade, Bedfordshire
Details See Biggleswade Antique Fair 16 Jan

Silhouette Fairs
Organizer Fat Cat Fairs
Location The Guildhall, Abbey Close, Abingdon, Oxfordshire, OX14 3JE
Details See Silhouette Fairs 16 Jan

The Old Brig Antique & Collectors' Fair
Organizer The Old Brig
Location The Highland Conference Centre, Nairn, Inverness
Details See The Old Brig Antique & Collectors' Fair 20 Mar

V&A Antique & Collectors Fair
Organizer V&A Fairs
Location The Civic Centre, High Street, Whitchurch, Shropshire
Details See V&A Antique & Collectors Fair 20 Feb

25

Scotfairs Antique and Collectors Fairs
Organizer Scotfairs
Location Citadel Leisure Centre, Ayr Baths,
South Harbour Street, Ayr
Details See Scotfairs Antique and Collectors Fairs 29 Jan

26

Biggleswade Antiques Fair
Organizer Biggleswade Antiques Fairs
Location Addison Centre, Kempton, Bedfordshire
Details See Biggleswade Antique Fair 23 Jan

Bloomsbury Postcard & Collectors Fair
Organizer IPM Promotions
Location Royal National Hotel, Bedford Way, London WC1
Details See Bloomsbury Postcard & Collectors Fair 3 Jan

Fat Cat Fairs
Organizer Fat Cat Fairs
Location Burford School, Burford, Oxfordshire
(on A40 to Cheltenham)
Details See Fat Cat Fairs 23 Jan

Newmarket International Antiques & Collectors Fair
Organizer DMG Antiques Fairs
Location Rowley Mile Racecourse, Newmarket, Suffolk
Details See Newmarket Antiques & Collectors Fair 20 Feb

Wessex Antiques Fairs
Organizer Wessex Antiques Fairs
Location Winter Gardens Pavilion, Weston-super-Mare
Details See Wessex Antiques Fair 23 Jan

30

V&A Antique & Collectors Fair
Organizer V&A Fairs
Location The Civic Hall, Nantwich, Cheshire
Details See V&A Antique & Collectors Fair 1 Jan

JULY

3

Antiques & Collectables Fair
Organizer Take Five Fairs
Location Canons Leisure Centre, Mitcham, Surrey
Details See Antiques & Collectables Fair 2 Jan

Cross Country Fairs
Organizer Cross Country Fairs Ltd
Location Effingham Park, West Sussex
Details See Cross Country Fairs 2 Jan

V&A Antique & Collectors Fair
Organizer V&A Fairs
Location The Village Hotel & Leisure Club, Cheadle Road, Cheadle, Cheshire
Details See V&A Antique & Collectors Fair 2 Jan

5

Fat Cat Fairs
Organizer Fat Cat Fairs
Location New Memorial Hall, Lechlade-on-Thames, Gloucestershire
Details See Fat Cat Fairs 2 Jan

Sandown Park Antiques Fairs
Organizer Wonder Whistle Enterprises
Location Sandown Park Racecourse, Portsmouth Road, Esher, Surrey
Details See Sandown Park Antiques Fairs 15 Feb

8–10

11th Cheshire Summer Antiques & Fine Art Fair
Organizer Robert Bailey Fairs Ltd

Location Tatton Park, Knutsford
Details See 13th Cheshire Antiques & Fine Art Fair 7–9 Jan

9

Antiques and Collectors Fair
Organizer West Country Fairs
Location The Town Hall, Market Square, Wells, Somerset
Details See Antiques and Collectors Fair 8 Jan

Scotfairs Antique and Collectors Fairs
Organizer Scotfairs
Location Albert Halls, Dumbarton Road, Stirling
Details See Scotfairs Antique and Collectors Fairs 15 Jan

9–10

Carmarthen Antiques Fair
Organizer Towy Antiques Fairs
Location United County Showground, Carmarthen
Details See Carmarthen Antiques Fair 12–13 March

10

Adams Antiques Fair
Organizer Adams Antiques Fairs
Location Lindley Hall, Royal Horticultural Hall, Elverton Street (off Vincent Square) Victoria, London SW1
Details See Adams Antiques Fair 23 Jan

Antiques & Collectables Fair
Organizer Take Five Fairs
Location Woking Leisure Centre, Kingfield Road, Woking, Surrey
Details See Antiques & Collectables Fair 9 Jan

Magna Carta Fayre
Organizer Magna Carta Country Fayres
Location St Leonard's Mansion, Legoland, Windsor, Berkshire
Details See Magna Carta Country Fayres 9 Jan

Malvern International Antiques & Collectors Fair
Organizer DMG Antiques Fairs
Location Three Counties Showground, Malvern, Worcestershire
Details See Malvern International Antiques & Collectors Fair 2 Jan

Scotfairs Antique and Collectors Fairs
Organizer Scotfairs
Location Meadowbank Stadium, London Road, Edinburgh
Entrance fee
Details See Scotfairs Antique and Collectors Fairs 9 Jan

V&A Antique & Collectors Fair
Organizer V&A Fairs
Location The Hanover International Hotel, Stretton, Nr Warrington, Cheshire (M56 junction 10)
Details See V&A Antique & Collectors Fair 9 Jan

12–14

The Highland Antiques Fair
Organizer The Old Brig
Location The Highland Conference Centre, Nairn, Inverness P
Est. 1984
Open 11am–4.30pm
Entrance fee £3

13–16

Albany Fairs
Organizer Albany Fairs
Location Victory Memorial Hall, St Andrews, Fife
Open 10am–4.30pm
Details Antiques and Collectables

15–17

Shepton Mallet Antiques & Collectors Fair
Organizer DMG Antiques Fairs
Location Royal Bath and West Showground, Shepton Mallet, Somerset
Details See Shepton Mallet Antiques & Collectors Fair 21–23 Jan

16

Coin Fair
Organizer Davidson Monk Fairs
Location Drury's Hotel, Great Russell Street, London WC1
Details See Coin Fair 15 Jan

16–17

Buxton Book Fair
Organizer Buxton Book Fair
Location Pavilion Gardens, Buxton, Derbyshire
Est. 1982
Details See Buxton Book Fair 20 Feb

17

Abergavenny Antiques & Collectors Fairs
Organizer Monmouthshire County Council
Location Abergavenny Market Hall, Abergavenny, Monmouthshire
Details See Abergavenny Antiques & Collectors Fairs 16 Jan

Biggleswade Antiques Fair
Organizer Biggleswade Antiques Fairs
Location Weatherley Centre, Biggleswade, Bedfordshire
Details See Biggleswade Antique Fair 16 Jan

Silhouette Fairs
Organizer Fat Cat Fairs
Location The Guildhall, Abbey Close, Abingdon, Oxfordshire, OX14 3JE
Details See Silhouette Fairs 16 Jan

The Big Weymouth Antiques & Collectors Fair
Organizer West Country Fairs
Location Weymouth Pavilion, The Esplanade, Weymouth, Dorset
Details See Antiques & Collectors Fair 21 Mar

The Old Brig Antique & Collectors' Fair
Organizer The Old Brig
Location The Highland Conference Centre, Nairn, Inverness
Est. 1984
Details See The Old Brig Antique & Collectors' Fair 20 Mar

19–20

Ardingly International Antiques & Collectors Fair
Organizer DMG Antiques Fairs
Location South of England Showground, Ardingly, West Sussex

Details See Ardingly International Antiques & Collectors Fair 11–12 Jan

22–24

The Great Northern International Antiques & Collectors Fair
Organizer Grosvenor Exhibitions Ltd
Location The Great Yorkshire Showground, Harrogate (A661 Harrogate–Wetherby Road)
Details See The Great Northern International Antiques & Collectors Fair 14–16 Jan

23

Camfair
Organizer Janba Fairs
Location Castle Hall, Hertford
Details See Camfair 22 Jan

23–24

Buxton Antique & Collectors Fair
Organizer Unicorn Fairs Ltd
Location Pavilion Gardens, Buxton, Derbyshire
Details See Buxton Antique & Collectors Fair 29–30 Jan

Detling International Antiques & Collectors Fair
Organizer DMG Antiques Fairs
Location Kent County Showground, Detling, Nr Maidstone, Kent
Details See Detling International Antiques & Collectors Fair 15–16 Jan

24

Bloomsbury Postcard & Collectors Fair
Organizer IPM Promotions
Location Royal National Hotel, Bedford Way, London WC1
Details See Bloomsbury Postcard & Collectors Fair 3 Jan

Fat Cat Fairs
Organizer Fat Cat Fairs
Location Burford School, Burford, Oxfordshire (on A40 to Cheltenham)
Details See Fat Cat Fairs 23 Jan

V&A Antique & Collectors Fair
Organizer V&A Fairs
Location The Community Hall, Low Town (on A442), Bridgnorth, Shropshire
Details See V&A Antique & Collectors Fair 23 Jan

Wessex Antiques Fairs
Organizer Wessex Antiques Fairs
Location Winter Gardens Pavilion, Weston-super-Mare
Details See Wessex Antiques Fair 23 Jan

28

V&A Antique & Collectors Fair
Organizer V&A Fairs
Location The Civic Hall, Nantwich, Cheshire
Details See V&A Antique & Collectors Fair 1 Jan

28–30

Antiques for Everyone
Organizer The NEC Group
Location NEC, Birmingham
Details See Antiques for Everyone 31 Mar1–Apr

29–31

The International Antiques & Collectors Fair at RAF Swinderby
Organizer Arthur Swallow Fairs
Location RAF Swinderby, A46 between Newark and Lincoln
Details See The International Antiques & Collectors Fair at RAF Swinderby 28–30 Jan

30

Scotfairs Antique and Collectors Fairs
Organizer Scotfairs
Location Citadel Leisure Centre, Ayr Baths, South Harbour Street, Ayr
Details See Scotfairs Antique and Collectors Fairs 29 Jan

AUGUST

4–6

Newark International Antiques & Collectors Fair
Organizer DMG Antiques Fairs
Location Newark & Notts Showground, Newark
Details See Newark International Antiques & Collectors Fair 3–5 Feb

6

Scotfairs Antique and Collectors Fairs
Organizer Scotfairs
Location Albert Halls, Dumbarton Road, Stirling
Details See Scotfairs Antique and Collectors Fairs 15 Jan

AUGUST

7

Antiques & Collectables Fair
Organizer Take Five Fairs
Location Canons Leisure Centre, Mitcham, Surrey
Details See Antiques & Collectables Fair 2 Jan

Cross Country Fairs
Organizer Cross Country Fairs Ltd
Location Effingham Park, West Sussex
Details See Cross Country Fairs 2 Jan

Fat Cat Fairs
Organizer Fat Cat Fairs
Location New Memorial Hall, Lechlade-on-Thames, Gloucestershire
Details See Fat Cat Fairs 2 Jan

Malvern International Antiques & Collectors Fair
Organizer DMG Antiques Fairs
Location Three Counties Showground, Malvern, Worcestershire
Details See Malvern International Antiques & Collectors Fair 2 Jan

Scotfairs Antique and Collectors Fairs
Organizer Scotfairs
Location Meadowbank Stadium, London Road, Edinburgh
Entrance fee
Details See Scotfairs Antique and Collectors Fairs 9 Jan

V&A Antique & Collectors Fair
Organizer V&A Fairs
Location The Village Hotel & Leisure Club, Cheadle Road, Cheadle, Cheshire
Details See V&A Antique & Collectors Fair 2 Jan

12–14

Stafford Bingley Hall Giant 3-Day Antiques Fair
Organizer Bowman Antiques Fairs Ltd
Location Bingley Hall, County Showground, Stafford
Details See Stafford Bingley Hall 12–14 February

13–14

6th Annual Weymouth Fleamarket
Organizer West Country Fairs
Location Weymouth Pavilion, The Esplanade, Weymouth, Dorset P
Open Trade 9am public 10am–5pm
Entrance fee Trade FWC public £1
Details 100 stands of collectables and antiques. Refreshments

14

Antiques & Collectables Fair
Organizer Take Five Fairs
Location Woking Leisure Centre, Kingfield Road, Woking, Surrey
Details See Antiques & Collectable Fair 9 Jan

Art Deco Fair
Organizer Abbey Fairs
Location Kelham Hall, Kelham, Newark, Nottinghamshire
Entrance fee
Details See The International Art Deco – Art Nouveau – Arts & Crafts Fair Fair 3 April

Magna Carta Fayre
Organizer Magna Carta Country Fayres
Location St Leonard's Mansion, Legoland, Windsor, Berkshire
Details See Magna Carta Country Fayres 9 Jan

Mark Carter Militaria & Medal Fair
Organizer Mark Carter Militaria & Medal Fairs
Location Yate Leisure Centre, Kennedy Way, Yate, Bristol
Details See Mark Carter Militaria & Medal Fair 6 Feb

Midas Antiques Fair
Organizer Midas Fairs
Location Bellhouse Hotel, Beaconsfield, Buckinghamshire
Details See Midas Antiques Fair 9 Jan

Midland Clock & Watch Fair
Organizer Brunel Clock & Watch Fair
Location National Motorcycle Museum, M42 junction 6, West Midlands
Details See Midland Clock & Watch Fair 16 Jan

V&A Antique & Collectors Fair
Organizer V&A Fairs
Location The Hanover International Hotel, Stretton, Nr Warrington, Cheshire (M56 junction 10)
Details See V&A Antique & Collectors Fair 9 Jan

18–21

Antiques for Everyone
Organizer The NEC Group
Location Earls Court, London P
Open Thurs 11am–8pm Fri–Sun 11am–6pm
Entrance fee £10

19–21

The Anglian Art Fair
Organizer Penman Antiques Fairs
Location The medieval Barns, Cressing temple, near Braintree, Essex
Est. 2005
Open Preview Thurs 6–9pm Fri Sat Sun 10.30am–5pm
Entrance fee £3.50
Details 40 galleries of paintings, prints and sculptures by famous and emerging artists

20

Camfair
Organizer Janba Fairs
Location Castle Hall, Hertford
Details See Camfair 22 Jan

21

Abergavenny Antiques & Collectors Fairs
Organizer Monmouthshire County Council
Location Abergavenny Market Hall, Abergavenny, Monmouthshire
Details See Abergavenny Antiques & Collectors Fairs 16 Jan

Ardingly Sunday Antiques & Collectors Fair
Organizer DMG Antiques Fairs
Location South of England Showground, Ardingly, West Sussex P
Open 10am–4pm
Entrance fee £3.50
Details Up to 350 stalls of antiques and collectables

Chipping Norton Toy Fair
Organizer Don Davidson
Location Chipping Norton School, Burford Road (A361), Chipping Norton, Oxfordshire
Details See Chipping Norton Toy Fair 20 February

Silhouette Fairs
Organizer Fat Cat Fairs
Location The Guildhall, Abbey Close, Abingdon, Oxfordshire, OX14 3JE
Details See Sihouette Fairs 16 Jan

The Old Brig Antique & Collectors' Fair
Organizer The Old Brig
Location The Highland Conference Centre, Nairn, Inverness
Details See The Old Brig Antique & Collectors' Fair 20 Mar

V&A Antique & Collectors Fair
Organizer V&A Fairs
Location The Civic Centre, High Street, Whitchurch, Shropshire
Details See V&A Antique & Collectors Fair 20 Feb

Wessex Antiques Fairs
Organizer Wessex Antiques Fairs
Location Coombe Lodge, Blagdon, Churchill, Somerset (A368 Churchill to Bath)
Details See Wessex Antiques Fair 16 Jan

27

Antiques and Collectors Fair
Organizer West Country Fairs
Location The Town Hall, Market Square, Wells, Somerset
Details See Antiques and Collectors Fair 8 Jan

Scotfairs Antique and Collectors Fairs
Organizer Scotfairs
Location Citadel Leisure Centre, Ayr Baths, South Harbour Street, Ayr
Details See Scotfairs Antique and Collectors Fairs 29 Jan

27–29

Beckett Antiques Fairs
Organizer Beckett Antiques Fairs
Location Doncaster Racecourse, Doncaster, South Yorkshire
Details See Beckett Antiques Fairs 19–20 Feb

Buxton Antique & Collectors Fair
Organizer Unicorn Fairs Ltd
Location Pavilion Gardens, Buxton, Derbyshire
Details See Buxton Antique & Collectors Fair 29–30 Jan

28

Bloomsbury Postcard & Collectors Fair
Organizer IPM Promotions
Location Royal National Hotel, Bedford Way, London WC1
Details See Bloomsbury Postcard & Collectors Fair 3 Jan

Newmarket International Antiques & Collectors Fair
Organizer DMG Antiques Fairs
Location Rowley Mile Racecourse, Newmarket, Suffolk
Details See Newmarket Antiques & Collectors Fair 22 Feb

Northern Clock & Watch Fair
Organizer Northern Clock & Watch Fairs
Location Haydock Park Racecourse, Merseyside
Details See Northern Clock & Watch Fair 30 Jan

28–29

Janba Fair
Organizer Janba Fairs
Location Burgess Hall, St Ivo Leisure Centre, St Ives, Cambridgeshire
Details See Janba Fair 1–2 Jan

Wessex Antiques Fairs
Organizer Wessex Antiques Fairs
Location Winter Gardens Pavilion, Weston-super-Mare
Details See Wessex Antiques Fair 23 Jan

29

16th Annual August Antique & Fine Art Fair
Organizer Castle Antique Fairs NI
Location Lissanoure Castle, Loughguille, between Ballymena and Ballymoney, Northern Ireland P
Est. 1989
Open 11am–7pm
Entrance fee £3 accompanied children free
Details 45 dealers

Art Nouveau/Deco Fair
Organizer Take Five Fairs
Location Woking Leisure Centre, Kingfield Road, Woking, Surrey
Details See Art Nouveau/Deco Fair 28 Mar

Bob Evans Fair
Organizer Bob Evans Fairs
Location Leisure Centre, Coventry Road, Hinckley, Leicestershire (tel. 01455 610011)
Details See Bob Evans Fair 1 Jan

Buxton Book Fair
Organizer Buxton Book Fair
Location Pavilion Gardens, Buxton, Derbyshire
Est. 1982
Details See Buxton Book Fair 20 Feb

V&A Antique & Collectors Fair
Organizer V&A Fairs
Location The Civic Hall, Nantwich, Cheshire
Details See V&A Antique & Collectors Fair 1 Jan

SEPTEMBER

2–4

The Annual Bury St Edmunds Antiques & Fine Art Fair
Organizer Penman Antiques Fairs
Location The Athenaeum, Angel Square, Bury St Edmunds, Suffolk
Open Fri 6–9pm Sat 10.30am–6pm Sun 10.30am–5pm
Entrance fee £4
Details A traditional antiques fair featuring 40 dealers from East Anglia and across the UK

The Great Northern International Antiques & Collectors Fair
Organizer Grosvenor Exhibitions Ltd
Location The Great Yorkshire Showground, Harrogate (A661 Harrogate–Wetherby Road)
Details See The Great Northern International Antiques & Collectors Fair 14–16 Jan

FAIRS: CALENDAR

SEPTEMBER

3

Frock Me!
Organizer Adams Antiques Fairs
Location Chelsea Town Hall, King's Road, Chelsea, London SW3
Details See Frock Me! 5 Feb

Scotfairs Antique and Collectors Fairs
Organizer Scotfairs
Location Albert Halls, Dumbarton Road, Stirling
Details See Scotfairs Antique and Collectors Fairs 15 Jan

3–4

6th South Bucks Antiques Fair
Organizer Gemsco Promotions
Location Missenden Abbey, High Street, Great Missenden, Buckinghamshire, HP16 0BD P
Est. 2002
Open Sat 11am–5pm Sun 10am–5pm
Details Dateline fair, restaurant

4

Antiques & Collectables Fair
Organizer Take Five Fairs
Location Canons Leisure Centre, Mitcham, Surrey
Details See Antiques & Collectables Fair 2 Jan

Bob Evans Fair
Organizer Bob Evans Fairs
Location Sports Connexion, Ryton on Dunsmore, Coventry
Details See Bob Evans Fair 6 Feb

Chiswick Art Deco Fair
Organizer London Art Deco Fairs
Location Chiswick Town Hall, Heathfield Terrace, London W4
Details See Chiswick Art Deco Fair 20 Mar

Cross Country Fairs
Organizer Cross Country Fairs Ltd
Location Effingham Park, West Sussex
Details See Cross Country Fairs 2 Jan

Fat Cat Fairs
Organizer Fat Cat Fairs
Location New Memorial Hall, Lechlade-on-Thames, Gloucestershire
Details See Fat Cat Fairs 2 Jan

Malvern International Antiques & Collectors Fair
Organizer DMG Antiques Fairs
Location Three Counties Showground, Malvern, Worcestershire
Details See Malvern International Antiques & Collectors Fair 2 Jan

Scotfairs Antique and Collectors Fairs
Organizer Scotfairs
Location Meadowbank Stadium, London Road, Edinburgh
Entrance fee
Details See Scotfairs Antique and Collectors Fairs 9 jan

V&A Antique & Collectors Fair
Organizer V&A Fairs
Location The Village Hotel & Leisure Club, Cheadle Road, Cheadle, Cheshire
Details See V&A Antique & Collectors Fair 2 Jan

Wessex Antiques Fairs
Organizer Wessex Antiques Fairs
Location The Holiday Inn, Taunton, Somerset
Details See Wessex Fairs 2 Jan

5

Art Deco Fair
Organizer Abbey Fairs
Location Battersea Town Hall
Details See Art Deco Fair 15 Feb

6–7

Ardingly International Antiques & Collectors Fair
Organizer DMG Antiques Fairs
Location South of England Showground, Ardingly, West Sussex
Details See Ardingly International Antiques & Collectors Fair 11–12 Jan

8–11

36th Cheshire Autumn Antiques & Fine Art Fair
Organizer Robert Bailey Fairs Ltd
Location Tatton Park, Knutsford P
Open Thurs 1–6pm Fri Sat 11am–6pm Sun 11–5pm
Entrance fee £5

9–11

The Antique Dealers Fair of Wales
Organizer Allen Lewis Fairs
Location The Orangery, Margam Park, South Wales, West Glamorgan
Details See The Antique Dealers Fair of Wales 14–16 Jan

The Petersfield Antiques Fair
Organizer Penman Antiques Fairs
Location The Festival Hall, Petersfield, Hampshire
Details See Petersfield Antiques Fair 11–13 February

10

Antiques and Collectors Fair
Organizer West Country Fairs
Location The Town Hall, Market Square, Wells, Somerset
Details See Antiques and Collectors Fair 8 Jan

11

Abergavenny Antiques & Collectors Fairs
Organizer Monmouthshire County Council
Location Abergavenny Market Hall
Details See Abergavenny Antiques & Collectors Fairs 16 Jan

Antiques & Collectables Fair
Organizer Take Five Fairs
Location Woking Leisure Centre, Kingfield Road, Woking, Surrey
Details See Antiques & Collectables Fair 9 Jan

Art Deco Fair
Organizer Abbey Fairs
Location Warwick Hilton Hotel, Warwick
Details See Art Deco Fair 27 Feb

Bob Evans Fair
Organizer Bob Evans Fairs
Location The Cresset, Bretton

Centre, Peterborough
(tel. 01733 265705)
Details See Bob Evans Fair 9 Jan

Magna Carta Fayre
Organizer Magna Carta Country Fayres
Location St Leonard's Mansion, Legoland, Windsor, Berkshire
Details See Magna Carta Country Fayres 9 Jan

Midas Antiques Fair
Organizer Midas Fairs
Location Bellhouse Hotel, Beaconsfield, Buckinghamshire
Details See Midas Antiques Fair 9 Jan

The Brocante & Decorative Living Show
Organizer Adams Antiques Fairs
Location Kensington Town Hall, Hornton Street, London SW7
Details See The Brocante & Decorative Living Show 6 Mar

V&A Antique & Collectors Fair
Organizer V&A Fairs
Location The Hanover International Hotel, Stretton, Nr Warrington, Cheshire (M56 junction 10)
Details See V&A Antique & Collectors Fair 9 Jan

16–25

Chelsea Antiques Fair
Organizer Penman Antiques Fairs
Location Chelsea Old Town Hall, Kings Road, Chelsea, London SW3
Est. 1950
Open Fri noon–9pm thereafter weekdays 10.30am–8pm Sat 10.30am–6pm Sun 10.30am–5pm
Entrance fee £6 (includes catalogue), double £10 (includes one catalogue)
Details Traditional antiques fair with quality period furniture and stylish artefacts

17

12th Annual Charity Antique & Collectors Fair
Organizer Castle Antique Fairs NI
Location Queens Hall, Newtownards, Northern Ireland P
Est. 1992
Open 11am–5pm
Entrance fee £2 children free
Details 34 dealers

17–18

Carmarthen Antiques Fair
Organizer Towy Antiques Fairs
Location United County Showground, Carmarthen
Details See Carmarthen Antiques Fair 12–13 March

Detling International Antiques & Collectors Fair
Organizer DMG Antiques Fairs
Location Kent County Showground, Detling, Nr Maidstone, Kent
Details See Detling International Antiques & Collectors Fair 15–16 Jan

18

Adams Antiques Fair
Organizer Adams Antiques Fairs
Location Lindley Hall, Royal Horticultural Hall, Elverton Street (off Vincent Square) Victoria, London SW1
Details See Adams Antiques Fair 23 Jan

Biggleswade Antiques Fair
Organizer Biggleswade Antiques Fairs
Location Weatherley Centre, Biggleswade, Bedfordshire
Details See Biggleswade Antique Fair 16 Jan

Bob Evans Fair
Organizer Bob Evans Fairs
Location Leisure Village, Thurston Drive, Kettering, Northamptonshire
(tel. 01536 414141)
Details See Bob Evans Fair 20 Feb

Dublin Toy and Train Fair
Organizer Dublin Toy and Train Fair
Location Clontarf Castle Hotel, Castle Avenue, Clontarf, Dublin 3
Details See Dublin Toy and Train Fair 6 February

Silhouette Fairs
Organizer Fat Cat Fairs
Location The Guildhall, Abbey Close, Abingdon, Oxfordshire, OX14 3JE
Details See Silhouette Fairs 16 Jan

The Big Weymouth Antiques & Collectors Fair
Organizer West Country Fairs
Location Weymouth Pavilion, The Esplanade, Weymouth, Dorset
Details See Antiques & Collectors Fair 20 Mar

The Old Brig Antique & Collectors' Fair
Organizer The Old Brig
Location The Highland Conference Centre, Nairn, Inverness
Details See The Old Brig Antique & Collectors' Fair 20 Mar

21–25

55th Northern Antiques Fair
Organizer Robert Bailey Fairs Ltd
Location Harewood House, West Yorkshire P
Open Wed 1–8pm Thurs–Sat 11am–6pm Sun 11am–5pm
Entrance fee £10

23–25

Shepton Mallet Antiques & Collectors Fair
Organizer DMG Antiques Fairs
Location Royal Bath and West Showground, Shepton Mallet, Somerset
Details See Shepton Mallet Antiques & Collectors Fair 21–23 Jan

24

Camfair
Organizer Janba Fairs
Location Castle Hall, Hertford
Details See Camfair 22 Jan

Scotfairs Antique and Collectors Fairs
Organizer Scotfairs
Location Citadel Leisure Centre, Ayr Baths, South Harbour Street, Ayr
Details See Scotfairs Antique and Collectors Fairs 29 Jan

24–25

Beckett Antiques Fairs
Organizer Beckett Antiques Fairs
Location Doncaster Racecourse,

Doncaster, South Yorkshire
Details See Beckett Antiques Fairs 19–20 Feb

Buxton Antique & Collectors Fair
Organizer Unicorn Fairs Ltd
Location Pavilion Gardens, Buxton, Derbyshire
Details See Buxton Antique & Collectors Fair 29–30 Jan

The 75th London Antique Arms Fair
Organizer Antique Arms Fairs Ltd
Location Thistle London Hotel Heathrow, Bath Road, Longford, West Drayton
Details See 74th London Antique Arms Fair 23–24 April

25

Alexandra Palace Antique & Collectors Fair
Organizer Pig & Whistle Promotions
Location The Great Hall, Alexandra Palace, Wood Green, London N22
Details See Alexandra Palace Antique & Collectors Fair 16 Jan

Biggleswade Antiques Fair
Organizer Biggleswade Antiques Fairs
Location Addison Centre, Kempton, Bedfordshire
Details See Biggleswade Antique Fair 23 Jan

Bloomsbury Postcard & Collectors Fair
Organizer IPM Promotions
Location Royal National Hotel, Bedford Way, London WC1
Details See Bloomsbury Postcard & Collectors Fair 3 Jan

Bob Evans Fair
Organizer Bob Evans Fairs
Location Sport Village, Drayton High Road, Hellesdon, Norwich (tel. 01603 278178)
Details See Bob Evans Fair 30 Jan

Buxton Book Fair
Organizer Buxton Book Fair
Location Pavilion Gardens, Buxton, Derbyshire
Est. 1982
Details See Buxton Book Fair 20 Feb

Fat Cat Fairs
Organizer Fat Cat Fairs
Location Burford School, Burford, Oxfordshire (on A40 to Cheltenham)
Details See Fat Cat Fairs 23 Jan

Janba Fair
Organizer Janba Fairs
Location Knights Hill Hotel, King's Lynn, Norfolk, (junction A148/A149)
Details See Janba Fair 30 Jan

V&A Antique & Collectors Fair
Organizer V&A Fairs
Location The Community Hall, Low Town (on A442), Bridgnorth, Shropshire
Details See V&A Antique & Collectors Fair 23 Jan

Wessex Antiques Fairs
Organizer Wessex Antiques Fairs
Location Winter Gardens Pavilion, Weston-super-Mare
Details See Wessex Antiques Fair 23 Jan

29

V&A Antique & Collectors Fair
Organizer V&A Fairs
Location The Civic Hall, Nantwich, Cheshire
Details See V&A Antique & Collectors Fair 1 Jan

30–1 OCTOBER

Coinex
Organizer British NumismaticTrade Association Ltd
Location The Platinum Suite, London Exhibition and Convention Centre, 1 Weston Gateway, Royal Victoria Docks, London E16
Est. 1978
Open 9.30am–5pm
Entrance fee Earlybird 10.30am–12.30pm £25 after 12.30 Fri £5 Sat £2
Details Annual fair organised by the BNTA, coins, banknotes, medals

Peterborough Festival of Antiques
Organizer Bob Evans Fairs
Location East of England Showground, Peterborough (tel. 01733 234451)
Details See Peterborough Festival of Antiques 8–9 Apr

30–2 OCTOBER

Stafford Bingley Hall Giant 3-Day Antiques Fair
Organizer Bowman Antiques Fairs Ltd
Location Bingley Hall, County Showground, Stafford
Details See Stafford Bingley Hall 12–14 February

OCTOBER

2

Antiques & Collectables Fair
Organizer Take Five Fairs
Location Canons Leisure Centre, Mitcham, Surrey
Details See Antiques & Collectables Fair 2 Jan

Battersea Vintage Fashion Fairs
Organizer Pre-empt Events
Location Battersea Art Centre, Lavender Hill, London SW11
Details See Battersea Vintage Fashion Fairs 6 Feb

Cross Country Fairs
Organizer Cross Country Fairs Ltd
Location Effingham Park, West Sussex
Details See Cross Country Fairs 2 Jan

Fat Cat Fairs
Organizer Fat Cat Fairs
Location New Memorial Hall, Lechlade-on-Thames, Gloucestershire
Details See Fat Cat Fairs 2 Jan

Mark Carter Militaria & Medal Fair
Organizer Mark Carter Militaria & Medal Fairs
Location Yate Leisure Centre, Kennedy Way, Yate, Bristol
Details See Mark Carter Militaria & Medal Fair 6 Feb

Scotfairs Antique and Collectors Fairs
Organizer Scotfairs

FOR FAIR ORGANIZERS SEE PAGE 522

Location Meadowbank Stadium, London Road, Edinburgh
Entrance fee
Details See Scotfairs Antique and Collectors Fairs 9 Jan

V&A Antique & Collectors Fair
Organizer V&A Fairs
Location The Village Hotel & Leisure Club, Cheadle Road, Cheadle, Cheshire
Details See V&A Antique & Collectors Fair 2 Jan

Wessex Antiques Fairs
Organizer Wessex Antiques Fairs
Location The Holiday Inn, Taunton, Somerset
Details See Wessex Fairs 2 Jan

3–5

33rd Bailey Antiques & Fine Art & Investment Fair
Organizer Robert Bailey Fairs Ltd
Location Seaford College, Petworth, West Sussex P
Open Fri 1–6pm Sat 11am–6pm Sun 11am–5pm
Entrance fee £5

4

Sandown Park Antiques Fairs
Organizer Wonder Whistle Enterprises
Location Sandown Park Racecourse, Portsmouth Road, Esher, Surrey
Details See Sandown Park Antiques Fairs 15 Feb

4–9

The Decorative Antiques and Textiles Fair
Organizer Harvey Management Services Ltd
Location The Marquee, Battersea Park, London
Details See The Decorative Antiques and Textiles Fair 18–23 Jan

6–9

The Milton Keynes Antiques Fair
Organizer E W Services
Location Milton Keynes Shopping Centre
Details See The Milton Keynes Antiques Fair 3–6 Mar

7–9

The International Antiques & Collectors Fair at RAF Swinderby
Organizer Arthur Swallow Fairs
Location RAF Swinderby, A46 between Newark and Lincoln
Details See The International Antiques & Collectors Fair at RAF Swinderby 30 Jan–1 Feb

8

Antiques and Collectors Fair
Organizer West Country Fairs
Location The Town Hall, Market Square, Wells, Somerset
Details See Antiques and Collectors Fair 8 Jan

Scotfairs Antique and Collectors Fairs
Organizer Scotfairs
Location Albert Halls, Dumbarton Road, Stirling
Details See Scotfairs Antique and Collectors Fairs 15 Jan

8–9

60th Luton Antiques Fair
Organizer Gemsco Promotions
Location Putteridge Bury House, Hitchin Road, Luton LU2 8LE (off A505)
Details See 59th Luton Antiques Fair 12–13 Feb

9

Adams Antiques Fair
Organizer Adams Antiques Fairs
Location Lindley Hall, Royal Horticultural Hall, Elverton Street (off Vincent Square) Victoria, London SW1
Details See Adams Antiques Fair 23 Jan

Antique & Collectors Fair
Organizer Blooms A1 Events
Location The Racecourse, Beverley, East Riding of Yorkshire
Details See Antique & Collectors Fair 13 Feb

Antiques & Collectables Fair
Organizer Take Five Fairs
Location Woking Leisure Centre, Kingfield Road, Woking, Surrey
Details See Antiques & Collectables Fair 9 Jan

Art Deco Fair
Organizer Abbey Fairs
Location The Grand Hall, Art Centre, Lavender Hill, Battersea, London SW11
Details See Art Deco Fair 13 Feb

Magna Carta Fayre
Organizer Magna Carta Country Fayres
Location St Leonard's Mansion, Legoland, Windsor, Berkshire
Details See Magna Carta Country Fayres 9 Jan

Malvern International Antiques & Collectors Fair
Organizer DMG Antiques Fairs
Location Three Counties Showground, Malvern, Worcestershire
Details See Malvern International Antiques & Collectors Fair 2 Jan

Midas Antiques Fair
Organizer Midas Fairs
Location Bellhouse Hotel, Beaconsfield, Buckinghamshire
Details See Midas Antiques Fair 9 Jan

Newmarket International Antiques & Collectors Fair
Organizer DMG Antiques Fairs
Location Rowley Mile Racecourse, Newmarket, Suffolk
Details See Newmarket Antiques & Collectors Fair 20 Feb

V&A Antique & Collectors Fair
Organizer V&A Fairs
Location The Hanover International Hotel, Stretton, Nr Warrington, Cheshire (M56 junction 10)
Details See V&A Antique & Collectors Fair 9 Jan

13–15

Newark International Antiques & Collectors Fair
Organizer DMG Antiques Fairs

FAIRS: CALENDAR

OCTOBER

Location Newark & Notts Showground, Newark
Details See Newark International Antiques & Collectors Fair 3–5 Feb

14–16

13th Buxton Autumn Antiques & Fine Art Fair
Organizer Robert Bailey Fairs Ltd
Location Pavilion Gardens, Buxton, Derbyshire P
Open Fri 1–6pm Sat 11am–6pm Sun 11am–5pm
Entrance fee £5
Details 50 dealers, vetted and datelined

The Fine Antiques Fairs of Scotland
Organizer Pantheon Fairs Ltd
Location Hopetoun House, South Queensferry, near Edinburgh
Details See The Fine Antiques Fairs of Scotland 11–13 Mar

16

Abergavenny Antiques & Collectors Fairs
Organizer Monmouthshire County Council
Location Abergavenny Market Hall, Abergavenny, Monmouthshire
Details See Abergavenny Antiques & Collectors Fairs 16 Jan

Biggleswade Antiques Fair
Organizer Biggleswade Antiques Fairs
Location Weatherley Centre, Biggleswade, Bedfordshire
Details See Biggleswade Antique Fair 16 Jan

Bob Evans Fair
Organizer Bob Evans Fairs
Location Leisure Centre, Coventry Road, Hinckley, Leicestershire
Details See Bob Evans Fair 1 Jan

Silhouette Fairs
Organizer Fat Cat Fairs
Location The Guildhall, Abbey Close, Abingdon, Oxfordshire, OX14 3JE
Details See Silhouette Fairs 16 Jan

The Old Brig Antique & Collectors' Fair
Organizer The Old Brig
Location The Highland Conference Centre, Nairn, Inverness
Details See The Old Brig Antique & Collectors' Fair 20 Mar

V&A Antique & Collectors Fair
Organizer V&A Fairs
Location The Civic Centre, High Street, Whitchurch, Shropshire
Details See V&A Antique & Collectors Fair 20 Feb

Wessex Antiques Fairs
Organizer Wessex Antiques Fairs
Location Coombe Lodge, Blagdon, Churchill, Somerset (A368 Churchill to Bath)
Details See Wessex Antiques Fair 16 Jan

20

Bob Evans Fair
Organizer Bob Evans Fairs
Location Leisure Centre, Holmer Road, Hereford (tel. 01432 278178)
Details See Bob Evans Fair 16 Jan

20–23

The LAPADA Antiques & Fine Art Fair
Organizer The Antique Dealers Fair Ltd
Location Cheltenham Racecourse, Cheltenham, Gloucestershire P
Est. 2004
Open Thur 11am–8pm Fri Sat 11am–6pm Sun 11am–5pm
Entrance fee £10
Details Showcase for members of LAPADA, with 90 stands

22–23

Cowbridge Antiques Fair
Organizer Towy Antiques Fairs
Location The Leisure Centre, Cowbridge, Vale of Glamorgan
Details See Cowbridge Antiques Fair 19–20 February

23

Art Deco Fair
Organizer Abbey Fairs
Location Twickenham Rugby Ground, Twickenham, Middlesex
Details See Art Deco Fair 27 Feb

Bloomsbury Postcard & Collectors Fair
Organizer IPM Promotions
Location Royal National Hotel, Bedford Way, London WC1
Details See Bloomsbury Postcard & Collectors Fair 3 Jan

Bob Evans Fair
Organizer Bob Evans Fairs
Location Sports Connexion, Ryton on Dunsmore, Coventry (tel. 02476 306155)
Details See Bob Evans Fair 6 Feb

Buxton Book Fair
Organizer Buxton Book Fair
Location Pavilion Gardens, Buxton, Derbyshire
Est. 1982
Details See Buxton Book Fair 20 Feb

Fat Cat Fairs
Organizer Fat Cat Fairs
Location Burford School, Burford, Oxfordshire (on A40 to Cheltenham)
Details See Fat Cat Fairs 23 Jan

Mark Carter Militaria & Medal Fair
Organizer Mark Carter Militaria & Medal Fairs
Location Stratford Leisure & Visitor Centre, Stratford-upon-Avon, Warwickshire
Details See Mark Carter Militaria & Medal Fair 6 Mar

27

V&A Antique & Collectors Fair
Organizer V&A Fairs
Location The Civic Hall, Nantwich, Cheshire
Details See V&A Antique & Collectors Fair 1 Jan

27–30

The Chester Antiques & Fine Art Show
Organizer Penman Antiques Fairs
Location The County Grandstand, Chester Racecourse, Chester
Details See The Chester Antiques & Fine Art Show 17–20 Feb

28–30

The East Anglian Antiques Dealers Fair
Organizer Lomax Antiques Fairs
Location Langley Park School, Loddon, Norfolk, NR14 6BJ P
Est. 1990
Open 28th noon–6pm 29th 10.30am–6pm 30th 10.30am–5pm
Entrance fee £3.50 including catalogue
Details Datelined antiques

29

Camfair
Organizer Janba Fairs
Location Castle Hall, Hertford
Details See Camfair 22 Jan

Scotfairs Antique and Collectors Fairs
Organizer Scotfairs
Location Citadel Leisure Centre, Ayr Baths, South Harbour Street, Ayr
Details See Scotfairs Antique and Collectors Fairs 29 Jan

29–30

Beckett Antiques Fairs
Organizer Beckett Antiques Fairs
Location Doncaster Racecourse, Doncaster, South Yorkshire
Details See Beckett Antiques Fairs 19–20 Feb

Detling International Antiques & Collectors Fair
Organizer DMG Antiques Fairs
Location Kent County Showground, Detling, Nr Maidstone, Kent
Details See Detling International Antiques & Collectors Fair 15–16 Jan

30

Art Nouveau/Deco Fair
Organizer Take Five Fairs
Location Woking Leisure Centre, Kingfield Road, Woking, Surrey
Details See Art Nouveau/Deco Fair 28 Mar

Biggleswade Antiques Fair
Organizer Biggleswade Antiques Fairs
Location Kimbolton Castle, Huntingdon
Details See Biggleswade Antiques Fair 13 Feb

Chipping Norton Toy Fair
Organizer Don Davidson
Location Chipping Norton School, Burford Road (A361), Chipping Norton, Oxfordshire
Details See Chipping Norton Toy Fair 20 February

Janba Fair
Organizer Janba Fairs
Location Knights Hill Hotel, King's Lynn, Norfolk, (junction A148/A149)
Details See Janba Fair 30 Jan

Midland Clock & Watch Fair
Organizer Brunel Clock & Watch Fair
Location National Motorcycle Museum, M42 junction 6, West Midlands
Details See Midland Clock & Watch Fair 16 Jan

The Big Weymouth Antiques & Collectors Fair
Organizer West Country Fairs
Location Weymouth Pavilion, The Esplanade, Weymouth, Dorset
Details See Antiques & Collectors Fair 20 Mar

Wessex Antiques Fairs
Organizer Wessex Antiques Fairs
Location Winter Gardens Pavilion, Weston-super-Mare
Details See Wessex Antiques Fair 23 Jan

NOVEMBER

1

Art Deco Fair
Organizer Abbey Fairs and E W Services
Location Novotel Hotel, No 1 West Keys, Southampton
Details See Art Deco Fair 1 May

1–2

Ardingly International Antiques & Collectors Fair
Organizer DMG Antiques Fairs
Location South of England Showground, Ardingly, West Sussex
Details See Ardingly International Antiques & Collectors Fair 11–12 Jan

4–5

The Chelsea Book Fair
Organizer Antiquarian Booksellers Association
Location Chelsea Old Town Hall, London SW3 (parking limited) P
Est. 1978
Open Fri 2–7pm Sat 11am–5pm
Entrance fee Fri £4 Sat £2
Complimentary tickets available on request or from web site
Details Antiquarian Books

4–6

23rd Hertfordshire Antiques & Fine Art Fair
Organizer Robert Bailey Fairs Ltd
Location Hatfield House, Hatfield, Hertfordshire P
Open Sat 11am–6pm Sun 11am–5pm
Entrance fee £5
Details 50 dealers, vetted and datelined

The Great Northern International Antiques & Collectors Fair
Organizer Grosvenor Exhibitions Ltd
Location The Great Yorkshire Showground, Harrogate (A661 Harrogate–Wetherby Road)
Details See The Great Northern International Antiques & Collectors Fair 14–16 Jan

5

London Coin Fair
Organizer Simmons Gallery
Location Holiday Inn, London Bloomsbury, Coram Street, London WC1
Details See London Coin Fair 5 Feb

Scotfairs Antique and Collectors Fairs
Organizer Scotfairs
Location Albert Halls, Dumbarton Road, Stirling
Details See Scotfairs Antique and Collectors Fairs 15 Jan

NOVEMBER

5–6

Buxton Antique & Collectors Fair
Organizer Unicorn Fairs Ltd
Location Pavilion Gardens, Buxton, Derbyshire
Details See Buxton Antique & Collectors Fair 29–30 Jan

5–7

The Portmeirion Antiques Fair
Organizer Allen Lewis Fairs
Location Portmeirion Village, Gwynedd, North Wales off A487
Entrance fee
Details See The Portmeirion Antiques Fair 25–27 Feb

6

Adams Antiques Fair
Organizer Adams Antiques Fairs
Location Lindley Hall, Royal Horticultural Hall, Elverton Street (off Vincent Square) Victoria, London SW1
Details See Adams Antiques Fair 23 Jan

Antiques & Collectables Fair
Organizer Take Five Fairs
Location Canons Leisure Centre, Mitcham, Surrey
Details See Antiques & Collectables Fair 2 Jan

Beckett Antiques Fairs
Organizer Beckett Antiques Fairs
Location York Racecourse P
Est. 2005
Open 10am–4.30pm
Entrance fee £2 concessions £1
Details Antiques and collectables

Bob Evans Fair
Organizer Bob Evans Fairs
Location Leisure Village, Thurston Drive, Kettering, Northamptonshire (tel. 01536 414141)
Details See Bob Evans Fair 20 Feb

Cross Country Fairs
Organizer Cross Country Fairs Ltd
Location Effingham Park, West Sussex
Details See Cross Country Fairs 2 Jan

Fat Cat Fairs
Organizer Fat Cat Fairs
Location New Memorial Hall, Lechlade-on-Thames, Gloucestershire
Details See Fat Cat Fairs 2 Jan

Malvern International Antiques & Collectors Fair
Organizer DMG Antiques Fairs
Location Three Counties Showground, Malvern, Worcestershire
Details See Malvern International Antiques & Collectors Fair 2 Jan

Scotfairs Antique and Collectors Fairs
Organizer Scotfairs
Location Meadowbank Stadium, London Road, Edinburgh
Entrance fee
Details See Scotfairs Antique and Collectors Fairs 9 Jan

V&A Antique & Collectors Fair
Organizer V&A Fairs
Location The Village Hotel & Leisure Club, Cheadle Road, Cheadle, Cheshire
Details See V&A Antique & Collectors Fair 2 Jan

Wessex Antiques Fairs
Organizer Wessex Antiques Fairs
Location The Holiday Inn, Taunton, Somerset
Details See Wessex Fairs 2 Jan

7–13

Winter Fine Art & Antiques Fair
Organizer Clarion Events Ltd
Location Olympia Exhibition Centre, London P
Est. 1992
Open Phone for details
Entrance fee £10 single £16 double
Details The rich variety of specialist stock will appeal to collectors and curators while connoisseurs and private buyers will find something unique. An exceptional choice of antique furniture and fine art is for sale.

11–13

2nd Bailey Yorkshire Affordable Fine Art Fair
Organizer Robert Bailey Fairs Ltd
Location Pavilions of Harrogate, Great Yorkshire Showground P
Open Sat 11am–6pm Sun 11am–5pm
Entrance fee £5

The Goodwood House Fine Antiques Fairs
Organizer Pantheon Fairs Ltd
Location Goodwood House, Chichester, West Sussex
Details See The Goodwood House Fine Antiques Fairs 18–20 Feb

12

23rd Annual Belfast Book Fair
Organizer Jiri Books
Location Wellington Park Hotel, Malone Road, Belfast P
Est. 1982
Open 10am–5pm
Entrance fee £2 concessions £1
Details 35 dealers exhibiting from NI, ROI and GB, much Irish interest stocks

12–13

Janba Fair
Organizer Janba Fairs
Location Burgess Hall, St Ivo Leisure Centre, St Ives, Cambridgeshire
Details See Janba Fair 1–2 Jan

13

Antique & Collectors Fair
Organizer Blooms A1 Events
Location The Racecourse, Beverley, East Riding of Yorkshire
Details See Antique & Collectors Fair 13 Feb

Bob Evans Fair
Organizer Bob Evans Fairs
Location The Cresset, Bretton Centre, Peterborough (tel. 01733 265705)
Details See Bob Evans Fair 9 Jan

Chiswick Art Deco Fair
Organizer London Art Deco Fairs
Location Chiswick Town Hall, Heathfield Terrace, London W4
Details See Chiswick Art Deco Fair 20 Mar

Magna Carta Fayre
Organizer Magna Carta Country Fayres

Location St Leonard's Mansion, Legoland, Windsor, Berkshire
Details See Magna Carta Country Fayres 9 Jan

Midas Antiques Fair
Organizer Midas Fairs
Location Bellhouse Hotel, Beaconsfield, Buckinghamshire
Details See Midas Antiques Fair 9 Jan

Newmarket International Antiques & Collectors Fair
Organizer DMG Antiques Fairs
Location Rowley Mile Racecourse, Newmarket, Suffolk
Details See Newmarket Antiques & Collectors Fair 20 Feb

The Brocante & Decorative Living Show
Organizer Adams Antiques Fairs
Location Kensington Town Hall, Hornton Street, London SW7
Details See The Brocante & Decorative Living Show 6 Mar

V&A Antique & Collectors Fair
Organizer V&A Fairs
Location The Hanover International Hotel, Stretton, Nr Warrington, Cheshire (M56 junction 10)
Details See V&A Antique & Collectors Fair 9 Jan

13–15

The Goodwood House Fine Antiques Fairs
Organizer Pantheon Fairs Ltd
Location Goodwood House, Chichester, West Sussex
Details See The Goodwood House Fine Antiques Fairs 18–20 Feb

15

Sandown Park Antiques Fairs
Organizer Wonder Whistle Enterprises
Location Sandown Park Racecourse, Portsmouth Road, Esher, Surrey
Details See Sandown Park Antiques Fairs 15 Feb

18–20

Shepton Mallet Antiques & Collectors Fair
Organizer DMG Antiques Fairs
Location Royal Bath and West Showground, Shepton Mallet, Somerset
Details See Shepton Mallet Antiques & Collectors Fair 21–23 Jan

19

Camfair
Organizer Janba Fairs
Location Castle Hall, Hertford
Details See Camfair 22 Jan

19–20

10th Mid Beds Antiques Fair
Organizer Gemsco Promotions
Location Silsoe Conference Centre (Cranfield University), Silsoe, Bedfordshire, MK45 4DT (off A6)
Details See 9th Mid Beds Antiques Fair 21–22 May

20

Abergavenny Antiques & Collectors Fairs
Organizer Monmouthshire County Council
Location Abergavenny Market Hall, Abergavenny, Monmouthshire
Details See Abergavenny Antiques & Collectors Fairs 16 Jan

Alexandra Palace Antique & Collectors Fair
Organizer Pig & Whistle Promotions
Location The Great Hall, Alexandra Palace, Wood Green, London N22
Details See Alexandra Palace Antique & Collectors Fair 16 Jan

Biggleswade Antiques Fair
Organizer Biggleswade Antiques Fairs
Location Weatherley Centre, Biggleswade, Bedfordshire
Details See Biggleswade Antique Fair 16 Jan

Bob Evans Fair
Organizer Bob Evans Fairs
Location Sport Village, Drayton High Road, Hellesdon, Norwich (tel. 01603 278178)
Details See Bob Evans Fair 30 Jan

Dublin Toy and Train Fair
Organizer Dublin Toy and Train Fair
Location Clontarf Castle Hotel, Castle Avenue, Clontarf, Dublin 3
Details See Dublin Toy and Train Fair 6 February

Northern Clock & Watch Fair
Organizer Northern Clock & Watch Fairs
Location Haydock Park Racecourse, Merseyside
Details See Northern Clock & Watch Fair 30 Jan

Silhouette Fairs
Organizer Fat Cat Fairs
Location The Guildhall, Abbey Close, Abingdon, Oxfordshire, OX14 3JE
Details See Sihouette Fairs 16 Jan

The Big Weymouth Antiques & Collectors Fair
Organizer West Country Fairs
Location Weymouth Pavilion, The Esplanade, Weymouth, Dorset
Details See Antiques & Collectors Fair 20 Mar

The Old Brig Antique & Collectors' Fair
Organizer The Old Brig
Location The Highland Conference Centre, Nairn, Inverness
Details See The Old Brig Antique & Collectors' Fair 20 Mar

Wessex Antiques Fairs
Organizer Wessex Antiques Fairs
Location Winter Gardens Pavilion, Weston-super-Mare
Details See Wessex Antiques Fair 23 Jan

24

V&A Antique & Collectors Fair
Organizer V&A Fairs
Location The Civic Hall, Nantwich, Cheshire
Details See V&A Antique & Collectors Fair 1 Jan

24–27

Antiques for Everyone
Organizer The NEC Group
Location Earls Court, London
Details See Antiques for Everyone 31 Mar1–Apr

FAIRS: CALENDAR

DECEMBER

25–27

The International Antiques & Collectors Fair at RAF Swinderby
Organizer Arthur Swallow Fairs
Location RAF Swinderby, A46 between Newark and Lincoln
Details See The International Antiques & Collectors Fair at RAF Swinderby 28–30 Jan

26

Scotfairs Antique and Collectors Fairs
Organizer Scotfairs
Location Citadel Leisure Centre, Ayr Baths, South Harbour Street, Ayr
Details See Scotfairs Antique and Collectors Fairs 29 Jan

27

Biggleswade Antiques Fair
Organizer Biggleswade Antiques Fairs
Location Addison Centre, Kempton, Bedfordshire
Details See Biggleswade Antique Fair 23 Jan

Bloomsbury Postcard & Collectors Fair
Organizer IPM Promotions
Location Galleon Suite, Royal National Hotel, Bedford Way, London WC1
Details See Bloomsbury Postcard & Collectors Fair 3 Jan

Bob Evans Fair
Organizer Bob Evans Fairs
Location Leisure Centre, Holmer Road, Hereford (tel. 01432 278178)
Details See Bob Evans Fair 16 Jan

Buxton Book Fair
Organizer Buxton Book Fair
Location Pavilion Gardens, Buxton, Derbyshire
Est. 1982
Details See Buxton Book Fair 20 Feb

Fat Cat Fairs
Organizer Fat Cat Fairs
Location Burford School, Burford, Oxfordshire (on A40 to Cheltenham)
Details See Fat Cat Fairs 23 Jan

Janba Fair
Organizer Janba Fairs
Location Knights Hill Hotel, King's Lynn, Norfolk, (junction A148/A149)
Details See Janba Fair 30 Jan

V&A Antique & Collectors Fair
Organizer V&A Fairs
Location The Community Hall, Low Town (on A442), Bridgnorth, Shropshire
Details See V&A Antique & Collectors Fair 23 Jan

Wessex Antiques Fairs
Organizer Wessex Antiques Fairs
Location Coombe Lodge, Blagdon, Churchill, Somerset (A368 Churchill to Bath)
Details See Wessex Antiques Fair 16 Jan

28

Art Deco Fair
Organizer Abbey Fairs
Location Battersea Town Hall
Details See Art Deco Fair 15 Feb

DECEMBER

1–3

Newark International Antiques & Collectors Fair
Organizer DMG Antiques Fairs
Location Newark & Notts Showground, Newark
Details See Newark International Antiques & Collectors Fair 3–5 Feb

3

Scotfairs Antique and Collectors Fairs
Organizer Scotfairs
Location Albert Halls, Dumbarton Road, Stirling
Details See Scotfairs Antique and Collectors Fairs 15 Jan

3–4

Buxton Antique & Collectors Fair
Organizer Unicorn Fairs Ltd
Location Pavilion Gardens, Buxton, Derbyshire
Details See Buxton Antique & Collectors Fair 29–30 Jan

4

Adams Antiques Fair
Organizer Adams Antiques Fairs
Location Lindley Hall, Royal Horticultural Hall, Elverton Street (off Vincent Square) Victoria, London SW1
Details See Adams Antiques Fair 23 Jan

Antique & Collectors Fair
Organizer Blooms A1 Events
Location The Racecourse, Beverley, East Riding of Yorkshire
Details See Antique & Collectors Fair 13 Feb

Antiques & Collectables Fair
Organizer Take Five Fairs
Location Canons Leisure Centre, Mitcham, Surrey
Details See Antiques & Collectables Fair 2 Jan

Art Deco Fair
Organizer Abbey Fairs
Location Warwick Hilton Hotel, Warwick
Details See Art Deco Fair 27 Feb

Battersea Vintage Fashion Fairs
Organizer Pre-empt Events
Location Battersea Art Centre, Lavender Hill, London SW11
Details See Battersea Vintage Fashion Fairs 6 Feb

Cross Country Fairs
Organizer Cross Country Fairs Ltd
Location Effingham Park, West Sussex
Details See Cross Country Fairs 2 Jan

Fat Cat Fairs
Organizer Fat Cat Fairs
Location New Memorial Hall, Lechlade-on-Thames, Gloucestershire
Details See Fat Cat Fairs 2 Jan

Malvern International Antiques & Collectors Fair
Organizer DMG Antiques Fairs
Location Three Counties Showground, Malvern, Worcestershire
Details See Malvern International Antiques & Collectors Fair 2 Jan

FOR FAIR ORGANIZERS SEE PAGE 522

Mark Carter Militaria & Medal Fair
Organizer Mark Carter Militaria & Medal Fairs
Location Yate Leisure Centre, Kennedy Way, Yate, Bristol
Details See Mark Carter Militaria & Medal Fair 6 Feb

Scotfairs Antique and Collectors Fairs
Organizer Scotfairs
Location Meadowbank Stadium, London Road, Edinburgh
Entrance fee
Details See Scotfairs Antique and Collectors Fairs 9 Jan

V&A Antique & Collectors Fair
Organizer V&A Fairs
Location The Civic Centre, High Street, Whitchurch, Shropshire
Details See V&A Antique & Collectors Fair 20 Feb

Wessex Antiques Fairs
Organizer Wessex Antiques Fairs
Location The Holiday Inn, Taunton, Somerset
Details See Wessex Fairs 2 Jan

6

Beckett Antiques Fairs
Organizer Beckett Antiques Fairs
Location York Racecourse
Details See Beckett Antiques Fairs 6 Nov

9–11

Stafford Bingley Hall Giant 3-Day Antiques Fair
Organizer Bowman Antiques Fairs Ltd
Location Bingley Hall, County Showground, Stafford
Details See Stafford Bingley Hall 12–14 February

10

Frock Me!
Organizer Adams Antiques Fairs
Location Chelsea Town Hall, King's Road, Chelsea, London SW3
Details See Frock Me! 5 Feb

10–11

Carmarthen Antiques Fair
Organizer Towy Antiques Fairs
Location United County Showground, Carmarthen
Open 10am–4pm
Details See Carmarthen Antiques Fair 6–7 March (although note earlier closing time)

11

Antiques & Collectables Fair
Organizer Take Five Fairs
Location Woking Leisure Centre, Kingfield Road, Woking, Surrey
Details See Antiques & Collectable Fair 9 Jan

Magna Carta Fayre
Organizer Magna Carta Country Fayres
Location St Leonard's Mansion, Legoland, Windsor, Berkshire
Details See Magna Carta Country Fayres 9 Jan

Midas Antiques Fair
Organizer Midas Fairs
Location Bellhouse Hotel, Beaconsfield, Buckinghamshire
Details See Midas Antiques Fair 9 Jan

V&A Antique & Collectors Fair
Organizer V&A Fairs
Location The Hanover International Hotel, Stretton, Nr Warrington, Cheshire (M56 junction 10)
Details See V&A Antique & Collectors Fair 9 Jan

Wessex Antiques Fairs
Organizer Wessex Antiques Fairs
Location Winter Gardens Pavilion, Weston-super-Mare
Details See Wessex Antiques Fair 23 Jan

15

V&A Antique & Collectors Fair
Organizer V&A Fairs
Location The Civic Hall, Nantwich, Cheshire
Details See V&A Antique & Collectors Fair 1 Jan

17

Camfair
Organizer Janba Fairs
Location Castle Hall, Hertford
Details See Camfair 22 Jan

Scotfairs Antique and Collectors Fairs
Organizer Scotfairs
Location Citadel Leisure Centre, Ayr Baths, South Harbour Street, Ayr
Details See Scotfairs Antique and Collectors Fairs 29 Jan

18

Abergavenny Antiques & Collectors Fairs
Organizer Monmouthshire County Council
Location Abergavenny Market Hall, Abergavenny, Monmouthshire
Details See Abergavenny Antiques & Collectors Fairs 16 Jan

Biggleswade Antiques Fair
Organizer Biggleswade Antiques Fairs
Location Weatherley Centre, Biggleswade, Bedfordshire
Details See Biggleswade Antique Fair 16 Jan

Bloomsbury Postcard & Collectors Fair
Organizer IPM Promotions
Location Galleon Suite, Royal National Hotel, Bedford Way, London WC1
Details See Bloomsbury Postcard & Collectors Fair 3 Jan

Buxton Book Fair
Organizer Buxton Book Fair
Location Pavilion Gardens, Buxton, Derbyshire
Est. 1982
Details See Buxton Book Fair 20 Feb

Janba Fair
Organizer Janba Fairs
Location Knights Hill Hotel, King's Lynn, Norfolk, (junction A148/A149)
Details See Janba Fair 30 Jan

Silhouette Fairs
Organizer Fat Cat Fairs
Location The Guildhall, Abbey Close, Abingdon, Oxfordshire, OX14 3JE
Details See Silhouette Fairs 16 Jan

DECEMBER

20

The Old Brig Antique & Collectors' Fair
Organizer The Old Brig
Location The Highland Conference Centre, Nairn, Inverness
Details See The Old Brig Antique & Collectors' Fair 20 Mar

27

Bob Evans Fair
Organizer Bob Evans Fairs
Location Sports Connexion, Ryton on Dunsmore, Coventry (tel. 02476 306155)
Details See Bob Evans Fair 6 Feb

27–28

Beckett Antiques Fairs
Organizer Beckett Antiques Fairs
Location Doncaster Racecourse, Doncaster, South Yorkshire
Details See Beckett Antiques Fairs 19–20 Feb

28

Art Nouveau/Deco Fair
Organizer Take Five Fairs
Location Woking Leisure Centre, Kingfield Road, Woking, Surrey
Details See Art Nouveau/Deco Fair 28 Mar

Bob Evans Fair
Organizer Bob Evans Fairs
Location Leisure Village, Thurston Drive, Kettering, Northamptonshire (tel. 01536 414141)
Details See Bob Evans Fair 22 Feb

29–30

2nd Northamptonshire Antiques Fair
Organizer Gemsco Promotions
Location The Grandstand, Towcester Racecourse, Easton Neston P
Est. 2004
Open Sat 11am–5pm Sun 10am–5pm
Details Datelined event

31–1 JANUARY

Buxton Antique & Collectors Fair
Organizer Unicorn Fairs Ltd
Location Pavilion Gardens, Buxton, Derbyshire
Details See Buxton Antique & Collectors Fair 29–30 Jan

Indexes

In the Index of Specialists and the General Index, shops and businesses beginning with a forename are listed alphabetically by surname: thus R G Archer Books is listed under A and Michael Saffell Antiques appears under S.

The county in which a city, town or village has been placed in the Directory is also given In the Index of Place Names. Note that this is not always the county given in the address that forms part of the entry.

KEY TO MEMBER ORGANIZATIONS

In order to make the information in this book more concise we have used the following abbreviations where applicable.

ABA Antiquarian Booksellers' Association
ADA Antique Dealers' Association
ADDA Art Deco Dealers' Association
AFRA Antique Furniture Repairers Association
AHS Antiquarian Horological Society
AMU Association Master Upholsterers
ANA American Numismatic Association
APS American Philatelic Society
ARVA Association of Regional Valuers & Auctioneers
ASDA American Stamp Dealers' Association
ASVA Association of Society of Valuers & Auctioneers
AU Association of Upholsterers
BA Booksellers' Association
BABAADA Bath & Bradford on Avon Antique Dealers' Association
BABI Booksellers' Association of Britain & Ireland
BACA British Antiques and Collectables Awards
BADA British Antique Dealers' Association
BAFRA British Antique Furniture Restorers' Association
BAR British Association of Removers
BCCA British Cheque Clearers Association
BCPAA British China & Porcelain Artists' Association
BCS British Cartographic Society
BGA British Gemologists' Association
BHI British Horological Institute
BIFA British International Freight Association
BJA British Jewellers' Association
BNTA British Numismatic Trade Association
BSMGP British Society of Master Glass Painters
BWCG British Watch & Clockmakers' Guild
CAAV Central Association of Agricultural Valuers
CADA Cotswold Antique Dealers' Association
CC Clockmakers' Company
CGLI City & Guilds of London Institute
CINOA Confédération Internationale des Négociants en Oeuvres d'Art
CLPGS City of London Phonograph & Gramophone Society
CPADA Camden Passage Antique Dealers' Association
CPTA Camden Passage Traders' Association
DADA Dorking Antique Dealers' Association
DGA Diamond member of the Gemmological Association
EADA Essex Antique Dealers' Association
ESoc Ephemera Society
FATG Fine Art Trade Guild
FIDI Fédération Internationale des Déménageurs Internationaux
FNAVA Federation of National Auctioneers & Valuers
FSVA Fellow of the Society of Valuers & Auctioneers
GADAR Guild of Antique Dealers & Restorers
GAGTL Gemmological Association and Gem Testing Laboratory of Great Britain
GCS Golf Collectors' Society (GB, USA)
GTA Gun Traders' Association
HADA Hudson Antique Dealers' Association
HHGFAA Household Goods Forwarders of America
IAA Institute of Antiques Auctioneers
IADA Irish Antique Dealers' Association
IADAA International Association of Dealers in Ancient Art
IAMA The International Antiquarian Map Sellers' Association
IAPN International Society of Professional Numismatists
IATA International Air Transport Association
IAVI Irish Auctioneers & Valuers Institute
IBNS International Bank Note Society
IBSS International Bond and Share Society
ICHAWI Institute for the Conservation of Historic & Artistic Works in Ireland
ICOM International Council of Museums (Committee for Conservation)
IDDA Interior Decorators' & Designers' Association
IIC International Institute for Conservation of Historic & Artistic Work
ILAB International League of Antiquarian Booksellers
IMA Irish Museums Association
IMCOS International Map Collectors' Society
IMTA International Map Trade Association
IPAA International Porcelain Artists' Association
IPAV Institute of Professional Auctioneers & Valuers
IPC Institute of Paper Conservation
IPCRA Irish Professional Conservators' & Restorers' Association
IPG Independent Publishers Guild
IRRV Institute of Revenues, Ratings & Valuation
ISVA Incorporated Society of Valuers & Auctioneers
ITA Islington Trading Association
KCSADA Kensington Church Street Antique Dealers' Association
LAPADA London & Provincial Antique Dealers' Association

KEY TO MEMBER ORGANIZATIONS

LJAJDA	London & Japan Antique Jewellery Dealers' Association
LSVA	London Silver Vaults Association
MAPH	Member of the Association of Professional Horologists
MBHI	Member of British Horological Society
MBWCG	Member of British Watch & Clockmakers' Guild
MGR	Museums and Galleries Register
NACF	National Art Collections Fund
NAEA	National Art Education Association
NAG	National Association of Goldsmiths
NAVA	National Association of Auctioneers & Valuers
NAWCC	National Association of Watch & Clock Collectors
NCCR	National Council for Conservation and Restoration
NIAVI	Northern Ireland Auctioneers & Valuers Institute
NPA	National Pawnbrokers Association
OCS	Oriental Ceramic Society
OMNI	Overseas Moving Network International
OMRS	Order Medals Research Society
OMSA	Orders and Medals Society of America
PAADA	Petworth Art & Antique Dealers' Association
PADA	Portobello Antique Dealers' Association
PBFA	Provincial Book Fair Association
PNG	Professional Numismatists' Guild
PTA	Postcard Traders' Association
PTS	Philatelic Traders' Society
RADS	Registered Antique Dealers' Association
RETRA	Radio, Electrical and Television Retailers' Association
RICS	Royal Institute of Chartered Surveyors
RWHA	Royal Warrant Holders' Association
SAA	Scottish Association of Auctioneers
SAADA	Sherborne Art & Antique Dealers' Association
SAPCON	South African Paper Conservation Group
SIS	Scientific Instrument Society
SLAD	Society of London Art Dealers
SOB	Society of Book Binders
SOC	Society of Cartographers
SOFAA	Society of Fine Art Auctioneers
SPAB	Society for the Protection of Ancient Buildings
SPTA	Scottish Philatelic Traders' Association
SSA	Sussex Saleroom Association
SSBA	Stony Stratford Business Association
SSCR	Scottish Society for Conservation & Restoration
TADA	Tetbury Antique Dealers' Association
TCS	Tennis Collectors' Society
TPCS	Torquay Pottery Collectors' Club
TRADA	Timber Research and Development Association
TVADA	Thames Valley Antique Dealers' Association
UACC	Universal Autograph Collectors' Club
UKIC	United Kingdom Institute for Conservation
WADA	Warwick Antique Dealers Association
WBA	Welsh Booksellers' Association
WKADA	West Kent Antique Dealers' Association

INDEX OF ADVERTISERS

INDEX OF SPECIALISTS

ADVERTISING

INDEX OF SPECIALISTS

BOOKS

INDEX OF SPECIALISTS

DECORATIVE ARTS

DECORATIVE ARTS

DESIGN

ELECTRICAL AND MECHANICAL

EPHEMERA

FANS

FURNITURE

17THC ENGLISH

17TH–18THC

17TH–19THC

18THC

18THC ENGLISH

18THC WALNUT, MAHOGANY

18TH–19THC

18TH–19THC CONTINENTAL

18TH–19THC ENGLISH

18TH–19THC MAHOGANY

INDEX OF SPECIALISTS
FURNITURE

GARDENING ANTIQUES

GLASS

INDEX OF PLACE NAMES

A

A

B

C

D

E

F

G

H

T

U

0–9

A

GENERAL INDEX

A

B

GENERAL INDEX

B

C

GENERAL INDEX

C

D

E

F

G

GENERAL INDEX

G

H

GENERAL INDEX

H

I

J

K

L

M

GENERAL INDEX

N

N

O

Q

R

S

GENERAL INDEX

S

T

GENERAL INDEX

T

U

V

W

GENERAL INDEX

W

X

Y

Z

MILLER'S

Antiques Shops, Fairs & Auctions in the UK & Ireland 2006

ENTRY FORM

Please return a signed copy of this form to: Miller's Publications (Directory 2006), The Cellars, High Street, Tenterden, Kent TN30 6BN or fax to 01580 766100.

Name of Business: ....

Type of Entry *(Dealer/Auction House/Market or Centre/Associated Service)*: ....

Contact Name: ....

Street: ....

Town: .... County: .... Postcode: ....

Address for mailing *(if different from above)*: ....

....

Telephone: .... Fax: .... Mobile: ....

Email: .... Web address: ....

Trade only *(Yes/No)*: .... Parking nearby *(Yes/No)*: ....

Member of: .... Established: ....

Opening/Office hours: ....

Dealers only

Principal Stock: ....

If a Specialist Dealer, please give speciality *(one only)*: ....

Services offered *(Valuation/Restoration/Shipping/Book Search)*: ....

....

Exhibitor at which fairs? *(two only)*: ....

Quantity of stock held *(Small/Medium/Large)*: ....

Auction Houses only

Sale details: ....

Catalogues *(Yes/No)*: .... Frequency of main sale: ....

Markets/Centres only

Number of stalls/shops/dealers: ....

Associated Service only

Specialist area: ....

Services offered: ....

I agree that the above data may be included in the 2006 and future editions of Miller's Antiques Shops, Fairs & Auctions in the UK & Ireland. I further acknowledge that it is my responsibility to keep this information up to date and agree to inform Octopus Publishing Group Ltd (OPG) of any changes to it.

Signature: ____________________ Name: ____________________ Date: __________

Paragraph A: We Octopus Publishing Group Ltd (OPG) wish to share the information you have provided with our business partners for promotional and product development purposes, via a range of media including web sites and digital television. If you do not wish us to use your information in this way, then please tick here: ❑

If you no longer want to be included in the above publication or if you have any queries concerning the personal information held about you, please contact: Valerie Lewis, Miller's Publications, The Cellars, High Street, Tenterden, Kent TN30 6BN.